THE
AMERICAN
PROMISE

A HISTORY OF THE UNITED STATES

Second Edition

CANADA

Lake Superior

Lake Michigan

Lake Huron

Lake Ontario

Lake Erie

St. Lawrence River

Mt. Washington
(6,288 ft.; 1,917 m)

Gulf of Maine

Cape Cod

Hudson River

Connecticut River

Long Island

Missouri River

Des Moines River

CENTRAL
LOWLAND

Wabash River

Illinois River

Ohio River

APPALACHIAN PLATEAU

APPALACHIAN MOUNTAINS

Delaware River

Susquehanna River

Potomac River

N

W   E

S

James River

Chesapeake
Bay

Cape
Hatteras

ATLANTIC
OCEAN

Cumberland River

Mt. Mitchell
(6,684 ft.; 2,037 m)

BLUE RIDGE MTS.

PIEDMONT

Roanoke River

OZARK
PLATEAU

Mississippi River

Tennessee River

Savannah River

Cape
Fear

Red River

Brazos River

Alabama River

Chattahoochee River

OKEEFENOKEE
SWAMP

C O A S T A L   P L A I N

Cape
Canaveral

THE
UNITED STATES

Elevation

Feet	Meters
Over 13,001	Over 3,001
6,561–13,000	2,001–3,000
3,281–6,560	1,001–2,000
1,641–3,280	501–1,000
661–1,640	201–500
0–660	0–200
Below sea level	Below sea level

Mississippi
River Delta

Gulf of Mexico

Lake
Okeechobee

THE
EVERGLADES

B A H A M A S

ATLANTIC
OCEAN

VIRGIN
ISLANDS

PUERTO
RICO

Caribbean Sea

0   50   100 miles
0   50   100 kilometers

FLORIDA
KEYS

0   150   300 miles
0   150   300 kilometers

**For a series of maps showing the territorial growth of the
United States, see pages M–2 to M–9 at the back of this book.**

CUBA

THE CONTEMPORARY WORLD

ARCTIC OCEAN

NORWAY
SWEDEN
FINLAND
DEN.
ESTONIA
LATVIA
LITHUANIA
NETH.
GERMANY
POLAND
BELARUS
BEL.
LUX.
CZ. REP.
SLK.
UKRAINE
SLN.
AUS.
HUNG.
ROMANIA
MOLDOVA
SWITZ.
CR.
YUG.
BULGARIA
ITALY
B.H.
MAC.
GEORGIA
ALB.
GREECE
ARMENIA
TURKEY
TUNISIA
MALTA
CYPRUS
SYRIA
LEBANON
AZERBAIJAN
ISRAEL
IRAQ

RUSSIAN FEDERATION

KAZAKHSTAN

UZBEKISTAN
KYRGYZSTAN
TURKMENISTAN
TAJIKISTAN
AFGHANISTAN

MONGOLIA

CHINA

N. KOREA
S. KOREA

JAPAN

PACIFIC OCEAN

ALGERIA
LIBYA
EGYPT

JORDAN
KUWAIT
SAUDI ARABIA
QATAR
UNITED ARAB
EMIRATES
BAHRAIN
OMAN
IRAN
PAKISTAN

NEPAL
BHUTAN
BANGLADESH
INDIA
MYANMAR
(BURMA)
LAOS
VIETNAM
THAILAND
CAMBODIA

TAIWAN

Mariana Is.
(U.S.)

Guam
(U.S.)

MARSHALL
IS.

NIGER
CHAD
SUDAN
ERITREA
DJIBOUTI
YEMEN

MALDIVES

SRI
LANKA

PHILIPPINES

PALAU

FEDERATED STATES
OF MICRONESIA

NIGERIA
BENIN
TOGO
CAMEROON
EQ.
GUINEA
GABON
CONGO
SÃO TOMÉ
& PRÍNCIPE
CENTRAL
AFRICAN REP.
RWANDA
DEM. REP. OF
THE CONGO
BURUNDI
UGANDA
KENYA
TANZANIA
ETHIOPIA
SOMALIA

BRUNEI

MALAYSIA

SINGAPORE

INDONESIA

PAPUA
NEW
GUINEA

NAURU

KIRIBATI

TUVALU

SOLOMON
IS.

COMOROS
SEYCHELLES

INDIAN OCEAN

ANGOLA
ZAMBIA
MALAWI
ZIMBABWE
NAMIBIA
BOTSWANA
MADAGASCAR
MAURITIUS

VANUATU

FIJI

AUSTRALIA

New Caledonia
(Fr.)

SOUTH
AFRICA
MOZAMBIQUE
SWAZILAND
LESOTHO

NEW
ZEALAND

Tasmania
(Aust.)

ABBREVIATIONS

ALB.	ALBANIA
AUS.	AUSTRIA
BEL.	BELGIUM
B.H.	BOSNIA AND HERZEGOVINA
CR.	CROATIA
CZ. REP.	CZECH REPUBLIC
DEN.	DENMARK
HUNG.	HUNGARY
LUX.	LUXEMBOURG
MAC.	MACEDONIA
NETH.	NETHERLANDS
SLK.	SLOVAKIA
SLN.	SLOVENIA
SWITZ.	SWITZERLAND
YUG.	YUGOSLAVIA

ANTARCTICA

20°E   40°E   60°E   80°E   100°E   120°E   140°E   160°E

THE AMERICAN PROMISE

A HISTORY OF THE UNITED STATES

Second Edition

PULLING DOWN THE STATUE OF GEORGE III *by William Walcutt. Private Collection.*

THE AMERICAN PROMISE

A HISTORY OF THE UNITED STATES

Volume I: To 1877

Second Edition

JAMES L. ROARK
Emory University

MICHAEL P. JOHNSON
Johns Hopkins University

PATRICIA CLINE COHEN
University of California at Santa Barbara

SARAH STAGE
Arizona State University West

ALAN LAWSON
Boston College

SUSAN M. HARTMANN
The Ohio State University

BEDFORD / ST. MARTIN'S
Boston • New York

FOR BEDFORD/ST. MARTIN'S

Publisher of History: Patricia A. Rossi
Senior Development Editor: Elizabeth M. Welch
Production Editor: Ara Salibian
Senior Production Supervisor: Catherine Hetmansky
Art Editors: Tina Samaha and Coleen O'Hanley
Marketing Manager: Jenna Bookin Barry
Associate Editor: Sarah Barrash
Editorial Assistant: Brianna R. Germain
Production Assistants: Coleen O'Hanley and Arthur Johnson
Copyeditors: Barbara G. Flanagan, Janet Renard, and Joy Sobeck
Proofreaders: Pauline Chin and Janet Cocker
Text Design: Wanda Kossak
Photo Research: Pembroke Herbert / Sandi Rygiel, Picture Research Consultants & Archives, Inc.
Cartography: Mapping Specialists Limited
Indexer: Maro Riofrancos
Cover Designer: Donna Lee Dennison
Composition: TechBooks East
Printing and Binding: RR Donnelley & Sons Company

President: Charles H. Christensen
Editorial Director: Joan E. Feinberg
Director of Marketing: Karen Melton
Director of Editing, Design, and Production: Marcia Cohen
Managing Editor: Elizabeth Schaaf

Library of Congress Control Number: 2001131214

Manufactured in the United States of America.

6 5 4 3 2
f e d c b

For information, contact: Bedford/St. Martin's, 75 Arlington Street, Boston, MA 02116
617-399-4000
www.bedfordstmartins.com

ISBN: 0–312–39124–2 (hardcover)
ISBN: 0–312–39419–5 (paperback Vol. I)
ISBN: 0–312–39418–7 (paperback Vol. II)

Cover art: Revolutionary War flag: David A. Schorsch, American Antiques, Inc. Painted wooden eagle drum: Fort Ticonderoga Museum. Beaver hat: Courtesy of Plimoth Plantation, Inc. Plymouth, MA. Lincoln's hat: National Museum of American History, Smithsonian Institution, Washington, D.C. Fancy over the ankle shoes: Lynn Historical Society.

BRIEF CONTENTS

CONTENTS

MAPS, FIGURES, AND TABLES

Maps

Figures

Tables

SPECIAL FEATURES

PREFACE

The American Promise grew out of the authors' experience as longtime teachers of the survey course. Collectively, we have logged more than a century in introductory American history classrooms in institutions that range from community colleges and state universities to private colleges and research institutions. We know firsthand that the survey course is the most difficult to teach and the most difficult to take. Our goal was an ambitious one: to publish the most teachable and readable textbook available.

Most survey texts emphasize either a social or political approach to history; by focusing on one, they inevitably slight the other. In our classrooms, students need **both** the structure a political narrative provides and the insights gained from examining social and cultural experiences. To write a comprehensive, balanced account of American history, we focused on the public arena—the place where politics intersects social and cultural developments—to show how Americans confronted the major issues of their day and created far-reaching historical change.

Our title, The American Promise, *reflects our emphasis on human agency and our conviction that American history is an unfinished story.*

We thought hard about the concerns most frequently voiced by instructors: that students often find history boring, unfocused, and difficult. How could our text help introductory students see and remember American history's main events and developments? We decided to explore fully the political, social, economic, and cultural changes that students need to understand, at the same time avoiding unnecessary detail that threatened to befuddle rather than inform them. We organized each chapter to emphasize the essential people, events, and themes of the period. To portray the power of human agency and the diversity of the American experience, we stitched into the narrative the voices of hundreds of contemporaries—from presidents to

pipefitters—whose ideas and actions shaped their times and whose efforts still affect our lives. By incorporating a rich selection of authentic American voices, we sought to create a vivid and compelling narrative that captures students' interest and sparks their historical imagination.

Our title, *The American Promise,* reflects our emphasis on human agency and our conviction that American history is an unfinished story. For millions, the nation held out the promise of a better life, unfettered worship, representative government, democratic politics, and other freedoms seldom found elsewhere on the globe. But none of these promises came with guarantees. And promises fulfilled for some meant promises denied to others. As we see it, much of American history is a continuing struggle over the definition and realization of the nation's promise. Abraham Lincoln, in the midst of what he termed the "fiery trial" of the Civil War, pronounced the nation "the last best hope of Earth." That hope, kept alive by countless sacrifices, has been marred by compromises, disappointments, and denials, but it lives still. Ideally, *The American Promise,* Second Edition, will help students become aware of the legacy of hope bequeathed to them by previous generations of Americans stretching back nearly four centuries, a legacy that is theirs to preserve and to build upon.

Features

Because students learn best when they find a subject engaging, we have made a special effort to incorporate features that bring American history to life and make it memorable. **Chapter-opening vignettes** invite students into the narrative with vivid accounts of individuals or groups who embody each chapter's main themes. Vignettes new to this edition include Pocahontas's "rescue" of John Smith, James Madison's coming of age during the American Revolution, and Nat Turner's holy war on slavery. **Two-tiered running heads** on every page remind students where the reading falls chronologically. Innovative **call-outs**—key points pulled from the main narrative and set in larger type—catch the student's eye and highlight the text's narrative power. At the close of each chapter, strengthened **conclusions** revisit central ideas and provide a bridge to the next chapter; annotated **chronologies** review the key events and developments explored in the chapter; and extensive **bibliographies,** updated to include recent studies, provide students with detailed suggestions for reading and research beyond the boundaries of the textbook. We have retained the well-received **appendices,** adding to our comprehensive collection of reference materials such important documents as the Articles of Confederation, the Seneca Falls Resolution, the Confederate Constitution, and Martin Luther King Jr.'s "I Have a Dream" speech; we have also expanded the section on research resources to include more information on Internet sites. Throughout the text **cross-references to the new Online Study Guide** encourage mastery of the text material and development of critical-thinking skills.

An enriched array of special features reinforces the narrative and offers teachers more points of departure for assignments and discussion. By adding new selections to the feature program, we now provide in every chapter two distinctive special features that captivate students' attention while helping them understand that history is both a body of knowledge and an ongoing process of investigation. **Documenting the American Promise** features (formerly "Texts in Historical Context") combine three or four primary documents that dramatize the human dimension of major events and controversies with brief interpretive commentary. For this edition we nearly doubled the number of primary-source selections, adding such topics as "King Philip Considers Christianity" and "The Destruction of the Tea." Questions for Analysis and Debate now follow the documents to help students analyze and squeeze meaning from primary sources. Illustrated **Historical Questions** pose and interpret specific questions of continuing interest so as to demonstrate the depth and variety of possible answers, thereby countering the belief of many beginning students that historians simply gather facts and string them together into a chronological narrative. **The Promise of Technology** features (formerly "Technology in America") examine the ramifications—positive and negative—of technological innovations in American society and culture. We have revised substantially all these illustrated essays to provide additional context and analysis, and again, we have nearly doubled the number of topics to in-

clude such significant technologies as the cultivation of corn, the telegraph, the cotton gin, and the daguerreotype.

We take great pride as well in our full-color design and rich art program. We have preserved the **award-winning design** and added many new **illustrations** to make *The American Promise* a visual feast. In all, more than 450 images, many in full color and all large enough to study in detail, reinforce and extend the narrative. To emphasize visually the text's sustained treatment of Western history, all chapters offer one or more images of the West. An illustration accompanies each chapter-opening vignette, providing a visual supplement to the narrative portrait that opens every chapter. All pictures are contemporaneous with the period of the chapter, with **comprehensive captions** that draw students into active engagement with the images and help them unpack the layers of meaning. Full-page **chapter-opening artifacts** combine with many other illustrations of artifacts to emphasize the importance of material culture in the study of the past.

Finally, we have extended and expanded our highly regarded **map program** to offer the most effective set of maps available in a survey text. Each chapter offers, on average, four **full-size maps** showing major developments in a wide range of areas, from environmental and technological issues to political, social, cultural, and diplomatic matters. New maps reflect this edition's increased attention to Native American peoples and to a sustained continental perspective. Each chapter includes as well two or three new **"spot maps,"** small, single-concept maps embedded in pertinent passages of the narrative to increase students' grasp of crucial issues. Unique to our text, the spot maps highlight such topics as ancient California, Pontiac's rebellion, the Haitian revolution, the Vicksburg campaign, and Pullman's company town. In addition, critical-thinking map exercises—one per chapter—combine for an **embedded map workbook.** Another unique feature is our **mini-atlas,** a series of full-color maps at the end of each volume that reveals the changing cartography of America and its role in the world.

Textual Changes

A new edition of a textbook is cause for celebration, for it proudly announces the successful reception of the previous edition. But as authors, we found little time for complacency, for we welcomed this opportunity to reconsider the original text, to take stock of what worked and what could be improved. In addition to the many changes already mentioned, we made several major revisions in organization and coverage.

To mesh better with most course calendars, we reduced the number of chapters from sixteen to fifteen, in the process highlighting a stronger thematic development. Specifically, coverage of ancient America now appears in a refashioned and richly illustrated prologue, to show students how and why the discussion of this crucial but obscured history differs from the historical narrative that follows in the remainder of the book. Discussion of antebellum society has been reorganized and revised to ensure a smooth, unified narrative. Throughout the text we have incorporated the most important recent scholarship, as reflected in chapter bibliographies.

Shortening the text by 15 percent permitted us to eliminate excessive political detail and to achieve a clearer, more focused narrative. To provide an even more dynamic and memorable narrative while reinforcing the text's central theme, we expanded the number of historical actors whose interpretations of "the American promise"—sometimes shared, often competing—drove historical change. More succinct coverage of politics also permitted us to expand discussion of cultural and social topics such as the diversity of West Africa, the experience of Native Americans, and Western history. We have also made an effort to better place American history in a global context. Discussions of early modern Europe's westward expansion and the Haitian revolution, for example, strengthen the text's balanced, braided coverage, contributing to our effort to provide the introductory classroom the most teachable and readable text available.

Supplements

Thoroughly revised to reflect changes in the new edition, our comprehensive collection of print and electronic supplements provides a wide range of resources for students and teachers. We are especially pleased to welcome the groundbreaking Online Study Guide to our broad and integrated program of teaching and learning.

For Students

Reading the American Past: Selected Historical Documents, **Second Edition.** This highly regarded primary-source collection, edited by Michael Johnson (Johns Hopkins University), one of the authors of *The American Promise,* complements the textbook by offering 4 or 5 documents for each chapter. The new edition provides a host of compelling features while retaining its low cost and brevity: a rich selection of over 125 documents (one-quarter of them new to this edition), balancing accounts by well-known figures with the voices of ordinary people; a wide array of sources that vividly illustrate the diversity of materials with which historians work; and user-friendly editorial apparatus such as chapter introductions, headnotes, questions, and an Introduction for Students on the goals and methods of source analysis.

Study Guide. For each chapter, this essential supplement for students, prepared by Rachel Standish (Foothill College), offers a summary; an annotated chronology followed by multiple-choice questions; a term-matching exercise; multiple-choice and short-answer questions; and map, illustration, and source exercises that help students synthesize the material they have learned as well as understand the skills historians use to make sense of the past. Answers for all exercises are provided, with cross-references to relevant discussion in the textbook.

Online Study Guide **www.bedfordstmartins .com/tap.** For each chapter, our free Online Study

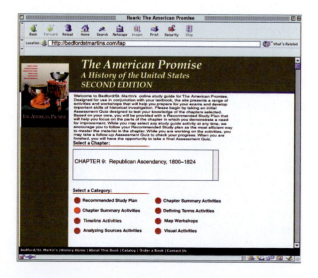

Guide offers an initial multiple-choice test that allows students to assess their comprehension of the material and a Recommended Study Plan that suggests specific exercises on the subject areas students still need to master. Two follow-up multiple-choice tests per chapter help students judge their command of the material. Additional exercises encourage students to think about chapter themes as well as help them develop skills of analysis. Results of multiple-choice tests can be e-mailed to instructors.

The Bedford Series in History and Culture. Over fifty American titles in this highly praised series combine first-rate scholarship, historical narrative, and important primary documents for undergraduate courses. Each book is brief, inexpensive, and focused on a specific topic or period. Package discounts are available.

Historians at Work Series. Brief enough for a single assignment yet substantive enough to provoke thoughtful discussion, each volume in this series combines the best thinking about an important historical issue with helpful learning aids. Selections by distinguished historians, each with a differing perspective, provide a unique structure within which to examine a single question. With headnotes and questions to guide their reading and the complete original footnotes, students are able to engage in discussion that captures the intellectual excitement of historical research and interpretation. Package discounts are available.

For Instructors

Instructor's Resource Manual. This popular manual by Sarah E. Gardner (Mercer University) offers extensive information for each chapter in the textbook: outlines of chapter themes and topics, lecture and discussion strategies, multiple-choice questions for quizzing, video and film resources, and advice on outside readings. The new edition offers as well suggestions on how to incorporate all the supplements to *The American Promise,* including the volumes in the Bedford Series relevant to each chapter, into teaching plans; "Using the Internet" exercises that reinforce and extend the text; and a wealth of practical offerings for first-time teaching assistants, ranging from suggestions on running discussion sections and designing assignments to advice on dealing with difficult students.

Online Instructor's Resource Manual www .bedfordstmartins.com/tap. For each chapter in the textbook, the Online Instructor's Resource Manual provides chapter outlines; lecture and discussion strategies; suggestions on how to incorporate all the supplements to *The American Promise,* including relevant volumes in the Bedford Series, into teaching plans; multiple-choice questions for quizzing; advice on outside readings; "Using the Internet" exercises, with links; and video and film resources. In addition, the Online Instructor's Manual offers annotated Web links for each chapter, PowerPoint slides for lectures, syllabus hosting, and the ability to track student work.

Test Bank. This thoroughly revised test bank by Norman C. McLeod (Dixie State College) and Valerie Hinton (Richland College) includes for each chapter in the text fifty multiple-choice questions (ranked as easy, medium, or difficult), an exercise in which students match important terms with definitions or examples, a chronology exercise, ten short-answer questions, four essay questions, and a two-part map exercise. Answers for objective questions are provided.

Computerized Test Bank CD-ROM for Windows or Macintosh provides easy-to-use software to create and administer tests on paper or over a network. Instructors can generate exams and quizzes from the print test bank or write their own. A grade-management function helps keep track of student progress.

Map Transparencies. Full-color transparencies of all full-size maps in the text help instructors present the materials and teach students important map-reading skills.

Presentation Manager Pro. This CD offers all the maps and chapter-opening artifacts as well as numerous other illustrations from the text in an electronic format designed to enhance class presentations. Extended captions for many of the maps and artifacts provide additional background information as well as suggestions for discussion.

Using the Bedford Series in the U.S. History Survey. This short guide by Scott Hovey (Boston University) gives practical suggestions for using more than sixty volumes from the Bedford Series with a core text in the survey classroom. The guide not only supplies links between the text and the supplements but also provides ideas for starting discussions focused on a single primary-source volume.

Map Central **www.bedfordstmartins.com /mapcentral.** Bedford/St. Martin's is proud to announce Map Central, a database of the more than 450 maps that appear in *The American Promise* and its other history survey texts. Designed to help instructors create more effective lecture presentations, Map Central is easily searchable by specific chapter or by keyword. Maps are in full color and downloadable for use in PowerPoint or other presentation software.

Videos. Available to all adopters of the text are segments drawn from the award-winning telecourse "Shaping America," developed and distributed by the LeCroy Center for Educational Telecommunications, Dallas County Community College District. Bedford/St. Martin's is proud to announce that *The American Promise: To 1877,* Second Edition, has been selected for use in this distinguished long-distance learning program.

Acknowledgments

We gratefully acknowledge all of the helpful suggestions that have come from those who have read and taught the first edition of *The American Promise,* and we hope that our many classroom collaborators will see their influence in this revision. In particular, we wish to thank the talented scholars and teachers who gave generously of their time and knowledge to review our manuscript; their critiques and suggestions have contributed greatly to the published work: Robert Allison, *Suffolk University;* Edward Baptist, *University of Miami;* Manuel Callahan, *University of Texas;* Marvin Cann, *Lander University;* Robert Cormier, *Shrewsbury High School;* Dolores Davison Peterson, *Foothill College;* Randy Finley, *Georgia Perimeter College;* Valerie Hinton, *Richland College;* Jill Lepore, *Boston College;* Barbara

Loomis, *San Francisco State University;* Norman Love, *El Paso Community College;* Joanne Maypole, *Front Range Community College;* Tom Nierman, *University of Kansas;* Robert Olwell, *University of Texas at Austin;* Terry Perrin, *Austin Community College;* Peggy Renner, *Glendale Community College;* James Schick, *Pittsburgh State University;* Michael Searles, *Augusta State College;* Rebecca Shoemaker, *Indiana State University;* Rachel Standish, *Foothill College;* Thomas Winn, *Austin Peay State University.*

A project as complex as this requires the talents of many individuals. First, the authors would like to acknowledge our families for their support, forbearance, and toleration of our textbook responsibilities. Pembroke Herbert and Sandi Rygiel of Picture Research Consultants, Inc., contributed their imagination and research to make possible the extraordinary illustration program. Thanks are also due to Louise Townsend, whose accomplished editing greatly improved the manuscript.

We would also like to thank the many people at Bedford/St. Martin's who have been crucial to this project. No one has done more than our friend, Senior Editor Elizabeth M. Welch, whose intelligence, knowledge of American history, commitment to excellence, and unfailing good judgment guided our every step. We thank as well Patricia Rossi, Publisher for History, and Jenna Bookin Barry, Marketing Manager, for their tireless efforts in marketing the book. With great skill and professionalism, Ara Salibian, Production Editor, pulled all the pieces together with the assistance of Arthur Johnson, Coleen O'Hanley, and Kerri Cardone, as well as the invaluable guidance of Project Consultant Tina Samaha. Managing Editor Elizabeth Schaaf, Assistant Managing Editor John Amburg, and Senior Production Supervisor Catherine Hetmansky oversaw production of the book, and Sarah Barrash and Brianna Germain helped with countless editorial tasks. Our original copyeditor, Barbara Flanagan, returned to the project, and her sharp eye improved our best efforts. Charles H. Christensen, President, and Joan E. Feinberg, Editorial Director, have taken a personal interest in *The American Promise* from the start and have guided all its editions through every stage of development.

ABOUT THE AUTHORS

James L. Roark

Born in Eunice, Louisiana, and raised in the West, James L. Roark received his B.A. from the University of California, Davis, in 1963 and his Ph.D. from Stanford University in 1973. His dissertation won the Allan Nevins Prize. He has taught at the University of Nigeria, Nsukka; the University of Nairobi, Kenya; the University of Missouri, St. Louis; and, since 1983, Emory University, where he is Samuel Candler Dobbs Professor of American History. In 1993, he received the Emory Williams Distinguished Teaching Award. He has written *Masters without Slaves: Southern Planters in the Civil War and Reconstruction* (1977). With Michael P. Johnson, he is author of *Black Masters: A Free Family of Color in the Old South* (1984) and editor of *No Chariot Let Down: Charleston's Free People of Color on the Eve of the Civil War* (1984). He has received research assistance from the American Philosophical Society, the National Endowment for the Humanities, and the Gilder Lehrman Institute of American History. Active in the Organization of American Historians and the Southern Historical Association, he is also a fellow of the Society of American Historians. He will be the Pitt Professor of American Institutions at Cambridge University for 2001–2002.

Michael P. Johnson

Born and raised in Ponca City, Oklahoma, Michael P. Johnson studied at Knox College in Galesburg, Illinois, where he received a B.A. in 1963, and at Stanford University in Palo Alto, California, earning a Ph.D. in 1973. He is currently professor of history at Johns Hopkins University in Baltimore, having previously taught at the University of California, Irvine, San Jose State University, and LeMoyne (now LeMoyne-Owen) College in Memphis. He is the author, co-author, or editor of *Toward a Patriarchal Republic: The Secession of Georgia* (1977); *Black Masters: A Free Family of Color in the Old South* (1984); *No Chariot Let Down: Charleston's Free People of Color on the Eve of the Civil War* (1984); *Reading the American Past: Selected Historical Documents* (1998); and *Abraham Lincoln, Slavery, and the Civil War: Selected Speeches and Writings* (2000); and articles that have appeared in the *William and Mary Quarterly,* the *Journal of Southern History, Labor History,* the *New York Review of Books,* the *New Republic,* the *Nation,* and other journals. Johnson has been awarded research fellowships by the American Council of Learned Societies, the National Endowment for the Humanities, and the Center for Advanced Study in the Behavioral Sciences. He directed a National Endowment for the Humanities Summer Seminar for College Teachers and has been honored with the University of California, Irvine, Academic Senate Distinguished Teaching Award and the University of California, Irvine, Alumni Association Outstanding Teaching Award. He is an active member of the American Historical Association, the Organization of American Historians, and the Southern Historical Association.

Patricia Cline Cohen

Born in Ann Arbor, Michigan, and raised in Palo Alto, California, Patricia Cline Cohen earned a B.A. at the University of Chicago in 1968 and a Ph.D. at the University of California, Berkeley in 1977. In 1976, she joined the history faculty at the University of California at Santa Barbara. Cohen has written *A Calculating People: The Spread of Numeracy in Early America* (1982; reissued 1999) and *The Murder of Helen Jewett: The Life and Death of a Prostitute in Nineteenth-Century New York* (1998). She has also published articles on numeracy, prostitution, sexual crime, and murder in journals including the *Journal of Women's History, Radical History Review,* the *William and Mary Quarterly,* and the *NWSA Journal.* Her scholarly work has received support from the National Endowment for the Humanities, the National Humanities Center, the Mellon Foundation, the American Antiquarian Society, the University of California President's Fellowship in the Humanities, the Schlesinger Library, and the Newberry Library. She sits on the council for the Omohundro Institute of Early American History and Culture and on the advisory council of the Society for the History of the Early American Republic. She has served as chair of the Women's Studies Program and as acting dean of the humanities and fine arts at the University of California at Santa Barbara.

Sarah Stage

Sarah Stage was born in Davenport, Iowa, and received a B.A. from the University of Iowa in 1966 and a Ph.D. in American studies from Yale University in 1975. She has taught U.S. history for more than twenty-five years at Williams College and the University of California, Riverside. Currently she is professor of Women's Studies at Arizona State University West, in Phoenix. Her books include *Female Complaints: Lydia Pinkham and the Business of Women's Medicine* (1979) and *Rethinking Home Economics: Women and the History of a Profession* (1997). Among the fellowships she has received are the Rockefeller Foundation Humanities Fellowship, the American Association of University Women dissertation fellowship, a fellowship from the Charles Warren Center for the Study of History at Harvard University, and the University of California President's Fellowship in the Humanities. She is at work on a book entitled *Women and the Progressive Impulse in American Politics, 1890–1914.*

Alan Lawson

Born in Providence, Rhode Island, Alan Lawson received his B.A. from Brown University in 1955 and his Ph.D. from the University of Michigan in 1967. Since winning the Allan Nevins Prize for his dissertation, Lawson has served on the faculties of the University of California, Irvine, Smith College, and, currently, Boston College. He has written *The Failure of Independent Liberalism* (1971) and coedited *From Revolution to Republic* (1976). While completing the forthcoming *The New Deal and the Mobilization of Progressive Experience,* he has published book chapters and essays on political economy and the cultural legacy of the New Deal. He has served as editor of the *Review of Education and the Intellectual History Newsletter* and contributed articles to those journals as well as to the *History Education Quarterly.* He has been active in the field of American studies as director of the Boston College American studies program and as a contributor to the *American Quarterly.* Under the auspices of the United States Information Agency, Lawson has been coordinator and lecturer for programs to instruct faculty from foreign nations in the state of American historical scholarship and teaching.

Susan M. Hartmann

Professor of history and women's studies at Ohio State University, Susan M. Hartmann received her B.A. from Washington University in 1961 and her Ph.D. from the University of Missouri in 1966. After specializing in the political economy of the post–World War II period and publishing *Truman and the 80th Congress* (1971), she expanded her interests to the field of women's history, publishing many articles and three books: *The Home Front and Beyond: American Women in the 1940s* (1982); *From Margin to Mainstream: American Women and Politics since 1960* (1989); and *The Other Feminists: Activists in the Liberal Establishment* (1998). She has won research fellowships from the Rockefeller Foundation, the National Endowment for the Humanities, and the American Council of Learned Societies. Hartmann has taught at the University of Missouri, St. Louis, and Boston University, and she has lectured on American history in Greece, France, Austria, Germany, Australia, New Zealand, and Nepal. She has served on book and article award committees of the American Historical Association, the Organization of American Historians, and the American Studies Association. At Ohio State she has served as director of women's studies, and in 1995 she won the Exemplary Faculty Award in the College of Humanities.

THE AMERICAN PROMISE

A HISTORY OF THE UNITED STATES

Second Edition

OLMEC RITUAL FIGURES

Ancient American artifacts sometimes portray human forms that probably bore a strong resemblance to the people for whom they were made. This astonishing group of Olmec men, crafted and buried between 900 and 600 B.C. in the ceremonial center at La Venta in what is now southern Mexico, is shown exactly as it was found when archaeologists excavated it in 1955. The men all exhibit cranial deformation, probably common among Olmecs of the era; it was created by wrapping tight bindings around the skulls of infants and children. These men seem to be engaged in an important ritual. The sandstone figure with his back to the upright stones, or celts, observes four men filing in front of him from his right, while eleven men of differing heights and distinctive physiognomies stand in a semicircle looking on. The significance of this ceremony is documented by its haunting artistry and careful burial, but exactly what the ceremony meant remains utterly mysterious, like so much else about ancient Americans.

Museo Nacional de Antropologia, Mexico City.

PROLOGUE:
ANCIENT AMERICA

Before 1492

I N AUGUST 1908, A VIOLENT STORM dumped thirteen inches of rain near Folsom, New Mexico, causing a devastating flood. Afterward, George McJunkin, the manager of the Crowfoot Ranch near Folsom, rode out to mend fences and to look for missing cattle. An African American, McJunkin had been born a slave in Texas forty years earlier and had been riding horses since he was a boy. After he became free at the end of the Civil War in 1865, McJunkin worked as a cowboy for ranchers in Colorado and New Mexico, becoming the Crowfoot manager in 1891. As he surveyed the damage done by the recent storm, McJunkin noticed that the floodwater had gouged Wild Horse Arroyo eight or nine feet deeper than ever before, exposing a deposit of stark white bones in the bank of the gulch. Curious, he dismounted and chipped away at the deposit until he uncovered an entire fossilized bone. Since the bone was considerably larger than the parched skeletons of range cattle and buffalo, McJunkin took it back to the ranch to see if it could be identified.

In 1912, McJunkin met a white man named Carl Schwachheim, a blacksmith in Raton, New Mexico, who shared his curiosity about fossils, and the two men became friends. McJunkin told Schwachheim about the fossil deposit—what he called the "Bone Pit"—but Schwachheim could not get out to the Crowfoot Ranch to take a look for himself. Ten years later, a few months after McJunkin's death, Schwachheim and some friends finally drove to the Bone Pit, dug out enough bones to fill a gunnysack, and brought them back to Raton. But they could not identify animals that had such big bones.

In 1926, when Schwachheim delivered cattle to the stockyards in Denver, he took some of the old bones to the Denver Museum of Natural History and showed them to J. D. Figgins, a paleontologist who was an expert on fossils of ancient animals. Figgins immediately recognized the significance of the fossils and a few months later began an excavation of the Folsom Bone Pit that revolutionized knowledge about the first Americans.

When Figgins began his dig at Folsom, archaeologists (individuals who study the artifacts of prehistoric peoples) believed that Native Americans had arrived relatively recently in the Western Hemisphere, probably no more than three or four thousand years earlier when, experts assumed, they had paddled small boats across the icy waters of the Bering Strait from what is now Siberia. At Folsom, Figgins learned that the bones McJunkin had first spotted belonged to twenty-three giant bison, a species known to have been extinct for at least 10,000 years. Far more startling, Figgins found nineteen flint projectile points (Folsom points, they have since been called) associated with the bones, proof that human beings had been alive at the same time as the giant bison. One flint point remained stuck

GEORGE MCJUNKIN
This photo shows McJunkin a few years after he discovered the Folsom site, but about fifteen years before anyone understood the significance of his find. He appears here in his work clothes on horseback, as he probably was when he made the discovery. The fossilized bones he discovered belonged to an extinct bison species that was much larger than modern bison; the horns of the ancient animal often spanned six feet, wide enough for McJunkin's horse to have stood sideways between the horns.
Eastern New Mexico University, Blackwater Draw Site, Portales, New Mexico 88130.

between two ribs of a giant bison, just where a Stone Age hunter had plunged it more than 10,000 years earlier. No longer could anyone doubt that human beings had inhabited North America for at least ten millennia.

The Folsom discovery sparked other major finds of ancient artifacts that continue to this day. Since the 1930s, archaeologists have tried to reconstruct the history of ancient Americans, making connections between the hunters who killed giant bison with flint points, their descendants who built southwestern pueblos and eastern burial mounds, and *their* descendants who encountered Christopher Columbus in 1492. Although the story they have assembled is incomplete and controversial, scholars have nonetheless learned enough about ancient Americans to bring into focus who they were, where they came from, and some basic features of their history in the thousands of years before that moment in 1492 when some of them stood on the beach of a small island in the Caribbean and watched Columbus and his men row ashore.

Archaeology and History

Archaeologists and historians share the desire to learn about people who lived in the past, but they usually employ different methods to obtain information. Both archaeologists and historians study artifacts as clues to the activities and ideas of the humans who created them. They concentrate, however, on different kinds of artifacts. Archaeologists tend to focus on physical objects such as bones, stones, pots, baskets, jewelry, textiles, clothing, graves, and buildings. Historians direct their attention mostly to writings, which encompass personal and private jottings such as diary entries and love letters, official and public pronouncements such as laws and speeches, as well as an enormous variety of other documents such as court records, censuses, business ledgers, newspapers, books, pamphlets, and even laundry lists. Although historians are interested in other artifacts and archaeologists do not neglect written sources if they exist, the characteristic concentration of historians on writings and

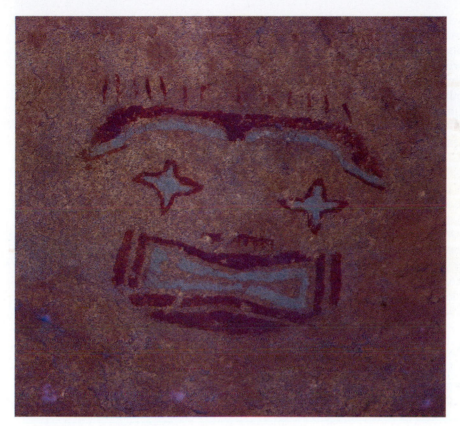

JORNADA PICTOGRAPH MASK
This mask and hundreds of others were painted on stones near El Paso, Texas, by artists of the Jornada people, a branch of the Mogollon culture, sometime between A.D. 900 and 1400. Ancient Americans had frequented this site for millennia because the large number of depressions in the hard rock served as reservoirs for rainwater. Perhaps the mask somehow signified a link between the Jornada and the thirst-slaking water.
Tom Todsen/Hueco Tanks State Historic Park.

archaeologists on other physical objects denotes a rough cultural and chronological boundary between the human beings studied by the two groups of scholars, a boundary marked by the use of writing.

A system of symbols that record spoken language, writing originated among ancient peoples in China, Egypt, and Central America about 8,000 years ago, within the most recent 3 percent of the 300 millennia that modern human beings (*Homo sapiens*) have existed. Writing came into use even later in most other places in the world. The ancient Americans who inhabited North America in 1492, for example, possessed many forms of symbolic representation, but not writing. The people who lived during the millennia before writing were biologically nearly identical to people today; after all, their DNA was the template for ours. But they differed from us in many other ways, among them in not using writing to communicate across space and time. The long era they inhabited before the invention of writing is often labeled *prehistory,* a term that is both revealing and somewhat misleading.

To the degree that *prehistory* suggests that these ancient people lived in some sort of twilight zone before human history began, it is misleading. They certainly had a history, both individually and collectively. They moved across the face of the globe; they invented more spoken languages than we will ever know; they learned to survive and even to thrive in almost every natural environment; they chose and honored leaders; they traded, warred, and worshiped; and, above all, they learned from and taught each other, not just old ways but, little by little, surprising new ways. Nonetheless, much of what we would like to know about their history remains unknown because it took place before the history that has been recorded in writing. The term *prehistory* reveals our muted knowledge of their history caused by their use of oral rather than written communication. They spoke to each other, but, without writing, time forever muffled their words and thus their history.

Archaeologists specialize in learning about people whose history was not documented in writing. They study the millions of artifacts created by these people, trying to decipher what the objects can tell us about their lives. To extract meanings from life-less objects, archaeologists also examine the natural environment that existed when the artifacts were made and used. By scrutinizing soil, geological strata, pollen, climate, and other environmental features, they attempt to reconstruct the outlines of the history of ancient peoples. But much of their history remains unknown and unknowable. Countless artifacts that would help disclose their history rotted away millennia ago while others probably still exist but have not yet been discovered. Above all, the absence of written sources means that ancient human beings remain anonymous. They doubtless had names, but nobody now knows or can know what they were. No documents chronicle their births and deaths, comings and goings, victories and defeats. No diaries chart their daily lives. No letters record their thoughts and emotions. No songs or stories capture their musings about who

they were and what was important to them. Despite these silences, archaeologists have learned to make ancient artifacts tell a great deal about the people who made them.

This prologue to a history of the United States relies on the work of archaeologists to sketch a brief overview of ancient America. Calling the long history of ancient Americans a *prologue* reflects our present-mindedness, an outgrowth of our desire to understand the origins and development of our own society over the last five centuries or so. Ancient Americans surely did not consider their history a prologue to a future that included us. They resided in North America for thousands of years before Europeans arrived. They created societies and cultures of amazing diversity and complexity. But because they did not use written records, it is impossible to identify the individuals and groups who experienced and contributed to the many changes that occurred in their long history. Nor can we know

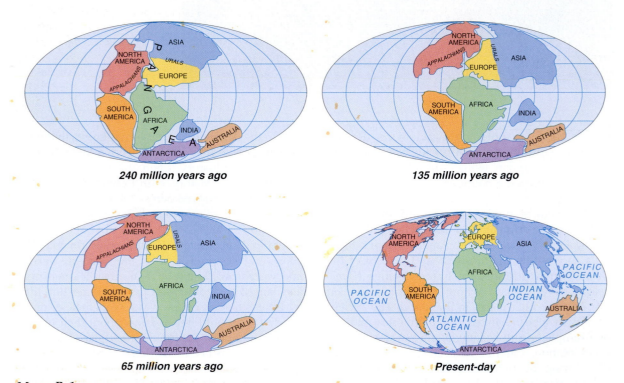

240 million years ago

135 million years ago

65 million years ago

Present-day

MAP P.1

Continental Drift

Massive geological forces separated North and South America from other continents eons before human beings evolved in Africa in the last 1.5 million years. This continental drift explains why human life developed elsewhere on the planet for hundreds of thousands of years before the first person entered the Western Hemisphere during the last fifteen thousand years.

with any certainty what they thought about themselves or one another. Although their history cannot be reconstructed with the detail and certainty made possible by written documents, their remarkable longevity and creativity make it far preferable to abbreviate and oversimplify their history than to ignore it.

The First Americans

Human beings existed elsewhere in the world long before they reached the Western Hemisphere. The basic reason for the prolonged absence of humans from the Western Hemisphere is that millions of years before human beings came into existence North and South America became detached from the gigantic continent scientists now call Pangaea. Beginning about 240 million years ago, powerful forces deep within the earth slowly pushed the continents apart to approximately their present positions (Map P.1). This process of continental drift encircled the land of the Western Hemisphere with large oceans and isolated it from the other continents, long before human beings (*Homo erectus*) evolved in Africa about 1.5 million years ago. Hundreds of thousands of years later, *Homo sapiens* migrated out of Africa and into Europe and Asia. For almost 95 percent of the time *Homo sapiens* existed, no one set foot in the Western Hemisphere.

Asian Origins

Two major developments made it possible for human beings to reach the Western Hemisphere. First, humans successfully adapted to the frigid environment near the Arctic Circle. Second, changes in the earth's climate reconnected North America to Asia.

By about 25,000 years ago, people had learned to use bone needles to sew animal skins into warm clothing that permitted humans to become permanent residents of extremely cold regions like northeastern Siberia. Today the Bering Strait, a body of water about sixty miles wide, separates easternmost Siberia from westernmost Alaska. But during the last great global cold spell—termed by scientists the Wisconsin glaciation, which endured from about 80,000 years ago to about 10,000 years ago—snow piled up in glaciers that did not melt, causing the sea level to drop as much as 350 feet below

The Bering Strait

its current level. The seafloor that is now submerged 120 feet below the surface of the Bering Strait was then dry land, forming what is often called a "land bridge" between Asian Siberia and American Alaska. However, the exposed land was not a narrow passageway. Instead, it was a region about a thousand miles wide that scientists call Beringia.

For most of the Wisconsin glacial period, Beringia stood above sea level. Grasses and small shrubs covered much of the land and supported herds of mammoth, bison, and horses as well as numerous smaller animals. Siberian hunters presumably roamed into Beringia for thousands of years in search of game animals. Archaeologists speculate that hunters traveled in small bands of perhaps twenty-five people. How many such bands arrived in North America before water once again covered Beringia will never be known. It may have been as few as one or two or three. When they arrived is hotly debated by experts. The first migrants probably arrived sometime after 15,000 years ago. Scattered and inconclusive evidence suggests that the first Americans may have arrived a few thousand years earlier.

Archaeologists refer to these first migrants and their descendants for the next few millennia as Paleo-Indians. Their Asian origins seem almost certain. Siberians hunted large game, and Beringia provided an attractive hunting ground that reached all the way to the Western Hemisphere, a wide avenue that existed for no other humans at the time. Some archaeologists have speculated that the first migrants may have come across the South Pacific from Polynesia or across the North Atlantic from Europe, but no physical evidence discovered so far conclusively supports such views. Furthermore, Native Americans today still share certain obvious physical characteristics of Asians, including straight black hair, light brown skin, relatively sparse facial and body hair, and incisor teeth that often have shovel-shaped indentations on their inner surface. Detailed analyses of Native American languages and of certain blood proteins provide additional compelling evidence of Asian origins.

FIGURE P.1

Human Habitation of the Western Hemisphere
This clock face illustrates the long history of ancient Americans. If the total period of human life in the New World is converted from millennia to a twelve-hour clock, then all history since Columbus occupies only the last half-hour. Ancient American history makes up the first eleven and a half hours.

Paleo-Indian Hunters

When humans first arrived in the Western Hemisphere, massive glaciers covered most of Canada. A narrow corridor not entirely obstructed by ice ran along the eastern side of the Canadian Rockies, and most archaeologists believe that Paleo-Indians migrated through it in pursuit of game. They may also have traveled along the coast in small boats, hopscotching from one desirable landing spot to another. At the southern edge of the glaciers, Paleo-Indians entered a hunters' paradise. North, Central, and South America teemed with wildlife that had never before confronted wily two-legged predators armed with razor-sharp spears. The abundance of game presumably made hunting relatively easy. Ample food permitted the Paleo-Indian population to grow. Within a thousand years or so, Paleo-Indians had reached the southern tip of South America and virtually everywhere else in the Western Hemisphere.

Paleo-Indians used a distinctively shaped spearhead known as a Clovis point, named for the place in New Mexico where it was first excavated. The discovery of Clovis points throughout North and Central America in sites dated between 11,500 and 11,000 years ago is powerful evidence that these nomadic hunters shared a common ancestry and way of life. The Paleo-Indians who used Clovis points to kill big animals probably also hunted smaller animals. Archaeologists have discovered a few sites that appear to predate the Clovis era and indicate that the inhabitants ate both small game and plants. But most of the artifacts that have survived from this era indicate that Paleo-Indians specialized in hunting big mammals. One mammoth kill supplied meat for weeks or, if dried, for months. In addition, the hide could be used for clothing and shelter. Bones and tusks could be used to erect a framework for small, hide-covered dwellings, fashioned into a variety of useful tools, or even burned for fuel.

About 11,000 years ago Paleo-Indians confronted a major crisis. The big-game animals they hunted became extinct. Scientists are not completely certain why the extinction occurred, although the changing environment probably triggered it. About this time the Wisconsin glacial period came to an end, glaciers melted, and sea levels rose. Large mammals presumably had difficulty adapting to the warmer climate. Many archaeologists also believe that Paleo-Indian hunters contributed to the New World extinctions by killing animals more rapidly than they could reproduce.

About 11,000 years ago Paleo-Indians confronted a major crisis. The big-game animals they hunted became extinct.

Paleo-Indians adapted to the big-game extinctions by making at least two important changes in

WOOLLY MAMMOTH SKELETON
This reconstructed skeleton of a woolly mammoth demonstrates the massive size of animals that Paleo-Indians hunted with stone-tipped spears. What hunting techniques might Paleo-Indians have used to kill such an enormous and dangerous beast?
Smithsonian Institution, Washington, D.C.

their way of life. First, throughout the hemisphere hunters necessarily focused their attention on smaller animals. Second, Paleo-Indians devoted more energy to foraging, that is, to collecting wild plant foods such as roots, seeds, nuts, berries, and fruits. When Paleo-Indians made these changes, the apparent uniformity of the big-game-oriented Clovis culture* was replaced by great cultural diversity.

---

*The word *culture* is used here to connote what is commonly called "way of life." It refers not only to how a group of people supplied themselves with food and shelter but also to their family relationships, social groupings, religious ideas, and other features of their way of life. For most prehistoric cultures—as for the Clovis people—more is known about food and shelter because of the artifacts that have survived. Ancient Americans' ideas, assumptions, hopes, dreams, and fantasies were undoubtedly important, but we know very little about them.

Paleo-Indians adapted to the many natural environments throughout the hemisphere, ranging from icy tundra to steamy jungles.

Post-Clovis adaptations to local environments led to the astounding variety of Native American cultures that existed when Columbus arrived in 1492. By then, more than three hundred major tribes and hundreds of lesser groups inhabited North America alone; hundreds more lived in Central and South America. These people spoke different languages, practiced different religions, lived in different dwellings, followed different subsistence strategies, and observed different rules of kinship and inheritance. Hundreds of other ancient American cultures had disappeared or transformed themselves as their members constantly adapted to changing environmental conditions. A full account of those changes and the cultural diversity they created is beyond the scope of this textbook. But we cannot ignore the most important changes and adaptations made by ancient Americans during the last eleven millennia.

Archaic Hunters and Gatherers

Archaeologists use the term *Archaic* to describe the many different hunting and gathering cultures that descended from Paleo-Indians. *Archaic* also refers to the long period of time when those cultures dominated the history of ancient America, roughly from 8000 B.C. to somewhere between 2000 and 1000 B.C. Although the cultural and the chronological boundaries of the Archaic era are not sharply defined, the term *Archaic* is still meaningful. It describes the important era in the history of ancient America that followed the Paleo-Indian big-game hunters and preceded the development of agriculture. It also denotes a hunter-gatherer way of life that persisted throughout most of North America well into the era of European colonization.

Like their Paleo-Indian ancestors, Archaic Indians hunted with spears; but they also took smaller game with traps, nets, and hooks. Unlike Paleo-Indians, most Archaic peoples used a variety of stone tools to prepare food from wild plants. A characteristic Archaic artifact is a grinding stone used to pulverize seeds into edible form. Most Archaic Indians migrated from place to place to harvest plants and hunt animals. They usually did not establish

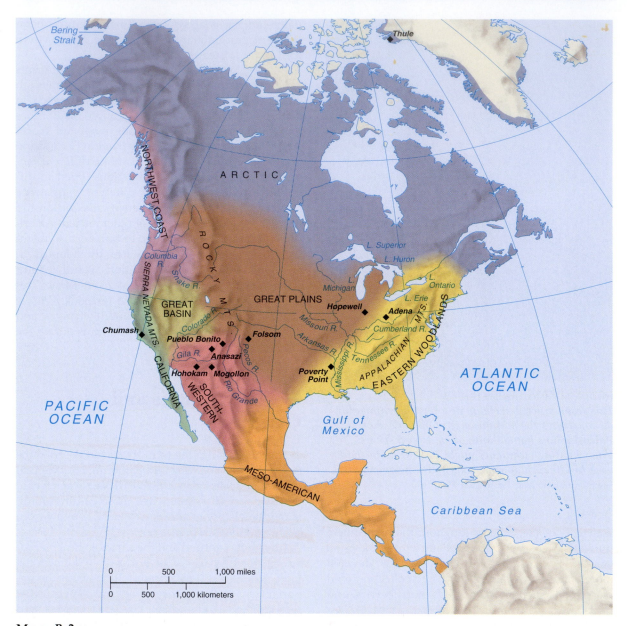

MAP P.2

Native North American Cultures
Environmental conditions defined the boundaries of the broad zones of cultural similarity among ancient North Americans. Using the map, try to specify the crucial environmental features that set the boundaries of each cultural region. The topography indicated on Map P.3, "Native North Americans about 1500," may be helpful.

permanent villages, although they often returned to the same river valley or fertile meadow from year to year to take advantage of abundant food resources. In certain regions where resources were especially rich—such as California and the Pacific Northwest— permanent settlements did develop. Many Archaic groups became highly proficient basket makers in order to collect and store plant food. Above all, Archaic folk did not depend on agriculture for food. Instead, they gathered wild plants and hunted wild

26 |

animals. These general traits of Archaic peoples were expressed in distinctive ways in the major environmental regions of North America (Map P.2).

Great Plains Bison Hunters

After the extinction of mammoths and other large game, hunters began to concentrate on huge herds of bison that grazed the grassy, arid plains stretching for hundreds of miles east of the Rocky Mountains. For almost a thousand years after the big-game extinctions, Archaic Indians hunted bison with Folsom points.

Like their predecessors, Folsom hunters were nomads who moved constantly to maintain contact with their prey. Often two or three hunters from a band of several families would single out a few bison from a herd and creep up close enough to spear them. Always the hunters were on foot. The ancient horses that had once existed in the Western Hemisphere were extinct; bison hunters walked to work until Spaniards reintroduced horses to the New World in the 1500s. Bison hunters developed trapping techniques that made it easier to kill large numbers of animals. At the original Folsom site, careful study of the bones McJunkin found suggests that early one winter hunters drove bison into the arroyo and speared twenty-three of them. At many other sites, hunters stampeded large numbers of bison over cliffs, killing some and injuring others, which could then be readily dispatched by waiting hunters.

Above all, Archaic folk did not depend on agriculture for food. Instead, they gathered wild plants and hunted wild animals.

Bows and arrows reached the Great Plains from the north by about A.D. 500 and largely replaced spears, which had been the hunters' weapon of choice for millennia. Bows permitted hunters to strike an animal from farther away, and arrows made it easy to shoot repeatedly. These new weapons did not much alter the age-old techniques of bison hunting that had been developing since the Folsom era.

Great Basin Cultures

Archaic peoples in the Great Basin between the Rocky Mountains and the Sierra Nevada inhabited

FOLSOM POINT AT WILD HORSE ARROYO
In 1927, paleontologist J. D. Figgins found this spear point (subsequently named a Folsom point) at the site discovered by George McJunkin. Embedded between the fossilized ribs of a bison that had been extinct for 10,000 years, this point proved that ancient Americans had inhabited the hemisphere at least that long. The importance of this find led one paleontologist to hold up several Folsom points and proclaim, "In my hand I hold the answer to the antiquity of man in America." Although he exaggerated (since Folsom was only part of the answer), this discovery in Wild Horse Arroyo stimulated archaeologists to rethink the history of ancient Americans and to uncover fresh evidence of their many cultures.

a region of great environmental diversity. Some Great Basin Indians lived along the shores of large marshes and lakes that formed during rainy periods. Other cultures survived in the foothills of mountains between the blistering heat in the desert floor and the cold, treeless mountain heights. These broadly defined zones of habitation changed constantly depending largely on the amount of rainfall.

Great Basin hunters took deer, antelope, and sometimes bison, as well as smaller game like rabbits, rodents, and snakes. At sites near water, Great Basin peoples hunted waterfowl with well-crafted decoys made of reeds. They also ate fish of every available size and type, taking them with bone hooks as well as with nets.

Despite the variety and occasional abundance of animals, plants were the most important source of food for Great Basin peoples. Unlike animal food, plant food could be collected in large quantities and stored in baskets for long periods to protect against shortages caused by the fickle rainfall. Piñon nuts became a dietary staple for many Great Basin peoples. By diversifying their food sources and migrating to favorable locations, Great Basin peoples adapted to environmental challenges and maintained their basic hunter-gatherer way of life until long after A.D. 1492.

Pacific Coast Cultures

The richness of the natural environment made California the most densely settled area in all of ancient North America. The abundant resources of both land and ocean offered such ample food that California groups remained hunters and gatherers for hundreds of years after Europeans arrived in the Western Hemisphere. The diversity of California's environment encouraged corresponding diversity among native peoples. By A.D. 1492, the mosaic of settlements in California included about five hundred separate tribes speaking some ninety languages, each with many local dialects. No other region of comparable size in North America exhibited such cultural variety.

The Chumash, one of the many California cultures, emerged near Santa Barbara about 5,000 years ago. Comparatively plentiful food resources per-

Ancient California

mitted Chumash people to establish relatively permanent villages. Conflict frequently broke out among Chumash villages, and skeletons from burials document a notable proportion of violent deaths. Archaeologists believe that such conflicts arose in part from efforts by Chumash villages to restrict access to their valuable acorn-gathering territory. Although few other California cultures achieved the population density and cultural complexity of the Chumash, all shared the hunter-gatherer way of life and reliance on acorns as a major food source.

Another rich natural environment lay along the Pacific Northwest coast. Abundant fish and marine life permitted the ancient Americans in this region to devote substantial time and energy to activities other than hunting and gathering. After about 5,500 years ago they concentrated on catching large quantities of salmon, halibut, and other fish, which they dried to last throughout the year. With time free from the demands of food gathering, Northwest peoples developed sophisticated woodworking skills. They

OZETTE WHALE EFFIGY
This carving of a whale fin decorated with hundreds of sea otter teeth was discovered along with thousands of other artifacts of daily life at Ozette, an ancient village on the tip of the Olympic Peninsula in present-day Washington that was inundated by a catastrophic mudslide about five hundred years ago. The fin illustrates the importance of whale hunting to the residents of Ozette, who set out in canoes carrying eight men armed with harpoons to catch and kill animals weighing twenty to thirty tons.
Makah Cultural and Resource Center.

fashioned huge canoes, some big enough to hold fifty people, which they used to fish, hunt, and conduct warfare against neighboring tribes. Much of the conflict among Archaic northwesterners seems to have arisen from attempts to defend good fishing sites from incursions by outsiders.

Like the Chumash, the Northwest peoples built more or less permanent villages. They constructed large, multifamily houses from cedar planks. Beginning around A.D. 500 they adorned their houses with *totems,* elaborately carved images of animals, supernatural beings, or their own ancestors (it is possible that similar carvings were made much earlier but disintegrated in the damp climate). These carvings honored the lineage of the family clan and displayed the clan's wealth and status.

Eastern Woodland Cultures

East of the Mississippi River, Archaic peoples adapted to a forest environment that included many local variants, such as the major river valleys of the Mississippi, Ohio, Tennessee, and Cumberland; the Great Lakes region; and the Atlantic coast (see Map P.2). Throughout these diverse locales, Archaic peoples adopted basic survival strategies.

Deer were the most important prey of nearly all Woodland hunters. At one Archaic dwelling site in Tennessee, deer accounted for 90 percent of the excavated remains. In addition to food, deer supplied hides and bones that were crafted into useful items such as clothing, weapons, needles, and other tools. Like Archaic peoples elsewhere, Woodland Indians gathered edible plants, seeds, and especially nuts. Hickory nuts were the most commonly gathered plant food, but pecans, walnuts, acorns, and hazelnuts were also collected. About 4000 B.C., some Woodland groups established more or less permanent settlements of 25 to 150 people, usually near a river or lake that offered a wide variety of plant and animal resources. The existence of semipermanent settlements has permitted archaeologists to locate numerous Archaic burial sites that provide fascinating insights into the character of Woodland cultures. (See "The Promise of Technology," page P-12.) At one site in western Kentucky, which dates to about 2500 to 2000 B.C., archaeologists found enough burials to allow them to calculate that the life expectancy at birth for these Woodland people was slightly over eighteen years.

Around 2000 B.C., the Woodland cultures incorporated two important features into their basic hunter-gatherer lifestyles: agriculture and pottery. Gourds and pumpkins that originated in Mexico began to be grown in parts of Missouri and Kentucky. After the introduction of these Mexican crops, Woodland peoples began to cultivate local species such as sunflowers. It is likely that they also grew tobacco, another import from South America, since stone pipes for smoking appeared by 1500 B.C. Corn, the most important plant food in Mexico, did not become a significant food crop until more than a thousand years later. These cultivated crops added to the quantity, variety, and predictability of Woodland food sources, but they did not fundamentally alter the hunter-gatherer way of life.

Techniques for making ceramic pots probably also originated in Mexico and may have been brought north along with Mexican seeds. Pots were more durable than baskets for food preparation and storage, but they were also much heavier, probably an outgrowth of more permanent settlements. Neither pottery nor agriculture caused Woodland peoples to turn away from their basic hunter-gatherer cultures, which persisted in most areas to A.D. 1492 and beyond.

Around 2000 B.C., the Woodland cultures incorporated two important features into their basic hunter-gatherer lifestyles: agriculture and pottery.

Perhaps the most spectacular Archaic Woodland site was Poverty Point near the Mississippi River in northeastern Louisiana. The Poverty Point culture existed from about 1700 B.C. to 700 B.C. These ancient Americans constructed an enormous earthworks consisting of six concentric half-circles more than a half-mile in diameter; each ring was built of dirt piled nine feet high and twenty-five feet wide. The purpose of this huge earthworks is unknown. It may have been used for astronomical observations since it seems aligned to view the spring and fall equinoxes. The labor and organization required to build such a massive structure suggest that important ceremonies were conducted at the site. The complex may also have served as a meeting place for traders. At least a thousand people lived in dwellings near the earthworks and almost one hundred villages clustered nearby.

Weaver's Workbasket

This workbasket of a master weaver illustrates the technology of ancient American textile production. Found in a woman's grave in the Andes dating from 500 years before the arrival of Columbus, the workbasket contains tools for every stage in the process of textile production. The weaver took fiber from cotton plants or animal wool (such as llama or alpaca) and spun it into thread. For colored threads, the weaver died the fibers before spinning, using different vegetable and mineral concoctions. The pointed sticks wrapped with thread (left center) are spindles on which the weaver spun. She used the small ceramic cup to hold one end of the spindle while she twisted the fiber through her fingers to create strong, thin thread. She used the two pieces of chalk (to the right of the ceramic cup) to make a powder that lubricated her fingers to allow the thread to pass smoothly onto the spindle. Skeins of finished thread removed from their spindles are just to the left of the ceramic cup. This small workbasket contained more than 150 spindles for the many varieties of thread a master weaver made and used. The beadlike objects at the center are whorls the weaver placed on spindles to anchor the thread and for decoration; the designs on the whorls probably had spiritual meaning. On the right, above the chalk and ceramic cup, are bobbins used to pass the thread through the weaving, a bone pick with fine teeth to press down on the closely woven threads and tighten the weave, and a long spine needle with a tiny hole, used for sewing and for embroidery. Mastery of this technology presumably took years of training and experience. Most likely, a master weaver passed on her skill and knowledge to her daughters or other kinswomen.

Gift of Charles H. White. Courtesy of Museum of Fine Arts, Boston.

Agricultural Settlements and Chiefdoms

Among Eastern Woodland peoples and other Archaic cultures, agriculture supplemented rather than replaced hunter-gatherer subsistence strategies. Reliance on wild animals and plants required most Archaic groups to remain small and mobile.

But in the centuries after 2000 B.C., distinctive southwestern cultures slowly came to rely on agriculture and to build permanent settlements. Later, around 500 B.C., Woodland peoples in the vast Mississippi valley began to construct burial mounds and other earthworks that suggest the existence of social and political hierarchies that archaeologists term *chiefdoms*. Although the hunter-gatherer lifestyle never entirely disappeared, the development of agricul-

ANCIENT AGRICULTURE
Dropping seeds into holes punched in cleared ground by a pointed stick, this ancient American farmer sows a new crop while previously planted seeds— including the corn and beans immediately opposite him—bear fruit for harvest. Created by a sixteenth-century European artist, the drawing misrepresents who did the agricultural work in many ancient American cultures, namely women rather than men.
Art Resource, NY.

tural settlements and chiefdoms represented important innovations to the Archaic way of life.

Southwestern Cultures

Ancient Americans in Arizona, New Mexico, and southern portions of Utah and Colorado developed cultures characterized by agriculture and eventually by multiunit dwellings called *pueblos.* All southwestern peoples confronted the challenge of a dry climate and unpredictable fluctuations in rainfall that made the supply of wild-plant food very unreliable. These ancient Americans probably adopted agriculture in response to this basic environmental condition.

Until about 5,000 years ago, the population of the Southwest appears to have been extremely sparse. Sometime within a few centuries of 1500 B.C., southwestern hunters and gatherers began to cultivate their signature food crop, corn. Over the next three thousand years, corn became the basic cultivated food crop for Native American peo-

ples throughout North America. The demands of corn cultivation encouraged southwestern hunter-gatherers to restrict their migratory habits in order to tend the crop. A vital consideration was access to water. Southwestern Indians became irrigation experts, conserving water from streams, springs, and rainfall and distributing it to thirsty crops.

Between about A.D. 200 and 900, small farming settlements appeared throughout southern New Mexico marking the emergence of the Mogollon culture. Typically a Mogollon settlement included about a dozen pit houses, made by digging out a rounded pit about fifteen feet in diameter and a foot or two deep and then erecting poles to support a roof of branches or dirt. Larger villages usually had one or two bigger pit houses that may have been the predecessors of the circular *kivas,* the ceremonial rooms that became a characteristic of nearly all southwestern settlements. About A.D. 1000, Mogollon culture began to decline, for reasons that remain obscure. Among its descendants

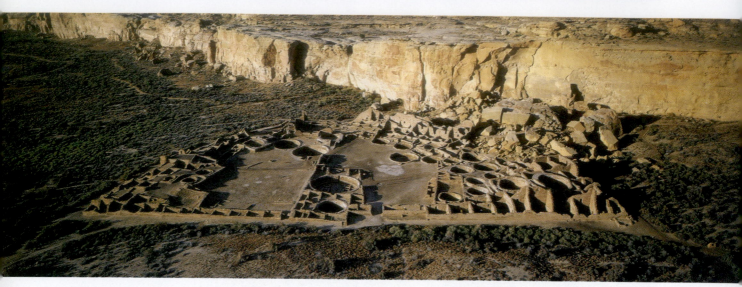

PUEBLO BONITO, CHACO CANYON
The ruins of Pueblo Bonito, the largest of many similar pueblos built centuries ago by the Anasazi in Chaco Canyon, New Mexico, can still be visited today. The numerous circular structures were kivas, underground ceremonial chambers that were originally covered with wooden roofs. What do the number, size, and arrangement of kivas at Pueblo Bonito suggest about the Anasazi who lived and visited there?
Richard Alexander Cooke III.

FLINT LIZARD
Ancient Americans' expertise in crafting stones into useful objects like knives, axes, and spear points reached amazing levels of virtuosity and artistry, as illustrated by this exquisite lizard meticulously shaped from a flint stone.
Dallas Art Museum.

were the Mimbres peoples in southwestern New Mexico, who produced spectacular pottery with designs that often portrayed human and animal forms. By about A.D. 1150, the Mimbres culture also disappeared.

All southwestern peoples confronted the challenge of a dry climate and unpredictable fluctuations in rainfall. These ancient Americans probably adopted agriculture in response to this basic environmental condition.

About A.D. 500, people who appear to have emigrated from Mexico established the distinctive Hohokam culture in southern Arizona. Hohokam peoples made extensive use of irrigation to plant and harvest twice a year. Their comparatively high crop yields allowed the Hohokam population to grow and seek out more land to settle. Hohokam culture continued to be strongly influenced by Mexico. The people built sizable platform mounds and ball courts characteristic of cultures to the south.

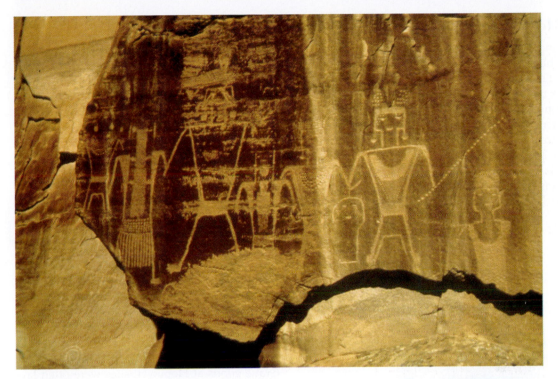

DRY FORK CANYON PETROGLYPHS
These life-size effigies are petroglyphs made by members of the Fremont culture, a northern branch of the Anasazi, who chipped these designs into a stone wall at a site in present-day Utah about 1,000 years ago. Ancient Americans left hundreds of thousands of petroglyphs ranging from large and elaborate images like these to simpler forms such as handprints and geometric shapes. The meaning of petroglyphs remains mysterious to archaeologists and historians alike.
Laboratory of Anthropology/Museum of Indian Arts and Cultures, Santa Fe, New Mexico, 70.1/365.

The Hohokam culture declined about A.D. 1400, for reasons that remain a mystery.

North of the Hohokam and Mogollon cultures, in a region that encompassed southern Utah and Colorado and northern Arizona and New Mexico, the Anasazi culture began to flourish during the first century A.D. The early Anasazi built pit houses on mesa tops and used irrigation much like their neighbors to the south. Beginning around A.D. 1000 (again, we do not know why), the Anasazi began to move to large, multistory cliff dwellings whose spectacular ruins can still be seen at Mesa Verde, Colorado, and Canyon de Chelly, Arizona. Other Anasazi communities, like the one whose impressive ruins can be visited at Chaco Canyon, New Mexico, erected huge, stone-walled pueblos with enough rooms to house the entire population of the settlement. Pueblo Bonito at Chaco Canyon, for example, contained more than eight hundred rooms. Anasazi pueblos and cliff dwellings typically contained one or more kivas used for secret ceremonies, restricted to men, that sought to communicate with the supernatural world.

Around A.D. 1130, drought began to plague the region, as proven by the growth rings of trees that Anasazi cut down and used in pueblo construction, where they still exist today. The drought lasted for half a century and triggered the disappearance of Anasazi culture. By 1200, the large Anasazi pueblos had been abandoned. The prolonged drought may have intensified conflict among pueblos and rendered ineffective the agricultural methods that had been developed in earlier centuries. Some Anasazi migrated toward regions with more reliable rainfall and settled in Hopi, Zuñi, and Acoma pueblos that their descendants in Arizona and New Mexico have occupied ever since.

Burial Mounds and Chiefdoms

No other ancient Americans created dwellings similar to pueblos, but around 500 B.C., Woodland cultures throughout the vast drainage of the Mississippi River began to build burial mounds. The size of the mounds, the labor and organization required to erect them, and the differences in the artifacts buried with certain individuals suggest the existence of a social and political hierarchy that archaeologists term a *chiefdom*.

Between about 500 and 100 B.C., Adena people built hundreds of burial mounds radiating from

WOODLAND EAGLE CARVING
This eagle effigy topped a post in a charnel house where Woodland Indians deposited the remains of their dead ancestors sometime between 1,500 and 1,000 years ago at a site in present-day Florida. The significance of the eagle is unknown; it may have represented the clan of the deceased in the charnel house.
Florida Museum of Natural History, photograph © 1985 The Detroit Institute of Arts.

central Ohio (see Map P.2). In the mounds the Adena usually deposited a wide variety of grave goods, including spear points and stone pipes as well as decorative and ritualistic items such as thin sheets of mica (a glasslike mineral) crafted into naturalistic shapes. Once the body and grave goods were in place, dirt was piled into a mound one basketful at a time. Sometimes mounds were constructed all at once, but often they were built up over many years.

About 100 B.C., Adena culture evolved into the more elaborate Hopewell culture, which lasted about 500 years. It too was centered in Ohio but extended throughout the Ohio and Mississippi valleys. Hopewell people built larger mounds and filled them with more magnificent grave goods than had their Adena predecessors. Burial was probably reserved for the most important members of Hopewell groups. Most people were cremated. Careful analysis of skeletons in one Hopewell mound suggests that the more important graves contained men who were hunters; they tended to have arthritis of the elbow associated with stress to the elbow joint from using spear-throwers.

Grave goods at Hopewell sites were often lavish. In one burial a young man and woman lay side by side, each adorned with copper jewelry, necklaces of grizzly bear teeth, and artificial copper noses; the woman was surrounded with thousands of buttons and pearl beads. Sites testify not only to the high quality of Hopewell crafts but also to the existence of a trade network ranging from Wyoming to Florida. After about A.D. 400, Hopewell culture declined, for reasons that are obscure. Some archaeologists believe that the bow and arrow and increasing reliance on agriculture may have made small settlements more self-sufficient and less dependent on the central authority of the chiefs responsible for the burial mounds.

Four hundred years later, another mound-building culture flourished. The Mississippian culture emerged in the floodplains of the major southeastern river

Major Mississippian Mounds, A.D. 800–1500

systems about A.D. 800 and lasted until about 1500. Major Mississippian sites included huge mounds with platforms on top for ceremonies and for the residences of great chiefs. The largest Mississippian site was Cahokia, Illinois, just across the Mississippi River from St. Louis, Missouri.

At Cahokia, more than one hundred mounds of different sizes and shapes were grouped around large open plazas. Monk's Mound, the largest, covered sixteen acres at its base and was one hundred feet tall. Dwellings at one time covered five square miles and may have housed as many as thirty thousand inhabitants, easily qualifying Cahokia as the largest settlement in North America. At Cahokia and other Mississippian sites, people evidently worshiped a sun god; perhaps the mounds were a way to elevate elites nearer to the sun.

One Cahokia burial mound suggests the authority a great chief exercised. One man—presumably the chief—was buried with the dismembered bodies of several people, perhaps enemies or slaves; three men and three women of high status, perhaps the chief's relatives; four men, perhaps servants or guards, whose heads and hands had been cut off; and fifty young women between the ages of eighteen and twenty-three who had evidently been strangled. Such a mass sacrifice shows the power a Cahokian chief wielded and the obedience he commanded.

Cahokia and other Mississippian sites had dwindled by A.D. 1500. By the time of European contact, most of the descendants of Mississippian cultures lived in small dispersed villages supported by agriculture, hunting, and gathering.

Native Americans in 1492

By the time Columbus arrived, North American tribes had incorporated and adapted many of the cultural achievements of their ancestors. The rigors of the continent's natural environments required that they maintain time-tested adaptations.

Eastern Woodland peoples clustered into three major groups. Algonquian tribes inhabited the Atlantic seaboard, the Great Lakes region, and much of the upper Midwest (Map P.3). The relatively mild climate along the Atlantic permitted the coastal Algonquians to grow corn and other crops as well as to hunt and fish. Around the Great Lakes and in northern New England, however, cool summers

and severe winters made agriculture impractical. Instead, the Abenaki, Penobscot, Chippewa, and other tribes hunted and fished, using canoes both for transportation and for gathering wild rice.

Inland from the Algonquians were the territories of the Iroquoian tribes, centered in Pennsylvania and upstate New York, as well as the hilly upland regions of the Carolinas and Georgia. Several features distinguished Iroquoian tribes from their neighbors. First, their success in cultivating corn and other crops allowed them to build permanent settlements, usually consisting of several bark-covered longhouses up to one hundred feet long and housing five to ten families. Second, Iroquoian societies were thoroughly matriarchal. Property of all sorts, including land, children, and inheritance, belonged to women. Women headed family clans and even selected the chiefs (normally men) who governed tribes. Third, for purposes of war and diplomacy, the Seneca, Onondaga, Mohawk, Oneida, and Cayuga tribes formed the League of Five Nations, an Iroquoian confederation that remained powerful well into the eighteenth century.

Iroquoian societies were thoroughly matriarchal. Property of all sorts, including land, children, and inheritance, belonged to women.

Muskogean peoples spread throughout the Southeast, south of the Ohio River and east of the Mississippi. Including Creek, Choctaw, Chickasaw, and Natchez tribes, Muskogeans inhabited a bountiful natural environment that provided abundant food both from agriculture and from hunting and gathering. Remnants of the Mississippian culture existed in the religious rites common among the Muskogean. They practiced a form of sun worship, and the Natchez even built temple mounds modeled after those of their Mississippian ancestors.

West of the Mississippi River, Great Plains peoples straddled the boundary between the Eastern Woodland and the western tribes. Many of the tribes had migrated to the plains within the century or two before 1500, forced westward by Iroquoian and Algonquian tribes. They were in the process of increasing their reliance on buffalo, although some tribes—especially the Mandan and Pawnee—were successful farmers, growing both

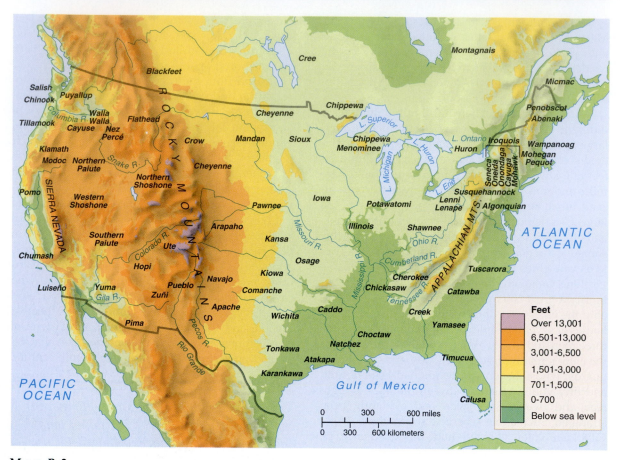

MAP P.3

Native North Americans about 1500
*Distinctive Native American peoples resided throughout the area that, centuries later,
would become the United States. This map indicates the approximate location of some
of the larger tribes about 1500. In the interest of legibility, many other peoples who
inhabited North America at the time are omitted from the map.*

corn and sunflowers. The Teton Sioux, Blackfeet,
Comanche, Cheyenne, and Crow on the northern
plains and the Apache and other nomadic tribes on
the southern plains depended on buffalo. Tribes in
the Great Basin region, such as the Comanche and
Shoshone, also continued to follow earlier subsistence practices, as did Pacific coast cultures.

In the Southwest, descendants of the Mogollon,
Hohokam, and Anasazi cultures lived in settled
agricultural communities, many of them pueblos.
However, a large number of warlike Athapascan
tribes had invaded the area within the two hundred
years before 1500. The Athapascans—principally
Apache and Navajo—were skillful warriors who

preyed on the sedentary pueblo Indians, reaping the
fruits of agriculture without the work of farming.

By the time Columbus arrived, the comparatively small Native American settlements in North
America supported a population estimated to be
about 4 million, slightly less than the population of
the British Isles at the time. All of them depended
on hunting and gathering for a major portion of
their food. Most of them also practiced agriculture,
some far more than others. All of them used bows
and arrows, as well as other weapons, for hunting
and warfare. None of them employed writing, expressing themselves instead in many other ways.
They made drawings on stones, wood, and animal

skins; wove patterns in baskets and textiles; painted designs on pottery; and crafted beadwork, pipes, and other decorative items. They danced, sang, and played music. They performed elaborate burial ceremonies and other religious rites.

Ancient Americans' rich and varied cultural resources did not include certain common features of life in late-fifteenth-century Europe: They did not use wheels; sailing ships were unknown; they had no large domesticated animals like horses, cows, or oxen; their use of metals was restricted to copper; and metallurgy did not exist in North America. However, the absence of these European conveniences was profoundly irrelevant to ancient North Americans. Their cultures had developed as adaptations to the natural environment local to each tribe. That great similarity underlay all the cultural diversity among native North Americans.

The Mexica: A Meso-American Culture

By 1492, the indigenous population of the New World numbered roughly 80 million, about the same as the population of Europe. All but about 4 million of these people lived in Central and South America. Like their North American counterparts, they too lived in a natural environment of tremendous diversity. They too developed hundreds of cultures, far too numerous to catalog here. But among all the Central and South American cultures, the Mexica stood out. (Europeans often called these people Aztecs, a name the Mexica did not use.) Their empire stretched from coast to coast across central Mexico, encompassing as many as 25 million people. We know more about the fifteenth-century Mexica than about any other Native American society of the time, principally because of their written sources, massive monuments, and their Spanish conquerors' well-documented interest in subduing them. Their significance in the history of the New World after 1492 dictates a brief consideration of their culture and society.

The Mexica began their rise to prominence about A.D. 1325 when small bands settled on a marshy island in Lake Texcoco, the site of the future city of Tenochtitlán. Resourceful, courageous, cold-blooded warriors, the Mexica were often hired as mercenaries by richer, more settled tribes. By 1430, the Mexica succeeded in asserting their dom-

inance over their former allies and leading their own military campaigns in an ever-widening arc of empire building. Despite pockets of resistance, by 1500 the Mexica ruled an empire that covered more land than Spain and Portugal combined and contained almost three times as many people.

The empire exemplified the central values of Mexican society. The Mexica worshiped the war god

HUMAN SACRIFICE
Many ancient American peoples practiced human sacrifice as a sacred rite of communion with the gods. The Inca, a powerful people whose empire stretched down the west coast of South America, required each village to send one or two especially beautiful children to the capital, where they were honored in religious ceremonies and other festivities and then given an intoxicating drink and buried in a prepared tomb, where they died. This mummy was probably a child sacrificed in such a ritual about 500 years ago. Discovered in Chile at an altitude of about 20,000 feet, where the dry, intense cold preserved the body, the mummy was accompanied by a tiny female votive figure wrapped in finely woven cloth and capped with a bright feather headdress, a llama figurine, a bag of coca leaves, and other objects.
Loren McIntyre.

Why Did the Mexica Practice Human Sacrifice?

MEXICAN CEREMONIAL SKULL

This human skull, decorated by Mexican artisans with a mosaic of turquoise, jet, and shell, represented Tezcatlipoca, the Mexican deity who governed human fate. A handsome young man was selected for the great honor of impersonating Tezcatlipoca for eighteen months. The Mexican emperor gave the impersonator riches and privileges of all sorts, and even allowed him to rule Tenochtitlán for the last five days of his life. On the last day, the impersonator climbed the steps of a temple where priests cut out his heart and decapitated him. This skull from the Tezcatlipoca ceremony presumably belonged to one of the impersonators. The skull is said to have been a gift from the emperor Montezuma to Cortés, leader of the Spanish conquest of Mexico.
Copyright © The British Museum.

THE MEXICA PRACTICED HUMAN SACRIFICE on a scale unequaled in human history. That does not mean, of course, that they intentionally killed more people than any other society. Plenty of other societies, both before and since, have systematically killed other human beings. Only a partial accounting of the years from 1930 to 1945, for example, would include millions of Jews and others murdered by the Nazis, millions of Russians killed by the Soviet leader Joseph Stalin, hundreds of thousands of Chinese slaughtered by the Japanese, and hundreds of thousands of Japanese annihilated by the atomic bombs dropped by the United States on Hiroshima and Nagasaki. Warfare of any kind involves intentional sacrifice of human life. However, the human sacrifice practiced by the Mexica was different. For them, human sacrifice was an act of worship—in fact, the ultimate act of worship.

Looking back from our vantage point five hundred years later, we may find it difficult to understand why the Mexica accepted human sacrifice as a normal and reasonable activity. Yet it is perfectly clear that they did. Although the precise number of victims is unknown, experts estimate that roughly 20,000 people were sacrificed each year throughout the Mexican empire. Celebration of an important victory or the appointment of a new emperor often involved the sacrifice of hundreds, sometimes thousands.

Most of the victims were prisoners captured in battle or rendered in tribute. Nonetheless, ordinary Mexican citizens—especially young men, women, and children—were often sacrificed in religious rituals. Every eighteen months, for example, a greatly honored young man was sacrificed to Tezcatlipoca, the god of human fate. From time to time, all Mexica practiced sacrificial bloodletting, piercing themselves with stingray spines or cactus thorns to demonstrate their religious devotion. Both as symbol and reality, human sacrifice was an integral part of daily life in Mexican communities.

Mexica employed several different techniques of sacrifice, all supervised and carried out by priests. By far the most common sacrifice was performed at an altar on the top of a temple where a priest cut out the still-beating heart of a victim and offered it to the gods. The victim's head and limbs were then severed and the torso fed to wild animals kept in cages in and near the temple. The heads were displayed on large racks at the base of the temple, while the limbs were cooked and eaten in sacred rituals. It is likely that participation in this ritualistic cannibalism was restricted to a minority of Mexica, principally warriors, priests, and wealthier merchants. However, every Mexica participated in symbolic cannibalism by eating small cakes made of flour mixed with blood and shaped into human forms.

To us, these rituals may seem ghoulish and disgusting, as they certainly did to sixteenth-century Europeans who eventually witnessed them. Yet the Mexica devoted so much time, energy, and resources to such rituals that it is impossible to doubt their importance to them. But why was human sacrifice so important?

In recent times, some scholars have argued that the Mexica practiced human sacrifice and cannibalism to remedy protein deficiencies in their diet. However, the Mexica's diet contained many sources of protein, including turkeys, chickens, fish, turtles, and eggs as well as corn and beans. For most Mexica, dietary protein was adequate or better. Protein deficiency interprets human sacrifice as a solution to a problem that, evidently, did not actually exist.

Mexican religious beliefs offer a far more persuasive explanation for human sacrifice. Scholars know a good deal about Mexican religion because, in the years immediately following European conquest, Catholic priests studied Mexican religion in order to convert the people more readily to Christianity. These sources make clear that the Mexica inhabited a world suffused with the power of supernatural beings. A special deity oversaw nearly every important activity. Mexica believed that their gods communicated with human beings through omens, signs that the gods were either happy or displeased. In turn, the people communicated their own reverence for the gods by observing appropriate rituals. Bad omens such as an unexplained fire or a lightning bolt striking a temple meant that a god was angry and needed to be appeased with the proper rituals. Since almost every occurrence could be interpreted as an omen that revealed the will of a god,

the routine events of daily life had a profound, supernatural dimension.

The Mexica's most powerful gods were Huitzilopochtli, the war god, and Quetzalcoatl, the god who gave sustenance to human beings. Mexica believed that these two gods had created the world, the sun, the moon, the first human beings, the whole array of lesser deities, and everything else in the universe. Since the moment of creation, the earth had passed through four different epochs, which Mexica called the Four Suns, each of which had ended in catastrophe. It fell to Quetzalcoatl and other potent deities to begin the Fifth Sun by re-creating human beings and all the other features of the universe. After years of work, Quetzalcoatl and the other gods had accomplished everything except the creation of the sun. Finally, two gods agreed to sacrifice themselves by jumping into a fire. Thereby they became the sun and the moon, and other gods quickly followed them into the fire to keep the sun burning. But the sacrifice of the gods was sufficient only to ignite the sun. To maintain the light of the sun and keep it moving across the sky every day required human beings to follow the example of the gods and to feed the sun with human blood. Without the sacrificial blood, the world would go dark and time would stop. Mexica considered the Fifth Sun the final stage of the universe, which would end when cataclysmic earthquakes destroyed the earth and supernatural monsters ravaged human life. By feeding the sun with human sacrifices, Mexica believed they could delay that horrible final reckoning.

For the Mexica, human sacrifice was absolutely necessary for the maintenance of life on earth. Victims of sacrifice fulfilled the most sacred of duties. Through the sacrifice of their own lives they fed the sun and permitted others to live. The living demonstrated their respect and reverence for victims of sacrifice by eating their flesh. As one sixteenth-century Catholic priest explained, "The flesh of all those who died in sacrifice was held truly to be consecrated and blessed. It was eaten with reverence, ritual, and fastidiousness—as if it were something from heaven." From the Mexica's perspective, it was not wrong to engage in human sacrifice; it was wrong not to.

Huitzilopochtli. Warriors held the most exalted positions in the Mexican social hierarchy, even above the priests who performed the sacred ceremonies that won Huitzilopochtli's favor. In the almost constant battles necessary to defend and extend the empire, young Mexican men exhibited the courage and daring that would allow them to rise in the carefully graduated ranks of warriors. The Mexica considered capturing prisoners the ultimate act of bravery. The captives were usually turned over to the priests, who sacrificed them to Huitzilopochtli by cutting out their hearts. (See "Historical Question," page P-20.)

The empire contributed far more to Mexican society than victims for sacrifice. At the most basic level, the empire was a military and political system for collecting tribute from subject peoples. The Mexica forced conquered tribes to pay tribute in goods, not money. Tribute redistributed to the Mexica as much as one-third of the goods produced by conquered tribes. It could include everything from candidates for human sacrifice to basic food products like corn and beans as well as exotic luxury items like gold, turquoise, and rare bird feathers.

On the whole, the Mexica did not interfere much with the internal government of conquered regions. Instead, they usually permitted the traditional ruling elite to stay in power—so long as they paid tribute. For their efforts, the conquered provinces received very little from the Mexica, except immunity from punitive raids by the dreaded Mexican warriors.

Tribute reflected the fundamental relations of power and wealth that pervaded the Mexican empire. The relatively small nobility of Mexican warriors, supported by a still smaller priesthood, possessed the military and religious power to command the obedience of thousands of nonnoble Mexicans and of millions of other non-Mexicans in subjugated provinces. The Mexican elite exercised their power to obtain tribute and thereby to redistribute wealth from the conquered to the conquerors, from the commoners to the nobility, from the poor to the rich. This redistribution of wealth made possible the achievements of Mexican society that eventually amazed Europeans: the fabulous temples, markets, bridges, waterworks, gardens, and zoos, not to mention the storehouses stuffed with gold and other treasures.

Subjugated communities felt exploited by the constant payment of tribute to the Mexica. By depending on military conquest and constant collection of tribute, the Mexica failed to create among their subjects a belief that Mexican domination was, at some level, legitimate and equitable. The high level of discontent among subject peoples constituted the soft, vulnerable underbelly of the Mexican empire. Instead of making friends for the Mexica, the empire created many bitter and resentful opponents, a fact Spanish conquerors eventually discovered.

SALADO RITUAL FIGURE
About A.D. 1350—more than a century before Columbus arrived in the New World—this figure was carefully wrapped in a reed mat with other items and stored in a cave in a mountainous region of New Mexico by people of the Salado culture, descendants of the Mimbres who had flourished three centuries earlier. The face of this figure is as close to a self-portrait of ancient Americans on the eve of their encounter with Europeans as we are ever likely to have. Adorned with vivid pigments, cotton string, bright feathers, and stones, the effigy testifies to the human complexity of all ancient Americans, a complexity visible in artifacts that have survived the millennia before the arrival of Europeans.
The Art Institute of Chicago.

Conclusion: The Legacy of Ancient America

Ancient Americans shaped the history of human beings in the New World for more than twelve thousand years. They established continuous human habitation in the Western Hemisphere from the time the first big-game hunters crossed Beringia until 1492 and beyond. Much of their history remains irretrievably lost, erased by reliance on oral rather than written communication. But much can be pieced together from artifacts they left behind, like the bones discovered at Folsom by George McJunkin. Ancient Americans achieved their success through resourceful adaptation to the hemisphere's many and ever-changing natural environments. They also adapted to social and cultural changes caused by human beings—such as marriages, deaths, political struggles, and warfare—but the sparse evidence that has survived renders those adaptations almost entirely unknowable. Their creativity and artistry are unmistakably documented in the artifacts they left behind at kill sites, camps, and burial mounds. Those artifacts sketch the only likenesses of ancient Americans we will ever have—blurred, shadowy images that are indisputably human but forever silent.

In the five hundred years after 1492—barely 4 percent of the time human beings have inhabited the Western Hemisphere—Europeans and their descendants began to shape and eventually to dominate American history. Native American peoples continued to influence major developments of American history after 1492. But the new wave of strangers that at first trickled and then flooded into the New World from Europe and Africa forever transformed the peoples and places of ancient America.

CHRONOLOGY

c. 80,000–10,000 B.C.	Wisconsin glaciation exposes Beringia, "land bridge" between Siberia and Alaska.
c. 13,000–10,000 B.C.	First humans arrive in North America.
c. 9500–9000 B.C.	Paleo-Indians in North and Central America use Clovis points to hunt big game.
c. 9000 B.C.	Mammoths and many other big-game prey of Paleo-Indians become extinct.
c. 8000–1000 B.C.	Archaic hunter-gatherer cultures dominate ancient America.
c. 5000 B.C.	Corn cultivation begins in Central and South America.
c. 2000 B.C.	Some Eastern Woodland people grow gourds and pumpkins and begin making pottery.
c. 1700–700 B.C.	Poverty Point culture flourishes in Louisiana.
c. 1500 B.C.	Southwestern cultures begin corn cultivation. Stone pipes for tobacco smoking appear in Eastern Woodland cultures.
c. 500 B.C.	Eastern Woodland cultures start to build burial mounds.
c. 500–100 B.C.	Adena culture develops in Ohio.
c. 300 B.C.	Some Eastern Woodland peoples begin to cultivate corn.
c. 100 B.C.–A.D. 400	Hopewell culture emerges in Ohio and Mississippi valleys.
c. A.D. 200–900	Mogollon culture emerges in New Mexico.
c. A.D. 500	Bows and arrows appear in North America south of Arctic. Pacific Northwest cultures denote wealth and status with elaborate wood carvings.
c. A.D. 500–1400	Hohokam culture develops in Arizona.
c. A.D. 800–1500	Mississippian culture flourishes in Southeast.
c. A.D. 1000–1150	Anasazi peoples build cliff dwellings at Mesa Verde, Colorado, and pueblos at Chaco Canyon, New Mexico. Mimbres culture thrives in New Mexico.
c. A.D. 1325–1500	Mexica conquer neighboring peoples and establish Mexican empire.
A.D. 1492	Columbus arrives, beginning European conquest of New World.

BIBLIOGRAPHY

GENERAL WORKS

Karen Olsen Bruhns, *Ancient South America* (1994).

Karen Olsen Bruhns and Karen E. Stothert, *Women in Ancient America* (1999).

Michael D. Coe, *Mexico: From the Olmecs to the Aztecs* (4th ed., 1994).

Michael Coe, Dean Snow, and Elizabeth Benson, *Atlas of Ancient America* (1986).

Thomas D. Dillehay, *The Settlement of the Americas: A New Prehistory* (2000).

E. James Dixon, *Quest for the Origins of the First Americans* (1993).

Roger Downey, *Riddle of the Bones: Politics, Science, Race, and the Story of Kennewick Man* (2000).

Brian M. Fagan, *The Journey from Eden: The Peopling of Our World* (1990).

Brian M. Fagan, *Ancient North America: The Archaeology of a Continent* (1991).

Brian M. Fagan, *Kingdoms of Gold, Kingdoms of Jade: The Americas before Columbus* (1991).

Stuart J. Fiedel, *Prehistory of the Americas* (2nd ed., 1992).

Robert L. Hall, *An Archaeology of the Soul: North American Indian Belief and Ritual* (1997).

David Henige, *Numbers from Nowhere: The American Indian Contact Population Debate* (1998).

Francis Jennings, *The Founders of America: How Indians Discovered the Land . . .* (1993).

Jesse D. Jennings, *Prehistory of North America* (1974).

Jesse D. Jennings, ed., *Ancient North Americans* (1983).

Alvin M. Josephy Jr., *America in 1492: The World of the Indian Peoples before the Arrival of Columbus* (1992).

David Hurst Thomas, *Skull Wars: Kennewick Man, Archaeology, and the Battle for Native American Identity* (2000).

Richard Townsend, ed., *The Ancient Americas: Art from Sacred Landscapes* (1992).

Frederick Hadleigh West, ed., *American Beginnings: The Prehistory and Paleoecology of Beringia* (1996).

NORTH AMERICAN CULTURES

Mary J. Adair, *Prehistoric Agriculture in the Central Plains* (1988).

Kenneth M. Ames and Herbert D. G. Maschner, *Peoples of the Northwest Coast: Their Archaeology and Prehistory* (1999).

David G. Anderson, *The Savannah River Chiefdoms: Political Change in the Late Prehistoric Southeast* (1994).

Alex W. Barker and Timothy R. Pauketat, eds., *Lords of the Southwest: Social Inequality and the Native Elites of Southeastern North America* (1992).

Timothy G. Baugh and Jonathon E. Ericson, eds., *Prehistoric Exchange Systems in North America* (1994).

John Howard Blitz, *Ancient Chiefdoms of the Tombigbee* (1993).

Linda S. Cordell, *Prehistory of the Southwest* (1984).

Linda S. Cordell and George R. Gumerman, eds., *Dynamics of Southwest Prehistory* (1989).

David Damas, ed., *Handbook of North American Indians*, vol. 5, *Arctic* (1984).

Warren L. D'Azevedo, ed., *Handbook of North American Indians*, vol. 11, *Great Basin* (1986).

Richard J. Dent Jr., *Chesapeake Prehistory: Old Traditions, New Directions* (1995).

E. James Dixon, *Bones, Boats, and Bison: Archeology and the First Colonization of Western North America* (1999).

Don Dumond, *Eskimos and Aleuts* (2nd ed., 1987).

Thomas E. Emerson and R. Barry Lewis, eds., *Cahokia and the Hinterlands: Middle Mississippian Cultures of the Midwest* (1991).

Thomas E. Emerson et al., eds., *Late Woodland Societies: Tradition and Transformation across the Midcontinent* (2000).

Brian M. Fagan, *The Great Journey: The Peopling of Ancient America* (1987).

William Fitzhugh, ed., *Crossroads of Continents: Cultures of Siberia and Alaska* (1988).

William W. Fitzhugh and Valerie Chaussonnet, eds., *Anthropology of the North Pacific Rim* (1994).

Franklin Folsom, *Black Cowboy: The Life and Legend of George McJunkin* (1992).

Nelson Foster and Linda S. Cordell, eds., *Chilies to Chocolate: Food the Americas Gave to the World* (1992).

Kendrick Frazier, *People of Chaco: A Canyon and Its Cultures* (1986).

George C. Frison, *Prehistoric Hunters of the High Plains* (2nd ed., 1991).

George Gumerman, *A View from Black Mesa* (1984).

George Gumerman, ed., *Themes in Southwest Prehistory* (1994).

Robert F. Heizer, ed., *Handbook of North American Indians,* vol. 8, *California* (1978).

June Helm, ed., *Handbook of North American Indians,* vol. 6, *Subarctic* (1981).

R. Douglas Hurt, *Indian Agriculture in America: Prehistory to the Present* (1987).

Barry L. Isaac, ed., *Prehistoric Economies of the Pacific Northwest Coast* (1988).

Sissel Johannessen and Christine A. Hastorf, eds., *Corn and Culture in the Prehistoric New World* (1994).

Roger G. Kennedy, *Hidden Cities: The Discovery and Loss of Ancient North American Civilization* (1994).

Ruth Kirk, *Hunters of the Whale* (1975).

Theodora Kroeber, *Ishi in Two Worlds* (1965).

Steven A. LeBlanc, *The Mimbres People: Ancient Pueblo Potters of the American Southwest* (1983).

Steven A. LeBlanc, *Prehistoric Warfare in the American Southwest* (1999).

Stephen H. Lekson, *The Chaco Meridian: Centers of Political Power in the Ancient Southwest* (1999).

Mary Ann Levine et al., eds., *The Archaeological Northeast* (1999).

Ronald J. Mason, *Great Lakes Archaeology* (1981).

R. G. Matson, *The Origins of Southwestern Agriculture* (1991).

William E. McGoun, *Prehistoric Peoples of South Florida* (1993).

Jerald T. Milanich, *Archaeology of Precolumbian Florida* (1994).

Claudia G. Mink, *Cahokia: City of the Sun: Prehistoric Urban Center in the American Bottom* (1992).

Michael J. Moratto, *California Archaeology* (1984).

William N. Morgan, *Precolumbian Architecture in Eastern North America* (1999).

Jon Muller, *Archaeology of the Lower Ohio Valley* (1986).

Alfonso Ortiz, ed., *Handbook of North American Indians,* vol. 9, *Southwest* (1979).

Alfonso Ortiz, ed., *Handbook of North American Indians,* vol. 10, *Southwest* (1983).

Timothy R. Pauketat, *The Ascent of Chiefs: Cahokia and Mississippian Politics in Native North America* (1994).

Timothy R. Pauketat and Thomas E. Emerson, eds., *Cahokia: Domination and Ideology in the Mississippian World* (2000).

Jefferson Reid and Stephanie Whittlesley, *The Archaeology of Ancient Arizona* (1997).

Karl H. Schlesier, *Plains Indians, A.D. 500–1500: The Archaeological Past of Historic Groups* (1994).

Lynne Sebastian, *The Chaco Anasazi: Sociopolitical Evolution in the Prehistoric Southwest* (1992).

Lynda Shaffer, *Native Americans before 1492: The Moundbuilding Centers of the Eastern Woodlands* (1992).

Dennis Slifer, *Signs of Life: Rock Art of the Upper Rio Grande* (1998).

Bruce D. Smith, ed., *The Mississippian Emergence* (1990).

Dean Snow, *The Archaeology of New England* (1980).

Katherine A. Spielmann, *Interdependence in the Prehistoric Southwest: An Ecological Analysis of Plain-Pueblo Interaction* (1991).

Kenneth B. Tankersley and Barry L. Isaan, eds., *Early Paleoindian Economies of Eastern North America* (1990).

Bruce G. Trigger, *The Children of Aataentsic: A History of the Huron People to 1660* (1972).

Bruce G. Trigger, *Natives and Newcomers* (1985).

Bruce G. Trigger, ed., *Handbook of North American Indians,* vol. 15, *Northeast* (1978).

J. A. Tuck, *Onondaga Iroquois Prehistory* (1971).

Christy G. Turner II and Jacqueline A. Turner, *Cannibalism and Violence in the Prehistoric American Southwest* (1999).

William Snyder Webb, *The Adena People* (1974).

Randolph J. Widmer, *The Evolution of the Calusa: A Nonagricultural Chiefdom on the Southwest Florida Coast* (1988).

Biloine Whiting Young and Melvin L. Fowler, *Cahokia: The Great Native American Metropolis* (1999).

THE MEXICA

Philip P. Arnold, *Eating Landscape: Aztec and European Occupation of Tlalocan* (1999).

BEFORE 1492

Frances Berdan, *The Aztecs of Central Mexico: An Imperial Society* (1982).

Elizabeth Hill Boone, *Stories in Red and Black: Pictorial Histories of the Aztecs and Mixtecs* (2000).

David Carrasco, *Quetzalcoatl and the Irony of Empire: Myths and Prophecies in the Aztec Tradition* (1992).

David Carrasco, *City of Sacrifice: The Aztec Empire and the Role of Violence in Civilization* (1999).

David Carrasco et al., eds., *Mesoamerica's Classic Heritage: From Teotihuacan to the Aztecs* (2000).

Inga Clendinnen, *Aztecs: An Interpretation* (1991).

Marty W. Eubanks, *Corn in Clay: Maize Paleoethnobotany in Pre-Columbian Art* (1999).

Brian M. Fagan, *The Aztecs* (1984).

Ross Hassig, *War and Society in Ancient Mesoamerica* (1992).

Richard F. Townsend, *The Aztecs* (1992).

Muriel Porter Weaver, *The Aztecs, Maya, and Their Predecessors: Archaeology of Mesoamerica* (1981).

THE
AMERICAN
PROMISE

A HISTORY OF THE UNITED STATES

Second Edition

TAINO ZEMI BASKET
This basket is an example of the effigies Tainos made to represent zemis, their deities. The effigy illustrates not only the artistry of the basket maker—probably a Taino woman— but also the basket maker's use of European mirrors in a sacred object. Crafted sometime between 1492 and about 1520, the effigy suggests that Tainos readily incorporated goods obtained through contacts with Europeans into their own traditional beliefs and practices.
Archìvio Fotogràfico del Museo Preistòrico Etnografico L. Pigorini, Rome.

EUROPEANS AND THE NEW WORLD

1492–1600

1

A HALF HOUR BEFORE SUNRISE ON AUGUST 3, 1492, Christopher Columbus commanded three ships to catch the tide out of a harbor in southern Spain and sail west. Just over two months later, in the predawn moonlight of October 12, 1492, Columbus glimpsed an island on the western horizon. At last, he believed, he had found what he had been looking for—the western end of a route across the Atlantic Ocean to Japan, China, and India. At daybreak, Columbus could see people on the shore who had spotted his ships. He rowed ashore and, as the curious islanders crowded around, he claimed possession of the land for Ferdinand and Isabella, king and queen of Spain, who had sponsored his voyage. He named the island San Salvador, in honor of the Savior, Jesus Christ.

A day or two afterward, Columbus described that first encounter with the inhabitants of San Salvador in an extensive diary he kept during his voyage. He called these people Indians, assuming that their island lay somewhere in the East Indies near Japan or China. The Indians were not dressed in the finery Columbus expected. "All of them go around as naked as their mothers bore them; and the women also," he observed. Their skin color was "neither black nor white." They were not familiar with the Spaniards' weapons. "I showed them swords," Columbus wrote, "and they took them by the edge and through ignorance cut themselves." This first encounter led Columbus to conclude, "They should be good and intelligent servants, for I see that they say very quickly everything that is said to them; and I believe that they would become Christians very easily, for it seemed to me that they had no religion."

The people Columbus called Indians called themselves Tainos, which to them meant "good" or "noble." They inhabited most of the islands Columbus visited on his first voyage, as had their ancestors for more than two centuries. The Tainos were an agricultural people who grew cassava, a nutritious root, as well as sweet potatoes, corn, cotton, tobacco, and other crops. To fish and to travel from island to island, they built canoes from hollowed-out logs. The Tainos worshiped gods they called *zemis*, the spirits of ancestors and of natural objects like trees and stones. They made effigies of *zemis* and performed rituals to honor them. "It seemed to me that they were a people very poor in everything," Columbus wrote. But the Tainos mined gold in small quantities, enough to catch the eye of Columbus and his men.

What the Tainos thought about Spaniards we can only surmise. At first, Columbus believed that the Tainos thought he and his men came from heaven. After six weeks of contact, Columbus concluded that in fact he did not understand Tainos. Late in November 1492, he wrote that "the people of these lands do not understand me nor do I, nor anyone else that I have with me, them. And many times I understand one thing said by these Indians . . . for another, its contrary."

CACIQUE'S CANOE
This sixteenth-century drawing of a large canoe carrying a cacique, or chief, and powered by twenty oarsmen probably resembles the canoes used by Tainos and the other native Americans who paddled out to visit the ships of Columbus and other European explorers. The influence of such European contacts may be reflected in the flags flying from the corners of the leafy awning that enthrones the cacique.
Art Resource, NY.

The confused communication between Europeans and Tainos suggests how different, how strange, each group seemed to the other. Columbus's perceptions of Tainos were shaped by European ideas, attitudes, and expectations, just as Tainos' perceptions of Europeans must have been colored by their own culture. Yet the word that Columbus coined for the Tainos—*Indians,* a word that originated in a colossal misunderstanding— hinted at the direction of the future. To Europeans, *Indians* came to mean all native inhabitants of the New World, the name they gave to the lands in the Western Hemisphere. After 1492 the perceptions, the cultures, and even the diseases of Europeans began to exert a transforming influence on the New World and its peoples.

Long before 1492, certain Europeans restlessly expanded the limits of the world known to them. Their efforts made possible Columbus's encounter with the Tainos. In turn, Columbus's landfall in the Caribbean changed the history not only of the Tainos, but also of Europe and the rest of the world. Beginning in 1492, the promise of the New World lured more and more Europeans to venture their lives and fortunes on the western shores of the Atlantic, a promise realized largely at the expense of New World peoples like Tainos.

Europe in the Age of Exploration

Historically, the East—not the West—attracted Europeans. Around the year 1000, Norsemen ventured west across the North Atlantic and founded a small fishing settlement in North America at L'Anse aux Meadows on the tip of Newfoundland. After a decade or so, the Norse left and did not return because the world's climate cooled, choking the North Atlantic with ice. Viking sagas memorialized the Norse "discovery," but it had virtually no other impact in the New World or in Europe. Instead, wealthy Europeans developed a taste for luxury goods from Asia and Africa, and merchants competed to satisfy that taste. As Europeans traded with the East and with one another, they acquired new information about the world they inhabited. Some learned that the known world was not all there was to know. A few people—sailors, merchants, aristocrats—took the risks of exploring beyond the limits of what was known. Those risks were genuine and could be deadly. But sometimes they paid off in new information, new opportunities, and eventually in the discovery of a world entirely new to Europeans.

Mediterranean Trade and European Expansion

From the twelfth through the fifteenth century, spices, silk, carpets, ivory, gold, and other exotic goods traveled overland from Persia, Asia Minor, India, and Africa and then were funneled into continental Europe through Mediterranean trade routes (Map 1.1). Dominated primarily by the Italian cities of Venice, Genoa, and Pisa, this lucrative trade enriched Italian merchants and bankers. Rival merchants and financiers in other European cities coveted a share of the Mediterranean trade, but the Italians battled to protect their near-monopoly of access to eastern goods. Instead of trying to displace the Italians, merchants in other European countries chose the far safer alternative of trading with them.

Late in the thirteenth century, a fleet of Genoese ships left the western Mediterranean through the narrow Strait of Gibraltar into the stormy waters of the North Atlantic, carrying goods from southern Europe to markets in northern Europe. Ocean-borne access to North Atlantic ports allowed Mediterranean traders to carry much larger quantities much less expensively than in the old overland trade. The vitality of the Mediterranean trade in the fourteenth and fifteenth centuries gave established merchants and governments few reasons to look for alternatives. New routes to the East and the discovery of new lands were the stuff of fantasy.

MAP 1.1

European Trade Routes and Portuguese Exploration in the Fifteenth Century
The strategic geographic position of Italian cities as a conduit for overland trade from Asia was slowly undermined during the fifteenth century by Portuguese explorers who hopscotched along the coast of Africa and eventually found a sea route that opened the rich trade of the East to Portuguese merchants.

The risks of exploring beyond the limits of what was known were genuine and could be deadly. But they paid off in new information, new opportunities, and eventually in the discovery of a world entirely new to Europeans.

Preconditions for turning fantasy into reality developed in fifteenth-century Europe. In the mid-fourteenth century, Europeans suffered a catastrophic epidemic of bubonic plague. The Black Death, as it was called, killed about a third of the European population. This devastating pestilence had repercussions that lasted for decades. So many people died that the pressure of population on Europe's food resources was significantly eased. Survivors, many of whom inherited property from those who had died, had greater opportunities for advancement. Many peasants moved from village to village and even to cities.

Most Europeans perceived the world as a place of alarming risks where the delicate balance of health, harvests, and peace could quickly be tipped toward disaster by epidemics, famine, and violence. They protected themselves from the constant threat of calamity by worshiping the supernatural, by living amid kinfolk and friends, and by maintaining good relations with the rich and powerful. Curiously, the insecurity and uncertainty of fifteenth-century European life encouraged a few people to take greater chances. A sailor's willingness to embark on a dangerous sea voyage through uncharted waters to points unknown was one of many European responses to the hazards of fifteenth-century life.

Some aristocrats, members of the most powerful class in European society, also had reasons to engage in exploration. Monarchs hoped to enlarge their realms and enrich their dynasties. More territory meant more subjects who could pay more taxes, provide more soldiers, and participate in more commerce, magnifying monarchs' power and prestige. Voyages of exploration also helped divert the military energies of lesser members of the nobility toward distant lands and rulers, stabilizing monarchs' regimes at home. Monarchs sponsored some explorers who were young sons of aristocratic families that had fallen on hard times. Other explorers, like Columbus, were not of noble birth but hoped to gain entrance to the aristocracy in return for their daring achievements. Exploration promised both monarchs and explorers rewards and status in European society.

Scientific and technological advances also helped set the stage for exploration. The invention of movable type stimulated diffusion of information among literate Europeans. By 1400, the crucial navigational aids employed by maritime explorers like Columbus were already available. Compasses were in widespread use. Hourglasses allowed fairly precise calculation of elapsed time, useful in estimating speed. The astrolabe and the quadrant, devices for determining latitude, were beginning to be adopted by sailors. Charts called *portulanos* included detailed drawings of the shoreline and compass settings for sailing from one point to another.

These and other technological advances were known to many people throughout fifteenth-century Europe. Only the Portuguese used them in a campaign to sail beyond the limits of the known world.

A Century of Portuguese Exploration

In many ways, Portugal was an unlikely candidate to take the lead in exploration. A small country, Portugal was populated by poor peasants governed by a tiny minority of noble families. Yet with less than 2 percent of the population of Christian Europe, the country devoted far more energy and wealth to the geographical exploration of the world between 1415 and 1460 than all the other countries of Europe combined.

Facing the Atlantic on the Iberian peninsula, the Portuguese lived on the fringes of the thriving Mediterranean trade. As a Christian kingdom, Portugal cooperated with Spain in the Reconquest, the centuries-long drive to expel Muslims from the Iberian peninsula. The religious zeal that propelled the Reconquest also justified continued expansion into what the Portuguese considered heathen lands. The key victory came in 1415 when Portuguese forces conquered Ceuta, the Muslim bastion at the mouth of the Strait of Gibraltar that had blocked Portugal's access to the Atlantic coast of Africa (see Map 1.1).

The most influential advocate of Portuguese exploration was Prince Henry the Navigator, son of the Portuguese king. From 1415 until his death in 1460, Henry collected the latest information about sailing techniques and geography, supported new crusades against the Muslims, encouraged fresh sources of trade to fatten Portuguese pocketbooks, and pushed explorers to go farther still. Henry had the backing of the king and the pope to extend the Reconquest down the African coast. Economic motives also fueled Portuguese exploration. African conquests promised to wrest wheat fields from their Moroccan owners and to obtain gold, the currency of European trade. Gold was scarce in Europe where the accelerating pace of commerce increased the need for currency, while purchases in the East drained gold away from European markets.

Neither the Portuguese nor anybody else in Europe knew how big Africa was. At first, Portuguese mariners cautiously hugged the west coast of Africa, seldom venturing beyond sight of land. By 1434, they had reached the northern edge of the Sahara Desert, where strong westerly currents swept them out to sea. They soon learned how to ride those currents far away from the coast before sailing back toward land, a technique that allowed them to reach Cape Verde by 1444 (see Map 1.1).

To stow the supplies necessary for long periods at sea and to withstand the battering of ocean waves, the Portuguese developed the caravel, a sturdy ship that became the workhorse of exploration. The caravel enabled Portuguese sailors to round Cape Verde by first sailing hundreds of miles west into the Atlantic before catching favorable trade winds and currents that swung them back along the African coast. Navigating these huge westward loops into the Atlantic, Portuguese caravels sailed into and around the Gulf of Guinea and as far south as the Congo by 1480.

Fierce African resistance confined the Portuguese to coastal trading posts where they bartered successfully for gold, slaves, and ivory. Portuguese merchants learned that relatively peaceful trading posts on the coast were far more profitable than violent conquests and attempts at colonization inland. In the 1460s, the Portuguese employed African slaves to develop sugar plantations on the Cape Verde Islands, inaugurating an association between African slaves and plantation labor that would be transplanted to the New World in the centuries to come.

About 1480, the Portuguese began a conscious search for a sea route to Asia. In 1488, Bartolomeu Dias sailed around the Cape of Good Hope at the southern tip of Africa and hurried back to Lisbon with the exciting news that it appeared to be possible to sail on to India and China. In 1498, after ten years of careful preparation, Vasco da Gama commanded the first Portuguese fleet to sail to India. Portugal quickly capitalized on the commercial potential of da Gama's new sea route. By the early sixteenth century, the Portuguese controlled a far-flung commercial empire in India, Indonesia, and China (collectively referred to as the East Indies). Their new sea route to the East eliminated overland travel and the numerous intermediate merchants and markups, integral parts of the old Mediterranean trade routes controlled by the Italians. As a result, Portuguese merchants could charge lower prices, and Europeans could purchase more eastern goods than ever before, to the great profit of Portugal.

Through its century of African explorations, Portugal broke the monopoly of the old Mediterranean trade with the East, dramatically expanded the known world, established a network of Portuguese outposts in Africa and Asia, and developed methods of sailing the high seas that Columbus employed on his revolutionary voyage west.

BENIN SALTCELLAR LID
This ivory saltcellar lid was carved in the sixteenth century by a highly skilled artist among the Benin people of western Africa. The carving portrays a Portuguese soldier wielding an intimidating gun and astride a warhorse that tramples upon the faces of Africans. Whatever the intentions of the carver, the saltcellar conveys a powerful message of the consequences of Portuguese exploration along the African coast.
Danish National Museum, Copenhagen (#128).

America required someone bold enough to believe that the experts were wrong, that despite the best available scientific knowledge the East Indies could be reached by sailing west. That person was Christopher Columbus.

The Explorations of Columbus

Born in 1451 into the family of an obscure master weaver in Genoa, Italy, Columbus went to sea when he was about fourteen. Sometime around 1476, he moved to Lisbon and two or three years later married Felipa Moniz. Felipa's father, Bartolomeu, had been raised in the household of Prince Henry the Navigator and had retained close ties to the prince. Columbus inherited Bartolomeu's maps and papers, which were crammed with information about the currents and winds of the Atlantic. Columbus himself sailed frequently to the Madeira Islands and at least twice all the way to the coast of central Africa.

Like other educated Europeans, Columbus believed that the earth was a sphere and that theoretically it was possible to reach the East Indies by sailing west. But according to Ptolemy, an ancient geographer whose writings were considered the final authority by most fifteenth-century Europeans, the earth was simply too big for anyone to sail west from Europe to Asia. Sailors would die of thirst and starvation long before they reached Asia.

Columbus rejected this conventional Ptolemaic wisdom. With flawed calculations, Columbus estimated the circumference of the earth to be 25 percent smaller than it really is. He reasoned that Asia lay about 2,500 miles from the westernmost boundary of the known world, a shorter distance than Portuguese ships routinely sailed between Lisbon and the Congo. In fact, the shortest distance to Japan from Europe's jumping off point in the Canary Islands was almost 11,000 miles. Convinced by his erroneous calculations, Columbus became obsessed with a scheme to prove he was right.

Columbus tried to convince the Portuguese king to sponsor an expedition west. But his peculiar notions about geography did not divert the Portuguese monarchy from its lucrative African explorations. Disappointed, Columbus moved to Spain in 1485 where he lobbied for his plan and even tried to interest the royal courts of England and France. He obtained a few modest but encouraging grants; then in 1492, Spain's King Ferdinand and Queen Isabella finally agreed to finance most of the journey. The

YORUBA QUEEN
This expressive terracotta head, discovered in Nigeria in 1957, was once part of a large sculpture of a Yoruba queen memorialized in a shrine built between 800 and 900 years ago, centuries before the arrival of Portuguese explorers.
The National Commission for Museums and Monuments & Life, Nigeria.

A Surprising New World in the Western Atlantic

In retrospect, the Portuguese seemed ideally qualified to venture across the Atlantic. They had pioneered the frontiers of seafaring, exploration, and geography for almost a century. However, the knowledge and experience that led them around Africa discouraged them from trying to sail across the Atlantic. They knew better than to undertake such a risky venture. The European discovery of

Spanish monarchs saw Columbus's venture as an inexpensive gamble: If it failed, not much was lost; if it succeeded, a great deal might be gained. They gave Columbus a letter of introduction to the Grand Khan of the Mongols, whom they hoped Columbus would meet soon after he arrived in China.

After barely three months of hurried preparation, Columbus and his small fleet—the *Niña* and *Pinta*, both caravels, and the *Santa María*, a larger merchant vessel—embarked for the Canary Islands. When he cast off from the Canaries, however, he did not head for the coast of Africa; instead he kept sailing west. Six weeks later, he landed on a tiny Caribbean island about three hundred miles north of the eastern tip of Cuba, which he named San Salvador.

Columbus and his men understood that they had made a momentous discovery. Yet they found it frustrating. Although the Tainos proved friendly, they did not have the riches Columbus expected to find in the East. For three months Columbus cruised from island to island, looking for the king of Japan. In mid-January 1493, he started back, taking seven Tainos with him. When he reached Isabella and Ferdinand, they were overjoyed by his news. With a voyage that had lasted barely eight months, Columbus appeared to have catapulted Spain from a secondary position in the race for a sea route to Asia into that of a serious challenger to Portugal, whose explorers had not yet sailed to India or China. Columbus and his Taino companions became the toast of the royal court. Ferdinand and Isabella appointed Columbus Admiral of the Ocean Sea and elevated him to the nobility. Ferdinand and his son became the godfathers of all seven Tainos, who were baptized as Christians.

The Spanish monarchs, following Portuguese precedent, rushed to the pope to obtain confirmation of their claim to Columbus's discoveries. Pope Alexander VI, a Spaniard, complied. In May 1493, he granted to Spain all land discovered west of an imaginary line three hundred miles west of the Azores. The decree alarmed the Portuguese, who believed that it violated their rights under previous papal grants. To protect their African claims, in 1494 the Portuguese negotiated the Treaty of Tordesillas with Spain, shifting the imaginary line eleven hundred miles west of the Canary Islands (Map 1.2). Land discovered west of the line belonged to Spain, while Portugal claimed land to the east. In effect, the treaty reassured Portugal and allowed Spain to follow up Columbus's discovery without interference from the menacing Portuguese.

In the fall of 1493, Isabella and Ferdinand sent Columbus west again to locate the Asian mainland. This time he commanded a fleet of seventeen ships and more than one thousand men who planned to settle, explore, find gold, and get rich. Near the end of his first voyage, a shipwreck had forced Columbus to leave behind thirty-nine of his sailors on the island of Hispaniola. When Columbus returned in 1493, he learned that his men had terrorized the Tainos, kidnapping local women and holding them in harems; in retaliation, Taino chiefs had killed all of the Spaniards. The brief history of that first group of Spaniards to reside in the New World prefigured much of what was to happen in the years ahead.

Columbus's First Voyage to the New World, 1492–1493

Before Columbus died in 1506, he returned to the New World two more times (1498–1500 and 1502–1504) without relinquishing his belief that the East Indies were there, someplace. Explorers continued to search for a passage to the East or some other source of profit. Before long, prospects of beating the Portuguese to Asia began to dim along with the hope of finding vast hoards of gold. For a generation after 1492, the yield from New World exploration disappointed the Spanish crown. Nonetheless, Columbus's discoveries forced sixteenth-century Europeans to think about the world in new ways. Columbus proved that it was possible to sail from Europe to the western rim of the Atlantic and return to Europe. Most important, Columbus made clear that beyond the western shores of the Atlantic lay lands entirely unknown to Europeans.

The Geographic Revolution and the Columbian Exchange

Within thirty years of Columbus's initial discovery, Europeans' understanding of world geography underwent a revolution. An elite of perhaps twenty thousand people surrounding the royal courts and trading centers of western Europe had access to information about the new geography of the world. It took a generation of additional exploration before

M A P   1 . 2

European Explorations in Sixteenth-Century America

This map illustrates the approximate routes of early European explorations of the New World.

READING THE MAP: Which countries were most actively exploring the New World? Which countries were exploring later than others?

CONNECTIONS: What were the motivations behind the explorations? What were the motivations for colonization?

www.bedfordstmartins.com/tap   SEE THE ONLINE STUDY GUIDE for more help in analyzing this map.

they could comprehend the general contours of what Columbus had found.

Columbus made clear that beyond the western shores of the Atlantic lay lands entirely unknown to Europeans.

In 1497, King Henry VII of England, who had spurned Columbus's request for sponsorship a decade earlier, sent another Genoese sailor, John Cabot, to look for a passage to the Indies across the North Atlantic, referred to as a "Northwest Passage" (see Map 1.2). Cabot managed to reach the tip of Newfoundland, which he believed was part of Asia. He hurried back to England, assembled a small fleet to follow up his discovery, and returned in 1498. But he was never heard from again. Three thousand miles to the south, in 1498 Columbus touched the mainland of Venezuela, near the mouth of the Orinoco River. A year later, another Spanish expedition landed about six hundred miles farther south, accompanied by Amerigo Vespucci, an Italian businessman whose avocation was geography. In 1500, Pedro Álvars Cabral commanded a Portuguese fleet bound for the Indian Ocean that accidentally made landfall on the coast of Brazil as it looped westward into the Atlantic. The next year the Portuguese sent Vespucci to learn whether Cabral's discovery lay on their side of the Tordesillas line, as in fact it did.

By 1500, it was clear that several large chunks of land cluttered the western Atlantic. A few cartographers speculated that these chunks were connected to one another in a landmass that was not Asia. In 1507, Martin Waldseemüller, a German cartographer, published the first map that showed the New World separate from Asia; he named the land America, in honor of Amerigo Vespucci.

Two additional discoveries confirmed Waldseemüller's speculation. In 1513, Vasco Núñez de Balboa crossed the isthmus of Panama and reached the Pacific Ocean. Clearly, more water lay between the New World and Asia. How much water Ferdinand Magellan discovered when he led an expedition to circumnavigate the globe in 1519. Sponsored by King Charles I of Spain, Magellan's voyage took him first to the New World, around Cape Horn at the southern tip of South America through what became known as the Straits of Magellan, and into the Pacific late in November 1520. Crossing the Pacific took almost four months. When he reached the Philippines, his crew had been decimated by extreme hunger and thirst. Magellan himself was killed by Philippine tribesmen. A remnant of his expedition continued into the Indian Ocean and managed to transport a cargo of spices back to Spain in 1522.

In most ways Magellan's voyage was a disaster. One ship and 18 men crawled back from an expedition that had begun with five ships and more than 250 men. But the geographic information it provided left no doubt that America was a continent separated from Asia by the enormous Pacific Ocean. The voyage made clear that Columbus was dead wrong about the identity of what he had discovered. It was possible to sail west to reach the East Indies, but that was a terrible way to go. After Magellan, most Europeans who sailed west had their sights set on the New World, not on Asia.

Columbus's arrival in the Caribbean anchored the western end of what might be imagined as a sea bridge spanning the Atlantic and connecting the New World to Europe. That sea bridge ended the age-old separation of the hemispheres and initiated the Columbian exchange, a transatlantic exchange of goods, people, and ideas that has continued ever since. Spaniards brought things that were novelties in the New World but commonplace in Europe, including Christianity, iron technology, sailing ships, firearms, wheeled vehicles, and horses and other domesticated animals. Smuggled along unknowingly were also Old World microorganisms that caused epidemics of smallpox, measles, and other diseases that killed the vast majority of Indian peoples during the sixteenth century and continued to decimate survivors in later centuries. The catastrophic effects of European diseases made the Columbian exchange far from equal.

After Magellan, most Europeans who sailed west had their sights set on the New World, not on Asia.

Ancient American goods, people, and ideas made the return trip across the Atlantic. Europeans were introduced to such vital New World crops as corn and potatoes as well as exotic items like pineapples, named for their resemblance to

COLUMBIAN EXCHANGE

The arrival of Columbus in the New World initiated an unending transatlantic exchange of goods, people, and ideas. Spaniards brought domesticated animals from the Old World, including horses, cattle, goats, chickens, cats, and sheep (left). The novelty of such animals is demonstrated by the Nahua words the Mexican people initially used to refer to these strange new beasts: for horses, they used the Nahua word for deer; a cow was "one with horns"; a goat was a "bearded one with horns"; a chicken was a "Spanish turkey hen"; a cat was a "little cougar"; a sheep was referred to with the word for cotton, linking the animal with its fibrous woolen coat. Spaniards brought many other alien items such as cannon, which the Mexica at first termed "fat fire trumpets," and guitars, which the Mexica called "rope drums." Spaniards also carried Old World microorganisms that caused devastating epidemics of smallpox, measles, and other diseases (center). Ancient American people, goods, and ideas made the return trip across the Atlantic. Columbus's sailors quickly learned to use Indian hammocks and became infected with syphilis in sexual encounters with Indian women; then they carried both hammocks and syphilis back to Europe. Smoking tobacco, like the cigar puffed by the ancient Mayan lord (right), became such a fashion in Europe that some came to believe, as a print of two men relaxing with their pipes was captioned, "Life Is Smoke." The strangeness of New World peoples and cultures also reinforced Europeans' notions of their own superiority. Although the Columbian exchange went in both directions, it was not a relationship of equality. Europeans seized and retained the upper hand.

The Bancroft Library; Arxiv Mas; Collection of Dr. Robicsek.

pinecones. Columbus's sailors became infected with syphilis in sexual encounters with New World women and then unwittingly carried the deadly parasite back to Europe. New World tobacco created a European rage for smoking that has yet to abate. But for almost a generation after 1492, this Columbian exchange did not reward Spaniards with the riches they longed to find.

Spanish Exploration and Conquest

During the sixteenth century, the New World helped Spain become the most powerful country in both Europe and the Americas. Initially, Spanish expeditions reconnoitered the Caribbean, scouted stretches of the Atlantic coast, and established settlements on the large islands of Hispaniola, Puerto Rico, Jamaica, and Cuba. Spaniards enslaved Caribbean tribes and put them to work growing crops and mining gold. But the profits from these early ventures barely covered the costs of maintaining the settlers. After almost thirty years of exploration, the promise of Columbus's discovery seemed illusory.

Soon after 1519, however, that promise was fulfilled, spectacularly. The mainland phase of exploration began in 1519 with Hernán Cortés's march into Mexico; by about 1545, Spanish conquests extended from northern Mexico to southern Chile, and New World riches filled Spanish treasure chests. Cortés's expedition served as the model for those to follow.

The Conquest of Mexico

Hernán Cortés, who would become the richest and most famous conquistador (conqueror), arrived in the New World in 1504, an obscure nineteen-year-old Spaniard seeking adventure and the chance to make a name for himself. He fought in the conquest of Cuba and elsewhere in the Caribbean. In 1519, the governor of Cuba authorized Cortés to organize an expedition to investigate rumors of a fabulously wealthy kingdom somewhere in the interior of the mainland. A charming, charismatic leader, Cortés quickly assembled a force of about six hundred men, loaded his ragtag army aboard eleven ships, and set out.

Hernán Cortés arrived in the New World in 1504, an obscure nineteen-year-old Spaniard seeking adventure and the chance to make a name for himself.

Cortés's confidence that he could talk his way out of most situations and fight his way out of the rest fortified the small band of Spaniards. Landing first on the Yucatán peninsula, Cortés had the good fortune to receive a gift from a Mayan chief: a young woman named Malinali who spoke both Mayan and Nahuatl, the language of most people in Mexico and Central America. Malinali, whom the Spaniards called Marina, soon learned Spanish and became Cortés's interpreter. (She also became one

of Cortés's mistresses and bore him a son.) Marina served as the essential conduit of communication between the Spaniards and the Indians. With her help, Cortés talked and fought with Indians along the Gulf coast of Mexico, trying to discover the location of the fabled kingdom (see Map 1.2).

In Tenochtitlán, the capital of the Mexican empire, the emperor Montezuma heard about some strange creatures along the coast. (Montezuma and his people are often called Aztecs, but they called themselves Mexica.) He feared that the strangers

CORTÉS'S CONQUEST OF MONTEZUMA
This postconquest drawing displays Spaniards' view of the major military and religious symbols of conquest. Cortés, wearing armor and mounted on a powerful steed, carries a crucifix defended by a battle shield. Behind him stands a worshipful Marina, exhibiting her devotion to Cortés, Christ, and presumably conquest. Montezuma, prodded by Cortés's lance, stands in shackles with his shattered crown at his feet, unable to resist the combined forces of the Spaniard's weapons and faith.
Hunterian Museum Library, University of Glasgow. Glasgow University Library, Department of Special Collections.

were led by the god Quetzalcoatl, who was returning to Tenochtitlán as predicted by Mexican religion. Montezuma sent emissaries, carrying gifts appropriate for a god, to meet with the intruders. Marina had told Cortés about Quetzalcoatl, and when the emissaries arrived Cortés donned the regalia they had brought, almost certain proof to the Mexica that he was indeed the god. For their part, the Spaniards astounded the emissaries by blasting their cannon, showing off their iron swords and armor, and exhibiting their horses, which the Mexica considered a bizarre kind of deer.

The emissaries hurried back to Montezuma with their amazing news. Montezuma arranged for large quantities of food to be brought to the coast to welcome the strangers and also to postpone (and perhaps prevent) Quetzalcoatl's arrival in Tenochtitlán. In addition, since Quetzalcoatl presumably hungered for blood, Montezuma sent numerous hostages for sacrifice. Before the food was served to the Spaniards, the Mexica sacrificed the hostages and soaked the food in their blood. This fare sickened the Spaniards and might have been enough to turn them back to Cuba. However, the Mexica also brought a gift, a "disk in the shape of the sun, as big as a cartwheel and made of very fine gold," as one Mexican recalled. Here was conclusive evidence that the rumors heard by Cortés and his army had some basis in fact.

In August 1519, Cortés embarked on a march to find Montezuma. Leading about 350 men armed with swords, lances, and muskets and supported by ten cannon, four smaller guns, and sixteen horses, Cortés had to live off the land, making friends with the indigenous tribes when he could and killing them when he thought necessary. On November 8, 1519, Montezuma came out to meet Cortés on a causeway leading into Tenochtitlán. After presenting Cortés with gifts, Montezuma welcomed the Spaniards to the royal palace and showered them with lavish hospitality. Quickly, Cortés took Montezuma hostage and held him under house arrest, hoping to make him a puppet through which the Spaniards could rule the Mexican empire. This uneasy peace existed for several months until, after a brutal massacre of many Mexican nobles by one of Cortés's subordinates, the population of Tenochtitlán revolted, murdered Montezuma, and mounted a ferocious assault on the Spaniards. On June 30, 1520, Cortés and about a hundred other Spaniards fought their way out of Tenochtitlán and retreated toward the coast about one hundred miles to Tlaxcala, a stronghold of bitter enemies of the Mexicans. The friendly Tlaxcalans allowed Cortés to regroup, obtain reinforcements, and plan a strategy to conquer Tenochtitlán.

In the spring of 1521, Cortés mounted a complex campaign against the Mexican capital. The Spaniards and tens of thousands of Indian allies laid siege to the city. With a relentless, scorched-earth strategy, Cortés finally defeated the last Mexican defenders on August 13, 1521. (See "Historical Question," page 16.) The great capital of the Mexican empire "looked as if it had been ploughed up," one of Cortés's soldiers remembered. A few years later, one of the Mexica described the utter despair of the defeated:

> Broken spears lie in the roads;
> we have torn our hair in grief.
> The houses are roofless now, and their walls
> are red with blood. . . .
> We have pounded our hands in despair
> against the adobe walls,
> for our inheritance, our city, is lost and dead.

The Search for Other Mexicos

Lured by their insatiable appetite for gold, conquistadors quickly fanned out from Tenochtitlán in search of other Mexicos. To the south, Guatemala, El Salvador, and Nicaragua came under Spanish control by 1524. The Mayan tribes of the Yucatán peninsula did not succumb for another twenty years. The most spectacular prize fell to Francisco Pizarro, who conquered the Incan empire in Peru. The Incas controlled a vast, complex region that contained more than nine million people and stretched along the western coast of South America for more than two thousand miles. In 1532, Pizarro and his army of fewer than two hundred men captured the Incan emperor Atahualpa and held him hostage. As ransom, the Incas gave Pizarro the largest treasure yet produced by the conquests: gold and silver equivalent to half a century's worth of precious-metal production in Europe. With the ransom safely in their hands, the Spaniards executed Atahualpa. The Incan treasure proved that at least one other Mexico did exist.

Cortés's Invasion of Tenochtitlán, 1519–1521

0   50   100 miles
0   50   100 kilometers

Gulf of Mexico

Otumba   Zautla   Jalapa
Texcoco
Tenochtitlán   Veracruz
Cholula

→ Cortés' original route, 1519
→ Cortés' retreat, 1520
→ Cortés' return route, 1520–1521

HUEJOTZINGO CODEX
The Nahua of Huejotzingo, who resided in one of Cortés's encomiendas, recorded in a codex—a page of which is shown here—the textiles, crops, animals, and laborers taken from them by other Spanish conquistadors while Cortés was visiting Spain. When Cortés returned to Mexico in 1531, the people of Huejotzingo gave him the codex. He used it to mount a successful lawsuit that forced the Spanish plunderers to compensate him—not the Huejotzingo—for the thefts from his encomienda. What other sign of conquest did the Huejotzingo document on this page of their codex?
Library of Congress, Hispanic Division.

www.bedfordstmartins.com/tap   SEE THE ONLINE STUDY GUIDE for more help in analyzing this image.

Lured by their insatiable appetite for gold, conquistadors quickly fanned out from Tenochtitlán in search of other Mexicos.

In the north, Juan Ponce de León, who had sailed around the Florida peninsula in 1513, was encouraged by Cortés's success to return to Florida in 1521, where he was killed in a battle with Calusa Indians. In 1525, Lucas Vázquez de Ayllón explored the Atlantic coast north of Florida to South Carolina. A year later, he established a small settlement on the Georgia coast that he named San Miguel de Gualdape, the first Spanish attempt to create a town in what is now the United States. Within a few months most of the settlers, including Ayllón, became sick and died, and the few survivors retreated to the Caribbean. In 1528, Pánfilo de Narváez surveyed the Gulf coast from Florida to Texas. The Narváez expedition ended disastrously on the Texas coast, near Galveston, where Indians enslaved the few survivors. After several years, four Spaniards managed to escape and were ultimately rescued by Spanish slave hunters in northern Mexico.

In 1539, Hernando de Soto, a seasoned conquistador who had taken part in the conquest of Peru, set out with nine ships and more than six

Why Did Cortés Win?

BY CONQUERING MEXICO, Hernán Cortés demonstrated that Columbus had in fact discovered a New World of enormous value to the Old. But how did a few hundred Spaniards so far away from home defeat millions of Indians fighting on their home turf?

First, several military factors favored the Spaniards. They possessed superior military technology, which partially offset the Mexica's numerical superiority. They fought with weapons of iron and steel against the Mexica's stone, wood, and copper; they charged on horseback against Mexican warriors on foot; they ignited gunpowder to fire cannon and muskets toward attacking Mexica, whose only source of power was human muscle. But the Mexica's immense numerical superiority could overpower the Spaniards' weaponry.

Spaniards also possessed superior military organization, although they were far from a highly disciplined, professional fighting force. Cortés's army was composed of soldiers of fortune, young men who hoped to fight for God and king and get rich. The unsteady discipline among the Spaniards is suggested by Cortés's decision to beach and dismantle the ships that had brought his small army to the Mexican mainland—after that, his men had no choice but to go forward.

Nonetheless, the Spaniards were a well-oiled military machine compared with the Mexica, who tended to attack from ambush or in waves of frontal assaults, with great courage but little organization or discipline. The Mexica seldom sustained attacks, even when they had the Spaniards on the run. In the siege of Tenochtitlán, for example, the Mexica often paused to sacrifice Spanish soldiers they had captured, taking time to skin "their faces," one Spaniard recalled, "which they afterward prepared like leather gloves, with their beards on." Spanish tactics, in contrast, concentrated their soldiers to magnify the effect of their firepower and to maintain communication during the thick of battle.

But perhaps the Spaniards' most fundamental military advantage was their concept of war. The Mexican concept was shaped by the nature of the empire. The Mexica fought to impose their tribute system on others and to take captives for sacrifices. From their viewpoint, war made their adversaries realize the high cost of continuing to fight and gave them a big incentive to surrender and pay tribute. For the Spaniards, war meant destroying the enemy's ability to fight. In short, the Spaniards sought total victory; the Mexica sought surrender. All these military factors weakened the Mexica's resistance, but they were insufficient to explain Cortés's victory.

Disease played a major part in the Mexica's defeat. When the Mexica confronted Cortés, they were not at full strength. An epidemic of smallpox and measles had struck the Caribbean in 1519, arrived in Mexico with Cortés and his men, and lasted through 1522. Thousands of Indians died, and many others became too sick to fight. When the Spaniards were regrouping in Tlaxcala after their disastrous evacuation of Tenochtitlán, a great plague broke out in the Mexican capital. As one Mexica explained to a Spaniard shortly after the conquest, the plague lasted for seventy days, "striking everywhere in the city and killing a vast number of our people. Sores erupted on our faces, our breasts, our bellies. . . . The illness was so dreadful that no one could walk or move. . . . They could not get up to search for food, and everybody else was too sick to care for them, so they starved to death in their beds."

The sickness was not confined to Tenochtitlán. It also killed and weakened people in the areas surrounding the city, spreading back along the network of trade and tribute that fed the city, reducing its food supply and further weakening the survivors. While the Mexica were decimated by their first exposure to smallpox and measles, the Spaniards were for all practical purposes immune, having previously been exposed to the diseases. European viruses probably played at least as large a role in the conquest as weapons and military tactics.

Religion also contributed to the Mexica's defeat. Mexican religious doctrine led Montezuma to be hesitant and uncertain in confronting the Spaniards during the months when they were most vulnerable. While Cortés marched toward Tenochtitlán, the Indians thought that the Spaniards and their horses were immortal deities. Cortés worked hard to maintain the illusion, hiding Spaniards who died. But by the time Cortés retreated from Tenochtitlán, the

MEXICAN COUNTERATTACK
This postconquest painting by a sixteenth-century Mexican artist is one of a series depicting crucial battles in the Spaniards' ultimate defeat of the Mexica. Here Mexican warriors attack the conquistadors, forcing the Spaniards to retreat from Tenochtitlán and regroup for the final siege. The distinctive shields and costumes of the Mexicans signified their military status, which was based on their battlefield prowess. The Spaniards wear uniform battle armor. The painting contrasts the colorful individuality of the Mexican warriors with the massed, anonymous Spaniards who level crossbows and firearms against the Mexicans' wooden spears. The painting does not show one of the Spaniards' deadliest weapons: steel swords.
Oronoz.

Mexica knew that the Spaniards could be killed, and their resistance stiffened accordingly.

While the Mexica's religion reduced their initial resistance to the conquistadors, Christianity strengthened the Spaniards. The Spaniards' Christianity was a confident and militant faith that commanded its followers to destroy idolatry, root out heresy, slay infidels, and subjugate nonbelievers. Their religious zeal had been honed for centuries in the battles of the Reconquest. Christianity was as much a part of the conquistadors' armory as swords and gunpowder.

Mexican military commanders often turned to their priests for military guidance. Spaniards routinely celebrated mass and prayed before battles, but their military and diplomatic decisions were made by Cortés and his subordinates—tough, practical, wily men. When the Spaniards suffered defeats, they did not worry that God had abandoned them. However, when the Mexica lost battles advised by their priests, they confronted the distressing fear that their gods no longer seemed to listen to them. The deadly sickness sweeping through the countryside also seemed to show that their gods

had abandoned them. "Cut us loose," one Mexica pleaded, "because the gods have died."

Finally, political factors proved decisive in the Mexica's defeat. Cortés shrewdly exploited the tensions between the Mexica and their subjects. With skillful diplomacy, Cortés obtained cooperation from thousands of Indian soldiers, porters, and food suppliers who were the crucial ingredient in the Spaniards' success. Besides fighting alongside Cortés, the Spaniards' Indian allies provided the invaders with a fairly secure base from which to maneuver against the Mexican stronghold. Cortés's small army was reinforced by thousands of Indians who were eager to seek revenge against the Mexica. Hundreds of thousands of other Indians helped the Spaniards by not contributing to the Mexica's defense. These passive allies of the Spaniards prevented the Mexica from fully capitalizing on their overwhelming numerical superiority. In the end, although many factors contributed to the conquest, Cortés won because the Mexican empire—the source of the Mexica's impressive wealth and power—was also their crippling weakness.

hundred companions to find another Peru in North America. Landing in Florida, de Soto literally slashed his way through much of southeastern North America for three years, searching for the rich, majestic civilizations he thought were there. After many brutal battles and much hardship, de Soto became sick and died in 1542, and his men buried him in the Mississippi River before turning back to Mexico, disappointed.

Tales of the fabulous wealth of the mythical Seven Cities of Cíbola also lured Francisco Vásquez de Coronado to search the Southwest and Great Plains of North America. In 1540, Coronado left northern Mexico with more than three hundred Spaniards, a thousand Indians, fifteen hundred horses, and a priest named Marcos de Niza who claimed to know the way to what he called "the greatest and best of the discoveries." Cíbola turned out to be a small Zuñi pueblo of about a hundred families. When the Zuñi shot arrows at the Spaniards, Coronado attacked the pueblo and routed the defenders after a hard battle. Convinced that the rich cities must lie somewhere over the horizon, Coronado kept moving all the way to central Kansas before deciding in 1542 that the rumors he had pursued were just that, nothing more.

Juan Rodríguez Cabrillo led an expedition in 1542 that sailed along the coast of California. Cabrillo died on Santa Catalina Island, offshore from present-day Los Angeles, but his men sailed on to the border of Oregon, where a ferocious storm forced them to turn back toward Mexico.

These probes into North America by de Soto, Coronado, and Cabrillo persuaded Spaniards that enormous territories stretched northward, yet their inhabitants had little to loot or exploit. After a generation of vigorous exploration, Spaniards concluded that there was only one Mexico and one Peru.

New Spain in the Sixteenth Century

For all practical purposes, Spain dominated the New World in the sixteenth century (Map 1.3). Portugal claimed the giant territory of Brazil under the Tordesillas treaty but was far more concerned with exploiting its hard-won trade with the East Indies than in colonizing the New World. England and France were absorbed in the affairs of Europe and largely lost interest in America until late in the century. In the decades after 1519, Spaniards created the distinctive colonial society of New Spain that gave other Europeans a striking illustration of how the New World could be made to serve the purposes of the Old.

The Spanish monarchy claimed ownership of most of the land in the Western Hemisphere and gave the conquistadors permission to explore and plunder. (See "Documenting the American Promise," page 22.) The crown took one-fifth, called the "royal fifth," of any loot confiscated by the conquerors and allowed the conquerors to divide the rest. In the end, the conquistadors themselves received very little. After the conquest of Tenochtitlán, Cortés decided to compensate his disappointed, battle-hardened men by giving them the towns the Spaniards had subdued.

ZUÑI DEFEND PUEBLO AGAINST CORONADO
This sixteenth-century drawing by a Mexican artist shows Zuñi bowmen fighting back against the arrows of Coronado's men and the entreaties of Christian missionaries. Intended to document the support some Mexican Indians gave to Spanish efforts to extend the conquest into North America, the drawing depicts the Zuñi defender at the bottom of the pueblo aiming his arrow at a Mexican missionary armed only with religious weaponry: a crucifix, a rosary, and a book—presumably the Bible.
Hunterian Museum Library, University of Glasgow. Glasgow University Library, Department of Special Collections.

Spaniards created the distinctive colonial society of New Spain that gave other Europeans a striking illustration of how the New World could be made to serve the purposes of the Old.

The distribution of conquered towns institutionalized the system of *encomienda,* which empowered conquistadors to rule the Indians and the lands in and around their towns. The concept of encomienda was familiar to the Spaniards, who had used it to govern regions recaptured from the Muslims during the Reconquest. In New Spain, encomienda transferred to the Spanish *encomendero* (the man who "owned" the town) the tribute that the town had previously paid to the Mexican empire.

In theory, encomienda involved a reciprocal relationship between the encomendero and "his" Indians. In return for the tribute and labor of the Indians, the encomendero was supposed to encourage the Indians to convert to Christianity, to

MAP 1.3

New Spain in the Sixteenth Century *Spanish control spread throughout Central and South America during the sixteenth century, with the important exception of Portuguese Brazil. North America, although claimed by Spain under the Treaty of Tordesillas, remained peripheral to Spain's New World empire.*

MISSIONARY CATECHISM

In the 1540s Franciscan missionaries tried to teach basic Christian rituals by using pictures that resembled the symbols in preconquest Mexican documents, hoping to appeal to the Mexicans' respect for the authority of the ancient texts. Known as Testerian manuscripts, these catechisms were read line by line, moving from left to right all the way across two facing pages (as shown here), then back from right to left on the next line, and so on. This catechism illustrates the prayer "Salve Regina"; the words below the pictures are in the Otomi language. Can you puzzle out some of the symbols that were intended to communicate the words of the prayer? Begin with the title "La Salve Regina" at the far left of the second line: "Hail to the Queen who reigns above / Mother of clemency and love! / Hail, thou our hope, life, sweetness! We / Eve's banished children cry to thee. / We, from this wretched vale of tears, / Send sighs and groans unto thy ears; / Oh then, sweet advocate, bestow / A pitying look on us below! / After this exile let us see / Our blessed Jesus, born of thee. / O merciful, O pious Maid / O gracious Mary, lend thy aid."

Bibliotheque Nationale, Paris / Arch. Photeb.

be responsible for their material well-being, and to guarantee order and justice in the town. Catholic missionaries labored earnestly to convert the Indians to Christianity. After baptizing tens of thousands of Indians, the missionaries discovered that the Indians continued to worship their own gods along with the Christian God. Some friars began to realize that authentic conversions could take place only if the Spaniards first learned about the Indians' religion. Fray Bernardino de Sahagún, for example, compiled a systematic account of Mexican society in his *General History of the Things of New Spain*. Most friars, however, came to believe that the Indians were lesser be-

MISSION SCHOOL
This early-seventeenth-century woodcut depicts a mission school in New Spain. A monk instructs Indian children in Christian doctrine by leading them word by word through a printed book, unlike a Testerian manuscript. The obedient students follow the monk's directions by pointing to the right passage in the book. A disobedient student is punished with a whipping administered by a fellow student at the monk's command. According to this woodcut, what lessons did mission school students learn in addition to Christian doctrine?
© Collection of the New-York Historical Society.

ings inherently incapable of fully understanding the Christian faith.

In practice, encomenderos were far more interested in what the Indians could do for them than in what they or missionaries could do for the Indians. Encomenderos subjected Indians to chronic overwork, mistreatment, and abuse without recompense. As one Spaniard remarked, "Everything [the Indians] do is slowly done and by compulsion. They are malicious, lying, thievish. . . . They are very ungrateful. . . . They are capital enemies of the Spaniards." Economically, however, encomienda recognized a fundamental reality of New Spain: The most important treasure the Spaniards could plunder from the New World was not gold, but Indian labor. To exploit that labor, the hemisphere's richest natural resource, encomienda gave encomenderos the right to force Indians to work when, where, and how the Spaniards pleased.

Encomienda engendered two groups of influential critics. A few of the missionaries were horrified at the brutal mistreatment of the Indians. The cruelty of the encomenderos made it difficult for priests to persuade Indians of the tender mercies of the Spaniards' God. "What will [the Indians] think about the God of the Christians," Fray Bartolomé de Las Casas asked, when they see their friends "with their heads split, their hands amputated, their intestines torn open? . . . Would they want to come to Christ's sheepfold after their homes had been destroyed, their children imprisoned, their wives raped, their cities devastated, their maidens deflowered, and their provinces laid waste?" Las Casas and other outspoken missionaries softened few hearts among the encomenderos, but they did win some sympathy for the Indians from the Spanish monarchy and royal bureaucracy. Royal officials, however, interpreted the encomenderos' brutal treatment of the Indians as part of a larger general problem: the autonomy of the encomenderos. The Spanish monarchy sought to abolish encomienda in an effort to take the government of New Spain away from swashbuckling old conquistadors and to put it in the hands of royal bureaucrats.

Justifying Conquest

*T*he immense riches Spain reaped from its New World empire came largely at the expense of Indians. A few individual Spaniards raised their voices against the brutal exploitation of Indians. Their criticisms prompted the Spanish monarchy to formulate an official justification of conquest that, in effect, blamed Indians for resisting Spanish dominion.

DOCUMENT 1. Montecino's 1511 Sermon

In 1511, a Dominican friar named Antón Montecino delivered a blistering sermon that astonished the Spaniards gathered in the church in Santo Domingo, headquarters of the Spanish Caribbean.

Your greed for gold is blind. Your pride, your lust, your anger, your envy, your sloth, all blind. . . . You are in mortal sin. And you are heading for damnation. . . . For you are destroying an innocent people. For they are God's people, these innocents, whom you destroyed. By what right do you make them die? Mining gold for you in your mines or working for you in your fields, by what right do you unleash enslaving wars upon them? They have lived in peace in this land before you came, in peace in their own homes. They did nothing to harm you to cause you to slaughter them wholesale. . . . Are you not under God's command to love them as you love yourselves? Are you out of your souls, out of your minds? Yes. And that will bring you to damnation.

SOURCE: Zvi Dor-Ner, *Columbus and the Age of Discovery* (New York: William Morrow, 1991), 220–21.

DOCUMENT 2. The *Requerimiento*

Montecino returned to Spain to bring the Indians' plight to the king's attention. In 1512 and 1513, King Ferdinand met with philosophers, theologians, and other advisers and concluded that the holy duty to spread the Christian faith justified conquest. To buttress this claim, the king had his advisers prepare the Requerimiento. *According to the* Requerimiento, *Indians who failed to welcome Spanish conquest and all its blessings deserved to die. Conquistadors were commanded to read the* Requerimiento *to Indians before any act of conquest. Beginning in 1514, they routinely did so, speaking in Spanish while other Spaniards brandishing unsheathed swords stood nearby.*

On the part of the king . . . [and] queen of [Spain], subduers of the barbarous nations, we their servants notify and make known to you, as best we can, that the Lord our God, living and eternal, created the heaven and the earth, and one man and one woman, of whom you and we, and all the men of the world, were and are descendants. . . .

God our lord gave charge to one man called St. Peter, that he should be lord and superior to all the men in the world, that all should obey him, and that he should be the head of the whole human race, wherever men should live . . . and he gave him the world for his kingdom and jurisdiction.

And he commanded him to place his seat in Rome, as the spot most fitting to rule the world from. . . . This man was called Pope, as if to say, Admirable Great Father and Governor of men. The men who lived in that time obeyed that St. Peter and took him for lord, king, and superior of the universe. So also they have regarded the others who after him have been elected to the pontificate, and so has it been continued even till now, and will continue till the end of the world.

One of these pontiffs, who succeeded that St. Peter as lord of the world . . . made donation of these islands and mainland to the aforesaid king and queen [of Spain] and to their successors. . . .

So their highnesses are kings and lords of these islands and mainland by virtue of this donation; and . . . almost all those to whom this has been notified, have received and served their highnesses, as

One of the most important blows against encomienda was the imposition in 1549 of a reform called the *repartimiento,* which limited the labor an encomendero could command from his Indians to forty-five days per year from each adult male. The repartimiento, however, did not challenge the principle of forced labor, nor did it prevent encomenderos from continuing to cheat, mistreat, and overwork their Indians. Enforcement was haphazard. Slowly, as the old encomenderos died, reparlords and kings, in the way that subjects ought to do, with good will, without any resistance, immediately, without delay, when they were informed of the aforesaid facts. And also they received and obeyed the priests whom their highnesses sent to preach to them and to teach them our holy faith; and all these, of their own free will, without any reward or condition have become Christians, and are so, and the highnesses have joyfully and graciously received them, and they have also commanded them to be treated as their subjects and vassals; and you too are held and obliged to do the same. Wherefore, as best we can, we ask and require that you consider what we have said to you, and that you take the time that shall be necessary to understand and deliberate upon it, and that you acknowledge the Church as the ruler and superior of the whole world, and the high priest called Pope, and in his name the king and queen [of Spain] our lords, in his place, as superiors and lords and kings of these islands and this mainland by virtue of the said donation, and that you consent and permit that these religious fathers declare and preach to you. . . .

If you do so . . . we . . . shall receive you in all love and charity, and shall leave you your wives and your children and your lands free without servitude, that you may do with them and with yourselves freely what you like and think best, and they shall not compel you to turn to Christians unless you yourselves, when informed of the truth, should wish to be converted to our holy Catholic faith. . . . And besides this, their highnesses award you many privileges and exemptions and will grant you many benefits.

But if you do not do this or if you maliciously delay in doing it, I certify to you that with the help of God we shall forcefully enter into your country and shall make war against you in all ways and manners that we can, and shall subject you to the yoke and obedience of the Church and of their highnesses; we shall take you and your wives and your children and shall make slaves of them, and as such shall sell and dispose of them as their highnesses may command; and we shall take away your goods and shall do to you all the harm and damage that we can, as to vassals who do not obey and refuse to receive their lord and resist and contradict him; and we protest that the deaths and losses which shall accrue from this are your fault, and not that of their highnesses, or ours, or of these soldiers who come with us.

Indians who heard the Requerimiento *could not understand Spanish, of course. No native documents survive to record the Indians' thoughts upon hearing the Spaniards' official justification for conquest, even when it was translated into a language they recognized. But one conquistador reported that when the* Requerimiento *was translated for two chiefs in Columbia, they responded that if the pope gave the king so much territory that belonged to other people, "the Pope must have been drunk."*

SOURCE: Adapted from A. Helps and M. Oppenheim, eds., *The Spanish Conquest in America and Its Relation to the History of Slavery and to the Government of the Colonies,* 4 vols. (London and New York, 1900–1904), 1:264–67.

QUESTIONS FOR ANALYSIS AND DEBATE

1. How did the *Requerimiento* answer the criticisms of Montecino? According to the *Requerimiento,* why was conquest justified? What was the source of Indians' resistance to conquest?

2. What arguments might a critic like Montecino have used to respond to the *Requerimiento*'s justification of conquest? What arguments might the Mexican leader Montezuma have made against those of the *Requerimiento*?

3. Was the *Requerimiento* a faithful expression or a cynical violation of Spaniards' Christian faith?

timiento replaced encomienda as the basic system of exploiting Indian labor.

The practice of coerced labor in New Spain grew directly out of the Spaniards' assumption that they were superior to the Indians. As one missionary put it, the Indians "are incapable of learning. . . . The Indians are more stupid than asses and refuse to improve in anything." Therefore, most Spaniards assumed, Indians' labor should be organized by and for their conquerors.

AFRICAN SLAVES MINING GOLD
This sixteenth-century illustration depicts African slaves mining gold in New Spain. Spaniards imported African slaves in substantial numbers after the native American population had been decimated by conquest and disease. Here, the two slaves on the right dig ore, from which the gold is separated by the slave in the center and then washed in hot water over the fire, before the clean nuggets are given to the Spaniard, who carefully weighs and saves them. How did the artist emphasize the differences between the Spaniard and the slaves? Is it possible to detect the artist's point of view about who was more "civilized"?

The Pierpont Morgan Library, New York. MA 3900, f.100.

From the viewpoint of Spain, the single most important economic activity in New Spain after 1540 was silver mining. Spain imported more New World gold than silver in the early decades of the century, but that changed with the discovery of major silver deposits at Potosí, Bolivia, in 1545 and Zacatecas, Mexico, in 1546. As the mines swung into large-scale production during the 1540s, an ever-growing stream of silver flowed from New Spain to Spain (Figure 1.1). Overall, exports of precious metals from New Spain during the sixteenth century were worth about twenty-five times more than hides, the next most important export. The silver mines required large capital investments and numerous workers. Typically, a mine was supervised by a handful of Spaniards, and the miners were mostly Indians, with some African slaves later in the sixteenth century. The mines exemplified the fundamental relationship between the colonists and Spain. The Indian miners worked for local Spanish bosses to produce silver for export to Spain. The mines and their products were valuable principally for their contribution to the wealth of Spain, not to that of the colony.

For Spaniards, life in New Spain was relatively easy. Only a few thousand Spaniards actually fought during the conquests. Although the riches the survivors won fell far short of their expectations, the benefits of encomienda provided a comfortable, leisurely existence that was the envy of many poorer noblemen in Spain. As one colonist wrote to his brother back in Spain, "Don't hesitate [to come]. . . . This land [New Spain] is as good as ours [Spain], for God has given us more here than there, and we shall be better off."

During the century after 1492, about 225,000 Spaniards settled in the colonies. Virtually all of them were poor young men of common (nonnoble) lineage who came directly from Spain. Laborers and artisans made up the largest proportion, but soldiers and sailors were also numerous. Throughout the sixteenth century, men vastly outnumbered

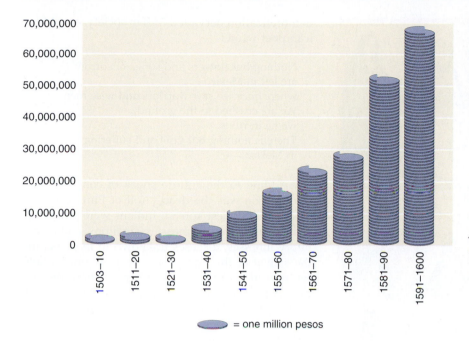

70,000,000
60,000,000
50,000,000
40,000,000
30,000,000
20,000,000
10,000,000
0

1503–10 1511–20 1521–30 1531–40 1541–50 1551–60 1561–70 1571–80 1581–90 1591–1600

= one million pesos

FIGURE 1.1

New World Gold and Silver Imported into Spain during the Sixteenth Century, in Pesos
Spain imported more gold than silver during the first three decades of the sixteenth century, but the total value of this treasure was quickly eclipsed during the 1530s and 1540s when rich silver mines were developed. Silver accounted for most of the enormous growth in Spain's precious-metal imports from the New World.

women, although the proportion of women grew from about one in twenty before 1519 to nearly one in three by the 1580s. The gender and number of Spanish settlers shaped two fundamental features of the society of New Spain. First, despite the thousands of immigrants, Europeans never made up more than 1 or 2 percent of the total population. Although Spaniards ruled New Spain, the population was almost wholly Indian. Second, the shortage of Spanish women meant that a great deal of concubinage and intermarriage took place between Spanish men and Indian women.

The highest social status in New Spain was reserved for natives of Spain, *peninsulares* (people born on the Iberian peninsula). Below them but still within the elite were *creoles* (from the Spanish word for "native," *criollo*), the children born in the New World to Spanish men and women. Together, peninsulares and creoles made up barely 1 or 2 percent of the population. Below them on the social pyramid was a larger group of *mestizos,* the offspring of Spanish men and Indian women, who made up 4 or 5 percent of the population. So many of the mestizos were illegitimate that the term *mestizo* (from the Spanish word for "mixed") was almost synonymous with *bastard* in the sixteenth century. Some mestizos worked as artisans and labor overseers and lived well, and a few rose into the ranks of the elite, especially if their Indian ancestry was not ob-

vious from their skin color. Most mestizos, however, were lumped with the Indians, the enormous bottom mass of the population.

The society of New Spain established the precedent for what would become a pronounced pattern in the European colonies of the New World: a society stratified sharply by social origin and race. All Europeans of whatever social origin considered themselves superior to the native Americans; in New Spain, they were a dominant minority in both power and status.

The Spanish monarchy administered New Spain for its own purposes, mostly to provide a large and growing source of revenue for the royal treasury. The principles of royal government were simple: Tax economic transactions and retain monopolies on essential goods. The result in New Spain was that competition was stifled, incentive was thwarted, and economic development was rigidly controlled for the benefit of Spain rather than the colonists.

The Toll of Spanish Conquest and Colonization

By 1560, the major centers of Indian civilization had been conquered, their leaders overthrown, their religion held in contempt, and their people forced to work for the Spaniards. Profound

Español con India, Mestizo.

Mestizo con Española, Castizo.

Castizo con Española, Español.

Español con Mora, Mulato.

Mulato con Española, Morisco.

Morisco con Española, Chino.

Chino con India, Salta atras.

Salta atras con Mulata, Lobo.

demoralization pervaded Indian society. As a Mexican poet wrote:

Nothing but flowers and songs of sorrow
are left in Mexico . . .
where once we saw warriors and wise men. . . .
We are crushed to the ground;
we lie in ruins.
There is nothing but grief and suffering
in Mexico.

Adding to the culture shock of conquest and colonization was the deadly toll of European diseases. As conquest spread, Indians were struck by virulent epidemics of measles, smallpox, and respiratory illnesses, diseases unknown to them before the arrival of the Europeans. By 1570, only a half century after Cortés entered Tenochtitlán, the Indian population of New Spain had fallen to about 10 percent of what it had been when Columbus arrived. In little more than fifty years, nine out of ten Indians had succumbed to the severity of colonial policies and even more deadly European diseases. The destruction of the Indian population was a catastrophe unequaled in human history. A Mayan Indian recalled that when sickness struck his village, "Great was the stench of the dead. . . . The dogs and vultures devoured the bodies. The mortality was terrible. . . . So it was that we became orphans. . . . We were born to die!" Natives of the New World had never been infected with and thus they had not developed immunities to the alien viruses from Europe, Africa, and Asia that the Spaniards unwit-

MIXED RACES
Residents of New Spain maintained a lively interest in each person's racial lineage. These eighteenth-century paintings illustrate forms of racial mixture common in the sixteenth century. In the first painting, a Spanish man and an Indian woman have a mestizo son; in the fourth, a Spanish man and a woman of African descent have a mulatto son; in the fifth, a Spanish woman and a mulatto man have a morisco daughter. The many racial permutations of parents led residents of New Spain to develop an elaborate vocabulary of ancestry. The child of a morisco and a Spaniard was a chino; the child of a chino and an Indian was a salta abas; the child of a salta abas and a mulatto was a lobo; and so on. Can you detect hints of some of the meanings of racial categories in the clothing depicted in these paintings?
Bob Schalkwijk/INAH.

tingly carried. For most Indians, New Spain was a graveyard.

New Spain established the precedent for what would become a pronounced pattern in the European colonies of the New World: a society stratified sharply by social origin and race.

For the Spaniards, Indian deaths meant that the most valuable resource of New Spain—Indian labor—dwindled rapidly. By the last quarter of the sixteenth century, Spanish colonists felt the pinch of a labor shortage. To help redress the need for laborers, the colonists began to import African slaves. Some Africans had come to Mexico with the conquistadors; one Mexica recalled that among Cortés's men were "some black-skinned ones with kinky hair." In the years before 1550, while Indian labor was still ample, only 15,000 slaves were imported from Africa. Even after Indian labor began to decline, the relatively high cost of African slaves kept imports low, approximately 36,000 from 1550 to the end of the century. During the sixteenth century, New Spain continued to rely primarily on a diminishing number of Indians.

Northern Outposts in Florida and New Mexico

After the explorations of de Soto, Coronado, and Cabrillo, officials in New Spain lost interest in North America. The monarchy claimed that Spain owned North America as part of the grant made by the pope in 1493 and insisted that a few North American settlements be established to give some tangible reality to its claims. Settlements in Florida would have the additional benefit of protecting Spanish ships from pirates and privateers who lurked along the southeastern coast, waiting for the Spanish treasure fleet sailing toward Spain.

In 1565, the Spanish king sent Pedro Menéndez de Avilés to create settlements along the Atlantic coast of North America. In early September, Menéndez founded St. Augustine in Florida and within a few weeks mounted a deadly attack that eliminated a nearby French settlement. In addition to St. Augustine, the first permanent European settlement within what became the United States, Menéndez established a series of small outposts along the Florida coast. In 1567, he founded the town of St. Elena, on what is now Parris Island, South Carolina. In 1570, Menéndez sent an expedition to settle on the Chesapeake Bay, but within a few months the settlers were killed by local Indians.

Antagonisms between Spaniards and native peoples also plagued the earlier settlements. In 1576, an Indian attack forced evacuation of St. Elena. Spanish officials destroyed St. Elena themselves in 1587 and fell back to St. Augustine, where they dug in. By 1600, the garrison town had a population of about five hundred, a token Spanish presence on the vast Atlantic shoreline of North America (see Map 1.3).

More than 1,600 miles west of St. Augustine, the Spaniards founded another outpost in 1598. During the 1580s, the Mexican mining frontier extended far into northern Mexico, and rumors of fabulous riches to be found just over the northern horizon still circulated, as they had in Coronado's time forty years earlier. In 1598, Juan de Oñate led an expedition of about five hundred people to settle northern Mexico, now called New Mexico, and claim the booty that supposedly awaited. Oñate had impeccable credentials for both conquest and mining. His father had helped discover the bonanza silver mines of Zacatecas, and his wife was Isabel Tolosa Cortés Montezuma, the granddaughter of Cortés—the conqueror of Mexico—and the great-granddaughter of the Mexican emperor Montezuma.

Oñate and his companions set out from Mexico and after two months reached a pueblo near present-day Albuquerque, where Oñate solemnly convened the pueblo's leaders and received their oath of loyalty to the Spanish king and to the Christian God. Oñate repeated these ceremonies at additional pueblos as he made his way to a pueblo that he named San Gabriel, north of present-day Santa Fe. He soon sent out scouting parties to find the legendary treasures of the region and to locate the ocean, which he reasoned had to be nearby. Meanwhile, a large contingent of his soldiers planned to mutiny, and relations with the Indians deteriorated. When the Acoma pueblo revolted, Oñate ruthlessly suppressed the uprising, killing some eight hundred men, women, and children. Although Oñate reconfirmed the Spaniards' military superiority, he did not bring peace or stability to San Gabriel. Another pueblo revolted in 1599, and many of Oñate's settlers returned to Mexico, disillusioned. A few held on, deserting San Gabriel early in the seventeenth century for the greater security of Santa Fe.

SIGN OF EMPIRE
The Spanish explorer Juan de Oñate scratched this inscription over an ancient American petroglyph on a huge sandstone in New Mexico, not far from the Zuñi and Acoma pueblos. For years, Oñate had searched the greater Southwest for the oceans he knew had to be nearby. In 1605, he trekked down the Colorado River to the Gulf of California, the sea he had long sought—or so he believed. On his return to New Mexico, he memorialized his success with this inscription: "There passed this way the Adelantado Don Juan de Oñate, from the discovery of the South Sea, on the 16th of April, 1605."
El Morro National Monument, photo by Brian Quigley.

New Mexico was so marginal to New Spain that officials talked repeatedly of abandoning it, but they did not. Instead, New Mexico lingered as a small, dusty token of Spanish claims to the North American Southwest.

The New World and Europe

The riches of New Spain helped make the sixteenth century the Golden Age of Spain. After the deaths of Queen Isabella and King Ferdinand, their sixteen-year-old grandson became King Charles I of Spain in 1516. Charles used the wealth of New Spain to pursue his vast ambitions in the fierce dynastic and religious battles of sixteenth-century Europe. Through the power of Spain, the New World had a major impact on Europeans.

In 1519, Charles I used judicious bribes to secure his selection as Holy Roman Emperor Charles V. His empire encompassed more than that of any other European monarch. With ambitions that matched his sprawling territories, Charles V confronted an unexpected challenge from Martin Luther, an obscure Catholic priest in central Germany.

The Protestant Reformation and the European Order

In 1517, Martin Luther initiated the Protestant Reformation by publicizing his criticisms of the Catholic Church. Luther's ideas, while shared by many other Catholics, were considered extremely dangerous by church officials and by many monarchs like Charles V who believed firmly that, just as the church spoke for God, they ruled for God.

Luther preached a doctrine known as *justification by faith:* Individual Christians could obtain salvation and life everlasting only by faith that God would save them. Giving offerings to the church, following the orders of the priest, or participating in church rituals did not put believers one step closer to heaven. The only true source of information about God's will was the Bible, not the church. By reading the Bible, any Christian could learn as much about God's commandments as any priest. Indeed, Luther called for a priesthood of all believers.

In effect, Luther charged that the Catholic Church was in many respects fraudulent. Contrary to the church's claims, priests were unnecessary for salvation; they even hindered it by engaging in religious practices not specifically commanded by the

Bible. The church had neglected its proper role—to help individual Christians understand the realm of faith revealed to them in the Bible—and instead had wasted its resources in the worldly realm of wars and politics. Although Luther hoped his ideas would reform the Catholic Church, instead they ruptured forever the unity of Christianity in western Europe.

Although Luther hoped his ideas would reform the Catholic Church, instead they ruptured forever the unity of Christianity in western Europe.

Charles V pledged to exterminate the Protestant heresies. The wealth pouring into Spain from the New World fueled his efforts to defend the Catholic faith against Protestants, Muslims in eastern Europe, and any nation bold or foolhardy enough to contest Spain's supremacy. As the wealthiest and most powerful monarch in Europe, Charles V, followed by his son and successor Philip II, assumed responsibility for upholding the existing order of sixteenth-century Europe.

New World Treasure and Spanish Ambitions

Both Charles V and Philip II fought wars throughout the world during the sixteenth century. Mexican silver funneled through the royal treasury into the hands of military suppliers, soldiers, and sailors wherever in the world Spain's forces happened to be fighting. New World treasure was dissipated in military adventures that served the goals of the monarchy but did little to benefit most Spaniards.

In a sense, American wealth made the Spanish monarchy too rich and too powerful among the states of Europe. The ambitions of Charles V and Philip II were so great that the expenses of constant warfare far outstripped the revenues arriving from New Spain. To help meet military expenditures, both kings continually raised taxes in Spain. Between 1527 and 1598, taxes levied on Spaniards increased more than fivefold. In accordance with the principle of privilege, the nobility—by far the wealthiest class in Spain—was completely exempt from direct taxation, so the increasing tax burden fell mostly on the peasantry. Not only did the ambitions of the monar-

chy impoverish the vast majority of Spain's population, but they also brought Spain to the brink of economic bankruptcy. When taxes did not provide enough funds to fight its wars, the monarchy was forced to borrow from European bankers. By the end of the century, interest paid on debts swallowed two-thirds of the crown's annual revenues. For Spain, the riches from New Spain proved a short-term blessing but a long-term curse.

But sixteenth-century Spaniards did not see it that way. As they looked at their accomplishments in the New World, they saw unmistakable signs of progress. They had added enormously to their knowledge and wealth. They had built mines, cities, churches, and even universities on the other side of the Atlantic. Their military, religious, and economic achievements gave them great pride and confidence.

Europe and the Spanish Example

The lessons of sixteenth-century Spain were not lost on Spain's European rivals. Spain proudly displayed the fruits of its New World conquests. In 1520, for instance, Charles V exhibited some of the gifts Montezuma had presented to Cortés. After seeing the objects, the German artist Albrecht Dürer wrote in his diary of his amazement at "the things which were brought to the King from the New Golden Land: a sun entirely of gold, a whole fathom [six feet] broad; likewise a moon, entirely of silver, just as big. . . . I have never seen in all my days what so rejoiced my heart, as these things. For I saw among them amazing objects, and I marvelled over the subtle ingenuity of the men in these distant lands." Dürer's reaction illustrates the intellectual excitement the New World generated among some Europeans. But the most exciting news about "the men in these distant lands" was that they could serve the interests of Europeans, as Spain had shown. With a few notable exceptions, Europeans saw the New World as a place for the expansion of European influence, a place where, as one Spaniard wrote, Europeans could "give to those strange lands the form of our own."

Spain's example proved that an empire in the New World could boost a nation's power and prestige in Europe and could reap financial profits from the new arena of transatlantic commerce. France and England tried to follow Spain's lead. Both nations warred with Spain in Europe, preyed on Spanish treasure fleets, and ventured to the New World, where they too hoped to find an undiscovered passageway to the East Indies or another Mexico or Peru.

Spain's example proved that an empire in the New World could boost a nation's power and prestige in Europe.

In 1524, France sent Giovanni da Verrazano to scout the Atlantic coast of North America from North Carolina to Canada, looking for a Northwest Passage (see Map 1.2). Eleven years later, France probed farther north with Jacques Cartier's voyage up the St. Lawrence River. Encouraged, Cartier returned to the region with a group of settlers in 1541, but the colony they established—like the search for a Northwest Passage—came to nothing. In 1564, a group of French Huguenots (Protestants fleeing from persecution in Catholic France) established a settlement near present-day Jacksonville, Florida, that was soon eliminated by Spaniards led by Pedro Menéndez de Avilés. French interest in North America did not revive until the seventeenth century.

English attempts to follow Spain's lead were slower but equally ill fated. Not until 1576, almost

ALGONQUIAN CEREMONIAL DANCE
When the English artist John White visited the coast of present-day North Carolina in 1585 as part of Raleigh's Roanoke expedition, he painted this watercolor portrait of an Algonquian ceremonial dance. This and White's other portraits are the only surviving likenesses of sixteenth-century North American Indians that were drawn from direct observation in the New World. White's portrait captures the individuality of these Indians' appearances and gestures while depicting a ceremony that must have appeared bizarre and alien to a sixteenth-century Englishman. The significance of this ceremonial dance is still a mystery, although the portrait's obvious signs of order, organization, and collective understanding show that the dancing Indians knew what it meant.

eighty years after John Cabot's voyages, did the English try again to find a Northwest Passage. This time Martin Frobisher sailed into the frigid waters of northern Canada; his sponsor was the Cathay Company, which hoped to open trade with China (see Map 1.2). Like many other explorers who preceded and followed him, Frobisher was mesmerized by the Spanish example and was sure he had found gold. But the tons of "ore" he hauled back to England proved worthless, the Cathay Company collapsed, and English interests shifted southward.

English attempts to establish North American settlements were no more fruitful than their search for a northern route to China. Sir Humphrey Gilbert led expeditions in 1578 and 1583 that made feeble efforts to found colonies in Newfoundland until Gilbert himself vanished at sea in 1583. Sir Walter Raleigh organized an expedition in 1585 to settle Roanoke Island off the coast of present-day North Carolina. The first group of explorers left no colonists on the island, but two years later Raleigh sent a contingent of more than one hundred settlers to Roanoke under John White's leadership. White returned to England for supplies and when he went back in 1590, the Roanoke colonists had disappeared, leaving only the word *Croatoan* (whose meaning is unknown) carved on a tree. The Roanoke colonists most likely died from a combination of natural causes and unfriendly Indians. By the end of the century, England had failed to secure a New World beachhead.

Roanoke Settlement, 1585–1590

Conclusion: The Legacy of the Sixteenth Century

The sixteenth century in the New World belonged to the Spaniards, who employed Columbus, and the Indians, who greeted him as he stepped ashore. Spaniards initiated the Columbian exchange between the New World and the Old that continues to this day. The exchange subjected native Americans to the ravages of European diseases and Spanish conquest. Spanish explorers, conquistadors, and colonists forced Indians to serve the interests of Spanish settlers and the Spanish monarchy. The exchange illustrated one of the most important legacies of the sixteenth century: After millions of years, the Atlantic no longer was an impermeable barrier separating the Eastern and Western Hemispheres. After the voyages of Columbus, European sailing ships regularly bridged the Atlantic and carried people, products, diseases, and ideas from one shore to the other.

No European monarch could forget the seductive lesson taught by Spain's example: The New World could vastly enrich the Old. Spain remained a New World power for almost four centuries, and its language, culture, and institutions left a permanent imprint. By the end of the sixteenth century, however, other European monarchies began to contest Spain's dominion in Europe and to make forays into the northern fringes of Spain's New World preserve. To reap some of the benefits the Spaniards enjoyed from their New World domain, the others had to learn a difficult lesson: how to deviate from Spain's example. That discovery lay ahead.

www.bedfordstmartins.com/tap SEE THE ONLINE STUDY GUIDE to assess your mastery of the material covered in this chapter.

CHRONOLOGY

1415 Portugal conquers Ceuta at Strait of Gibraltar, gaining access to western coast of Africa.

1444 Portuguese explorers reach Cape Verde.

1451 Columbus born in Genoa.

1480 Portuguese ships reach Congo.

1488 Bartolomeu Dias rounds Cape of Good Hope.

1492 Columbus lands on Caribbean island that he names San Salvador.

1493 Columbus makes second voyage to New World.

1494 Portugal and Spain negotiate Treaty of Tordesillas to divide New World between them.

1497 John Cabot searches for Northwest Passage.

1498 Columbus makes third voyage to New World and lands in Venezuela.

Vasco da Gama sails to India.

1500 Pedro Álvars Cabral makes landfall in Brazil.

1502 Columbus makes fourth voyage to New World.

1507 German mapmaker Waldseemüller names New World *America*.

1513 Vasco Núñez de Balboa crosses isthmus of Panama.

1517 Protestant Reformation begins in Europe.

1519 Hernán Cortés leads expedition to find and conquer Mexico.

Ferdinand Magellan sets out to sail around the world.

Charles I of Spain becomes Holy Roman Emperor Charles V.

1521 Cortés conquers Mexico at Tenochtitlán.

Juan Ponce de León lands in Florida.

1524 Guatemala, El Salvador, and Nicaragua come under Spanish control; Giovanni da Verrazano scouts Atlantic coast of North America for France.

Franciscan missionaries arrive in Mexico.

1526 Lucas Vázquez de Ayllón establishes San Miguel de Gualdape on Georgia coast.

1528 Pánfilo de Narváez leads expedition to survey Gulf coast from Florida to Texas.

1532 Francisco Pizarro begins conquest of Peru.

1535 Jacques Cartier explores St. Lawrence River.

1539 Hernando de Soto launches exploration of southeastern North America.

1540 Francisco Vásquez de Coronado starts to explore Southwest and Great Plains of North America.

1542 Juan Rodríguez Cabrillo explores California coast.

1549 Repartimiento reforms begin to replace encomienda.

1565 Pedro Menéndez de Avilés establishes St. Augustine, Florida.

1576 Martin Frobisher sails into northern Canadian waters.

1578 Sir Humphrey Gilbert attempts to found colonies in Newfoundland.

1587 English colonists under Sir Walter Raleigh settle Roanoke Island.

1598 Juan de Oñate leads expedition into New Mexico.

BIBLIOGRAPHY

GENERAL WORKS

Richard Boyer and Geoffrey Spurling, eds., *Colonial Lives: Documents on Latin American History, 1550–1850* (2000).

Alfred W. Crosby Jr., *The Columbian Exchange: Biological and Cultural Consequences of 1492* (1972).

Zvi Dor-Ner, *Columbus and the Age of Discovery* (1991).

Felipe Fernández-Armesto, *Before Columbus: Exploration and Colonization from the Mediterranean to the Atlantic, 1229–1492* (1987).

J. H. Elliott, *The Old World and the New, 1462–1650* (1970).

D. W. Meinig, *The Shaping of America* (1986).

Samuel E. Morison, *The European Discovery of America: The Northern Voyages,* A.D. *500–1600* (1971).

Samuel E. Morison, *The European Discovery of America: The Southern Voyages,* A.D. *1492–1616* (1974).

William D. Phillips and Carla Rahn Phillips, *The Worlds of Christopher Columbus* (1992).

David B. Quinn, *North America from Earliest Discovery to First Settlements* (1977).

David B. Quinn, ed., *New American World: A Documentary History of North America to 1612,* 5 vols. (1970).

A. J. R. Russell-Wood, *The Portuguese Empire, 1415–1808: A World on the Move* (1998).

Hugh Thomas, *Conquest: Montezuma, Cortés, and the Fall of Old Mexico* (1993).

John Thornton, *Africa and Africans in the Making of the Atlantic World, 1400–1680* (1992).

David J. Weber, *The Spanish Frontier in North America* (1992).

EXPLORERS AND EMPIRES

Charles Boxer, *The Portuguese Seaborne Empire, 1415–1825* (1969).

Miles H. Davidson, *Columbus Then and Now: A Life Reexamined* (1997).

Jan De Vries, *The Economy of Europe in an Age of Crisis, 1600–1750* (1976).

William Eccles, *Canadian Frontier, 1534–1760* (1969).

Karen Ordahl Kupperman, *Roanoke: The Abandoned Colony* (1984).

Peggy K. Liss, *Isabel the Queen: Life and Times* (1992).

John Lynch, *Spain, 1516–1598: From Nation State to World Empire* (1992).

Harry A. Miskimin, *The Economy of Later Renaissance Europe, 1460–1600* (1977).

John H. Parry, *The Spanish Seaborne Empire* (1966).

David B. Quinn, *England and the Discovery of America, 1481–1620* (1974).

David B. Quinn, *Set Fair for Roanoke* (1985).

David B. Quinn, ed., *North American Discovery, 1000-1612* (1971).

Carl O. Sauer, *Sixteenth-Century North America: The Land and the People as Seen by the Europeans* (1971).

A. C. de C. M. Saunders, *A Social History of Black Slaves and Freedmen in Portugal, 1441–1555* (1982).

Roger C. Smith, *Vanguard of Empire: Ships of Exploration in the Age of Columbus* (1993).

Robert S. Weddle, *The Gulf of Mexico in North American Discovery, 1500–1685* (1985).

EUROPEANS ENCOUNTER THE NEW WORLD

James Axtell, *Beyond 1492: Encounters in Colonial North America* (1992).

Robert F. Berkhofer Jr., *The White Man's Indian: Images of the American Indian from Columbus to the Present* (1978).

Philip P. Boucher, *Cannibal Encounters: Europeans and Island Caribs, 1492–1763* (1992).

Nicholas Canny and Anthony Pagden, *Colonial Identity in the Atlantic World, 1500–1800* (1987).

Rebecca Catz, *Christopher Columbus and the Portuguese, 1476–1498* (1993).

Alfred W. Crosby, *Ecological Imperialism: The Biological Expansion of Europe, 900–1900* (1986).

Alfred W. Crosby, *Germs, Seeds, and Animals: Studies in Ecological History* (1994).

Valerie J. Flint, *The Imaginative Landscape of Christopher Columbus* (1992).

William W. Fitzhugh, ed., *Cultures in Contact: The Impact of European Contacts on Native American Cultural Institutions, 1000–1800* (1985).

Anthony Grafton, *New Worlds, Ancient Texts: The Power of Tradition and the Shock of Discovery* (1992).

David Henige, *In Search of Columbus: The Sources for the First Voyage* (1991).

Peter Hulme, *Colonial Encounters: Europe and the Native Caribbean, 1492–1797* (1986).

Peter Hulme and Neil L. Whitehead, eds., *Wild Majesty: Encounters with Caribs from Columbus to the Present Day* (1992).

William F. Keegan, *The People Who Discovered Columbus: An Introduction to the Prehistory of the Bahamas* (1992).

Anthony Pagden, *The Fall of Natural Man: The American Indian and the Origins of Comparative Ethnology* (1981).

Anthony Pagden, *European Encounters with the New World: From Renaissance to Romanticism* (1993).

Anthony Pagden, *Lords of All the World: Ideologies of Empire in Spain, Britain, and France, 1500–1800* (1995).

Irving Rouse, *The Tainos: Rise and Decline of the People Who Greeted Columbus* (1992).

David Hurst Thomas, ed., *Columbian Consequences*, 3 vols. (1991).

Samuel M. Wilson, *Hispaniola: Caribbean Chiefdoms in the Age of Columbus* (1990).

CONQUEST AND NEW SPAIN

Ida Altman, *Emigrants and Society: Extremadura and Spanish America in the Sixteenth Century* (1989).

Gary Clayton Anderson, *The Indian Southwest, 1580–1830: Ethnogenesis and Reinvention* (1999).

Kenneth J. Andrien and Rolena Adorno, eds., *Transatlantic Encounters: Europeans and Andeans in the Sixteenth Century* (1991).

Frances Berdan, *The Aztecs of Central Mexico: An Imperial Society* (1982).

Peter J. Blackwell, *Silver Mining and Society in Colonial Mexico: Zacatecas, 1546–1700* (1971).

Peter J. Blackwell, *Miners of the Red Mountain: Indian Labor in Potosí, 1545–1650* (1984).

Frederick P. Bowser, *The African Slave in Colonial Peru, 1524–1650* (1974).

Gordon Brotherston, *Image of the New World: The American Continent Portrayed in Native Texts* (1979).

Louise M. Burkhart, *The Slippery Earth: Nahua-Christian Moral Dialogue in Sixteenth-Century Mexico* (1989).

Inga Clendinnen, *Aztecs: An Interpretation* (1991).

Noble David Cook, *Born to Die: Disease and New World Conquest, 1492–1650* (1998).

Kathleen A. Deegan, ed., *America's Ancient City: Spanish St. Augustine, 1565–1763* (1991).

Charles Gibson, *The Aztecs under Spanish Rule* (1964).

Charles Gibson, *Spain in America* (1966).

Serge Gruzinski, *The Conquest of Mexico: The Incorporation of Indian Societies into the Western World, Sixteenth–Eighteenth Centuries* (1993).

Ramon A. Gutiérrez, *When Jesus Came, the Corn Mothers Went Away: Marriage, Sexuality, and Power in New Mexico, 1500–1846* (1991).

Lewis Hanke, *All Mankind is One: A Study of the Disputation between Bartolomé de Las Casas and Juan Ginés de Sepúlveda in 1550 on the Intellectual and Religious Capacity of the American Indians* (1974).

Robert T. Himmerich, *The Encomenderos of New Spain, 1521–1555* (1991).

Paul E. Hoffman, *A New Andalacía and a Way to the Orient: The American Southeast during the Sixteenth Century* (1990).

Robert H. Jackson, *Race, Caste, and Status: Indians in Colonial Spanish America* (1999).

Robert H. Jackson, ed., *Indians, Franciscans, and Spanish Colonization: The Impact of the Mission System on California Indians* (1995).

Kenneth F. Kiple and Stephen V. Beck, eds., *Biological Consequences of European Expansion, 1450–1800* (1997).

Andrew L. Knaut, *The Pueblo Revolt of 1680: Conquest and Resistance in Seventeenth-Century New Mexico* (1995).

James Lang, *Conquest and Commerce: Spain and England in the Americas* (1975).

Clark Spencer Larsen and George R. Milner, eds., *In the Wake of Contact: Biological Responses to Conquest* (1994).

Bartolomé de Las Casas, *In Defense of the Indians*, trans. Stafford Poole (1974).

Miguel Leon-Portilla, ed., *The Broken Spears: The Aztec Account of the Conquest of Mexico* (1962).

James Lockhart, *The Nahuas After Conquest: A Social and Cultural History of the Indians of Central Mexico, Sixteenth through Eighteenth Centuries* (1992).

James Lockhart, ed., *We People Here: Nahuatl Accounts of the Conquest of Mexico* (1993).

James Lockhart and Enrique Otte, eds., *Letters and People of the Spanish Indies: Sixteenth Century* (1976).

James Lockhart and Stuart B. Schwartz, *Early Latin America: A History of Colonial Spanish America and Brazil* (1983).

Lyle N. McAlister, *Spain and Portugal in the New World, 1492–1700* (1984).

Sabine McCormack, *Religion in the Andes: Vision and Imagination in Early Colonial Peru* (1991).

Bonnie G. McEwan, *The Spanish Missions of La Florida* (1993).

Jerald T. Milanich, *Florida Indians and the Invasion from Europe* (1995).

Jerald T. Milanich, ed., *Earliest Hispanic/Native American Interactions in the American Southeast* (1991).

Jerald T. Milanich and Susan Milrath, eds., *First Encounters: Spanish Explorations in the Caribbean and the United States* (1989).

Jerald T. Milanich and Charles Hudson, *Hernando De Soto and the Indians of Florida* (1993).

Kenneth Mills and William B. Taylor, eds., *Colonial Spanish America: A Documentary History* (1998).

Colin A. Palmer, *Slaves of the White God: Blacks in Mexico, 1570–1650* (1976).

Carroll L. Riley, *Rio del Norte: People of the Upper Rio Grande from Earliest Times to the Pueblo Revolt* (1995).

Susan Schroeder, *Native Resistance and the Pax Colonial in New Spain* (1998).

Robert Silverberg, *The Pueblo Revolt* (1994).

Steve J. Stern, *Peru's Indian Peoples and the Challenge of Spanish Conquest: Huamanga to 1640* (1982).

David Hurst Thomas, ed., *Ethnology of the Indians of Spanish Florida* (1991).

David Hurst Thomas, ed., *The Missions of Spanish Florida* (1991).

TOBACCO JAR

This tobacco storage jar combines a product and place name from the southern colonies with the fine craft of decorative ceramics designed for Europeans to use in their everyday lives. The jar illustrates the many ways tobacco grown in the New World influenced life beyond tobacco fields. Grown principally by servants and slaves, the tobacco stored in this jar was transported to port in barrels made by coopers, ferried across the Atlantic in ships—constructed by shipbuilders and equipped with sails, ropes, and specialized fittings made by skilled workmen—and insured by financiers and insurance companies. Upon arrival on the eastern shores of the Atlantic, the tobacco barrels were off-loaded and opened. Tobacconists chopped, ground, and flavored the tobacco, then sold it in shops to consumers avid for tobacco to smoke, sniff, or chew. They also sold jars like the one pictured here for attractive repositories both to store the stimulant and to display buyers' sophisticated taste. Most tobacco came from the Chesapeake region; the label "Carolina" was a brand name rather than an accurate indication of the origin of the tobacco.

Colonial Williamsburg Foundation.

THE SOUTHERN COLONIES IN THE SEVENTEENTH CENTURY

1601–1700

2

I N DECEMBER 1607, BARELY SIX MONTHS AFTER ARRIVING AT JAMESTOWN with the first English colonists, Captain John Smith was captured by warriors of Powhatan, the supreme chief of about fourteen thousand Algonquian people who inhabited the coastal plain of present-day Virginia, near the Chesapeake Bay. According to Smith, Powhatan "feasted him after their best barbarous manner." Then, after the chief consulted with his men, "two great stones were brought before Powhatan: then as many [Indians] as could layd hands on [Smith], dragged him to [the stones], and thereon laid his head, and being ready with their clubs, to beate out his braines." At that moment, Pocahontas, Powhatan's eleven-year-old daughter, rushed forward and "got [Smith's] head in her armes, and laid her owne upon his to save him from death." Pocahontas, Smith wrote, "hazarded the beating out of her owne braines to save mine, and . . . so prevailed with her father, that I was safely conducted [back] to James towne."

This romantic story of an Indian maiden rescuing a white soldier and saving not only his life but also Jamestown and ultimately English colonization of North America has been enshrined in the writing of American history since 1624 when Smith published his *Generall Historie of Virginia* and has even been dramatized in a recent Disney movie. Historians believe that this episode actually happened more or less as Smith described it. But Smith did not understand why Pocahontas acted as she did. Many commentators have claimed that her love for Smith caused her to rebel against her father's authority. Pocahontas left no document that explains her motives; most likely she could not write. Everything known about her was written by Smith or other Englishmen. When their writings are considered in the context of what is known about the Algonquian society Pocahontas was born into, her actions appear in an entirely different light.

When Pocahontas intervened to save Smith, she almost certainly was participating in an Algonquian ceremony that expressed Powhatan's supremacy and his ritualistic adoption of a subordinate chief, or *werowance*. Most likely, what Smith interpreted as Pocahontas's saving him from certain death was a ceremonial enactment of Powhatan's willingness to incorporate Smith and the white strangers at Jamestown into Powhatan's empire. The ceremony displayed Powhatan's power of life or death over a subordinate chief—Smith—and Powhatan's willingness to give protection to those who acknowledged his supremacy—in this case, the interlopers at Jamestown. By appearing to save Smith, Pocahontas was probably acting out Smith's new status as an adopted member of Powhatan's extended

POCAHONTAS IN ENGLAND
Shortly after Pocahontas and her husband John Rolfe arrived in England in 1616, an engraver made this portrait of her dressed in English clothing suitable for a princess. The portrait captures the dual novelty of England for Pocahontas and of Pocahontas for the English. Ornate, courtly clothing probably signified to English observers that Pocahontas was royalty and to Pocahontas that the English were accepting her as befitted the "Emperor" Powhatan's daughter. The mutability of Pocahontas's identity is displayed in the engraving's identification of her as "Matoaka" or "Rebecca."
Library of Congress.

family. Rather than a rebellious, love-struck girl, Pocahontas was almost certainly a dutiful daughter playing the part prescribed for her by her father and her culture.

About two years after the adoption ritual, Smith went back to England. In the meantime, Pocahontas frequented the English settlement, often bringing Powhatan's gifts of food to the colonists. Powhatan often placed his sons and daughters in

subordinate tribes as an expression of both his dominance and his protection. It appears that Pocahontas's relationship to the English colonists grew out of Powhatan's attempt to treat the tribe of white strangers at Jamestown as he did other tribes in his empire, an attempt that failed.

In 1613, after relations between Powhatan and the English colonists had deteriorated into bloody raids by both parties, Pocahontas was captured and held hostage at Jamestown. Within a year she converted to Christianity and married one of the colonists, a widower named John Rolfe. After giving birth to a son, Thomas, Pocahontas, her husband, and the new baby sailed for England in the spring of 1616. There, promoters of the Virginia colony dressed her as a proper Englishwoman and arranged for her to meet dignitaries and even to attend a ball that included among its guests King James I and Queen Anne.

Hearing that Pocahontas was in London, John Smith went to see her. According to Smith, Pocahontas said, "You did promise Powhatan what was yours should bee his, and he the like to you; you called him father, being in his land a stranger, and by the same reason so must I doe you." Pocahontas's words may well have expressed her understanding of both Smith's subordination to her father and her own subordination to Smith as her adopted father in this strange land of England. It seems likely, in other words, that Pocahontas understood what was happening to her in England as a counterpart to the ritual John Smith had experienced in Virginia back in 1607.

Pocahontas died in England in 1617. Her son, Thomas, ultimately returned to Virginia and by the time of the American Revolution his descendants numbered in the hundreds. But the world Thomas Rolfe and his descendants inhabited was shaped by a reversal of the power ritualized when his mother "saved" John Smith. By the end of the seventeenth century, native Americans were far from vanquished, but—unlike Powhatan—they no longer dominated the newcomers who had arrived in the Chesapeake with John Smith.

During the seventeenth century, the English colonists learned how to make a living growing tobacco, a crop native Americans had cultivated in small quantities for centuries. The new settlers, however, grew enormous crops of tobacco, far more than they could smoke, chew, or sniff themselves, and they exported most of it to Europe. Rather than incorporating Powhatan's people into their new society, the

SECOTAN VILLAGE

This engraving, published in 1612, was copied from an original drawing John White made in 1585 when he visited the village of Secotan on the coast of North Carolina. The drawing provides a schematic view of daily life in the village, which may have resembled one of Powhatan's settlements. White noted on the original that the fire burning behind the line of crouching men was "the place of solemne prayer." The large building in the lower left was a tomb where the bodies of important leaders were kept. Dwellings similar to those illustrated on Smith's map of Virginia lined a central space, where men and women ate. Corn is growing in the fields along the right side of the village. The engraver included hunters shooting deer at the upper left. Hunting was probably never so convenient—no such hunters or deer appear in White's original drawing. This drawing conveys the message that Secotan was orderly, settled, religious, harmonious, and peaceful (note the absence of fortifications), and very different from English villages. Princeton University Libraries.

www.bedfordstmartins.com/tap
SEE THE ONLINE STUDY GUIDE for more help in analyzing this image.

settlers appropriated lands surrounding the Chesapeake Bay that had supported ancient Americans for millennia and built new societies on the foundation of tobacco agriculture and transatlantic trade.

To produce large crop surpluses for export required hard labor and people who were willing—or could be forced—to do it. For the most part, native Americans refused to be conscripted into the colonists' fields. Instead, the settlers depended on the labor of family members, indentured servants, and, by the last third of the seventeenth century, African slaves. By the end of the century, the southern colonies had become sharply different both from the world dominated by Powhatan when the Jamestown settlers first arrived and from contemporary English society. In ways unimaginable to Powhatan, Pocahontas, or John Smith, the colonists paid homage to the international market and the English monarch by working mightily to make a good living growing crops for sale to the Old World.

An English Colony on the Chesapeake

By 1600, King James I eyed North America as a possible location for English colonies. England's defeat of the Spanish Armada in 1588 made it seem likely that England could also prevail against Spain in North America, a distant hinterland of Spain's colonial heartland in Mexico and South America.

In 1606, a number of "knightes, gentlemen, merchauntes, and other adventurers of our cittie of London" organized a joint stock company, the Virginia Company of London, and petitioned King James to grant them permission to establish a colony in North America. The king gave the company a charter authorizing the group to settle on the coast of Virginia and to possess all that lay within fifty miles north and south of their settlement and one hundred miles inland (later extended to the Pacific). James boldly granted the Virginia Company over six million acres and everything they might contain, in large measure because they were not his to grant. In effect, the charter was a royal license to poach on Spanish claims and on Powhatan's chiefdom.

The adventurers in the Virginia Company hoped to found an empire that would strengthen England not only overseas but also at home. Richard Hakluyt, a strong proponent of colonization, argued that a colony would provide a convenient outlet for the swarms of poor "valiant youthes rusting and hurtfull by lacke of employement" in England. These jobless Englishmen would be put to work in the colony, producing goods that England currently had to import from other nations. They would also provide a ready market in the colony for English woolens. But the main reason the Virginia Company adventurers were willing to risk (or "adventure") their capital in Virginia was their fervent hope for quick profits. One way or another, Virginia promised to reward the adventurers. Or so they thought.

The Fragile Jamestown Settlement

In December 1606, the *Susan Constant, Discovery,* and *Godspeed* carried 144 Englishmen toward Virginia. Delayed by storms and a stopover in the West Indies, they arrived at the mouth of the Chesapeake Bay on April 26, 1607. That night while the colonists rested onshore, one of them later recalled, a band of Indi-ans "creeping upon all foure, from the Hills like Beares, with their Bowes in their mouthes," attacked and dangerously wounded two men. The attack gave the colonists an early warning that the North American wilderness was not quite the paradise described by the Virginia Company's publications in England. For the next three weeks, the 105 colonists (39 had died at sea) explored the bay for a suitable place to settle. On May 14, they put ashore on a small peninsula in the midst of Powhatan's chiefdom. With the memory of their first night in America fresh in their minds, they quickly built a fort, the first building in the settlement they named Jamestown.

† The Church
1. Marketplace
2. Storehouse and Court of Guard
3. Streets of "Settled" Houses
4. Palisades of Posts
5. Bulwarks of half-moon shape
6. Principal entrance, or "South Gate"
7. Other gates
8. Trench or moat around palisade

Jamestown, 1607
"Jamestown in 1607." From *Jamestown and St. Mary's: Buried Cities of Romance* by Henry Chandler (p. 39). © 1938 The Johns Hopkins University Press. Reprinted with permission of the publisher.

The Jamestown fort showed the colonists' awareness that native peoples were prepared to defend Virginia as their own. During May and June 1607, the settlers and Powhatan's warriors skirmished repeatedly. English muskets and cannon repelled Indian attacks on Jamestown, but the Indians' superior numbers and knowledge of the Virginia wilderness made it risky for the settlers to venture far beyond the peninsula. Late in June, Powhatan sensed a stalemate and made peace overtures.

The settlers soon confronted far more dangerous, invisible threats: disease and starvation. By September, fifty of the colonists had died. "Our men were destroyed with [such] cruell diseases as Swellings, Fluxes, Burning Fevers," George Percy recalled. The colonists increased their misery by constant bickering and plotting, leaving crops unplanted and food supplies diminishing; some died "of meere famine," according to Percy. Powhatan's people came to the rescue of the weakened and distracted colonists. Early in September 1607, they began to bring corn to the colony for barter. When that was insufficient to keep the colonists fed, the settlers sent Captain John Smith to trade for corn with tribes upriver from Jamestown. More soldier

JOHN SMITH'S MAP OF VIRGINIA
In 1612, John Smith published a detailed map of early Virginia that showed not only geographic features but also the limits of exploration (indicated by small crosses), the locations of the houses of the Indian "kings" (indicated by dwellings that look like Quonset huts), and "ordinary houses" of indigenous people (indicated by dots). The map shows the early settlers' intense interest in knowing where the Indians were—and were not. Note the location of Jamestown (upriver from Point Comfort) and of Powhatan's residence at the falls (just to the right of the large P outside the hut in the upper left corner). The drawing of Powhatan surrounded by some of his many wives (upper left corner) was almost certainly made by an English artist who had never been to Virginia or seen Powhatan but who tried to imagine the scene as described by John Smith.
Princeton University Libraries.

than merchant, Smith did not hesitate to take hostages and shoot to kill when Indians were reluctant to trade. His efforts managed to keep 38 of the original settlers alive until a fresh supply of food and 120 more colonists arrived from England in January 1608.

It is difficult to exaggerate the precarious state of the early Jamestown settlement. Although the Virginia Company sent hundreds of new settlers to Jamestown each year, few survived. During the "starving time" winter of 1609–10, food was so short that one or two famished settlers resorted to eating their recently deceased neighbors.

Encounters between Natives and Newcomers

In retrospect, the weakened condition of the settlers raises the question of why Powhatan did not strike to eliminate them. We cannot be certain about Powhatan's motives: Since native Americans relied on spoken rather than written language, they left no documents that record their ideas. All our information about them comes filtered through the distorting lenses of English eyes and ears. However, we can be certain what the Indians did. They maintained contact with the English settlers, and most of the time the contact was peaceful. But they also kept their distance.

The Virginia Company boasted that the settlers bought from the Indians "the pearles of earth [corn] and [sold] to them the pearles of heaven [Christianity]." In fact, few Indians converted to Christianity, and the English devoted scant effort to proselytizing. Marriage between Indian women and English men was also rare, despite the acute shortage of English women in Virginia in the early years. One of the few settlers who troubled to learn the Indians' language was John Smith. From his notes on Indian vocabulary, we know that the settlers quickly adopted several Virginia Algonquian words. We remain ignorant of English words that may have entered the Indians' vocabulary. It is safe to speculate that such words were few, given the cultural distance the Indians maintained.

Powhatan's people regarded the English with suspicion, and for good reason. While the settlers often exhibited friendship toward the Indians, they did not hesitate to use their superior weapons—muskets, swords, and cannon—to enforce English notions of proper Indian behavior. More than once the Indians refused to trade corn to the settlers,

Becaufe many doe defire to know the manner

of their Language, I haue inferted thefe few words.

KA katorawincs yowo. What call you this.

Nemarough, a man.

Crenepo, a woman.

Marowancheffo, a boy.

Yehawkans, Houfes.

Matchcores, Skins, or garments.

Mockafins, Shooes.

Tuffan, Beds. *Pokatawer*, Fire.

Attawp, A bow. *Attonce*, Arrowes.

Monacookes, Swords.

Aumouhhowgh, A Target.

Pawcuffacks, Gunnes.

Tomahacks, Axes.

Tockahacks, Pickaxes.

Pamefacks, Kniues.

Accowprets, Sheares.

Pawpecones, Pipes. *Mattaßin*, Copper

Vffawaffin, Iron, Braffe, Silver, or any white mettall. *Muffes*, Woods.

Attaffkuff, Leaues, weeds, or graffe.

Chepfin, Land. *Shacquohocan*. A ftone.

Wepenter, A cookold.

Suckahanna, Water. *Noughmaff*, Fifh.

Copotone, Sturgeon.

Weghfhaughes, Flefh.

Sawwehone, Bloud.

Netoppew, Friends.

Marrapough, Enemies.

Maskapow, the worft of the enemies.

Mawchick chammay, The beft of friends

Cafacunnakack, peya quagh acquintan vttafantafough, In how many daies will there come hither any more Englifh Ships.

Their Numbers.

Necut, 1. *Ningh*, 2. *Nuff*, 3. *Yowgh*, 4. *Paranske*, 5. *Comotinch*, 6. *Toppawoff*, 7 *Nuffwafh*, 8. *Kekatawgh*, 9. *Kaskeke* 10 They count no more but by tennes as followeth.

Cafe, how many.

Ninghfapooeksku, 20.

Nuffapooeksku, 30.

Yowghapooeksku, 40.

Parankeftaffapoockfku, 50.

Comatinchtaffapoockfku, 60.

Nuffwafhtaffapoockfku, 70.

Kekataughtaffapoockfku, 90.

Necuttoughtyfinough, 100.

Necuttwevnquaaough, 1000.

Rawcofowghs, Dayes.

Kefkowghes, Sunnes:

Toppquough. Nights.

Nepawwefhowghs, Moones.

Pawpaxfoughes, Yeares.

Pummahumps, Starres.

Ofies, Heauens.

Okees, Gods.

Quiyoughcofoughs, Pettie Gods, and their affinities.

Righcomoughes, Deaths.

Kekughes, Liues.

Mowchick woyawgh tawgh noeragh kaquere mecher, I am very hungry? what fhall I eate?

Tawnor nehiegh Powhatan, Where dwels Powhatan.

Mache, nehiegh yourowgh, Orapaks. Now he dwelsa great way hence at Orapaks.

Vittapitchewayne anpechitchs nehawper Werowacomoco, You lie, he ftaid ever at Werowacomoco.

Kator nehiegh mattagh neer vttapitchewayne, Truely he is there I doe not lie.

Spaughtynere keragh werowance mawmarinough kekatë wawgh peyaquaugh. Run you then to the King Mawmarynough and bid him come hither.

Vtteke, e peya weyack wighwhip, Get you gone, & come againe quickly.

Kekaten Pokahontas patiaquagh ningh tanks manotyens neer mowchick rawrenock audowgh, Bid Pokahontas bring hither two little Baskets, and I will giue her white Beads to make her a Chaine. *FINIS*.

JOHN SMITH'S DICTIONARY OF POWHATAN'S LANGUAGE *In 1612, John Smith published this list of the English equivalents of words used by Powhatan's people, almost the only record of the coastal Algonquian language that exists. Smith probably compiled this list by pointing and listening carefully. Can you find any of Powhatan's words that made their way into common English usage? What do the words in the list suggest about Smith's encounters with Powhatan's people? What interested Smith? What compelled the interest of his informants?* Princeton University Libraries.

evidently hoping to starve them out. But each time, the English broke the boycott by pillaging uncooperative villages and confiscating their corn. The Indians retaliated against English violence, but for fifteen years they did not organize an all-out assault on the European intruders, probably for several reasons. Although the Indians felt no attraction to Christianity, they were impressed by the power of the settlers' God. One chief told John Smith that "he did believe that our God as much exceeded theirs as our guns did their bows and arrows." Powhatan and his werowances probably concluded that these powerful strangers would make better allies than enemies. As allies, the English not only strengthened Powhatan's dominance over the tribes in the region; they also supplied his people with European goods, usually in exchange for corn. Although the native Virginians possessed copper before the English arrived, they immediately recognized the superiority of the settlers' iron and steel weapons and tools, and they could not get enough of them.

While the settlers often exhibited friendship toward the Indians, they did not hesitate to use their superior weapons—muskets, swords, and cannon—to enforce English notions of proper Indian behavior.

The trade that supplied Indians with European conveniences provided the English settlers with a prime necessity: food. But why did the settlers prove unable to feed themselves for more than a decade? First, as the staggering death rate suggests, many settlers were too sick to be productive members of the colony. Second, very few farmers came to Virginia in the early years. Instead, most of the newcomers were gentlemen and their servants, men who, in John Smith's words, "never did know what a day's work was." In fact, the proportion of gentlemen in Virginia in the early years was six times greater than in England, a reflection of the Virginia Company's urgent need for both investors and settlers. Instead of seeing gentlemen as a liability to the colony, the company tried to attract them. In a

ADVERTISEMENT FOR JAMESTOWN SETTLERS
While Virginia imported thousands of indentured servants to labor in tobacco fields, the colony advertised in 1631 for settlers like those pictured here. The notice features men and women equally, although men heavily outnumbered women among actual newcomers to the Chesapeake. How would the English experiences of the individuals portrayed in the advertisement be useful in Virginia? Why would such individuals want to leave England and go to Virginia? If indentured servants were pictured, how might their appearances differ from these people?
Houghton Library, Harvard Map Collection, Harvard University.

1610 pamphlet, the company declared that nobody should believe that Virginia "excludeth Gentlemen . . . for though they cannot digge, use the square, nor practise the axe and chizell, yet [they know] . . . how to employ the force of knowledge, the exercise of counsell, the operation and power of their best breeding and qualities." In Virginia, however, breeding and quality were worthless for growing corn, catching fish, or even hunting deer. Nevertheless, for more than a decade, the colonists clung to English notions that gentlemen were not supposed to work with their hands and tradesmen were not supposed to work at trades for which they had not been trained, ideas about labor that made more sense in labor-rich England than in labor-poor Virginia. In the meantime, the colonists depended on the Indians' corn for food. (See "The Promise of Technology," page 46.)

The persistence of the Virginia colony, precarious as it was, created difficulties for Powhatan's chiefdom. The steady contact between natives and newcomers spread European viruses among the Indians, who suffered deadly epidemics in 1608 and between 1617 and 1619. While epidemics weakened the Indians, trade with the settlers distorted native American culture. If the Indians produced only enough corn for self-sufficiency, as they had for centuries, they risked famine when the English commandeered it to feed the settlers. The need to produce corn both for their own survival and for trade probably introduced tensions within Powhatan's villages, increasing the significance of agriculture and women's work. But from the Indians' viewpoint, the most important fact about the Virginia colony was that it was surviving. Instead of a temporary outpost, it was proving to be a permanent settlement.

Powhatan died in 1618, and his brother Opechancanough replaced him as supreme chief. In 1622, Opechancanough organized an all-out assault on the English settlers. Striking on March 22, the Indians killed 347 settlers, nearly a third of the English population. But the attack failed to dislodge the colonists. In the aftermath, the settlers unleashed a murderous campaign of Indian extermination that in a few years pushed Indians beyond the small circumference of white settlement. Before 1622, the settlers knew that the Indians, though dangerous, were necessary to keep the colony alive. After 1622, the settlers concluded that the life of the colony required the death of the Indians, at least in the vicinity of white settlement. After 1622, most colonists considered Indians their perpetual enemies.

From Private Company to Royal Government

The 1622 uprising came close to achieving Opechancanough's goal of pushing the colonists back into the Atlantic—so close that it prompted a royal investigation of affairs in Virginia. The investigators discovered that the appalling mortality among the colonists was caused by disease and mismanagement more than by Indian raids. In 1624, King James revoked the charter of the Virginia Company and made Virginia a royal colony, subject to the direction of the royal government rather than to the company's private investors, an arrangement that lasted until 1776.

The king now appointed the governor of Virginia and his council, but most other features of local government established under the Virginia Company remained intact. In 1619, for example, the company had inaugurated the House of Burgesses, an assembly of representatives (called burgesses) elected by the colony's inhabitants. (Historians do not know exactly which settlers were considered inhabitants and were thus qualified to vote for burgesses.) The company authorized the burgesses to propose laws that, when approved by company officials in London, would become enforceable. Under the new royal government, laws had to be approved by the king's bureaucrats in England rather than by the company. Otherwise, the House of Burgesses continued as before, acquiring distinction as the oldest representative legislative assembly in the British colonies. In addition, under the royal government in Virginia, all free adult men could vote for burgesses, giving the House of Burgesses a far broader and more representative constituency than the English House of Commons.

All free adult men could vote for burgesses, giving the House of Burgesses a far broader and more representative constituency than the English House of Commons.

The demise of the Virginia Company marked the end of the first phase of colonization of the Chesapeake. From the 105 adventurers who had landed in 1607 and the hundreds more who followed, the population had grown to about 1,200 by 1624. Mortality rates among newcomers continued at levels higher than those in the worst epidemics in London, but new settlers still arrived. Their arrival and King James's willingness to take over the struggling colony signaled a fundamental change in Virginia. After years of fruitless experimentation, it was becoming clear that English settlers could make a fortune in Virginia by growing tobacco.

A Tobacco Society

Tobacco did not figure in the initial plans of the Virginia Company. "As for tobacco," John Smith wrote later, "we never then dreamt of it." John Rolfe began to plant West Indian tobacco seeds in 1612. His experiments showed that the plant could be grown successfully in Virginia. The first commercial shipment of tobacco to England left the colony in 1617. When it sold for a high price, the same Virginia colonists who had difficulty growing enough corn to feed themselves quickly tried to learn how to grow as much tobacco as possible. In a sense, that first commercial cargo was a pivot on which Virginia turned from a colony of rather aimless adventurers into a society of dedicated planters.

Dedicated they were. In 1620, with fewer than a thousand colonists, Virginia shipped 60,000 pounds of tobacco to England. By 1700, tobacco exports from the Chesapeake region (encompassing Virginia and Maryland) topped 35 million pounds, and more than 98,000 colonists lived in the region. Per capita tobacco exports grew fivefold, demonstrating that Chesapeake colonists had mastered the demands of tobacco agriculture. Tobacco planters' endless need for labor attracted droves of indentured servants from England to work in tobacco fields and settle the Chesapeake (Map 2.1).

TOBACCO WRAPPER
This wrapper labeled a container of "Virginia Planters Best Tobacco." It shows a colonial planter supervising slaves who hold hoes used to chop weeds that robbed the leafy tobacco plants of nutrients and moisture. The planter enjoys a pipe in the shade of an umbrella held by a slave. After the tobacco was harvested and dried, it was pressed tightly into barrels, like those shown here, for shipment overseas. How does this illustration indicate the differences between the planter and the slaves?
Colonial Williamsburg Foundation.

Tobacco Agriculture

Tobacco was a demanding crop. It required close attention and a great deal of hand labor year-round. By the time one year's crop was being readied for market, the next year's crop was already in the ground. Food crops had to be grown in the midst of the tobacco crop cycle, so the colonists had little time for idleness. But in spare moments they enjoyed the fruits of their labor. As a traveler observed, "Everyone smokes while working or idling . . . men, women, girls, and boys from the age of seven years."

English settlers were willing to work hard because they could expect to do much better in the Chesapeake than in England. One colonist declared that "the dirt of this Province affords as great a profit to the general Inhabitant, as the Gold of Peru doth to . . . the Spaniard." Although that observation was exaggerated, it was true that a hired man would have to work two or three years in England to earn as much as he could in just one year in Chesapeake tobacco fields. Better still, in Virginia land was so abundant that, by English standards, it was extremely cheap. In the mid-seventeenth-

Corn, the "Life-Giver"

Europeans first learned about corn from Columbus. As soon as he returned to Spain in 1493, he told the royal court about amazing things he had seen on his voyage to the other side of the Atlantic, including a plant he called *maize,* his version of *mahiz,* the Taino word for corn, which meant "life-giver." Ancient Americans had been growing corn for about seven thousand years. From its origin in central Mexico, corn had spread throughout the Western Hemisphere by the time Columbus arrived. Although the rest of the world had never seen or heard of corn, within a generation after 1493 travelers carried seeds throughout the Old World. By the early sixteenth century, corn seeds sprouted in Europe, the Middle East, Africa, India, and China.

Accustomed to growing wheat and eating foods derived from it, Europeans at first did not like corn. A few years before the settlers arrived in Jamestown, an English botanist expressed the common European view that "the barbarous Indians which know no better, are constrained to make a vertue of necessitie, and think [corn is] a good food; whereas we may easily judge that it nourisheth but little, and is of hard and evill digestion, a more convenient foode for swine than for man."

Early in the seventeenth century, English settlers in North America discovered that hunger quickly made a virtue of necessity. John Smith wrote that during the spring of 1609 Jamestown residents became so hungry that "they would have sould their soules" for a half-basket of Powhatan's corn. Before settlers could reliably subsist in the Chesapeake region, they had to learn the technology of corn.

From the perspective of the twenty-first century, it may seem odd to speak of the technology of corn. Today, we tend to think that technology refers only to machinery such as engines, computer chips, or airplanes. But technology also refers to a much broader range of human experience. *Webster's* defines technology as "the science of the application of knowledge to practical purposes." Nowadays, technological knowledge has found countless practical uses for corn as food, sweetener, and oil, as well as in such products as medicines, tires, batteries, and lipstick. The roots of these modern-day uses of corn stretch back to ancient Americans who first developed the technology of growing, processing, and consuming corn, a technology English settlers of North America sought to learn for the practical purpose of eating.

Corn needs help to grow. Bury an ear of corn in the soil and the seeds that sprout strangle each other in an overcrowded quest for light. But strip the husk from a ripe ear of corn, rub the seeds out of the cob, plant the separated seeds on a spring day in a spot with sufficient heat, light, and water, and during the summer each seed is capable of producing a stalk with two or more ears, each bearing hundreds of edible corn seeds. An awestruck English visitor described corn's "marveillous great increase; of a thousand, fifteene hundred and some two thousand fold."

To obtain this impressive yield, early-seventeenth-century European settlers throughout North America watched native Americans cultivate corn. "In place of ploughs" commonly used in England, one observer reported, "they use an instrument of hard wood, shaped like a spade" to break up the soil and prepare it for planting, work usually done by men. Then women used a stick to "make a hole [in the soil] wherein they put out four grains . . . and cover them." Another colonist acknowledged that native Americans were "our first instructors for the planting of their Indian Corne, by teaching us to cull out the finest seede, to observe the fittest season, to keepe distance for holes, and fit measure for hills, to worme it, and weede it; to prune it, and dresse it as occasion shall require." Jamestown's early settlers did not depend on chance observations of this planting technology. John Smith boasted that two hostages the colonists captured from Powhatan "taught us how to order and plant our fields" while they were held as "fettered prisoners."

Along with corn, Indians usually planted beans. "When they [beans] grow up they interlace with the corn . . . and they keep the ground very free from weeds," one newcomer noticed. Ancient Americans' association of beans with corn had a sound biochemical basis. Beans fixed nitrogen in the soil, a function corn roots cannot perform. Corn plants then absorbed the nitrogen to produce higher yields. Beans also made corn more nutritious. Beans contain niacin, an essential nutrient lacking in corn. Together, corn and beans provided the basic ingredients for a healthy diet.

As every popcorn eater knows, corn kernels are hard enough to crack a tooth. European settlers had no difficulty eating green or sweet corn, the immature form of ripening corn commonly consumed today as corn on the cob. But to obtain the nutritious interior of mature corn kernels without cracking their teeth they had to learn ancient American technology. For millennia native Americans had soaked or boiled corn kernels with wood ash or other alkaline material. The alkali softened and loosened the tough hull protecting the corn's nutrients. Treated in this way, corn kernels that otherwise were rock-hard could be separated from their hulls and readily mashed into dough for tortillas or mixed with beans or other foods in tasty stews. Early colonists copied this process to make softened corn foods they called samp, or hominy, or grits.

Since settlers were accustomed to wheat ground into a fine flour, they preferred cornmeal obtained by the much more laborious process of pulverizing corn kernels with a mortar and pestle or grinding them between stones, both processes familiar to native Americans. From cornmeal dough cooked on an iron griddle or baked in the coals of a cookfire, Europeans made corn bread, corn pone, hoecake, and johnnycake—English names for ancient American food.

Unlike wheat, many varieties of corn pop open when heated, an astonishing trait Columbus duly reported to his Spanish sponsors. Archaeologists speculate that ancient Americans first thought to cultivate corn when a few grains accidentally landed in a campfire and out popped a morsel of readily edible food. For millennia ancient Americans enjoyed popcorn, not least because it so easily avoided the need to soak, boil, or grind hard corn kernels. They also ground popped corn into a nu-

ANCIENT CORN POPPER

Long before movies and microwaves, ancient Americans munched popcorn. This corn popper comes from the Mochica culture, which thrived on the northern coast of Peru for about 600 years after the birth of Christ. The Mochica presumably nestled the popper on a bed of coals with the opening facing up, placed corn inside, and covered the opening with a lid (not shown) while the kernels popped. The Mochica and other ancient Americans did not pop most of the corn they grew. Instead they ground it into corn meal which they incorporated in a wide variety of dishes, probably including ancient counterparts of modern tortillas.

The Field Museum #A112961c, Chicago. Photographer: Diane Alexander White.

tritious and portable powder that could be mixed with water and other foods for a satisfying meal. The New England minister Roger Williams wrote that he "made a good dinner and supper" with "a *spoonfull* of this *meale* and a *spoonfull* of water from the *Brooke.*" Other colonists, too, learned the ancient technology of popcorn. Today, at the cineplex and on the couch, every American consumes about fifty quarts of popped corn each year, participating— usually unwittingly—in a technology that reaches back in unbroken continuity to a campfire in central Mexico about seven thousand years ago.

MAP 2.1
**The Chesapeake Colonies
in the Seventeenth Century**
*The intimate association of
land and water in the settlement of the Chesapeake
in the seventeenth century
is illustrated by this map.
Why was access to navi-
gable water so important?*

century Chesapeake, even common laborers could buy one hundred acres of land for less than their annual wages—an impossibility in England. New settlers who paid their own transportation to the Chesapeake received a grant of fifty acres of free land (a headright), a policy begun by the Virginia Company and continued by the royal government to encourage settlement.

A Servant Labor System

Headrights, cheap land, and high wages gave poor English folk powerful incentives to immigrate to the New World. Yet many potential immigrants could not scrape together the fare to cross the Atlantic.

Their poverty and the colonists' crying need for labor formed the basic context for the creation of a servant labor system.

Today, people think of the colonial South as a slave society. The seventeenth-century Chesapeake, however, was fundamentally a servant society. Twenty Africans arrived in Virginia in 1619, but until the last quarter of the seventeenth century, only a small number of slaves labored in Chesapeake to-bacco fields. (Large numbers of slaves came later, as chapter 4 explains.) About 80 percent of the immi-grants to the Chesapeake during the seventeenth century were indentured servants. Along with to-bacco, the servant labor system profoundly influ-enced nearly every feature of Chesapeake society.

To buy passage aboard a ship bound for the Chesapeake, an English immigrant had to come up with about £5, roughly a year's wages for an English servant or laborer. Saving a year's wages was no easier at that time than it is now. Opportunities for work were shrinking in seventeenth-century England. Many country gentlemen fenced fields they had formerly planted with crops and began to pasture sheep in the enclosures, which required fewer farmhands. Even the employed found the purchasing power of their wages slowly deteriorating as prices rose.

The seventeenth-century Chesapeake was fundamentally a servant society.

Lacking the money to get across the Atlantic, poor immigrants signed a contract, called an *indenture,* with a local shopkeeper, mariner, or merchant specifying that the merchant would pay for the immigrant's transportation to the Chesapeake. In return, the immigrant agreed to work for a period—usually four to seven years—without pay. During this period of indentured servitude, the immigrant received food and shelter from an employer in the colonies. When the indenture expired, the employer was required to give the former servant "freedom dues," usually three barrels of corn and a suit of clothes. In effect, indentures allowed poor immigrants to trade their most valuable asset—their ability to work—for a trip to the New World.

Most planters were willing to pay about twice the cost of transportation for the right to four to seven years of an immigrant's labor. Most of the planter's payment was returned as a handsome profit to the English merchant who had indentured the immigrant. And the planters profited as well. As one Virginian noted, "our principall wealth . . . consisteth in servants." More servants meant more hands to grow more tobacco. More servants also meant more land. For every servant purchased, a planter received from the colonial government a headright of another fifty acres of land. Even without the land, a servant was a good investment. A servant was expected to grow enough tobacco in one year to cover the cost of the indenture plus enough corn to feed himself or herself. The servant's labor for the rest of the indenture gave the planter a substantial return on investment.

At least it did if all went well. Bad weather, crop disease, or insects could ruin a harvest. But the biggest risk to both the planter and the servant was that the servant would get sick and die before serving out the term of the indenture. Among one group of 275 servant men who arrived in Maryland before midcentury, 40 percent died before their servitude ended. Less than a third of the original group remained in the colony for ten years after their indentures expired. Eight out of ten of these men managed to acquire small farms, and a few possessed servants of their own.

For the most part, servants were simply poor young English men seeking work. More than two-thirds of them were between fifteen and twenty-five when they came to the Chesapeake. Many were orphans. Most had no special training or skills, although the majority had some experience with agricultural work. "Hunger and fear of prisons bring to us onely such servants as have been brought up to no Art or Trade," a Virginia planter complained in 1662. A skilled craftsman could obtain a shorter indenture, but few risked coming to the colonies since their prospects were better at home.

LEARNING TO INHALE
It took a while for Europeans to master the many refinements of smoking. This Dutch ceramic tile made early in the seventeenth century shows a smoker accomplishing the remarkable feat (at that time) of blowing smoke through his nose. Other fashionable Europeans inhaled snuff, finely ground tobacco powder that delivered a stiff jolt of nicotine to nasal membranes.
Niemeyer Tabaksmuseum.

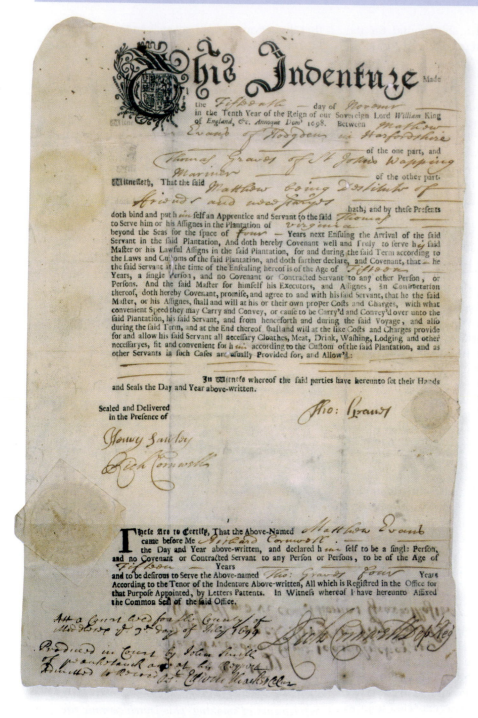

INDENTURE CONTRACT
Indenture contracts were so common that forms were printed, leaving blank spaces for the details. Here, in mid-November 1698, fifteen-year-old Mathew Evans, a friendless boy from Harfordshire, agreed to serve mariner Thomas Graves, or anybody to whom Graves sold his rights, for four years in Virginia. The contract specified that Graves would carry Evans to Virginia and provide during the term of the indenture, "all necessary Cloathes, Meat, Drink, Washing, Lodging and other necessaryes, fit and convenient for him according to the Custom of the said Plantation, as other Servants in such Cases are usually Provided for. . . ."
The Library of Virginia.

Women were almost as rare as skilled craftsmen in the Chesapeake and more ardently desired. In the early days of the tobacco boom, the Virginia Company shipped unattached young women to the colony as prospective wives for male settlers willing to pay "120 weight [pounds] of the best leaf tobacco for each of them." The company reasoned that, as one official wrote in 1622, "the plantation can never flourish till families be planted, and the respect of wives and children fix the people on the soil." The company's efforts as a marriage broker proved no more successful than its other ventures.

Men continued to outnumber women by a wide margin until late in the seventeenth century. The servant labor system perpetuated the gender imbalance. Although female servants cost about the same as males and generally served for the same length of time, only about one indentured servant in four was a woman. Planters preferred male servants for field work, although many women also hoed tobacco fields. Most women servants, however, did household chores such as cooking, washing, cleaning, gardening, and milking.

Servant life was harsh by the standards of seventeenth-century England and even by the rougher frontier standards of the Chesapeake. Unlike their English counterparts, Chesapeake servants had virtually no control over who purchased their labor—and thus them—for the period of the indenture. A servant might be bought and sold several times before the indenture expired. One servant wrote from Virginia in 1623 that his master "hath sold me for £150 sterling like a damnd slave." The colonial practice of treating servants as property alarmed some Englishmen. But the colonists' need for labor and the profits to be made in supplying it quickly muffled such qualms.

Servant life was harsh by the standards of seventeenth-century England and even by the rougher frontier standards of the Chesapeake.

Some former servants argued that indentured servitude had advantages, despite its rigors. But most found otherwise. James Revel, an eighteen-year-old thief who was punished by being indentured to a Virginia tobacco planter, described experiences common to most servants. In verse, Revel chronicled what happened when he arrived at his new master's plantation:

My Europian clothes were took from me,
Which never after I again could see.

A canvas shirt and trowsers then they gave,
With a hop-sack frock in which I was to slave:
No shoes nor stockings had I for to wear,
Nor hat, nor cap, both head and feet were bare.

Thus dress'd into the Field I next must go,
Amongst tobacco plants all day to hoe,
At day break in the morn our work began,
And so held to the setting of the Sun.

Severe laws were designed to keep servants in their place in more ways than one. Punishments for petty crimes like running away or stealing a pig stretched servitude far beyond the original terms of indenture. Servant Christopher Adams, for example, had to serve three extra years for running away for six months; Richard Higby received six extra years of servitude for killing three hogs. Just after midcentury, the Virginia legislature added at least three years to the servitude of most servants by requiring them to serve until they were twenty-four years old.

Women servants were subject to special restrictions and risks. They were prohibited from marrying until their servitude had expired. A servant woman, the law assumed, could not serve two masters at the same time: one who owned her indentured labor and another who was her husband. However, the overwhelming predominance of men in the Chesapeake population inevitably pressured women to engage in sexual relations. The pressure was strong enough that about a third of immigrant women were pregnant when they got married. Pregnancy and childbirth sapped a woman's strength, and a new child diverted her attention, reducing her usefulness to her master. As a rule, if a woman servant gave birth to a child, she had to serve two extra years and pay a fine.

Such punishments reflected four fundamental realities of the servant labor system. First, masters' hunger for labor led them to demand as much work from their servants as possible, and they did not hesitate to devise legal ways to extend the period of servitude. Second, servants hoped to survive their period of servitude and then use their freedom to start a family and obtain land. They worked as hard as they had to rather than—as their masters wanted—as hard as they could. Third, servants saw themselves as free people in a temporary status of servitude, and they frequently resisted their masters' orders. Fourth, both servants and masters put up with this contentious arrangement because the alternatives were less desirable.

Masters could not easily hire free men and women because land was so readily available that those who were free preferred to work on their own land for themselves. Furthermore, most masters could not depend on much labor from family members. The preponderance of men meant that families were few, were started late, and thus had few children. And, until the 1680s and 1690s, slaves were expensive and hard to come by. Before then,

TOBACCO PLANTATION
This print illustrates the tobacco harvest on a seventeenth century plantation. Workers cut the mature plants and put the leaves in piles to wilt (left foreground and center background). After the leaves had dried somewhat, they were suspended from poles in a drying barn (right foreground), where they were seasoned before being packed in casks for shipping. Sometimes they were also dried in the fields (center background). The print suggests the labor demands of tobacco by showing twenty-two individuals, all but two of them actively at work with the crop. The one woman depicted (hand in hand with a man in the left foreground) may be on her way to work in the harvest, but it appears more likely that she and the man are overseeing the labor of their servants or employees.
From "About Tobacco," Lehman Brothers.

masters who wanted to expand their labor force and grow more tobacco had few alternatives to buying indentured servants.

The Evolution of Chesapeake Society

The colonists' incessant desire to grow more tobacco propelled the evolution of Chesapeake society. The requirements of tobacco agriculture shaped patterns of settlement, making the landscape of the English colonies in the Chesapeake quite different from that of rural England. English colonists professed the Protestant and Catholic faiths, but they governed their daily lives less by the dictates of religious doctrine than by the demands of tobacco cultivation.

The system of indentured servitude sharpened inequality in Chesapeake society by the mid-seventeenth century. Social and political polarization culminated in 1676 with Bacon's Rebellion. The rebellion ultimately prompted reforms that stabilized relations between elite planters and their lesser neighbors and paved the way for a social hierarchy based less overtly on land and wealth than on race. (See "Historical Question," page 54.) Amidst this social and political evolution, one thing did not change: the dedication of Chesapeake colonists to growing tobacco.

Life, Faith, and Labor

Villages and small towns dotted the rural landscape of seventeenth-century England, but colonists did not reproduce that English pattern in the Chesapeake. Instead, acres of wilderness were interrupted here and there by tobacco farms. This landscape arose from the settlers' determination to profit from tobacco, even at the expense of familiar patterns of English community life.

Tobacco was such a labor-intensive crop that one field worker could tend only about two acres of the plants in a year (an acre is slightly smaller than a football field). A family farmer needed to devote a few more acres to food crops, but a total of five or ten acres under cultivation sufficed to make a working tobacco farm. However, a successful farmer needed a great deal more land because tobacco quickly exhausted the fertility of the soil. Since each farmer cultivated only 5 or 10 percent of his land at any one time, a "settled" area comprised swatches of cultivated land surrounded by virgin forest.

Settlement Patterns along the James River

Arrangements for marketing tobacco also contributed to the dispersion of settlements. Ideally, tobacco planters sought land that fronted a navigable river. Ocean-going ships could then dock at the planter's doorstep and minimize the work of transporting and loading the heavy hogsheads of tobacco leaves. A settled region resembled a lacework of farms stitched around waterways.

On individual farmsteads, farmers built their houses from beams and planks hewn from felled timber. Although serviceable, the houses were by no means grand, or even particularly sturdy. A typical seventeenth-century tobacco farmer lived with his family and servants (if he had them) in a one- or two-room box of about four hundred square feet.

Most Chesapeake colonists were nominally Protestants. Attendance at Sunday services and conformity to the doctrines of the Church of England were required of all English men and women. However, clergymen were difficult to attract to the Chesapeake, and many of those who came were no more pious or righteous than their parishioners. Certainly some colonists took their religion seriously. Church courts punished fornicators, censured blasphemers, and served notice on those who spent Sundays "goeing a fishing." But on the whole, religion did not awaken the zeal of Chesapeake settlers, certainly not as it did the New England settlers in these same years (see chapter 3). What quickened the pulse of most Chesapeake folk was a close-run horse race, a bloody cockfight, or—most of all—an exceptionally fine tobacco crop. The religion of the Chesapeake colonists was Anglican, but their faith lay in the turbulent, competitive, high-stakes gamble of survival as tobacco planters.

The situation was similar in the Catholic colony of Maryland. In 1632, King Charles I (who had succeeded James I in 1625) granted his Catholic friend Lord Baltimore about six and a half million acres in the northern Chesapeake region. Lord Baltimore intended to create a refuge for Catholics, who suffered severe discrimination in England. He fitted out two ships, the *Ark* and the *Dove*, gathered about 150 settlers, and sent them to the new colony, where they arrived on March 25, 1634. However, the population of Maryland grew very slowly for the next twenty years, and most settlers were Protestants rather than Catholics. The religious turmoil of the Puritan Revolution in England (discussed in chapter 4) spilled across the Atlantic, creating conflict between Maryland's few Catholics—most of them wealthy and prominent—and the Protestant majority, most of them neither wealthy nor prominent. During the 1660s, Maryland began to attract settlers as readily as Virginia, mostly Protestants. Although Catholics and the Catholic faith continued to exert influence in Maryland, the colony's society, economy, politics, and culture became virtually indistinguishable from Virginia's. Both colonies shared a devotion to tobacco, the true faith of the Chesapeake.

The religion of the Chesapeake colonists was Anglican, but their faith lay in the turbulent, competitive, high-stakes gamble of survival as tobacco planters.

One historian has aptly termed this the era of the yeoman planter—that is, a farmer who owned a small plot of land sufficient to support a family and tilled largely by family members and perhaps a few servants. A few elite planters had larger estates

Why Did English Colonists Consider Themselves Superior to Indians and Africans?

WERE SEEDS OF THE RACIAL PREJUDICE that has been such a powerful force in American history planted in the seventeenth-century Chesapeake? To answer that question, historians have paid close attention to the words the colonists used to describe Indians, Africans, and themselves.

In the mid-1500s, the English adopted the words *Indian* and *Negro* from Spanish, where they had come to mean, respectively, an aboriginal inhabitant of the New World and a black person of African ancestry. Both terms were generic, homogenizing an enormous diversity of tribal affiliations, languages, and cultures. Neither term originated with the people to whom it referred. The New England minister Roger Williams, who published a book on Indian languages in 1643, reported, "They have often asked mee, why we call them Indians," a poignant question that reveals the European origins of the term.

After *Indians,* the word the settlers used most frequently to describe native Americans was *savages.* The Indians were savages in the colonists' eyes because they lacked the traits of English civilization. As one Englishman put it in 1625, the natives of Virginia were "so bad a people, having little of humanitie but shape, ignorant of Civilitie, of Arts, of Religion; more brutish than the beasts they hunt, more wild and unmanly than that unmanned wild countrey, which they range rather than inhabite; captivated also to Satans tyranny in foolish pieties, mad impieties, wicked idlenesse, busie and bloudy wickednesse." Some English colonists counterbalanced this harsh indictment with admiration for certain features of Indian behavior. They praised Indians' calm dignity and poise, their tender love and care for family members, and their simple, independent way of life in apparent harmony with nature.

Color was not a feature of the Indians' savagery. During the seventeenth century, colonists never referred to Indians as "red." Instead, they saw Indians' skin color as tawny or tanned, the "Sun's livery," as one settler wrote. Many settlers held the view that Indians were innately white like the English but in every other way woefully un-English.

In effect, the English colonists defined the Indians as "them," not "us." The colonists assumed that this distinction expressed a hierarchy of power and status: "We" are superior and should be dominant; "they" are inferior and should be subordinate. They enforced the distinction ferociously. In the early years of settlement, the colonists allowed a few young men to live for a while in Indian villages to learn native languages and then serve as interpreters. However, settlers who deserted English settlements in preference for Indian society were punished with a vengeance.

The colonists identified Africans quite differently. Only a few Africans lived in the Chesapeake early in the seventeenth century. The first recorded arrival of Africans occurred in 1619, when a Dutch man-of-war brought to Virginia "20. and odd Negroes," as John Rolfe wrote. Rolfe's usage illustrates the colonists' most common term for Africans: *Negroes.* But the other word the colonists frequently used to refer to Africans was not *savage* or *heathen,* but *black.* What struck English colonists most forcefully about Africans was not their un-English ways but their un-English skin color.

Black was not a neutral color to the colonists. According to the *Oxford English Dictionary* (which catalogs the changing meaning of words), *black* meant to the English people who settled the Chesapeake "deeply stained with dirt; soiled, dirty, foul . . . having dark or deadly purposes, malignant; pertaining to or involving death, deadly; baneful, disastrous, sinister . . . foul, iniquitous, atrocious, horrible, wicked." Black was the opposite of white, which connoted purity, beauty, and goodness—attributes the colonists identified with themselves. In fact, by the middle of the seventeenth century, the colonists referred to themselves not only as English but also as free, implying that people who were not English were not free. After about 1680, the colonists stated that implication in racial terms by referring to themselves as white. By the end of the seventeenth century, blacks were "them"—un-English, unwhite, and unfree.

A few of the English dissented from such views. Thomas Phillips, a slave ship captain, declared in 1694 that he could not "imagine why they [blacks] should be despis'd for their colour, being what they cannot help, and the effect of the climate it has pleas'd God

KATARINA, "MOORISH WOMAN"

Albrecht Dürer, one of the foremost artists of the Renaissance, drew this portrait of Katarina early in the sixteenth century. It is among the first portraits of Africans made in Renaissance Europe. Katarina was the servant of a Portuguese merchant Dürer visited in the Netherlands, in the spring of 1521. The portrait was completed before the Atlantic slave trade had begun to boom, but well after Portuguese merchants had brought thousands of African slaves to Europe. Dürer's meticulous portrait betrays no trace of racial prejudice. Katarina wears European clothing and is depicted with the same respect and dignity Dürer accorded Europeans whose likenesses he drew. In what ways might this portrait have been different if it had been executed by an artist in the southern colonies of North America in the late seventeenth century?

Foto Marburg/Art Resource, NY.

A YOUNG VIRGINIAN

In 1645, the Dutch artist Wenceslaus Hollar drew this portrait of a twenty-three-year-old Indian man from Virginia. The young man had evidently been brought to London where he posed for this likeness. Hollar portrayed the exotic adornment of the man—the animal claw headband, shell earrings and necklace, facial markings, Mohawk haircut, and bare-chested torso. Yet these distinctly non-European features did not cause Hollar to compromise his humane, dignified depiction of this man, whose gaze seems to be fixed steadily and shamelessly upon the observer. If this young Virginian had been back in the Chesapeake rather than in London, he would probably have been engaged in the deadly warfare triggered by Opechancanough's 1644 uprising. How might this portrait have been different if it had been drawn by a Virginia colonist in 1645?

Copyright © The British Museum.

to appoint them. I can't think there is any intrinsick value in one colour more than another, nor that white is better than black, only we think it so because we are so, and are prone to judge favourably in our own case, as well as the blacks, who in odium of the colour, say, the devil is white, and so paint him."

Virginians did not legally define slavery until 1660, but the sparse surviving evidence (*Continued*) demonstrates that they practiced slavery long before that. Although there is no way to be certain, it is likely that the "20. and odd Negroes" who arrived in 1619 were slaves. And the punishments handed out to blacks who broke the law usually took for granted that their servitude could not be extended, presumably because they were already in bondage for life, not—like servants—for several years.

The debased status of slavery strengthened the colonists' prejudice toward blacks, just as racial prejudice buttressed slavery. A Virginia law of 1662, for instance, provided that "if any christian shall committ Fornication with a negro man or woman, hee or shee soe offending" had to pay a double fine. The law also demonstrates that, despite racial prejudice, sexual relations between white and black settlers were prevalent enough to attract the attention of the legislature.

For most of the seventeenth century, possession of a black skin did not automatically and necessarily condemn a person to the status of slave in the eyes of whites. Some Africans in the Chesapeake served for limited periods of time like white servants, became free like white servants, and even acquired land, reared families, and participated in local affairs like former white servants. In fact, white colonists' prejudice against blacks represented an extreme form of wealthy colonists' attitudes toward servants and other poor white people. White servants, like blacks, were often considered "the vile and brutish part of mankind" by their masters.

The colonists hardened and exaggerated English attitudes about social hierarchy, about "us" and "them." Part of the reason is that, when colonists left England, they worried that they were separating themselves from "us"—the English—and risking becoming "them"—those uncivilized people found in the colonial wilds. To temper those fears and reduce those risks, colonists defined "us" and "them" in terms that emphasized their own Englishness in both color and civilization, providing a fertile seedbed for the growth of racial prejudice.

and commanded ten or more servants. But for the first thirty or forty years, few men lived long enough to accumulate a fortune sufficient to set them much apart from their neighbors. Until midcentury, the principal division in Chesapeake society was less between rich and poor planters than between free farmers and unfree servants. While these two groups contrasted sharply in their legal and economic status, their daily lives had many similarities: Most of them worked at the same tasks in the same fields, ate the same food, often at the same table, and slept in the same house. Although servants were required to be subordinate, they nonetheless looked forward to the time when their indentures would expire and they would be free. Once free, they usually had to work several more years as hired hands or tenant farmers to earn enough to buy land. Nonetheless, they readily assimilated into free society. On the whole, a rough, frontier equality characterized free families in the Chesapeake until about 1650.

Three major developments splintered that equality during the third quarter of the century. First, as tobacco production increased, prices declined. Cheap tobacco reduced planters' profits and made it more difficult for freed servants to save enough to become landowners. Second, because the mortality rate dropped, more and more servants survived their indentures. As landless freemen became more numerous, they grew more discontent. Third, declining mortality also encouraged the formation of a planter elite. By living longer, the most successful planters compounded their success. The wealthiest planters also began to serve as merchants, marketing crops for their less successful neighbors, importing English goods for sale, and above all giving credit to hard-pressed customers.

By the 1670s, the social structure of the Chesapeake had become polarized. Landowners—the planter elite and the more numerous yeoman planters—clustered around one pole. Landless colonists, mainly freed servants, gathered at the other. Each group eyed the other with suspicion and mistrust. For the most part, planters saw landless freemen as a dangerous rabble rather than as fellow colonists with legitimate grievances.

Government, Politics, and Polarization

In general, government and politics amplified the distinctions in Chesapeake society. The most vital distinction separated servants and masters, and the colonial government enforced it with an iron fist. Quick to prosecute critics, the governor's council hesitated to censure masters who brutalized their servants. No wonder poor men like William Tyler complained that "nether the Governor nor Counsell could or would

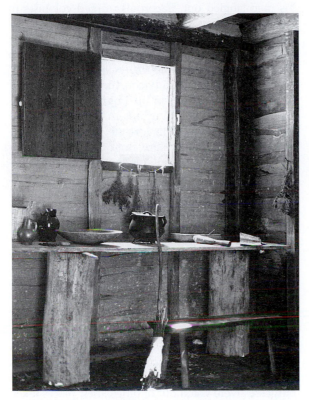

INSIDE A POOR PLANTER'S HOUSE
The houses of seventeenth-century Chesapeake settlers were typically "earth-fast"—that is, the structural timbers that framed the house were simply placed in holes in the ground and the floor was packed dirt. No seventeenth-century house was substantial enough to survive until today. This photo shows a carefully documented historical reconstruction of the interior of a poor planter's house at St. Mary's City, Maryland. The wall of this one-room dwelling with a loft features a window with a shutter, but no glass; when the shutter was closed, the only source of light was a candle or a fire. Note the rustic, unfinished bench, table, and walls. These meager furnishings were usually accompanied by a storage chest and some bedding, but not a bed. If and when the planters became more prosperous, they often made a bed their first acquisition, suggesting that the lack of a good night's sleep was one of their major discomforts.
Paul Leibe, Historic St. Mary's City.

doe any poore men right, but that they would shew favor to great men and wronge the poore." The poor had plenty of ammunition for such views. After 1640, no former servant ever served in either the governor's council or the House of Burgesses. Until 1670, all freemen could vote, and they routinely elected prosperous planters to the legislature. Most Chesapeake colonists, like most Europeans, assumed that the responsibilities of government were best borne by men of wealth and status.

In the 1660s and 1670s, colonial officials began to seek additional security as discontent mounted among the poor. Beginning in 1661, for example, Governor Berkeley did not call an election for the House of Burgesses for fifteen years. In 1670, the House of Burgesses limited voting rights to landowners and householders. Poor men with neither land nor homes were prohibited from voting.

The governor and other colonial officials also exploited their powers to squeeze colonists for personal gain. Tax agents, for example, received a slice of the revenues they collected. During his seven years as governor of Virginia, Lord Thomas Culpeper lived in England for all but nine months, pocketed the governor's annual salary, and hired a substitute to do the dirty work of governing the colony. Other governors spent more time in the colony, but they too expected to make their office pay.

In 1660, the king himself began to tighten the royal government's control of trade and to collect substantial revenue from the Chesapeake. The Navigation Act passed that year required all tobacco and other colonial products to be sent only to English ports. The act supplemented laws of 1650 and 1651 that specified that colonial goods had to be transported in English ships with predominantly English crews. A 1663 law stipulated that all goods sent to the colonies must pass through English ports and be carried in English ships by English sailors. Together, these navigation acts were designed to funnel the colonial import trade exclusively into the hands of English merchants, shippers, and seamen and reflected the English government's mercantilist assumptions about the colonies: What was good for England should determine policies toward the colonies.

These mercantilist assumptions underlay the import duty on tobacco inaugurated by the 1660 Navigation Act. The law assessed a duty of two pence on every pound of colonial tobacco imported into England, about the price a Chesapeake tobacco farmer received at the time. The duty gave the king a major financial interest in the size of the tobacco crop. In the 1660s, tobacco revenues amounted to about one-quarter of all English customs duties, and they continued to grow.

Hierarchy and inequality permeated all levels of government and politics, from the relation between king and colonies to that between master and servant. At every level, rulers expected to rule and to be obeyed; subjects expected to be ruled and to be punished for disobeying. To our ears, these expectations sound like a recipe for tyranny. In the seventeenth century, however, they were counterbalanced by other expectations that moderated their severity. Both rulers and subjects expected government to be administered for the good of the society as a whole. However, if rulers violated this precept, subjects might justifiably rebel, not so much to contest the principles of inequality and hierarchy but to protest their rulers' failure to govern for the general good.

Bacon's Rebellion

In 1676, Bacon's Rebellion erupted as a dispute over Indian policy. Before it was over, the rebellion convulsed Chesapeake politics and society, leaving in its wake death, destruction, and a legacy of hostility between the great planters and their poorer neighbors.

Opechancanough, the old chief who had led the Indian uprising of 1622 in Virginia, mounted another surprise attack in 1644 and killed about five hundred colonists in two days. During the next two years of bitter fighting, the colonists captured and murdered Opechancanough, eventually gaining the upper hand. The treaty that concluded the war established policies toward the Indians that the government tried to maintain for the next thirty years. The Indians relinquished all claims to land already settled by the English. Wilderness land beyond the fringe of English settlement was supposed to be reserved exclusively for Indian use. The government hoped to minimize contact between settlers and Indians and thereby maintain the peace.

Had the Chesapeake population remained constant, the policy might have worked. But the number of land-hungry colonists, especially poor, recently freed servants, continued to multiply. In their quest for land, they pushed beyond the treaty limits of English settlement and encroached steadily on Indian land. During the 1660s and 1670s, violence between colonists and Indians repeatedly flared along the advancing frontier. The government, headquartered in the tidewater region near the coast, far from the danger of Indian raids, took steps to calm the disputes

and reestablish the peace. Frontier settlers thirsted for revenge against what their leader, Nathaniel Bacon, termed "the protected and Darling Indians." Bacon minced no words about his intention: "Our Design [is] not only to ruine and extirpate all Indians in Generall but all Manner of Trade and Commerce with them." Indians were not the only enemies Bacon and his men singled out. Bacon also urged colonists to "see what spounges have suckt up the Publique Treasure." He charged that "Grandees," or elite planters, operated the government for their private gain, a charge that made sense to many colonists.

By most measures, Bacon himself was one of the grandees. The son of an English country gentleman, Bacon came to Virginia in 1674 at the age of twenty-seven to make his fortune. A cousin of Governor Berkeley and a relative of other colonial officials, Bacon remained outside the inner circle of established planters who ran things in Jamestown and in county governments. Within two years, he had crystallized the grievances of the small planters and poor farmers against both the Indians and the colonial rulers in Jamestown.

At first, Bacon insisted that Governor Berkeley appoint him to lead a small army against the Indians. Berkeley refused, hoping to maintain the fragile peace on the frontier. To put Bacon in his place, Berkeley pronounced him a rebel, threatened to punish him for treason, and called for new elections of burgesses who, Berkeley believed, would endorse his get-tough policy toward Bacon and his followers. To Berkeley's surprise, the elections backfired. Almost all the old burgesses were voted out of office, their places taken by local leaders, including Bacon. The legislature was now in the hands of minor grandees who, like Bacon, chafed at the rule of the elite planters.

In June 1676, the new legislature passed a series of reform measures known as Bacon's Laws. Among other changes, the laws gave local settlers a voice in setting tax levies, forbade officeholders from demanding bribes or other extra fees for carrying out their duties, placed limits on holding multiple offices, required officials to be native-born or resident for at least three years, and restored the vote to all freemen. When Bacon marched into Jamestown at the head of five hundred armed men demanding a commission to fight the Indians, Berkeley sensed that it was time to compromise. He pardoned Bacon and authorized his campaign of frontier warfare.

After Bacon trekked off to fight the Indians, elite planters convinced Berkeley that it was extremely dangerous to have hundreds of armed men marauding through the countryside. What if they should decide to attack the grandees as well as the Indians? What if they should call for servants, about half the population, to join them? Bacon's followers were desperate men, the secretary of the colony pointed out. Berkeley agreed that Bacon and his men were a greater threat than Indians.

Bacon challenged the ruthless exploitation of the many outsiders by the few insiders.

When Bacon learned that Berkeley had once again branded him a traitor, he declared war against Berkeley and the other grandees. For three months, Bacon's forces fought the Indians and sacked the grandees' plantations. Berkeley's loyalists retaliated by plundering the homes of Bacon's supporters. To obtain fresh recruits, both Bacon and Berkeley promised freedom to servants and slaves who would aid their cause. In mid-September, Bacon marched on Jamestown, routed Berkeley's forces, and burned the town. The fighting continued until late October, when Bacon unexpectedly died, most likely from dysentery, and several English ships arrived to bolster Berkeley's strength. Back in power, Berkeley hanged several of Bacon's allies and destroyed farms that belonged to Bacon's supporters.

The crucial distinction between Bacon's rebels and Berkeley's loyalists was less between poor and rich than between outsiders and insiders. Bacon's supporters generally were less wealthy than Berkeley's allies, but they included planters and small farmers as well as landless freemen. Bacon did not intend to overturn the hierarchy of Chesapeake politics and society. Instead, he challenged the ruthless and callous exploitation of the many outsiders by the few insiders. The rebellion did not dislodge the grandees from their seats of power. If anything, it strengthened their position. When the king learned of the turmoil in the Chesapeake and its devastating effect on tobacco exports and customs duties, he ordered an investigation. The royal officials replaced Berkeley with a governor more attentive to the king's interests, nullified Bacon's Laws, and instituted an export tax on every hogshead of tobacco as a way of paying the expenses of government without having to obtain the consent of the tightfisted House of Burgesses. In a sense, the grandees of the Chesapeake were put in their place by still grander royal officials.

In the aftermath of Bacon's Rebellion, tensions between great planters and small farmers gradually lessened. By 1700, the new export duty on tobacco allowed the government to cut other taxes to just one-fourth what they had been in 1660, a move welcomed by all freemen. In the long run, however, the most important contribution to political stability was the declining importance of the servant labor system. During the 1680s and 1690s, fewer servants arrived in the Chesapeake, partly because of improving economic conditions in England. Accordingly, the number of poor, newly freed servants also declined, reducing the size of the lowest stratum of free society. In 1700, as many as one-third of the free colonists still worked as tenants on land owned by others, but the social and political distance between them and the great planters, enormous as it was, did not seem as profound as it had been in 1660. The main reason was that by 1700 the Chesapeake was in the midst of transition to a slave labor system that minimized the differences between poor farmers and rich planters and magnified the differences between whites and blacks.

Toward a Slave Labor System

Spaniards and Portuguese engaged in an extensive African slave trade in the sixteenth century, and they established slavery as a major form of coerced labor in the New World. In the seventeenth century, British colonies in the West Indies followed the Spanish and Portuguese examples and developed sugar plantations with slave labor. In the British North American colonies, however, a slave labor system did not emerge until the last quarter of the seventeenth century. During the 1670s, settlers from Barbados brought slavery to the new English mainland colony of Carolina, where the imprint of the West Indies remained strong for decades. In Chesapeake tobacco fields at about the same time, slave labor began to replace servant labor, marking the transition toward a society of freedom for whites and slavery for Africans.

The West Indies: Sugar and Slavery

The most profitable part of the British New World empire in the seventeenth century lay in the Caribbean (Map 2.2). The tiny island of Barbados,

M A P 2.2

The West Indies and Carolina in the Seventeenth Century
*Although Carolina was geographically closer to the Chesapeake colonies, it was cultur-
ally closer to the West Indies in the seventeenth century since its early settlers—both
blacks and whites—came from Barbados. South Carolina retained close ties to the West
Indies for more than a century, long after many of its subsequent settlers came from
England, Ireland, France, and elsewhere.*

READING THE MAP: Locate English colonies in America and English holdings in the
Caribbean. Which European country controlled most of the mainland bordering the
Caribbean? Where was the closest mainland English territory?

CONNECTIONS: Why were colonists in Carolina so interested in Barbados? What goods
did they export? Describe the relationship between Carolina and Barbados in 1700.

www.bedfordstmartins.com/tap   SEE THE ONLINE STUDY GUIDE for more help in analyzing
this map.

SUGAR MILL

This seventeenth-century drawing of a Brazilian sugar mill highlights the heavy equipment needed to extract the juice from sugarcane. A vertical waterwheel turns a large horizontal gear that exerts force on the jaws of a press, which squeezes the cane. Workers constantly remove crushed cane from the press and replenish it with freshly harvested cane as it is unloaded from an oxcart. Note that except for the overseer (just to the right of the waterwheel), all of the workers are black, presumably slaves from Africa, as suggested by their clothing. All of the mill workers appear to be men, a hint of the predominance of men among newly imported African slaves.
Musées Royaux des Beaux-Arts de Belgique.

colonized in the 1630s, was the jewel of the British West Indies. During the 1640s, Barbadian planters began to grow sugarcane, with such success that a colonial official proclaimed Barbados "the most flourishing Island in all those American parts, and I verily beleive in all the world for the production of sugar." Sugar commanded high prices in England, and planters rushed to grow as much as they could. By midcentury, annual sugar exports from the British Caribbean totaled about 150,000 pounds; by 1700, exports reached nearly 50 million pounds.

Sugar transformed Barbados and other West Indian islands. Poor farmers could not afford the expensive machinery that extracted and refined the sugarcane juice. So many farmers left Barbados in quest of better opportunities that the white population in 1700 was only half what it had been in 1650. Planters who remained and had the necessary capital to grow sugar got rich. By 1680, the wealthiest

Barbadian sugar planters were, on average, four times richer than tobacco grandees in the Chesapeake. The sugar grandees differed from their Chesapeake counterparts in another crucial way: The average sugar baron in Barbados in 1680 owned 115 slaves.

African slaves planted, cultivated, and harvested the sugarcane that made West Indian planters wealthy. Beginning in the 1640s, Barbadian planters purchased thousands of slaves to work their plantations, and the African population on the island mushroomed. During the 1650s, when blacks made up only 3 percent of the Chesapeake population, they had already become the majority on Barbados. By 1700, slaves constituted more than three-fourths of the island's population. Barbados was literally a slave society that belonged to white men.

For slaves, work on a sugar plantation was a life sentence to brutal, unremitting labor. Slaves' life expectancy was short and their death rate high. Furthermore, since slave men outnumbered slave women two to one, the vast majority of slaves could not form a family and have children. These grim realities meant that in Barbados and elsewhere in the West Indies, the slave population did not grow by natural reproduction. Instead, planters continually purchased slaves from Africa who tended to be bitter, unruly, and hostile, and sugar planters became all the more ruthless in enforcing obedience.

By 1700, Barbados was literally a slave society that belonged to white men.

As the sugar boom moved from island to island in the Caribbean, this distinctively West Indian colonial society was reproduced repeatedly. Although sugar plantations did not gain a foothold in North America in the seventeenth century, the West Indies nonetheless exerted a powerful influence on the development of slavery in the mainland colonies.

Carolina: A West Indian Frontier

The early settlers of what became South Carolina were immigrants from Barbados. In 1663, a Barbadian planter named John Colleton and a group of seven other men obtained a charter from King Charles II to establish a colony south of the Chesapeake and north of the Spanish territories in Florida. Colleton and his colleagues, known as the "proprietors," hoped to siphon settlers from Barbados and other colonies and encourage them to develop a profitable export crop comparable to West Indian sugar and Chesapeake tobacco. Following the Chesapeake example, the proprietors offered headrights of up to 150 acres of land for each settler. In 1670, they established the first permanent English beachhead in the colony, on the west bank of the Ashley River just across from the peninsula where the king's namesake city, Charles Towne (later spelled Charleston), was founded (see Map 2.2).

As the proprietors had planned, most of the settlers were from Barbados. In fact, Carolina was the only seventeenth-century English colony to be settled principally by colonists from other colonies rather than from England. The Barbadian immigrants brought their slaves with them. More than a fourth of the early settlers were black, and as the

BELL OF SLAVE SHIP
This bronze bell was cast for the English slave ship **Henrietta Marie.** *The ship sailed from England to the west African coast in 1699, loaded a cargo of slaves and made the Middle Passage to the West Indies where the slaves were sold, then started back to England only to sink with all aboard off the Florida Keys. Centuries later, the bell was recovered from the wreckage.*
Mel Fisher Maritime Heritage Society, Key West, FL © 1991. Photo: Dylan Kibler.

colony continued to attract settlers from Barbados, the black population multiplied. By 1700, blacks made up about half the population of Carolina. English officials associated the colony so closely with Barbados that as late as 1700 they referred to "Carolina in ye West Indies."

Both economically and socially, seventeenth-century Carolina was a frontier outpost of the West Indian sugar economy.

The Carolinians experimented with tobacco, cotton, indigo, olives, and rice as potentially prof-

BARBADOS SHIPPING REGISTER

This shipping register page records the arrival of the slave ship **Henrietta Marie** *in late June 1699 in Barbados, where the ship's captain, William Deacon, consigned 188 slaves to a slave broker, William Shuller, to be sold. The* **Henrietta Marie's** *slaves were just over 10 percent of the 1,772 slaves Shuller received for sale in the three-year period recorded on this page.*

Public Records Office, London.

itable export crops. But until the end of the seventeenth century, the experiments proved disappointing. Finally, in the mid-1690s, colonists identified a hardy strain of rice and worked out successful methods of cultivation that inaugurated a flourishing industry. During the first generation of settlement in the seventeenth century, however, Carolina remained an economic colony of Barbados. Settlers sold livestock and timber to the West Indies. They also exploited another "natural resource": They captured and enslaved several thousand local Indians and sold them to Caribbean planters. Both economically and socially, seventeenth-century Carolina was a frontier outpost of the West Indian sugar economy.

The Chesapeake: Tobacco and Slaves

By 1700, more than eight out of ten people in the southern colonies of British North America lived in the Chesapeake. Until the 1670s, almost all Chesapeake colonists were white people from England. In 1700, however, one out of eight people in the region was a black person from Africa (Figure 2.1). Although a few blacks had lived in the Chesapeake since the 1620s, the black population increased fivefold between 1670 and 1700 as hundreds of tobacco planters made the transition from servant to slave labor, purchasing slaves rather than servants to work in their tobacco fields. For planters, slaves had several obvious advantages over servants. Although slaves cost

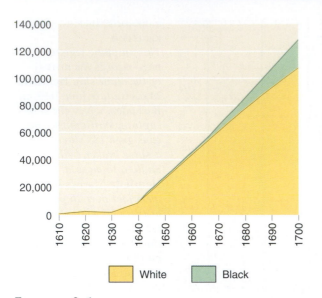

FIGURE 2.1

White and Black Populations in the Southern Colonies in the Seventeenth Century
Although the first Africans arrived in the southern colonies in 1619, Africans and their descendants remained a small fraction of the population throughout the seventeenth century. What features of this chart reflect the servant labor system, the transition to slave labor, and the settlement of Carolina?

three to five times more than servants, slaves never became free. Since the mortality rate had declined by the 1680s, planters could reasonably expect slaves to live longer than a servant's period of indenture. Slaves also promised to be a perpetual labor force. Children of slave mothers inherited the status of slavery. As William Fitzhugh, a wealthy Chesapeake planter, pointed out to a friend, his "Negroes increase being all young, & a considerable parcel of breeders, will keep that Stock [of slaves] good for ever."

For planters like Fitzhugh, slaves had another important advantage over servants: They could be controlled politically. Servants came to the Chesapeake expecting to become free, obtain land, and participate in colonial society. Bacon's Rebellion had demonstrated how disruptive former servants could be when their expectations were not met. A slave labor system promised to avoid the political problems caused by the servant labor system. Slavery kept discontented laborers in permanent servitude, and their color was a badge of their bondage. Slaves were even prohibited from defending themselves. A 1680 Virginia law provided that "any negroe or other slave

[who] shall presume to lift up his hand in opposition against any [white] christian" would be punished with "thirty lashes on his bare back well laid on."

The slave labor system polarized Chesapeake society along lines of race and status: All slaves were black and nearly all blacks were slaves; almost all free people were white and all whites were free or only temporarily bound in indentured servitude. Unlike Barbados, however, the Chesapeake retained a vast white majority. Among whites, huge differences of wealth and status still existed. In fact, the emerging slave labor system sharpened the economic differences among whites because only prosperous planters could afford to buy slaves. By 1700, more than three-quarters of white families had neither servants nor slaves. Nonetheless, poorer white farmers enjoyed the privileges of free status. They could own property of all sorts; they could marry, have families, and bequeath their property and free status to their descendants; they could move when and where they wanted; they could associate freely with other people; they could serve on juries, vote, and even hold political office; they could work, loaf, or sleep as they chose.

All these privileges and more were prohibited to slaves. These distinctions between slaves and free people made lesser white folk feel they had a genuine stake in the existence of slavery, even if they did not own a single slave. By emphasizing the privileges of freedom shared by all white people, the slave labor system reduced the tensions between poor folk and grandees that had plagued the Chesapeake region in the 1670s.

The slaves purchased by Chesapeake planters in the seventeenth century came mostly from the West Indies. Chesapeake planters made a leisurely transition to slave labor with Africans who had already been "seasoned," that is, acclimated to the natural environment of the New World and the repressive confines of slavery. Many of the slaves probably had already learned some English. The transition was still under way in 1700, but by then the majority of laborers found in Chesapeake tobacco fields were slaves.

In contrast to Barbados, most slaves in the seventeenth-century Chesapeake colonies had frequent and close contact with white people. Slaves and white servants performed the same tasks on tobacco plantations, often working side by side in the fields. For slaves, work on a tobacco plantation was less onerous than on a sugar plantation. But slaves' constant exposure to white surveillance made Chesapeake slavery especially confining. Slaves took advantage of every opportunity to slip away from white supervision and seek out the company of other slaves, "going abroad" to visit slaves on neighboring plantations. Planters did not like such visiting, but they often permitted it. More than once, slaves turned such seemingly innocent social pleasures to political ends, either to run away or to conspire to strike against their masters. In 1680, for example, Virginia planters uncovered a "Negro Plott, formed . . . for the Distroying and killing [of] his Majesties Subjects . . . with a designe of Carrying it through the whole Collony of Virginia." An investigation concluded that masters were at fault for allowing slaves to travel between plantations and to meet for funerals and admonished masters to be more vigilant.

While slavery resolved the political unrest caused by the servant labor system, it created new political problems. By 1700, the bedrock political issue in the Chesapeake was keeping slaves in their place, at the business end of a hoe in a tobacco field. The Chesapeake was well on its way to developing a slave labor system that stood midway, both geographically and socially, between the sugar plantations and black majority of Barbados to the south and the small farms and homogeneous villages that developed in seventeenth-century New England to the north.

Conclusion: Status and Race in the Southern Economy

By 1700, the colonies of Virginia, Maryland, and Carolina were firmly established. The staple crops they grew for export provided a livelihood for many, a fortune for a few, and valuable revenues for shippers, merchants, and the English monarchy. Their societies differed markedly from English society in most respects, yet the colonists considered themselves English people who happened to live in North America. They claimed the same rights and privileges of English men and women while they denied those rights and privileges to native Americans and African slaves.

The English colonies also differed from the sixteenth-century example of New Spain. Large quantities of gold and silver never materialized in the Chesapeake. The system of encomienda was never adopted because Indians were too few and too hostile and their communities too small and decentralized compared with those of the Mexica. Yet forms of coerced labor and racial distinction that developed in New Spain had North American counterparts, as English colonists employed servants and slaves and defined themselves as superior to Indians and Africans.

By 1700, the remnants of Powhatan's people still survived. As English settlement pushed north, west, and south of the Chesapeake Bay, the various Indian peoples were faced with the new colonial world that Powhatan and Pocahontas had encountered when John Smith and the first settlers arrived at Jamestown. By 1700, the many descendants of Pocahontas's son, Thomas, as well as other colonists and native Americans understood that the English had come to stay.

www.bedfordstmartins.com/tap   SEE THE ONLINE STUDY GUIDE to assess your mastery of the material covered in this chapter.

CHRONOLOGY

1588 England defeats Spanish Armada.

1606 Virginia Company of London receives royal charter to establish colony in North America.

1607 English colonists found Jamestown settlement; Pocahontas "rescues" John Smith.

1609 Starvation plagues Jamestown.

1612 John Rolfe begins to plant tobacco in Virginia.

1617 First commercial tobacco shipment leaves Virginia for England. Pocahontas dies in England.

1618 Powhatan dies; Opechancanough becomes supreme chief.

1619 First Africans arrive in Virginia. House of Burgesses begins to meet in Virginia.

1622 Opechancanough leads Indian uprising against Virginia colonists.

1624 Virginia becomes royal colony.

1632 King Charles I grants Lord Baltimore land for colony of Maryland.

1634 Colonists begin to arrive in Maryland.

1644 Opechancanough leads Indian uprising against Virginia colonists.

1660 Navigation Act requires colonial tobacco to be shipped to English ports and to be assessed customs tax.

1663 Carolina proprietors receive charter from King Charles II for Carolina colony.

1670 Charles Towne, South Carolina, founded. Slave labor system emerges first in Carolina and more gradually in Chesapeake colonies.

1676 Bacon's Rebellion convulses Virginia.

BIBLIOGRAPHY

Please consult the bibliographies of chapters 1 and 3 for additional suggested readings.

GENERAL WORKS

Kenneth R. Andrews, *Trade, Plunder, and Settlement: Maritime Enterprise and the Genesis of the British Empire* (1984).

Bernard Bailyn and Philip D. Morgan, eds., *Strangers within the Realm: Cultural Margins of the First British Empire* (1991).

Robert M. Bliss, *Revolution and Empire: English Politics and the American Colonies in the Seventeenth Century* (1990).

Wesley Frank Craven, *The Southern Colonies in the Seventeenth Century, 1607–1689* (1949).

K. G. Davies, *The North Atlantic World in the Seventeenth Century* (1974).

Richard Beale Davis, *Intellectual Life in the Colonial South, 1585–1763*, 3 vols. (1978).

Seymour Drescher and Stanley L. Engerman, eds., *A Historical Guide to World Slavery* (1998).

Betty Fussell, *The Story of Corn* (1992).

Alison Games, *Migration and the Origins of the English Atlantic World* (1999).

Lewis Cecil Gray, *History of Agriculture in the Southern United States to 1860,* 2 vols. (1933).

Jack P. Greene and J. R. Pole, eds., *Colonial British America: Essays in the New History of the Early Modern Era* (1984).

Winthrop D. Jordan, *White over Black: American Attitudes towards the Negro, 1550–1812* (1968).

Karen Ordahl Kupperman, *Indians and English: Facing Off in Early America* (2000).

John J. McCusker and Russell R. Menard, *The Economy of British America, 1607–1789* (1985).

Edmund S. Morgan, *American Slavery, American Freedom: The Ordeal of Colonial Virginia* (1975).

INDIANS

James Axtell, *The European and the Indian: Essays in the Ethnohistory of Colonial North America* (1981).

James Axtell, *The Invasion Within: The Contest of Cultures in Colonial North America* (1985).

James Axtell, *The Indians' New South: Cultural Change in the Colonial Southeast* (1997).

Philip L. Barbour, *Pocahontas and Her World* (1970).

Kathryn E. Holland Braund, *Deerskins and Duffels: The Creek Indian Trade with Anglo-America, 1685–1815* (1993).

Wesley Frank Craven, *White, Red, and Black: The Seventeenth-Century Virginian* (1971).

Frederic W. Gleach, *Powhatan's World and Colonial Virginia: A Conflict of Cultures* (1997).

Charles Hudson and Carmen Chaves Tesser, eds., *The Forgotten Centuries: Indians and Europeans in the American South, 1521–1704* (1994).

Karen Ordahl Kupperman, *Settling with the Indians: The Meeting of English and Indian Cultures in America, 1580–1640* (1981).

J. A. Leo Lemay, *Did Pocahontas Save Captain John Smith?* (1992).

James H. Merrell, *The Indians' New World: Catawbas and Their Neighbors from European Contact through the Era of Removal* (1989).

Helen C. Rountree, *The Powhatan Indians of Virginia: Their Traditional Culture* (1989).

Helen C. Rountree, *Pocahontas's People: The Powhatan Indians of Virginia through Four Centuries* (1990).

Helen C. Rountree, ed., *Powhatan Foreign Relations, 1500–1722* (1993).

Helen C. Rountree and Thomas E. Davidson, *Eastern Shore Indians of Virginia and Maryland* (1997).

Bernard W. Sheehan, *Savagism and Civility: Indians and Englishmen in Colonial Virginia* (1980).

Timothy Silver, *A New Face on the Countryside: Indians, Colonists, and Slaves in South Atlantic Forests, 1500–1800* (1990).

Peter H. Wood, Gregory A. Waselkov, and M. Thomas Hatley, eds., *Powhatan's Mantle: Indians in the Colonial Southeast* (1989).

CHESAPEAKE SOCIETY

Philip L. Barbour, ed., *The Complete Works of Captain John Smith,* 3 vols. (1986).

Warren M. Billings, *The Old Dominion in the Seventeenth Century: A Documentary History of Virginia, 1606–1689* (1975).

Warren M. Billings, John E. Selby, and Thad W. Tate, *Colonial Virginia: A History* (1986).

Kathleen Brown, *Good Wives, Nasty Wenches, and Anxious Patriarchs: Gender, Race, and Power in Colonial Virginia* (1996).

Carl Bridenbaugh, *Jamestown, 1544–1699* (1980).

Lois Green Carr, Russell R. Menard, and Lorena S. Walsh, *Robert Cole's World: Agriculture and Society in Early Maryland* (1991).

Lois Green Carr, Philip D. Morgan, and Jean B. Russo, eds., *Colonial Chesapeake Society* (1988).

Richard Beale Davis, ed., *William Fitzhugh and His Chesapeake World, 1676–1701* (1963).

James Deetz, *Flowerdew Hundred: The Archaeology of a Virginia Plantation, 1619–1864* (1993).

Carville Earle, *The Evolution of a Tidewater Settlement System: All Hallow's Parish, Maryland, 1650–1783* (1975).

James Horn, *Adapting to a New World: English Society in the Seventeenth-Century Chesapeake* (1994).

David William Jordan, *Maryland's Revolution of Government, 1689–1692* (1974).

David W. Jordan, *Foundations of Representative Government in Maryland, 1632–1715* (1987).

Jon Kukla, *Political Institutions in Virginia, 1619–1660* (1989).

Aubrey C. Land, *Colonial Maryland: A History* (1981).

Aubrey C. Land, Lois Green Carr, and Edward C. Papenfuse, eds., *Law, Society, and Politics in Early Maryland* (1977).

Kenneth A. Lockridge, *The Diary, and Life, of William Byrd II of Virginia, 1674–1744* (1987).

Gloria Lund Main, *Tobacco Colony: Life in Early Maryland, 1650–1720* (1982).

James Perry, *The Formation of a Society on Virginia's Eastern Shore, 1615–1655* (1990).

Jacob M. Price, *Perry of London: A Family and a Firm on the Seaborne Frontier, 1615–1753* (1992).

Darrett B. Rutman and Anita H. Rutman, *A Place in Time: Middlesex County, Virginia, 1650–1750*, 2 vols. (1984).

James F. Shepherd and Gary M. Walton, *Shipping, Maritime Trade, and the Economic Development of Colonial North America* (1972).

Thad W. Tate and David L. Ammerman, eds., *The Chesapeake in the Seventeenth Century: Essays on Anglo-American Society* (1979).

SERVANTS AND SLAVES

Ira Berlin, *Many Thousands Gone: The First Two Centuries of Slavery in North America* (1998).

Robin Blackburn, *The Making of New World Slavery: From the Baroque to the Modern, 1492–1800* (1997).

David W. Galenson, *White Servitude in Colonial America: An Economic Analysis* (1981).

David W. Galenson, *Traders, Planters, and Slaves: Market Behavior in Early English America* (1986).

Marcus W. Jernegan, *Laboring and Dependent Classes in Colonial America, 1607–1783* (1931).

Herbert S. Klein, *The Middle Passage: Comparative Studies of the Atlantic Slave Trade* (1978).

Paul E. Lovejoy, ed., *Africans in Bondage: Studies in Slavery and the Slave Trade* (1986).

Richard B. Morris, *Government and Labor in Early America* (1946).

James A. Rawley, *The Transatlantic Slave Trade: A History* (1981).

Abbot Emerson Smith, *Colonists in Bondage: White Servitude and Convict Labor in America, 1607–1776* (1947).

Hugh Thomas, *The Slave Trade* (1997).

CAROLINA SOCIETY

Alan Vance Briceland, *Westward from Virginia: The Exploration of the Virginia-Carolina Frontier, 1650–1710* (1987).

Converse D. Clowse, *Economic Beginnings in Colonial South Carolina, 1670–1730* (1971).

Daniel C. Littlefield, *Race and Slaves: Ethnicity and the Slave Trade in Colonial South Carolina* (1981).

Leland G. Ferguson, *Uncommon Ground: Archaeology and Early African America, 1650–1800* (1992).

Thomas M. Hatley, *The Dividing Paths: Cherokees and South Carolinians through the Era of the American Revolution* (1993).

Alexander S. Salley Jr., ed., *Narratives of Early Carolina, 1650–1708* (1911).

Aaron M. Shatzmann, *Servants into Planters: The Origin of an American Image: Land Acquisition and Status Mobility in Seventeenth-Century South Carolina* (1989).

Richard Waterhouse, *A New World Gentry: The Making of a Merchant and Planter Class in South Carolina, 1670–1770* (1989).

Robert M. Weir, *Colonial South Carolina: A History* (1983).

Peter H. Wood, *Black Majority: Negroes in Colonial South Carolina from 1670 through the Stono Rebellion* (1974).

THE WEST INDIES

Carl Bridenbaugh and Roberta Bridenbaugh, *No Peace Beyond the Line: The English in the Caribbean, 1624–1690* (1972).

Michael Craton, *Sinews of Empire: A Short History of British Slavery* (1974).

Richard S. Dunn, *Sugar and Slaves: The Rise of the Planter Class in the English West Indies, 1624–1713* (1972).

Jerome S. Handler and Frederick W. Lange, *Plantation Slavery in Barbados* (1978).

Kenneth F. Kiple, *The Caribbean Slave: A Biological History* (1984).

Herbert S. Klein, *African Slavery in Latin America and the Caribbean* (1986).

Sidney W. Mintz, *Sweetness and Power: The Place of Sugar in Modern History* (1985).

Richard B. Sheridan, *Sugar and Slavery: An Economic History of the British West Indies, 1623–1775* (1974).

Eric Williams, *From Columbus to Castro: The History of the Caribbean, 1492–1969* (1970).

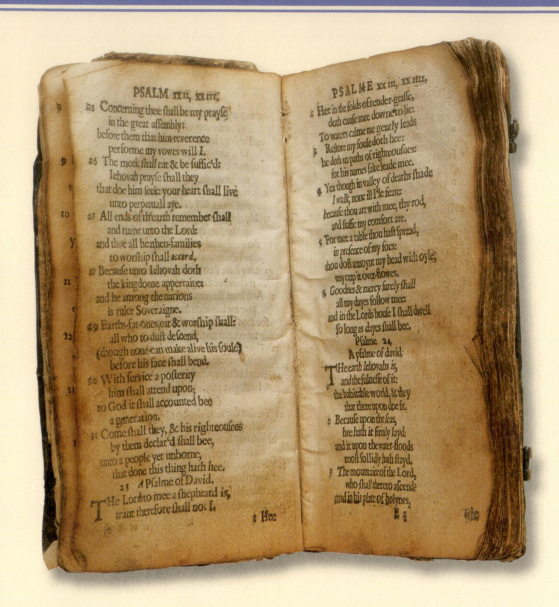

AMERICA'S FIRST BOOK

The first book printed in what is now the United States, this well-thumbed copy of **The Whole Booke of Psalmes Faithfully Translated into English Metre** *was published in Cambridge, Massachusetts, in 1640. Puritan services banned musical instruments and other diversions from God's holy word. Worshippers used this book and others to sing psalms, celebrating with a chorus of voices the wonders of God's Truth. The famous Twenty-third Psalm begins near the bottom of the left-hand page and concludes on the facing page. Read the psalm aloud to re-create the experience of seventeenth-century New England Puritan congregations.*

Library of Congress.

THE NORTHERN COLONIES IN THE SEVENTEENTH CENTURY

1601–1700

3

ANNE HUTCHINSON ARRIVED IN THE MASSACHUSETTS BAY COLONY from England in 1634 with her husband and family. A brilliant woman, Hutchinson had received an excellent education from her father. The mother of fourteen children, she served her neighbors as a skilled midwife. She was a devout Puritan, steeped in Scripture and absorbed by sermons. After she settled into her home in Boston, women gathered there to hear her Thursday lectures on recent sermons, a proper female activity since, according to one minister, it "water[ed] the seeds *publikely* sowen." But as the months passed, the meetings increased to twice a week and the crowds grew to sixty or more women and men. One of those who attended praised Hutchinson as a "Woman that Preaches better Gospell then any of your black-coates that have been at the Ninneversity."

Hutchinson expounded on the sermons of John Cotton, her favorite minister. Cotton emphasized that individuals could be saved only by God's grace in choosing them to be members of the elect, a doctrine Cotton termed the "covenant of grace." Cotton contrasted this familiar Puritan tenet with the "covenant of works," the belief that one's behavior—one's works—could win God's favor and, ultimately, salvation. Cotton's sermons strongly hinted that many Puritans, even ministers, leaned toward this heretical "covenant of works." Anne Hutchinson agreed. In her lectures to the groups assembled at her home, she amplified Cotton's somewhat muted message that the leaders of Massachusetts were repudiating the covenant of grace, the true basis of Puritan faith.

The meetings at Hutchinson's house alarmed her nearest neighbor, former governor John Winthrop, who believed that she was subverting the good order of the colony. In 1637, Winthrop had formal charges brought against Hutchinson and confronted her in court as her chief accuser. "You have stept out of your place," he said, "*you have rather bine a Husband than a Wife and a preacher than a Hearer; and a Magistrate than a Subject.*"

Winthrop, however, proved to be no match for Hutchinson's learning, wit, and insight. Hutchinson pointed to passages in the Bible that instructed women to meet and teach one another. When Winthrop claimed those Scriptures did not apply to her, she asked him: If it is "not lawful for me to teach women . . . why do you call me to teach the court?" Outsmarted and off-balance, Winthrop pressed forward with the investigation, fishing for some heresy that he could pin on Hutchinson.

Winthrop and other Puritan elders referred to Hutchinson and her followers as "Antinomians," that is, people who opposed the law. Hutchinson's opponents charged that she believed that Christians could be saved by faith alone and that they therefore did not need to act according to God's law as stated in the Bible and as interpreted by the colony's leaders. Hutchinson nimbly defended herself against this accusation. Yes, she believed that men and women were saved by faith alone; but no, she did not deny the need to obey God's law. "The Lord hath let me see which was the clear ministry and which the wrong," she said. Finally, her interrogators cornered her. How could she tell which was which? "By an immediate revelation," she replied, "by the voice of [God's] own spirit to my soul." Here was the crime Winthrop had been searching for, the heresy of prophecy, the erroneous claim that God revealed his will directly to a believer instead of exclusively through the Bible, as every good Puritan knew.

In 1638, the Boston church formally excommunicated Hutchinson. The minister decreed, "I doe cast you out and . . . deliver you up to Satan that you may learne no more to blaspheme to seduce and to lye. . . . I command you . . . as a Leper to withdraw your selfe out of the Congregation." Banished, Hutchinson and her family moved first to Rhode Island and then to Long Island, where all but her ten-year-old daughter were killed by Indians.

Hutchinson's admission of divine revelation was a departure from standard Puritan belief. Yet by urging believers to search for evidence of God's grace, Puritanism encouraged the faithful to listen for a whisper from God. Puritanism was a volatile combination of rigid insistence on conformity to God's law and aching uncertainty about how to identify and act upon it. Despite the best efforts of Winthrop and other New England leaders to render God's instructions in no uncertain terms, Puritanism inspired believers like Anne Hutchinson to draw their own conclusions and stick to them.

During the seventeenth century, New England's Puritan zeal—exemplified by both Anne Hutchinson and her persecutors—cooled, and the goal of founding a holy new England faded. Late in the century, new colonies—New York, New Jersey, and Pennsylvania—were founded that differed sharply from New England. All the new colonies featured greater religious and ethnic diversity than New England, an outgrowth of their welcome of new settlers. Religion remained important throughout all the colonies, but it competed with a growing faith that the promise of a better life required less of the Puritan's intense focus on salvation and more attention to the mundane affairs of family, work, and trade.

By 1700, all the North American colonies—the new middle colonies as well as New England and the southern colonies—had become more integrated into the English empire. Although located an ocean away from England, the colonists shipped North American wares east and off-loaded Old World goods on western shores. The continual exchange of products, people, and ideas was the lifeblood of empire that pulsed between England and the colonies, energizing both.

Puritan Origins: The English Reformation

In 1500, the church in England, like the church in other European countries, owed allegiance to the pope in Rome. The Roman church was a catholic, or universal, church. It was also a unified church. But when the Protestant Reformation arose in Germany in 1517 and spread to other countries soon afterward, that unity shattered forever.

During the early years of the Reformation, the English church remained within the Catholic fold. King Henry VIII, who reigned from 1509 to 1547, was such a loyal Catholic that the pope bestowed on him the honorific title Defender of the Faith. Henry's faith, like that of other European monarchs, was strongly influenced by political considerations. He witnessed the bitter religious disputes and popular unrest the Reformation brought to the European continent and hoped to prevent both from spreading to England. He also understood that the Reformation offered him an opportunity to break with Rome and take control of the church in England.

In 1534, Henry completed the break with Rome and formally initiated the English Reformation. At his insistence, Parliament passed the Act of Supremacy, which outlawed the Catholic Church and proclaimed the king "the only supreme head on earth of the Church of England." The vast properties of the Catholic Church in England were now the king's, as was the privilege of appointing bishops and other members of the church hierarchy. But Protestant doctrines advocated by Martin Luther and his followers held no attraction for Henry. In almost all matters of theology and religious practice, he remained an orthodox Catholic.

In the short run, the English Reformation allowed Henry VIII to achieve his political goal of

PERSECUTION OF ENGLISH PROTESTANTS
This sixteenth-century drawing shows the persecution of Protestants during the reign of Queen Mary, a staunch Catholic. Here Protestant prisoners are being marched to London to be tried for heresy. This pro-Protestant drawing emphasizes the severity of royal tyranny by depicting four well-armed guards, two of them mounted, escorting some fifteen prisoners, including at least five women. The women are roped together, but not because they appear to be menacing or likely to run away. The guards seem to be necessary less to maintain order among the prisoners than to prevent sympathetic citizens from rushing toward the marchers and freeing the prisoners. The drawing assumes that most citizens opposed the queen's persecution of Protestants. The Bible verse from the Book of Matthew underscored Protestants' fealty to Christ rather than to mere "Princes and Rulers" like Queen Mary.
Folger Shakespeare Library.

controlling the church. In the long run, however, the English Reformation brought to England the political and religious turmoil that Henry had hoped to avoid. Henry himself sought no more than a halfway Reformation. Many English Catholics wanted no Reformation at all; they hoped to return the Church of England to the pope and to maintain Catholic doctrines and ceremonies. But many other English people insisted on a genuine, thoroughgoing Reformation; these people came to be called Puritans.

During the sixteenth century, Puritanism was less an organized movement than a set of ideas and religious principles that appealed strongly to many dissenting members of the Church of England. Puritans adhered to the doctrines of Protestantism developed by Martin Luther, John Calvin, and others on the European continent. They sought to purify the Church of England by eliminating what they considered the offensive features of Catholicism. For example, they demanded that the church hierarchy be abolished and that ordinary Christians be given greater control over religious life. They wanted to do away with the rituals of Catholic worship and instead emphasize an individual's relationship with God developed through Bible study, prayer, and introspection. Although there were many varieties and degrees of Puritanism, all

Puritans shared a desire to carry the Reformation to its logical Protestant conclusion.

Many English Catholics wanted no Reformation at all. But other English people insisted on a genuine, thoroughgoing Reformation; these people came to be called Puritans.

When Henry VIII died in 1547, the advisers of the new king, Edward VI—Henry's nine-year-old son—initiated religious reforms that moved in a Protestant direction. The tide of reform reversed in 1553 when Edward died and was succeeded by Mary I, the daughter of Henry and Catherine of Aragon. Mary had remained a steadfast Catholic, and shortly after she became queen she married Europe's most powerful guardian of Catholicism, Philip II of Spain. Mary attempted to return England to a pre-Reformation Catholic Church. She outlawed Protestantism and persecuted those who refused to conform, sentencing almost three hundred to burn at the stake.

The tide turned again in 1558 when Mary died and was succeeded by Elizabeth I, the daughter of Henry and Anne Boleyn. Elizabeth tried to consolidate the English Reformation midway between the extremes of Catholicism and Puritanism. She legalized Protestantism, reaffirmed the breach with Rome, and asserted her control over the Church of England. Like her father, she was less concerned with theology than with politics. Above all, she desired a church that would strengthen the monarchy and the nation. By the time Elizabeth died in 1603, many people in England looked on Protestantism as a defining feature of national identity.

Shortly after Elizabeth's successor, James I, came to the throne, English Puritans petitioned for further reform of the Church of England. The king authorized a new translation of the Bible, known ever since as the King James version. However, neither James I nor his son Charles I, who became king in 1625, was receptive to the ideas of Puritan reformers. James and Charles moved the Church of England away from Puritanism rather than toward it. They enforced conformity to the Church of England and punished dissenters, both ordinary Christians and ministers. In 1629, Charles I dissolved Parliament—where Puritans were well represented—and initiated aggressive anti-Puritan policies. Many Puritans despaired about continuing to defend their faith in England and began to make plans to emigrate. Some left for Europe, others for the West Indies. The largest number set out for America.

Puritans and the Settlement of New England

Puritans who emigrated aspired to escape the turmoil of England and to build a new, orderly society that resembled a Puritan version of England. Their faith shaped the colonies they established in New England in virtually every way. Although many New England colonists were not Puritans, Puritanism remained the paramount influence in New England's religion, politics, and community life.

The Pilgrims and Plymouth Colony

One of the earliest groups to emigrate, known subsequently as Pilgrims, espoused a heresy known as separatism: They sought to withdraw and separate from the Church of England, actions that would be punished severely in England. They moved first to Holland, in 1608, but by 1620 they found they could not establish the life they envisioned. William Bradford, a leading member of the group, recalled that "many of their children, by . . . the great licentiousness of youth in [Holland], and the manifold temptations of the place, were drawn away by evil examples." Determining that America was a place where they might protect their children's piety and preserve their community, the Pilgrims obtained permission to settle in the extensive lands granted to the Virginia Company. To finance their journey, they formed a joint stock company with London investors. The investors provided the capital; the Pilgrims, their labor, lives, and a share in all profits for seven years. In August 1620, following months of delay in Holland and England, 102 prospective settlers finally boarded the *Mayflower*. After eleven weeks at sea, all but one of them arrived at the outermost tip of Cape Cod, in present-day Massachusetts.

The Pilgrims realized immediately that they had landed far north of the Virginia grant and had no legal authority from the king to settle in the area. To provide order and security as well as a claim to

PLYMOUTH FORT AND MEETINGHOUSE
This building is a careful historical reconstruction of a fort built by the Plymouth settlers in 1622, shortly after they heard of Powhatan's uprising against English colonists in Virginia (discussed in chapter 2). Adapted from the traditional design of a seventeenth-century granary, ports lined the second story not for stacking sheaves of grain but for firing on attacking Indians or on hostile Spaniards or Frenchmen. In fact, no attack ever came. The Pilgrims nonetheless made good use of the fort as a meetinghouse. Sermons, prayers, and worldly testimony—not cannon—echoed through the fort. Colonists gathered on the first floor for church services and court sessions. The building evokes the Plymouth colonists' military vulnerability and religious security.
Courtesy of Plimoth Plantation, Inc., Plymouth, MA USA/Ted Curtin, photographer.

legitimacy until the king granted them legal rights, they drew up the Mayflower Compact on the day they arrived. In signing the document, they agreed to "covenant and combine ourselves together into a civil Body Politick, for our better Ordering and Preservation"; the signers (all men) agreed to enact and obey necessary and just laws.

Early in December, the Pilgrims settled at Plymouth and elected William Bradford as their governor, a position he held almost continuously until his death in 1657. That first winter "was most sad and lamentable," Bradford wrote later. "In two or three months' time half of [our] company [including Bradford's wife] died . . . being the depth of winter, and wanting houses and other comforts [and] being infected with scurvy and other diseases."

In the spring, Indians rescued the floundering Plymouth settlement. First Samoset, then Squanto—both of whom understood English—befriended the settlers. Samoset arranged for the Pilgrims to meet and establish good relations with Massasoit, the chief of the Wampanoags, whose ter-

ritory included Plymouth. Squanto, Bradford recalled, "was a special instrument sent of God for their [the Pilgrims'] good beyond their expectation. He directed them how to set their corn, where to take fish, and to procure other commodities, and was also their pilot to bring them to unknown places." With Squanto's help and their own hard labor, the Pilgrims managed to store enough food to guarantee their survival through the coming winter, an occasion they celebrated in the fall of 1621 with a feast of thanksgiving attended by Massasoit and many of his warriors.

The colony's status remained precarious. Only seven dwellings had been erected that first year, half the original colonists had died, and a new group of thirty-six threadbare, sickly settlers arrived in November 1621, requiring the colony to adopt stringent food rationing. The colonists quarreled with their London investors, who became frustrated when the colony failed to produce the expected profits. But the Pilgrims lived quietly and simply, coexisting in relative peace with the Indians, paying Massasoit when settlers gradually encroached on Wampanoag territory. By 1630, Plymouth had become a permanent settlement.

Having succeeded in founding a small Puritan haven from the religious turmoil of England and the secular temptations of Holland, the Plymouth colonists nevertheless failed to attract many other English Puritans. That did not alarm the Plymouth separatists. They had given up on reforming the English church and simply wanted to live godly lives as they saw fit.

The Founding of Massachusetts Bay Colony

In 1629, shortly before Charles I dissolved Parliament, a group of Puritan merchants and country gentlemen obtained a royal charter for the Massachusetts Bay Company. The charter provided the usual privileges granted to joint stock companies. It granted land for colonization from sea to sea, including the present-day states of Massachusetts, New Hampshire, Vermont, Maine, and upstate New York. In addition, the charter contained a unique provision that allowed the government of the company to be located in the colony rather than in England. Exactly how the Massachusetts Bay Company slipped this innovation past the king's advisers remains unknown. But the Puritan stockholders understood its significance. With royal permission, Puritans could exchange their position as a harassed minority in England for self-government in Massachusetts—which, in practice, meant Puritan government.

To lead the emigrants, the stockholders of the Massachusetts Bay Company elected John Winthrop, a prosperous, respected lawyer and landowner, to serve as governor. In March 1630, eleven ships crammed with seven hundred passengers and assorted livestock, tools, and food sailed for Massachusetts; six more ships and another five hundred emigrants followed a few months later.

Winthrop's fleet arrived in Massachusetts Bay in early June. The new arrivals did not want to be associated with the heretical separatism of the struggling colony at Plymouth. Unlike the Pilgrims, Winthrop's Puritans aspired to reform the corrupt Church of England (rather than separate from it) by setting an example of godliness in the New World. Winthrop and a small group chose to settle on the peninsula that became Boston, and other settlers clustered at promising locations nearby (Map 3.1).

SEAL OF MASSACHUSETTS BAY COLONY
In 1629 the Massachusetts Bay Company designed this seal depicting an Indian man inviting English settlers to "Come Over And Help Us." Of course, such an invitation was never issued. Instead, the seal was an attempt to lend an aura of altruism to the Massachusetts Bay Company's colonization efforts. In English eyes the Indian man obviously needed help. The only signs that he was more civilized than the pine trees flanking him were his girdle of leaves, his bow and arrow, and his miraculous use of English. In reality, colonists in Massachusetts and elsewhere were far less interested in helping Indians than in helping themselves. For the most part that suited Indians, since they did not want the colonists' "help."
Courtesy of Massachusetts Archives.

www.bedfordstmartins.com/tap SEE THE ONLINE STUDY GUIDE for more help in analyzing this image.

In a sermon to his companions aboard the *Arbella* while they were still at sea—probably the most famous sermon in American history—Winthrop explained the cosmic significance of their journey. The Puritans had "entered into a covenant" with God to "work out our salvation under the

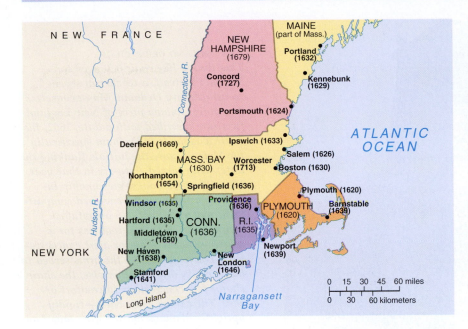

MAP 3.1

New England Colonies in the Seventeenth Century *New Englanders spread across the landscape town by town during the seventeenth century. (For the sake of legibility, only a few of the more important towns are shown on the map.) Why were towns so much more a feature of seventeenth-century New England than of the Chesapeake?*

power and purity of his holy ordinances," Winthrop proclaimed. This sanctified agreement with God meant that "the Lord will [not] bear with such failings at our hands as he doth from those among whom we have lived" in England. The Puritans had to make "extraordinary" efforts to "bring into familiar and constant practice" religious principles that most people in England merely preached. They had to subordinate their individual interests to the common good. "We must be knit together in this work as one man," Winthrop declared. "We must delight in each other, make others' conditions our own, rejoice together, mourn together, labor and suffer together, always having before our eyes . . . our community as members of the same body." To do otherwise discredited God in the eyes of humankind, jeopardized God's plan for the world, and would surely cause him to "break out in wrath against us." The stakes could not be higher, Winthrop told his listeners. "We must consider that we shall be as a city upon a hill. The eyes of all people are upon us."

That belief shaped seventeenth-century New England as profoundly as tobacco shaped the Chesapeake. The vision of a city on a hill announced the Puritans' fierce determination to keep their covenant and live according to God's laws, unlike the backsliders and compromisers who accommodated to the Church of England. The Puritans believed that God had one perfect plan, and they re-

solved to do their best to discover it through prayer, Bible study, and church attendance. Their determination to adhere strictly to God's plan charged nearly every feature of life in seventeenth-century New England with a distinctive, high-voltage piety.

The vision of a city on a hill announced the Puritans' fierce determination to keep their covenant and live according to God's laws.

The new colonists, as Winthrop's son John wrote later, had "all things to do, as in the beginning of the world." Unlike the early Chesapeake settlers, the first Massachusetts Bay colonists encountered few Indians because the local population had been almost exterminated by an epidemic more than a decade earlier. Still, as in the Chesapeake, the colonists fell victim to deadly ailments. More than two hundred settlers died during the first year, including one of Winthrop's sons and eleven of his servants. About the same number decided by the spring of 1631 that they had had enough and returned to England. But Winthrop maintained a confidence that proved infectious. Each year from 1630 to 1640, ship after ship followed Winthrop's fleet. In all, more than twenty thousand new settlers came, their eyes fixed on the Puritans' city on a hill.

NEW ENGLAND GREAT CHAIR
This throne-like chair belonged to Michael Metcalf, a teacher in seventeenth-century Dedham, Massachusetts. The oldest known piece of New England furniture inscribed with a date, 1652, the chair was made in Dedham specifically for Metcalf (note the initials flanking the date), who turned sixty-six in that year. Metcalf stored books, presumably including a Bible, in the enclosed compartment under the seat. No overstuffed recliner, the chair is suited less for a relaxing snooze than for alert concentration. The panels under the arms served to block chilly drafts. Otherwise, the chair shows few concessions to comfort or ease. The carved chair back—rigidly upright—displays motifs often found on Puritan tombstones. The grand austerity of the chair hints at the importance of serious Bible study and unflinching introspection in Puritan New England.
Dedham Historical Society/photo by Forrest Frazier.

Often, when the Anglican Church cracked down on a Puritan minister in England, he and many of his followers uprooted and moved together to New England. By 1640, New England had one of the highest ratios of preachers to population in all of Christendom: 129 preachers had settled in New England, among them such eminences of Puritanism as John Cotton, Richard Mather, Thomas Shepard, and Thomas Hooker. But the ratio was still not high enough to provide a trained minister for every band of settlers who hungered for religious instruction; one colonist complained that ordinary "fellowes which keepe hogges all weeke preach on the Saboth." A few ministers sought to carry the message of Christianity to Indians, accompanied by instructions about proper civilized (that is, English) behavior to replace what missionary John Eliot termed their "unfixed, confused, and ungoverned . . . life, uncivilized and unsubdued to labor and order." (See "Documenting the American Promise," page 80.)

The occupations of the New England immigrants reflected the social origins of English Puritans. On the whole, the immigrants came from the middle ranks of English society. Few representatives of the nobility or the landed gentry came to Massachusetts; Winthrop was an exception. Instead, the vast majority of immigrants were either farmers or tradesmen, including carpenters, tailors, textile workers, and many others. Servants, whose numbers dominated the Chesapeake settlers, accounted for only about a fifth of those headed for New England. Most of the New England imminied by a servant or two. In this group, women and children made up a solid majority.

These families were not democracies, of course. As Winthrop reminded the first settlers in his *Arbella* sermon, each family was a "little commonwealth" that mirrored the hierarchy among all God's creatures. Just as humankind was subordinate to God, so young people were subordinate to their elders, children to their parents, and wives to their husbands. The immigrants' family ties reinforced their religious beliefs with an effective and universally understood form of government. While immigrants to the Chesapeake were disciplined mostly by the coercions of servitude and the caprices of the tobacco market, immigrants to New England entered a social order defined by the interlocking institutions of family, church, and community.

The Evolution of New England Society

The New England colonists, unlike their counterparts in the Chesapeake, settled in small towns, usually located on the coast or a river. Massachusetts Bay colonists founded 133 towns during the seventeenth century, each with one or more churches.

grants had paid their way to Massachusetts, even though the journey often took their life savings. To such people, reports like the one Winthrop sent his son must have been encouraging: "Here is as good land as I have seen there [in England]. . . . Here can be no want of anything to those who bring means to raise out of the earth and sea."

In contrast to the Chesapeake, where immigrant women and children were nearly as rare as atheists in Boston, New England immigrants usually arrived as a family. In fact, more Puritans came with family members than did any other group of immigrants in all of American history. A ship that left Weymouth, England, in 1635 carried 106 passengers, 98 of whom belonged to one of the 14 families aboard, typically a husband, wife, and children, sometimes accompa-

King Philip Considers Christianity

Beginning in 1646, Puritan minister John Eliot served as a missionary to New England's Indians, trying to teach both the doctrines of Christianity and the orthodoxies of proper English behavior. During his half-century tenure as the leader of the Puritan congregation in Roxbury, Massachusetts, Eliot studied the languages, customs, and beliefs of native Americans, hoping to help them along the path to Christian piety and to strengthen them against colonists' unscrupulous encroachment on their lands. The efforts of Eliot and other missionaries convinced some Indians to leave their own communities and settle in "praying towns" populated by native Americans who had agreed to live in conformity with English ways. Most Indians, however, did not move into praying towns or adopt the faith or manners of the colonists.

In Indian Dialogues, *a book published in 1671, Eliot illustrated the challenge he and other missionaries confronted as they tried to convince native Americans of the errors of their ways. Based upon his decades of missionary experience, Eliot created imaginary conversations between converted Indians and those who resisted Christianity. Eliot's invented conversations echoed arguments he and other missionaries had encountered repeatedly. The following selection from an imaginary dialogue between two praying Indians, Anthony and William, and King Philip (or Metacomet), the chief (or sachem) of the powerful Wampanoags, documents Eliot's perception of the attractions of Christianity and one Indian leader's doubts about it, doubts that ultimately prevailed when King Philip led the Wampanoags in an all-out attack against the settlers in 1675.*

Anthony: Sachem, we salute you in the Lord, and we declare unto you, that we are sent by the church, in the name of our Lord Jesus Christ, to call you, and beseech you to turn from your vain conversation unto God, to pray unto God, and to believe in Jesus Christ for the pardon of your sins, and for the salvation of your soul. . . . So we are come this day unto you, in the name of Jesus Christ, to call you to come unto the Lord, and serve him. . . . We hear that many of your people do desire to pray to God, only they depend on you. We pray you to consider that your love to your people should oblige you to do them all the good you can. . . . You will not only yourself turn from sin unto God . . . , but all your people will turn to God with you, so that you may say unto the Lord, oh Lord Jesus, behold here am I, and all the people which thou hast given me. We all come unto thy service, and promise to pray unto God so long as we live. . . . Oh how happy will all your people be. . . . It will be a joy to all the English magistrates, and ministers, and churches, and good people of the land, to hear that Philip and all his people are turned to God, and become praying Indians. . . .

Philip: Often have I heard of this great matter of praying unto God, and hitherto I have refused. . . . Mr. Eliot himself did come unto me. He was in this town, and did persuade me. But we were then in our sports, wherein I have much delighted, and in that temptation, I confess, I did neglect and despise the offer, and lost that opportunity. Since that time God hath afflicted and chastised me, and my heart doth begin to break. And I have some serious thoughts of accepting the offer, and turning to God, to become a praying Indian, I myself and all my people. But I have some great objections, which I cannot tell how to get over, which are still like great rocks in my way, over which I cannot climb. And if I should, I fear I shall fall down the precipice on the further side, and be spoiled and undone. By venturing to climb, I shall catch a deadly fall to me and my posterity.

The first objection that I have is this, because you praying Indians do reject your sachems, and refuse to pay them tribute, in so much that if any of my people turn to pray unto God, I do reckon that I have lost him. He will no longer own me for his sachem, nor pay me any tribute. And hence it will come to pass, that if I should pray to God, and all my people with me, I must become as a common man among them, and so lose all my power and authority over them. This is such a temptation as . . . I, nor any of the other great sachems, can tell how to get over. Were this temptation removed, the way would be more easy and open for me to turn praying Indian. I begin to have some good likance of the way, but I am loth to buy it at so dear a rate.

William: . . . I say, if any of the praying Indians should be disobedient (in lawful things) and refuse to pay tribute unto their sachems, it is not their religion and praying to God that teaches them so to do, but their corruptions. . . . I am sure the word of God commandeth all to be subject to the higher powers, and pay them tribute. . . . And therefore, beloved sachem, let not your heart fear that praying to God will alienate your people from you. . . . for the more beneficent you are unto them, the more obligation you lay upon them. And what greater beneficence can you do unto them than to further them in religion, whereby they may be converted, pardoned, sanctified, and saved? . . .

Philip: I have another objection stronger than this, and that is, if I pray to God, then all my men that are willing to pray to God will (as you say) stick to me, and be true to me. But all such as love not and care not to pray to God, especially such as hate praying to God, all these will forsake me, yea will go and adjoin themselves unto other sachems that pray not to God. And so it will come to pass, that if I be a praying sachem, I shall be a poor and weak one, and easily trod upon by others, who are like to be more potent and numerous. And by this means my tribute will be small, and my people few, and I shall be a great loser by praying to God. In the way I am now, I am full and potent, but if I change my way and pray to God, I shall be empty and weak. . . .

William: . . . Suppose all your subjects that hate praying to God should leave you. What shall you lose by it? You are rid of such as by their sins vitiate others, and multiply transgression, and provoke the wrath of God against you and yours. But consider what you shall gain by praying to God. . . . All the praying Indians will rejoice at it, and be your friends, and they are not a few. . . . [And] you shall gain a more intimate love of the Governor, and Magistrates. . . . They will more honor, respect, and love you, than ever they did. . . . The Governor and Magistrates of the Massachusetts will own

you, and be fatherly and friendly to you. . . . Yea more, the King of England, and the great peers who . . . yearly send over means to encourage and promote our praying to God, they will take notice of you.

Philip: I perceive that in your praying to God, and in your churches, all are brought to an equality. Sachems and people they are all fellow brethren in your churches. Poor and rich are equally privileged. The vote of the lowest of the people hath as much weight as the vote of the sachem. Now I doubt [worry] that this way will lift up the heart of the poor to too much boldness, and debase the rulers to[o] low. This bringing all to an equality will bring all to a confusion. . . . [T]here is yet another thing that I am much afraid of, and that is your church admonitions and excommunications. I hear that your sachems are under that yoke. I am a sinful man as well as others, but if I must be admonished by the church, who are my subjects, I know not how I shall like that. I doubt [worry] it will be a bitter pill, too hard for me to get down and swallow. . . . I feel your words sink into my heart and stick there. You speak arrows. . . . I desire to ponder and consider of these things. . . . I am willing they should still lie soaking in my heart and mind.

SOURCE: John Eliot, *Indian Dialogues* (Cambridge, 1671) in Henry W. Bowden and James P. Ronda, eds., *John Eliot's Indian Dialogues: A Study in Cultural Interaction* (Westport, Conn.: Greenwood Press, 1980), 120–31.

QUESTIONS FOR ANALYSIS AND DEBATE

1. To what degree is Eliot's dialogue a reliable guide to Philip's doubts about the wisdom of becoming a praying Indian?

2. According to Eliot, was Philip's religion a stumbling block to his acceptance of Christianity? What made Philip fear that he would "fall down the precipice"?

3. If Philip had written a dialogue proposing that Eliot convert to the Wampanoag way of life, what arguments might it have made?

Church members' fervent piety, buttressed by the institutions of local government, enforced remarkable religious and social conformity in the small New England settlements. During the century, tensions within the Puritan faith and changes in New England communities splintered religious orthodoxy and weakened Puritan zeal. By 1700, however, Puritanism still maintained a distinctive influence in New England.

Church, Covenant, and Conformity

To Puritans, the church was not the building where the services were preached on Sundays and usually on Thursdays, too. Instead, the church was composed of men and women who had entered a solemn covenant with one another and with God. Winthrop and three other men signed the original covenant of the first Boston church in 1630, agreeing to "Promisse, and bind our selves, to walke in all our wayes according to the Rule of the Gospell, and in all sincere Conformity to His holy Ordinaunces, and in mutuall love, and respect to each other, so neere as God shall give us grace." A new member of the covenant also had to persuade existing members that she or he had fully experienced conversion. The fervent Puritans among the early colonists, whose faith had been tempered by persecution in England and by the journey to Massachusetts, had little difficulty meeting the test of covenant membership. By 1635, the Boston church had added more than 250 names to the four original subscribers to the covenant.

Puritan views on church membership derived from John Calvin, a sixteenth-century Swiss Protestant theologian. Calvin stressed the doctrine of predestination, which held that before the creation of the world, God exercised his divine grace and chose a few human beings to receive eternal life. Only God knew who these fortunate individuals—the "elect" or "visible saints"—were. Nothing a person did could change God's inscrutable choice.

Puritans, however, believed that if one were among the elect, then one would surely act like it. To a certain extent, one's sainthood would become visible in one's behavior, especially if one were privileged to know God's Word as revealed in the Bible. However, the connection between sainthood and saintly behavior was far from firm. Some members of the elect, for example, had never heard God's Word and did not know how to manifest their sainthood in their behavior. One reason the Puritans required all town residents to attend church services was to enlighten visible saints who remained ignorant of God's truth. Other people might act as if they were saints, yet in fact not be one of the chosen few. But the Puritans thought that passing the demanding test of membership in one of their churches was a promising clue that one was in fact among God's elect.

THE
World turn'd upside down:
OR,
A briefe description of the ridiculous Fashions of these distracted Times.
By T.J. a well-willer to King, Parliament and Kingdom.

London : Printed for John Smith. 1647.

THE PURITAN CHALLENGE TO THE STATUS QUO
This title page of "The World Turn'd Upside Down," satirizes the Puritan notion that the contemporary world was deeply flawed. Printed in London in 1647, the pamphlet refers to the "distracted Times" of the Puritan Revolution in England. The drawing ridicules criticisms of English society that were also common among New England Puritans. The drawing shows at least a dozen examples of the conventional world of seventeenth-century England turned upside down. Can you identify them? Puritans, of course, would claim that the drawing had it wrong—that instead the conventional world turned God's order upside down. How might the drawing have been different if a devout Puritan had drawn it?
By permission of The British Library.

Members of Puritan churches ardently hoped that they were visible saints and tried to act that way. Their covenant bound them to help each other attain this lofty goal and to discipline the entire community by saintly standards. Church members kept an eye on the behavior of everybody in town. Infractions of morality, order, or propriety were reported to the elders, who summoned the wayward to a church inquiry. The watchfulness that set the tone of life in Puritan communities is suggested by a minister's note that "the church was satisfied with Mrs. Carlton as to the weight of her butter." By saintly surveillance of every aspect of life, including Mrs. Carlton's butter, church members enforced a remarkable degree of righteous conformity in Puritan communities. Perfect conformity was never achieved, however. A servant in Roxbury, for example, declared that "if hell were ten times hotter, he had rather be there than he would serve his master," illustrating how Puritan doctrine defined the fiery punishment for failure to conform.

Despite the central importance of religion, churches had no direct role in the civil government of New England communities. Puritans did not want to emulate the Church of England, which they considered a puppet of the king rather than an independent body that served the Lord. They were determined to insulate New England churches from the contaminating influence of the civil state and its merely human laws. Although ministers were the most highly respected figures in New England towns, they were prohibited from holding government office.

As much as possible, the Puritans tried to bring public life into conformity with their view of God's law.

Puritans had no qualms, however, about their own beliefs influencing New England governments. As much as possible, the Puritans tried to bring public life into conformity with their view of God's law. Most Puritans agreed that the Sabbath began at sunset on Saturday evening, and enforcement of proper Sabbath behavior was taken seriously. After the Sabbath began, townsfolk could not work, play, or travel. Fines were issued for transgressions such as playing a flute, smoking a pipe, and visiting neighbors. Puritans mandated other purifications of what

they considered corrupt English practices. They refused to celebrate either Christmas or Easter. They outlawed religious wedding ceremonies; couples were married by a magistrate in a civil ceremony— the first Massachusetts wedding to be performed by a minister did not occur until 1686. They prohibited elaborate, colorful clothing, censuring such fineries as lace trim, short sleeves—"whereby the nakedness of the arm may be discovered"—and long hair. Cards, dice, shuffleboard, and other games of chance were banned, as were music and dancing. The distinguished minister Increase Mather insisted that "Mixt or Promiscuous Dancing . . . of Men and Women" could not be tolerated since "the unchaste Touches and Gesticulations used by Dancers have a palpable tendency to that which is evil." On special occasions, Puritans proclaimed days of fasting and humiliation, which, as one preacher boasted, amounted to "so many Sabbaths more."

Government by Puritans for Puritanism

It is only a slight exaggeration to say that seventeenth-century New England was governed by Puritans for Puritanism. The charter of the Massachusetts Bay Company empowered the company's stockholders (freemen) to meet as a body known as the General Court and make the laws to govern the company's affairs. The colonists transformed this arrangement for running a joint stock company into a structure for governing the colony. In 1631, the General Court expanded the small number of original stockholders by admitting almost 120 settlers to the status of freemen. At the same time, the court ruled that freemen must be male church members, hoping to ensure that godly men would decide government policies. Only freemen had the right to vote for governor, deputy governor, and other colonial officials. When new settlers continued to be admitted as freemen, the number became too large for the group to meet conveniently. In 1634, the freemen in each town agreed to send two deputies to the General Court to act as the colony's legislative assembly.

All other men were classified as "inhabitants," and they had the right to vote, hold office, and participate fully in town government. A "town meeting," composed of all the town's inhabitants and freemen, chose the selectmen and other officials who administered local affairs. New England town meetings routinely practiced a level of popular

DR. JOHN CLARK

The earliest known New England portrait, this 1664 painting shows Dr. John Clark, who practiced medicine, performed surgery, and dispensed drugs for thirty years in Massachusetts, as well as farmed and owned a wharf and warehouse. Clark is shown holding a surgical saw used to open a patient's skull and remove bone fragments caused by injury, an operation he became renowned for performing. Clark immigrated to New England in 1638 and lived there until his death shortly after this portrait was made. His somber clothing documents the continuing influence of Puritanism long after the Great Migration of the 1630s.
Boston Medical Library, Francis A. Countway Library of Medicine, Boston, MA.

One of the most important functions of New England government was land distribution. Settlers who desired to establish a new town entered a covenant and petitioned the General Court for a grant of land. The court granted town sites to suitably pious petitioners but did not allow settlement until the Indians who inhabited a grant agreed to relinquish their claim to the land, usually in exchange for manufactured goods. For instance, William Pynchon purchased the site of Springfield, Massachusetts, from the Agawam Indians for "eighteen fathams [arm's lengths] of Wampam, eighteen coates, 18 hatchets, 18 hoes, [and] 18 knives."

Having obtained their grant, town founders apportioned land among themselves and any newcomers they permitted to join them. Normally, each family received a house lot large enough for an adjacent garden as well as one or more strips of agricultural land on the perimeter of the town. Although there was a considerable difference between the largest and smallest grants, most allocations clustered in the middle—typically 50, 100, or 150 acres—giving New England a more homogeneous distribution of wealth than the Chesapeake. Towns usually allotted only a fraction of their total grant. They reserved some common land, which all inhabitants could use for grazing livestock and cutting wood, and saved the rest for new settlers and the descendants of the founders. The physical layout of the towns encouraged settlers to look inward toward their neighbors, multiplying the opportunities for godly vigilance. Most people considered the forest that lay just beyond every settler's house an alien environment that was interrupted here and there by those oases of civilization, towns. The footpaths connecting one town to another were so rudimentary that even John Winthrop once got lost within half a mile of his house and spent a sleepless night in the forest, circling the light of his small campfire and singing psalms.

The Splintering of Puritanism

Almost from the beginning, John Winthrop and other leaders discovered that Puritans sang with more than one voice. In England, persecution as a dissenting minority unified Puritan voices in opposition to the Church of England. But in New England, the promise of a godly society and the Puritans' emphasis on individual Bible study led New Englanders toward different visions of godliness. Puritan leaders, however, interpreted dissent as an error caused either by a misguided believer or by the malevolent power of Satan.

participation in political life that was unprecedented elsewhere during the seventeenth century. Almost every adult man could speak out in town meetings and fortify his voice with a vote. However, town meetings were far from democratic. All women—even church members—were prohibited from voting, and towns did not permit "contrary-minded" men to become or remain inhabitants. Although town meetings wrangled from time to time, widespread political participation tended to reinforce conformity to Puritan ideals.

Whatever the cause, errors could not be tolerated. As one Puritan minister proclaimed, "God doth no where in his word tolerate Christian States, to give Tolerations to . . . adversaries of his Truth, if they have power in their hands to suppress them. The Scripture saith . . . there is no Truth but one."

Among the immigrants who arrived in Massachusetts in 1630 was Roger Williams, a lively young minister who counted Winthrop and other Puritan elders among his friends. From the start, Williams needled the colony's leadership with his outspoken views that their church was fatally impure. He pronounced that requiring people who were not full church members to attend sermons was a policy that "stinks in God's nostrils." Worse from the viewpoint of Winthrop and other leaders, Williams declared that the government of Massachusetts contaminated the purity of the church, which had to be kept absolutely separate from civil influence. For these opinions and others, Massachusetts banished Williams in 1635. He helped found the colony of Rhode Island, which became a refuge for dissenters from Puritan orthodoxies.

Almost from the beginning, John Winthrop and other leaders discovered that Puritans sang with more than one voice.

Strains within Puritanism exemplified by Williams and Anne Hutchinson caused it to splinter repeatedly during the seventeenth century. The prominent minister Thomas Hooker, for example, clashed with Winthrop and John Cotton over the composition of the church. Hooker argued that men and women who lived godly lives should be admitted to church membership, even if they had not experienced conversion. This question, like most others in New England, had both religious and political dimensions, since only church members could vote in Massachusetts. In 1636, Hooker led an exodus of more than eight hundred colonists from Massachusetts to the Connecticut River valley, where they founded Hartford and neighboring towns. In 1639, the towns adopted the Fundamental Orders of Connecticut, a quasi-constitution that could be altered by vote of the freemen, who did not have to be church members, though nearly all of them were.

Puritan churches divided and subdivided throughout the seventeenth century as acrimony developed over doctrine and church government. Sometimes churches split over the appointment of a controversial minister. Sometimes families who had a long walk to the meetinghouse simply decided to form their own church nearer their houses. The schism of Puritan churches arose from the ambiguities and tensions within Puritan belief. As the colonies matured, other tensions developed as well.

Growth, Change, and Controversy

In England, disputes between King Charles I and Parliament escalated in 1642 to civil war, known as the Puritan Revolution. The king and his supporters were defeated both politically and militarily by the parliamentary forces led by the staunch Puritan Oliver Cromwell. In 1649, Cromwell's forces crowned their victories by executing Charles I and proclaiming a Puritan Republic. From 1649 to 1660, England's rulers were not monarchs who tried to suppress Puritanism but believers who tried to champion it. In a half century, English Puritans rose from a harassed group of religious dissenters to a dominant power in English government.

Such a revolutionary transformation in the fortunes of English Puritans had profound consequences in New England. When the Puritan Revolution began, the stream of immigrants to New England dwindled to a trickle, creating hard times for the colonists. They could no longer consider themselves a city on a hill setting a godly example for humankind. English society was being reformed by Puritans in England, not New England. Furthermore, the steady current of immigrants during the 1630s had stimulated the New England economy. Newcomers brought money and English goods to exchange for the food, supplies, and services they needed to put down roots in New England. When that immigrant trade came to a halt, the colonists faced sky-high prices for scarce English goods and few customers for their plentiful colonial products. As they searched to find a substitute for the immigrant trade, they marked out the basic patterns of the New England economy.

New England's rocky soil and short growing season ruled out cultivating the southern colonies' crops of tobacco and rice that found a ready market in Atlantic ports. Exports that New Englanders could not get from the soil they took instead from the forest and the sea. During the first decade of settlement, colonists traded with Indians for animal pelts, which were in demand in Europe. By the 1640s, fur-bearing

A NEW ENGLAND CHILD

This 1668 painting of young Alice Mason illustrates the drift away from the intense piety and plain dress of New England's founding generation. The elaborately decorated dress, especially the slashed sleeves, reflects the prosperity that some New Englanders had achieved by the 1600s, prosperity they displayed in their clothing and homes in ways the founders would have deemed profane.

Adams National Historic Site.

animals were scarce unless traders ventured far beyond the frontiers of English settlement. Trees from the seemingly limitless forests of New England proved a longer-lasting resource. Masts for ships and staves for barrels of Spanish wine and West Indian sugar were crafted from New England timber.

But the most important New England export was fish. During the religious and political turmoil of the 1640s, English ships withdrew from the rich North Atlantic fishing grounds and New England fishermen quickly took their place. Dried, salted codfish found markets in southern Europe and the West Indies. The fish trade also stimulated colonial shipbuilding and trained generations of fishermen, sailors, and merchants. New England fishermen and merchants built a commercial network that endured for more than a century. But the export econ-

omy remained peripheral to most New England colonists. Their lives revolved around their farms, their churches, and their families.

Families were the source of one of the most important long-term changes in seventeenth-century New England. Although immigration came to a standstill in the 1640s, the population continued to boom, doubling every twenty years. In New England, universal marriage and frequent births (a woman often had eight or nine children) created an ever-growing population. Long, cold winters eliminated the warm-weather ailments of the southern colonies and reduced New England mortality. New England children survived the hazards of infancy and childhood at a higher rate than children elsewhere. Thus the descendants of the immigrants of the 1630s multiplied and remultiplied, boosting the New England population to roughly equal that of the southern colonies (Figure 3.1).

Under the pressures of steady population growth and integration into the Atlantic economy, the white-hot piety of the founders cooled during the last half of the seventeenth century. After 1640, the population grew faster than church membership. All residents attended sermons on pain of fines and punishment, but many could not find seats in the meetinghouses. Boston's two churches in 1650 could house only about a third of the population. By the 1680s, women were the majority among full church members throughout New England. In some towns, only 15 percent of the adult men were members. Puritan minister Michael Wigglesworth asked:

How is it that I find
  In stead of holiness Carnality,
In stead of heavenly frames an Earthly mind,
  For burning zeal luke-warm Indifferency,
For flaming love, key-cold Dead-heartedness,
  For temperance (in meat, and drinke, and cloaths)
  excess?
Whence cometh it, that Pride, and Luxurie
  Debate, Deceit, Contention, and Strife,
False-dealing, Covetousness, Hypocrisie
  (With such Crimes) amongst them are so rife,
That one of them doth over-reach another?
  And that an honest man can hardly trust his
  Brother?

Most alarming to Puritan leaders, the children of visible saints often failed to experience conversion and attain full church membership. Puritans

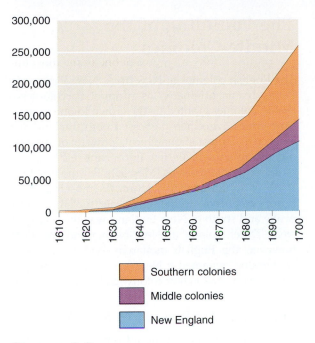

Southern colonies

Middle colonies

New England

F I G U R E   3 . 1

Population of British North American Colonies in the Seventeenth Century

The colonial population grew at a steadily accelerating rate during the seventeenth century. On the whole, New England and the southern colonies each comprised about half the total colonial population until after 1680, when the growth in Pennsylvania and New York contributed to a surge in the population of the middle colonies.

tended to assume that sainthood was inherited—that the children of the elect were probably also among the elect. Acting on this premise, churches permitted saints to baptize their babies, symbolically cleansing the infants of their contamination with original sin. Yet during the 1640s and 1650s, children of visible saints seldom experienced the inward transformation that signaled conversion and qualification for church membership. The problem became urgent during the 1650s when the children of saints—people who had grown to adulthood in New England but who had not experienced conversion—began to have children themselves. These babies, the grandchildren of visible saints, could not receive baptism and the protection it afforded against the terrors of death before baptism.

Puritan churches debated what to do. To allow anyone, even the child of a saint, to become a church

member without conversion was an unthinkable retreat from the most fundamental Puritan doctrine. In 1662, a synod of Massachusetts ministers reached a compromise known as the Halfway Covenant. The unconverted children of saints were permitted to become halfway church members. They could baptize their infants, but they could not participate in communion or have the voting privileges of church membership. The Halfway Covenant generated a controversy that sputtered through Puritan churches for the remainder of the century. Opponents protested the "many chaffy hypocrites" the compromise brought into the covenant, if only halfway. Defenders argued that the Halfway Covenant permitted the church to "nurse up still successively another Generation of Subjects to Christ." With the Halfway Covenant, Puritan churches came to terms with the replacement of "burning zeal" by "luke-warm Indifferency."

During the last half of the seventeenth century, New England communities continued to enforce piety with holy rigor. Beginning in 1656, small bands of Quakers began to arrive in Massachusetts determined to bear witness for their faith. Quakers—or members of the Society of Friends, as they called themselves—believed that God spoke directly to each individual through an "inner light." Neither a preacher nor the Bible was necessary to discover God's Word. Furthermore, since all human beings were equal in God's eyes, subordination to mere temporal authority should be refused unless God, speaking through each person's inner light, requested otherwise. Quakers affronted Puritan doctrines of faith and social order. They refused to observe the Sabbath, for example, because they insisted that God did not set aside any special day for worship but instead expected the faithful to worship every day.

New England communities treated Quakers with ruthless severity. Some Quakers were branded on the face "with a red-hot iron with [an] H. for heresie." Several Quaker women were stripped to the waist, tied to the back of a cart, and whipped as they were paraded through towns. When Quakers refused to leave Massachusetts, the Boston magistrates sentenced two men and a woman to be hanged in 1659. The three Quakers walked to the gallows "Hand in Hand, all three of them, as to a Weding-day, with great cheerfulness of Heart," one colonist observed.

New Englanders' partial success in realizing the promise of a godly society ultimately undermined the intense appeal of Puritanism. In the pious communities of New England, leaders tried to eliminate sin. In

VALUABLES CHEST
This sturdy chest used to hold jewelry and valuable papers commemorated the wedding of Joseph and Bathsheba Pope in 1679. Quakers, the Popes lived in Salem, Massachusetts. Thirteen years after acquiring this chest, the Popes became participants in the 1692 Salem witch trials. They both accused neighbors of being witches. Bathsheba succumbed to fits that she attributed to the witchcraft of Martha Corey. Joseph testified that John Proctor claimed to have powers to exorcise Satan. Both Corey and Proctor were convicted of witchcraft and hanged.
Peabody and Essex Museum.

the process, they diminished the sense of utter human depravity that was the wellspring of Puritanism. By 1700, New Englanders did not doubt that human beings sinned, but they were far more concerned with the sins of others than with their own, as the Salem witch trials demonstrated. (See "Historical Question," page 90.) The Brattle Street Church, founded in Boston in 1699, symbolized the change in Puritanism. Any person who contributed money to the Brattle Street Church could participate in the selection of a minister. The contrast between the financial contributors to the Brattle Street Church and the members of the covenant John Winthrop described in his *Arbella* sermon was one measure of the change in Puritanism during the seventeenth century.

The Founding of the Middle Colonies

The English colonies of New York, New Jersey, and Pennsylvania originated as proprietary colonies—that is, colonies granted by the crown to one or more proprietors, who then possessed both the land and extensive, almost monarchical, powers of government. Before the 1670s, few Europeans settled in any of these middle colonies (Map 3.2). For the first two-thirds of the seventeenth century, the most important European outpost in the region north of the Chesapeake and south of New England was the relatively small Dutch colony of New Netherland. By 1700, however, the English monarchy had seized New Netherland, renamed it New York, and encouraged the creation of a Quaker colony led by William Penn.

From New Netherland to New York

In 1609, the Dutch East India Company dispatched Henry Hudson to search for a Northwest Passage

MAP 3.2
Middle Colonies in the Seventeenth Century
For the most part, the middle colonies in the seventeenth century were inhabited by settlers who clustered along the Hudson or Delaware River. The vast geographic extent of the colonies shown in this map represented land grants authorized in England but still inhabited by native Americans rather than settled by colonists.

to the Orient. Hudson sailed along the Atlantic coast and ventured up the large river that now bears his name until it dwindled to a stream that obviously did not lead to China.

A decade later, the Dutch government granted the West India Company—a group of Dutch merchants and shippers seeking to mimic the success of the East India Company—exclusive rights to trade with the Western Hemisphere. In 1624, the West India Company established fur trading posts on the Hudson River as well as along the Connecticut and Delaware Rivers. Two years later, Peter Minuit, the resident director of the company, purchased Manhattan Island from the Manhate Indians for trade goods worth sixty florins, the equivalent of a dozen beaver pelts. New Amsterdam, the small settlement established at the southern tip of Manhattan island, became the principal

NEW AMSTERDAM, NEW YORK
This map was made for the Duke of York, whose small fleet seized New Amsterdam in 1664. The map reflects the early transition from Dutch to English rule. Although the map still uses the Dutch name New Amsterdam, the fort at the tip of Manhattan ("the Towne of Mannados") flies an English flag, as do at least six ships in the harbor, making clear that the colony is New York in all but name. Even then Manhattanites were seeking refuge in the suburbs, indicated here as the enclosures along the top of the peninsula, to the left of the city wall (the vertical line dividing city streets from the wilds of upper Manhattan).
By permission of The British Library.

Why Were Some New Englanders Accused of Being Witches?

ALMOST EVERYBODY IN SEVENTEENTH-CENTURY NORTH AMERICA—whether native American, slave, or colonist—believed that supernatural spirits could cause harm and misfortune. Outside New England, however, few colonists were legally accused of being witches, that is, persons who had become possessed by evil spirits. More than 95 percent of all legal accusations of witchcraft in the North American colonies occurred in New England. In 1691 and 1692, an epidemic of witchcraft accusations broke out in Salem, Massachusetts, where accusers formally charged more than one hundred individuals with witchcraft. Many other New Englanders whispered privately that a particular person was a witch, but to charge a person with witchcraft was a serious matter. As a 1641 Massachusetts law stated, "If any man or woman be a witch . . . they shall be put to death." The other New England colonies had identical laws. During the seventeenth century, courts carried out the letter of the law: Thirty-four accused witches were legally executed, nineteen of them during the Salem outbreak.

To understand the peculiar New England preoccupation with witchcraft, historians have gathered a great deal of information about accused witches and the dark deeds their accusers attributed to them. Almost anyone could be accused of being a witch, but 80 percent of the accusations were leveled against women. About two-thirds of the accused women were over forty years old, past the normal age of childbearing. About half the men who were accused as witches were relatives of accused women. Normally one family member did not accuse another. Nor did accusers single out a stranger as a witch. Instead, accusers pointed to a neighbor they knew well.

Almost always the accused witch denied the charge. Occasionally, the accused confessed. A confession could sometimes win sympathy and a reduced punishment from officials. During the Salem witch-hunt, those who confessed usually saved their own skins by naming other people as witches. The testimony of the confessed witch was then used to accuse others.

Accusers of all descriptions stepped forward to testify against alleged witches. Witchcraft investigations often stretched over weeks, months, or even years as courts accumulated evidence against (and sometimes in favor of) the accused. About 90 percent of accusers were adults, about six out of ten of them men. Young women between the ages of sixteen and twenty-five made up almost all of the remaining 10 percent of accusers; they claimed to be tortured by the accused witches.

At Salem, for example, afflicted young girls shrieked in pain, their limbs twisted into strange, involuntary contortions as they pointed out the witches who tortured them. At the trial of accused witch Bridget Bishop in Salem, the court record noted that if Bishop "but cast her eyes on them [the afflicted], they were presently struck down. . . . But upon the touch of her hand upon them, when they lay in their swoons, they would immediately revive." The bewitched girls testified that "the shape of the prisoner did oftentimes very grievously pinch them, choke them, bite them, and afflict them; urging them to write their names in a book," the devil's book.

Such sensational evidence of torture by a witch was relatively rare in witch-hunts and trials. Usually, accusers attributed some inexplicable misfortune they had suffered to the evil influence of an accused witch. One woman testified against a woman who had bewitched her cow, causing it to give discolored milk. Another woman accused a witch whom she feared would "smite my chickens," and "quickly after [the suspected witch went away] one chicken died." A man was accused as a witch because his "spirit bewitched the pudding," which was inexplicably "cut lengthwise . . . as smooth as any knife could cut it." Mary Parsons testified that she suspected her husband, Hugh, of being a witch "because almost all that he sells to anybody does not prosper."

WITCHES SHOW THEIR LOVE FOR SATAN
Mocking pious Christians' humble obeisance to God, witches hideously debased themselves by standing in line to kneel and kiss Satan's buttocks—or so it was popularly believed. This seventeenth-century print portrays Satan with hands, feet, and tail of a rodent, wings of a bat, and head of a lustful ram attached to the torso of a man. Note that women predominate among the witches eager to express their devotion to Satan and to do his bidding.
The Library and Center for Knowledge Management, University of California, San Francisco.

From our present-day perspective, the accusers seem to have been victims not of witches but of simple accidents, of overheated imaginations, or—in the case of the possessed young women—of emotional distress. But why did seventeenth-century New Englanders find the testimony of accusers persuasive?

Seventeenth-century New Englanders believed that almost nothing happened by chance. Supernatural power, whether God's or Satan's, suffused the world and influenced the smallest event, even the color of a cow's milk. When something bad happened, an unhappy God may have caused it to show his displeasure with the victim, who had perhaps sinned in some way. But maybe the victim was not in fact responsible for the misfortune; maybe Satan, acting through a witch, had caused it. If misfortunes could be pinned on a witch in thrall to Satan, the accuser was absolved from responsibility; the accuser became a helpless victim rather than a guilty party. Witches were an explanation for the disorder that continually crept into New England communities, an explanation that attributed the disorder not to chance or to the faults of individuals but to the witches' evil purposes.

Accusers usually targeted a vulnerable neighbor, such as an older, often poor woman. Historians have noted that accusers often complained that accused witches were quarrelsome, grumbled about being mistreated, muttered vague threats about getting even, and seemed to be dissatisfied with their lives. Researchers have pointed out that many New Englanders had such feelings after about 1650, but most people did not express them openly or, if they did, felt guilty about doing so. Accused witches often expressed and acted on feelings that other people shared but considered inappropriate, shameful, or sinful in their zeal to lead the saintly lives prescribed by their Puritan religion. Witches made it somewhat easier for New Englanders to consider themselves saints rather than sinners.

trading center in New Netherland and the colony's headquarters.

Unlike the English colonies, New Netherland did not attract many European immigrants. The company tried to stimulate immigration by granting patroonships—allotments of eighteen miles of land along the Hudson River—to wealthy stockholders who would bring fifty families to the colony and settle them as serflike tenants on their huge domains. Only one patroonship succeeded; the others failed to attract settlers, and much of the land was sold back to the company. Like New England and the Chesapeake colonies, New Netherland never realized the profits of its sponsors' dreams.

Although few in number, the New Netherlanders were remarkably diverse, especially compared with the homogeneous English settlers to the north and south. Religious dissenters and immigrants from Holland, Sweden, France, Germany, and elsewhere made their way to the colony. A minister of the Dutch Reformed Church complained to his superiors in Holland that several groups of Jews had recently arrived, adding to the religious mixture of "Papists, Mennonites and Lutherans among the Dutch . . . [and] many Puritans . . . and many other atheists . . . who conceal themselves under the name of Christians."

The West India Company struggled to govern the motley colonists for its own purposes. Under the stern leadership of Peter Stuyvesant, governor from 1647 to 1664, the population slowly grew, but it remained intractable. Stuyvesant tried to enforce conformity to the Dutch Reformed Church, but the company declared that "the consciences of men should be free and unshackled," making a virtue of New Netherland necessity. The company never permitted the colony's settlers to form a representative government. Instead, the company appointed government officials who set policies, including taxes, which many colonists deeply resented.

Although few in number, the New Netherlanders were remarkably diverse. Religious dissenters and immigrants from Holland, Sweden, France, Germany, and elsewhere made their way to the colony.

In 1664, New Netherland became New York. Charles II, who became king of England in 1660, gave his brother James, the Duke of York, an enormous grant of land that included New Netherland. Of course, the Dutch colony did not belong to the king of England. But that legal technicality did not impede the king or his brother. The duke quickly organized a small fleet of warships, which appeared off Manhattan island in late summer 1664, and demanded that Stuyvesant surrender. With little choice, he did.

As the new proprietor of the colony, the Duke of York exercised almost the same unlimited authority over the colony as had the West India Company. The duke himself never set foot in New York, but his governors struggled to impose order on the unruly colonists. Like the Dutch, the duke permitted "all persons of what Religion soever, quietly to inhabit . . . provided they give no disturbance to the publique peace, nor doe molest or disquiet others in the free exercise of their religion." This policy of religious toleration was less an affirmation of liberty of conscience and more a recognition of the reality of the most heterogeneous colony in seventeenth-century North America.

New Jersey and Pennsylvania

The creation of New York led indirectly to the founding of two other middle colonies, New Jersey and Pennsylvania (see Map 3.2). In 1664, the Duke of York subdivided his grant and gave the portion between the Hudson and Delaware Rivers to two of his friends. The proprietors of this new colony, New Jersey, soon discovered that Puritan and Dutch settlers already in the region stubbornly resisted the new government. The continuing strife persuaded one of the proprietors to sell his share to two Quakers. When the Quaker proprietors began to quarrel, they called in a prominent English Quaker, William Penn, to arbitrate their dispute. Penn eventually worked out a settlement that continued New Jersey's proprietary government but did little to end the conflict with the settlers. In the process, Penn became intensely interested in what he termed a "holy experiment" of establishing a genuinely Quaker colony in America.

Unlike most Quakers, William Penn came from an eminent family. His father served both Cromwell and Charles II and had been knighted. Born in 1644, the younger Penn trained for a military career, but the ideas of dissenters from the reestablished Anglican Church appealed to him, and he became a devout Quaker. By 1680, he had published fifty books and pamphlets and spoken at countless pub-

WILLIAM PENN
This portrait of William Penn was drawn about a decade after the founding of Pennsylvania. At a time when extravagant clothing and fancy wigs proclaimed that their wearer was an important person, Penn is portrayed informally, lacking even a coat, his natural hair neat but undressed—all a reflection of his Quaker faith. Penn's full face and double chin show that his faith did not make him a stranger to the pleasures of the table. No hollow-cheeked ascetic or wild-eyed enthusiast, Penn appears sober and observant, as if sizing up the viewer and reserving judgment. The portrait captures the calm determination—anchored in his faith—that inspired Penn's hopes for his new colony.
Historical Society of Pennsylvania.

lic meetings, although he had not won official toleration for Quakers in England.

The Quakers' concept of an open, generous God who made his love equally available to all people manifested itself in unusually egalitarian worship services and in social behavior that continually brought Quakers into conflict with the English government. Quaker leaders were ordinary men and women, not specially trained preachers. More than any other seventeenth-century sect, Quakers allowed women to assume positions of religious leadership. "In souls there is no sex," they said. Since all people were equal in the spiritual realm, Quakers considered social hierarchy false and evil. They called everyone "friend" and shook hands instead of curtsying or removing their hats—even when meeting the king. These customs enraged many non-Quakers and provoked innumerable beatings and worse. Penn himself was jailed four times, once for nine months.

Despite his many run-ins with the government, Penn remained on good terms with Charles II, who granted him land to found a Quaker colony in America. Partly to rid England of the troublesome Quakers, in 1681 Charles made Penn the proprietor of 45,000 square miles for his new colony, called Pennsylvania.

Toleration and Diversity in Pennsylvania

When Penn announced the creation of his colony, Quakers flocked to English ports in numbers exceeded only by the great Puritan migration to New England fifty years earlier. Between 1682 and 1685, nearly eight thousand immigrants arrived in Pennsylvania, most of them Quakers from England, Ireland, and Wales. They represented a cross section of the artisans, farmers, and laborers who predominated among English Quakers. Quaker missionaries also encouraged immigrants from the European continent, and many came, giving Pennsylvania greater ethnic diversity than any other English colony except New York.

Penn was determined to live in peace with the Indians who inhabited the region. His Indian policy expressed his Quaker ideals and contrasted sharply with the hostile policies of the other English colonies. On the eve of colonization, he explained to the chief of the Lenni Lenape (or Delaware) Indians that "God has written his law in our hearts, by which we are taught and commanded to love and help and do good to one another . . . [and] this great God has been pleased to make me concerned in your parts of the world, and the king of the country where I live has given unto me a great province therein, but I desire to enjoy it with your love and consent." Penn instructed his agents to obtain the Indians' consent by purchasing their land, respecting their claims, and dealing with them fairly.

Penn declared that the first principle of government was that every settler would "enjoy the free possession of his or her faith and exercise of worship towards God." Accordingly, Pennsylvania tolerated Protestant sects of all kinds as well as Roman Catholics. All voters and officeholders had to be Christians, but the government did not compel settlers to attend religious services or to pay taxes to maintain a state-supported church.

Despite its toleration and diversity, Pennsylvania was as much a Quaker colony as New England was a stronghold of Puritanism. Penn had no hesitation about using civil government to enforce religious morality. One of the colony's first laws provided severe punishment for "all such offenses against God, as swearing, cursing, lying, profane talking, drunkenness, drinking of healths, obscene words . . . all prizes, stage plays, cards, dice, May games, gamesters, masques, revels, bull-baitings, cock-fightings, bear-baitings, and the like, which excite the people to rudeness, cruelty, looseness, and irreligion." The ethnic and religious diversity of Pennsylvania prevented strict enforcement of these prohibitions, but the Quaker expectations of godly order and sobriety set the tone of Pennsylvania society.

Pennsylvania prospered and the capital city, Philadelphia, soon rivaled New York—though not yet Boston—as a center of commerce. By 1700, the city's five thousand inhabitants participated in a thriving trade exporting flour and other food products to the West Indies and importing textiles and manufactured goods. In less than two decades, Philadelphia had become one of the most important cities in British North America.

Despite its toleration and diversity, Pennsylvania was as much a Quaker colony as New England was a stronghold of Puritanism.

As proprietor, Penn had extensive powers, subject only to review by the king. But he did not want a proprietary government in which "the will of one man may . . . hinder the good of an whole country." Penn proposed instead to appoint a governor who would maintain the proprietor's power to veto any laws passed by the colonial council, which was elected by property owners who possessed at least one hundred acres of land or who paid taxes. The council had the power to originate laws and administer all the affairs of government. An elected assembly served as a check on the council; its members had the authority to reject or approve laws framed by the council.

Penn stressed that the exact form of government mattered less than the men who served in it.

PINE TREE SHILLING

Currency was in short supply in the colonies. Since England prohibited the export of its coins, the precious currency circulating in the North American colonies tended to be Spanish, Dutch, French, or Portuguese. In violation of English rules that forbade colonies from issuing their own currency, John Hull, a wealthy Boston merchant and shipowner, began to mint coins in 1652. Shown here is one of his pine tree shillings, both sides boldly announcing its Massachusetts origins. A shilling was worth twelve pennies; twenty shillings equaled a pound sterling. Despite Hull's attempt to ease the currency shortage, the legal tender most colonists used consisted of such commonly available items as bushels of corn or wheat, skins of beaver or deer, and, following Native American practice, wampum.

Courtesy of the Museum of the American Numismatic Association.

In Penn's eyes, "good men" staffed Pennsylvania's government because Quakers dominated elective and appointive offices. Quakers, of course, differed among themselves. Members of the assembly struggled to win the right to debate and amend laws, especially tax laws. They finally won the battle in 1701 when a new Charter of Privileges gave the proprietor the power to appoint the council and in turn stripped the council of all its former powers and gave them to the assembly, which became the only unicameral legislature in all the British colonies.

The Colonies and the British Empire

The creation of proprietary colonies permitted the king to reward his friends with faraway lands to which he had tenuous claims and over which he exercised almost no real control. From the king's point of view, the proprietary grants were, in a sense, cheap gifts. As the colonies grew, however, the gifts became more valuable. After 1660, the king took initiatives to channel colonial trade through English hands and to consolidate royal authority over colonial governments. These initiatives defined the basic relationship between the colonies and England that endured until the American Revolution (Map 3.3).

Royal Regulation of Colonial Trade

English economic policies toward the colonies were designed to yield customs revenues for the monarchy and profitable business for English merchants and shippers. In addition, the policies were intended to divert the colonies' trade from England's enemies, the Dutch and the French.

The Navigation Acts of 1650, 1651, and 1660 set forth two fundamental regulations governing colonial trade. First, all colonial goods imported into England had to be transported in English ships. Second, the Navigation Acts "enumerated" (listed) specific colonial products that could be shipped only to England or to other English colonies. While enumeration prevented Chesapeake planters from shipping their tobacco directly to the European continent, it did not interfere with the commerce of New England and the middle colonies. Their principal exports—fish, lumber, and flour—were not enumerated and could still be shipped to their most important market in the West Indies.

The Staple Act of 1663 imposed a third regulation on colonial trade. It required all goods imported into the colonies to pass through England. Goods manufactured in France or Italy, for example, had to be shipped first to England, unloaded and taxed, and then reloaded in English ships before they could be sent to the colonies. The Staple Act gave English merchants a monopoly on exports to the colonies and, by raising the prices of non-English goods, gave English manufacturers a competitive edge in colonial markets.

By the end of the seventeenth century, colonial commerce was defined by regulations that subjected merchants and shippers to royal supervision and gave them access to markets throughout the British Empire on the same terms as residents of England. In addition, colonial commerce came under the protection of the British navy, the world's strongest. By 1700, colonial goods (including those from the West Indies) accounted for one-fifth of all British imports and for two-thirds of all goods re-exported from England to the continent. In turn, the colonies absorbed more than one-tenth of British exports. The commercial regulations gave economic meaning to England's proprietorship of American colonies.

Consolidation of Royal Authority

The monarchy also took steps to exercise greater control over colonial governments. Virginia had been a royal colony since 1624; Maryland, South Carolina, and the middle colonies were proprietary colonies with close ties to the crown. The New England colonies possessed royal charters, but they had developed their own distinctively Puritan governments. Charles II, whose father, Charles I, had been executed by Puritans in England, took a particular interest in harnessing the New England colonies more firmly to the British Empire. The occasion was a royal investigation following King Philip's War between colonists and Indians.

In 1675, warfare between Indians and colonists erupted in the Chesapeake and in New England. Almost a half century earlier, in 1637, Massachusetts settlers had massacred hundreds of Pequot Indians, establishing relatively peaceful relations with the more potent Wampanoags. Afterward, New Englanders encroached steadily on Indian lands and, in 1675, the Wampanoags struck back with

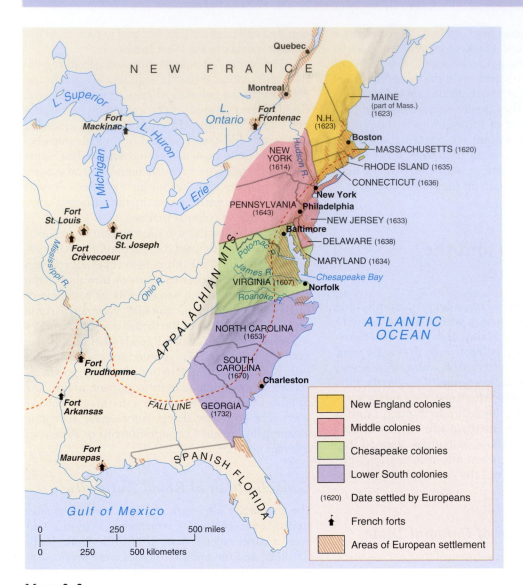

MAP 3.3

American Colonies at the End of the Seventeenth Century

By the end of the seventeenth century, settlers inhabited a narrow band of land that stretched more or less continuously from Boston to Norfolk, with pockets of settlement farther south. The colonies' claims to enormous tracts of land to the west were contested by native Americans as well as the ambitions of France and Spain.

READING THE MAP: What geographic feature acted as the boundary for colonial territorial claims? Which colonies were the most settled and which the least?

CONNECTIONS: The map divides the colonies into four regions; can you think of an alternative organizations? On what criteria would they be based?

www.bedfordstmartins.com/tap SEE THE ONLINE STUDY GUIDE for more help in analyzing this map.

KING PHILIP

No portrait of Metacomet, or King Philip, was made during his lifetime. This likeness imagines him as a proud warrior wrapped in a shawl and armed with a musket, a symbol of both his adoption of this European weapon and his willingness to use it against English colonists.

Library of Congress.

King Philip's War, 1675

gland colonies counterattacked all three tribes, a deadly sequence of battles killed over a thousand colonists and thousands more Indians. The Indians utterly destroyed thirteen English settlements and partially burned another half dozen. By the spring of 1676, Indian warriors ranged freely within seventeen miles of Boston. The colonists finally forced the Indians to stop fighting, principally with a scorched-earth policy of burning their food supplies. King Philip's War left the New England colonists with an enduring hatred of Indians, a large war debt, and a devastated frontier. And in 1676, Edward Randolph, an agent of the king, arrived to investigate whether New England abided by English laws.

Not surprisingly, Randolph found all sorts of deviations from English rules, and the English government decided to govern New England more directly. In 1684, an English court revoked the Massachusetts charter, the foundation of the distinctive Puritan government. Two years later, royal officials incorporated Massachusetts and the other colonies north of Maryland into the Dominion of New England. To govern the dominion, the English sent Sir Edmund Andros to Boston. Some New England merchants cooperated with Andros, but most colonists were offended by his flagrant disregard of such Puritan traditions as keeping the Sabbath. Worst of all, the Dominion of New England invalidated all land titles, confronting every landowner in New England with the horrifying prospect of losing his or her land.

King Philip's War left the New England colonists with an enduring hatred of Indians, a large war debt, and a devastated frontier.

Events in England, however, permitted Massachusetts colonists to overthrow Andros and retain title to their property. When Charles II died in 1685, he was succeeded by his brother James II, a zealous

attacks on settlements in western Massachusetts. Metacomet—whom the colonists called King Philip—was the chief of the Wampanoags and the son of Massasoit, who had befriended William Bradford and his original band of Pilgrims. Metacomet probably neither planned the attacks nor masterminded a conspiracy with the Nipmucks and the Narragansetts, as the colonists feared. But when militias from Massachusetts and other New En-

KING PHILIP'S SASH
This woolen sash belonged to Metacomet, or King Philip. Small white glass beads, obtained through trade with Europeans, embroider the sash in the shape of a serpent.
Peabody Museum, Harvard University.

Catholic. James's aggressive campaign to appoint Catholics to government posts engendered such unrest that in 1688 a group of Protestant noblemen invited the Dutch ruler William of Orange to claim the English throne. When William landed in England at the head of a large army, James fled to France and William became king in the bloodless Glorious Revolution, which reasserted Protestant influence in England and its empire. Rumors of the revolution raced across the Atlantic and emboldened colonial uprisings against royal authority in Massachusetts, New York, and Maryland.

In Boston, colonists seized Andros and other English officials and tossed them in jail. The rebels reestablished the former charter government, destroying the Dominion of New England. New Yorkers followed the Massachusetts example. Under the leadership of Jacob Leisler, rebels seized the royal governor and ruled the colony for more than a year. When King William's new governor arrived in 1691, Leisler relinquished control of the government without violence, but the governor executed him for treason. In Maryland, the Protestant Association, led by John Coode, overthrew the colony's pro-Catholic government in 1689, fearing it would not recognize the new Protestant king. Coode's men ruled until the new royal governor arrived in 1692 and ended both Coode's rebellion and Lord Baltimore's proprietary government.

Much as they chafed under increasing royal control, the colonists still valued English protection from hostile neighbors. While the northern colonies were distracted by the Glorious Revolution, French forces from the fur trading regions along the Great Lakes and in Canada attacked villages in New England and New York. Known as King William's War, the conflict with the French was a colonial outgrowth of William's war against France in Europe. The war dragged on until 1697 and ended inconclusively in both Europe and the colonies. But it made clear to many colonists that along with English royal government came a welcome measure of military security.

In Massachusetts, John Winthrop's city on a hill became another royal colony in 1691, when a new charter was issued. Under the charter, the governor was appointed by the king rather than elected by the colonists' representatives. But perhaps the most unsettling change was the new qualification for voting. Possession of property replaced church membership as a prerequisite for voting in colony-wide elections. Wealth replaced God's grace as the defining characteristic of Massachusetts citizenship.

Conclusion: The Seventeenth-Century Legacy of English North America

By 1700, the diverse English colonies in North America had developed along lines quite different from the example New Spain had set in 1600. In the

North American colonies, English immigrants and their descendants created societies of settlers, unlike the largely Indian societies in New Spain ruled by a tiny group of Spaniards. Although many settlers came to North America from other parts of Europe and a growing number of Africans arrived in bondage, English laws, habits, ideas, and language dominated all the colonies.

Economically, the English colonies thrived on agriculture and trade instead of mining silver and exploiting Indian labor as in New Spain. Southern colonies grew huge crops of tobacco and rice with the labor of indentured servants and slaves, while farmers in the middle colonies planted wheat and New England fishermen harvested the sea. Although servants and slaves could be found throughout the North American colonies, many settlers depended principally on the labor of family members. Relations between settlers and native Americans often exploded in bloody warfare, but Indians seldom served as an important source of labor for settlers, as they did in New Spain.

Protestantism prevailed in the North American settlements, relaxed in some colonies and straitlaced in others. The convictions of Puritanism that motivated John Winthrop and others to build a new England in the colonies became muted as the New England colonies matured and dissenters like Anne Hutchinson multiplied. Catholics, Quakers, Anglicans, Jews, and others settled in the middle and southern colonies, creating considerable religious toleration, especially in Pennsylvania and New York.

Politics and government differed from colony to colony, although the imprint of English institutions and practices existed everywhere. And everywhere local settlers who were free adult white men had an extraordinary degree of political influence, far beyond that of colonists in New Spain or ordinary citizens in England. A new world of settlers that Columbus could not have imagined, that Powhatan only glimpsed, had been firmly established in English North America by 1700. During the next half century, that world would undergo surprising new developments built upon the legacies of the seventeenth-century colonies.

www.bedfordstmartins.com/tap SEE THE ONLINE STUDY GUIDE to assess your mastery of the material covered in this chapter.

CHRONOLOGY

1534 Henry VIII breaks with Roman Catholic Church and initiates English Reformation.

1609 Henry Hudson searches for Northwest Passage for Dutch East India Company.

1620 English Pilgrims found Plymouth colony and elect William Bradford governor.

1626 Peter Minuit purchases Manhattan island for Dutch West India Company and founds New Amsterdam.

1629 Massachusetts Bay Company receives royal charter for colony.

1630 John Winthrop leads Puritan settlers to Massachusetts Bay.

1635 Roger Williams, banished from Massachusetts, establishes Rhode Island colony.

1636 Thomas Hooker leaves Massachusetts and helps found Connecticut colony.

1637 Anne Hutchinson accused of Antinomianism; excommunicated from Boston church in 1638.

1642 Civil war inflames England, pitting Puritans against royalists.

1649 English Puritans win civil war and execute King Charles I.

1656 Quakers arrive in Massachusetts and are persecuted there.

1660 Monarchy restored in England; Charles II becomes king.
Navigation Act requires colonial goods to be shipped in English vessels through English ports.

1662 Many Puritan congregations adopt Halfway Covenant.

1663 Staple Act requires all colonial imports to come from England.

1664 English seize New Netherland colony from Dutch, rename it New York.
Duke of York subdivides colony, creating colony of New Jersey.

1675 Indians and colonists clash in King Philip's War.

1681 King Charles II grants William Penn charter for colony of Pennsylvania.

1686 Royal officials create Dominion of New England.

1688 James II overthrown by Glorious Revolution; William III becomes king.

1691 Massachusetts becomes royal colony.

1692 Witch trials flourish at Salem, Massachusetts.

BIBLIOGRAPHY

Please consult the bibliographies of chapters 1 and 2 for additional suggested readings.

GENERAL WORKS

Patricia U. Bonomi, *Under the Cope of Heaven: Religion, Society, and Politics in Colonial America* (1986).

Jon Butler, *Awash in a Sea of Faith: Christianizing the American People* (1990).

Colin G. Calloway, *New Worlds for All: Indians, Europeans, and the Remaking of Early America* (1998).

Patrick Collinson, *The Birthpangs of Protestant England: Religious and Cultural Change in the Sixteenth and Seventeenth Centuries* (1988).

David Hackett Fischer, *Albion's Seed: Four British Folkways in America* (1989).

Stephen Foster, *The Long Argument: English Puritanism and the Shaping of New England Culture, 1570–1700* (1991).

Jack P. Greene, *Pursuits of Happiness: The Social Development of Early Modern British Colonies and the Formation of American Culture* (1988).

David D. Hall, *Worlds of Wonder, Days of Judgment: Popular Religious Belief in Early New England* (1989).

Stephen Innes, *Creating the Commonwealth: The Economic Culture of Puritan New England* (1995).

David Jaffee, *People of the Wachusett: Greater New England in History and Memory, 1630–1860* (1999).

David S. Lovejoy, *Religious Enthusiasm in the New World: Heresy to Revolution* (1985).

Perry Miller, *The New England Mind: From Colony to Province* (1953).

Robert Blair St. George, *Possible Pasts: Becoming Colonial in Early America* (2000).

Helena M. Wall, *Fierce Communalism: Family and Community in the American Colonies in the Seventeenth Century* (1990).

Keith Wrightson, *English Society, 1580–1680* (1982).

INDIANS

Colin G. Calloway, *The Western Abenaki of Vermont, 1600–1800: War, Migration, and the Survival of an Indian People* (1990).

Richard W. Cogley, *John Eliot's Mission to the Indians before King Philip's War* (1999).

William Cronon, *Changes in the Land: Indians, Colonists, and the Ecology of New England* (1983).

Matthew Dennis, *Cultivating a Landscape of Peace: Iroquois-European Encounters in Seventeenth-Century America* (1993).

Carol Devens, *Countering Colonization: Native American Women and Great Lakes Missions, 1630–1900* (1992).

James David Drake, *King Philip's War: Civil War in New England, 1675–1676* (2000).

Nicholas Griffiths and Fernando Cervantes, eds., *Spiritual Encounters: Interactions between Christianity and Native Religions in Colonial America* (1999).

Francis Jennings, *The Ambiguous Iroquois Empire: The Covenant Chain Confederation of Indian Tribes with English Colonies from Its Beginnings to the Lancaster Treaty of 1744* (1983).

Yasughide Kawashima, *Puritan Justice and the Indian: White Man's Law in Massachusetts, 1630–1763* (1986).

Jill Lepore, *The Name of War: King Philip's War and the Origins of American Identity* (1998).

James W. Mavor, *Manitou: The Sacred Landscape of New England's Native Civilization* (1989).

Michael Leroy Oberg, *Dominion and Civility: English Imperialism and Native America, 1585–1685* (1999).

Jean M. O'Brien, *Dispossession by Degrees: Indian Land and Identity in Natick, Massachusetts, 1650–1790* (1997).

Ann Marie Plane, *Colonial Intimacies: Indian Marriages in Early New England* (2000).

Daniel K. Richter, *The Ordeal of the Longhouse: The Peoples of the Iroquois League in the Era of European Colonization* (1992).

Daniel K. Richter and James H. Merrell, *Beyond the Covenant Chain: The Iroquois and Their Neighbors in Indian North America, 1600–1800* (1987).

Neal Salisbury, *Manitou and Providence: Indians, Europeans, and the Making of New England, 1500–1643* (1982).

Alden T. Vaughan, ed., *New England Encounters: Indians and Euroamericans, ca. 1600–1850* (2000).

Richard White, *The Middle Ground: Indians, Empires, and Republics in the Great Lakes Region, 1650–1815* (1991).

NEW ENGLAND

David Grayson Allen, *In English Ways: The Movement of Societies and the Transferal of English Local Law and Custom to Massachusetts Bay in the Seventeenth Century* (1981).

Virginia Dejohn Anderson, *New England's Generation: The Great Migration and the Formation of Society and Culture in the Seventeenth Century* (1991).

Paul Boyer and Stephen Nissenbaum, *Salem Possessed: The Social Origins of Witchcraft* (1974).

Theodore Dwight Bozeman, *To Live Ancient Lives: The Primitivist Dimension in Puritanism* (1988).

T. H. Breen, *Puritans and Adventurers: Change and Persistence in Early America* (1980).

Francis J. Bremer, *Shaping New Englands: Puritan Clergymen in Seventeenth-Century England and New England* (1994).

Richard Bushman, *From Puritan to Yankee: Character and the Social Order in Connecticut, 1690–1765* (1967).

Jonathan M. Chu, *Neighbors, Friends, or Madmen: The Puritan Adjustment to Quakerism in Seventeenth-Century Massachusetts Bay* (1985).

Charles Lloyd Cohen, *God's Caress: The Psychology of Puritan Religious Experience* (1986).

James F. Cooper Jr., *Tenacious of Their Liberties: The Congregationalists in Colonial Massachusetts* (1999).

David Cressy, *Coming Over: Migration and Communication between England and New England in the Seventeenth Century* (1987).

Bruce C. Daniels, *The Connecticut Town: Growth and Development, 1635–1790* (1979).

Bruce Colin Daniels, *Puritans at Play: Leisure and Recreation in Colonial New England* (1995).

Cornelia Hughes Dayton, *Women Before the Bar: Gender, Law, and Society in Connecticut, 1639–1789* (1995).

John Demos, *A Little Commonwealth: Family Life in Plymouth Colony* (1970).

John Putnam Demos, *Entertaining Satan: Witchcraft and the Culture of Early New England* (1982).

Stephen Foster, *Their Solitary Way: The Puritan Social Ethic in the First Century of Settlement in New England* (1971).

Stephen Foster, *The Long Argument: English Puritanism and the Shaping of New England Culture, 1570–1700* (1991).

Richard P. Gildrie, *The Profane, the Civil, and the Godly: The Reformation of Manners in Orthodox New England, 1679–1749* (1994).

Richard Godbeer, *The Devil's Dominion: Magic and Religion in Early New England* (1992).

Judith S. Graham, *Puritan Family Life: The Diary of Samuel Sewall* (2000).

Philip J. Greven Jr., *Four Generations: Population, Land, and Family in Colonial Andover, Massachusetts* (1970).

Philip Gura, *A Glimpse of Sion's Glory: Puritan Radicalism in Seventeenth-Century New England, 1620–1660* (1984).

Michael G. Hall, *The Last American Puritan: The Life of Increase Mather, 1639–1723* (1988).

Stephen Innes, *Labor in a New Land: Economy and Society in Seventeenth-Century Springfield* (1983).

Sydney V. James, *The Colonial Metamorphoses in Rhode Island: A Study of Institutions in Change* (2000).

Jane Kamensky, *Governing the Tongue: The Politics of Speech in Early New England* (1997).

Carol F. Karlsen, *The Devil in the Shape of a Woman: Witchcraft in Colonial New England* (1987).

Karen Ordahl Kupperman, *Providence Island, 1630–1641: The Other Puritan Colony* (1993).

Kenneth A. Lockridge, *A New England Town: The First Hundred Years, Dedham, Massachusetts, 1636–1736* (1970).

Kenneth A. Lockridge, *Literacy in Colonial New England: An Enquiry into the Social Context of Literacy in the Early Modern West* (1974).

Jackson Turner Main, *Society and Economy in Colonial Connecticut* (1985).

Bruce H. Mann, *Neighbors and Strangers: Law and Community in Early Connecticut* (1987).

Carolyn Merchant, *Ecological Revolutions: Nature, Gender, and Science in New England* (1989).

Edmund S. Morgan, *The Puritan Dilemma: The Story of John Winthrop* (1958).

Edmund S. Morgan, *Visible Saints: The History of a Puritan Idea* (1963).

Edmund S. Morgan, *Roger Williams: The Church and the State* (1967).

James G. Mosely, *John Winthrop's World: History as a Story, the Story as History* (1992).

Margaret Ellen Newell, *From Dependency to Independence: Economic Revolution in Colonial New England* (1999).

Carla Gardina Pestana, *Quakers and Baptists in Colonial Massachusetts* (1991).

Mark A. Peterson, *The Price of Redemption: The Spiritual Economy of Puritan New England* (1998).

Amanda Porterfield, *Female Piety in Puritan New England: The Emergence of Religious Humanism* (1992).

Michael J. Puglisi, *Puritans Besieged: The Legacies of King Philip's War in the Massachusetts Bay Colony* (1991).

Phillip H. Round, *By Nature and by Custom Cursed: Transatlantic Civil Discourse and New England Cultural Production, 1620–1660* (1999).

Robert Blair St. George, *Conversing by Signs: Poetics of Implication in Colonial New England Culture* (1998).

Timothy J. Sehr, *Colony and Commonwealth: Massachusetts Bay, 1649–1660* (1989).

Kenneth Silverman, *The Life and Times of Cotton Mather* (1984).

Richard C. Simmons, *Studies in the Massachusetts Franchise, 1631–1691* (1989).

Darren Staloff, *The Making of an American Thinking Class: Intellectuals and Intelligentsia in Puritan Massachusetts* (1997).

David E. Stannard, *The Puritan Way of Death: A Study in Religion, Culture, and Social Change* (1977).

Harry S. Stout, *The New England Soul: Preaching and Religious Culture in Colonial New England* (1986).

Lawrence William Towner, *A Good Master Well Served: Masters and Servants in Colonial Massachusetts, 1620–1750* (1998).

Laurel Thatcher Ulrich, *Good Wives: Image and Reality in the Lives of Women in Northern New England, 1650–1750* (1982).

Robert E. Wall Jr., *Massachusetts Bay: The Crucial Decade, 1640–1650* (1972).

Lisa Wilson, *Ye Heart of a Man: The Domestic Life of Men in Colonial New England* (1999).

Michael P. Winship, *Seers of God: Puritan Providentialism in the Restoration and Early Enlightenment* (1996).

Avihu Zakai, *Exile and Kingdom: History and Apocalypse in the Puritan Migration to America* (1992).

MIDDLE COLONIES

Thomas J. Archdeacon, *New York City, 1664–1710: Conquest and Change* (1976).

Patricia U. Bonomi, *A Factious People: Politics and Society in Colonial New York* (1971).

Richard S. Dunn and Mary Maples Dunn, eds., *The World of William Penn* (1986).

Joseph E. Illick, *Colonial Pennsylvania: A History* (1976).

Michael G. Kammen, *Colonial New York: A History* (1975).

Sung Bok Kim, *Landlord and Tenant in Colonial New York: Manorial Society, 1664–1775* (1978).

Cathy Matson, *Merchants and Empire: Trading in Colonial New York* (1998).

Donna Merwick, *Possessing Albany, 1630–1710: The Dutch and English Experiences* (1990).

Donna Merwick, *Death of a Notary: Conquest and Change in Colonial New York* (1999).

David E. Narrett, *Inheritance and Family Life in Colonial New York City* (1992).

Gary B. Nash, *Quakers and Politics: Pennsylvania, 1681–1726* (1968).

John E. Pomfret, *Colonial New Jersey: A History* (1973).

Oliver A. Rink, *Holland on the Hudson: An Economic and Social History of Dutch New York* (1986).

Robert C. Ritchie, *The Duke's Province: A Study of New York Politics and Society, 1664–1691* (1977).

Allen Tully, *Forming American Politics: Ideals, Interests, and Institutions in Colonial New York and Pennsylvania* (1994).

Stephanie Grauman Wolf, *Urban Village: Population, Community, and Family Structure in Germantown, Pennsylvania, 1683–1800* (1976).

Karin A. Wulf, *Not All Wives: Women of Colonial Philadelphia* (2000).

"DUMMY BOARD" OF PHYLLIS, A
NEW ENGLAND SLAVE
*This life-size portrait of a slave
woman named Phyllis, a mulatto who
worked as a domestic servant for her
owner, Elizabeth Hunt Wendell, was
painted sometime before 1753. Known
as a "dummy board," it was evidently
propped against a wall or placed in a
doorway or window to suggest that
the residence was occupied and to discourage thieves. Phyllis is portrayed as a demure,
well-groomed woman whose dress and demeanor suggest that she was capable, orderly,
and efficient. Although tens of thousands of slaves were brought from Africa to the British
North American colonies during the eighteenth century, it does not appear that Phyllis was
one of them. Instead, she was probably born in the colonies of mixed black and white
parentage. Like thousands of other slave women who labored in the homes of prosperous
white families, Phyllis illustrates the integration of the mundane tasks of housekeeping
with the shifting currents of transatlantic commerce.*
Courtesy of the Society for the Preservation of New England Antiquities/photo by David Bohl.

COLONIAL AMERICA IN THE EIGHTEENTH CENTURY

1701–1770

4

Early on a Sunday morning in October 1723, young Benjamin Franklin stepped from a wharf along the Delaware River onto the streets of Philadelphia. As he wrote later in his autobiography, "I was dirty from my Journey; my Pockets were stuff'd out with Shirts and Stockings; I knew no Soul, nor where to look for Lodging. I was fatigu'd with Travelling, Rowing and Want of Rest. I was very hungry."

Born in 1706, Benjamin Franklin grew up in Boston, where his father, Josiah, worked as a tallow chandler, making soap and candles. The father of seventeen children, Josiah apprenticed each of his sons to learn a trade. At the age of twelve, Benjamin signed an indenture to serve for nine years as an apprentice to his brother James, a printer. In James's shop, Benjamin learned the printer's trade and had access to the latest books and pamphlets, which he read avidly. In 1721, James inaugurated the *New England Courant,* avowing to "expose the Vice and Follies of Persons of all Ranks and Degrees" with articles written "in a very easy and familiar manner, so that the meanest ploughman, the very meanest of God's people may understand them."

Benjamin's responsibilities in the print shop grew quickly, but he chafed under his brother's supervision. James "considered himself as my Master, and me as his Apprentice," Benjamin remembered; "I thought he demean'd me too much. . . . My Brother was passionate and had often beaten me, which I took extreamly amiss." Benjamin resolved to escape from his apprenticeship and "to assert my Freedom."

Benjamin secretly traveled to New York, nearly three hundred miles from anyone he knew. When he could not find work, he wandered to the Delaware River and then talked his way aboard a small boat heading toward Philadelphia. After rowing half the night, Franklin arrived in the city and went straight to a bakery where he purchased "three great Puffy Rolls." He began to eat one and "having no room in my Pockets," which were stuffed with shirts and socks, he set off for the wharf, "with a Roll under each Arm," to wash down the bread with "a Draught of the River Water." After quenching his thirst, Franklin followed "many clean dress'd People . . . to the great Meeting House of the Quakers. . . . I sat down among them, and . . . I fell fast asleep, and continu'd so till the Meeting broke up."

Franklin's account of his life in Boston and his arrival in Philadelphia is probably the most well known portrait of life in eighteenth-century America. It illustrates everyday experiences that Franklin shared with many other colonists: a large family; long hours of labor subject to the authority of a parent, relative, or employer; and a restless quest for escape from the ties that bound, for freedom. Franklin's

PHILADELPHIA WHARF
This early-nineteenth-century drawing of the Arch Street wharf in Philadelphia approxi-
mates the world Benjamin Franklin entered when he stepped ashore in 1723. The wharf
was a center of industrious activity; almost everyone depicted appears to be working. The
pulse of Atlantic commerce propels casks of products from the deck of the small local
sailboat (right) toward the hold of large oceangoing ships (center) bound for England and
Europe. The small rowboat carrying four people (just to the right of the large ships) is
probably similar to the boat Franklin rowed to the city. Coordinating the complicated
comings and goings of people and goods that moved through the wharf required individu-
als who combined intelligence, energy, and discipline with efficiency, reliability, and trust-
worthiness—traits Franklin and other eighteenth-century colonists sought to cultivate.
Rare Book Department, The Free Library of Philadelphia.

account hints at other, less tangible trends: an ambition to make something of oneself in this world
rather than worry too much about the hereafter; an
eagerness to subvert orthodox opinion by publishing dissenting views expressed in simple, clear language understandable by "the meanest ploughman"; a confidence that, with a valued skill and a
few coins, a young man could make his way in the
world, a confidence few young women could dare
assert; and a slackening of religious fervor displayed both in open dissent and in Franklin's quiet
snooze—rather than rapt attention—during the
Quaker meeting he wandered into on his first day
in Philadelphia.

Franklin's story introduces some of the major
changes that affected all the colonies in eighteenth-
century British North America. Social and economic changes tended to reinforce the differences
among New England, the middle colonies, and the
southern colonies, while important cultural and political developments tugged in the opposite direction, creating common experiences, aspirations,
and identities. In 1776, when *E Pluribus Unum*
(Latin meaning "From Many, One") was adopted
as the motto for the Great Seal of the United States,
the changes in eighteenth-century America that
strengthened *Pluribus* also planted the seeds of
Unum.

A Growing Population and Expanding Economy

The most important fact about eighteenth-century colonial America was its phenomenal population growth. In 1700, colonists numbered about 250,000; by 1770, they tallied well over 2 million. An index of the emerging significance of colonial America is that in 1700 there were 19 people in England for every American colonist, whereas by 1770 there were only 3. The eightfold growth of the colonial population signaled the maturation of a distinctive colonial society. That society was by no means homogeneous. Colonists of different ethnic groups, races, and religions lived in varied environments under thirteen different colonial governments, all of them part of the British Empire.

In general, the growth and diversity of the eighteenth-century colonial population derived from two sources: immigration and natural increase (that is, growth through reproduction). Natural increase contributed about three-fourths of the population growth, immigration about one-fourth. Immigration shifted the ethnic and racial balance among the colonists, making them by 1770 less English and less white than ever before. Fewer than 10 percent of eighteenth-century immigrants came from England; about 36 percent were Scots-Irish, mostly from northern Ireland; 33 percent arrived from Africa, almost all of them slaves; nearly 15 percent had left the many German principalities (the nation of Germany did not exist until 1871); and almost 10 percent came from Scotland. In 1670, more than 9 out of 10 colonists were of English ancestry, and only 1 out of 25 was of African ancestry. By 1770, only about half the colonists were of English descent, while more than 20 percent descended from Africans. By 1770, the people of the colonies had a distinctive *colonial*—rather than English—profile (Map 4.1).

The booming population of the colonies hints at a second major feature of eighteenth-century colonial society: an expanding economy. Today, societies with rapidly growing populations often have more people than they can adequately feed; or, put another way, they have a high ratio of people to land. In the eighteenth-century colonies, very different conditions prevailed.

In 1700, after almost a century of settlement, nearly all the colonists lived within fifty miles of the Atlantic coast, on the edge of a vast wilderness peo-

MAP 4.1

Europeans and Africans in the Eighteenth Century
This map illustrates regions where Africans and certain immigrant groups clustered. It is important to avoid misreading the map. Predominantly European regions, for example, also contained colonists from other places. Likewise, regions where African slaves resided in large numbers also included many whites, their masters among them. The map suggests the polyglot diversity of eighteenth-century colonial society.

pled by native Indians and a few trappers and traders. The almost limitless wilderness gave the colonies an extremely low ratio of people to land. Consequently, land was cheap. Of course, it was never so cheap that every colonist owned some. But land in the colonies commonly sold for a fraction of its price in the Old World, often for only a shilling an acre, at a time when a carpenter could earn three shillings a day. Along the frontiers of settlement, newcomers who lacked the money to buy land often lived as squatters on unoccupied land, hoping it might eventually become theirs.

Without labor, land was almost worthless for agriculture. The abundance of land in the colonies made labor precious, and the colonists always needed more. The colonists' insatiable demand for labor was the fundamental economic environment that sustained the mushrooming population, that made it possible for the colonial population to grow rapidly without producing widespread poverty. Economic historians estimate that the standard of living of free colonists (that is, those who were not indentured servants or slaves) improved during the eighteenth century: By 1770, most free colonists had a higher standard of living than the majority of people elsewhere in the Atlantic world. That did not mean that most colonists were rich but that their rare social and economic environment permitted them to live well. Many colonists did get rich during the eighteenth century, but the unique achievement of the eighteenth-century colonial economy was not the wealth of the most successful colonists but the modest economic welfare of the vast bulk of the free population. In Europe, pinnacles of wealth stood on foundations of poverty; in the eighteenth-century colonies, the pyramid of wealth was impressive not for its height but for its broad, solid base in the free population.

New England: From Puritan Settlers to Yankee Traders

The New England population grew sixfold during the eighteenth century, but it lagged behind the growth in the other colonies. The main reason New England failed to keep pace was that most immigrants chose other destinations, partly because Puritan orthodoxy made these colonies comparatively inhospitable for both religious dissenters and those indifferent to religion. But the most important reason immigrants avoided New England was that its growth of population produced a higher and less desirable ratio of people to land than in the other colonies. As the population grew, many settlers in

search of farmland dispersed from towns, and Puritan communities lost much of their cohesion. Nonetheless, networks of economic exchange laced rural settlers to their neighbors, local market towns, Boston merchants, and the broad currents of Atlantic commerce. In many ways, trade became a faith that competed strongly with the traditions of Puritanism.

Natural Increase and Land Distribution

The New England population grew mostly by natural increase, much as it had during the seventeenth century. Nearly every adult woman married. Most married women had children and, thanks to the relatively low mortality rate in New England, often many children. The perils of childbirth gave wives a shorter life expectancy than husbands, but wives often lived to have six, seven, or eight babies. When a wife died, her husband usually remarried quickly. A wife's labor and companionship were too vital for a family to do without. Benjamin Franklin's father had seven children with his first wife and ten (including Benjamin) with his second.

The burgeoning New England population pressed against a limited amount of land. The interior of New England was smaller than that of colonies farther south (see Map 4.1). Moreover, as the northernmost group of colonies, New England had a contested northern and western frontier. Powerful Indian tribes, especially the Iroquois and Mahicans, jealously guarded their territories. When provoked by colonial or European disputes, the French (and Catholic) colony of Quebec also menaced the English (and Protestant) colonies of New England.

During the seventeenth century, New England towns parceled out land to individual families. In most cases, the original settlers practiced partible inheritance (that is, they subdivided the land more or less equally among sons). By the eighteenth century, the original land allotments had to be further subdivided to accommodate grandsons and great-grandsons, and many plots of land became too small for a family to make a living. Sons who could not hope to inherit sufficient land to farm had to move away from the town where they were born.

During the eighteenth century, colonial governments in New England abandoned the seventeenth-century policy of granting land to towns. Needing revenue, the governments of both Connecticut and Massachusetts sold land directly to individuals, including speculators. Now money, rather than membership in a community bound by a church covenant, determined whether a person could obtain land. The new land policy also caused the disintegration of the seventeenth-century pattern of settlement. As colonists moved into western Massachusetts and Connecticut and north into New Hampshire and Maine, they tended to settle on individual farms rather than in the towns and villages that characterized the seventeenth century. New Englanders still depended on their relatives and neighbors for help in clearing land, raising a house, worshiping God, and having a good time. But far more than in the seventeenth century, they regulated their behavior in newly settled areas by their own individual dictates.

Farms, Fish, and Trade

The relative scarcity of land in New England encouraged agricultural diversification. New England farmers grew food for their families, but their fields did not produce a huge marketable surplus. Without one big crop, farmers grew many small ones and, if they had extra, sold to or traded with neighbors. Poor roads made travel difficult, time-consuming, and expensive, especially with bulky and heavy agricultural goods. The one major agricultural product the New England colonies exported—livestock—walked to market on its own legs. A New England farm was a place to get by, not to get rich. By 1770, for example, New Englanders had only one-fourth as much wealth as free colonists in the southern colonies.

New Englanders still depended on relatives and neighbors, but far more than in the seventeenth century, they regulated their behavior in newly settled areas by their own individual dictates.

As consumers, New England farmers made up the foundation of a diversified commercial economy that linked remote farms to markets throughout the world. Merchants large and small stocked imported goods—English textiles, ceramics, and metal goods; Chinese tea; West Indian sugar; and Chesapeake tobacco. Farmers' needs for sturdy shoes, a warm coat, a sound cart, and a solid building supported local

shoemakers, tailors, wheelwrights, and carpenters. In the larger towns and especially in Boston, specialized artisans such as cabinetmakers and silversmiths could be found, along with tallow chandlers and printers, like Benjamin Franklin's father and brother. Shipbuilders tended to do better than other artisans because they served the most dynamic sector of the New England economy.

As they had since the seventeenth century, many New Englanders made their fortunes at sea. Fish accounted for more than a third of New England's eighteenth-century exports, with livestock and timber making up another third. The West Indies absorbed two-thirds of all New England's

A YOUNG MAN
This mid-eighteenth-century portrait by an unknown artist of an open-faced young man emphasizes his individuality and prominence in an almost empty and placid landscape, except for the two chickens jealously facing off against each other. Unlike the tunnel-visioned chickens, the artist seems to say, the youth gazes on a promising future in a benign and receptive natural environment.
Christie's Images, Inc.

MAP 4.2

Atlantic Trade in the Eighteenth Century

This map illustrates the economic outlook of the colonies in the eighteenth century: that is, east toward the Atlantic world rather than west toward the interior of North America. The long distances involved in the Atlantic trade and the uncertainties of seaborne travel suggest the difficulties Britain experienced governing the colonies and regulating colonial commerce.

READING THE MAP: What were the major markets for trade coming out of Europe? What goods did the English colonies import and export?

CONNECTIONS: In what ways did the flow of raw materials from the colonies affect English industry? How did English colonial trade policies influence the Atlantic trade?

www.bedfordstmartins.com/tap   SEE THE ONLINE STUDY GUIDE for more help in analyzing this map.

exports. Slaves on Caribbean sugar plantations ate dried, salted codfish caught by New England fishermen, filled barrels crafted from New England timber with molasses and refined sugar, and loaded them aboard ships bound ultimately for Europeans with a sweet tooth (Map 4.2). Almost all the rest of New England's exports went to England and continental Europe. This Atlantic commerce benefited the entire New England economy, providing jobs for laborers and tradesmen as

CAPTAIN ASHLEY BOWEN'S DIARY
This page from mariner Captain Ashley Bowen's diary vividly documents the importance of seafaring in the New England colonies. Bowen drew these ships in the harbor of Marblehead, Massachusetts, a center of the fishing industry, depicting the town as a backdrop to the ships, the focus of interest and action. To Bowen, each ship had distinctive features. Can you spot the differences that caught his eye? Why might such differences be important to Bowen?
Marblehead Historical Society.

well as for ship captains, clerks, and, especially, merchants.

Merchants dominated the commercial economy of New England. Whether in inland communities like Hartford, Connecticut, or seaports like Providence, Rhode Island, merchants stood at the hub of trade between local folk and the international market. The largest and most successful merchants lived in Boston, where they not only bought and sold imported goods but also owned and insured the ships that carried the merchandise. When John Adams, a Massachusetts lawyer who became a leader during the American Revolution and ultimately the second president of the United States, was invited to a wealthy Boston merchant's home, he was stunned by its magnificence. It was a house "for a noble Man, a Prince," he wrote: "The Turkey Carpets, the painted Hangings, the Marble Tables, the rich Beds with crimson Damask Curtains and Counterpins, the beautiful Chimney Clock, the Spacious Garden, are the most magnificent of any Thing I have ever seen." The contrast Adams noted between the luxurious home of this merchant prince and the lives of other New Englanders indicates the polarization of wealth that occurred in Boston and other seaports during the eighteenth century. In the late seventeenth century, the richest 5 percent of Bostonians owned about one-third of the city's wealth; by 1770, they owned about half. At the other end of the spectrum, the share of the city's wealth possessed by the poorest two-thirds of the population declined from about one-sixth to less than one-tenth.

The rich got richer, and everybody else had a smaller share of the total wealth, but the incidence of genuine poverty did not change much. Roughly 5 or 6 percent of the New England population qualified for poor relief throughout the eighteenth century. The colonies' growing population increased the sheer numbers of unemployed or sick, but compared with the poverty in England, the colonists were better off. As a Connecticut traveler wrote from England in 1764, "We in New England know nothing of poverty and want, we have no idea of the thing, how much better do our poor people live than 7/8 of the people on this much famed island."

The contrast with English poverty had meaning since the overwhelming majority of New Englanders traced their ancestry to England, making the region more homogeneous than any other. The population of African ancestry (almost all slaves) in the region remained small. New Englanders had no hesitation about acquiring slaves, and many Puritan ministers owned one or two. In the Narragansett region of Rhode Island, numerous slaves were imported by the colony's prominent slave traders to work raising livestock. But New England's family farms were unsuited for slave labor. Instead, the region's slaves concentrated in towns, especially Boston, where most of them worked as domestic servants and laborers. Although the black population of New England grew to over 15,000 by 1770, it barely diluted the region's 97 percent white majority.

By 1770, the population, wealth, and commercial activity of New England differed from what they had been in 1700. Ministers still enjoyed high status in New England, but Yankee traders had replaced Puritan settlers as the symbolic New Englanders.

The Middle Colonies: Immigrants, Wheat, and Work

In 1700, almost twice as many people lived in New England as in the middle colonies—Pennsylvania, New York, New Jersey, and Delaware. But by 1770, the population of the middle colonies had multiplied tenfold—mainly from an influx of German, Irish, Scotch, and other immigrants—and nearly equaled the population of New England. Immigrants made the middle colonies a uniquely diverse society. By 1800, barely one-third of Pennsylvanians and less than half the total population of the middle colonies traced their ancestry to England.

German and Scots-Irish Immigrants

Germans made up the largest contingent of migrants from the European continent to the middle colonies. By 1770, about 85,000 Germans had arrived in the colonies. Their fellow colonists often referred to them as "Pennsylvania Dutch," an English corruption of *Deutsch,* the word the immigrants used to describe themselves.

Most German immigrants came from a region in southwestern Germany called the Palatinate, although some hailed from German-speaking parts of Switzerland, Austria, and the Netherlands. Throughout Europe, peasants suffered from exploitation by landowners and governments, and they had few opportunities to improve their lives. Palatine peasants in particular, one observer noted, were "not as well off as cattle elsewhere." Devastating French invasions of the Palatinate during Queen Anne's War (1702–1713) made ordinarily bad conditions even worse and triggered the first large-scale migration. German immigrants to the middle colonies included numerous artisans and a few merchants, but the great majority were farmers and laborers. Economically, they represented "middling" folk, neither the poorest (who could not afford the trip) nor the better off (who did not want to leave).

By the 1720s, Germans who had established themselves in the colonies wrote back to their friends and relatives, as one reported, "of the civil and religious liberties [and] privileges, and of all the goodness I have heard and seen." Such letters prompted still more Germans to pull up stakes and embark for America, to exchange the miserable certainties of their lives in Germany for the uncertain attractions of life in the colonies.

Similar motives propelled the Scots-Irish, who considerably outnumbered German immigrants. The term *Scots-Irish,* like *Pennsylvania Dutch,* was a misleading label coined in the colonies. Immigrants labeled Scots-Irish actually hailed from the north of Ireland, Scotland, and northern England. Some of the Scots-Irish were Irish natives who had no personal or ancestral connection whatever with Scotland.

Like the Germans, the Scots-Irish were Protestants, but with a difference. Most German immigrants worshiped in Lutheran or German Reformed churches; many others belonged to dissenting sects like the Mennonites, Moravians, and Amish, whose adherents sought relief from persecution they had suffered in Europe for their refusal to bear arms and to swear oaths, practices they shared with Quakers. In contrast, the Scots-Irish tended to be militant Presbyterians who seldom hesitated to swear oaths or bear arms. Like German settlers, however, Scots-Irish immigrants were clannish, residing when they could among relatives or neighbors from the old country.

In the eighteenth century, wave after wave of Scots-Irish immigrants arrived, beginning in 1717, cresting every twelve or fifteen years thereafter and culminating in a flood of immigration in the years just before the American Revolution. Deteriorating economic conditions in northern Ireland, Scotland, and England pushed many toward America. Most of the immigrants were farm laborers or tenant farmers fleeing droughts, crop failures, high food prices, or rising rents. By 1773, British officials became so concerned about the drain of people to the colonies that they began to quiz prospective settlers about why they were leaving. The answers Scots-Irish gave echoed the motives of their predecessors: "out of work"; "poverty"; "tyranny of landlords"; and the desire to "do better in America."

Both Scots-Irish and Germans probably heard the common saying that "Pennsylvania is heaven for farmers [and] paradise for artisans," but they almost certainly did not fully understand the risks of their decision to leave their native lands. Gottfried Mittelberger, a musician who traveled from Germany to Philadelphia in 1750, described the grueling passage to America commonly experienced by eighteenth-century emigrants. Mittelberger's trip from his home village in the interior to the port of Rotterdam took seven weeks and cost four times more than the trip from Rotterdam to Philadelphia. Nearly two-thirds of all German emigrants arrived at their port of departure with no money to stock up on extra provisions for the trip or even to buy a ticket. Likewise, they could not afford to go back home. Ship captains, aware of the hunger for labor in the colonies, eagerly signed up the penniless emigrants as "redemptioners," a variant of indentured servants. A captain would agree to provide transportation to Philadelphia, where redemptioners would obtain the money to pay for their passage from a friend or relative who was already in the colonies or, as most did, by selling themselves as servants. Impoverished Scots-Irish emigrants, especially the majority who traveled alone rather than with families, typically paid for their passage by contracting to become indentured servants before they sailed.

Mittelberger enjoyed the amenities reserved for passengers who paid their way to Pennsylvania, but he witnessed the distress among the four hundred other Germans aboard his ship, most of them redemptioners. They were packed "as closely as herring," in bunks two feet by six feet. Seasickness compounded by exhaustion, poverty, poor food, bad water, inadequate sanitation, and tight quarters encouraged the spread of disease. The dismal conditions on Mittelberger's ship were not unusual. One historian has noted that on the sixteen immigrant ships arriving in Philadelphia in 1738, over half of all passengers died en route.

Both Scots-Irish and Germans heard the saying that "Pennsylvania is heaven for farmers [and] paradise for artisans," but they almost certainly did not fully understand the risks of their decision to leave home.

When his ship finally approached land, Mittelberger wrote, "everyone crawls from below to the deck . . . and people cry for joy, pray, and sing praises and thanks to God." Unfortunately, their troubles were far from over. Once the ship docked, passengers who had paid their fare could go ashore, as could redemptioners who provided the captain some collateral while they tried to raise the funds for their passage. All the other redemptioners and indentured servants—the majority of passengers—had to stay on board until someone came to purchase their labor. Unlike indentured servants, redemptioners negotiated independently with their purchasers about their period of servitude. Typically, a healthy adult redemptioner agreed to four years of labor. Indentured servants commonly served five, six, or seven years, as did weaker, younger, and less skilled redemptioners. Children ten years old or younger usually had to become indentured servants until they were twenty-one.

Pennsylvania: "The Best Poor [White] Man's Country"

New settlers, whether free or in servitude, poured into the middle colonies because they perceived unparalleled opportunities, particularly in Pennsylvania, "the best poor Man's Country in the World," as indentured servant William Moraley wrote in 1743. Although

Moraley reported that "the Condition of bought Servants is very hard" and masters often failed to live up to their promise to provide decent food and clothing, opportunity abounded because there was more work to be done than workers to do it.

Most servants toiled in Philadelphia, New York City, or one of the smaller towns or villages. Artisans, small manufacturers, and shopkeepers prized the labor of male servants. Female servants made valuable additions to households, where nearly all of them cleaned, washed, cooked, or minded children. From the masters' viewpoint, servants were a bargain. A master could purchase five or six years of a servant's labor for approximately the wages a common laborer would earn in four months. Wage workers could walk away from their jobs when they pleased, and they did so often enough to be troublesome to employers. Servants, however, were legally bound to work for their masters until their terms expired. The restrictions and confinements of bondage were genuine, and they were vigorously enforced.

New settlers, whether free or in servitude, poured into the middle colonies because they perceived unparalleled opportunities.

A few black slaves worked in shops and homes in Philadelphia and New York City. For example, after Benjamin Franklin became prosperous, he purchased five slaves. Since a slave cost at least three times as much as a servant, only affluent colonists could afford the long-term investment in slave labor. While the population of African ancestry (almost all slaves) in the middle colonies grew to over thirty thousand in 1770, it represented only about 7 percent of the total population, and in most of the region much less. The reason more slaves were not brought to the middle colonies was that farmers, the vast majority of the population, had little use for them. Most farms operated with family labor.

> TO be Sold, a Young Negro Woman, about 20 Year old, fhe dos all fortr of Houfe work; fhe can Brew, Bake, boyle foaft Soap, Wafh, Iron & Starch; and is a good darey Women fhe can Card and Spin at the great Wheel, Cotten, Lennen and Wollen, fhe has another good Property fhe neither drinks Rum nor fmoaks Tobacco, and fhe is a ftrong hale healthy Wench, fhe can Cook pretty well for Roft and Boyld; fhe can fpeak no other Language but Englifh; fhe had the fmall Pox in *Barbados* when a Child.   Enquire of the Printer here of and know the Purchafe.
> N.B. She is well Clothed.

ADVERTISEMENT TO SELL A SLAVE WOMAN
This advertisement appeared in a New York newspaper in 1734. (Note that in the printing of the era, a lowercase s somewhat resembles an f.) What does this woman's owner think might make her valuable to a buyer? Reading between the lines of the notice, one can glimpse the outlines of the woman's biography, at least from her owner's point of view. Try to reconstruct the life history of this woman, based on the information provided. How might the advertisement have been different if she had described herself?
© Collection of the New-York Historical Society.

Wheat, the most widely grown crop, did not require more labor than farmers could typically muster from relatives, neighbors, and a hired hand or two.

During the eighteenth century, most slaves came to the middle colonies as they did to New England, in ships returning from the West Indies. Enough arrived to prompt colonial assemblies to pass slave codes that punished slaves much more severely than servants for the same transgressions. "For the least trespass," servant Moraley reported, slaves "undergo the severest Punishment." In practice, both servants and slaves were governed more by their masters than by the laws. But in cases of abuse, servants could and did charge masters with violating the terms of their indenture contracts. The terms of a slave's bondage were set forth in a master's commands, not in a written contract.

Small numbers of slaves managed to obtain their freedom, but free African Americans did not escape whites' firm convictions about black inferiority and white supremacy. Whites' racism and blacks' lowly social status made African Americans scapegoats for European Americans' suspicions and anxieties. In 1741, when arson and several unexplained thefts plagued New York City, officials suspected a murderous slave conspiracy. On the basis of little more than evidence of slaves' "insolence" (that is, refusal to conform fully to whites' expectations of servile behavior), city authorities had thirteen slaves burned at the stake and eighteen others hanged. Although slaves were certifiably poor (they usually had no property whatever), they were not included among the poor for whom the middle colonies were reputed to be the best country in the world.

Immigrants swarmed to the middle colonies because of the availability of land. The Penn family encouraged immigration to bring in potential buyers for their enormous tracts of land in Pennsylvania. From the beginning, Pennsylvania followed a policy of negotiating with Indian tribes to purchase additional land. This policy greatly reduced the violent frontier clashes evident elsewhere in the colonies. Yet the Penn family did not shrink from pushing its agreements with Indian tribes to the limit and beyond. In a dispute with tribes on the northern Delaware River in 1737, the Penn family pulled out a deed showing that local tribes had in 1686 granted the Penns land that stretched as far as a man could walk in a day and a half. Under the terms of this infamous "Walking Purchase," the Penns sent out three runners, two of whom collapsed before the

NEW YORK STREET SCENE
This painting depicts John Street, a residential neighborhood of New York, in 1768, as recalled by artist Joseph B. Smith early in the nineteenth century. The painting highlights the urbane pleasures of casual encounters and friendly conversations on the street. Unlike urban streets today, noise on John Street was limited to human voices, a few yipping dogs, and the clatter of horses' hooves. The street appears safe and secure; the people show no sign of caution about theft or assault, nor do they appear to be in a hurry to seek refuge indoors. What do the clusters of people suggest about patterns of sociability on John Street in the eighteenth century? Standing at the door of Wesley Chapel is Peter Williams, an African American who served as sexton of the church. Williams later earned enough money buying and selling tobacco to help build New York's first African American Methodist church.
Old John Street United Methodist Church.

thirty-six hours expired. The third runner managed to cover sixty miles of wilderness, approximately doubling the size of the Penns' claim.

Few colonists drifted beyond the northern boundaries of Pennsylvania. Owners of the huge estates in New York's Hudson valley preferred to rent rather than sell their land, and thus they attracted fewer immigrants. The Iroquois dominated the lucrative fur trade of the St. Lawrence valley and eastern Great Lakes, and they had the political and

BETHLEHEM, PENNSYLVANIA

This view of the small community of Bethlehem, Pennsylvania, in 1757 dramatizes the profound transformation of the natural landscape in the eighteenth century by highly motivated human labor. Founded by Moravian immigrants in 1740, Bethlehem must have appeared at first like the dense woods on the upper left horizon. In fewer than twenty years, precisely laid-out orchards and fields had replaced forests and glades. Carefully penned livestock (lower center right) and fenced fields (lower left) kept the handiwork of farmers separate from the risks and disorders of untamed nature. Not only individual farmsteads (lower center) but impressive multistory brick town buildings (upper center) combined the bounty of the land with the delights of community life. Few eighteenth-century communities were as orderly as Bethlehem, but many effected a comparable transformation of the environment.

Miriam and Ira D. Walsh Division of Art, Prints, and Photographs, The New York Public Library. Astor, Lenox, and Tilden Foundations.

www.bedfordstmartins.com/tap   SEE THE ONLINE STUDY GUIDE for more help in analyzing this image.

military strength to defend their territory from colonial encroachment. Few settlers wanted to risk having their scalps lifted by Iroquois warriors in northern New York when they could choose to settle instead in the comparatively safe environs of Pennsylvania.

The price of farmland varied depending on soil quality, access to water, distance from a market town, and the extent of improvements. One hundred acres

of improved land that had been cleared, plowed, fenced, ditched, and perhaps had a house and barn built on it might cost three or four times more than the same acreage of uncleared, unimproved land. Since the cheapest unimproved land always lay at the margin of settlement, would-be farmers tended to migrate to promising areas just beyond already improved farms. From Philadelphia, settlers moved north along the Delaware River and west along the Schuylkill and Susquehanna Rivers. By midcentury, settlement had reached the eastern slopes of the Appalachian Mountains, and newcomers spilled down the fertile valley of the Shenandoah River into western Virginia and the Carolinas. Thousands of settlers migrated from the middle colonies through this back door to the South.

Patterns of Settlement, 1700–1777

Farmers made the middle colonies the breadbasket of North America. They planted a wide variety of crops to feed their families, but they grew wheat in abundance. Flour milling was the number one industry and flour the number one export, constituting nearly three-fourths of all exports from the middle colonies. Pennsylvania flour fed residents in other colonies, in southern Europe, and, above all, in the West Indies (see Map 4.2). For farmers, the world grain market proved risky but profitable. Grain prices rose steadily after 1720; by 1770, a bushel of wheat was worth twice (in real terms, that is, adjusted for inflation) what it had been fifty years earlier.

The standard of living in rural Pennsylvania was probably higher than in any other agricultural region of the eighteenth-century world. The comparatively widespread prosperity of all the middle colonies permitted residents to indulge in a half-century shopping spree for English imports. The middle colonies' per capita consumption of imported goods from England more than doubled between 1720 and 1770, far outstripping the per capita consumption of English goods in New England and the southern colonies.

At the crossroads of trade in wheat exports and English imports stood Philadelphia. By 1776, Philadelphia had a larger population than any other city in the entire British Empire except London. Merchants occupied the top stratum of Philadelphia society. They made fortunes in trade,

Farmers made the middle colonies the breadbasket of North America.

shipping, insurance, land, and law. In a city where only 2 percent of the residents owned enough property to qualify to vote, merchants built grand homes and dominated local government. They sent their sons to Europe for education and refinement; their daughters learned enough at home, they believed. Many of Philadelphia's wealthiest merchants were Quakers. Quaker traits of industry, thrift, honesty, and sobriety encouraged the accumulation of wealth. A colonist complained that a Quaker "prays for his neighbor on First Days [the Sabbath] and then preys on him the other six."

The ranks of merchants reached downward to aspiring tradesmen like Benjamin Franklin. After he started to publish the *Pennsylvania Gazette* in 1728, Franklin opened a shop, run mostly by his wife, Deborah, that sold a little bit of everything: cheese, codfish, coffee, goose feathers, sealing wax, soap, and now and then a slave. In 1733, Franklin began to publish *Poor Richard's Almanack*, a calendar of weather predictions, astrological alignments, and pithy epigrams. Poor Richard preached the likelihood of long-term rewards for tireless labor. The *Almanack* sold thousands of copies, quickly becoming Franklin's most profitable product.

The popularity of *Poor Richard's Almanack* suggests that many Pennsylvanians thought less about the pearly gates than about their pocketbooks. Where were the mysteries of divine providence in what might be considered Poor Richard's motto for the middle colonies, "God gives all Things to Industry"? The promise of a worldly payoff made work a secular faith in the middle colonies. Poor Richard advised, "Work as if you were to live 100 years, Pray as if you were to die Tomorrow."

William Penn's Quaker utopia became a center of worldly affluence whose most famous citizen, Franklin, was neither a Quaker nor a utopian. Quakers remained influential, but Franklin spoke for most colonists with his aphorisms of work, discipline, and thrift that echoed Quaker rules for outward behavior. Franklin's maxims did not look to the Quakers' divine inner light for guidance. They depended instead on the spark of ambition and the glow of gain.

BENJAMIN FRANKLIN
This is the earliest known portrait of Benjamin Franklin. Painted by Robert Feke about 1748 when Franklin was in his early forties, the portrait illustrates Franklin's status as an aspiring printer, merchant, and citizen of Philadelphia. To the present-day viewer, Franklin appears prim, foppish, and mannered, with an elaborately curled wig framing a composed, satisfied face. However, compare Franklin's demeanor and dress with that of the young man (page 109) and of Mrs. Barnard Elliott (page 126). Franklin appears more pretentious than the unformed boy and less elegant than Mrs. Elliott, a rough index of his in-progress social mobility from a hardworking printer to a prominent and wealthy thinker and statesman.
Courtesy of the Harvard University Portrait Collection, Bequest, Dr. John C. Warren, 1856.

The Southern Colonies: Land of Slavery

Between 1700 and 1770, the population of the southern colonies—Virginia, Maryland, North Carolina, South Carolina, and Georgia—grew almost ninefold. By 1770, about twice as many people lived in the South as in either the middle colonies or New England. As elsewhere, natural increase and immigration accounted for this rapid population growth. Many Scots-Irish and German immigrants funneled from the middle colonies into the southern backcountry. Other immigrants were indentured servants (mostly English and Scots-Irish) who followed their seventeenth-century predecessors.

But involuntary immigrants—slaves—made the most striking contribution to the booming southern colonies, transforming the racial and ethnic composition of the population and shaping the region's economy, society, and politics.

The Atlantic Slave Trade and the Growth of Slavery

The number of southerners of African ancestry (nearly all of them slaves) rocketed from just over 20,000 in 1700 to well over 400,000 in 1770. The black population increased nearly three times faster than the South's briskly growing white population. Consequently, the proportion of southerners who were black grew from 20 percent in 1700 to 40 percent in 1770. By then, the number of slaves in the South considerably exceeded the entire population (white and black) of New England in 1750 or the middle colonies in 1760. Slavery became the defining characteristic of the southern colonies during the eighteenth century.

Southern colonists clustered into two distinct geographic and agricultural zones. The colonies in the upper South, surrounding the Chesapeake Bay, specialized in growing tobacco, as they had since the early seventeenth century. Throughout the eighteenth century, nine out of ten southern whites and eight out of ten southern blacks lived in the Chesapeake region. The upper South retained a white majority during the eighteenth century, although it dwindled from four-fifths to two-thirds because the slave population grew so dramatically.

In the lower South, a much smaller cluster of colonists inhabited the coastal region and specialized in the production of rice and indigo (a plant used to make blue dye). Lower South colonists made up only 5 percent of the total population of the southern colonies in 1700 but inched upward to 15 percent by 1770. South Carolina was the sole British colony along the South Atlantic coast until 1732 when Georgia was founded. In contrast to every other British mainland colony, blacks in South Carolina outnumbered whites almost two to one; in some low country districts, the ratio of blacks to whites exceeded ten to one.

The enormous growth in the South's slave population occurred through natural increase and the flourishing Atlantic slave trade (Map 4.3 and Table 4.1). Slave ships brought almost 300,000 Africans to British North America between 1619 and 1780. Of those Africans, 95 percent arrived in the South and 96 percent arrived during the eighteenth century. Unlike indentured servants or redemptioners, the Africans did not choose to come to the colonies. They were imported. The word *imported*—a word normally used to describe the shipment of goods for sale—accurately conveys their status. Most of them had been born into free families in villages located within a few hundred miles of the West African coast. Although they shared African origins, they came from many different

African cultures, including Akan, Angolan, Asante, Bambara, Gambian, Igbo, Mandinga, and others. They spoke different languages, worshiped different deities, followed different rules of kinship, grew different crops, and recognized different rulers. The most important experience they had in common was the process of enslavement. Captured in war, kidnapped, or sold into slavery by other Africans, they were brought to the coast, sold to African traders who assembled slaves for sale, and sold again to European or colonial slave traders or ship captains who bought them for shipment to the New World. Packed aboard a slave ship with two to three hundred or more other slaves, they were subjected to the infamous Middle Passage—the crossing of the Atlantic in the hold of a

MAP 4.3

The Atlantic Slave Trade

Although the Atlantic slave trade endured from about 1450 to 1870, its heyday occurred during the eighteenth century, when more than six million African slaves were imported to the New World. Only a small fraction of the African slaves imported to the Western Hemisphere were taken to British North America; most went to sugar plantations in Brazil and the Caribbean. Why were so many more African slaves sent to the West Indies and Brazil than to British North America?

slave ship—and then sold yet again by the ship captain to a colonial slave merchant or to a southern planter.

The voices of Africans who were swept up in the slave trade have been enveloped by a deafening historical silence, with one major exception. In 1789, Olaudah Equiano published *The Interesting Narrative,* an account of his own enslavement that hints at the stories that might have been told by the thousands of silenced Africans. Equiano was born in 1745 in the interior of what is now Nigeria. "I had never heard of white men or Europeans, nor of the sea," he recalled. One day when Equiano was eleven years old, two men and a woman, all Africans, broke into his home, seized him and his sister, and carried them off. The kidnappers soon separated Equiano from his sister, leaving him "in a state of distraction not to be described. I cried and grieved continually, and for several days did not eat anything but what they forced into my mouth."

Unlike indentured servants or redemptioners, the Africans did not choose to come to the colonies. They were imported.

During the next six or seven months, Equiano was sold to several different African masters, each of whom moved him closer to the coast. When Equiano arrived at the coast, a slave ship waited offshore. Equiano feared that he had "gotten into a world of bad spirits," that he was going to be killed and "eaten by those white men with horrible looks, red faces, and loose hair." Once the ship set sail, the slaves were confined to the hold, which "became absolutely pestilential." Many slaves died from sickness, crowded together in suffocating heat fouled by filth of all descriptions. "The shrieks of the women and the groans of the dying rendered the whole a scene of horror almost inconceivable," Equiano recalled. The ship finally arrived in Barbados, and merchants and planters came on board to examine the slaves. In a few days, white masters in Barbados had purchased most of Equiano's shipmates, but he was "not saleable," probably because he was so young. He and other leftovers "were shipped off in a sloop for North America." The sloop sailed to Virginia, where Equiano "saw few or none of our native Africans and not one soul who could talk to me." Soon all the other slaves had been sold "and only

TABLE 4.1	
SLAVE IMPORTS, 1451–1870	
Estimated Slave Imports to the Western Hemisphere	
1451–1600	275,000
1601–1700	1,341,000
1701–1810	6,100,000
1811–1870	1,900,000

myself was left. I was now exceedingly miserable and thought myself worse off than any of the rest of my companions, for they could talk to each other, but I had no person to speak to that I could understand." Equiano finally was sold to a white man, the captain of a tobacco ship bound for England. Equiano remained a slave for ten years, traveling frequently from England to the West Indies and North America until he bought his freedom in 1766.

Some of the slaves brought into the southern colonies came as Equiano did, aboard ships from the West Indies. Merchants in the North American colonies often specialized in this trade; Equiano himself was owned for several years by a Quaker merchant from Philadelphia who traded extensively with the West Indies. But slaves arriving from the West Indies accounted for only about 15 percent of all the Africans brought into the southern colonies during the eighteenth century. All the rest came directly from Africa, and almost all the ships that brought them (roughly 90 percent) belonged to British merchants. Most slaves on board were young adults, men usually outnumbering women two to one. Children under the age of fourteen, like Equiano, were typically no more than 10 or 15 percent of a cargo.

Mortality during the Middle Passage varied considerably from ship to ship. On average, about 15 percent of the slaves died, but sometimes half or more perished. The average mortality among the white crew of slave ships was often nearly as bad. In general, the longer the voyage, the larger the number of deaths. Recent studies suggest that many slaves succumbed not only to virulent epidemic diseases such as smallpox and dysentery but also to acute dehydration caused by fluid loss from heavy perspiration, vomiting, and diarrhea combined with a severe shortage of drinking water.

Normally an individual planter purchased at any one time a relatively small number of newly arrived Africans, or "new Negroes," as they were called. In the Chesapeake in 1735, for example, a healthy adult slave cost about the same as nineteen head of cattle. Slave prices escalated with surging demand for their labor; by 1770, a comparable slave cost as much as thirty head of cattle. Planters often bought slaves on credit, hoping to pay off their debt with the boost in production they anticipated from their new laborers.

Another reason planters preferred to purchase small groups of slaves was to permit the newcomers to be trained by the planters' other slaves. Like Equiano, newly arrived Africans were often profoundly depressed, demoralized, and disoriented. Planters counted on their other slaves—either those born into slavery in the colonies (often called "country-born" or "creole" slaves) or Africans who had arrived earlier—to help new Negroes become accustomed to their strange new surroundings.

Planters' preferences for slaves from specific regions of Africa aided the process of acculturation (or "seasoning," as it was called) to the routines of slave life in the southern colonies. Chesapeake planters preferred slaves from Senegambia, the Gold Coast, or—like Equiano—the Bight of Biafra, the origin of 40 percent of all Africans imported to the Chesapeake. South Carolina planters favored slaves from the central African Congo and Angola regions, the origin of about 40 percent of the African slaves they imported. Although slaves within each of these regions spoke many different languages, enough linguistic and cultural similarities existed that they could communicate with other Africans from the same region.

Seasoning acclimated new Africans to the physical as well as the cultural environment of the southern colonies. Slaves who had just endured the Middle Passage were poorly nourished, weak, and sick. In this vulnerable state they encountered the alien diseases of North America without having developed a biological arsenal of acquired immunities. As many as 10 or 15 percent of newly arrived Africans, sometimes more, died during their first year in the southern colonies. New arrivals who survived for a year or two were considered seasoned.

While newly enslaved Africans poured into the southern colonies, slave women made an even greater contribution to the growth of the black population. Both country-born women and seasoned Africans gave birth to slave babies, which caused the slave population to mushroom. Slave owners encouraged these births. Thomas Jefferson explained, "I consider the labor of a breeding [slave]

OLAUDAH EQUIANO
This portrait of Olaudah Equiano was painted by an unknown English artist about 1780, when Equiano was in his mid-thirties, more than a decade after he had bought his freedom. The portrait evokes Equiano's successful acculturation to the customs of eighteenth-century England. His clothing and hairstyle reflect the fashions of respectable young Englishmen. In his **Interesting Narrative,** *Equiano explained that he had learned to speak and understand English while he was a slave. He wrote that he "looked upon [the English] . . . as men superior to us [Africans], and therefore I had the stronger desire to resemble them, to imbibe their spirit and imitate their manners; I therefore embraced every occasion of improvement, and every new thing that I observed I treasured up in my memory." Equiano's embrace of English culture did not cause him to forsake his African roots. He honored his dual identity by campaigning against slavery. His* **Narrative** *was one of the most important and powerful antislavery documents of the time.*
EX 17082 *Portrait of a Negro Man, Olaudah Equiano,* 1780s by English School (18th century). Royal Albert Memorial Museum, Exeter, England.

woman as no object, that a [slave] child raised every 2 years is of more profit than the crop of the best laboring [slave] man." The growing number of slave babies set the southern colonies apart from other

THE AFRICAN SLAVE TRADE

The African slave trade supplied the New World's demand for labor and Europe's voracious appetite for such New World products as sugar, tobacco, and rice with millions of enslaved Africans to work for their New World purchasers. African men, women, and children, like those pictured in this early-eighteenth-century engraving of a family residence in Sierra Leone, were kidnapped or captured in wars—typically by other Africans—and enslaved. Uprooted from their homes and kin, they were usually taken to coastal enclaves where African traders and European ship captains negotiated prices, made deals, and often branded the newly enslaved people. The significance of this diabolical collaboration between Europeans and their African trading partners is illustrated by the seventeenth-century Benin bronze box, which depicts a royal palace in Nigeria, whose slave trading and other activities are guarded by massive birds and two Portuguese soldiers. Jammed into the holds of slave ships, enslaved Africans made the dreaded Middle Passage to the New World. The model of a slave ship shown here was used in parliamentary debates by antislavery leaders in Britain to demonstrate the inhumanity of shipping people as if they were just so much tightly packed cargo. The model does not show another typical feature of slave ships: weapons. Slaves vastly outnumbered the crews aboard the ships, and crew members justifiably feared slave uprisings.

Museum für Volkerkunde, Berlin / Courtesy, Earl Gregg Swen Library, College of William and Mary, Williamsburg, Virginia / Wilberforce House Museum, Hull City Museum, Art Gallery, and Archives.

New World slave societies, which experienced natural decrease; that is, slave deaths exceeded births. The high rate of natural increase in the southern colonies meant that by the 1740s the majority of southern slaves were country-born. But the large numbers of newly enslaved Africans made the influence of African culture in the eighteenth-century South stronger than ever before—or since.

Slave Labor and African American Culture

Planters expected slaves to work from sunup to sundown and beyond. George Washington wrote that his slaves should "be at their work as soon as it is light, work til it is dark, and be diligent while they are at it." The conflict between the masters' desire for maximum labor and the slaves' reluctance to do more than necessary made the threat of physical punishment a constant for eighteenth-century slaves. Masters preferred black slaves over white indentured servants not just because slaves served for life, but also because colonial laws did not limit the force masters could use against slaves. Masters often reached for their whips, or worse. As a traveler observed in 1740, "A new negro . . . will require more discipline than a young spaniel. . . . let a hundred men show him how to hoe, or drive a wheelbarrow; he'll still take the one by the bottom and the other by the wheel and . . . often die before [he] . . . can be conquered." Slaves, the traveler noted, were not stupid or simply obstinate; despite the inevitable punishment, they resisted their masters' demands because of their "greatness of soul," their stubborn unwillingness to conform to their masters' definition of them as merely slaves.

The large numbers of newly enslaved Africans made the influence of African culture in the eighteenth-century South stronger than ever before—or since.

Some slaves escalated their acts of resistance to direct physical confrontation with the master, mistress, or an overseer. But a hoe raised in anger, a punch in the face, or a desperate swipe with a knife led to swift and predictable retaliation by whites. Throughout the southern colonies, the balance of physical power rested securely in the hands of whites.

Rebellion occurred, however, at Stono, South Carolina, in 1739. Before dawn on a September Sunday, a group of about twenty slaves attacked a country store, killed the two storekeepers, confiscated the store's guns, ammunition, and powder, and set out toward Spanish Florida after pausing to set the severed heads of their victims on the store's front steps. Enticing other rebel slaves to join the march south, the group plundered and burned more than a half dozen plantations and killed more than twenty white men, women, and children. As their numbers grew, the rebels stopped to rest, to beat drums to signal more slaves to join them, and to dance and sing in celebration. A mounted force of whites attacked the exultant slaves and killed many of them. They placed rebels' heads atop mileposts along the road, grim reminders of the consequences of rebellion. The Stono rebellion illustrated that eighteenth-century slaves, no matter how determined, had no chance of overturning slavery and very little chance of defending themselves in any bold strike for freedom. After the rebellion, South Carolina legislators enacted repressive laws designed to guarantee that whites would always have the upper hand. (See "Documenting the American Promise," page 124.) No other similar uprising occurred during the colonial period.

Day-to-day experience convinced most slaves that survival lay within the boundaries of slavery. But slaves maneuvered constantly to protect themselves and to gain a measure of autonomy. In Chesapeake tobacco fields, most slaves were subject to close supervision by whites. In the lower South, the task system gave slaves some control over the pace of their work and some discretion in the use of the rest of their time. A task was typically defined as a certain area of ground to be planted, cultivated, and harvested or a specific job to be completed. A slave who completed the assigned task could use the remainder of the day to work in a garden, fish, hunt, spin, weave, sew, or cook. If a master sought to increase productivity by changing the definition of tasks, slaves did their best to defend customary practices.

Eighteenth-century slaves planted the roots of African American lineages that branch out to the present. Historians are only beginning to explore the kin networks slaves built; much remains unknown. But it is clear that slaves valued family ties and that, as in West African societies, kinship structured slaves' relations with one another. Slave parents often gave a child the name of a grandparent,

Regulating Slavery

The slave rebellion at Stono, South Carolina, in 1739 alarmed white South Carolinians. The colony's legislators responded in the spring of 1740, only a few months after the rebellion had been suppressed, by enacting new regulations governing slavery. The laws disclosed widespread perceptions among whites of the dangers posed by slaves and of the remedies that would maintain order.

DOCUMENT 1. Act Requiring White Men to Serve on Patrols, 1740

To maintain order among slaves, a law required white men to serve on patrols that had summary power to punish slaves engaged in suspicious activity. The law inadvertently revealed that slaves routinely found ways to evade their masters' control, at least from time to time.

Forasmuch as many late horrible and barbarous massacres have been actually committed, and many more designed, on the white inhabitants of this Province, by negro slaves, who are generally prone to such cruel practices, which makes it highly necessary that constant patrols should be established . . . for the better preventing any future insurrections or cabals of said slaves; we therefore humbly pray his most sacred Majesty that it may be enacted. . . .

That every patrol shall go to and examine the several plantations in their districts . . . at least once in a fortnight, and may take up all slaves which they shall see without the fences or cleared ground of their owners' plantations, who have not a ticket or letter to shew the reasonableness of their absence, or who have not some white person in company to give an account of his, her, or their business, and such patrol may correct every such slave or slaves by whipping with a switch or cowskin, not exceeding twenty lashes; provided no patrol man shall beat or abuse any slave quietly and peaceably being in his master's plantation. . . . And the said patrols

shall have full power to search and examine all negro houses for offensive weapons and ammunition . . . [and] to enter into any disorderly tipling houses or other houses suspected of harbouring, trafficking or dealing with negroes, either of white persons, free negroes or others, and to apprehend and correct all disorderly slaves there found, by whipping.

SOURCE: Thomas Cooper and David McCord, comps., *The Statutes at Large of South Carolina,* 10 vols. (Columbia, 1836–1841), 556–63.

DOCUMENT 2. Act to Tax Imported Slaves, 1740

Another act sought to increase the security of the white population by imposing a tax on purchasers of African slaves and using the revenue to attract white immigrants to settle in the colony. The act contrasted the dangers of "barbarous and savage" slaves, regardless of their size and age, with the expected benefits of "poor protestants."

Whereas, the great importation of negroes from the coast of Africa, who are generally of a barbarous and savage disposition, may hereafter prove of very dangerous consequence to the peace and safety of this Province, and which we have now more reason to be apprehensive of from the late rising in rebellion of a great number of the negroes lately imported into this Province from the coast of Africa . . . and whereas, the best way to prevent those fatal mischiefs for the future, will be to establish a method . . . for the better settling . . . of this Province with white inhabitants, by which we may be the better enabled to suppress any future insurrection of negroes and slaves. . . . There shall be imposed and paid by all and every [one of] the inhabitants of this Province . . . first purchasing any negro or other slave . . . , a certain tax or sum of ten pounds current money for every such negro and other slave of the height of four feet and two inches and upwards; and for every one under that height, and above three feet two inches, the sum of five pounds like money; and for all under three feet two inches, (sucking children excepted) two pounds ten shillings like money. . . . And . . . that out of the said tax or duty on negroes and slaves . . . two-third parts . . . of the net sum arising by the tax . . . [be used] for defraying the charge of transportation or carriage of poor protestants from Charlestown to the townships or other place where they shall settle . . . and for purchasing tools necessary for planting and settling, and for provisions for one year for each of such poor protestants, (not being upwards of fifty years of age) and also for purchasing one cow and calf over and besides such provisions, for every five persons who shall actually become settlers.

SOURCE: Thomas Cooper and David McCord, comps., *The Statutes at Large of South Carolina,* 10 vols. (Columbia, 1836–1841), 568–73.

DOCUMENT 3. South Carolina Slave Code Provisions, 1740

The legislators also enacted a comprehensive slave code containing fifty-eight provisions. All the regulations indirectly acknowledged the lesson whites learned from the Stono rebels—namely, that slaves must be controlled and disciplined more rigorously if masters were to continue to reap the economic and social benefits of slaveholding.

XVI. Be it . . . enacted . . . That . . . if any slave, free negro, mulattoe, Indian or mustizoe [mestizo, a person of mixed white and Indian ancestry], shall wilfully and maliciously burn or destroy any stack of rice, corn, or other grain, of the product, growth or manufacture of this Province, or shall wilfully and maliciously set fire to, burn or destroy any tar kiln, barrels of pitch, tar, turpentine or rosin, or any other [of] the goods or commodities of the growth, produce or manufacture of this Province, or shall feloniously steal, take or carry away any slaves, being the property of another, with intent to carry such slave out of this Province, or shall wilfully or maliciously poison or administer any poison to any person, free man, woman, servant or slave, every such slave, free negro, mulattoe, Indian . . . and mustizoe, shall suffer death as a felon. . . .

XXIV. And be it further enacted . . . That if any slave shall presume to strike any white person, such slave, upon trial and conviction . . . shall for the first and second offence, suffer such punishment as the said justice [of the peace] and freeholders . . . shall, in their discretion think fit, not extending to life or limb; and for the third offence, shall suffer death. But in case any such slave shall grievously wound, maim or bruise any white person, though it be only the first offence, such slave shall suffer death. . . .

LVI. And whereas, several negroes did lately rise in rebellion, and did commit many barbarous murders at Stono and other parts adjacent thereto; and whereas, in suppressing the said rebels, several of them were killed and others taken alive and executed; and as the exigence and danger the inhabitants at that time were in and exposed to, would not admit of the formality of a legal trial of such rebellious negroes, but for their own security, the said inhabitants were obliged to put such negroes to immediate death. . . . Be it enacted . . . That all and every act . . . done, committed and executed, in and about the suppressing and putting all and every [one of] the said . . . negroes to death, is and are hereby declared lawful . . . as fully and amply as if such rebellious negroes had undergone a formal trial and condemnation.

SOURCE: Thomas Cooper and David McCord, comps., *The Statutes at Large of South Carolina,* 10 vols. (Columbia, 1836–1841), 397–417.

QUESTIONS FOR ANALYSIS AND DEBATE

1. Why did legislators believe laws like these were necessary?

2. Did these laws apply only to slaves? To what degree were the laws designed to regulate the behavior of slave owners?

3. According to the laws, what kinds of slave behavior were most threatening?

4. Why did the legislators pass special laws that governed slaves instead of simply governing slaves by the same laws that applied to all other colonists?

PLANTATION MISTRESS
Enslaved Africans made possible the opulence of Mrs. Barnard Elliott, the wife of a wealthy South Carolina rice planter. Mrs. Elliott appears to be a discriminating consumer. Although she probably made most of her purchases in the best Charleston shops, her custom-made fashions would not have been out of place in the drawing rooms of the English gentry. Sensuous textiles, billowing lace-encrusted sleeves, a daring neckline, and dazzling jewels demonstrate Mrs. Elliott's cosmopolitan tastes despite her colonial residence. Her formal, almost regal pose evokes the enormous distance between the luxurious refinements of elite planters and workaday plantation realities. Contrast the appearance of Mrs. Elliott with that of her approximate contemporary, the New England household slave Phyllis (page 104).
The Gibbes Museum of Art, Carolina Art Association.

aunt, or uncle. In selecting a husband or wife (when the master permitted a choice), slaves avoided first cousins or closer relatives, further evidence of their awareness of kin connections.

In West Africa, kinship not only identified a person's place among living relatives; it also linked the person to ancestors among the dead and to descendants in the future. Kinship rooted people in both society and time. Newly imported African slaves usually arrived alone, without kin; like Equiano, they had been snatched away from their relatives in Africa. Often slaves who had traversed the Middle Passage on the same ship adopted one another as "brothers" and "sisters." Likewise, as new Negroes were seasoned and incorporated into existing slave communities, established families often adopted them as kin and recognized them as aunts or uncles.

When possible, slaves expressed many other features of their West African origins in their lives on New World plantations. They gave their children African names such as Cudjo or Quash, Minda or Fuladi. They grew food crops familiar to them in Africa such as yams and okra. They constructed huts with mud walls and thatched roofs similar to African residences. They fashioned banjos, drums, and other musical instruments, held dances, and observed funeral rites that echoed African practices. In these and many other ways, slaves drew upon their African heritages to endow their personal lives with relationships and meanings that they controlled, as much as the circumstances of slavery permitted.

Tobacco, Rice, and Prosperity

Slaves' labor bestowed prosperity on their masters, British merchants, and the monarchy. The southern colonies supplied 90 percent of all North American exports to England. Rice exports from the lower South exploded from less than half a million pounds in 1700 to eighty million pounds in 1770, virtually all of it grown by slaves. Exports of indigo also boomed. Together, rice and indigo made up three-fourths of lower South exports, nearly two-thirds of them going to England and most of the rest to the West Indies, where sugar-growing slaves ate slave-grown rice. Tobacco exports from the Chesapeake did not accelerate as rapidly as rice exports, but they still leaped from about thirty million pounds in 1700 to a hundred million pounds in 1770. Tobacco was by far the most important export from British North America; by 1770, it represented almost one-third of all colonial exports and three-fourths of all Chesapeake exports. And under the provisions of the Navigation Acts (see chapter 3), nearly all of it went to England, where the monarchy collected a lucrative tax on each pound. British merchants then re-exported more than 80 percent of the tobacco to the European continent, pocketing a nice markup for their troubles.

These products of slave labor made the southern colonies by far the richest in North America. The per capita wealth of free whites in the South was four times greater than that in New England and three times that in the middle colonies. At the top of the wealth pyramid stood the rice grandees of the lower South and the tobacco gentry of the Chesapeake. These elite families commonly resided on large estates adorned by handsome mansions and luxurious gardens, maintained and supported by slaves. The extravagant lifestyle of one gentry family astonished a young tutor from New Jersey who noted that during the winter months the family kept twenty-eight large fires roaring, requiring six oxen to haul in a heavy cartload of slave-cut wood four times a day. By contrast, yeoman families—who supported themselves on a small plot of land without slaves and cut their own wood—normally warmed themselves around one fire.

The vast differences in wealth among white southerners engendered envy and occasional tension between rich and poor, but remarkably little open hostility. The gentry looked down upon the "meaner sort" and spoke of them disparagingly in private. In public, the planter elite acknowledged humble whites as their equals, at least in belonging to the superior—in their minds—white race. Looking upward, white yeomen and tenants (who owned neither land nor slaves) sensed the gentry's condescension and veiled contempt. But they also appreciated the gentry for granting favors, upholding white supremacy, and keeping slaves in their place. While racial slavery made a few whites much richer than others, it also gave those who did not get rich a powerful reason to feel similar (in race) to those who were so different (in wealth).

The slaveholding gentry dominated the politics and economy of the southern colonies. In Virginia, only adult white men who owned at least one hundred acres of unimproved land or twenty-five acres of land with a house could vote. This property-holding requirement prevented about 40 percent of white men in Virginia from voting for representatives to the House of Burgesses. In South Carolina, only fifty acres of land were required to vote, and most adult white men qualified. But in both colonies, voters elected members of the gentry to serve in the colonial legislature. The gentry passed elected political offices from generation to generation, almost as if they were hereditary. Politically, the gentry built a self-perpetuating oligarchy—rule by the elite few—with the votes of their many humble neighbors.

The gentry also set the cultural standard in the southern colonies. They bought fine wines from France and the latest fashions and books from London. They entertained lavishly, gambled regularly, and attended Anglican church services more for social than religious reasons. Above all they cultivated a life of leisurely pursuit of happiness. They did not condone idleness, however. Their pleasures and their responsibilities kept them busy. Thomas Jefferson, a phenomenally productive member of the gentry, recalled that his earliest childhood memory was of being carried on a pillow by a family slave—a powerful image of the slave hands beneath the gentry's leisure and achievement.

Unifying Experiences

While the societies of New England, the middle colonies, and the southern colonies became more sharply differentiated during the eighteenth century, colonists throughout British North America shared certain unifying experiences. The first was economic: The economies of all three regions had their roots in agriculture. But the tempo of commerce quickened during the eighteenth century. Colonists sold their distinctive products in markets that, in turn, offered to consumers throughout the colonies a more or less uniform array of goods. A second unifying experience was a decline in the importance of religion. Although some settlers called for a revival of religious intensity, for most people throughout the colonies religion mattered less, the affairs of the world more, than they did in the seventeenth century. Third, white inhabitants throughout North America became aware that they shared a distinctive identity as British colonists. Thirteen different governments presided over the North American colonies, but all of them answered to the British monarchy. Royal officials who expected loyalty from the colonists often had difficulty obtaining obedience. The North American colonists asserted their prerogatives as British subjects to defend their special colonial interests.

Commerce and Consumption

Eighteenth-century commerce whetted the appetite to consume. Colonial products spurred the development of mass markets throughout the Atlantic world. Huge increases in the supply of colonial

CONSPICUOUS CONSUMPTION
An eighteenth-century South Carolina rice planter and his wife purchased this exquisite silver epergne during a visit to London. Designed to grace the table at formal dinners, the lacy silver baskets held delicacies to tempt the eye and palate. The epergne, finer than any American silversmith could make, conspicuously displayed its owners' wealth and sophistication. The design shows the delicate balance required to keep the epergne upright: A little too much taken from one basket or added to another could tumble everything into a well-dressed lap. Its fragile equilibrium hints at the significance of social order and stability if slaveholders were to maintain their exalted position atop a society resting on the labor of slaves. Middleton Place Foundation, Charleston.

The Atlantic commerce that took colonial goods to markets in England brought objects of consumer desire back to the colonies. English merchants and manufacturers recognized that colonists made excellent customers, and the Navigation Acts gave English exporters privileged access to the colonial market. By midcentury, export-oriented industries in England were growing ten times faster than firms attuned to the home market. Most English exports went to the vast European market, where potential customers outnumbered those in the colonies by more than one hundred to one. But as European competition stiffened, colonial markets became increasingly important. English exports to North America multiplied eightfold between 1700 and 1770, outpacing the rate of population growth after midcentury (Figure 4.1). When the colonists' eagerness to consume exceeded their ability to pay, English exporters willingly extended credit, and colonial debts soared.

Imported mirrors, silver plate, spices, bed and table linens, clocks, tea services, wigs, books, and more infiltrated parlors, kitchens, and bedrooms throughout the colonies. Despite the many differences among the colonists, the consumption of English exports built a certain material uniformity across region, religion, class, and status. Consumption of English exports did not simply tie the colonists to the British economy. It also made the colonists look and feel more British, even though they lived at the edge of a wilderness an ocean away from England.

Colonial goods brought into focus an important lesson of eighteenth-century commerce. Ordinary people, not just the wealthy elite, would buy the things that they desired in addition to what they absolutely needed.

The rising tide of colonial consumption had other less visible but no less important consequences. Because consumption so often arose from desire rather than necessity, it presented colonists—both women and men—with a novel array of choices. In many respects the choices were seemingly trivial: whether to buy knives and forks, teacups, or a clock. But such small choices confronted eighteenth-century consumers with a big

tobacco and sugar brought the price of these small luxuries within reach of most free whites, at least from time to time. Colonial goods brought into focus an important lesson of eighteenth-century commerce. Ordinary people, not just the wealthy elite, would buy the things that they desired in addition to what they absolutely needed. Even news, formerly restricted mostly to a few people through face-to-face conversations or private letters, became an object of public consumption through the innovation of newspapers. (See "The Promise of Technology," page 130.) With the appropriate stimulus to desire, markets seemed unlimited.

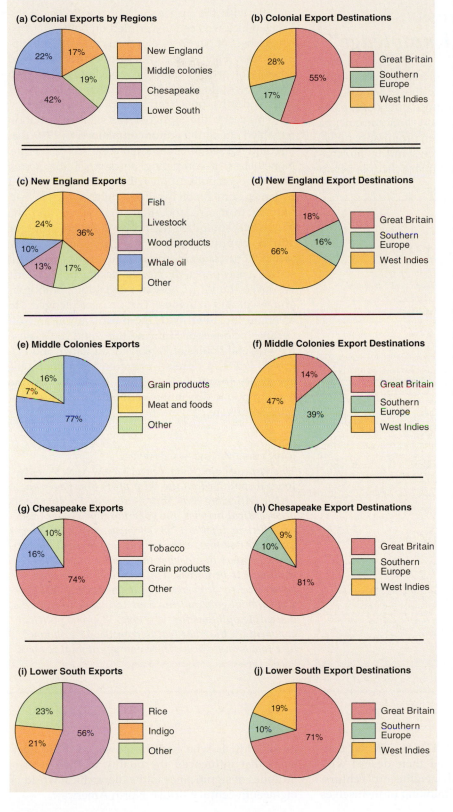

(a) Colonial Exports by Regions

- 17% New England
- 19% Middle colonies
- 42% Chesapeake
- 22% Lower South

(b) Colonial Export Destinations

- 55% Great Britain
- 17% Southern Europe
- 28% West Indies

(c) New England Exports

- 36% Fish
- 17% Livestock
- 13% Wood products
- 10% Whale oil
- 24% Other

(d) New England Export Destinations

- 18% Great Britain
- 16% Southern Europe
- 66% West Indies

(e) Middle Colonies Exports

- 77% Grain products
- 7% Meat and foods
- 16% Other

(f) Middle Colonies Export Destinations

- 14% Great Britain
- 39% Southern Europe
- 47% West Indies

(g) Chesapeake Exports

- 74% Tobacco
- 16% Grain products
- 10% Other

(h) Chesapeake Export Destinations

- 81% Great Britain
- 10% Southern Europe
- 9% West Indies

(i) Lower South Exports

- 56% Rice
- 21% Indigo
- 23% Other

(j) Lower South Export Destinations

- 71% Great Britain
- 10% Southern Europe
- 19% West Indies

FIGURE 4.1

Colonial Exports, 1768–1772

These pie charts provide an overview of the colonial export economy in the 1760s. The first two show that almost two-thirds of colonial exports came from the South and that the majority of the colonies' exports went to Great Britain. The remaining charts illustrate the distinctive patterns of exports in each colonial region. Fish, livestock, and wood products were New England's most important exports; they were sent primarily to the West Indies, only a small fraction going to Great Britain. From the colonial breadbasket in the middle colonies, grain products made up three-fourths of all exports, most of which went to the West Indies or to southern Europe. The Chesapeake also exported some grain, but tobacco accounted for three-fourths of the region's export trade, nearly all of it bound for Great Britain as mandated by the Navigation Acts. Rice and indigo comprised three-fourths of the exports from the lower South, the bulk of which was sent to Great Britain. Taken together, these charts reveal Britain's economic interest in the exports of the North American colonies.

The Printing Press: "The Spring of Knowledge"

IN THE EIGHTEENTH CENTURY, colonial printers began to publish newspapers. Since the 1630s, colonial printers had used presses to churn out books, pamphlets, broadsides, government announcements, legal forms, invitations, and even promissory notes. The innovation of compiling newsworthy information and publishing it on a regular schedule began in 1704 with the appearance of the *Boston News-Letter,* which was usually printed on both sides of a single sheet of paper smaller than conventional typing paper. Each week the *News-Letter* contained reprints of articles that had appeared in English newspapers, along with a few tidbits of local news such as deaths, fires, storms, and ship arrivals.

For years, the audience for such information remained small; the editor complained in 1719 that he could not sell three hundred copies of each issue. Nonetheless, a competing newspaper, the *Boston Gazette,* began publication in that year. It was printed by James Franklin on his press (right), which he had brought from England. Both the *Gazette* and the *News-Letter* submitted their copy to the governor for official approval before the newspapers were printed. Frustrated by this official scrutiny, Franklin started a new paper, the *New England Courant,* which set out to thumb its nose at officialdom, both governmental and religious. The *Courant* pledged "to entertain the Town with the most comical and diverting Incidents of Humane Life" and to "expose the Vice and Follies of Persons of all Ranks and Degrees." Franklin's press—operated faithfully by his apprentice brother, Benjamin—broadcast to the reading public dissenting opinions previously confined to private conversations.

JOHN PETER ZENGER'S NEWSPAPER
This issue of John Peter Zenger's New-York Weekly Journal *contained on the third of its four pages an article criticizing New York's governor. For this and other critical articles, the governor had Zenger tried for seditious libel in 1735. The jury sided with Zenger and acquitted him, although the law favored the governor. Printers like Zenger throughout the colonies continued to be harassed by public officials who tried to censor irreverent and independent publishers. But colonial governments were too weak to suppress dissenting opinions for very long. Vigorous political commentary like that featured on the page shown here found an avid audience among colonial readers.*
Courtesy, American Antiquarian Society.

question: "What do you want?" As colonial consumers defined and expressed their desires with greater frequency during the eighteenth century, they became accustomed to thinking of themselves as individuals who had the power to make decisions that influenced the quality of their lives—attitudes of significance in the hierarchical world of eighteenth-century British North America.

By 1740, more than a dozen newspapers were published in the colonies and their numbers continued to increase. The relatively high rates of literacy gave them a large reading audience. In the northern colonies, readers included well over half of adult men and nearly half of adult women. In the southern colonies, literacy rates among whites were slightly lower, but still considerably above those in Europe. Since whites tried to prevent slaves from learning to read, literacy rates remained low among southern blacks.

But the information printed by newspapers spread far beyond readers. Newspapers were often read aloud not just at home but in workshops, taverns, and courthouses. In these public places people who could not read listened to the controversial ideas, partisan accusations, and salacious rumors that printers relished. An eighteenth-century poem illustrates the many connections between news and audiences cultivated by colonial newspapers:

News'papers are the spring of knowledge,
The gen'ral source throughout the nation.
Of ev'ry modern conversation.
What would this mighty people do,
If there, alas! were nothing new?
   A New-paper is like a feast,
Some dish there is for ev'ry guest;
Some large, some small, some strong, some tender,
For ev'ry stomach, stout or slender;
Those who roast beef and ale delight in,
Are pleas'd with trumpets, drums, and fighting;
For those who are more puny made,
Are arts and sciences, and trade;
For fanciful and am'rous blood,
We have a soft poetic food;
For witty and satyric folks,
High-season'd, acid, BITTER JOKES;
And when we strive to please the mob,
A jest, a quarrel, or a job.
   If any gentleman wants a wife,
(A partner, as 'tis termed, for life)
An advertisement does the thing,
And quickly brings the pretty thing.

JAMES FRANKLIN'S PRINTING PRESS
Newport Historical Society.

If you want health, consult our pages,
You shall be well, and live for ages. . . .
   Our services you can't express,
The good we do you hardly guess;
There's not a want of human kind,
But we a remedy can find.

When newspapers employed the technology of printing to publish everything from political news to advertisements for a spouse, all kinds of information and ideas began to diffuse more readily beyond official channels and to help form public opinion. Eighteenth-century newspapers combined the old technology of printing with the new currents of commerce, dissent, and enlightenment, creating a novel awareness of the problems and possibilities of public life.

Religion, Enlightenment, and Revival

Eighteenth-century colonists could choose from almost as many religions as consumer goods. Virtually all of the bewildering variety of religious denominations represented some form of Christianity, almost all of them Protestant. Roman Catholics concentrated in Maryland as they had since the seventeenth century, but even there they were outnumbered by

Protestants. Slaves made up the largest group of non-Christians. A few slaves converted to Christianity in Africa or after they arrived in North America, but most continued to embrace elements of indigenous African religions.

The varieties of Protestant faith and practice ranged across an extremely broad spectrum. Throughout the plantation South and in urban centers like Charleston, New York, and Philadelphia, prominent colonists belonged to the Anglican Church, conforming to the rituals and relaxed worldliness of the king's faith. In New England, old-style Puritanism splintered into strands of Congregationalism that differed over fine points of theological doctrine. The thousands of immigrants in the middle colonies and the southern backcountry included militant Baptists and Presbyterians. Huguenots who had fled persecution in Catholic France peopled congregations in several cities. In New England, the Congregational Church was the official established church and all residents paid taxes for its support. In the South, the Anglican Church enjoyed a similar status. But in both regions, dissenting faiths grew, and in most colonies adherents of other faiths won the right to worship publicly, although the established churches retained official sanction.

Rivalry and competition for converts often developed among Protestant churches. A faith that affirmed the "priesthood of all believers" (in Martin Luther's famous phrase) empowered Christians to look into their Bibles and their hearts to find God's Way. Not surprisingly, faithful and well-meaning Protestants identified different Ways, denouncing the Ways of others as misguided heresies. The strife engendered by the core of Protestant belief led many colonists to favor toleration of religious differences and peaceful coexistence among disputing churches.

Many educated colonists became deists, looking for God's plan in nature more than in the Bible. Deists shared the ideas of eighteenth-century European Enlightenment thinkers. Representing a multifaceted intellectual movement that challenged many conventional ideas, Enlightenment thinkers tended to agree that science and reason could disclose God's laws in the natural order. During the seventeenth century, Isaac Newton, the brilliant English scientist, demonstrated that all physical objects obeyed precise mathematical laws, such as the law of gravity. Newton's ideas suggested a new vision of the universe and the place of human beings in it. In the Newtonian universe, order was maintained not by the constant intervention of God but by basic mathematical laws. God had presumably created those laws and set the universe in motion, but then he had stepped back, like a watchmaker who assembled a watch and then let it run. To eighteenth-century thinkers, a watchmaker God seemed more distant from the world, less interested in the minutiae of each person's vices and virtues. A watchmaker God was not arbitrary, capricious, or vengeful, plaguing the world with flood, famine, or fire to express his displeasure. Instead, God was orderly and predictable, although still mysterious because the deepest underlying principles of his order remained unknown.

The ideas associated with a Newtonian universe percolated through the Atlantic world during the eighteenth century, influencing devout Christians as well as skeptical deists. In the colonies as well as in Europe, these and other Enlightenment ideas encouraged people to study the world around them, to think for themselves, and to ask whether the disorderly appearance of things masked the principles of a deeper, more profound order. From New England towns to southern drawing rooms, individuals met to discuss such matters. Philadelphia was the center of these conversations, especially after the formation of the American Philosophical Society in 1769, an outgrowth of an earlier discussion group organized by Benjamin Franklin, who was a deist. The American Philosophical Society fostered communication among leading colonial thinkers; Benjamin Franklin was its first president, Thomas Jefferson its third. Among the purposes of these discussions was to find ways to improve society. Franklin's interest in electricity, stoves, and eyeglasses exemplified the shift of focus among many eighteenth-century colonists from heaven to the here and now.

Most eighteenth-century colonists went to church seldom or not at all, although they probably considered themselves Christians. A minister in Charleston observed that on the Sabbath "the Taverns have more Visitants than the Churches." In the leading colonial cities, church members were a small minority of eligible adults, no more than 10 or 15 percent. Anglican parishes in the South rarely claimed more than one-fifth of eligible adults as members. In some regions of rural New England and the middle colonies, church membership embraced two-thirds of eligible adults, while in other areas only one-quarter of the residents belonged to a church. The dominant faith overall was religious indifference. As a late-eighteenth-century traveler observed, "Religious indifference is imperceptibly disseminated from one end of the continent to the other."

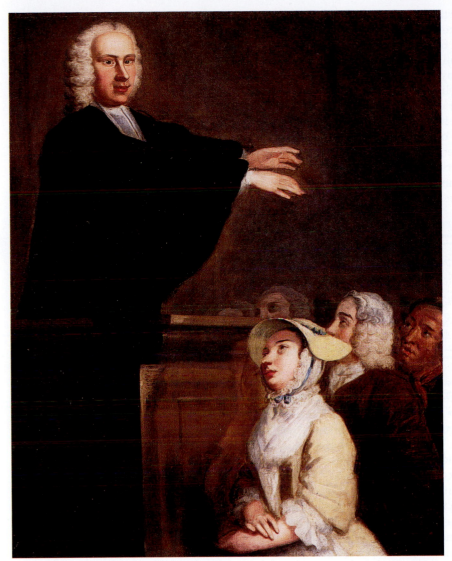

GEORGE WHITEFIELD

An anonymous artist portrayed George Whitefield preaching, emphasizing the power of his sermons to transport his audience to a revived awareness of divine spirituality. Light from above gleams off Whitefield's forehead. His crossed eyes and faraway gaze suggest that he spoke in a semihypnotic trance. Note the absence of a Bible at the pulpit. Rather than elaborating on God's word as revealed in Scripture, Whitefield speaks from his own inner awareness. The young woman bathed in light below his hands appears transfixed, her focus not on Whitefield but on some inner realm illuminated by his words. Her eyes and Whitefield's do not meet, yet the artist's use of light suggests that she and Whitefield see the same core of holy Truth. The other people in Whitefield's audience appear not to have achieved this state. They remain intent on Whitefield's words, failing so far to be ignited by the divine spark. National Portrait Gallery, London.

The spread of religious indifference, of deism, of denominational rivalry, and of comfortable backsliding profoundly concerned many ministers. A few despaired that, as one wrote, "religion . . . lay a-dying and ready to expire its last breath of life." To combat what one preacher called the "dead formality" of church services, some ministers set out to convert nonbelievers and to revive the piety of the faithful with a new style of preaching that appealed more to the heart than to the head. Historians have termed this wave of revivals the "Great Awakening." In Massachusetts during the mid-1730s, the fiery Puritan minister Jonathan Edwards reaped a harvest of souls by reemphasizing tradi-

tional Puritan doctrines of humanity's utter depravity and God's vengeful omnipotence. The title of Edwards's most famous sermon, "Sinners in the Hands of an Angry God," conveys the flavor of his message. In Pennsylvania and New Jersey, Presbyterian William Tennent led revivals dramatizing conventional appeals for spiritual rebirth with accounts of God's miraculous powers—such as raising his son William Tennent Jr. from the dead.

The most famous revivalist in the eighteenth-century Atlantic world was George Whitefield. An Anglican, Whitefield preached well-worn messages of sin and salvation to large audiences in England using his spellbinding, unforgettable voice.

Whitefield visited the North American colonies seven times, staying for more than three years during the mid-1740s and attracting tens of thousands, including Benjamin Franklin, to his sermons. His preaching transported many in his audience to emotion-choked states of religious ecstasy. At one revival, he wrote, "the bitter cries and groans were enough to pierce the hardest heart. Some of the people were as pale as death; others were wringing their hands; others lying on the ground; others sinking into the arms of their friends; and most lifting their eyes to heaven, and crying to God for mercy. They seemed like persons . . . coming out of their graves to judgment."

To combat what one preacher called the "dead formality" of church services, some ministers set out to convert nonbelievers and to revive the faithful with preaching that appealed more to the heart than to the head.

Whitefield's successful revivals spawned many lesser imitations. Itinerant preachers, many of them poorly educated, toured the colonial backcountry after midcentury, echoing Whitefield's medium and message as best they could. Educated and established ministers often regarded them with disgust. But in fact, the revivals that they deplored awakened and refreshed the spiritual energies of thousands of colonists struggling with the uncertainties and anxieties of eighteenth-century America. The conversions at revivals did not substantially boost the total number of church members, however. After the revivalists moved on, the routines and pressures of everyday existence reasserted their primacy in the lives of many converts. But revivals imparted an important message to colonists, both converted and unconverted. They communicated that every soul mattered, that men and women could choose to be saved, that individuals had the power to make a decision for everlasting life or death. Colonial revivals expressed in religious terms many of the same democratic and egalitarian values expressed in economic terms by colonists' patterns of consumption. One colonist noted the analogy by referring to itinerant revivalists as "Pedlars in divinity." Like consumption, revivals contributed to a set of common experiences that bridged colonial divides of faith, region, class, and status.

Bonds of Empire

The plurality of peoples, faiths, and communities that characterized the North American colonies arose from the somewhat haphazard policies of the eighteenth-century British Empire. Since the Puritan Revolution of the mid-seventeenth century, British monarchs had valued the colonies' contributions to trade and encouraged their growth and development. Unlike France—whose policy of excluding Protestants and foreigners kept the population of its territory tiny—Britain kept the door to its colonies open to anyone, and tens of thousands of non-British immigrants settled in the North American colonies and raised families. The open door did not extend to trade, however, as the seventeenth-century Navigation Acts restricted colonial trade to British ships and traders. These policies evolved because they served the interests of the monarchy and of influential groups in England and the colonies. The policies of empire gave the colonists a common framework of political expectations and experiences.

At a minimum, British power defended the colonists from foreign enemies. Each colony organized a militia, and privateers sailed from every port to prey on foreign ships. But the British navy and army bore responsibility for colonial defense. Royal officials warily eyed the settlements of New France and New Spain for signs of threats to the colonies. Alone, neither New France nor Spanish Florida jeopardized British North America, but with Indian allies they became a potent force that kept colonists on their guard.

All along the ragged edge of settlement, colonists encountered Indians. Indians' impulse to defend their territory from colonial incursions warred with their desire for trade, which tugged them toward the settlers. The fur trade was the principal medium of exchange between the two groups. To trade for goods manufactured largely by the British—knives, axes, blankets, guns, powder—Indians trapped animals throughout the interior, and colonial traders competed for the furs. British officials monitored the trade to prevent French, Spanish, and Dutch competitors from deflecting the flow of hides toward their own markets. Indians took advantage of this competition to improve their own prospects, playing one trader off against another. And Indian tribes and confederacies competed for favored trading rights with one colony or another, a competition colonists encouraged.

HURON BONNET
This dazzling bonnet illustrates the trade between Native Americans and colonists. Beads of Venetian glass were one of the many items colonists imported from Europe to exchange for animal skins offered by Indian hunters and trappers. Native American women in turn incorporated these European beads into designs they had previously wrought with porcupine quills, shells, and bones. European needle and thread were also used to craft this bonnet. Native American artistry transformed these simple trade goods into a beautiful bonnet useful and valuable among the Huron, who lived near the Great Lakes.
Musée de l'Homme.

The shifting alliances and complex dynamics of the fur trade struck a fragile balance along the frontier. The threat of violence from all sides was ever present, and the threat became reality often enough for all parties to be prepared for the worst. In the Yamasee War of 1715, Yamasee and Creek Indians—with French encouragement—mounted a coordinated attack against colonial settlements in South Carolina and inflicted heavy casualties. The Cherokees, traditional enemies of the Creeks, refused to join the attack. Instead, they protected their access to British trade goods by allying with the colonists and turning the tide of battle, thus triggering a murderous rampage of revenge by the colonists against the Creeks and Yamasees.

Relations between Indians and the colonists differed from colony to colony and from year to year. But the colonists' nagging perception of menace on the frontier kept them continually hoping for help from the British in keeping the Indians at bay and in maintaining the essential flow of trade. In 1754,

the colonists' endemic competition with the French flared into the French and Indian War, which would inflame the frontier for years (see chapter 5). Before the 1760s, neither the colonists nor the British developed a coherent policy toward Indians. But both agreed that Indians made profitable trading partners, powerful allies, and deadly enemies.

British attempts to exercise their political power in colonial governments met with success so long as British officials were on or very near the sea. Colonists acknowledged—although they did not always readily comply with—British authority to collect customs duties, inspect cargoes, and enforce trade regulations. But when royal officials tried to wield their authority on land, in the internal affairs of colonies, they invariably encountered colonial resistance. A governor appointed by the king in each of the nine royal colonies (Rhode Island and Connecticut selected their own governors) or by the proprietors in Maryland and Pennsylvania headed the government of each colony. The British envisioned colonial governors as mini-monarchs able to

BEAVER HAT
European colonists, like Native Americans, adapted items obtained in trade to their own purposes. The beaver hat shown here is a careful reproduction of a seventeenth-century design. Although a colonial hat-maker pressed and molded beaver skin in the process of manufacture, the animal origins of the hat were still evident in the finished product. A good-quality beaver hat like this one was sturdy, water-repellent, and warm. But compared to the Huron bonnet opposite, it was drab and utilitarian. Women colonists sewed garments of all kinds, but they did not create intricate designs of beadwork on hats or other items.
Courtesy of Plimoth Plantation, Inc., Plymouth, Ma.

exert influence in the colonies much as the king did in England. But colonial governors were not kings and the colonies were not England.

Eight out of ten colonial governors had been born in England, not in the colonies. Some governors—like the two men who served as governors of Virginia for the first half of the eighteenth century—stayed in England, close to the source of royal patronage, and delegated the grubby details of colonial affairs to subordinates. Even the best-intentioned colonial governors had difficulty developing relations of trust and respect with influential colonists because their terms of office averaged just five years and could be terminated at any time. Too, colonial governors did not have access to many patronage positions to secure political friendships. The officials who administered the colonial customs service, for example, received their positions through patronage networks centered in England rather than in the hands of colonial governors. In obedience to their instructions from England, colonial governors fought incessantly with representatives in the colonial assemblies. They battled over governors' vetoes of colonial legislation, removal of colonial judges, creation of new courts, dismissal of the representative assemblies themselves, and other local issues. Some governors developed a working relationship with the assemblies. But during the eighteenth century, the assemblies gained the upper hand.

The British envisioned colonial governors as mini-monarchs able to exert influence in the colonies much as the king did in England. But colonial governors were not kings and the colonies were not England.

British policies did not clearly define the powers and responsibilities of colonial assemblies. In effect, the assemblies made many of their own rules and established a strong tradition of representative government analogous, in their eyes, to the English Parliament. Voters often returned representatives to the assemblies year after year, building continuity in power and leadership that far exceeded those of the governor. By 1720, colonial assemblies had won the power to initiate legislation, including tax laws and authorizations to spend public funds. Although all laws passed by the assemblies (except in Maryland, Rhode Island, and Connecticut) had to be approved by the governor and then by the Board

of Trade in England, the difficulties in communication about complex subjects over long distances effectively ratified the assemblies' decisions. Years often passed before laws were repealed, and in the meantime the assemblies' laws prevailed.

The heated political struggles between royal governors and colonial assemblies that occurred throughout the eighteenth century taught colonists a common set of political lessons. They learned to employ traditionally British ideas of representative government to defend their own interests. They learned that power in the British colonies rarely belonged to the British government.

Conclusion: The Dual Identity of British North American Colonists

During the eighteenth century, a distinctive society emerged in British North America, a society that was both distinctively colonial and distinctively British. Tens of thousands of immigrants and slaves gave the colonies an unmistakably colonial complexion. People of different ethnicities and faiths sought their fortunes in the colonies, where land was cheap, labor was dear, and—as Benjamin Franklin preached—work promised to be rewarding. Indentured servants and redemptioners risked a temporary period of bondage for the potential reward of better opportunities than on the Atlantic's eastern shore. Slaves endured lifetime servitude that they neither chose nor desired, and their masters benefited.

Identifiably colonial products from New England, the middle colonies, and the southern colonies flowed across the Atlantic. Back came unquestionably British consumer goods along with fashions in ideas, faith, and politics. The bonds of the British Empire required colonists to think of themselves as British subjects and, at the same time, encouraged them to consider their status as colonists.

By the 1750s, colonists could not imagine that their distinctively dual identity—as British and as colonists—would soon become a source of intense conflict. But by 1776, colonists in British North America had to choose whether they were British or American.

www.bedfordstmartins.com/tap   SEE THE ONLINE STUDY GUIDE to assess your mastery of the material covered in this chapter.

CHRONOLOGY

1702	Queen Anne's War triggers large German migration to American colonies.
1715	Yamasee War pits South Carolina colonists against Yamasee and Creek Indians.
1717	Scots-Irish immigration to American colonies begins to increase.
1721	*New England Courant* begins publication.
1723	Benjamin Franklin arrives in Philadelphia.
1730s	Jonathan Edwards leads New England religious awakening.
1732	Georgia founded.
1733	Benjamin Franklin begins to publish *Poor Richard's Almanack*.
1737	The Penn family takes advantage of "Walking Purchase" to claim twice as much land as originally agreed upon with Indians.
1739	Slave insurrection occurs at Stono, South Carolina.
1740s	George Whitefield preaches revival of religion throughout colonies. Majority of southern slaves are born in colonies rather than in Africa.
1741	New York officials suspect slave conspiracy and execute thirty-one slaves.
1745	Olaudah Equiano born in present-day Nigeria.
1750s	Colonists begin to move down Shenandoah valley from Pennsylvania into southern backcountry. Colonists increasingly become indebted to English merchants.
1754	French and Indian War.
1769	American Philosophical Society founded in Philadelphia.

BIBLIOGRAPHY

Please consult the bibliographies of chapters 1–3 for additional suggested readings.

GENERAL WORKS

Douglas Anderson, *The Radical Enlightenment of Benjamin Franklin* (1997).

Richard Aquila, *The Iroquois Restoration: Iroquois Diplomacy on the Colonial Frontier, 1701–1754* (1997).

Bernard Bailyn, *The Peopling of British North America* (1986).

Bernard Bailyn, *Voyagers to the West: A Passage in the Peopling of America on the Eve of the Revolution* (1986).

Richard D. Brown, *Knowledge Is Power: The Diffusion of Information in Early America, 1700–1865* (1989).

Jon Butler, *Becoming America: The Revolution before 1776* (2000).

Colin G. Calloway, *New Worlds for All: Indians, Europeans, and the Remaking of Early America* (1997).

A. Roger Ekirch, *Bound for America: The Transportation of British Convicts to the Colonies, 1718–1775* (1987).

Jack P. Greene, *Peripheries and Center: Constitutional Development in the Extended Polities of the British Empire and the United States, 1607–1788* (1986).

Jack P. Greene, *The Intellectual Construction of America: Exceptionalism and Identity from 1492 to 1800* (1993).

Timothy D. Hall, *Contested Boundaries: Itineracy and the Reshaping of the Colonial American Religious World* (1994).

Alice Hanson Jones, *Wealth of a Nation to Be: The American Colonies on the Eve of the Revolution* (1980).

Nancy F. Koehn, *The Power of Commerce: Economy and Governance in the First British Empire* (1994).

Shepard Krech III, *The Ecological Indian: Myth and History* (1999).

Frank Lambert, *"Pedlar in Divinity": George Whitefield and the Transatlantic Revivals, 1723–1770* (1994).

Frank Lambert, *Inventing the "Great Awakening"* (1999).

Michael N. McConnell, *A Country Between: The Upper Ohio Valley and Its People, 1724–1774* (1997).

Robert D. Mitchell, *Appalachian Frontiers: Settlement, Society, and Development in the Preindustrial Era* (1991).

Gregory H. Nobles, *American Frontiers: Cultural Encounters and Continental Conquest* (1997).

Mary Beth Norton, *Founding Mothers and Fathers: Gendered Power and the Forming of American Society* (1996).

Alison Gilbert Olson, *Making the Empire Work: London and American Interest Groups, 1690–1790* (1992).

A. G. Roeber, *Palatines, Liberty, and Property: German Lutherans in Colonial British America* (1993).

Michael Schudson, *The Good Citizen: A History of American Civic Life* (1998).

Carole Shammas, *The Pre-Industrial Consumer in England and America* (1990).

David S. Shields, *Civil Tongues and Polite Letters in British America* (1997).

Nancy L. Struna, *People of Prowess: Sport, Leisure, and Labor in Early Anglo-America* (1996).

Marianne E. Wokeck, *Trade in Strangers: The Beginnings of Mass Migration to North America* (1999).

Stephanie Grauman Wolf, *As Various as Their Land: The Everyday Lives of Eighteenth-Century Americans* (1993).

NEW ENGLAND

John L. Brooke, *The Heart of the Commonwealth: Society and Political Culture in Worcester County, Massachusetts, 1713–1861* (1989).

Richard Bushman, *From Puritan to Yankee: Character and the Social Order in Connecticut, 1690–1765* (1967).

David W. Conroy, *In Public Houses: Drink and the Revolution of Authority in Colonial Massachusetts* (1995).

Jay Coughtry, *The Notorious Triangle: Rhode Island and the African Slave Trade, 1700–1807* (1981).

Elaine Forman Crane, *Ebb Tide in New England: Women, Seaports, and Social Change, 1630–1800* (1998).

Christopher Grasso, *A Speaking Aristocracy: Transforming Public Discourse in Eighteenth-Century Connecticut* (1999).

Christine Leigh Heyrman, *Commerce and Culture: The Maritime Communities of Colonial Massachusetts, 1690–1750* (1984).

Douglas Lamar Jones, *Village and Seaport: Migration and Society in Eighteenth-Century Massachusetts* (1981).

Daniel R. Mandell, *Behind the Frontier: Indians in Eighteenth-Century Eastern Massachusetts* (1996).

Carolyn Merchant, *Ecological Revolutions: Nature, Gender, and Science in New England* (1989).

Gregory H. Nobles, *Divisions throughout the Whole: Politics and Society in Hampshire County, Massachusetts, 1740–1775* (1983).

William D. Piersen, *Black Yankees: The Development of an Afro-American Subculture in Eighteenth-Century New England* (1988).

Patricia J. Tracy, *Jonathan Edwards, Pastor: Religion and Society in Eighteenth-Century Northampton* (1979).

Lynne Withey, *Urban Growth in Colonial Rhode Island: Newport and Providence in the Eighteenth Century* (1984).

MIDDLE COLONIES

Randall H. Balmer, *A Perfect Babel of Confusion: Dutch Religion and English Culture in the Middle Colonies* (1989).

Thomas J. Davis, *A Rumor of Revolt: The "Great Negro Plot" in Colonial New York* (1985).

Thomas M. Doerflinger, *A Vigorous Spirit of Enterprise: Merchants and Economic Development in Revolutionary Philadelphia* (1986).

Aaron Spencer Fogelman, *Hopeful Journeys: German Immigration, Settlement, and Political Culture in Colonial America, 1717–1775* (1996).

J. William Frost, *A Perfect Freedom: Religious Liberty in Pennsylvania* (1990).

Eric Hinderaker, *Elusive Empires: Constructing Colonialism in the Ohio Valley, 1673–1800* (1997).

Sung Bok Kim, *Landlord and Tenant in Colonial New York: Manorial Society, 1664–1775* (1978).

Jessica Kross, *The Evolution of an American Town: Newtown, New York, 1642–1775* (1983).

Ned C. Landsman, *Scotland and Its First American Colony, 1683–1765* (1985).

Hartmut Lehmann, et al., eds. *In Search of Peace and Prosperity: New German Settlements in Eighteenth-Century Europe and America* (2000).

James T. Lemon, *The Best Poor Man's Country: A Geographical Study of Early Southeastern Pennsylvania* (1972).

Stephen L. Longenecker, *Piety and Tolerance: Pennsylvania German Religion, 1700–1850* (1994).

Brendan J. McConville, *These Darling Disturbers of the Public Peace: The Struggle for Property and Power in Early New Jersey* (1999).

Edward J. McManus, *A History of Negro Slavery in New York* (1970).

Peter C. Mancall, *Valley of Opportunity: Economic Culture along the Upper Susquehanna, 1700–1800* (1991).

James H. Merrell, *Into the American Woods: Negotiators on the Pennsylvania Frontier* (1999).

Gary B. Nash and Jean R. Soderlund, *Freedom by Degrees: Emancipation in Pennsylvania and Its Aftermath* (1991).

Benjamin H. Newcomb, *Political Partisanship in the American Middle Colonies, 1700–1776* (1995).

Sharon V. Salinger, *"To Serve Well and Faithfully": Labor and Indentured Servitude in Pennsylvania, 1682–1800* (1987).

Sally Schwartz, *"A Mixed Multitude": The Struggle for Toleration in Colonial Pennsylvania* (1987).

Mary M. Schweitzer, *Custom and Contract: Household, Government, and the Economy in Colonial Pennsylvania* (1987).

Beverly Prior Smaby, *The Transformation of Moravian Bethlehem: From Communal Mission to Family Economy* (1988).

Billy G. Smith, *The "Lower Sort": Philadelphia's Laboring People, 1750–1800* (1990).

Merrill D. Smith, *Breaking the Bonds: Marital Discord in Pennsylvania, 1730–1830* (1991).

Jean R. Soderlund, *Quakers and Slavery: A Divided Spirit* (1985).

Peter Thompson, *Rum Punch and Revolution: Taverngoing and Public Life in Eighteenth-Century Philadelphia* (1999).

Alan Tully, *William Penn's Legacy: Politics and Social Structure in Provincial Pennsylvania, 1726–1755* (1977).

SOUTHERN COLONIES

Richard R. Beeman, *The Evolution of the Southern Backcountry: A Case Study of Lunenburg County, Virginia, 1746–1832* (1984).

Edward J. Cashin, *Lachlan McGillivray, Indian Trader: The Shaping of the Southern Colonial Frontier* (1992).

Edward J. Cashin, *Governor Henry Ellis and the Transformation of British North America* (1994).

David R. Chesnutt, *South Carolina's Expansion into Colonial Georgia, 1720–1765* (1989).

Paul G. E. Clemons, *The Atlantic Economy and Colonial Maryland's Eastern Shore: From Tobacco to Grain* (1980).

Peter A. Coclanis, *The Shadow of a Dream: Economic Life and Death in the South Carolina Low Country, 1670–1920* (1989).

Harold E. Davis, *The Fledgling Province: Social and Cultural Life in Colonial Georgia, 1733–1776* (1976).

A. Roger Ekirch, *Poor Carolina: Politics and Society in Colonial North Carolina, 1729–1776* (1981).

David Hackett Fischer and James C. Kelly, *Bound Away: Virginia and the Westward Movement* (2000).

Sylvia R. Frey and Betty Wood, *Come Shouting to Zion: African American Protestantism in the American South and British Caribbean to 1830* (1998).

Allan Gallay, *The Formation of a Planter Elite: Jonathan Bryan and the Southern Colonial Frontier* (1989).

Michael Angelo Gomez, *Exchanging Our Country Marks: The Transformation of African Identities in the Colonial and Antebellum South* (1998).

Gwendolyn Midlo Hall, *Africans in Colonial Louisiana: The Development of Afro-Creole Culture in the Eighteenth Century* (1992).

Rhys Isaac, *The Transformation of Virginia, 1740–1790* (1982).

George Johnson, *The Frontier in the Colonial South: South Carolina Backcountry, 1736–1800* (1997).

Alan L. Karras, *Sojourners in the Sun: Scottish Migrants in Jamaica and the Chesapeake, 1740–1800* (1992).

Marvin L. Michael Kay, *Slavery in North Carolina, 1748–1775* (1995).

Cynthia A. Kierner, *Beyond the Household: Women's Place in the Early South, 1700–1835* (1998).

John Gilman Kolp, *Gentlemen and Freeholders: Electoral Politics and Political Commentary in Colonial Virginia* (1998).

Allan Kulikoff, *Tobacco and Slaves: The Development of Southern Cultures in the Chesapeake, 1680–1800* (1986).

Hugo Prosper Leaming, *Hidden Americans: Maroons of Virginia and the Carolinas* (1995).

Jan Lewis, *The Pursuit of Happiness: Family and Values in Jeffersonian Virginia* (1983).

Gloria L. Main, *Tobacco Colony: Life in Early Maryland, 1650–1720* (1982).

Philip D. Morgan, *Slave Counterpoint: Black Culture in the Eighteenth-Century Chesapeake and Low Country* (1998).

Michael Mullin, *Africa in America: Slave Acculturation and Resistance in the American South and the British Caribbean, 1736–1831* (1992).

Robert Olwell, *Masters, Slaves, and Subjects: The Culture of Power in the South Carolina Low Country, 1740–1790* (1998).

A. G. Roeber, *Faithful Magistrates and Republican Lawyers: Creators of Virginia Legal Culture, 1680–1810* (1981).

Michael J. Rozbicki, *The Complete Colonial Gentleman: Cultural Legitimacy in Plantation America* (1998).

Jon F. Sensbach, *A Separate Canaan: The Making of an Afro-Moravian World in North Carolina, 1763–1840* (1997).

Daniel Blake Smith, *Inside the Great House: Planter Family Life in Eighteenth-Century Chesapeake Society* (1980).

Donna Spindel, *Crime and Society in North Carolina, 1663–1776* (1989).

Mechal Sobel, *The World They Made Together: Black and White Values in Eighteenth-Century Virginia* (1987).

Daniel B. Thorp, *The Moravian Community in Colonial North Carolina: Pluralism on the Southern Frontier* (1989).

Lorena S. Walsh, *From Calabar to Carter's Grove: The History of a Virginia Slave Community* (1997).

Betty Wood, *The Origins of American Slavery: Freedom and Bondage in the English Colonies* (1997).

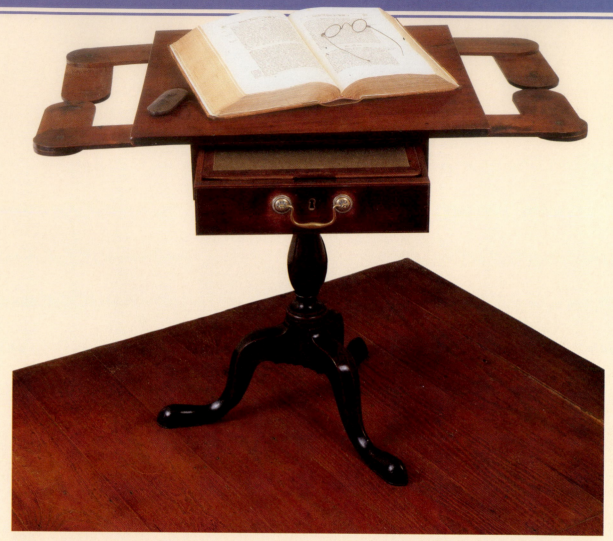

PATRICK HENRY'S MAP DESK

Patrick Henry's father, John Henry of Virginia, was both a county judge and a surveyor, and his son absorbed well the importance of both professions. Patrick studied law, and in 1763, he stunned a courtroom crowd by exclaiming that the king was a tyrant, for voiding an act of the Virginia House of Burgesses relating to ministers' salaries. Shocked onlookers muttered "treason," but the judge in the case—none other than John Henry—allowed his son's incendiary remark to stand. Two years later, Patrick's reputation for brilliant, unrestrained oratory was well established, and his county elected him to the House of Burgesses where he immediately created another sensation, skillfully maneuvering the burgesses into a startling repudiation of British power known as the Virginia Resolves. But Patrick Henry was not a reckless firebrand fulltime. His father's surveying and mapmaking skills inclined him to attend to frontier real estate, the sure way to wealth in eighteenth-century Virginia. This map desk sat in Henry's law office. Its fold-out extensions provided support for the large maps required to represent Virginia's vast western land claims. Its light weight allowed Henry to move it near the window with the best light, depending on the time of day and year. Patrick Henry ultimately had seventeen children, fourteen of whom survived to adulthood. Through astute land purchases, he managed to establish each with a landed estate.

Courtesy of Scotchtown, photo by Katherine Wetzel.

THE BRITISH EMPIRE AND THE COLONIAL CRISIS

1754–1775

5

Thomas Hutchinson was a fifth-generation descendant of Anne Hutchinson, the woman of conscience who so rattled the Puritan town of Boston in the 1630s. Thomas Hutchinson likewise was a man of conscience, but there the resemblance to his famous ancestor ended. A Harvard-educated member of the Massachusetts elite, from a family of successful merchants, Hutchinson was also a measured and cautious man. "My temper does not incline to enthusiasm," he once wrote.

After serving two decades in the Massachusetts general assembly, Hutchinson was appointed lieutenant governor in 1758, as well as chief justice of the highest court in 1760. In 1771, with Boston politics a powder keg, he agreed to become the royal governor, knowing full well the risks. Despite his family's deep roots in American soil, Hutchinson remained steadfastly loyal to England. His love of order and tradition inclined him to unconditional support of the British Empire, but loyalty was a dangerous choice in Boston after 1765. Hutchinson faced agitated crowds during demonstrations over the Stamp Act, the Townshend duties, the Boston Massacre, and the Boston Tea Party, all landmark events on the road to the American Revolution. Privately he lamented the stupidity of the British acts that provoked trouble, but his sense of duty required him to defend the king's policies, however misguided. Quickly, he became an inspiring villain to the emerging revolutionary movement. The man not inclined to enthusiasm unleashed popular enthusiasm all around him. He never appreciated that irony.

As early as anyone, Thomas Hutchinson recognized the difficulties of maintaining full rights and privileges for Americans so far from their supreme government, the king and Parliament in England. In 1769, soon after British troops had come to occupy Boston, he wrote privately to a friend in England, "There must be an abridgement of what are called English liberties. . . . I doubt whether it is possible to project a system of government in which a colony three thousand miles distant from the parent state shall enjoy all the liberty of the parent state." What he could not imagine was the possibility of giving up the parent state altogether and creating an independent government closer to home.

Thomas Hutchinson was a loyalist; in the 1750s, most English-speaking colonists were affectionately loyal to England. But the French and Indian War, which England and its colonies fought together as allies, shook that affection, and imperial policies in the decade following the war (1763–1773) shattered it completely. Over the course of that decade, serious questions about American liberties and rights were raised insistently and repeatedly, especially over the issues of taxation and representation. Many on the American side came to believe what

THOMAS HUTCHINSON
The only formal portrait of Thomas Hutchinson still in existence shows an assured young man in ruffles and hair ribbons. Decades of turmoil in Boston failed to puncture his self-confidence. Doubtless he sat for other portraits, as did all the Boston leaders in the 1760s to 1780s, but no other likeness has survived. Hutchinson was hated; any portrait that fell into his enemies' hands would probably have been mutilated.
Courtesy of the Massachusetts Historical Society ©.

Thomas Hutchinson could never credit, that a tyrannical Britain had embarked on a course to enslave the colonists by depriving them of their traditional English liberty. The opposite of liberty was slavery, a condition of unfreedom and of coercion. Political rhetoric about liberty, tyranny, and slavery heated up emotions during the many crises of the 1760s and 1770s. But this rhetoric turned out to be a two-edged sword. The call for an end to tyrannical slavery meant one thing when sounded by Boston merchants whose commercial shipping rights had been revoked; the same call meant something quite different when sounded by black Americans in 1775, locked in the bondage of perpetual slavery.

The French and Indian War, 1754–1763

For nearly half of the first fifty years of the eighteenth century, England was at war intermittently, with either France or Spain. Often the colonists in America experienced reverberations from these conflicts, most acutely along the frontier in northern New England which bumped up against French settlements in Quebec and Montreal. In the 1750s, tensions mounted again, but this time the spark setting off war originated in America. The conflict involved contested land in the Ohio valley, variously claimed by colonial land speculators from Virginia, by traders from Pennsylvania, by the French in Canada—and of course by the Indians resident on that land. The competition touched off nearly a decade of war, drawing in much of Europe, the Caribbean, and even India. In its American setting, this worldwide conflict was known as the French and Indian War. From 1754 to 1763, British and American soldiers shared the hardships of battle and the glory of victory over the French and their Indian allies. But the immense costs of the war—in money, in deaths, in desires for revenge by losers and even winners—laid the groundwork for the imperial crisis of the 1760s between British leaders and American colonists.

French-English Rivalry in the Ohio Valley

In 1753, French military forces advanced from Canada south into Indian territory in the Ohio valley, a region encompassing present-day western Pennsylvania and eastern Ohio. For more than a decade, the French had cultivated alliances with the Indian tribes there, cementing their relationship with trade and gifts. But in the late 1740s, aggressive Pennsylvania traders pushed into the Ohio valley and began to poach on their business, underselling French goods and threatening to

Ohio River Valley, 1753

reorient Indian loyalties. In response, the French embarked on building a series of forts, hoping to create a western barrier to British-American expansion. Ultimately, they wished to link Canadian and Ohio valley settlements with existing French towns along the Mississippi River at St. Louis, Natchez, and New Orleans.

The same region was also claimed by Virginia, based on its seventeenth-century charter that had granted Virginia all lands west to the Mississippi River and far north to Lake Superior. In 1747, a group of wealthy Virginians, including the brothers Lawrence and Augustine Washington, formed the Ohio Company and obtained a grant from the English king to some 200,000 acres of forests. The Virginians were interested in profits from the eventual resale of the land; the British government authorizing the Virginians' speculative real estate development was more interested in blocking the French. By 1753, the enterprising Virginians had blazed an eighty-mile road and built a trading post near present-day Pittsburgh. The royal governor of Virginia, Robert Dinwiddie, himself a major shareholder in the Ohio Company, sent a messenger to warn the French that they were trespassing on Virginia land.

The man who volunteered to be the messenger on this dangerous mission was George Washington, younger half-brother of the Ohio Company leaders. Although he was only twenty-one, Washington was an ambitious youth whose imposing height (six foot two) and air of silent competence convinced the governor he could do the job. A middle child in a large family of the gentry class, Washington was eager to gain public reputation and to curry favor with the wealthiest Virginia planters. Leading a mission to the French would give him the visibility he craved. Accompanied by six other Virginians (one of whom spoke French), Washington delivered Dinwiddie's letter to a French outpost near Lake Erie in late 1753 and returned from his assignment with crucial intelligence about French military strength, along with a scornful reply to Dinwiddie from the French.

Within weeks, the governor commissioned Washington to lead a small military force west to defend Virginia's claim. Young Washington returned to the Ohio country, this time with 160 armed men. In late May 1754, some allies from the Mingo tribe led a detachment of Washington's force numbering about forty to a small French encampment of about three dozen French soldiers. A brief skirmish ensued, during which fourteen Frenchmen were

THE

JOURNAL

OF

Major *George Washington,*

SENT BY THE

Hon. *ROBERT DINWIDDIE,* Esq;
His Majesty's Lieutenant-Governor, and
Commander in Chief of *VIRGINIA,*

TO THE

COMMANDANT

OF THE

FRENCH FORCES

ON

OHIO.

To WHICH ARE ADDED, THE

GOVERNOR's LETTER,

AND A TRANSLATION OF THE
FRENCH OFFICER's ANSWER.

WILLIAMSBURG:

Printed by WILLIAM HUNTER. 1754

WASHINGTON'S JOURNAL, 1754
When George Washington returned from his first mission to the French, Governor Dinwiddie asked him to write a full report of what he had seen of the countryside, of the Indians, and of French troop strength. Washington obliged, writing about 7,000 words in less than two days (about equivalent to a 30-page paper of today). He coolly narrated scenes of personal danger: of traveling in deep snow and freezing temperatures, of falling off a raft into an icy river, of being shot at by a lone Indian. Dinwiddie printed Washington's report, along with his own letter and the French commander's defiant answer, in a 32-page pamphlet; shortly thereafter it was reprinted in London. The governor's aim was to inform Virginians and British leaders about the French threat in the west. But the pamphlet suited Washington's aims as well: at age 22, he was now known on both sides of the Atlantic for resolute and rugged courage.
Huntington Library.

wounded. While Washington struggled to communicate with the injured French commander, the Mingo allies proceeded to kill and then scalp the wounded Frenchmen, including the commander. This unintended massacre raised the stakes considerably. Washington, now very anxious about French retaliation, reassembled his entire force and ordered the men to build a defensive fort, dubbed Fort Necessity. Built in just a week, the fortification was flimsy. Reinforcements arrived, amounting to several hundred more men, but local Indian tribes now backed off from supporting the Virginians. In early July, over 600 French soldiers attacked Fort Necessity, aided by some of the tribes the Virginians had assumed were on their side. After a third of the fort's occupants were killed or wounded, Washington capitulated. The French sent him back to his governor carrying a message of defeat: The French had no intention of departing from the disputed territory.

Thus began the French and Indian War, as well as young Washington's military career. By 1756, the war had escalated to include a half dozen countries. In Europe it would be known as the Seven Years' War, after it concluded in 1763. But for Americans, with their two-year head start, it actually lasted nine years.

The Albany Congress and Intercolonial Defense

To succeed in even a limited war, the British needed help from the colonists as well as some prospect of Indian support, or at least neutrality. Colonies from Virginia northward were instructed to send delegates to a meeting in Albany, New York. One goal of the Albany Congress was to construct an intercolonial agency to coordinate the mutual defense of the colonies. A second and perhaps more crucial goal was to woo with gifts and promises selected tribes of the powerful Iroquois Nation of western New York.

In June 1754, twenty-four delegates from seven colonies met in Albany, among them Benjamin Franklin of Pennsylvania and Thomas Hutchinson of Massachusetts, both rising political stars in their home colonies. For several years Franklin had urged closer connections among the colonies because he feared the military alliance of the French and Native American peoples in the west. Hutchinson was more interested in restructuring and streamlining imperial authority. At Albany, these two drew up a document, the Albany Plan of Union, which proposed a unified but limited governmental agency to coordinate colonial defense and Indian affairs. The Albany Plan called for a crown-appointed president

general who met annually with a grand council, composed of 48 representatives, to consider questions of war, peace, and trade with the Indians. This new government would have taxation powers, to pay for soldiers and defense. The Albany Plan humbly reaffirmed Parliament's authority over the colonies; this was no bid for enlarged autonomy of the colonies.

To Franklin's surprise, not a single colony approved the Albany Plan. The Massachusetts assembly feared it was "a Design of gaining power over the Colonies," especially the power of taxation. Others objected that it would be impossible to agree on unified policies toward hundreds of quite different Indian tribes. Oddly enough, the British government never backed the Albany Plan either, which perplexed both Franklin and Hutchinson, who were earnestly trying to solidify British authority. Many years later, after the Revolution, Franklin wistfully reflected that if the Albany Plan "had been adopted and carried into Execution, the subsequent Separation of the Colonies from the Mother Country might not so soon have happened."

To Franklin's surprise, not a single colony approved the Albany Plan. The Massachusetts assembly feared it was "a Design of gaining power over the Colonies," especially the power of taxation.

Representatives of the Iroquois League, embracing the Seneca, Mohawk, Onondaga, Cayuga, Oneida, and Tuscarora tribes, also attended the Albany Congress. They collected thirty wagon loads of gifts and made ambiguous promises to the colonists, but left without pledging to fight the French. The Iroquois preferred to stall and play off the English against the French, for their interests were best served by being on the winning side, which in 1754 looked to be the French.

The War and Its Consequences

By 1755, Washington's frontier skirmish had turned into a major mobilization of British and American troops against the French. At first the British hoped for quick victory by throwing armies at the French in three strategic places. General Edward Braddock from England was to attack the French at Fort

Duquesne in western Pennsylvania, accompanied by George Washington's Virginia militia. In Massachusetts, Governor William Shirley aimed his soldiers at Fort Niagara, critically located between Lakes Erie and Ontario. And finally, forces under William Johnson of New York moved north toward Lake Champlain to push the French back to Canada (Map 5.1).

Unfortunately for the British, the French were prepared to fight. In July 1755, General Braddock's army of 2,000 British and Virginian troops was ambushed by a combined French and Indian force a day short of their march to Fort Duquesne, leaving 976 killed or wounded. Washington was unhurt, though two horses in succession were shot from under him; Braddock was killed. Despite the humiliation of defeat, Washington's bravery in battle caused the governor to promote him to commander of the Virginia army. At age twenty-two, Washington was beginning to realize his ambitions.

News of Braddock's defeat alarmed the other two British armies, then hacking their way through dense New York forests. Shirley's forces gave up their mission, and Johnson's troops were put on the run before reaching Lake Champlain. For the next two years, the British stumbled badly on the American front, with inadequate soldiers and supplies. The American colonies perversely refused to coordinate their military strategies, while all the major Indian tribes allied themselves with what they anticipated would be the winning side, the French.

What finally turned the war around was the rise to power in 1757 of William Pitt, England's secretary of state, a man willing to commit massive resources to an all-out war. Within two years, Pitt's strategy resulted in a string of resounding successes, including the capture of Fort Duquesne in 1758 and Fort Niagara and Fort Ticonderoga in 1759. With Niagara and Ticonderoga gone and the British navy now advancing up the St. Lawrence River, the French cities of Montreal and Quebec were isolated from help. The decisive victory was the capture of the seemingly invincible fortress city of Quebec in September 1759 by the young British general James Wolfe.

The fall of Quebec broke the backbone of the French in North America. The victory was completed by the surrender of the French at Montreal to Sir Jeffrey Amherst in late 1760. American colonists rejoiced, but the French and Indian War was not officially over yet. Battles continued in the Caribbean, where the French sugar islands Mar-

tinique and Guadeloupe fell to the English. A costly siege of Spanish Cuba, requiring some four thousand provincial soldiers from New York and New England, finally succeeded in 1762. After further fighting in Europe and India, France and Spain capitulated, and the Treaty of Paris was signed in 1763.

GEORGE WASHINGTON BY CHARLES WILLSON PEALE
In 1772, George Washington posed for the artist Charles Willson Peale in his splendid vintage uniform from the French and Indian War. The vest buttons, but not the jacket buttons, still meet buttonholes over Washington's forty-year-old girth. Note the ornamental gorget hung around his neck, a miniature symbol of the throat-piece of a medieval suit of armor. Both English and Indian leaders in the eighteenth century often sported gorgets. Washington's pocket contains an "Order of March," implying that military duty still lies ahead. Peale captured Washington's grandeur in his clothes but not his face, which appears plain, simple, and still very youthful. Washington wrote a friend that he was "in so grave—so sullen a mood" and often so sleepy during the portrait sitting "that I fancy the skill of this gentleman's pencil will be hard put to it, in describing to the world what manner of man I am."
Washington and Lee University.

The triumph of victory was sweet but short-lived. The complex peace negotiations reorganized the map of North America but stopped short of providing the full spoils of victory to England. Canada was turned over to England, which eliminated the French threat from the north and west. But this was not a devastating loss for the French, relieved of a colony that had generally been a drain on imperial resources. English and American title was confirmed for the eastern half of North America, precisely what England had claimed before the war. But all French territory west of the Mississippi River, including New Orleans, was transferred to Spain as compensation for its assistance to France during the war. Stranger still, Cuba was returned to Spain, and Martinique and Guadeloupe, the Caribbean islands captured late in the war, were returned to France (Map 5.2).

In truth, the French islands in the Caribbean were hardly a threat to Americans, for they provided a profitable trade in smuggled molasses. The main threat to the safety of colonists came instead from Indians disheartened by England's victory. The Treaty of Paris completely ignored the Indians and assigned their lands to English rule. With the French gone, the Indians had lost the advantage of having two opponents to play off against each other, and they now had to cope with the westward-moving Americans. Indian policy would soon become a serious bone of contention between the British government and the colonists.

Other cracks in the English-American alliance were soon evident. England's version of the victory of 1763 awarded all credit to the mighty British army. In this version, ungrateful colonists had provided inadequate support for a war fought to save them from the French. In defiance of British law, colonists had engaged in smuggling. A lively trade

in beaver pelts, conducted by Albany merchants with French fur traders, continued throughout the war. And a British informant counted more than a hundred American ships anchored at one of the French islands, no doubt picking up cargoes of cheap molasses. American traders, grumbled the British leaders, were really traitors. William Pitt was convinced that the illegal trade "principally, if not alone, enabled France to sustain and protract this long and expensive war."

Colonists read the lessons of the war differently. American provincial soldiers had turned out in force, they claimed, but the troops had been relegated to grunt work by arrogant British military leaders. Worse yet, they experienced unexpectedly harsh military discipline at British hands, ranging from floggings to executions that seemed unnecessarily cruel. Americans bristled at encountering British disdain, such as the remark of the impetuous General Wolfe, the British hero of Quebec, who said the American soldiers were "contemptible dogs." The overconfident General Braddock had foolishly bragged to Benjamin Franklin that "these savages may, indeed, be a formidable enemy to your raw American militia, but upon the king's regular and disciplined troops, sir, it is impossible they should make any impression." Braddock's defeat "gave us Americans," Franklin wrote, "the first suspicion that our exalted ideas of the prowess of British regulars had not been well founded."

England's version of the victory of 1763 awarded all credit to the mighty British army. Colonists read the lessons of the war differently.

The human costs of the war were also etched sharply in the minds of New England colonists, who had contributed most of the colonial troops. About one-third of all Massachusetts men between age fifteen and thirty had seen service. Many families lost loved ones, and this cost would not soon be forgotten. The assault on Havana, for example, took the lives of some two thousand Americans, more than half the provincial soldiers who had been sent there.

The enormous expense of the war caused by Pitt's no-holds-barred military strategy cast another huge shadow over the victory. By 1763, England's

MAP 5.1

European Areas of Influence and the French and Indian War, 1754–1763

In the mid-eighteenth century, France, England, and Spain claimed vast areas of North America, many of them already inhabited by various Indian peoples. The early flash points of the French and Indian War occurred in regions of disputed claims where the French had allied with powerful native groups—the Iroquois and the Algonquin—to put pressure on the westward-moving English.

MAP 5.2
North America before and after the French and Indian War
In the peace treaty of 1763, France ceded its interior lands but retained fishing rights and tiny islands in the far north and, more important, several sugar islands in the Caribbean. A large part of France's claim—to land called Louisiana west of the Mississippi River—went not to England but to Spain.

READING THE MAP: How did European land claims change from 1750 to 1763? Which country's claims did not change?

CONNECTIONS: What was the goal of the Proclamation Act of 1763? What was the eventual fate of Louisbourg following the French and Indian War?

www.bedfordstmartins.com /tap SEE THE ONLINE STUDY GUIDE for more help in analyzing these maps.

national debt, double what it had been when Pitt took office, posed a formidable challenge to the next decade of leadership in England. At the heart of the matter was disagreement about the relative responsibility the colonists should bear in helping to pay off that debt.

Tightening the Bonds of Empire

Throughout the 1760s, inconsistent leadership in England pursued a hodgepodge of policies toward the colonies. A new and inexperienced king gained the throne in 1760, and he spent the next ten years searching for a prime minister he could trust. Nearly half a dozen ministers in succession took their turns formulating policies designed to address one basic, underlying British reality: A huge war debt needed to be serviced, and the colonists, as British subjects, should expect to pay. From the American side, however, these policies deeply violated what colonists perceived to be their rights and liberties as British subjects.

British Leadership and the Indian Question

In 1760, in the middle of the French and Indian War, George III, age twenty-two, came to the British throne, quite underprepared for his monarchical duties. The previous king, George II, was his grandfather; his father's death, when young George was thirteen, thrust the boy suddenly into the role of heir apparent. Timid and insecure, the new King George trusted only his tutor, John Stuart, earl of Bute, a Scotsman who was an outsider to power circles in London. George III immediately installed Bute as head of his cabinet of ministers.

Bute opposed Pitt's strategy for the war in America as "too bloody and expensive." He next squandered England's war victory by negotiating the unfavorable Treaty of Paris. Within two years, the best talents in the cabinet had resigned, leaving Bute isolated. In his short remaining time in office, Bute made one other significant decision—to keep a standing army in the colonies. In terms of money and political tension, this was a costly move.

The ostensible reason for keeping ten thousand British troops in America was to maintain the peace

MOHAWK WARRIOR
This rear view of a Mohawk warrior highlights clothes and body decoration: arm and ankle bracelets, earrings, a hair ornament, and body paint. The English watercolor artist includes an important element of frontal display—the warrior's tomahawk.
Ville de la Rochelle.

between the colonists and the Indians. This was not a misplaced concern. The defeat and withdrawal of the French from North America had left their Indian allies—who did not accept defeat—in suspension. In the early 1760s, a religious revival sparked by several Delaware prophesies had swept through many tribes, from western New York through Pennsylvania and Ohio, up into the Great Lakes area and down below the Ohio River. The prophetic message explained the hardships and disease associated with the late war as sacred signs that Indians should reject all whites and the trade goods they brought, especially alcohol, and return to the customs of old.

For the first time, a pan-Indian movement was underway, linking at least a dozen tribes in a plotted uprising. Three months after the Treaty of Paris was signed, Pontiac, chief of the Ottawa tribe in the northern Ohio region, inaugurated the uprising by attacking the British garrison near Detroit in late April 1763. By early June, six more attacks had occurred on British forts. Joining the Ottawa were Chippewa, Huron, Potawatomi, Miami, Kickapoo, Mascouten, Wea, Shawnee, Mingo, Delaware, and Seneca tribes. By July every fort west of Detroit had been captured, and attacks on isolated settlements were frequent. By fall, more than four hundred British soldiers were dead, and another two thousand colonists had been killed or taken captive.

Pontiac's Rebellion, 1763

American colonial assemblies generally let the British army strategize a response, but in one alarmed region in central Pennsylvania, the Scots-Irish inhabitants decided that their colonial assembly was shirking its responsibility to defend them against the Indian threat. Calling themselves the Paxton Boys, after the name of a nearby creek, some fifty men attacked an Indian village called Conestoga and murdered twenty Christian Indians. Their style of vigilante action proved popular and gained support, and within a few months some five hundred Paxton Boys marched toward Philadelphia to demand better protection and a larger voice in the colonial assembly. Leaders of the government party, including Benjamin Franklin, persuaded them to go home in exchange for a promise not to prosecute them for murder of the friendly Indians. Pontiac's uprising was finally quelled in December 1763 by the combined efforts of British and colonial soldiers, plus the news that French aid to the Indians would not materialize. Pontiac later wrote to the British, "All my young men have buried their hatchets."

The potential for continued and costly wars with the Indians, so well illustrated by Pontiac's uprising, caused the British government to issue an order, called the Proclamation Act of 1763, which forbade colonists to settle west of a line drawn from Canada to Georgia along the crest of the Appalachian Mountains. The ten thousand British

For the first time, a pan-Indian movement was underway, linking at least a dozen tribes in a plotted uprising.

troops were to police this line. Meant as a temporary expedient rather than a permanent boundary, the line promised to protect not only the Indians but also the lucrative fur trade, now in British rather than French hands. But the pressure of population growth meant that the proclamation line would be very difficult to enforce. Settlers had already moved west of the line, as had land speculators, such as those of Virginia's Ohio Company, who stood to lose opportunities for profitable resale of their claims. Bute's decision to leave a standing army in the colonies was thus a cause for concern for western settlers and eastern speculators alike.

Growing Resentment of British Authority

The mission of George Grenville, the king's next chief minister, was to tackle the problem of the war debt, which in 1763 amounted to £123 million, a shockingly high figure. The annual interest alone on the debt was nearly £5 million, owed to anxious London bankers. To find increased revenue, Grenville first scrutinized the customs service, a division of the government responsible for monitoring the flow of ships and collecting duties on specified trade items in both England and America. Grenville found that customs officers' salaries cost the government four times what was collected in revenue. The revenue shortfall was due in part to bribery and smuggling, and so Grenville began to insist on rigorous attention to paperwork and a strict accounting of collected duties.

The hardest duty for Grenville to enforce was the one imposed by the Molasses Act of 1733—a stiff tax of six pence per gallon on any molasses purchased from non-British sources. The purpose of the tax was to discourage trade with French Caribbean islands and redirect the molasses trade to British sugar islands. But it did not work: French molasses remained cheap and abundant because French planters on Martinique and Guadeloupe had no use for it. A by-product of sugar production, molasses was a key ingredient in making rum, a drink the French scorned. Rum-loving Americans were eager to buy French molasses, and they flouted the tax law for decades.

Grenville's ingenious solution to this problem was the Revenue Act of 1764, popularly dubbed the Sugar Act. It lowered the duty on French molasses to three pence, making it more attractive for shippers to obey the law, and at the same time raised penalties for smuggling. The act appeared to be in the tradition of navigation acts, meant to regulate trade. But Grenville had added a new twist: His actual intent was to raise revenue, not redirect trade. He was using an established form of law for new ends, and he was doing it by the novel means of lowering a duty.

The Sugar Act set out tougher enforcement policies. From now on, Grenville announced, all British naval crews could act as impromptu customs officers, boarding ships suspected of smuggling and seizing cargoes found to be in violation. Smugglers caught without proper paperwork would be prosecuted, not in a friendly civil court with a local jury, but in a vice-admiralty court located in Halifax, Nova Scotia, where a single judge presided without a jury. The implication was that justice would be more sure and severe.

Grenville hoped that his tightening of the customs service and the lowered duties of the Sugar Act would reform American smugglers into law-abiding shippers and in turn generate income for the empire. Unfortunately, the decrease in duty was not sufficient to offset the attractions of smuggling, which continued unabated, and the vigilant enforcement of the act greatly annoyed American shippers. The increased numbers of customs officers made it harder for shippers to rely on the old system of bribery, and several ugly confrontations occurred in key port cities such as Newport, Rhode Island, and New York City. Reaction to the Sugar Act foreshadowed questions about England's right to tax Americans, but in 1764 objections to the act came principally from Americans in the shipping trades inconvenienced by the law.

Another new act engineered by Grenville added to the growing resentment of British authority. The Currency Act of 1764 flatly prohibited the colonies from printing any paper money. During the French and Indian War, colonies had resorted to paper money to finance wartime expenses. In modest amounts, colonial currency lubricated the economy by increasing the volume of money in a society perpetually short of silver and gold coins. But London merchants squawked about not getting full value for their goods, and Grenville persuaded Parliament to ban new paper money. Colonies were left

PAPER CURRENCY OF THE 1750S TO 1770S

Colonial paper currencies contained text that stipulated the legality and value of the money, accompanied by elaborate designs that discouraged counterfeiting. Handwritten numbers and signatures authenticated each paper. Parliament's Currency Act of 1764 prohibited paper money, but some colonies continued to print it, and it returned with force in 1775 when the Continental Congress began printing dollars (lower left).

Courtesy of the Decorative & Industrial Arts Collection of the Chicago Historical Society.

with no short-term financing flexibility and a re-duced flow of money.

From the British point of view, the 1763 Procla-mation Act, the Sugar Act, and the Currency Act all seemed to be reasonable efforts to administer the colonies. To the Americans, however, the British su-pervision appeared to be a disturbing intrusion into colonial practices.

The Stamp Act Crisis, 1765

By his second year in office, Grenville had made al-most no dent in the national debt. Continued evasion prevented the Sugar Act from becoming the money-maker he had hoped it would be. So in February 1765, he significantly escalated his revenue program by se-curing passage of the Stamp Act, which precipitated the first major conflict between England and the colonies over Parliament's right to tax.

Taxation and Consent

The Stamp Act imposed a tax on paper used for various colonial documents—newspapers, pam-phlets, contracts, court documents, licenses, deeds,

wills, ships' bills of lading—and required that a spe-cial stamp be affixed to the paper proving that the tax had been paid. Unlike the Sugar Act, which was part of a trade regulation system, the Stamp Act broke new ground by instituting a tax whose purpose was plainly and simply to raise money. It affected people in all walks of life, such as apprentices and masters who signed indentured service contracts, and all who read newspapers or bought almanacs. But it dispro-portionately targeted the business and legal commu-nities, whose repeated use of documents would now tax them the most. Stamp taxes, long in use in Britain, were designed to produce revenue from the classes and regions most able to pay.

Grenville further required that the tax be paid in sterling silver, a condition that made the Stamp Act even more unpopular, because hard money was in short supply. But Grenville was no fool; antici-pating that the stamp tax would be unpopular, he delegated the administration of the act to Ameri-cans, to avoid the problem of hostility to British en-forcers. In each colony, local stamp distributors would be hired at a handsome salary of 8 percent of the revenue collected.

Grenville's forewarnings came partly from Thomas Hutchinson, lieutenant governor of Mass-

TAX ASSESSMENT BOOK
American colonists rou-tinely paid property taxes to local authorities. This 1772 tax book from Rowley, Massachusetts, records amounts due in pounds, shillings, and pence. The several entries for each name indicate assessments on real estate, personal property, and a poll (per head) tax. Notice that two women identified as Mrs. owe taxes. Since married women by law owned no property, we can conclude that these were widows. Several specific numbers are frequently repeated (3–8 and 82); what might that suggest?
Chicago Historical Society.

achusetts, who privately lobbied against the tax. Hutchinson immediately appreciated the key legal issue at stake. Aside from the navigation acts, which were intended primarily to regulate trade, Parliament had levied no previous taxes on the colonists. Hutchinson warned that the colonies could reasonably conclude that Parliament had conceded to them the right to tax themselves. On practical grounds, he also urged the British officials to consider whether trade disruptions caused by the Stamp Act might cost more than the revenue the act generated. But Hutchinson's warnings went unheeded.

The colonists already paid taxes to support their local governments, but the taxing bodies were always the colonial assemblies, composed of elected representatives. An old English tradition held that taxation was a gift of the people to the king offered by the people's representatives. This view of taxes, as a freely given gift, preserved an essential concept of English political theory, the idea that citizens have the liberty to enjoy and use their property without fear of confiscation. The king could not simply demand money; only the House of Commons could grant it. Grenville quite agreed with the notion of taxation by consent, but he argued that the colonists were already "virtually" represented in Parliament; the House of Commons represented all British subjects, wherever they were.

This view of taxes, as a freely given gift, preserved an essential concept of English political theory, the idea that citizens have the liberty to enjoy and use their property without fear of confiscation.

Colonial leaders emphatically rejected this British view of representation. A Maryland lawyer named Daniel Dulany wrote a best-selling pamphlet explaining that virtual representation, while it might work within England, could not withstand the stretch across the Atlantic. The stamp tax itself illustrated the problem: It was levied by a distant Parliament on unwilling colonies. Dulany debunked the notion of virtual representation as "a mere cob-web, spread to catch the unwary, and entangle the weak."

Resistance Strategies and Crowd Politics

The Stamp Act was to take effect on November 1, 1765. News of its passage arrived in the colonies in April 1765, leaving colonial leaders seven months to contemplate a response. Colonial governors were unlikely to challenge the law, since most of them owed their office to the king. Instead, the colonial assemblies took the lead; eight of them held discussions on objections to the Stamp Act.

Virginia's assembly, the House of Burgesses, waded into the implications of objecting to the Stamp Act and learned where that road led. At the very end of the May 1765 session, when two-thirds of the members had already gone home, a twenty-nine-year-old lawyer and political newcomer named Patrick Henry presented a series of resolutions on the Stamp Act that were debated and passed, one by one. They came to be called the Virginia Resolves.

Henry's successive resolutions inched the assembly toward radical opposition to the Stamp Act. The first three resolutions stated the obvious: that Virginians were British citizens, that they enjoyed the same rights and privileges as Britons, and that self-taxation was one of those rights. The fourth resolution noted that Virginians had always taxed themselves, via their representatives in the House of Burgesses. The fifth took the radical leap, by pushing the other four unexceptional statements to one logical conclusion—that the Virginia assembly alone had the sole right to tax Virginians. Henry persuaded the small group of burgesses present to endorse this declaration, but the ebbing numbers of positive votes indicated shrinking support.

Two more fiery resolutions were debated, but majority support eroded as Henry pressed the logic of his case to the extreme. The sixth resolution denied legitimacy to any tax law originating outside Virginia, and a seventh boldly called anyone who disagreed with these propositions an enemy of Virginia. This was too much for the burgesses. They backed away from resolutions six and seven and the following day, after Henry had left, rescinded their vote on number five as well.

Their caution hardly mattered, however, because newspapers in other colonies printed all seven Virginia Resolves, creating the impression that a daring first challenge to the Stamp Act had taken place in Virginia. This made it easier for other assemblies to consider more radical questions, and a few finally debated the thorniest of all: By what authority could Parliament legislate for the colonies without also taxing them? No one disagreed, in 1765, that Parliament had legislative power over the colonists, who were, after all, British subjects. Several assemblies advanced the argument that there was a distinction between *external* taxes, imposed to regulate trade, and *internal* taxes, such as a stamp tax or a property tax, which could only be self-imposed.

Reaction to the Stamp Act ran far deeper than the politicians in assemblies. Every person whose livelihood required the use of official paper had to decide whether to comply with the act. Hence, local communities strategized their responses. Should they boycott all paper use? While this kept non-compliance within the law, it also was very inconvenient; if enough people ceased using stamped paper, the information network of newspapers, the legal system, and the world of trade might grind to a halt. Should they defy the law and conduct business as usual on unstamped paper? That way ran the risk of fines or jail. A third strategy promised the safest, surest success: to destroy the stamped paper or prevent its distribution at the source, before the law took effect. This tactic would ensure universal noncompliance.

The first concerted effort to resist the Stamp Act began in Boston, capital of Massachusetts and port city of about seventeen thousand people packed into a square-mile peninsula. Virtually all Boston's major occupational groups—lawyers and politicians, merchants and shipowners, tradesmen and artisans, dockworkers and sailors—depended on official papers to conduct business. In June 1765, the *Boston Gazette* offered its readers all seven Virginia Resolves as an example of a "spirited" response. The *Gazette* exuberantly appropriated the language of the seventh resolution, calling anyone who agreed that Parliament could tax Massachusetts "An Enemy to This His Majesty's Colony."

Over the summer a plan took shape to head off the Boston stamp distribution at its source. The leadership behind the plan came from a small group of shopkeepers and master craftsmen, working closely with Samuel Adams, a forty-three-year-old town politician. The protesters called themselves—and anyone who joined them—the Sons of Liberty, picking up a term first used by a pro-American member of Parliament who had argued strongly against the Stamp Act back in February. Adams, the

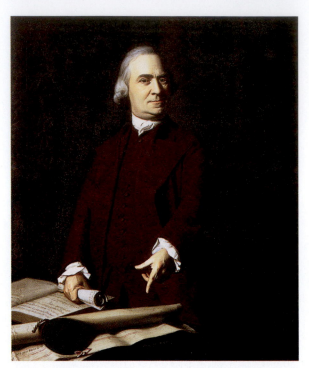

SAMUEL ADAMS BY JOHN COPLEY
Samuel Adams consented to pose for Boston artist John Singleton Copley in 1770. The portrait highlights Adams's face, which projects a dramatic intensity and dominates the bulky body, subdued by dark clothes. Adams stares thoughtfully and silently at the viewer and points to important legal documents before him, including the Massachusetts charter of 1689. Wealthy merchant John Hancock commissioned the portrait, which hung in his house. Copley painted scores of Boston's leaders in the 1760s, both loyalists and patriots. He maintained neutrality until 1773, when his father-in-law became an official East India tea distributor. Copley's home was threatened by a crowd, and he left for England in 1774.
Deposited by the City of Boston, Museum of Fine Arts, Boston.

Harvard-educated son of a prosperous brewer, devoted himself to politics in the Boston town meeting and in the Massachusetts assembly. In distinct contrast to Thomas Hutchinson, he cared nothing for status, high office, or fine material goods. He was oblivious to his daily clothing, a matter that occasionally distressed his friends. What Adams did value were his shrewd political instincts and gift for organizing.

The plan hatched by Samuel Adams and others called for a large street demonstration highlighting a ritualized mock execution, designed to convince Andrew Oliver, the stamp distributor, that his personal safety would best be served by resigning. With no stamp distributor, no stamps could be sold. On the morning of August 14, 1765, an effigy (stuffed dummy) of Oliver was found hanging from a tree. The royal governor of Massachusetts, Francis Bernard, met with Hutchinson and the governor's council and decided to take no action, in an effort to keep tensions under control. By evening, a large crowd of two to three thousand people paraded the effigy around town, using it as a prop in short plays demonstrating the dangers of selling stamps. The crowd then pulled down a small building on Oliver's dock, reported to be the future stamp office. Next, at Oliver's house, they beheaded and burned the effigy and broke some windows. The flesh-and-blood Oliver was in hiding; the next

ANDREW OLIVER
This portrait shows Bostonian Andrew Oliver at age twenty-two, just a few years after his graduation from Harvard College. The powdered wig and stern look add years to his face; the blousy clothing adds substance to his body. He was fifty-nine and probably even more imposing in appearance when he ran afoul of the stamp act rioters in Boston in 1765.
Collection of the Oliver Family, photo by Clive Russ.

SEAL OF ANDREW OLIVER
This amethyst seal suggests that important business was a routine event for its owner, Andrew Oliver. Long before he became the unfortunate stamp distributor in 1765, Oliver held a succession of offices—overseer of the poor, collector of taxes, member of the provincial council, and secretary of Massachusetts. He thus had many occasions to press the unique seal into melted wax to authenticate documents. The stone bears the tough-minded motto **Pax Quaeritur Bello** *(Peace is Obtained by War), an appropriate maxim for the man willing to become the royal lieutenant governor of Massachusetts in 1770.*
Collection of the Oliver Family, photo by Clive Russ.

day he resigned his office in a well-publicized announcement.

There were lessons from the August 14 demonstration for everyone. Oliver learned that stamp distributors would be very unpopular people. Bernard and Hutchinson learned the limitations of their own powers to govern, with no police to call on. The demonstration's leaders learned that street action was very effective. And hundreds of laborers, sailors, and apprentices not only learned what the Stamp Act was all about but also gained pride in their ability to have a decisive impact on politics.

Twelve days later, a second crowd action, more properly termed a riot, showed just how well some of these lessons had been learned. On August 26, a crowd visited the houses of four detested officials. One was a customs officer and two others were officers of the admiralty courts, where smugglers were tried; the crowd broke windows and raided wine cellars. The fourth house was the finest dwelling in Massachusetts, owned by the stiff-necked Thomas Hutchinson. Rumors abounded that Hutchinson had urged Grenville to adopt the Stamp Act. In fact, he had done the opposite, but he refused to set the record straight, saying curtly, "I am not obliged to give an answer to all the questions that may be put me by every lawless person." The crowd attacked his house, and by daybreak only the exterior walls were standing.

The destruction of Hutchinson's house brought a temporary halt to crowd activities in Boston. The Boston town meeting issued a statement of sympathy; but a reward of £300 for the arrest and conviction of riot organizers failed to produce a single lead. The Sons of Liberty denied planning the event.

Essentially, the opponents of the Stamp Act in Boston had won the day; no one volunteered to replace Oliver as distributor. When November 1 arrived, the day the Stamp Act took effect, the customs officers allowed ships to pass through the harbor without properly stamped clearance papers. They had little choice; they simply did not have the staff to force the ships to halt. Hutchinson, in his role as chief justice of the Massachusetts court, could not tolerate this defiance of the law, but also could not bring the lawbreakers to justice in his court. So he did the only thing he could do as a principled man: He resigned his judgeship. Hutchinson did not escape continuing tension, however. He was still the lieutenant governor, and within five years he would agree to become the royal governor.

Liberty and Property

Boston's crowd actions of August sparked similar eruptions by groups calling themselves Sons of Liberty in nearly fifty towns throughout the colonies, and stamp distributors everywhere hastened to resign. A New Hampshire distributor resigned three times in public places, to make sure that the word got out. A Connecticut distributor was forced by a crowd to throw his hat and powdered wig in the air while shouting a cheer for "Liberty and property!" This man fared better than another Connecticut stamp agent, who was nailed in a coffin and lowered in the ground by the local Sons of Liberty. Only when the thuds of dirt sounded on the box did he have a sudden change of heart, shouting out his resignation to the crowd above. In Charleston, South Carolina, the stamp distributor resigned in late October after crowds burned effigies and chanted "Liberty! Liberty!"

Some colonial leaders, as worried about the riots of the summer and fall as they were about the Stamp Act, hastened to mount a more measured and moderate challenge to Parliamentary authority. Nine colonial assemblies sent a total of twenty-seven delegates to New York City in October 1765, to a meeting called the Stamp Act Congress. The men met for two weeks, hammering out a declaration of principles about taxation and addressing petitions to the king, the House of Lords, and the House of Commons. Their formal statement closely resembled the first five Virginia Resolves, claiming taxes were "free gifts of the people" which only the people's representatives could give. They dismissed virtual representation: "The people of these colonies are not, and from their local circumstances, cannot be represented in the House of Commons." But the delegates also took great care to affirm their subordination and loyalty to Parliament and monarch in deferential and convoluted language. They also met in secret and declined to make public their petitions; not until six months later did a Boston newspaper give them unauthorized circulation. Although timid, the Stamp Act Congress by the mere fact of its meeting advanced a radical potential, the notion of intercolonial political action. And by insisting that liberty and property were linked, the cautious congress echoed the sentiments of the boisterous street crowds.

The rallying cry "Liberty and property" made perfect sense to many white Americans of all social ranks, who feared that the Stamp Act threatened their traditional rights as British subjects. Englishmen claimed liberty as a birthright, meaning that they had a right to be free from interference by other people. The opposite of liberty was slavery, the condition of being under the total control of someone else. Civil society required some interference in perfect freedom in the form of laws, but Englishmen preserved liberty by making sure that only representative governments passed the laws. Up to 1765, Americans consented to accept Parliament as a body that in some way represented them, at least for purposes of legislation. But the right to own property was a special kind of liberty, requiring even stricter safeguards, given the possibility that a greedy ruler might try to deprive citizens of their property. This was why the tradition arose that only a representative body could tax British subjects.

The rallying cry "Liberty and property" made perfect sense to many white Americans of all social ranks, who feared that the Stamp Act threatened their traditional rights as British subjects.

To Americans, the Stamp Act violated this principle of liberty and property, and some Americans began to speak and write about a plot by British leaders to enslave them. One Pennsylvania pamphlet writer asserted that the Stamp Act threatened to plunge the colonies into "a state of slavery." A Maryland writer warned that if the colonies lost "the right of exemption from all taxes without their consent," that loss would "deprive them of every privilege distinguishing freemen from slaves." The opposite meanings of *liberty* and *slavery* were utterly clear to white Americans, but they stopped short of applying similar logic to the one million black Americans they held in bondage. Many blacks, however, could see the contradiction. A crowd of Charleston blacks paraded with shouts of "Liberty!" just a few months after white Sons of Liberty had done the same; the town militia turned out to break up the demonstration.

Politicians and merchants in England reacted with alarm to the American demonstrations and petitions. Merchants particularly feared trade disruptions and pressured Parliament to repeal the Stamp Act. In the summer of 1765, yet another new minister, Charles Watson-Wentworth, the marquess of

Rockingham, headed the king's cabinet. His dilemma was to find a dignified way to repeal the act that did not yield to the Americans' claim that Parliament could not tax them.

Parliament debated repeal, and George Grenville, now a member of that body, seized the occasion to deliver an impassioned condemnation of American ingratitude, which also served to justify his stamp tax policy. "When they want the protection of this kingdom, they are always ready to ask for it. . . . The nation has run itself into an immense debt to give them their protection; and now [when] they are called upon to contribute a small share towards the public expence, an expence arising from themselves, they renounce your authority, insult your officers, and break out, I might almost say, into open rebellion."

No doubt many in the British government shared Grenville's anger, but economic considerations won out. In March 1766, the Stamp Act was repealed, but Parliament at the same time passed the Declaratory Act, which asserted Parliament's right to legislate for the colonies "in all cases whatsoever." Perhaps the stamp tax had been inexpedient, but the power to tax—one prime case of a legislative power—was stoutly upheld.

The Townshend Acts and Economic Retaliation, 1767–1770

Rockingham did not last long as prime minister. By the summer of 1766, George III had persuaded William Pitt to resume that role. Pitt then appointed Charles Townshend to be chancellor of the exchequer, the chief financial minister. Townshend faced both the old war debt problem and the continuing cost of stationing the British army in America, and he turned again to taxation. But Townshend's knowledge of the developing political climate in the colonies was unfortunately limited; his simple idea to raise revenue turned into a major blunder.

The Townshend Duties

Townshend proposed new taxes in the old form of a navigation act. Officially called the Revenue Act of 1767, it established new duties on tea, glass, lead, paper, and painters' colors imported into the colonies, to be paid by the importer but surely passed on to consumers in the retail price. A year before, the duty on French molasses had been reduced from three pence down to one pence per gallon, and finally the Sugar Act was pulling in a tidy revenue of about £45,000 annually. So it was not unreasonable to suppose that duties on additional trade goods might also improve the cash flow. Townshend assumed that external taxes—that is, duties levied on the transatlantic trade—would be more acceptable to Americans than internal taxes, such as the stamp tax. He also established an American Board of Customs Commissioners, to oversee the customs service, but he located it in combustible Boston, a decision that showed Townshend was not very shrewd about colonial protest politics.

The Townshend duties by themselves were not especially burdensome, but the principle they embodied—taxation extracted through trade duties—looked different to the colonists now, when seen against the backdrop of the Stamp Act crisis. If Americans once distinguished between external and internal taxes, that distinction was wiped out by an external tax meant only to raise money. John Dickinson, a Philadelphia lawyer, articulated this view in a series of articles titled *Letters from a Farmer in Pennsylvania*, widely reprinted in the winter of 1767–68. "We are taxed without our consent. . . . We are therefore—SLAVES," Dickinson wrote, calling for "a total denial of the power of Parliament to lay upon these colonies any 'tax' whatever."

A controversial provision of the Townshend duties directed that some of the revenue generated would be used to pay the salaries of royal governors. Before 1767, local assemblies set the salaries of their own officials, giving them significant influence over crown-appointed officeholders. But the assemblies seemed to Townshend to be getting out of hand, and he wanted to strengthen the independence of the governors.

In New York, for example, the assembly had refused to enforce a British rule of 1765 called the Quartering Act, which directed the colonies to furnish shelter and provisions for the British army, and the royal governor was unable to make them comply. The assembly argued that the Quartering Act was really a tax measure because it required New Yorkers to pay money by order of Parliament. Townshend came down hard on the New York assembly: He orchestrated a parliamentary order, the New York Suspending Act, which declared all the assembly's acts null and void until it met its obligations to the army.

Both these measures—the new way to pay royal governors' salaries and the suspension of the governance functions of the New York assembly—struck a chill throughout the colonies. Many Americans wondered if their legislative government was at all secure.

"We are taxed without our consent. . . . We are therefore—SLAVES," wrote Philadelphia lawyer John Dickinson, calling for "a total denial of the power of Parliament to lay upon these colonies any 'tax' whatever."

The Massachusetts assembly quickly took the lead in protesting the Townshend duties. Samuel Adams, a member from Boston, argued that any form of parliamentary taxation was unjust because Americans were not represented in Parliament. He also declared that the new way to pay the governors' salaries subverted the proper relationship between the people and their rulers. The assembly circulated a letter with Adams's arguments to other colonial assemblies and urged their endorsement. Not since the Stamp Act Congress of 1765 had there been any similar attempt to coordinate the response of the colonies to British measures.

In response to Adams's letter, the new man in charge of colonial affairs in Britain, Wills Hill, Lord Hillsborough, instructed the Massachusetts governor, Francis Bernard, to dissolve the assembly if it refused to rescind its statement. The assembly refused, by a vote of 92 to 17, and Governor Bernard carried out his instruction. In the summer of 1768, Boston was in an uproar.

Nonconsumption and the Daughters of Liberty

The Boston town meeting had already passed resolutions, termed "nonconsumption agreements," calling for a boycott of British-made goods. Dozens of other towns passed similar resolutions in 1767 and 1768. For example, prohibited purchases in the town of New Haven, Connecticut, included carriages, furniture, hats, clothing, shoes, lace, iron plate, clocks, jewelry, toys, textiles, velvets, linseed oil, malt liquors, and cheese. The idea was to encourage home manufacture of such items and to hurt trade with Britain, causing London merchants to pressure Parliament for repeal of the duties.

But nonconsumption agreements were very hard to enforce. With the Stamp Act, there was one hated item, a stamp, and a limited number of official distributors. In contrast, an agreement to boycott all British goods required serious personal sacrifice from many individuals. Some merchants were wary of nonconsumption because it hurt their pocketbooks, and a few continued to import in readiness for the end of nonconsumption (or to sell on the side to people choosing to ignore nonconsumption). In Boston, such merchants found themselves blacklisted in newspapers and broadsides.

A more direct blow to trade came from nonimportation agreements, but it proved even more difficult to get merchants to agree to these. There was always the risk that merchants in other colonies might continue to trade and thus receive handsome profits if neighboring colonies prohibited trade. Not until late 1768 could Boston merchants agree to suspend trade through nonimportation agreements. Sixty men signed the agreement, to be in effect exactly one year—from January 1, 1769, to January 1, 1770. New York merchants soon followed suit, as did Philadelphia and Charleston merchants in 1769.

Doing without British products, whether they were luxury goods or basics such as tea or textiles, no doubt was a hardship for the American population. But it also presented an opportunity, for many of the British goods specified in nonconsumption agreements were household items and goods traditionally under the control of women. By 1769, male leaders in the patriot cause clearly understood that women's cooperation in nonconsumption and home manufacture was essential. The Townshend duties thus provided an unparalleled opportunity for developing and showcasing female patriotism. During the Stamp Act crisis, Sons of Liberty took to the streets in protest. During the difficulties of 1768–1769, the Daughters of Liberty emerged to give shape to a new idea—that women could play a role in public affairs.

Any individual woman could express affiliation with the colonial protest by complying with the nonconsumption agreements and by taking up home manufacture of items previously imported from England. One young Philadelphia woman inscribed some "patriotic poesy" in her notebook in 1768, the gist of which was that women can take up the patriotic cause even if men falter and stumble: "If the Sons (so degenerate) the Blessing despise, / Let the Daughters of Liberty nobly arise, / And tho' we've no Voice, but a negative here, / The use of

EDENTON TEA LADIES
American women in many communities renounced British apparel and tea during the early 1770s. Women in Edenton, North Carolina, publicized their pledge and drew hostile fire in the form of a British cartoon. The cartoon's message is that brazen women who meddle in politics will undermine their femininity. Neglected babies, urinating dogs, wanton sexuality, and mean-looking women are some of the dire consequences, according to the artist. The cartoon works as humor for the British because of the gender inversions it predicts and because of the insult it poses to American men.
Library of Congress.

the Taxables, let us forbear, / (Then Merchants import till yr. Stores are all full / May the Buyers be few and yr. Traffick be dull.) / Stand firmly resolved and bid Grenville to see / That rather than Freedom, we'll part with our Tea." Women in at least three towns met together formally to sign nonconsumption agreements. In Boston, over three hundred women signed a petition to abstain from tea, "sickness excepted." A nine-year-old girl on a social visit to the royal governor's house in New Jersey took the tea she was offered, curtsied, and tossed the beverage out a nearby window.

Homespun cloth became a prominent symbol of patriotism. In the latter half of 1769, dozens of towns organized public spinning "frolicks" or bees where women staged competitions in spinning and weaving. Cloth making was no longer simply a chore of family service but a task invested with political content. A Connecticut girl who spun ten knots of wool in one day proclaimed in her journal that her work made her feel "Nationly."

During the difficulties of 1768–1769, the Daughters of Liberty emerged to give shape to a new idea—that women could play a role in public affairs.

On the whole, the year of boycotts was a success. British imports fell by more than 40 percent, and British merchants felt the pinch.

Military Occupation and "Massacre" in Boston

By the summer of 1768, Boston's royal officials felt alarm. Townshend's new customs commissioners had fled to an island in Boston harbor for safety. On August 15, a rollicking celebration of the Stamp Act demonstration of 1765 put crowds in the street and apprehension in the hearts of Governor Bernard and Lieutenant Governor Hutchinson. With no police force and no reasonable hope of controlling the town militia, Bernard concluded that he needed British soldiers to keep the peace.

In the fall of 1768, three thousand uniformed troops arrived to occupy Boston. The soldiers drilled conspicuously on the Common, played loud music on the Sabbath, and in general grated on the nerves of Bostonians. To occupy their spare time, some soldiers took casual day-labor work, putting themselves in direct competition with laboring Bostonians for low-wage jobs.

Although the situation was frequently tense, no major troubles occurred during that winter and through most of 1769. But as January 1 approached, marking the end of the nonimportation agreement, it was clear that some merchants could no longer be kept in line. Thomas Hutchinson's two sons, for example, were both importers hostile to the boycott,

and they had already ordered new goods from England. The early months of 1770 were thus bound to be an eventful and conflict-ridden period in Boston.

Serious troubles began in January. The shop of the Hutchinson sons was visited by a crowd that smeared "Hillsborough paint," a potent mixture of human excrement and urine, on the door. In mid-February, a crowd surrounded the house of Ebenezer Richardson, a cranky, low-level customs official. Richardson panicked and fired his musket to scare off the crowd, but he accidentally hit an eleven-year-old boy on the fringes of the crowd; the boy died within hours. The Sons of Liberty mounted a massive funeral procession to mark this first instance of violent death in the struggle with England.

For the next week, heightened tensions gripped Boston, and frequent brawls occurred. The climax came on Monday evening, March 5, 1770, when a small crowd taunted a soldier guarding the customs house. Among other things, he was called a "damned rascally Scoundrel Lobster Son of a Bitch." (The red uniforms of the British were often likened to lobsters.) British Captain Thomas Preston decided to send a seven-man guard to join the lone sentry. Meanwhile, the hostile crowd grew, and the soldiers raised their loaded muskets in defense. Onlookers threw snowballs and sticks, daring the soldiers to fire. Finally one of the soldiers, hit by some object, pulled his trigger. After a short pause, during which time someone yelled "Fire!" the other soldiers fired as well. Eleven men in the crowd were hit, five of them fatally. The victims had funerals befitting martyrs, with elaborate orations by leaders of the Sons of Liberty about the threat to all Americans posed by the British army.

The Boston Massacre, as it quickly became called, was over in minutes, but its repercussions were serious and long-lasting. In the immediate aftermath, Hutchinson (now acting governor after Bernard's recall to England) showed courage in confronting the crowd personally, from the balcony of the customs house. By daybreak of March 6, he ordered the removal of the regiments to an island in the harbor to prevent further bloodshed. Hutchinson also jailed Preston and the eight soldiers, as much for their own protection as to appease the townspeople, and promised they would be held accountable for their actions.

Preston and the soldiers came to trial in the fall of 1770, defended by two young attorneys, Samuel Adams's cousin John Adams and Josiah Quincy. Because Adams and Quincy had direct ties to the lead-

THE BLOODY MASSACRE PERPETRATED IN KING STREET, BOSTON, ON MARCH 5, 1770 **This mass-produced engraving by Paul Revere sold for six pence per copy. In this patriot version, the soldiers fire on an unarmed crowd under orders of their captain. The tranquil dog is an artistic device to signal the crowd's peaceful intent; not even a deaf dog could actually hold that pose during the melee. Among the five killed was Crispus Attucks, a black sailor, but Revere shows only whites among the casualties.**
Anne S. K. Brown Military Collection, Providence, R.I.

www.bedfordstmartins.com /tap SEE THE ONLINE STUDY GUIDE for more help in analyzing this image.

ership of the Boston Sons of Liberty, their decision to defend the British soldiers at first seems odd. But John Adams was deeply committed to the idea that even unpopular defendants deserve a fair trial. Samuel Adams respected his cousin's decision to take the case, for there was a tactical benefit as well. It showed that the Boston leadership was not lawless but could be seen as defenders of British liberty and law.

The Boston "Massacre" was over in minutes, but its repercussions were serious and long-lasting.

The five-day trial, with dozens of witnesses, resulted in acquittal for Preston and for all but two of the soldiers. Those two were convicted of manslaughter and then branded on the thumbs and released. Nothing materialized in the trial to indicate a conspiracy or concerted plan, either by the British or by the leaders of the Sons of Liberty, to provoke trouble. To this day, the question of who was responsible for the Boston Massacre remains obscure.

The years from 1767 to 1770 propelled the growing crisis into deeper and murkier channels. The nebulous Townshend duties lacked the symbolic punch of the Stamp Act, and the decision to try the tactics of nonimportation and nonconsumption created serious divisions in the American population. A military occupation of Boston brought the first fatalities in the coming Revolution, but, electrifying as that was to Bostonians, colonists distant from that city could still indulge the luxury of thinking that the crisis was perhaps not all that serious.

The Tea Party and the Coercive Acts, 1770–1774

In the same week as the Boston Massacre, the new British prime minister, Frederick North, contemplated the decrease in trade caused by the Townshend duties and recommended repeal. A skillful politician, Lord North took office in 1770 and kept it for twelve years; at last King George had stability at the helm. North sought peace with the colonies and prosperity for British merchants, so all the Townshend duties were removed, except the tax on tea, a pointed reminder of Parliament's ultimate power. North hoped to cool tensions without sacrificing principles.

Those few Americans who could not abide the symbolism of the tea tax turned to smuggled Dutch tea. The renewal of trade and the return of cooperation between England and the colonies gave men like Thomas Hutchinson hope that the worst of the crisis was behind them. For nearly two years, it looked as though Hutchinson's hope might be realized.

The Calm before the Storm

With the repeal of the Townshend duties came an end to the nonimportation agreements, despite the tax on tea. Trade boomed in 1770 and 1771. Moreover, the leaders of the popular movement seemed to be losing their power. Samuel Adams, for example, ran for a minor local office in Boston and lost to a conservative merchant.

In 1772, however, several incidents brought the conflict with England into focus again. One was the burning of the *Gaspée*, a Royal Navy ship chasing down suspected smugglers off the coast of Rhode Island. Although a royal investigating commission failed to arrest anyone, it announced that it would send suspects, if it found any, to England for trial for high treason.

This decision seemed to fly in the face of the traditional English right to a trial by a jury of one's peers. When the news of the *Gaspée* investigation spread, it was greeted with disbelief in other colonies. Patrick Henry, Thomas Jefferson, and Richard Henry Lee from the Virginia House of Burgesses proposed that a network of standing committees be established to link the colonies and pass along alarming news. By mid-1773, every colonial assembly except Pennsylvania had a "committee of correspondence." The British handling of the *Gaspée* incident had backfired, for it provoked the first serious effort to create semiofficial links among the American colonial governments.

Another British action in 1772 further spread the communications network of committees of correspondence. Lord North proposed to pay the salaries of superior court justices out of the tea revenue, in a move parallel to Townshend's earlier plan for royal governors. The Boston town meeting, alarmed that judges would now be in the pockets of their new paymasters, established a committee of correspondence and urged other towns to do likewise. The first vital message, circulated far and wide in December 1772, attacked the judges' salary policy as the latest proof of a British plot to undermine traditional English "liberties": unjust taxation, military occupation, massacre, now capped by the subversion of justice. By spring 1773, half the towns in Massachusetts had set up their own committees of correspondence, providing local forums for debate stimulated by letters sent out by the more radical Boston group. Committees of correspondence politicized ordinary townspeople and bypassed the official flow of political power and information through the colony's royal government.

The third and final incident that irrevocably shattered the relative calm of the early 1770s was the Tea Act of 1773. Americans had been drinking moderate amounts of English tea and paying the tea duty without objection, but they were also smuggling large quantities of Dutch tea, causing the British East India Company to experience sagging sales. So Lord North proposed special legislation giving favored status to the East India Company, allowing it to sell its tea through special agents, appointed by the government, rather than through public auction to independent merchants. The hope was that the price of the East India tea, even with the duty, would then fall below that of the smuggled Dutch tea, creating an incentive for Americans to obey the law as well as boosting sales for the East India Company.

Tea in Boston Harbor

In the fall of 1773, news of the Tea Act reached the colonies. Parliamentary legislation to make tea inexpensive struck many colonists as an insidious plot to trick Americans into buying large quantities of the duties tea. The real goal, some argued, was the increased revenue, which would then be used to pay the royal governors and judges. The Tea Act was thus a sudden and painful reminder of Parliament's claim to the power to tax and legislate for the colonies.

As with the Stamp Act and the Townshend duties, the colonists' strategy was crucial. Nonimportation was not a viable option, because the trade was too lucrative to expect colonial merchants to give it up willingly. Consumer boycotts of tea had proved ineffective since 1770, chiefly because it was impossible to distinguish between dutied tea (the object of the boycott) and smuggled tea (illegal but politically clean) once it was in the teapot. Like the Stamp Act, the Tea Act mandated special agents to handle the tea sales, and that requirement pointed to the solution for anti-tea activists. In nearly every port city, revived Sons of Liberty found ways to pressure tea agents to resign.

The Boston Sons of Liberty were slower to act than their compatriots in other cities, but their action—more direct and illegal than anywhere else—ultimately provoked the most alarmed and alarming reprisals from England. Three ships bearing tea arrived in Boston in late November 1773. They cleared customs and unloaded their other cargoes, but not the tea. Sensing the extreme tension, the captains wished to return to England, but because the ships had already entered the harbor, they could not get clearance to leave without first paying the tea duty. On top of that, there was a twenty-day limit on the stay allowed in the harbor, by which time either the duty had to be paid or the tea would be confiscated and sold by the authorities. Governor Hutchinson refused to bend any rules.

The Boston Sons of Liberty were slower to act than their compatriots in other cities, but their action ultimately provoked the most alarmed and alarming reprisals from England.

For the full twenty days, pressure built in Boston. Daily mass meetings energized the citizenry not only from Boston but from surrounding towns,

TOSSING THE TEA
This colored engraving appeared in an English book published in 1789, recounting the history of North America from its earliest settlement to "becoming united, free, and independent states." Men on the ship break into the chests and dump the contents; a few are depicted in Indian disguise, with feathers on their heads or topknots of hair. A large crowd on the shore looks on. The red rowboat is clearly stacked with tea chests, suggesting that some of the raiders were stealing rather than destroying the tea. However, the artist, perhaps careless, shows the rowboat heading toward the ship instead of away. This event was not dubbed the "Tea Party" until the 1830s when a later generation celebrated the illegal destruction of the tea and made heroes out of the few surviving participants, by then men in their eighties.
Library of Congress.

alerted by the committees of correspondence. On the final day, December 16, a large crowd gathered at Old South Church to hear Samuel Adams declare, "This meeting can do nothing more to save the country." This was a signal to initiate the end of the stalemate. The meeting adjourned to the harbor, where between 100 and 150 men, many dressed as Indians, destroyed the tea while a crowd of two thousand watched. It took three hours to dump 342 chests of tea—weighing ninety thousand pounds—into Boston harbor; its value was £10,000 sterling. (See "Documenting the American Promise," page 168.)

The Coercive Acts

Lord North's response was swift and stern. Within three months he persuaded Parliament to issue the first of the Coercive Acts, a series of four laws meant to punish Massachusetts for the destruction of the tea. The laws were soon known as the Intolerable Acts in America, along with a fifth one not aimed at Massachusetts alone, the Quebec Act.

The first, the Boston Port Act, closed Boston harbor to all shipping traffic as of June 1, 1774, for as long as the destroyed tea was not paid for. In ef-

BOSTONIANS IN DISTRESS
This British cartoon portrays the effects of the closure of the port of Boston in 1774. Men in a cage hang from the "Liberty Tree," an actual tree in central Boston so named by the crowds that staged rallies there. The prisoners, surrounded by cannons and British soldiers, act like animals eating raw fish. The three fishermen get a bundle labeled "promises" in return. Is this cartoon sympathetic to the distress of Boston, or is it scornful?
Courtesy of the John Carter Brown Library at Brown University.

fect, England was obliterating the commercial life of the city.

The second act, called the Massachusetts Government Act, altered the colony's charter (in itself an unprecedented step, underscoring Parliament's claim to supremacy over Massachusetts). The royal governor's powers were greatly augmented; the council became an appointive, not elective, body; and no town meeting beyond the annual spring election of town selectmen could be held unless the governor expressly permitted it. Not only Boston but every Massachusetts town felt the punitive sting.

The third of the Coercive Acts, the Impartial Administration of Justice Act, stipulated that any royal official accused of a capital crime—for example, Captain Preston and his soldiers at the Boston Massacre—would now be tried in a court in England. It did not matter that Preston in fact got a fair trial in Boston. What this act ominously suggested was that down the road, there might be more Captain Prestons and soldiers firing into crowds.

The fourth of the Coercive Acts was a new amendment to the 1765 Quartering Act, permitting military commanders to lodge soldiers wherever necessary, even in private households. For Boston this was no idle gesture, for in a related move Lord North appointed General Thomas Gage, commander of the Royal Army in New York, to be the new governor of Massachusetts. Thomas Hutchinson was out, relieved at long last of his duties, and military rule, including soldiers, returned once more to Boston.

The fifth Intolerable Act, the Quebec Act, had little to do with the first four but, ill-timed, it greatly fed the fear of Americans. It confirmed the continuation of French civil law, government form, and Catholicism for Quebec, all an affront to Protestant New Englanders denied their own representative government. The act also gave Quebec control of disputed lands (and hence control of the lucrative fur trade) throughout the Ohio River valley, lands claimed variously by Virginia, Pennsylvania, and Connecticut.

The Coercive Acts spread alarm to all the colonies. If England could step on Massachusetts and change its charter, suspend government, inaugurate military rule, and on top of that give Ohio to Catholic Quebec, then what liberties were secure? Fearful royal governors in a half dozen colonies suspended sitting assemblies, adding to the sense of urgency; some suspended assemblies defiantly continued to meet in new locations. Via the committees of correspondence, the colonies agreed to meet in Philadelphia in the fall of 1774 to respond to the crisis.

The First Continental Congress

Every colony except Georgia sent delegates to Philadelphia for the meeting of the First Continental Congress in September 1774. The gathering included the leading patriots, such as Samuel and John Adams from Massachusetts and George Washington and Patrick Henry from Virginia. A few colonies sent men who were cool to provoking a crisis with England, like Pennsylvania's Joseph Galloway. Whatever their views, most of the delegates were the leading statesmen of their localities. John Adams wrote to his wife, Abigail, that "the magnanimity and public spirit which I see here make me blush for the sordid, venal herd which I have seen in my own Province."

Two difficult tasks confronted the congress: The delegates wanted to agree on exactly what liberties they claimed as English subjects and what rights Parliament held over them, and they needed to make a unified response to the Coercive Acts. Some delegates wanted a total ban on trade with England, to force a repeal of the Coercive Acts, but others—especially those from the southern colonies heavily dependent on the export of tobacco and rice—could not afford such a comprehensive stoppage. Samuel Adams and Patrick Henry were more than eager for a ringing denunciation of all parliamentary control, whereas the conservative Joseph Galloway proposed a plan (quickly defeated) to create a colonial miniparliament in America to assist the British Parliament in ruling the colonies.

The congress met for seven weeks in Carpenter's Hall, Philadelphia, and eventually hammered out a declaration of rights, couched in traditional language: "We ask only for peace, liberty and security. We wish no diminution of royal prerogatives, we demand no new rights." Yet the rights assumed already to exist were in fact radical, from England's point of view. Chief among them was the claim that Americans were not represented in Parliament and so each colonial government had the sole right to legislate for and tax its own people. The one slight concession to England was a carefully worded agreement that the colonists would "cheerfully consent" to trade regulations for the larger good of the empire—so long as trade regulation was not a

The Destruction of the Tea

*T*he night of December 16, 1773, when over a hundred men disguised as Indians threw many chests of tea into Boston harbor, provided the incendiary spark that propelled Britain and the colonies into a raging and ever-escalating conflict. Different participants in the events leading up to that night had radically different analyses of the causes and consequences of this momentous event.

DOCUMENT 1. Governor Hutchinson's Account, Published in 1828

Thomas Hutchinson had long intended to write an extensive history of his beloved Massachusetts colony, and he collected materials for that work throughout his administrative career in Boston. He wrote the manuscript in the years after he fled to England; it was not published until 1828, after his death, in a massive three-volume work. The third volume covered the revolutionary decades in Massachusetts, when Hutchinson himself became a historical figure in his own book. He always referred to himself in the third person, but his point of view was definitely weighted towards self-vindication.

As a permit . . . was always required at the castle, for all vessels except small coasters, and there were several men of war in the harbour, which it was supposed would stop the ship from proceeding any other way, the destruction of the tea was considered as necessary to prevent the payment of it. A demand was made of the collector, . . . of a clearance for the ship, which he could not grant until the goods which were imported, . . . were landed and the duties paid. . . . It was expected, that, in twenty days after the arrival of the tea, a demand of the duty would be made by the collector, and the ship or goods be seized; which would occasion additional difficulties. Another meeting . . . was therefore called. . . . The people came into Boston from the adjacent towns within 20 miles, . . . and, as soon as they were assembled, enjoined the owner of the ship, at his peril, to demand of the collector of the customs a clearance for the ship, and appointed ten of their number a committee to accompany him; and adjourned for two days to receive the report. Being

re-assembled and informed by the owner, that a clearance was refused, he was then enjoined immediately to apply to the governor for a pass by the castle. He made an apology to the governor, for coming upon such an errand, having been compelled to it; and received an answer, that no pass ever had been, or lawfully could be, given to any vessel which had not first been cleared at the custom-house. . . . The governor was unable to judge what would be the next step. . . . But he was relieved from his suspense, the same evening, by the intelligence from town of the total destruction of the tea.

It was not expected the governor would comply with the demand; and, before it was possible for the owner of the ship to return . . . with an answer, about fifty men had prepared themselves, and passed by the house where the people were assembled, to the wharf where the vessels lay, being covered with blankets, and making the appearance of Indians. The body of the people remained until they had received the governor's answer; and then, after it had been observed to them, that, every thing else in their power having been done, it now remained to proceed in the only way left . . . the meeting was declared to be dissolved, and the body of the people repaired to the wharf, and surrounded the immediate actors, as a guard and security, until they finished their work. In two or three hours, they hoisted out of the holds of the ships, three hundred and forty-two chests of tea, and emptied them into the sea. The governor was unjustly censured by many people in the province, and much abused by the pamphlet and newspaper writers in England, for refusing his pass, which, it was said, would have saved the property thus destroyed; but he would have been justly censured, if he had granted it. He was bound, as all the king's governors were, by oath, faithfully to observe the acts of trade. . . . His granting a pass to a vessel which had not cleared at the custom-house, would have been a direct violation of his oath, by making himself an accessory in the breach of those laws which he had sworn to observe. It was out of his power to have prevented this mischief, without the most imminent hazard of much greater mischief. The tea could have been secured in the town in no other way than by landing marines from the men of war, or bringing to town the regiment which was at the castle, to remove the guards from the ships, and to take their places. This would have brought on a greater convulsion than there was any danger of in 1770, and it would not have been possible . . . for so small a body of troops to have kept possession of the town. Such a measure the governor had no reason to suppose would have been approved of in England. He was not sure of support from any one person in authority. The house of representatives openly avowed principles which implied complete independency. The council, appointed by charter to be assisting to him, declared against any advice from which might be inferred an acknowledgment of the authority of parliament in imposing taxes. . . . There was not a justice of peace, sheriff, constable, or peace officer in the province, who would venture to take cognizance of any breach of law, against the general bent of the people.

SOURCE: Thomas Hutchinson, *The History of the Colony and Province of Massachusetts-Bay* (Cambridge, Mass.: Harvard University Press, 1936), 3:311–14.

DOCUMENT 2: George Robert Twelves Hewes's Recollection, Transcribed in 1834

George Robert Twelves Hewes, a thirty-one-year-old Boston shoemaker, was first stirred to political action by witnessing the Boston Massacre. During the struggle over tea, he joined the "Indian" boarding party and found himself thrust into a leadership role, a singular moment of glory which he proudly recounted when he was in his nineties. As one of the last surviving participants of that famous event, he enjoyed enormous celebrity in the 1830s. His life came to symbolize the Revolution's power to lift up the common man and endow him with a sense of political significance.

The commander of the division to which I belonged, as soon as we were on board the ship, appointed me boatswain, and ordered me to go to the captain and demand of him the keys to the hatches and a dozen candles. I made the demand accordingly, and the captain promptly replied, and delivered the articles; but requested me at the same time to do no damage to the ship or rigging. We then were ordered by our commander to open the hatches, and take out all the chests of tea and throw them overboard, and we immediately proceeded to execute

his orders; first cutting and splitting the chests with our tomahawks, so as thoroughly to expose them to the effects of the water. In about three hours from the time we went on board, we had thus broken and thrown overboard every tea chest to be found in the ship; while those in the other ships were disposing of the tea in the same way, at the same time. We were surrounded by British armed ships, but no attempt was made to resist us. We then quietly retired to our several places of residence, without having any conversation with each other, or taking any measures to discover who were our associates.

SOURCE: [James Hawkes], *A Retrospect of the Boston Tea-Party, with a Memoir of George R. T. Hewes, a Survivor of the Little Band of Patriots Who Drowned the Tea in Boston Harbour in 1773* (New York, 1834), reprinted in Alfred F. Young, *The Shoemaker and the Tea Party: Memory and the American Revolution* (Boston: Beacon Press, 1999), 44.

DOCUMENT 3: John Adams's Diary Entry of December 17, 1773

John Adams reveled in the bold destruction of the tea in his diary the day after the event. He also gave thought to the legal consequences that might follow, rehearsing the justifications that motivated "the People."

Last Night 3 Cargoes of Bohea Tea were emptied into the Sea. This Morning a Man of War sails.

This is the most magnificent Movement of all. There is a Dignity, a Majesty, a Sublimity, in this last Effort of the Patriots, that I greatly admire. The people should never rise, without doing something to be remembered—something notable And striking. This Destruction of the Tea is so bold, so daring, so firm, intrepid and inflexible, and it must have so important Consequences, and so lasting, that I cant but consider it as an Epocha in History.

This however is but an Attack upon Property. Another similar Exertion of popular Power, may produce the destruction of Lives. Many Persons wish, that as many dead Carcasses were floating in the Harbour, as there are Chests of Tea:—a much less Number of Lives however would remove the Causes of all our Calamities.

The malicious Pleasure with which Hutchinson the Governor, the Consignees of the Tea, and the officers of the Customs, have stood and (*Continued*) looked upon the distresses of the People, and their Struggles to get the Tea back to London, and at last the destruction of it, is amazing. Tis hard to believe Persons so hardened and abandoned.

What Measures will the Ministry take, in Consequence of this?—Will they resent it? will they dare to resent it? will they punish Us? How? By quartering Troops upon Us?—by annulling our Charter?—by laying on more duties? By restraining our Trade? By Sacrifice of Individuals, or how.

The Question is whether the Destruction of this Tea was necessary? I apprehend it was absolutely and indispensably so.—They could not send it back, the Governor, Admiral, and Collector and Comptroller would not suffer it. It was in their Power to have saved it—but in no other. It could not get by the Castle, the Men of War &c. Then there was no other Alternative but to destroy it or let it be landed. To let it be landed, would be giving up the Principle of Taxation by Parliamentary Authority, against which the Continent have struggled for 10 years, it was loosing all our labour for 10 years and subjecting ourselves and our Posterity forever to Egyptian Taskmasters—to Burthens, Indignities, to Ignominy, Reproach and Contempt, to Desolation and Oppression, to Poverty and Servitude.

But it will be said it might have been left in the Care of a Committee of the Town, or in Castle William. To this many Objections may be made. . . . The Tories blame the Consignees, as much as the Whiggs do—and say that the Governor will loose his Place, for not taking the Tea into his protection before, by Means of the Ships of War, I suppose, and the Troops at the Castle.

SOURCE: L. H. Butterfield, ed., *Diary and Autobiography of John Adams* (Cambridge, Mass.: Harvard University Press, 1961), 2:85–86.

DOCUMENT 4: Samuel Adams's Letter to Arthur Lee, January 25, 1774

Samuel Adams explained his views of the real causes of the tea destruction in this letter to his friend Arthur Lee.

The sending the East India Companies Tea into America appears evidently to have been with Design of the British Administration, and to complete the favorite plan of establishing a Revenue in America. . . . Governor Hutchinson & the other Crown officers having the Command of the Castle by which the Ships must have passed, & other powers in their Hands, made use of these Powers to defeat the Intentions of the people & succeeded; in short the Governor who for Art & Cunning as well as an inveterate hatred of the people was inferior to no one of the Cabal; both encouragd & provoked the people to destroy the Tea. By refusing the grant a Passport he held up to them the alternative of destroying the property of the East India Company or suffering that to be the sure means of unhinging the Security of property in general in America, and by delaying to call on the naval power to protect the Tea, he led them to determine their Choice of Difficulties. In this View of the Matter the Question is easily decided who ought in Justice to pay for the Tea if it ought to be paid for at all.

SOURCE: Harry Alonzo Cushing, ed., *Writings of Samuel Adams* (New York: Putnam's, 1904–07), 3:78–79.

QUESTIONS FOR ANALYSIS AND DEBATE

1. Does Thomas Hutchinson persuade you that he had no other option than to refuse to let the ship either leave or land? Why did he reject the use of troops to guard the tea?

2. How might men like Hewes be politicized by hacking open chests of tea?

3. John Adams says that Hutchinson took a malicious pleasure in forcing the tea crisis to its conclusion. Was he right or wrong in your judgment? Why?

4. What is at stake, for John Adams, in the showdown over tea, when he speaks of ten years of struggle by "the Continent" and of poverty and servitude to "Egyptian Taskmasters"? How does he feel about the possibility of deaths in the building struggle?

5. Who does Samuel Adams think is really responsible for the destruction of the tea? Why?

covert means of raising revenue. By consenting to this one power, however, the patriots were implying their right to revoke consent at any time.

To put pressure on England, the delegates agreed to a staggered and limited boycott of trade—imports prohibited this year, exports the following year, and rice totally exempted, to keep South Carolinians happy. To enforce the boycott, they created a mechanism called the Continental Association, with chapters in each town. Local associations, variously called committees of public safety or of inspection, would monitor all commerce and confront suspected violators of the boycott. (Violators might face a bucket of tar and a bag of feathers; see "Historical Question," page 172.) Its work done, the congress disbanded on October 26, 1774, with a vote to reconvene the following May in a Second Continental Congress.

The committees of public safety, the committees of correspondence, the regrouped colonial assemblies, and the Continental Congresses were all functioning political bodies without any formal constitutional authority. British officials did not recognize them as legitimate, but many Americans who supported the patriot cause instantly accepted them. A key reason for the stability of such unauthorized bodies throughout the Revolutionary period was that they were composed of the same men, by and large, who had composed the official bodies now disbanded.

England's severe reaction to Boston's destruction of the tea finally succeeded in making many colonists from New Hampshire to Georgia realize that the problems of British rule went far beyond questions of taxation. The Coercive Acts infringed on liberty and denied self-government; they could not be ignored. With one colony subordinated to military rule now, and a British army at the ready in Boston, the threat of a general war was at the doorstep.

Domestic Insurrections, 1774–1775

Before the Second Continental Congress could meet, war broke out in Massachusetts. General Thomas Gage, military commander and new governor, at first thought he faced a domestic insurrection that needed only a show of force to quiet it. The rebels saw things differently: They were defending their homes and liberties against an intrusive power bent on enslaving them. To the south, a different and inverted version of the same story began to unfold, as thousands of enslaved black men and women seized an unprecedented opportunity to mount a different kind of domestic insurrection, against planter-patriots who looked over their shoulders uneasily whenever they called out for liberty from the British.

Lexington and Concord

Over the winter of 1774–75 Americans pressed on with boycotts. Some hoped for the repeal of the Coercive Acts, while pessimists started accumulating arms and ammunition. In Massachusetts, gunpowder and shot were secretly stored, and militia units called "minutemen" prepared to respond on a minute's notice to any threat from the British in Boston.

Thomas Gage soon realized how desperate the British position was. The people, Gage wrote Lord North, were "numerous, worked up to a fury, and not a Boston rabble but the freeholders and farmers of the country." Gage requested twenty thousand reinforcements. He also strongly advised repeal of the Coercive Acts, to defuse a very tense situation, but leaders in England could not admit failure. Instead Gage was ordered in mid-April 1775 to arrest the troublemakers immediately, before the Americans got better organized.

The people, Gage wrote Lord North, were "numerous, worked up to a fury, and not a Boston rabble but the freeholders and farmers of the country."

Gage quickly planned a surprise attack on a suspected ammunition storage site at Concord, a village about eighteen miles west of Boston (Map 5.3). Near midnight on April 18, 1775, British soldiers moved west across the Charles River. Boston silversmith Paul Revere raced ahead to alert the minutemen. When the British soldiers got to Lexington, a village five miles east of Concord, they met with some seventy armed American men assembled on the village green. The British commander barked out, "Lay down your arms, you damned rebels and disperse." The militiamen hesitated and began to comply, turning to leave the green, but then someone fired; who it was has never been clear. In the next two minutes, more firing left eight

Who Got Tarred and Feathered, and Why?

TARRING AND FEATHERING as a form of vigilante brutality has long been associated with the American Revolution. British political cartoons gave wide currency to images of befeathered victims in humiliating postures. Boston loyalist Peter Oliver (brother-in-law of Thomas Hutchinson) claimed that tarring and feathering was an American invention and supplied shocked British friends with the "recipe," as he termed it:

> First, strip a Person naked, then heat the Tar until it is thin, & pour it upon the naked Flesh, or rub it over with a Tar Brush, *quantum sufficit*. After which, sprinkle decently upon the Tar, whilst it is yet warm, as many Feathers as will stick to it. Then hold a lighted Candle to the Feathers, & try to set it all on Fire; if it will burn so much the better.

Both the cartoon depictions and Oliver's recipe for this messy ritual must be taken cautiously, however, for they were promulgated by pro-British men who had a stake in portraying Americans as barbarians. How often did tarring and feathering really occur? Who were the victims? Was actual harm done? Answers to such questions allow historians to evaluate the role of violence and terrorism as tactics of revolutionary struggle.

Recorded incidents of tarring and feathering do not support Oliver's assertion that the practice was frequent. Probably fewer than a dozen instances occurred between 1765 and the outbreak of war in April 1775. The practice peaked in popularity in the turbulent year 1775, making a total of perhaps two to three dozen cases in all the colonies.

Tarred and feathered victims were *not* British officials. Instead, they were colonists who openly identified with British authority. Often, more moderate demonstrations of crowd displeasure prevailed, such as hanging or burning an effigy of the victim's body or conducting a mock funeral. Using a body substitute made a chilling point and released anger without doing any real physical harm.

Tarring and feathering pushed the boundaries of restraint, for the act involved considerable bodily discomfort. Victims of the sticky, feathery assault were usually community members suspected of being informers, violators of agreements to spurn British goods, or men conspicuous for their animosity toward the revolutionary point of view.

TAR AND FEATHERING CARTOON
John Malcolm, a customs official in Boston, becomes a feathery chicken forced to drink tea. A tar bucket sits in the left foreground; the Boston Tea Party—which happened a month before Malcolm's humiliation—proceeds in the rear. The Liberty Tree has become a gallows; posted to it is the Stamp Act, upside down. The hated Malcolm had been tarred two months earlier, in Portsmouth, New Hampshire, but in that attack he remained clothed. In Boston he was stripped naked first.
Courtesy of John Carter Brown at Brown University.

They were men *of* the community who had to be ritually distanced from the community for breaking a moral code, not a law. The standard treatment for lawbreakers was a flogging, fine, or jail, imposed by a judge. Transgressors of the moral code, in contrast, got symbolic punishments from their neighbors on the local committee of public safety, without benefit of legal procedures.

Tarring and feathering was a severe variant in a long tradition of ritual humiliations for transgressive people. Typical humiliations imposed on fornicators, adulterers, or other deceivers included dressing victims in clothes of the opposite sex, riding them around town backward on an ass, or making them stand in public wrapped in white sheets. The object was to shame them into apologizing for their bad behavior as a condition of acceptance back into the community. Tarring and feathering introduced a new variation on the theme: A person was rendered into an animal—a fowl or chicken—and paraded around in a state of near nakedness, the better to garner public shame.

For example, in 1771 a Providence, Rhode Island, man suspected of informing on smugglers was stripped, tied up, painted with warm tar, and feathered, after which dirt was thrown in his face. A man in Charleston, South Carolina, snarled, "Damnation to the Committee and their proceedings" and was soon tarred and feathered for his outburst. A New Jersey artisan who reviled the Continental Congress in late 1775 was set upon by townsmen, stripped, tarred and feathered, and paraded in a wagon for a half hour until he begged pardon. Probably the most famous case occurred in 1774, involving the Bostonian John Malcolm, a dishonest customs collector who extorted extra money from shippers. Malcolm's horrid fate was immortalized in a London cartoon showing five cruelly gleeful Americans forcing tea into his mouth, yanking his hair, and terrorizing him with a noose about his neck.

Peter Oliver's assertion that feathers were set on fire was a serious exaggeration. Hot tar of course hurt, and the eventual removal of the suit of feathers posed the risk of additional pain. It mattered what feathers were used. Soft goose down was an expensive household item in the eighteenth century; few Revolutionary women would relinquish treasured quilts and pillows easily. A more prevalent source of feathers, scratchy ones at that, was the chicken coop. Powerful humiliation, not serious injury, was the goal. In one of the few known instances of a female-inspired sticky assault, girls at a quilting frolic in a small Hudson River village in fall 1775 reportedly stripped to the waist a young man of loyalist sympathies and adorned him with molasses and weeds.

In one unusual case, British soldiers in Boston in March 1775 turned the tables and attacked a rural man who had tried to buy a gun from a soldier. The man was stripped, tarred, feathered, and hauled around on a cart, with a sign affixed to his back proclaiming, "American Liberty, or a Specimen of Democracy"—meaning, a sorry specimen. A fife and drum accompanied him, playing "Yankee Doodle" to irritate the Bostonian onlookers, and twenty bayonet-bearing British soldiers surrounded him, to prevent a rescue attempt. The soldiers' inversion fundamentally changed the ritual: No longer community-confirming, the event became in their hands a mockery of the civilian population.

Tarring and feathering was not practiced often. Other tactics involving less personal violence were more frequently used: publishing offenders' names in the newspaper, boycotting businesses, intimidating their families, and breaking windows. Sometimes just the threat of a tar and feather treatment was sufficient, as when a Pennsylvania loyalist had his nose pushed up to a barrel of tar or when a warning directed at an individual mysteriously appeared in a newspaper, signed by a fictional "Committee for Tarring and Feathering."

Peter Oliver did not think so, but historians generally agree that the years of revolutionary turmoil from 1765 to the 1770s were remarkably free of serious personal violence, aside from organized warfare. The Boston Massacre of five people hardly qualifies as a massacre by twentieth-century war zone standards. Tarring and feathering was rough stuff, but it did not cause death. The American Revolution, even in its aspects that resemble a civil war, stopped short of the kind of massive bloodshed and torture of civilians by civilians that would characterize revolutions from the 1789 French Revolution onward.

MAP 5.3
Lexington and Concord, April 1775
Under pressure from England, British forces at Boston staged a raid on a suspected rebel arms supply in Concord, Massachusetts, starting the first battle of the Revolutionary War.

Americans dead and ten wounded. One British soldier suffered a slight wound.

The British units then moved on to Concord, no longer under cover of dark or with any pretense of surprise. Three companies of minutemen nervously occupied the center of Concord but offered no challenge to the British troops as they searched in vain for the ammunition storage. Finally, at the Old North Bridge in Concord, shots were exchanged, killing two Americans and three British soldiers.

By now both sides were very apprehensive. The British had failed to find the expected arms storage, and the Americans had failed to stop their raid. As the British returned to Boston along a narrow road, militia units attacked from the sides in the bloodiest fighting of the day. In the end, 273 British soldiers were wounded or dead; the toll for the Americans stood at about 95. It was April 19, 1775, and the war had begun.

Another Rebellion against Slavery

News of the battles of Lexington and Concord spread rapidly. Within eight days, Virginians had heard of the fighting, and, as Thomas Jefferson reflected, "A phrenzy of revenge seems to have seized all ranks of people." The royal governor of Virginia, Lord Dunmore, had just removed a large quantity of gunpowder from the Williamsburg powder house and put it on a ship in the dead of night, out of reach of any frenzied Virginians. Next, Dunmore

threatened to arm the slaves, if necessary, to ward off attacks by colonists.

This was clearly Dunmore's ace card, for he understood full well how to produce panic among the planters. Yet he did not play the card until November 1775, when he issued an official proclamation promising freedom to defecting, able-bodied slaves who would fight for the British. Dunmore's dilemma was that while he wanted to scare the planters, he had no intention of liberating all slaves or of starting a real slave rebellion. So his offer was limited to able-bodied men. Female, young, and elderly slaves were not welcome behind British lines, and many were sent back to face irate masters. Astute blacks noticed that Dunmore neglected to free his own slaves. A Virginia barber named Caesar declared that "he did not know any one foolish enough to believe him [Dunmore], for if he intended to do so, he ought first to set his own free."

In the northern colonies as well, slaves clearly recognized the evolving political struggle with England as an ideal moment to bid for freedom. A twenty-one-year-old Boston domestic slave employed biting sarcasm in a 1774 newspaper essay to call attention to the hypocrisy of local slave owners: "How well the Cry for Liberty, and the reverse Disposition for exercise of oppressive Power over others agree,—I humbly think it does not require the Penetration of a Philosopher to Determine." This extraordinary young woman, Phillis Wheatley, had already gained international recognition

BRITISH TROOPS IN CONCORD CENTER
In this contemporary engraving by Amos Doolittle, based on a painting done on the spot by Ralph Earl, two British officers seek the high ground of the cemetery in Concord, Massachusetts, to orient themselves to the unfamiliar town at around 9 A.M. on April 19, 1775. Their troops march in formation, fresh from the skirmish at Lexington. American militiamen had amassed at the Old North Bridge, off to the right about a mile from the town center. The officer with the telescope is undoubtedly scanning for them.
Miriam and Ira D. Walsh Division of Art, Print and Photographs, The New York Public Library. Astor, Lenox and Tilden Foundations.

through a book of poems published in London in 1773. Kidnapped from Africa at age eight, sold to a Boston merchant named John Wheatley in 1761, fully literate in English within sixteen months and in Latin by age twelve, Phillis Wheatley became an accomplished poet by age sixteen. She earned the regard of both Governor Thomas Hutchinson and Boston merchant John Hancock, whose testimonials endorsed her book and affirmed her remarkable life story. Possibly neither man fully appreciated the irony of his endorsement, however, for Wheatley's poems spoke of "Fair Freedom" as the "Goddess long desir'd" by Africans enslaved in America. At the urging of his wife, Wheatley's master freed the young poet in 1775.

Wheatley's poetic ideas about freedom found concrete expression among other discontented groups. Some slaves in Boston petitioned Thomas Gage, promising to fight for the British if he would liberate them. Gage turned them down. In Ulster County, New York, along the Hudson River, two blacks were overheard discussing gunpowder, and thus a plot unraveled that involved at least twenty slaves in four villages discovered to have ammunition stashed away.

Slaves clearly recognized the evolving political struggle with England as an ideal moment to bid for freedom.

The numerical preponderance of black slaves in the southern colonies deepened white fears of rebellion. In Maryland, soon after the news of the Lexington battle arrived, slaves exhibited impatience with their status, in light of the revolutionary movement unfolding around them. One Maryland planter reported that "the insolence of the Negroes in this county is come to such a height, that we are under a necessity of disarming them. . . . We took about eighty guns, some bayonets, swords, etc." In North Carolina, a planned uprising was

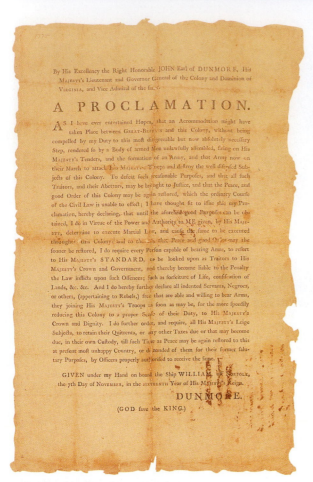

LORD DUNMORE'S PROCLAMATION
In November 1775, Lord Dunmore of Virginia offered freedom to "all indented Servants, Negroes, or others (appertaining to Rebels)" who would help put down the rebellion. Dunmore issued multiple printed copies in broadside form from the safety of a ship anchored at Norfolk, Virginia.
Special Collections, University of Virginia, Alderman Library.

uncovered and scores of slaves were arrested. No one seemed to see any irony in the fact that it was the revolutionary committee of public safety that dealt severely with this quest for liberty: Each conspiring slave suffered eighty lashes on the back and had both ears cropped.

Understandably, Lord Dunmore's proclamation to encourage slave defection was not reported in southern newspapers. Blacks, however, did not depend on newspapers for their information. John Adams was assured by southern delegates to the Continental Congress that a proclamation like Dunmore's would quickly draw twenty thousand slaves in South Carolina because "the Negroes have a wonderful art of communicating Intelligence among themselves; it will run several hundreds of miles in a week or fortnight." The contagion of liberty spread quickly by newspaper, by word of mouth, and even by drumbeat.

In 1775, probably several thousand slaves in Virginia took Lord Dunmore up on his offer, and by 1778 the number had escalated to as many as thirty thousand. Possibly eighty thousand southern blacks over the course of the Revolutionary War voted against slavery with their feet. Some failed to achieve the liberation they were seeking. The British army generally used them for menial labor; and disease, especially smallpox, devastated encampments of runaways. More than five hundred blacks died of smallpox on an island off the Virginia coast in 1776. Twenty years later the skeletons were still there, where the refugees had been abandoned by the British.

In South Carolina, Sullivan's Island became a magnet for fleeing slaves. One black man went there after delivering to his white master a grand speech. The master reported, "Though he is my property, he has the audacity to tell me, he will be free, that he will serve no Man, and that he will be conquered or governed by no Man." But the Charleston committee of public safety decided otherwise. The encampment, with an estimated five hundred slaves, was raided by Charleston revolutionaries. They killed about fifty blacks, burned their tents, and sent hundreds back to slavery.

Eventually, some thousands of blacks managed to secure freedom as a result of the Revolution. About three thousand who persisted in their support of the British were allowed to set sail from New York in 1783 under the protection of the British navy to start new lives in Nova Scotia, Canada, or in Sierra Leone in Africa, while unknown numbers of others set sail from Charleston.

Conclusion: How Far Does Liberty Go?

The French and Indian War set the stage for the imperial crisis of the 1760s and 1770s by creating distrust between England and its colonies and by running up a huge deficit in the British treasury. The years from 1763 to 1775 brought repeated attempts by the British government to subordinate the colonies into taxpaying partners in the larger scheme of empire.

American resistance grew slowly but steadily over those years. In 1765, Thomas Hutchinson shared with Samuel Adams the belief that it was exceedingly unwise for England to assert a right to taxation, because Parliament did not adequately represent Americans. But Hutchinson, a proud royal officer and a staunch believer in British authority, felt compelled to uphold Parliament's policy; Adams, in contrast, protested the policy and made political activists out of thousands in the process.

By 1775, events propelled many Americans to the conclusion that a concerted effort was afoot to deprive them of all their liberties, the most important of which were the right to self-taxation, the right to live free of an occupying army, and finally their right to self-rule. It appeared to them that England was trying to enslave them, and they used the term "abject slavery" very often to describe the ultimate and most horrible stage of being unfree, deprived of all liberty and property. Hundreds of minutemen converged on Concord, prepared to die for these American liberties. April 19 marked the start of their rebellion.

Another rebellion under way in 1775 was doomed to be short-circuited. Black Americans who had experienced actual slavery now listened to shouts of "Liberty!" from white crowds and appropriated the language of revolution swirling around them that spoke to their deepest needs and hopes. Defiance of authority was indeed contagious.

The emerging leaders of the patriot cause were mindful of a delicate balance they felt they had to strike. To energize the American public about the crisis with England, they had to politicize masses of men—and eventually women too—and infuse them with a keen sense of their rights and liberties. But in so doing, they became fearful of the unintended consequences of teaching a vocabulary of rights and liberties. They worried that the rhetoric of enslavement might go too far.

The question of how far the crisis could be stretched before something snapped was largely unexamined in 1765. Patriot leaders in that year wanted a correction, a restoration of an ancient liberty of self-taxation that Parliament seemed to be ignoring. But events from 1765 to 1775 convinced many that no return to the old ways was possible. A challenge to Parliament's right to tax had led, step by step, to a challenge to Parliament's right to legislate over the colonies in any matter. If Parliament's sovereignty was set aside, then who actually had authority over the American colonies? By 1775, with the outbreak of fighting and the specter of slave rebellions, American leaders turned to the king for the answer to that question.

www.bedfordstmartins.com/tap SEE THE ONLINE STUDY GUIDE to assess your mastery of the material covered in this chapter.

CHRONOLOGY

1747 Ohio Company of Virginia formed.

1754 French and Indian War begins in America.

Albany Congress proposes Plan of Union and courts Iroquois support.

1755 General Braddock defeated by French and Indians in Pennsylvania.

1757 William Pitt, prime minister in Britain, fully commits to war effort.

1759 Quebec falls to British.

1760 George III becomes king.

1763 Treaty of Paris ends French and Indian War.

Pontiac's uprising provokes fear and destruction in western frontier settlements.

Proclamation Act of 1763 prohibits settlement west of Appalachians.

1764 The Revenue (Sugar) Act lowers tax on foreign molasses to promote compliance with trade duty.

Currency Act prohibits issuance of colonial paper money.

1765 Stamp Act imposes tax on documents.

May. Patrick Henry sponsors Virginia Resolves.

August. Crowd actions in Boston inaugurate Sons of Liberty.

October. Stamp Act Congress meets in New York City.

1766 Stamp Act repealed; Declaratory Act asserts Parliament's control over colonies.

1767 Townshend duties reinstate revenue-raising taxes.

1768 **Fall.** British troops stationed in Boston.

1769 Year of nonimportation agreements; Daughters of Liberty appear.

1770 **March 5.** Boston Massacre.

Townshend duties repealed; Lord North comes to power.

1772 **June.** *Gaspée* attacked off Rhode Island.

Committees of correspondence formed.

1773 Tea Act lowers price of tea to encourage Americans to purchase legal rather than smuggled tea.

December 16. Boston Tea Party.

1774 Parliament passes Coercive Acts (Intolerable Acts): Boston Port Act, Massachusetts Government Act, Impartial Administration of Justice Act, Quartering Act, Quebec Act.

September. First Continental Congress meets. Continental Association formed.

1775 **April 19.** Battles of Lexington and Concord.

Virginia's Lord Dunmore promises freedom to defecting slaves.

BIBLIOGRAPHY

GENERAL WORKS

John R. Alden, *A History of the American Revolution* (1989).

Edward Countryman, *The American Revolution* (1985).

Marc Egnal, *A Mighty Empire: The Origins of the American Revolution* (1988).

Francis Jennings, *The Creation of America through Revolution to Empire* (2000).

Merrill Jensen, *The Founding of a Nation: A History of the American Revolution, 1763–1776* (1968).

A. J. Langguth, *Patriots: The Men Who Started the American Revolution* (1989).

James Kirby Martin, *In the Course of Human Events: An Interpretive Exploration of the American Revolution* (1979).

Robert Middlekauff, *The Glorious Cause: The American Revolution, 1763–1789* (1982).

Edmund S. Morgan, *The Challenge of the American Revolution* (1976).

Gordon Wood, *The Radicalism of the American Revolution* (1992).

Alfred F. Young, *The American Revolution: Explorations in the History of American Radicalism* (1976).

NATIVE AMERICANS AND THE FRENCH AND INDIAN WAR

Fred Anderson, *A People's Army: Massachusetts Soldiers and Society in the Seven Years' War* (1984).

Fred Anderson, *Crucible of War: The Seven Years' War and the Fate of Empire in British North America, 1754–1766* (2000).

Francis Jennings, *Empire of Fortune: Crowns, Colonies, and Tribes in the Seven Years' War in America* (1988).

Douglas E. Leach, *Roots of Conflict: British Armed Forces and Colonial Americans, 1677–1763* (1986).

Michael N. McConnell, *A Country Between: The Upper Ohio Valley and Its Peoples, 1724–1774* (1992).

James H. Merrell, *Into the American Woods: Negotiators on the Pennsylvania Frontier* (1999).

Timothy J. Shannon, *Indians and Colonists at the Crossroads of Empire: The Albany Congress of 1754* (1999).

Richard White, *The Middle Ground: Indians, Empires, and Republics in the Great Lakes Region, 1650–1815* (1991).

THE BRITISH VIEW OF EMPIRE

Bernard Bailyn, *The Origins of American Politics* (1968).

Thomas C. Barrow, *Trade and Empire: The British Customs Service in America, 1660–1775* (1967).

John L. Bullion, *A Great and Necessary Measure: George Grenville and the Genesis of the Stamp Act, 1763–1765* (1983).

Don Cook, *The Long Fuse: How England Lost the American Colonies, 1760–1785* (1996).

Jack P. Greene, *Peripheries and Center: Constitutional Development in the Extended Politics of the British Empire and the United States, 1607–1788* (1986).

James A. Henretta, *"Salutary Neglect": Colonial Administration under the Duke of Newcastle* (1972).

Michael Kammen, *A Rope of Sand: Colonial Agents, British Politics, and the American Revolution* (1968).

Michael Kammen, *Empire and Interest: The American Colonies and the Politics of Mercantilism* (1970).

Philip Lawson, *George Grenville: A Political Life* (1984).

Alison Gilbert Olson, *Making the Empire Work: London and American Interest Groups, 1690–1790* (1992).

Alan Rogers, *Empire and Liberty: American Resistance to British Authority, 1755–1763* (1974).

THE REVOLUTIONARY CRISIS OF THE 1760S AND 1770S

David Ammerman, *In the Common Cause: American Response to the Coercive Acts of 1774* (1975).

Bernard Bailyn, *The Ideological Origins of the American Revolution* (1967).

Bernard Bailyn, *The Ordeal of Thomas Hutchinson* (1974).

Bernard Bailyn, *Faces of Revolution: Personalities and Themes in the Struggle for American Independence* (1990).

Richard R. Beeman, *Patrick Henry* (1974).

Ruth H. Bloch, *Visionary Republic: Millennial Themes in American Thought, 1750–1800* (1985).

John L. Brooke, *The Heart of the Commonwealth: Society and Political Culture in Worcester County, Massachusetts, 1713–1861* (1989).

John E. Ferling, *The First of Men: A Life of George Washington* (1988).

David Hackett Fischer, *Paul Revere's Ride* (1994).

Jay Fliegelman, *Prodigals and Pilgrims: The American Revolution against Patriarchal Authority, 1750–1800* (1982).

Dirk Hoerder, *Crowd Action in Revolutionary Massachusetts, 1765–1780* (1977).

Woody Holton, *Forced Founders: Indians, Debtors, Slaves, and the Making of the American Revolution in Virginia* (1999).

Thomas A. Lewis, *For King and Country: The Maturing of George Washington, 1748–1760* (1993).

Pauline Maier, *From Resistance to Revolution: Colonial Radicals and the Development of American Opposition to Britain, 1765–1776* (1972).

Pauline Maier, *The Old Revolutionaries: Political Lives in the Age of Samuel Adams* (1980).

Edmund S. Morgan, *The Genius of George Washington* (1980).

Edmund S. Morgan, *Inventing the People: The Rise of Popular Sovereignty in England and America* (1988).

Edmund S. Morgan and Helen M. Morgan, *The Stamp Act Crisis: Prologue to Revolution* (1962).

Gary B. Nash, *The Urban Crucible: Social Change, Political Consciousness, and the Origins of the American Revolution* (1979).

Peter Shaw, *American Patriots and the Rituals of Revolution* (1981).

John W. Tyler, *Smugglers and Patriots: Boston Merchants and the Advent of the American Revolution* (1986).

Ann Fairfax Withington, *Toward a More Perfect Union: Virtue and the Formation of American Republics* (1991).

Alfred F. Young, *The Shoemaker and the Tea Party: Memory and the American Revolution* (1999).

Hiller B. Zobel, *The Boston Massacre* (1970).

WOMEN

Richard Buel and Joy Day Buel, *The Way of Duty: A Woman and Her Family in Revolutionary America* (1984).

Joan Gundersen, *To Be Useful to the World: Women in Revolutionary America, 1740–1790* (1996).

Ronald Hoffman and Peter J. Albert, eds., *Women in the Age of the American Revolution* (1989).

Linda Kerber, *Women of the Republic: Intellect and Ideology in Revolutionary America* (1980).

Mary Beth Norton, *Liberty's Daughters: The Revolutionary Experience of American Women, 1750–1800* (1980).

SLAVERY

Ira Berlin and Ronald Hoffman, *Slavery and Freedom in the Age of the American Revolution* (1983).

Jeffrey Crow, *The Black Experience in Revolutionary North Carolina* (1977).

David Brion Davis, *The Problem of Slavery in the Age of Revolution, 1770–1823* (1975).

Sylvia Frey, *Water from the Rock: Black Resistance in a Revolutionary Age* (1991).

Winthrop D. Jordan, *White over Black: American Attitudes toward the Negro, 1550–1812* (1968).

Sidney Kaplan and Emma Nogrady Kaplan, *The Black Presence in the Era of the American Revolution* (1989).

Duncan J. Macleod, *Slavery, Race, and the American Revolution* (1974).

Philip Morgan, *Slave Counterpoint* (1998).

Donald L. Robinson, *Slavery in the Structure of American Politics, 1765–1820* (1971).

REGIONAL STUDIES

Richard R. Beeman, *The Evolution of the Southern Backcountry: A Case Study of Lunenburg County, Virginia, 1746–1832* (1984).

T. H. Breen, *Tobacco Culture: The Mentality of the Great Tidewater Planters on the Eve of the American Revolution* (1985).

Richard D. Brown, *Revolutionary Politics in Massachusetts: The Boston Committee of Correspondence and the Towns, 1772–1774* (1970).

Richard Bushman, *King and People in Provincial Massachusetts* (1985).

Edward Countryman, *A People in Revolution: The American Revolution and Political Society in New York, 1760–1790* (1981).

Jere R. Daniell, *Experiment in Republicanism: New Hampshire Politics and the Revolution, 1741–1794* (1970).

A. Roger Ekirch, *"Poor Carolina": Politics and Society in North Carolina, 1729–1776* (1981).

Larry R. Gerlach, *Prologue to Independence: New Jersey in the Coming of the Revolution* (1976).

Paul Gilje, *Road to Mobocracy: Popular Disorder in New York City, 1763–1834* (1987).

Robert A. Gross, *The Minutemen and Their World* (1976).

Ronald Hoffman, *A Spirit of Dissension: Economics, Politics, and the Revolution in Maryland* (1973).

Rhys Isaac, *The Transformation of Virginia, 1740–1790* (1982).

Stephen E. Lucas, *Portents of Rebellion: Rhetoric and Revolution in Philadelphia, 1765–1776* (1976).

William Pencak, *Politics and Revolution in Provincial Massachusetts* (1981).

Bruce A. Ragsdale, *A Planters' Republic: The Search for Economic Independence in Revolutionary Virginia* (1996).

Steven Rossman, *Arms, Country, and Class: The Philadelphia Militia and the "Lower Sort" during the American Revolution* (1987).

Albert H. Tillson, *Gentry and Common Folk: Political Culture on a Virginia Frontier, 1740–1789* (1991).

Richard Walsh, *Charleston's Sons of Liberty: A Study of the Artisans, 1763–1789* (1959).

PAINTED DRUM

Drums were essential military equipment in eighteenth-century wars. Small to carry but loud in use, they provided a percussive beat that penetrated the din of the battlefield to signal troop advances, retreats, or other field movements. Drummers often stood right behind soldiers in firing formation, regulating the timing of each volley of shots. The eagle painted on this Revolutionary-era drum from Fort Ticonderoga in New York holds a banner inscribed "Sons of Liberty," a name adopted in 1765 to distinguish protesters of British policies toward the colonies.
Fort Ticonderoga Museum.

THE WAR FOR AMERICA
1775–1783

6

ABIGAIL ADAMS WAS IMPATIENT for American independence. While her husband, John, was away in Philadelphia as a member of the Second Continental Congress, Abigail tended house and farm in Braintree, Massachusetts, just south of British-occupied Boston. She had four young children to look after, and in addition to her female duties, such as cooking, sewing, and making soap, she also had to shoulder male duties in her husband's absence—hiring farm help, managing rental property, selling the crop. John wrote to her often, approving of the fine "Farmeress" who was conducting his business so well. She replied, conveying news of the family along with shrewd commentary on revolutionary politics. In December 1775, she chastised the congress for being too timid and urged that independence be declared. A few months later, she astutely observed to John that southern slave owners might shrink from a war in the name of liberty: "I have sometimes been ready to think that the passion for Liberty cannot be Equally strong in the Breasts of those who have been accustomed to deprive their fellow Creatures of theirs."

"I long to hear that you have declared an independency," she wrote in March 1776. "And by the way in the new Code of Laws which I suppose it will be necessary for you to make I desire you would Remember the Ladies, and be more generous and favourable to them than your ancestors." If Abigail was politically precocious for being in favor of independence and for being suspicious of slave owners' devotion to liberty, she showed herself to be positively visionary in this extraordinary plea to her husband to "Remember the Ladies." "Do not put such unlimited power into the hands of the Husbands," she advised. "Remember all Men would be tyrants if they could." Abigail had put her finger on another form of tyranny that was rarely remarked on in her society: that of men over women. "If particular care and attention is not paid to the Ladies," she jokingly threatened, "we are determined to foment a Rebellion, and will not hold ourselves bound by any Laws in which we have no voice, or Representation."

John Adams dismissed his wife's provocative idea as a "saucy" suggestion: "As to your extraordinary Code of Laws, I cannot but Laugh." The Revolution had perhaps unleashed discontent among other dependent groups, he allowed; children, apprentices, students, Indians, and blacks had grown "disobedient" and "insolent." "But your Letter was the first Intimation that another Tribe more numerous and powerful than all the rest were grown discontented." Men were too smart to repeal their "Masculine Systems," John assured her, for otherwise they would find themselves living under a "despotism of the petticoat."

This clever exchange between husband and wife in 1776 says much about the cautious, limited radicalism of the American Revolution. Both John and Abigail Adams understood (Abigail probably far more than John) that ungluing the hierarchical bond between the king and his subjects potentially unglued other kinds of social inequalities. John was surely joking in listing the groups made unruly in the

ABIGAIL ADAMS

Abigail Smith Adams was twenty-two when she sat for this pastel portrait in 1766. A wife for two years and a mother for one, Adams exhibits a steady, intelligent gaze. Pearls and a lace collar anchor her femininity, while her facial expression projects a confidence and maturity not often credited to young women of the 1760s.

Courtesy of the Massachusetts Historical Society ©.

more cautiously hoping for reconciliation, had their hands full in 1775 and 1776. The war had already begun, and it fell to the congress to raise an army, finance it, and explore diplomatic alliances with foreign countries. For the next six years, the war for America engrossed everyone's attention. In part, it was a classic war with professional armies and textbook battles. But it was also a civil war in America, at times even a brutal guerrilla war, of committed rebels versus loyalists.

Only in one glorious moment did the congress issue a ringing statement about social hierarchy and how it would be rearranged in America after submission to the king was undone. That was on July 4, 1776, when the Declaration of Independence asserted in its preamble that "all men are created equal." This striking phrase went completely unremarked in the two days of congressional debate spent tinkering with the language of the Declaration. The solvent to dissolve social inequalities in America was created at that moment, but none of the men at the congress, or even Abigail Adams up in Braintree, fully realized it at the time.

The Second Continental Congress

On May 10, 1775, nearly one month after the fighting at Lexington and Concord, the Second Continental Congress assembled in Philadelphia. The congress immediately set to work on two crucial and seemingly contradictory tasks: to raise and supply an army and to negotiate a reconciliation with England. But as the war progressed and hopes of reconciliation faded, delegates at the congress began to ponder the treasonous act of declaring independence.

Assuming Political and Military Authority

Like the First Continental Congress, the second had no legal authority for existing. Neither did most of the legislatures that had selected the delegates to go to Philadelphia. The political leadership of one colony after another subverted British authority by simply assuming power on its own. The same pattern was replicated in town after town as well: Men who had once been the selectmen or town councillors now called themselves the committee of public

spirit of a challenge to authority, for children, apprentices, and students were hardly rebellious in the 1770s. But it would soon prove to be an uncomfortable joke, because Indians and blacks did take up the cause of their own liberty during the Revolution, and the great majority of them saw their liberty best served by joining the British side in the war.

Though Abigail Adams was impatient for independence, many other Americans feared separation from Britain. What kind of civilized country had no king? Who, if not Britain, would protect Americans from the French and Spanish? How could the colonies possibly win a war against the most powerful military machine on the globe? Reconciliation, not independence, was favored by many.

Members of the Continental Congress, whether they were pro-independence like John Adams or safety, of inspection, or of correspondence, and took it upon themselves to be the ruling body of the town. The inspiration for such creative government came initially from the Coercive Acts that had crippled town government in Massachusetts in 1774. Government by committee spread to other colonies when the First Continental Congress implemented the Continental Association and recommended that local committees of public safety form to enforce economic boycotts of British goods.

Royal administrators found there was little they could do to stop such actions, with no police force and a militia of, at best, uncertain loyalty. For their own protection, most governors packed their bags and sailed for England. By the end of 1775, royal authority was virtually dead in the colonies, a feat accomplished with hardly a single act of violence.

The delegates to the Second Continental Congress were well-established political figures in their home colonies, but they still had to learn to know and trust each other, and they found that they were not of similar minds about the political issues facing them. The Adams cousins John and Samuel defined the radical end of the spectrum, favoring independence from England. John Dickinson of Pennsylvania, no longer the eager revolutionary who had dashed off *Letters from a Farmer* back in 1767, was now a moderate, seeking reconciliation with England. George Washington showed up wearing his old military uniform from the French and Indian War, a conspicuous hawkish declaration. Benjamin Franklin, in contrast, was feared by some to be a British spy. He had returned from an eleven-year residence in England just five days before the congress met. His long sojourn abroad, plus his long silences in the congress in the first months, made his loyalty suspect. Mutual suspicions flourished easily when the undertaking was so dangerous, opinions were so varied, and a misstep could spell disaster.

Most of the delegates were not yet prepared to break with England. Total independence was an alarming idea to many, and some legislatures, chiefly those in the middle colonies such as New York and Pennsylvania, had instructed their delegates to oppose any such move. Some felt that government without a monarchical element was surely unworkable. Others feared that the colonies would always need the protection of England against their traditional enemies, France and Spain, and that independence would therefore be suicidal. Colonies that traded actively with England feared undermining their economies. Nor were the vast majority of ordinary Americans ready or able to envision independence from the British monarchy. From the Stamp Act of 1765 to the Coercive Acts of 1774, the constitutional struggle with England had turned on the issue of parliamentary power. During that decade almost no one had questioned the legitimacy of the monarchy.

The few men at the Continental Congress who did think that independence was desirable were, not surprisingly, the Massachusetts delegates. Their colony had been stripped of civil government under the Coercive Acts and their capital was occupied by the British army. Even so, those men knew that it was premature to push for a break with England. John Adams wrote to Abigail in June 1775: "America is a great, unwieldy body. Its progress must be slow. It is like a large fleet sailing under convoy. The fleetest sailors must wait for the dullest and slowest."

From the Stamp Act of 1765 to the Coercive Acts of 1774, the constitutional struggle with England had turned on the issue of parliamentary power. Almost no one had questioned the legitimacy of the monarchy.

As slow as the American colonies were in sailing toward political independence, they needed to take swift action to coordinate a military defense, for the Massachusetts countryside was under threat of further attack and the New England militias were clearly inadequate. Even the hesitant moderates in the congress agreed that a military buildup was necessary. Around the country, militia units from New York to Georgia collected arms and drilled on village greens in anticipation. On June 14, the congress voted to create an army, which mainly meant proclaiming that the New England soldiers dug in around Boston *were* the American army, henceforth called the Continental army and directed and paid by the congress. The congress also called for ten companies of riflemen from Virginia, Maryland, and Pennsylvania to join the New England troops.

Choosing a commander in chief to lead the army presented the congress with an opportunity to demonstrate that this was no local war of a single rebellious colony. The most obvious candidate for the job was Artemas Ward from Massachusetts, a veteran officer from the French and Indian War, who was already commanding the soldiers massed around Boston. But congress instead turned to a southerner, George Washington, a man not much known beyond his native Virginia. Washington's appointment sent the message to England that there was widespread commitment to war beyond New England.

Next a committee of the congress drew up a document titled "A Declaration of the Causes and Necessity of Taking Up Arms," which rehearsed familiar arguments about the tyranny of Parliament and the need to defend traditional English liberties. This declaration was first drafted by a young Virginia planter, Thomas Jefferson, a newcomer to the congress and a radical on the question of independence. The moderate John Dickinson, fearing that the declaration would offend England and rule out reconciliation, was allowed to rewrite it; however, he still left much of Jefferson's highly charged language about choosing "to die freemen rather than to live slaves." Even a man as reluctant for independence as Dickinson acknowledged the necessity of military defense against an invading army.

To pay for the military buildup, the congress authorized a currency issue of two million dollars. The Continental dollars were merely paper; they did not represent gold or silver, for the congress owned no precious metals. The delegates somewhat naively expected that the currency would be accepted as valuable on trust as it spread in the population through the hands of soldiers, farmers, munitions suppliers, and beyond.

In just two months, the Second Continental Congress had created an army, declared war, and issued its own currency. It had taken on the major functions of a legitimate government, both military and financial, without any legal basis for its authority, for it had not—and would not for a full year—declare independence from the legitimate authority of the king. Equally unnoticed, the congress's assumption of governance lacked any real power to compel compliance by Americans. Enthusiasm for the cause drew recruits to the army, and optimism kept the newly printed Continental dollars afloat at full value for a time. But when that initial enthusiasm waned, the congress and the war effort fell on hard times.

Pursuing Both War and Peace

Three days after the congress voted to raise the Continental army, one of the bloodiest battles of the entire Revolution occurred. The British commander in Boston, Thomas Gage, had recently received troop reinforcements, three talented major generals (William Howe, John Burgoyne, and Henry Clinton), and new instructions to root out the rebels around Boston. But before Gage could take the offensive, Massachusetts and Connecticut militias fortified the hilly terrain of Charlestown, a peninsula just north of Boston, on the night of June 16, 1775.

The British generals could have nipped off the peninsula where it met the mainland, to box in the Americans. But General Howe insisted on a bold frontal assault, sending his 2,500 soldiers across the water and up the hill, in an intimidating but potentially costly attack. The American troops, 1,400 strong, held their fire until the British were about twenty yards away. At that distance the musket volley was sure and deadly, and the British turned back. Twice more General Howe sent his men up the hill to receive the same blast of firepower; each time they had to step around the bodies felled in the previous attempts.

On the third assault, the British took the hill, mainly because the American ammunition supply gave out, and the defenders quickly retreated across the Charlestown neck. The Battle of Bunker Hill was thus a British victory, but an expensive one. The dead numbered 226 on the British side, with more than 800 wounded; the Americans suffered 140 dead, 271 wounded, and 30 captured. As General Clinton later remarked, "It was a dear bought victory; another such would have ruined us."

General Clinton wanted to pursue the fleeing Americans to their headquarters at Cambridge, a few miles away, but Howe overruled him and pulled the army back to Boston. There they sat, penned up, unwilling to risk more raids into the countryside. Their food had to be shipped in by British naval vessels. If the British had had any grasp of the basic instability of the

The Battle of Bunker Hill, 1775

AN EXACT VIEW OF THE LATE BATTLE AT CHARLESTOWN
This dramatic panorama is the earliest visual representation of the Battle of Bunker Hill. On sale to the public just six weeks after the battle, the engraving shows Charlestown in flames and the British regiments in retreat after their first assault on the Americans, who are dug in along the crest of the hill. The artist, Bernard Romans, was a noted cartographer, military engineer, linguist, and mathematician. Born in the Netherlands, he came to America as a British-paid surveyor, but he took the American side in the Revolution. Romans produced maps of the war zones, bought by Americans eager to track the geography of war. His 11" by 16" eyewitness depiction of Bunker Hill, produced in multiple copies, some of which were hand painted like this one, likely deco-rated many a patriot's wall. A halfsize copy was engraved and inserted in an issue of the **Pennsylvania Magazine,** *a monthly periodical edited by Thomas Paine.*
Courtesy of the John Carter Brown Library at Brown University.

American units gathered at Cambridge, they might have pushed westward and perhaps decisively de-feated the core of the Continental army in its in-fancy. Instead they lingered in Boston, abandoning it without a fight nine months later.

A week after Bunker Hill, when General Wash-ington arrived to take charge of the new Continen-tal army, he found enthusiastic but undisciplined troops. Sanitation was an unknown concept, with in-adequate latrines fouling the campground. Drunk-enness on duty was common, and soldiers appeared to be free to come and go at will. The amazed gen-eral attributed the disarray to the New England cus-tom of letting militia units elect their own officers, a custom he felt undermined deference and respect. A captain from a Connecticut regiment was spotted shaving one of his own men, an inappropriate ges-ture of personal service on the part of a superior of-ficer. But in civilian life the captain was a barber; he had been chosen as an officer by the men of his town, who saw nothing strange in his practicing his trade in the camp. Washington moved quickly to establish military discipline, staging whippings and frequent courts-martial to impress on the soldiers the impor-tance of obedience to superiors. "Discipline is the soul of the army," he stated.

While military plans moved forward, the Sec-ond Continental Congress pursued its second, contradictory objective, reconciliation with England. Delegates from the middle colonies, especially Pennsylvania, Delaware, and New York, whose merchants depended on trade with England, urged that channels for negotiation remain open. Congressional moderates led by John Dickinson engineered an appeal to the king, called the Olive Branch Petition, in July 1775. The petition affirmed loyalty to the monarchy and resorted to a convenient fiction of blaming all the troubles on bad advice from the king's ministers and on Parliament. It proposed that the American colonial assemblies be recognized as individual parliaments, all under the umbrella of the monarchy. That Dickinson himself could write both the "Declaration on the Causes and Necessity of Taking Up Arms" and the Olive Branch Petition within a few days of each other shows how ambivalent the American position was in the summer of 1775.

By late fall 1775, however, reconciliation was out of the question. King George rejected the Olive Branch Petition and heatedly condemned the Americans, calling them rebels, traitors, and enemies. It was thereafter hard to maintain the illusion that ministers and not the king himself were to blame for the conflict. And while the Continental Congress still shied away from an official declaration of independence, moderates like Dickinson would not be able to keep a lid on revolutionary sentiments much longer.

Thomas Paine and the Case for Independence

Pressure for independence was pushed into high gear starting in January of 1776, when a pamphlet titled *Common Sense* appeared in Philadelphia. Thomas Paine, its author, was an English artisan and coffeehouse intellectual who had befriended Benjamin Franklin in London. He came to America in the fall of 1774 with letters of introduction from Franklin to several Philadelphia printers. He landed a job with the *Pennsylvania Magazine* and soon met delegates from the Second Continental Congress. With their encouragement, he wrote *Common Sense* to lay out a lively and compelling case for complete independence.

In simple yet forceful language, Paine elaborated on the absurdities of the British monarchy. Why should one man, by accident of birth, claim extensive power over others? he asked. A king might be foolish or wicked. "One of the strongest natural proofs of the folly of hereditary right in

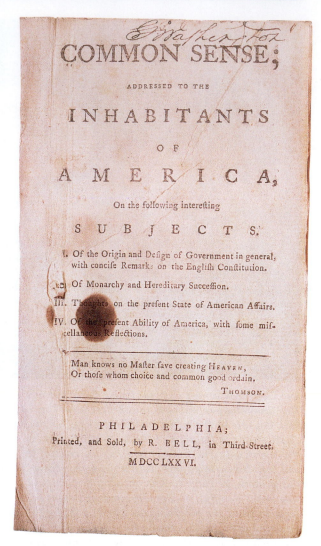

WASHINGTON'S INSCRIBED COPY OF *COMMON SENSE*
Thomas Paine's incendiary pamphlet **Common Sense** *was widely read after its publication in Philadelphia in January 1776. Copies were passed from hand to hand and read aloud in public. Virginian George Washington, a member of the Second Continental Congress, inscribed his name on the title page to declare his ownership of Paine's booklet.*
Boston Athenaeum.

kings," Paine wrote, "is that nature disapproves it; otherwise she would not so frequently turn it into ridicule by giving mankind an *ass for a lion*."

Calling the king of England an ass broke through the automatic deference most Americans still had for the monarchy. And by moving the focus from Parliament to the king, Paine succeeded in making a case for independence. To replace monarchy, he advocated republican government, based on the consent of the people. Rulers, according to Paine, were only representatives of the people, and the best form of government relied on frequent elections to achieve the most direct democracy possible.

Paine's pamphlet sold more than 150,000 copies in a matter of weeks. Newspapers reprinted it; men read it aloud in taverns and coffeehouses; John Adams sent a copy to Abigail Adams, who passed it around to neighbors. Another of John Adams's correspondents wrote him in late February that ninety-nine out of a hundred New Englanders desired an official declaration of independence. But of course New England had two armies on its doorstep to fire its spirit. The middle and southern colonies, under no immediate threat of violence, remained cautious.

In simple yet forceful language, Paine elaborated on the absurdities of the British monarchy. Why should one man, by accident of birth, claim extensive power over others? he asked.

One factor hastening official independence was the prospect of an alliance with France, Britain's archrival. France was willing to provide military supplies as well as naval power, but not without firm assurance that the Americans would separate from England. News that the British were negotiating for German mercenary soldiers further solidified support for independence. By May, all but four colonies were agitating for a declaration. The exceptions were Pennsylvania, Maryland, New York, and South Carolina, the latter two containing large loyalist populations.

Finally on June 7, 1776, the Virginia delegation introduced a resolution calling for independence. Here was the assertion everyone had been anticipating, some with impatience, others with dread. (See "Documenting the American Promise," page 190.) The moderates still commanded enough support to postpone a vote on the measure until July, which allowed them time to go home and consult about this extreme step. In the meantime, the congress appointed a committee, with Thomas Jefferson and others, to draft a longer document setting out the justification for independence.

On June 7, 1776, the Virginia delegation introduced a resolution calling for independence. Here was the assertion everyone had been anticipating, some with impatience, others with dread.

On July 1, the first vote was taken on the resolution of June 7. Pennsylvania and South Carolina voted against it, while the two-man Delaware delegation was split and the New Yorkers abstained. On July 2, after a night of politicking, a second vote shifted South Carolina and Pennsylvania into the pro-independence camp, and a newly elected delegate from Delaware rode all night to cast the deciding pro-independence vote. The New Yorkers still abstained, but since they had not voted negatively, the congress could truthfully claim that the resolution for independence had passed without a negative vote.

On July 2 and 3, the congress turned to the document drafted by Thomas Jefferson and his committee. Jefferson began with a preamble that articulated philosophical principles about natural rights, equality, the right of revolution, and the consent of the governed as the only true basis for government. He then listed more than two dozen specific grievances against King George. The congress merely glanced at the political philosophy, finding nothing exceptional in it; the ideas about natural rights and the consent of the governed were seen as "self-evident truths," just as the document claimed. In itself, this absence of comment showed a remarkable transformation in political thinking since the end of the French and Indian War. The single phrase declaring the natural equality of "all men" was also passed over without comment; no one elaborated on its radical implications.

What the congress did wrangle over were the specific grievances, especially the issue of slavery. Jefferson had included an impassioned statement blaming the king for slavery, which delegates from Georgia and South Carolina struck out. They had no intention of denouncing their labor system as an evil practice. But the congress let stand another of Jefferson's fervent grievances, blaming the king for mobilizing "the merciless Indian Savages" into bloody frontier warfare.

On July 4, the amendments to Jefferson's text were complete and the document was formally

The Issue of Independence

*I*n May and June 1776, talk of independence gripped Americans everywhere. When would it come? What would it mean? Why was the congress so slow to declare it? Town meetings all over Massachusetts were voting for immediate action; with war already on their doorstep, they saw no reason to delay. In contrast, political leaders in New York City were ambivalent and divided, and they did their best to avert calls for action. Independence-minded planters in Virginia worried that the common people might take a completely different meaning from the rush for independence. And merchants everywhere expressed anxiety that a declaration would kill all chances at reconciliation. While the congress no doubt hoped that the July 4 Declaration of Independence would help unite the country, the reality was that disunity was fearfully evident.

DOCUMENT 1. The Town Meeting of Scituate, Massachusetts, Pledges to Fight for Independence, June 4, 1776

Men of Scituate debated independence on June 4 and conveyed their remarks to their town representative.

The Inhabitants of this Town being called together on the recommendation of our General Assembly to Signify our minds on the great point of Independence on Great-Britain, think fit to Instruct you on that head.

The Ministry of that Kingdom, having formed a design of Subjecting the Colonies to a distant, external and absolute power in all Cases whatsoever, wherein the Colonies have not, nor in the nature of things can have any share by Representation, have, for a course of years past, exerted their utmost Art and Endeavours to put the same plan, so destructive to both Countries, into Execution. But finding it, through the noble and virtuous opposition of the Sons of Freedom, impracticable by means of mere political Artifice and Corruption, they have at length had a fatal Recourse to a Standing Army, so repugnant to the nature of a free Government, to fire and Sword, to Bloodshed and Devastation, calling in the aid of foreign Troops, as well as endeavouring to stir up the Savages of the wilderness to exercise their barbarities upon us, being deter-

mined, by all appearances, if practicable, to extirpate the Americans from the face of the Earth, unless they tamely resign the Rights of humanity, and to repeople this once happy Country with the ready Sons of Vassalage, if such can be found.

We therefor, Apprehending such a subjection utterly inconsistant with the just rights and blessings of Society, unanimously Instruct you to endeavour that our Delegates in Congress be informed, in case that Representative Body of the Continent should think fit to declare the Colonies Independant of Great Britain, of our readiness and determination to assist with our Lives and Fortunes in Support of that, we apprehend, necessary Measure.

SOURCE: Henry S. Commager and Richard B. Morris, eds., *The Spirit of Seventy-Six* (1958; reprint, 1975), 298–99. Original in the Massachusetts Archives, CLVI, 103.

DOCUMENT 2. Minutes of the New York Assembly, June 3, 1776

In New York, a group of craftsmen drafted their own document justifying independence. They delivered it to the assembly and encountered a chilly reception.

A number of citizens, who style themselves a Committee of Mechanicks, having come into the Congress-Chamber . . . and delivered at the Chair a paper which they style an Address, the House was ordered to be cleared, in order that the said paper may be inspected, to discover whether it is proper for this Congress to receive the same. . . . The door was opened, and the said citizens were desired to come into the Chamber, . . . the said paper being read by Lewis Thibou.

They therein set forth that they are devoted friends to their bleeding country; that they are afflicted by beholding her struggling under heavy loads of oppression and tyranny; . . . that their Prince is deaf to petitions for redressing our grievances; that one year has not sufficed to satisfy the rage of a cruel Ministry in their bloody pursuits, designed to reduce us to be slaves, and to be taxed by them without our consent; that, therefore, they rather wish to separate from such oppressors; and declare that, if this Congress should think proper to instruct their Delegates in Continental Congress to cause these United Colonies to become independent of Great Britain, it would give them the highest satisfaction.

We are of opinion that the Continental Congress alone have that enlarged view of our political circumstances which will enable them to decide upon those measures which are necessary for the general welfare. We cannot presume . . . to make or declare any resolutions upon so momentous a concern; but are determined patiently to await and firmly to abide by whatever a majority of that august body shall think needful.

SOURCE: Peter Force, *American Archives*, 4th ser., vol. 6 (1846), 1362–63.

DOCUMENT 3. Virginian Landon Carter Writes to Fellow Planter George Washington, May 9, 1776

In Virginia, ordinary citizens circulated petitions pressing for a Declaration of Independence in May 1776. Landon Carter, a wealthy and worried planter, feared that what they meant by independence might be far more radical than he could accept. In a letter to George Washington, Carter expressed his concerns.

I need only tell you of one definition that I heard of Independency: It was expected to be a form of Government that, by being independent of the rich men, every man would then be able to do as he pleased. . . . One of the Delegates [to the Virginia assembly] I heard exclaim against the Patrolling law, because a poor man was made to pay for keeping a rich man's slaves in order. I shamed the fool so much for it that he slunk away; but he got elected by it. . . . I know who I am writing to, and therefore I am not quite so confined in my expressions. . . . And from hence it is that our independency is to arise! Papers, it seems, are everywhere circulating about for poor ignorant creatures to sign, as directions to their Delegates to endeavour at an independency. In vain do we ask to let it be explained what is designed by it!

SOURCE: Peter Force, *American Archives*, 4th ser., vol. 6 (1846), 389–92.

DOCUMENT 4. Merchants Joseph Reed and Robert Morris Exchange Fading Hopes for Reconciliation, July 1776

Even after July 4, many merchants remained dubious about the wisdom of independence. The Philadelphia merchant Joseph Reed wrote to Robert Morris on July 18.

I fear the die is irrevocably cast, and that we must play out the game, however doubtful and desperate. . . . My private judgment led me to think that if the two great cardinal points of exemption from British taxation and charge of internal government could have been secured, our happiness and prosperity would have been best promoted by preserving the dependence. The Declaration of Independence is a new and very strong objection to entering into any negotiation. . . . But I fancy there are numbers, and some of them firm in the interests of America, who would think an overture ought not to be rejected.

Robert Morris replied to Reed on July 21.

I am sorry to say there are some amongst us that cannot bear the thought of Reconciliation on any terms. I cannot help Condemning this disposition as it must be founded in keen Resentment or on interested Views. . . . I have uniformly voted against & opposed the declaration of Independance because in my poor oppinion it was an improper time and will neither promote the interest or redound to the honor of America, for it has caused division when we wanted Union.

SOURCE: John H. Hazelton, *The Declaration of Independence: Its History* (1906), 226–28.

QUESTIONS FOR ANALYSIS AND DEBATE

1. What reasons did the men of Scituate, Massachusetts, give for favoring immediate independence? Who asked them to vote on this matter?

2. Did the mechanics of New York agree in their reasoning with the men of Scituate? What evidence is there in this document that the New York Assembly was not friendly to their petition?

3. Document 3 alludes to petitions circulating in Virginia that make these elite men uneasy. Why?

4. Why do the two Philadelphia merchants in Document 4 oppose independence at this juncture?

DECLARATION OF INDEPENDENCE READ TO A CROWD
Printed copies of the Declaration of Independence were read aloud in public places throughout America in the week after July 4, 1776, often accompanied by carefully orchestrated celebrations.
Library of Congress.

www.bedfordstmartins.com/tap SEE THE ONLINE STUDY GUIDE for more help in analyzing this image.

adopted. Nearly a month later, on August 2, the delegates formally affixed their signatures to the official parchment copy, handwritten by an exacting scribe. Four men, including John Dickinson, declined to sign; several others "signed with regret . . . and with many doubts," according to John Adams. The document was printed and widely distributed. In celebrations in towns and cities it was read aloud. A crowd in New York listened to a public reading of it and then toppled a lead statue of George III on horseback to melt it down for bullets. On July 15, the New York delegation switched from abstention

to endorsement, making the vote on independence truly unanimous.

Printed copies of the Declaration of Independence did not include the signers' names, for they had committed treason, a crime punishable by death. On the day of signing, they had indulged in gallows humor. When Benjamin Franklin paused before signing to look over the Declaration, John Hancock teased him, "Come, come, sir. We must be unanimous. No pulling different ways. We must all hang together." Franklin replied, "Indeed we must all hang together. Otherwise we shall most assuredly hang separately."

The First Year of War, 1775–1776

Both sides had cause to approach the war for America with uneasiness. The Americans, with only inexperienced and undertrained militias, opposed the mightiest military power in the world, and many thought it was foolhardy to expect victory. Further, pockets of loyalism remained strong; the country was not united. But the British faced serious obstacles as well. Their utter disdain for the fighting abilities of the Americans had to be reevaluated in light of their costly Bunker Hill victory. The logistics of supplying an army with food across three thousand miles of water were daunting. And since the British goal was to regain allegiance, not to destroy and conquer, the army was often constrained in its actions.

The American Military Forces

Americans claimed that the initial months of war were purely defensive, triggered by the British army's invasion. But quickly the war also became a rebellion, an overthrowing of long-established authority. As both defenders and rebels, Americans were generally highly motivated to fight, and the potential manpower that could be mobilized was in theory very great.

From the earliest decades of settlement, local defense in the colonies rested with a militia requiring participation from nearly every able-bodied man over age sixteen. When the main threat to public safety was the occasional Indian attack, the local militia made sense. But such attacks were now very rare and mostly limited to the frontier. Southern militias trained with potential slave rebellions in mind, but these too were very rare. The annual muster day in most communities had evolved into a holiday, amounting to a day of drinking, marching, and perhaps shooting practice with small fowling guns or old muskets left over from the French and Indian War.

Militias were best suited to limited engagements, when a local community was under immediate attack. But they were not appropriate for extended wars requiring military campaigns far from home. In forming the Continental army, the congress set enlistment at one year, but army leaders soon learned that that was not enough time to train soldiers and carry out campaigns. A three-year enlistment earned a new soldier a twenty-dollar bonus, paid up front, while men who committed for the duration of the war were promised a postwar land grant of one hundred acres. To make this inducement effective, of course, recruits had to believe that the Americans would win. By early 1777, the army was the largest it would ever be—29,000 troops; it was still not enough.

The Continental Congress assigned troop quotas to each state; local committees of public safety began to function like draft boards. Draftees tended to be the marginal men in a community, such as servants or the unemployed; thus the army had a very different look from the state militias. In some towns, suspected loyalists were drafted first, either as an effective way to smoke them out or as a way to punish them. Although it proved hard to get adequate numbers of men to enlist, the total number of individual enlistments over the course of the war totaled 231,950 men, or roughly one-quarter of the white male population over age sixteen.

Women also served in the Continental army. They were needed to do the daily cooking and washing, and after battle they nursed wounded men. The professional British army established a ratio of one woman to every ten men; in the Continental army, the ratio was set at one woman to fifteen men. Close to twenty thousand women served during the war, probably most of them wives of men in service. Children tagged along as well, and babies were born in the camps and on the road.

Black Americans were at first excluded from the Continental army, a rule that slave owner George Washington made on his fifth day as commander in chief. But as manpower needs increased, the northern states began to welcome free blacks into service; even slaves could serve in some states, with their masters' permission. About five thousand black men served in the Revolutionary War on the rebel side, mostly from the northern states. Black Continental soldiers sometimes were segregated into separate units; two battalions from Rhode Island were entirely black. Just under three hundred blacks joined regiments from Connecticut. While some of these were draftees, others were clearly men inspired by the ideals of freedom being voiced in a war against tyranny. For example, five Connecticut blacks gave "Liberty" as their surname at the time of enlistment, and another eighteen said their name was "Freedom" or "Freeman."

Military service helped to politicize Americans during the early stages of the war. In early 1776, independence was a risky idea, potentially treasonous. But as the war heated up and leaders and

BLACK REVOLUTIONARY WAR SAILOR
Thousands of black men served on the patriot side as soldiers and sailors, usually at the rank of private or ordinary seaman. Their names are preserved in regiment records and crew lists; rarely, however, were their faces preserved. This 1780 portrait by an unknown artist shows an unnamed man, sword and scabbard at hand, dressed in military finery with a ship in view to establish his naval connection.
Collection of A. A. McBurney.

recruiters demanded commitment, some apathetic Americans discovered that apathy had its dangers as well. Anyone who refused to serve ran the risk of being called a traitor to the cause. Military service established one's credentials as a patriot; it became a prime way of defining and demonstrating political allegiance.

Five Connecticut blacks gave "Liberty" as their surname at the time of enlistment, and another eighteen said their name was "Freedom" or "Freeman."

The American army was at times raw and inexperienced and much of the time woefully undermanned. It never had the precision and discipline of European professional armies. But it was never as bad as the British continually assumed. The British were to learn that it was a serious mistake to underrate the enemy.

The British Strategy

The American strategy was relatively straightforward—to repulse and defeat an invading army. The British strategy was not nearly so clear. England wanted to put down a rebellion and restore monarchical power in the colonies, but the question was how to accomplish this. A decisive defeat of the Continental army was essential but not sufficient to end the rebellion, for there were all those militiamen around the countryside to contend with. An armed and highly motivated insurgent population proved a tough enemy.

Furthermore, there was no single political nerve center whose capture would spell certain victory. The Continental Congress floated from place to place, staying just out of reach of the British. During the course of the war, the British captured and for a time occupied every major port city—Boston, New York, Newport, Philadelphia, and Charleston—but with no significant gain. The British needed these harbor cities for their constant caravan of supply ships, but capturing them brought no serious loss to the Americans, 95 percent of whom lived in the countryside.

England's delicate task was to restore the old governments, not to destroy an enemy country. Hence, the British generals were usually reluctant to ravage the countryside, confiscate food, or burn villages and towns. There were thirteen distinct political entities to capture, pacify, and then restore to the crown, and they were spread out in a very long line from New Hampshire to Georgia. Clearly a large land army was required for the job. Without the willingness to seize food from the locals, such an army needed hundreds of supply ships that could keep several months' worth of food in storage. Another ingredient of the British strategy was the assumption (quite untested) that large numbers of Americans remained loyal to the king and would come to the aid of the British army. Without substantial numbers of loyal subjects, the plan to restore old royal governments made no sense.

The overall British plan was a divide-and-conquer approach to recapturing the thirteen colonies. The plan focused first on New York, the state judged to harbor the greatest number of loyal subjects, perhaps as much as half the population. New York offered a geographic advantage as well: Control of the Hudson River would allow the British to isolate the most troublesome states, those in New England. Armies could descend from Canada and move up from New York City along the Hudson River into western Massachusetts. Between a naval blockade on the eastern coast and army raids in the west, Massachusetts would be driven to surrender. Or so the British hoped.

South of New York, in New Jersey and Pennsylvania, the British also expected to find large pockets of loyalist strength to secure their advances. Rebellious citizens would be pressured to sign loyalty oaths to the crown. Virginia was a problem, like Massachusetts, but the British were confident that the Carolinas contained many loyalists and that they could thus isolate and subdue Virginia.

Quebec, New York, and New Jersey

While Washington disciplined his troops in Massachusetts, an American expedition was launched in late 1775 to capture the British cities Montreal and Quebec, a clear sign that the war was not merely a defensive reaction to the invasion of Massachusetts. The two cities were symbolic as well as strategic goals, having been sites of contest in the French-British wars of the 1740s and 1750s. American commanders moved swiftly north to attack before British reinforcements could arrive. A force of New York Continentals commanded by General Richard Montgomery took Montreal easily in September

1775 and then advanced on Quebec. Meanwhile, a second contingent of Continentals led by Colonel Benedict Arnold moved through Maine along the Kennebec River to Quebec, a punishing trek through freezing rain with woefully inadequate food and boats; many men died. Arnold's fierce determination to get to Quebec was heroic, but in human costs the campaign was a tragedy. Arnold and Montgomery jointly attacked Quebec in December but suffered heavy losses and failed to take the city (Map 6.1).

The main action of the first year of war came not in Canada, however, but in New York, the state deemed crucial to England. In August 1776, some 20,000 fresh British troops (including 8,000 German mercenary soldiers, called Hessians) landed on Staten Island, south of New York City. They were joined by regiments from Nova Scotia, bringing the total to nearly 45,000 soldiers, under the command of General Howe. General Washington had anticipated that New York would be Howe's target and had moved his army, numbering about 20,000, from Massachusetts to an area of fortified ground on Long Island.

The Battle of Long Island, in late August 1776, pitted the well-trained British redcoats against a very green Continental army. Howe attacked the American fortifications, inflicting many casualties (1,500 dead and wounded) and spreading panic among the American soldiers, who fled under fire to the eastern edge of Long Island. Howe failed to press forward, however, perhaps remembering the costly victory of Bunker Hill, and in the meantime Washington evacuated his troops to Manhattan Island in the dead of night, under cover of an unusually thick fog.

Washington knew it would be hard to hold Manhattan against a British attack. One of his generals recommended burning the city; two-thirds of the buildings belonged to loyalists anyway, and burning it would prevent the British from housing troops there. Washington vetoed this idea, preferring instead to strip it of ammunition and supplies and leave quickly. He left, moving north out of the city, with the British close on his heels.

From September to November, the two armies jockeyed for position and engaged in limited fighting. In November, Howe finally attacked and captured two critical forts on either side of the Hudson River, Fort Washington and Fort Lee, taking thousands of prisoners. Washington retreated quickly across New Jersey into Pennsylvania. The British

army followed him; at one point, Howe was only one hour behind Washington, but he rested his men for a day and widened the gap. As Howe moved through New Jersey, the Continental Congress, meeting in Philadelphia, fled to Baltimore.

Yet again, Howe unaccountably failed to take advantage of the situation. Had he attacked Washington's army at Philadelphia, he would probably have taken the city. Instead he parked his German troops in winter quarters along the Delaware River. Perhaps he knew that many of the Continental soldiers' enlistment periods ended on December 31, so he felt confident that the Americans would not attack him. But he was wrong. On Christmas—a holiday Germans celebrated with much more spirit (and spirits) than did Americans—Washington recrossed the Delaware River at night with 2,400 men and made a quick capture of the unsuspecting German soldiers at Trenton. The victory was impressively executed, and it did much to restore the sagging morale of the patriot side. For the next two weeks, Washington remained on the offensive, dancing just ahead of the British army, capturing supplies in a clever attack on British units at Princeton on January 3. Soon he was safe in Morristown, in northern New Jersey, settled in for the winter.

All in all, in the first year of declared war, the rebellious Americans had a few isolated moments to feel proud of but also much to worry about. The very inexperienced Continental army had barely hung on in the New York campaign. Washington had shown exceptional daring as well as admirable restraint, but what really saved the American army may have been the repeated reluctance of the British to follow through militarily when they had the advantage.

The Home Front

Battlefields alone did not determine the outcome of the war. Struggles on the home front were equally important. In 1776, each community contained small numbers of highly committed people on both sides and far larger numbers who were either apolitical or uncertain about whether independence was worth a war. The contest for the allegiance of the many neutrals thus was a major factor, and both persuasion and force were used. Revolutionaries who took control of local government often used it to punish loyalists and intimidate neutrals. On their side, loyalists worked to reestablish British

BRITISH NORTH AMERICA

Battle of Quebec
Dec. 31, 1775

Siege of Quebec
Nov. 1775–Mar. 1776

Trois Rivières
June 7, 1776

Arnold 1775

Montgomery 1775

Montgomery 1775

Montreal

St. Lawrence R.

St. Leger

L. Ontario

Fort Stanwix
Held by Americans
under Benedict Arnold,
Aug., 1777

Fort Oswego

Oriskany
Aug. 6, 1777

Mohawk R.

NEW YORK

L. Champlain

Burgoyne

Fort Ticonderoga
Captured by British
July, 1777

L. George

Saratoga
Burgoyne surrenders,
Oct. 17, 1777

Bemis Heights
Oct. 7, 1777

Gates

Albany

Hudson R.

VERMONT
(Claimed by
N.Y. & N.H.)

NEW
HAMPSHIRE

Bennington
Aug. 16, 1777

MASSACHUSETTS

CONNECTICUT

R.I.

MAINE
(part of MASS.)

Kennebec R.

Arnold 1775

Newburyport

Bunker Hill
June 17, 1775

Concord
April 19, 1775

Lexington
April 19, 1775

Siege of Boston
July 1775–March 1776

Howe, 1776

British leave Boston
March 17, 1776

Morristown
American winter quarters
1776–77

Fort Washington

**Fort
Lee**

Long Island

Brooklyn
Aug. 27, 1776

Manhattan

Howe, 1776

N.J.

Princeton
Jan. 3, 1777

Germantown
Oct. 4, 1777

Valley Forge
American winter quarters
1777–78

Washington

Clinton

Trenton
Dec. 26, 1776

Staten Island

Monmouth Court House
June 28, 1778

PENNSYLVANIA

Brandywine Creek
Sept. 11, 1777

Philadelphia
captured by British
under Howe,
Sept. 26, 1777

Delaware R.

MARYLAND

DEL.

Chesapeake Bay

Howe, 1777

VIRGINIA

ATLANTIC
OCEAN

→ American forces
→ British forces
✦ American victories
✦ British victories

0   25   50   75   100 miles
0   50   100 kilometers

authority. The struggle to secure political allegiance was complicated greatly by the wartime instability of the economy. The creative financing of the fledgling government brought hardships as well as opportunities, forcing Americans to confront new manifestations of virtue and corruption.

Patriotism at the Local Level

Committees of correspondence, of public safety, and of inspection dominated the political landscape in patriot communities. These committees took on more than customary local governance; they enforced boycotts, picked army draftees, and policed suspected traitors. They sometimes invaded homes to search for contraband goods.

Loyalists were dismayed by what seemed to them to be excessive or arbitrary power taken on by committees. On occasion, secret and resourceful loyalists managed to win election to these committees in order to subvert them. Others were open with their denunciations. A man in Westchester, New York, described his response to intrusions by committees: "Choose your committee or suffer it to be chosen by a half dozen fools in your neighborhood—open your doors to them—let them examine your tea-cannisters and molasses-jugs, and your wives' and daughters' petty coats—bow and cringe and tremble and quake—fall down and worship our sovereign lord the mob.... Should any pragmatical committee-gentleman come to my house and give himself airs, I shall show him the door, and if he does not soon take himself away, a good hickory cudgel shall teach him better manners." Excessive or not, the powers of the local committees were rarely challenged. Committees of safety and of correspondence became the local governing agencies, and their persuasive powers convinced many middle-of-the-road citizens that neutrality was not a comfortable option.

MAP 6.1

The War in the North, 1775–1778

After the early battles in Massachusetts in 1775, rebel forces invaded Canada but failed to capture Quebec. A large British army landed in New York in August 1776, turning New Jersey into a continual site of battle in 1777 and 1778. Burgoyne arrived to secure Canada and made his attempt to pinch off New England along the Hudson River line, but he was stopped at Saratoga in 1777 in the key battle of the early war years.

Another group new to political life—white women—increasingly demonstrated a capacity for patriotism at the local level as wartime hardships dramatically altered their work routines. Like Abigail Adams on her Braintree farm, many wives with husbands away on military or political service found themselves taking on masculine duties. Their increased competence to tend farms and make business decisions appears to have encouraged some to assert competence in political matters as well. Eliza Wilkinson managed a plantation on the South Carolina coast and talked revolutionary politics with her women friends. "None were greater politicians than the several knots of ladies who met together," she remarked, alert to the unusual turn female conversations had taken. "We commenced perfect statesmen."

Committees of safety and of correspondence became the local governing agencies, and their powers convinced many citizens that neutrality was not a comfortable option.

Women from prominent Philadelphia families went a step beyond political talk to action. In 1780, they formed the Ladies Association, going door to door collecting a substantial sum of money to help support the Continental soldiers. A published broadside, "The Sentiments of an American Woman," defended their female patriotism. "The time is arrived to display the same sentiments which animated us at the beginning of the Revolution, when we renounced the use of teas . . . [and] when our republican and laborious hands spun the flax."

The Loyalists

Between 20 and 30 percent of the American population remained openly loyal to the British monarchy in 1776, and another 20 to 40 percent could be described as neutral. Such a large population base could have sustained the British Empire in America, if only the British army leaders had known how to use it (Map 6.2). In general, loyalists were people who still found the idea of the British Empire, with all its historical, cultural, and economic ties, an appealing vision. They were convinced that American prosperity and stability depended on British rule and on a government anchored by monarchy

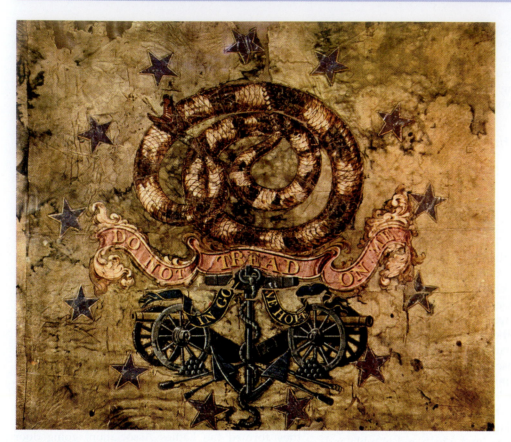

RHODE ISLAND REGIMENT FLAG
In the absence of an official American flag, regiments often created their own symbolic banners. One very popular theme portrayed a coiled rattlesnake paired with the slogan "Don't Tread on Me." Such a flag conveyed a dire warning and a clear point of view about who had started the war in America: the rattler, uniquely American, was deadly only when aroused or provoked. This 1775 flag of an artillery company in Rhode Island offers an unusual variant, using the more formal "do not" instead of "don't." The slogan endures today, showing up on state license plates and as lyrics in popular songs. The Rhode Island flag displays another nearly familiar motto: "In God We Hope." It precedes by almost a century the Civil War–era origins of the modern-day motto on U.S. coinage, "In God We Trust."
Collection of Mr. and Mrs. Boleslaw Mastai.

and aristocracy. Perhaps most of all, they feared democratic tyranny. Like Abigail Adams, they understood that dissolving the automatic respect that submissive subjects had for their king could potentially lead to a society in which all deference and hierarchy came unglued. Adams welcomed this chance to identify tyranny in unequal power relations, as between men and women; loyalists feared it. Patriots seemed to them to be unscrupulous, violent, self-interested men who simply wanted power for themselves.

The most visible and dedicated loyalists (also called Tories by their enemies) were royal officials,

not only top officeholders like Thomas Hutchinson in Massachusetts, but also local judges and customs officers. Wealthy merchants with commercial ties to England were made uneasy by the thought of abandoning the trade protections of navigation acts and the British navy. Urban lawyers of a conservative temperament often found it impossible to imagine forgoing the stability of British law and order. The early-eighteenth-century grants of religious liberty to grateful groups like the Palatine Germans in upstate New York and the French Huguenots in the Carolinas influenced some of them to remain loyal to Britain. Two other religious enclaves, the Quak-

MAP 6.2
Loyalist Strength and Rebel Support
The exact number of loyalists can never be known. No one could have made an accurate count at the time; in addition, political allegiance often shifted with the winds. This map shows the pockets of loyalist strength on which the British relied— the lower Hudson valley and the Carolina piedmont.

READING THE MAP: Which forces were stronger, those loyal to Britain or those rebelling? What areas were contested? If the contested areas ultimately sided with the British, how would the balance of power change? CONNECTIONS: Who was more likely to be a loyalist, and why? How many loyalists left the United States, and where did they go?

www.bedfordstmartins.com /tap   SEE THE ONLINE STUDY GUIDE for more help in analyzing this map.

ers and the Moravians, located in Pennsylvania and North Carolina, were pacifists by religious conviction and were therefore often treated as though they were loyalists.

Some were loyalists merely as a product of oppositional politics with leading patriot men. For example, backcountry farmers in the Carolinas gravitated toward loyalism out of resentment over the political and economic power of the lowlands gentry. Southern slaves had their own resentments against the white slave-owning class. Many thousands in Virginia responded to Lord Dunmore's promise of eventual freedom if they would defect and aid the British, and more still in South Carolina ran off to Charleston to seek refuge with the British army when it occupied the city.

Many Indian tribes attempted to maintain neutrality at the start of the war, seeing it as a civil war between English and American brothers. But eventually most were drawn in, many taking the British side. The powerful Iroquois confederacy divided, with Mohawks, Cayugas, Senecas, and Onondagas lining up with the British, while the Oneidas and Tuscaroras aided the Americans. One young Mohawk leader, Thayendanegea (known to Americans as Joseph Brant), traveled to England in 1775 to complain to King George about how the colonists repeatedly deceived the Mohawks. "It is very hard when we have let the King's subjects have so much of our lands for so little value," he wrote, "they should want to cheat us in this manner of the small spots we have left for our women and children to live on. We are tired out in making complaints & getting no redress." Thayendanegea negotiated Indian support for the king in exchange for protection from encroaching settlers, under a revived implementation of the Proclamation Act of 1763. In western Pennsylvania and Ohio, the Shawnees and

JOSEPH BRANT
The Mohawk leader Thayendanegea, called Joseph Brant by Americans, had been educated in English ways at Eleazar Wheelock's New England school (which became Dartmouth College in 1769). In 1775, Brant traveled to England with another warrior to negotiate Mohawk support for the British. There he had his portrait painted by George Romney. The thirty-four-year-old Brant wears a feudal gorget around his neck over his English shirt (compare with Washington, page 147), along with Indian armbands and headdress.
National Gallery of Canada, Ottawa.

lenged the emerging patriot side using pamphlets, broadsides, and newspapers; every major city had one or sometimes two loyalist printers. In New York City in 1776, some loyalists even circulated a broadside titled "A Declaration of Dependence," in rebuttal to the Congress's July 4 manifesto, denouncing this "most unnatural, unprovoked Rebellion that ever disgraced the annals of Time."

Pockets of loyalism existed everywhere, in the middle colonies, in the backcountry of the southern colonies, and out beyond the Appalachian Mountains in Indian country.

Speeches and rallies amplified the spread of loyalism in backcountry areas where print culture had not fully penetrated. Loyalist ministers used their pulpits, while other defenders of the empire staged rallies or disrupted patriot gatherings. At an open-air rally in backcountry South Carolina in 1775, a loyalist elbowed his way to the platform to remind the audience of the superior might of the British army and of the damage to trade independence would surely bring. But his winning argument was to invoke the backcountry's resentments of the coastal planters' wealth and political power: It is ironic, he said, that "the charge of our intending to enslave you should come oftenest from the mouths of those lawyers who in your southern provinces, at least, have long made you slaves to themselves."

Who Is a Traitor?

The rough treatment that loyalists experienced at the hands of the revolutionaries seemed to substantiate their worst fears. In June 1775, the First Continental Congress passed a resolution declaring loyalists to be traitors. Over the next year, state after state wrote laws defining treasonable acts, such as joining the British army or providing it with food or ammunition. In some states, it was treason to discourage men from enlisting in the Continental army or to say or print anything undermining patriot morale. Punishments ranged from house arrest and suspension of voting privileges to confiscation of property and deportation. And sometimes self-appointed committees of Tory hunters bypassed the

Delawares started out as pro-American but shifted to the British by 1778–1779 in the face of repeated depredations by Americans.

Pockets of loyalism thus existed everywhere, in the middle colonies, in the backcountry of the southern colonies, and out beyond the Appalachian Mountains in Indian country. Even New England towns at the heart of turmoil, like Concord, Massachusetts, had a small and increasingly silenced core of loyalists who refused to countenance armed revolution.

The loyalists were most vocal between 1774 and 1776, when the possibility of a full-scale rebellion against England was still uncertain. Loyalists chaljudicial niceties and terrorized loyalists, raiding their houses or tarring and feathering them.

A question rarely asked in the heat of the revolutionary moment was whether the wives of loyalists were traitors as well. When loyalist families fled the country, they usually fled together, and property held in the name of the family patriarch was then confiscated. But what if the wife stayed? One Connecticut woman brought witnesses before a justice of the peace to testify that she was "a steady and true and faithful friend to the American states in opposition to her husband, who has been of quite a different character." In such cases, the court typically allowed the woman to keep her dower rights (one-third of the property, the amount she was due if widowed) and confiscated the rest. But even when the wife fled with her husband, was she necessarily a traitor? Could she have independent political beliefs apart from her husband's? If he ordered her to flee with him, was she not obligated to go? Such questions came up in several lawsuits after the Revolution, where descendants of refugee loyalists sued to regain property that had entered the family through the mother's line of inheritance. In one well-publicized case in Massachusetts in 1805, the issue of female responsibility for political acts was debated by some of the best legal minds of the time. The outcome confirmed the traditional view of women as political blank slates; the American son of

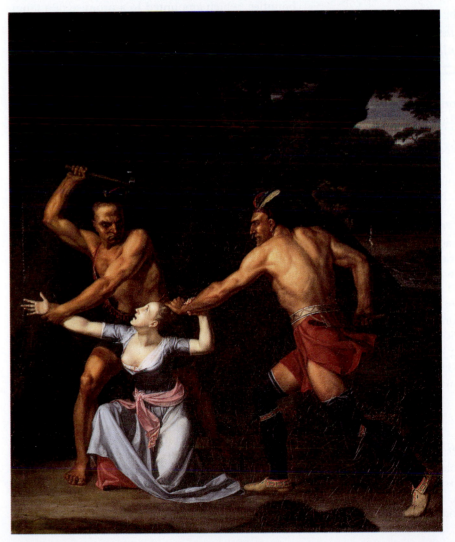

DEATH OF JANE MCCREA
This 1804 painting by John Vanderlyn memorializes the martyr legend of Jane McCrea. McCrea lived with her patriot family in upstate New York, but in July 1777 she fled to join her fiancé, a loyalist fighting with Burgoyne's army. She was murdered en route, allegedly by Iroquois allies of the British. The American general Horatio Gates sent Burgoyne an accusatory letter. "The miserable fate of Miss McCrea was particularly aggravated by her being dressed to meet her promised husband," Gates wrote, "but she met her murderers employed by you." Gates skillfully used the story of the vulnerable, innocent maiden dressed in alluring clothes as propaganda to inspire his soldiers' drive for victory at Saratoga. Vanderlyn's work, and other similar pictorial representations, emphasized McCrea's helplessness and sexuality. Yet had McCrea been a man, her flight would have been traitorous. Why this different treatment of a woman?
Wadsworth Atheneum, Hartford.

loyalist refugee Anna Martin recovered her property on the grounds that she had no independent will to be a loyalist.

Tarring and feathering, property confiscation, deportation, terrorism—to the loyalists, such denials of liberty of conscience and of freedom to own private property proved that democratic tyranny was more to be feared than the monarchical variety. A Boston loyalist, Mather Byles, aptly expressed this point: "They call me a brainless Tory, but tell me . . . which is better—to be ruled by one tyrant three thousand miles away, or by three thousand tyrants not a mile away?" Byles, a minister, was soon sentenced to deportation.

"They call me a brainless Tory, but tell me . . . which is better—to be ruled by one tyrant three thousand miles away, or by three thousand tyrants not a mile away?"

Throughout the war, probably 7,000 to 8,000 loyalists fled to England, while 28,000 found closer haven in Canada. But many chose to remain in the new United States and tried to swing with the changing political fortunes of their communities as best they could. In some places, that proved extremely hard to manage. In New Jersey, for example, 3,000 Jerseyites felt protected enough by the occupying British army in 1776 to swear an oath of allegiance to the king. Even a man who just months before had signed the Declaration of Independence, Richard Stockton, came forward to beg pardon for his action. What those 3,000 publicly sworn loyalists could not foresee was that General Howe would draw back to New York City and leave them at the mercy of local patriot committees. British strategy depended on using loyalists to hold occupied territory, but the New Jersey experience showed just how poorly that strategy was put into practice.

Financial Instability and Corruption

Wars cost money—to pay soldiers; to pay suppliers for food, clothing, and housing; to pay manufacturers for muskets, cannon, and gunpowder. The Continental Congress printed money, but within a few short years its value had deteriorated, since the congress held no reserves of gold or silver to back the currency. In practice, the currency was worth only what a buyer and seller agreed it was worth. The dollar eventually bottomed out at one-fortieth of its face value; a loaf of bread that once sold for two and a half cents now sold for a dollar. States too were printing their own paper money to pay for wartime expenses, further complicating the economy.

Soon the congress had to resort to other means to procure supplies and labor. One method was to borrow hard money (not paper) from wealthy men, who would get certificates of debt (also called public securities) promising repayment with interest. In effect, the wealthy men had bought government bonds. To pay soldiers, the congress offered land bounties, which amounted to a promise of a tangible form of wealth. Public securities and land bounties quickly became a form of negotiable currency. For example, a soldier with no paycheck or cash might sell his land bounty certificate to get food for his family. These certificates also fluctuated in value, mainly depreciating.

Depreciating currency inevitably led to rising prices, as sellers compensated for the falling value of the money. The wartime economy of the late 1770s, with its unreliable currency and price inflation, was unprecedented and extremely demoralizing to Americans everywhere. So local committees of public safety in 1778 began to fix prices on goods such as flour, bread, and other essentials for short periods in an effort to impose some brief stability. Such short-run expectations for holding down prices testify to the wild character of the economy.

Inevitably, some Americans turned this roller-coaster situation to their advantage. Money that fell fast in value needed to be spent quickly; being in debt was suddenly advantageous because the debt could be repaid weeks later in devalued currency. A brisk black market sprang up in prohibited luxury imports, such as tea, sugar, textiles, and wines. No matter that these items came from Britain. A New Hampshire delegate to the congress denounced the extravagance that flew in the face of the virtuous homespun association agreements of just a few years before: "We are a crooked and perverse generation, longing for the fineries and follies of those Egyptian task masters from whom we have so lately freed ourselves."

The Campaigns of 1777–1779: Highs and Lows

In early 1777, the Continental army had a bleak road ahead. Washington had shown considerable skill in avoiding outright military defeat, but the minor victories in New Jersey lent only faint optimism to the American side. The British moved large numbers of soldiers into Quebec, readying their plan to isolate New England by controlling the Hudson River.

Burgoyne's Army and the Battle of Saratoga

In 1777, British General John Burgoyne assumed command of an army of 7,800 soldiers in Canada and began the northern squeeze on the Hudson River valley. His goal was to capture Albany, a town 150 miles north of New York City near the intersection of the Hudson and Mohawk Rivers (see Map 6.1). In addition to his soldiers, Burgoyne traveled with another 1,000 assorted "camp followers" (cooks, laundresses, musicians) and some 400 Indian warriors and scouts. This very large army did not travel light, requiring food supplies not only for 9,200 people but also for the more than 400 horses needed to haul heavy artillery. Burgoyne, who was nicknamed "Gentleman Johnny," also carted thirty trunks of personal belongings, including fine wines and elegant clothing.

Burgoyne first captured Fort Ticonderoga with ease. Some 3,000 American troops stationed there spotted the approaching British and, low on food and supplies, abandoned the fort without a fight. The British continued to move south, but the large army moved slowly on primitive roads through forest land. Local farmers created obstacles by felling trees in the army's path. Burgoyne lost a critical month hacking his way down the road, and meanwhile his supply lines back to Canada were severely stretched. Soldiers sent out to forage food were beaten back by local militia units.

The logical second step in isolating New England should have been to advance troops up the Hudson from New York City to meet Burgoyne. American surveillance indicated that General Howe in Manhattan was readying his men for a major move in August 1777. George Washington, watching from New Jersey, was astonished to see Howe's men sail south; Howe had decided to try to capture Philadelphia.

The third prong of British strategy involved troops moving east from the Great Lakes down the Mohawk River, aided by Mohawks and Senecas of Joseph Brant's Iroquois League. The British believed that the Palatine Germans of the Mohawk valley were heavily loyalist, so they expected little trouble getting to Albany. But a hundred miles west of their goal they encountered American soldiers at Fort Stanwix, reinforced by militia units composed of local Palatine Germans and by Oneida Indians. The Seneca ambushed the Germans and their onetime allies the Oneida in a narrow ravine called Oriskany and inflicted heavy losses. But Fort Stanwix held back the British and Seneca and eventually sent them into retreat (see Map 6.1).

Burgoyne thus did not have the additional troops he expected. Camped at a small village called Saratoga, he was isolated and stuck; his food supplies were dwindling, and his men were deserting. His adversary at Albany, General Horatio Gates, began moving 7,000 Continental soldiers north in search of the British. Burgoyne decided to attack first, since every day his army weakened. The first Battle of Saratoga was a British victory, but an expensive one, leaving 600 dead and wounded redcoats. Only three weeks later, a second Battle of Saratoga cost Burgoyne another 600 men and most of his cannon as well. Burgoyne tried to retreat, but Gates's army blocked his path. With food running out and many of his men wounded and demoralized, Burgoyne finally surrendered officially to the Americans on October 17, 1777.

Battle of Saratoga, 1777

Americans on the side of the rebellion were jubilant. After Saratoga, the first decisive victory for the Continental army, a popular dance called "General Burgoyne's Surrender" swept through the country, and bookies in the major cities set odds at five to one that the war would be won in just six months.

THE SURRENDER OF BURGOYNE AT SARATOGA
Artist John Trumbull completed this large scene of Burgoyne's surrender in 1817 as part of a four-picture commission he won to decorate the Rotunda of the U.S. Capitol in Washington. As a youth Trumbull had served briefly in the Continental Army as an officer; his father was the revolutionary governor of Connecticut. He did not witness Saratoga, but he interviewed participants forty years later to reconstruct a version of the ritual scene. To the left, the British general "Gentleman Johnny" hands his sword over to the American commander, General Horatio Gates, at the center. Virginian Daniel Morgan, in white buckskin, looks on from the right. Trumbull's three other paintings, also each 12' by 18', depicted the writing of the Declaration of Independence, the surrender of Cornwallis at Yorktown, and the resignation of General Washington from the army. That context enshrines Saratoga as the second most crucial military event of the war, next to the finality of the Yorktown surrender. Saratoga was not only the most decisive early victory in the war; it was the victory needed to trigger the French alliance.
Yale University Art Gallery, Mabel Brady Garven Collection.

General Howe, meanwhile, had succeeded in occupying Philadelphia in September 1777. Washington had moved his army south of the city to defend it, but he lost a crucial battle at Brandywine Creek. The British government figured that Burgoyne's surrender was evenly balanced by the capture of Philadelphia and thus proposed a negotiated settlement—not including independence—to end the war. But the American side refused.

Their optimism was not well founded, however, in the winter of 1777–78; spirits ran high, but finances, arms, and food supplies ran precariously low. (See "The Promise of Technology," page 206.) Washington moved his troops into winter quarters at Valley Forge, a day's march west of occupied Philadelphia. Quartered in drafty sheds, the men lacked blankets, boots, and stockings. Washington complained to the congress that nearly 3,000 of his men were "unfit for duty because they are bare foot and otherwise naked"; without blankets, large numbers were forced to "set up all Night by fires, instead of taking comfortable rest in a natural way." Food was also scarce. Standard rations dwindled for a time to "firecake," a tasteless pancake made of flour and water, and in one week in February there were no food rations at all. Local farms had produced adequate food that year, but Washington was sure that the farmers were selling their grain to the British, who could pay with the king's silver. His young aide-de-camp Alexander Hamilton openly wondered if the country was even worth fighting for, so corrupt did it seem.

The evidence of corruption indeed appeared abundant. Army suppliers too often provided defective food, clothing, and gunpowder. Washington's men unfolded a shipment of blankets only to discover that they were a quarter of their customary size. Teamsters who hauled barrels of preserved salted meat might drain out the brine to lighten their load and then refill the barrels later, allowing the meat to rot in transit. Selfishness and greed seemed to infect the American side. As one Continental officer said, "The people at home are destroying the Army by their conduct much faster than Howe and all his army can possibly do by fighting us."

The War in Indian Country

By 1779, it was clear that neutrality was not a viable option for the multitudes of Indian tribes, most of whom lived west of the Appalachian Mountains. Somewhere between 150,000 and 200,000 Indians inhabited that region and, despite the 1763 Proclamation Act, by 1778 something like 50,000 American settlers, many of them recent Scots-Irish immigrants to the colonies, had penetrated Indian country. The British maintained military outposts at Niagara and Detroit, but Fort Pitt was now an American garrison.

Even though the 1776 Declaration of Independence blamed the British for inciting "Savages," there was a significant group of Delaware and Shawnee Indians who sought peace with the Americans—until 1778, when a series of murderous events provoked by frontier soldiers began turning the Indians into enemies. A Delaware leader named White Eyes negotiated a treaty with the Americans at Fort Pitt in mid-1778, pledging Indian support in the war in exchange for supplies and trade goods. But supplies and goods were not forthcoming, and escalating violence undermined the agreement. In one incident, American soldiers captured, held, and killed friendly Shawnee chiefs Cornstalk and Red Hawk. A short time later, White Eyes himself was ambushed and killed by militiamen. Despite Indian professions of support, American military leaders repeatedly had trouble honoring distinctions between allied and enemy Indians.

By 1779, it was clear that neutrality was not a viable option for the multitudes of Indian tribes.

Soon, isolated instances of violence escalated into anti-Indian campaigns. In North Carolina, militias attacked Cherokee settlements, destroying 36 villages and burning fields and livestock. To the north, Continental army troops under the command of General John Sullivan carried out a planned campaign of terror and destruction against the Iroquois in western New York in August and September 1779. Forty well-established Indian towns met with total destruction; the soldiers looted and torched the dwellings, then burned cornfields and fruit orchards. In a few towns women and children were slaughtered, but in others, the inhabitants managed to escape. The Delaware and Shawnee town of Coshocton, west of Fort Pitt, consisting of some 2,000 inhabitants and still, amazingly, pro-American, was attacked and burned to the ground by militiamen in 1781. In these and other violent raids, Indians were driven into the hills, into starvation, and into the arms of the British at Detroit and Niagara, or into the arms of the Spanish in Florida or west of the Mississippi River. Said one officer on the Sullivan campaign, "Their nests are destroyed but the birds are still on the wing." Sometimes the "birds" returned: The Shawnee town of Chillicothe, in modern-day Ohio, was destroyed and rebuilt three times between 1779 and 1786.

Rare as it was, the occasional Indian support for the American side persisted out of a strategic sense that the Americans were unstoppable in their westward pressure, and that it was better to work out an alliance than to lose in a war. But American treatment of even friendly Indians showed that there really was no winning strategy to be had for the Indians.

Arming the Soldiers: Muskets and Rifles

How combat-ready was the American side of the Revolutionary War? Were there adequate numbers of firearms along with men trained in their use? These are lively and important questions that have generated sharp debate among twenty-first-century historians and that speak to the issue of whether the United States had, in its founding days, a national gun culture.

In theory, all towns in the colonies were expected to maintain a local militia, at the ready to protect their own communities. All able-bodied adult men were supposed to participate in annual training days, bringing their own guns, but in many communities, such "muster" or "train-band" days had been gradually transformed into festive town holidays. Male camaraderie as expressed in displays of parading and shooting competitions often took precedence over military drill and serious musket practice, an altogether understandable relaxation in coastal or northern towns not feeling any imminent threat of Indian attack or slave rebellion.

Furthermore, gun ownership, despite militia assumptions, was far from universal. Table meat came mainly from domesticated animals slaughtered with knives, and wild-game hunting was a frontier activity, not something that men in Lexington and Concord, not to mention Boston, would typically pursue. Men who turned out on muster days could take turns firing the available muskets. Even in non-frontier areas, many men owned small shotguns known as fowling pieces, which were used to shoot birds and turkeys, creatures easily felled at close range. But such guns were of limited use in warfare.

Muskets were the preferred weapon of eighteenth-century warfare. Muskets were a sixteenth-century invention, featuring by the mid-eighteenth century an improved flintlock ignition system in which the trigger released a spring-held cock that caused a hammer to strike a flint, a special rock that sparks easily. The sparks set off a small charge in a priming pan leading directly to a larger explosion in the barrel. To load the gun, a soldier first put the gun on half-cock, to prevent an accidental firing. He might also remove the bayonet, a knife-like blade affixed to the end of the barrel, to prevent sliced fingers. He next put a small quantity of powder (carried in a powder horn) in the priming pan and closed it, poured more powder down the smooth gun barrel, dropped in the lead projectile (a ball weighing about one ounce), and then wadded paper down the barrel with a ramrod to hold the loose ball in place. He would then replace the bayonet, raise the gun to firing position, put it on full cock, and fire. The whole procedure took highly experienced shooters from 45 to 90 seconds.

The range of muskets extended only about 50 to 100 yards. They were notoriously inaccurate, owing to the poor fit between ball and barrel and

POWDER HORN

James Pike, a twenty-three-year-old New England militiaman, made and then personalized this powder horn, a hollow cow's horn capped on both ends with leather. The stopper was designed to be pulled off by the teeth, leaving the hands to hold the musket barrel and pour the powder. Pike's carvings suggest his motivation for fighting. Above his name he depicts a scene dated April 19, 1775, in which British soldiers, labeled "the Aggressors," fire through the Liberty Tree at "Provincials, Defending." Pike was not at Lexington or Concord; his first combat experience came two months later at the Battle of Bunker Hill, where he saw his brother killed and was himself wounded in the shoulder.

Chicago Historical Society.

to the considerable kick produced by firing, which interfered with aiming. Far more accurate were longer-barreled rifles, the weapons of choice in frontier regions, where hunting was more common. The interior of a rifle barrel carried spiral grooves that imparted spin to the ball as it traversed the barrel, stabilizing and lengthening its flight, and enabling expert marksmen to hit small game at 150 or 200 yards. Yet military commanders much preferred muskets to rifles. Rifles took twice as long to load and fire, and their longer barrels made them unwieldy for soldiers on the march. Inaccurate muskets were quite deadly enough when fired in unison at 50 yards.

How many American men actually owned muskets or rifles? Evidence on this point is complicated and controversial. One way to get at the question is through an analysis of probate inventories. An inventory, taken soon after the owner's death, listed the contents of an estate in order to establish its value, both for inheritance purposes and for paying off the deceased person's creditors. There are many thousands of revolutionary-era probate inventories preserved as legal records in courthouses, and they seem to promise an unparalleled opportunity for learning about material belongings in history. Yet they are fraught with thorny problems that make them something less than an accurate indicator of possessions. For one thing, they are often not complete: if few inventories itemize clothing, can we conclude the decedents went nude? Clearly not. Further, they list possessions of a recently deceased person who owned property of interest to creditors and heirs; so they are biased by age (older), sex (male), and wealth (more). No doubt many men and women died without having their property inventoried at all.

Despite these and other complexities, scholars have worked with probate inventories as the best available source of information. Current studies yield estimates on gun ownership in the early 1770s

that range from one-seventh to just over one-half of all households, with significant regional variations.

A second way to assess gun ownership rates is to look at the arms procurement experiences of state legislatures and the Continental Congress as they geared up for war. Soldiers were requested to report for duty with muskets, gunpowder, and cartridges, but many failed to comply. A New Hampshire captain complained of his unit's plight in June 1775: "We are in want of both arms and ammunition. There is but very little, or none worth mentioning—perhaps one pound of powder to twenty men, and not one-half our men have arms." A militia officer in Pennsylvania noted that even when men owned firearms, they were reluctant to report for duty with them unless assured they would be reimbursed in the event of loss of the valuable possession. Lacking muskets, soldiers often fought with whatever weapon was available. A Prussian general, who volunteered his expertise to the Continental army, arrived at Valley Forge in 1778 and was shocked to find "muskets, carbines, fowling pieces, and rifles" all in the same company of troops.

Purchasing or manufacturing new guns was essential to the war effort. A scattering of ironworks artisans, mostly concentrated in Pennsylvania (where iron ore was abundant), repaired old muskets or handcrafted new ones by adding a wooden stock and an iron barrel to a British-made gunlock, the central firing mechanism. But the British Parliament, anticipating trouble, prohibited all gunlock and firearm exports to the colonies in October 1774. The Continental Congress thus turned to French and Dutch suppliers to purchase gunlocks, gunpowder, and finished muskets.

Whether one-seventh or one-half of all American households had guns at the start of the Revolution may be less important than the fact that a musket or a fowling piece is by itself fairly inefficient as a lethal weapon. Muskets worked in military settings because of the massed fire of shots discharged in unison and at fairly close range. Not until the fourth and fifth decades of the nineteenth century would the United States begin to manufacture firearms whose components were machine-tooled rather than handcrafted, leading to a faster and cheaper manufacturing process and a more deadly and accurate weapon. At that point, muskets, rifles, and handguns set the stage for a national gun culture far more lethal than any degree of gun ownership in the 1770s.

The French Alliance

On their own, the Americans could not have defeated England, and the additional western pressure from hostile Indians magnified their task. But essential help arrived as a result of the victory at Saratoga, which convinced the French to enter the war; a formal alliance was signed in February 1778. France recognized the United States as an independent nation and promised full military and commercial support throughout the war. The most crucial support was the French navy, which now could challenge England's transatlantic pipeline of supplies and troops.

Although France had been waiting for a promising American victory to justify a formal declaration of war, since 1776 the French had aided the Americans in many ways. They had provided military goods—cannons, muskets, gunpowder—and highly trained French military experts who had advised the American army in the field. Still, monarchical France was understandably cautious about endorsing a democratic revolution that attacked the principles of kingship. The main attraction of an alliance for France was simply the opportunity to defeat England, its archrival. A victory would also open pathways to trade and perhaps result in France acquiring the coveted British West Indies. Even American defeat was not a full disaster for France, if the war took many years and drained England of men, money, and psychological energy.

On their own, the Americans could not have defeated England. Essential help arrived as a result of the victory at Saratoga, which convinced the French to enter the war.

The French navy arrived off the coast of Virginia in July 1778 and then sailed north to threaten (but not attack) the British in New York. In August, the allied ships went farther north to Newport, Rhode Island, also held by the British, and engaged in limited and inconclusive battle. By 1781, the French proved indispensable to the American victory, but the first months of the alliance brought no dramatic victories, leading some Americans to grumble that the partnership would prove worthless. Indeed, by late fall 1778, the French fleet had sailed off for the West Indies to defend the French sugar islands, ripe for seizing by the British as rich compensation in the event they lost their mainland colonies.

PROMISSORY NOTE NEGOTIATED BY FRANKLIN
Benjamin Franklin, in France in 1778, negotiated loans from the French government to the United States. The preprinted loan form calls Franklin a "Minister Plenipotentiary" with authority to act on behalf of the thirteen United States. The fact that the form is printed suggests that the French anticipated making several, or even many, such loans; this one is numbered 2. It called for repayment in 1779 at 5 percent interest.
American Philosophical Society Library.

The Southern Strategy and the End of the War

When France joined the war, some British officials paused to consider whether the fight was worth continuing. A troop commander, arguing for an immediate negotiated settlement, shrewdly observed that "we are far from an anticipated peace, because the bitterness of the rebels is too widespread, and in regions where we are masters the rebellious spirit is still in them. The land is too large, and there are too many people. The more land we win, the weaker our army gets in the field." The commander of the British navy argued for abandoning the war, and even Lord North, the prime minister of King George's cabinet, was believed to be in favor of ending it quickly. But the king was determined to crush the rebellion, the French notwithstanding, and he encouraged the development of a new strategy for victory. It was a brilliant but desperate plan.

Georgia and South Carolina

The new strategy shelved the plan to isolate New England and instead focused on the South, thought to be easier to recapture for the crown. The southern region had valuable crops—tobacco, rice, and indigo—worth struggling to keep under the British flag. Further, the large slave population was a powerful destabilizing factor from which the British hoped to benefit. White southerners could ill afford the instability of all-out war, for it might unleash violence from two sides—from the British and from slaves seizing the moment to claim freedom themselves. Georgia and the Carolinas also looked promising for victory because of the large pockets of loyalism presumed to be prevalent and, most important, militant. The British hoped to recapture the southern colonies one by one, restore the loyalists to power, and then move north to the more problematic middle colonies, saving prickly New England for last.

Georgia, the first target, fell at the end of December 1778. A small army of British soldiers occupied Savannah and Augusta, and a new royal governor and loyalist assembly were quickly installed. Taking Georgia was easy because the bulk of the Continental army was in New York and New Jersey, keeping an eye on General Clinton, Howe's replacement as commander in chief, and the French were in the West Indies. The British in Georgia quickly organized twenty loyal militia units, and 1,400 Georgians swore an oath of allegiance to the king. So far, the plan looked as if it might work.

The next target was South Carolina. General Clinton moved British troops south from New York, while the Continental army put ten regiments into Charleston to defend the capital city. For five weeks in early 1780, the British laid siege to the city, which finally surrendered in mid-May 1780, sending 3,300 soldiers, a tremendous loss, into British captivity. Again, the king's new strategy seemed to be working as planned.

Clinton returned to New York, leaving the task of pacifying South Carolina to General Charles Cornwallis and 4,000 troops. The boldest of all the British generals in the war for America, Lord Cornwallis quickly moved into action. He chased out the remaining Continental army units and established military control of the province by midsummer 1780. He purged rebels from government office and disarmed potential rebel militias. The export of South Carolina's main crop, rice, resumed, suggesting an easy normalization of relations between England and the colony. As in Georgia, pardons were offered to Carolinians who swore loyalty oaths to the crown and then proved their loyalty by taking up arms for the British.

In August 1780, the Continental army was ready to strike back at Cornwallis. General Gates, the hero of the Battle of Saratoga, arrived in South Carolina with more than 3,000 troops, some of them experienced army units and others green militiamen. They met Cornwallis's army at Camden, South Carolina, on August 16 (Map 6.3). Gates put the militiamen into the center of the battle, where a contagious panic gripped them at the sight of the approaching enemy cavalry. Men threw down unfired muskets and ran from the field of battle. When regiment leaders tried to regroup the next day, only 700 showed up. The rest were either dead, captured, or still in flight—including Gates, who traversed a speedy 180 miles in three days before he stopped to file a report on the battle. Camden was a devastating defeat; prospects now seemed very grim for the Americans.

Benedict Arnold's Treason

The new British strategy succeeded in 1780 partly as a product of improved information about American troop movements and supplies that was secretly furnished to the British by Benedict Arnold, a Connecticut general and acknowledged hero of several battles. Arnold was a brilliant military talent but also a deeply insecure man who never felt he got his due, in either honor or financial reward. Often argumentative and grasping, he bickered with military colleagues, insulted civilians, and made secret pacts with war profiteers. For Arnold, the war represented an opportunity to gain fame and reputation and to line his pockets.

After being wounded at Saratoga, Arnold was appointed to an inactive command, as military commandant of Philadelphia in June 1778 soon after the British had vacated it. During his months there, he used his power to continue his private financial speculations. He also married an eighteen-year-old woman, Peggy Shippen, from a wealthy, loyalist-leaning family. When his business irregularities came to light, he found himself on the defensive in a court-martial that challenged his integrity and led to an official rebuke. Probably the final straw for Arnold came when he failed to earn promotion to higher rank, while men he considered inferior were pro-

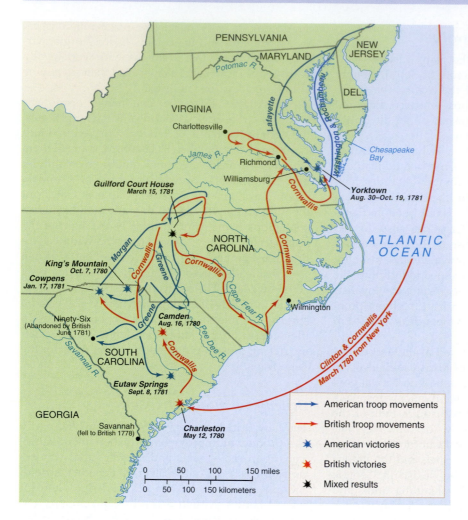

MAP 6.3

The War in the South, 1780–1781
After taking Charleston in 1780, the British advanced into South Carolina and the foothill region of North Carolina, leaving a bloody civil war in their wake. Cornwallis next invaded Virginia but was overpowered by American and French forces at Yorktown in 1781 in the final battle of the Revolutionary War.

moted over him. Sometime in 1779, he opened secret negotiations with the British commander in New York, Henry Clinton, trading information for money and hinting he could deliver far more of value.

The ever-hesitant Clinton remained cautious about Arnold for more than a year. Arnold had named an enormous sum for his reward, £8,000, but it was not clear what he could deliver from his inactive duty in Philadelphia. Meanwhile, to show good faith, Arnold passed along whatever he learned from Washington—about the arrival of the French fleet, about the weak state of Charleston's defenses, even about a planned invasion of Canada that was actually deliberate disinformation on Washington's part. Arnold's main task throughout 1779 and early 1780 was to acquire an active command that would be worth something to the British. In the meantime he quietly closed out his property

holdings in Connecticut and Philadelphia in anticipation of flight.

Arnold lobbied Washington for the command of West Point, a fortress guarding a narrows in the Hudson River about sixty miles north of New York City. West Point's critical function was to protect against the original and still ultimate British goal, controlling the Hudson and isolating New England. Its easy seizure might well spell imminent victory for the British. Arnold could make Clinton's victory effortless by revealing full information on the Americans' defensive plans.

Granted command in the spring of 1780, Arnold entered into serious negotiations over his payoff with the British. He demanded to meet an emissary from Clinton, to argue the terms; Clinton hesitated for weeks, knowing the danger. Finally Clinton sent a trusted aide, Major John André, behind enemy

PEGGY SHIPPEN ARNOLD
The British major John André met the pert, flirtatious Peggy Shippen in 1778, when the British occupied Philadelphia. He frequently escorted the seventeen-year-old to social events and the theater. He sketched Peggy, showing her in a beribboned dress with an even more extravagant, gravity-defying hairstyle. If the two were romantically involved, it was not serious on André's part. The gallant officer socialized with several other young women as well. In 1779, Peggy married the American general Benedict Arnold. Through Peggy, Arnold gained access to André's superiors.
Yale University Art Gallery.

lines at night, and Arnold detained him until daybreak haggling over the payment. André, unescorted and burdened with plans for the fort's defense, was arrested for spying on his return flight by Americans. After a quick trial, André went to the gallows ten days later, lamented by his British friends and by American officers as well, who were moved by his honorable acceptance of his fate. Arnold narrowly escaped to the British in New York City, safe but not sound, being surrounded by British officers who despised him for luring André

into the danger that caused his death and, equally, for bungling the delivery of West Point.

News of the Arnold treason created shock waves. Arnold represented all of the patriots' worst fears: greedy self-interest like that of the war profiteers, unprincipled abandonment of war aims like that of the turncoat Tories of the South, panic like that of the terrified soldiers with Gates at Camden. But instead of symbolizing all that was troubling about the American side of the war, the treachery of Arnold became celebrated in a kind of displacement of the anxieties of the moment. Vilifying Arnold allowed Americans to stake out a wide distance between themselves and dastardly conduct. It inspired a renewal of patriotism at a particularly low moment.

The Other Southern War: Guerrillas

Shock over Gates's defeat at Camden and the treason of Benedict Arnold revitalized rebel support in

BENEDICT ARNOLD
This portrait shows Benedict Arnold in 1776, when he was the hero of the Quebec campaign. Probably the final straw for Arnold came when he failed to earn promotion, while men he considered inferior were elevated to higher rank.
Anne S. K. Brown Military Collection, Providence, R.I.

western South Carolina, an area that Cornwallis had believed to be pacified and loyal. The backcountry of the South soon became the site of a guerrilla war. In hit-and-run attacks, both sides burned and ravaged not only opponents' property but the property of anyone claiming to be neutral. The loyalist militia units organized by the British were met by fierce rebel militia units who now figured they had little to lose. Guerrilla warfare soon spread to Georgia and North Carolina. In South Carolina, some 6,000 men became active partisan fighters, and they entered into at least twenty-six engagements with loyalist units. Some of these were classic battles; but on other occasions the fighters were more like bandits than soldiers. Both sides committed murders and atrocities and plundered property, clear deviations from standard military practice.

In hit-and-run attacks, both sides burned and ravaged not only opponents' property but the property of anyone claiming to be neutral.

The British southern strategy counted on sufficient loyalist strength—in terms of both numbers of people and the respect and authority they could command—to hold reconquered territory as the army moved north. The backcountry civil war proved this assumption false. The Americans won few major battles in the South, but they ultimately succeeded by dogging the British forces, harassing them, and thus preventing them from foraging for food. Cornwallis boldly moved the war into North Carolina in late 1780, not because he thought South Carolina was secure—it was not—but because the North Carolinians were supplying the South Carolina rebels with arms and men. (See Map 6.3.) But news of a brutal defeat—a massacre, actually—of loyalist units in western South Carolina at Kings Mountain, at the hands of 1,400 frontier riflemen, sent him hurrying back. The British were stretched too thin to hold even two of their onetime colonies.

Surrender at Yorktown

In the early months of 1781, Cornwallis set out to try his North Carolina plan again; if successful, it would isolate South Carolina and Georgia. For months, he moved his army around the province, taking land but not holding it. In February 1781,

Cornwallis proclaimed, prematurely, that North Carolina was reconquered, a move calculated to increase loyalist support. But he found few loyalists who were willing to take up arms against the energized rebel forces.

Cornwallis decided to push the war farther north, into Virginia. He captured Williamsburg, which had been the colony's seat of government until the previous year. Then he raided Charlottesville, where Virginia's revolutionary government was meeting, and seized members of the assembly; Governor Thomas Jefferson narrowly avoided capture. (More than a dozen slaves of the drafter of the Declaration of Independence chose this moment to seek refuge with the British.) As late as the start of September, Cornwallis was not wrong to think he had the upper hand in Virginia.

What changed the picture dramatically was an infusion of French military support. A large French army under the command of the comte de Rochambeau had joined Washington in Rhode Island in mid-1780. News that a large fleet had sailed from France in the spring of 1781 set in motion Washington's plan to defeat the British. The fleet, commanded by the comte de Grasse, went first to the West Indies. In August de Grasse sailed twenty-eight ships to the Chesapeake, to box in Cornwallis's army in Virginia. In a coordinated move Washington and Rochambeau fixed their attention on Virginia. Bypassing New York (where Clinton had been expecting an attack), thousands of American and French soldiers headed south in the last week of August 1781, traveling on four separate roads to confuse the British.

British intelligence about the French fleet movement had been delayed, and by the time British ships arrived at the mouth of the Chesapeake, the French had already taken control of it. A five-day naval battle in early September sent the British ships limping away and left the French in clear command of the bay and the Virginia and North Carolina coasts. This proved to be the decisive factor in ending the war, because it eliminated a water escape route for Cornwallis's land army, encamped at Yorktown, Virginia.

General Cornwallis and his 7,500 troops now faced a combined French and American army numbering over 16,000. For twelve days, the Americans and French bombarded the British fortifications at Yorktown; Cornwallis ran low on food and ammunition. An American observer keeping a diary noted that "the enemy, from want of forage, are killing off their horses in great numbers. Six or seven hundred of these valuable animals have been killed, and their

Siege of Yorktown, 1781

carcasses are almost continually floating down the river." Realizing escape was impossible, Cornwallis signaled his intention to surrender.

On October 19, 1781, the British leaders formally capitulated. Cornwallis claimed "indisposition" and sent a subordinate as substitute. The defeated troops marched through a double line of American and French soldiers to relinquish their weapons; an American diarist reported that "their mortification could not be concealed. . . . Many of the soldiers manifested a sullen temper, throwing their arms on the pile with violence as if determined to render them useless." Washington allowed Cornwallis his personal liberty, and he sailed off to New York City with as many loyalists as could fit on one ship. The remaining British soldiers were packed off to prison camps in Virginia and Maryland.

What had begun as a promising southern strategy by the British in 1778 had turned into a discouraging defeat by 1781. British attacks in the South energized American resistance, as did the timely exposure of Benedict Arnold's treason. The arrival of the French fleet sealed the fate of Cornwallis at Yorktown, and the military war quickly came to a halt.

The Losers and the Winners

The surrender at Yorktown proved to be the end of the war, but it took some time for the principals to realize that. The peace treaty was nearly two years in the making, and in the meantime both the American and the British armies remained in the field, in case the treaty fell through. Clinton continued to occupy New York; Charleston and Savannah, too, stayed under British control, although the British had been chased out of the rest of the South. King George tenaciously clung to the idea of pursuing the war, but the sentiment for a formal peace was growing in Parliament. The war had become unpopular among the British citizenry in general, and support for it dwindled until finally the king had to realize it was over.

It took six months for the three American commissioners, Benjamin Franklin, John Adams, and John Jay of New York, to negotiate the three-way settlement in Paris. The British tried to exploit differences between French and American interests. For example, the French had no problem with dividing up the colonies, giving New York, the Carolinas, and Georgia back to the British; the Americans wanted not only all thirteen colonies but Canada as well.

In late November 1782, eighty-two articles of peace were agreed to. The first article went to the heart of the matter: "His Britannic Majesty acknowledges the said United States to be free Sovereign and independent States." Other articles described the boundaries of the new country: a northern line separating Canada, which remained British, a western line along the Mississippi River, and a southern line sectioning off Florida, which England soon handed over to Spain in a separate treaty. Creditors on both sides were entitled to collect debts owed them, in sterling money; this was an important provision for British merchants, especially those in the southern trade, who claimed that commercial debts owed them had gone uncollected during the war. England agreed to withdraw its troops quickly; more than a decade later, this promise would still not be fully kept. The final, official peace treaty—the Treaty of Paris—was signed nearly a year later, on September 2, 1783.

In late November 1782, eighty-two articles of peace were agreed to. The first article went to the heart of the matter: "His Britannic Majesty acknowledges the said United States to be free Sovereign and independent States."

As at the end of the French and Indian War, no article in this treaty recognized the Indians as players in the war. Indian lands were assigned to the victors as though they were uninhabited. Many Indian refugees had fled, some west into Missouri and Arkansas, others into Canada, and yet others into Spanish Florida. But significant numbers remained, displaced from their ancestral homelands. For them, especially the tribes gravitating to what would soon be called the Northwest Territory (and later the states of Ohio, Indiana, Illinois, Michigan, and

A FRENCH OFFICER'S VIEW OF THE FRENCH BLOCKADE
A young naval officer named Pierre Joseph Jeunot sketched the lines of British and French ships shortly before they clashed at the battle of the Chesapeake Capes, at the entrance to Chesapeake Bay on September 5, 1781. More than two dozen French ships sealed the bay and the York River, preventing the escape of Cornwallis's army at Yorktown. Notice that Jeunot showed some ships in action, totally obscured by the impenetrable smoke of the fired cannons.
Huntington Library.

Wisconsin), the peace of 1783 was only a temporary lull in a much longer war that would extend at least until 1795. A delegation of some 270 Indians representing tribes spanning the regions from New York, through Ohio, and down to the Carolinas reported to the Spanish governor at St. Louis in 1784 that the Revolutionary War was "the greatest blow that could have been dealt us, unless it had been our total destruction."

With the treaty finally signed, the British began their evacuation of New York, Charleston, and Savannah, a process made complicated by the sheer numbers involved—soldiers, fearful loyalists, and runaway blacks by the thousands. In New York City, more than 27,000 soldiers and 30,000 loyalists sailed on hundreds of ships for England in late fall 1783. In a final act of mischief, on the November day when the last ships left, the losing side raised the British flag at the southern tip of Manhattan, cut away the ropes used to hoist it, and greased the flagpole.

Conclusion: Why the British Lost

The British began the war for America convinced that they could not lose. They had the strongest and best-trained army and navy in the world; they were familiar with the American landscape from the French and Indian War; and they outnumbered their opponents in uniform. They easily captured the capital and every other port city of consequence in America. Probably one-fifth of the population was loyalist, and another two-fifths were undecided. Why, then, did they lose?

One continuing problem the British faced was the uncertainty of food and supplies. Unwilling to ravage the countryside, the army depended on a steady stream of supply ships from home. Insecurity about food helps explain the repeated reluctance of Howe and Clinton to pursue the Continental army aggressively.

A second obstacle to British success was their continual misuse of loyalist energies. Any plan to repacify the colonies required the cooperation of the loyalists as well as new support from the many neutrals. But again and again, the British failed to back the loyalists, leaving them to the mercy of vengeful rebels. In the South, they allowed loyalist militias to engage in vicious guerrilla warfare that drove away potential converts among the rest of the population. There was no real program to court the neutrals and to show them that the stability of British rule was preferable to the rebel government. If the British had been more lenient and forgiving, they might have succeeded in retaking the South.

The French alliance looms large in any explanation of the British defeat. The artillery and ammunition the French supplied throughout the war, even before 1778, were critical necessities for the Continental army. In 1780, the French army brought a fresh infusion of troops to a war-weary America, and the French navy made the Yorktown victory possible. The symbolic impact of the major naval defeat in the Chesapeake, just before the Yorktown siege, dissolved the pro-war spirit in England and forced the king to admit it was over.

Finally, the British abdicated civil power in the colonies in 1775 and 1776, when royal officials were forced to flee to safety, and they never really regained it. For nearly seven years, the Americans of necessity created their own government structures, from the Continental Congress to local committees and militias. Staffed by many who before 1775 had been the political elites, these new government agencies had remarkably little trouble establishing their credentials and authority to rule. The single effort in Georgia to appoint a new royal governor was not successful, and the British did not try to repeat the experiment. The basic British goal in the war—to turn back the clock to imperial rule—receded into impossibility as the war dragged on.

The war for America had taken five and a half years to fight, from Lexington to Yorktown; negotiations and the evacuation took two more. It profoundly disrupted the lives of Americans everywhere, from Canada to Georgia. It was a war for independence from England, but it was also much more. It was a war that required men and women to think about politics and the legitimacy of authority. Americans had to forge new government structures to fill the vacuum left by the departing British. The precise disagreement with England about representation and political participation had profound implications for the kinds of governance the Americans would choose to adopt, both in the moment of emergency, as extralegal committees and bodies took charge, and in the longer run of the late 1770s and early 1780s when states began to write their constitutions and the Continental Congress pondered its own legitimacy. The rhetoric employed to justify the revolution against England put words like *liberty, tyranny, slavery, independence,* and *equality* into common usage. These words carried far deeper meanings than a mere complaint over taxation without representation. As Abigail Adams and others saw, the Revolution unleashed a dynamic of equality and liberty. That it was largely unintended and unwanted by the revolutionary leaders of 1776 made it all the more potent a force in American life in the decades to come.

www.bedfordstmartins.com/tap   SEE THE ONLINE STUDY GUIDE to assess your mastery of the material covered in this chapter.

CHRONOLOGY

1775 **May 10.** Second Continental Congress convenes in Philadelphia.

June 14. Continental Congress creates Continental army.

June 17. Battle of Bunker Hill.

July. Congress offers Olive Branch Petition in attempt at reconciliation with king.

September. American armies march on Montreal and Quebec.

1776 **January.** Americans lose assault on Quebec.

Thomas Paine's *Common Sense* published.

March. British evacuate Boston.

July 4. Declaration of Independence adopted.

August 27. Battle of Long Island.

September. British take Manhattan.

November. Americans retreat to Philadelphia.

December 26. Washington surprises British and Hessians at Trenton.

1777 **January.** Washington winters at Morristown, New Jersey.

July. Burgoyne takes Fort Ticonderoga for British.

August. Fort Stanwix ambush.

September. British occupy Philadelphia.

October. Burgoyne surrenders at Saratoga.

December. Washington goes into winter quarters at Valley Forge, Pennsylvania.

1778 **February.** France enters war on American side.

July–August. French fleet threatens New York and Newport, Rhode Island.

December. Savannah, Georgia, falls to British.

1779 **January–June.** Skirmishes in South Carolina and Georgia.

October. British evacuate Newport.

1780 Philadelphia Ladies Association raises money for soldiers.

March–May. British lay siege to Charleston, South Carolina.

July. Comte de Rochambeau and French army arrive at Newport.

August 16. Battle of Camden, South Carolina, dims hopes for Americans.

September–October. Benedict Arnold's treason exposed.

September–December. Guerrilla warfare in South.

October 7. Battle of Kings Mountain, South Carolina.

1781 **January 17.** Battle of Cowpens, South Carolina.

May–August. Cornwallis in Virginia.

August. Cornwallis occupies Yorktown, Virginia.

September 5. French fleet takes Chesapeake Bay.

September 28–October 19. Siege of Yorktown.

October 19. Cornwallis surrenders.

1783 Treaty of Paris ends war.

BIBLIOGRAPHY

GENERAL WORKS

Michael A. Bellesiles, *Arming America: The Origins of a National Gun Culture* (2000).

Benson Bobrick, *Angel in the Whirlwind: The Triumph of the American Revolution* (1997).

Edward Countryman, *The American Revolution* (1985).

Don Higginbotham, *The War of Independence: Military Attitudes, Policies, and Practices, 1763–1789* (1983).

Don Higginbotham, *War and Society in Revolutionary America: The Wider Dimensions of Conflict* (1988).

Ronald Hoffman and Peter J. Albert, *Arms and Independence: The Military Character of the American Revolution* (1984).

Mark V. Kwasny, *Washington's Partisan War, 1775–1783* (1996).

Piers Mackesy, *The War for America, 1775–1783* (1964).

Charles Royster, *A Revolutionary People at War: The Continental Army and American Character, 1775–1783* (1979).

Geoffrey Scheer, *Rebels and Redcoats: The American Revolution through the Eyes of Those Who Fought and Lived It* (1988).

John Shy, *A People Numerous and Armed: Reflections on the Military Struggle for American Independence* (rev. ed., 1990).

James L. Stokesbury, *A Short History of the American Revolution* (1991).

THE WARTIME CONFEDERATION

John Alden, *George Washington* (1984).

Joseph J. Ellis, *Passionate Sage: The Character and Legacy of John Adams* (1993).

John Ferling, *John Adams: A Life* (1992).

Jay Fliegelman, *Declaring Independence: Jefferson, Natural Language, and the Culture of Performance* (1993).

Eric Foner, *Tom Paine and Revolutionary America* (1976).

Edith Gelles, *Portia: The World of Abigail Adams* (1992).

James H. Hutson, *John Adams and the Diplomacy of the American Revolution* (1980).

Pauline Maier, *American Scripture: Making the Declaration of Independence* (1997).

Jackson Turner Main, *The Sovereign States, 1775–1783* (1973).

Jack N. Rakove, *The Beginnings of National Politics: An Interpretive History of the Continental Congress* (1979).

Peter Shaw, *The Character of John Adams* (1976).

Garry Wills, *Inventing America: Jefferson's Declaration of Independence* (1978).

Lynne Withey, *Dearest Friend: A Life of Abigail Adams* (1981).

THE LOYALISTS

Wallace Brown, *The Good Americans: The Loyalists in the American Revolution* (1969).

Robert M. Calhoon, *The Loyalists of Revolutionary America* (1973).

Robert M. Calhoon, *The Loyalist Perception and Other Essays* (1989).

John Ferling, *The Loyalist Mind: Joseph Galloway and the American Revolution* (1977).

Malcolm Frieberg, *Prelude to Purgatory: Thomas Hutchinson in Provincial Massachusetts Politics, 1760–1770* (1990).

Adele Hast, *Loyalism in Revolutionary Virginia* (1982).

William N. Nelson, *The American Tory* (1961).

Mary Beth Norton, *The British-American: The Loyalist Exiles in England, 1774–1789* (1972).

William Pencak, *American's Burke: The Mind of Thomas Hutchinson* (1982).

Janice Potter, *The Liberty We Seek: Loyalist Ideology in Colonial New York and Massachusetts* (1983).

James W. St. G. Walker, *The Black Loyalists: The Search for a Promised Land in Nova Scotia and Sierra Leone, 1783–1870* (1976).

THE WAR IN THE NORTH

Michael A. Bellesiles, *Revolutionary Outlaws: Ethan Allen and the Struggle for Independence on the Early American Frontier* (1993).

W. Jeffrey Bolster, *Black Jacks: African American Seamen in the Age of Sail* (1998).

Clare Brandt, *The Man in the Mirror: A Life of Benedict Arnold* (1994).

Richard Buel Jr., *Dear Liberty: Connecticut's Mobilization for the Revolutionary War* (1980).

Colin G. Calloway, *The American Revolution in Indian Country: Crisis and Diversity in Native American Communities* (1995).

E. Wayne Carp, *To Starve the Army at Pleasure: Continental Army Administration and American Political Culture, 1775–1783* (1984).

Edward Countryman, *A People in Revolution: The American Revolution and Political Society in New York, 1760–1790* (1981).

John C. Dann, ed., *The Revolution Remembered: Eyewitness Accounts of the War for Independence* (1980).

Gregory E. Dowd, *A Spirited Resistance: The North American Indian Struggle for Unity, 1745–1815* (1992).

Joseph R. Fischer, *A Well-Executed Failure: The Sullivan Campaign against the Iroquois, July–September 1779* (1997).

William M. Fowler Jr., *Rebels under Sail: The American Navy during the Revolution* (1976).

Sylvia Frey, *The British Soldier in America: A Social History of Military Life in the Revolutionary Period* (1965).

Barbara Graymont, *The Iroquois in the American Revolution* (1972).

Robert Gross, *The Minutemen and Their World* (1976).

Ira D. Gruber, *The Howe Brothers and the American Revolution* (1972).

Richard J. Hargrove Jr., *General John Burgoyne* (1983).

Sidney Kaplan and Emma Nogrady Kaplan, *The Black Presence in the Era of the American Revolution* (1989).

Isabel T. Kelsay, *Joseph Brant, 1743–1807* (1984).

Richard M. Ketchum, *Saratoga: Turning Point of America's Revolutionary War* (1997).

Donald R. Lennon and Charles E. Bennett, *A Quest for Glory: Robert Howe and the American Revolution* (1991).

James Kirby Martin, *Benedict Arnold, Revolutionary Hero: An American Warrior Reconsidered* (1997).

James Kirby Martin and Edward Mark Lender, *A Respectable Army: The Military Origins of the Republic, 1763–1789* (1982).

David B. Mattern, *Benjamin Lincoln and the American Revolution* (1995).

Holly A. Mayer, *Belonging to the Army: Camp Followers and Community during the American Revolution* (1996).

Dave R. Palmer, *The Way of the Fox: American Strategy in the War for America, 1775–1783* (1975).

Gary A. Puckrein, *The Black Regiment in the American Revolution* (1978).

John Shy, *Toward Lexington: The Role of the British Army in the Coming of the American Revolution* (1965).

John A. Tilley, *The British Navy and the American Revolution* (1987).

Donald Wallace White, *A Village at War: Chatham, New Jersey, and the American Revolution* (1979).

Robert K. Wright Jr., *The Continental Army* (1983).

DIPLOMACY

Jonathan R. Dull, *A Diplomatic History of the American Revolution* (1985).

R. Ernest Dupuy et al., *The American Revolution: A Global War* (1977).

Ronald Hoffman and Peter Albert, eds., *Peace and the Peacemakers: The Treaty of 1783* (1986).

Reginald Horsman, *The Diplomacy of the New Republic, 1776–1815* (1985).

James H. Hutson, *John Adams and the Diplomacy of the American Revolution* (1980).

Lee Kennett, *The French Forces in America, 1780–1783* (1977).

THE SOUTHERN STRATEGY

Lawrence E. Babits, *A Devil of a Whipping: The Battle of Cowpens* (1998).

W. Arthur Bowler, *Logistics and the Failure of the British Army in America, 1775–1783* (1975).

Jeffrey J. Crow and Larry Tise, eds., *The Southern Experience in the American Revolution* (1978).

John Ferling, ed., *The World Turned Upside Down: The American Victory in the War of Independence* (1988).

M. Thomas Hatley, *The Dividing Paths: Cherokees and South Carolinians through the Era of Revolution* (1993).

W. Robert Higgins, ed., *The Revolutionary War in the South* (1979).

Ronald Hoffman, Thad W. Tate, and Peter J. Albert, eds., *An Uncivil War: The Southern Backcountry during the American Revolution* (1985).

Henry Lumpkin, *From Savannah to Yorktown* (1981).

Jerome J. Nadelhaft, *The Disorders of War: The Revolution in South Carolina* (1981).

James H. O'Donnell III, *Southern Indians in the American Revolution* (1973).

John S. Pancake, *This Destructive War: The British Campaign in the Carolinas, 1780–1782* (1985).

Hugh Rankin, *The North Carolina Continentals* (1971).

John E. Selby, *The Revolution in Virginia, 1775–1783* (1988).

Timothy Silver, *A New Face on the Countryside: Indians, Colonists, and Slaves in South Atlantic Forests, 1500–1800* (1990).

Russell F. Weigley, *The Partisan War: The South Carolina Campaign of 1780–1782* (1970).

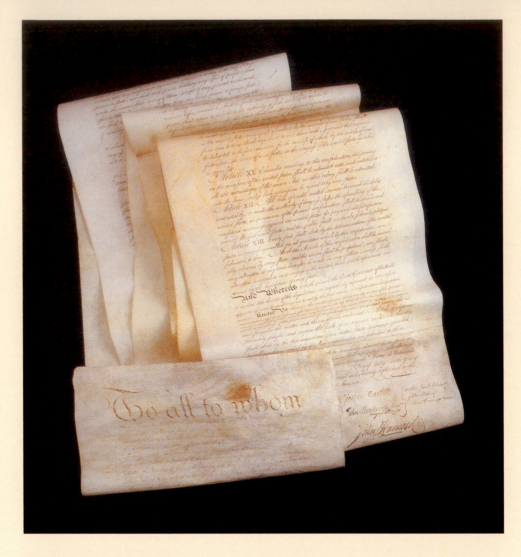

ARTICLES OF CONFEDERATION

The first written frame of government that bound together the thirteen rebelling provinces was called the Articles of Confederation. Delegates to the Second Continental Congress hammered out the plan over many months in 1776 and 1777, working on it when there was time free from the more pressing problems of pursuing the war. Once Congress agreed on it, the plan was printed and distributed to state legislatures for ratification, a process that took more than three years because it required the assent of all thirteen. After ratification, in February 1781, this parchment copy became the official original version. As was often done with significant manuscript documents, the professional scribe wrote the opening words of the Articles in very large print, to proclaim the news. How do you think TO ALL TO WHOM compares with such famous opening words that have taken on special resonance in the country's history as IN CONGRESS, JULY 4, 1776—the start of the Declaration of Independence—and later, WE THE PEOPLE for the United States Constitution, which replaced the Articles in 1788? Can you imagine TO ALL TO WHOM turned into any kind of slogan or catchword, had the Articles persisted as the country's sacred text?

National Archives.

BUILDING A REPUBLIC
1775–1789

7

JAMES MADISON GRADUATED FROM PRINCETON COLLEGE in New Jersey in 1771, at a loss to know what to do next with his life. Certainly the twenty-year-old had an easy fallback position. As the firstborn son of a wealthy plantation master, he could return to Montpelier in the rolling foothills of Virginia and take his place in the ranks of substantial landowners, eventually inheriting a large force of slaves. But James was a bookish young man, uninterested in plantation management, studious to an extreme, and reluctant to leave the intense collegiate environment. Five years at a boarding school had given him fluency in Greek, Latin, French, and higher mathematics, and three years at Princeton had brought him extensive knowledge of the great thinkers, both ancient and modern. Driven by a thirst for learning, young Madison slept only four or five hours a night, perhaps undermining his health. Protesting he was too ill to travel, he lingered in Princeton for six months after graduation.

In 1772, he went home to recuperate, spending his days tutoring siblings and nights reading books. He tried studying law, but his unimpressive oratorical talents discouraged him. Political theory greatly attracted him, and he swapped reading lists and ideas by letter with a Princeton classmate. While Madison drifted and struggled for direction, the powerful winds before the storm of the American Revolution swirled through the colonies, portending significant change for Americans. The young Virginian's postcollege moratorium was about to end abruptly. In May 1774, Madison traveled north to deliver his brother to boarding school and was thus in Philadelphia when the startling news broke that Britain had closed the port of Boston in retaliation for the destruction of the tea. A month in Philadelphia and New York City during that turbulent time of protest over the Coercive Acts turned him into a committed revolutionary.

Back in Virginia, Madison joined his father and others on the newly formed Committee of Public Safety. For a few days in early 1775, the twenty-four-year-old took up musket shooting and bragged of his ability to hit small targets at one hundred yards, an implausible boast given the limited range and notorious inaccuracy of muskets. But his continued poor health ruled out the militia soldier's life, and he quickly gave it up. His special contribution to the revolution lay along a different path.

The first step on that path came in spring 1776, when he was elected from his county to the Virginia Convention, an extralegal body replacing the defunct royal government. The convention's main task was to hammer out a state constitution featuring revolutionary goals such as frequent elections and a limited executive power. Madison, shy, self-effacing, and still learning the ropes, mostly stayed on the sidelines. Still, Virginia's elder statesmen noted the young man's logical, thoughtful contributions. When his county failed to return him to the assembly in the next election, he was instead appointed to the governor's council, where he spent two years gaining practical experience helping to manage a government under crisis of war.

In early 1780, Madison was ready for the next big step: representing his state in the Continental Congress. Not quite twenty-nine, unmarried, and supported by his father's money, Madison was free of the common burdens that made distant political service onerous for so many others. Madison stayed in the North for three years, working with men like

JAMES MADISON BY CHARLES WILLSON PEALE
James Madison, a short and slight man, was often mistaken for being younger than he was. With natural hair (no wig) and smooth face, as shown here, he could pass for a youth of 20. This miniature portrait was made in 1783 when Madison was 32. That year he experienced his first serious romance, with a young woman who was just 16. She lived in his boarding house in Philadelphia, along with her father, a congressional delegate from New York. But the girl dropped him for another suitor. Madison waited eleven years to try romance again. New York congressman Aaron Burr introduced him to a Quaker widow named Dolley Payne Todd, who came from Virginia but lived in Philadelphia. Madison was 43 and Dolley was 26; they married four months after meeting.
Library of Congress.

Alexander Hamilton of New York and Robert Morris of Pennsylvania as the congress wrestled with the chaotic economy and the ever-precarious war effort. In one crisis Madison's negotiating skills proved crucial: He broke the deadlock over the ratification of the Articles of Confederation by arranging for the cession of Virginia's western lands. More often, service in the congress proved frustrating to Madison because the confederation government seemed to lack essential powers.

Madison returned to Virginia in 1784 and resumed his seat in the state assembly. But he did not retreat to a local point of view. He urged the assembly to call an all-state meeting to discuss ways to confer powers of taxation on the tottering confederation government. That meeting led soon to a second larger gathering, in Philadelphia in the late spring of 1787, a convention of delegates steered by Madison into totally rewriting the structure of government for the infant country. True to form, Madison spent the months before the convention in feverish study of the great thinkers he had read in college, searching out the best way to constitute a government on republican principles. His lifelong passion for scholarly study, seasoned by a dozen years of energetic political experience, paid off handsomely. The United States Constitution was the result.

By the end of the 1780s, James Madison had had his finger in every kind of political pie, on the local, state, confederation, and finally national level. He had transformed himself from a directionless youth of unassuming and solitary ways into one of the leading political thinkers of the Revolutionary period. His personal history over the 1780s mirrored the path of the emerging United States.

The Articles of Confederation

For five years, from independence in 1776 until 1781, the Second Continental Congress continued to meet in Philadelphia and other cities. It existed without any formal constitutional basis, while its members groped to establish a government on principles congruent with the themes of the Revolution. With monarchy gone, where did sovereignty lie? What was the nature of representation? Who held the power of taxation? If distant governments inevitably lost sight of the interests of the people, what was the proper size for a political entity? And just who were "the people" anyway?

The initial answers to these questions took the form of a plan called the Articles of Confederation. (See page A-4.) The plan, however, proved to be surprisingly difficult to implement.

Congress and Confederation

The Second Continental Congress assumed power in May 1775, when the British attack on Lexington and Concord required a unified colonial response. Only as they fashioned the Declaration of Independence a year later did the delegates consider the need for a written document that would specify what powers the congress had, by what authority it existed, and how it was to be constituted. It finally fell to John Dickinson, the moderate conciliator from Pennsylvania, to chair the committee entrusted with the important task of drafting such a document.

With monarchy gone, where did sovereignty lie? What was the nature of representation? And just who were "the people" anyway?

Dickinson's draft of the Articles of Confederation reveals that the delegates, unified by their opposition to England, agreed that the congress should handle functions such as pursuing war and peace, conducting foreign relations, regulating trade, and running a postal service. The draft also gave the congress the authority to issue bills of credit and to borrow money, to settle all disputes between states, and to administer the unsettled western lands. It was these final two points that proved to be the major sources of disagreement over the draft. Some states, such as Virginia and Connecticut, had very old colonial charters that located their western boundaries many hundreds of miles to the west. States without extensive land grants could not abide such grandiose claims. Dickinson's draft granted the congress final authority on this and many other matters.

Off and on over the next sixteen months, the congress tinkered with the Articles. Its immediate attention, however, was focused on the war, and a final version of the Articles of Confederation emerged only in November 1777. This second draft

departed from Dickinson's by identifying the union as a loose confederation of states. Gone was the provision giving the congress control of state boundaries and western lands. Also, each state retained all powers and rights not expressly delegated to the congress, and the union was characterized as "a firm league of friendship" existing mainly to foster a common defense. There was no national executive (that is, no president) and no national judiciary.

The structure of the government paralleled that of the existing Continental Congress. The confederation was embodied in a congress, composed of two to seven delegates from each state, selected annually by the state legislatures and prohibited from serving more than three years out of any six. The actual number of delegates was not critical, since each state delegation cast a single vote.

Routine decisions in the congress required a simple majority of seven states; for momentous powers, such as declaring war, nine states needed to agree. But to approve or amend the Articles required the unanimous consent both of the thirteen state delegations and of the thirteen state legislatures. The congressional delegates undoubtedly thought they were guaranteeing that no individual state could be railroaded by the other twelve in fundamental constitutional matters. But what this requirement really did was to hamstring the government. One renegade state could—and did—hold the rest of the country hostage to its demands.

On the delicate question of deriving revenue to run the government, specifically to finance the war, the Articles provided an ingenious but ultimately troublesome solution. Each state was to contribute to the common treasury in proportion to the current property value of the state's land. Large and populous states would contribute more than small or sparsely populated states whose land was not settled and improved. The actual taxes would be levied by the state legislatures, not by the congress, to preserve the Revolution's principle of taxation only by direct representation. However, no mechanism was created to compel states to contribute their fair share.

In general, the lack of centralized authority in the confederation government was exactly what many state leaders wanted in the late 1770s. A league of states with rotating personnel, no executive branch, no power of taxation, and a requirement of unanimity for any major change seemed to be a good way to avoid the potential tyranny of government. But soon the inherent weaknesses of these features became apparent.

The Problem of Western Lands

Once approved by the congress in 1777, the Articles of Confederation had to be approved unanimously by the state legislatures. Newspapers published the plan, but there was little public discussion because the war monopolized the news.

The most important proposed change that occupied the delegates in the final debate over the Articles was a plea by five states to give the congress administrative control of the western lands up to the Mississippi River as a national domain that could eventually constitute new states. Not surprisingly, these five states were small, with boundaries at most a few hundred miles from the coast: Maryland, Delaware, New Jersey, Rhode Island, and Pennsylvania. Though Pennsylvania was much larger than the others, about one-fifth of its area was simultaneously claimed by Connecticut, which asserted that its western boundary was the Mississippi River.

The remaining eight states claimed boundaries extending far to the west on the basis of early colonial charters from the British government (Map 7.1). Virginia's view of the map put the name Virginia over territory stretching west to the Mississippi River and north to Lake Superior, taking in present-day West Virginia, Kentucky, Ohio, Indiana, Illinois, Michigan, and Wisconsin. Massachusetts claimed a strip of present-day Michigan and Wisconsin, while the Carolinas and Georgia drew their western boundaries at the Mississippi River. A great portion of the contested western lands actually fell under the control of another group that was not party to the disputes in the Continental Congress: the many thousands of Indians who inhabited that region.

The eight states with western land claims were ready to sign the Articles of Confederation as approved by the congress in 1777. Rhode Island, Pennsylvania, and New Jersey eventually capitulated and signed, "not from a Conviction of the Equality and Justness of it," said a New Jersey delegate, "but merely from an absolute Necessity there was of complying to save the Continent." But Delaware and Maryland continued to hold out for many months, insisting on a national domain policy. Compromise finally came near the end of 1779 when the congress agreed that any "unappropriated lands that may be ceded or relinquished to the United States, by any particular state, . . . shall be disposed of for the common benefit of the United States and be settled and formed into distinct Republican States, which shall become members of the federal union." The logjam finally broke in early 1781 when the Virginia congressmen James Madison and Thomas Jefferson agreed to cede all lands to the confederation except the area that later became West Virginia. The compromise undercut Virginia's economic interests but made sense in terms of republican principles. Both Madison and Jefferson recognized that such a large area as Virginia claimed could not really be governed successfully, because the seat of state government would be too far from its citizens to represent them adequately.

The western lands issue demonstrated that powerful interests divided the thirteen new states; the apparent unity of purpose inspired by fighting the war against England papered over sizable cracks in the new confederation.

Running the New Government

No fanfare greeted the long-awaited inauguration of the new government. The congress continued to sputter along, its problems far from solved by the signing of the Articles. Day-to-day activities were often hampered by the lack of a quorum. The Articles required representation from seven states to conduct business, with a minimum of two men from each state's delegation. But some days fewer than fourteen men in total showed up.

State legislatures were slow to select delegates; those appointed were often reluctant to attend, especially if they had wives and children at home, and absenteeism was a constant problem. Consequently, some of the most effective and committed delegates were young bachelors like James Madison and men in their fifties and sixties whose families were grown, like Samuel Adams. Other delegates came for very short terms, barely learning the business of congress before they were on their way home. Many active politicians preferred to devote their energies to their state governments, especially when the congress seemed deadlocked or, worse, irrelevant. It also did not help that the congress had no permanent home. During the war, when the British army threatened Philadelphia, the congress relocated to small Pennsylvania towns like Lancaster and York and then to Baltimore. After hostilities ceased, the congress moved from Trenton to Princeton to Annapolis to New York City.

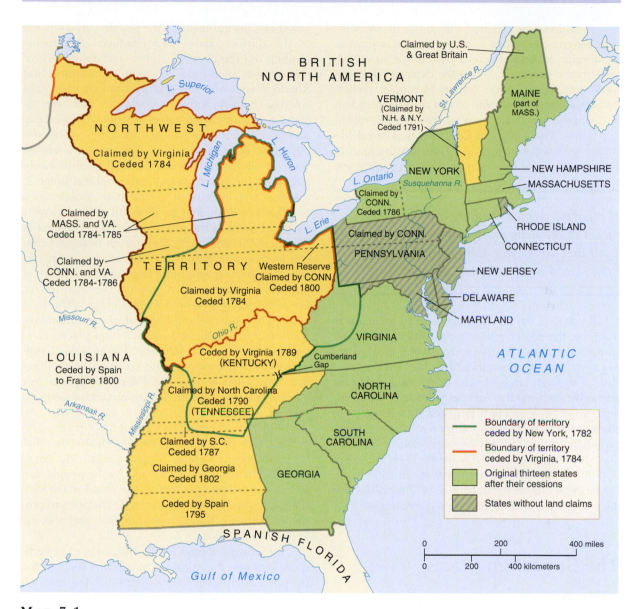

MAP 7.1

Cession of Western Lands, 1782–1802

The thirteen new states found it hard to ratify the Articles of Confederation without settling their conflicting land claims in the west, an area larger than the original states and occupied by Indian tribes.

READING THE MAP: Which states had the largest claims on western territory? What disputed territory became the fourteenth state?

CONNECTIONS: In what context did the first dispute regarding western lands arise; how was it resolved? How did the experience of the 1760s and the institution of democratic rule influence the decision of Virginia to give up its western lands?

www.bedfordstmartins.com/tap   SEE THE ONLINE STUDY GUIDE for more help in analyzing this map.

To address the inherent difficulties of an inefficient congress, executive departments of war, finance, and foreign affairs were created to handle purely administrative functions. When the department heads were ambitious—as was Robert Morris, a wealthy Philadelphia merchant who served as superintendent of finance—they could exercise considerable executive power. The Articles of Confederation had deliberately refrained from setting up an executive branch, but a modest one was being invented by necessity.

No fanfare greeted the long-awaited inauguration of the new government. The congress continued to sputter along, its problems far from solved by the signing of the Articles.

Because of the pressing needs of running a war machine, the confederation government got a slow start on writing its justifying document, the Articles of Confederation. Then the difficulties over ownership of western lands slowed down ratification for years. By the time the Articles were fully functioning, yet another problem emerged. Much more exciting political work was going on at the state level, especially during the creative burst of state constitution writing in the late 1770s. Before 1776, the cream of political talent in the country was attracted to the Continental Congress, but between 1776 and 1780 the talent flowed instead to the state governments.

The Sovereign States

In the first decade of independence, the states were sovereign and all-powerful. Only a few functions, like that of declaring war and peace, had been transferred to the confederation government. Familiar and close to home, state governments claimed the allegiance of their citizens. As Americans discarded their English identity, they thought of themselves instead as Virginians or New Yorkers or Rhode Islanders. State government was thus the arena where the Revolution's innovations would first be tried.

The State Constitutions

In May 1776, the congress in Philadelphia recommended that all the states draw up constitutions based on "the authority of the people." By 1778, ten of the thirteen states had produced documents spelling out the liberties, rights, and obligations of citizens and rulers, and two more (Connecticut and Rhode Island) adopted and updated their original colonial charters. Americans felt they had been injured by the unwritten nature of British political traditions; liberties they had assumed they were entitled to had been denied them. They wanted a written contract whose basic principles could not be easily altered by the government in power at the moment.

A shared feature of all the state constitutions was the conviction that government ultimately rests on the consent of the governed. Political writers in the late 1770s embraced the concept of republicanism as the underpinning of the new governments. Republicanism meant more than just the practice of popular elections and representative institutions. For some, republicanism invoked a way of thinking about who leaders should be—ideally autonomous, virtuous, public-minded citizens who placed civic values above private interests. For others, it suggested direct democracy, with not much of anything standing in the way of the will of the people. For all, it meant government that promoted the people's welfare.

Widespread agreement about the virtues of republicanism went hand in hand with the idea that republics could succeed only in relatively small units. A government run for and by the people had to be near at hand, so the people could make sure their interests were being served. Distant governments could easily become tyrannical; that was the lesson of the 1760s.

It followed, then, that the best form of government was one that allowed maximum voice to the people. Nearly every state continued the colonial practice of a two-chamber assembly but greatly augmented the powers of the lower house. Two states, Pennsylvania and Georgia, did away with the upper house altogether. Virtually all of the state constitutions severely limited the powers of the governor, identified in most people's minds with the royal governor of colonial days. Governors could no longer convene or dismiss legislatures at will, veto legislation, or buy loyalty through land grants or job patronage. Most states also restricted the governor's term to one year, with limited eligibility for reelection. Pennsylvania and Georgia abolished the office of governor altogether.

Daily governance of the state rested with the lower house, whose most important decisions were economic: printing, borrowing, taxing, and spending money to finance each state's war effort. Most states made their lower houses very responsive to popular majorities. Annual elections and guaranteed rotation in office prevented anyone from monopolizing power; if a representative displeased his constituents, he could be out of office in a matter of months. James Madison's second attempt to win election to the Virginia assembly offers an example. After only one year in office, the fledgling politician was defeated in 1777; he was sure it was because he failed to campaign in the traditional style with abundant liquor and the gladhanding his constituents had come to expect. Madison, shy and retiring, was not capable of electioneering in this manner. His series of increasingly significant political posts from 1778 to 1787 all came as a result of appointment, not popular election.

Six of the state constitutions included bills of rights, lists of basic individual liberties that governments could not abridge. Virginia debated and passed the first bill of rights in June 1776, and many of the other states borrowed from it. Its language also bears a close resemblance to the wording of the Declaration of Independence, which Thomas Jefferson was composing that same June in Philadelphia: "That all men are by nature equally free and independent, and have certain inherent rights, of which, when they enter into a state of society, they cannot by any compact deprive or divest their posterity; namely, the enjoyment of life and liberty, with the means of acquiring and possessing property, and pursuing and obtaining happiness and safety." Along with these inherent rights went more specific rights to freedom of speech, freedom of the press, and trial by jury.

Who Are "the People"?

When the Continental Congress called for state constitutions based on "the authority of the people," and when the Virginia bill of rights granted "all men" certain rights, who was meant by "the people"? Who exactly were the citizens of this new country, and how far did the principle of democratic government extend? Different people answered these questions differently, but in the 1770s certain limits to full political participation by all Americans were widely agreed upon.

Every state set property qualifications for voters and candidates. The idea prevailed everywhere that the propertied classes were the only legitimate participants in government. In nearly every state,

the highest offices—the governorship and membership in the upper house—drew only on the richest segment of the population. In Maryland, for example, a candidate for governor had to be worth £5,000, quite a large sum of money. Voters in Maryland had to own fifty acres of land or £30, a sum that would screen out perhaps one-third of adult white males. In the most democratic state, Pennsylvania, voters and candidates alike needed only to be taxpayers—that is, to own enough property to owe taxes.

Who exactly were the citizens of this new country, and how far did the principle of democratic government extend? Different people answered these questions differently.

The justification for restricting political participation to property owners was so widely accepted that it rarely needed to be explained. Only property owners were presumed to possess the necessary independence of mind to make wise political choices. Are not propertyless men, asked John Adams, "too little acquainted with public affairs to form a right judgment, and too dependent upon other men to have a will of their own?" Adams and others assumed that only property owners would feel a keen sense of community and thus be able to think clearly about the public interest. Besides, it did not seem right to give a propertyless man a voice in decisions to levy taxes if he was not going to be paying taxes himself.

Probably one-quarter to one-half of all adult white males were disfranchised by property qualifications. Not all of them took their nonvoter status quietly. One Maryland man wondered what was so special about being worth £30: "Every poor man has a life, a personal liberty, and a right to his earnings; and is in danger of being injured by government in a variety of ways." Why then restrict such a man from voting for his representatives? Others pointed out that propertyless men were fighting and dying in the Revolutionary War; surely they were expressing an active concern about politics. Finally, a very few radical voices challenged the notion that owning property automatically transformed men into good citizens. Perhaps it did the opposite: The richest men might well be greedy and selfish, the worst kind of citizen.

But ideas like this were clearly outside the mainstream. The writers of the new constitutions were themselves men of property and often considerable wealth, and they viewed the Revolution as an effort to guarantee people the right to own property and to prevent unjust governments from appropriating it through taxation. John Adams urged the framers of the Massachusetts constitution not even to discuss the scope of suffrage but simply to adopt the traditional colonial property qualifications. If suffrage is brought up for debate, he warned, "there will be no end of it. New claims will arise; women will demand a vote; lads from twelve to twenty-one will think their rights not enough attended to; and every man who has not a farthing, will demand an equal voice with any other." Adams was astute enough to anticipate complaints about excluding women, youth, and poor men from political life, but it did not even occur to him to worry about another excluded group: slaves.

Equality and Slavery

Restrictions on political participation did not mean that propertyless people enjoyed no civil rights and liberties. The various state bills of rights applied to all individuals who had, as the Virginia bill so carefully phrased it, "enter[ed] into a state of society." No matter how poor, a free person was entitled to life, liberty, property, and freedom of conscience. Unfree people, however, were another matter.

The author of the Virginia bill of rights was George Mason, a plantation owner with 118 slaves. When he penned the sentence "all men are by nature equally free and independent," he did not have his slaves in mind. He was doubtless invoking this principle of equality to argue that Americans were the equals of the British and could not be denied the liberties of British citizens. Other members of the Virginia legislature, however, feared that the words could be construed to apply to slaves. These aristocratic slaveholders were finally put at ease by the addition of the phrase specifying that rights belonged only to people who had entered civil society. As one wrote, with relief, "Slaves, not being constituent members of our society, could never pretend to any benefit from such a maxim."

One month later, the Declaration of Independence used essentially the same phrase about equality, this time without the modifying clause about entering society. Two state constitutions, for Pennsylvania and Massachusetts, also included the inspiring language about equality, again without limiting it as in Virginia. In Massachusetts, where the state constitution was sent around to be ratified town by town, the town of Hardwick suggested that the sentence on equality be reworded to read "All men, whites and blacks, are born free and equal." But the suggestion fell on deaf ears.

PAUL CUFFE'S SILHOUETTE
Captain Paul Cuffe of Martha's Vineyard, off the Massachusetts coast, was the son of a Wampanoag Indian woman and an African man who had purchased his own freedom from a Quaker owner. Cuffe studied navigation and went to sea at age sixteen during the American Revolution (enduring several months of imprisonment by the British). After the war, he and his brother petitioned for tax relief, a move that foreshadowed Cuffe's life of dedication to racial issues. In his thirty-year career as a shipbuilder and master mariner, Cuffe traveled extensively. By 1812, when this engraving with silhouette was made, Cuffe had explored the African country of Sierra Leone as a possible site for resettlement of American blacks and had met with African kings, English dukes, and an American president.
Library of Congress.

The only other state to draft language about equality was Vermont, whose 1777 constitution explicitly made slavery illegal and based its logic on the equality phrase. (Vermont had almost no slaves within its borders. Its statehood was not recognized until 1791 because New York and New Hampshire, each of whom claimed the Vermont land as its own, had many friends in the Continental Congress.) A reluctance to include equality language in other state bills of rights and constitutions probably means that its radical implication for the institution of slavery was beginning to be recognized.

Yet inevitably, after 1776, the ideals of the Revolution about natural equality and rights and liberty began to erode the institution of slavery. In some cases, enslaved blacks themselves challenged their legal status. (See "Documenting the American Promise," page 230.) In 1777, some Massachusetts slaves petitioned the state legislature, claiming a "natural & unalienable right to that freedom which the great Parent of the Universe hath bestowed equally on all mankind." They modestly asked for freedom for their children at age twenty-one and were turned down. In 1779, similar petitions in Connecticut and New Hampshire met with no success. Seven Massachusetts freemen, including the mariner brothers Paul and John Cuffe, refused to pay taxes for three years on the grounds that they could not vote and so were not represented. The Cuffe brothers landed in jail in 1780 for tax evasion, but their petition to the state legislature spurred the extension of suffrage to taxpaying free blacks in that state.

A reluctance to include equality language in state bills of rights and constitutions probably means that its radical implication for the institution of slavery was beginning to be recognized.

Another way to bring the issue before lawmakers was to sue in court. In 1781, a Massachusetts slave named Quok Walker ran away from his master, who pursued and beat him. Walker pressed charges for assault and battery, and his lawyer argued in court that he was a free man, under the Massachusetts constitution's preamble that stated "all men are born free and equal." Walker won and was set free, a decision confirmed in an appeal to

the state's superior court in 1783. Several similar cases followed, and by 1789 judges agreed that slavery had been effectively abolished by judicial decision in Massachusetts.

In other northern states, untold numbers of blacks simply ran away from owners and claimed their freedom, sometimes with the help of sympathetic whites. In Philadelphia, one estimate holds that more than half of young slave men took flight in the 1780s to join the ranks of free blacks. By 1790, free blacks outnumbered slaves in Pennsylvania by nearly a factor of two.

Pennsylvania was the first state to legislate an end to slavery by statute, in 1780. Yet the law provided for a very gradual emancipation: Only infants born to a slave mother on or after March 1, 1780, had a future opportunity to be freed, and then not until age twenty-eight. That meant that no current slave in Pennsylvania would be freed until 1808, and well into the nineteenth century some blacks would still be slaves. (Not until 1847 did Pennsylvania fully abolish slavery.) Rhode Island and Connecticut adopted gradual emancipation laws in 1784. In 1785, New York liberalized its manumission law, expanding the terms under which individual owners could free slaves. Only in 1799 did New York adopt a gradual emancipation law; New Jersey followed suit in 1804. These were the two northern states with the largest number of slaves: New York in 1800 was home to 20,000 slaves, and New Jersey, more than 12,000. In contrast, Pennsylvania had just 1,706. Gradual emancipation illustrates the tension between radical and conservative implications of republican ideology. Republican government was designed to protect people's liberties and property; yet slaves were both people and property. Gradual emancipation balanced the civil rights of blacks and the property

Legal Changes to Slavery, 1777–1804

Blacks Petition for Freedom and Rights

In the 1780s, a language of rights and liberty was in the air and on many lips. Extraordinary times encouraged extraordinary actions, and enslaved as well as newly freed African Americans everywhere felt emboldened to make bids to enlarge their own liberty. Brand-new state governments held out the potential for revolutionary change in legal and social relations, encouraging some blacks to take up their pens to petition for various freedoms. To be effective, petitions generally needed to beg or persuade rather than assert. Notice the kinds of argument made by these three sets of petitioners, the ways they describe themselves, and the promises they make about how they will use their hoped-for freedom.

DOCUMENT 1. Four Men Petition the Massachusetts Assembly for Their Freedom, 1773

Massachusetts law in the 1770s allowed even slaves to present petitions to the government. These four enslaved men arranged for a printing of their petition so they could send a separate copy to each town representative instead of submitting a single copy to the assembly. (The document was entirely set in type except the last word—Thompson—which was written in by hand.) Making a separate appeal to each representative was perhaps a way to maximize the impact of the petition.

Boston, April 20th, 1773

Sir, The efforts made by the legislative of this province in their last sessions to free themselves from slavery, gave us, who are in that deplorable state, a high degree of satisfaction. We expect great things from men who have made such a noble stand against the designs of their *fellow-men* to enslave them. We cannot but wish and hope Sir, that you will have the same grand object, we mean civil and religious liberty, in view in your next session. The divine spirit of *freedom*, seems to fire every humane breast on this continent, except such as are bribed to assist in executing the execrable plan.

We are very sensible that it would be highly detrimental to our present masters, if we were allowed to demand all that of *right* belongs to us for past services; this we disclaim. Even the *Spaniards*, who have not those sublime ideas of freedom that English men have, are conscious that they have no right to all the services of their fellow-men, we mean the *Africans*, whom they have purchased with their money; therefore they allow them one day in a week to work for themselves, to enable them to earn money to purchase the residue of their time, which they have a right to demand in such portions as they are able to pay for (a due appraizement of their services being first made, which always stands at the purchase money.) We do not pretend to dictate to you Sir, or to the Honorable Assembly, of which you are a member. We acknowledge our obligations to you for what you have already done, but as the people of this province seem to be actuated by the principles of equity and justice, we cannot but expect your house will again take our deplorable case into serious consideration, and give us that ample relief which, *as men*, we have a natural right to.

But since the wise and righteous governor of the universe, has permitted our fellow men to make us slaves, we bow in submission to him, and determine to behave in such a manner as that we may have reason to expect the divine approbation of, and assistance in, our peaceable and lawful attempts to gain our freedom.

We are willing to submit to such regulations and laws, as may be made relative to us, until we leave the province, which we determine to do as soon as we can, from our joynt labours procure money to transport ourselves to some part of the Coast of *Africa*, where we propose a settlement. We are very desirous that you should have instructions relative to us, from your town, therefore we pray you to communicate this letter to them, and ask this favor for us.

In behalf of our fellow slaves in this province, and by order of their Committee.

Peter Bestes,
Sambo Freeman,
Felix Holbrook,
Chester Joie.

For the Representative of the town of *Thompson*.

SOURCE: Herbert Aptheker, ed., *A Documentary History of the Negro People in the United States* (New York: Citadel Press, 1968), 1:7–8. Copyright © by Citadel Press. Reprinted with permission.

Document 2. Paul and John Cuffe Protest Taxation in Massachusetts, 1780

After judicial emancipation in Massachusetts, Paul and John Cuffe, together with five other freed men from the town of Dartmouth, sent this petition to the Massachusetts legislature.

To the Honouerable Councel and House of Representatives in General Court assembled for the State of the Massachusetts Bay in New England—March 14th AD 1780—

The petition of several poor Negroes & molattoes who are Inhabitant of the Town of Dartmouth Humbly Sheweth—That we being Chiefly of the African Extract and by Reason of Long Bondag and hard Slavery we have been deprived of Injoying the Profits of our Labouer or the advantage of Inheriting Estates from our Parents as our Neighbouers the white peopel do haveing some of us not long Injoyed our own freedom & yet of late, Contrary to the invariable Custom & Practice of the Country we have been & now are Taxed both in our Polls and that small Pittance of Estate which through much hard Labour & Industry we have got together to Sustain our selves & families withal—We apprehand it therefore to be hard usag and will doubtless if Continued will Reduce us to a State of Beggary whereby we shall become a Berthan to others if not timely prevented by the Interposition of your Justice & power & yor Petitioners farther sheweth that we apprehand ourselves to be Aggreeved, in that while we are not allowed the Privilage of freemen of the State having no vote or Influence in the Election of those that Tax us yet many of our Colour (as is well known) have cheerfully Entered the field of Battle in the defence of the Common Cause and that (as we conceive) against a similar Exertion of Power (in Regard to taxation) too well Known to need a recital in this place—

That these the Most honouerable Court we Humbley Beseech they would take this into Considerration and Let us aside from Paying tax or taxes or cause us to Be Cleaired for we ever have Been a people that was fair from all these thing ever since the days of our four fathers and therefore we take it as aheard ship that we should be so delt By now in these Difficulty times for there is not to exceed more then five or six that hath a cow in this town and theirfore in our Distress we send unto the peaceableness of thee people and the mercy of God that we may be Releaved for we are not alowed in voating in the town meating in nur to chuse an oficer Neither their was not one ever heard in the active Court of the General Asembly the poor Dispised miserable Black people, & we have not an equal chance with white people neither by Sear nur by Land therefore we take it as a heard ship that poor old Negroes should be Rated which have been in Bondage some thirty some forty and some fifty years and now just got their Liberty some by going into the serviese and some by going to Sea and others by good fortan and also poor Distressed mungrels which have no larning and no land. . . . Neither where to put their head but some shelter them selves into an old rotten hut which thy dogs would not lay in.

Therefore we pray that these may give no offence at all By no means But that thee most Honouerable Court will take it in to consideration as if it were their own case for we think it as to be a heard ship that we should be assessed and not be a lowed as we may say to Eat Bread therefore we Humbley Beg and pray thee to plead our Case for us with thy people O God; that those who have the rule in their hands may be mercyfull unto the poor and needy give unto those who ask of thee and he that would Borrow of thee turn not away empty. . . . Neither with lieing Lips therefore we think that we may be clear from being called tories tho some few of our Colour hath Rebelled and Done Wickedly however we think that there is more of our Collour gone into the wars according to the Number of them into the Respepiktive towns then any other nation here. . . . We most humbley Request therefore that you would take our unhappy Case into your serious Consideration and in your wisdom and Power grant us Relief from Taxation while under our Present depressed Circumstances and your poor Petioners as in duty bound shall ever pray &c.

SOURCE: Herbert Aptheker, ed., *A Documentary History of the Negro People in the United States* (New York: Citadel Press, 1968), 1:15–16. Copyright © 1968 by Citadel Press. Reprinted with permission.

(Continued)

Document 3. The Connecticut Assembly Answers a Petition from a Husband and Wife, 1789

Fifteen years after their loyalist owner fled the country, this black couple petitioned the state assembly to clarify their legal status. After a hearing, the assembly reviewed the evidence and granted them and their children freedom.

Upon the Petition of Cesar a Negro and Lowis his Wife both of Hebron in the County of Tolland Shewing to this Assembly that by the Laws of this State they were Slaves to the Revd Samuel Peters late of said Hebron but now of the City of London in Great Britain who left Said Hebron in Septembr 1774 and hath ever since remained in the Kingdom of Great Britain, and that the Petitioners have during the absence of the said Peters been at Liberty to provide for themselves, and that the Petitioners now have eight Children, which they have by their Industry maintained in a decent Manner, and the Petitioners in April 1784, wrote to the said Peters then at London requesting that he would give to the Petitioners and their Children their Freedom. And that the said Peters in answer to the request of the Petitioners on the 26th Day of July 1784 Wrote a Letter to the Petitioners declaring his willingness to grant the request of the Petitioners if it was in his Power, but supposed that the Petitioners were Claimed by the State of Connecticut as forfeited by the said Peters to said State, and that some Persons have lately been endeavouring to sell the Petitioners and their Children out of this State, and that the Petitioners are in continual fear of being secretly taken with their Children and sold out of this State to some foreign Country. Praying that they and their said eight Children may be emancipated and declared free from the said Peters as per Petition on File, And upon the Tryal of said Cause and a full hearing of the said Petition and the Evidence produced to support the same, it appears that the said Peters by his Letter dated at London the 26th Day of July 1784, to the Petitioners in answer to their request that he has in said Letter declared that he is willing to emancipate the Petitioners and their Children, and that he would do all in his Power to effect the same.

Whereupon it is Resolved by this Assembly that the Petitioners and their said eight Children be and they are hereby emancipated and declared free from the said Peters and all others from by or under his former Claim to the Petitioners and their said eight Children as Slaves.

Source: Herbert Aptheker, ed., *A Documentary History of the Negro People in the United States* (New York: Citadel Press, 1968), 1:21–22. Copyright © 1968 by Citadel Press. Reprinted with permission.

QUESTIONS FOR ANALYSIS AND DEBATE

1. What do the four Massachusetts petitioners mean when they congratulate the state legislators for their recent efforts "to free themselves from slavery"? Are they contradictory when they claim a natural right "*as men*" to relief from slavery but then also "bow in submission" to the "governor of the universe" who has allowed their slavery? What is it they "disclaim" out of consideration to their present masters? Why do they raise the case of a Spanish version of slavery?

2. Is the Cuffe petition essentially a call for "no taxation without representation"? Does it differ from the revolutionaries' stand on taxation in relation to Britain? Do the petitioners want representation—or relief from taxation? Why do they mention their military service?

3. Why do you think the Connecticut couple waited until 1784 to contact their former owner, who had left in 1774? Who might be scaring the family with threats to sell them out of state? What is the basis of their petition to the state government? On what grounds were they finally freed? How might you account for the assembly's additional five-year delay to arrive at this decision in 1789?

4. What can you conclude about the options available to northern blacks to secure freedom or rights under law? Are the petitioners confident about their rights, or about the outcome they expect? How have they had to shape their petitions to appeal to an all-white legislature? Do you see instances of subtle irony or sarcasm employed?

rights of their owners by delaying the promise of freedom.

South of Pennsylvania, in Delaware, Maryland, and Virginia, general emancipation bills were rejected; slavery was too deeply entrenched and too important to the economy to abolish. All three states, however, eased legal restrictions and allowed individual acts of emancipation for adult slaves below the age of forty-five, under new manumission laws passed by Virginia in 1782, Delaware in 1787, and Maryland in 1790. By 1790 close to ten thousand freed Virginia slaves had formed local free black communities complete with schools and churches, a visible alternative to the system of slavery.

In the deep South—the Carolinas and Georgia—freedom for slaves was unthinkable for whites. Yet more than ten thousand slaves from South Carolina—more than in all the northern states combined—achieved immediate freedom in 1783 by leaving with the British army from Charleston, and another six thousand set sail under the British flag from Savannah, Georgia. In sheer numbers alone, this was by far the largest emancipation of blacks in the entire country. Some went to Canada, some to England, and a small number relocated in the 1790s to Sierra Leone, on the west coast of Africa. Additionally, many hundreds of ex-slaves took refuge with Seminole and Creek Indians, becoming permanent members of their communities in Spanish Florida and western Georgia.

Although emancipation affected fewer blacks in the North, simply because there were fewer of them to begin with, its symbolic importance was enormous. Every state from Pennsylvania northward acknowledged that the enslavement of blacks was fundamentally inconsistent with revolutionary ideology; "all men are created equal" was beginning to acquire real force as a basic principle. On some level, southerners also understood this, but their inability to imagine a free biracial society prevented them from taking action. George Washington owned 390 slaves and freed not one of them in the 1780s, even when his friend the French general Lafayette urged him to do so as a model for others. In his will, Washington provided for the eventual freedom of his slaves—but only after his wife, Martha, died. (Upon his death, Martha Washington promptly freed them all, preferring loss of income to the uneasy situation of her life being her slaves' only barrier to freedom.) From the 1780s on, the North was associated with freedom and the South with slavery. This geographical pattern would have profound consequences for the next two centuries of American history.

The Critical Period

From 1781 to 1786, a sense of crisis gripped some of the revolutionary leaders who feared the Articles of Confederation were too weak. But others defended the Articles as the best guarantee of individual liberty, because real governance occurred at the state level, closer to the people. Political theorizing about the proper relation among citizen, state, and confederation remained active and controversial throughout the decade as Americans confronted questions of finance, territorial expansion, and civil disorder.

Financial Chaos and Paper Money

Seven years of war produced a booming but chaotic economy in the 1780s. The confederation and the individual states had run up huge war debts, financed by printing paper money and borrowing from private sources. Some $400 to $500 million in paper currency had been injected into the economy, and prices and wages fluctuated wildly. Private debt and rapid expenditure flourished. Newspapers bemoaned the rampant spending on imported items—hats, silks, china, tea—indulged in even by ordinary people. Some political leaders warned that the economy was headed for disaster. Legal suits between debtors and creditors quadrupled in many localities over prewar levels, and debtors' prisons became crowded. A serious postwar depression settled in by the mid-1780s and did not lift until the 1790s.

The confederation government was itself in a terrible financial fix in 1781. Continental dollars had lost almost all value: It took 146 of them to buy what a dollar had bought in 1775. Desperate times required desperate measures. The congress turned to Robert Morris, a merchant and newly reelected delegate from Pennsylvania, appointing him superintendent of finance for the confederation. Six years earlier, the wealthy Morris had procured from Europe much-needed muskets for the army, which were shipped to his private firm in crates disguised as routine merchandise. Morris had resigned from the congress in 1778 under suspicion that he had unfairly profited from his public service efforts;

RHODE ISLAND MONEY

In an effort to prevent currency deflation or infla-tion, Rhode Island's paper money in 1786 stated di-rectly on each bill that an act passed in May by the state assembly required the acceptance of such paper for all payments at face value.

Rhode Island Historical Society.

Rhode Island, with its active wharves at Newport and Providence, absolutely refused. When Morris pushed the impost amendment again in 1783, it was New York (whose premier port had just been freed from British occupation) that refused.

Morris's next idea was the creation of a private bank, the Bank of North America, which would enjoy a special relationship with the confederation government. It would hold the government's hard-

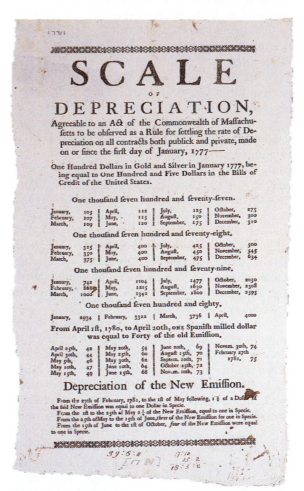

SCALE OF DEPRECIATION

This chart shows the monthly value of United States Continental dollars from January 1777 to February 1781, as stipulated by the government of Massachu-setts. For example, in March 1780, it took 3,736 Con-tinental dollars to equal the buying power of $100 in gold or silver, up from $3,322 the month before. Such a chart was needed when debtors and creditors set-tled accounts contracted at one time and paid off later in greatly depreciated dollars.

Courtesy, American Antiquarian Society.

indeed, he had left public life many thousands of dollars richer than he had entered it. Nevertheless, the congress called on him from 1781 to 1784 to apply his considerable talent to the confederation's economic problems.

To augment the revenue of the confederation government, Morris first proposed a 5 percent im-port tax (called an *impost*). Since there was no au-thority in the Articles of Confederation for such a tax, Morris's plan required an amendment to the Ar-ticles approved unanimously by the thirteen states. But unanimous agreement was impossible. States with bustling ports already collected taxes on imports and were loath to share that income.

money deposits (insofar as there were any) as well as private deposits, and it would make short-term loans to the government. The bank's contribution to economic stability came in the form of banknotes, pieces of paper inscribed with a dollar value. Unlike paper money, banknotes were backed by hard money in the bank's vaults and thus would not depreciate. Morris hoped that the new banknotes would perform the functions of paper money without its drawbacks. Congress agreed and voted to approve the bank in 1781.

The Bank of North America, located in Philadelphia, had limited success curing the confederation's economic woes. In the short run, the bank supplied the government with a currency that held its value, but it issued so little that the impact was very small. It mainly enriched Morris and three close associates who owned 40 percent of the bank stock. When its charter expired in 1786, the Pennsylvania legislature refused to renew it.

If Morris could not resuscitate the economy in the 1780s, probably no one could have done it. Because the Articles of Confederation reserved most economic functions to the states, congress was helpless to tax trade, control inflation, curb the flow of state-issued paper money, or pay the mounting public debt. But the confederation had acquired one source of potential enormous wealth: the huge territory ceded by Virginia, which in 1784 became the national domain.

Land Ordinances and the Northwest Territory

The Continental Congress appointed Thomas Jefferson to draft a policy for handling the national domain. Jefferson proposed dividing the territory north of the Ohio River and east of the Mississippi— called the Northwest Territory—into ten new states, with each state divided into townships ten miles square. He advocated giving the land to settlers, rather than selling it, on the grounds that the improved lands would so enrich the country through property taxes over the years that there was no need to make the settlers contribute to the government twice. Jefferson's aim was to encourage rapid and democratic settlement of the land, to build a nation of freeholders (as opposed to renters), and to avoid speculative frenzy.

Jefferson also insisted that the new states have representative governments equal in status to those of the original states once they reached a cer-

tain population. This ensured that the new United States, so recently released from colonial dependency, would not itself become a colonial power. Finally, Jefferson's draft prohibited slavery and involuntary servitude in all of the ten new states.

The congress adopted parts of Jefferson's plan in the Ordinance of 1784: the rectangular grid, the ten states, and the guarantee of self-government

THOMAS JEFFERSON BY JOHN TRUMBULL
This miniature shows Thomas Jefferson at age forty-five, during his years as a diplomat in Paris. The American artist John Trumbull visited France in 1788 and painted Jefferson's likeness in this five-by-four-inch format so he could later copy it into his planned large canvas depicting the signing of the Declaration of Independence. Jefferson requested three replicas of the miniature to bestow as gifts, a common and intimate item of exchange. One went to his daughter Martha, another to an American woman in London, and the third to Maria Cosway, a British artist of whom the widower Jefferson had grown very fond during his stay in France.
Monticello.

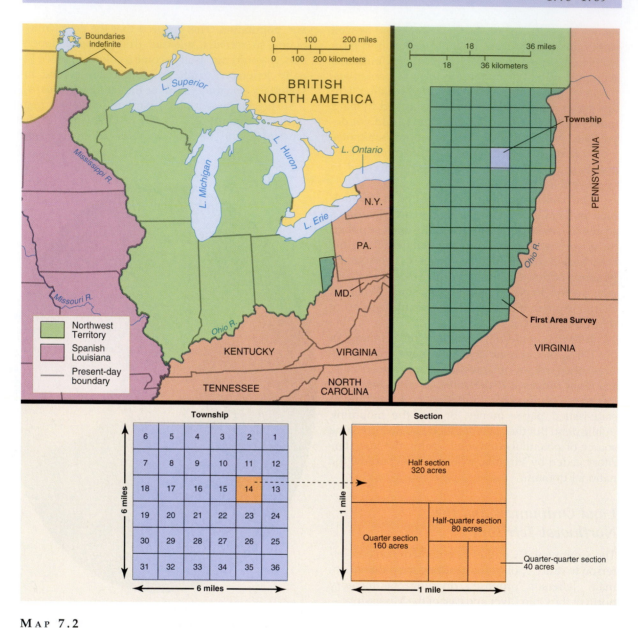

M A P   7 . 2

The Northwest Territory and Ordinance of 1785

Surveyors mapping the eastern edge of the Northwest Territory followed the Ordinance of 1785, using the stars as well as poles and chains (standard surveying equipment) to run long boundary lines. The result was a blanket of six-mile-square townships, further subdivided into one-mile squares each containing sixteen forty-acre farms.

and eventual statehood. What the congress found too radical was the proposal to give away the land; the national domain was the confederation's only source of independent wealth. And the slavery prohibition failed by only one state's vote.

A year later, the congress reconsidered the land act and passed a new version, the Ordinance of 1785 (Map 7.2). The new plan called for walkable townships six miles square, each containing thirty-six sections; each section contained 640 acres, enough

JEFFERSON'S MAP OF THE NORTHWEST TERRITORY
Thomas Jefferson sketched out borders for ten new states in his initial plan for the North-west Territory in 1784. Straight lines and right angles held a strong appeal for him. But such regularity ignored inconvenient geographic features like rivers and even more inconvenient political features like Indian territorial claims, most unlikely to be ceded by treaty in orderly blocks. Jefferson also submitted ten distinctive names for the states. Number 9, for example, was Polypotamia, or "land of many rivers" in Greek.
William L. Clements Library.

www.bedfordstmartins.com/tap SEE THE ONLINE STUDY GUIDE for more help in analyzing this image.

for four family farms. One lot in each township was set aside for educational purposes. The 1785 ordinance reduced Jefferson's plan for ten rectangular states down to three to five states, with boundaries conforming to natural geographic features like the Great Lakes and major rivers instead of abstractly drawn survey lines. Land sales would occur by public auction; the minimum price was set at one dollar an acre, but market forces could drive up the prices of the most desirable land. Two further restrictions applied: Land was sold in minimum parcels of 640 acres each, and payment had to be in hard money or in certificates of debt issued by the confederation government.

To join in the land boom, a purchaser thus had to have at least 640 hard dollars or an equivalent amount in debt certificates. Like every other currency substitute in the war years, debt certificates had been circulated, depreciated, and purchased by speculators at a small fraction of their face value. The speculators tended to be wealthy easterners who could afford the risk that the certificates would become worthless—or suddenly be worth a handsome amount. The Land Ordinance of 1785 made good their bet.

Jefferson's aim was to encourage rapid and democratic settlement, to build a nation of freeholders, and to avoid speculative frenzy.

Speculators purchasing the Northwest Territory acreage usually held the land for resale rather than settling on it. Thus they avoided direct contact with the most serious obstacle to settlement: the dozens of Indian tribes that occupied the land. Treaties signed at Fort Stanwix in 1784 and Fort McIntosh in 1785 coerced partial cessions of land from Iroquois, Delaware, Huron, and Miami tribes, but a united Indian meeting near Detroit in 1786 issued an ultimatum: No cession would be valid without unanimous consent. The Indians advised the United States to "prevent your surveyors and other people from coming upon our side of the Ohio river"—precisely the land claimed as the new national domain. For two more decades, violent and terrible Indian wars in Ohio and Indiana would continue to impede white settlement.

In 1787, a third land act, called the Northwest Ordinance, promised eventual self-government for a territory when the white male population reached five thousand, but it devised an interim plan for sparsely settled territories with a congressionally appointed governor. The other landmark feature of the 1787 act was a prohibition on slavery in the entire region, which this time passed without any debate. Something less than a fervent antislavery sentiment was at work in the passage of this provision, as shown by an accompanying warning that fugitive southern slaves caught in the Northwest Territory would be returned to their owners. And the prohibition applied only to the area north of the Ohio River; plenty of territory south of the river and west of Georgia was still available for the spread of slavery. Still, the prohibition on slavery in the Northwest Territory perpetuated the dynamic of gradual emancipation in the North: A North-South sectionalism, based on slavery, was slowly taking shape.

Shays's Rebellion, 1786–1787

Without an impost amendment, the confederation turned to the states to contribute revenue voluntarily. The states were struggling with their own war debts, and most state legislatures were reluctant to tax their constituents too heavily. Some segments of society did favor heavier taxation: The holders of the public debt certificates wanted to be paid, and wealthy people in general hoped taxation would counteract the alarming depreciation of paper money that was eroding their net worth. But the vast majority of ordinary Americans preferred low taxes, cheap money, and easy credit. And popularly elected representatives, facing annual elections, liked to give voters what they wanted.

Massachusetts, however, had a tough-minded, fiscally conservative upper house with veto power over its lower house. The upper house, dominated by the commercial centers of eastern Massachusetts, wanted to retire the state debt by raising taxes; to make matters worse, it insisted that taxes be paid in hard money, not cheap paper. Farmers in the western half of the state found it difficult to comply, and by 1786 sheriffs frequently confiscated property and put tax delinquents in jail.

However, the western farmers had learned from the American Revolution how to respond to oppressive taxation. They called conventions to discuss their grievances and circulated petitions demanding tax reductions, paper money, and debt relief legislation. In the fall of 1786, about 2,500 armed men marched on the courthouses in three western Massachusetts counties. The leader of this tax revolt was a farmer and onetime captain in the Continental army, Daniel Shays.

The governor of Massachusetts, James Bowdoin, who had once organized protests against British taxes, now characterized the Shaysites as illegal rebels. Another former rebel, Samuel Adams, defined the protest movement as a treasonous rebellion and took the extreme position that "the man who dares rebel against the laws of a republic ought to suffer death."

Why did the protesting farmers so upset the aging tax protesters of an earlier era? The Shaysites challenged the idea that popularly elected governments would always be fair and just. The revolutionary generation, and particularly its most democratically inclined members, had given little thought to the possibility that popular majorities,

SILVER BOWL FOR ANTI-SHAYS GENERAL

The militia of Springfield in western Massachusetts presented its leader, General William Shepard, with this silver bowl to honor his victory over the insurgents in Shays's Rebellion. Presentational silver conveyed a double message. It announced gratitude and praise in engraved words, and it transmitted considerable monetary value in the silver itself. General Shepard could display his trophy on a shelf, use it as a punch bowl, will it to descendants to keep his famous moment alive in memory, or melt it down in hard times. Not only is Shepard's name commemorated on the silver; SHAYS too appears in the last line, there for the ages to remember.

Yale University Art Gallery, Mabel Brady Garvan Collection.

embodied in a state legislature, could be oppressive, just as monarchs could. The farmers now felt they were an oppressed minority in Massachusetts with no hope of altering the composition of the state legislature, dominated by eastern counties.

The western farmers had learned from the American Revolution how to respond to oppressive taxation, and they challenged the idea that popularly elected governments would always be fair and just.

In January 1787, Governor Bowdoin recruited a volunteer army, 4,000 strong and composed of eastern Massachusetts men, to quell the rebellion. When Shaysites numbering about 1,500 attacked a federal armory in Springfield, where weapons were stored, they were met with gunfire; 4 rebels were killed and another 20 wounded. The governor's army then chased the dissidents north out of Springfield. The

final and bloodless encounter came a week later, at Petersham, where the army surprised the rebels on a freezing winter morning and took 150 prisoners; the others fled into the woods. Shays took off for Canada and other leaders left the state, but more than a thousand dissidents were rounded up and jailed. No one was executed for rebellion. The legislature passed the Disqualifying Act prohibiting the rebels from ever again voting, holding public office, working as schoolmasters, or operating taverns.

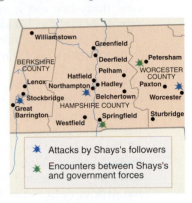

Shays's Rebellion, 1786–1787

The first two prohibitions denied the men a political voice, and the second two denied them occupations in which they could instruct or influence others.

Shays's Rebellion caused leaders throughout the country to worry whether the confederation could handle problems of civil disorder. Perhaps there were similar "combustibles" in other states, awaiting the spark that would set off a dreadful political conflagration. New York lawyer and diplomat John Jay wrote to George Washington, "Our affairs seem to lead to some crisis, some revolution—something I cannot foresee or conjecture. I am uneasy and apprehensive; more so than during the war." Benjamin Franklin, in his eighties, shrewdly observed that in 1776 Americans had feared "an excess of power in the rulers," whereas now the problem was "a defect of obedience" in the subjects. To some, the sense of crisis in the confederation had greatly deepened.

The United States Constitution

Events in the fall of 1786 provoked an odd mixture of fear and hope that the government under the Articles of Confederation was losing its grip on power. A small circle of Virginians decided to try one last time to augment the powers granted to the government by the Articles. Their call for a meeting to discuss trade regulation led, more quickly than they could have imagined in 1786, to a total reworking of the national government.

From Annapolis to Philadelphia

The Virginians took their lead from James Madison, now thirty-five and a member of the Virginia assembly. Madison persuaded the Virginia assembly to call for a meeting of delegates at Annapolis, Maryland, to revise the trade regulation powers of the Articles. Delegates from only five states actually showed up in September 1786. Like Madison, the dozen men who attended were deeply troubled by a sense of impending crisis, and they rescheduled the meeting for Philadelphia in May 1787. The congress of the confederation government reluctantly endorsed the Philadelphia meeting and tried to limit its scope to "the sole and express purpose of revising the Articles of Confederation." But at least one representative at the Annapolis meeting had far more ambitious plans. Alexander Hamilton of New York hoped the Philadelphia meeting would do whatever was necessary to strengthen the federal government.

Alexander Hamilton by character was suited for such bold steps. Born the illegitimate son of a poor mother in the West Indies, Hamilton trained as a bookkeeper and prospered under the intellectual mentorship of a local minister. At age sixteen the exceptionally bright lad greatly impressed an American trader, who brought him to New York City in 1773 and enrolled him at King's College (soon renamed Columbia). While at college, Hamilton got swept up in the military enthusiasm of 1776. By 1777 he had joined General Washington's staff, where he remained through much of the Revolution. After the war, he studied law, married into a wealthy New York mercantile family, and sat in the Continental Congress for two years. Despite his stigmatized and impoverished childhood, the aspiring Hamilton identified with the elite classes and their fear of democratic disorder.

The fifty-five men who assembled at Philadelphia in the spring of 1787 to consider the shortcomings of the Articles of Confederation were generally those most concerned about weaknesses in the present government. Few attended who were opposed to revising the Articles. Patrick Henry, author of the Virginia Resolves in 1765 and more recently the governer of his state, refused to go, saying he "smelled a rat." Rhode Island refused to send delegates. Two New York delegates, strongly opposed to revising the Articles, left in dismay in the middle of the convention, leaving Hamilton as the sole New York representative.

This gathering of white men included no artisans or day laborers or even farmers of middling wealth. Two-thirds of the delegates were lawyers. The majority had served in the Continental Congress and were intimately familiar with the workings of that government. Fully half had been officers in the Continental army, giving them a practical perspective on the financial difficulties faced by the confederation government. Seven men had been governors of their states and knew firsthand the frustrations of thwarted executive power. A few elder statesmen attended, such as Benjamin Franklin and George Washington, who was elected to preside over the meeting. But on the whole, the delegates were young, like Madison and Hamilton.

The Virginia and New Jersey Plans

The convention pursued its work in secrecy, so the men could freely explore alternatives without fear that their honest opinions would come back to haunt them. They even nailed the windows of the State House shut, to eliminate the chance of being heard by eavesdroppers.

The Virginia delegation first laid out a fifteen-point plan for a complete restructuring of the government. The Virginia Plan, as it became known, was a total repudiation of the principle of a confederation of states. Largely the work of Madison, the plan set out a three-branch government composed of a two-chamber legislature, a powerful executive, and a judiciary. It virtually eliminated the voices of the smaller states by pegging representation in both houses of the congress to population. The theory was that government operated directly on people, not on states. Among the breathtaking powers assigned to the congress were the rights to veto state legislation and to coerce states militarily to obey national laws. To prevent the congress from having absolute power, the executive and judiciary could jointly veto the actions of the congress.

In mid-June, delegates from New Jersey, Connecticut, Delaware, and New Hampshire, all small states, unveiled an alternative proposal. The New Jersey Plan, as it was called, resembled the existing Articles of Confederation in that it set out a single-house congress in which each state had one vote. Acknowledging the need for an executive, it created a plural presidency to be shared by three men elected by the congress from among its membership. Where it sharply departed from the existing government was in the sweeping powers it gave to the congress: the right to tax, to regulate trade, and to use force on unruly state governments. In favoring national

THE PENNSYLVANIA STATEHOUSE

The constitutional convention assembled at the Pennsylvania statehouse to sweat out the summer of 1787 with the windows tightly closed. Built in the 1740s to house the colony's assembly, the statehouse accommodated the Continental Congress at various times in the 1770s and 1780s. The building is now called Independence Hall, in honor of the signing of the Declaration of Independence within its walls in 1776.

Free Library of Philadelphia.

power over states' rights, it aligned itself with the Virginia Plan. But the New Jersey Plan retained the confederation principle that the national government was to be an assembly of states, not of people.

For two weeks, delegates debated the two plans, focusing on the key issue of representation. The small-state delegates were willing to concede that one house in a two-house legislature could be apportioned by population, but they would never agree that both houses could be. Madison was equally vehement about bypassing representation by state, which he viewed as the fundamental flaw in the Articles.

The debate seemed deadlocked, and for a while the convention was "on the verge of dissolution, scarce held together by the strength of a hair," according to one delegate. Only in mid-July did the so-called Great Compromise break the logjam and produce the basic structural features of the emerging United States Constitution. Proponents of the competing plans agreed on a bicameral legislature; representation in the lower house, the House of Representatives, would be apportioned by population, and representation in the upper house, the Senate, would come from all the states equally. But instead of one vote per state in the upper house, as in the New Jersey Plan, the compromise provided two senators who voted independently of each other.

Representation by population turned out to be an ambiguous concept once it was subjected to rigorous discussion. Who counted? Were slaves, for example, people or property? As people, they added weight to the southern delegations in the House of

Representatives, but as property they added to the tax burdens of those states. What emerged was the compromise known as the three-fifths clause: All free persons plus "three-fifths of all other Persons" constituted the numerical base for the apportionment of representatives.

Using "all other Persons" as a substitute for "slaves" indicates the discomfort delegates felt in acknowledging the existence of slavery in a republican constitution. The words *slave* and *slavery* appear nowhere in the document, but slavery figured in two other places besides the three-fifths clause. Trade regulation, for example, a power of the new House of Representatives, naturally included regulation of the slave trade. In euphemistic language, a compromise between southern and northern states specified that "the Migration or Importation of such Persons as any of the States now shall think proper to admit, shall not be prohibited by the Congress prior to the Year one thousand eight hundred and eight." And a third provision guaranteed the return of fugitive slaves: "No person, held to Service or Labour in one State, under the Laws thereof, escaping into another, shall, in Consequence of any Law or Regulation therein, be discharged from such Service or Labour but shall be delivered up on Claim of the party to whom such Service or Labour may be due." Slavery was nowhere named, but it was recognized, guaranteed, and thereby perpetuated by the U.S. Constitution.

The words slave *and* slavery *appear nowhere in the document, but slavery was recognized, guaranteed, and thereby perpetuated by the U.S. Constitution.*

Plenty of fine-tuning followed the Great Compromise of mid-July, but the most difficult problem—that of representation—had been solved. The small states worked to consolidate power in the Senate, where their weight would be proportionately greater than in the lower house, and Madison slowly recovered from his initial crushing sense of defeat. He had entered the convention convinced that the major flaw in the old government was that it had relied on unreliable states, and he feared that the Great Compromise perpetuated that flaw. But as the respective powers of the House and Senate were hammered out, he lent his support to the package as the most reasonable of political outcomes.

Democracy versus Republicanism

The delegates at the Philadelphia convention made a distinction between democracy and republicanism new to American political vocabulary. Pure democracy was now taken to be a dangerous thing. As a Massachusetts delegate put it, "the evils we experience flow from the excess of democracy." The delegates still claimed to favor republican institutions, but they created a government that gave direct voice to the people only in the House and that granted a check on that voice to the Senate, which would be composed of men more removed from the control of the people.

In the final document, senators would hold office for six years, with no limit on reelection. They were to be elected not by direct popular vote but by the state legislatures. In a country that was itself only eleven years old, a guaranteed six years in office was a very long time. Senators were protected from the whims of democratic majorities, and their long terms fostered experience and maturity in office.

Similarly, the presidency evolved into a powerful office out of the reach of direct democracy. The delegates devised an electoral college whose only function was to elect the president and vice president. Each state's legislature would choose the electors, whose number was the sum of representatives and senators for the state, an interesting melding of the two principles of representation. The president thus would owe his office not to the Congress, the states, or the people, but to an ephemeral body of distinguished citizens who could vote their own judgment on the candidates.

The convention carefully listed the powers of Congress and of the president. The president could initiate policy and propose legislation; he could veto acts of Congress; he could command the military and direct foreign policy; and he could make appointments to numerous lesser executive offices and to the entire judiciary, subject only to the approval of the Senate. Congress held the purse strings: the power to levy taxes, to regulate trade, and to coin money and control the currency. States were expressly forbidden to issue paper money. Two further powers of Congress—to "provide for the common defence and general Welfare" of the country and "to make all laws which shall be necessary and proper" for carrying out its powers—provided elastic language that came closest to Madison's wish to grant sweeping powers to the new government.

The framers had developed a far more complex form of federal government than that provided by the Articles of Confederation. To curb the excesses of democracy, they devised a government with limits and checks on all branches. They set forth a powerful president who could veto Congress but then gave Congress power to override presidential vetoes. They set up a national judiciary to settle disputes between states and citizens of different states. They made each branch of government as independent from the other branches as they could, by basing election on different universes of voters—voting citizens, state legislators, the electoral college.

The Constitution was a product of lengthy debate and compromise; no one was entirely satisfied with every line. Madison himself, who soon became its staunchest defender and has been called the Father of the Constitution, remained unsure that the most serious flaws of the Articles had been expunged. But when the final vote was taken at the Philadelphia convention in September 1787, only three dissenters refused to endorse the Constitution. The thirty-nine who signed it (thirteen others had gone home early) no doubt wondered how to sell this plan, with its powerful executive and Congress and its deliberate limits on pure democracy, to the American public. The Constitution specified a mechanism for ratification that avoided the dilemma faced earlier by the confederation government: Nine states, not all thirteen, had to ratify it, and special ratifying conventions, not state legislatures, would make the crucial decision. The innovation of debating the Constitution in special bodies elected only for that purpose drew attention to a major theme of the proposed plan: that the national government was no longer a league of states, but a government for all the people. But who could predict how the people, through the ratifying conventions, would react?

Ratification of the Constitution

Had a popular vote been taken on the Constitution in the late fall of 1787, it would probably have been rejected. In the three most populous states—Virginia, Massachusetts, and New York—substantial majorities opposed a powerful new national government. North Carolina and Rhode Island refused to call ratifying conventions. In only a few of the eight remaining states could the proponents of the Constitution count on an easy victory. Securing the approval of nine states appeared to be a formidable task.

The Federalists

The proponents of the Constitution plotted their course carefully and moved into action swiftly. To silence the charge that they had illegally bypassed the confederation government (which indeed they had, by failing to adhere to the legal procedure for amending the government and overstepping their charge only to revise the Articles), they sent the new document to the Continental Congress for approval. The congress, at first reluctant, finally resolved to send the Constitution to the states for their consideration. It helped that James Madison was then a member of the congress and was able to speak persuasively for the plan.

The pro-Constitution forces shrewdly secured another advantage by calling themselves Federalists. By all logic, this label was more suitable for the backers of the confederation concept, since the Latin root of the word *federal* means "league." The new Federalists, however, preempted the term and its positive Revolutionary-era associations and applied it to a comparatively nonfederalist plan that diminished the power of the states in a national government. Their opponents became known as Antifederalists, a label that made them sound defensive and negative, lacking a program of their own.

The Federalists identified the states most likely to ratify quickly, and they immediately scheduled special local elections to select delegates to ratifying conventions in those states. Delaware managed to push through elections, a convention, and unanimous ratification by early December, before the Antifederalists had barely begun a campaign. Pennsylvania, New Jersey, and Georgia followed within a month (Map 7.3). In the latter two states, voter turnout was extremely low; apathy favored the Federalists. Delaware and New Jersey were small states that lived in the shadows of more powerful neighbors; a government that would regulate trade and set taxes according to population was an attractive proposition to them. Georgia had a different reason for ratifying: A powerful national government would afford greater protection against hostile Indians and Spanish Florida, which bordered the state. "If a weak State with the Indians on its back and the Spaniards on its flank does not see the necessity of a General Government there must I think

MAP 7.3
Ratification of the Constitution, 1788–1790
Populated areas cast votes for delegates to state ratification conventions. This map shows Antifederalist strength generally concentrated in backcountry, noncoastal, and nonurban areas, but with significant exceptions (for example, Rhode Island).

be wickedness or insanity in the way," said Federalist George Washington.

Another three states to ratify with relative ease were Connecticut, Maryland, and South Carolina. As in Pennsylvania, merchants, lawyers, and urban artisans in general favored the new Constitution, as did large landowners and slaveholders. This tendency for the established political elite to be Federalist enhanced the prospects of victory, for Federalists already had power disproportionate to their numbers. Antifederalists in these states tended to be rural, western, and noncommercial, men whose access to news was limited and whose participation in state government was tenuous. (See "Historical Question," page 246.)

Massachusetts was the only early state in which the Federalists encountered difficulty. The popular vote for delegates gave a twenty-man advantage to the Antifederalists, whose strength came mainly from the western areas, home to Shays's Rebellion. Others opposed the Constitution as well. One rural delegate from the town of Sutton, in Worcester County, voiced widely shared suspicions: "These lawyers and men of learning and money men that talk so finely, and gloss over matters so smoothly, to make us poor illiterate people swallow down the pill, expect to get into Congress themselves; they expect to be the managers of the Constitution and get all the power and all the money into their own hands, and then they will swallow up all us little folks." Nevertheless, the Antifederalist lead was slowly eroded by a vigorous newspaper campaign. In the final vote, the Federalists won by a very slim margin and only with promises that amendments to the Constitution suggested by the Massachusetts Antifederalists would be taken up in the first Congress.

By May 1788, eight states had ratified; only one more was needed. The Federalists knew that North Carolina and Rhode Island were hopeless for their cause, and New Hampshire looked nearly as bleak. More worrisome was their failure to win over the largest and most important states. In Virginia and New York, Antifederalists emerged distinctly and coherently as opponents of the Constitution.

The Antifederalists

Antifederalists were a composite group, united mainly in their desire to block the Constitution. Much Antifederalist strength came from rural and backcountry areas with a long tradition of suspicion of the motives of eastern elites. Yet clearly many Antifederalist leaders came from the same social background as Federalist leaders; economic class alone did not differentiate them. Antifederalism also drew strength in states already on a sure economic footing, like New York, that could afford to remain in-dependent. Probably the biggest appeal of antifederalism lay in the long-nurtured fear that distant power might infringe on people's liberties. The language of the 1760s and 1770s revolutionary movement was not easily forgotten.

But by the time eight states had ratified, the Antifederalists faced a far harder task than they had at first imagined. First, they were no longer defending the status quo, now that the momentum lay with the Federalists. Second, it was difficult to defend the confederation government with its admitted flaws. Even so, they remained genuinely fearful that the new government would be too distant from the people and could thus become corrupt or tyrannical.

The new government was indeed distant. In the House of Representatives, the only directly democratic element of the government, one member represented some thirty thousand people. How could such a representative really know or communicate with his constituency, the Antifederalists wondered. And how could the constituents judge their representative's service to them? Clearly the status quo was preferable, as one Antifederalist explained: "The members of our state legislatures are annually elected—they are subject to instructions—they are chosen within small circles—they are sent but a small distance from their respective homes. Their conduct is constantly known to their constituents.

THE TENSIONS OF 1787
A New Haven engraver named Amos Doolittle captured the tensions of 1787. A wagon named **Connecticut** *sinks in the mud. To the left, under sunshine, men spouting nationalist ideas try to pull it out: "Pay Commutation" (pensions to veteran officers), "Comply with Congress." To the right, under severe weather, localist men call out "Tax Luxury," "Success to Shays," and "The People Are Opres'd."*
The Connecticut Historical Society, Hartford.

Was the New United States a Christian Country?

REBECCA SAMUEL, a Jewish resident of Virginia, conveyed her excitement about the new U.S. Constitution when she wrote her German parents in 1791 that finally "Jew and Gentile are as one" in the realm of politics and citizenship. Other voices were distinctly less approving. An Antifederalist pamphlet warned that the pope could become president; another feared that "a Turk, a Jew, a Roman Catholic, and what is worse than all, a Universalist, may be President."

The document that produced such wildly different readings was indeed remarkable in its handling of religion. The Constitution did not invoke Christianity as a state religion. It made no reference to an almighty being, and it specifically promised, in Article 6, section 3, that "no religious test shall ever be required as a qualification to any office or public trust under the United States." The six largest congregations of Jews—numbering about two thousand and located in Newport, New York, Philadelphia, Baltimore, Charleston, and Savannah—were delighted with this nearly unprecedented statement of political equality and wrote George Washington to express their hearty thanks.

But more than a few Christian leaders were stunned at the Constitution's near silence on religion. It seemed to represent a complete turnabout from the state constitutions of the 1770s and 1780s. A New Yorker warned that, "should the Citizens of America be as irreligious as her Constitution, we will have reason to tremble, lest the Governor of the universe . . . crush us to atoms." A delegate to North Carolina's ratifying convention played on anti-immigrant fears by predicting that the Constitution was "an invitation for Jews and pagans of every kind to come among us." A concerned Presbyterian minister asked Alexander Hamilton why religion was not in the Constitution, and Hamilton reportedly quipped, "Indeed, Doctor, we forgot it."

Measured against the practices of state governments, Hamilton's observation is hardly credible.

The men who wrote and debated the state and federal constitutions from 1775 to 1787 actively thought about principles of inclusion and exclusion when they defined citizenship, voting rights, and office-holding. They carefully considered property ownership, race, gender, and age in formulating rules about who could participate. And they also thought about religious qualifications.

Most leaders of the 1780s took for granted that Christianity was the one true faith and the essential foundation of morality. All but two state constitutions assumed the primacy of Protestantism, and one-third of them collected public taxes to support Christian churches. Every state but New York required a Christian oath as a condition for office-holding. Every member of Pennsylvania's legislature swore to "acknowledge the Scripture of the Old and New Testament to be given by divine inspiration." North Carolina's rule was even more restrictive, since it omitted Catholics: "No person who shall deny the being of God or the truth of the Protestant religion, or the divine authority of the Old or New Testaments" could hold office. In South Carolina all *voters* had to be Protestants.

Other common political practices affirmed that the United States was a Christian country. Governors proclaimed days of public thanksgiving in the name of the Holy Trinity. Chaplains led legislatures in Christian prayer. Jurors and witnesses in court swore Christian oaths. New England states passed Sabbath laws prohibiting all work or travel on Sunday. Blasphemy laws punished people who cursed the Christian God or Jesus.

Close to half the state constitutions included the right to freedom of religion as an explicit guarantee. But freedom of religion meant only that difference would be tolerated; it did not guarantee political equality. How then did the U.S. Constitution come to be such a break from the immediate past? Had the framers really just forgotten about religion?

Not James Madison of Virginia. Madison arrived at the 1787 convention fresh from a hard-won victory in Virginia to establish religious liberty. At the end of 1786, he had finally secured passage of a bill written by Thomas Jefferson seven years earlier called the Virginia Statute of Religious Freedom. "All men shall be free to profess, and by argument to maintain, their opinions in matters of religion, and that the same shall in no wise diminish, enlarge, or affect their civil capacities," the bill read.

TOURO SYNAGOGUE
A Jewish community inhabited the coastal shipping city of Newport, Rhode Island, as early as the 1650s. In 1759, the thriving group built a synagogue, the oldest Jewish house of worship still standing in the United States. The building blends a Georgian brick exterior with elements of Sephardic Jewish origin, and is sited diagonally on its property so that worshipers face east, the direction of Jerusalem. President Washington visited Newport in 1790 and wrote to "the Hebrew Congregation" a few days later: "It is now no more that toleration is spoken of, as if it was by the indulgence of one class of people, that another enjoyed the exercise of their inherent natural rights."
Touro Synagogue/photo John T. Hopf.

Madison had convinced both the Episcopalians and the Baptist dissenters, at war with each other over state support, that to grant either or both churches tax money would be to concede to the state the authority to endorse one religion—and by implication to crush another. The statute separated church from state to protect religion. Further, it went beyond mere toleration to guarantee that religious choice was independent of civil rights.

In Madison's judgment, it was best for the U.S. Constitution to say as little as possible about religion, especially since state laws reflected a variety of positions. When Antifederalists demanded a bill of rights, Madison drew up a list for the first Congress to consider. Two items dealt with religion, but only one was approved. One became part of the First Amendment: "Congress shall make no law respecting an establishment of religion, or prohibiting the free exercise thereof." In a stroke, Madison set religious worship and the privileging of any one church beyond Congress's power. Significantly, his second proposal failed to pass: "No State shall violate the equal rights of conscience." Evidently, the states wanted to be able to keep their Christian-only rules without federal interference. Different faiths would be tolerated—but not guaranteed equal standing. And the very same session of Congress proceeded to hire Christian chaplains and proclaim days of thanksgiving.

Gradually, states deleted restrictive laws, but as late as 1840 Jews still could not hold public office in four states. Into the twentieth century, some states maintained Sunday laws that forced business closings on the Christian Sabbath, working enormous hardship on those whose religion required Saturday closings. The guarantee of freedom of religion was embedded in state and federal founding documents in the 1770s and 1780s, but it has taken many years to fulfill Jefferson's vision of what true religious liberty means: the freedom for religious belief to be independent of civil status.

They frequently see, and are seen, by the men whose servants they are."

Probably the biggest appeal of antifederalism lay in the long-nurtured fear that distant power might infringe on people's liberties. The language of the 1760s and 1770s revolutionary movement was not easily forgotten.

In addition, the Antifederalists were convinced that elected representatives would always be members of the elite. Such men "will be ignorant of the sentiments of the middling and much more of the lower class of citizens, strangers to their ability, unacquainted with their wants, difficulties, and distress," worried a Maryland man. None of this would be a problem under a confederation system, according to the Antifederalists, because real power would continue to reside in the state governments.

The Federalists generally agreed with the Antifederalist assumption that the elite would be favored for election to the House of Representatives, not to mention the Senate and the presidency. That was precisely what they hoped. The Federalists wanted power to flow to intelligent, virtuous, public-spirited leaders like themselves. They did not envision a government constituted of every class of people. "Fools and knaves have voice enough in government already," argued a New York Federalist, without being guaranteed representation in proportion to the total population of fools. Alexander Hamilton claimed that mechanics and laborers preferred to have their social betters represent them. The Antifederalists challenged the notion that any class of men could be sufficiently free of selfish interests to rule disinterestedly for others. They feared that the Federalists were merely resurrecting rule by a wealthy aristocracy.

Antifederalists fretted over many specific features of the Constitution. It prohibited state-issued paper money. It regulated the time and place of congressional elections, leading to fears that only one inconvenient polling place might be authorized, to disfranchise rural voters. Probably the most widespread objection to the Constitution was its lack of any guarantees of individual liberties. Unlike nearly half of the state constitutions, the proposed Constitution did not contain a bill of rights.

Despite the Federalists' campaigns in the large states, it was a small state—New Hampshire—that provided the decisive ninth vote for ratification, on June 21, 1788. Federalists there succeeded in getting the convention postponed from February to June and in the interim conducted an intense and successful lobbying effort on specific delegates.

The Big Holdouts: Virginia and New York

Four states still remained outside the new union, and a glance at a map demonstrated the necessity of pressing the Federalist case in the two largest, Virginia and New York (see Map 7.3). Though Virginia was home to Madison and Washington, an influential Antifederalist group led by Patrick Henry and George Mason made the outcome uncertain. Mason had been present throughout the Philadelphia convention and was one of the three delegates who refused to sign the Constitution; this made him an especially effective opponent. The Federalists finally won his support by including a resolution that certain individual rights and republican principles were inviolate in the new government and by proposing twenty specific amendments that the new government would promise to consider. By a 10-vote margin, out of 168 votes cast, the Federalists got their ratification in Virginia.

In New York, Governor George Clinton represented agrarian interests in the northern part of the state, but more central to his antifederalism was a sense that a state as large and powerful as New York did not need to relinquish so much authority to the new federal government. New York was also home to some of the most persuasive and resourceful Federalists. Starting in October 1787, Alexander Hamilton collaborated with James Madison and New York lawyer John Jay on a series of essays on the political philosophy of the new Constitution. Ultimately numbering eighty-five, the essays were published in New York newspapers and later republished as *The Federalist*. The essays brilliantly set out the failures of the Articles of Confederation and offered an analysis of the complex nature of federalism. In one of the most compelling essays, number 10, Madison challenged one of the Antifederalists' most heartfelt convictions that republican government had to be small scale. Madison argued that a large and diverse population was itself a guarantee of liberty. In a national government, no single faction or self-interested group could ever be large enough to subvert the freedom of other groups. "Extend the sphere, and you take in a greater variety of parties and interests; you make it less probable that a majority of the whole will have a common motive to invade the rights of other citizens," Madison asserted. He called it "a republican remedy for the diseases most incident to republican government."

New York's ratifying convention met at Poughkeepsie, a town halfway between New York City and Albany, deep in the heart of Antifederalist country. An unmistakable majority of the delegates were Antifederalist, but newspaper debate and heavy lobbying produced some switches in votes. The last-minute arrival of news that Virginia had ratified finally tipped the balance in favor of the Federalists. New York's ratification assured the solidity and legitimacy of the new government. It took another year and a half for the Antifederalists in North Carolina to come around. Fiercely independent Rhode Island held out until May 1790, and even then it ratified by only a two-vote margin.

In less than twelve months, the U.S. Constitution was both written and ratified. An amazingly short time by twentieth-century standards, it is equally remarkable for the late eighteenth century, with its horse-powered transportation and hand-printed communications. The Federalists had faced a formidable task, but by building momentum and assuring a bill of rights, they did indeed carry the day.

Conclusion:
Decade of Decision

Thus ended one of the most intellectually tumultuous and creative decades in American history. Americans experimented with ideas and drew up plans to embody their evolving and conflicting notions of how a society and a government ought to be formulated. Widespread agreement supported the concept of a republican government in which the people are sovereign and government leaders derive their power and authority from the people. State constitutions, the Articles of Confederation, and finally the federal Constitution wrestled with different conceptions of the degree of democracy— of the amount of direct control of government by the people—that was truly workable in American society and that was consistent with the ideal of republicanism.

The decade began in 1776 with a confederation government that could barely be ratified because of its requirement of unanimity, but there was no reaching unanimity on the western lands, on the impost amendment, or on the proper way to respond to unfair taxation in a republican state. The new Constitution offered one set of solutions to these problems, but it drew intense opposition from Antifederalists. Once it was ratified, the Antifederalists accepted it but continued to worry that the government might fail. Only a relative few—men like James Madison—could anticipate that diversity of opinion was not only an unavoidable reality but a hidden strength of the new society beginning to take shape. This was the message of Madison's tenth *Federalist* essay.

The Federalists still hoped for a society in which leaders of exceptional wisdom would discern the best path for public policy. They looked backward to a society of hierarchy, rank, and benevolent rule by an aristocracy of talent, but they created a government with forward-looking checks and balances as a guard against corruption, which they figured would most likely emanate from the people. The Antifederalists also looked backward, but to an old order of small-scale direct democracy and local control, where virtuous people kept a close eye on potentially corruptible rulers. Antifederalists feared a national government led by distant, heterogeneous, self-interested leaders who needed to be held in check. In the 1790s, these two conceptions of republicanism and of leadership would be tested in real life.

www.bedfordstmartins.com/tap   SEE THE ONLINE STUDY GUIDE to test your mastery of the material covered in this chapter.

CHRONOLOGY

1775 **May.** Second Continental Congress begins.

1776 Virginia adopts state bill of rights.

John Dickinson of Pennsylvania drafts Articles of Confederation.

1777 **November.** Final draft of Articles of Confederation approved by congress and sent to states.

1778 State constitutions completed.

1780 Pennsylvania institutes gradual emancipation.

1781 Articles of Confederation ratified.

Creation of executive departments; Robert Morris appointed superintendent of finance.

Bank of North America formed.

Slave Quok Walker sues for freedom in Massachusetts.

1782 Virginia relaxes state manumission law.

1783 Treaty of Paris signed.

1784 Gradual emancipation laws passed in Rhode Island and Connecticut.

Treaty of Fort Stanwix cedes Iroquois land to confederation government.

1786 Bank of North America expires, not renewed.

Virginia adopts Statute of Religious Freedom.

Farmer Shays leads rebellion in western Massachusetts.

Annapolis meeting proposes convention to revise Articles of Confederation.

1787 Northwest Ordinance allows self-government and prohibits slavery in Northwest Territory.

Delaware provides manumission law.

May–September. Constitutional convention meets in Philadelphia.

1788 United States Constitution ratified.

1790 Maryland provides manumission law.

1799 Gradual emancipation in New York.

1804 Gradual emancipation in New Jersey.

BIBLIOGRAPHY

GENERAL WORKS

Lance Banning, *The Sacred Fire of Liberty: James Madison and the Founding of the Federal Republic* (1995).

Jacob E. Cooke, *Alexander Hamilton* (1982).

Joseph J. Ellis, *After the Revolution: Profiles of Early American Culture* (1979).

Merrill Jensen, *The New Nation: A History of the United States during the Confederation, 1781–1789* (1950).

Ralph Ketcham, *James Madison: A Biography* (1971).

Edmund S. Morgan, *Inventing the People: The Rise of Popular Sovereignty in England and America* (1988).

Richard B. Morris, *The Forging of the Union, 1781–1789* (1987).

Peter S. Onuf and Cathy D. Matson, *A Union of Interests: Political and Economic Thought in Revolutionary America* (1990).

John Phillip Reid, *The Concept of Liberty in the Age of the American Revolution* (1988).

Robert E. Shalhope, *The Roots of Democracy: American Thought and Culture, 1760–1800* (1990).

Gordon Wood, *The Creation of the American Republic, 1776–1787* (1969).

Alfred F. Young, ed., *Beyond the American Revolution: Explorations in the History of American Radicalism* (1993).

THE CONFEDERATION GOVERNMENT

Joseph L. Davis, *Sectionalism in American Politics, 1774–1787* (1977).

Daniel M. Friedenberg, *Life, Liberty, and the Pursuit of Land: The Plunder of Early America* (1992).

J. James Henderson, *Party Politics in the Continental Congress* (1974).

Merrill Jensen, *The Articles of Confederation: An Interpretation of the Social-Constitutional History of the American Revolution, 1774–1781* (1940).

Jackson Turner Main, *Political Parties before the Constitution* (1973).

Peter S. Onuf, *Statehood and Union: A History of the Northwest Ordinance* (1987).

Jack N. Rakove, *The Beginnings of National Politics: An Interpretive History of the Continental Congress* (1979).

Rosemarie Zagarri, *The Politics of Size: Representation in the United States, 1776–1850* (1987).

THE SOVEREIGN STATES

Willi Paul Adams, *The First American Constitutions: Republican Ideology and the Making of the State Constitutions in the Revolutionary Era* (1980).

Van Beck Hall, *Politics without Parties: Massachusetts, 1780–1791* (1972).

Ronald Hoffman and Peter J. Albert, eds., *Sovereign States in an Age of Uncertainty* (1981).

Marc W. Kruman, *Between Authority and Liberty: State Constitution Making in Revolutionary America* (1997).

Jackson Turner Main, *The Sovereign States, 1775–1783* (1973).

Richard P. McCormick, *Experiment in Independence: New Jersey in the Critical Period, 1781–1789* (1950).

Alfred Young, *The Democratic-Republicans of New York: The Origins, 1763–1797* (1967).

CITIZENSHIP

Ira Berlin, *Many Thousands Gone: The First Two Centuries of Slavery in North America* (1998).

Robert Dinkin, *Voting in Revolutionary America* (1982).

Linda K. Kerber, *Women of the Republic: Intellect and Ideology in Revolutionary America* (1980).

Linda K. Kerber, *No Constitutional Right to Be Ladies: Women and the Obligations of Citizenship* (1998).

James H. Kettner, *The Development of American Citizenship, 1608–1870* (1978).

Joanne Pope Melish, *Disowning Slavery: Gradual Emancipation and "Race" in New England, 1780–1860* (1998).

Gary B. Nash and Jean R. Sonderlund, *Freedom by Degrees: Emancipation in Pennsylvania and Its Aftermath* (1991).

Marylynn Salmon, *Women and the Law of Property in Early America* (1986).

Rogers M. Smith, *Civic Ideals: Conflicting Visions of Citizenship in U.S. History* (1997).

Rosemarie Zagarri, *A Woman's Dilemma: Mercy Otis Warren and the American Revolution* (1995).

THE CRITICAL PERIOD

William G. Anderson, *The Price of Liberty: The Public Debt of the American Revolution* (1983).

Robert A. Becker, *Revolution, Reform, and the Politics of American Taxation, 1763–1783* (1980).

John L. Brooke, *The Heart of the Commonwealth: Society and Political Culture in Worcester County, Massachusetts, 1713–1861* (1989).

E. James Ferguson, *The Power of the Purse: A History of American Public Finance, 1776–1790* (1961).

Robert A. Gross, ed., *In Debt to Shays: The Bicentennial of an Agrarian Rebellion* (1993).

James R. Morrill, *The Practice and Politics of Fiat Finance: North Carolina in the Confederation, 1783–1789* (1969).

David P. Szatmary, *Shays' Rebellion: The Making of an Agrarian Insurrection* (1980).

Alan Taylor, *Liberty Men and Great Proprietors: The Revolutionary Settlement on the Maine Frontier, 1760–1820* (1990).

THE CONSTITUTION AND RATIFICATION

John K. Alexander, *The Selling of the Constitutional Convention: A History of News Coverage* (1990).

Lance Banning, *The Sacred Fire of Liberty: James Madison and the Founding of the Federal Republic* (1995).

Charles Beard, *An Economic Interpretation of the Constitution* (1913).

Richard Beeman, Stephen Botein, and Edward C. Carter II, eds., *Beyond Confederation: Origins of the Constitution and American National Identity* (1987).

Herman Belz, Ronald Hoffman, and Peter J. Albert, eds., *To Form a More Perfect Union: The Critical Ideas of the Constitution* (1992).

Richard B. Bernstein and Kym S. Rice, *Are We to Be a Nation? The Making of the Constitution* (1987).

Stephen R. Boyd, *The Politics of Opposition: Antifederalists and the Acceptance of the Constitution* (1979).

M. E. Bradford, *Original Intentions: On the Making and Ratification of the United States Constitution* (1993).

Robert E. Brown, *Charles Beard and the Constitution* (1956).

Roger H. Brown, *Redeeming the Republic: Federalists, Taxation, and the Origins of the Constitution* (1993).

Christopher Collier and James Lincoln Collier, *Decision in Philadelphia: The Constitutional Convention of 1787* (1987).

Patrick T. Conley and John P. Kaminski, eds., *The Bill of Rights and the States: The Colonial and Revolutionary Origins of American Liberties* (1992).

Saul Cornell, *The Other Founders: Anti-Federalism and the Dissenting Tradition in America, 1788–1828* (1999).

Linda Grant DePauw, *The Eleventh Pillar: New York State and the Federal Constitution* (1966).

Michael Allen Gillespie and Michael Lienesch, eds., *Ratifying the Constitution* (1989).

John P. Kaminski and Richard Leffler, *Federalists and Antifederalists: The Debate over the Constitution* (1998).

Michael Kammen, *A Machine That Would Go of Itself: The Constitution in American Culture* (1986).

Cecelia M. Kenyon, ed., *The Antifederalists* (1966).

Ralph Ketcham, *Framed for Posterity: The Enduring Philosophy of the Constitution* (1993).

Peter B. Knupfer, *The Union As It Is: Constitutional Unionism and Sectional Compromise, 1787–1861* (1991).

Leonard W. Levy and Dennis J. Mahoney, eds., *The Framing and Ratification of the Constitution* (1987).

Jackson Turner Main, *The Antifederalists: Critics of the Constitution, 1781–1788* (1961).

Elizabeth P. McCaughey, *Government by Choice: Inventing the United States Constitution* (1987).

Forrest McDonald, *We the People: The Economic Origins of the Constitution* (1958).

William Lee Miller, *The Business of May Next: James Madison and the Founding* (1992).

Richard B. Morris, *Witnesses at the Creation: Hamilton, Madison, Jay, and the Constitution* (1985).

Ellen Franken Paul and Howard Dickman, eds., *Liberty, Property, and the Foundations of the American Constitution* (1989).

Jack N. Rakove, *James Madison and the Creation of the American Republic* (1990).

Jack N. Rakove, *Original Meanings: Politics and Ideas in the Making of the Constitution* (1996).

John Phillip Reid, *Constitutional History of the American Revolution: The Authority of Rights* (1986).

William H. Riker, *The Strategy of Rhetoric: Campaigning for the American Constitution* (1996).

Robert A. Rutland, *The Ordeal of the Constitution: The Antifederalists and the Ratification Struggle of 1787–1788* (1966).

Stephen L. Schechter, *The Reluctant Pillar: New York and the Adoption of the Federal Constitution* (1985).

Bernard Schwartz, *The Great Rights of Mankind: A History of the American Bill of Rights* (1992).

Garry Wills, *Explaining America: The Federalist* (1981).

RELIGION

Ruth H. Bloch, *Visionary Republic: Millennial Themes in American Thought, 1756–1800* (1985).

Morton Borden, *Jews, Turks, and Infidels* (1984).

Thomas E. Buckley, *Church and State in Revolutionary Virginia, 1776–1787* (1977).

Jon Butler, *Awash in a Sea of Faith: Christianizing the American People* (1990).

Naomi W. Cohen, *Jews in Christian America: The Pursuit of Religious Equality* (1992).

Thomas J. Curry, *The First Freedoms: Church and State in America to the Passage of the First Amendment* (1986).

Nathan O. Hatch, *The Sacred Cause of Liberty: Republican Thought and the Millennium in Revolutionary New England* (1977).

Nathan O. Hatch, *The Democratization of American Christianity* (1989).

Ronald Hoffman and Peter Albert, eds., *Religion in a Revolutionary Age* (1994).

Rhys Isaac, *The Transformation of Virginia, 1740–1790* (1982).

Leonard W. Levy, *The Establishment Clause: Religion and the First Amendment* (1994).

Jacob Marcus, *United States Jewry, 1776–1985* (1989).

William G. McLoughlin, *New England Dissent, 1630–1833: The Baptists and the Separation of Church and State* (1971).

William Lee Miller, *The First Liberty: Religion and the American Republic* (1986).

Sally Schwartz, *A Mixed Multitude: The Struggle for Toleration in Colonial Pennsylvania* (1987).

WASHINGTON STANDS OUTSIDE OF TIME

    A French clockmaker and artist produced this piece
of Washington memorabilia after the death of the president. Washington's trim
figure, rendered in gilt bronze, sports a spiffy uniform complete with epaulets
on the shoulders. One gloved hand rests on a sword while the other holds a
rolled parchment, offered up in front of an eagle, the symbol of America's
strength. Below the eagle a familiar motto is inscribed: "E Pluribus Unum,"
or, out of many, one, a reference to the political unity of the sovereign states.
Below the clock is another motto that quickly became a commonplace about
Washington: "First in War, First in Peace, and First in the Hearts of his Coun-
trymen." In his lifetime and for years after, Washington attained celebrity status, and Americans immortalized him in many souvenirs.

The Warner Collection of Gulf States Paper Corporation.

THE NEW NATION TAKES FORM

1789–1800

8

THE ELECTION OF GEORGE WASHINGTON in February 1789 was quick work. Seven months earlier, right after Virginia and New Hampshire ratified the Constitution, many July 4 orators and newspaper editors considered the Virginia planter as good as president, and the tallying of the unanimous votes by the electoral college became a mere formality. Washington was everyone's first choice. He perfectly embodied the republican ideal of disinterested, public-spirited leadership; indeed, he cultivated that image. His self-sacrificing leadership during the Revolutionary War had earned him the gratitude of many Americans. Here was a general who had refused all salary for his war service and who wintered with his army in the field, instead of retiring to more privileged housing. At the end of the war, he had dramatically surrendered his sword to the Continental Congress, symbolizing the subservience of military power to the law.

Washington professed an attractive reluctance to accept the presidency; that way no one could accuse him of lusting for power. In his diary he wrote that his impending inauguration made him feel like "a culprit who is going to the place of his execution, so unwilling am I, in the evening of a life nearly consumed in public cares, to quit a peaceful abode for an Ocean of difficulties." His diary, of course, was not really a private document, as Washington knew full well; his sense of his place in history already controlled his pen. Instead, he entrusted his real confidences to Alexander Hamilton, the young New Yorker who had served at his side in the army. Could he really profess reluctance and then accept the presidency, he wrote Hamilton, and still avoid the charge of excessive ambition? Hamilton replied that he must accept the office: Public sentiment was universally for it.

Washington accepted, and in April he journeyed from Virginia to the capital, New York City, in six days, encountering cheering crowds, large triumphal arches, and military parades at many villages en route. In New York City, he mounted a white horse and headed a procession down Broadway to the applause of thirty thousand. He took the oath of office at the newly built Federal Hall at Broad and Wall Streets; a cannon salute in the harbor signaled his inauguration.

The pageantry was a kind of hero worship for Washington as an individual. But the question, as yet unresolved, was whether the office of the presidency itself would be grandly heroic. The arches, the grand entry on a white horse, the gun salute—all this was an uneasy reminder of the trappings of monarchy. In its first month, Congress debated the proper form of address for the president, raising explicitly the issue of how kingly this new presidency was to be. Titles such as "His Highness, the President of the United States of America and Protector of Their Liberties" and "His Majesty, the President" were floated as possibilities, while Washington himself was known to favor "His High Mightiness." Several former

GEORGE WASHINGTON BY JOSEPH WRIGHT
George Washington wears a laurel wreath, the traditional mark of honor in ancient times. Carved in beeswax in 1784, the work elevates Washington to the status of a Greek or Roman hero.
Courtesy of the Mount Vernon Ladies' Association.

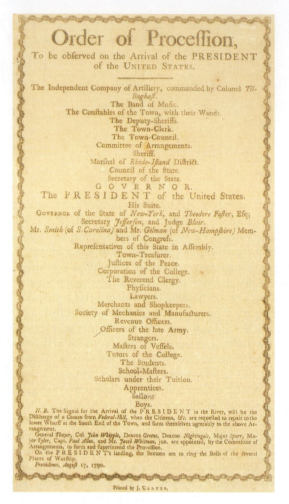

Antifederalists sitting in Congress held out for a less exalted title. The final version was simply "President of the United States of America," and the established form of address became "Mr. President," a subdued yet dignified title in a society where only independent, property-owning adult white males could presume to be called "Mister."

Washington's genius in establishing the presidency lay in his capacity for implanting his own reputation for integrity into the office itself. He was not a particularly brilliant thinker, nor was he a shrewd political strategist. He was not even a very congenial man. In the political language of the day, he was virtuous. Washington was studiously aloof, resolute, and dignified, to the point of appearing wooden at times. He encouraged pomp and ceremony to create respect for the authority of his office, traveling with no fewer than six horses drawing his coach, hosting formal balls, and surrounding himself with servants in livery. He even held weekly

ORDER OF PROCESSION
When President Washington visited Providence, Rhode Island, the town government prepared an "Order of Procession" to inform citizens of their exact place in the welcoming parade. Soldiers, a band, and town officers preceded the honored guest, whose immediate entourage included two governors, a cabinet member, a judge, and two members of Congress. Next came town politicians, professors in the local college (Brown), clergy, doctors, lawyers, and merchants. Further along came masters of ships, tutors at Brown, college students, and, bringing up the rear, apprentices, sailors, and boys. Who was excluded from the procession? How might merchants or sailors feel about their place in line? Several such "orders of procession" exist for other towns; were such elaborate rituals consistent with a non-monarchical political system? In what other ways might President Washington have entered a town?
The Huntington Library and Art Collections, San Marino, California.

levees, as European monarchs did, hour-long audiences granted to distinguished visitors, at which Washington appeared attired in black velvet, a feathered hat, and a polished sword. The president and his guests bowed, avoiding the egalitarian familiarity of handshakes. But he always managed, perhaps just barely, to avoid the extreme of royal splendor.

The thirteen American states had just come through a difficult decade, swinging between a distrust of executive power on the one hand and a fear of turbulent factional politics on the other. The first task of the new government was to establish its legitimacy and authority. Washington's reputation for integrity boosted confidence that executive power could be compatible with the public good. And his strong pronouncements about the evils of divisive factions raised hopes that at last America was on a steady course.

National harmony proved elusive, however. Political divisions emerged in the 1790s, despite the best intentions of the decade's statesmen. Even men who had worked together to ratify the Constitution found that the process of implementing it exposed serious disagreement. Economic policy and foreign affairs proved to be the two most significant fissures in the political leadership of the 1790s. The disagreements were articulated around particular events and policies, but at heart they arose out of opposing ideological stances about the value of democracy, the nature of leadership, and the limits of federal power. By 1800, these divisions had begun to crystallize into political parties, the Federalists and the Republicans.

The Search for Stability

Conventional wisdom today praises the development of a party system: Parties organize conflict, legitimize disagreement, and mediate among competing political strategies. Yet they were entirely unanticipated by the writers of the Constitution. James Madison had argued in *The Federalist* in 1788 that a superior feature of the national government was precisely that its extensive size would prevent small, selfish factions from becoming dangerously dominant. Thomas Jefferson wrote in 1789 that "if he could not go to heaven but with a party" then he would waive all hopes of heaven. Parties were thought of as being destructive. No one was pre-

pared for the intense and passionate polarization of the mid-1790s.

Instead, leaders in the early 1790s sought stability to heal divisions of the 1780s. Veneration for President Washington provided one powerful source of unity. People trusted him to initiate the untested and perhaps elastic powers of the presidency. Congress quickly agreed on passage of the Bill of Rights in 1791, which satisfied many Antifederalist critics. And the private virtue of women was mobilized to bolster the public virtue of male citizens; republicanism was forcing a rethinking of women's relation to the state.

Washington's Cabinet

Congress immediately set up departments of war, treasury, and state, leaving to Washington the selection of secretaries over each. The president picked talented and experienced individuals for each post, regardless of their deep philosophical differences. For the Department of War, he chose former General Henry Knox, who had been secretary of war in the confederation government. For the Treasury, he turned to Alexander Hamilton of New York, known for his general brilliance and financial astuteness. Washington understood that heading the Treasury would be the hardest job; revenue problems excited discontent and had largely caused the confederation government to fail. To lead the Department of State, the foreign policy arm of the executive branch, Washington chose Thomas Jefferson, recalling him from his confederation post as minister to France, a country now in the early stages of a democratic revolution. No one understood the intricacy of diplomatic relations better than Jefferson.

In addition, for attorney general Washington picked Edmund Randolph, a Virginian who had attended the Constitutional Convention but had turned Antifederalist during ratification. For chief justice of the Supreme Court, Washington designated John Jay, the New York lawyer who vigorously defended the Constitution along with Madison and Hamilton in *The Federalist*.

Washington liked and trusted all these men, and by 1793, in his second term, he was meeting regularly with them, thereby establishing the precedent of a presidential cabinet. (Vice President John Adams did not join these meetings; his only official duty was to preside over the Senate, a job he found "a punishment" because he could not actually participate in legislative debates. He complained to his wife, Abigail, "My country has in its wisdom contrived for me the most insignificant office.") No one anticipated that two decades of party turbulence would emerge from the brilliant but explosive mix of Washington's first cabinet.

The Bill of Rights

Many Antifederalists had complained about the absence of guarantees of individual liberties and limitations to federal power in the Constitution, and seven states had ratified on the condition that a bill of rights be swiftly incorporated. Delegates at the 1787 Philadelphia convention had decided that an enumeration of rights was not necessary, since many state constitutions already protected freedom of speech, press, peaceable assembly, and the rights to petition and to have jury trials. But the complaint surfaced continually in the ratification process, and so in 1789, in response to Antifederalist criticisms, James Madison drew up a set of amendments.

Final agreement from both House and Senate on the first ten amendments to the Constitution, collectively known as the Bill of Rights, came in September 1789. Amendments 1–8 dealt with individual liberties, and 9 and 10 concerned the boundary between federal and state authority. The amendments had the immediate effect of cementing a sense of national unity. The process of state ratification of the amendments took another two years, but there was no serious doubt about the outcome.

The Bill of Rights had the immediate effect of cementing a sense of national unity.

Still, not everyone was entirely satisfied. Some eighty proposed amendments had been submitted by state ratifying conventions. Those that would change the structural details of the new government were never considered by Congress. Madison had no intention of reopening debates settled at the Philadelphia convention about the length of term for the president or the power to levy excise taxes or the power of Congress to maintain a peacetime army.

Significantly, no one complained about a striking omission in the Bill of Rights: the right to vote.

Only much later was voting seen as a fundamental liberty requiring protection by constitutional amendment—indeed, by four amendments. The 1788 Constitution deliberately left all decisions about defining voters to individual states, to promote stability in the new federal government. Any uniform federal voting law would run the double risk of excluding some who could already vote in state elections or including too many new voters deemed undesirable in the more restrictive states. Most states maintained property qualifications for voting, thus excluding slaves, servants, apprentices, tenants, wives, and a new and growing class of propertyless wage laborers at the lower end of the social scale.

The New Jersey state constitution of 1776, however, enfranchised all free inhabitants worth over £50, thereby including free blacks as well as unmarried women who met the property requirement. (Married women owned no property, for by law their husbands held title to everything.) Little fanfare accompanied this radical shift, and some historians have inferred that the inclusion of blacks and unmarried women was accidental, the result of an unstated assumption that the voters would be white and male. Yet other parts of the suffrage clause pertaining to residency and property were extensively debated when it was put in the state constitution, and no objections were raised at that time to its gender- and race-free language. Other historians have concluded that the law was intentionally inclusive. By 1790, a revised election law used the words *he or she* in reference to voters, thus making woman suffrage explicit. As one New Jersey legislator boasted, "Our Constitution gives this right to maids or widows *black or white*."

In 1790, only about 1,000 free black adults of both sexes lived in New Jersey, a state with a population of 184,000. The number of unmarried adult white women is unknown but was probably likewise small and predominantly widows. Considering the property requirement, the voter bloc enfranchised under this law could not have been decisive in elections. Still, this highly unusual state of affairs lasted until 1807, when a new state law specifically disfranchised both blacks and women. Henceforth, independence of mind, that essential precondition of voting, was redefined to be sex- and race-specific. After 1807, free black men could not vote in New Jersey until 1870, with the passage of the Fifteenth Amendment to the U.S. Constitution; for women, white and black, it took until 1920, when the Nineteenth Amendment became law.

The Republican Wife and Mother

The general exclusion of women from political activity did not mean they had no civic role or responsibility. A flood of periodical articles of the 1790s by both male and female writers reevaluated courtship, marriage, and motherhood in light of republican ideals. Tyrannical power in the ruler, whether king or husband, was now declared a thing of the past. Affection, not duty, bound wives to their husbands and citizens to their government. In republican marriages, the writers claimed, women had the capacity to reform the morals and manners of men. One male author promised women that "the solidity and stability of the liberties of your country rest with you; since Liberty is never sure, 'till Virtue reigns triumphant." By upholding public virtue, women bolstered political liberty.

Until the 1790s, public virtue was strictly a masculine quality. But another sort of virtue loomed in importance: sexual chastity, a private asset prized as a feminine quality. Essayists of the 1790s explicitly advised young women to use sexual virtue to produce more public virtue in men. "Love and courtship . . . invest a lady with more authority than in any other situation that falls to the lot of human beings," one male essayist proclaimed. If women spurned selfish suitors, they could promote good morals more than any social institution could, essayists promised.

Republican ideals cast motherhood in a new light, centering on the importance of mothers as the teachers of virtuous sons.

Republican ideals also cast motherhood in a new light, centering on the importance of mothers as the teachers of virtuous sons. Benjamin Rush, a Pennsylvania physician and educator, called for female education because "our ladies should be qualified . . . to concur in instructing their sons in the principles of liberty and government." Throughout the 1790s, advocates legitimized female education, still a controversial proposition, through the claim of significant maternal influence on the future male citizenry. A series of essays by Judith Sargent Murray of Massachusetts, using the pen name Constantia, favored education that would remake women into self-confident, competent, rational beings, poised to become the equals of men. But even

REPUBLICAN WOMANHOOD:
MRS. REUBEN HUMPHREY OF CONNECTICUT
This late-eighteenth-century American mother displayed her gentility by the objects she chose to grace her portrait: an intricate wood frame mirror, a silver tea service, a plumed hat incongruously worn indoors while tending the baby. Mrs. Reuben Humphrey of East Granby, Connecticut, was married to the superintendent of a state prison; this painting was done by a prisoner.
The Connecticut Historical Society, Hartford.

Murray had to dress her advanced ideas in the cloak of republican motherhood, justifying female education in the context of family duty.

This shift in understanding about women's relation to the state was subtle but profoundly important. Politics was still a masculine preserve, but now women's domestic obligations as lovers, wives, and mothers were infused with political meaning, and a few women became so bold as to claim an expanded scope for women's intellectual development as well. But nothing about this shift altered traditional gender relations. The analogy between marriage and civil society worked precisely because of the self-subordination inherent in the term *virtue*. Men should put the public good first, before selfish desires, just as women must put their husbands and families first, before themselves. Women might gain literacy and knowledge, but only in the service of improved domestic duty. Many of the essayists troubled to caution wives that they must still defer to their husbands. In Federalist America, wives and citizens alike should feel affection for and trust in their rulers and should never rebel.

Sources of Economic Change

Following a decade of severe economic instability, the 1790s ushered in a period of prosperity and sustained economic growth. New agricultural opportunities, transportation improvements, and innovations in finance were beginning to transform not only the economy but the way ordinary men and women thought about their work and their chances for bettering their lives.

Commercial Agriculture

From at least the mid-eighteenth century, most farmers had participated in market transactions at local stores and in nearby towns. Self-sufficiency was simply not possible in a society where a taste for some of the luxuries of life had taken hold. For example, a store in the village of Brookfield, in central Massachusetts, stocked fine cloth from England and India; watch chains and shoe buckles; teapots and dishware; and raisins, allspice, salt, sugar, and tea. Rarely was cash exchanged at the moment of purchase. Instead, the store owner recorded transactions in his account book, keeping a running total of each customer's debt, which was periodically paid off in either cash or, more likely, "country goods"—a surplus of cheese, butter, or grain from the farmer's production.

This pattern of local market exchange was altered in the 1790s, when dramatic increases in the international price of grain motivated farmers to step up their grain production. Food prices, driven by population growth, were generally rising in Europe in the late eighteenth century. After 1793, prices rose even more sharply, when France and England entered two decades of conflict known as the Napoleonic Wars. Soon all the major European powers were embroiled in war, leaving the United States, the only neutral shipper, with a near-monopoly on the Atlantic trade. American grain farmers from the Connecticut River valley to the Chesapeake responded by growing more wheat. The increase in overseas grain trade generated a host of new jobs in related areas as the number of millers, coopers, and ship and wagon builders expanded.

Cotton production also underwent a boom, spurred by market growth and a mechanical invention. Limited amounts of smooth-seed cotton had long been grown in the low-lying coastal areas of the South; but this variety of cotton did not prosper in the drier, inland regions. Green-seed cotton grew well inland, but it contained many rough seeds that adhered tenaciously to the cotton fibers. Typically, it took an entire day to clean a pound of cotton by hand. In 1793, a Yale graduate named Eli Whitney, visiting a Georgia plantation, turned his mechanical talents to the task of reducing the labor in cotton production. His invention, the cotton gin, could clean fifty pounds of cotton per day. The English textile industry provided a ready market for raw cotton; now the southern states could meet the increasing demand. The figures of cotton production tell the story: 138,228 pounds of cotton were grown in the South in 1792; two years later, the number was 1,601,000, eleven times as much, and by 1800, the figure was 35 million pounds. Cotton fever had gripped the South, with momentous and chilling consequences for the one million enslaved black Americans living there.

Transportation

The prosperous cash economy made possible by grain exports and cotton culture was initially confined to areas within thirty miles of navigable waterways or the coast. The high cost of transporting goods over muddy or rutted paths barely wide enough for a wagon was the single biggest obstacle to the spread of commercial farming. The only major continuous road existing at the beginning of the 1790s was the Post Road, running near the East Coast for sixteen hundred miles from Maine to Georgia. It consisted of local country roads, linked together in the 1780s, and it carried an increasing load of passenger traffic in stagecoaches as well as freight and the U.S. mail.

In the 1790s, east-to-west road building commenced. In 1794, the Lancaster Turnpike, the first private toll road in the nation, connected Philadelphia with Lancaster, sixty-five miles west, and later with Pittsburgh in western Pennsylvania. Soon another turnpike connected Boston with Albany, New

York. Private companies under charter by state governments financed these turnpikes; a company built the road and collected fees from all vehicles. In areas away from the coast, a major road extended southwest down the Shenandoah Valley, while a road called Zane's Trace moved across southern Ohio. A new road linked Richmond, Virginia, with the Tennessee towns of Knoxville and Nashville. An early Ohio law reveals the primitive character of the western roads compared with state-of-the-art gravel turnpikes in the East: The law prohibited stumps in the roadway higher than one foot.

Major Roads in the 1790s

By 1800, a dense network of dirt, gravel, or plank roadways connected cities and towns in southern New England and the Middle Atlantic states, while isolated roadways and old Indian trails fanned out to the west. Commercial stage lines connected major eastern cities, offering four-day travel time between New York and Boston and an exhausting but speedy one-and-one-half-day trip between New York and Philadelphia (Map 8.1). In 1790, only three stagecoach companies operated out of Boston, but by 1800 there were twenty-four. Western roads facilitated the migration of settlers—Kentucky and Tennessee became sufficiently populated to join the Union by 1800—but the roads were generally too slow to allow an economical movement of heavy, bulky agricultural products like grain.

South of the Potomac River, road building and commercial stagecoach travel remained rudimentary, chiefly because of low passenger demand. Two-thirds of the southern population—the enslaved blacks and the poorer whites—were unlikely to travel, and the elite planters generally owned their own coaches and wagons. Growers of cotton and tobacco continued to rely on the many southern rivers to move produce to market, a practice that reinforced the economic dominance of property owners fronting on the eastern waterways.

STAGECOACH ADVERTISEMENT
Stagecoach lines publicized their schedules and terms in newspapers. This advertisement appeared in the **New York Journal and Patriotic Register** *for August 21, 1793. It promises to accommodate passengers in the most agreeable manner and to reach Philadelphia in "about" twenty-four hours.*
Courtesy, American Antiquarian Society.

Merchants and Capital

The surge in the overseas grain and cotton trades stimulated the growth of the commercial classes in seacoast cities. At the pinnacle of the business community were the merchants, often men with multiple financial dealings in both wholesale and retail operations. The richest merchants not only bought and sold foreign goods; they typically owned some fraction of the ships that carried the goods.

In the 1780s, states could and did erect trade barriers, but the creation of the federal government finally removed all obstacles to interstate business alliances and guaranteed the free movement of goods across state borders. The horizons of the business community widened, and the volume of trade mushroomed. New investment opportunities beck-

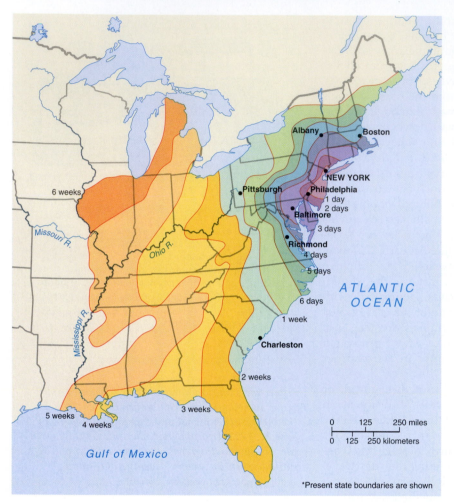

MAP 8.1

Travel Times from New York City in 1800
Notice that the first week of travel out of New York extends over a much greater distance than subsequent weeks because of poor or nonexistent roads in the West, mountain barriers, and Indian dangers. River corridors in the West and East speeded up travel— only if one were going downriver. Also note that travel by sea (north and south along the coast) was much faster than land travel.

oned in mercantile trades and in such areas as the chartering of turnpike companies and stagecoach lines and the development of textile mills.

These opportunities required a larger and longer commitment of capital than did a joint venture for a single cargo in a ship. The need for investment capital was met by the development of commercial banking, a financial innovation that had not existed in America before the Revolution. During the 1790s, the number of banks multiplied nearly tenfold, from three at the beginning of the decade to twenty-nine in 1800. Banks drew in money chiefly through the sale of stock. They then made loans in the form of banknotes, paper currency backed by the gold and silver paid in by stockholders. Because they issued two or three times as much money in banknotes as they held in hard money, banks were really creating new money for the economy.

Rich merchants embraced banking opportunities with enthusiasm. In one feverish week in New York City in 1792, three rival banks were proposed, with prospective stock subscriptions totaling about $4 million. Isaac Roosevelt, the president of the Bank of New York, typified the multiventure involvement of this new breed of merchants. Roosevelt owned a sugar refinery, financed overseas shipping, and speculated heavily in confiscated loyalist real estate. As bank president, he had ready access to investments (buying stock in the bank) and to credit. Not everyone appreciated the virtues of commercial banking, however. When Roosevelt and his fellow merchants applied for a state charter for their bank, one New York newspaper condemned the bank as "an odious combination of wealthy men."

Hamilton's Political Economy

In late 1790, the government moved from New York City to Philadelphia, which was more centrally located. This too was a temporary home; the long-range plan entailed construction of the capital on the Potomac River between Maryland and Virginia, independent of any state. (See "Historical Question," page 264.) Serious economic choices faced the country, and the young secretary of the treasury, Alexander Hamilton, proposed a wide-ranging, three-part economic program as innovative as it was controversial.

ALEXANDER HAMILTON BY JOHN TRUMBULL
Alexander Hamilton posed for this portrait in 1792, at age thirty-seven and at his height of power. Ever a prodigy, Hamilton at age nineteen became an indispensable wartime aide to George Washington. In his midtwenties he gained admission to the bar after only three months of study. In 1789, he became Washington's youngest cabinet member.
Yale University Art Gallery.

The Public Debt and Taxes

Hamilton first turned his attention to the very large public debt, nearly $52 million. About $11.7 million was owed to foreign creditors, while a tangled web of domestic IOUs and interest-bearing public securities amounted to a further $40.4 million. The debt dated from the difficult war years, when the government needed supplies and manpower but had no independent source of revenue. In the 1780s, the actual paper IOUs and certificates of debt had fallen in value, in some states to as little as one-twentieth of the original value; this drop reflected the widespread belief that the confederation government could never make good on them. The question now was open: What exactly should be done about the debt?

Hamilton's answer, elaborated in his *Report on Public Credit* in January 1790, was that the debt, both foreign and domestic, be funded at full value. This meant that an old IOU or a certificate of debt would be rolled over into a new bond, at the same value, with a schedule of regular interest payments from government to holder and a promise to retire the debt in forty years. Thus there would still be a public debt, but it would be secure, supported by the confidence of Americans in their new government. The new bonds would circulate as a stable medium of exchange, injecting new and more valuable money into the economy. "A national debt if not excessive will be to us a national blessing; it will be a powerfull cement of our union," Hamilton wrote to a financier.

Probably about 2 percent of the white population held the largest portions of the debt. Many of them were wealthy speculators who had bought up the IOUs cheaply, betting that they might rise in value in the long run. Now these influential men would have a direct financial stake in the new government, support that Hamilton regarded as essential to the country's stability. He was also providing those same few men with more than $40 million released for new investment, a distinct improvement over the old depreciated bonds, which had circulated in daily transactions at only a small fraction of their face value.

If the *Report on Public Credit* had gone only this far, it would have been somewhat controversial. But Hamilton took a much bolder step by adding into the federal debt another $25 million still owed by some state governments to individuals. All the states had obtained supplies during the war by

How Did Washington, D.C., Become the Federal Capital?

WHY DIDN'T BOSTON, Philadelphia, or New York City become the capital of the United States? The great cities of London and Paris were great precisely because political power was situated at the heart of commerce and culture in those European countries. Although much smaller in scale, the several American cities boasted elegant houses, cultural institutions, lively economies, newspapers, food markets, taverns, coffeehouses, and stagecoach and shipping lines—nearly everything necessary to accommodate the political elites who would be running the new government. Instead, the infant United States chose marshy, vacant acreage along the Maryland shore of the Potomac River for its permanent capital.

While the choice of that particular site was by no means inevitable, the country's leaders agreed that there should be only one site. During the war years, the Continental Congress had jumped around many times, from Philadelphia, Lancaster, and York in Pennsylvania to Princeton and Trenton in New Jersey, and down to Baltimore, often on the run from the British army. Even after the war, the congress continued to circulate, meeting in Trenton, in Annapolis and Georgetown in Maryland, and finally in New York City. When the confederation government commissioned an equestrian statue of George Washington to inspire and dignify its meetings, a humorist suggested that the marble horse be fitted with wheels so it could be towed from place to place.

For some, a floating capital symbolized the precarious status of the confederation. But the alternative, a fixed location, put the federal government at the mercy of the particular state it sat in. If irate citizens stormed the congress, as had happened once in Philadelphia in 1783, could the local state's militia always be counted on to protect it? The writers of the Constitution thus came up with a novel solution. They decided to locate the capital on land not controlled by any state. The 1788 Constitution specified a square district, not exceeding ten miles on a side, where Congress would have sole jurisdiction; but they deferred the complicated choice of the exact site to the First Congress.

In 1790, more than forty cities and towns clamored for consideration, from Kingston and Newburgh in New York's Hudson River valley down to Richmond and Williamsburg in Virginia. Eleven contenders clustered along the Delaware River between New Jersey and Pennsylvania, roughly the demographic center of the country. Six more sites fell in the interior of Pennsylvania, along the Susquehanna River, each claiming to be the future geographic center as the country grew westward. Another eleven locations dotted the Potomac River from the Chesapeake to the Appalachians. Clearly, river transportation figured heavily in all these plans, and investors in canal and river navigation companies took special notice.

The First Congress struggled to reconcile private interests, regional jealousies, and genuine dilemmas of citizen access. A Pennsylvania proposal naming a Susquehanna River site finally passed the House but not the Senate. Virginians held out for the Potomac, drawing objections from New Englanders fearful of disease-laden southern swamps. Philadelphians insisted that their city, the premier cultural and economic center of America, was the only logical choice. In short, the situation was at a stalemate.

Another, unrelated stalemate obstructed Congress in early 1790. Alexander Hamilton presented Congress with his controversial plan to fund the public debt by assuming state debts. James Madison objected and wrested the necessary votes from Hamilton—at first.

Hamilton approached Robert Morris of Pennsylvania to propose a deal: If Morris would deliver votes for Hamilton's assumption plan, the influential Hamilton would back a capital site in Pennsylvania. But Morris could not command enough congressional votes, so Hamilton next approached Thomas Jefferson, secretary of state, who invited him to dinner with James Madison. There the three reached agreement: enough southern votes for assumption in exchange for a Potomac River site. Madison could not bring himself to vote for assumption, but he rounded up the necessary votes

PLAN FOR WASHINGTON, D.C., ON A HANDKERCHIEF
In 1791 and 1792, the pressure was high to get a detailed map of the proposed capital city into circulation so that prospective land buyers could be lined up. Finally a Philadelphia engraving firm produced this plan of the future city with each block numbered. It was reproduced on large handkerchiefs in an early marketing strategy to entice buyers. The actual site in 1792 consisted of fields and marshes.
Library of Congress.

from men representing districts along the river. In the final bill, Philadelphia was named the interim capital until 1800, by which time a site on the Potomac River, to be selected by President Washington, would be constructed and open for business. Robert Morris gloated that the Virginians had been tricked; he felt sure that Philadelphia's charms would ensnare the government permanently. Assumption quickly passed, by six votes.

Washington, drawing on his surveying expertise, took another year to select the hill-banked plain east of Georgetown, after scouting far up the river. For any location he chose, the Potomac Company—of which Washington himself was president and principal investor—stood to benefit, but this was

not considered a conflict of interest in the 1790s. What made the Potomac advantageous both for a capital site and for investment in navigation was that it penetrated the farthest inland of any East Coast river, traversing the lowest point in the Appalachian Mountains. Washington's scouting trips convinced him that with short portages, water routes could connect the Chesapeake Bay to western Pennsylvania and beyond to the Ohio and Mississippi Rivers.

Next, the rural site had to be purchased from the Maryland farmers who owned it. Washington and Jefferson purposely deployed surveyors in widely scattered locations up and down the river, to keep local owners from guessing where the government center would finally rest within the district—and thus to keep a lid on land prices. The president also deputized friends to purchase the land, "as if for yourselves, and to conduct your propositions so as to excite no suspicion that they are on behalf of the public."

Washington then hired a French-born master designer to plan the capital. Pierre L'Enfant, an architect living in New York City, mapped out a grid of streets slashed dramatically by wide diagonal boulevards. L'Enfant envisioned a mall surrounded by grand government buildings. The rest of his map showed small lots intended for private buyers, who, it was hoped, would provide housing and services for the government population. The proceeds of the land sales would fund the government construction, so that a city could be built without having to draw on the U.S. Treasury at all.

In the end, the capital landed in the South because a major east–west river was there and because the South had crucial votes to trade on the assumption bill. Washington, D.C., represented the geographic but not the demographic center of the thirteen states. Its placement exerted a southern tug on the federal government, augmented by the fact that five of the first seven presidents were also southerners. In all the political horse trading over choosing the site, nobody thought it worthy to note that the capital of the Republic sat in the heart of a slave society. But it would turn out to be of major significance some sixty years later, when the capital of President Abraham Lincoln's Union was surrounded by slavery, with many of its inhabitants of doubtful loyalty to the Union.

debt. His "assumption plan" in effect consolidated federal power over the states.

The assumption of state debts required the federal government to exercise even stronger powers of taxation. To meet the interest payments on a national debt swollen to some $77 million, Hamilton did not propose raising import duties, for that would have been unacceptable to the merchant class whose support he was seeking. Instead, he convinced Congress in 1791 to pass a 25 percent excise tax on distilled spirits, to be paid by the farmer when he brought his grain to the distillery. Members of Congress favored the tax, especially those from New England where the favorite drink was rum, an imported beverage already taxed under the import laws. A New Hampshire representative pointed out that the country would be "drinking down the national debt," an idea he evidently thought was good.

> *Hamilton called for the federal government to assume the state debts and add them to the federal debt. His "assumption plan" in effect consolidated federal power over the states.*

Congressman James Madison objected to Hamilton's funding plan, fearing that windfall profits would go mainly to speculators who had bought the original IOUs at bargain prices. He also strenuously objected to assumption of all the states' debts. A large debt was dangerous, Madison warned, especially because it would lead to high taxation. But he lost the vote in Congress. Madison and Hamilton, so recently allies in writing *The Federalist,* were becoming opponents.

Secretary of State Jefferson also was fearful of Hamilton's proposals. Cabinet meetings had become disagreeable and uncomfortable, and President Washington rebuked them both. Hamilton misread the motives of Madison and Jefferson, thinking they were rivals for his power. Jefferson had a clearer picture of the problem: "No man is more ardently intent to see the public debt soon and sacredly paid off than I am. This exactly marks the difference between Colonel Hamilton's views and mine, that I would wish the debt paid tomorrow; he wishes it never to be paid, but always to be a thing where with to corrupt and manage the legislature."

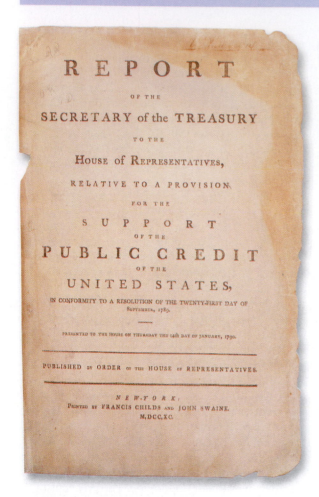

HAMILTON'S REPORT ON PUBLIC CREDIT
Hamilton wrote this report in just over three months, in response to a resolution by Congress, but he had been thinking about the problem of the public debt for many years. He proposed funding the debt— that is, rolling it over into a new debt instead of paying it off. As with all reports and resolutions before the government, his report was printed, to ensure easy distribution to the nearly sixty members of Congress.
The Gilder Lehrman Collection, Pierpont Morgan Library.

issuing IOUs to farmers, merchants, and moneylenders. Some states, such as Virginia and New York, had paid off these debts entirely, while others, like Massachusetts, had partially paid them through heavy and painful taxation of the inhabitants; about half the states had made little headway. Hamilton called for the federal government to assume these state debts and add them to the federal

The First Bank of the United States and the Report on Manufactures

The second and third major elements of Hamilton's economic plan were his proposal for a national bank, the Bank of the United States, and his program to encourage domestic manufacturing. Believing that banks were the "nurseries of national wealth," Hamilton modeled his plan on the Bank of England, a private corporation that worked primarily for the public good. In Hamilton's plan, 20 percent of the bank's stock would be bought by the federal government. In effect, the bank would become the fiscal agent of the new government, holding and handling its revenues derived from import duties, land sales, and the whiskey excise tax. The other 80 percent of the bank's capital would come from private investors, who could buy stock in the bank with either hard money (silver or gold) or federal securities. By its size and the privilege of being the only national bank, the bank would help stabilize the economy by exerting prudent control over credit, interest rates, and the value of the currency. Five of the twenty-five directors of the bank would be appointed by the government, to look out for the public interest. Hamilton had extraordinarily good faith in the virtue of the other twenty directors, who would be chosen from among the private stockholders, merchants from the world of commerce and high finance.

Madison, concerned that the bank gave a handful of rich men undue influence over the economy, tried but failed to stop the plan in Congress. An equally concerned Jefferson advised Washington that creating a national bank was unconstitutional because there was nothing about chartering banks in the list of specified powers granted to Congress. Hamilton, however, argued that the same list specified many powers to regulate commerce and ended with a broad grant of the right "to make all laws which shall be necessary and proper for carrying into execution the foregoing powers." Washington, who studied the arguments for two weeks, ultimately agreed with Hamilton and signed the Bank of the United States into law in February 1791, providing it with a charter to operate for twenty years. When the bank's privately held stock went on sale in New York City in July, it sold out in a few hours, touching off an immediate mania of speculation in resale. A discouraged Madison reported that "the Coffee House is an eternal buzz with the gamblers," some of them self-interested congressmen intent on "public plunder."

The third component of Hamilton's plan was issued in December 1791 in the *Report on Manufactures*, a proposal to encourage the production of American-made goods. Manufacturing was in its infancy in 1790, the result of years of dependence on British imports. Hamilton recognized that a balanced and self-reliant economy required the United States to produce its own cloth and iron products. His plan mobilized the new powers of the federal government to impose tariffs and grant subsidies to encourage the growth of local manufacturing. Hamilton had to be careful not to undercut his important merchant allies who traded with England and generated over half the government's income. A high tariff would either seriously dampen that trade or force merchants into smuggling. So Hamilton favored a moderate tariff, with extra bounties paid to American manufacturers to encourage production. The *Report on Manufactures* was the one Hamiltonian plan that was not approved by Congress.

The Whiskey Rebellion

Hamilton's excise tax on whiskey showed that he could make serious political mistakes. Many more voters were grain farmers and whiskey drinkers than were merchants. Western farmers with an abundance of wheat and rye suddenly faced high taxes that had to be paid up front at the distillery. Cash-short farmers deeply resented their assigned role in Hamilton's plan for economic recovery.

In 1791, angry grain farmers in the western parts of Pennsylvania, Virginia, Maryland, and the Carolinas and throughout Kentucky conveyed to Congress their resentment of Hamilton's tax. One farmer complained that he already paid half his grain to the local distillery for distilling his rye, and now the distiller was taking the new whiskey tax out of the farmer's remaining half. This "reduces the balance to less than one-third of the original quantity. If this is not an oppressive tax, I am at a loss to describe what is so." Congress responded with modest modifications in the tax in 1792; but even so, discontent was rampant.

Simple evasion of the law was the most common response from the farmer. And indeed, the tax proved hard to collect. Federally appointed tax inspectors soon learned the unpleasant consequences, as crowds threatened to tar and feather them. Even in

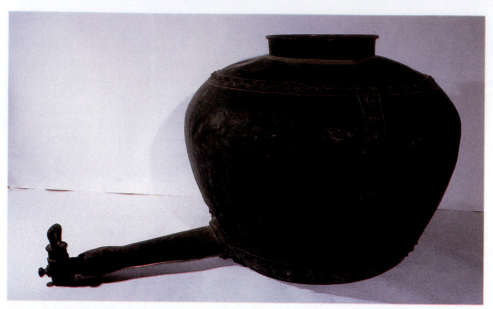

WHISKEY REBELLION "FIRE COPPER"
This forty-gallon "fire copper" produced Monongahela rye whiskey in the 1790s in western Pennsylvania. Mashed rye grain was mixed and heated with mash from a previously distilled brew. The distiller next added yeast and water and let the mixture ferment for several days. The mixture was then heated to 175 degrees, the boiling point of alcohol, in this three-foot copper vessel (called a "still"). Alcohol-laden vapor from the boiling brew cooled and condensed in a spiral copper tubing that dripped whiskey into a jug. High-proof, expensive whiskey required a second processing in the still to concentrate the vapors. The owner of this fire copper was James Miller, whose nephew Oliver Miller Jr. was an early fatality in the Whiskey Rebellion.
Oliver Miller Homestead/Photo by Andrew Wagner; Courtesy of *American History* magazine.

Philadelphia, the nation's capital, major distilleries right under Hamilton's nose were evading the tax by underreporting their production by nearly half. With embarrassment, Hamilton admitted to Congress that the revenue yield from the tax was far less than anticipated. But rather than abandon the law, he tightened up on the prosecution of tax evaders.

In western Pennsylvania, Hamilton had one ally, a stubborn tax collector named John Neville who had refused to quit even after a group of spirited farmers had burned him in effigy. In late May 1794, Neville filed charges against seventy-five farmers and distillers for tax evasion. In mid-July, he and a federal marshal were ambushed in Allegheny County by a group of forty men, and during the next two days Neville's house was burned to the ground by a crowd estimated at five hundred. At the end of July, seven thousand farmers staged a march on Pittsburgh to express their hostility to the hated tax.

An angry Hamilton convinced President Washington to respond with a show of force. Washington nationalized the Pennsylvania militia, donned his old military garb, and set out, with Hamilton at his side urging him on, at the head of fifteen thousand soldiers. By the time the military force arrived, in late September, the demonstrators had all gone home. No battles were fought, and no fire was exchanged. Twenty men were rounded up as rebels and charged with high treason, but only two were convicted, and both were soon pardoned by Washington.

Had the government overreacted? Or was Hamilton right to think that the whiskey rioters posed a serious threat to the stability of the federal government? At the core of the Whiskey Rebellion lay the question of what citizens can and cannot do when they think a law is unjust and what governments can and cannot do when groups of citizens resort to extralegal and even violent means to express their grievances.

The long colonial tradition of crowd action to protest unfair practices or to express public opinion had worked comfortably when colonists had limited formal access to power. But in a republic, laws were passed by the supposed representatives of the people, not by tyrannical kings or distant parliaments. Burning effigies of stamp tax collectors in 1765 made sense as an effective contribution to the political process. Burning effigies of whiskey tax collectors in 1792 appeared to many to be an unlawful rejection of the will of the people as expressed through Congress.

At the core of the Whiskey Rebellion lay the question of what citizens can and cannot do when they think a law is unjust and what governments can and cannot do when groups of citizens resort to extralegal and even violent means to express their grievances.

The whiskey rebels, however, recognized oppressive taxes for what they were and felt entitled to resort to protest and demonstration. Representative government had not worked to their benefit. The Whiskey Rebellion was an early example of what would prove to be a long-term conflict: the tension between minority rights and majority rule.

Conflicts West, East, and South

Washington's second term began in 1793, after a smooth and unanimous reelection. But as the Whiskey Rebellion demonstrated, the widespread admiration for the individual man did not translate to complete domestic tranquility. While the whiskey rebels challenged federal leadership from within the country, disorder threatened the United States from external sources as well. To the west, a powerful confederation of Indian tribes in the Ohio country resisted white encroachment. The result was a brutal war. At the same time, conflicts between the major European powers forced Americans to take sides and nearly thrust the country into another war, this time across the Atlantic. And to the south, a Caribbean slave rebellion raised fears of racial war imported to the United States.

To the West: The Indians

By the Treaty of Paris of 1783, England had given up all land east of the Mississippi River to the United States. But this area was not entirely England's to give; the English neglected to consult their allies in the Revolutionary War, the Indian tribes who inhabited 25,000 square miles of that territory. As recently as 1768, England had formally guaranteed the Indians their rights to all land north of the Ohio River, but the Treaty of Paris simply ignored that obligation.

WASHINGTON'S PROCLAMATION PROTECTING INDIAN TERRITORY

The president's name, in bold print, prefaces a warning that American citizens were forbidden to injure Indians or trespass their lands in the Northwest Territory. When the federal government signed treaties with tribes ceding land, it often guaranteed protections for land not ceded. This poster of 1793, designed to be tacked up on trees, announced federal protection for Indians around the Eel River in Ohio. Such warnings were not very effective, however. Washington wrote in 1796, "I believe scarcely any thing short of a Chinese Wall, or line of Troops will restrain Land Jobbers, and the Incroachment of Settlers, upon Indian Territory."

The Huntington Library and Art Collections, San Marino, California.

MAP 8.2
Western Expansion and Indian Land Cessions to 1810
By the first decade of the nineteenth century, the period of intense Indian wars had resulted in significant cessions of land to the U.S. government by treaty.

READING THE MAP: Locate the Appalachians. What line of 1763 ran along the mountains? What was that line's purpose and how well was that purpose met?
CONNECTIONS: How much did the population of the United States grow between 1750 and 1790? How did this growth affect western settlement?

www.bedfordstmartins.com /tap SEE THE ONLINE STUDY GUIDE for more help in analyzing this map.

When the British commanders at forts in North America finally told their Indian neighbors about the treaty terms, the Indians expressed astonishment. "They told me they never could believe that our king could pretend to cede to America what was not his own to give," the commander at Fort Niagara wrote of the Iroquois. In southern Ohio, British Indian agents assured the Shawnees and Delawares that England had relinquished only political control to the United States but that Indians still had the right to occupy the land over the claims of American settlers. Such confusion and misrepresentation aggravated an already volatile situation.

A doubled American population, from two million in 1770 to nearly four million in 1790, created an insistent pressure for western land. Several thousand settlers a year moved down the Ohio River in the mid-1780s, some bound for Kentucky but many others eyeing the fresh forests and fields north of the Ohio River. By the late 1780s, government land sales in eastern Ohio commenced (Map 8.2).

Even western Ohio was not safe from American incursions. Downriver, at the site of present-day Cincinnati, an outpost named Fort Washington was constructed in 1789 and put under the command of General Arthur St. Clair, who was also named governor of the entire Northwest Territory. St. Clair's mission was to displace the Indians and clear the way for permanent American settlement in Ohio. He first tried peaceful tactics and got an assortment of Indians to sign a treaty yielding land near the Muskingum River in eastern Ohio. But the signing Indians were not chiefs authorized to undertake negotiations, so the dubious treaty did nothing to improve the chances for peace in the region.

By the Treaty of Paris, England had given up all land east of the Mississippi River to the United States. But the English neglected to consult their allies in the Revolutionary War, the Indian tribes who inhabited 25,000 square miles of that territory.

Bloody frontier raids and skirmishes between settlers and Indians led the United States to expand its military force. Finally, St. Clair took direct action. In the fall of 1791, more than 2,000 men (and 200 women camp followers) marched north from Fort Washington to engage in battle with Miami and Shawnee Indians. The Indians attacked first, at daybreak on November 4, at the headwaters of the Wabash River in western Ohio. The ferocious battle was a total disaster for the Americans. Fifty-five percent of the force were dead or wounded before noon; only three of the women escaped alive. It was the worst American defeat in the entire history of the U.S.-Indian wars. The Indians captured valuable guns and artillery and scalped and dismembered the dead and dying. They pursued fleeing survivors for miles into the forest. The grisly tales of St. Clair's defeat became instantly infamous, increasing, if this were possible, the level of sheer terror that Americans brought to their confrontations with the Indians.

President Washington doubled the American military presence in Ohio and appointed a new commander, General Anthony Wayne of Pennsylvania. An officer in the Continental army during the Revolution, Wayne had earned the nickname "Mad Anthony" for his headstrong and rambunctious style of leadership. He was a heavy drinker, inclined to incautious decisions, and severe with disobedient soldiers. About the Ohio natives he wrote, "I have always been of the opinion that we never should have a permanent peace with those Indians until they were made to experience our superiority." With some 3,500 men, Wayne established two new military camps, Fort Greenville and Fort Recovery, deep in Indian territory in western Ohio.

In December 1793, Wayne was ready to seize the initiative, and by spring his army had engaged in several skirmishes with the Shawnees and Delawares. The decisive action came in August 1794 at the Battle of Fallen Timbers, near the Maumee River where a recent severe rainstorm had felled many trees. The confederated Indians—mainly Ottawas, Potawatomis, and Delawares, numbering around 800—first ambushed the Americans, but they were underarmed, many having only tomahawks. Wayne's well-disciplined troops made effective use of their guns and bayonets, and in just over an hour the Indians had retreated and scattered.

Fallen Timbers was a major defeat for the Indians. The Americans had destroyed cornfields and villages on the march north, and, with winter approaching, the Indians' confidence was sapped. They reentered negotiations in a much less powerful bargaining position. In 1795, about a thousand Indians representing a confederacy of nearly a dozen tribes met with Wayne and other American emissaries to work out the Treaty of Greenville. The Americans offered $25,000 worth of treaty goods (calico shirts, axes, knives, blankets, kettles, mirrors, ribbons, thimbles, and abundant wine and liquor casks) and promised additional shipments every year. The government's idea was to create a dependency on American goods to keep the Indians friendly. In exchange, the Indians ceded most of Ohio to the Americans; only the northwest region of the territory was reserved solely for the Indians (see Map 8.2).

The treaty brought peace to the region, but it did not bring back a peaceful life to the Indians. The annual allowance from the United States too often came in the form of liquor. "More of us have died since the Treaty of Greenville than we lost by the years of war before, and it is all owing to the introduction of liquor among us," said Little Turtle, chief of the Miami people, in 1800. "This liquor that they introduce into our country is more to be feared than the gun and tomahawk."

Across the Atlantic: France and England

Since 1789, a violent revolution had been raging in France. At first, the general American reaction was positive, for it was flattering to think that the American Revolution had inspired imitation in France.

TREATY OF GREENVILLE, 1795
*General Anthony Wayne meets with Chief Little Turtle of the Miamis and Chief Tarhe
the Crane of the Wyandots to sign the Treaty of Greenville, in Ohio in 1795.*
Chicago Historical Society.

Monarchy and privilege were overthrown in the name of republicanism; towns throughout America celebrated the victory of the French people with civic feasts and public festivities. For example, townspeople in the village of Augusta, Maine, staged a French banquet under the tricolor flag of the French Republic and banners proclaiming "France, Liberty, Equality."

But news of the beheading of King Louis XVI quickly dampened the uncritical enthusiasm for everything French. Now Americans were divided in their sentiments. Those who fondly remembered the excitement and risk of the American Revolution were still apt to regard France with the same kind of optimism. However, the reluctant revolutionaries of the 1770s and 1780s, who had worried about excessive democracy and social upheaval in America, deplored the far greater violence occurring in the name of republicanism as France moved into the Reign of Terror.

Support for the French Revolution could remain a matter of personal conviction until 1793, when England and France went to war and French versus British loyalty became a very delicate and critical foreign policy question. France had helped America substantially during the American Revolution, and the confederate government had signed an alliance in 1778 promising aid if France were ever under attack. Americans still optimistic about the eventual outcome of the French Revolution wanted to deliver on that promise now. But others, including those shaken by the guillotining of thousands of French people as well as those with strong commercial ties to England, sought ways to stay neutral.

In May 1793, President Washington issued a Neutrality Proclamation, with friendly assurances to both sides. His aim was to cool the tensions abroad and protect American interests in both countries. But tensions at home flared in response to official neutrality. "The cause of France is the cause of man, and neutrality is desertion," wrote H. H. Brackenridge, a western Pennsylvanian, voicing the sentiments of thousands. Dozens of popular pro-French political clubs sprang up around the country, called Democratic or Republican Societies.

The societies mobilized farmers and mechanics, issued circular letters, injected pro-French and anti-British feelings into local elections, and in general heightened popular participation and public interest in foreign policy. The activities of these societies made Washington and Hamilton intensely uncomfortable, for they vented opposition to the policies of the president.

Support for the French Revolution could remain a matter of personal conviction until 1793, when England and France went to war.

The Neutrality Proclamation was in theory a fine idea, in view of Washington's goal of staying out of European wars. Yet American ships continued to trade between the French West Indies and France, carrying primarily grains, sugar, and other foodstuffs. In late 1793 and early 1794, England expressed displeasure with the limited American interpretation of neutrality by capturing more than three hundred of these ships near the West Indies. A crisis ensued, and even pro-British politicians like Hamilton agreed that it was necessary to make a formal agreement with England. Washington sent John Jay, the chief justice of the Supreme Court and a man known to have very strong pro-British sentiments, to negotiate a treaty.

The Jay Treaty

John Jay's assignment was to secure agreement about general commercial ties between the two countries and to negotiate compensation for the seizure of American ships. In addition, he was supposed to resolve several long-standing problems dating from the end of the Revolution. Southern planters wanted reimbursement for the slaves lured away by the British army during the war, and western settlers wanted England to vacate the western forts still occupied for their strategic proximity to the Indian fur trade.

Jay returned from his diplomatic mission with a treaty that almost no one liked because of several major concessions to the British. First, the treaty made no direct provision for the captured ships or the lost property in slaves. Second, the

treaty granted the British eighteen months to withdraw from the western forts while guaranteeing them continued rights in the fur trade. Many Americans felt that the British had already retained the forts for twelve years too long; a continued British presence in the Great Lakes region would only offer their Indian allies hope of making Michigan into a territory of terror, as Ohio had been. Finally, the Jay Treaty called for repayment with interest of the debts some American planters still owed to British firms dating from the Revolutionary War. In exchange for granting such generous terms to England, Jay secured some favorable commercial agreements for the United States, but even there the results were mixed. The treaty was widely regarded as exchanging the country's strong moral bargaining power (the outrage over the seized ships) for an improved trading status beneficial to only a handful of merchants in the overseas trade.

Washington sent the Jay Treaty to the Senate for approval. He tried to keep its terms secret, but a newspaper editor got hold of it and printed it, with damning commentary. In short order, powerful opposition to the treaty emerged from Maine to Georgia. In Massachusetts, graffiti appeared on a wall: "Damn John Jay! Damn everyone who won't damn John Jay! Damn everyone who won't stay up all night damning John Jay!" A newspaper in New Jersey used accessible gender imagery to explain to its readers the implications of the Jay Treaty:

> The nation has been secretly, I will not say treacherously, divorced from France, and most clandestinely married to Great Britain: we are taken from the embraces of a loving wife, and find ourselves in the arms of a detestable and abandoned whore, covered with crimes, rottenness, and corruption.

Nevertheless, the Jay Treaty passed the Senate in 1795 by a vote of twenty to ten. Some representatives in the House, led by Madison, tried to undermine the Senate's approval by insisting on a separate vote on the funding provisions of the treaty, on the grounds that the House controlled all money bills. Finally, in 1796, the House approved funds to implement the various commissions mandated by the treaty, but by only a three-vote margin. The cleavage of votes in both houses of Congress divided along the same lines as the Hamilton-Jefferson split on economic policy.

To the South: The Haitian Revolution

In addition to the Indian wars in Ohio and the European wars across the Atlantic, a third bloody conflict to the south polarized and even terrorized many Americans in the 1790s. The western third of the large Caribbean island of Hispaniola, just to the east of Cuba, became engulfed in revolution starting in 1791. The eastern portion of the island was a Spanish colony called Santo Domingo; the western part, in bloody conflagration, was the French Saint Domingue. War

Haitian Revolution, 1790–1804

raged there for over a decade, resulting in the birth of the Haitian Republic in 1804, distinguished as the first and only independent black state to arise out of a successful revolution by slaves.

The Haitian Revolution was a complex event involving many participants, including the diverse local population and, eventually, armies of three European countries. Some 30,000 whites ruled the island in 1790, running sugar and coffee plantations with close to half a million slaves, two-thirds of them of African birth. The white French colonists were not the only plantation owners, however. About 28,000 free coloreds (*gens de couleur*) of mixed race also lived in Saint Domingue; they owned one-third of the island's plantations and nearly a quarter of the slave labor force. Despite their economic status, the free coloreds were barred from political power; but they aspired to it.

The French Revolution of 1789 was the immediate catalyst for rebellion in this already tense society. First, white colonists challenged the white royalist government in an effort to link Saint Domingue with the new revolutionary government in France. Next the free coloreds rebelled in 1791, demanding equal civil rights with the whites. No sooner was this revolt viciously suppressed than another part of the island exploded, this time involving thousands of slaves armed with machetes and torches who wreaked devastation and slaughter. In 1793, the civil war escalated to include French, Spanish, and British troops fighting the inhabitants and also each other. The slaves, led by Toussaint L'Ouverture

in alliance with Spain, destroyed the northern regions of the island, leaving a thousand plantations in ruins and tens of thousands of people dead. Thousands of whites and free coloreds, along with some of their slaves, fled to Spanish Louisiana and southern cities of the United States.

White Americans followed the revolution in fascinated horror through newspapers and refugees' accounts. A few sympathized with the impulse for liberty, but many more shuddered at the violent atrocities. White refugees were welcomed in Charleston, Norfolk, and Richmond; but French-speaking blacks were eventually barred from entry in all southern states except Virginia. Southerners clearly feared that violent black insurrection might be exported into their own society.

Many black American slaves also followed the revolution, hearing about it from dockworkers, from black sailors, from anxious whites who spoke of it over dinner or at the tavern, where blacks waited on table, and from the French blacks themselves, arriving in Virginia ports in significant numbers after 1793. Amazing news—the success of a first-ever, massive revolution by slaves—traveled quickly in this oral culture. Whites complained of behaviors that might prefigure plots and conspiracies, such as increased insolence and higher runaway rates among slaves. A letter accidentally dropped in the streets of Yorktown, Virginia, in 1793 seemed to reveal a shadow world of "Secret Keepers" in southern cities who were stockpiling arms and readying thousands of slaves for rebellion. But no rebellion ensued.

Southerners clearly feared that violent black insurrection might be exported into their own society.

The Haitian Revolution provoked naked fear in white Americans. Jefferson, agonizing over the contagion of liberty in 1797, wrote another Virginia slaveholder that "if something is not done, and soon done, we shall be the murderers of our own children . . . ; the revolutionary storm, now sweeping the globe, will be upon us, and happy if we make timely provision to give it an easy passage over our land. From the present state of things in Europe and America, the day which brings our combustion must be near at hand; and only a single spark is wanting to make that day to-morrow."

Federalists and Republicans

Political statesmen of the early 1790s had always believed that a division into political factions was a sign of failure, but this assumption was soon put to a severe test. In Washington's second term, consistent voting blocs first appeared in Congress on economic issues. By the time of the Jay Treaty, distinctive labels—Federalist and Republican—had come into use for rival politicians and rival newspapers. These words summarized conflicting ideologies and principles; they did not yet describe organized political parties. Washington's decision not to seek a third term opened the floodgates to serious partisan electioneering.

The Election of 1796

Washington struggled to appear to be above party politics, and in his farewell address of September 1796 he stressed the need to maintain a "unity of government" reflecting a unified body politic. He also urged the country to "steer clear of permanent alliances with any portion of the foreign world." The leading contenders for his position, John Adams of Massachusetts and Thomas Jefferson of Virginia, in theory agreed with him: Political parties were deplorable, and neutrality toward England and France was essential. But around them raged a party contest split along pro-English versus pro-French lines.

Adams and Jefferson were not adept politicians in the modern sense, skilled in the arts of persuasion and intrigue. Bruised by his conflicts with Hamilton, Jefferson had resigned as secretary of state in 1793 and retreated to Monticello, his home in Virginia. Adams's job as vice president kept him closer to the political action, but his personality often put people off. He was temperamental, thin-skinned, and quick to take offense.

The leading Federalists and Republicans informally caucused to choose candidates. The Federalists picked Thomas Pinckney of South Carolina to run with Adams; the Republicans settled on Aaron Burr of New York to pair with Jefferson. The Constitution did not anticipate parties and tickets. Instead, each electoral college voter could cast two votes for any two candidates, but on only one ballot; the top vote-getter became president and the next highest assumed the vice presidency. (This procedural flaw was corrected by the Twelfth Amendment, adopted in 1804.) With only one ballot, care-

JOHN ADAMS BY JOHN TRUMBULL
In 1793, a year after the youthful Secretary of the Treasury Alexander Hamilton posed for him (see page 263), John Trumbull painted Vice President John Adams, then age fifty-eight. A friend once listed Adams's shortcomings as a politician: "He can't dance, drink, game, flatter, promise, dress, swear with gentlemen, and small talk and flirt with the ladies."
National Portrait Gallery, Smithsonian Institution/Art Resources, N.Y.

ful maneuvering was required to make sure the chief rivals for the presidency did not land in the top two spots.

Into that maneuverable moment stepped Alexander Hamilton. No longer in the cabinet, Hamilton had returned to his law practice in 1795, but he kept a firm hand on political developments. Hamilton did not trust Adams; he preferred Pinckney, and he tried to influence electors to throw their support to the South Carolinian. But his plan backfired: Adams was elected president with seventy-one electoral votes, and Jefferson came in second with sixty-eight and thus became vice president. Pinckney got fifty-nine votes, while Burr trailed with thirty.

Adams's inaugural speech before Congress emphasized his determination to rise above party strife. He promised to be neutral in foreign affairs and lifted Republican hopes by noting his great respect for the French people based on seven years' residence there. To solidify Federalist support, he retained the same three cabinet members from Washington's administration, the secretaries of state, treasury, and war, without fully realizing that all three were Hamilton loyalists. They wrote Hamilton for advice, which they then passed on to the unwitting Adams as their own. Thus, private citizen Hamilton exercised a great deal of power in the Adams administration.

Vice President Jefferson, a gracious loser to Adams after the electoral college balloting, extended a conciliatory arm when the two old friends met in Philadelphia, still the capital. They took temporary lodging in the same boardinghouse as if expecting to work closely together. But quickly the Hamiltonian cabinet ruined the honeymoon. Jefferson's advice was spurned, and he withdrew from active counsel of the president.

The XYZ Affair

Foreign policy lay at the heart of the rift between Adams and Jefferson and between Federalists and Republicans. If the Jay Treaty heated American tempers initially, the French response in 1797 was like oil added to the fire.

France read the Jay Treaty as the Republicans did: as a document giving so many concessions to the British that it made America a British satellite. In retaliation, France abandoned the terms of the 1778 wartime alliance with the United States and allowed privateers—armed private vessels—to seize American ships carrying British goods. By March 1797, when Adams's inaugural address promised evenhanded neutrality, French privateers had already detained more than three hundred American vessels and seized the goods on board. In a related move, in the winter of 1796–97, France refused to recognize a new minister sent by President Washington, Charles Cotesworth Pinckney.

To avenge these insults, Federalists started murmuring openly about war with France. Adams preferred negotiations and dispatched a three-man commission to France in the fall of 1797. But at the same time, the president recommended new expenditures for military defense. Negotiations, it appeared, would be backed by the muscle of military preparedness. Congress approved money for build-ing three new naval frigates, for arming merchant vessels, and for reinforcing and improving defenses in coastal cities.

Foreign policy lay at the heart of the rift between Adams and Jefferson and between Federalists and Republicans. If the Jay Treaty heated American tempers initially, the French response was like oil added to the fire.

When the three Americans arrived in Paris, French officials would not receive them. Finally the French minister of foreign affairs, Talleyrand, sent three French agents, unnamed and later known to the American public as X, Y, and Z, to the American commissioners with the recommendation that $250,000 might grease the wheels of diplomacy and that a $12 million loan to the French government would be the price of a peace treaty. The three Americans were incensed by Talleyrand's suggestion of a bribe, and they departed to inform the president.

Americans reacted to the XYZ affair with shock and anger. Even staunch pro-French Republicans began to reevaluate their allegiance. The Federalists' demand for military action became more insistent. Congress repealed all prior treaties with France, and in 1798 twenty naval warships launched the United States into its first undeclared war, called the Quasi War by historians to underscore its uncertain legal status. The main scene of action was the Caribbean, where more than one hundred French privateers were captured.

The Federalist-dominated Congress also appropriated funds to recruit an army of ten thousand men immediately, with a further plan for a provisional army of fifty thousand. Republicans feared—with justification—that the Federalists' real aim might be to use the army to threaten domestic dissenters, since there seemed to be little chance of a land invasion by France. Some claimed that Hamilton had masterminded the army buildup and was lobbying to be second in command of the army, behind the aging Washington. President Adams was increasingly mistrustful, but his cabinet pressured for Hamilton, and Adams was too weak politically to prevail. He was, however, beginning to suspect that his cabinet was more loyal to Hamilton than to the presidency.

Antagonism intensified between Federalists and Republicans. Republican newspapers launched heated attacks on Adams: One denounced him as "a person without patriotism, without philosophy, and a mock monarch." On July 4, 1798, a pro-French mob roamed the streets in Philadelphia wearing hats with cockades, small ribbon florets that indicated solidarity with the radical revolutionaries of France. An alarmed Adams stocked guns and ammunition in his house, fearing attack by a Republican mob.

Federalists too were taking the offensive. In Newburyport, Massachusetts, they staged a huge bonfire, burning issues of the state's Republican newspapers. Officers in a New York militia unit drank a menacing toast on July 4, 1798: "One and but one party in the United States." A leading Federalist newspaper declared that "he who is not for us is against us."

The Alien and Sedition Acts

If the United States had actually declared war on France, the pro-French Republicans could have been labeled traitors, subject to laws of treason.

CARTOON OF MATTHEW LYON FIGHT IN CONGRESS

The political tensions of 1798 were not merely intellectual. A February session in Congress degenerated from name-calling to a brawl. Roger Griswold, a Connecticut Federalist, called Matthew Lyon, a Vermont Republican, a coward. Lyon responded with some well-aimed spit, the first departure from the gentleman's code of honor. Griswold responded by raising his cane to Lyon, whereupon Lyon grabbed nearby fire tongs to beat back his assailant. Madison wrote to Jefferson that the two should have dueled: "No man ought to reproach another with cowardice, who is not ready to give proof of his own courage" by negotiating a duel, the honorable way to avenge insults. What is the picture on the wall of the House chambers?

Library of Congress.

www.bedfordstmartins.com/tap   SEE THE ONLINE STUDY GUIDE for more help in analyzing this image.

The Crisis of 1798: Sedition

As President John Adams inched toward an undeclared war on France, criticism of his foreign policy reached an all-time high. Newspaper editors and politicians favorable to France blasted him with such intemperate language that his supporters feared the country could be pushed to the brink of civil war. Federalists in Congress tried to muffle the opposition by criminalizing seditious words, believing it the only path to preserve the country. Republicans just redoubled their opposition.

DOCUMENT 1. Abigail Adams Complains of Sedition, 1798

Throughout the spring of 1798, a beleaguered Abigail Adams complained repeatedly in confidential letters to her sister Mary Cranch about the need for a sedition law to put a stop to the political criticisms of her husband, the president, by Benjamin Bache, pro-French editor of the Philadelphia Aurora.

(April 26): . . . Yet dairingly do the vile incendaries keep up in Baches paper the most wicked and base, voilent & caluminiating abuse—It was formerly considerd as leveld against the Government, but now it . . . insults the Majesty of the Sovereign People. But nothing will have an Effect untill congress pass a Sedition Bill. . . . (April 28): . . . we are now wonderfully popular except with Bache & Co who in his paper calls the President old, querilous, Bald, blind, cripled, Toothless Adams. (May 10): . . . This Bache is cursing & abusing daily. If that fellow . . . is not surpressd, we shall come to a civil war. (May 26): . . . I wish the Laws of our Country were competant to punish the stirer up of sedition, the writer and Printer of base and unfounded calumny. This would contribute as much to the Peace and harmony of our Country as any measure. . . . (June 19): . . . in any other Country Bache & all his papers would have been seazd and ought to be here, but congress are dilly dallying about passing a Bill enabling the President to seize suspisious persons, and their papers. (June 23): . . . I wish our Legislature would set the example & make a sedition act, to hold in order the base Newspaper calumniators. In this State, you could not get a verdict, if a prosecution was to be commenced.

SOURCE: Stewart Mitchell, ed., *New Letters of Abigail Adams, 1788–1801* (Boston: Houghton Mifflin, 1947), 165, 167, 172, 179, 193, 196.

DOCUMENT 2. The Sedition Act of 1798

On July 14, 1798, the Congress approved a bill making sedition with malicious intent a crime.

SECTION 1. . . . if any persons shall unlawfully combine or conspire together, with intent to oppose any measure or measures of the government of the United States . . . , or to impede the operation of any law of the United States, or to intimidate or prevent any person holding . . . office in or under the government of the United States, from undertaking, performing or executing his trust or duty, and if any person or persons, with intent as aforesaid, shall counsel, advise or attempt to procure any insurrection, riot, unlawful assembly, or combination . . . , he or they shall be deemed guilty of a high misdemeanor, and on conviction . . . shall be punished by a fine not exceeding five thousand dollars, and by imprisonment during a term not less than six months nor exceeding five years. . . .

   SEC. 2. . . . if any person shall write, print, utter or publish, or shall cause or procure to be written, printed, uttered or published . . . , any false, scandalous and malicious writing or writings against the government of the United States, or either house of the Congress of the United States, or the President of the United States, with intent to defame the said government . . . or to bring them . . . into contempt or disrepute; or to excite against them . . . the hatred of the good people of the United States . . . , or to aid, encourage or abet any hostile designs of any foreign nation against the United States . . . , then such person, being thereof convicted thereof . . . shall be punished by a fine not exceeding two thousand dollars, and by imprisonment not exceeding two years.

SOURCE: *United States Statutes at Large; Containing the Laws and Concurrent Resolutions . . . and Proclamations, Treaties, International Agreements Other Than Treaties and Reorganized Plans* (Washington: U.S. Government Printing Office, 1789–1845). Avalon Project, Yale Law School, 1996, <www.yale.edu/lawweb/avalon/statutes/sedact.htm>

DOCUMENT 3. Matthew Lyon Criticizes John Adams, 1798

Matthew Lyon, a member of Congress from Vermont, published this criticism of President Adams in a letter to the editor of Spooner's Vermont Journal *(July 31, 1798). It became the first of three counts against him in a sedition trial. Lyon drew a four-month sentence and a fine of $1,000. From jail he ran for reelection to Congress—and won.*

As to the Executive, when I shall see the efforts of that power bent on the promotion of the comfort, the happiness, and the accommodation of the people, that Executive shall have my zealous and uniform support. But when I see every consideration of the public welfare swallowed up in a continual grasp for power, in an unbounded thirst for ridiculous pomp, foolish adulation, or selfish avarice; when I shall behold men of real merit daily turned out of office for no other cause but independence of sentiment; when I shall see men of firmness, merit, years, abilities, and experience, discarded on their application for office, for fear they possess that independence; and men of meanness preferred for the ease with which they take up and advocate opinions, the consequence of which they know but little of; when I shall see the sacred name of religion employed as a State engine to make mankind hate and persecute one another, I shall not be their humble advocate.

SOURCE: Matthew Lyon, Letter in *Spooner's Vermont Journal*, July 31, 1798. Quoted in Aleine Austin, *Matthew Lyon: New Man of the Democratic Revolution, 1749–1822* (Pennsylvania State University Press, 1981), 108–9.

DOCUMENT 4. James Bayard Defends the Law, 1799

James Bayard, a Federalist representative from Delaware, led the charge in the House to expel Matthew Lyon from his seat in Congress. Bayard argued that Lyon was guilty of subverting the government.

This Government . . . depends for its existence upon the good will of the people. That good will is maintained by their good opinion. But, how is that good opinion to be preserved, if wicked and unprincipled men, men of inordinate and desperate ambition, are allowed to state facts to the people which are not true, which they know at the time to be false, and which are stated with the criminal intention of bringing the Government into disrepute among the people? This was falsely and deceitfully stealing public opinion; it was a felony of the worst and most dangerous nature.

SOURCE: *Annals of Congress* (1799). Quoted in Richard Buel, *Securing the Revolution: Ideology in American Politics* (Ithaca, N.Y.: Cornell University Press, 1972), 256.

DOCUMENT 5. The Virginia Resolution, December 24, 1798

James Madison drafted the Virginia Resolution and had a trusted ally present it to the Virginia legislature, which was dominated by Republicans. (Jefferson did the same for Kentucky.) The Virginia document denounces the Alien and Sedition Acts and declares that states have the right to "interpose" to stop unconstitutional actions by the federal government.

RESOLVED . . . That this assembly most solemnly declares a warm attachment to the Union of the States, to maintain which it pledges all its powers; and that for this end, it is their duty to watch over and oppose every infraction of those principles which constitute the only basis of that Union, because a faithful observance of them, can alone secure its existence and the public happiness.

That this Assembly doth explicitly and peremptorily declare, that it views the powers of the federal government, as resulting from the compact, to which the states are parties; as limited by the plain sense and intention of the instrument constituting the compact; as no further valid that they are authorized by the grants enumerated in that compact; and that in case of a deliberate, palpable, and dangerous exercise of other powers, not granted by the said compact, the states who are parties thereto, have the right, and are in duty bound, to interpose for arresting the progress of the evil, and for maintaining within their respective limits, the authorities, rights and liberties appertaining to them. . . .

That the General Assembly doth particularly protest against the palpable and alarming infractions of the Constitution, in the two late cases of the "Alien and Sedition Acts" . . . ; the first of which exercises a power no where delegated to the federal government . . . ; and the other of which acts, *(Continued)* exercises in like manner, a power not delegated by the constitution, but on the contrary, expressly and positively forbidden by one of the amendments thereto; a power, which more than any other, ought to produce universal alarm, because it is levelled against that right of freely examining public characters and measures, and of free communication among the people thereon, which has ever been justly deemed, the only effectual guardian of every other right.

SOURCE: Avalon Project, Yale Law School, 1996, <www.yale.edu/lawweb/avalon/virres.htm>.

QUESTIONS FOR ANALYSIS AND DEBATE

1. Why did Federalists believe a Sedition Act was necessary? What exactly was the threat, according to Abigail Adams? James Bayard? What is the threat implied by the wording of the act?

2. Does Matthew Lyon's criticism of President Adams rise to the level of threat that Federalists feared? How do you explain his guilty verdict? His reelection to Congress?

3. What might Madison have meant by "interpose" as the desired action by states? What could states actually do?

4. How would Adams and Bayard square the Sedition Act with the First Amendment's protection of free speech? Did critics of the law invoke freedom of speech and press?

5. Which side had the stronger argument in 1798–1799? Do you think there should be limits on what can be said publicly about high government officials?

But without a declared war, Federalists had to invent another law to muffle opposition. In June and July 1798, Congress hammered out a Sedition Act that mandated a heavy fine or a jail sentence for anyone engaged in conspiracies or revolts against the government or convicted of "speaking, writing, or publishing any false, scandalous, or malicious statement, with the intent to defame or bring into contempt or disrepute the President, the Congress, or the Government." In other words, spoken or written words that falsely criticized government leaders were now criminal utterances. (See "Documenting the American Promise," page 278.)

Congress also passed two Alien Acts. The first extended the waiting period required for an alien to achieve status as a naturalized citizen from five to fourteen years and required all aliens to register with the federal government. The second empowered the president in time of war to deport or imprison without trial any foreigner suspected of being a danger to the United States. The clear intent of the alien laws was to harass French immigrants in the United States and discourage others from coming.

The main targets of the Sedition Act were the Republican newspaper editors who were free and abusive in their criticism of the Adams administration. One Federalist in Congress justified his vote for the law with reference to the Republican press: "Let gentlemen look at certain papers printed in this city and elsewhere, and ask themselves whether an unwarrantable and dangerous combination does not exist to overturn and ruin the government by publishing the most shameless falsehoods against the representatives of the people." In all, twenty-five men, almost all newspaper editors, were charged with sedition; twelve were convicted by juries.

Jefferson, Madison, and other Republicans strongly opposed the Alien and Sedition Acts on the grounds that they were in conflict with the Bill of Rights, but they did not have the votes to revoke the acts in Congress, nor could the federal judiciary, dominated by Federalist judges, be counted on to challenge them. So Jefferson and Madison turned to the state legislatures, the only other competing political arena, to mount their opposition. They each drafted a set of resolutions condemning the acts and had the legislatures of

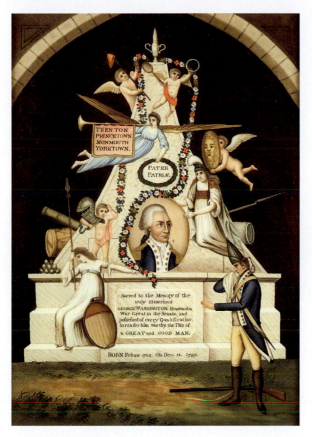

WASHINGTON'S DEATH

The death of George Washington in 1799 occasioned many memorial souvenirs. This painting on glass represents Washington as the **Pater Patriae,** *the father of his country. A soldier weeps, while Columbia with her shield and spear looks stunned with grief. Minerva, the goddess of war, holds the great man's portrait, and an angel trumpets his famous military victories. Nothing in the memorial notes his service as president, except the oblique statement that he was "Great in the Senate," a reference to ancient Roman government service. Notice as well that the amateur artist failed to capture Washington's actual likeness.*

The Metropolitan Museum of Art, Gift of Edgar William and Bernice Chrysler Garblach, 1964 (64.309.6).

Virginia and Kentucky present them to the federal government in late fall 1798. The Virginia and Kentucky Resolutions tested the novel argument that state legislatures have the right to judge the constitutionality of federal laws and to nullify laws that infringe on the liberties of the people as de-

fined in the Bill of Rights. The resolutions made little dent in the application of the Alien and Sedition Acts, but the idea of a state's right to nullify federal law did not disappear. The theme of states' rights to challenge federal power surfaced many times in decades to come, most notably in a major tariff dispute in 1832 and in the sectional arguments that led to the Civil War.

Jefferson, Madison, and other Republicans strongly opposed the Alien and Sedition Acts on the grounds that they were in conflict with the Bill of Rights.

Amidst all the war hysteria, sedition fears, and party conflict in 1798, President Adams somehow managed to regain a measure of caution. Uncharacteristically, he was remarkably restrained in pursuing opponents under the Sedition Act, and he finally refused to be pushed into a hasty declaration of war by the extreme Federalists. No doubt he was beginning to realize how much he had been the dupe of Hamilton. He also shrewdly realized that France was in fact not eager for war and that a peaceful settlement might be close at hand. In January 1799, a peace initiative from France arrived, in the form of a letter assuring Adams that diplomatic channels were open again and that new commissioners would be welcomed in France. Adams accepted this overture and appointed a new negotiator; by late 1799, the Quasi War with France had subsided. But in responding to the French initiative, Adams lost the support of a significant part of his own party and sealed his fate as the first one-term president of the United States.

The election of 1800 was openly organized along party lines, with the self-designated national leaders of each group meeting to handpick their candidates for president and vice president. Adams's chief opponent was Thomas Jefferson. When the election was finally over, President Jefferson mounted the inaugural platform to announce, "We are all republicans, we are all federalists," an appealing rhetoric of harmony appropriate to an inaugural address. But his formulation perpetuated a denial of the validity of party politics, a denial that ran deep in the founding generation of political leaders.

Conclusion: Parties Nonetheless

The Federalists had dominated Congress and the presidency throughout the 1790s and persisted in thinking of themselves as the legitimate, disinterested rulers who could give the country enlightened leadership. President Washington sought unity for the new Union and deplored party strife, which in his view resulted from a misguided but vocal minority. Yet under Federalist presidencies, the issues that divided the country—Hamilton's economic program, the whiskey tax, the Jay Treaty, the Quasi War, and the Alien and Sedition Acts—engendered serious opposition.

The emerging Republicans were not a small minority. Many were onetime Federalists in Congress, like Madison, now in strenuous disagreement with Federalist policies. Others were 1780s Antifederalists, still suspicious of a powerful federal government; the Sedition Act seemed an especially clear example of what the Republicans feared. The Federalists were pro-British, pro-commerce, and ever alarmed about the potential excesses of democracy, while the Republicans celebrated, up to a point, the radical republicanism of France.

When Jefferson offered his conciliatory assurance that Americans were at the same time "all republicans" and "all federalists," he was possibly thinking of widely shared ideas that undergirded the country's political institutions. Certainly his listeners favored republican government, where power derived from the people, and likewise they favored the unique federal system of shared governance structured by the Constitution. But by 1800, these same two words, adapted to be the proper names of parties, had come to signify competing philosophies of government. Federalists and Republicans had strong disagreements that had developed over a decade of decision making. Jefferson's speech was spoken aloud; his listeners could not hear the presence or absence of capital letters. For at least some of his listeners, Jefferson's assertion of harmony across party lines could only have seemed bizarre.

www.bedfordstmartins.com/tap   SEE THE ONLINE STUDY GUIDE to test your mastery of the material covered in this chapter.

CHRONOLOGY

1789	George Washington inaugurated first president.
	French Revolution begins.
	First Congress meets in New York City.
1790	Alexander Hamilton's plans for funding the government: debts and assuming states' debts approved.
	Government moves from New York to Philadelphia.
1791	Bill of Rights ratified by states.
	Bank of the United States chartered by Congress.
	General Arthur St. Clair's forces defeated by Ohio Indians.
	Congress passes whiskey tax.
	Haitian Revolution begins.

1793	Washington's second term begins.
	Napoleonic Wars break out between France and England.
	Washington issues Neutrality Proclamation over war between France and England.
	General Anthony Wayne's forces defeat Ohio Indians at Fallen Timbers.
	Eli Whitney invents cotton gin.
1794	Farmers stage Whiskey Rebellion in western Pennsylvania.
	Lancaster Turnpike, first private toll road, constructed.
1795	Treaty of Greenville cedes most Indian land in Ohio to United States.
	Jay Treaty with England.

1796	John Adams elected president, Thomas Jefferson vice president.		Virginia and Kentucky Resolutions press for states' rights in judging constitutionality of federal laws.
1797	XYZ affair with France.	**1800**	Thomas Jefferson elected third president.
1798	Quasi War with France. Alien and Sedition Acts passed to suppress pro-French sentiments.		

BIBLIOGRAPHY

GENERAL WORKS

Doron Ben-Atar and Barbara B. Oberg, eds., *Federalists Reconsidered* (1998).

Richard Buel, *Securing the Revolution: Ideology in American Politics, 1789–1815* (1972).

William Nisbet Chambers, *Political Parties in a New Nation: The American Experience, 1776–1809* (1963).

David P. Currie, *The Constitution in Congress: The Federalist Period, 1789–1801* (1997).

Stanley Elkins and Eric McKitrick, *The Age of Federalism: The Early American Republic, 1788–1800* (1993).

John F. Hoadley, *Origins of American Political Parties, 1789–1803* (1986).

Ronald Hoffman and Peter J. Albert, eds., *Launching the "Extended Republic": The Federalist Era* (1996).

Donald R. Kennon, ed., *A Republic for the Ages: The United States Capitol and the Political Culture in the Early Republic* (1999).

Ralph Ketcham, *Presidents above Party: The First American Presidency, 1789–1829* (1984).

John R. Nelson, *Liberty and Property: Political Economy and Policymaking in the New Nation, 1789–1812* (1987).

James Rogers Sharp, *American Politics in the Early Republic: The New Nation in Crisis* (1993).

Larry E. Tise, *The American Counterrevolution: A Retreat from Liberty, 1783–1800* (1999).

David Waldstreicher, *In the Midst of Perpetual Fetes: The Making of American Nationalism, 1776–1820* (1997).

WASHINGTON'S ADMINISTRATION

Carl Abbott, *Political Terrain: Washington, D.C., from Tidewater Town to Global Metropolis* (1999).

Bob Arnebeck, *Through a Fiery Trial: Building Washington, 1790–1800* (1991).

Kenneth R. Bowling, *Politics in the First Congress, 1789–1791* (1990).

Kenneth R. Bowling, *The Creation of Washington, D.C.: The Idea and Location of the American Capital* (1991).

Steven R. Boyd, ed., *The Whiskey Rebellion: Past and Present Perspectives* (1985).

Jerry A. Clouse, *The Whiskey Rebellion: Southwestern Pennsylvania's Frontier People Test the American Constitution* (1995).

James T. Flexner, *George Washington and the New Nation, 1783–1793* (1970).

James T. Flexner, *George Washington: Anguish and Farewell, 1793–1799* (1972).

Forrest McDonald, *The Presidency of George Washington* (1974).

Forrest McDonald, *The American Presidency: An Intellectual History* (1994).

Robert A. Rutland, *The Birth of the Bill of Rights, 1776–1791* (1991).

Thomas P. Slaughter, *The Whiskey Rebellion: Frontier Epilogue to the American Revolution* (1986).

THE ECONOMY AND HAMILTON'S PROGRAM

Joyce Appleby, *Capitalism and a New Social Order: The Republican Vision of the 1790s* (1984).

Richard Brookhiser, *Alexander Hamilton, American* (2000).

Christopher Clark, *The Roots of Rural Capitalism: Western Massachusetts, 1780–1860* (1990).

Jacob E. Cooke, *Alexander Hamilton* (1982).

Paul A. Gilje, ed., *Wages of Independence: Capitalism in the Early American Republic* (1997).

James A. Henretta, *The Origins of American Capitalism: Collected Essays* (1991).

Joan Jensen, *Loosening the Bonds: Mid-Atlantic Farm Women, 1750–1850* (1986).

Allan Kulikoff, *The Agrarian Origins of American Capitalism* (1992).

James Lemon, *The Best Poor Man's Country: A Geographical Study of Early Southeastern Pennsylvania* (1972).

Forrest McDonald, *Alexander Hamilton: A Biography* (1982).

Winifred Rothenberg, *From Market-Places to a Market Economy: The Transformation of Rural Massachusetts, 1750–1850* (1992).

Herbert E. Sloan, *Principle and Interest: Thomas Jefferson and the Problem of Debt* (1995).

SOCIETY AND CULTURE

Richard D. Brown, *Knowledge Is Power: The Diffusion of Information in Early America, 1700–1865* (1989).

Patricia Cline Cohen, *A Calculating People: The Spread of Numeracy in Early America* (1999).

Nancy Cott, *The Bonds of Womanhood: Women's Sphere in New England, 1780–1835* (1977).

Cathy N. Davidson, *Revolution and the Word: The Rise of the Novel in America* (1986).

Emory Elliott, *Revolutionary Writers: Literature and Authority in the New Republic, 1725–1810* (1982).

Richard B. Kielbowicz, *News in the Mail: The Press, the Post Office, and Public Information, 1700–1860* (1989).

NATIVE AMERICANS AND THE FRONTIER

Robert F. Berkhofer Jr., *Salvation and the Savage: An Analysis of Protestant Missions and American Indian Response, 1787–1862* (1965).

Colin G. Calloway, *Crown and Calumet: British-Indian Relations, 1783–1815* (1987).

Andrew R. L. Cayton, *Frontier Republic: Ideology and Politics in the Ohio Century, 1780–1825* (1989).

Gregory E. Dowd, *A Spirited Resistance: The North American Indian Struggle for Unity, 1745–1815* (1992).

R. Douglas Hurt, *The Ohio Frontier: Crucible of the Old Northwest, 1720–1830* (1998).

Francis Paul Prucha, *American Indian Policy in the Formative Years: The Indian Trade and Intercourse Acts, 1780–1834* (1962).

Malcolm J. Rohrbough, *The Transappalachian Frontier: People, Societies, and Institutions, 1775–1850* (1978).

Wiley Sword, *President Washington's Indian War: The Struggle for the Old Northwest, 1790–1795* (1985).

Richard White, *The Middle Ground: Indians, Empires, and Republics in the Great Lakes Region, 1650–1815* (1991).

FOREIGN RELATIONS

Albert H. Bowman, *The Struggle for Neutrality: Franco-American Diplomacy during the Federalist Era* (1974).

Jerald A. Combs, *The Jay Treaty: Political Battleground of the Founding Fathers* (1970).

Alexander DeConde, *The Quasi-War: The Politics and Diplomacy of the Undeclared War with France, 1797–1801* (1966).

Carolyn E. Fick, *The Making of Haiti: The Saint Domingue Revolution from Below* (1991).

David Barry Gaspar and David Patrick Geggus, eds., *A Turbulent Time: The French Revolution and the Greater Caribbean* (1997).

Peter P. Hill, *French Perceptions of the Early American Republic, 1783–1793* (1988).

Daniel G. Lang, *Foreign Policy in the Early Republic* (1985).

Martin Ros, *Night of Fire: The Black Napoleon and the Battle for Haiti* (1993).

William Stinchcombe, *The XYZ Affair* (1981).

Richard J. Twomey, *Jacobins and Jeffersonians: Anglo-American Radicalism in the United States, 1790–1820* (1989).

FEDERALISTS AND REPUBLICANS

Ralph A. Brown, *The Presidency of John Adams* (1975).

Noble Cunningham, *The Jeffersonian Republicans: The Formation of Party Organization, 1789–1801* (1957).

Larry D. Eldridge, *A Distant Heritage: The Growth of Free Speech in Early America* (1994).

Joseph J. Ellis, *Passionate Sage: The Character and Legacy of John Adams* (1993).

John Ferling, *John Adams: A Life* (1992).

Richard Hofstadter, *The Idea of a Party System: The Rise of Legitimate Opposition in the United States, 1780–1840* (1969).

Richard H. Kohn, *Eagle and Sword: The Federalists and the Creation of the Military Establishment in America, 1783–1802* (1975).

Leonard Levy, *The Emergence of a Free Press* (1985).

Drew McCoy, *The Elusive Republic: Political Economy in Jeffersonian America* (1980).

Peter Shaw, *The Character of John Adams* (1976).

James Morton Smith, *Freedom's Fetters: The Alien and Sedition Laws and American Civil Liberties* (1966).

John Zvesper, *Political Philosophy and Rhetoric: A Study of the Origins of American Party Politics* (1977).

STATE HISTORIES

Richard R. Beeman, *The Old Dominion and the New Nation, 1788–1801* (1972).

Andrew R. L. Cayton, *Frontier Indiana* (1996).

Paul Goodman, *The Democratic-Republicans of Massachusetts* (1964).

Christopher Grasso, *A Speaking Aristocracy: Transforming Public Discourse in Eighteenth-Century Connecticut* (1999).

Norman Risjord, *Chesapeake Politics, 1781–1800* (1978).

Charles Steffen, *The Mechanics of Baltimore: Workers and Politics in the Age of Revolution, 1763–1812* (1984).

Alan Taylor, *Liberty Men and Great Proprietors: The Revolutionary Settlement on the Maine Frontier, 1760–1820* (1990).

Alfred Young, *The Democratic-Republicans of New York: The Origins, 1763–1797* (1967).

A JEFFERSON FAN

Ladies' fans became increasingly popular fashion accessories in the late eighteenth and early nineteenth centuries. This folding fan of vellum and carved ivory, made in the early 1800s, features a medallion portrait of President Thomas Jefferson. Carried by the ribbon on a woman's wrist, the fan could be flicked open to announce a partisan political statement. Fans and other handheld articles such as parasols and handkerchiefs expanded the repertoire of nonverbal expression for women, who by the custom and training of the time were expected to be less assertive than men in mixed conversation. Many emotions and messages—from modesty, coyness, and flirtatiousness to anger, irritability, and boredom— could be communicated by the expert deployment of this delicate emblem of femininity.
Collection of David J. and Janice L. Frent.

REPUBLICAN ASCENDANCY

1800–1824

9

T HE NAME *TECUMSEH* translates to "the Shooting Star"; certainly the Shawnee chief Tecumseh lived up to his name, reaching meteoric heights of fame among Indians well beyond his native Ohio. From Canada to Georgia and west to the Mississippi, Tecumseh was accounted a charismatic leader. Some Americans, too, praised (and feared) him as a would-be Moses of the Indians. Graceful, attractive, eloquent, compelling, magnetic, astute: Tecumseh was all these things and more, a gifted natural leader, equal parts politician and warrior.

Tecumseh was born in 1768 into a family of six sons and one daughter in the Ohio country. His parents had migrated there around 1760 from present-day Alabama along with hundreds of Shawnees. The Northwest Territory had become home to some dozen Indian tribes, several of them displaced newcomers. But now Ohio had become ground zero in the incessant wars with the Big Knives, as the Shawnees called the Americans.

Tecumseh's childhood during the American Revolution was marked by violence and loss. Battles took the lives of his father and two brothers. Five times between 1774 and 1782 the boy fled raids by American soldiers that left his homes in flames and his villages destroyed. When he was ten, his widowed mother returned to the South, leaving her remaining children in the care of an aunt.

The establishment of the United States government brought no peace to the Indians' country. George Washington's administration could not stem the flow of eager but foolhardy American settlers floating down the Ohio River, and the youthful Tecumseh honed his warrior skills in ambushing flatboat pioneers. He did not take part in the Indians' 1791 dramatic victory over General St. Clair, but he fought at the Battle of Fallen Timbers, a major Indian defeat. He avoided the 1795 negotiations of the Treaty of Greenville, in which a half dozen depleted and dispirited tribes ceded most of the future state of Ohio to the Big Knives. And with growing frustration he watched the remaining Indian land shrink, as seven further treaties between 1802 and 1805 whittled away ever more territory.

Some Indians, resigned and tired, looked for ways to accommodate to new realities, taking up farming, trade, and even intermarriage with the Big Knives. Others turned their treaty payments into deadly quantities of alcohol. By the reckoning of one American trader, six hundred warriors consumed six thousand gallons of liquor per year. Tecumseh's younger brother Tenskwatawa led an embittered life of idleness and excessive drink. But Tecumseh rejected assimilation and inebriation. Instead he embarked on a campaign to return his people to their ancient ways.

Donning traditional animal-skin garb and crowned by scalp locks, he began to travel around the Great Lakes area, persuading tribes to join his pan-Indian confederacy. The American territorial governor of Indiana, William Henry Harrison, reported,

"For four years he has been in constant motion. You see him today on the Wabash, and in a short time hear of him on the shores of Lake Erie or Michigan, or on the banks of the Mississippi, and wherever he goes he makes an impression favorable to his purpose." In 1811, he toured the South for six months, visiting the powerful Creek, Chickasaw, Cherokee, and Choctaw tribes from Mississippi to Georgia, while a brilliant comet with a tail a hundred million miles long illuminated the night sky. The Shooting Star understood that only a powerful alliance of Indians could block the path of the westward-moving Big Knives.

Even his once-dissolute brother was born anew. After a near-death experience in 1805, Tenskwatawa miraculously revived and recounted a startling vision, a meeting with the Master of Life. He now claimed to have prophetic powers, which he demonstrated by identifying witches plaguing troubled tribes and by correctly predicting an eclipse of the sun. Like Tecumseh, the Prophet (as Tenskwatawa was called) urged Indians everywhere to return to the customs of their ancestors and to give up cultural borrowings, such as European dress, firearms, plows, bread, and alcohol. He preached that the Americans were children of the Evil Spirit and therefore destined in the end to be destroyed. The Prophet established a new village called Prophetstown, located in present-day Indiana along Tippecanoe Creek, soon inhabited by a thousand warriors. Tecumseh and his brother pledged a potent blend of spiritual regeneration and political unity that attracted adherents throughout the territories. Harrison, the territorial governor, was skeptical of the Prophet's supernatural powers but granted Tecumseh admiration mingled with apprehension: He is "one of those uncommon geniuses which spring up occasionally to produce revolutions," Harrison said.

Harrison and his boss, President Thomas Jefferson, had special reason to fear such a leader. Not only might Tecumseh organize a widespread Indian opposition to white Americans, he might also revive the old Indian-English alliance by teaming up with Canada. Jefferson's first term in office was marked by notable successes, like the Louisiana Purchase and the Lewis and Clark expedition, but his second term was consumed by the threat of war with Britain and France. Insults over shipping rights, the capture of vessels, and impressment of sailors escalated tensions. Jefferson tried to avoid war by invoking economic sanctions in the form of trade embargoes against both coun-

TECUMSEH
Several portraits of Tecumseh exist, but they all present a different visage, and none of them enjoys a verified authenticity. This one perhaps comes closest: it is an engraving adapted from an earlier drawing that no longer exists, sketched by a French artist named Pierre Le Dru in a live sitting with the Indian leader. The engraver has given Tecumseh a British army officer's uniform, showing that Tecumseh fought on the British side in the War of 1812. Note the head covering and the medallion around the neck, marking Tecumseh's Indian identity.
Library of Congress.

tries, but this policy greatly alienated Federalist New England, whose economy depended on overseas trade. New Englanders wanted neither war nor trade embargo, but some western politicians in areas like Kentucky were actually eager for armed conflict with Britain, hoping it would provide an opportunity to seize extensive land not only from Indians confederated under Tecumseh but also from Canadians.

Jefferson managed to avoid war, but James Madison, his successor, was not able to contain the opposing forces and deepening party strife. As had happened in the late 1790s, the country teetered in a crisis as it struggled to identify the real enemy, England or France. Congress finally declared war on England in 1812.

As expected, Tecumseh allied his confederacy with the British and delivered eight hundred warriors to augment British strength. Unfortunately for the Indians, the British concentrated on protecting Canada, not the Indians' country. Tecumseh lost his life on Canadian soil at the Battle of the Thames in the fall of 1813, defending Canada against an army led by General William Henry Harrison. In the end, the War of 1812 settled little between the Americans and the British, but it was tragically conclusive for the Indians. No Indian leader like Tecumseh would emerge again in the area east of the Mississippi.

Jefferson's Presidency

Thomas Jefferson later called his election the "revolution of 1800." Certainly the tumultuous events of John Adams's last years in office suggested to some that violence might erupt. The election itself—inconclusive in the electoral college, triggering a cliffhanger vote in the House of Representatives—was highly suspenseful.

At the same time, a different and far more deadly "revolution of 1800" crystallized. A literate slave named Gabriel who worked in Richmond, Virginia's capital, followed the scurrilous rhetoric of the presidential campaign and figured that when white men were so badly divided, the time was right to strike for freedom. Rebellion perhaps seemed logical to Gabriel, but it took Federalists and Republicans alike by surprise.

What Jefferson likely meant when he recalled 1800 as a moment of revolution was the emergence of a fundamentally new idea: that even amidst great strife there could be a peaceful transfer of power from one group of leaders to another. But Jefferson may also have been referring to his transformation of the presidency, which amounted to a rejection of the Federalists' vision of a powerful, even regal, executive branch. Jefferson favored republican simplicity and aimed for a more limited government. Yet he found that circumstances sometimes required him to draw on the expansive powers of the presidency.

The Election of 1800

John Adams assumed the head of the Federalist ticket for reelection in 1800, even though he had angered and demoralized a significant number of Federalist politicians in Congress by his diplomatic overtures with France, puncturing the crisis of 1798–99. New England Federalists supported him, but others from the middle and southern states hoped to ease him out in favor of his running mate, Charles Cotesworth Pinckney of South Carolina, through a careful manipulation of the electoral college votes. Alexander Hamilton went public with a contemptuous and abusive condemnation of Adams, revealing the deep divisions in the Federalist camp. The surprise in the election tally thus was not that Adams lost but that the two Republican candidates tied each other, an outcome possible because of the single balloting to choose both president and vice president. Thomas Jefferson and his running mate, Senator Aaron Burr of New York, both got seventy-three votes (Map 9.1). Despite having been the second man on the ticket, Burr, driven by ambition and vanity, now declined to concede

Candidate	Electoral Vote*
Thomas Jefferson** (Republican)	73
Aaron Burr*** (Republican)	73
John Adams (Federalist)	65
C.C. Pinckney (Federalist)	64
John Jay (Federalist)	1

*Before 1824, most presidential electors were chosen by state legislatures rather than by popular vote.
**Chosen president by House of Representatives.
***Chosen vice president by House of Representatives.

MAP 9.1
The Election of 1800

the presidency to Jefferson. So the election was thrown into the House of Representatives, where a Federalist-dominated chamber would make the final choice. In the newly elected House, Jefferson's party had secured sixty-five seats, the Federalists forty-one. But it was the existing House, not the new one, that would determine the new president.

In February 1801, the House met to choose. Each state delegation commanded one vote, and the winner needed nine votes. Some Federalists preferred Burr, believing his character flaws made him more susceptible to Federalist pressure. "His very selfishness prevents his entertaining any mischievous predilections for foreign nations," wrote one senator privately. But Hamilton, although no friend to Jefferson, recognized that the high-strung and arrogant Burr would be more dangerous in the presidency than Jefferson, with his hated but steady habits of republicanism. Jefferson was a fanatic and a "contemptible hypocrite" to Hamilton, but at least he was not corrupt. Jefferson had the votes of eight states on the first ballot; it took thirty-six more ballots and six days to get a ninth vote (and also a tenth) in his column. In the end, anti-Burr Federalist representatives in three states abstained from voting to allow Jefferson the victory without actually having to cast a ballot for him.

The election of 1800 demonstrated a remarkable feature of the new constitutional government. No matter how hard-fought the campaign, this election showed that leadership of the nation could shift from one group to a distinctly different one, in a peaceful transfer of power effected by ballots, not bullets.

Gabriel's Rebellion

As the country struggled over its white political leadership, a twenty-four-year-old blacksmith named Gabriel plotted his own revolution of 1800 in Virginia. Gabriel, the slave of Thomas Prosser, recruited hundreds of coconspirators from five Virginia counties over the spring and summer of 1800. Inspired by the model of the Haitian Revolution, and perhaps directly informed of it by French slaves new to the Richmond area, Gabriel and his followers planned to march on the state capitol at Richmond, set diversionary fires, capture a major arsenal, and then take the governor, James Monroe, hostage. Gabriel ordered his followers to spare Methodists and Quakers, known to hold antislavery views, and he also expected Indians and "the

poor white people" of Richmond and Norfolk to join him. Knowing that Governor Monroe was a pro-French (and thus liberty-loving) Republican, Gabriel assumed he might prove sympathetic to their cause. Gabriel, it appears, took the Federalist rhetoric about Republican Francophiles too seriously.

As the country struggled over its white political leadership, a twenty-four-year-old blacksmith named Gabriel plotted his own revolution of 1800 in Virginia.

Gabriel's revolt never actually materialized. A massive thunderstorm scuttled it on the appointed day at the end of August, and a few nervous slaves spilled the secret. Within days, scores of implicated conspirators were locked in jail and brought to trial. One of the accused, Jack Ditcher, declared in court, "We have as much right to fight for our liberty as any men." Another jailed rebel compared himself to the most venerated icon of the early Republic: "I have nothing more to offer than what General Washington would have had to offer, had he been taken by the British and put to trial by them."

Such talk invoking the specter of a black George Washington made James Monroe and Thomas Jefferson exceedingly uneasy. Persistent rumors implicated two white Frenchmen in the plot as well; if that connection had been established, it would have strengthened the Federalists' claims that slave insurrections were a logical outcome of Republican slogans about liberty and equality. Meanwhile, Virginia judges were keeping the Richmond gallows busy. Over September and October, twenty-seven black men were hanged for contemplating rebellion. Finally, Vice President Jefferson advised Governor Monroe that the hangings had gone far enough and that deportation was a better alternative. "The world at large will forever condemn us if we indulge a principle of revenge," Jefferson wrote Monroe. Hanging so many men for their desire to be free was a disturbing idea for these two particular Virginia planters. Deportation proved difficult, however; Caribbean ports as well as Spanish New Orleans did not welcome slaves inclined to revolution. Some eventually were sold into Spanish Florida.

Gabriel's near-rebellion failed, but it scared Virginia politicians into a serious—but secret—effort to identify a site to which future troublesome slaves could be expatriated. In 1801, the Virginia legislature pressed the federal government for help, since deportation required cooperation with a foreign power. As a Virginia planter troubled by slavery, Jefferson was at first sympathetic to this effort. But as the new president, he let the idea drop. To remove insubordinate slaves, by deporting them to Sierra Leone in Africa or to some imagined Spanish colony west of the Mississippi, would perhaps reduce tensions in Virginia, but it might also encourage defiance because the eventual payoff was freedom. The shock of Gabriel's rebellion brought some Virginia leaders as close as they would ever come to embracing a plan to reduce slavery in their midst; and yet it was not nearly close enough to have any effect.

The Jefferson Vision of Republican Simplicity

Jefferson sidestepped the problem of slavery and turned his attention to establishing a mode of governing that was a clear contrast to that of the Federalists. He was the first president inaugurated in Washington, D.C., still a mere village of three thousand inhabitants. On inauguration day, he dressed in everyday wear, to strike the tone of republican simplicity, and walked to the Senate chamber in the Capitol for the modest swearing-in ceremony.

Once in office, Jefferson continued to emphasize simplicity and frugality. He scaled back on Federalist building plans for Washington and cut the government budget. He wore plain clothes and presented an appearance that was "neglected but not slovenly," according to one onlooker. He cultivated a casual style, wearing slippers to greet important guests and seating them haphazardly at his table, avoiding the formality of state dinner parties or liveried servants like Washington's. Jefferson's studied carelessness was very deliberate.

Jefferson was no Antifederalist. He had supported the Constitution in 1788 from his diplomatic post in France, although he had some qualms about the unrestricted reelection allowed to the president. But his political service of the 1790s, first as Washington's secretary of state and then as Adams's vice president, caused him to fear what he regarded as an inappropriate stretching of governmental powers in the executive branch.

Jefferson had watched with mounting distrust as Hamilton led the Federalists to fund the public

JEFFERSON'S RED WAISTCOAT

During his presidency, Jefferson often wore this red silk waistcoat as informal daywear. The garment had a velvet collar, woolen sleeves, and a thick lining made from recycled cotton and wool stockings. The thrifty Jefferson preferred to conserve firewood by wearing layers of warm clothes. A senator visiting in 1802 reported in dismay that the president was "dressed, or rather undressed, with an old brown coat, red waistcoat, old corduroy small clothes, much soiled, woolen hose, and slippers without heels." Another guest in 1804 found him in the red waistcoat, green velveteen breeches with pearl buttons, and "slippers down at the heels" which made him look like an ordinary farmer. Such colorful clothing in silk and velveteen carries dressy or feminine connotations in the twenty-first century, but not in 1800. Jefferson did dress up in silk stockings and clean linen for fancy dinner parties; and when he lived in Paris in the 1780s, he wore an elaborately embroidered silk waistcoat under a greatcoat trimmed with gold lace. But in the 1800s, he used his simple, colorful clothes to make a point about republican manners.

Courtesy Monticello, photo by Colonial Williamsburg.

JEFFERSON'S INDEPENDENT FARMER

A Jeffersonian vision of rustic virtue; a farmer plows his field on the outskirts of Salem, North Carolina. The farmer wears a hat, coat, and long trousers to protect his legs; he also appears to be barefoot. Collection of the Wachovia Historical Society.

debt, establish a national bank, and secure commercial ties with England. The Hamiltonian program seemed to Jefferson to be wrongly promoting the interests of a small circle of money-hungry speculators at the expense of the rest of the country. Jefferson was not at all anticommerce. But financial schemes that seemed merely to allow rich men to become richer, without enhancing the vast and natural productivity of America, were corrupt and worthless, he believed, and their promotion had no authority under the Constitution.

In Jefferson's vision, the source of true freedom in America was the independent farmer, someone who owned and worked his land both for himself and for the market. Widespread landownership, which would support unsubservient and therefore virtuous citizens, was Jefferson's cornerstone of liberty. He had embedded the idea of easy access to land in the various land ordinances he designed in the 1780s for the Northwest Territory, even going so far as to suggest that western lands be given away free, in fifty-acre parcels, to any landless white man. Members of the Virginia legislature, substantial landowners who had gotten their land the old-fashioned way (inheritance, shrewd marriage, or outright purchase), found his idea too radical and

rejected it. But Jefferson remained committed to the idea of cheaply available land as the insurance policy that guaranteed American freedom.

In Jefferson's vision, the source of true freedom in America was the independent farmer, someone who owned and worked his land both for himself and for the market.

Distrusting Hamiltonian plans, Jefferson as president set about to dismantle many Federalist innovations. He reduced the size of the army by a third, leaving only three thousand soldiers, and cut back the navy from twenty-five to seven ships. Peacetime defense, he felt, should rest with "a well-disciplined militia," not a standing army. With the consent of Congress, he abolished all federal internal taxes, including both those based on population and the hated whiskey tax; government revenue would now derive solely from customs duties and from the sale of western lands. (This maneuver was of particular benefit to the South, where the three-fifths clause of the Constitution counted slaves for both representation and taxation. Now the South enjoyed its extra weight in the House of Representatives without having to pay any extra taxes.) By the end of his first term, Jefferson had deeply reduced Hamilton's cherished national debt.

A properly limited federal government, according to Jefferson, was responsible merely for running a postal system, maintaining the federal courts, staffing lighthouses, collecting customs duties, and conducting a census once every ten years. Government jobs were kept to a minimum. The president had just one private secretary, a young man named Meriwether Lewis, to help with his correspondence, and Jefferson paid him out of his own pocket. (Another 14 servants performed domestic and valet chores for the president, and they were also paid—or owned—by Jefferson.) The Department of State employed only 8 people: Secretary James Madison, 6 clerks, and a messenger. The Treasury Department was by far the largest unit, with 73 revenue commissioners, auditors, and clerks and 2 watchmen. The entire payroll of the executive branch amounted to a mere 130 people in 1801. In the hot summer months, it shrank to just a few dozen men.

The Judiciary and the Midnight Judges

There was one set of government workers not under Jefferson's control to appoint. His predecessor, John Adams, seized the short time between his election defeat and Jefferson's inauguration to appoint 217 Federalist men to various judicial, diplomatic, and military posts.

Some of this windfall of appointments came to Adams as a result of the Judiciary Act of 1801, passed in the final month of his presidency. The new law revised the Judiciary Act of 1789, which had established a six-man Supreme Court and six circuit courts, each presided over by a Supreme Court justice. The new act set up sixteen circuit courts, each headed by a new judge. A fast-acting Adams could appoint sixteen new judges with lifetime tenure, plus dozens more state attorneys, marshals, and clerks for each court. The 1801 act also reduced the size of the Supreme Court, from six to five justices. Adams had recently appointed John Marshall, a Virginia lawyer and solid Federalist, to a vacant sixth seat, but once the Judiciary Act became law, the Republican president would not be able to fill the next empty seat.

Adams and Marshall worked feverishly in the last weeks of February to secure agreements from the new appointees. In view of the slowness of mail and travel, their getting 217 acceptances was astonishing. The two men were still at work until 9 P.M. on the last night Adams was president, signing and delivering commissions to the new officeholders.

The appointment of "midnight judges" infuriated the Republicans. Jefferson, upon taking office, immediately canceled the appointments of the nontenured men. A few commissions had not yet been delivered, by Marshall's oversight, and Jefferson refused to send them out. One of them was addressed to William Marbury, who soon decided to sue the new secretary of state, James Madison, for failure to make good on the appointment. This action gave rise to a landmark Supreme Court case, *Marbury v. Madison,* decided in 1803. The Court, presided over by John Marshall, ruled that although Marbury's commission was valid and the new president should have delivered it, the Court could not compel him to do so. What made the case significant was little noted at the time: The Court found that the grounds of Marbury's suit, resting in the Judiciary Act of 1789, were in conflict with the Constitution. For the first time, the Court acted to disallow a law (part of the 1789 act) on the grounds that it was unconstitutional. John Marshall quietly established the concept of judicial review; the Supreme Court in effect assumed the legal authority to nullify acts of the other branches of the federal government.

The reach of the *Marbury* decision went largely unnoticed in 1803 because the president and Congress were completely preoccupied with other major issues. One was a concerted effort to repeal via Congress the Judiciary Act of 1801. Republicans argued that so many new courts were expensive. Federalists argued that removing the judges was unconstitutional because they had been guaranteed lifetime tenure, and nothing but a criminal trial could unseat them. At issue was the power relation between Congress and the judiciary, with the Republicans claiming that if Congress could create courts, it could abolish them. The Judiciary Act was finally repealed in 1802.

The Promise of the West: The Louisiana Purchase and the Lewis and Clark Expedition

Jefferson's vision of a limited federal government could be sustained as long as international affairs remained peaceful. The rise of Napoleon to power in France in 1799 soon brought France and England into open warfare again. And renewed European tensions created an unexpected opportunity for Jefferson's administration.

In 1800, the Mississippi River formed the western boundary of the United States; the expanse of land west of the river was under the flag of Spain. For a century before the French and Indian War, France had claimed and partly settled the territory, only to lose it to Spain in the 1763 Treaty of Paris. Spain never sent adequate forces to control or settle the land, however; Spanish power remained precarious everywhere outside New Orleans.

Meanwhile, American farming families were advancing west, to Kentucky and Tennessee, in the 1790s. They settled along rivers emptying into the upper Mississippi, on which they depended for shipping their agricultural produce. For a while the Spanish governor of New Orleans allowed free navigational rights on the Mississippi, and American farmers supplied the city with flour, whiskey, and other foodstuffs. The Spanish crown even encouraged Americans to settle across the river, in an effort to augment the population, and by 1801 Americans made up a sizable minority of the population around the lower Mississippi. Publicly, Jefferson protested the luring of Americans into Spanish territory, but privately he wrote, "I wish a hundred thousand of our inhabitants would accept the invitation; it will be the means of delivering to us peaceably, what may otherwise cost us a war." Jefferson's fears of war were not unrealistic. In 1802, the Spanish governor of New Orleans revoked American shipping privileges through or past his city. Congressmen began muttering about taking the city by force; talk of war, especially in Federalist newspapers, became commonplace.

In the same year, rumors reached Jefferson that Spain had struck a secret bargain with France to hand over a large part of Spain's trans-Mississippi territory to Napoleon in exchange for a duchy in Italy. Spain had proved a weak western neighbor, but France was another story. Jefferson was sufficiently alarmed that he instructed Robert R. Livingston, America's minister in France, to try to buy New Orleans. At first the French denied they owned the city, but Livingston politely announced that he had seen the treaty with Spain. Livingston hinted that the United States might simply seize New Orleans if buying it was not an option. The French negotiator suddenly asked Livingston to name

his price for the entire Louisiana Territory, stretching from the Gulf of Mexico north to Canada. Livingston stalled, and the Frenchman made suggestions: $125 million? $60 million? Livingston shrewdly stalled some more, and within days the French sold the entire territory for the bargain price of $15 million (Map 9.2).

Jefferson and most of Congress were delighted with the outcome of the diplomatic mission. Congress quickly approved the purchase and voted for a bond issue to raise money for the price. However, all but one of New England's representatives voted against it. Federalist-dominated New England had been willing to consider war to seize New Orleans and control navigation rights on the Mississippi, but the unexpectedly huge territory raised anxiety about the ultimate geographic balance of power in the United States. So much land, sure to be carved into states one day, made some fear the eventual marginalization of New England.

Jefferson had his own reason to be reluctant about the Louisiana Purchase. The price was right, and the enormous territory fulfilled Jefferson's dream of abundant farmland for generations of Americans to come. But by what authority in the Constitution could he justify the purchase? His frequent criticism of the Hamiltonian stretching of the Constitution came back to haunt him. His legal reasoning told him he needed a constitutional amendment to fully authorize the addition of territory; more expedient minds told him the treaty-making powers of the president could cover his action. Expediency won out. In late 1803, the American army took formal control of the Louisiana Territory, and the United States was now 828,000 square miles larger.

Even before the Louisiana Territory fell in his lap, Jefferson had eyed the trans-Mississippi west with intense curiosity. In early 1803, he had arranged congressional funding for a secret exploration into Spanish and Indian territory whose object was both scientific and military. Jefferson appointed twenty-eight-year-old Meriwether Lewis, his personal secretary, to head the expedition. Jefferson, ever the scientist, instructed Lewis to investigate Indian cultures, to collect plant and animal specimens, and to chart the geography of the West. Congress had more traditional goals in mind: The expedition was to scout out locations for military posts, open commercial agreements for the fur trade, and locate any possible waterway between the East and West Coasts (see Map 9.2).

MAP 9.2

The Louisiana Purchase and the Lewis and Clark Expedition
Robert Livingston's bargain buy of 1803 far exceeded his initial assignment, to acquire just the city of New Orleans. Federalists of New England, worried that their own geographically based power in the federal government would someday be eclipsed by the West, voted against the purchase. The Indians who inhabited the vast region, unaware that their land had been sold, got their first look at Anglo-American and African American men when the Lewis and Clark expedition came exploring in 1804–1806.

For his co-leader, Lewis chose Kentuckian William Clark, a fellow veteran of the 1790s Indian wars. Together they handpicked a crew of forty-five, including expert rivermen, gunsmiths, fishermen, hunters, interpreters, a cook, and a slave in his thirties named York who belonged to Clark. The explorers left St. Louis in the spring of 1804, working their way northwest up the Missouri River. They camped for the winter at a Mandan village in what is now central North Dakota. The Mandan Indians were familiar with British and French traders from Canada, but the black man York created a sensation. Reportedly, Indians rubbed moistened fin-

gers over the man's skin to see if the color was painted on.

Even before the Louisiana Territory fell in his lap, Jefferson had eyed the trans-Mississippi west with intense curiosity.

The following spring, the explorers headed west, aided by a French trapper accompanied by his wife, a sixteen-year-old Indian woman named

SACAJAWEA

Sacajawea is pictured here with her baby, as imagined by mid-nineteenth-century artist Edgar S. Paxson, who produced a series of paintings of grand moments on the Lewis and Clark expedition. The young Shoshone mother was also called Janey by the two explorers, who admired her courage and fortitude. Her baby, Jean Baptiste Charbonneau, was nicknamed Pompey. William Clark brought the boy to St. Louis when he was six years old to educate him. In the 1820s, the youth was taken to Germany by the prince of Württemberg; he returned six years later, fluent in German, French, Spanish, and English. Half Shoshone and half French, Charbonneau became a guide and interpreter for numerous trading expeditions throughout the West until his death in the 1860s.

Sacajawea oil painting by Edgar S. Paxson. The University of Montana Museum of Fine Arts Collection.

Sacajawea, who had just had a baby. Sacajawea's presence was to prove unexpectedly helpful. Indian tribes encountered en route withdrew their suspicion that the Americans were hostile because, as Lewis wrote in his journal, "no woman ever accompanies a war party of Indians in this quarter."

The Lewis and Clark expedition reached the Pacific Ocean at the mouth of the Columbia River in November 1805. When they returned home the following year, they were greeted as national heroes. They had established favorable relations with dozens of Indian tribes; they had collected invaluable information on the peoples, soils, plants, animals, and geography of the West; and they had inspired a nation of restless explorers and solitary imitators.

Republicans in a Dangerous World

The election of 1804 proved an easy triumph for the Republican Party. The Federalist candidate, Charles Cotesworth Pinckney of South Carolina, secured only 14 votes in the electoral college, in contrast to 162 for the president. Just months before the election, the Federalists had lost their shrewdest statesman: Alexander Hamilton, called by some "the brains of the Federalist Party," was tragically killed in a duel with Aaron Burr. (See "Historical Question," page 298.) Republicans would hold the presidency for another twenty years.

Jefferson's second term was dominated by the ongoing war between France and England, which continually threatened to involve the United States. As peaceful alternatives to war, the president experimented with economic sanctions and trade embargoes. Jefferson and his successors faced war threats not only across the Atlantic but also in the new states of the old Northwest Territory, where the powerful new Indian confederacy led by Tecumseh challenged the westward press of American settlement.

Troubles at Sea and the Embargo Act of 1807

In the 1790s, American shipping had prospered when the two leading European powers, France and England, were at war, for they left trade routes and markets wide open. Determined not to make that

TWO CAPTAINS AT SEA
The captains of two sailing ships confer at sea, using horns to amplify their voices, in this watercolor by Benjamin Latrobe (the architect of the Capitol). New England coastal towns like Salem, Newburyport, Portsmouth, and Portland played a major role in the shipping trade and extended their routes to China and India in the early nineteenth century, in addition to traversing the West Indies–Europe circuit. Some schooners really were as small as these depicted, measuring fifteen to eighteen feet wide and as little as forty feet long. Jefferson's embargo worked a great hardship on the New England shipping industry.
Maryland Historical Society, Baltimore.

mistake again when war broke out between them in 1803, the two countries established independent restrictions on American trade with the enemy, backed up by threats to blockade routes and seize ships.

British enforcement of their threats beginning in 1806 affected many hundreds of Americans. In addition to searching for prohibited goods, British naval patrols claimed the right to seize (and impress into service) sailors whom they accused of being deserters from the British navy. In fact, some of those captured in the impressment sweeps *were* deserters, but hundreds of native-born Americans were caught up as well. Between 1807 and 1812, about 2,500 men were taken captive and impressed

into royal naval service. Jefferson and the American public were outraged.

One incident in particular made the usually cautious Jefferson nearly belligerent. In June 1807, an American ship, the *Chesapeake,* harboring some British deserters, was ordered to stop for inspection by a British frigate. The *Chesapeake* refused, and the British opened fire, killing three Americans. What was worse, this incident took place in Chesapeake Bay, well within U.S. territory. President Jefferson prepared a heated manifesto to send to Great Britain, demanding an end to impressment. But the United States was not actually prepared for war— the much-reduced army and navy presented a serious problem—and Jefferson's advisers toned down

How Could a Vice President Get Away with Murder?

ON JULY 11, 1804, the vice president of the United States, Aaron Burr, shot Alexander Hamilton, the architect of the Federalist Party, in a duel on a narrow ledge below the cliffs of Weehawken, New Jersey, across the Hudson River from New York City. The pistol blast tore through a rib, demolished Hamilton's liver, and splintered his spine. The forty-seven-year-old Hamilton died the next day, in agonizing pain.

How could it happen that a sitting vice president and a prominent political leader could put themselves at such risk? Why did men who made their living by the legal system go outside the law and turn to the centuries-old ritual of the duel? Here were two eminent attorneys, skilled in the legalistic negotiations meant to substitute for violent resolution of disputes, firing .54-caliber hair-trigger weapons at ten paces. Did anyone try to stop them? How did the public react? Was Hamilton's death a criminal act? How could Burr continue to fulfill his federal office, presiding over the U.S. Senate?

Burr challenged Hamilton in late June after learning about a newspaper report that Hamilton "looked upon Mr. Burr to be a dangerous man, and one who ought not be trusted with the reins of government." Burr knew that Hamilton had long held a very low opinion of him and had never hesitated to say so in private, but now his private disparagement had made its way into print. Compounding the insult were political consequences: Burr was sure that Hamilton's remark cost him election to the governorship of New York.

Quite possibly he was right. Knowing that Jefferson planned to dump him from the federal ticket in the 1804 election, Burr had chosen to run for New York's highest office. His opponent was an obscure Republican judge; Burr's success depended on the support of the old Federalist leadership in the state. Up to the eve of the election, he appeared to have it—until Hamilton's remark was circulated.

So on June 18, Burr challenged Hamilton to a duel if he did not disavow his comment. Over the next three weeks, the men exchanged several letters clarifying the nature of the insult that aggrieved Burr. Hamilton the lawyer evasively quibbled over words, causing Burr finally to rail against his focus on syntax and grammar. At heart, Hamilton could not deny the insult, nor could he spurn the challenge without injury to his reputation for integrity and bravery. Both Burr and Hamilton were locked in a highly ritualized procedure meant to uphold a gentleman's code of honor.

Each man had a trusted "second," in accord with the code of dueling, who helped frame and deliver the letters and finally assisted at the duel site. Only a handful of close friends knew of the challenge, and no one tried to stop it. Hamilton did not tell his wife. He wrote her a tender farewell letter the night before, to be opened in the event of his death. He knew full well the pain dueling brought to loved ones, for his nineteen-year-old son Philip had been killed in a duel three years earlier, at the same ledge at Weehawken, as a result of hotheaded words exchanged at a New York theater. Even when Hamilton's wife was called to her husband's deathbed, she was first told he had terrible spasms from an illness. Women were completely shut out of the masculine world of dueling.

AARON BURR BY JOHN VANDERLYN
Aaron Burr was fifty-three years old at the time of this portrait, painted in 1809 by the New York artist John Vanderlyn.
Collection of The New-York Historical Society.

News of Hamilton's death spread quickly in New York and then throughout the nation. On the day of the funeral, church bells tolled continuously and New York merchants shut down all business. Thousands joined the procession, and the city council declared a six-week mourning period. Burr fled to Philadelphia, fearing retribution by the crowd.

Northern newspapers expressed indignation over the illegal duel and the tragic death of so prominent a man. (Response in the South was more subdued. Dueling was fully accepted there as an extralegal remedy for insult, and Burr's grievance fit perfectly the sense of violated honor that legitimated duels. In addition, southerners had never been particularly fond of the Federalist Hamilton.) Many northern states had criminalized dueling recently, treating a challenge as a misdemeanor and a dueling death as a homicide. Even after death, the loser of an illegal duel could endure one final penalty—being buried without a coffin, having a stake driven through the body, being strung up in public until the body rotted, or, more horrible still for the time, being donated to medical students for dissection. Such prescribed mutilation of the dead showed that northern lawmakers themselves participated in the code of honor by using threats of postmortem humiliation to discourage dueling. Hamilton's body was spared such a fate. But two ministers in succession refused to administer Holy Communion to him in his dying hours because he was a duelist; finally, one relented.

The public demanded to know the reasons for the duel, so the seconds prepared the correspondence between the principals for publication. A coroner's jury in New York soon indicted Burr on misdemeanor charges for issuing a challenge; a grand jury in New Jersey indicted him for murder. By that time, Burr was a fugitive from justice hiding out with sympathetic friends in South Carolina.

But not for long. Amazingly, he returned to Washington, D.C., in November 1804 to resume presiding over sessions of the Senate, a role he continued to assume until his term ended in March 1805. Federalists snubbed him, but eleven Republican senators petitioned New Jersey to drop its indictment on the grounds that "civilized nations" do not treat dueling deaths as "common murders." New Jersey did not pursue the murder charge. Burr freely visited New Jersey and New York for three more decades, paying no penalty for killing Hamilton.

Few would doubt that Burr was a scoundrel, albeit a brilliant one. A few years later, he was in-

PISTOLS FROM THE BURR–HAMILTON DUEL
Alexander Hamilton's brother-in-law John B. Church purchased this pair of dueling pistols in London in 1797. Church used them once in a duel with Aaron Burr, occasioned by Church's calling Burr a scoundrel in public; neither man was hurt. Hamilton's son Philip had borrowed them for his own fatal duel, three years before. When Burr challenged Hamilton, the latter also turned to John Church for the weapons. The guns stayed in the Church family until 1930, when they were given to the Chase Manhattan Bank in New York City, chartered in 1799 as the Manhattan Company. (Burr, Church, and Hamilton all served on the bank's board of directors.) When the pistols were cleaned in 1874, a hidden hair trigger came to light. It could be cocked by moving the trigger forward one-eighth inch. It then required only a half-pound pull, instead of ten pounds, to fire the gun. Hamilton gained no advantage from the hair trigger, if he knew of it.
Courtesy of Chase Manhattan Archives.

dicted for treason against the U.S. government in a presumed plot to break off part of the United States and start his own country in the Southwest. (He dodged that bullet too, in a spectacular trial presided over by John Marshall, chief justice of the Supreme Court.) Hamilton certainly thought Burr a scoundrel, and when that opinion reached print, Burr had cause to defend his honor under the etiquette of dueling. The accuracy of Hamilton's charge was of absolutely no account. Dueling redressed questions of honor, not questions of fact.

Dueling continued to be a feature of southern society for many more decades, but in the North the custom became extremely rare by the 1820s, helped along by the disrepute of Hamilton's death and by the rise of a legalistic society that now preferred evidence, interrogation, and monetary judgments to avenge injury.

his challenge to England, limiting it to a ban on British warships in American waters.

Before the *Chesapeake* incident, Jefferson had convinced Congress to pass nonimportation laws banning a select list of British-made goods. But after the *Chesapeake* incident, Jefferson and Secretary of State James Madison pushed the idea of a total embargo, passed by Congress as the Embargo Act in December 1807. American ships were forbidden from engaging in trade with any foreign port. It was a drastic measure, but it was intended as economic coercion rather than the far more drastic possibility of war. The immediate goal was to make England suffer, and all foreign ports were included in the ban so as to discourage illegal trading through secondary ports. The two Republican leaders were convinced that England needed America's trade goods, mainly agricultural products, far more than America needed British goods.

The *Chesapeake* Incident, June 22, 1807

The Embargo Act of 1807 was a total disaster. From 1790 to 1807, U.S. exports had increased fivefold, and in an instant the Embargo Act wiped out all commerce. Worse, it was ineffective; instead of suffering, England simply turned to South American countries for agricultural supplies, sailing on seas now empty of American vessels. In New England, the heart of the shipping industry, trade came to a standstill, and unemployment began to rise. Protest petitions flooded Washington. Federalists in Barre, Massachusetts, pointed out that farmers were also hurt: "We consider the interest of Agriculture and Commerce as inseparable"; the "belief that the farmer can flourish, while [the merchant] is neglected and depressed" was a serious error, they warned. In the South, tobacco rotted on the docks and cotton went unpicked. The wheat crop of the central and western states plummeted in value, and river traffic came to a halt. The federal government itself suffered too, for import duties were a significant source of national revenue. Jefferson paid political costs as well. The Federalist Party, in danger of fading away after its very weak showing in the election of 1804, began to pick up strength from the anti-Jefferson protest.

The embargo stayed in place until the last day of Jefferson's presidency, in March 1809, but it created a very rocky final year for the administration. Congress at last replaced it with the Non-Intercourse Act of 1809, which prohibited trade only with England and France and their colonial possessions. In effect, the new law opened the way for legal, indirect trade, so the economic anguish of New England shippers and southern planters was greatly diminished, for the moment.

Madison Gets Entangled

In mid-1808, Jefferson indicated that he would not run for a third term. James Madison, the secretary of state for eight years and Jefferson's closest ally, was the clear heir apparent. Disgruntled Republicans from hurting tobacco regions of the South made a move to support James Monroe, a Virginia planter with wide experience as a diplomat to England, but Madison was the favorite among the various state caucuses of Republicans. At this point, party politics, still held to be a bad thing by leading statesmen, operated through informal coalition building and statewide caucuses that orchestrated state and local elections. The Federalist caucuses, thinking they would gain strength from the unpopular Embargo Act, chose Charles Cotesworth Pinckney again to run against Madison. Pinckney did much better than in 1804; he received forty-seven electoral votes, nearly half Madison's total. Support for the Federalists remained centered in the New England states, but Republicans still held the balance of power nationwide.

The attacks on American ships continued, by both the British and the French. In 1810, the Non-Intercourse Act expired, and Congress replaced it with a law that permitted direct trade with either France or England, whichever first gave assurance that it would stop harassing American ships. Napoleon seized the initiative and declared that France would comply. Madison too hastily accepted Napoleon's offer, reopened trade with France, and notified England that he intended to reinstate the embargo in the spring of 1811 unless England rescinded its search-and-seizure policy.

Unfortunately for Madison, the duplicitous French leaders continued to seize American ships. Furthermore, the British made no move to stop impressments or to repeal trade restrictions, and Madison was forced to reactivate the embargo, much to the great displeasure of the New England shipping industry. In 1811, the country was seriously divided and in a deep quandary. To some, it seemed the United States must be on the verge of war; but was the enemy to be France or England? To others, war meant disaster, for it would surely finish off the grievously hurting shipping industry.

A new Congress, elected in the fall of 1810, arrived in Washington in March 1811 just as Madison's threatened embargo was to take effect. Some of the new and much younger members were eager to avenge the insults from abroad. In particular, Henry Clay, thirty-four, from Kentucky, and John C. Calhoun, twenty-nine, from South Carolina, became the center of a group informally known as the War Hawks. Though calling themselves Republicans, like Madison, these younger men had much more expansive ideas of the way the United States should meet the challenge of enemies abroad.

Indian Troubles in the West

In the atmosphere of indecision about war with European powers, tensions mounted over difficulties with Indian tribes coalescing under the Shawnee chief Tecumseh's leadership. Northernmost tribes were already renewing ties with supportive British Indian agents and fur traders in Canada, a potential source of food and weapons. If the United States embarked on war with England, there would likely be serious repercussions on the frontier.

Shifting demographics raised the stakes for both sides. The 1810 census counted some 230,000 Americans living in Ohio, only seven years after statehood. Another 40,000 Americans had moved into the territories of Indiana, Illinois, and Michigan. The Indian population of the entire region (the old Northwest Territory) was much smaller, probably about 70,000, a number unknown (because uncounted) to the Americans but within the mental grasp of Tecumseh, based on his extensive travels.

Up to 1805, Indiana's territorial governor, William Henry Harrison, had managed to negotiate a series of treaties in a divide-and-conquer strategy

TENSKWATAWA

Tenskwatawa, the Shawnee Prophet, and his brother Tecumseh led the spiritual and political efforts of a number of Indian tribes to resist land-hungry Americans moving west in the decade before the War of 1812. The Prophet is shown in a portrait by George Catlin with beaded necklaces, metal arm- and wristbands, and earrings. Compare the metal gorget here with ones worn by George Washington (p. 147) and Joseph Brant (p. 200).

National Museum of American Art, Washington, D.C./Art Resource, New York.

extracting Indian lands for paltry payments. But with the rise to power of Tecumseh and his brother Tenskwatawa, the Prophet, Harrison's strategy became harder to carry out. A fundamental part of Tecumseh's message was the assertion that all Indian lands were held in common by all the tribes: "No tribe has the right to sell, even to each other, much less to strangers. . . . Sell a country! Why not sell the air, the great sea, as well as the earth? Didn't the Great Spirit make them all for the use of his children? The way, the only way to stop this evil is for the red man to unite in claiming a common and equal right in the land, as it was first, and should be now, for it was never divided."

> *A fundamental part of Tecumseh's message was the assertion that all Indian lands were held in common by all the tribes.*

In 1809, while Tecumseh was away on a recruiting trip, Harrison called together some of the leaders of the Potawatomi, Miami, and Delaware tribes to negotiate the Treaty of Fort Wayne. As required, Harrison first sought approval from President Madison, who authorized negotiations so long as all "who have or pretend right to these lands" were party to the agreement. Harrison sidestepped that requirement, calling in chiefs who in some cases had no pretense of claims to the land in question, along the Wabash River in southern Indiana. After promising (falsely) that this was the last cession of land the United States would seek, Harrison secured title to more than three million acres of land for the United States, in exchange for payments that amounted to two cents per acre (Map 9.3).

When he returned, Tecumseh was furious, both at Harrison and at the tribal leaders, and he redoubled his efforts to recruit for his confederacy. Leaving his brother in charge at Prophetstown, with the warning that he should avoid all warfare until Tecumseh returned, the Shawnee chief left on a trip that would take him throughout the South for much of 1811. While he was away, Harrison decided to march on Prophetstown. With one thousand armed

MAP 9.3

Indian Lands Ceded by Treaties in the Old Northwest Territory, 1795–1809
Two-thirds of Ohio was transferred to the Americans in the Treaty of Greenville of 1795. For more than a decade thereafter, officials like William Henry Harrison managed to acquire vast tracts along the Ohio and up the Mississippi, by negotiating with Indians whose authority to speak for their tribes was often unclear or dubious.

"Land Cessions in the Old Northwest 1795–1809." From *Tecumseh: A Life* by John Sugden. Copyright 1997 by John Sugden. Reprinted with the permission of Henry Holt and Company LLC.

men he approached Tippecanoe Creek, but Tenskwatawa decided to attack first. The two-hour battle resulted in about a hundred deaths—sixty-two Americans and forty Indians—before the Prophet's forces fled the town, which Harrison's men set on fire. The November 1811 Battle of Tippecanoe was heralded as a glorious victory for the Americans; Harrison acquired the nickname "Tippecanoe" and used it as a patriotic rallying cry when he ran for the presidency in 1840. The Indians' faith in the Prophet's magical powers diminished sharply; Tenskwatawa never again enjoyed such influence. But Tecumseh was now more ready than ever to make war on the Americans.

Battle of Tippecanoe, 1811

The War of 1812

The Indian conflicts in the Northwest Territory in 1811 soon merged into the wider conflict with England known as the War of 1812. The defeat at Tippecanoe propelled Tecumseh into a renewal of the old alliance with British military commanders stationed at outposts in lower Canada. If there had been doubt before about who should be the target of a declaration of war, France or England, it was now abundantly clear, especially to westerners living near the frontier, that the British should get the honor.

The War Begins

The several dozen young War Hawks new to Congress saluted Harrison's Tippecanoe victory and continued to urge the country on to war. Mostly lawyers by profession, they came from the West and South, and they welcomed a war with England both to legitimize attacks on the Indians and to bring an end to impressment. Many were also expansionists,

looking to occupy Florida and threaten Canada. And they captured prominent posts in Congress from which to wield influence. Henry Clay was elected Speaker of the House, an extraordinary honor for a young newcomer. John C. Calhoun won a seat on the Foreign Relations Committee. The War Hawks approved major defense expenditures; the army, for example, was quadrupled in size. New England Federalists in Congress staunchly refused to endorse any of these war preparations, just as they had opposed the embargo in 1807.

In June 1812, Congress declared war on Great Britain in a vote that divided on sectional lines: New England and some of the Middle Atlantic states opposed the war, while the South and West were strongly for it. Ironically, Great Britain had just formally decided to stop the search and seizure of American ships. News of that diplomatic breakthrough arrived too late, however; the war machine would not be stopped. The Foreign Relations Committee issued an elaborate justification titled *Report on the Causes and Reasons for War*, written mainly by Calhoun. The report went far beyond a condemnation of Britain's naval actions to assert that war was necessary to avenge British insults in treating the United States like a third-rate power. Extravagant language about Britain's "lust for power," "unbounded tyranny," and "mad ambition" suggested that America was actually engaged in a second revolution for independence. These were fighting words, in a war that was in large measure about insult and honor.

The War Hawks proposed an invasion of Canada, confidently predicting victory in four weeks, before the fall elections. Instead, the war lasted two and a half years, and Canada never fell. The northern invasion turned out to be a series of strategic blunders that revealed the grave unpreparedness of the United States for war. The combined British and Indian forces were unexpectedly powerful, and the United States made no attempt at the outset to create a naval presence on the Great Lakes. Detroit quickly fell, as did Fort Dearborn (site of the future Chicago). By the fall of 1812, the war was in a dismal state.

Worse, the New England states dragged their feet in raising troops, while New England merchants carried on illegal trade with Great Britain. Britain encouraged friendly overtures with New England, hoping to divide and conquer the Americans. New Englanders drank India tea in Liverpool cups, while President Madison fumed in Washington about Federalist disloyalty.

A BOXING MATCH, or Another Bloody Nose for JOHN BULL.

WAR OF 1812: BOXING MATCH
A battle between the American ship Enterprise *and the British ship* Boxer *off the Maine coast sparked this wishful-thinking cartoon. A bare-knuckled James Madison has just punched King George III, blackened his eye, and made his nose bleed. The king begs "Mercy, mercy on me," and acknowledges "your [Madison's] superior skill." Madison asserts "we are an* Enterpriseing Nation" *capable of "equal force any day." This Madison clearly does not anticipate the humiliating burning of Washington in 1814.*
Courtesy, American Antiquarian Society.

The presidential election in 1812 solidified Federalist discontent with the war. Madison stood for a second term, opposed by DeWitt Clinton of New York. The nephew of Madison's first-term vice president, George Clinton, the younger Clinton was nominally Republican but able to attract the Federalist vote. He picked up all of New England's electoral votes, with the exception of Vermont's, and also took New York, New Jersey, and part of Maryland. Madison won in the electoral college, 128 to 89, but his margin of victory was considerably smaller than in the 1808 election.

In late 1812 and early 1813, the tide began to turn in the Americans' favor. First came some reassuring victories at sea, but little lasting gain. Americans attacked York (now Toronto), the capital of Upper Canada, and burned it in April 1813. A few months later, Commodore Oliver Hazard Perry defeated the British fleet at the western end of Lake Erie. Emboldened, General Harrison drove an army into Canada from Detroit and in October 1813 defeated the British and Indians at the Battle of the Thames, where Tecumseh met his death (Map 9.4).

Indians also met defeat in the South, where a general named Andrew Jackson led 2,500 Tennessee militiamen in an attack on Creek Indians, who were fighting in solidarity with Tecumseh's confederacy. At the Battle of Horseshoe Bend in March 1814, Jackson's militia killed more than 550 Indians, including women and children.

The British Offensives of 1814

In August 1814, British ships sailed into Chesapeake Bay toward Washington, D.C., throwing Washington dwellers into a panic. Families evacuated, banks removed their money, and government clerks carted away boxes of important papers. One State Department worker quickly located the Declaration of Independence and removed it to safety.

When five thousand British troops landed and marched toward the city, the only defense came from inexperienced militia units from Maryland. President Madison and his cabinet mounted horses and vainly tried to inspire the militia, who fled in disorder as the British advanced. The British entered the city, set fire to the president's house, and burned the Capitol building, a newspaper office, some dockyards, and a well-stocked arsenal. August 24 was a low moment for the American side.

Instead of trying to hold the city, the British headed north for the port of Baltimore. They attacked the city on September 11, 1814, but a fierce defense by the Maryland militia and a steady barrage of gunfire from Fort McHenry in the harbor kept them at bay. The firing continued until mid-

M A P   9.4

The War of 1812
Battles in the War of 1812 were fought along the border of Canada and in the Chesapeake region. The most important American victory came in New Orleans, two weeks after peace had been agreed to in England.

night, motivating Francis Scott Key to compose a poem he called "The Star-Spangled Banner" the next day. The British pulled back, unwilling to try to take the city.

September 1814 brought another powerful British offensive. Marching from Canada into New York State, the British seemed to have every advantage—trained soldiers, superior artillery, cavalry, professional leaders. But a series of blunders cost them a naval skirmish at Plattsburgh on the northern end of Lake Champlain. It also cost them

their nerve; without ever engaging the astonished American troops, the British general turned his huge army around and retreated to Canada. This nonbattle was in fact a decisive military event, for British leaders in England, hearing the news of the retreat, concluded that incursions by land into the United States would be costly, difficult, and perhaps ineffective.

This point was confirmed when a large British army landed in lower Louisiana and encountered General Andrew Jackson and his militia just outside New Orleans, in early January 1815. Jackson's forces dramatically carried the day. The British suffered between two and three thousand casualties, the Americans less than eighty. Jackson became an instant hero, and the Battle of New Orleans was the most glorious and decisive victory the Americans had experienced. Ironically, negotiators in Europe had already signed a peace agreement two weeks earlier.

The War Ends

The Treaty of Ghent, signed in December 1814, settled few of the surface issues that had led to war. Neither country could claim the role of victor, and no land traded hands. Instead, the treaty reflected a mutual agreement to give up certain goals. The Americans yielded on impressment and gave up any claim to Canada; and the British agreed to evacuate western forts and abandoned their aid to Indians. Nothing was said about shipping rights, but both sides agreed to submit lingering trade disputes to arbitration at a future time. The most concrete result was an agreement to set up a commission to determine the exact boundary between the United States and Canada.

The Battle of New Orleans was the most glorious and decisive victory the Americans had experienced. Ironically, negotiators in Europe had already signed a peace agreement.

New England Federalists, united in opposition to the war, did not enjoy a sense of triumph over its ambiguous conclusion. Instead they felt a sting of disgrace because of an antiwar meeting convened by New England politicians in Hartford, Connecticut, in December 1814. Delegates to the Hartford Convention discussed but did not agree on secession from the Union. The main thrust of the convention was to protect New England's sectional interests by amending the Constitution. Proposed amendments would abolish the three-fifths clause as a basis of representation; specify that congressional powers to pass embargoes, admit states, or declare war should require a two-thirds vote instead of a simple majority; and limit the president to one term and prohibit successive presidents from the same state. The cumulative effect of these proposals would be to reduce the South's political power and break the lock of the Virginia dynasty on national office. New England wanted to make sure that no sectional party or group could again lead the country into war against the clear interests of some other section.

Just as the Hartford Convention broke up, news came first of Jackson's victory at New Orleans and then of the formal peace treaty. The combative list of amendments suddenly looked very unpatriotic and were dismissed by the U.S. Congress. The Federalist Party never recovered its grip, and within a few years its hold even in New England was reduced to a shadow.

No one really won the War of 1812. Americans celebrated as though they had, however, with parades and fireworks. The war gave rise to a new spirit of nationalism, even in New England. The paranoia over British tyranny evident in the 1812 declaration of war was laid to rest, replaced by pride in a more equal relationship with the old mother country.

Perhaps the biggest winners in the War of 1812 were the young men, once called War Hawks, who took up the banner of the Republican Party and carried it in new, expansive directions. These younger politicians favored trade, western expansion, internal improvements, and the energetic development of new economic markets after the war. The biggest losers of the war were the Indians. Tecumseh was dead, the Prophet discredited, the prospects of an Indian confederacy dashed, and the British protectors vanished.

Women's Status in the Early Republic

Unlike the American Revolution, the War of 1812 had little impact on the status of women. Developments in women's status in the early Republic came not as a result of wartime emergency but instead in incremental steps. As state legislatures and the courts grappled with the legal dependency of married white women in a country whose defining characteristic was independence, religious organizations struggled to redefine the role of women in church governance.

Women and the Law

The Anglo-American view of women, implanted in British common law, was that wives had no independent legal or political personhood. The legal doctrine of *feme covert* held that a wife's civic life was completely subsumed by her husband's: A wife was obligated to obey her husband; her property was his; her domestic and sexual services were his; and even their children were legally his. If the husband died, the court assigned responsibility for children to a guardian, usually a near male relative. Women had no right to keep their wages, to make contracts, or to sue or be sued. Any crime committed by a wife in the presence of her husband was chargeable to him, with two exceptions: treason against the state and keeping a brothel. The fundamental assumption of coverture was that husbands did—and ought to—control their wives.

> *The Anglo-American view of women, implanted in British common law, was that wives had no independent legal or political personhood. A wife's civic life was completely subsumed by her husband's.*

State legislatures, when codifying their laws, generally passed up the opportunity to rewrite the laws of domestic relations, even though they redrafted so much other British law in light of republican principles. The standard treatise on family law, published in 1816 in Connecticut, was titled *The Law of Baron and Feme* ("lord and woman"). Lawyers never paused even to defend, much less to challenge, the assumption that unequal power relations lay at the heart of marriage. The early Republic's conception of the "republican wife and mother" in no way altered the basic legal framework inherited from British law. The virtuous wife whose obedience was earned by a husband's affection and the enlightened mother who acquired intellectual skills to transmit to her citizen sons still operated well within the boundaries of expected female subservience and obligation to men.

The one aspect of family law that changed in the early Republic was divorce. Before the Revolution, only New England jurisdictions had recognized a right to divorce; by 1820, every state except South Carolina had set up divorce procedures. Divorce was uncommon and difficult, however. In many states, divorce could be obtained only by petition to the state's legislature, a daunting obstacle for many ordinary people. A mutual wish to terminate a marriage was never sufficient grounds for divorce. A New York judge affirmed that "it would be aiming a deadly blow at public morals to decree a dissolution of the marriage contract merely because the parties requested it. Divorces should never be allowed, except for the protection of the innocent party, and for the punishment of the guilty." States upheld the institution of marriage both to protect persons they thought of as naturally dependent (women and children) and to regulate the use and inheritance of property. The state's enforcement of marriage as an unequal relationship played a major role in maintaining gender inequality in the nineteenth century.

HOME AND AWAY: THE NEW BOARDING SCHOOL *These two engravings show "before" and "after" pictures of a young woman circa 1820 whose family has enrolled her in one of the new female academies that were springing up by the scores in the decades after 1800. What seem to be the family's expectations as they send her off? How is she changed when she returns? Did she acquire a practical or an ornamental education? Note the various emblems of women's household work. What do these pictures reveal about the options for young women in this period? Is the artist, John Lewis Krimmel, making a joke? Or does this picture betray anxieties about women's education? Krimmel himself was a Philadelphia painter who worked as a drawing master at a girls' academy.* Library Company of Philadelphia.

Single adult women could own and convey property, make contracts, initiate suits, and pay taxes. They could not vote (except in New Jersey until 1807), serve on juries, or practice law, so their civil status was limited. Single women's economic status was often limited as well: Unless she had inherited adequate property, a single adult woman in the early Republic was often a poor woman.

None of the legal institutions that structured white gender relations applied to black slaves. As property themselves, slaves could not freely consent to any contractual obligations, including marriage. The protective features of state-sponsored unions were thus denied to black men and women in slavery. Husbands could not guarantee support, nor could wives guarantee exclusive services, because both were controlled by a more powerful authority, the slave owner. But this also meant that slave unions did not establish unequal power relations backed by the force of law, as did free marriages.

Women and Church Governance

In most Protestant denominations around 1800, white women made up the majority of congregants, as they had for some time. Yet the church hierarchy—ordained ministers and elders—was exclusively male, and the governance of most denominations rested in men's hands.

There were some exceptions, however. In several small evangelical groups, notably Baptist congregations in New England that had been strongly affected by the Great Awakening, women served along with men on church governance committees, where they decided admission of new members, voted on the hiring of ministers, participated in disciplinary proceedings, and even debated doctrinal points. Quakers, too, had a history of recognizing that women's spiritual talents could equal men's. Quaker women who felt a special call were accorded the status of minister, which among Quakers meant they were capable of leading and speaking in religious meetings. Quaker governance, however, proceeded along sex-segregated lines: Separate men's and women's committees heard disciplinary cases and formulated church policy.

Between 1790 and 1820, a small and highly unusual set of women emerged who actively engaged in open preaching. Most were from the Freewill Baptist groups centered in Maine, New Hampshire, Vermont, and upstate New York. Others were from small Methodist sects, and yet others rejected any formal religious affiliation. Probably fewer than a hundred such women existed, most of them single or widowed, but several dozen became known beyond their local communities because they traveled, making converts and creating controversy wherever they went. They spoke from the heart, without prepared speeches, often exhibiting trances and claiming to exhort (counsel or warn) rather than to preach. But none of these women were ordained ministers, with official credentials to preach or perform baptisms.

Perhaps the most well known exhorting woman was Jemima Wilkinson, who called herself

WOMEN AND THE CHURCH: JEMIMA WILKINSON
Jemima Wilkinson, the "Publick Universal Friend," in an early woodcut, wears a clerical collar and body-obscuring robe, in keeping with the claim that the former Jemima was now a person without sex or gender. Her hair is pulled back tight on her head and curled at the neck in a masculine style of the 1790s.
Rhode Island Historical Society.

the "Publick Universal Friend." After a near-death experience from high fever in 1776, Wilkinson awoke to proclaim that her body was no longer female *or* male, but the incarnation of the "Spirit of Light." She dressed in men's clothes, wore her hair in a masculine style, shunned gender-specific pronouns, and preached openly in Rhode Island and Philadelphia. In the early nineteenth century, Wilkinson withdrew to a settlement called New Jerusalem in western New York with more than 250 followers, her fame sustained by periodic newspaper articles that fed a public curiosity about her lifelong transvestism and her unfeminine forcefulness.

As more women exhorters cropped up, their behavior came under increasing fire. A Baptist periodical in Massachusetts printed frequent reminders of the biblical prohibition "Let your women learn to keep silence in the churches" (1 Corinthians 14:34). Female preachers well knew such scriptural passages and were ready with biblical interpretations of their own, as in Deborah Pierce's 1817 book *A Scriptural Vindication of Female Preaching, Prophesying, and Exhortation.*

The decades from 1790 to the 1820s marked a period of unusual confusion, ferment, and creativity in American religion. New denominations blossomed, new styles of religiosity gripped adherents, and an extensive periodical press devoted to religion popularized all manner of theological and institutional innovations. In such a climate, the age-old tradition of gender subordination came into question here and there among the most radically democratic of the churches. But the presumption of male authority over women was deeply entrenched in American culture. Even denominations that had allowed women to participate in church governance began to pull back, and most churches reinstated patterns of dominance and subordination along gender lines.

Madison's Successors

Through the elections of 1812, 1816, and 1820, Virginians extended their lock on the presidency to twenty-four years. In 1816, James Monroe beat Federalist Rufus King of New York for the presidency by an electoral vote of 183 to 34. When Monroe stood for reelection in 1820, the national presence of the Federalists was fully eclipsed, with all but one electoral vote going to the president. The unanimity of the 1820 election did not reflect voter sat-

isfaction with the status quo, however, for barely one-quarter of eligible voters bothered to vote.

Monroe's two terms were dubbed the "Era of Good Feelings" by a contemporary newspaper. Yet during Monroe's presidency, a major constitutional crisis emerged over the admission of Missouri to the Union. Foreign policy questions animated sharp disagreements as well. The election of 1824 brought forth an abundance of candidates, all claiming to be Republicans. A one-party political system was put to the test of practical circumstances; it failed and then fractured.

The Missouri Compromise

In February 1819, Missouri applied for statehood. In the years since 1815, four other states had joined the Union (Indiana, Mississippi, Illinois, and Alabama), following the smooth pathway from territory to statehood that had operated since the 1790s. But Missouri's path was not smooth. While the northern part of Missouri lined up geographically with Illinois, Indiana, Ohio, and Pennsylvania, the territory already contained ten thousand slaves, brought by southern whites migrating from Virginia, Kentucky, and Tennessee. They constituted about one-sixth of the territory's population.

Missouri's unusual combination of geography and demography led a New York representative in Congress named James Tallmadge Jr. to propose two amendments to the Missouri statehood bill. The first stipulated that slaves born in Missouri after enactment of the law would be free at age twenty-five, and the second declared that no new slaves could be imported into the state. Tallmadge modeled the first amendment on New York's gradual emancipation law of 1799. It did not strip slave owners of their current property, even giving them full use of the labor of newborn slaves well into their prime productive years, at which point a profit-minded owner could sell his property in the South rather than let twenty-fifth birthdays rob him of his investment. Still, southerners in Congress loudly protested Tallmadge's amendments. Although gradual emancipation protected slave owners from immediate financial loss, in the long run it made Missouri a free state, and southerners were increasingly sensitive to the national balance of power between free and slave states. Just as southern economic power rested on slave labor, southern political power drew extra strength from the slave population, which was counted at three-fifths the

A VIEW OF ST. LOUIS FROM AN ILLINOIS TOWN
Just fifteen years after the Missouri Compromise, St. Louis was already a booming city, having gotten its start in the eighteenth century as a French fur trading village. It was incorporated as a town in 1809 and chartered as a city in 1822. In this 1835 view, commercial buildings and steamships line the riverfront; a ferry on the Illinois shore prepares to transport travelers across the Mississippi River. Black laborers (in the foreground) handle loading tasks. The Illinois side is a free state; Missouri, where their ferry lands, is a slave state.
Private Collection.

www.bedfordstmartins.com/tap   SEE THE ONLINE STUDY GUIDE for more help in analyzing this image.

weight of the free population. In 1820, the South as a region had seventeen more representatives in Congress than it would have had if only whites were counted.

Both of Tallmadge's amendments passed in the House of Representatives, but with a close and sharply sectional vote of North against South (with a few northern Republicans taking the side of the South). The debate was ferocious and explosive,

nearly a complete dress rehearsal for the arguments that would surface a generation later in the struggle leading to civil war. A Georgia representative predicted that the Missouri slavery question had started "a fire which all the waters of the ocean could not extinguish. It can be extinguished only in blood." The Senate, with an even number of slave and free states, voted down the amendments, with some border states joining the proslavery line. The deadlock meant that determination of Missouri statehood was set aside for the next congressional term.

In 1820, the components of a compromise slowly took shape in the Senate debate. Maine, once a part of Massachusetts, applied for statehood as a free state; it would balance Missouri as a slave state in the Senate. To quiet northern fears about the slave state Missouri reaching so far into the North, the Senate agreed that the southern boundary of Missouri, latitude 36°30′, extended west would become the permanent line dividing slave from free. All of the Louisiana Territory north of the line—except Missouri—would be closed to slavery (Map 9.5). The compromise plan passed in the Senate and, after vigorous debate, also passed in the House thanks to some expert deal brokering by Kentucky's Henry Clay, who earned a lifetime nickname—the "Great Pacificator"—for his superb negotiating skills. The North secured a large area where federal prohibition of slavery was guaranteed and got Maine as a counterbalance to Missouri. The South got Missouri without any interference with slavery. The whole pack-

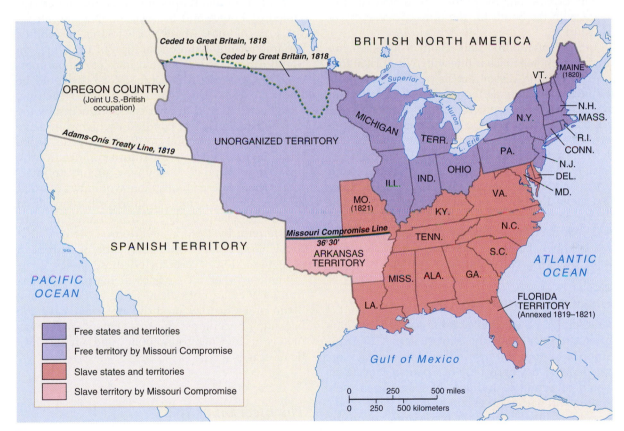

M A P 9.5

The Missouri Compromise, 1820

After a difficult battle in Congress, Missouri entered the Union in 1821 as part of a package of compromises. Maine was admitted as a free state to balance slavery in Missouri; and a line drawn at latitude 36°30′ put most of the rest of the Louisiana Territory off limits to slavery in the future.

READING THE MAP: How many free and how many slave states were there prior to the Missouri Compromise? What did the admission of Missouri as a slave state threaten to do?

CONNECTIONS: Who precipitated the crisis over Missouri, what did he propose, and where did the idea come from? What was the Missouri Compromise and who proposed it?

www.bedfordstmartins.com/tap SEE THE ONLINE STUDY GUIDE for more help in analyzing this map.

Just as southern economic power rested on slave labor, southern political power drew extra strength from the slave population, which was counted at three-fifths the weight of the free population.

age passed only because seventeen northern representatives decided that minimizing sectional conflict was in the best interests of the United States and so voted with the South for the unrestricted entry of Missouri.

President Monroe and Thomas Jefferson, retired to his home in Charlottesville, Virginia, at first worried that the Missouri crisis would reinvigorate the Federalist Party as the party of the North. But even ex-Federalists agreed that the division of free versus slave states was too dangerous a fault line to let shape national politics. When new parties did develop in the 1830s, they took pains to bridge geography, each party developing a presence in both North and South. Monroe and Jefferson also worried about the future of slavery. Each understood slavery to be deeply problematic, but, as Jefferson said, "We have the wolf by the ears, and we can neither hold him, nor safely let him go. Justice is in one scale, and self-preservation in the other."

The Monroe Doctrine

New foreign policy challenges arose even as Congress struggled with the slavery issue. In 1816, American troops led by General Andrew Jackson invaded the northern part of Spanish Florida in search of Seminole Indians who had been welcoming and harboring escaped slaves. Once there, Jackson declared himself the commander of northern Florida, demonstrating his power in 1818 by executing two British men who he claimed were dangerous enemies. In asserting rule over the territory, and surely in executing the two British subjects on Spanish land, Jackson had gone too far. Privately, President Monroe was grievously distressed and pondered court-martialing Jackson. But Jackson's immense popularity as a war hero dissuaded the president. Instead, John Quincy Adams, the secretary of state, opened negotiations with Spain to acquire the territory. The result was the Adams-Onís Treaty, which delivered Florida to the United States in 1819. In exchange, the Amer-

icans agreed to abandon any claim to Texas or Cuba. The South took this as a large concession, since southerners had eyed both places as potential slave states. Adams's treaty also established a boundary between New Spain to the west and the Louisiana Territory.

Spain at that moment was preoccupied with its colonies in South America, several of which were on the verge of breaking away. One after another—Chile, Colombia, Peru, and finally Mexico—declared itself independent in the early 1820s. For a time, it appeared that Spain, perhaps joined by France and Prussia, might try to regain the lost colonies. In response to this possibility, Monroe formulated a declaration of principles on South America, incorporated into his annual message to Congress in December 1823. It would be known in decades to come as the Monroe Doctrine. He asserted that "the American Continents, by the free and independent condition which they have assumed and maintain, are henceforth not to be considered as subjects for future colonization by any European power." Any new attempt to interfere in the Western Hemisphere would be regarded as "the manifestation of an unfriendly disposition towards the United States." In exchange for noninterference by Europeans, Monroe pledged that the United States would stay out of European struggles. Monroe articulated these policy goals without any real force to back them up. The American navy could not defend Chile or Peru against Spain or France. Monroe did not even have the backing of Congress for his statement; it was merely his idea of a sound policy laid out in a public message.

The Election of 1824

Monroe's nonpartisan administration was the last of its kind, a fitting throwback to eighteenth-century ideals, led by a president who was the last in that office to wear a powdered wig and knee breeches. Monroe's cabinet contained men of sharply different philosophies, all calling themselves Republicans. Secretary of State John Quincy Adams represented the urban Northeast, South Carolinian John C. Calhoun spoke for the commercial planter aristocracy as secretary of war, and William H. Crawford of Georgia, secretary of the treasury, was a proponent of Jeffersonian states' rights and limited federal power. Well before the end of Monroe's second term, these men and others began to maneuver for the presidency.

Since 1800, the congressional caucus of each party had met to identify and lend its considerable but still informal support to its party's leading candidate. In 1824, with only one party, the caucus system splintered. Some New York and Virginia representatives met and endorsed Crawford, but the fifty-one-year-old planter had just suffered a serious stroke, which left him largely incapacitated.

John Quincy Adams had headed the State Department for eight years; since 1800, every secretary of state had become the next president, and so Adams felt he had a claim on the office. Henry Clay,

Speaker of the House, also was a declared candidate. A man of vast congressional experience, he had engaged in high-level diplomacy, having accompanied John Quincy Adams to Ghent to negotiate the 1814 peace treaty with Britain. The Kentuckian put forth a set of policies he called the American System, a package of protective tariffs to promote manufacturing and federal expenditures for extensive internal improvements, many of them roads and canals in the western states. Secretary of War John Calhoun, who combined the riches of a well-off Carolina planter with the agile mind of a bright Yale-trained lawyer, was another serious contender. Calhoun had served in Congress and in

THE ELECTION OF 1824: THREAD BOX FOR JOHN QUINCY ADAMS

Purchasers of this thread box confirmed their loyalty to John Quincy Adams, presidential candidate in 1824. The inside cover carried a picture of Adams, created by a lithographic process just coming into wide use in the 1820s that made possible the production of thousands of pictures from a single master stone plate. (Wood and copper plates, the earlier technology, produced prints numbering only in the hundreds before deteriorating under pressure.) The velvet pincushion on the outside cover is printed with the slogan "BE FIRM FOR ADAMS."

Collection of Janice L. and David J. Frent.

THE ELECTION OF 1824: JACKSON CUP PLATE

A ceramic saucer of 1824 doubles as an object of veneration for General Andrew Jackson in his first bid for the presidency. It shows Jackson in civilian clothes, even though his reputation was largely military. This particular image of Jackson was mass-produced on housewares, using a newly developed transfer process. Even the English pottery industry made articles for the specialized election market, attaching Jackson's face to expensive pitchers imported to America. Both the saucer and the thread box were household implements associated with women's daily lives. The thread box was, then, no longer just a thread box; it was a commodity that allowed its purchaser to imagine a partisan identity for herself, even though the rules of politics formally excluded her.

Collection of Janice L. and David J. Frent.

several cabinets. Like Clay, he favored internal improvements, protective tariffs, and banking measures, which he figured would gain him support in northern states.

The final candidate was an outsider: General Andrew Jackson of Tennessee. Jackson had much less national political experience than the others. He had served a total of one year in the House and two in the Senate, plus a three-month term as territorial governor of Florida. His fame rested mainly on his reputation as a military leader, but that was sufficient to give him a huge surge of support, much to the surprise of the experienced politicians. Calhoun soon dropped out of the race and shifted his attention to winning the vice presidency.

The 1824 election was the first presidential contest in which popularity with ordinary voters could be measured. Recent changes in state constitutions gave voters in all but six states the power to choose electors for the electoral college. (Before, state legislatures had held this power.) Jackson was by far the most popular candidate with voters. He won more than 153,000 votes, while Adams was second with 109,000; Clay won 47,000 votes and the incapacitated Crawford garnered 46,600. This was not a large voter turnout, probably amounting to only a quarter of adult white males. Many more voters participated regularly in local and state elections, where the real political action generally lay.

The 1824 election was the first presidential contest in which popularity with ordinary voters could be measured.

Translated to the electoral college, Jackson had 99 votes, Adams 84, Crawford 41, and Clay 37. Jackson did not have a majority, so the election was thrown into the House of Representatives, for the second (and last) time in American history. Each state delegation voted as one vote, and only the top three candidates could enter the runoff, under the terms of the Twelfth Amendment to the Constitution, passed in 1804. Thus Henry Clay, Speaker of the House, was out of the race and in a position now to throw his support to another candidate.

The election of 1824 came to be characterized as the "corrupt bargain" in the eyes of Jackson's supporters. Clay backed Adams, and Adams won

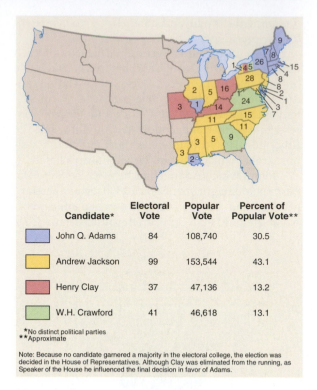

Candidate*	Electoral Vote	Popular Vote	Percent of Popular Vote**
John Q. Adams	84	108,740	30.5
Andrew Jackson	99	153,544	43.1
Henry Clay	37	47,136	13.2
W.H. Crawford	41	46,618	13.1

*No distinct political parties
**Approximate

Note: Because no candidate garnered a majority in the electoral college, the election was decided in the House of Representatives. Although Clay was eliminated from the running, as Speaker of the House he influenced the final decision in favor of Adams.

MAP 9.6
The Election of 1824

by one vote in the House (Map 9.6). Clay's support made sense on several levels. He and Adams were close on many issues, particularly on Clay's American System and Adams's backing of internal improvements. Clay was uneasy with Jackson's volatile temperament and unstated political views and with Crawford's diminished capacity. But Clay's choice still was not easy because of a strong personal animosity he felt for Adams.

What made Clay's decision look unseemly was that three days after the election, Adams offered to appoint Clay secretary of state—and Clay accepted. In the weeks before the vote in the House, rumors of exactly such a deal were whispered about and breezily dismissed by Adams and Clay supporters, confident that two such archenemies could never cooperate. There probably was no actual bargain; Adams's subsequent cabinet appointments abundantly demonstrated that he was incapable of making appointments for purely political reasons. But the Clay appointment looked bad, and a storm of public protest greeted it. Andrew Jackson felt that the election had been stolen from him and wrote bitterly that "the Judas of the West has closed the contract and will receive the thirty pieces of silver."

The Adams Administration

John Quincy Adams, like his father before him, was a one-term president. His career had been built on diplomacy, not electoral politics, and his political horse sense was not well developed. His choices for cabinet posts drew his opposition into his inner circle. He asked Crawford to stay on in the Treasury, and he retained the postmaster general, an openly pro-Jackson man, even though that position controlled thousands of patronage appointments all over the country. Most amazingly, he asked Jackson to become secretary of war. With Calhoun as vice president (elected without opposition by the electoral college) and Clay at State, the whole argumentative crew would be thrust into the executive branch. Crawford and Jackson had the good sense to decline appointments.

Adams had lofty ideas for federal action during his presidency, and the plan he put before Congress was so sweeping that it took Henry Clay aback. Adams called for federally built roads, canals, and harbors. He proposed a national university in Washington as well as government-sponsored scientific research. He wanted to build observatories to advance astronomical knowledge and to promote precision in timekeeping. (See "The Promise of Technology," page 316.) He issued a massive report promoting a decimal-based system of weights and measures, written when he was secretary of state. In all these endeavors, Adams believed he was picking up where both Jefferson and Madison had left off, using the powers of government to advance knowledge. But his opponents feared he was taking too much from Hamilton's legacy, using federal power inappropriately to advance commercial interests.

Whether he was more truly Federalist or Republican was a moot point, however. Lacking political skills, Adams was unable to implement much of his program. He scorned the idea of courting voters to gain support and the use of the patronage system to enhance his power. He often made appointments (to posts like customs house collectors) to placate enemies rather than reward friends. A story of a toast offered to the president may well have been mythical, but as humorous folklore it made the rounds during his term and came to summarize Adams's precarious hold on leadership. A dignitary raised a glass and pledged, "May he strike confusion to his foes . . . ," to which another voice scornfully chimed in, "as he has already done to his friends."

Conclusion: From Jefferson to Adams

The nineteenth century opened with the Jeffersonian Republicans in power, trying to undo much of the Federalist structure created in the 1790s. But Jefferson's desire for a more limited government, in size, scope, and power, finally gave way to the realities of increasing interaction with foreign powers as well as steady expansion westward. Jefferson sent Lewis and Clark to explore for scientific knowledge the far reaches of the continent, and then unexpectedly that region dropped into his hands as the Louisiana Purchase. Jefferson and Madison tried valiantly to avoid war with England and France, experimenting with high-minded but costly trade embargoes, but nonetheless the War of 1812 came, caused less by concrete economic or political issues than by questions of honor. Its conclusion at the Battle of New Orleans allowed Americans to feel they had fought a second war of independence.

Tecumseh's valiant attempt to promote a large confederacy of Indian tribes was cut short both by the war and by his untimely death. Without British support, the Indians probably could not have successfully challenged for long the westward dynamic of American settlement, aided by the devious treaty-making efforts of men like William Henry Harrison. But British support came at a time when Canada was under attack, and the British put their own self-defense higher than their promises to help the Indians. If the War of 1812 was a second war of independence for the whites, how much more so it was for the Indians, who lost both times.

The war elevated to national prominence General Andrew Jackson, whose sudden popularity with voters in the 1824 election surprised traditional politicians and threw the one-party rule of Republicans into a tailspin. John Quincy Adams barely secured the presidency in the early months of 1825 before the election campaign of 1828 was off and running. Appeals to the people—the mass of white

Eli Terry's Clock

AT THE AGE OF FOURTEEN, Eli Terry of East Windsor, Connecticut, apprenticed to learn the high art of clockmaking. In the late eighteenth century, tallcase clocks were luxury items for the well-to-do, made by a highly skilled master craftsman turning out one at a time, usually in response to a customer's order. An apprentice had to work for years to develop the exacting techniques of cutting and fitting the wheels, cogs, and gears made of brass that together formed a precision mechanism called the clock's movement. Weights pulled by gravity supplied the motive force that kept a long pendulum going for a week. As befit luxury items, tallcase clocks were mounted in fine wooden cases made by an expert cabinetmaker. Young Terry had chosen a craft featuring slow, painstaking production for a very select clientele.

However much a clock owner might pride himself on knowing the passage of exact minutes and hours, these expensive clocks were really extravagant curiosities. Exactitude in time measurement simply was not of paramount importance in the everyday life of the eighteenth century. Before 1800, people reckoned time accurately enough by the sun and the moon. Almanacs listed the daily rising and setting time of those celestial bodies, and sundials measured out the hours. Something as simple as a stick could indicate when it was high noon, the point when the sun was directly overhead and the stick's shadow pointed north. In the larger towns, a perfectly adequate method of synchrony was provided by clocks and bells mounted on a church or town hall. The hourglass, a device in use since ancient times, marked out the allotted span for a minister's sermon or a schoolmaster's lesson. Relatively few families owned a mechanical clock.

As Eli Terry grew to adulthood, he brought an entrepreneurial spirit to his chosen calling. He began to envision clocks as affordable household fixtures instead of individual artworks. His particular genius was to anticipate a growing market for home timepieces in the early nineteenth century, once they were cheaply priced. In 1793 the twenty-one-year-old clockmaker opened his own business in the village of Plymouth, Connecticut, and began experimenting by combining wood with brass in the movements. When Jefferson's embargo of 1807 dried up the supply of brass from England, Terry switched to all-wood parts. Wooden movements were bulkier than brass and they swelled in humid weather, a condition that made the clocks less accurate timepieces. But they were easier to cut and much cheaper to produce.

Convinced he could do it, Terry boldly contracted in 1807 to deliver four thousand tallcase clocks in three years. He bought an old mill building and devoted the first year to designing water-powered machinery (lathes and saws) to cut the wooden parts. In the next year he produced one thousand clocks, and in the third, three thousand, in a novel feat of mass production aided by skilled woodworkers and assemblers. This was the first successful implementation of a system of manufacturing called "interchangeable parts." Instead of building each clock individually, using custom-cut metal parts laboriously fitted together, Terry patterned and machine-cut inexpensive wooden cogs and wheels that fit interchangeably into any of his clocks. Under the old handcraft system, a small clockmaker's shop might produce ten tallcase clocks a year. Terry's shop had made three thousand.

To broaden further the market for clocks, Terry next applied his mechanical gifts to a complete redesign of the wooden movement to develop a compact version, the shelf clock, which he marketed starting in 1814. By the 1820s, shelf clocks were sold all over the United States, priced from five to ten dollars. Terry's most famous model was the pillar and scroll clock (pictured here), with its fancy scrolled woodwork and decorative painting, which his factory produced at the rate of ten to twelve thousand per year in the 1820s. Other eager entrepreneurs rushed to join the business. By 1830, there were two hundred clock factories in Connecticut producing many thousands of clocks per year. Connecticut clocks graced mantels and walls all over the United States.

Terry's shelf clock revolutionized timekeeping by bringing fairly accurate measurement of time—off by only a few minutes each day—into the reach of many householders. Within a local area, me-did not merely measure time; they helped speed up the pace of life.

In its peak year, 1836, Terry's company made eighty thousand clocks that sold for about ten dollars each. A year later, a onetime apprentice of Terry named Chauncey Jerome pioneered a cheap shelf clock with a brass movement which within a few years supplanted the less accurate wooden clocks. Railroad building in the 1830s in particular sharpened the need for greater precision in timekeeping, since trains rolled through stations with minutes-long stops, far shorter than rest stops for horse-drawn stagecoaches; the margin for passenger error had shrunk considerably. One Massachusetts writer and social critic, Henry David Thoreau, remarked with heavy sarcasm, "Have not men improved somewhat in punctuality since the railroad was invented? Do they not talk and think faster in the depot than they did in the stage office?"

But railroads with their speed and reliability brought to light an entirely new wrinkle in time measurement. With every village on its own local time, determined by the sun, railroads could not produce simple departure and arrival schedules for east–west lines. A conductor leaving Boston would arrive in Worcester, forty miles to the west, with a pocket watch set to Boston time—but that time differed from Worcester's local time by about five minutes. One solution was for a railroad company to standardize its schedule to the time of its home city. But that meant that railroad stations had to display multiple clocks, one for the local sun time and an additional clock for every company that used the station. This problem would not be solved until the late 1880s when the United States abandoned sun time completely and adopted standardized time zones.

The pervasiveness of regularized time brought about by Eli Terry's clocks paved the way for a future of rapid transport, of factory discipline, of industrial capitalism, of a hurried rhythm of life in American cities. Yet the paintings on Eli Terry's famous pillar and scroll clocks of the 1820s invariably featured a pastoral scene—a farmyard, a rural dwelling, a country landscape—linking time to the natural order of the universe. Perhaps Terry did not anticipate how his clocks would come to symbolize speed, progress, and change.

ELI TERRY'S PILLAR AND SCROLL CLOCK
This typical Terry clock was made in Connecticut in 1825. Note the rural scene showing a grand house and pastoral landscape.
American Clock & Watch Museum.

chanical clocks could periodically be set to the nooning of the sun, bringing a town or city into congruence. Clocks enabled factory workers to coordinate household schedules with the factory bell, bankers and businessmen to set meetings on a brisk schedule, and travelers to make stagecoach and canal boat departure times. Employers could demand and expect punctuality, a newly esteemed moral virtue made possible by the pervasiveness of clocks. Clocks imposed regularity and uniformity in the mundane chores and pleasures of life alike. They male voters—would be the hallmark of all elections after 1824. It was a game at which Adams was at quite a disadvantage.

The War of 1812 started another chain of events that would prove momentous in later decades. Jefferson's long embargo and Madison's wartime trade stoppages gave strong encouragement to American manufacturing, momentarily protected from competition with English factories. When peace resumed in 1815, the years of independent development burst forth into a period of sustained economic growth that continued nearly unabated into the mid-nineteenth century.

www.bedfordstmartins.com/tap SEE THE ONLINE STUDY GUIDE to assess your mastery of the material covered in this chapter.

CHRONOLOGY

1789	Judiciary Act establishes six Supreme Court justices, who preside over circuit courts.
1800	Thomas Jefferson and Aaron Burr tie in electoral college.
	Gabriel's slave rebellion fails in Virginia.
1801	Judiciary Act reduces Supreme Court justices to five and allows for sixteen circuit judges.
	Jefferson elected president by House of Representatives.
1802	Judiciary Act of 1801 repealed.
1803	*Marbury v. Madison* declares part of Judiciary Act of 1789 unconstitutional.
	Embargoes on American shipping by England and France.
	Louisiana Purchase from France.
1804	Jefferson reelected president.
	Burr-Hamilton duel ends in Hamilton's death.
1804–1806	Lewis and Clark expedition.
1807	**June.** *Chesapeake* attacked and searched by British in Chesapeake Bay.
	December. Embargo Act forbids any American ship from engaging in trade with any foreign port.
1808	James Madison elected president.
1809	Treaty of Fort Wayne with Indians in Indiana Territory.

	Non-Intercourse Act forbids American trade with England, France, and their colonies.
1811	Battle of Tippecanoe won by William Henry Harrison's troops.
1812	**June.** War declared on Great Britain.
	Madison reelected president.
1813	Death of Tecumseh at the Battle of the Thames.
1814	British attack Washington, D.C., burning several buildings.
	Treaty of Ghent ends War of 1812.
	Hartford Convention proposes constitutional amendments.
	Battle of New Orleans won by Andrew Jackson's forces.
1816	James Monroe elected president.
1819	Spain cedes Florida to United States.
1820	Missouri Compromise admits Missouri as slave state and Maine as free state.
	Monroe reelected president.
1823	Monroe Doctrine asserts independence of Western Hemisphere from European intervention.
1824	"Corrupt bargain" election of John Quincy Adams.

BIBLIOGRAPHY

GENERAL WORKS

Lance Banning, *The Jeffersonian Persuasion: Evolution of a Party Ideology* (1978).

James Broussard, *The Southern Federalists, 1800–1816* (1978).

Saul Cornell, *The Other Founders: Anti-Federalism and the Dissenting Tradition in America, 1788–1828* (1999).

Noble E. Cunningham, *In Pursuit of Reason: The Life of Thomas Jefferson* (1987).

John R. Howe, *From the Revolution through the Age of Jackson* (1973).

Ralph Ketcham, *Presidents above Party: The First American Presidency, 1789–1829* (1984).

David Waldstreicher, *In the Midst of Perpetual Fetes: The Making of American Nationalism, 1776–1820* (1997).

Stephen Watts, *The Republic Reborn: War and the Making of Liberal America, 1790–1820* (1987).

JEFFERSON AND REPUBLICANS

Doron S. Ben-Atar, *The Origins of Jeffersonian Commercial Policy and Diplomacy* (1993).

Noble E. Cunningham, *The Jeffersonian Republicans in Power: Party Operations, 1801–1809* (1963).

Alexander DeConde, *This Affair of Louisiana* (1976).

Joseph J. Ellis, *American Sphinx: The Character of Thomas Jefferson* (1997).

Richard E. Ellis, *The Jeffersonian Crisis: Courts and Politics in the Young Republic* (1971).

David Hackett Fischer, *The Revolution of American Conservatism: The Federalist Party in the Era of Jeffersonian Democracy* (1965).

Annette Gordon-Reed, *Thomas Jefferson and Sally Hemings: An American Controversy* (1997).

Morton J. Horwitz, *The Transformation of American Law, 1780–1860* (1977).

Herbert A. Johnson, *The Chief Justiceship of John Marshall, 1801–1835* (1997).

Lawrence S. Kaplan, *"Entangling Alliances with None": American Foreign Policy in the Age of Jefferson* (1987).

Jan Ellen Lewis and Peter S. Onuf, eds., *Sally Hemings and Thomas Jefferson: History, Memory, and Civic Culture* (1999).

Milton Lomask, *Aaron Burr* (1982).

Dumas Malone, *Jefferson the President: First Term, 1801–1805* (1970).

Dumas Malone, *Jefferson the President: Second Term, 1805–1809* (1974).

Richard K. Matthews, *The Radical Politics of Thomas Jefferson: A Revisionist View* (1984).

Drew R. McCoy, *The Elusive Republic: Political Economy in Jeffersonian America* (1980).

Drew R. McCoy, *The Last of the Fathers: James Madison and the Republican Legacy* (1989).

R. Kent Newmyer, *The Supreme Court under Marshall and Taney* (1986).

Peter Onuf, ed., *Jeffersonian Legacies* (1993).

Merrill Peterson, *Thomas Jefferson and the New Nation: A Biography* (1970).

Arnold A. Rogow, *A Fatal Friendship: Alexander Hamilton and Aaron Burr* (1998).

Robert A. Rutland, *The Presidency of James Madison* (1990).

Thomas C. Shevory, ed., *John Marshall's Achievement: Law, Politics, and Constitutional Interpretations* (1989).

Jack M. Sosin, *The Aristocracy of the Long Robe: The Origins of Judicial Review in America* (1989).

Francis N. Stites, *John Marshall: Defender of the Constitution* (1981).

Robert W. Tucker, *Empire of Liberty: The Statecraft of Thomas Jefferson* (1990).

G. E. White, *The Marshall Court and Cultural Change, 1815–1835* (1988).

LEWIS AND CLARK AND THE WEST

Stephen E. Ambrose, *Undaunted Courage: Meriwether Lewis, Thomas Jefferson, and the Opening of the American West* (1996).

Albert Furtwangler, *Acts of Discovery: Visions of America in the Lewis and Clark Journals* (1993).

David Freeman Hawke, *Those Tremendous Mountains: The Story of the Lewis and Clark Expedition* (1980).

James P. Ronda, *Lewis and Clark among the Indians* (1984).

FOREIGN POLICY AND THE WAR OF 1812

James M. Banner, *To the Hartford Convention: The Federalists and the Origins of Party Politics in Massachusetts, 1789–1815* (1969).

Carl Benn, *The Iroquois in the War of 1812* (1998).

Pierre Berton, *The Invasion of Canada* (1980).

Harry L. Coles, *The War of 1812* (1965).

Ronald L. Hatzenbuehler and Robert L. Ivie, *Congress Declares War: Rhetoric, Leadership, and Partisanship in the Early Republic* (1983).

Donald R. Hickey, *The War of 1812: A Forgotten Conflict* (1989).

Reginald Horsman, *The Causes of the War of 1812* (1962).

Linda K. Kerber, *Federalists in Dissent: Imagery and Ideology in Jeffersonian America* (1970).

C. Edward Skeen, *Citizen Soldiers in the War of 1812* (1999).

Burton Spivak, *Jefferson's English Crisis: Commerce, Embargo, and the Republican Revolution* (1979).

J. C. A. Stagg, *Mr. Madison's War: Politics, Diplomacy, and Warfare in the Early American Republic, 1783–1830* (1983).

SLAVERY

David Brion Davis, *The Problem of Slavery in the Age of Revolution, 1770–1823* (1975).

Douglas Egerton, *Gabriel's Rebellion* (1993).

Sylvia Frey, *Water from the Rock* (1991).

James Oliver Horton and Lois E. Horton, *In Hope of Liberty: Culture, Community, and Protest among Northern Free Blacks, 1700–1860* (1997).

Robert McColley, *Slavery and Jeffersonian Virginia* (1964).

Gary B. Nash, *Forging Freedom: The Formation of Philadelphia's Black Community, 1720–1840* (1988).

Donald L. Robinson, *Slavery in the Structure of American Politics, 1765–1820* (1971).

James Sidbury, *Ploughshares into Swords: Race, Rebellion, and Identity in Gabriel's Virginia* (1997).

Shane White, *Somewhat More Independent: The End of Slavery in New York City, 1710–1810* (1991).

NATIVE AMERICANS

Henry Warner Bowden, *American Indians and Christian Missions: Studies in Cultural Conflict* (1981).

Christopher Densmore, *Red Jacket: Iroquois Diplomat and Orator* (1999).

Gregory E. Dowd, *A Spirited Resistance: The North American Indian Struggle for Unity, 1745–1815* (1992).

R. David Edmunds, *The Shawnee Prophet* (1983).

R. David Edmunds, *Tecumseh and the Quest for Indian Leadership* (1984).

Bil Gilbert, *God Gave Us This Country: Tekamthi and the First American Civil War* (1989).

H. S. Halbert and T. H. Ball, *The Creek War of 1813 and 1814* (1969).

William G. McLoughlin, *Cherokees and Missionaries, 1789–1839* (1984).

James Merrell, *The Indians' New World: Catawbas and Their Neighbors from European Contact through the Era of Removal* (1989).

Paul Francis Prucha, *The Great Father: The United States Government and the American Indians* (1984).

Bernard W. Sheehan, *Seeds of Extinction: Jeffersonian Philanthropy and the American Indians* (1973).

John Sugden, *Tecumseh: A Life* (1997).

Richard White, *The Middle Ground: Indians, Empires, and Republics in the Great Lakes Region, 1650–1815* (1991).

WOMEN, MARRIAGE, AND RELIGION

Norma Basch, *In the Eyes of the Law: Women, Marriage, and Property in Nineteenth-Century New York* (1982).

Norma Basch, *Framing American Divorce: From the Revolutionary Generation to the Victorians* (1999).

Catherine A. Brekus, *Strangers and Pilgrims: Female Preaching in America, 1740–1845* (1998).

Jon Butler, *Awash in a Sea of Faith: Christianizing the American People* (1990).

Nancy Cott, *Public Vows: A History of Marriage and the Nation* (2001).

Philip Greven, *The Protestant Temperament: Patterns of Child-rearing, Religious Experience, and the Self in Early America* (1977).

Michael Grossberg, *Governing the Hearth: Law and the Family in Nineteenth-Century America* (1985).

Nathan Hatch, *The Democratization of American Christianity* (1989).

Hendrik Hartog, *Man and Wife in America: A History* (2000).

Susan Juster, *Disorderly Women: Sexual Politics and Evangelicalism in Revolutionary New England* (1994).

Linda Kerber, *Women of the Republic* (1980).

Jan Lewis, *The Pursuit of Happiness: Family and Values in Jefferson's Virginia* (1983).

Carla Pestana, *Quakers and Baptists in Colonial Massachusetts* (1991).

Marylynn Salmon, *Women and the Law of Property in Early America* (1986).

Laurel Thatcher Ulrich, *A Midwife's Tale: The Life of Martha Ballard, Based on Her Diary, 1786–1812* (1990).

MONROE AND ADAMS PRESIDENCIES

Harry Ammon, *James Monroe: The Quest for National Identity* (1971).

Noble E. Cunningham Jr., *The Presidency of James Monroe* (1996).

George Dangerfield, *The Era of Good Feelings* (1952).

Don E. Fehrenbacher, *The South and Three Sectional Crises* (1980).

Mary W. M. Hargreaves, *The Presidency of John Quincy Adams* (1986).

Shaw Livermore, *The Twilight of Federalism: The Disintegration of the Federalist Party, 1815–1830* (1962).

Paul C. Nagel, *John Quincy Adams: A Public Life, A Private Life* (1997).

Ernest R. May, *The Making of the Monroe Doctrine* (1975).

SHIP'S FIGUREHEAD OF ANDREW JACKSON

Carved in 1834 and affixed to the bow of the revered navy frigate Constitution, *this figurehead of Andrew Jackson symbolized national pride by putting "the image of the most popular man of the West upon the favorite ship of the East," according to the commodore who commissioned it. But when Jackson introduced a new, strict banking policy, his popularity in the urban East quickly plummeted. In Boston, where the* Constitution *was docked, protesters complained that the figurehead of a tyrant corrupted their ship. On the night of July 3, 1834, the eve of the national holiday, a twenty-seven-year-old mariner and ardent Whig stole on board and decapitated the figurehead, sawing it through just below the ears. Jackson deflected the insult with humor, declaring "I never did like that image! Give the man a postmaster's job." The commodore, himself alert to symbolic actions, wrapped the headless statue in a flag and sent it to New York City where woodworkers fashioned a new head in 1835. It was reattached to the ship in another port: Jackson's banking policies still rankled in urban financial centers, and naval authorities did not want to risk a second mutilation of the president's image. In 1990, the original head was recovered from a private collector in France and restored to view in the museum that now owns the figurehead.* Museum of the City of New York.

THE EXPANDING REPUBLIC 10

1815–1840

PRESIDENT ANDREW JACKSON WAS THE DOMINANT FIGURE of his age, yet his precarious childhood little foretold the fame, fortune, and influence he would enjoy in the years after 1815. Jackson was born in the Carolina backcountry in 1767. His Scots-Irish father had recently died, leaving a poor, struggling mother to support three small boys. During the Revolution, young Andrew followed his brothers into the militia, where both died of disease, as did his mother. Orphaned at fourteen, Jackson drifted around, drinking, gambling, and brawling.

But at seventeen, his prospects improved. He studied law for three years with a North Carolina lawyer and then moved west to Nashville, a frontier community full of opportunities for a young man of legal training and aggressive temperament. He became a public prosecutor, married into a leading family, and acquired land and slaves. When Tennessee became a state in 1796, Jackson, then twenty-nine, was elected to Congress for a single term.

Jackson captured national attention in 1815 by leading the victory at the Battle of New Orleans. With little else to celebrate about the War of 1812, many Americans seized on the Tennessee general as the champion of the day. Songs, broadsides, and an admiring biography set him up as the original self-made man, the parentless child magically responsible for his own destiny. Jackson seemed to have created himself, a gritty, forceful personality extracting opportunities from the dynamic, turbulent frontier.

Jackson enhanced his military reputation by fighting Creek and Seminole Indians. He was more than a belligerent man of action, however. He was also strong-willed, reckless, and quick to anger, impulsively challenging men to duels, sometimes on slight pretexts. In one legendary fight in 1806, Jackson deliberately let his opponent, an expert marksman, shoot first. The bullet hit him in a rib, but Jackson masked all sign of injury under a loose cloak and immobile face. He then took careful aim at the astonished man and killed him. Such steely courage chilled his political opponents.

Jackson's image as a tough frontier hero set him apart from the learned and privileged gentlemen from Virginia and Massachusetts who had monopolized the presidency up to 1828. When he lost the 1824 election to John Quincy Adams, an infuriated Jackson vowed to fight a rematch and started running for the office immediately. He won in 1828 and again in 1832, capturing large majorities. His appeal stretched across the urban working classes of the East, frontier voters of the West, and slaveholders in the South, who all saw something of themselves in Jackson. Once elected, he brought a combative style to politics and enlarged the powers of the presidency.

The confidence and even recklessness of Jackson's personality mirrored the new confidence of American society in the years after 1815. An entrepreneurial spirit gripped the country, producing a market revolution of unprecedented scale. Old social hierarchies eroded; the most ordinary men could dream of moving high on the wheel of fortune, just as Jackson had done. Stunning advances in transportation and economic productivity fueled such dreams and propelled thousands to move west and many thousands more to move to cities. Urban growth and technological change fostered the diffusion of a distinctive and vibrant public culture, spread through newspapers and the spoken word. The development of rapid print allowed popular opinions to coalesce and intensify; Jackson's sudden nationwide celebrity was a case in point.

Expanded communication transformed politics dramatically. Sharp disagreements over the best way to promote individual liberty, economic opportunity, and national prosperity in the new market economy defined key differences between Jackson and Adams and the parties they gave rise to in the 1830s. The process of party formation brought new habits of political participation and party loyalty to many thousands more adult white males. Religion became democratized as well: An evangelical revival of national proportions brought its adherents the confidence that salvation and perfection were now available to all.

As president from 1828 to 1836, Jackson presided over all these changes, fighting some and supporting others in his vigorous and volatile way. As with his own stubborn personality, there was a dark underside to the confidence and expansiveness of American society. Steamboats blew up, banks and businesses periodically collapsed, alcoholism rates soared, Indians were killed or relocated farther west, and slavery continued to expand. The brash confidence that turned some people into rugged, self-promoting, Jackson-like individuals inspired others to think about the human costs of rapid economic expansion and thus about reforming society in dramatic ways. The common denominator was a faith that people and societies can shape their own destinies.

The Market Revolution

The return of peace in 1815 unleashed powerful economic and social forces that revolutionized the organization of the market. Spectacular changes in transportation facilitated the movement of com-modities, information, and people, while textile mills and other factories created many new jobs, especially for young unmarried women. Innovations in banking functions, legal practices, and tariff policies promoted swift economic growth.

This was not yet an industrial revolution, but a market revolution. The energy to fuel development still came from traditional sources—water, wood, beasts of burden, and human muscle. What was new was the accelerated pace of economic activity and the scale of distribution of goods. Men and women were drawn out of old patterns of rural self-sufficiency into the wider realm of national market relations. At the same time, the nation's money supply enlarged considerably, leading to speculative investments in commerce, manufacturing, transportation, and land. The new nature and scale of production and consumption changed Americans' behavior, attitudes, and expectations.

Improvements in Transportation

Before 1815, transportation in the United States was slow, difficult, and expensive; it cost as much to ship freight over thirty miles of domestic roads as it did to send the same weight of cargo across the Atlantic Ocean. A stagecoach trip from Boston to New York took an uncomfortable four days. But between 1815 and 1840, networks of roads, canals, steamboats, and finally railroads dramatically raised the speed and lowered the cost of travel (Map 10.1). Migrants like Andrew Jackson went west to Nashville in the 1790s by walking or riding horseback for weeks along old Indian trails. But when he returned east in 1829 for his inauguration, the newly elected President Jackson traveled by steamboat and turnpike to the capital city in a matter of days.

The benefits of improved transportation to economic development were abundantly clear: Products could be sold more cheaply in a wider market. Equally important, transportation facilitated the flow of political information; traffic in newspapers had profound consequences for Jacksonian-era elections. Travel encouraged cultural change as well. Easily accessible passenger travel lifted men and women out of their local communities, brought country merchants on buying trips to urban centers, and pulled adolescents of both sexes into employment opportunities in cities or factory towns, often far from home.

Enhanced public transport was very expensive to build, and it produced uneven economic benefits. (A canal in New York or a road in Kentucky

MAP 10.1

Routes of Transportation in 1840
Transportation advances by the 1830s had cut travel times significantly. Goods and people could move from New York City to Buffalo, New York, in four days via the Erie Canal, a trip that took two weeks by road in 1800. A trip from New York to New Orleans that took four weeks in 1800 could now be accomplished in less than half that time on steamboats on the western rivers.

produced no benefit for South Carolina.) Administrations from Jefferson to Monroe were therefore reluctant to undertake federally funded transportation. During Jefferson's presidency, Congress approved start-up funding for the National Road, to connect Baltimore with the heart of Ohio, provided that the money came from the sale of Ohio public lands, the area that would ultimately and directly benefit. Laying the roadbed went slowly; by 1818, the National Road extended to Wheeling, West Virginia, reaching Ohio only in the 1830s. President John Quincy Adams departed from previous presidents and adopted the pro-development view of Henry Clay's American System, which would commit federal dollars to building roads and canals, but Congress would not go along.

The new nature and scale of production and consumption changed Americans' behavior, attitudes, and expectations.

Instead, private investors sponsored transportation improvements. They pooled resources and chartered stagecoach, canal, and railroad companies, with significant aid from state governments in the form of subsidies and guarantees of monopoly rights. Turnpike and roadway mileage dramatically increased after 1815, reducing the cost of land shipment of goods. Stagecoach lines proliferated in an extensive network of passenger corridors dense in the populated East and fanning out to the Mississippi River. Travel time on main routes was cut in half; Boston to New York now took two days.

Steamboats signaled an important advance in the technology of transportation. In 1807, Robert Fulton adapted a steam engine to propel a 133-foot boat, the *Clermont*. Its first voyage, up the Hudson River from New York City to Albany, took thirty-two hours against a head wind, compared with two days for the land route. Soon a steamboat craze was in full swing, and by 1820 a dozen steamboats left New York City daily, churning up the Hudson to Albany in half a day or moving east on Long Island Sound to Providence, Rhode Island. Traffic soon spread to the western rivers and the Great Lakes. A voyager on one of the first steamboats to go down the Mississippi reported that the Chickasaw Indians called the vessel a "fire canoe" and considered it "an omen of evil . . . the sparks from the chimney of the boat being likened to the train of the celestial visitant"—that is, a comet, also feared as an evil omen. By the early 1830s, more than seven hundred steamboats had been swiftly launched into operation on the Ohio and Mississippi Rivers. A journey upriver from New Orleans to Louisville, Kentucky, took only one week.

Such speed came with costs, however. Repeatedly, boiler explosions revealed the risks of steam transport; by 1830, close to eighty vessels had been blasted out of the water and hundreds of passengers killed. Despite such horrors, the public remained excited over fast travel. (See "The Promise of Technology," page 328.)

The early practice of states granting monopolies to encourage investment in steam transportation came to seem restrictive and unfair to newcomers in the business. In a landmark decision of 1824, *Gibbon v. Ogden*, the Supreme Court under John Marshall ruled that navigation on the Hudson River was actually a form of interstate commerce and thus was under the jurisdiction of the federal government; state-granted monopolies were therefore declared invalid on rivers that traversed two or more states.

Canals were another major innovation of the transportation revolution. These two-way highways of water could be shallow; usually four feet of water sufficed to float a flat-bottomed barge, powered by horses or mules trudging along a towpath beside the canal, between locks. Travel speed was slow, under five miles per hour, but the economy came from increased loads: The low-friction water allowed one horse to pull a fifty-ton barge. In winter, canals froze over and became smooth, stump- and rock-free highways for sleighs.

Pennsylvania in 1815 and New York in 1817 commenced major state-sponsored canal enterprises intended to create large regional markets for goods. Pennsylvania's Schuylkill Canal stretched 108 miles west into the state when it was completed in 1826. It was overshadowed by the impressive Erie Canal in New York, begun in 1817 and finished in 1825, connecting the 350 miles between Albany on the Hudson River and Buffalo on Lake Erie. In effect, the Erie Canal linked the port of New York City with the inland region of New York State and, via the Great Lakes, the entire Northwest Territory. Wheat and flour moved east, while textiles and books moved west, joined by heavy passenger traffic in both directions. By the 1830s, the cost of shipping by canal fell to less than a tenth of the cost of overland transport, and New York City quickly blossomed into the premier city of trade and commerce in the United States.

In the 1830s, private railroad companies began to give canals stiff competition, and by the mid-1840s the canal-building era was over. (However, use of the canals for freight continued well into the twentieth century.) The nation's first railroad, the Baltimore and Ohio, boasted thirteen miles of track in 1829, laid out west from Baltimore and pointing toward Ohio. During the 1830s, three thousand more miles of track materialized nationwide, the result of a speculative fever in railroad construction masterminded by bankers, locomotive and iron manufacturers, and state legislators, who provided subsidies, charters, and land rights-of-way. Rail lines in the 1830s were generally short, on the order of twenty to one hundred miles; they were not yet an efficient distribution system for goods. But passengers flocked to experience the marvelous travel speeds of fifteen to twenty miles per hour, enduring the frightful noise and cascades of ashes and cinders that rained on them.

Factories, Workingwomen, and Wage Labor

Transportation advances promoted a rapid expansion of manufacturing after 1815. Teamsters, wagoners, and bargemen hauled consumer products like shoes, textiles, clocks, and books into nationwide distribution. Some of the gain in manufacturing, especially in the textile industry, came from the

LANDSCAPE WITH FREIGHT TRAIN AND TOW BOAT
*A canal boat and train pass through a village, each transporting goods, not passengers.
Three horses on a tow path power the boat; a coal-burning locomotive steam engine
drives the train. The utility poles along the train tracks (probably telegraph wires)
indicate that this anonymous watercolor dates no earlier than the late 1840s.*
Gift of Maxim Karolik. Courtesy, Museum of Fine Arts, Boston.

development of water-driven machinery, built near
fast-coursing rivers. (The steam power harnessed
for steamboats and railroads had limited application in industry until the 1840s.) But much of the
new manufacturing involved only a reorganization
of production, still using the power and skill of
human hands. Both mechanized and manual manufacturing pulled young women into the labor market for the first time and greatly enlarged the segment of the population earning a living by selling
labor for hourly wages.

The earliest factory, built by British immigrant
Samuel Slater in Pawtucket, Rhode Island, in the
1790s, featured a mechanical spinning machine that
produced thread and yarn. By 1815, nearly 170 spinning mills dotted lower New England. Unlike Eng-

lish manufacturing cities, where entire families
worked in low-wage, health-threatening factories,
American spinning and textile factories targeted
young women as employees. The assumption was
that adolescent girls would gladly work for minimal wages in view of their limited options for paid
employment. After a few years, they would retire
to marriage, their jobs taken by fresh recruits from
the countryside earning a beginner's wage. There
would thus be no class of permanent poor clustered
around factories, and factory labor would remain
cheap.

A female labor force came to be called the
"Waltham system" after 1814, when a group of Boston entrepreneurs headed by Francis Cabot Lowell
consolidated and mechanized all aspects of cloth

Early Steamboats

STEAMBOATS REVOLUTIONIZED TRAVEL in the early nineteenth century. The basic technology consisted of a steam engine, powered by the steam from a boiler heated by a wood-burning furnace. The steam first collected in a cylinder and then cooled and condensed to create a vacuum that drove a piston, which in turn propelled a paddlewheel mounted either at the side or in the stern of the boat. From the 1780s to 1807, perhaps a dozen experimental steamboats had been launched in eastern waters, as inventors sought the ideal combination of engine size, boat size, and paddlewheel type. Robert Fulton's *Clermont* of 1807 was not the first American steamboat, but it was the first long-distance, commercially successful endeavor. The *Clermont* made the trip upriver from New York City to Albany in thirty-two hours, a trip that by land took two days at that time.

Two advantages marked Fulton's effort: He imported a superior British-made engine, a low-pressure model built with many precision parts, and he formed a partnership with wealthy New York businessman Robert R. Livingston. The precocious Livingston had acquired from the New York state legislature in 1798 the right to a twenty-year monopoly on all steam transportation on the Hudson River, on the condition that he produce a boat capable of traveling four miles per hour upriver. The *Clermont* met that test, and in 1808 Fulton and Livingston extended their monopoly for another thirty years.

In 1811, Fulton and Livingston launched the first steamboat on the Mississippi River. Their low-pressure engine, operating at about two pounds per square inch of pressure in the cylinder, failed to maneuver against the river's shifting currents and many obstructions. A high-pressure steam engine developed by Delaware entrepreneur Oliver Evans proved far more suitable. It was much lighter in weight and made of fewer parts and so was easier to keep in repair. The powerful engine generated pressures from eighty to one hundred pounds per square inch; it required 30 percent more fuel, but

wood was plentiful along western waterways. By the 1830s, there were many hundreds of boats on the Mississippi, the Ohio, and the lower Missouri Rivers, run by companies all competing to reduce travel time. An upriver trip from New Orleans to Louisville that took nearly a month in the 1810s took less than a week in the 1830s. The American traveling public fell in love with steamboats for their speed and power.

Steamboats offered luxury as well as speed. Boats often were floating palaces, providing swank accommodations to ladies and gentlemen paying first-class fares. A few boats had private cabins, but most often there were two large rooms, one for each sex, filled with chairs that converted to beds. (The separation of sexes answered an important need in addition to bodily modesty: Women travelers often expressed their disgust over the spit-drenched carpets in the men's cabin.) Dining rooms with elegant appointments served elaborate meals. Many steamboats had gambling rooms as well. Low-fare passengers, typically men, occupied the lower decks of the boats, taking sleeping space out in the open or in crowded berths in public rooms. The largest boats could accommodate four hundred passengers.

The fire and smoke of a steamboat proved awesome and even terrifying to many. An older gent making his first trip in 1836 wrote that "I went on board, and passing the fireroom, where they were just *firing up*, I stopped, with unfeigned horror, and asked myself if, indeed, I was prepared to die! I almost fancied myself at the entrance of the infernal regions, and the firemen, all begrimed and black and covered with sweat, seemed like the imps of the devil, tossing the damned spirits into the flames." But many others were enthralled by the unprecedented power represented by the belching smoke. Impromptu boat racing became a popular sport. A German traveler identified a competitive streak in American passengers: "When two steamboats happen to get alongside each other, the passengers will encourage the captains to run a race. . . . The boilers intended for a pressure of only 100 pounds per square inch, are by the accelerated generation of steam, exposed to a pressure of 150, and even 200 pounds, and this goes sometimes so far, that the trials end with an explosion."

Steamboats in fact were far from safe. Between 1811 and 1851, accidents destroyed nearly a thousand boats, a third of all steam vessels built in that

THE *LEXINGTON* EXPLODES IN FLAMES ON LONG ISLAND SOUND, 1840
The **Lexington** *was six years old in 1840 and equipped with many extra safety features, such as a fire engine and pump. Three lifeboats contained enough room for only half the passengers; they were quickly swamped in the emergency and rendered useless. Only four people survived; many froze to death in the cold waters. Consider this lithograph as an object made for sale: Who would buy this kind of artistic production?*
Library of Congress.

period. More than half the steamboat accidents resulted from underwater snags—tree trunks or other debris—which penetrated hulls and sank boats. Fires, too, were fearsome hazards in wooden boats that commonly carried highly combustible cargoes, such as raw cotton in burlap bags. The development of sheet metal, which strengthened hulls and protected wooden surfaces near the smokestacks from sparks, was a major safety advance.

Boiler explosions were the most horrifying cause of accidents. As so powerfully shown in the lithograph of the steamboat *Lexington*, whose boiler blew up in Long Island Sound in January 1840, by far the greatest loss of life on steamboats came from scalding steam, flying wreckage, and the fire that would engulf a boat in a matter of minutes. In the 1830s alone, eighty-nine boiler explosions caused 861 deaths and many more injuries. The cause of

explosion was often mysterious: Was it excessive steam pressure or weak metal? Exactly how much pressure could plate iron fastened with rivets really withstand? Did a dangerous or explosive gas develop in the boiler when the water level fell too low? Or was it principally human error—reckless or drunk engineers (none of them licensed) or captains bent on breaking speed records or bowing to the economics of competition?

And who was responsible for public safety? In the wake of one accident, a newspaper called for a citizens' investigation to be conducted by a committee of twenty disinterested men with mechanical aptitude. When the three-week-old *Moselle* blew up near Cincinnati in 1838, with the loss of 150 lives, an investigative committee fixed blame on the twenty-eight-year-old captain, who had ordered the fires stoked with pitch and the safety valves (Continued) shut to build up a bigger head of steam. "Such disasters have their foundation in the present mammoth evil of our country, an inordinate love of gain," said the committee. "We are not satisfied with getting rich, but we must get rich in a day. We are not satisfied with traveling at a speed of ten miles an hour, but we must fly. Such is the effect of competition that everything must be done cheap; boiler iron must be cheap, traveling must be done cheap, freight must be cheap, yet everything must be speedy. A steamboat must establish a reputation of a few minutes 'swifter' in a hundred miles than others, before she can make fortunes fast enough to satisfy the owners."

In 1830, the federal government awarded a grant to the Franklin Institute of Philadelphia to study the causes of boiler explosions, but it was not until 1852 that public safety became a federal responsibility with passage of regulations by the U.S. Congress mandating steamboat inspections. After the Civil War, affordable sheet steel and the development of new welding techniques produced boilers that were much stronger and safer.

But by then, railway travel had stolen the glamour from steamboats, offering much faster speeds, more passenger seats, and overland travel to the West Coast. The grand era of steamboating gradually came to a close, but it would remain deeply embedded in the American imagination for a century and more through the literary works of Samuel Clemens, better known as Mark Twain. In his early twenties, Clemens, a Missouri-born boy who grew up along the Mississippi, piloted steamboats from New Orleans to St. Louis and back again. "Mark Twain," Clemens once explained, was "an old river term, a leads-man's call, signifying two fathoms—twelve feet. . . . It was always a pleasant sound for a pilot to hear on a dark night; it meant safe water." In his four years of piloting, Clemens earned a perfect safety record, never experiencing snag, fire, or boiler explosion.

production—carding, fulling, spinning, weaving, and dyeing—in one location, in Waltham, Massachusetts, and hired young women. A decade later, Lowell improved on the Waltham system at Lowell, Massachusetts, a new manufacturing town he and his associates built along the Merrimack River. By 1830, the eight mills in Lowell employed more than six thousand young women. A key innovation was the close moral supervision of the female workers, who lived in company-owned boardinghouses run by middle-aged women. Both parents and mill owners alike gained assurance that the mill workers were watched, guarded, and disciplined to be an industrious and orderly group. Soon the Waltham system was replicated in many towns in New Hampshire and Maine.

Cotton Textile Industry, 1839

The vast majority of mill workers were women age sixteen to twenty-three who worked for a year or two before leaving. Pay averaged two to three dollars a week, more than what a seamstress or domestic servant could earn but less than a young man's wages. The hours were long, typically eleven to thirteen hours a day, six days a week. The mill workers tended noisy machines in large rooms kept hot and humid (ideal for yarn, not so comfortable for people). The boardinghouses were often crowded, sometimes with six to a bedroom.

Despite the discomforts, young women flocked to obtain textile jobs. Animated by the same energy that moved Andrew Jackson westward—the faith that people can shape their own destinies—the mill workers left rural farms behind and traveled to new factory towns in the hope of becoming more autonomous individuals. They welcomed the unprecedented if still limited personal freedom of living in an all-female social space, away from parents, excused from domestic tasks, and with the exhilarating bonus of a little pocket money. In Lowell, the women workers could engage in evening self-improvement activities, like attending lectures, and the company established a newspaper, *The Lowell Offering*, written and edited by some of the workingwomen.

MILL WORKER TENDING A POWER LOOM, 1850
This daguerreotype—the earliest form of photograph (see page 458)—shows a young woman weaver tending a power loom in a textile mill. Her main task was to replace the shuttle bobbin, a wooden cradle that held spooled yarn, when it was empty. She also had to be constantly alert for sudden breaks in the warp yarn which then required a quick repair. In the 1830s, women weavers generally tended two machines at a time; in the 1840s, some companies increased the workload to four.
American Textile History Museum.

In the mid-1830s, worldwide changes in the cotton market impelled the mill owners to increase productivity from their labor force by adding more machines per worker and by lowering wages. The workers protested, emboldened by their communal living arrangements and by their relative independence from the job, being only temporary, not lifelong, employees. In 1834 and again in 1836, several hundred women at Lowell went out on strike. At mill sites all around New England, young women were the leaders in planning strikes and forming labor unions. Women strikers at a mill in Dover, New Hampshire, in 1834 denounced their owners for trying to turn them into "slaves": "However freely the epithet of 'factory slaves' may be bestowed upon us, we will never deserve it by a base and cringing submission to proud wealth or haughty insolence." Their assertiveness surprised many; but ultimately their easy replaceability undermined their bargaining power. Still, the owners gradually realized that an all-female labor force could not be counted on to be compliant and submissive. In the 1840s, mill owners began to shift to immigrant families as their labor source, and factory towns came to resemble Euro-

pean industrial sites with their permanent working class.

The mill workers welcomed the unprecedented if still limited personal freedom of living in an all-female social space, away from parents, excused from domestic tasks, and with the exhilarating bonus of a little pocket money.

Other manufacturing enterprises of the 1820s and 1830s, such as shoemaking, employed women in ever larger numbers. No new machinery transformed the actual work, but new modes of organizing the work allowed the manufacturers to step up production, control wastage and quality, and lower wages by subdividing the tasks and by hiring women. Male workers cut leather and made soles, while the stitching of the upper part of the shoe, called shoebinding, became women's work, performed at home so that it could mesh with women's domestic chores. Women shoebinders

FANCY WEDDING SHOES MADE IN LYNN, MASSACHUSETTS
These shoes were part of the wedding outfit of Emily Lucinda Alden when she married Addison Davis in 1840. The soles are flat, with no heel, and the upper shoe is hand-stitched of white satin. Nothing except the ankle lacing distinguishes right from left shoe. (Most footwear from the period was made with identical rights and lefts; only usage over time differentiated the shoes.) An extraordinary clue about women and marriage is revealed in the bride's name-to-be affixed to the shoe box. Etiquette books of the 1840s uniformly decreed that the correct public name should be Mrs. Addison Davis. We might surmise that Emily, on the verge of marriage, had not entirely internalized the eclipse of her own public and legal personage that marriage would soon impose on her. When Elizabeth Cady married Henry Stanton in 1840, she had to do battle to be called Mrs. Elizabeth Cady Stanton when she became a leader of the emerging women's rights movement in 1848 (see page 380).
Lynn Historical Society/photo by Lightstream.

earned piecework wages—that is, a payment per item completed. Women's wages were much smaller than men's, but their contribution to family income was now tangible, in cash. By 1830, there were more women shoebinders in Massachusetts than mill workers.

The new shoe entrepreneurs who had reorganized the industry moved to cut shoebinder wages in the economically turbulent 1830s. Unlike the mill workers, women shoebinders worked in relative isolation, a serious hindrance to organized protest. In Lynn, Massachusetts, a major shoemaking center, women turned to other female networks, mainly churches, as sites for meetings and religious newspapers as forums for communication. The Lynn shoebinders who demanded higher wages in 1834 built on a collective sense of themselves as women even though they did not share daily work lives. "Equal rights should be extended to all—to the weaker sex as well as the stronger," they wrote in a document forming the Female Society of Lynn.

Yet ultimately, the Lynn shoebinders' protests of the 1830s failed to achieve wage increases. Isolated workers all over New England continued to accept low wages, undercutting attempts to establish a minimum rate. And even within the town of Lynn, many shoebinders shied away from organized protest, preferring to situate their work in the context of family duty (helping their menfolk to finish shoes) instead of market relations.

Bankers and Lawyers

Entrepreneurs like the Lowell factory owners relied on innovations in the banking system to finance their ventures. The number of state-chartered banks in the country more than doubled in the boom years 1814–1816, from fewer than 90 to 208; by 1830, there were 330, and hundreds more by 1840. Banks stimulated the economy both by making loans to merchants, manufacturers, and real estate purchasers and by enlarging the country's money supply. Borrowers were issued loans in the form of banknotes, certificates unique to each bank. The borrowers then used the notes exactly like money, good for all transactions. Neither federal nor state governments issued paper money, so banknotes became the currency of the country.

In theory, a note could always be traded in at the bank for its equivalent in gold or silver (in a transaction known as "specie payment"). A note from a solid local bank might be worth exactly what it was written for, but if the note came from a distant or questionable bank, its value would be discounted by some variable fraction. The money market of Jacksonian America definitely required knowledge, caution, and trust. Not surprisingly, counterfeiting flourished under these conditions.

Bankers exercised great power over the economy in their decisions about who would get loans and what the discount rates would be. The most powerful bankers sat on the board of directors for the second Bank of the United States, headquartered in Philadelphia. (The first Bank of the United States, chartered in 1791 for twenty years, had lapsed in

United States; by 1817, there were eighteen hundred.

The legal revolution of these decades reformulated older concepts of contract to reflect the burgeoning entrepreneurial marketplace. Courts had enforced business contracts in the eighteenth century in light of notions of fairness. If a seller foolishly contracted to sell a barrel of wheat for half its true or accepted value and then had regrets, he could rely on the courts to declare the agreement void. In the nineteenth century, courts moved toward an interpretation of contracts as freely negotiated, legally binding agreements, regardless of the fairness of the outcome; the law now presumed that a price was, simply, what a buyer and seller agreed it should be.

Ever-increasing numbers of young men were drawn to legal training in the years after the War of 1812. By 1820, most representatives in the U.S. Congress were lawyers, and a similar wave of legal professionals moved into state politics. Articulate and legalistic, lawyers brought formidable skills to the job of writing and enforcing the new laws governing commerce.

Working through legislatures and courts, lawyers established rights to contract without state interference and designed the model of the business corporation that would carry the United States through the commercial and industrial transformation of the nineteenth century. Lawyers outlawed the use of strikes by aggrieved employees on the grounds that strikes constituted illegal conspiracies. They wrote the laws of eminent domain, empowering states to buy land for roads and canals, even from unwilling sellers. They drafted legislation on contributory negligence, relieving employers from responsibility for workplace injuries if it could be shown that the employees exercised inadequate caution and thus contributed to the injuries. In these ways and many others, entrepreneurial lawyers of the 1820s and 1830s created the legal foundation for an economy that gave priority to ambitious individuals interested in maximizing their own wealth.

Not everyone applauded these developments. Andrew Jackson, himself a skillful lawyer-turned-politician, spoke for a large and mistrustful segment of the population when he warned about the abuses of power "which the moneyed interest derives from a paper currency which they are able to control, from the multitude of corporations with exclusive privileges which they have succeeded in obtaining in the different states, and which are employed altogether for their benefit." Jacksonians believed that

OFFICE SAFE
Financial records, ledgers, banknotes, and stock certificates required safekeeping in the stepped-up commercial world of the 1830s. This small office safe opened by key.
Eric Long/Smithsonian Institution.

1811.) The second bank opened for business in 1816 under a twenty-year charter with eighteen branches throughout the country. The rechartering of this second bank would prove to be a major issue in Andrew Jackson's reelection campaign in 1832.

Accompanying the market revolution was a revolution in commercial law. In the decades after 1815, lawyers fashioned a legal system that advanced the interests of commercial activity and enhanced the prospects of private investment. Of particular significance was the changing practice of legal incorporation, the chartering of businesses by states. Earlier, charters were generally limited to businesses formed to serve the public good, such as to build a bridge. Under new state laws dating from 1811 on, corporations could be formed for any reasonable purpose; a key value of incorporation was legal protections for individual investors. In 1800, there were perhaps twenty corporations in the ending government-granted privileges was the way to maximize individual liberty and economic opportunity.

Booms and Busts

One aspect of the economy that the lawyer-politicians could not control was the threat of financial collapse. The boom years from 1815 to 1818 exhibited an energy and volatility that resulted in the first sharp, large-scale economic downturn in U.S. history, a depression that Americans in the early Republic called a "panic"; the pattern was repeated in the 1830s. Rapidly rising consumer demand stimulated rising prices for goods, and speculative investment opportunities with high payoffs abounded—in bank stocks, western land sales, urban real estate, and commodities markets. Steep inflation made some people wealthy but created hardships for workers on fixed incomes.

When the bubble first burst in 1819, the overnight rich suddenly became the overnight poor. Some suspected that a precipitating cause of the panic of 1819 was the second Bank of the United States. For too long, the bank had neglected to exercise control over state banks, many of which had suspended specie payments—the exchange of gold or silver for banknotes—in their eagerness to make loans and expand the economic bubble. Then, in mid-1818, the Bank of the United States started to call in its loans and insisted that state banks do likewise. The contraction of the money supply created tremors throughout the economy, a foretaste of the catastrophe to come.

What made the crunch worse was a parallel financial crisis in Europe in the spring of 1819. Overseas prices of agricultural products plummeted; cotton, tobacco, and wheat suddenly fell in value by more than 50 percent. Now when the Bank of the United States and state banks tried to call in their outstanding loans, debtors involved in the commodities trade could not pay. The number of business and personal bankruptcies skyrocketed.

The intricate web of credit and debt relationships meant that almost everyone with even a toe in the new commercial economy was affected by the panic of 1819. Thousands of Americans lost their savings and property. Estimates of unemployment suggest that a half million people lost their livelihoods nationwide.

It took several years for the country to recover from the panic of 1819. Unemployment rates slowly improved, but the emotional shock and bitterness lingered, ready to be mobilized by politicians in the decades to come. The dangers of a system that depended on extensive credit were now clear: In one memorable, folksy formulation that gained circulation around 1820, a farmer was said to compare credit to "a man pissing in his breeches on a cold day to keep his arse warm—very comfortable at first but I dare say . . . you know how it feels afterwards."

By the mid-1820s, the booming economy was back on track, driven by high productivity, a resumed consumer demand for goods, a greatly accelerating volume of international trade, and a restless and calculating people moving goods, human labor, and investment capital in ever larger and expanding circles of commerce. But an undercurrent of fear and anxiety about rapid economic change continued to shape the political views of many Americans.

The Spread of Democracy

Just as the market revolution held out the promise, if not the reality, of economic opportunity for anyone who worked hard, the political transformation of the 1830s held out the promise of political opportunity for hundreds of thousands of new voters. Between 1828 and 1836, the years of Andrew Jackson's presidency, the second American party system took shape, although not until 1836 would the parties have distinct names and consistent programs that transcended the particular personalities running for office. Over those years, more men could and did vote, responding to new methods of arousing voter interest. In 1828, Jackson's charismatic personality defined his party. By 1836, both parties had institutionalized one of his most successful themes: that politicians had to appear to have the common touch in an era when popularity with voters drove the electoral process.

Popular Politics and Partisan Identity

The election of 1828 was the first presidential contest in which popular votes determined the outcome; in twenty-two out of twenty-four states, voters—and not state legislatures—now designated electors committed to a particular candidate. More than a million voters participated, nearly three times the number in 1824, reflecting the high stakes voters perceived in the Adams-Jackson rematch. Throughout the 1830s, the number of voters rose to all-time highs. This increase resulted partly from relaxed voting restrictions; by the mid-1830s, all but three states allowed universal white male suffrage, without property qualifications. But the higher turnout also indicated increased political interest. In contrast to the sleepy Monroe elections of 1816 and 1820, more than half the electorate voted in 1828, and in some states the turnout ran as high as 70 percent. By 1840, national elections generated unprecedented voter turnouts.

Just as the market revolution held out the promise, if not the reality, of economic opportunity for anyone who worked hard, the political transformation of the 1830s held out the promise of political opportunity for hundreds of thousands of new voters.

The 1828 election inaugurated new campaign styles as well. State-level candidates routinely gave speeches to woo the voters, appearing at picnics and public banquets. (Adams and Jackson still declined such activities as too undignified; but Henry Clay of Kentucky, campaigning for Adams, earned the nicknames the "Barbecue Orator" and the "Gastronomic Cicero.") Campaign rhetoric, under the necessity to create popular appeal, became more informal and often blunt.

As party rivalry evolved, political leaders in the 1830s orchestrated public events such as rallies and parades. The Jackson camp established many Hickory Clubs, trading on Jackson's popular nickname, "Old Hickory," from a common Tennessee tree suggesting resilience and toughness. (Jackson was the first presidential candidate to have an affectionate and widely used nickname.) Political committees made sure their supporters got to the polls, which could be a day's ride or more away for some voters.

Partisan newspapers defined issues and publicized political personalities as never before. Party leaders cultivated editors and judiciously dispensed subsidies and other favors to secure the loyalties of papers, even in remote towns and villages. In New York State, where party development was

most advanced, a pro-Jackson group called the Bucktails had fifty weekly publications under its control. Stories from the leading Jacksonian paper in Washington, D.C., would be reprinted two days later in a Boston or Cincinnati paper, as fast as the mail stage could carry them. Presidential campaigns were now coordinated in a national arena.

Parties declined to adopt official names in 1828, still honoring the fiction of Republican Party unity. Instead, they called themselves the Jackson party or the Adams party. By the 1832 election, labels began to appear; Adams's political heir, Henry Clay, represented the National Republicans, while Jackson's supporters called themselves Democratic Republicans. Both parties were still claiming the mantle of the Jefferson-to-Monroe heritage by keeping "Republican" in the name, but the National Republicans favored national action to promote commercial development, while the Democratic Republicans promised to be responsive to the will of the majority. By 1834, a few state-level National Republicans shortened their name to the Whig Party, a term that was gradually accepted and in common use by 1836, the same year that Jackson's party became simply the Democrats. Thus, Whig and Democrat crystallized as names only at the end of an eight-year evolutionary process.

The Election of 1828 and the Character Issue

The campaign of 1828 was modern in more ways than just the drawn-out electioneering and the importance of popular votes. It was also the first national election in which scandal and character questions reigned supreme.

John Quincy Adams was vilified by his opponents as a hopeless elitist, a bookish academic, and perhaps even a monarchist. Critics pointed to a billiard table and an ivory chess set in Adams's White House as symbols of his aristocratic degeneracy along with the "corrupt bargain" of 1824, the alleged election deal between Adams and Henry Clay. Jackson men were especially happy to malign Clay because they viewed him as the chief architect of anti-Jackson propaganda as well as the most credible threat in future elections.

The Adams men returned fire with fire. They portrayed Jackson as the bastard son of a prostitute, a story made remotely plausible by his fatherless childhood. Worse, the cloudy, undocumented circumstances around his marriage to Rachel

Donelson Robards in 1791 gave rise to the story that Jackson was a seducer and an adulterer, having married a woman whose divorce from her first husband was not entirely legal. Pro-Adams newspapers howled that Jackson was a sinful and impulsive man, while Adams was portrayed as a man of restraint, piety, learning, and virtue.

Editors in favor of Adams played up Jackson's notorious violent temper, evidenced by the many duels, brawls, and canings they could recount. Jackson men, of course, used the same stories to project the old man as a tough frontier hero who knew how to command obedience. As for learning, Jackson's rough frontier education gave him a "natural sense," wrote a Boston editor, which "can never be acquired by reading books—it can only be acquired, in perfection, by reading men."

These stories were not smoke screens to obscure the "real" issues in the election. They became real issues themselves because voters used them to comprehend the kind of public officer each man would make. Character issues conveyed in shorthand larger questions about morality, honor, discipline, and the sanctity of contracts. Jackson and Adams presented two radically different styles of masculinity, and the voters, all men, concluded that the behavior of these candidates foreshadowed their presidential styles and policies.

The campaign of 1828 was the first in which scandal and character questions reigned supreme.

Throughout the campaign, Jackson was vague on economic and political issues; he was famous for his support of a "judicious tariff," a position that could be endorsed by proponents of both higher and lower taxes on imports. His supporters were thus a diverse group who could be sure only that Jackson favored western expansion and more limited federal powers than Adams. As the incumbent, Adams stood by his record, mainly his promise to promote commerce through federal action, which brought him strength in New England and parts of New York.

Jackson won a sweeping victory, with 56 percent of the popular vote and 178 electoral votes, compared with Adams's 83 (Map 10.2). The victor took most of the South and West and carried Pennsylvania and New York as well. Jackson's vice pres-

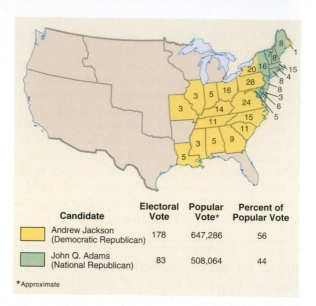

Candidate	Electoral Vote	Popular Vote*	Percent of Popular Vote
Andrew Jackson (Democratic Republican)	178	647,286	56
John Q. Adams (National Republican)	83	508,064	44

*Approximate

MAP 10.2
The Election of 1828

ident was John C. Calhoun, who had just served as vice president under Adams but had broken with Adams's policies.

After 1828, national politicians no longer deplored the existence of political parties. They were coming to see that parties mobilized and delivered voters, sharpened the focus of differences in candidates, and created loyalty to the party that surpassed loyalty to individual candidates and elections. Jackson was an especially charismatic man, and his election did much to solidify voter loyalty to what would soon be called the Democratic Party. An election over personalities went far to create a party system that could withstand and override personality contests. This apparent contradiction makes sense because the personalities of Adams and Jackson clearly symbolized and defined for voters the competing ideas of the emerging parties: a moralistic, top-down party ready to make major decisions to promote economic growth competing against a contentious, energetic party ready to embrace liberty-loving individualism.

Jackson's Democratic Agenda

Between the November election and the inauguration in March 1829, Rachel Jackson died. An embittered Andrew Jackson, certain that the ugly campaign had hastened her death, went into deep mourning. His depression was worsened by con-

PRESIDENT JACKSON'S KITCHEN CABINET
Jackson's official cabinet, consisting of party loyalists who were heads of executive depart-
ments, did not inspire the president's trust and confidence. Instead, Jackson turned to a set
of close friends, quickly dubbed the Kitchen Cabinet by the press, for advice, for patronage
decisions, and even for the drafting of state papers. Several were newspapermen; one was
an old Tennessee friend, William B. Lewis, who moved into the White House with Jackson.
Martin Van Buren was also in this inner circle. This cartoon purports to show a meeting
of the Kitchen Cabinet: raucous, argumentative, violently employing the tools of women's
work. How does its pointed message reflect the new partisan politics of the time?
Granger Collection.

stant pain from the 1806 bullet still lodged in his chest and by lead and mercury poisoning unwittingly caused by the medicines he took constantly. Sixty-two years old, he carried only 140 pounds on his six-foot-one frame. His adversaries doubted he would make it to a second term.

His supporters, however, went wild at the inauguration. Thousands cheered his ten-minute inaugural address, the shortest in history. An open reception at the White House turned into a near-riot as well-wishers jammed the premises, used windows as doors, stood on furniture for a better view of the great man, and broke thousands of dollars' worth of china and glasses.

During his presidency, Jackson continued to offer unprecedented hospitality to the public.

Twenty spittoons newly installed in the East Room of the White House accommodated the spit of the throngs that arrived daily to see the president. Some visitors came without invitation to seek jobs in the new administration. Others were tourists just calling to chat. The courteous Jackson, committed to his image as the president of the "common man," held audience with unannounced visitors throughout his two terms.

Jackson's cabinet appointments marked a departure. Whereas past presidents had tried to lessen party conflict by including men of different factions in their cabinets, Jackson would have only Jackson loyalists, a political tactic followed by most later presidents. The most important position, secretary of state, he offered to Martin Van Buren, one of the shrewdest politicians of the day and newly elected governor of New York.

The courteous Jackson, committed to his image as the president of the "common man," held audience with unannounced visitors throughout his two terms.

Jackson's agenda quickly came into focus once he was in office. He favored a Jeffersonian limited federal government, fearing that intervention in the economy inevitably favored some groups at the expense of others. He therefore opposed federal support of transportation and grants of monopolies and charters that privileged wealthy investors. Like Jefferson, he anticipated rapid settlement of the interior of the country, where land sales would spread economic democracy to settlers. Establishing a federal Indian policy thus had high priority.

Unlike Jefferson, however, Jackson exercised full presidential powers over Congress. In 1830, he vetoed a highway project in Kentucky that Congress voted to support with federal dollars. In addition to his principled objection that it was unconstitutional, Jackson took satisfaction from the fact that the project was located in the home state of Henry Clay, who was fast becoming the center of the opposition party. Jackson used the veto twelve times during his tenure in office; all previous presidents had exercised that right a total of nine times.

Cultural Shifts

Despite differences about the best or fairest way to enhance commercial development, Jackson's Democratic Republicans and Henry Clay's National Republicans shared enthusiasm for the outcome—a growing, booming economy. For increasing numbers of families, especially in the highly commercialized Northeast, the standard of living rose, consumption patterns changed, and the nature and location of work altered.

All of these changes had a direct impact on the roles and duties of men and women in families and on the training of youth for the economy of the future. New ideas about gender relations in a commercial economy surfaced in printed material and in public behavior. In Jacksonian America, a widely shared public culture came into being, originating within the new commercial classes and spreading rapidly through rising levels of literacy, an explosion of print, and an increase in all of the performance arts.

The Family and Separate Spheres

The centerpiece of new ideas about gender relations held that husbands found their status and authority in the new world of work, leaving wives to tend the hearth and home. Sermons, advice books, periodical articles, and novels reinforced the idea that men and women inhabited separate spheres with separate duties. "To woman it belongs . . . to elevate the intellectual character of her household [and] to kindle the fires of mental activity in childhood," wrote Mrs. A. J. Graves in a popular book titled *Advice to American Women.* For men, in contrast, "the absorbing passion for gain, and the pressing demands of business, engross their whole attention." In particular, the private home, now the exclusive domain of women, was sentimentalized as the source of intimacy, love, and safety, an island of refuge from the cruel and competitive world of market relations.

Some new aspects of society gave substance to this formulation of separate spheres. Men's work, especially in the manufacturing, urban Northeast, was undergoing profound change after 1815. Increasingly, men's jobs brought cash to the household. Farmers and tradesmen sold products in a market, and bankers, bookkeepers, shoemakers, and canal diggers got pay envelopes. Furthermore, many men's jobs were performed outside of the home, at an office or store. For men who were not farmers, work indeed seemed newly disconnected from the home.

The private home, now the exclusive domain of women, was sentimentalized as an island of refuge from the cruel and competitive world of market relations.

A woman's role in the home was more complicated than the cultural prescriptions indicated. Although the vast majority of married white women did not hold paying jobs, the home continued to be a site of time-consuming labor. But the advice books treated household tasks as loving familial duties; housework as *work* was thereby rendered invisible in an economy that evaluated work by how much cash it generated.

In reality, wives directly contributed to family income in many ways. Some took in boarders, while others engaged in outwork, earning pay for shoe-binding, hatmaking, or needlework done at home. Even among the most comfortable classes, the market intruded whenever wives hired domestic servants to perform the heavy household tasks no true lady would consider doing, like laundry. Most middle- and upper-income families hired servants; households striving to meet a respectable level of class display simply could not be run on the labor of one woman. A wife was therefore also an employer, facing tensions similar to those of her husband in supervising unruly, underpaid workers.

These idealized notions about the sentimental, noncommercial, feminine home and the masculine world of work gained acceptance in the 1830s (and well beyond) because of the cultural dominance of the middle and upper classes of the Northeast. The doctrine of separate spheres unambiguously defined masculinity and femininity. Men achieved a sense of manhood through work and pay; women established a sense of femininity through duty to the home and family and service to others. The convenient fiction of this formulation of gender difference helped smooth the path for the first generation of Americans experiencing the market revolution. The doctrine of separate spheres ordained that men would absorb and display the values appropriate to the market economy—competition, acquisitiveness—while women would exemplify and foster older, noncommercial values of loving service to family and community. Both men and women of the middle classes benefited from this bargain; men were set free to pursue wealth, while women gained moral authority within the home. Beyond the middle and upper classes, these new gender ideals had limited applicability. Despite their apparent dominance in printed material of the period, they were never monolithic.

The Education and Training of Youth

The market economy with its new expectations for men and women required fresh methods of training youth of both sexes. The generation that came of age in the 1820s and 1830s had opportunities for education and work unparalleled in previous eras.

Northern states adopted public schooling between 1790 and the 1820s, and within another decade southern states began to provide "common schools" for white children. The curriculum produced pupils who were able, by age twelve or fourteen, to read and to participate in marketplace calculations. Remarkably, girls usually received the same basic education as boys. Literacy rates for white females climbed dramatically, rivaling the rates for white males for the first time.

The generation that came of age in the 1820s and 1830s had opportunities for education and work unparalleled in previous eras.

The fact that taxpayers paid for children's education created an incentive to seek an inexpensive teaching force. By the 1830s, northeastern school districts had replaced male teachers with young females. Like mill workers, teachers were in their late teens and regarded the work as temporary. Some had acquired education in private girls' academies that were springing up to meet the middle-class ambition for polished daughters. In the 1840s, several states opened teacher training schools ("normal" schools) for women students. Only one college in the 1830s admitted women: Oberlin College in Ohio in 1837 opened a Ladies' Department. The school also admitted black male students, so clearly it was unusually progressive. No other colleges admitted women until after the Civil War, but a handful of private "female seminaries" established a rigorous curriculum that rivaled that of the best men's colleges. The three most prominent were the Troy Seminary in New York, founded by Emma Willard in 1821; the Hartford Seminary in Connecticut, founded by Catharine Beecher in 1822; and Mount Holyoke in Massachusetts, founded by Mary Lyon in 1837. These women educators argued that women made better teachers than men: "If men have more knowledge, they have less talent at communicating it. Nor have they the patience, the long-suffering, and gentleness necessary to superintend the formation of character," said the author Harriet Beecher Stowe, who taught at her sister's Hartford school.

Male youths leaving the common school faced two paths. A small percentage continued at private boys' academies (numbering in the several hundreds nationwide), and a far smaller number

PHILADELPHIA FAMILY MEMBERS IN THEIR SUNDAY BEST, 1820

The Philadelphia artist John Lewis Krimmel painted this cozy domestic scene of a middle-class family, with mother at the center, presiding over children, grandmother, dog, and doll. What appears to be a conventional family portrait is a little more peculiar, however. Five of the people in the picture were dead when Krimmel composed the painting: the mother and baby and the three girls nearest to them, all with unusually intense, shining eyes. Each is portrayed at the age when death took them; the surviving family members are shown at the age they were when the mother died. Professional and amateur artists did a brisk business making portraits of recently deceased family members, to provide tokens of remembrance for the survivors. This improbable, ghostly grouping takes that common custom to another level. Krimmel himself was part of this family, and he painted himself in the back left. A year later, he died at age thirty-four in a drowning accident.

The National Gallery of Art, Washington, D.C.

WOMEN GRADUATES OF OBERLIN COLLEGE, CLASS OF 1855
*Oberlin College was founded in Ohio by evangelical and abolitionist activists in the
1830s; it admitted white and black men and women, although in the early years the
black students were all male and the women students were all white. Admission was
not exactly equal: the women entered a separate Ladies' Department. By 1855, as this
daguerreotype shows, black women had integrated the Ladies' Department. The two
older women with bonnets were the principal and a member of the board. The students
wear the latest fashion: dark taffeta dresses with sloping shoulders and tight bodice,
topped by detachable white lace collars. Hair fashions were similarly uniform for
women of all ages throughout the 1850s: a central part, hair dressed with oil and
lustrously coiled over the ears.*
Oberlin College Archives, Oberlin, Ohio.

matriculated at the country's two dozen colleges.
More typically, boys left school at fourteen to apprentice to a specific trade or to seek business ca-
reers in entry-level clerkships, abundant in the
growing urban centers. Young girls also headed for
mill towns or for the cities in unprecedented numbers, seeking work in the expanding service sector
as seamstresses and domestic servants.

Changes in patterns of youth employment and
training meant that large numbers of youngsters in
the 1830s and later escaped the watchful eyes of
their families. Moralists fretted about the dangers
of unsupervised youth, and, following the lead of
the Lowell mill owners, some established appren-

tices' libraries and uplifting lecture series to keep
young people honorably occupied. Advice books
published by the hundreds instructed youth in the
virtues of hard work and delayed gratification.

Public Life, the Press, and Popular Amusements

Many new forms of inexpensive reading matter and
public entertainments competed with the moralistic messages for youth. Innovations in printing technology as well as rising literacy rates created a brisk
market in the 1830s for publications appealing to
popular tastes: adventure and mystery pamphlets,

LURID COVER OF A CRIME PAMPHLET, NEW YORK
Cheap and easy printing in the early nineteenth century gave rise to new genres of popular reading matter, including large pamphlet literature detailing horrific murder stories that invited readers to contemplate the nature of evil. This woodcut cover from 1836 promises to reveal the "interesting particulars" of the murder of Ellen Jewett, a New York City prostitute axed to death in her brothel bed. The pamphlet claims to constitute "an impressive warning" to youth about the tragedies of "dens of infamy." But the crude picture of the female corpse, with bare legs and breasts fully exposed, suggests that alternative, less moralistic readings of the same material were certainly possible for the purchasers.
William L. Clements Library.

dime novels, and penny press newspapers. In cities, theaters were nightly magnets for audiences in the thousands.

In the 1790s, fewer than ninety newspapers, each printing a few thousand copies per issue, provided the knowledge base of current events. By 1830, there were eight hundred papers, sixty-five of them urban dailies, and in the 1830s the most successful of these, the new penny press papers, gained circulations of ten to twenty thousand copies daily (Table 10.1). Such huge print runs were made possible only by the development of steam-driven rotary presses with automatic paper feed devices replacing the old-style handpresses. Six-cent papers covered politics, banking, and shipping news; the one-cent papers featured breezy political coverage, irreverent editorializing on current events, racetrack results, and crime reporting.

New York had three penny papers by 1835, and Philadelphia, Boston, and Baltimore each had one or two. Their influence extended throughout the nation, facilitated by a regular system of newspaper exchange via the postal system. Town and village papers reprinted the snappy political editorials and sensationalized crime stories, putting very undeferential ideas into the heads of readers new to politics.

Newspapers were not the only new medium for spreading a shared American culture. Starting in the 1830s, traveling lecturers crisscrossed the country, bringing entertainment and instruction to small-town audiences. Speakers gave dramatic readings of plays or poetry or lectured on history, current events, popular science, or controversial topics like advanced female education or anatomy and physiology.

Theater blossomed in the 1830s, providing Americans with their most common form of shared entertainment. An increase in the number and size of theaters along with a drop in ticket prices put theatergoing within the reach of many ordinary Americans. The major cities each had a half dozen or more theaters, with as many as three thousand seats apiece. Audiences mostly comprised white men of all classes, but women and blacks attended as well, in smaller numbers and in segregated seating. Theater etiquette allowed for much interaction between performers and audiences, who applauded, hissed, jeered, whistled, hooted, and stomped as the spirit moved them.

Shakespeare's plays were an all-round favorite. In just one year, 1835, in Philadelphia, no fewer than

TABLE 10.1

THE GROWTH OF NEWSPAPERS, 1820–1840

	1820	1830	1835	1840
U.S. population (in millions)	9.6	12.8	15.0	17.1
Number of newspapers published	500	800	1200	1400
Daily newspapers	42	65	—	138

sixty-five separate Shakespeare productions were staged. Other English and American productions of tragedies, comedies, and melodramas rotated nightly. Before and after plays, theaters provided short acts featuring singers, dancers, and, increasingly, minstrelsy, a blackface musical comedy first performed in New York City in 1831. White performers with blackened faces parodied everything from romance to Shakespeare, trading on and reinforcing racist stereotypes about African Americans' speech, dress, and conduct.

The public culture of the theater demonstrates a fluidity of cultural styles in the 1830s. In the era of the "common man," ordinary men and women showed a surprising familiarity with Shakespeare, knowing the plays so well that they could hoot when actors muffed their lines or laugh at clever satires of the Bard. Not until the 1840s and beyond would a kind of market segmentation appear in public amusements, with some theaters targeting the cultural elite and others the working classes.

The theater world also promoted a new vision of what a public woman could be. Traditionally, a "public woman" meant a prostitute, and actresses risked having their sexual respectability called into question. (In Shakespeare's day, boys played the female roles to avoid the indecency of female exposure.) But the spectacular success of American theaters in the 1830s made some women stars of the stage, drawing fans and fame as well as a measure of respectability. Celebrated actresses enlarged the scope of the possible for female behavior. They could speak commanding words in a loud voice; some even dressed in breeches and played male parts. The trade-off was that theaters also offered actresses' bodies for viewing by the largely male audience.

The popularity of theaters exemplified a general cultural turn toward the celebration of brilliant public speech. In this golden age of oration, actors, lawyers, politicians, and ministers could hold crowds spellbound for hours with their flawless elocution and elegant turns of phrase. Criminal trials, for example, were very short by modern standards, but the lawyers' closing arguments might consume many hours, with crowds of spectators hanging on every word. Senator Daniel Webster of Massachusetts was the acknowledged genius of political oration, putting grown men into raptures. At a Webster speech commemorating the Pilgrims' arrival, one man in a crowd of fifteen hundred recalled that "three or four times I thought my temples would burst with the gush of blood." Ministers with gifted tongues could in the space of an evening transform crowds of skeptics into deeply moved believers. Skillful speakers demanded and generally got skillful, attentive listeners. Catchy slogans had little place in this oratorical style.

Democracy and Religion

An unprecedented revival of evangelical religion peaked in the early 1830s, after gathering three decades of momentum in states across the North and the upper South. Known as the Second Great Awakening, the outpouring of religious fervor changed the shape of American Protestantism. The heart of the evangelical message was that salvation was available to anyone willing to eradicate individual sin and accept faith in God's grace. Just as universal male suffrage allowed all white men to vote, democratized religion offered salvation to all who chose to embrace it.

Among the most serious adherents of evangelical Protestantism were men and women of the new mercantile classes whose self-discipline in pursuing market ambitions meshed well with the message of self-discipline in pursuit of spiritual perfection. Not content with individual perfection, many of these men and women sought to perfect society as well.

The Second Great Awakening

The earliest manifestations of an unusual outbreak of fervent piety appeared in 1801 in Kentucky. A crowd of ten to fifteen thousand people camped out on a hillside at Cane Ridge for an evangelical revival meeting that lasted several weeks. By the 1810s and 1820s, camp meetings had spread to the

Atlantic seaboard states, finding especially enthusiastic audiences in western New York and Pennsylvania. The outdoor settings permitted huge attendance, which itself intensified the emotional impact of the experience. "For more than a half mile, I could see people on their knees before God in humble prayer," recalled one Cane Ridge worshiper.

Just as universal male suffrage allowed all white men to vote, democratized religion offered salvation to all who chose to embrace it.

The gatherings attracted women and men hungry for a more immediate access to spiritual peace, one not requiring years of soul-searching preparation. Ministers adopted an emotional style and invited an immediate experience of conversion and salvation. One eyewitness at a revival reported that "some of the people were singing, others praying, some crying for mercy in the most piteous accents. . . . At one time I saw at least 500 swept down in a moment as if a battery of a thousand guns had been opened upon them, and then immediately followed shrieks and shouts that rent the very heavens."

From 1800 to 1820, church membership doubled in the United States, much of it among the evangelical groups. Methodists, Baptists, and Presbyterians formed the core of the new movement, while Episcopalians, Congregationalists, Unitarians, Dutch Reformed, Lutherans, and Catholics maintained strong skepticism about the emotional enthusiasm. Women more than men were attracted to the evangelical movement, and wives and mothers typically recruited husbands and sons to join them.

The leading exemplar of the Second Great Awakening was a lawyer-turned-minister named Charles Grandison Finney. Finney lived in western New York, where the completion of the Erie Canal in 1825 fundamentally altered the social and economic landscape overnight. Towns swelled with new inhabitants who brought in remarkable prosperity along with other, less admirable aspects of urban growth, such as prostitution, drinking, and gaming. Finney saw New York canal towns like Utica, Rome, and Buffalo as ripe for evangelical awakening. In Rochester, New York, he sustained a six-month revival through the long winter of 1830–31, generating thousands of new converts.

The message that Finney preached was directed primarily at women and men of the business classes, and, true to his training, Finney couched his message in legal metaphors. "The world is divided into two great political parties," he announced in a sermon—the party of Satan and the party of Jehovah. "Ministers should labor with sinners, as a lawyer does with a jury . . . ; and the sinner should weigh his arguments, and make up his mind as upon oath and for his life, and give a verdict upon the spot." Finney urged his listeners to take control of their own salvation, arguing that a reign of Christian perfection loomed. The promise of perfection required a public-spirited outreach to the less than perfect to foster their salvation. Christian benevolence, or do-good action, was demanded of all believers. Evangelicals promoted Sunday schools to bring piety to children; they battled to end mail delivery, stop public transport, and close shops on Sundays to honor the Sabbath. Many women formed missionary societies, which printed and distributed millions of Bibles and religious tracts. Maternal associations sprang up to promote a new style of moral mothering. Through such avenues, evangelical religion offered women expanded spheres of influence.

In 1832, Finney moved to New York City and renovated a disreputable theater into a Free Presbyterian church. His dynamic, theatrical performances were taken down by scribes and published in the New York *Evangelist*, a weekly paper of national distribution. Finney adopted tactics of Jacksonian-era politicians to sell his cause: publicity, argumentation, rallies, and speeches. His object, he said, was to get Americans to "vote in the Lord Jesus Christ as the governor of the Universe."

The Temperance Movement and the Campaign for Moral Reform

The evangelical disposition—a combination of righteousness, energy, self-discipline, and faith—animated vigorous campaigns to eliminate alcohol abuse and eradicate sexual sins. Millions of Americans took the temperance pledge to abstain from strong drink, and hundreds became involved in efforts to end prostitution.

Alcohol consumption had steadily risen in the decades up to 1830, when the average person over age thirteen consumed an astonishing 9.5 gallons of hard liquor plus 30.3 gallons of hard cider, beer, and wine per year. To a degree, consumption of bottled,

THE BROADWAY TABERNACLE.

CHARLES G. FINNEY'S BROADWAY TABERNACLE
The Reverend Charles G. Finney took his evangelical movement to New York City in the early 1830s, operating first out of a renovated theater. In 1836, the Broadway Tabernacle was built for his pastorate. In its use of space the Tabernacle resembled a theater more than a traditional church, but in one respect it departed radically from one very theater-like tradition of churches—the custom of charging pew rents. In effect, most churches required worshipers to purchase their seats. In contrast, Finney insisted that all seats in his house were free, unreserved, and open to all.
Oberlin College Archives, Oberlin, Ohio.

www.bedfordstmartins.com/tap   SEE THE ONLINE STUDY GUIDE for more help in analyzing this image.

fermented drinks made a certain amount of sense, in view of unsafe urban water sources and the lack of reliable refrigeration. However, alcohol abuse was on the rise.

All classes imbibed. Leisure-time drinking flourished in urban streets in saloons, barbershops, and groceries selling liquor by the glass. A lively saloon culture fostered masculine camaraderie among laborers along with extensive alcohol consumption and a new style of binge drinking that alarmed older proponents of moderate drinking. In elite homes, the after-dinner whiskey or sherry was com-

monplace. Colleges before 1820 routinely served students a pint of ale with meals, and the army and navy included rum in the standard daily ration.

Organized opposition to drinking first surfaced in the 1810s among health reformers in New England. In 1826, Lyman Beecher, a Connecticut minister of an "awakened" church, founded the American Temperance Society, which condemned drinking as a moral vice leading to poverty, idleness, crime, and family violence. Adopting the methods of evangelical ministers, temperance lecturers traveled the country expounding the damage

TEMPERANCE WOMEN SERVING TEA
The woodcut artist titled this picture Women Enjoying a Seated Tea While Making a Strong Stand in Favor of Temperance. *No actual tea is in sight in the drawing; the menu seems to consist of fruit and pie. The guests look on with approval as the hostess empties a wine bottle out the window; wineglasses on the table are turned upside down, and more bottles await their fate in the basket at the lower right. The drawing, dating from 1840, symbolizes women's rejection of alcohol; it seems highly unlikely that such a scene was actually played out.*
Courtesy, American Antiquarian Society.

of drink; by 1833, some six thousand local affiliates of the American Temperance Society boasted more than a million members. Middle-class drinking began a steep decline. One powerful tool of persuasion was the temperance pledge, which many manufacturers and business owners began to require of employees.

In 1836, the temperance leaders regrouped into a new society, the American Temperance Union, which demanded total abstinence of its adherents; even sacramental wine was condemned. The intensified war against alcohol moved beyond individual moral suasion into the realm of politics, as reformers sought to deny taverns liquor licenses and to wipe out the dram shops selling liquor by the

glass. By 1845, temperance advocates had put an impressive dent in alcohol consumption, which had diminished to one-quarter of the per capita consumption of 1830. In 1851, Maine became the first state to ban entirely the sale or manufacture of all alcoholic beverages.

More controversial than evangelical temperance was a social movement called "moral reform," which first aimed at public morals in general but quickly narrowed to a campaign to eradicate sexual sin, especially prostitution. In 1833, a group of Finneyite women started the New York Female Moral Reform Society. Its members insisted that male sexual expression, which they considered the ultimate in lack of self-control, posed a serious threat to society in general and to women in particular.

The women reformers published a newspaper, *The Advocate of Moral Reform*, that quickly established a national circulation. It was the first major woman-edited, woman-written, and woman-typeset paper in the country. Columns were devoted to first-person tales of woe and to advice about curbing sexual sin. The reformers condemned clerks who visited brothels and traveling businessmen who befriended and then allegedly seduced girls away from home. Within five years, more than four thousand auxiliary groups had sprung up, mostly in New England, New York, Pennsylvania, and Ohio, all areas where evangelical religion was strong. Not content merely to publicize sin, the New York group engaged in direct action, stationing women outside brothels to intimidate the patrons. They urged chaste women to sign pledges, like the pledges of the temperance movement, promising to accept only virtuous men in courtship.

The Female Moral Reform Society drew on the evangelicals' familiar themes of self-control and suppression of sin. But in its analysis of the causes of licentiousness and its conviction that women had a duty to speak out about unspeakable things, it pushed the limits of what even the men in the evangelical movement could tolerate. Yet the moral reformers did not regard themselves as radicals of any kind. They were simply pursuing the logic of a gender system that defined home protection and morality as women's special sphere and a religious conviction that called for the eradication of sin.

Organizing against Slavery

Even more radical than moral reform was the evangelicals' effort in the 1830s to eradicate the sin of slavery. The abolition movement was also far more radical than the only previous antislavery organization, the American Colonization Society. In 1817, a group of Maryland and Virginia planters had promoted gradual emancipation by individual plantation owners followed by colonization of African Americans in Africa; by the early 1820s, several thousand ex-slaves had been transported to Liberia on the West African coast. But not surprisingly, newly freed men and women were often not eager to move to Liberia; their African roots were three or more generations in the past. Emigration to Africa proved to be so gradual (and expensive) as to have a negligible impact on American slavery.

A more insistent attention to the evils of slavery emerged in 1831, spurred by the perfectionist impulse of the Second Great Awakening. Charles Finney's religious campaigns in Rochester and New York City identified slavery as a major obstacle to America's progress toward perfection. Both of those cities quickly became centers of antislavery agitation.

Even more radical than moral reform was the evangelicals' effort in the 1830s to eradicate the sin of slavery.

In Boston, an antislavery movement developed around William Lloyd Garrison, who started publishing a weekly newspaper called the *Liberator* in 1831. Garrison, then twenty-six, launched a drive for immediate abolition, promising that his paper would be "as harsh as truth, and as uncompromising as justice. On this subject, I do not wish to think, or speak, or write, with moderation. No! No! Tell a man whose house is on fire to give a moderate alarm; tell him to moderately rescue his wife from the hands of the ravisher; tell the mother to gradually extricate her babe from the fire into which it has fallen;—but urge me not to use moderation in a cause like the present." No gradualist plan could ever be acceptable to Garrison.

Garrison's visibility in Boston built on several years of growing local antislavery sentiment. In 1829, a black printer named David Walker published *An Appeal to the Colored Citizens of the World*, which condemned racism, invoked the egalitarian language of the Declaration of Independence, and hinted at racial violence if whites did not change their prejudiced ways. Walker's fervent *Appeal* electrified Garrison, pushing him into a more radical stance on slavery. It electrified the South as well, and several southern states prohibited the circulation of both Walker's *Appeal* and the *Liberator*.

In 1831, a young black woman, Maria Stewart, began a series of public lectures for black audiences in Boston on slavery and racial prejudice. While her arguments against slavery were welcomed, her voice—that of a woman—created problems. Few American-born women had yet engaged in public speaking beyond ceremonial or theatrical performance; Stewart was breaking a social taboo. Boston's elite black men in the audience discouraged her

ABOLITIONIST PURSES
Female antislavery societies raised many thousands of dollars to support the abolitionist cause by selling handcrafted items at giant antislavery fairs. Toys, infant clothes, quilts, caps and collars, purses, needlebooks, wax flowers, inlaid boxes: the list was endless. Items were often emblazoned with abolitionist mottoes, such as "Let My People Go," "Liberty," and "Loose the Bonds of Wickedness." These pink silk drawstring bags were decorated with pictures of the hapless slave woman, an object of compassion. Dollars raised at these fairs supported the travels of abolitionist speakers as well as the publication and distribution of many antislavery books and articles.
The Daughters of the American Revolution Museum, Washington, D.C. Gift of Mrs. Erwin L. Broecker.

career, and she retired from the platform in 1833. Garrison published her lectures, giving them wider circulation.

In 1832 and 1833, the antislavery movement got organized. The New England Anti-Slavery Society coalesced in 1832 around Garrison, and New York and Philadelphia Anti-Slavery Societies became active in 1833. The print media were fully enlisted, with a dozen antislavery newspapers as well as pamphlets and books in circulation. Effective antislavery speakers embarked on lecture tours and inspired the formation of new societies. By 1837, thirteen hundred local antislavery societies had sprung up all over the North, with a membership totaling a quarter of a million men and women. This was a significant number but by no means a large one in relation to the North's population, just under ten million.

Many northerners were not prepared to embrace the abolitionist call for emancipation, imme-diate or gradual. They might oppose slavery as a blot on the country's ideals or as a rival to the free-labor system of the North, but at the same time most white northerners remained antiblack and therefore antiabolition. From 1834 to 1838, there were more than a hundred eruptions of serious mob violence against abolitionists or free blacks. On one occasion, antislavery headquarters in Philadelphia and a black church and orphanage were burned to the ground; in another incident, Illinois abolitionist editor Elijah Lovejoy was killed by a rioting crowd that tried to destroy his printing press.

Women played a prominent role in abolition, just as they did in moral reform and evangelical religion. They formed women's auxiliaries and engaged in fundraising to support agents in the field and the expenses of pamphlet publication. In the political realm, women circulated antislavery petitions, which they presented to the U.S. Congress with tens of thousands of signatures.

Garrison particularly welcomed women's activity. When a southern plantation daughter named Angelina Grimké wrote him about her personal repugnance for slavery, Garrison published the letter in the *Liberator* and brought her overnight fame. Grimké and her older sister, Sarah, now living in Philadelphia, quickly became lecturers for the antislavery movement and started a speaking tour to women's groups in Massachusetts in 1837. Grimké's powerful eyewitness speeches attracted men as well, causing the Congregational church leadership of Massachusetts to issue a warning to all its ministers not to let the Grimké sisters use their pulpits. As with Maria Stewart, the Grimkés had violated a gender norm by presuming to instruct men.

In the late 1830s, the cause of abolition divided the nation as no other issue did. Even among the abolitionists, significant divisions emerged. The Grimké sisters, radicalized by the public reaction to their speaking tour, began to write and speak about women's rights. They were opposed by moderate abolitionists who were unwilling to mix a new and controversial issue about women with their first cause, the rights of blacks. A few radical men, like Garrison, embraced women's rights fully, working to get women leadership positions in the national antislavery group. Out of the New England antislavery movement came the first organized women's rights movement in U.S. history, in the 1840s.

The many men and women active in reform movements in the 1830s found their initial inspiration in evangelical Protestantism's dual message: Salvation was open to all and society needed to be perfected. Their activist mentality squared well with the interventionist tendencies of the party forming in opposition to Andrew Jackson's Democrats. On the whole, reformers gravitated to the Whig Party.

Jackson Defines the Democratic Party

In his eight years in office, Andrew Jackson worked to implement his vision of a politics of opportunity for all white men. He also greatly enhanced the power of the presidency. He favored rapid western land settlement, which led to conflict with Indian tribes. He had a dramatic confrontation with John C. Calhoun and South Carolina when that state tried to nullify the tariff of 1828. Disapproving of all government-granted privilege, Jackson challenged what he called the "monster" Bank of the United States and took it down to defeat. Jackson's legacy to his successor, Martin Van Buren, was a Democratic Party strong enough to withstand the passing of the powerful old man.

Indian Policy and the Trail of Tears

Improved transportation after 1815 greatly accelerated the westward flow of white settlers, and states containing Indian tribes rapidly joined the Union. But fundamental questions remained unresolved: What was the legal status of the quarter of a million Indians now resident in the United States? Were they subject to state and federal law?

From the 1790s to the 1820s, the federal government negotiated treaties with tribes on the assumption that the tribes were foreign nations. The Indians, though within state borders, asserted their sovereignty and communal rights to their land. Treaty making, however, proved a precarious practice. American negotiators found it hard to strike terms that whole tribes would accept, and all too often a few Indians with no legitimacy to speak for their tribes signed treaties ceding vast acreage.

As an army general, Andrew Jackson had negotiated many such treaties, but he privately thought it was "absurd" to call the Indians foreigners. In his view, they were really subjects of the United States, entitled perhaps to keep small areas of their improved land but not their large hunting grounds. Jackson also did not think it feasible to promote assimilation of the Indians. From 1790 to the 1820s, various missionary associations had tried to "civilize" native peoples by converting them to Christianity, and presidents from Jefferson to Monroe had promoted assimilation as a peaceable alternative to warfare. In 1819, Congress authorized $10,000 a year for interdenominational missions to instruct Indians in religion, reading and writing, and agricultural practices. Missionaries also tried to get Indians to adopt white gender customs, but Indian women were reluctant to embrace practices that accorded them less power than their tribal system did. The general failure

CHEROKEE PHOENIX
Around 1820, Sequoyah, about forty-five years old and nephew of a Cherokee chief, invented written symbols to convey the Cherokee language. Each symbol represented a syllable of sound. In 1828, the Cherokees in New Echota, Georgia, ordered custom-made type embodying the new symbols and began printing a newspaper, the **Cherokee Phoenix,** *the first newspaper published by Native Americans, printed in both English and Cherokee.*
Special Collections Division, Georgetown University Library, Washington, D.C.

of assimilation moved Jackson to a more drastic policy.

In his first message to Congress in 1829, Jackson declared that Indians within the United States borders could not remain independent and in sovereign control of tribal lands. Congress agreed and passed the Removal Act of 1830, appropriating $500,000 to relocate tribes west of the Mississippi River (Map 10.3).

For northern tribes, their numbers greatly diminished by years of war, gradual removal was already well under way. But not all the Indians went quietly. In 1832 in western Illinois, Black Hawk, a leader of the Sac and Fox Indians, resisted. Volunteer militias attacked and chased the Indians into southern Wisconsin, where, after several skirmishes and a deadly battle, Black Hawk was captured and more than nine hundred of his people massacred.

In his first message to Congress in 1829, Jackson declared that Indians within the United States borders could not remain independent and in sovereign control of tribal lands. Congress agreed and passed the Removal Act of 1830.

Southern tribes proved to be even more resistant to removal. The powerful Creek, Chickasaw, Choctaw, and Cherokee tribes, whose lands encompassed parts of North Carolina, Tennessee, and northern Georgia, Alabama, and Mississippi, at first refused to relocate. But their land attracted cotton-hungry white settlers, and a rumor of gold on

MAP 10.3

Indian Removal and the Trail of Tears

The federal government under President Andrew Jackson pursued a vigorous policy of Indian removal in the 1830s. Southern tribes were forcibly moved west to land known as the Indian Territory (in present-day Oklahoma). As many as a quarter of the Cherokee Indians died in 1838 on their route, known as the Trail of Tears.

READING THE MAP: From which states were most of the Native Americans removed? Through what states did the Trail of Tears go?

CONNECTIONS: Before Jackson's presidency, how did the federal government view Native Americans and what policy initiatives were undertaken by the government and private groups? How did Jackson change the government's Native American policies?

www.bedfordstmartins.com/tap   SEE THE ONLINE STUDY GUIDE for more help in analyzing this map.

Cherokee land in Georgia in 1829 only intensified the pressure.

Ironically, the seventeen thousand members of the Cherokee tribe had "assimilated" most successfully, spurred by dedicated missionaries living with them. Starting in 1808, they had adopted written laws, culminating in 1827 in a constitution that provided for a bicameral legislature, an executive office, and a court system modeled on that of the United

States. More than two hundred of the wealthiest Cherokees had intermarried with whites and had adopted white styles of housing, dress, and cotton agriculture, including the ownership of more than a thousand African American slaves. They had developed a written alphabet and published a newspaper as well as Christian prayerbooks in their language.

In 1831, after Georgia announced it would subject the Indians to state law, the Cherokee tribe responded by suing Georgia before the U.S. Supreme Court. Chief Justice John Marshall set aside the suit on technicalities but encouraged the Cherokees to seek further legal redress. When Georgia jailed two missionaries under an 1830 law forbidding missionary aid to Indians without state permission, the Cherokees brought suit again. In the 1832 case, *Worcester v. Georgia*, the Supreme Court found for the missionaries and also recognized the Cherokees' existence as "a distinct community, occupying its own territory, in which the laws of Georgia can have no force."

An angry President Jackson made it clear that he would ignore the Supreme Court's decision and proceeded to enforce the Removal Act. "If they [the Cherokees] now refuse to accept the liberal terms offered, they can only be liable for whatever evils and difficulties may arise. I feel conscious of having done my duty to my red children."

Still, the Cherokee tribe remained in Georgia for two more years without significant violence. Then in 1835, a small, unauthorized part of the tribe signed a treaty ceding all the tribal lands to the state, and Georgia rapidly sold off the land to whites. Several thousand Cherokees petitioned the U.S. Congress to ignore the bogus treaty, but their pleas went unheard.

The disputed treaty relinquished a large piece of northern Georgia in exchange for $5 million and equal acreage west of Arkansas, in present-day Oklahoma. But most of the Cherokee Indians refused to move, and in May 1838, the deadline for voluntary evacuation, federal troops arrived to deport them. Under armed guard, the Cherokees embarked on a twelve-hundred-mile journey that came to be called the Trail of Tears. A newspaperman in Kentucky described the forced march: "Even aged females, apparently, nearly ready to drop into the grave, were traveling with heavy burdens attached to the back. . . . They buried fourteen to fifteen at every stopping place." Nearly a quarter of the Cherokees died en route, from hardship and starvation. They joined fifteen thousand Creek, twelve thousand Choctaw, and five thousand Chickasaw Indians also forcibly relocated to what is now Oklahoma (see Map 10.3).

In his farewell address to the nation in 1837, Jackson justified Indian removal with high-minded language about the benefit of the policy to the forlorn natives: "This unhappy race . . . are now placed in a situation where we may well hope that they will share in the blessings of civilization and be saved from the degradation and destruction to which they were rapidly hastening while they remained in the states." Jackson genuinely believed that exile to the West was necessary to save Indian culture from destruction.

The Tariff of Abominations and Nullification

Jackson's Indian policy happened to harmonize with the principle of states' rights: The president supported Georgia's right to ignore the Supreme Court decision in *Worcester v. Georgia*. But in another pressing question of states' rights, Jackson contested South Carolina's claim to ignore federal tariff policy.

Federal tariffs as high as 33 percent on imports like textiles and iron goods had been passed in 1816 and again in 1824, in an effort to favor new American manufactures and shelter them from foreign competition as well as to raise federal revenue. But some southern congressmen opposed steep tariffs, fearing they would decrease overseas shipping and hurt the South's export of raw cotton. During John Quincy Adams's administration (1825–1829), tariff policy generated heated debate. In 1828, Congress passed a revised tariff that came to be known as the Tariff of Abominations. A bundle of conflicting duties, the set of tariffs—some as high as 50 percent—had something for *and* against every economic and sectional interest. Assembled mostly by pro-Jackson congressmen, who loaded it with duties on raw materials needed by New England, it also contained protectionist elements favored by northern manufacturers. One wealthy cotton mill owner laughed that the tariff would "keep the South and West in debt to New England the next hundred years."

South Carolina in particular suffered from the Tariff of Abominations. Worldwide prices for cotton were already in sharp decline in the late 1820s and early 1830s, and the further depression of shipping caused by the high tariffs hurt the South's export market. In 1828, a group of South Carolina politicians headed by John C. Calhoun drew up a statement outlining a doctrine called "nullification." The Union, they argued, was a confederation of states that had yielded some but not all power to the federal government. When Congress overstepped its powers, states had the right to nullify Congress's acts; as precedents they pointed to the Virginia and Kentucky Resolutions of 1798, which had attempted to invalidate the Alien and Sedition Acts (see chapter 8). Congress had erred in using tariff policy as an instrument to benefit specific industries, the South Carolinians claimed; tariffs should be used only to raise revenue.

On assuming the presidency in 1829, Jackson ignored the South Carolina statement of nullification and proceeded to shut out Calhoun, his new vice president, from influence or power. Tariff revisions in early 1832 brought little relief to the South. Sensing futility, Calhoun resigned from the vice presidency in 1832 and accepted election by the South Carolina legislature to a seat in the U.S. Senate, where he could better protect his state's anti-tariff stance. Strained to their limit, the South Carolina leaders took the radical step of declaring the federal tariffs to be null and void in their state as of February 1, 1833.

Finally, the constitutional crisis was out in the open. Opting for a dramatic confrontation, Jackson sent armed ships to Charleston's harbor and threatened to invade the state. He pushed through Congress a bill, called the Force Bill, defining the Carolina stance as treason and authorizing military action to collect federal tariffs.

At the same time, Congress moved quickly to pass a revised tariff more acceptable to the South. The astute Senator Henry Clay rallied support for a moderate bill that gradually lowered tariffs by half, back to the level prevailing in 1816. Both the new tariff and the Force Bill were passed by Congress on March 1, 1833. South Carolina responded by withdrawing its nullification of the old tariff—and then nullifying the Force Bill. It was a symbolic gesture, since Jackson's show of muscle was no longer necessary. Both sides took a measure of satisfaction in the immediate outcome. Federal power had prevailed over a dangerous assertion of states' rights; and South Carolina got the lower tariff it wanted.

Yet the question of federal power versus states' rights was far from settled. The implied threat behind nullification was secession, a position articulated in 1832 by some South Carolinians whose concerns went beyond tariff policy. The growing voice of antislavery activism in the North threatened the South's economic system. If and when a northern-dominated federal government decided to end slavery, the South Carolinians thought, the South must have the right to remove itself from the Union.

The Bank War and the Panic of 1837

Along with the tariff and nullification, President Jackson had another political battle on his hands over the Bank of the United States. After riding out the panic of 1819, the bank had prospered under the leadership of Philadelphian Nicholas Biddle. It handled the federal government's deposits, extended credit and loans, and issued banknotes—by 1830 the most secure and steady circulating currency in the country. With twenty-nine branches, it spread its stabilizing benefits to the whole nation. Jackson, however, did not find the bank's temperate functions sufficiently valuable to offset his criticism of the concept of a national bank. In his first and second messages to Congress, in 1829 and 1830, Jackson claimed that the bank concentrated undue economic power in the hands of a few. His Democratic allies privately hoped he would be content with antibank rhetoric, without taking concrete action.

National Republican senators Daniel Webster and Henry Clay decided to force the issue. They convinced Biddle to apply for renewal of the bank's federal charter in 1832, well before the fall election, even though the bank's twenty-year charter ran until 1836. They fully expected that Congress's renewal would force Jackson to follow through on his rhetoric with a veto. The unpopular veto would then cause Jackson to lose the election, while the bank would survive on an override vote from a new Congress swept into power in the anti-Jackson tide.

At first the plan seemed to work. Biddle applied for recharter, Congress voted to renew, and Jackson, angry over being manipulated, issued his veto. But it was a brilliantly written veto, full of fierce language about privileges of the moneyed elite who oppress the liberties of the democratic masses in order to concentrate wealth in their own hands. "Many of our rich men have not been content with equal protection and equal benefits, but have besought us to make them richer by act of Congress," Jackson wrote.

Biddle and Clay thought that Jackson's economic ideas were so absurd and his language of class antagonism so shocking that they distributed thousands of copies of the bank veto as campaign material for the National Republicans. A confident Henry Clay headed the ticket for the presidency. But they miscalculated. Jackson had translated the bank controversy into a language of class antagonism and

Darken his day lights Nick
Pat the Screw to him my Tulip!!

Blowme right if Nick ain't
been crammed too much.
You see how he 's losing
his wind.

Hurrah Nick my kiddy
let him a pelt in the
Smellers!!

Go it Hickory, my Old buffer!
give it to him in the bread
basket, it will make him
throw up his deposits !

I swan if the Ginral
haint been taken
lessons from Fuller!

Hurrah my old yallow
flower of the forrest,
walk into him like a streak
of Greased lightning through
a gooseberry bush!

FISTFIGHT BETWEEN OLD HICKORY AND BULLY NICK
This 1834 cartoon represents President Andrew Jackson squaring off to fight Nicholas Biddle, the director of the Bank of the United States. Pugilism as a semiprofessional sport gained great popularity in the 1830s; the joke here is that the aged Jackson and the aristocratic Biddle would strip to such revealing tight pants and engage in open combat. To Biddle's left are his seconds, Daniel Webster and Henry Clay; behind the president is his vice president, Martin Van Buren. Whiskey and port lubricate the action.
The Library Company of Philadelphia.

egalitarian ideals that strongly resonated with many Americans. Old Hickory won the election easily, gaining 55 percent of the popular vote and a lopsided electoral college vote of 219 to only 49 for Clay. The Jackson party still controlled Congress, so no override was possible. The bank's fate was sealed; it would cease to exist after 1836.

But Jackson took his reelection as a mandate to destroy the bank sooner. Calling the bank a "monster," he ordered the secretary of the treasury to remove the federal deposits from Biddle's vaults, ignoring the opposition of nearly his entire cabinet. The money was redeposited into "pet banks," Democratic-leaning institutions throughout the country; because of the high tariffs and high-volume sales of public lands, this government nest egg was quite sizable. In retaliation, Biddle raised interest rates and called in loans, claiming the bank's dangerously low deposits forced him to do so. This action caused a minor recession in 1833 and actually enhanced Jackson's claim that the bank was too powerful for the good of the country.

Unleashed and unregulated, the economy went into high gear, to Jackson's dismay. Perhaps only a small part of the problem arose from irresponsible banking practices; just at this moment, an excess of silver from Mexican mines had made its way into American banks, giving bankers license to print ever more banknotes. Inflation soared from 1834 to 1837; prices of basic goods rose more than 50 percent. Southern planters bought land and slaves fast, paying as much as 30 percent interest on bank loans for their purchases. Many hundreds of new private banks were quickly chartered by the states, each bank issuing its own banknotes and setting interest rates as high as the market would bear. Entrepreneurs borrowed and invested money, much of it funneled into privately financed railroads and canals.

Jackson had translated the bank controversy into a language of class antagonism and egalitarian ideals that strongly resonated with many Americans.

The market in western land sales heated up. In 1834, about 4.5 million acres of the public domain had been sold, the highest annual volume since the peak year 1819; by 1836, the total reached an astonishing 20 million acres (Figure 10.1). Some of these acres were in the South, where slave owners

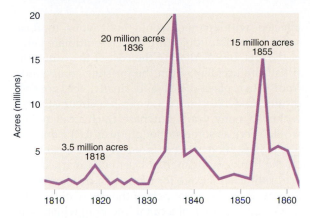

F I G U R E **10.1**

Western Land Sales, 1810–1860
Land sales peaked in the 1810s, 1830s, and 1850s as Americans rushed to speculate in western lands sold by the federal government. In particular the surges in 1818 and 1836 demonstrate the volatile, speculative economy that suddenly collapsed in the panics of 1819 and 1837.

rushed to bring under cultivation large tracts in Mississippi and Louisiana, but many more were in the North, where land offices were deluged with buyers. The Jackson administration worried that the purchasers were overwhelmingly eastern capitalists, land speculators instead of self-reliant yeoman farmers who intended to settle on the land.

In one respect, the economy attained an admirable goal: The national debt disappeared and, for the first and only time in American history, from 1835 to 1837, the government had a surplus of money. But much of it consisted of questionable bank currencies—"bloated, diseased" currencies, in Jackson's vivid terminology.

Jackson decided to restrain the economy. In 1836, the Treasury Department issued the Specie Circular, an order that public land could be purchased only with hard money, federally coined gold and silver. In response, bankers started to reduce their loans, fearing a general contraction of the economy. Compounding the difficulty, the Bank of England also now insisted on hard-money payments for American loans, which had grown large in the years since 1831 because of a trade imbalance. Some short-run failures in various crop markets, a downturn in the price of cotton on the international market, and the silver glut, all unrelated to Jackson's fiscal policies, fed the growing economic crisis.

The familiar events of the panic of 1819 unfolded again, with terrifying rapidity. In April 1837, a wave of bank and business failures ensued, and the credit market tumbled like a house of cards. (See "Documenting the American Promise," page 356.) The Specie Circular was only one precipitating cause, but the Whig Party held it and Jackson responsible for the depression. For more than five years after the panic of 1837, the United States suffered from economic hard times.

Van Buren's One-Term Presidency

The election of 1836, which preceded the panic by six months, demonstrated the transformation of the Democrats from coalition to party. The personality of Jackson had stamped the elections of 1824, 1828, and 1832, but now the party apparatus was sufficiently developed to support itself. Local and state committees existed throughout the country. Democratic candidates ran in every state election, succeeding even in old Federalist states like Maine and New Hampshire. More than four hundred newspapers declared themselves Democratic. In 1836, the Democrats repeated an innovation begun in 1832, holding a national convention that nominated Vice President Martin Van Buren of New York for president. Van Buren's running mate was Richard M. Johnson, a slave owner from Kentucky whose principal claim to fame in the campaign was the unverifiable boast that he had been the actual killer of Shawnee chief Tecumseh in 1813.

Sophisticated party organization was Martin Van Buren's specialty. Nicknamed the "Little Magician" for his consummate political skills, the Dutch New Yorker had built his career by heading the Bucktails in his state, a political coalition that pioneered many of the loyalty-enhancing techniques the Democrats used in the 1830s. After engineering a revision of his state's constitution in 1821, which implemented dramatic democratic reforms, Van Buren served as senator and then governor, leaving the latter post to become Jackson's secretary of state in 1828. He replaced Calhoun as vice president on the 1832 ticket. His eight years in the volatile Jackson administration required the full measure of his political deftness, as he sought repeatedly to save Jackson both from his enemies and from his own obstinacy.

Van Buren was a backroom politician, not a popular public figure, and the Whigs hoped that he might be defeatable. In many states, Whigs had

The Panic of 1837

*T*he wild take-off of the American economy in the mid-1830s in the wake of Jackson's bank veto was alarming to some but exhilarating to many others. Speculative fever gripped the nation, as millions hurried to lock in the promise of easy money through get-rich-quick investments in real estate, in transportation companies, in banks, and in businesses. Then suddenly, the panic of 1837 punctured the bubble. Crowds of hundreds thronged banks in many cities to try to recover their money. Business came to a standstill and many merchants appeared to be ruined overnight.

DOCUMENT 1. An English Visitor Describes the "Mania" for Speculation, 1836

Harriet Martineau traveled throughout the United States and described booming land sales in the infant city of Chicago.

I never saw a busier place than Chicago was at the time of our arrival. The streets were crowded with land speculators, hurrying from one sale to another. A negro, dressed up in scarlet, bearing a scarlet flag, and riding a white horse with housings of scarlet, announced the times of sale. At every street-corner where he stopped, the crowd flocked round him; and it seemed as if some prevalent mania infected the whole people. The rage for speculation might fairly be so regarded. As the gentlemen of our party walked the streets, store-keepers hailed them from their doors, with offers of farms, and all manner of land-lots, advising them to speculate before the price of land rose higher. A young lawyer of my acquaintance there, had realised five hundred dollars per day, the five preceding days, by merely making out titles to land. . . . Of course, this rapid money-making is a merely temporary evil. A bursting of the bubble must come soon. The absurdity of the speculation is so striking, that the wonder is that the fever should have attained such a height as I witnessed. The immediate occasion of the bustle which prevailed, the week we were at Chicago, was the sale of lots . . . along the course of a projected canal. . . . Persons not intending to game, and not infected with mania, would endeavour to form some reasonable conjecture as to the ultimate value of the lots, by calculating the cost of the canal, the risks from accident, from the possible competition from other places, &c., and finally, the possible profits, under the most favourable circumstances, within so many years' purchase. Such a calculation would serve as some sort of guide as to the amount of purchase-money to be risked. Whereas, wild land on the banks of a canal, not yet even marked out, was selling at Chicago for more than rich land, well improved, in the finest part of the valley of the Mohawk, on the banks of a canal [the Erie] which is already the medium of an almost inestimable amount of traffic. If sharpers and gamblers were to be the sufferers by the impending crash at Chicago, no one would feel much concerned: but they, unfortunately, are the people who encourage the delusion, in order to profit by it. Many a high-spirited, but inexperienced, young man; many a simple settler, will be ruined for the advantage of knaves.

SOURCE: Harriet Martineau, *Society in America* (London, 1837), 350–52, reprinted in David Brion Davis, *Antebellum American Culture: An Interpretive Anthology* (Lexington, Mass.: D. C. Heath, 1979), 121–22.

DOCUMENT 2. The Diary of Philip Hone, March–May 1837

Philip Hone, a wealthy New York Whig, had an early taste of the crash to come when his son's business failed in March, on the last day of President Jackson's term. By May, the national house of cards was in total ruins.

Saturday, March 4.—This is the end of Gen. Jackson's administration—the most disastrous in the annals of the country. . . .

This is a dark and melancholy day in the annals of my family. Brown & Hone stopped payment to-day, and called a meeting of their creditors. My eldest son has lost the capital I gave him, and I am implicated as endorser for them to a fearful amount. The pressure of the times, the immense amount they have paid of extra interest, and the almost total failure of remittances have been the causes of their ruin. . . .

Friday, March 17.—The great crisis is near at hand, if it has not already arrived. The banking house of I. and L. Joseph . . . stopped payment to-day, and occasioned great consternation in Wall Street, for their business has been enormous. . . . The immediate cause of this disaster was the intelligence received from New Orleans by this day's mail of the stoppage of the House of Hermann & Co. and others connected with them, for whom the Josephs are under acceptances to the amount of two millions of dollars. This is another evidence of the reckless manner in which business has been conducted, or rather, to speak more charitably, of the straits to which men have been driven by the wicked interference of the government with the currency of the country. . . .

Wednesday, May 10.— . . . The volcano has burst and overwhelmed New York; the glory of her merchants is departed. After a day of unexampled excitement, and a ruthless run upon all the banks, which drew from their vaults $600,000 in specie yesterday, nearly as much having been drawn on Monday, the officers held a meeting last evening and resolved to *suspend specie payments*. . . .

Thursday, May 11.—A dead calm has succeeded the stormy weather of Wall Street and the other places of active business. All is still as death. No business is transacted, no bargains made, no negotiations entered into; men's spirits are better because the danger of universal ruin is thought to be less imminent. A slight ray of hope is to be seen in countenances where despair only dwelt for the last fortnight, but all is wrapped up in uncertainty. Nobody can foretell the course matters will take. The fever is broken, but the patient lies in a sort of syncope, exhausted by the violence of the disease and the severity of the remedies.

SOURCE: Allan Nevins, ed., *The Diary of Philip Hone, 1828–1851* (New York: Dodd Mead, 1936), 244, 248–49, 257, 259.

DOCUMENT 3. A Religious View of "Existing Commercial Embarrassments," July 1837

The July 1837 issue of the Christian Examiner, *a Boston monthly, counseled that some good would come from the catastrophe.*

There will be then much individual improvement of character. . . . One of the first and most valuable . . . will be a check upon that extravagant estimate and overstrained pursuit of wealth, which are marked features in the character of the nation and the times. That such a check was needed and will be a blessing to the social and moral condition of the community, cannot be doubted. We were getting to be almost insane upon the subject of wealth. The lust of accumulation has ever been the root of much evil among men, but in this country several causes have naturally operated to give a strong impulse to this passion. Our political organization is that which offers the widest scope to enterprise, and applies the strongest stimulus to ambition and exertion, while, at the same time, it produces a state of society in which wealth is necessarily the principal distinction, the surest and readiest of attainment, and therefore the first and most eagerly sought. . . . A new country like ours, of almost unbounded extent, rich beyond comparison in resources, . . . naturally awakens in its inhabitants earnest and insatiable desires. . . .

. . . Great benefits have . . . flowed from . . . enterprise. . . . Towns have been built and cities reared, mountains levelled, and valleys filled, and distant places brought near, and the wide wilderness of nature changed to a garden of human civilization, comfort, and luxury. . . .

But the moral influence of these causes has not all been good. They were making us proud, presumptuous, extravagant, luxurious, visionary. We were getting to think that there was no end to the wealth, and could be no check to the progress of our country; that economy was not needed, that prudence was weakness, that moderation was a sinful neglect of the golden chances by which many were winning fortunes. The tardy gains of honorable enterprise were spurned, that the lucky speculation of an hour might bestow a fortune. We needed a check, a restraint, a rebuke. Many felt that it was needed and foresaw that it must come, and he who ruleth over the nations has at length sent it. As in other general calamities, the evil in many individual cases falls on those who may not themselves have been guilty, but the benefit will be reaped by all. The fever which has raged in society will abate.

SOURCE: "Existing Commercial Embarrassments," *Christian Examiner and General Review* 22, 3rd ser., vol. 4 (1837): 395–96. *(Continued)*

QUESTIONS FOR ANALYSIS AND DEBATE

1. How could Martineau, a foreigner, so readily predict that the economic bubble would soon burst? Do you think the buyers and sellers in Chicago whom she describes could also predict it? Who really was making money in the Chicago she observed?

2. What does Hone's diary entry tell you about the interconnections among many businesses? Who or what does Hone blame for the crash?

3. In the *Christian Examiner*'s interpretation, what caused the panic? Are American enterprise and ambition good or bad, in this view? What characteristics of American society stimulated the "lust of accumulation"?

---

captured high office in 1834, shedding the awkward National Republican label and developing statewide organizations to rival those of the Democrats. However, no figure at the national level could command support in all regions; Massachusetts Senator Daniel Webster, for example, had no following in the South, a heavily pro-Jackson region. The result was that three candidates opposed Van Buren in 1836, each with a solid popular regional base. Webster could deliver New England; Tennessee Senator Hugh Lawson White attracted proslavery, pro-Jackson, but anti–Van Buren voters in the South; and the aging General William Henry Harrison of Indiana, memorable for his Indian war heroics in 1811, pulled in the western, anti-Indian vote. Not one of the three candidates could have won the presidency, but together they came close to denying Van Buren a majority vote. Their combined strength pulled many Whigs into office at the state level and laid the groundwork for an alternative to the Democrats in the South, an area that had been solidly pro-Jackson until 1836. In the end, Van Buren had 170 electoral votes, while the other three received a total of 113.

Van Buren took office in March 1837, and a month later the panic hit. The new president called a special session of Congress to consider creating an independent treasury system to fulfill some of the functions of the defunct Bank of the United States. Such a system, funded by the government's deposits, would deal only in hard money, and gold and silver would flow out of commercial banks, with restrictions on their issuance of paper currency. Equally important, the new system would not make loans and would thus avoid the danger of speculative meddling in the economy. In short, an independent treasury system could exert a powerful moderating influence on inflation and the credit market without itself being directly involved in the market. But Van Buren encountered strong resistance in Congress, even from Democrats. The treasury system finally won approval in 1840; by then, however, Van Buren's chances of a second term in office were virtually nil. The four years had proved to be tumultuous for the economy, with federal bank policy at a stalemate while twenty-six separate state legislatures battled over controversial bank regulation.

In 1840, the Whigs settled on William Henry Harrison, sixty-seven, as their single candidate to oppose Van Buren. The campaign drew on voter involvement as no other presidential campaign ever had. The Whigs took tricks out of the Democrats' book: Harrison was touted as a common man born in a log cabin, although a Virginia plantation was the real site. His Indian-fighting days, now thirty years behind him, were played up to give him an aura like that of Jackson. Whigs staged festive rallies all over the country, drumming up mass appeal with candlelight parades and song shows. Women participated in Whig campaign rallies as never before. Some 78 percent of eligible voters cast ballots—the highest percentage ever in American history. Even so, the campaign was not really close. Harrison took 53 percent of the popular vote and won a resounding 234 electoral college votes, to Van Buren's 60. A Democratic editor lamented, "We have taught them how to conquer us!"

Conclusion: Democrats and Whigs

From 1828 to 1840, the Democrats put together an unlikely, tenuous, but ultimately workable coalition of rural western farmers, urban laborers, pro–state bank commercial men, and wealthy southern slave owners. These groups embraced personal liberty, free competition, and egalitarian opportunity for all white men, all values symbolized by Andrew Jackson. Jacksonian Democrats accepted drinking and tolerated Sabbath violations, preferring not to legislate morality. They avoided debating the wisdom of slavery at all costs.

In contrast, the Whigs were the party of activist moralism and state-sponsored entrepreneurship. Wealthy merchants from Boston to Savannah who appreciated a national bank and protective tariffs tended to be Whigs, as did the evangelical middle classes. Personal liberty must be tempered by self-discipline and backed by government controls over moral issues, Whigs asserted, favoring laws that prohibited liquor sales or stagecoach travel on Sundays. Abolitionists tended to vote for Whigs, even though most Whig politicians shied away from antislavery ideas.

National politics in the 1830s were more heated and divisive than at any other time since the 1790s. The party system of Democrats and Whigs cut far deeper into the electorate than had the system of Federalists and Republicans. Innovations in transportation and communication disseminated political information from the city to the backwoods, politicizing voters who now understood what they might gain or lose under the competing economic policies of the two parties. Politics acquired immediacy and excitement, causing nearly four out of five white men to cast a ballot in 1840.

High rates of voter participation would continue into the 1840s and 1850s, because politics remained the arena where different choices about economic development and social change were contested. Unprecedented urban growth, westward expansion, and early industrialism marked those decades, sustaining the Jacksonian-Whig split in the electorate. But other new challenges not easily dealt with by those two parties—critiques of slavery, concerns for free labor, and an emerging protest against women's second-class citizenship—complicated the political scene of the 1840s, leading to third-party movements that splintered from the two parties of the 1830s. One of these third parties, called the Republican Party, would achieve dominance in 1860 with the election of an Illinois lawyer, Abraham Lincoln, to the presidency.

www.bedfordstmartins.com/tap   SEE THE ONLINE STUDY GUIDE to assess your mastery of the material covered in this chapter.

CHRONOLOGY

1807 Robert Fulton develops first commercially successful steamboat, *Clermont*.

1814 Francis Cabot Lowell and others establish textile mill at Waltham, Massachusetts.

1816 Second Bank of the United States chartered for twenty years.

Import tariff imposed on foreign textiles.

1817 American Colonization Society founded to promote gradual emancipation and removal of African Americans to Liberia.

1818 National Road links Baltimore and Wheeling, West Virginia.

1819 Economic collapse and panic nationwide.

1821 F. C. Lowell and business associates start to build mills with power looms at Lowell, Massachusetts.

1824 Congress passes expanded tariff bill.

1825 Erie Canal spans 350 miles in New York State.

1826 Schuylkill Canal—108 miles long— opens in Pennsylvania.

1828 Tariff of Abominations passed.

Andrew Jackson elected president.

1829 David Walker's *An Appeal to the Colored Citizens of the World* published in Boston.

Baltimore and Ohio Railroad lays 13 miles of tracks.

1830 Indian Removal Act appropriates money to relocate Indian tribes west of Mississippi River.

1831 William Lloyd Garrison begins publishing abolitionist newspaper *Liberator*.

Charles G. Finney stages evangelical revival in Rochester, New York.

Supreme Court allows Georgia to continue to subject Indians to state laws.

1832 Supreme Court in *Worcester v. Georgia* recognizes Cherokees as distinct community outside legal jurisdiction of Georgia.

Jackson vetoes Bank of the United States charter.

New England Anti-Slavery Society founded.

Andrew Jackson reelected president.

1833 Nullification crisis: South Carolina declares federal tariffs void in the state.

New York and Philadelphia Anti-Slavery Societies founded.

1834, 1836 Female mill workers strike in Lowell, Massachusetts.

1836 Jackson issues Specie Circular.

Martin Van Buren elected president.

1837 Economic panic.

1838 Trail of Tears—Cherokees forced to relocate west.

1840 William Henry Harrison elected president.

BIBLIOGRAPHY

GENERAL WORKS

Daniel Feller, *The Jacksonian Promise: America, 1815–1840* (1995).

Michael F. Holt, *Political Parties and American Political Development from the Age of Jackson to the Age of Lincoln* (1992).

Merrill D. Peterson, *The Great Triumvirate: Webster, Clay, and Calhoun* (1987).

Charles G. Sellers, *The Market Revolution: Jacksonian America, 1815–1846* (1991).

Harry L. Watson, *Liberty and Power: The Politics of Jacksonian America* (1990).

Robert H. Wiebe, *The Opening of American Society: From the Adoption of the Constitution to the Eve of Disunion* (1984).

THE MARKET REVOLUTION

Elizabeth Blackmar, *Manhattan for Rent, 1785–1850* (1989).

Mary H. Blewett, *Men, Women, and Work: Class, Gender, and Protest in the New England Shoe Industry, 1780–1910* (1988).

Jeanne Boydston, *Home and Work: Housework, Wages, and the Ideology of Labor in the Early Republic* (1990).

Christopher Clark, *The Roots of Rural Capitalism: Worcester, Massachusetts, 1780–1860* (1990).

Alan Dawley, *Class and Community: The Industrial Revolution in Lynn* (1976).

Thomas Dublin, *Women at Work: The Transformation of Work and Community in Lowell, Massachusetts, 1826–1860* (1979).

Thomas Dublin, *Transforming Women's Work: New England Lives in the Industrial Revolution* (1994).

Tony A. Freyer, *Producers versus Capitalists: Constitutional Conflict in Antebellum America* (1994).

Paul A. Gilje, ed., *Wages of Independence: Capitalism in the Early Republic* (1997).

Erik F. Haites, James Mak, and Gary M. Walton, *Western River Transportation: The Era of Early Internal Development, 1800–1860* (1975).

Morton J. Horwitz, *The Transformation of American Law, 1780–1860* (1977).

Bruce Laurie, *Artisans into Workers: Labor in Nineteenth-Century America* (1989).

John D. Majewski, *A House Dividing: Economic Development in Pennsylvania and Virginia before the Civil War* (2000).

Otto Mayr and Robert C. Post, eds., *Yankee Enterprise: The Rise of the American System of Manufactures* (1981).

Carol Sheriff, *The Artificial River: The Erie Canal and the Paradox of Progress, 1817–1862* (1996).

Richard B. Stott, *Workers in the Metropolis: Class, Ethnicity, and Youth in Antebellum New York City* (1990).

Christopher L. Tomlins, *Law, Labor, and Ideology in the Early American Republic* (1993).

Barbara Tucker, *Samuel Slater and the Origins of the American Textile Industry, 1790–1860* (1984).

THE SPREAD OF DEMOCRACY

Ronald P. Formisano, *The Birth of Mass Political Parties: Michigan, 1827–1861* (1971).

Paul Goodman, *Towards a Christian Republic: Antimasonry and the Great Transition in New England, 1826–1836* (1988).

Daniel W. Howe, *The Political Culture of the American Whigs* (1980).

Lawrence Frederick Kohl, *The Politics of Individualism: Parties and the American Character in the Jacksonian Era* (1989).

Robert V. Remini, *Andrew Jackson and the Course of American Freedom, 1822–1832* (1981).

Alexander Saxton, *The Rise and Fall of the White Republic: Class Politics and Mass Culture in Nineteenth-Century America* (1990).

Sean Wilentz, *Chants Democratic: New York City and the Rise of the American Working Class, 1788–1850* (1984).

CULTURE AND SOCIETY

Gerald J. Baldasty, *The Commercialization of News in the Nineteenth Century* (1992).

Stuart M. Blumin, *The Emergence of the Middle Class: Social Experience in the American City, 1760–1900* (1989).

Richard L. Bushman, *The Refinement of America: Persons, Houses, Cities* (1992).

Kenneth Cmiel, *Democratic Eloquence: The Fight over Popular Speech in Nineteenth-Century America* (1990).

Patricia Cline Cohen, *The Murder of Helen Jewett: The Life and Death of a Prostitute in Nineteenth-Century New York* (1998).

Faye E. Dudden, *Women in the American Theatre: Actresses and Audiences, 1790–1870* (1994).

Ann Fabian, *Card-Sharps, Dream Books, and Bucket Shops: Gambling in Nineteenth-Century America* (1990).

Timothy J. Gilfoyle, *City of Eros: New York City, Prostitution, and the Commercialization of Sex, 1790–1920* (1992).

Karen Halttunen, *Confidence Men and Painted Women: A Study of Middle-Class Culture in America, 1830–1870* (1982).

Richard R. John, *Spreading the News: The American Postal System from Franklin to Morse* (1995).

Carl F. Kaestle, *Pillars of the Republic: Common Schools and American Society, 1780–1860* (1983).

John F. Kasson, *Rudeness and Civility: Manners in Nineteenth-Century America* (1990).

Lawrence W. Levine, *Highbrow/Lowbrow: The Emergence of Cultural Hierarchy in America* (1988).

Lewis Perry, *Boats against the Current: American Culture between Revolution and Modernity, 1820–1860* (1993).

E. Anthony Rotundo, *American Manhood: Transformations in Masculinity from the Revolution to the Modern Era* (1993).

Mary P. Ryan, *Women in Public: Between Banners and Ballots, 1825–1880* (1990).

Carroll Smith-Rosenberg, *Disorderly Conduct: Visions of Gender in Victorian America* (1985).

Christine Stansell, *City of Women: Sex and Class in New York, 1789–1860* (1986).

Alan Taylor, *William Cooper's Town: Power and Persuasion on the Frontier of the Early American Republic* (1995).

Ronald J. Zboray, *A Fictive People: Antebellum Development and the American Reading Public* (1993).

REFORM AND RELIGION

Robert Abzug, *Cosmos Crumbling: American Reform and the Religious Imagination* (1994).

R. J. M. Blackett, *Building an Antislavery Wall: Black Americans in the Atlantic Abolitionist Movement, 1830–1860* (1983).

Ellen Eslinger, *Citizens of Zion: The Social Origins of Camp Meeting Revivalism* (1999).

Lawrence J. Friedman, *Gregarious Saints: Self and Community in American Abolitionism, 1830–1870* (1982).

Lori D. Ginzberg, *Women and the Work of Benevolence: Morality, Politics, and Class in the Nineteenth-Century United States* (1990).

Charles E. Hambrick-Stowe, *Charles G. Finney and the Spirit of American Evangelicalism* (1996).

Nathan O. Hatch, *The Democratization of American Christianity* (1989).

Nancy A. Hewitt, *Women's Activism and Social Change: Rochester, New York, 1822–1872* (1984).

Christine Leigh Heyrman, *Southern Cross: The Beginnings of the Bible Belt* (1997).

Donald M. Jacobs, ed., *Courage and Conscience: Black and White Abolitionists in Boston* (1993).

Julie Roy Jeffrey, *The Great Silent Army of Abolitionism: Ordinary Women in the Antislavery Movement* (1998).

Paul Johnson, *A Shopkeeper's Millennium: Society and Revivals in Rochester, New York, 1815–1837* (1978).

Katharine Du Pré Lumpkin, *The Emancipation of Angelina Grimké* (1974).

Steven Mintz, *Moralists and Modernizers: America's Pre–Civil War Reformers* (1995).

Mary P. Ryan, *Cradle of the Middle Class: The Family in Oneida County, New York, 1790–1865* (1981).

Ian Tyrrell, *Sobering Up: From Temperance to Prohibition in Antebellum America, 1800–1860* (1979).

Jean Fagan Yellin and John C. Van Horne, eds., *The Abolitionist Sisterhood: Women's Political Culture in Antebellum America* (1994).

JACKSONIAN POLITICS

Irving H. Bartlett, *John C. Calhoun: A Biography* (1993).

Maurice G. Baxter, *Henry Clay and the American System* (1995).

Donald B. Cole, *The Presidency of Andrew Jackson* (1993).

Richard E. Ellis, *The Union at Risk: Jacksonian Democracy, States' Rights, and the Nullification Crisis* (1987).

Daniel Feller, *The Public Lands in Jacksonian Politics* (1984).

William W. Freehling, *Prelude to Civil War: The Nullification Controversy in South Carolina, 1816–1836* (1965).

Michael F. Holt, *The Rise and Fall of the American Whig Party: Jacksonian Politics and the Onset of the Civil War* (1999).

Peter B. Knupfer, *The Union as It Is: Constitutional Unionism and Sectional Compromise, 1787–1861* (1991).

Richard B. Latner, *The Presidency of Andrew Jackson: White House Politics, 1829–1837* (1979).

John Niven, *Martin Van Buren: The Romantic Age of American Politics* (1983).

John Niven, *John C. Calhoun and the Price of Union: A Biography* (1988).

Lynn Hudson Parsons, *John Quincy Adams* (1998).

Robert V. Remini, *Henry Clay: Statesman for the Union* (1991).

Robert V. Remini, *Daniel Webster: The Man and His Time* (1997).

Leonard Richards, *The Life and Times of Congressman John Quincy Adams* (1986).

NATIVE AMERICANS

John A. Andrew, *From Revivals to Removal: Jeremiah Evarts, the Cherokee Nation, and the Search for the Soul of America* (1992).

Theda Perdue, *Cherokee Women: Gender and Culture Change, 1700–1835* (1998).

Theda Perdue and Michael D. Green, eds., *The Cherokee Removal: A Brief History with Documents* (1995).

Michael Paul Rogin, *Fathers and Children: Andrew Jackson and the Subjugation of the American Indian* (1975).

Anthony F. C. Wallace, *The Long, Bitter Trail: Andrew Jackson and the Indians* (1993).

Philip Weeks, *Farewell, My Nation: The American Indian and the United States, 1820–1890* (1990).

J. Leitch Wright, *The Only Land They Knew: The Tragic Story of the American Indians in the Old South* (1981).

SHAKO HAT

American soldiers fighting in the Mexican War were a colorful lot. Their dress uniform was a dark blue wool tailcoat worn with sky-blue wool trousers and topped with the shako, a full-dress cap made of leather, crowned with black feathers, and adorned with a decorative plate showing the eagle spreading its wings—the symbol of manifest destiny. Even everyday uniforms often included lace on collars and cuffs, silk sashes and scarves, and fringed epaulettes.

One veteran criticized the army for "dressing up men within an inch of their lives, until they looked more like a flock of eastern flamingos . . . than the descendants of the race of men who fought and bled to establish civil liberty and republican simplicity in our country." General Winfield Scott, "Old Fuss and Feathers," expected his troops to follow "regulations of dress, hair, whiskers, and so forth." Other commanders, most notably General Zachary Taylor, were notoriously lax. One junior officer serving under Taylor observed: "We wear all kinds of uniforms here, each one to his taste, some shirtsleeves, some white, some purple, some fancy jackets and all colors of cottonelle pants, some straw and some Quaker hats, and that is just the way, too, that our fellows went into battle." However they dressed, American soldiers in Mexico employed some of the world's most modern and innovative weapons.

Chicago Historical Society.

THE FREE NORTH AND WEST

11

1840–1860

EARLY IN NOVEMBER 1842, Abraham Lincoln and his new wife, Mary, moved into their first home in Springfield, Illinois, a rented room measuring eight by fourteen feet on the second floor of the Globe Tavern, the nicest place Abraham had ever lived. Next door a busy blacksmith shop filled the Lincoln's small room with the cacophony of iron being pounded into horseshoes, hinges, and other useful shapes. Mary Todd Lincoln had grown up in Lexington, Kentucky, attended by slaves in the elegant home of her father, a prosperous merchant, banker, and politician. The small, noisy room above the Globe Tavern was the worst place she had ever lived. Fewer than twenty years later, in March 1861, the Lincolns moved into what would prove to be their last home, the presidential mansion in Washington, D.C. Abraham Lincoln climbed from the Globe Tavern to the White House by relentless work, unslaked ambition, and immense talent, traits he had honed since boyhood.

Born in a Kentucky log cabin in 1809, Lincoln grew up on small, struggling farms. His father, Thomas, never learned to read and, Abraham explained, "never did more in the way of writing than to bunglingly sign his own name." Lincoln's mother, Nancy, could neither read nor write. In December 1816, Thomas Lincoln moved his young family out of Kentucky, crossing the Ohio River to the Indiana wilderness. They lived for two frozen months in a crude lean-to only partially enclosed by limbs and bushes while Thomas, a skilled carpenter, built a new cabin. There Abraham learned the arts of farming practiced by families throughout the nation. Although only eight years old, Abraham "had an axe put into his hands at once" and used it "almost constantly" for the next fifteen years, he recalled. He worked for neighbors for twenty-five cents a day and gave the money to his father. When he could be spared from work, the boy attended school, less than a year in all. "There was absolutely nothing to excite ambition for education," Lincoln recollected. In contrast, Mary Todd, his future wife, received ten years of schooling in Lexington's best academies for young women.

By 1830, Thomas Lincoln decided to start over once again. With Abraham astraddle one of the family's oxen, the Lincolns moved two hundred miles west to central Illinois. Once again the Lincolns built a log cabin and Abraham pitched in to make "sufficient of rails to fence ten acres of ground . . . [then] broke the ground, and raised a crop of sown corn upon it the same year." The next spring Thomas Lincoln moved again, and this time Abraham set out on his own, a "friendless, uneducated, penniless boy," as he described himself.

By dogged striving, Lincoln gained an education and the respect of his Illinois neighbors, although a steady income eluded him for years. He also received help from his father-in-law. Shortly after Lincoln married, Mary's father gave the young

ABRAHAM LINCOLN'S HAT
Abraham Lincoln wore this stovepipe hat, made of beaver pelt, during his years as president of the United States. Stovepipe hats were worn by established, respectable, middle-class men in the 1850s. Workingmen and farmers would have felt out of place wearing such a hat, except perhaps on special occasions like weddings or funerals. Growing up in Kentucky, Indiana, and Illinois, Lincoln may have seen stovepipe hats on the leading men of his community, but he probably never owned one until he became an aspiring Illinois lawyer and politician. Wearing such a hat was a mark that one had achieved a certain success in life, in Lincoln's case the enormous social distance he had traveled from his backwoods origins to the White House. But even as president he continued a backwoods practice he had begun as a young postmaster in New Salem, Illinois, using his hat as a place to store letters and papers. Lincoln's law partner William Herndon termed Lincoln's hat "an extraordinary receptacle [that] served as his desk and memorandum book."
Smithsonian Institution.

couple eighty acres of land and promised a yearly allowance of about $1,100 for six years, helping them to move out of their room above the Globe Tavern after one year. Lincoln eventually built a prosperous law practice in Springfield and served in the Illinois legislature and in Congress. Even though he did not hold office during the 1850s, his political activity and hard-driving ambition won him a large and admiring following that ultimately catapulted him into the White House.

Like Lincoln, millions of Americans believed they could make something of themselves, what-

ever their origins, so long as they were willing to work. Individuals who refused to work—who were lazy, improvident, or foolish—had only themselves to blame if they failed. Work was a prerequisite for success, not a guarantee. The promise of rewards from hard work spurred efforts that shaped the contours of America, pushing the boundaries of the nation south to the Rio Grande and west to the Pacific Ocean. That expansion—economic, political, and geographic—also raised anew the question of slavery that Lincoln ultimately confronted as president.

Economic and Industrial Evolution

During the 1840s and 1850s, Lincoln and other Americans lived amidst profound economic transformation that had been under way since the start of the nineteenth century. By 1860, the nation's population numbered over 31 million and the total output of the American economy had multiplied twelvefold since 1800. Four fundamental changes in American society fueled this phenomenal economic growth.

First, Americans began to move from farms to cities, a long-term shift that would continue well into the twentieth century. In 1860, farmers still made up 80 percent of the nation's population. But Abraham Lincoln and millions of other Americans left farms behind, boosting the urban population. By 1860, the nation had 186 towns about the size of Springfield, Illinois (9,500 people), and 16 cities with 50,000 or more.

A second major change, closely related to the movement away from farms, was that a growing number of Americans worked in factories, by 1860 almost 20 percent of the labor force. This trend contributed to the nation's economic growth because, in general, factory workers were twice as productive (in output per unit of labor input) as agricultural workers.

A third fundamental change—from water to steam as a source of energy—permitted factories to be more productive. Beginning around 1840, steam became harnessed to manufacturing, but the transition was slow, delayed by the continued effectiveness of water and animal power. By 1850, for example, animal and human muscles still provided thirty-three times more energy for manufacturing than steam.

The shortage of cheap, plentiful fuel had prevented earlier use of steam in factories. But during the 1830s, extensive mining began in Pennsylvania coal fields and massive quantities of coal became available for industrial fuel. Not only did coal provide heat to power steam engines in factories, it also coupled steam power to land transportation with the building of railroads.

This cascade of interrelated developments— steam, coal, iron, mechanization, railroads—had begun to transform the character of the American economy by the 1850s. Historians have often referred to this transformation as an industrial revolution. Certainly the profound changes in the American economy in these years pushed the nation toward industrialization. Yet those changes did not cause a revolutionary discontinuity in the economy or society. The United States remained overwhelmingly agricultural. Old methods of production continued alongside the new. Changes in production tended to be evolutionary and cumulative. Before 1860, the American economy underwent a process that might best be termed "industrial evolution."

That evolution was made possible by a fourth fundamental development that propelled American economic growth. Agricultural productivity (defined as crop output per unit of labor input) nearly doubled during Lincoln's lifetime. This dramatic increase contributed more than any other single factor to the economic growth of the era. While cities, factories, and steam engines blossomed throughout the nation—especially in the North and West— the roots of American economic growth lay in agriculture.

Agriculture and Land Policy

It may seem odd to consider an ax a basic agricultural tool, like a hoe or a shovel. Yet farmers needed axes. A French traveler observed that Americans had "a general feeling of hatred against trees" and taught their children "at an early age to use the axe against the trees, their enemies." Although the traveler exaggerated, his observation contained an important truth. Forests impeded agriculture. With axes—which Lincoln termed "that most useful instrument"—farmers leveled trees, cleared land for planting, and built cabins, fences, and barns.

The sheer physical labor required to convert forest to field limited agricultural productivity. Energy that might have gone to growing crops went instead to felling trees. But as farmers pushed west-

ward, they encountered thinner forests and eventually the Midwest's comparatively treeless prairie, where they could spend less time with an ax and more time at the plow or hoe, significantly boosting agricultural productivity. Rich prairie soils also gave somewhat higher crop yields than eastern farms, and farmers migrated to the Midwest by the tens of thousands between 1830 and 1860. The population of Indiana, Illinois, Michigan, Wisconsin, and Iowa exploded tenfold, growing from 500,000 in 1830 to more than 5 million by 1860, four times faster than the growth of the nation as a whole. During the 1850s, Illinois added more people than any other state in the Union.

While cities, factories, and steam engines blossomed throughout the nation—especially in the North and West—the roots of American economic growth lay in agriculture.

Labor-saving improvements in other farm implements also hiked agricultural productivity. Frontier farmers commonly planted their first crop by chopping a hole in the ground with an ax or hoe and then dropping in a few kernels of corn. The cast-iron plow in use since the 1820s proved too weak for the thick turf and dense soil of the midwestern prairie. In 1837, John Deere patented a strong, smooth steel plow that sliced through prairie soil so cleanly that farmers called it the "singing plow." Deere's company became the leading plow manufacturer in the Midwest, turning out more than ten thousand plows a year by the late 1850s. By 1860, the energy for plowing still came from two- and four-legged animals, but better plows permitted that energy to break more ground and plant more crops.

Improvements in wheat harvesting also multiplied farmers' productivity. Early in the nineteenth century, farmers harvested wheat by cutting the stalks with a sharp-bladed scythe. Working hard, a farmer could scythe three-fourths of an acre of wheat a day. By 1850, most farmers had adopted scythes with cradles (a frame that projected above the scythe). The long fingers of the cradles gathered more grain to be cut by each stroke of the attached blade. Farmers could now harvest two or three acres of wheat a day, but the work remained backbreaking. Tinkerers throughout the nation tried to

HARVESTING GRAIN WITH CRADLES
This late-nineteenth-century painting shows the grain harvest during the mid-nineteenth century at Bishop Hill, Illinois, a Swedish community where the artist, Olof Krans, and his parents settled in 1850. The men swing cradles, slowly cutting a swath through the grain; the women gather the cut grain into sheaves to be hauled away later for threshing. As a well-organized community, Bishop Hill could call upon the labor of a large number of men and women at harvest time. Most farmers had only a few family members and a hired hand or two to help with the harvest. Note that although the grain field appears level enough to be ideal for a mechanical reaper, all the work is done by hand; no machine is in sight.
Bishop Hill State Historic Site, Illinois Historic Preservation Agency.

fashion a mechanical reaper that would make the wheat harvest easier and quicker. Cyrus Mc-Cormick and others experimented with designs until the late 1840s, when mechanical reapers began to appear in American wheat fields. A McCormick reaper that cost between $100 and $150 allowed a farmer to harvest up to twelve acres a day, at least when it worked. By 1860, about eighty thousand reapers had been sold. Although reapers represented the cutting edge of agricultural technology, they still had to be powered by a horse or an ox. Most farmers continued to muscle the heavy cradle through their grain. Neither reapers nor plows in-

creased the yield of a given acre of cultivated land. Instead, they allowed more land to be brought into cultivation: The labor farmers saved could be used to plow and plant more land. Without access to fresh, uncultivated land, farmers could not have doubled the corn and wheat harvests between 1840 and 1860, as they did.

In the end, the agricultural productivity that fueled the nation's economy was an outgrowth of federal land policy. Up to 1860, the United States continued to be land rich and labor poor. During the nineteenth century, the nation became a great deal richer in land, acquiring more than a billion acres with the Louisiana Purchase and the annexation of Florida, Oregon, and vast territories following the Mexican War (discussed later in this chapter). The federal government made the land available for purchase to attract settlers and to generate revenues. Although federal land cost only $1.25 an acre, millions of Americans could not afford to pay $50 for a forty-acre farm. They squatted on unclaimed federal land and carved out a farm they neither rented nor owned. Many poor farmers never accumulated enough money to purchase the land on which they squatted, and eventually they moved elsewhere, often to squat again on unclaimed federal land.

In addition to aiding small farmers, government land policy enriched wily speculators who found ways to claim large tracts of the most desirable plots and sell them to settlers at a generous markup. Nonetheless, by making land available to millions of ordinary people, the federal government achieved the goal of attracting settlers to the new territories in the West, which in due course joined the Union as new states. Above all, federal land policy created the basic precondition for the increase in agricultural productivity that underlay the nation's impressive economic growth.

Manufacturing and Mechanization

Changes in manufacturing arose in the context of the nation's land-rich, labor-poor economy. England and other European countries had land-poor, labor-rich economies; there, meager opportunities in agriculture kept factory laborers plentiful and wages low. In the United States, geographical expansion and government land policies buoyed agriculture, keeping millions of people on the farm and thereby limiting the supply of workers for manufacturing and elevating wages. Because of this shortage of workers, manufacturers searched constantly for ways to save labor.

Mechanization marched forward as quickly as manufacturers could turn innovative ideas into workable combinations of gears, levers, screws, and pulleys. Outside the textile industry (see chapter 10), homegrown machines set the pace. The practice of manufacturing and then assembling interchangeable parts spread from gun making to other industries and became known as the "American system." Clock makers used it; sewing machine makers used it; even ax makers used it. Mechanization became so integral to American manufacturing that some machinists specialized in what was

called the machine tool industry. That is, they built machines that made parts for other machines that in turn produced goods for general consumption. Nothing better illustrated the transformation in American manufacturing than this mechanization of machine making.

Manufacturing and agriculture meshed into a dynamic national economy. New England led the nation in manufacturing, shipping products like clocks, guns, and axes west and south, while commodities like wheat, pork, whiskey, tobacco, and cotton flowed north and east. Manufacturers specialized in producing for the gigantic domestic market rather than for export. British goods dominated the international market and, on the whole, they were cheaper and better than American-made products. U.S. manufacturers supported tariffs to minimize British competition, but their best protection from British competitors was to strive harder to please their American customers, the vast majority of whom were farmers.

Throughout American manufacturing, hand labor continued to be an essential component of production, despite the advances in mechanization. Even in heavily mechanized industries, factories remained fairly small, few having more than twenty or thirty employees. But the industrial evolution under way before 1860 would quicken later in the nineteenth century; railroads were a harbinger of that future.

Railroads: Breaking the Bonds of Nature

To a degree unequaled by any other industry, railroads incorporated the most advanced developments of the age: steam energy; massive locomotives; mile after mile of iron rails; boldly engineered bridges vaulting rivers and chasms; unprecedented sums of money to undertake these tasks; and large, complex organizations to keep the trains running efficiently, safely, and on time. No wonder a Swedish visitor in 1849 noticed that American schoolboys constantly doodled sketches of locomotives, always smoking, always in motion.

Railroads captured Americans' imaginations in part because they seemed to break the bonds of nature. When canals and rivers froze in winter or became impassable during summer droughts, trains steamed ahead. When becalmed sailing ships went nowhere, locomotives kept on chugging, averaging over twenty miles an hour during the 1850s. Above

RAILROAD TRAVEL
In addition to carrying people and goods more quickly and reliably than ever before, railroads also brought many Americans face to face for the first time with machinery that was much larger and more powerful than any human being. This painting of a train leaving Rochester, New York, in 1852 contrasts the size and power of human beings and machines. The huge, lovingly portrayed, steam-belching locomotive is barely held back by some unseen brake against which the massive engine strains, ready to pull the long train through the columns of the station, out of the past and into the future. The people, in contrast, appear indistinct, passive, and dependent. Except for the two women and child in the foreground, the people face backward, and all of them avoid looking directly at the locomotive. The painting evokes the way the almost incomprehensible power of the railroads dwarfed human effort.
From the photographic collection of the Rochester Historical Society.

all, railroads offered cities not blessed with canals or navigable rivers a way to compete for the trade of the countryside.

By 1850, trains steamed along 9,000 miles of track, almost two-thirds of it in New England and the Middle Atlantic states. By 1860, several railroads had crossed the Mississippi River to link frontier farmers to the nation's 30,000 miles of track, approximately as much as in all the rest of the world combined. (In 1857, for example, France had 3,700 miles of track; England and Wales had a total of 6,400 miles.) Chicago stood at the hub of eleven railroads, including the Illinois Central, the longest railroad in the world (Map 11.1). This massive expan-

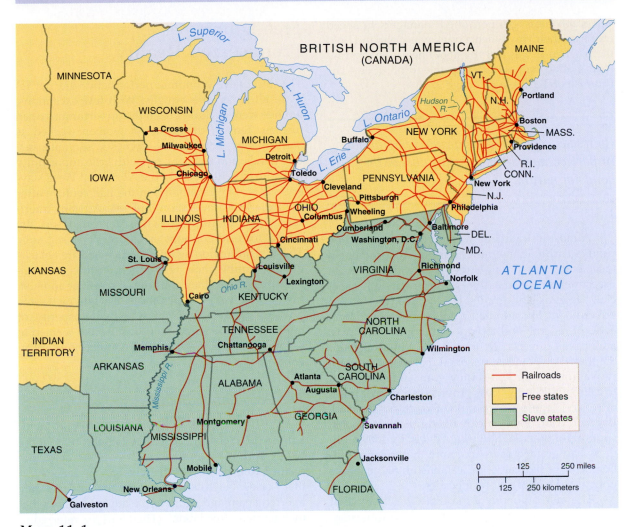

M AP 11.1

Railroads in 1860

Railroads were a crucial component of the revolutions in transportation and communications that transformed nineteenth-century America. The railroad system reflected the differences that had developed in the economies of the North and South.

sion of railroads helped the United States catapult into position as the world's second leading industrial power, behind Great Britain.

In addition to speeding transportation, railroads also fostered the growth of other industries. Iron production grew five times faster than the population during the decades up to 1860, in part to meet the demand for rails, wheels, axles, locomotives, and heavy, gravity-defying iron bridges. Likewise, coal production more than doubled during the 1850s to provide fuel for iron furnaces and locomotive boilers.

Railroads also stimulated the fledgling tele-graph industry. In 1844, Samuel F. B. Morse persuasively demonstrated the potential of his telegraph by transmitting a series of dots and dashes that instantly conveyed an electronic message along forty miles of wire between Washington and Baltimore. By 1861, more than 50,000 miles of wire stretched across the continent to the Pacific. Often telegraph lines ran alongside railroad tracks, and railroad managers soon discovered the advantages of instantaneous communication. Since most railroads had only one set of tracks, careful scheduling was required to avoid disastrous head-on collisions.

Telegraph messages permitted managers to speed trains on their way when a track was clear and hold them when it was not. By 1860, nearly every railroad station had a clattering telegraph. (See "The Promise of Technology," page 374.)

Railroads captured Americans' imaginations in part because they seemed to break the bonds of nature.

Almost all railroads were built and owned by private corporations rather than by government—local, state, or federal. Undergirding these private investments was massive government aid, especially federal land grants. Up to 1850, the federal government had granted a total of seven million acres of federal land to various turnpike, highway, and canal projects. In that year, Illinois Senator Stephen A. Douglas obtained congressional approval for a precedent-setting grant of federal land to railroads. The 1850 law provided six square miles of federal land for each mile of track constructed. Railroad companies quickly lined up congressional support for other lucrative land deals. By 1860, Congress had granted railroads more than twenty million acres of federal lands, establishing a generous policy that would last for decades.

The railroad boom of the 1850s was a signal of the growing industrial might of the American economy. But railroads, like other industries, succeeded because they served farms as well as cities. Passengers and freight routinely sped along tracks during the 1850s, but the continued significance of older forms of transportation is suggested by the operation of the federal postal system, which reached into every village and hamlet. By 1857, trains carried about one-third of the mail; most of the rest still went by stagecoach or horseback. In 1860, most Americans were still far more familiar with horses than with iron horses.

The economy of the 1840s and 1850s linked axes, muscles, animals, and farms to machines, steam, railroads, and cities. Abraham Lincoln split rails as a young man and defended railroad corporations as a successful attorney. His legendary upward mobility illustrated the direction of economic change and the opportunities that change offered to enterprising individuals.

Free Labor: Promise and Reality

The impressive economic performance did not reward all Americans equally. With few exceptions, women were excluded from the opportunities open to men. Tens of thousands of women worked as seamstresses, laundresses, domestic servants, factory hands, and teachers, but with little opportunity to aspire to better jobs. In the North and West, slavery was slowly eliminated in the half century after the American Revolution, but free African Americans there found themselves relegated, on the whole, to dead-end jobs as laborers and servants. This discrimination against women and free blacks did not trouble most white men. With certain notable exceptions, they considered it proper and just. Instead, the varied experiences of white men—the presence of poverty in the midst of prosperity, of failure alongside success, of the bust that seemed to follow every boom—caught the attention of influential spokesmen.

The Free-Labor Ideal: Freedom plus Labor

During the 1840s and 1850s, leaders throughout the North and West emphasized a set of ideas that seemed to explain why the changes under way in their society benefited some more than others. They referred again and again to the advantages of what they termed "free labor." (The word *free* referred to laborers who were not slaves; it did not mean laborers who worked for nothing.) By the 1850s, free labor identified the basic character of the economy and society taking shape in the North and West. Free-labor ideas proposed a social and economic ideal that accounted for both the successes and the shortcomings of American society.

Free-labor spokesmen celebrated hard work, self-reliance, and independence. They proclaimed that the door to success was open not just to those who inherited wealth or status but also to self-made men like Abraham Lincoln. Lincoln himself declared, "Free labor—the just and generous, and prosperous system, which opens the way for all—gives hope to all, and energy, and progress, and improvement of condition to all." The free-labor system permitted farmers and artisans to enjoy the products of their own labor. Free labor also benefited individuals who worked for wages, Lincoln

A YOUNG MECHANIC
This 1848 painting shows a young boy, a mechanic or tradesman, sitting behind the counter of a cluttered and worn woodworking shop. The painting hints that the young boy is an apprentice or perhaps the son of the mechanic who owns the shop. The better-dressed boys on the opposite side of the counter appear to be talking with the young mechanic about whittling a new mast for their toy boat. The barefoot young girl in the foreground appears to be the sister of the young mechanic; her attention is focused on the customers. The painting evokes the physical setting of a none-too-prosperous tradesman's workshop and the social differences that separated an open-faced young artisan and his better-off, shadowed customers. The image suggests that such routine encounters of the free-labor system were so commonplace that children reenacted them in play.
Los Angeles County Museum of Art, Gift of the American Art Council and Mr. and Mrs. J. Douglas Pardee.

and others pointed out. Unlike slaves, wage laborers were not fixed in perpetual bondage, and they received compensation for their labor.

Ultimately, the free-labor system made it possible for hired laborers to become independent property owners, proponents argued. "The pru-

dent, penniless beginner in the world," Lincoln asserted, "labors for wages awhile, saves a surplus with which to buy tools or land, for himself; then labors on his own account another while, and at length hires another new beginner to help him." Wage labor was the first rung on the ladder that reached upward toward self-employment and, eventually, to hiring others.

Free-labor spokesmen proclaimed that the door to success was open not just to those who inherited wealth or status but also to self-made men like Abraham Lincoln.

The free-labor ideal affirmed an egalitarian vision of human potential. Lincoln and other spokesmen stressed the importance of universal education to permit "heads and hands . . . [to] cooperate as friends." Throughout the North and West, communities supported public schools to make the rudiments of learning available to young children. By 1860, many cities and towns boasted that up to 80 percent of children age seven to thirteen attended school, at least for a few days each year. In rural areas, where the labor of children was more difficult to spare, schools typically enrolled no more than half the school-age children. Lessons included more than arithmetic, penmanship, and a smattering of other subjects. Textbooks and teachers—most of whom were young women—drummed into students the virtues of the free-labor system: self-reliance, discipline, and, above all, hard work. "Remember that all the ignorance, degradation, and misery in the world is the result of indolence and vice," one textbook intoned. Free-labor ideology, whether in school or out, emphasized labor as much as freedom.

Economic Inequality

The free-labor ideal made sense to many Americans, especially in the North and West, because it seemed to describe their own experience. Lincoln frequently referred to his humble beginnings as a hired laborer and silently invited his listeners to consider how far he had come. In 1860, his wealth of $17,000 easily placed him in the top 5 percent of the population. The opportunities presented by the expanding economy made a few men much, much richer. In 1860, the nation had about forty millionaires, including Cyrus

TELEGRAPH TRANSMITTER
This is Samuel Morse's telegraph key, the one that sent the first telegraph in 1844.
Division of Political History, Smithsonian Institution, Washington, D.C.

TELEGRAPH RECEIVER
Early receivers pressed dots and dashes into a moving paper strip attached to the machine.

Division of Political History, Smithsonian Institution, Washington, D.C.

The Telegraph: "The Wonder Working Wire"

THE TELEGRAPH PLAYED as important a role as the railroad in opening the West and uniting the nation. In fact, telegraph wires often followed railroad lines, and the two developments were allies in the nineteenth-century communications revolution. Both delivered what nineteenth-century Americans craved—speed and efficiency and the ability to overcome vast distances.

Samuel F. B. Morse is credited with inventing the telegraph because of his patent of June 20, 1840, but, as is the case with many inventions, the assumption of "one man, one invention" exaggerates the contribution of a single individual. The telegraph grew out of scientific knowledge gradually acquired in the eighteenth and nineteenth centuries by a number of scientists, especially André Ampère

of France, Alessandro Volta of Italy, and Joseph Henry of the United States, who pioneered in the field of electromagnetism and experimented with sending electrical signals through wires.

Morse was no scientist—in fact, he was an acclaimed painter—but beginning in the early 1830s he devoted himself to creating a machine that transmitted messages electrically. As one contemporary observed, Morse's talent consisted of "combining and applying the discoveries of others in the invention of a particular instrument and process for telegraphic purposes." This was no small achievement. In addition, Morse's system depended on a code he devised that represented each letter and number with dots and dashes. With a series of taps on a telegraph key, operators sent short and long

McCormick, whose wealth exceeded $2 million. Most Americans, however, measured success in far more modest terms. The average wealth of adult white men in the North in 1860 barely topped $2,000. Only about a quarter of American men possessed that much.

Nearly one-half had no wealth at all; almost 60 percent owned no land. It is difficult to estimate the wealth of adult white women since property possessed by married women was normally considered to belong to their husbands, but certainly women had pulses of electricity—a dash being three times as long as a dot. (The Morse code became the universal language of the telegraph.) At the receiver's end, the code was originally written out by an electrically activated stylus on a moving strip of paper and then read off. But soon skilled operators found that by listening to the taps they could interpret the message and write it down.

The breakthrough moment for Morse's invention came in 1842 when Congress voted $30,000 to build an experimental line between Washington and Baltimore. Four years earlier, a congressional report had declared that if Morse's invention succeeded, "space will be, to all practical purposes of information, completely annihilated between the States of the Union," and Congress was eager to find out if it would work. With the federal subsidy, Morse strung the line, and from the Supreme Court in Washington on May 22, 1844, he tapped out a biblical phrase; in Baltimore forty-one miles away, a receiver transcribed: "What hath God wrought!" The trial was a stunning technical success, and it was also a public relations coup, for the entire nation stood awed by the speed and precision of the "wonder working wire."

The telegraph spread almost as swiftly as news of its existence. By 1846, most eastern cities were connected by telegraph. By 1850, of the states east of the Mississippi River, only Florida remained without it. More than fifty thousand miles of wires webbed the nation by 1861 when the telegraph reached California. Despite the cost—initially, an astronomical dollar a word—the line between San Francisco and the East chattered with dots and dashes.

The telegraph obliterated distance, and cheap, efficient, and fast communication changed American businesses, newspapers, government, and everyday life. Telegraphs made it possible to synchronize clocks, which in turn allowed railroads to run safely according to precise schedules. Businesses of every kind could send and receive information and orders almost instantaneously. Investors from across the country could learn the latest stock prices from the New York Stock Exchange. In 1852, an English visitor reported:

> If, on the arrival of an European mail at one of the northern ports, the news from Europe report that the supply of cotton or of corn is inadequate to meet the existing demand, almost before the vessel can be moored intelligence is spread by the Electric Telegraph, and the merchants and shippers of New Orleans are busied in the preparation of freights, or the corn-factors of St. Louis and Chicago, in the far west, are emptying their granaries and forwarding their contents by rail or by canal to the Atlantic ports.

Newspapers could gather information from around the country and have it in the headlines within hours. As early as 1848, Americans followed the war in Mexico not from reports brought by messengers on horseback or on ships, but by the magical wire. After 1866, when an underwater transatlantic cable linked Europe and America, the federal government used the telegraph to monitor international affairs and to respond swiftly to crises. On a personal level, families scattered across the continent could communicate more quickly than letter writing allowed. The telegraph fit the needs of the vigorous, sprawling nation.

It is one thing to conceive of and build an innovative device. It is another to develop the idea into a profitable business. Unlike the unlucky inventor of the cotton gin, Eli Whitney, Morse was a skilled entrepreneur who grew rich off his invention. Patent rights, which he defended vigorously and successfully, allowed the Morse telegraph to dominate the United States and most of the non-British world. Morse's technology made him wealthy and worked powerfully to draw the far-flung young nation together, even as it began to pull apart politically.

less wealth than men. Free African Americans had still less; 90 percent were propertyless.

Free-labor spokesmen considered these economic inequalities a natural outgrowth of freedom, the inevitable result of some individuals being more able, more willing to work, and luckier. These inequalities suggest, however, the gap between the promise and the performance of the free-labor ideal in this era. Economic growth permitted many men to move from landless squatters to landowning farmers and from hired laborers to independent, self-employed producers. But many more Americans remained behind, landless and working for wages. Even those who realized their aspirations had a precarious hold on their independence; bad debts, crop failure, sickness, or death could quickly eliminate a family's gains.

Since the free-labor ideal pointed to individuals as the sources of both success and failure, many Americans felt anxious about their prospects. Seeking out new opportunities in pursuit of free-labor ideals created restless social and geographic mobility. Commonly up to two-thirds of the residents of a rural area moved every decade, and the population turnover in cities was even greater. Such constant coming and going weakened community ties to neighbors and friends and threw individuals even more upon their own resources for help in times of trouble. The stress on individual achievement encouraged personal introspection that often turned into intense self-doubt. Abraham Lincoln managed to get out of the log cabin in which he grew up, but that log cabin—with its economic insecurities, educational deficiencies, an illiterate mother, and a semiliterate father—remained with him, reminding him how far he had come and how few had come so far.

Immigrants and the Free-Labor Ladder

The risks and uncertainties of free labor did not deter millions of immigrants from entering the United States during the 1840s and 1850s. Almost four and a half million immigrants arrived between 1840 and 1860, six times more than had come during the previous two decades (Figure 11.1). The half million immigrants who came in 1854 accounted for nearly 2 percent of the entire population, a higher proportion than in any other single year of the nation's history. By 1860, foreign-born residents made up about one-eighth of the American population, a fraction that held steady well into the twentieth century.

Nearly three out of four of the immigrants who arrived between 1840 and 1860 came from either Germany or Ireland. The vast majority of the 1.4 million Germans who entered the United States during these years were skilled tradesmen and their families. They left Germany to escape deteriorating economic conditions and to seize opportunities of-fered by the expanding economy, where skilled artisans had little difficulty finding work. German butchers, bakers, beer makers, carpenters, shopkeepers, machinists, and others tended to congregate in cities, particularly in the Midwest. Roughly a quarter of German immigrants were farmers, most of whom scattered throughout the Midwest, although some settled in Texas. On the whole, German Americans settled into that middle stratum of sturdy independent producers celebrated by free-labor spokesmen; relatively few Germans occupied the bottom rung of the free-labor ladder as wage laborers or domestic servants.

The risks and uncertainties of free labor did not deter millions of immigrants from entering the United States during the 1840s and 1850s.

Irish immigrants, in contrast, entered at the bottom of the free-labor ladder and had difficulty climbing up. Nearly 1.7 million Irish immigrants arrived between 1840 and 1860, nearly all of them desperately poor and often weakened by hunger and disease. Potato blight struck Ireland in 1845 and returned repeatedly in subsequent years, spreading a catastrophic famine throughout the island. Millions of poor farmers and hired hands depended on potatoes as their principal source of food. When the blight ruined the potatoes, tens of thousands literally starved to death. The lucky ones, half-starved, crowded into the holds of ships and set out for America. As one immigrant group declared, "All we want is to get out of Ireland; we must be better anywhere than here." Death trailed after them. So many died crossing the Atlantic that ships from Ireland were often termed "coffin ships."

Roughly three out of four Irish immigrants worked as laborers or domestic servants. Irish men dug canals, loaded ships, built railroad tracks, and took what other work they could find. Irish women hired out to cook, wash and iron, mind children, and clean house. Slaveholders often preferred to hire Irish laborers for heavy, dangerous jobs rather than risk injury to their valuable slaves. Most Irish immigrants, however, congregated in northeastern cities. Almost all Irish immigrants were Catholic, a fact that set them apart from the

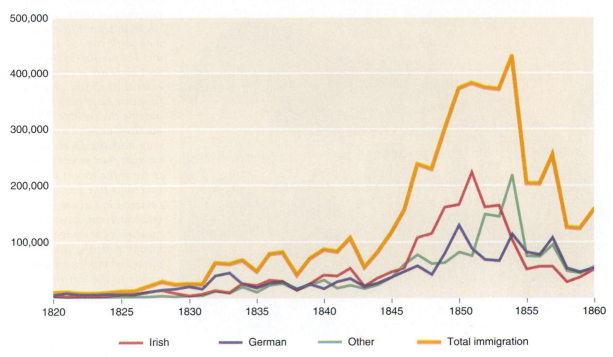

FIGURE 11.1
Antebellum Immigration, 1820–1860
After increasing gradually for several decades, immigration shot up in the mid-1840s.
Between 1848 and 1860, nearly 3.5 million immigrants entered the United States.

overwhelmingly Protestant native-born residents. Many natives regarded the Irish as hard-drinking, obstreperous, half-civilized folk. Such views lay behind the discrimination that often excluded Irish immigrants from better jobs. Job announcements commonly stated, "No Irish need apply." Despite these prejudices, native residents hired Irish immigrants because they accepted low pay and worked hard.

In America's labor-poor economy, Irish laborers could earn in one day wages that would require several weeks' work in Ireland, if work could be found there. In America, one immigrant explained in 1853, there was "plenty of work and plenty of wages plenty to eat and no land lords thats enough what more does a man want." But some immigrants wanted more, especially respect and decent working conditions. One immigrant prayed, "May heaven save me from ever again being compelled to labour so severely . . . driven like horses . . . a slave for the Americans as the generality of the Irish . . . are."

Such testimony illustrates that the free-labor system, whether for immigrants or native-born laborers, often did not live up to the optimistic vision outlined by Abraham Lincoln and others. If wage laborers could not realistically aspire to become independent, self-sufficient property holders—if wage laborers became a permanent rather than a temporary working class—what would become of the free-labor ideal? By 1860, a few workingmen asked such questions, but the continuing economic expansion muted their voices.

Reforming Self and Society

The emphasis on self-discipline and individual effort at the core of the free-labor ideal pervaded America in the 1840s and 1850s. Many Americans believed that insufficient self-control caused the most important social problems of the era. Evangelical Protestants struggled to control individu-

EVICTION OF IRISH TENANT
An Irish tenant (the seated man with crossed arms) and his family (two barefoot boys are shown) are evicted; their few pieces of furniture have been piled outside the cottage. The landlord or his agent (the man near the doorway) has brought four armed police to force the tenant to leave. Evictions like this were common in Ireland in the mid-nineteenth century, an example of the poverty and human suffering that pushed many Irish immigrants to the United States.
Lawrence Collection, National Library of Ireland.

als' propensity to sin, and temperance advocates exhorted drinkers to control their urge for alcohol. In the midst of the worldly disruptions of geographic expansion and economic change, evangelicals brought more Americans than ever before into churches. Historians estimate that church members accounted for about one-third of the American population by midcentury. Most Americans remained outside churches, as did Abraham Lincoln. But the influence of evangelical religion reached far beyond those who belonged to churches. The evangelical temperament—a conviction of righteousness coupled with energy, self-discipline, and faith that the world could be improved—animated most reformers to one degree or another.

A few activists pointed out that certain fundamental injustices lay beyond the reach of self-control. Transcendentalists and utopians believed that perfection could be attained only by rejecting the competitive values of the larger society. Women's rights activists and abolitionists sought to reverse the subordination of women and to eliminate the enslavement of blacks by changing society. They confronted the daunting challenge of repudiating widespread assumptions about male supremacy and white supremacy and somehow subverting the entrenched institutions that reinforced those assumptions: the family and slavery.

The Pursuit of Perfection: Transcendentalists and Utopians

A group of New England writers that came to be known as transcendentalists believed that individuals should not conform to the materialistic world or to some abstract notion of religion. Instead, people should look within themselves for truth and guidance. The leading transcendentalist, Ralph Waldo Emerson—an essayist, poet, and lecturer—proclaimed that most Americans failed to lift their eyes from the mundane task of making a living. "We hear . . . too much of the results of machinery, commerce, and the useful arts," Emerson wrote. The power of the solitary individual was nearly limitless. Henry David Thoreau, Margaret Fuller, and other transcendentalists agreed with Emerson that "if the single man plant himself indomitably on his instincts, and there abide, the huge world will come round to him." In many ways, transcendentalism represented less an alternative to the values of mainstream society than an exaggerated form of the rampant individualism of the age.

Unlike transcendentalists, a few reformers tried to change the world by organizing utopian communities. Although these communities never involved more than a few thousand people, the activities of their members demonstrated both their dissatisfactions with the larger society and their efforts to realize their visions of perfection. Some communities functioned essentially as retreats for those who did not want to sever their ties with the larger society. Brook Farm, organized in 1841 in West Roxbury, Massachusetts, provided a short-lived haven for literary and artistic New Englanders who agreed to balance bookish pursuits with manual labor.

Other communities set out to become models of perfection that they hoped would point the way toward a better life for everyone. During the 1840s, more than two dozen communities—principally in New York, New Jersey, Pennsylvania, and Ohio—organized around the ideas of Charles Fourier, a French critic of contemporary society. Members of these Fourierist communities (or phalanxes, as they were called) believed that individualism and competition were evils that denied the basic truth that "men . . . are brothers and not competitors." Fourierist phalanxes tried to replace competition with harmonious cooperation based on communal ownership of property. In addition, members were supposed to work not because they had to but because their work was satisfying and fulfilling. One former member complained that "there was plenty of discussion, and an abundance of variety, which is called the spice of life. This spice however constituted the greater part of the fare, as we sometimes had scarcely anything to eat." Such complaints signaled the failure of the Fourierist communities to achieve their ambitious goals. Few survived more than two or three years.

The Oneida community went beyond the Fourierist notion of communalism. John Humphrey Noyes, the charismatic leader of Oneida, believed that individuals who had achieved salvation were literally without sin. The larger society's commitment to private property, however, made even saints greedy and selfish. Noyes believed that the root of the evil of private property lay in marriage, in men's conviction that their wives were their exclusive property. With a substantial inheritance, Noyes organized the Oneida community in New York in 1848 to practice what he called "complex marriage." Sexual intercourse was permissible between any man and woman in the community who

MARY CRAGIN, ONEIDA WOMAN
Mary Cragin, one of the founding members of the Oneida community, had a passionate sexual relationship with John Humphrey Noyes even before the community was organized. Within the bounds of complex marriage as practiced by the Oneidans, Cragin's magnetic sexuality made her a favorite partner of many men. In her journal, Cragin confessed that "every evil passion was very strong in me from my childhood, sexual desire, love of dress and admiration, deceit, anger, pride." Oneida, however, transformed evil passion to holy piety. Cragin wrote, "In view of [God's] goodness to me and of his desire that I should let him fill me with himself, I yield and offer myself, to be penetrated by his spirit, and desire that love and gratitude may inspire my heart so that I shall sympathize with his pleasure in the thing, before my personal pleasure begins, knowing that it will increase my capability for happiness." Oneida's sexual practices were considered outrageous and sinful by almost all other Americans. Even Oneidans did not agree with all of Noyes's ideas about sex. "There is no reason why [sex] should not be done in public as much as music and dancing," he declared. It would display the art of sex, he explained, and watching "would give pleasure to a great many of the older people who now have nothing to do with the matter." Nonetheless, public sex never caught on among Oneidans.
Oneida Community Mansion House/James Demarest.

had been saved; in effect, every saved man in the community was married to every saved woman. Noyes usually reserved for himself the duties of "first husband," namely introducing sanctified young virgins to complex marriage. To prevent a population explosion and to promote health and self-control, Noyes insisted that Oneida men practice "male continence," that is, sexual intercourse without ejaculation. Noyes also required all members to relinquish their economic property to the community, which developed a lucrative business manufacturing animal traps. Oneida's sexual and economic communalism attracted several hundred members, but most of their neighbors considered Oneidans adulterers, blasphemers, and worse. Yet the practices that set Oneida apart from its mainstream neighbors also strengthened the community, and it survived long after the Civil War.

Women's Rights Activists

Women participated in the many reform activities that grew out of evangelical churches. Women church members outnumbered men two to one, and they worked to put their religious ideas into practice by joining peace, temperance, antislavery, and other societies. Although women supplied much energy and membership in these societies, men normally headed the groups. Assumptions of male supremacy were so strong and pervasive that even women's rights activists feared the consequences of openly confronting them. Involvement in reform organizations gave a few women activists practical experience in such political arts as speaking in public, running a meeting, drafting resolutions, and circulating petitions. Along with such experience came confidence. Abolitionist Lydia Maria Child pointed out in 1841 that "those who urged women to become missionaries and form tract societies . . . have changed the household utensil to a living energetic being and they have no spell to turn it into a broom again."

In 1848, about one hundred "living energetic beings," led by reformers Elizabeth Cady Stanton and Lucretia Mott, gathered at Seneca Falls, New York, for the first women's rights convention in the United States. The Seneca Falls Declaration of Sentiments proclaimed that "the history of mankind is a history of repeated injuries and usurpations on the part of man toward woman, having in direct

object the establishment of an absolute tyranny over her." In the style of the Declaration of Independence, the Seneca Falls Declaration listed the ways women had been discriminated against. Through the tyranny of male supremacy, men "endeavored in every way that [they] could to destroy her confidence in her own powers, to lessen her self-respect, and to make her willing to lead a dependent and abject life." The Seneca Falls Declaration insisted that women "have immediate admission to all the rights and privileges which belong to them as citizens of the United States," particularly the "inalienable right to the elective franchise."

In 1848, about one hundred "living energetic beings," led by reformers Elizabeth Cady Stanton and Lucretia Mott, gathered at Seneca Falls, New York, for the first women's rights convention in the United States.

Nearly two dozen other women's rights conventions assembled before 1860, repeatedly calling for suffrage. But they had difficulty receiving a respectful hearing, much less obtaining legislative action. No state came close to permitting women to vote. Politicians and editorialists hooted at the idea. Everyone knew, they sneered, that a woman's place was in the home, rearing her children and civilizing her man. Nonetheless, the Seneca Falls Declaration served as a path-breaking manifesto of dissent against male supremacy and of support for woman suffrage, which would become the focus of the women's rights movement during the next seventy years.

Abolitionists and the American Ideal

During the 1840s and 1850s, abolitionists continued to struggle to draw the nation's attention to the plight of slaves and the need for emancipation. Former slaves like Frederick Douglass, Henry Bibb, and Sojourner Truth lectured to reform audiences throughout the North about the cruelties, horrors, and indignities of slavery. Abolitionists published newspapers, held conventions, and petitioned Congress. But they never attracted a mass following

ABOLITIONIST MEETING
This rare daguerreotype was made by Ezra Greenleaf Weld in August 1850 at an abolitionist meeting in Cazenovia, New York. Frederick Douglass, who had escaped from slavery in Maryland twelve years earlier, is seated on the platform next to the woman at the table. One of the nation's most brilliant and eloquent abolitionists, Douglass also supported equal rights for women. The man immediately behind Douglass gesturing with his outstretched arm is Gerrit Smith, a wealthy New Yorker and militant abolitionist whose funds supported many reform activities. Note the two black women in similar clothing on either side of Smith and the white woman next to Douglass. Most white Americans considered such voluntary racial proximity scandalous and promiscuous. Clearly, what scandalized these respectable-appearing Americans was slavery, not biracial protest meetings.
Collection of the J. Paul Getty Museum, Malibu, Calif.

among white Americans. Many white Northerners became convinced that slavery was wrong, but they still believed that blacks were inferior. Many other white Northerners shared the common view of white Southerners that because blacks were inferior, slavery was necessary and even desirable. The geographic expansion of the nation during the 1840s offered abolitionists an opportunity to link their unpopular ideal to a goal that many white Northerners found much more attractive—limiting the geographic expansion of slavery, an issue that moved to the center of national politics during the 1850s (see chapter 13).

Black leaders rose to prominence in the abolitionist movement during the 1840s and 1850s. African Americans had actively opposed slavery for decades, but a new generation of leaders came to the forefront in these years. Men like Douglass, Henry Highland Garnet, William Wells Brown, and Martin R. Delany became impatient with white abolitionists' appeals to the conscience of the white majority. Garnet, for example, proclaimed in 1843 that slaves should rise in insurrection against their masters, an idea that alienated almost all white people. To express their own uncompromising ideas, black abolitionists founded their own newspapers and held their own antislavery conventions, although they still cooperated with sympathetic whites.

The commitment of black abolitionists to battling slavery grew out of their own experiences with white supremacy. The 250,000 free African Americans in the North and West constituted less than 2 percent of the total population. They confronted the humiliations of racial discrimination in virtually every arena of daily life: at work, at school, at church, in shops, in the streets, on trains, in hotels. Only four states (Maine, Massachusetts, New Hampshire, and Vermont) permitted black men to vote; New York imposed a special property-holding requirement on black—but not white—voters, effectively excluding most black men from the franchise. All other states prohibited black voting. The pervasive racial discrimination both handicapped and energized black abolitionists. African American leaders organized campaigns against segregation, particularly in transportation and education. Their most notable success came in 1855 when Massachusetts integrated public schools. Elsewhere white supremacy continued unabated.

The commitment of black abolitionists to battling slavery grew out of their own experiences with white supremacy.

Outside the public spotlight, free African Americans in the North and West contributed to the antislavery cause by quietly aiding fugitive slaves. Harriet Tubman escaped from slavery in Maryland in 1849 and repeatedly risked her freedom and her life to return to the South and escort slaves to freedom. Few matched Tubman's heroic courage, but when the opportunity arose, free blacks in the North provided fugitive slaves with food, a safe place to rest, and a helping hand. This "underground railroad" ran mainly through black neighborhoods, black churches, and black homes, an outgrowth of the antislavery sentiment and opposition to white supremacy that unified virtually all African Americans in the North. While a few fortunate southern slaves rode the underground railroad to freedom in the North, millions of other Americans uprooted their families and headed west.

The Westward Movement

The 1840s ushered in an era of rapid westward movement. Until then, the overwhelming majority of Americans lived east of the Mississippi River. To the west, Native Americans inhabited the plains, prairies, and deserts to the rugged coasts of the Pacific. The British claimed Oregon Country, and the Mexican flag flew over the vast expanse of the Southwest. But by 1850, the boundaries of the United States stretched to the Pacific, and the nation had more than doubled its size. By 1860, the great migration had carried four million Americans west of the Mississippi River.

Thomas Jefferson, John Quincy Adams, and other government officials had helped clear the way for the march across the continent. The nation's revolution in transportation and communication, its swelling population, and its booming economy propelled the westward surge. But the emigrants themselves conquered the continent. Farmer-settlers craved land and stubbornly shoved ahead. Shock troops of the American empire, frontier settlers took the soil and then lobbied their government to follow them with the flag. The human cost of westward expansion was high. Two centuries of Indian wars east of the Mississippi ended during the 1830s, but the old, fierce struggle between native inhabitant and invader continued for another half century in the West.

Manifest Destiny

Most Americans believed that the superiority of their institutions and white culture bestowed on them a God-given right to spread their civilization across the continent. They imagined the West as a howling wilderness, empty and undeveloped. If they recognized Indians and Mexicans at all, they dismissed them as primitive drags on progress who would have to be redeemed, shoved aside and isolated, or exterminated. The sense of uniqueness and mission was as old as the Puritans, but by the 1840s the conviction of superiority had been bolstered by the young nation's amazing success. What right had Americans, they asked, to keep the blessings of liberty, democracy, and prosperity to themselves? The West needed the civilizing power of the hammer and plow, the ballot box and pulpit, that had transformed the East.

In the summer of 1845, New York journalist John L. O'Sullivan coined the term *manifest destiny*

WIND RIVER COUNTRY, ALBERT BIERSTADT, 1860
Born and trained in Germany, Albert Bierstadt visited the American West for the first time in 1859 with a U.S. government expedition searching for shortcuts along the Oregon Trail. The Wind River range of the central Rockies captured his imagination. He portrays a new Eden, an epic landscape of spectacular beauty that silently beckons a restless, questing young nation. Bountiful, empty, without a single mark of civilization, Bierstadt's West shimmers in golden light, a kind of divine sanction for manifest destiny. Writer Mark Twain claimed that Bierstadt's landscapes were more beautiful than even the Creator's, but he lamented the fact that the artist strayed from factual accuracy. Indeed, Bierstadt painted his dramatic landscapes back in his New York studio, where he was less interested in accuracy than in creating a romantic metaphor for America's national potential.
Denver Art Museum.

as the latest justification for white settlers to take the land they coveted. O'Sullivan was an armchair expansionist, but he took second place to no one in his passion for conquest of the West. O'Sullivan called on Americans to resist any foreign power— British, French, or Mexican—that attempted to thwart "the fulfillment of our manifest destiny to overspread the continent allotted by Providence for the free development of our yearly multiplying mil-lions . . . [and] for the development of the great experiment of liberty and federative self-government entrusted to us." Almost overnight, the magic phrase *manifest destiny* swept the nation and provided an ideological shield for conquering the West.

As important as national pride and racial arrogance were to manifest destiny, economic gain made up its core. Land hunger drew hundreds of thousands of average Americans westward. Some politicians, moreover, had become convinced that national prosperity depended on capturing the rich trade of the Far East. To trade with Asia, the United States needed the Pacific ports that stretched from San Francisco to Puget Sound. No one was more eager to extend American trade in the Pacific than Missouri Senator Thomas Hart Benton. "The sun of civilization must shine across the sea: socially and commercially," he declared. The United States and Asia must "talk together, and trade together. Commerce is a great civilizer." In the 1840s, American economic expansion came wrapped in the rhetoric of uplift and civilization.

"Oregon Fever" and the Overland Trail

Oregon Country, that vast region bounded on the west by the Pacific, on the east by the Rockies, on the south by the forty-second parallel, and on the north by Russian Alaska, caused the pulse of American expansionists to race (Map 11.2). But Americans were not alone in hungrily eyeing the Pacific Northwest. The British traced their interest—and their rights—to the voyage of Sir Francis Drake, who, they argued, discovered the Oregon coast in 1579. Americans matched the British assertion with historic claims of their own. Unable

MAP 11.2
Trails to the West
In the 1830s, wagon trains began snaking their way to the Southwest and the Pacific coast. Deep ruts, some of which can still be seen today, soon marked the most popular routes.

to agree on ownership, the United States and Great Britain decided in 1818 on a "joint occupation" that would leave Oregon "free and open" to settlement by both countries. A handful of American fur traders and "mountain men" roamed the region in the 1820s, but in the 1830s and 1840s expansionists made Oregon Country an early target of manifest destiny.

"Oregon fever" broke out in 1833 when a Methodist journal published a fictitious letter from an Indian in the Northwest begging for the Bible. Pulpits across the East broadcast the plea, and soon earnest missionaries responded to the call. The Indians they encountered displayed a decided lack of enthusiasm for Christianity, but the missionaries' letters home glowed with astonishment at the bounty nature had bestowed on Oregon. By the late 1830s, settlers began to trickle along the Oregon Trail, following a path blazed by the mountain men (see Map 11.2). The first Oregon wagon trains hit the trail in 1841, and by 1843 about 1,000 emigrants a year set out from Independence, Missouri. By 1869, when the first transcontinental railroad was completed, something like 350,000 migrants had traveled west to the Pacific in wagon trains.

As important as national pride and racial arrogance were to manifest destiny, economic gain made up its core. Land hunger drew hundreds of thousands of average Americans westward.

Emigrants encountered Plains Indians, whose cultures differed markedly from those of the Eastern Woodlands tribes. The quarter of a million Native Americans who populated the area between the Rocky Mountains and the Mississippi River defy easy generalization. Some were farmers who lived peaceful, sedentary lives, but a majority of Plains Indians—the Sioux, Cheyenne, Shoshoni, and Arapaho of the Central Plains and the Kiowa, Wichita, Apache, and Comanche in the Southwest—were horse-mounted, nomadic, nonagricultural peoples whose warriors symbolized the "savage Indian" in the minds of whites.

Horses, which had been brought to the continent by Spaniards in the sixteenth century, permitted the Plains tribes to become highly mobile hunters of buffalo. In time they came to depend on

buffalo for most of their food, clothing, shelter, and fuel. As they followed the huge herds over the plains, these peoples bumped into one another. Competition and warfare became a crucial component of their way of life. Young men were introduced to the art of war early, learning to ride ponies at breakneck speed while firing off arrows and, later, rifles with astounding accuracy. "A Comanche on his feet is out of his element," observed George Catlin, an artist of the West, "but the moment he lays his hands upon his horse, I doubt very much whether any people in the world can surpass [him]."

Plains Indians struck fear in the hearts of whites who rode on the wagon trains. But Native Americans had far more to fear from whites. Indians killed fewer than four hundred emigrants on the trail between 1840 and 1860, while whites proved to be deadly to the Indians. Even though they were usually just passing through on their way to the Pacific slope, whites brought alcohol and disease, especially destructive epidemics of smallpox, measles, cholera, and scarlet fever. Moreover, whites killed the buffalo, slaughtering hundreds of thousands for sport and leaving their carcasses to rot in the sun. Buffalo still numbered some twelve million in 1860, but the herds were shrinking rapidly, intensifying conflict among the Plains Indians. Intertribal warfare weakened the Indians and made them more vulnerable to conquest.

As the number of wagon trains increased, emigrants insisted that the federal government provide them more protection. The government responded by constructing a chain of forts along the trail. More important, the United States adopted a new Indian policy of "concentration." To clear the way, the government rescinded the "permanent" frontier it had granted the Indians west of the ninety-fifth meridian, which was only two or three hundred miles west of the Mississippi River. Then, in 1851, it

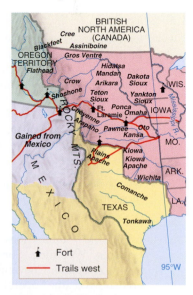

Plains Indians and Trails West in the 1840s and 1850s

WI-JUN-JON, AN ASSINIBOIN CHIEF
Pennsylvania-born artist George Catlin, the painter of this 1845 dual portrait, was present in the Assiniboin village when Wi-Jun-Jon returned from Washington, D.C., wearing the military uniform that President Andrew Jackson had presented to him. His uniform and ceaseless boasting bred so much dislike and distrust that a young warrior from a nearby tribe murdered him. Catlin was convinced that the western Indian cultures he had begun observing in the 1830s would soon disappear, and he sought to document Indian life through hundreds of paintings and prints.
Library of Congress.

www.bedfordstmartins.com/tap   SEE THE ONLINE STUDY GUIDE for more help in analyzing these images.

called the Plains tribes to a conference at Fort Laramie, Wyoming. Some ten thousand Dakota, Sioux, Arapaho, Cheyenne, Crow, and other Indians showed up, hopeful that something could be done to protect them from the ravages of the wagon trains. Instead, government negotiators persuaded the chiefs to sign agreements restricting their peo-ple to specific areas that whites promised they would never violate. This policy of isolation became the seedbed for the subsequent policy of reserva-tions. But whites would not keep out of Indian ter-ritory, and Indians would not easily give up their traditional way of life. Competition meant warfare for decades to come.

Still, Indians threatened emigrants less than life on the trail did. The men, women, and children who headed west each spring could count on four to six months of grueling travel. Until 1860, maps labeled the vast area between the Rockies and the Mississippi River as the "Great American Desert." With nearly two thousand miles to go and traveling no more than fifteen miles a day, the pioneers endured parching heat, drought, treacherous rivers, disease, physical and emotional exhaustion, and, if the snows closed the mountain passes before they got through, freezing and starvation. Women sometimes faced the dangers of trailside childbirth. It was said that one could walk from Missouri to the Pacific stepping only on the graves of those who had failed to make it.

Everyone experienced hardships on the trail, but no one felt the burden quite as much as the women who made the trip. Since husbands usually decided to pull up stakes and go west, many wives went involuntarily. One miserable woman, trying to keep her children dry in a rainstorm and to calm them as they listened to Indian shouts, wondered "what had possessed my husband, anyway, that he should have thought of bringing us away out through this God forsaken country." Men viewed the privation as a necessary step to land of their own and an independent life; women tended to judge it by the homes, kin, and friends they had left behind to take up what one called "this wild goose chase."

When men reached Oregon, they usually liked what they found. Oregon is "one of the greatest countries in the world," Richard R. Howard declared. From "the Cascade mountains to the Pacific, the whole country can be cultivated." When women reached Oregon, they found a wilderness. "I had all I could do to keep from asking George to turn around and bring me back home," one woman wrote to her mother in Missouri. Neighbors were few and far between, and the isolation weighed heavily. Moreover, things were in a "primitive state." One young wife set up housekeeping with her new husband with only one stew kettle and three knives. Necessity blurred the traditional division between men's and women's work. "I am maid of all traids," one busy woman remarked in 1853. Work seemed unending. "I am a very old woman," remarked twenty-nine-year-old Sarah Everett. "My face is thin sunken and wrinkled, my hands bony withered and hard." Pioneer life left little room for leisure or refinement. As one wife observed, "A woman that can not endure almost as much as a horse has no business here."

Despite the ordeal of the trail and the difficulties of starting from scratch, emigrants kept coming. By 1845, Oregon counted five thousand American settlers. And from the beginning, they clamored for the protection of the U.S. government.

The Mormon Migration

Not every wagon train heading west had the Pacific slope as its destination. One remarkable group of religious emigrants chose to settle in the heart of the arid West. Halting near the Great Salt Lake in what was then Mexican territory, the Mormons deliberately chose the remote site as a refuge. After years of persecution in the East, they sought religious freedom and communal security in the West. Protected by mountains and deserts, Deseret, as they called their kingdom, lay a thousand miles from the Kansas frontier.

In 1830, Joseph Smith Jr., who was only twenty-four, published *The Book of Mormon* and founded the Church of Jesus Christ of Latter-Day Saints (the Mormons). A decade earlier, the upstate New York farm boy had begun to have uncommon religious experiences. His visions and revelations were followed, he said, by a visit from an angel who led him to golden tablets buried near his home. With the aid of magic stones, he translated the mysterious language on the tablets. What was revealed was *The Book of Mormon*. It told the story of an ancient Christian civilization in the New World and predicted the appearance of an American prophet who would reestablish Jesus Christ's undefiled kingdom in America. Converts, attracted to the promise of a pure faith in the midst of antebellum America's social turmoil and rampant materialism, flocked to the new church.

Not every wagon train heading west had the Pacific slope as its destination. One remarkable group of religious emigrants chose to settle in the heart of the arid West: the Mormons.

"Gentile" neighbors branded Mormons heretics and resented their close-knit community, what they considered the Mormons' religious self-righteousness, and their sympathy toward abolitionists and Indians. Persecution drove Smith and his followers

PIONEER FAMILY ON THE TRAIL WEST

In 1860, W. G. Chamberlain photographed these unidentified travelers momentarily at rest by the Upper Arkansas River in Colorado. We do not know their fates, but we can hope that they fared better than the Sager family, Henry, Naomi, and their six daughters, who set out from St. Joseph, Missouri, in 1844. "Father," one of his daughters remembered, "was one of those restless men who are not content to remain in one place long at a time. . . . [He] had been talking of going to Texas. But mother, hearing much said about the healthfulness of Oregon, preferred to go there." Still far from Oregon, Henry Sager died of fever, and twenty-six days later, Naomi died, leaving seven children, the last delivered on the trail. The Sager children, under the care of other families in the wagon train, pressed on. After traveling 2,000 miles in seven months, the migrants arrived in Oregon, where a couple named the Whitmans, whose daughter had drowned, adopted all of the Sager children.

Denver Public Library, Western History Division # F3226.

from New York to Ohio, then to Missouri, and finally in 1839 to Nauvoo, Illinois, where they built a prosperous community of fifteen thousand. But the Mormons had not outrun trouble. Dissenters within the church accused Smith of advocating plural marriage (polygamy) and published an exposé of the practice. Non-Mormons caught wind of the controversy and eventually arrested Smith and

his brother. On June 27, 1844, a mob stormed the jail and shot both men dead.

The embattled church turned to an extraordinary new leader, Brigham Young, who immediately began to plan the exodus of his people from Illinois. In 1846, traveling in 3,700 wagons, twelve thousand Mormons made their way to eastern Iowa, where they established refugee camps. In 1847, Young led an advance party to their new home beside the Great Salt Lake. Young described it as a barren waste, "the paradise of the lizard, the cricket and the rattlesnake." Within ten years, however, the Mormons developed an efficient irrigation system and made the desert bloom. They accomplished the feat through cooperative labor, not the individualistic and competitive enterprise common among most emigrants. Under the stern leadership of Young and other church leaders, the Mormons built a thriving community.

In 1850, only three years after its founding, Deseret became annexed to the United States as Utah Territory. But what focused the nation's attention on the Latter-Day Saints was the announcement by Brigham Young in 1852 that many Mormons practiced polygamy. Although only one Mormon man in five had more than one wife (Young had twenty-three), Young's public statement caused an outcry that forced the government to establish its authority in Utah. In 1857, twenty-five hundred U.S. troops invaded Salt Lake City in what was known as the Mormon War. The bloodless occupation illustrates that most Americans viewed the Mormons as a threat to American morality, law, and institutions. The invasion did not dislodge the Mormon Church from its central place in Utah, however, and for years to come most Americans perceived the Mormon settlement as a strange, and suitably isolated, place.

The Mexican Borderlands

In the Mexican Southwest, westward-moving Anglo-American pioneers confronted northern-moving Spanish-speaking frontiersmen. On this frontier as elsewhere, cultures, interests, and aspirations collided. Since 1821, when Mexico won its independence from Spain, the Mexican flag had flown over the vast expanse that stretched from the Gulf of Mexico to the Pacific and from Oregon Country to Guatemala. Mexico's borders remained ill defined, and its northern provinces were sparsely populated. Moreover, severe problems plagued the young nation: civil wars, economic crises, quarrels between the Roman Catholic Church and the state, and devastating raids by the Comanche, Apache, and Kiowa. Mexico found it increasingly difficult to defend its borderlands, especially when faced with a northern neighbor that was convinced of its superiority and bent on territorial acquisition.

The American assault began quietly. In the 1820s, when Anglo-American trappers, traders, and settlers began drifting into Mexico's far northern provinces, they discovered that their newly independent neighbor was eager for American business. Santa Fe, a remote outpost in the province of New Mexico, became a magnet for American enterprise. American traders gathered each spring at Independence, Missouri, for the long trek southwest along the Santa Fe Trail (see Map 11.2). They crammed their wagons with inexpensive American manufactured goods and returned with Mexican silver, furs, and mules.

In the Mexican Southwest, Anglo-American pioneers confronted Spanish-speaking frontiersmen. On this frontier as elsewhere, cultures, interests, and aspirations collided.

The Mexican province of Texas attracted a flood of Americans who had settlement, not long-distance trade, on their minds (Map 11.3). The Mexican government, which wanted to populate and develop its northern territory, granted the American Stephen F. Austin a huge tract of land, and in the 1820s he established a thriving settlement along the Brazos River. Land was cheap—only ten cents an acre—and thousands of farmers poured over the border. Most of the migrants were Southerners, who brought cotton and slaves with them. By 1835, the number of American settlers—free and slave—in Texas had reached thirty thousand, while the *Tejano* (Spanish-speaking) population was less than eight thousand. By and large, Anglo-American settlers were not Roman Catholic, did not speak Spanish, and cared little about assimilating into a culture that was so different from their own. The Mexican government realized it had a problem on its hands. In 1829, it sought to arrest further immigration with an emancipation proclamation, which it hoped would make Texas less attractive. The settlers sidestepped the decree by calling their slaves servants, but settlers had other grievances, most significantly the puny voice they had in local government. General Antonio López de Santa Anna all but extinguished that voice when he seized political power and concentrated authority in Mexico City.

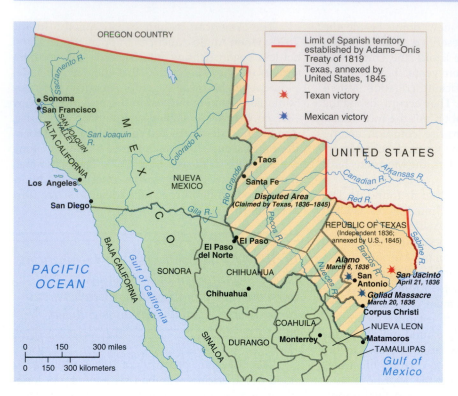

MAP 11.3
**Texas and Mexico
in the 1830s**
*As Americans spilled into
lightly populated and
loosely governed northern
Mexico, Texas and then
other Mexican provinces
became contested territory.*

Faced with what they considered tyranny, the Texan settlers rebelled and declared the independent Republic of Texas. Santa Anna took the field and in February 1836 arrived at the outskirts of San Antonio with nearly 6,000 troops. The rebels, who included the Tennessee frontiersman Davy Crockett and the Louisiana adventurer Jim Bowie, as well as a number of *Tejanos,* took refuge in the old Franciscan mission, the Alamo. Wave after wave of Mexicans crashed against the walls until the attackers finally broke through and killed all 187 defenders. A few weeks later in the small town of Goliad, Mexican forces surrounded and captured a garrison of 365 Texans. Following orders from Santa Anna, Mexican firing squads executed the

**Texas War for
Independence, 1836**

men as pirates. But in April 1836 at San Jacinto, Santa Anna suffered a crushing defeat at the hands of forces under General Sam Houston. Texans had succeeded in establishing their Lone Star Republic, and the following year the United States recognized the independence of Texas from Mexico.

The distant Mexican province of California also caught the eye of a few Anglo-Americans. Spain had first extended its influence into California in 1769, when it sent a naval expedition north from Mexico to San Francisco Bay in an effort to block Russian fur traders who were moving south along the Pacific Coast from their base in Alaska. The Spanish built garrisoned towns (*presidios*), but, more important, they constructed a string of twenty-one missions, spaced a day's journey apart, along the coast from San Diego to Sonoma. Junípero Serra and other Franciscan friars converted the Indians to Christianity and drew them into the life and often hard agricultural labor of the missions. In 1824, in an effort to increase Mexican migration to thinly settled California, the Mexican government granted *ranchos*—huge estates devoted to cattle raising—to new settlers. *Rancheros* ruled over near-feudal empires worked by Indians whose condition sometimes approached that of slaves. Not satisfied,

SURVEYING TEXAS LAND
Land has always bred conflict in Texas. The new republic (1836–1845) wrestled with a confusing variety of Spanish, Mexican, and Texas claims, surveys, and titles. This painting by Theodore Gentilz in about 1844 documents the efforts of surveyor John James to settle the thorny issues. Five years later, however, Texas governor P. H. Bell could still observe: "There is no subject which addresses itself more forcibly . . . than that of settling upon a secure and permanent basis the land titles of the country."
Courtesy, Mr. Larry Sheerin.

rancheros coveted the vast lands controlled by the Franciscan missions. In 1834, they persuaded the government to confiscate the missions and make their lands available to new settlement. Some seven hundred new *ranchos* followed, a development that accelerated the decline of California Indians. Devastated by disease, the Indians, who numbered approximately 300,000 when the Spanish arrived in 1769, declined to half that number by 1846.

Despite the efforts of the Mexican government, California in 1840 counted a population of only 7,000 Mexican settlers. Non-Mexican settlers numbered only 380, but among them were Americans who championed manifest destiny. Thomas O. Larkin, a prosperous merchant, John Marsh, a successful *ranchero* in the San Joaquin Valley, and others became boosters who sought to attract Americans from Oregon Country to California. The first overland party arrived in California in 1841. Thereafter, wagon after wagon followed the California Trail, which forked off from the Oregon Trail near the Snake River and led through the Sierra Nevada at Lake Tahoe (see Map 11.2). As the trickle of Americans became a river, Mexican officials grew alarmed. California, they feared, would go the way of Texas. As a New York newspaper put it in 1845, "Let the tide of emigration flow toward California and the American population will soon be sufficiently numerous to play the Texas game." Indeed, many Americans in California continued to live apart, unassimilated, and to view themselves as superior to their Mexican neighbors. Not all Americans in California wanted to play the "Texas game," but many dreamed of living again under the American flag.

The U.S. government made no secret of its desire to acquire California. In 1835, President Andrew Jackson tried to purchase it. In 1842, Commodore Thomas Catesby Jones, hearing a rumor that the United States and Mexico were at war, seized the port of Monterey and ran up the American flag. The red-faced officer promptly ran it down again when he learned of his error. But his actions left no doubt about Washington's intentions. In 1846, American settlers in the Sacramento Valley took matters into their own hands. Prodded by John C. Frémont, a former army captain and explorer who had arrived in December 1845 with a party of sixty buckskin-clad frontiersmen spoiling for a fight, the Californians raised an independence movement known as the Bear Flag Revolt. By then, James K. Polk, a champion of expansion, sat in the White House.

The Politics of Expansion

Although emigrants were the advance guard of American empire, there was nothing automatic about the U.S. annexation of territory in the West. Acquiring territory required political action, and in the 1840s the difficult problems of Texas, Oregon, and the Mexican borderlands intruded into national politics. The politics of expansion thrust the United States into dangerous diplomatic crises with Great Britain and Mexico. Even more ominous, expansion became hopelessly entangled with sectionalism and the slavery question.

Tyler and the Whig Fiasco

The complicated issues of westward expansion and the nation's boundaries ended up on the desk of John Tyler when he became president in April 1841. William Henry Harrison, a Whig, had been elected president in 1840, but one month after he took office, he died, the victim of pneumonia caught as he delivered his long inaugural address. For the first time in American history, a president had died in office, and it was not clear whether Vice President Tyler—"His Accidency," as his opponents called him—could legally exercise the full powers of an elected president.

Worse for the Whigs, Tyler was really a Democrat in Whig clothing. The fifty-one-year-old Virginian was a Whig only because he had fallen out with Andrew Jackson during the South Carolina nullification crisis. Tyler had consistently opposed all the measures of the Whig Henry Clay's American System: protective tariffs, the national bank, and internal improvements at federal expense. Tyler favored strict interpretation of the Constitution and states' rights, positions closer to those of the Democrats than of the Whigs. Whigs had placed Tyler on the ballot to appeal to Southerners, but they never expected that he would wield power. Even after Tyler moved into the White House, they assumed that he would bow to the party's leader, Kentucky Senator Henry Clay.

Clay viewed the Whig victory in 1840 as "a great civil revolution." After twelve years of Democratic rule, he could hardly wait to translate Whig programs and principles into law. Clay guided a raft of legislation through Congress. Tyler accepted the repeal of the Democrats' independent treasury and grudgingly approved a slightly higher tariff, but he vetoed a bill for internal improvements. Clay pressed on, emerging from Congress with a bill for a new national bank. The president promptly rejected it with a Jackson-like argument that it was "unconstitutional."

With his second veto, Tyler forfeited all claim to Whig leadership. His opposition left Clay's economic plan in shambles. The Whigs formally expelled Tyler from the party, and, in an unprecedented move, most of the cabinet resigned. Secretary of State Daniel Webster, however, stayed on to settle the boundary between Canada and the United States, still undetermined after fifty-six years. Observers dubbed the negotiations with Britain the "battle of the maps," but the Webster-Ashburton Treaty of 1842 settled all border issues with Canada, except Oregon.

Even Webster's success could not redeem the Tyler administration. Tyler betrayed the economic

For the first time in American history, a president had died in office, and it was not clear whether Vice President Tyler could legally exercise the full powers of an elected president.

principles of his supposed party, and Clay did not hesitate to compare John Tyler to Benedict Arnold. "Tyler is on his way to the Democratic camp," Clay declared. "They will give him lodgings in some outhouse, but they will never trust him. He will stand here, like Arnold in England, a monument of his own perfidy and disgrace." Writing off Tyler, Clay's followers hoisted Clay's banner for the presidency in 1844. Tyler dove into a quest for the Democratic nomination, but he needed an issue that could provide a bridge back to his former party.

Texas, Oregon, and the Election of 1844

The issue that stirred John Tyler's blood, and that of much of the nation, was Texas. Texans had sought admission to the Union almost since their independence from Mexico in 1836, and Tyler, an ardent expansionist, knew that the acquisition of Texas would appeal strongly to southern and western Democrats. He also understood that Texas was a dangerous issue. Any suggestion of adding another slave state to the Union brought many Northerners to a boil. Annexing Texas also risked precipitating war because Mexico had never relinquished its claim to its lost province.

Inhabitants of the Lone Star Republic lived a precarious existence. They often exchanged shots with Mexicans along the border, and they worried that Mexico would launch an invasion. Cold-shouldered by the United States, Texans explored Great Britain's interest in recognition and trade. They discovered that the British were eager to keep Texas independent. In Britain's eyes, Texas provided a buffer against American expansion and a new market for English manufactured goods. Moreover, Britain hoped to persuade Texas to adopt gradual emancipation. American officials worried that Britain's real object was adding Texas to the British Empire. This fluid mix of threat, fear, and opportunity convinced Tyler to risk negotiations with Texas,

and he worked vigorously to annex the republic before his term expired. His efforts pushed Texas and the slavery issue to the center of national politics.

In April 1844, after months of secret negotiations between Texas and the Tyler administration, the new secretary of state, South Carolinian John C. Calhoun, laid an annexation treaty before the Senate. But when Calhoun publicly linked annexation to the defense of slavery, he doomed the treaty. His statement strengthened the abolitionist claim that annexation was merely a proslavery plot, and howls of protest against annexation erupted everywhere north of the "Mason-Dixon line," the line drawn in 1763 by the English surveyors Charles Mason and Jeremiah Dixon to decide the boundary between the bickering colonies of Maryland and Pennsylvania. When the Senate soundly rejected the treaty, it appeared that Tyler had succeeded only in inflaming sectional conflict.

The issue of Texas had not died down by the 1844 elections. Henry Clay looked forward to waging his campaign on the old Whig economic principles that Tyler had frustrated. But everywhere he spoke, he confronted a barrage of questions about Texas. Finally, to appeal to northern voters, he came out against the immediate annexation of Texas. "Annexation and war with Mexico are identical," Clay declared. When news of Clay's statement reached Andrew Jackson at his plantation in Tennessee, he chuckled, "Clay [is] a dead political Duck." In Jackson's shrewd judgment, no man who opposed annexation could be elected president. But the Whig Party paid no attention, nominated Clay, and adopted a platform that proclaimed the principles of Clay's American System while remaining silent on Texas.

Among Democrats, Martin Van Buren expected to receive the party's nomination, but when he announced his opposition to Texas annexation, his candidacy collapsed in the South. Van Buren's demise opened the door at the Democratic convention. After John Tyler generated little support, James K. Polk of Tennessee gained his party's presidential nomination. Polk was as strong for the annexation of Texas as Clay was against it.

In the 1844 election, Democrats sought to champion Texas annexation without splitting their party or the nation. They succeeded by yoking Texas to Oregon, thus tapping the desire for expansion in the free states of the North as well as in the slave states of the South. The Democratic platform pulled out all the stops on behalf of manifest destiny. It called for the "reannexation of Texas" and the "reoccupation of Oregon." The suggestion that the United States was merely reasserting its existing rights was poor history but good politics. According to the Democratic formula, Texas annexation did not give an advantage to slavery and the South. Linked to Oregon, Texas expanded America to the advantage of the entire nation.

Much to Henry Clay's discomfort, Texas, not the tariff, emerged as the dominant issue of the 1844 campaign. When Clay finally recognized the groundswell for expansion, he lost his nerve. He waffled on Texas, hinting that he might accept annexation under certain circumstances. His retreat won little support in the South and only succeeded in alienating antislavery opinion in the North. James G. Birney, the candidate of the fledgling Liberty Party, picked up the votes of thousands of disillusioned Clay supporters. In the November election, Polk received 170 electoral votes and Clay 105. New York's 35 electoral votes proved critical to Clay's defeat. Birney received 15,000 votes in New York, but since Clay lost the state by only 5,000, a shift of just one-third of Birney's votes to Clay would have given him the state and the presidency.

Much to Henry Clay's discomfort, Texas, not the tariff, emerged as the dominant issue of the 1844 campaign.

The nation did not have to wait for Polk's inauguration to see results from his victory. One month after the election, President Tyler announced that the Democratic triumph provided a mandate for the annexation of Texas "promptly and immediately." In February 1845, after a fierce debate between antislavery and proslavery forces, Congress approved a joint resolution offering the Republic of Texas admission to the United States. Texas entered as the fifteenth slave state.

Tyler had delivered Texas, but James Polk had promised Oregon, too. Settlers in the West and expansionists elsewhere demanded that the new president make good on the Democrats' campaign slogan—"Fifty-four Forty or Fight"—that is, all of Oregon, right up to Alaska (54°40' being the southern latitude of Russian Alaska). But Polk was close to war with Mexico and could not afford a simultaneous war with Britain over its claims to Canada.

After the initial bluster, therefore, Polk buried the Democrats' campaign promise and renewed an old offer to divide Oregon along the forty-ninth parallel. After some hesitation, the British accepted the compromise. Westerners cried betrayal, but most Americans celebrated the agreement that gave the nation an enormous territory peacefully. Besides, when the Senate finally approved the treaty in June 1846, the United States and Mexico were already at war.

The Mexican War, 1846–1848

From its independence in 1821, Mexico realized that its security and success in nation building depended on harmonious relations with its northern neighbor. The United States, however, exhibited expansionist tendencies from the beginning. Aggravation between the two nations escalated to open antagonism in 1845 when the United States annexed Texas. Absorbing territory still claimed by Mexico ruptured diplomatic relations between the United States and Mexico and set the stage for war. But it was President James K. Polk's insistence on having Mexico's other northern provinces that made war certain. The war was not as easy as Polk anticipated, but it ended in American victory and acquisition of a new American West. Mexicans could only lament, "Poor Mexico, so far from God, so near the United States."

"Mr. Polk's War"

From the day he entered the White House, Polk craved Mexico's remaining northern provinces: California and New Mexico, land that today makes up California, Nevada, and Utah, most of New Mexico and Arizona, and parts of Wyoming and Colorado. Polk hoped to buy the territory. But the Mexicans refused to sell off their country, and in March 1846 they sent Polk's envoy, John Slidell, packing. A furious Polk concluded that it would take military force to realize the United States' manifest destiny.

Polk had already ordered General Zachary Taylor to march his 4,000-man Army of Occupation of Texas from its position on the Nueces River, the southern boundary of Texas according to the Mexicans, to the banks of the Rio Grande 150 miles south, the boundary claimed by Texans. Lieutenant George G. Meade, who would command troops at Gettysburg a few years later, admitted, "I hope for a war and a speedy battle, and I think one good fight will settle the business; and really, after coming so far . . . it would hardly be the thing to come back without some laurels." The Mexican general in Matamoros viewed the American advance as aggression and ordered Taylor back to the Nueces. Taylor refused, and on April 25 Mexican cavalry attacked a party of American soldiers, killing or wounding 16 and capturing the rest. Even before news of the battle arrived in Washington, Polk had already obtained his cabinet's approval of a war message.

On May 11, 1846, the president told Congress, "Mexico has passed the boundary of the United States, has invaded our territory, and shed American blood upon American soil." Thus "war exists, and, notwithstanding all our efforts to avoid it, exists by the act of Mexico herself." Two days later, Congress passed a declaration of war and began raising an army. Despite years of saber rattling toward Mexico and Britain, the American army was pitifully small, only 7,400 soldiers. Faced with the nation's first foreign war, up against a Mexican army that numbered more than 30,000, Polk called for volunteers who would serve for six to twelve months. Men everywhere rushed to the colors. More than 30,000 Tennesseans competed for the state's 3,000 allotted positions. Even Massachusetts, where many citizens denounced the war as a plot to extend slavery, filled its quota within a month. Eventually, more than 112,000 white Americans (blacks were banned) joined the army to fight in Mexico.

Despite the outpouring of support, the war divided the nation. Northerners were not nearly as hot-blooded about the war as Southerners. Although some Northerners kept their opposition to themselves because they did not want to appear unpatriotic or unwilling to support American soldiers in the field, a hard core of northern Whigs loudly condemned the war as the unwarranted bullying of a weak nation by its greedy expansionist neighbor.

On January 12, 1848, a gangly freshman representative from Illinois rose from his back-row seat in the House of Representatives to deliver his first important speech in Congress. Abraham Lincoln took direct aim at the president and his war. Polk's defense of the war, Lincoln declared, was from beginning to end the "sheerest deception." He challenged the president's version of the incident that precipitated war and sought to disprove Polk's claim that the territory between the Nueces and the Rio Grande was indisputably American soil. He likened the president's views to "the half-insane mumbling of a fever dream" and proclaimed Polk

"a bewildered, confounded, and miserably perplexed man." Before he sat down, Lincoln had questioned the president's intelligence, honesty, and sanity. President Polk simply ignored the upstart representative, but antislavery, antiwar Whigs kept up the attack throughout the conflict. In their effort to undercut national support, they labeled it "Mr. Polk's War."

Since most Americans backed the war, it was not really Polk's war, but the president acted as if it were. Although he had no military experience, he directed the war personally. Working eighteen hours a day, Polk established overall strategy and oversaw the details of military campaigns. He planned a short war in which American armies would occupy Mexico's northern provinces and defeat the Mexican army in a decisive battle or two, after which Mexico would sue for peace and the United States would keep the territory its armies occupied.

And, indeed, Polk's strategy seemed to work at first. In May 1846, Zachary Taylor's troops drove south from the Rio Grande and routed the Mexican army, first on the plain of Palo Alto and then in a palm-filled ravine known as Resaca de la Palma (Map 11.4). Taylor became an instant war hero. At sixty-two years, "Old Rough and Ready," as he was affectionately known, had an undistinguished career behind him. But his simplicity and informality, as well as his cool behavior under fire, endeared him to his men. Polk rewarded Taylor for his victories by making him commander for the conquest of Mexico.

A second prong of the campaign to occupy Mexico's northern provinces centered on Colonel Stephen Watts Kearny, who led a 1,700-man army from Missouri into New Mexico. Without firing a shot, American forces took Santa Fe in August 1846. Kearny promptly proclaimed New Mexico American territory and with 300 troops headed for California. On the trail, incredibly, he met Kit Carson, part of John C. Frémont's buckskin army, who was hurrying east with the news of the American seizure of California. After three months on the trail, Kearny's army marched into San Diego and into a major Mexican rebellion against American rule. In January 1847, after several clashes, the American forces occupied Los Angeles. California and New Mexico were in American hands.

By then, Taylor had driven deep into the interior of Mexico. In September 1846, after a five-day siege and house-to-house fighting, he took the fortified city of Monterrey. With reinforcements and fresh supplies, Taylor pushed his 5,000 troops

MAP 11.4

The Mexican War, 1846–1848

American and Mexican soldiers skirmished across much of northern Mexico, but the major battles took place between the Rio Grande and Mexico City.

southwest, where the Mexican hero of the Alamo, General Antonio López de Santa Anna, was concentrating a huge army of 21,000, which he hoped would strike a decisive blow against the invaders from the north.

On Washington's birthday 1847, Taylor's troops met Santa Anna's at Buena Vista. Superior American artillery and accurate musket fire won the day, but the Americans suffered heavy casualties, including Henry Clay Jr., the son of the man who had opposed Texas annexation for fear it would precipitate war. But the Mexicans suffered even greater

losses, and during the night Santa Anna removed his battered army from the battlefield, much to the "profound disgust of the troops," one Mexican officer remembered. "They are filled with grief that they were going to lose the benefit of all the sacrifices that they had made; that the conquered field would be abandoned, and that the victory would be given to the enemy." Retreat fed the belief "that it was impossible to conquer the Americans."

The series of uninterrupted victories in northern Mexico fed the American troops' sense of superiority and very nearly led to a feeling of invin-

BATTLE OF PALO ALTO

The battle of Palo Alto, fought in May 1846 and captured here by lithographer Carl Nebel, was the first full-scale battle the U.S. Army had fought since the War of 1812. Here we see General Zachary Taylor astride Old Whitey, as he directs the action from the right foreground. On the extreme right Colonel David Twiggs's infantry repulses Anastasio Torrejon's cavalry. On the left smoke from the grass fire conceals 150 additional Mexican cavalrymen. Ferocious American artillery won the day. "The American artillery," one Mexican reported, "much superior to ours, made terrible ravages in the Mexican ranks. . . . The troops, drained by the needless deaths, pleaded to go before the enemy's bayonets and die bravely in close range."

Amon Carter Museum of Western Art, Fort Worth, Texas.

cibility. "No American force has ever thought of being defeated by any amount of Mexican troops," one soldier declared. The Americans worried about other hazards, however. "I can assure you that fighting is the least dangerous & arduous part of a soldier's life," one young man said. Letters home told of torturous marches across burning, arid wastes alive with tarantulas, scorpions, and rattlesnakes. Others recounted dysentery, malaria, smallpox, cholera, and yellow fever. Of the 13,000 American soldiers who died in Mexico (some 50,000 Mexicans died), only 2,000 fell to Mexican bullets and shells. Disease killed most of the others. Medicine was so primitive and conditions so harsh that army doctors could do little. As a Tennessee man observed, "nearly all who take sick die."

Victory in Mexico

Although Americans won battle after battle, President Polk's strategy misfired. Despite its loss of territory and men, Mexico determinedly refused to trade land for peace. One American soldier captured the Mexican mood: "They cannot submit to be deprived of California after the loss of Texas, and nothing but the conquest of their Capital will force them to such a humiliation." Polk had arrived at the same conclusion. Zachary Taylor had not proven decisive enough for Polk, and the president tapped another general to carry the war to Mexico City. While Taylor occupied the north, General Winfield Scott would land his army on the Gulf coast of Mexico and march 250 miles inland to the capital. Polk's plan entailed enormous risk; it meant that Scott would have to cut himself off from supplies on the coast and lead his men deep into enemy country against a numerically superior foe.

The series of uninterrupted victories in northern Mexico fed the American troops' sense of superiority and very nearly led to a feeling of invincibility.

After months of careful planning and the skillful coordination of army and navy, an amphibious landing near Veracruz put 8,600 American troops ashore in five hours without the loss of a single life. The Americans encircled the city, and after eighty-eight hours of furious shelling, Veracruz surrendered. Scott immediately began preparations for the march west. Transportation alone posed enormous problems. His army required 9,300 wagons and 17,000 pack mules, 500,000 bushels of oats and corn, and 100 pounds of blister ointment before it could begin the mountainous journey. In early April 1847, the army moved out, following the path that had been trodden more than three centuries earlier by Hernán Cortés.

Meanwhile, after the frightful defeat at Buena Vista, Santa Anna had returned to Mexico City. He rallied his ragged troops and marched them east to set a trap for Scott in the mountain pass at Cerro Gordo. But the Americans knifed through Mexican lines, almost capturing Santa Anna, who fled the field on foot. So complete was the victory that Scott gloated to Taylor, "Mexico no longer has an army." But Scott barely had one either. One-third of his troops—some 3,000 men—were volunteers whose year's service had expired. Scott had no choice but to release them and wait for reinforcements. In July 1847, with the army topping 14,000 soldiers, Scott resumed his march. Ever resilient, Santa Anna again rallied the Mexican army. Some 30,000 troops took up defensive positions on the outskirts of Mexico City, where they hurriedly began melting down church bells to cast new cannon.

In August, Scott began his assault on the Mexican capital. The fighting proved the most brutal of the war. Santa Anna backed his army into the city, fighting each step of the way. At the battle of Churubusco, the Mexicans took 4,000 casualties in a single day and the Americans more than 1,000. At the castle of Chapultepec, American troops scaled the walls and fought the Mexican defenders hand to hand. After Chapultepec, Santa Anna evacuated

MEXICAN FAMILY
This family had its portrait taken in 1847, in the middle of the war. Where were the adult males? Mexican civilians were vulnerable to atrocities committed by the invading army. Volunteers, a large portion of American troops, received little training and resisted discipline. The "lawless Volunteers stop at no outrage," Brigadier General William Worth declared. "Innocent blood has been basely, cowardly, and barbarously shed in cold blood." Generals Zachary Taylor and Winfield Scott gradually tamed the volunteers with stern military justice.
Courtesy Amon Carter Museum, Fort Worth, Texas.

Mexico City, and on September 14, 1847, General Winfield Scott rode in triumphantly. The ancient capital of the Aztecs had fallen once again to an invading army.

With Mexico City in American hands, Polk sent Nicholas P. Trist, the chief clerk in the State Department, to Mexico to negotiate the peace. On February 2, 1848, Trist and Mexican officials signed the Treaty of Guadalupe Hidalgo. Mexico agreed to give up all claims to Texas above the Rio Grande and to cede the huge provinces of New Mexico and California to the United States. The United States agreed to pay Mexico $15 million and to assume

$3.25 million in claims that American citizens had against Mexico. Some Americans clamored for all of Mexico, and others for less, but the Senate ratified the treaty by a vote of thirty-eight to fourteen in March 1848. The last American soldiers left Mexico a few months later.

The American triumph in the Mexican War had enormous consequences. Less than three-quarters of a century after its founding, the United States achieved its self-proclaimed manifest destiny to stretch from the Atlantic to the Pacific (Map 11.5). With the northern half of Mexico in American hands, California gold, which was discovered almost

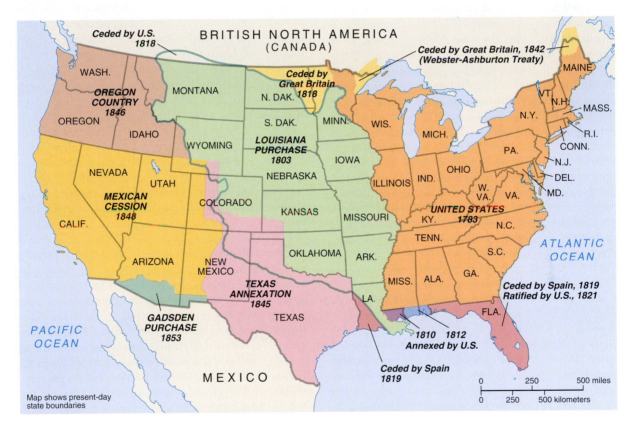

MAP 11.5

Territorial Expansion by 1860
Less than a century after its founding, the United States had spread from the Atlantic seaboard to the Pacific Ocean. War, purchase, and diplomacy had gained a continent.

READING THE MAP: List the countries from which the United States acquired land. Which nation lost the most land because of U.S. expansion?

CONNECTIONS: Who coined the phrase *manifest destiny?* When? What does it mean? What areas targeted for expansion were debated during the presidential campaign of 1844?

www.bedfordstmartins.com/tap SEE THE ONLINE STUDY GUIDE for more help in analyzing this map.

Who Rushed for California Gold?

ON A COLD JANUARY morning in 1848, while James Marshall was walking along the American River in the foothills of the Sierra Nevada, he detected the glint of yellow metal in the stream. The flakes he found set off the California gold rush, one of the wildest mining stampedes in the world's history. Between 1849 and 1852, more than 250,000 "forty-niners," as the would-be miners were known, descended on the Golden State.

Marshall discovered gold in the same year that the Treaty of Guadalupe Hidalgo transferred California and other northern provinces of Mexico to the United States. Americans did not find it surprising that the discovery coincided with American acquisition. "God kept that coast for a people of the Pilgrim blood," one minister intoned. "He would not permit any other to be fully developed there."

Gold proved irresistible to easterners. Newspapers went crazy with stories about prospectors who extracted half a pan of gold from every pan of gravel they scooped from western streams. Soon, cities reverberated with men singing:

Oh Susannah, don't you cry for me;
I'm gone to California with my wash-bowl on
   my knee.

Scores of ships sailed from East Coast ports, headed either around South America to San Francisco or across the Gulf of Mexico to Panama, where the passengers made their way by foot and canoe to the Pacific and waited for a ship to carry them north. Even larger numbers of gold seekers took riverboats to the Missouri River and then set out in wagons, on horseback, or by foot for the West.

But young men everywhere contracted gold fever. As stories of California gold circled the globe, Chinese and Germans, Mexicans and Irish, Australians and French, Chileans and Italians, and people of dozens of other nationalities set out to strike it rich. Louisa Knapp Clappe, wife of a minister and one of the few women in gold country, remarked that when she walked through Indian Bar, the little mining town where she lived, she heard English, French, Spanish, German, Italian, Kanaka (Hawaiian), Asian Indian, and American Indian languages. Hangtown, Hell's Delight, Gouge Eye, and a hundred other crude mining camps became temporary home to a diverse throng of nationalities and peoples.

One of the largest groups of new arrivals was the Chinese. Between 1848 and 1854, Chinese men numbering 45,000 (but almost no Chinese women) arrived in California. Most considered themselves "sojourners," temporary residents who planned to return home as soon as their savings allowed. The majority came under a Chinese-controlled contract labor system in which the immigrant worked out the cost of his transportation. In the early years, most became wage laborers in mining. By the 1860s, they dominated railroad construction in the West. Ninety percent of the Central Pacific Railroad's 10,000 workers were Chinese. The Chinese also made up nearly one-half of San Francisco's labor force, working in the shoe, tobacco, woolen, laundry, and sewing trades. By 1870, the Chinese population had grown to 63,200, including 4,500 women. They constituted nearly 10 percent of the state's people and 25 percent of its wage-earning force.

The presence of peoples from around the world shattered the Anglo-American dream of a racially and ethnically homogeneous West, but ethnic diversity did nothing to increase the tolerance of Anglo-American prospectors. In their eyes, no "foreigner" had a right to dig gold. In 1850, the California legislature passed the Foreign Miners' Tax Law, which levied high taxes on non-Americans to drive them from the gold fields, except as hired laborers working on claims owned by Americans. Stubborn foreign miners were sometimes hauled before "Judge Lynch." One of the earliest lynchings in the gold fields was of a Frenchman and a Chilean.

Anglo-Americans considered the Chinese devious and unassimilable. They also feared that hardworking, self-denying Chinese labor would undercut white labor and drive it from the country. As a consequence, the Chinese were segregated residentially and occupationally and made ineligible for citizenship. Along with blacks and Indians, Chinese were denied public education and the right to testify in court. In addition to exclusion, they suffered from violence. Mobs drove them from Eureka, Truckee, and other mining towns.

American prospectors swamped the *Californios*, the Spanish and Mexican settlers who had lived in California for generations. On the eve of the American takeover, *Californios* included *rancheros*, professionals, merchants, artisans, and laborers. Raging prejudice and discriminatory laws increasingly pushed Hispanics into the ranks of unskilled labor. Americans took their land, even though the federal government had pledged to protect Mexican and Spanish land titles after the cession of 1848. Anglo forty-niners branded Spanish-speaking miners, even native-born *Californios*, "foreigners" and drove them from the diggings. Mariano Vallejo, a leading *Californio*, said of the forty-niners: "The good ones were few and the wicked many."

For Native Americans, the gold rush was a catastrophe. Numbering about 150,000 in 1848, the Indian population fell to 25,000 in 1856. *Californios* had exploited the native peoples, but the forty-niners wanted to eradicate them. Starvation, disease, and a declining birthrate took a heavy toll. Indians also fell victim to wholesale murder. "That a war of extermination will continue to be waged between the two races until the Indian race becomes extinct must

be expected," declared California governor Peter W. Burnett in 1851. Nineteenth-century historian Hubert Howe Bancroft described white behavior toward Indians during the gold rush as "one of the last human hunts of civilization, and the basest and most brutal of them all." To survive, Indians moved to the most remote areas of the state and tried to stay out of the way.

The forty-niners created dazzling wealth—in 1852, eighty-one million ounces of gold, nearly one-half of the world's production. But because Anglo-Americans made the rules, not everyone shared equally. And only a few prospectors—of whatever race and nationality—struck it rich. The era of the individual prospector panning in streams quickly gave way to corporate-owned deep-shaft mining. Most forty-niners eventually took up farming or worked for wages for the corporations that pushed them out. But because of gold, an avalanche of people had roared across California. Anglo-Americans were most numerous, and Anglo dominance developed early. But the gold rush also brought a rainbow of nationalities. Anglo-American ascendancy and ethnic and racial diversity in the West both count among the most significant legacies of the gold rush.

The American triumph in the Mexican War had enormous consequences. Less than three-quarters of a century after its founding, the United States achieved its self-proclaimed manifest destiny to stretch from the Atlantic to the Pacific.

simultaneously with the transfer of territory, neither made Mexicans rich nor bankrolled Mexico's economic development. Instead, the West became an enclave for Anglo-American enterprise and wealth. (See "Historical Question," page 400.) The war also reinforced the worst stereotypes Mexicans and Americans had of each other. A virulent anti-Yankee sentiment took root in Mexico, while deeply prejudiced views of Mexicans and Mexican culture flourished in the fertile soil of American victory. For Mexico, defeat meant national humiliation, but it also had a positive effect. It generated for the first time a genuine nationalism, no small thing in a country still trying to build a nation. In America, victory increased the sense of superiority that was already deeply ingrained.

Conclusion: Free Labor, Free Men

In the 1840s, diplomacy and war handed the United States 1.2 million square miles and more than 1,000 miles of Pacific coastline. To most Americans, vast geographical expansion seemed to be the natural companion of a stunning economic transformation. A cluster of interrelated developments—steam power, railroads, and the growing mechanization of agriculture and manufacturing—resulted in greater productivity, a burst of output from farms and factories, and prosperity for many.

To Northerners, their industrial evolution confirmed the choice they had made to put slavery on the road to extinction and to promote free labor as the key to independence, equality, and prosperity. Millions of Northerners, like Abraham Lincoln, could point to personal experience as evidence of the practical truth of the free-labor ideal. But millions of others had different stories to tell. Rather than producing economic equality, the free-labor system saw wealth and poverty continue to rub shoulders. Instead of social independence, more than half of the nation's free-labor workforce toiled for someone else by 1860. Free-labor enthusiasts denied that the problems were built into the system. They argued that most social ills—including poverty and dependency—sprang from individual deficiencies. Consequently, reformers usually focused on the lack of self-control and discipline, on sin and alcohol. They denied that free labor meant exploitation. Slaves, not free workers, suffered, they argued.

White Southerners pitied northern free workers, not slaves. They denied that slaves suffered and instead claimed that slavery had built a superior civilization, for both whites and blacks. Differences between North and South had appeared early in the nation's history, but by midcentury the distinctive ways in which North and South organized their labor systems left their mark on all aspects of regional life. Each region was increasingly animated by economic interests, cultural values, and political aims that were antithetical to those of the other. The nation was half slave and half free, and not even victory over Mexico could bridge the deepening differences between North and South.

www.bedfordstmartins.com/tap SEE THE ONLINE STUDY GUIDE to assess your mastery of the material covered in this chapter.

CHRONOLOGY

1836 Texas declares independence from Mexico.

1837 John Deere patents his steel plow.

1840s Americans begin harnessing steam power to manufacturing.

Cyrus McCormick and others create practical mechanical reapers.

1841 First wagon trains set out for West on Oregon Trail.

Vice President John Tyler becomes president of the United States when William Henry Harrison dies in office after one month.

1842 Webster-Ashburton Treaty settles all border issues with British Canada except Oregon.

1844 Democrat James K. Polk elected president on platform calling for annexation of Texas and Oregon.

Samuel F. B. Morse invents telegraph.

1845 Term *manifest destiny* coined by New York journalist John L. O'Sullivan; used as justification for Anglo-American settlers to take land in West.

United States annexes Texas, which enters Union as slave state.

1846 Bear Flag Revolt, independence movement to secede from Mexico, takes place in California.

May 13. Congress declares war on Mexico.

United States and Great Britain agree to divide Oregon Country at forty-ninth parallel.

1847 Brigham Young leads advance party of Mormons to Great Salt Lake in Utah.

1848 Treaty of Guadalupe Hidalgo ends Mexican War. Mexico gives up all claims to Texas north of Rio Grande and cedes provinces of New Mexico and California to United States.

Oneida community organized in New York.

First women's rights convention in United States takes place at Seneca Falls, New York.

1849 California gold rush begins.

Harriet Tubman escapes from slavery in Maryland.

1850 Mormon community of Deseret annexed to United States as Utah Territory.

1851 Conference in Laramie, Wyoming, between U.S. government and Plains tribes marks beginning of government policy of forcing Indians onto reservations.

1855 Massachusetts integrates public schools as result of campaigns led by African Americans.

BIBLIOGRAPHY

GENERAL WORKS

Glenn C. Altschuler and Stuart M. Blumin, *Rude Republic: Americans and Their Politics in the Nineteenth Century* (2000).

Stuart Bruchey, *Enterprise: The Dynamic Economy of a Free People* (1990).

David B. Danbom, *Born in the Country: A History of Rural America* (1995).

David Herbert Donald, *Lincoln* (1995).

John Mack Faragher, *Sugar Creek: Life on the Illinois Frontier* (1986).

Lori D. Ginzberg, *Women and the Work of Benevolence: Morality, Politics, and Class in the Nineteenth-Century United States* (1990).

Jon Gjerde, *The Minds of the West: Ethnocultural Evolution in the Rural Middle West, 1830–1917* (1997).

Nathan O. Hatch, *The Democratization of American Christianity* (1991).

Bruce Laurie, *Artisans into Workers: Labor in Nineteenth-Century America* (1989).

Patricia Nelson Limerick, *The Legacy of Conquest: The Unbroken Past of the American West* (1987).

Malcolm Rohrbough, *Days of Gold: The California Gold Rush and the American Nation* (1997).

Robert M. Utley, *The Indian Frontier of the American West, 1846–1890* (1984).

Richard White, *"It's Your Misfortune and None of My Own": A New History of the American West* (1993).

THE ECONOMY AND FREE LABOR

Howard Bodenhorn, *A History of Banking in Antebellum America: Financial Markets and Economic Development in an Era of Nation Building* (2000).

Allan G. Bogue, *From Prairie to Corn Belt: Farming on the Illinois and Iowa Prairies in the Nineteenth Century* (1963).

Paul G. Faler, *Mechanics and Manufacturers in the Early Industrial Revolution: Lynn, Massachusetts, 1780–1860* (1981).

J. Matthew Gallman, *Receiving Erin's Children: Philadelphia, Liverpool, and the Irish Famine Migration, 1854–1855* (2000).

Paul W. Gates, *The Farmer's Age: Agriculture, 1815–1860* (1960).

Jonathan A. Glickstein, *Concepts of Free Labor in Antebellum America* (1991).

Brooke Hindle and Steven Lubar, *Engines of Change: The American Industrial Revolution, 1790–1860* (1986).

Susan E. Hirsch, *Roots of the American Working Class: The Industrialization of Crafts in Newark, 1800–1860* (1978).

Donald R. Hoke, *Ingenious Yankees: The Rise of the American System of Manufactures in the Private Sector* (1990).

David A. Hounshell, *From the American System to Mass Production, 1800–1932: The Development of Manufacturing Technology in the United States* (1984).

Reeve Huston, *Land and Freedom: Rural Society, Popular Protest, and Party Politics in Antebellum New York* (2000).

Paul Israel, *From Machine Shop to Industrial Laboratory: Telegraphy and the Changing Context of American Invention, 1830–1920* (1992).

Allan Kulikoff, *The Agrarian Origins of American Capitalism* (1992).

Bruce Laurie, *Working People of Philadelphia, 1800–1850* (1980).

Edward Laxton, *The Famine Ships: The Irish Exodus to America* (1998).

Robert A. Margo, *Wages and Labor Markets in the United States, 1820–1860* (2000).

Jonathan Prude, *The Coming of Industrial Order: Town and Factory Life in Rural Massachusetts, 1810–1860* (1983).

W. J. Rorabaugh, *The Craft Apprentice: From Franklin to the Machine Age in America* (1986).

John F. Stover, *Iron Road to the West: American Railroads in the 1850s* (1978).

George Rogers Taylor, *The Transportation Revolution, 1815–1860* (1951).

ANTEBELLUM CULTURE AND REFORM

Norman Basch, *In the Eyes of the Law: Women, Marriage, and Property in Nineteenth-Century New York* (1982).

Stuart Blumin, *The Emergence of the Middle Class: Social Experience in the American City, 1790–1900* (1989).

Jeanne Boydston, *Home and Work: Housework, Wages, and the Ideology of Labor in the Early Republic* (1990).

Ellen Carol DuBois, *Feminism and Suffrage: The Emergence of an Independent Women's Suffrage Movement in America, 1848–1869* (1978).

Michael Fellman, *The Unbounded Frame: Freedom and Community on Nineteenth Century American Utopianism* (1973).

Joseph P. Ferrie, *Yankeys Now: Immigrants in the Antebellum United States, 1840–1860* (1999).

Lawrence Foster, *Women, Family, and Utopia: Communal Experiments of the Shakers, the Oneida Community, and the Mormons* (1991).

Rhoda Golden Freeman, *The Free Negro in New York City in the Era Before the Civil War* (1994).

Paul Goodman, *Of One Blood: Abolitionism and the Origins of Racial Equality* (1998).

Karen Halttunen, *Confidence Men and Painted Women: A Study of Middle-Class Culture in America, 1830–1870* (1982).

Debra Gold Hansen, *Strained Sisterhood: Gender and Class in the Boston Female Anti-Slavery Society* (1993).

Nancy A. Hewitt, *Women's Activism and Social Change: Rochester, New York, 1822–1872* (1984).

Leo P. Himel, *Children of Wrath: New School Calvinism and Antebellum Reform* (1998).

Sylvia D. Hoffert, *When Hens Crow: The Women's Rights Movement in Antebellum America* (1995).

James O. Horton and Lois E. Horton, *In Hope of Liberty: Culture, Community, and Protest Among Northern Free Blacks, 1700–1860* (1998).

Nancy Isenberg, *Sex and Citizenship in Antebellum America* (1998).

Julie Roy Jeffrey, *The Great Silent Army of Abolitionism: Ordinary Women in the Antislavery Movement* (1998).

Joan M. Jensen, *Loosening the Bonds: Mid-Atlantic Farm Women, 1750–1850* (1986).

Carl F. Kaestle, *Pillars of the Republic: Common Schools and American Society, 1780–1860* (1983).

Spencer Klaw, *Without Sin: The Life and Death of the Oneida Community* (1993).

William J. McFeely, *Frederick Douglass* (1991).

Henry Mayer, *All On Fire: William Lloyd Garrison and the Abolition of Slavery* (1998).

Kerby A. Miller, *Emigrants and Exiles: Ireland and the Irish Exodus to North America* (1985).

Steven Mintz, *Moralists and Modernizers: America's Pre-Civil War Reformers* (1995).

John W. Quist, *Restless Visionaries: The Social Roots of Antebellum Reform in Alabama and Michigan* (1998).

Mary P. Ryan, *Civic Wars: Democracy and Public Life in the American City during the Nineteenth Century* (1998).

Mark S. Schantz, *Piety in Providence: Class Dimensions of Religious Experience in Antebellum Rhode Island* (2000).

Albert J. Von Frank, *The Trials of Anthony Burns: Freedom and Slavery in Emerson's Boston* (1998).

Edward L. Widmer, *Young America: The Flowering of Democracy in New York City* (1998).

Shirley Yee, *Black Women Abolitionists: A Study in Activism, 1828–1860* (1992).

Jean Fagan Yellin, *Women and Sisters: The Antislavery Feminists in American Culture* (1989).

Jean Fagan Yellin and John C. Van Horne, eds., *The Abolitionist Sisterhood: Women's Political Culture in Antebellum America* (1994).

POLITICS AND EXPANSION

Leonard J. Arrington and Davis Bitton, *The Mormon Experience: A History of the Latter-Day Saints* (1979).

Irving H. Bartlett, *John C. Calhoun: A Biography* (1993).

Richard A. Bartlett, *The New Country: A Social History of the American Frontier, 1776–1890* (1974).

Peter J. Blodgett, *Land of Golden Dreams: California in the Gold Rush Decade, 1848–1858* (1999).

William A. Bowen, *The Willamette Valley: Migration and Settlement on the Oregon Frontier* (1978).

Gene Brack, *Mexico Views Manifest Destiny, 1821–1846: An Essay on the Origins of the Mexican War* (1975).

Yong Chen, *Chinese San Francisco, 1850–1943: A Trans-Pacific Community* (2000).

Donald E. Chipman, *Spanish Texas, 1519–1821* (1992).

Arnoldo De Leon, *The Tejano Community, 1836–1900* (1982).

John Mack Faragher, *Women and Men on the Overland Trail* (1979).

James R. Gibson, *Farming the Frontier: The Agricultural Opening of the Oregon Country, 1786–1846* (1985).

William H. Goetzmann, *New Lands, New Men: America and the Second Great Age of Discovery* (1986).

William S. Greever, *Bonanza West: The Story of the Western Mining Rushes, 1848–1900* (1963).

Thomas R. Hietala, *Manifest Design: Anxious Aggrandizement in Late Jacksonian America* (1985).

Reginald Horsman, *Race and Manifest Destiny: The Origins of American Racial Anglo-Saxonism* (1981).

Albert L. Hurtado, *Indian Survival on the California Frontier* (1988).

Robert H. Jackson and Edward Castillo, *Indians, Franciscans, and Spanish Colonization: The Impact of the Mission System on California Indians* (1995).

Julie Roy Jeffrey, *Frontier Women: The Trans-Mississippi West, 1840–1880* (1979).

David Alan Johnson, *Founding the Far West: California, Oregon, and Nevada, 1840–1890* (1992).

Rudolph M. Lapp, *Blacks in Gold Rush California* (1977).

Charles J. McClain, *In Search of Equality: The Chinese Struggle against Discrimination in Nineteenth-Century America* (1994).

D. W. Meinig, *The Shaping of America: A Geographical Perspective on 500 Years of History*, vol. 2, *Continental America, 1800–1867* (1993).

Frederick Merk, *Manifest Destiny and Mission in American History: A Reinterpretation* (1963).

Michael C. Meyer and William L. Sherman, *The Course of Mexican History* (4th ed., 1991).

David Montejano, *Anglos and Mexicans in the Making of Texas, 1836–1986* (1987).

Gregory H. Nobles, *American Frontiers: Cultural Encounters and Continental Conquest* (1997).

Rodman W. Paul, *Mining Frontiers of the Far West, 1848–1880* (1963).

David M. Pletcher, *The Diplomacy of Annexation: Texas, Oregon, and the Mexican War* (1973).

Glenda Riley, *The Female Frontier: A Comparative View of Women on the Prairie and the Plains* (1988).

Malcolm J. Rohrbough, *The Trans-Appalachian Frontier* (1978).

Joel H. Silbey, *The American Political Nation, 1838–1915* (1991).

Ronald Takaki, *Iron Cages: Race and Culture in 19th-Century America* (1979).

John D. Unruh, *The Plains Across: The Overland Emigrants and the Trans-Mississippi West, 1840–1860* (1979).

David J. Weber, *The Mexican Frontier, 1821–1846: The American Southwest under Mexico* (1982).

Sanford Wexler, ed., *Westward Expansion: An Eyewitness History* (1991).

THE MEXICAN WAR

K. Jack Bauer, *The Mexican War, 1846–1848* (1974).

Seymour V. Conner and Odie B. Faulk, *North America Divided: The Mexican War, 1846–1848* (1971).

John S. D. Eisenhower, *So Far from God: The U.S. War with Mexico, 1846–1848* (1989).

Donald S. Frazier, ed., *The United States and Mexico at War: Nineteenth-Century Expansionism and Conflict* (1998).

Robert W. Johannsen, *To the Halls of the Montezumas: The Mexican War in the American Imagination* (1985).

Ernest M. Lander Jr., *Reluctant Imperialists: Calhoun, the South Carolinians, and the Mexican War* (1980).

Ward McAfee and J. Cordell Robinson, eds., *Origins of the Mexican War: A Documentary Source Book*, 2 vols. (1982).

James M. McCaffrey, *Army of Manifest Destiny: The American Soldier in the Mexican War, 1846–1848* (1992).

Ramon Eduardo Ruiz, ed., *The Mexican War: Was It Manifest Destiny?* (1963).

Richard Bruce Winders, *Mr. Polk's Army: The American Military Experience in the Mexican War* (1997).

SLAVE JUG

This ceramic water cooler, made in about 1840, is attributed to Thomas Chandler, a famous slave potter of Edgefield District, South Carolina. The relatively fine clothes of the African American man and woman portrayed on the vessel suggest that they are house servants. On the wall of the home of Alexander Stephens in Crawfordsville, Georgia, an intriguing letter from Stephens states that two of his favorite slaves are getting married and orders the plantation manager to butcher a hog for their wedding. With its portrait of a couple, a hog, and a jug, it is possible that Stephens commissioned this cooler to commemorate the union.

Potters made vessels for use—they held water and food. Analysis of the form, decoration, and glazes of southern pottery suggests a blend of European, African, and Native American ceramic traditions. Some pottery went beyond the utilitarian and became art. The most renowned slave potter was another Edgefield man by the name of Dave, who skillfully fashioned huge vessels, inscribed poems on their surfaces, and proudly and boldly signed them, "Dave the potter." Although a slave, Dave self-consciously left his mark.

Collection of the High Museum of Art, Atlanta. Purchase in honor of Audrey Shilt, President of the Members Guild of the High Museum of Art, 1996–1997, with funds from the Decorative Arts Endowment & Acquisition Trust 1996.

THE SLAVE SOUTH

1820–1860

12

BORN A SLAVE IN SOUTHAMPTON COUNTY, VIRGINIA, on October 1, 1800, Nat Turner had always been seen as different. His parents had noticed special marks on his body, which they said were signs that he was "intended for some great purpose." As a boy, he learned to read without being taught, and his master said that he was too intelligent to be a slave. As an adolescent, he adopted a severe lifestyle of Christian devotion and fasting. In his twenties, he received visits from the "Spirit," the same spirit, he believed, which had spoken to the ancient prophets. In time, Nat Turner began to interpret these things to mean that God had appointed him an instrument of divine vengeance for the sin of slaveholding. On February 12, 1831, a solar eclipse confirmed his suspicions, and a green-tinted sun on August 13 erased any lingering doubts he might have had about his purpose on this earth.

On Sunday, August 21, he gathered six trusted friends—Hark, Henry, Sam, Nelson, Will, and Jack—and early the next morning, they set out to punish slave owners and free their suffering slaves. The first blow was that of Nat Turner's ax to the head of his master, Joseph Travis. The rebels killed all of the whites—men, women, and children—in each household they attacked and then moved on to the next. By noon, they had visited eleven farms and slaughtered fifty-seven whites and, along the way, added fifty or sixty men to their army. Word spread quickly, however, and soon the militia and hundreds of local whites gathered. By the next day, whites had captured or killed all of the insurgents, except for Nat Turner, who successfully hid out for about ten weeks before being captured in nearby woods. Within a week, he was tried, convicted, and executed. By then, forty-five slaves had stood trial; twenty had been convicted and hanged and another ten had been transported from Virginia. Another hundred or more blacks—rebels and innocent bystanders—had been killed in the whites' frenzied counterattack against the insurrection.

Slave revolts were white Southerners' worst nightmare. "They lie down to sleep with fear," a sympathetic Northerner reported of Virginians. "Bolts and bars were tried, but the horrid fear haunted the whole population day and night." Virginia's governor John Floyd asked how this "murderous Bandit" with his band of "assassins and murderers" could have assaulted in their sleep the "unsuspecting and defenseless" citizens of "one of the fairest counties in the Commonwealth." Virginians prided themselves on having the "mildest" slavery in the South, but sixty black rebels on a rampage challenged the comforting theory of the contented slave. Nonetheless, whites found explanations that allowed them to sleep again. Often, they put the blame on outside agitators. In 1829, David Walker, a freeborn black man from North Carolina, had published his *Appeal . . . to the Colored Citizens of the World*, an invitation to slaves to rise up in bloody rebellion, and copies had fallen into the hands of Virginia slaves. In addition, William Lloyd Garrison, the Massachusetts abolitionist, had on January 1, 1831, published the first issue of his fiery newspaper, the *Liberator*. Most important, white Virginians dismissed the rebellion's

NAT TURNER

There are no known contemporary images of Nat Turner. This imagined portrait comes from William Still's **The Underground Railroad,** *which was published in 1872. Meeting secretly at night deep in a forest and thus well out of earshot of whites, an intense Turner passionately tries to convince four other slaves to join him in rebellion. What do their faces reveal? What considerations do you suppose entered their calculations about whether to join Turner? Significantly perhaps, they are holding work tools, not arms.*
Library of Congress.

leader, Nat Turner, as insane. "He is a complete fanatic, or plays his part admirably," wrote Thomas R. Gray, the lawyer who was assigned to defend Turner.

In the months following the insurrection, white Virginians debated the future of slavery in their state. While some expressed substantial doubts, the Virginia legislature reaffirmed the state's determination to beat back any threat to white supremacy. Delegates passed a raft of laws strengthening the institution of slavery and further restricting free blacks. A thirty-year-old professor at the College of William and Mary, Thomas R. Dew, published a vigorous defense of slavery that became the bible of Southerners' proslavery arguments. More than ever, the nation was divided along the "Mason-Dixon line" between Maryland and Pennsylvania. Half a century later, the English surveyors' mark divided the free North and slave South. Northern states had either abolished slavery or put it on the road to extinction while southern states were aggressively building the largest slave society in the New World.

Black slavery increasingly dominated southern society and shaped the South into a distinctive region. In the decades after 1820, Southerners, like Northerners, raced westward, but they spread slavery, cotton, and plantations. Geographic expansion meant that slavery became more vigorous and profitable than ever, embraced more people, and increased the South's political power. Antebellum Southerners included diverse peoples who at times found themselves at odds with one another—not only slaves and free people, but also women and men; Indians, Africans, and Europeans; and aristocrats and common folk. Nevertheless, beneath this diversity of Southerners there was also forming a distinctively southern society and culture. The South became a slave society, and most white Southerners were proud of it.

In the end, the South's identification with slavery and insistence on its preservation culminated in the creation of a separate Confederacy that ultimately brought about what Nat Turner had tried in vain to achieve in 1831: the end of slavery.

The Southern Difference

The Mason-Dixon line was a surveyor's mark on a map, not a physical barrier dividing North and South. No impenetrable jungle, insurmountable mountain range, or impassable desert separated the regions. From the earliest settlements, inhabitants of southern colonies had shared a great deal with northern colonists. Most whites in both sections were British and Protestant, and they spoke a common language, even if a regional twang or drawl flavored their speech. They shared an exuberant pride in their victorious revolution against British rule. The creation of the new nation under the Constitution in 1789 forged strong political ties that bound all Americans. In the nineteenth century, an incipient national economy helped foster economic interdependence and communication across regional boundaries. White Americans everywhere celebrated the achievements of the prosperous young nation, and they looked forward to its seemingly boundless future.

Despite these national similarities, Southerners and Northerners grew increasingly different. The French political observer Alexis de Tocqueville believed he knew why. "I could easily prove," he asserted in 1831, "that almost all the differences which may be noticed between the character of the Americans in the Southern and Northern states have originated in slavery." A quarter century later, most Americans agreed with the Frenchman. And neither Northerners nor Southerners liked what they saw on the other side of the Mason-Dixon line. "On the subject of slavery," the Charleston *Mercury* declared, "the North and South . . . are not only two Peoples, but they are rival, hostile Peoples." Slavery made the South different, and it was the differences between the North and the South, not the similarities, that came to shape antebellum American history.

Cotton Kingdom, Slave Empire

In the first half of the nineteenth century, legions of Southerners and Northerners migrated west, but the southern surge westward was propelled by an insatiable hunger for more and better cotton land. The stampede began in 1815 with the end of the War of 1812 against Great Britain and with the start of Indian removal east of the Mississippi River. Eager slaveholders seeking virgin acreage for new plantations, struggling yeomen looking for patches of good land for small farms, herders and drovers pushing their hogs and cattle toward fresh pastures—anyone who was restless and ambitious felt the pull. Southerners pushed into the territories of Alabama, Mississippi, Louisiana, Texas, and Arkansas, until by midcentury the South encompassed nearly a million square miles, much of it planted in cotton.

Slavery made the South different, and it was the differences between the North and the South, not the similarities, that came to shape antebellum American history.

The South's climate and geography were ideally suited for the cultivation of cotton. As Southerners advanced a thousand miles west from the Atlantic, they encountered a variety of terrain, soil, and weather, but the cotton seeds they carried with them were very adaptable. They grew in the sandy plains of the tidewater, the red clay of the Piedmont, and especially the rich soils of the black belt (named for the dark color of the soil) and the alluvial deltas. Cotton requires two hundred frost-free days from planting to picking and prefers rains that are plentiful in spring and lighter in fall, conditions found in much of the South. In less than half a century, cotton fields stretched from southern Virginia to central Texas. Production soared, and by 1860 the South produced three-fourths of the world's supply. The South—especially that tier of states from South Carolina west to Texas known as the Lower South—had become the cotton kingdom (Map 12.1).

The cotton kingdom was also a slave empire. The South's cotton boom rested on the backs of slaves, who grew 75 percent of the crop on plantations, toiling in gangs in broad fields under the di-

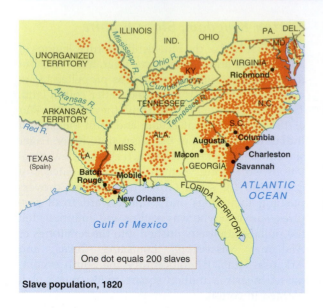

Slave population, 1820

One dot equals 200 slaves

Slave population, 1860

One dot equals 200 slaves

Cotton production, 1820

One dot equals 1,000 bales

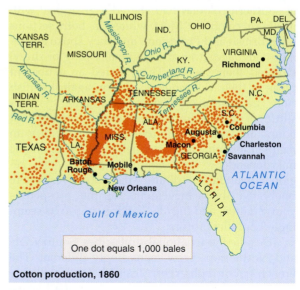

Cotton production, 1860

One dot equals 1,000 bales

MAP 12.1

Cotton Kingdom, Slave Empire: 1820 and 1860

As the production of cotton soared, the slave population increased dramatically. Slaves continued to toil in tobacco and rice fields along the Atlantic seaboard, but increasingly they worked on cotton plantations in Alabama, Mississippi, and Louisiana.

READING THE MAP: Where was slavery most prevalent in 1820? In 1860? How did the spread of slavery compare with the spread of cotton?

CONNECTIONS: How much of the world's cotton was produced in the American South in 1860? While most slaves worked in agriculture, how else were slaves employed?

www.bedfordstmartins.com/tap   SEE THE ONLINE STUDY GUIDE for more help in analyzing these maps.

Arise! Arise! and weep no more dry up your tears, we shall part no more, Come rose we go to Tennessee, that happy Shore. to old virginia never — never — return.

SLAVE TRADERS: SOLD TO TENNESSEE
Slave trading, or "Negro speculation" as it was called by contemporaries, was a boom-
ing business in the antebellum South. This color drawing by Lewis Miller portrays
slaves on their way from Virginia to Tennessee under the watchful eyes of professional
slave traders. A few children accompany the adults, some of whom presumably are their
parents, but forced migrations almost always resulted in separation of black families.
Abby Aldrich Rockefeller Folk Art Center, Williamsburg, Va.

rect supervision of whites. As cotton agriculture expanded westward, more than 300,000 slaves moved
away from the old seaboard states. Some accompanied masters who were leaving behind worn-out,
eroded plantations in the East, but at least two-
thirds were victims of a brutal but thriving domestic slave trade. Traders advertised for slaves who
were "hearty and well made" and marched black
men, women, and children hundreds of miles to the
new plantation regions of the Lower South. Cotton,
slaves, and plantations moved west together.

The slave population also grew enormously.
Southern slaves numbered fewer than 700,000 in
1790, about 2 million in 1830, and about 4 million
by 1860, an increase of almost 600 percent in seven
decades. By 1860, the South contained more slaves
than all the other slave societies in the New World

combined. The extraordinary growth was not the
result of huge purchases in the international slave
trade. The United States outlawed the importation
of slaves in 1808, after which only about 50,000
slaves were smuggled into the South illegally. The
main reason for the growth in the slave population
was natural reproduction. By the nineteenth century, most slaves were southern-born. They were
black Southerners.

The South in Black and White

White Southerners' continuing commitment to
slavery created a biracial population. By 1860, one
in every three Southerners was black (about 4 million blacks and 8 million whites). In the Lower
South, the proportion was higher, for whites and

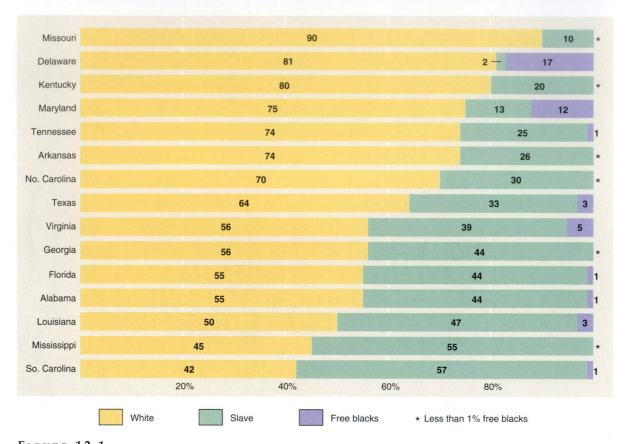

	White	Slave	Free blacks	* Less than 1% free blacks

Missouri 90 / 10 *
Delaware 81 / 2 / 17
Kentucky 80 / 20 *
Maryland 75 / 13 / 12
Tennessee 74 / 25 / 1
Arkansas 74 / 26 *
No. Carolina 70 / 30 *
Texas 64 / 33 / 3
Virginia 56 / 39 / 5
Georgia 56 / 44 *
Florida 55 / 44 / 1
Alabama 55 / 44 / 1
Louisiana 50 / 47 / 3
Mississippi 45 / 55 *
So. Carolina 42 / 57 / 1

FIGURE 12.1

Black and White Population in the South, 1860
Blacks represented a much larger fraction of the population in the South than in the North, but considerable variation existed from state to state. Only one Missourian in ten, for example, was black, while Mississippi and South Carolina had black majorities. States in the Upper South were "whiter" than in the Lower South, despite the Upper South's greater number of free blacks.

blacks lived there in almost equal numbers. In Mississippi and South Carolina, blacks were the majority (Figure 12.1). The contrast with the North was striking: In 1860, only one Northerner in 76 was black (about 250,000 blacks to 19 million whites).

The presence of large numbers of African Americans had profound consequences for the South. Southern culture—language, food, music, religion, and even accents—was in part shaped by blacks. But the most direct consequence of the South's biracialism was the response it stimulated in the region's white majority. Southern whites were dedicated to white supremacy. Northern whites were, too, but they lived in a society in which blacks made up barely more than 1 percent of the popula-

tion. Their commitment to white supremacy lacked the intensity and urgency increasingly felt by white Southerners. White Southerners lived among millions of blacks, whom they simultaneously despised and feared. They despised blacks because they considered them members of an inferior race, further degraded by their status as slaves. They feared blacks because they realized that slaves had every reason to hate their oppressors and to seek to end their oppression, as Nat Turner had, by any means necessary.

Attacks on slavery after 1820—from blacks within and from abolitionists without—jolted southern slaveholders into a distressing awareness that they lived in a dangerous world. In response, southern leaders in the 1820s and 1830s initiated fresh efforts to strengthen slavery and ward off threats. State legislatures constructed elaborate slave codes that required the total submission of slaves to their masters and to white society in general. As the Louisiana code stated, a slave "owes his master . . . a respect without bounds, and an absolute obedience." The laws underlined the authority of all whites, not just masters. Any white could stop a slave on a road and demand to see the slave's written permission to be away from home. Any white could "correct" slaves who did not stay "in their place" and show the proper deference.

Intellectuals joined legislators in the campaign to strengthen slavery. The South's academics, writers, and clergy constructed a proslavery argument that sought to unify the region's whites around slavery and provide ammunition for the emerging war of words with northern abolitionists. Under the intellectuals' tutelage, the white South gradually moved away from defending slavery as a "necessary evil"—the halfhearted argument popular in Jefferson's day—and toward a full-throated, aggressive defense of slavery as a "positive good."

Slavery's champions employed every imaginable defense. The law protected slavery, they observed, for slaves were legal property. And wasn't the security of property the bedrock of American liberty? History also endorsed slavery. Weren't the great civilizations—like those of the Hebrews, Greeks, and Romans—slave societies? In addition, the Bible, properly interpreted, sanctioned slavery. Didn't the Old Testament patriarchs own slaves? Didn't Paul in the New Testament return the runaway slave Onesimus to his master? Some proslavery spokesmen went on the offensive and attacked the economy and society of the North. The Virginia writer George Fitzhugh argued that behind the North's grand slogans—free labor, individualism, and egalitarianism—lay a heartless philosophy: "Every man for himself, and the devil take the hindmost." Gouging capitalists exploited wage workers unmercifully, Fitzhugh said, and he contrasted the vicious capitalist-laborer relationship with the humane relations that prevailed between masters and slaves because slaves were valuable capital that masters sought to protect.

Since slavery was a condition Southerners reserved exclusively for African Americans, at bottom the white defense of slavery rested on claims of black inferiority. Black enslavement was both necessary and proper, antebellum defenders argued, because Africans were inferior beings. Rather than exploitative, slavery was a mass civilizing effort that lifted lowly blacks from barbarism and savagery, taught them disciplined work, and converted them to soul-saving Christianity. According to Virginian Thomas R. Dew, most slaves were grateful. "The slaves of a good master are his warmest, most constant, and most devoted friends," he declared. Freeing blacks, the Charleston *Mercury* declared, would mean their destruction as well as the destruction of southern "civilization, society, and government."

The presence of large numbers of African Americans had profound consequences for the South. Southern culture—language, food, music, religion, and even accents—was in part shaped by blacks.

Black slavery encouraged whites to unify around race rather than to divide by class. The grubbiest, most tobacco-stained white man could proudly proclaim his superiority to blacks and his equality with the most refined southern patrician. Because slaves were not recognized as citizens in the South, Georgia attorney Thomas R. R. Cobb observed, everyone who was a citizen "feels that he belongs to an elevated class. It matters not that he is no slaveholder; he is not of the inferior race; he is a freeborn citizen." Consequently, the "poorest meets the richest as an equal; sits at his table with him; salutes him as a neighbor; meets him in every public assembly, and stands on the same social platform." In the South, Cobb boasted, "there is no war of classes."

In reality, slavery did not create perfect harmony among whites or ease every strain along class lines. But by providing every antebellum white Southerner symbolic membership in the ruling class, racial slavery helped whites bridge differences in class, wealth, education, and culture. Slavery meant white dominance, white superiority, and white equality.

The Plantation Economy

Race was important in unifying white Southerners because most whites did not own slaves. The majority of the South's whites worked small farms with just the help of family members. Only about one-quarter of the white population lived in slaveholding families. A majority of masters owned fewer than five. About 12 percent of slave owners owned twenty or more slaves, the number historians consider necessary to distinguish a planter from a farmer. Fewer than 1 percent of slaveholders owned one hundred or more slaves and thus could be considered "great planters." Although hugely outnumbered by nonslaveholders and small slaveholders, planters dominated the southern economy. In 1860, 52 percent of the South's slaves lived and worked on plantations. Plantation slaves produced more than 75 percent of the South's export crops, the backbone of the region's economy.

Patterns of plantation slavery established along the Atlantic seaboard persisted as Southerners raced westward in the nineteenth century. Fresh land reinvigorated plantation slavery by providing an escape hatch for slaveholders in the Southeast who limped along on exhausted acreage and by creating a vigorous market for the East's surplus slaves. Although slavery was slowly dying elsewhere in the New World, slave plantations increased their domination of southern agriculture with each antebellum decade.

Agriculture, in turn, remained the central feature of the southern economy.

The dominant cash crops of southern agriculture were the four major staples grown on plantations: tobacco, sugar, rice, and cotton. All plantations had similar features, but they differed depending on the staple crop they produced (Map 12.2). Tobacco was the original plantation crop in North America, but by the nineteenth century tobacco had shifted westward from the Chesapeake to Tennessee and Kentucky. Work in the tobacco fields was labor-intensive. Most phases of the process—planting, transplanting, thinning, picking off caterpillars, cutting, drying, packing—required field hands to stoop or bend down in painful labor over the tobacco plants.

Large-scale sugar production began in 1795, when Étienne de Boré built a modern sugar mill in what is today New Orleans. Labor on sugarcane plantations was reputed to be the most physically demanding in the antebellum South. During the fall, slaves worked eighteen hours a day to cut the cane and haul it to the sugar mill, where they would grind and boil it. Sugar plantations, which were

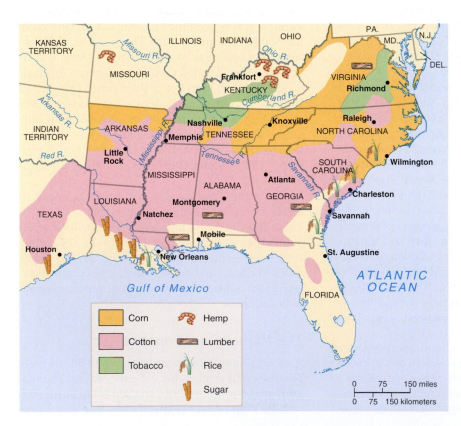

MAP 12.2

The Agricultural Economy of the South, 1860
Cotton dominated the South's agricultural economy, but the region grew a diversity of crops and was largely self-sufficient in foodstuffs.

THE *HENRY FRANK,* **NEW ORLEANS**
The steamboat **Henry Frank** *sits dangerously overloaded with cotton bales at the New Orleans levee in 1854. The banner flying from the flagstaff indicates that captains boasted about the number of bales their boats carried. The magnitude of the cotton trade in the South's largest city and major port is difficult to capture. Six years earlier, visitor Solon Robinson expressed his awe: "It must be seen to be believed; and even then, it will require an active mind to comprehend acres of cotton bales standing upon the levee, while miles of drays [carts] are constantly taking it off to the cotton presses. . . . Boats are constantly arriving, so piled up with cotton, that the lower tier of bales on deck are in the water." Amidst the mountains of cotton, few Southerners doubted that cotton was king.*
Historic New Orleans Collection.

www.bedfordstmartins.com/tap   SEE THE ONLINE STUDY GUIDE for more help in analyzing this image.

confined almost entirely to Louisiana, required large sums for expensive refining equipment to turn cane juice into sugar and for large gangs of slaves.

Commercial rice production began in seventeenth-century South Carolina. Like sugar, rice was confined to a small geographic area, a narrow strip of the tidewater stretching from the Carolinas into southern Georgia. Because of the need for canals, dikes, and gates to flood rice fields with water and then drain them and to protect the ripening plant from saltwater, rice planting was an expensive undertaking. Since rice plantations required huge numbers of slaves, blacks accounted for 90 percent of the population in the coastal region. For slaves, rice meant danger and extreme discomfort. Working in water and mud in the heat of a Carolina summer regularly threatened slaves with malaria, yellow fever, and other diseases.

The Cotton Gin: "Engine of the South"

I N 1792, A YOUNG NEW ENGLANDER accepted a position as tutor to the children of a Georgia planter. The teaching post did not work out, but Eli Whitney stayed on at the Savannah River plantation of Mrs. Catherine Greene, widow of Nathanael Greene, hero of the American Revolution. On September 11, 1793, Whitney wrote his sister: "I have . . . heard much said of the extreme difficulty of ginning cotton. That is, separating it from its seed." He had met "a number of respectable Gentlemen at Mrs Greene's who all agreed that if a machine could be invented which would clean the cotton with expedition, it would be a great thing both to the country and the inventor." Whitney was a Yale graduate who could read Latin, but he was also a practical man, and he turned his attention to the problem.

Cotton gins (the word *gin* is short for *engine*) already existed in 1793. One model in which cotton was fed between two rollers to squeeze out the seeds operated efficiently on the sea-island cotton that grew on the South Carolina and Georgia coasts. But the variety of cotton that grew in the upcountry—green seed, or short staple—was filled with seeds that clung to the fiber like ticks to the skin. Many a pioneer family spent the long winter evenings seated

THE COTTON GIN

By the 1790s, the English had succeeded in mechanizing the manufacture of cotton cloth, but they were unable to get enough raw cotton. The South could grow cotton in unimaginable quantities, but cotton that was stuck to seeds was useless in English textile mills. In 1793, Eli Whitney, a Northerner who was living on a Savannah River plantation, built a simple device for separating the cotton from the seed. Widespread use of the cotton gin broke the bottleneck in the commercial production of cotton and eventually bound millions of African Americans to slavery.

Smithsonian Institution.

If tobacco, sugar, and rice were princes of plantation agriculture, cotton was king. Cotton became commercially significant after the advent of Eli Whitney's cotton gin in 1793. (See "The Promise of Technology," above.) By the early years of the nineteenth century, cotton had displaced tobacco and had begun to dominate the southern economy. The white fluffy stuff was grown almost everywhere in the South and by almost everyone, small farmer and planter alike. It was relatively easy to grow and took little capital to get started— just enough for land, seed, and simple tools. Nonetheless, plantations produced three-quarters of the South's cotton, and planters received a dis-proportionate slice of the region's income. While hardscrabble farmer Jessup Snopes grew half a bale, Mississippian Frederick Stanton, who owned more than fifteen thousand prime acres, produced 3,054 bales of cotton worth $122,000 in 1859. With a record-breaking crop of 4,861,000 bales in 1859, the South's planters were, as they liked to put it, in "high cotton."

For slaveholders, then, the Old South's economy was productive and profitable. Further, plantation slavery benefited the national economy. Throughout the antebellum years, the products of southern plantations made up the greatest part of America's exports. By 1840, cotton alone accounted around the fire tediously plucking the fluff from each seed. The few pounds of clean cotton produced by evenings of handpicking got made up into homespun on family spinning wheels and handlooms.

The problem of sticky seeds attracted the attention of mechanics from India to Santo Domingo, but it was Whitney who succeeded in building a simple little device for separating cotton from the green seeds—just wire teeth set in a wooden cylinder that, when rotated, reached through narrow slats to pull cotton fibers away from the seeds, while a brush swept the fibers from the revolving teeth. It was crude, but news of the invention spread like a wildfire. Just days later, South Carolina planter Pierce Butler wrote a friend, "There is a young Man at Mrs Greene's in Georgia, who has made a Cotton Ginn that with two Boys cleans of the green seed cotton 64 pds of clean cotton in about 9 hours." Planters understood that Whitney's invention had succeeded in breaking the bottleneck in the commercial production of cotton. They also understood that his invention would allow them to produce vast amounts of clean cotton and satisfy the cotton-hungry English market. Eager to cash in on his invention, Whitney rushed back to Connecticut, where he took out a patent and began manufacturing cotton gins.

Planters clamored for the machines, and southern craftsmen who understood Whitney's basic design could reproduce it (and enlarge and improve it) without needing a model or drawings. No mere patent could stop them, and nothing could force them to pay Whitney royalties. The new Patent Act of 1793 stressed that proof of invention and proof of infringement were the burden of the inventor. Although Whitney's gin was pirated time and again, he found that it was difficult and costly to gain proof. At one time Whitney had more than sixty lawsuits pending, and the revenue from his gin factory in New Haven could scarcely keep up with his legal bills.

While Whitney made little money from the cotton gin, planters did. Cotton quickly pushed out indigo, then tobacco, as the upcountry's major cash crop. In just a few years, the gin helped transform the entire economy of the South. The commercial production of cotton bound millions of African Americans to perpetual slavery. For them, the promise of this particular piece of technology proved tragically hollow. Whitney's invention also spawned a cotton industry that changed the face of northern Britain and New England as mill towns sprang up everywhere. The cotton mills of Lancashire and Lowell brought cotton cloth within the reach of everyone. Before the gin, the world was clothed in flax and wool, and cotton fabrics were luxury items, but cotton soon became the poor man's cloth.

The great nineteenth-century British historian Lord Macaulay hardly exaggerated when he declared: "What Peter the Great did to make Russia dominant, Eli Whitney's invention of the cotton gin has more than equaled in relation to the power and progress of the United States."

for more than 60 percent of the nation's sales abroad. Much of the profit from sales of cotton overseas returned to planters, but some did not. Cotton had to be bought, sold, insured, warehoused, and shipped before it reached the mills in Great Britain and elsewhere. Increasingly, these services were in the hands of northern middlemen, each of whom made a profit from slave-grown southern crops. As these profits were invested in the burgeoning northern economy, industrial development there received much-needed capital. Furthermore, planters provided an important market for northern textiles, agricultural tools, and other manufactured goods. Without cotton, one economist has estimated, American industrial development would have been retarded a generation.

If tobacco, sugar, and rice were princes of plantation agriculture, cotton was king.

The economies of North and South steadily diverged. While the North developed a mixed economy—agriculture, commerce, and manufacturing—the South remained overwhelmingly agricultural. Since planters were earning healthy profits, they saw little reason to diversify. Moreover, economic change could threaten plantation slavery, the key to the social and economic order that planters dominated. Planters knew that if the southern economy followed the path blazed by the North, then manufacturing in the South would mean the rise of an urban, industrial working class without direct ties to slavery and the plantation. Would city-dwelling factory workers accept rural planter rule and give their hearty support to slavery, or would they favor free labor, as northern workers did? Planters did not want to find out. Year after year, they funneled the profits they earned from land and slaves back into more land and slaves.

With its capital flowing into agriculture, the Old South did not develop many factories. By 1860, only 10 percent of the nation's industrial workers were in the South. Indiana and Illinois, two midwestern states known for agriculture, had more capital invested in industry than the seven Lower South states, including Louisiana with its sugar mills. Southern factories usually processed agricultural products and raw materials produced in the region. Cotton mills, for example, developed where cotton, water power, and cheap labor existed. Still, in 1860 the region that produced 100 percent of the nation's cotton manufactured less than 7 percent of its cotton textiles.

Without significant economic diversification, the South developed fewer cities than the North. In 1860, it was the least urban region in the country (Map 12.3). While nearly 37 percent of New England's population lived in cities, less than 12 percent of Southerners were urban dwellers. That figure would have been dramatically smaller without Maryland's 34 percent urban population (because of Baltimore) and Louisiana's 26 percent (because

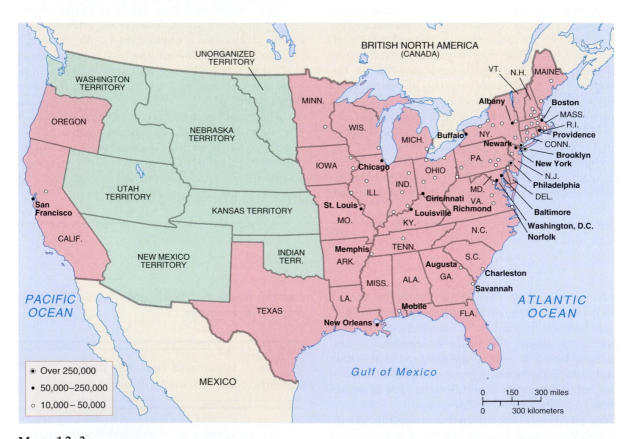

MAP 12.3

Major Cities in 1860

By 1860, northern cities were both more numerous and larger than southern cities. In the slave states, cities were usually seaports or river ports that served the needs of agriculture, especially cotton.

of New Orleans). In fact, nine southern states had 5 percent or fewer of their people in cities.

Not only were cities less common in the South, but they were also different from those in the North. They were mostly port cities on the periphery of the region and busy principally with exporting the agricultural products of plantations in the interior. The region's urban merchants provided agriculture with indispensable economic services, such as hauling, insuring, and selling the South's cotton, rice, and sugar. But as the tail of the plantation dog, southern cities did not become significant manufacturing centers or important independent centers of social and economic innovation.

Because the South had so few cities and industrial jobs, it attracted relatively small numbers of European immigrants. Seeking economic opportunity, not competition with slaves, immigrants steered well north of the South's slave-dominated, agricultural economy. In 1860, 13 percent of all Americans were foreign-born. But in nine of the fifteen slave states, only 2 percent or fewer were born abroad. Immigrants who did venture below the Mason-Dixon line concentrated in cities, as they did in the North.

Not every Southerner celebrated the region's plantation economy. Critics railed against the excessive commitment to cotton and slaves and bemoaned the "deplorable scarcity" of factories. Diversification, reformers promised, would make the South not only economically independent but more prosperous and healthy as well. State governments encouraged economic development by helping to create banking systems that supplied credit for a wide range of projects, industrial as well as agricultural. Government joined private investors in building an extensive railroad network. Alabama constructed its first railroad in 1830, just five years after the first modern railroad in the world was constructed in England and only three years after the inauguration of

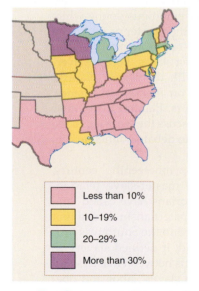

Immigrants as a Percent of State Populations, 1860

- Less than 10%
- 10–19%
- 20–29%
- More than 30%

the first railroad in America. Thirty years later, 9,280 miles of track spanned the South.

But encouragement of a diversified economy had clear limits. State governments failed to create some of the essential services modern economies require. By midcentury, for example, no southern legislature had created a statewide public school system. Consequently, the South's illiteracy rate for whites topped 20 percent. Dominant slaveholders failed to see any benefit in educating the region's labor force. Indeed, after the 1830s it was illegal in the South to teach slaves to read. Despite the flurry of railroad building, the South's mileage in 1860 was less than half that of the North. Moreover, northern railroads crisscrossed the region, connecting towns and cities and carrying manufactured goods as well as agricultural products. In the South, most rail lines ran from port cities back into farming areas and were built to export staple crops (see Map 11.1).

Northerners claimed that slavery was outmoded and doomed, but few Southerners perceived economic weakness in their region. In fact, the planters' pockets were never fuller than at the end of the antebellum period. But planters' individual profits did not automatically translate into long-term regional economic health. When white Southerners bet on plantation agriculture, especially cotton, they not only committed themselves to slavery but also left themselves vulnerable to the fickle world market. Compared with antebellum Northerners, Southerners committed less of their capital to investment in industry, transportation, and public education. Planters' decisions to reinvest in staple agriculture ensured the momentum of the plantation economy and the social and political relationships that were rooted in it.

Masters, Mistresses, and the Big House

Nowhere was the contrast between northern and southern life more vivid than in the plantations of the South. Located on a patchwork of cleared fields and dense forests, a plantation typically included a "big house" and slave quarters. Scattered about were numerous outbuildings, each with a special function. Near the big house were the kitchen, storehouse, smokehouse (for curing and preserving meat), and hen coop. More distant were the barns,

SAVANNAH RIVER

BRICK WALL

PLOT PLAN

LEGEND

1	MANSION	6	LOT
2	KITCHEN	7	SUNKEN GARDEN
3	SMOKE HOUSE	8	OVERSEER'S HOUSE
4	STABLES	9	HOSPITAL
5	COACH HOUSE	10	SLAVE HUTS

F I G U R E 12.2

A Southern Plantation

Slavery determined how masters laid out their plantations, where they situated their "big houses" and the slave quarters, and what kinds of buildings they constructed. This model of the Hermitage, the mansion built for Georgia rice planter Henry McAlpin in 1830, shows the overseer's house poised in the grove of oak trees halfway between the owner's mansion and the houses of his slaves. The mansion at the end of the extended road underscored McAlpin's great affluence and authority.

Adapted from *Back of the Big House: The Architecture of Plantation Slavery* by John Michael Vlach. Copyright © 1993 by the University of North Carolina Press. Original illustration property of the Historic American Buildings Survey, a division of the National Park Service.

toolsheds, artisans' workshops, and overseer's house. Large plantations sometimes had separate buildings for an infirmary, nursery, and chapel for the slaves. Depending on the crop, there was a tobacco shed, a rice mill, a sugar refinery, or a cotton gin house. Lavish or plain, plantations everywhere had an underlying similarity (Figure 12.2).

The plantation was the home of masters, mistresses, and slaves. Slavery shaped the lives of all the plantation's inhabitants, but it affected each differently. A hierarchy of rigid roles and duties governed relationships. Presiding was the master, who ruled his wife, children, and slaves, none of whom had many legal rights and all of whom were designated by the state as dependents under his dominion and protection.

Plantation Masters

Plantations were usually organized quite simply. Smaller planters supervised the labor of their slaves themselves. Larger planters usually hired an overseer. Overseers were either ambitious young white men—perhaps relatives of the planter or poor men from the neighborhood—or professionals who made a career of supervising slaves. Because overseers went to the fields with the slaves, planters could concentrate instead on marketing, finance, and general plantation affairs. Planters also found time to escape to town to discuss the weather, to the courthouse and legislature to debate politics, and to the woods to hunt and fish.

Increasingly in the nineteenth century, planters characterized the master-slave relationship in terms of what historians have called "paternalism." The concept of paternalism denied that the form of slavery practiced in the South was brutal and exploitative. Instead, it defined slavery as a set of reciprocal obligations between masters and slaves. In exchange for the slaves' labor and obedience, masters provided basic care and necessary guidance. To northern claims that they were tyrants and exploiters, slaveholders responded that they were stewards and guardians. As owners of blacks, masters argued, they had the heavy responsibility of caring for a childlike, dependent people. In 1814, Thomas Jefferson captured the essence of the advancing ideal: "We should endeavor, with those whom fortune has thrown on our hands, to feed & clothe them well, protect them from ill usage, require such reasonable labor only as is performed voluntarily by freemen, and be led

**SOUTHERN MAN WITH CHIL-
DREN AND THEIR MAMMY**
*Obviously prosperous and
projecting the aura of a
man accustomed to giving
orders and to being obeyed,
this patriarch poses around
1848 with his young daughters and their nurse. The
absent mother may have
been dead, which might in
part explain the inclusion
of the slave woman in the
family circle. But her presence also confirms her importance in the household.
Fathers left the raising of
children to mothers and
nurses. However important,
the black woman is clearly
a servant, a status indi-
cated by both her race and
her attire.*
Collection of the J. Paul Getty
Museum, Malibu, Calif.

by no repugnancies to abdicate them, and our duties to them."

Paternalism was part propaganda and part self-
delusion. But it was more. Indeed, there was some
truth in the assertion that master-slave relationships
in the South were unique. Unlike planters elsewhere
in the New World, most southern planters lived
year-round where their slaves worked, which
meant that the relationship between master and
slave was face to face, direct, and personal. In addition, slavery in the South reached its prime in the
nineteenth century, after the nation had closed its
external slave trade in 1808. Masters realized that
the expansion of the slave labor force could come
only from natural reproduction. Thus, masters had
to provide slaves with a certain minimum level of
physical welfare if they wanted more slaves, and
they certainly did want more slaves.

One consequence was a relative improvement
in slaves' material welfare. The nineteenth-century
slaves' diet still consisted mainly of fatty pork and
cornmeal. The cabins still had cracks large enough,
slaves said, for cats to slip through. Slaves' clothing
seldom amounted to much more than two crude
outfits a year. Nevertheless, conditions in the quar-

ters got better. In the fields, workdays remained
sunup to sundown, but planters often provided a
rest period in the heat of the day. And most owners ceased the eighteenth-century practices of punishing slaves by branding, castrating, and other
forms of mutilation.

Paternalism should not be mistaken for "Ol'
Massa's" kindness and goodwill. It had nothing to
do with gentleness and niceness. It encouraged better treatment, but it was essentially self-interested
and self-serving: It made economic sense to provide
at least minimal care for valuable slaves. Nor did
paternalism require that planters put aside their
whips. They could lay on the leather and claim that
they were only fulfilling their responsibilities as
guardians of their naturally lazy and at times insubordinate dependents. Paternalism gave slaves
some protection against the most brutal punishments, but whipping remained the planters' essential coercion. (See "Historical Question," page 424.)

The Virginia statesman Edmund Randolph argued that slavery created in white southern men a
"quick and acute sense of personal liberty" and a
"disdain for every abridgement of personal independence." Indeed, prickly individualism and ag-

How Often Were Slaves Whipped?

As important as this question is to historians, and obviously was to slaves, we have very little reliable evidence on the frequency of whipping. We know from white sources that whipping was the prescribed method of physical punishment on most antebellum plantations. Masters' instructions to overseers authorized whippings and often set limits on the number of strokes an overseer could administer. Some planters allowed fifteen lashes, some fifty, and some one hundred. But slave owners' instructions, as revealing as they are, tell us more about the severity of beatings than their frequency.

Remembrances of former slaves confirm that whipping was widespread and frequent. In the 1930s, a government program gathered testimony from more than 2,300 elderly African Americans about their experiences as slaves. Their accounts offered grisly evidence of the cruelty of slavery. "You say how did our Master treat his slaves?" asked one woman. "Scandalous, they treated them just like dogs." She was herself whipped "till the blood dripped to the ground." A few slaves remembered kind masters and never personally felt the sting of the lash. Bert Strong was one such slave, but he also recalled hearing slaves on other farms "hollering when they get beat." He said, "They beat them till it a pity." Beatings occurred often, but how often?

A remarkably systematic record of whippings over a sustained period of time comes from the diary of Bennet H. Barrow, the master of Highland plantation in West Feliciana Parish, Louisiana. For a twenty-three-month period in 1840–1841, Barrow meticulously recorded every whipping he administered or ordered. On most large plantations, overseers handled the business of day-to-day management, but in 1838 Barrow concluded that overseers were "good for nothing" and "a perfect nuisance." He dismissed his white overseer and, assisted only by a black driver, began managing his own plantation.

What does the Barrow evidence show? In 1840, according to the federal census, Barrow owned 129 slaves. In the twenty-three-month period, Barrow recorded 160 whippings. That means that, on the average, a slave was whipped every four and a half days. Sixty of the 77 slaves who worked in the fields were whipped at least once. Most of the 17 field slaves who escaped being beaten were children and pregnant women. Eighty percent of male cotton pickers and 70 percent of the female cotton pickers were whipped at least once in this period. Dave Barley received eight floggings, more than any other Barrow slave, and Patience received six whippings, more than any other female slave.

In most instances, Barrow recorded not only the fact of a whipping but also its cause. All sorts of "misconduct," "rascality," and "disorderly acts" made Barrow reach for his whip. The provocations included family quarrels in the slave quarters, impudence, running away, and failure to keep curfew. But nearly 80 percent of the acts he recorded were related to poor work. Barrow gave beatings for "not picking as well as he can," for picking "very trashy cotton," and for failing to pick the prescribed weight of cotton. One slave claimed to have lost his eyesight and for months refused to work until Barrow "gave him 25 cuts yesterday morning & ordered him to work Blind or not."

Whippings should not be mistaken for spankings. Some planters used whips that raised welts, caused blisters, and bruised. Others resorted to rawhide and cowhide whips that broke the skin, caused scarring, and sometimes permanently maimed. Occasionally, slaves were beaten to death. Whipping was not Barrow's only means of inflicting pain. His diary mentions confining slaves to a plantation jail, putting them in chains, shooting them, breaking a "sword cane" over one slave's head, having slaves mauled by dogs, placing them in stocks, "staking down" slaves for hours, "hand sawing" them, holding their heads under water, and a variety of punishments intending to ridicule and to shame, including making men wear women's clothing and do "women's work," such as the laundry. Still, Barrow's preferred instrument of punishment was the whip.

GORDON

This photograph of Gordon, a runaway slave from Baton Rouge, Louisiana, was taken on April 2, 1863, and sent home from the Civil War by Frederick W. Mercer, an assistant surgeon with the Forty-seventh Massachusetts Regiment. Mercer examined four hundred other runaways and found many "to be as badly lacerated." Masters claimed that they whipped only when they had to and only as hard as they had to, but slave testimony and photographic evidence refute their defense of slavery as a benign institution.
Courtesy of the Massachusetts Historical Society.

On the Barrow plantation, as on many others, whipping was public. Victims were often tied to a stake in the quarters, and the other slaves were made to watch. In a real sense the entire slave population on the plantation experienced a whipping every four and a half days. Even though some never felt the lash personally, all were familiar with its terror and agony.

Was whipping effective? Did it produce a hardworking, efficient, and conscientious labor force? Not according to Barrow's own record. No evidence indicates that whipping changed the slaves' behavior. What Barrow considered bad work continued. Unabated whipping is itself evidence of the failure of punishment to achieve the master's will. Slaves knew the rules. Yet they continued to act "badly." And they continued to suffer. It was a gruesome drama—the master seeking from his slaves hard labor and slaves denying their master what he most wanted, day after day.

Did Barrow whip with the same frequency as other planters? We simply do not know. As much as we would like to answer the question precisely, because of the lack of quantifiable evidence we will never know exactly how often whippings occurred. Still, the Barrow evidence allows us to speculate profitably on the frequency of whipping by large planters. We do know that Barrow did not consider himself a cruel man. He bitterly denounced his neighbor as "the most cruel Master i ever knew of" for castrating three of his slaves. Moreover, Barrow had dispensed with the overseers in part because of their "brutal feelings" toward slaves. Like most whites, he believed that the lash was essential to get work done. He used it no more than he believed absolutely necessary.

Most masters, including Barrow, tried to encourage work with promises of small gifts and brief holidays, but punishment was their most important motivator. We will never know if the typical slave was beaten once a year as on the Barrow plantation, but the admittedly scanty evidence suggests that on large plantations the whip fell on someone's back every few days.

And former slaves remembered. More than half a century after emancipation, their sharpest recollections usually involved punishment. They remembered the pain, the injustice, and their bitter resentment. They evaluated their former masters according to how frequently they reached for the whip. According to one former slave, "some was good and some was bad, and about the most of them was bad."

gressive independence became crucial features of the southern concept of honor. Social standing, political advancement, and even self-esteem rested on a reputation of honor. Defending honor became a male passion. Andrew Jackson's mother reportedly told her son, "Never tell a lie, nor take what is not your own, nor sue anybody for slander or assault and battery. *Always settle them cases yourself.*" Southern boys were expected to master the "manly" arts, and among planters such advice sometimes led to duels. Dueling arrived from Europe in the eighteenth century. It died out in the North, but in the South, even after legislatures banned it, gentlemen continued to defend their honor with pistols at ten paces.

Southerners also expected an honorable gentleman to be a proper patriarch. Nowhere in America was patriarchy more accentuated. In the South, slavery buttressed the power of husbands and fathers. Planters described the plantation as a single social unit, incorporating their "white and black families"—their personal households and the slave quarters. Attempts by family members to assert themselves against the patriarch—the head of the family, the master of slaves—threatened slavery itself. The master's absolute dominion sometimes led to miscegenation, the sexual mixing of the races. Laws prohibited interracial sex, and some masters condemned sex with slaves as immoral and practiced self-restraint. Others merely urged discretion. How many trips masters and their sons made to slave cabins is impossible to tell, but as long as slavery gave white men extraordinary power over black women, liaisons occurred.

Individualistic impulses were strong among planters, but duty to family was paramount. In time, as the children of one elite family married the children of another, ties of blood and kinship as well as ideology and economic interest linked planters to one another. Conscious of what they shared as slaveholders, planters worked together to defend their common interests. The values of the big house—slavery, honor, male domination—washed over the boundaries of plantations and flooded all of southern life.

Plantation Mistresses

Like their northern counterparts, southern ladies were expected to possess feminine virtues of piety, purity, chastity, and obedience within the context of marriage, motherhood, and domesticity. Southerners also expected ladies to exemplify all that was

best in plantation society. Countless toasts praised the southern lady as the perfect complement to her husband, the patriarch. She was physically weak, "formed only for the less laborious occupations," and thus dependent on male protection. To gain this protection, she was modest and delicate, beautiful and graceful, cultured and charming. The lady, southern men said proudly, was an "ornament."

The values of the big house—slavery, honor, male domination—washed over the boundaries of plantations and flooded all of southern life.

But for women, the image of the lady, which rigidly prescribed proper character and behavior, was no blessing. Chivalry—the South's romantic ideal of male-female relationships—glorified the lady while it subordinated her. Chivalry's underlying assumptions about the weakness of women and the protective authority of men resembled the paternalistic defense of slavery. Indeed, the most articulate proslavery advocates also eloquently defended the subordination of women. Just as the slaveholder's mastery was written into law, so too were the paramount rights of husbands. Once married, antebellum southern women found divorce almost impossible.

Daughters of planters confronted chivalry's demands at an early age. Their educations aimed at fitting them to become southern ladies. At their private boarding schools they read literature, learned languages, and struggled to master the requisite drawing-room arts. Elite women married early, usually before they were twenty. Kate Carney exaggerated only slightly when she wrote in her diary: "Today, I am seventeen, getting quite old, and am not married." Elizabeth Ruffin, who was about the same age, complained of being pushed into a wedding. Everyone, she said, seemed determined to "deter me from all the anticipated horrors of *old-maidenhood.*" When they married, elite women usually made enormous efforts to live up to their region's lofty ideal.

In fact, elite women faced an impossible task. The ideal of the southern lady clashed with the daily reality of the plantation mistress. Rather than being freed from labor by servants, she discovered that having servants required her to work long hours. Like her husband, the mistress had managerial responsibilities. She managed the big house, often su-

BIRD STORE, 626 ROYAL STREET, NEW ORLEANS

Most elite white women in the antebellum South lived isolated existences on rural plantations. But some lived in cities, where others visited them from time to time, and going shopping was a prominent feature of such visits. Teenager Gertrude Clanton, who lived in Augusta, Georgia, wore store-bought clothes that she described endlessly in letters to her friends. Here a wealthy mother and daughter shop for a pet in a New Orleans bird store. The attentive proprietor and attractive shop provide everything they need—birds, cages, bird food, even an inviting couch and blanket in case they wanted to rest before moving on. Elite white women were in a way themselves birds in golden cages. Could it be that they were attracted to the thought of owning birds of their own, something they could care for, train, and control?

Historic New Orleans Collection.

pervising anywhere from two or three to more than a dozen servants. But unlike her husband, who was often insulated from the aggravations of direct supervision of slaves, the mistress had no overseer. All the house servants answered to her. She assigned them tasks each morning, directed their work throughout the day, and punished them when she found fault. In addition to supervising a complex household, she had responsibility for the henhouse and dairy. And on some plantations, she directed the slave hospital and nursery and rationed supplies for the slave quarters. In addition, she bore

the burdens of childbearing and child rearing. Southern ladies did not lead lives of leisure.

The mistress's life was circumscribed by the plantation, as was the slave's life. Masters used their status as slaveholders as a springboard into public affairs, but their wives served the family, not the community. Masters left the plantation when they pleased, but plantation mistresses needed chaperones to travel. When they could, they went to church, for their faith was important to them. But women spent most days on the plantation, where they often became lonely. In 1853, Mary Kendall wrote how much she enjoyed her sister's letter: "For about three weeks I did not have the pleasure of seeing *one white female face,* there being no white family except our own upon the plantation." When a parade of family, friends, and strangers broke the isolation, the burden of hospitality fell on the mistress and the house slaves, not the master.

As members of slaveholding families, mistresses lived privileged lives. But they also had significant grounds for discontent, and a few independent-minded women protested. Some complained of their exhausting burdens as mistresses. Others protested their tiring and dangerous cycle of childbearing. Two decades of childbearing could mean ten or eleven children. And some women denounced slavery itself. In the early 1820s, Sarah and Angelina Grimké, daughters of a Charleston planter, fled their home for the North, where they wrote blistering attacks on slavery. Sarah Grimké's *Letters on the Equality of the Sexes* also protested the South's "image of women."

No feature of plantation life generated more rage and anguish among mistresses than miscegenation. Mary Boykin Chesnut of Camden, South Carolina, wrote in her diary, "God forgive us, but ours is a monstrous system, a wrong and iniquity. Like the patriarchs of old, our men live all in one house with their wives and their concubines; and the mulattos one sees in every family partly resemble the white children. Any lady is ready to tell you who is the father of all the mulatto children in everybody's household but her own. Those, she seems to think drop from the clouds."

But most planters' wives—including Mary Boykin Chesnut—found ways to accept slavery. According to the southern ideal, the white man ruled over all in his household—wife, children, and slaves. Thus the mistress's world rested on slavery, just as the master's did.

Slaves and the Quarters

On most plantations, only a few hundred yards separated the big house and the slave quarters. The distance was short enough to assure whites easy access to the labor of blacks. Yet the distance was great enough to provide slaves with some privacy, despite increased paternalistic intrusion. Out of eyesight and earshot of the big house, slaves drew together and built lives of their own.

The rise of plantations still left a substantial minority of slaves living and working elsewhere. Most labored on small farms, where they wielded a hoe alongside another slave or two and perhaps their master. But by 1850, as many as half a million slaves (one in eight) did not work in agriculture at all. Some were employed in towns and cities as domestics, day laborers, bakers, barbers, tailors, and more. Others, far from urban centers, toiled as fishermen, lumbermen, railroad workers, and deckhands and stokers on riverboats. Slavery was a flexible labor system, and slaves could be found in virtually every skilled and unskilled occupation throughout the South, including the region's few factories. Nevertheless, a majority of slaves (52 percent) counted plantations as their homes and workplaces.

Work

Above all, what masters wanted from slaves was work. The desire for exploitable labor was the chief explanation of slavery's origin in the New World and the principal reason it persisted into the nineteenth century. Slaves understood clearly the motive for their enslavement. As ex-slave Albert Todd recalled, "Work was a religion we was taught."

Out of eyesight and earshot of the big house, slaves drew together and built lives of their own.

All slaves who were capable of productive labor worked. Young children were introduced to the world of work as early as age five or six. Ex-slave Carrie Hudson recalled that children who were "knee high to a duck" had to work. Some were sent to the fields to carry water to thirsty workers or to protect ripening crops from hungry birds. Others helped in the slave nursery, caring for children even younger than themselves, or in the big house, where they did simple chores, such as sweeping floors or shooing flies in the dining room. When slave boys and girls reached the age of eleven or twelve, masters sent most of them to the fields, where they learned farmwork by laboring alongside their parents. After a lifetime of labor, old women left the fields to care for the small children and spin yarn and old men to mind livestock and clean stables.

THE PRICE OF BLOOD
This 1868 painting by T. S. Noble depicts a transaction between a slave trader and a rich planter. The trader nervously pretends to study the contract, while the planter waits impatiently for the completion of the sale. The planter's mulatto son, who is being sold, looks away. The children of white men and slave women were property and could be sold by the father/master. But the tragedy of miscegenation extended beyond the son shown here. Who is absent from the painting? Whose marriage has been betrayed? Who else's son is being sold away?
Morris Museum of Art, Augusta, Ga.

The overwhelming majority of slaves in 1860 were field hands. Planters sometimes assigned men and women to separate gangs, the women working at lighter tasks and the men doing the heavy work of clearing and breaking the land. But women also did heavy work. "I had to work hard," Nancy Boudry remembered, "plow and go and split wood just like a man." Although the daily tasks of slaves working in tobacco, rice, and sugar fields differed from those of slaves laboring in cotton fields, the backbreaking labor and the monotonous year-round routines made for grim similarity. As one ex-slave observed, on the plantation the "history of one day is the history of every day."

A few slaves (only one or two in every ten) became house servants. And virtually all of those who did (nine of ten) were women. There, under the critical eye of the white mistress, they cooked, cleaned house, babysat, washed clothes, and did the dozens of other tasks the master and mistress required. House servants enjoyed certain advantages over field hands, such as somewhat less physically demanding work, better food, and more comfortable quarters. But working in the big house had significant drawbacks. House servants were constantly on call, with no time that was entirely their own. Since no servant could please constantly, most bore the brunt of white frustration and rage. Ex-slave Jacob

NANCY FORT, HOUSE SERVANT
This rare portrait of a slave woman at the turn of the nineteenth century depicts a strong and dignified person. Some who worked in domestic service took pride in their superior status and identified more with the master than with the slaves. "Honey, I wan't no common eve'day slave," one former servant recalled proudly. "I [helped] de white folks in de big house." But intense interaction with whites did not necessarily breed affection. Most domestic servants remained bound by ties of kinship and friendship, as well as by common oppression, to the slave quarters.
Courtesy of Georgia Department of Archives and History.

SLAVE CARPENTER
Haywood Dixon (1826–c. 1889) was a slave carpenter who worked in Greene County, North Carolina. In this 1854 daguerreotype, he is posed with a symbol of his craft, the carpenter's square. When work was slow on the home plantation, masters could hire out their skilled artisans to neighbors who needed a carpenter, blacksmith, or mason.
Collection of William L. Murphy.

Branch of Texas remembered, "My poor mama! Every washday old Missy give her a beating." No wonder some house servants wished they could trade places with field hands.

Even rarer than house servants were skilled artisans. In the cotton South, no more than one slave in twenty (almost all men) worked in a skilled trade. Most were blacksmiths and carpenters, but slaves also worked as masons, mechanics, millers, and shoemakers. Slave craftsmen took pride in their skills and often exhibited an independence of spirit that caused slaveholder James H. Hammond of

South Carolina to declare in disgust that when a slave became a skilled artisan, "he is more than half freed." Skilled slave fathers often taught their crafts to their sons. "My pappy was one of the black smiths and worked in the shop," John Mathews remembered. "I had to help my pappy in the shop when I was a child and I learnt how to beat out the iron and make wagon tires, and make plows."

Rarest of all slave occupations was that of driver. Probably no more than one slave in a hundred—all men—worked in this capacity. These men were well named, for their primary task was driving other slaves to greater efforts in the fields. In some drivers' hands, the whip never rested. Ex-slave Jane Johnson of South Carolina called her driver the "meanest man, white or black, I ever see." But other drivers showed all the restraint they could. "Ole Gabe didn't like that whippin' business," West Turner of Virginia remembered. "When Marsa was there, he would lay it on 'cause he had to. But when old Marsa wasn't lookin', he never would beat them slaves."

Work dominated the slaves' daylight hours. Normally, slaves worked from what they called "can to can't," from "can see" in the morning to "can't see" at night. Even with a break at noon for a meal and rest, it made for a long day. For slaves, Lewis Young recalled, "work, work, work, 'twas all they do."

Family, Religion, and Community

From dawn to dusk, slaves worked for the master. But from dusk to dawn, when the labor was done, and all day Sundays and usually Saturday afternoons, slaves were left largely to themselves. Bone tired perhaps, they nonetheless used the time and space to develop and enjoy what mattered most: family, religion, and community.

In the quarters, slaves lived lives that their masters were hardly aware of. Temporarily leaving the master-slave relationship at their cabin doors, slaves became husbands and wives, mothers and fathers, sons and daughters, preachers and singers, storytellers and conjurers. Over the generations, they created a community and a culture of their own that buoyed them up during long hours in the fields and brought them joy and hope in the few hours they had to themselves.

One of the most important consequences of the slaves' limited autonomy was the preservation and persistence of the family. Perhaps the most serious charge abolitionists leveled against slavery was that it wrecked black family life, a telling indictment in a society that put family at the heart of decent society. Slaveholders sometimes agreed that blacks had no family life, but they placed the blame on the slaves themselves, claiming that blacks chose to lead licentious, promiscuous lives.

Contrary to both abolitionists' and slaveholders' claims, the black family survived slavery. Indeed, family was the chief fact of life in the quarters. Owners sometimes encouraged the creation and maintenance of families, but as often they were indifferent to the living arrangements of their slaves, as long as the quarters were quiet. Slave family life grew primarily from black commitment. While no laws recognized slave marriage, and therefore no master or slave was legally obligated to honor the bond, plantation records show that slave marriages were often long-lasting. Young men and women in the slave quarters fell in love, married, and set up housekeeping in cabins of their own. The primary cause of the ending of slave marriages was death, just as it was in white families. But the second most frequent cause of the end of slave marriages was the sale of the husband or wife, something no white family ever had to fear. Precise figures are unavailable, but one scholar estimates that in the years 1820–1860, sales destroyed 300,000 slave marriages. Years after Moses Grandy was parted from his slave wife, he said, "I have never seen or heard of her from that day to this." And he added, "I loved her as I love my life."

Plantation records also reveal the importance of slave fathers. Not all fathers could live with their children—some men had been sold away and others had married women on neighboring plantations—but most fathers were present. Despite their inability to fulfill the traditional roles of provider and protector, slave fathers gained status by doing what they could to provide for their families: hunting, raising hogs, cultivating a garden, making furniture. In the eyes of slaves, an ex-bondsman recalled, "the man who does this is a great man amongst them." Although patriarchal masters sharply circumscribed the authority of slave husbands, ex-slaves held both their mothers and fathers in high esteem, grateful for the refuge they had provided from the rigors of slavery.

Contrary to both abolitionists' and slave-holders' claims, the black family survived slavery. Indeed, family was the chief fact of life in the quarters.

Like families, religion also provided slaves with a refuge and a reason for living. In the seventeenth century and for most of the eighteenth, masters cared little about the spiritual lives of their slaves, and most blacks clung to their African beliefs. Beginning about the time of the American Revolution, however, Protestant evangelical sects, particularly the Baptists and Methodists, began trying to con-

SLAVE QUARTER, SOUTH CAROLINA
On large plantations, several score of African Americans lived in cabins that were often arranged along what slaves called "the street." The dwellings pictured in this image by Civil War photographer George N. Barnard of a South Carolina plantation were better built than the typical rickety, one-room, dirt-floored slave cabin. Although this photograph is almost certainly posed, it captures the inhabitants of the slave quarter—little children playing in the dirt, girls and women sitting on the steps talking and working at something, and older boys and men driving carts and wagons. During the daylight hours of the work week when most men and women labored in the fields, the quarter was largely empty. But at night and on Sundays, it was a busy place.
Collection of the New-York Historical Society.

vert slaves. Evangelicals offered an emotional "religion of the heart" to which blacks (and many whites as well) responded enthusiastically. By the mid-nineteenth century, perhaps as many as one-quarter of all slaves claimed church membership, and many of the rest would not have objected to being called Christians.

Planters began promoting Christianity in the quarters because they came to see the slaves' salvation as part of their obligation and to believe that religion made slaves more obedient. Certainly, the Christianity that masters broadcast to slaves emphasized the meeker virtues. White preachers admonished their black congregants to love God and

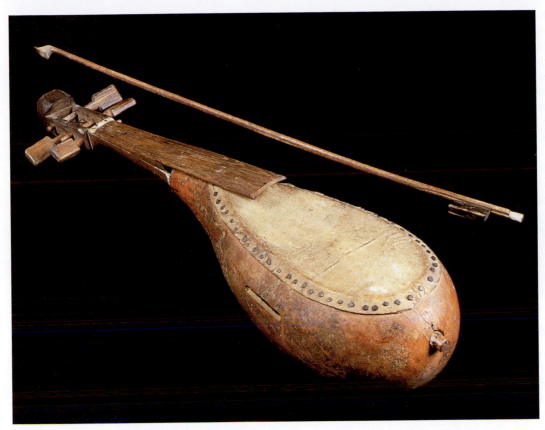

GOURD FIDDLE

Found in St. Mary's County, Maryland, this slave-made gourd fiddle is an example of the many musical instruments that African Americans crafted and played throughout the South. Henry Wright, an ex-slave from Georgia, remembered: "I made a fiddle out of a large sized gourd—a long wooden handle was used as a neck, and the hair from a horse's tail was used for the bow. The strings were made of catgut." A hybrid of African and European elements, this fiddle offers material evidence of the cultural transformation of African slaves. While Africans lost much in their forced journey to the Americas, Africa remained in their cultural memory. Black men and women drew on the traditions of their homeland and the South to create something new—an African American culture. Music, a crucial component of that sustaining culture, provided slaves with a creative outlet and relief from the rigors of slavery.

Smithsonian Institution/Aldo Tutino/Folio, Inc.

to obey their owners. Many slaves laughed up their sleeves at the message. "That old white preacher just was telling us slaves to be good to our masters," a Virginia ex-slave chuckled. "We ain't cared a bit about that stuff he was telling us 'cause we wanted to sing, pray, and serve God in our own way."

Meeting in their cabins or secretly in the woods, slaves created an African American Christianity that served their needs, not the masters'. Beginning in the 1830s, laws prohibited teaching slaves to read, but some slaves could read enough to struggle with the Bible. With the help of black preachers, they interpreted the Christian message themselves. Rather than obedience, their faith emphasized justice. Nat Turner felt himself to be an avenging angel who would punish whites and end bondage. More often, slaves believed that God kept score, and accounts of this world would be settled in the next. "God is punishing some of them old suckers and their children right now for the way they use to treat us poor colored folks," an ex-slave declared. But the slaves' faith involved more than retribution. It also spoke to their experiences in this world. In the Old Testament they discovered Moses, who delivered his people from slavery, and in the New Testament they found Jesus, who offered salvation to all and thereby established the equality of all people. Jesus' message of equality provided a potent antidote to the planters' claim that blacks were an inferior people whom God condemned to slavery and was a crucial buttress to the slaves' self-esteem.

Christianity did not entirely drive out traditional African beliefs. Even Christians in the quarters often continued to believe that conjurers, witches, and spirits possessed the power to protect and defend. Moreover, Christian music, preaching, and rituals showed the influence of Africa, as did much of the slaves' secular activities, such as wood carving, quilt making, and storytelling.

Resistance and Rebellion

Slaves did not suffer slavery passively. They were, as whites said, "troublesome property." Slaves understood that accommodation to what they could not change was the price of survival, but in a hundred ways they protested their bondage. Theoretically, the master was all-powerful and the slave powerless. But sustained by their culture and emboldened by the slave community, slaves engaged in day-to-day resistance against their enslavers.

The spectrum of slave resistance ranged from mild to extreme. Telling a pointed story by the fireside in a slave cabin was probably the mildest form of protest. But when the weak got the better of the strong, as they did in tales of Brer Rabbit and Brer Fox (*Brer* is a contraction of *Brother*), listeners could enjoy the thrill of a vicarious victory over their masters. Protest in the fields was more active than that around firesides. Slaves were particularly inventive in resisting their master's demand that they work. They dragged their feet getting to the fields, put rocks in their cotton bags before putting them on the scale to be weighed, feigned illness, and pretended to be so thickheaded that they could not understand the simplest instruction. Slaves broke so many hoe handles that owners outfitted the hoes with oversized handles. Slaves so mistreated the work animals that masters switched from horses to mules, which could absorb more abuse. While slaves worked hard in the master's fields, they also sabotaged his interests.

Running away, a widespread form of protest, particularly angered masters. By escaping the plantation, runaways denied masters what they wanted most from their slaves—work. Sometimes runaways sought the ultimate prize: freedom in the North or in Canada. Over the decades, thousands of slaves, mostly from the Upper South, made it. But from the Lower South, escape to freedom was almost impossible. At most, runaways could hope to escape for a few weeks. They usually stayed close to the plantation, keeping to the deep woods or swamps and slipping back into the quarters at night to get food. "Lying out," as it was known, usually ended when the runaway, worn out and ragged, gave up or was finally chased down by slave-hunting dogs.

While resistance was common, outright rebellion—a violent assault on slavery by large numbers of slaves—was rare. The scarcity of revolts in the antebellum South is not evidence of the slaves' contentedness. Rather, existing conditions gave rebels virtually no chance of success. By 1860, whites outnumbered blacks two to one and were heavily armed. Moreover, communication between plantations was difficult, and the South provided little protective wilderness into which rebels could retreat and defend themselves. Organized rebellion in the American South, as Nat Turner's experience showed, was virtual suicide.

Given the odds, it is perhaps surprising to find any organized rebellion. But slaves in the antebellum South did rise up. Nat Turner's revolt in 1831 was one of the bloodiest. And whites believed that conspiracies to rebel were everywhere. In 1822, Charleston was rocked by a revolt that never occurred. Denmark Vesey, a free black carpenter, was accused of planning to storm Charleston's arsenal, capture its weapons, kill any white who stood in the way, and set fire to the city. But slaves and other free blacks betrayed Vesey. One arrest led to another as suspects, prodded by torture and the threat of death, implicated others. Shaken badly by the disclosures, whites feverishly tracked down every one of the accused. After three months, the authorities had banished thirty-seven blacks from the state and executed thirty-five more, including Denmark Vesey.

Although masters often boasted that their slaves were "instinctively contented," steady resistance and occasional rebellion proved otherwise. Slaves did not have the power to end their bondage, but by asserting themselves, they affirmed their humanity and worth. By resisting their masters' will, slaves also helped shape their own destiny. They became actors in the plantation drama, helping to establish limits beyond which planters and overseers hesitated to go.

It would be false to the historical record to minimize what the lack of freedom meant to slaves. Because the essence of slavery was the inability to shape one's own life, slavery blunted and thwarted African Americans' hopes and aspirations. Slavery broke some and crippled others. But slavery's destructive power had to contend with the resiliency of the human spirit. Slaves fought back physically, culturally, and spiritually. Slaves not only survived bondage but created in the quarter a vibrant African American culture and community that would sustain them through more than two centuries of slavery and after.

Black and Free: On the Middle Ground

Not every black Southerner was a slave. In 1860, some 260,000 (approximately 6 percent) of the region's 4.1 million African Americans were free (see Figure 12.1). What is surprising is not that their numbers were small but that they existed at all. "Free black" seemed increasingly a contradiction to most white Southerners. According to the emerging racial thinking, blacks were supposed to be slaves; only whites were supposed to be free. Blacks who were free did not fit neatly into the South's idealized social order. They stood out, and whites made them more and more objects of special scrutiny. Free blacks realized that they stood precariously between slavery and full freedom, on what a young free black artisan in Charleston characterized in 1848 as "a middle ground."

Free Blacks and the White Response

Free blacks were rare in the colonial era, but their numbers swelled after the Revolution, when the natural rights philosophy of the Declaration of Independence and the egalitarian message of evangelical Protestantism joined to challenge slavery. Although probably not more than one slaveholder in a hundred freed his slaves, a brief flurry of emancipation visited the Upper South, where the ideo-

logical assault on slavery coincided with a deep depression in the tobacco economy. Other planters permitted favorite slaves to work after hours to accumulate money with which to buy their freedom. By 1810, free blacks numbered more than 100,000 and had become the fastest-growing element of the southern population. Burgeoning numbers of free blacks worried white Southerners, who, because of the cotton boom, wanted desperately to see more slaves, not more free blacks.

Free blacks were rare in the colonial era, but their numbers swelled after the Revolution, when the natural rights philosophy of the Declaration of Independence and the egalitarian message of evangelical Protestantism joined to challenge slavery.

In the 1820s and 1830s, state legislatures acted to stem the growth of the free black population and to shrink the liberty of those blacks who had already gained their freedom. Laws denied masters the right to free their slaves. Other laws humiliated and restricted free blacks by subjecting them to special taxes, requiring them to register annually with the state or to choose a white guardian, prohibiting them from interstate travel, denying them the right to have schools and to participate in politics, and requiring them to carry "freedom papers" to prove they were not slaves. Increasingly, whites subjected free blacks to many of the same laws as slaves. They could not testify under oath in a court of law or serve on juries. They were liable to punishment meted out to slaves such as whipping and the treadmill. Like slaves, free blacks were forbidden to strike whites, even to defend themselves. "Free negroes belong to a degraded caste of society," a South Carolina judge summed up in 1848. "They are in no respect on a perfect equality with the white man. . . . They ought, by law, to be compelled to demean themselves as inferiors."

The elaborate system of regulations confined most free African Americans to a constricted life of poverty and dependence, which led most whites to despise them as degraded parasites. Typically, free blacks were rural, uneducated, unskilled agricultural laborers and domestic servants, scrambling to find work and eke out a living. Opportunities of all kinds—for work, education, community—were slim. Planters looked upon free blacks as worthless rascals, likely to set a bad example for slaves. They believed that free blacks subverted the racial subordination that was the essence of slavery.

Achievement despite Restrictions

Despite increasingly harsh laws and stepped-up persecution, free African Americans made the most of the advantages their status offered. Unlike slaves, free blacks could legally marry. They could protect their families from arbitrary disruption by whites and pass on their heritage of freedom to their children. Freedom also meant that they could choose occupations and own property. For most, however, these economic rights proved only theoretical, for whites allowed most free blacks few opportunities. Unlike whites, a majority of the antebellum South's free blacks remained propertyless.

Still, some free blacks escaped the poverty and degradation whites thrust upon them. Particularly in urban areas—especially the cities of Charleston, Mobile, and New Orleans—a small elite of free blacks developed and even flourished. Urban whites enforced many of the restrictive laws only sporadically, allowing free blacks room to maneuver. The elite consisted overwhelmingly of light-skinned African Americans who worked at skilled trades, as tailors, carpenters, mechanics, and the like. Their customers were prominent whites—planters, merchants, and judges—who appreciated their able, respectful service. The free black elite operated schools for their children and traveled in and out of their states, despite the laws. They worshiped with whites (in separate seating) in the finest churches and lived scattered about in white neighborhoods, not in ghettos. And like elite whites, some owned slaves. Blacks could own blacks because, despite all of the restrictions whites placed on free African Americans, whites did not deny them the right to own property, which in the South included human property. Of the 3,200 black slaveholders (barely 1 percent of the free black population), most owned only a few, who were sometimes family members whom they could not legally free. But others owned slaves in large numbers, none of whom were family and all of whom were exploited for labor.

One such free black slave owner was William Ellison of South Carolina. Ellison was himself born a slave in 1790, but in 1816 he bought his freedom from his white master (who may have been his fa-

BUREAU BY THOMAS DAY, FREE MAN OF COLOR
Thomas Day was North Carolina's best-known cabinet maker. The basis of his reputation is clear in this stunning example of his craftsmanship. Day was also a free black man who owned and operated his own business and who sometimes even employed white journeymen. Most free blacks found jobs of any kind hard to come by, and only a few especially gifted and lucky men like Thomas Day escaped the poverty and grinding labor that most experienced.
© North Carolina Museum of History.

ther) and moved to a thriving plantation district about one hundred miles north of Charleston. He set up business as a cotton gin maker, a trade he had learned as a slave. Ellison's gin business grew with the cotton boom until by 1835 he was prosperous enough to purchase the home of a former governor of the state. Ellison lived in the house until his death in 1861. By then he had become the wealthiest free black in his state, a big planter who made a hundred bales of cotton a year with sixty-three slaves on an eight-hundred-acre plantation.

Not every free black was willing to accommodate to whites and enslave other blacks. At the very time Ellison was building his slave empire, Denmark Vesey talked rebellion with slaves. Most free blacks neither became slaveholders nor sought to raise a slave rebellion. Rather, they simply tried to preserve their freedom. Increasingly under attack from planters who wanted to eliminate or enslave them and from white artisans who coveted their jobs, they sought to impress whites with their reliability, their economic progress, and their good behavior.

The Plain Folk

Most whites in the South did not own slaves, not even one. In 1860, more than six million of the South's eight million whites lived in slaveless families. Some slaveless Southerners lived in cities and worked as artisans, traders, and mechanics, but their numbers were relatively small because the South had few cities. Others lived in the country but worked outside agriculture as storekeepers, parsons, and schoolteachers. But most "plain folk" were small farmers. Perhaps three out of four were yeomen, small farmers who owned their own land. As in the North, farm ownership provided a family with an economic foundation, social respectability, and political standing. Unlike their northern counterparts, however, southern yeomen lived in a region whose economy and society were increasingly dominated by unfree labor. By no means did the nonslaveholding white majority escape the influence of slavery.

In an important sense, the South had more than one white yeomanry. The huge southern landscape provided space enough for two yeoman societies, separated roughly along geographical lines. Yeomen throughout the South had a good deal in common, but the life of a small farm family in the plantation belt—the flatlands that included the black belt and delta regions—differed from the life of one in the upcountry—the area of hills and mountains.

Plantation Belt Yeomen

Plantation belt yeomen lived within the orbit of the planter class. Small landholdings actually outnumbered the larger plantations in that great arc of fertile land that spread from South Carolina to east Texas, but they were dwarfed in importance. Small farmers grew food crops, particularly corn, but like planters, yeomen devoted a significant portion of their land to growing cotton. With only family labor to draw upon, however, they produced only a couple of four-hundred-pound bales each year, whereas large planters measured their crop in hundreds of bales. The small farmers' cotton tied them to planters. Unable to afford cotton gins or baling presses of their own, they relied on helpful neighborhood slave owners to gin and bale their small crops. With no link to merchants in the port cities, yeomen turned to better-connected planters to ship and sell their cotton.

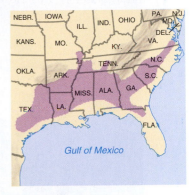

The Cotton Belt

A dense network of personal relationships laced small farmers and planters together in patterns of reciprocity and mutual obligation. A planter might send his slaves to help a newcomer build a house or a sick farmer get in his crop. He hired out surplus slaves to ambitious yeomen who wanted to expand cotton production. He sometimes chose his overseers from among the sons of local farm families. Plantation mistresses sometimes nursed ailing neighbors. Family ties could span class lines, making rich and poor kin as well as neighbors. Yeomen shared the planters' commitment to white supremacy and actively defended black subordination. Rural counties required adult white males to ride in slave patrols, which nightly scoured country roads to make certain that no slaves were moving about without permission. On Sundays, plantation dwellers and plain folk came together in church to worship and afterward lingered to gossip and to transact small business.

Yeomen may have envied, and at times even resented, wealthy slaveholders, but in general small farmers learned to accommodate. Planters made accommodation easier by going out of their way to provide necessary services, behave as good neighbors, and avoid direct exploitation of slaveless whites in their community. As a consequence, rather than raging at the oppression of the planter regime, the typical plantation belt yeoman sought entry into

GATHERING CORN IN VIRGINIA, C. 1870
In this romanticized agricultural scene, painter Felix Darley depicts a white farm family as it gathers its harvest by hand. A young black drover, who before the war would have been the property of the white man or rented by him from a neighboring planter, steadies the team of oxen while another man fills the wagon. Sitting before the bundled stalks, the couple shucks the ripened ears of corn. The happy moment is made complete by playful and dozing children and a sleeping dog. In reality, growing corn was hard work. Even those yeomen who grew considerable cotton also grew lots of corn, usually producing about twice the corn they needed for their families and livestock and marketing the rest. But the artist is less concerned with realism than with extolling rural family labor as virtuous and noble. Darley surrounds the southern yeomen with an aura of republican independence, dignity, and freedom.
Warner Collection of Gulf States Paper Corporation.

it. He dreamed of adding acreage to his farm, buying a few slaves of his own, retiring from field work, and perhaps even joining his prosperous neighbors on their shady verandas for a cool drink.

Upcountry Yeomen

By contrast, the hills and mountains of the South resisted the penetration of slavery and plantations. While increasing participation in the market was a trend everywhere in the South, the western parts of Virginia, North Carolina, and South Carolina, northern Georgia and Alabama, and eastern Ten-

nessee and Kentucky retained a quite different economy and society. The higher elevation, colder climate, rugged terrain, and poor transportation made it difficult for commercial agriculture to make headway. For yeomen who lived in the hills and mountains, planters and slaves were not everyday acquaintances. Geographically isolated, the upcountry was a yeoman stronghold.

At the core of the distinctive upcountry culture was the independent farm family working its own patch of land; raising a considerable number of hogs, cattle, and sheep; and seeking self-sufficiency and independence. Toward that end, all members of the family worked, their tasks depending on their sex and age. Husbands labored in the fields, and with their sons they cleared, plowed, planted, and cultivated primarily food crops—corn, wheat, sweet potatoes, and perhaps some fruit. Although pressed into field labor at harvest time, wives and daughters worked in and about the cabin most of the year. One upcountry farmer remembered that his mother "worked in the house cooking, spinning, weaving [and doing] patchwork." Women also tended the vegetable garden, kept a cow and some chickens, preserved foods, cleaned their homes, fed their families, and cared for their children. Male and female tasks were equally crucial to the farm's success, but as in other white southern households, the female domestic sphere was subordinated to the will of the male patriarch.

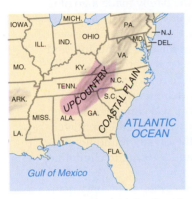

Upcountry of the South

The typical upcountry yeoman also grew a little cotton or tobacco, but production for home consumption was more important than production for the market. Not much currency changed hands in the upcountry. Credit was common, as was direct barter. A yeoman might trade his small commercial crop to a country store owner for a little salt, lead shot, needles, and nails. Or he might swap extra sweet potatoes with the blacksmith for a plow or with the tanner for leather. Networks of exchange and mutual assistance tied individual homesteads to the larger community. Farm families swapped goods and work and joined together in logrolling, house- or barn-raising, and cornhusking. Strong communal ties made the yeoman's goal of maintaining his family's independence realistic.

Yeomen did not have the upcountry entirely to themselves. Even the hills had some plantations and slaves. But they existed in much smaller numbers than in the plantation belt. Farmers and farms, not planters and plantations, dominated upcountry culture. Most upcountry counties were less than a quarter black, whereas counties in the plantation belt were more than half black. The few upcountry folks who owned slaves usually had only two or three. As a result, slaveholders had much less direct social and economic power, and yeomen had more.

But yeoman domination did not mean that the upcountry opposed slavery. As long as they were free to lead their own lives, upcountry plain folk defended slavery and white supremacy just as staunchly as did other white Southerners.

Whether plain folk lived in the hills or in the flatlands, they did not usually associate "book learning" with the basic needs of life. In any case, the children of yeomen had limited opportunity for schooling. A northern woman visiting the South in the 1850s observed, "Education is not extended to the masses here as at the North." Private academies charged fees that yeomen could not afford, and public schools were scarce. Even where public schools existed, terms were short, only about 50 or 60 days a year in the South compared with 100 to 150 days in the North. Although most people managed to pick up a basic knowledge of the "three R's," approximately one southern white man in five was illiterate in 1860, and the rate for white women was even higher. "People here prefer talking to reading," a Virginian remarked. Telling stories, reciting ballads, and singing hymns were important activities in yeoman folk culture.

At the core of the distinctive upcountry culture was the independent farm family working its own patch of land and seeking self-sufficiency and independence.

Plain folk everywhere spent more hours in revival tents than in classrooms. By no means were all rural whites religious, but many were, and the most characteristic feature of their evangelical Christian faith was the revival. The greatest of the early-nineteenth-century revivals occurred in 1801 at Cane Ridge, Kentucky, where some twenty thousand people gathered to listen to a host of evangelical preachers who spoke day and night for a week. Ministers sought to convert and save souls by bringing individuals to a personal conviction of sin. Revivalism crossed denominational lines; Baptists and Methodists adopted it wholeheartedly and by mid-century had become the South's largest religious groups. By emphasizing free choice and individual worth, the plain folk's religion was hopeful and affirming. Hymns and spirituals provided guides to right and wrong—praising modesty and steadfastness, condemning drinking and devilish activity like dancing. Above all, hymns spoke of eventual release from worldly sorrows and the assurance of eternal salvation.

Poor Whites

Northerners denied the claim that the South's white majority constituted a sturdy yeomanry—hard-working, landholding small farmers. Instead, they charged that the institution of slavery had pushed slaveless whites so far down the social and economic ladder that they had lost heart, ambition, and energy. The majority of the South's whites, according to northern critics, were landless, shiftless, and degraded. Contemporaries called these Southerners a variety of derogatory names: hillbillies, crackers, rednecks, and poor white trash. Even slaves were known to chant: "I'd rather be a nigger an' plow ol' Beck,/Than a white hill-billy with a long red neck." Poor whites were not just whites who were poor. The label carried a moral as well as a material meaning. Poor whites were supposedly ignorant and inbred, sick in body and degenerate in culture.

Significant numbers of Southerners were poor, as the critics claimed. Perhaps one in four farmers was landless. Landless farm families lived as tenants, renting rather than owning land, or as unskilled day laborers working for wages. Other poor rural Southerners made their living as hunters, herders, and fishermen. Living on the periphery of the southern economy, some barely made a go of it. Wits could declare that "poor whites were born lazy and had a relapse." In fact, poor whites subsisted on unhealthy diets, lived in miserable housing, and spent summers going barefooted around animals, consequently suffering high incidences of hookworm, pellagra, and other debilitating diseases that thrived in the South's warm, wet climate. Although impoverished, most poor white Southerners were not degenerate. Instead, they were ambitious people scratching to survive and aspiring to climb into the yeomanry.

Poor whites were sometimes poor only temporarily. The Lipscomb family illustrates the possibility of upward mobility. In 1845, Smith and Sally Lipscomb and their children abandoned tired land in South Carolina for Benton County, Alabama. "Benton is a mountainous country but ther is a heep of good levil land to tend in it," Smith wrote back to his brother. Alabama, Smith said, "will be better

A BAPTISING ON THE SOUTH BRANCH OF THE POTOMAC NEAR FRANKLIN, VIRGINIA (DETAIL), 1844
In 1844, noted painter William Thompson Russell Smith undertook a geological expedition to Virginia, and there he encountered this rural baptism. Primarily a landscape painter, Smith in this painting relegates the human figures to minor characters. If one of the participants had sketched the baptism, he or she might have emphasized the human drama, the emotional pitch of what was for evangelical Christians throughout the South a profound religious moment.
The Charleston Renaissance Gallery, Robert M. Hicklin Jr., Inc., Charleston, South Carolina.

for the rising generation if not for ourselves but I think it will be the best for us all that live any length of time." Indeed, primitive living conditions made life precarious. All of the Lipscombs fell ill, but all recovered, and the entire family went to work. Because they had no money to buy land, they squatted on seven acres. With the help of neighbors, they built a 22-by-24-foot cabin, a detached kitchen, and two stables. From daylight to dark, Smith and his sons worked the land. Nature cooperated, and they produced enough food for the table and several bales of cotton. The women worked as hard in the cabin, and Sally contributed to the family's income by selling homemade shirts and socks. In time, the Lipscombs bought land of their own. They joined Hebron Baptist Church and completed their transformation from landless poor whites to respectable yeomen.

Although impoverished, most poor white Southerners were ambitious people scratching to survive and aspiring to climb into the yeomanry.

The upward mobility demonstrated by the Lipscombs became rarer in the 1850s. The cotton boom of that decade encouraged planters to expand their operations, driving the price of land beyond the reach of poor families. Squeezed by competition with plantation slavery and pushed to the least fertile regions of the South, such as the pine barrens along the Atlantic coast, poor whites were likely to remain poor.

The Politics of Slavery

Like every other significant feature of southern society, politics showed the impress of slavery. Even after the South's politics became democratic in form for the white male population, political power remained unevenly distributed. The nonslaveholding white majority wielded less political power than their numbers indicated. The slaveholding white minority wielded more. Self-conscious, cohesive, and with a well-developed sense of class interest, slaveholders busied themselves with party politics, campaigns, and officeholding and made demands

of state governments. As a result, they received significant benefits. But nonslaveholding whites were concerned mainly with preserving their liberties and keeping their taxes low. Collectively, they asked government for little of an economic nature, and they received little.

Slaveholders worried about nonslaveholders' political loyalty to slavery. Ultimately, they need not have fretted. Since the eighteenth century, the mass of whites had accepted the planters' argument that the existing social order served *all* Southerners' interests. Slavery compensated every white man—no matter how poor—with membership in the South's white ruling class. It also provided the means by which nonslaveholders might someday advance into the ranks of the planters. White men in the South fought furiously about many things, but they agreed that they should take land from Indians, promote agriculture, uphold white supremacy, and defend slavery from its enemies.

The Democratization of the Political Arena

The political reforms that swept the nation in the first half of the nineteenth century reached deeply into the South. Southern politics became democratic politics—for white men. State by state, Southerners eliminated the wealth and property requirements that had restricted political participation. By the early 1850s (but in most cases much earlier) every state had extended suffrage to all white males who were at least twenty-one years of age. Most southern states also removed the property requirements for holding state offices. In addition, increasing numbers of local and state officials—justices of the peace, judges, militia officers, and others—were chosen by the voters. To be sure, undemocratic features lingered. Plantation districts still wielded disproportionate power in several state legislatures. Nevertheless, southern politics increasingly took place within a democratic political structure.

White male suffrage ushered in an era of vigorous electoral competition. Eager voters rushed to the polls to exercise their new rights. In South Carolina, for example, in the 1810 election—the last election with voting restrictions in place—only 43 percent of white men cast ballots. In 1824, a remarkable 76 percent of white men voted. High turnouts became a hallmark of southern electoral politics. Candidates crisscrossed their electoral district, speaking to groups several times a day. Voters displayed considerable political savvy and expected solid argument as well as stirring oratory. They also demanded good entertainment—barbecues and bands, rum and races. The candidates competed in producing extravaganzas, hoping to attract attention as well as votes.

As politics became aggressively democratic, it also grew fiercely partisan. From the 1830s to the 1850s, Whigs and Democrats battled for the electorate's favor. Whigs and Democrats both presented themselves as the plain white folk's best friend. All candidates declared their fervent commitment to republican equality and pledged to defend the people's liberty. Each party sought to portray the other as a collection of rich, snobbish, selfish men who had antidemocratic designs up their silk sleeves. Each, in turn, claimed for itself the mantle of humble "servant of the people."

By the early 1850s, southern politics became democratic politics—for white men.

The Whig and Democratic Parties sought to serve the people differently, however. Southern Whigs tended, as Whigs did elsewhere in the nation, to favor government intervention in the economy, and Democrats tended to oppose it. Whigs generally backed state support of banks, railroads, and corporations, arguing that government aid would stimulate the economy, enlarge opportunity, and thus increase the general welfare. Democrats emphasized the threat to individual liberty that government intervention posed, claiming that granting favors to special economic interests would result in concentrated power, which would in turn jeopardize the common man's opportunity and equality. Beginning with the panic of 1837, the parties clashed repeatedly on concrete economic and financial issues.

Planter Power

Whether Whig or Democrat, southern officeholders were likely to be slave owners. The power slaveholders exerted over slaves did not translate directly into political authority over whites, however. In the nineteenth century, political power could be won only at the ballot box, and almost everywhere

nonslaveholders were in the majority. Yet year after year, proud and noisily egalitarian common men elected wealthy slaveholders (Table 12.1).

And wealthy slaveholders increased their power in state legislatures. By 1860, the percentage of slave owners in state legislatures ranged from 41 percent in Missouri to nearly 86 percent in North Carolina. Legislators not only tended to own slaves—they often owned large numbers. The percentage of planters (individuals with twenty or more slaves) in southern legislatures in 1860 ranged from 5.3 percent in Missouri to 55.4 percent in South Carolina. In North Carolina, where only 3 percent of the state's white families belonged to the planter class, 36.6 percent of the legislature were planters. The democratization of politics in the nineteenth century meant that more ordinary citizens participated in elections, but yeomen and artisans remained rare sights in the halls of southern legislatures.

Upper-class dominance of southern politics reflected, in part, the strength of the rural folk culture, which valued tradition and stability. In the colonial era, yeomen had looked to the upper class for political leadership. Large planters possessed great wealth, education, oratorical gifts, experience in public affairs, the habit of command, and eagerness to serve. Notions of hierarchy and habits of deference declined in the nineteenth century as democracy rose, but planter status remained important in the South and the surest ticket to political advancement.

But tradition was not enough to ensure planter rule. Slaveholders had to persuade the white majority that what was good for slaveholders was also good for them. Slaveless whites proved to be receptive to the planters' argument. The South had, on the whole, done well by them. Most had farms of their own. They participated as equals in a democratic political system. As white men, they enjoyed an elevated social status, above all blacks and in theory equal to all other whites. As long as slavery existed, they could dream of joining the planter class, of rising above the drudgery of field labor. Slaveless white men found much to celebrate in the slave South.

Most slaveholders took pains to win the plain folk's trust and to nurture their respect. In the plantation districts especially, where slaveholders and nonslaveholders lived side by side, planters learned that flexing their economic muscle was a poor way to win the political allegiance of common men. Instead, they developed a lighter touch, fully atten-

TABLE 12.1

SLAVEHOLDERS AND PLANTERS IN
LEGISLATURES, 1860

Legislature	Percent of Slaveholders	Percent of Planters*
Virginia	67.3	24.2
Maryland	53.4	19.3
North Carolina	85.8	36.6
Kentucky	60.6	8.4
Tennessee	66.0	14.0
Missouri	41.2	5.3
Arkansas	42.0	13.0
South Carolina	81.7	55.4
Georgia	71.6	29.0
Florida	55.4	20.0
Alabama	76.3	40.8
Mississippi	73.4	49.5
Louisiana	63.8	23.5
Texas	54.1	18.1

*Planters: Owned 20 or more slaves.

Source: Adapted from Ralph A. Wooster, *The People in Power: Courthouse and Statehouse in the Lower South, 1850–1860* (1969), 41; *Politicians, Planters, and Plain Folks: Courthouse and Statehouse in the Upper South* (1975), 40.

Courtesy of the University of Tennessee Press.

tive to their own interests but aware of the personal feelings of poorer whites. One South Carolinian told his wealthy neighbor that he had a bright political future because he never thought himself "too good to sit down & talk to a poor man."

Not all of the gentry behaved astutely, however. Plain folk still encountered strutting slaveholders. A slaveless farmer in Tennessee declared that in his neighborhood, "all who owned as much as one negro seemed to feel that they were in a separate and higher class than the common people." But no slave master with political ambitions could afford to play the aristocrat. Even if he believed that the hierarchical social relations of plantations should extend to the broader community, he could not treat white men like slaves. Open elitism was political suicide.

Smart candidates found ways to convince wary yeomen of their democratic convictions and egalitarian sentiments, whether they were genuine or not. When young John A. Quitman ran for a seat in

the Mississippi legislature, he amazed a boisterous crowd of small farmers at one campaign stop by not only entering but winning contests in jumping, boxing, wrestling, and sprinting. For his finale he outshot the area's champion marksman. Then, demonstrating his deft political touch, he gave his prize, a fat ox, to the defeated rifleman. The electorate showed its approval by sending Quitman to the state capital. When Walter L. Steele ran for a seat in the North Carolina legislature in 1846, he commented sarcastically to a friend that he was "busily engaged in proving to the people, the soundness of my political faith, and the purity of my personal character & playing the fool to a considerable extent, as you know, all candidates are obliged to do." He detested pandering to the electorate, but he had learned to speak with "a candied tongue."

The massive representation of slaveholders ensured that southern legislatures would make every effort to preserve slavery. Georgia politics show how well the planters protected themselves in the political struggle. In 1850, about half of the state's revenues came from taxes on slave property, the characteristic form of planter wealth. However, the tax rate on slaves was trifling, only about one-fifth the rate on land. Moreover, planters benefited far more than other social groups from public spending: Financing railroads—which carried cotton to market—was the largest state expenditure in the late antebellum period. The legislature established low tax rates on land, the characteristic form of yeoman wealth, which meant that the typical yeoman's annual tax bill was small. Still, relative to their wealth, large slaveholders paid less than did other whites. Relative to their numbers, they got more. A sympathetic slaveholding legislature protected planters' interests and gave the impression of protecting the small farmers' interests as well.

The South's elite protected slavery in other ways. In the 1830s, whites decided that slavery was too important to debate, especially with the specter of abolitionism in the North. "So interwoven is [slavery] with our interest, our manners, our climate and our very being," one man declared in 1833, "that no change can ever possibly be effected without a civil commotion from which the heart of a patriot must turn with horror." A "cotton curtain" descended along the Mason-Dixon line that ended free speech on the slavery question. Slavery's critics were dismissed from college faculties, driven from pulpits, and hounded from political life. Sometimes they fell victim to vigilantes and mob violence. One could defend slavery; one could even delicately suggest mild reforms. But no Southerner could safely call slavery evil or sinful or advocate its destruction.

By gagging slavery's critics, slaveholders gained real advantage. In 1857, for example, Hinton Rowan Helper, a North Carolinian who moved north, published *The Impending Crisis of the South*, in which he argued that slavery denied nonslaveholding whites the opportunities for economic advancement that free-labor societies offered. Rather than confront the book's deeply disquieting arguments, southern legislatures simply banned it. The South's small farmers, whose economic advancement had stalled in the 1850s, remained unaware of Helper's broadside against slavery. Instead, they heard the South's politicians, academics, and clergy celebrate slavery's benefits.

In the antebellum South, therefore, the rise of the common man occurred alongside the continuing, even growing, power of the planter class. Rather than pitting slaveholders against nonslaveholders, elections remained an effective means of binding the region's whites together. Elections affirmed the sovereignty of white men, whether genteel planter or plain folk, and the subordination of African Americans. Those twin themes played well among white women as well. Although unable to vote, white women supported equality for whites and slavery for blacks.

Conclusion: A Slave Society

Southerners and Northerners came to see the South as fundamentally different from the rest of the nation. It was a rural region with a biracial population that reflected the dominance of plantation slavery. Regional differences generally increased over time, not merely because the South became more and more dominated by slavery, but also because developments in the North rapidly propelled it in a very different direction.

In 1860, nearly four million black Southerners, one-third of the South's population, were enslaved.

Bondage saddled blacks with enormous physical and spiritual burdens: hard labor, poor treatment, broken families, and, most important, the denial of freedom itself. Although degraded and exploited, they were not defeated. Out of African memories and New World realities, blacks created a life-affirming African American culture that sustained and strengthened them. Their families, religion, and community provided antidotes to white racist ideas and even to white power. Defined as property, they refused to be reduced to things. Perceived as inferior beings, they rejected the notion that they were natural slaves. The imbalance of power made Nat Turner's path of outright rebellion suicidal, but most slaves rebelled inwardly. They engaged in a war of wills with masters who sought their labor while they sought to live dignified, autonomous lives.

Much more than racial slavery contributed to the South's distinctiveness and to the loyalty and regional identification of its whites. White Southerners felt strong attachments to local communities, to extended families, to personal, face-to-face relationships, to rural life, to evangelical Protestantism, and to codes of honor and chivalry, among other things. But slavery was crucial to the South's economy, society, and culture, as well as to its developing sectional consciousness. After the 1830s, little disturbed the white consensus south of the Mason-Dixon line that racial slavery was necessary and just. By making all blacks a pariah class, all whites gained a measure of equality and harmony.

Racism did not erase stress along class lines. Nor did the other features of southern life that helped confine class tensions: the wide availability of land, rapid economic mobility, the democratic nature of political life, the shrewd behavior of slaveholders toward poorer whites, kinship ties between rich and poor, and rural traditions. Anxious slaveholders continued to worry that yeomen would defect from the proslavery consensus. But during the 1850s a far more ominous division emerged—that between the "slave states" and the "free states."

www.bedfordstmartins.com/tap SEE THE ONLINE STUDY GUIDE to test your mastery of the material covered in this chapter.

CHRONOLOGY

1808	External slave trade outlawed.
1810s–1850s	Suffrage gradually extended throughout South to white males over twenty-one years of age.
1820s–1830s	Southern legislatures enact slave codes to strengthen slavery.
	Southern legislatures enact laws to restrict growth of free black population and to limit freedom of free blacks.
	Southern intellectuals begin to fashion systematic defense of slavery.
1820–1860	Cotton production soars from about 300,000 bales to nearly 5 million bales.
1822	Denmark Vesey executed for conspiring to lead a slave rebellion in South Carolina.
1831	Nat Turner's slave rebellion occurs in Virginia.
1860	The slave population of South approaches 4 million, an increase of 600 percent in seven decades.

BIBLIOGRAPHY

GENERAL WORKS

John B. Boles, *The South through Time: A History of an American Region* (2nd ed., 1999).

W. J. Cash, *The Mind of the South* (1941).

William J. Cooper Jr. and Thomas E. Terrill, *The American South: A History* (2nd ed., 1996).

Carl N. Degler, *Place over Time: The Continuity of Southern Distinctiveness* (1977).

James Oakes, *Slavery and Freedom: An Interpretation of the Old South* (1990).

C. Vann Woodward, *The Burden of Southern History* (rev. ed., 1968).

THE ECONOMY

Fred Bateman and Thomas Weiss, *A Deplorable Scarcity: The Failure of Industrialization in the Slave Economy* (1981).

Peter A. Coclanis, *The Shadow of a Dream: Economic Life and Death in the South Carolina Low Country, 1670–1920* (1989).

Charles B. Dew, *Ironmaker to the Confederacy: Joseph R. Anderson and the Tredegar Iron Works* (1966).

Daniel S. Dupre, *Transforming the Cotton Frontier: Madison County, Alabama, 1800–1840* (1997).

Robert W. Fogel, *Without Consent or Contract: The Rise and Fall of American Slavery* (1989).

Lewis C. Gray, *History of Agriculture in the Southern United States to 1860,* 2 vols. (1933).

Sam B. Hilliard, *Atlas of Antebellum Southern Agriculture* (1984).

Joseph P. Reidy, *From Slavery to Agrarian Capitalism in the Cotton Plantation South: Central Georgia, 1800–1880* (1992).

Larry Schweikart, *Banking in the American South from the Age of Jackson to Reconstruction* (1987).

Harold D. Woodman, *King Cotton and His Retainers: Financing and Marketing the Cotton Crop of the South, 1800–1925* (1968).

Gavin Wright, *Old South, New South: Revolutions in the Southern Economy Since the Civil War* (1986).

SLAVEHOLDERS

Jane T. Censer, *North Carolina Planters and Their Children, 1800–1860* (1984).

Catherine Clinton, *The Plantation Mistress: Woman's World in the Old South* (1982).

Drew G. Faust, *James Henry Hammond and the Old South: A Design for Mastery* (1982).

Elizabeth Fox-Genovese, *Within the Plantation Household: Black and White Women of the Old South* (1988).

Eugene D. Genovese, *The World the Slaveholders Made: Two Essays in Interpretation* (1969).

James Oakes, *The Ruling Race: A History of American Slaveholders* (1982).

Anne F. Scott, *The Southern Lady: From Pedestal to Politics, 1830–1930* (1970).

Steven M. Stowe, *Intimacy and Power in the Old South: Ritual in the Lives of the Planters* (1987).

Michael Tadman, *Speculators and Slaves: Masters, Traders, and Slaves in the Old South* (1989).

Larry E. Tise, *Proslavery: A History of the Defense of Slavery in America, 1701–1840* (1987).

Marli F. Weiner, *Mistresses and Slaves: Plantation Women in South Carolina, 1830–1880* (1998).

SLAVES, SLAVERY, AND RACE RELATIONS

General works

John W. Blassingame, *The Slave Community: Plantation Life in the Antebellum South* (1972).

John B. Boles, *Black Southerners, 1619–1869* (1983).

Carl N. Degler, *Neither Black nor White: Slavery and Race Relations in Brazil and the United States* (1971).

Paul D. Escott, *Slavery Remembered: A Record of Twentieth-Century Slave Narratives* (1979).

George M. Fredrickson, *The Black Image in the White Mind: The Debate on Afro-American Character and Destiny, 1817–1914* (1971).

George M. Fredrickson, *The Arrogance of Race: Historical Perspectives on Slavery, Racism, and Social Inequality* (1988).

Eugene D. Genovese, *Roll, Jordan, Roll: The World the Slaves Made* (1974).

Peter Kolchin, *American Slavery, 1619–1877* (1993).

Lawrence W. Levine, *Black Culture and Black Consciousness: Afro-American Folk Thought from Slavery to Freedom* (1977).

Leslie H. Owens, *This Species of Property: Slave Life and Culture in the Old South* (1976).

George P. Rawick, ed., *The American Slave: A Composite Autobiography*, 41 vols. (1972–1979).

Willie Lee Rose, ed., *A Documentary History of Slavery in North America* (1976).

Kenneth M. Stampp, *The Peculiar Institution: Slavery in the Antebellum South* (1956).

Sterling Stuckey, *Slave Culture: Nationalist Theory and the Foundations of Black America* (1987).

Important aspects of slavery

John Hope Franklin and Loren Schweninger, *Runaway Slaves: Rebels on the Plantation* (1999).

David Barry Gaspar and Darlene Clark Hine, eds., *More Than Chattel: Black Women and Slavery in the Americas* (1996).

Eugene D. Genovese, *From Rebellion to Revolution: Afro-American Slave Revolts in the Making of the Modern World* (1979).

Herbert G. Gutman, *The Black Family in Slavery and Freedom, 1750–1925* (1976).

Ann Patton Malone, *Sweet Chariot: Slavery, Family, and Household Structure in Nineteenth-Century Louisiana* (1992).

Thomas D. Morris, *Southern Slavery and the Law, 1619–1860* (1996).

Albert J. Raboteau, *Slave Religion: The "Invisible Institution" in the Antebellum South* (1978).

William K. Scarborough, *The Overseer: Plantation Management in the Old South* (1966).

Robert S. Starobin, *Industrial Slavery in the Old South* (1970).

Brenda E. Stevenson, *Life in Black and White: Family and Community in the Slave South* (1996).

William L. Van Deburg, *The Slave Drivers: Black Agricultural Labor Supervisors in the Antebellum South* (1979).

Richard C. Wade, *Slavery in the Cities: The South, 1820–1860* (1964).

Deborah G. White, *Ar'n't I a Woman? Female Slaves in the Plantation South* (1985).

States and local studies

Randolph B. Campbell, *An Empire for Slavery: The Peculiar Institution in Texas, 1821–1865* (1989).

Margaret W. Creel, *"A Peculiar People": Slave Religion and Community-Culture among the Gullahs* (1988).

Charles B. Dew, *Bond of Iron: Master and Slave at Buffalo Forge* (1994).

Douglas R. Egerton, *Gabriel's Rebellion: The Virginia Slave Conspiracies of 1800 and 1802* (1993).

Barbara J. Fields, *Slavery and Freedom on the Middle Ground: Maryland during the Nineteenth Century* (1985).

John C. Inscoe, *Mountain Masters, Slavery, and the Sectional Crisis in Western North Carolina* (1989).

Charles W. Joyner, *Down by the Riverside: A South Carolina Slave Community* (1984).

Melton A. McLaurin, *Celia, a Slave* (1991).

Stephen B. Oates, *The Fires of Jubilee: Nat Turner's Fierce Rebellion* (1975).

SOCIETY AND CULTURE

Edward L. Ayers, *Vengeance and Justice: Crime and Punishment in the 19th Century American South* (1984).

Fred Arthur Bailey, *Class and Tennessee's Confederate Generation* (1987).

Peter W. Bardaglio, *Reconstructing the Household: Families, Sex, and the Law in the Nineteenth-Century South* (1995).

Ira Berlin, *Slaves without Masters: The Free Negro in the Antebellum South* (1974).

Dickson D. Bruce Jr., *Violence and Culture in the Antebellum South* (1979).

Orville Vernon Burton, *In My Father's House Are Many Mansions: Family and Community in Edgefield, South Carolina* (1985).

Victoria E. Bynum, *Unruly Women: The Politics of Social and Sexual Control in the Old South* (1992).

Bruce Collins, *White Society in the Antebellum South* (1985).

James O. Farmer Jr., *The Metaphysical Confederacy: James Henley Thornwell and the Synthesis of Southern Values* (1986).

Drew G. Faust, *A Sacred Circle: The Dilemma of the Intellectual in the Old South, 1840–1860* (1977).

David R. Goldfield, *Cotton Fields and Skyscrapers: Southern City and Region, 1607–1980* (rev. ed., 1989).

Steven Hahn, *The Roots of Southern Populism: Yeoman Farmers and the Transformation of the Georgia Upcountry, 1850–1890* (1983).

J. William Harris, *Plain Folk and Gentry in a Slave Society: White Liberty and Black Slavery in Augusta's Hinterlands* (1985).

Christine Leigh Heyrman, *Southern Cross: The Beginnings of the Bible Belt* (1997).

Samuel C. Hyde Jr., ed., *Plain Folk of the South Revisited* (1997).

Michael P. Johnson and James L. Roark, *Black Masters: A Free Family of Color in the Old South* (1984).

Robert C. Kenser, *Kinship and Neighborhood in a Southern Community: Orange County, North Carolina, 1849–1881* (1987).

Suzanne Lebsock, *The Free Women of Petersburg: Status and Culture in a Southern Town, 1784–1860* (1984).

Donald G. Mathews, *Religion in the Old South* (1977).

Stephanie McCurry, *Masters of Small Worlds: Yeoman Households, Gender Relations, and the Political Culture of the Antebellum South Carolina Low Country* (1995).

Christopher Morris, *Becoming Southern: The Evolution of a Way of Life, Warren County and Vicksburg, Mississippi, 1770–1860* (1995).

John Solomon Otto, *The Southern Frontiers, 1607–1860* (1989).

Christopher H. Owen, *The Sacred Flame of Love: Methodism and Society in Nineteenth-Century Georgia* (1998).

Mark M. Smith, *Mastered by the Clock: Time, Slavery, and Freedom in the American South* (1997).

Mitchell Snay, *Gospel of Disunion: Religion and Separatism in the Antebellum South* (1993).

Randy J. Sparks, *On Jordan's Stormy Banks: Evangelicalism in Mississippi, 1773–1876* (1994).

Bertram Wyatt-Brown, *Southern Honor: Ethics and Behavior in the Old South* (1982).

POLITICS AND POLITICAL CULTURE

Anthony Gene Carey, *Parties, Slavery, and the Union in Antebellum Georgia* (1997).

William J. Cooper Jr., *Liberty and Slavery: Southern Politics to 1860* (1983).

Lacy K. Ford Jr., *Origins of Southern Radicalism: The South Carolina Upcountry, 1800–1860* (1988).

William W. Freehling, *Prelude to Civil War: The Nullification Controversy in South Carolina, 1816–1836* (1966).

Kenneth S. Greenberg, *Masters and Statesmen: The Political Culture of American Slavery* (1985).

Robert E. May, *John A. Quitman: Old South Crusader* (1985).

Craig M. Simpson, *A Good Southerner: The Life of Henry A. Wise of Virginia* (1985).

J. Mills Thornton III, *Politics and Power in a Slave Society: Alabama, 1800–1860* (1978).

Elizabeth R. Varon, *We Mean to Be Counted: White Women and Politics in Antebellum Virginia* (1998).

Peter Wallenstein, *From the Slave South to New South: Public Policy in Nineteenth-Century Georgia* (1987).

Harry L. Watson, *Jacksonian Politics and Community Conflict* (1981).

Ralph A. Wooster, *The People in Power: Courthouse and Statehouse in the Lower South, 1850–1860* (1969).

Ralph A. Wooster, *Politicians, Planters, and Plain Folks: Courthouse and Statehouse in the Upper South, 1850–1860* (1975).

JOHN BROWN'S PIKES

Scorning what he called "milk-and-water" abolitionists who only talked about slavery, John Brown favored "action!" In 1859 when he brought his abolitionist war to Virginia, he carried with him 950 pikes, handsome but deadly spears made by a Connecticut blacksmith, which he expected to put into the hands of rebelling slaves. Bloody pikes, he thought, would end slavery in America. But after Brown's failure at Harpers Ferry, townspeople sold many of the weapons as souvenirs. Chicago Historical Society.

THE HOUSE DIVIDED

1846–1861

13

OTHER THAN TWENTY CHILDREN, John Brown did not have much to show for his life in 1859. Grizzled, gnarled, and fifty-nine years old, he had for decades lived like a nomad, hauling his large family back and forth across six states as he tried desperately to better himself. He turned his hand to farming, raising sheep, running a tannery, and selling wool, but failure followed failure. The world had given John Brown some hard licks, but it had not budged his conviction that slavery was wrong and ought to be destroyed. He had learned to hate slavery at his father's knee, and in the wake of the fighting that erupted over the issue in Kansas in the 1850s, his beliefs turned violent. On May 24, 1856, he led an eight-man antislavery posse in the midnight slaughter of five allegedly proslavery men at Pottawatomie, Kansas. He told Mahala Doyle, whose husband and two oldest sons he killed, that if a man stood between him and what he thought right, he would take that man's life as calmly as he would eat breakfast.

Kansans knew that John Brown and his men were the Pottawatomie killers, but Brown admitted nothing, slipped away from the territory, and reemerged in the East. More than ever, he was a man on fire for abolition. He spent thirty months begging money from New England abolitionists to support his vague plan for military operations against slavery, perhaps in Kansas, perhaps in the South itself. The rough-hewn fighting man captivated the genteel Easterners, particularly the Boston elite. They shared his antislavery convictions and were awed by his iron-willed determination and courage. They listened when the hypnotic-eyed Brown told them that God had touched him for a great purpose. Although he won more hearts than pocketbooks, Brown received enough in gifts to gather a small band of antislavery warriors.

On the night of October 16, 1859, John Brown took his war against slavery into the South. With only twenty-one men, including five African Americans, he crossed the Potomac River and invaded Harpers Ferry, Virginia. Sixty miles from Washington, D.C., the small town had little to recommend it except its federal arsenal, which bristled with rifles. Brown's band quickly seized the armory and rifle works, but the invaders were immediately surrounded, first by local militia and then by Colonel Robert E. Lee, who commanded the U.S. troops in the area. When Brown refused to surrender, federal soldiers charged with bayonets. It was all over in less than thirty-six hours. In all, seventeen men, two of whom were slaves, lost their lives. Although a few of Brown's raiders escaped, federal forces killed ten (including two of his sons) and captured seven, among them Brown himself, who suffered a painful but not life-threatening sword wound.

John Brown's precise objective remains somewhat hazy, but he apparently wanted to initiate a slave insurrection. "When I strike, the bees will begin to swarm," Brown told Frederick Douglass a few months before the raid. As slaves rushed to Harpers Ferry, Brown would arm them with the pikes (long spears) he carried with him and with weapons stolen from the armory. They would then fight a war of lib-

JOHN BROWN
Was John Brown crazy? The debate about Brown's mental state began with his contemporaries and has raged ever since. Those who argue that he was a madman have asked: Would a sane man have butchered innocent victims at Pottawatomie Creek and set out for Harpers Ferry to overthrow slavery with fewer than two dozen men? But others see a resolute and selfless hero, not a psychotic. Moreover, they ask: If John Brown was a lunatic, what does that make the proper New England abolitionists who supported him?
Boston Athenaeum.

to incite slaves in bloody rebellion. For more than a decade, Northerners and Southerners had hurled accusations at one another, and by 1859, emotions were raw. Sectional tension was as old as the United States, but hostility escalated to unprecedented heights with the outbreak of war with Mexico in May 1846. Only three months after the war began, national expansion and the slavery issue intersected when Representative David Wilmot introduced a bill to prohibit slavery from any territory that might be acquired as a result of the war. After that, the problem of slavery in the territories bitterly divided the nation.

South Carolina senator John C. Calhoun saw the sad truth of Mexican land earlier than most. "Mexico is to us the forbidden fruit," he declared at the war's outset. "The penalty of eating it [is] to subject our institutions to political death." For a decade and a half, the slavery issue poisoned national political debate and contaminated issues that were only distantly related. Slavery proved powerful enough to transform party politics into sectional politics. Rather than Whigs and Democrats confronting one another across party lines, Northerners and Southerners eyed one another hostilely across the Mason-Dixon line. Sectional politics encouraged the South's separatist impulses. A fitful tendency before the Mexican War, southern separatism gained strength with each confrontation. As the nation lurched from crisis to crisis, southern disaffection and alienation mounted. Year by year, support for compromise and conciliation eroded. The era ended as it began—with a crisis of the Union. As Abraham Lincoln predicted in 1858, "A house divided against itself cannot stand."

eration. The revolution would roll southward over the Carolinas, Georgia, and even Alabama, sweeping slavery before it. In reality, however, Brown had neglected to inform the slaves that he had arrived in Harpers Ferry, and the few who knew wanted nothing to do with the suicidal enterprise. "It was not a slave insurrection," Abraham Lincoln observed. "It was an attempt by white men to get up a revolt among slaves, in which the slaves refused to participate. In fact, it was so absurd that the slaves, with all their ignorance, saw plainly enough it could not succeed."

Although Brown's raid ended in utter defeat, it provided white Southerners with proof of their growing suspicion that Northerners actively sought

Fruits of War

Congress had faced the question of slavery in the national territories before the Mexican War, but history provided contradictory precedents. In 1787, Congress passed the Northwest Ordinance, which banned slavery in territory north of the Ohio River. In 1803, when the United States acquired the Louisiana Territory, where slavery was already legal, Congress allowed slavery to remain. As part of the Missouri Compromise of 1820, Congress voted to prohibit slavery in part of the territory and allow it in the rest.

In 1846, when it appeared that the war with Mexico would mean new U.S. territories, politicians put on the table a variety of different plans, but when the war ended in 1848, Congress had made no headway in solving the great issue of slavery in the territories. Nor did the presidential election that year produce an answer. Instead, the territorial issue battered the Whig and Democratic Parties and raised the political temperature of the nation to the boiling point. In 1850, after four years of strife, Congress patched together a settlement, one that most Americans hoped would be permanent.

The Wilmot Proviso and the Expansion of Slavery

In the years leading up to the Civil War, Americans did not focus on slavery where it existed but on the possibility that it might expand into areas where it did not exist. Except for a few abolitionists who strove to uproot slavery wherever they found it, most Americans agreed that the Constitution had left the issue of slavery to the individual states to decide. One by one, northern states had done away with slavery, while southern states had retained it. But what about slavery in the nation's territories? The Constitution stated that "Congress shall have power to . . . make all needful rules and regulations respecting the territory . . . belonging to the United States." The debate between the North and South about slavery, then, turned toward Congress and the definition of its authority over western lands.

The spark for the national debate was provided in August 1846 by a young Democratic representative from Pennsylvania, David Wilmot, who proposed that Congress bar slavery from all lands ac-

PINE FOREST, OREGON
This 1844 engraving by William E. Tucker illustrates the gargantuan size of the Northwest's timber. Some Easterners were awed by the size of nature's bounty; others calculated the board feet in a single tree. Images such as this inspired hundreds of thousands of white men to dream of land in the West.
Library of Congress.

quired in the war with Mexico. He modeled his proposal, which became known as the Wilmot Proviso, after the Northwest Ordinance of 1787, which prohibited slavery in the Northwest Territory. Wilmot explained that the Mexicans had already abolished slavery in all of their territory. "God forbid," he declared, "that we should be the means of planting this institution upon it."

Wilmot had his finger on the pulse of northern sentiment. Regardless of party affiliation, Northerners wanted to stop the spread of slavery. The Wilmot Proviso rallied an interesting assortment of antislavery Northerners. Abolitionists, of course, supported "free soil," that is, territory from which slavery was prohibited. Many Whigs also stepped forward on the basis of principle. They often denounced slavery as a sin and emphasized Congress's authority to ban it from the territories.

But not all Northerners who opposed slavery's extension did so out of sympathy for slaves. Some Democratic politicians feared that the Whigs would pick up voters by claiming that the Mexican War was a landgrab for slaveholders. By denying slavery a place in the territory the United States took from Mexico, Democrats could support territorial expansion without offending antislavery constituents. One Northerner declared that the "adoption of the principle of the 'Wilmot proviso' is the only way to save the Democratic Party in the free states." Without coming out against slavery's expansion, Democrats "are destined to defeat and doomed . . . from Iowa to Maine."

Support for blocking slavery's expansion also came from Northerners who were not so much antislavery as they were anti-South. New slave territories would eventually mean new slave states, and they opposed any act that would magnify the power of Southerners. From experience, they knew that proslavery Southerners in Congress backed economic policies radically different from their own, especially in banking, internal improvements, and the tariff. Further support came from Northerners who were hostile to African Americans and wanted to reserve new lands for whites. Wilmot himself had blatantly encouraged racist support when he declared, "I would preserve for free white labor a fair country, a rich inheritance, where the sons of toil, of my own race and own color, can live without the disgrace which association with negro slavery brings upon free labor." Hundreds of thousands of white men dreamed of land in the West, and few wanted to work shoulder to shoulder with blacks, whether slave or free. It is no wonder that some called the Wilmot Proviso the White Man's Proviso.

While the specter of new slave territory alarmed most Northerners, the thought that slavery might be excluded outraged almost all white Southerners. From the colonial era, yeoman and planter alike regarded the West as a ladder for economic and social opportunity. Although they knew that the arid West was not ideal plantation country, southern whites still agreed that the exclusion of slavery was a slap in the face. An Alabama observed that at least half of the American soldiers in Mexico were Southerners. "When the war-worn soldier returns home," he asked, "is he to be told that he cannot carry his property to the country won by his blood?" But beyond economic opportunity, social mobility, and honor, southern leaders approached the territorial issue with an eye on political clout. They understood the need for political parity with the North to protect the South's interests, especially slavery. The need never seemed more urgent than in the 1840s, when the North's population and wealth were booming. James Henry Hammond of South Carolina predicted that ten new states would be carved from the acquired Mexican land. If free soil won, the North would "ride over us rough shod" in Congress, he claimed. "Our only safety is in *equality* of POWER."

In the nation's capital, the two sides squared off. Because Northerners had a majority in the House, they easily passed the Wilmot Proviso over the united opposition of Southerners. In the Senate, John C. Calhoun denied that Congress had constitutional authority to exclude slavery from the nation's territories. He argued that the territories were the "joint and common property" of all the states, that Congress could not justly deprive any state of equal rights in the territories, and that Congress therefore could not bar citizens of one state from migrating with their property (including slaves) to the territories. Where Wilmot demanded that Congress slam shut the door to slavery, Calhoun called on Congress to hold the door wide open. Because slave states in the Senate outnumbered free states fifteen to fourteen, southern senators stopped the proviso.

Between these extremes there appeared to be little middle ground. One plan proposed by President James K. Polk and others—to extend the Missouri Compromise line to the Pacific—generated no significant enthusiasm. But Senator Lewis Cass of Michigan offered a compromise that he hoped would find support among moderates everywhere.

He proposed the doctrine of "popular sovereignty": letting the people who actually settled the territories decide for themselves slavery's fate. This solution, Cass argued, sat squarely in the American tradition of democracy and local self-government. It had the added attraction of removing the incendiary issue of the expansion of slavery from the nation's capital and lodging it in distant, sleepy territorial legislatures, where it would excite fewer passions.

While the specter of new slave territory alarmed most Northerners, the thought that slavery might be excluded outraged almost all white Southerners.

But the most attractive feature of this plan was its ambiguity about the precise moment when settlers could determine slavery's fate. That imprecision made possible different predictions about the plan's consequences. Northern advocates of popular sovereignty told their constituents that the decision on slavery could be made as soon as the first territorial legislature assembled. With free-soil majorities likely, they would shut the door to slavery almost before the first slave arrived. Southern supporters declared that popular sovereignty guaranteed that slavery would be unrestricted throughout the entire settlement period. Only at the very end, when settlers in the territory drew up a constitution and applied for statehood, could they decide the issue of slavery or freedom. By then, slavery would have sunk deep roots. As long as the matter of timing remained vague, popular sovereignty provided some Northerners and some Southerners with common ground.

When Congress ended its session in 1848, no plan had won a majority in both houses. Northerners who demanded no new slave territory anywhere, ever, and Southerners who demanded free entry for their slave property into all territories, or else, staked out their extreme positions. Unresolved in Congress, the territorial question naturally intruded into the presidential election of 1848.

The Election of 1848

The Democratic and Whig Parties were both hurting in 1848. The territorial debate revealed free-soil factions in both parties. Antislavery northern Democrats challenged Democratic President Polk and the dominant southern element of their party. Northern Whigs split between an antislavery faction, Conscience Whigs, and a more conservative group called Cotton Whigs (because many of them were textile mill owners), who sought compromise to hold the party together. Conscience Whigs denounced the evil alliance of northern "lords of the loom" and southern "lords of the lash" and threatened to bolt the party.

Polk—worn out, ailing, and unable to unite the Democratic Party—chose not to seek reelection. The Democratic convention nominated Lewis Cass of Michigan, the man most closely associated with popular sovereignty, but the party platform avoided a firm position on slavery in the territories. The Whigs followed a different strategy in their effort to patch the fissure within the party over slavery. They passed over "Mr. Whig"—Henry Clay, the seventy-one-year-old founder of the party and chief spokesman for its American System—and nominated the hero of Buena Vista, "Old Rough and Ready," General Zachary Taylor. They declined to adopt any party platform, no matter how vague. The Whigs bet that selection of a military hero combined with total silence on the central issue facing the country would carry the day. Taylor, who owned more than one hundred slaves on plantations in Mississippi and Louisiana, was hailed by Georgia politician Robert Toombs as a "Southern man, a slaveholder, a cotton planter." Conscience Whigs balked and looked for an alternative.

As old party allegiances unraveled, the time seemed ripe for a major political realignment. Senator Charles Sumner called for "one grand Northern party of Freedom," and in the summer of 1848 antislavery Democrats and antislavery Whigs founded the Free-Soil Party. Nearly fifteen thousand noisy Free-Soilers gathered in Buffalo, New York, where they welded the factions together by nominating a dissident Democrat, Martin Van Buren, for president and a Conscience Whig, Charles Francis Adams, for vice president. The platform boldly proclaimed, "Free soil, free speech, free labor, and free men."

The November election dashed the hopes of the Free-Soilers. Although they succeeded in making slavery the campaign's central issue, they did not carry a single state. The major parties went through contortions to present their candidates favorably in both the North and the South, and their evasions

GENERAL TAYLOR CIGAR CASE
This papier-mâché cigar case portrays General Zachary Taylor, Whig presidential candidate in 1848, in a colorful scene from the Mexican War. Shown as a dashing, elegant officer, Taylor was in fact a short, thickset, and roughly dressed Indian fighter who had spent his career commanding small frontier garrisons. The inscription reminds voters that Taylor was a victor in the first four battles fought in the war and directs attention away from the fact that in politics he was a rank amateur.
Collection of Janice L. and David J. Frent.

tions and apply immediately for admission to the Union as states. Predominantly antislavery, the settlers began writing free-state constitutions. "For the first time," Jefferson Davis lamented, "we are about permanently to destroy the balance of power between the sections."

When Congress convened in December 1849, anxious citizens packed the galleries, eager for the "Great Debate." They witnessed what proved to be one of the longest, most contentious, and most significant sessions in the history of Congress. For seven months, politicians orated, debated, buttonholed, cajoled, and threatened in efforts to fashion a solution to the problems that divided the nation.

Foremost was the territorial issue. In January 1850, President Taylor urged Congress to admit California as a free state immediately and to admit New Mexico, which lagged behind by a few months, as soon as it applied. Southerners exploded. In their eyes, Taylor had betrayed his region. Southerners who would "consent to be thus degraded and enslaved," a North Carolinian declared, "ought to be whipped through their fields by their own negroes." Calhoun almost lost heart. "As things now stand," he said in February, the South "cannot with safety remain in the Union."

succeeded. Taylor won the all-important electoral vote, 163 to 127, carrying eight of the fifteen slave states and seven of the fifteen free states (Map 13.1). (Wisconsin had entered the Union earlier in 1848 as the fifteenth free state.) Northern voters proved they were not yet ready for Sumner's "one grand Northern party of Freedom," but the struggle over slavery in the territories had shaken the major parties badly.

Debate and Compromise

Zachary Taylor was very much a mystery when he entered the White House in March 1849. He surprised almost everyone—and he infuriated Southerners. Who among them had imagined that the slaveholding father-in-law of Mississippi senator Jefferson Davis would champion a free-soil solution to the problem of western land? But he did. The discovery of gold in California and the rush of 1849 made the existing military rule of California and New Mexico pitifully inadequate and the need for competent civil government urgent. Taylor sent agents west to persuade settlers to frame constitu-

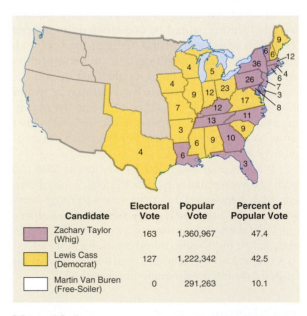

Candidate	Electoral Vote	Popular Vote	Percent of Popular Vote
Zachary Taylor (Whig)	163	1,360,967	47.4
Lewis Cass (Democrat)	127	1,222,342	42.5
Martin Van Buren (Free-Soiler)	0	291,263	10.1

M A P 1 3 . 1

The Election of 1848

When Congress convened in December 1849, anxious citizens packed the galleries, eager for the "Great Debate." They witnessed what proved to be one of the longest, most contentious, and most significant sessions in the history of Congress.

Into this rancorous scene stepped Henry Clay, recently returned to the Senate by his home state of Kentucky. His reputation preceded him: the "Great Pacificator," master of accommodation, architect of Union-saving compromises in the Missouri and nullification crises. Now seventy-two, Clay remained a powerful public speaker, and he had no doubt that the South's desperate mood threatened the nation.

"Mr. President," Clay declared when he took the floor on January 29, 1850, "I hold in my hand a series of resolutions which I desire to submit to the consideration of this body. Taken together, in combination, they propose an amicable arrangement of all questions in controversy between the free and slave states, growing out of the subject of slavery." His comprehensive plan sought to balance the interests of the slave and free states. Admit California as a free state, he proposed, but organize the rest of the Southwest without restrictions on slavery. Require Texas to abandon its claim to parts of New Mexico, but compensate it by assuming its preannexation debt. Abolish the slave trade in Washington, D.C., but confirm slavery itself in the nation's capital. Reassert Congress's lack of authority to interfere with the interstate slave trade. And enact a more effective fugitive slave law.

Abolitionists and "fire-eaters" (as radical southern secessionists were called) stumbled over one another in their rush to condemn Clay's plan. Senator Salmon Chase of Ohio ridiculed it as "sentiment for the North, substance for the South." Senator Henry S. Foote of Mississippi denounced it as more offensive to the South than the speeches of abolitionists William Lloyd Garrison, Wendell Phillips, and Frederick Douglass combined. The most ominous response came from the mighty Calhoun. Too weakened by consumption to deliver his own speech, he slumped in his Senate chair, wrapped his black cloak around him, and listened as a colleague read his gloomy words concluding that the time for com-

JOHN C. CALHOUN
Hollow-cheeked and dark-eyed in this 1850 daguerreotype by Mathew Brady, Calhoun had only months to live. Still, his passion and indomitable will come through. British writer Harriet Martineau once described the champion of southern rights as "the cast-iron man who looks as if he had never been born and could never be extinguished."
National Portrait Gallery, Smithsonian Institution/Art Resource, N.Y.

promise had passed. Unending northern agitation on the slavery question, Calhoun said, had "snapped" many of the "cords which bind these states together in one common Union . . . and has greatly weakened all the others." The fragile political equilibrium between North and South depended on continued equal representation in the Senate, which Clay's plan for a free California destroyed. Without equality, Calhoun declared, Southerners were defenseless and could not remain in the Union.

After Clay and Calhoun had spoken, it was time for the third member of the "great triumvirate," Daniel Webster of Massachusetts. Like Clay, Webster sought to balance the grievances of the North and South and build a constituency for compromise among moderates. Admitting that the South had complaints that required attention, he argued forcefully that secession from the Union would mean civil war. He appealed for an end to reckless proposals and, to the dismay of many Northerners, mentioned by name the Wilmot Proviso. A legal ban on slavery in the territories was unnecessary, he said, because nature prohibited the expansion of cotton and slaves into the Southwest. He added that there was no need to "taunt" or "reproach" Southerners with the proviso. "I would not take pains to reaffirm an ordinance of nature nor to reenact the will of God," Webster said.

Free-soil forces recoiled from what they saw as Webster's desertion. Theodore Parker, a Boston clergyman and abolitionist, could only conclude that "the Southern men" must have offered Webster the presidency. Senator William H. Seward of New York responded that Webster's and Clay's compromise with slavery was "radically wrong and essentially vicious." He flatly rejected Calhoun's argument that Congress lacked constitutional authority to exclude slavery from the territories. In any case, Seward said, in the most sensational moment in his address, there was a "higher law than the Constitution"— the law of God—to ensure freedom in all the public domain. Claiming that God was a Free-Soiler did nothing to cool the superheated atmosphere of Washington.

In May, a Senate committee (with the tireless Clay at its head) reported a bill that joined Clay's resolutions into a single comprehensive package, known as the Omnibus Bill because it was a vehicle on which "every sort of passenger" could ride. Clay bet that a majority of Congress wanted compromise and that while the omnibus contained items individuals disliked, each would vote for the package to gain an overall settlement of sectional issues. But the omnibus strategy backfired. Free-Soilers, Conscience Whigs, and proslavery Southerners would support separate parts of Clay's bill, but they would not endorse the whole. After making seventy speeches to defend his plan, Clay saw it go down to defeat.

Fortunately for those who favored a settlement, Senator Stephen A. Douglas, a rising Democratic star from Illinois, stepped into Clay's shoes. Rejecting the omnibus strategy, he broke the bill into its various parts and skillfully ushered each through Congress by fashioning a different coalition for its support. The agreement Douglas won in September 1850 was very much the one Clay had proposed in January. California entered the Union as a free state. New Mexico and Utah became territories in which the question of slavery would be decided by popular sovereignty. Texas accepted its present-day boundary with New Mexico and received $10 million from the federal government. Congress ended the slave trade in the District of Columbia yet enacted a more stringent fugitive slave law. In September, Millard Fillmore, who had become president upon the death of Zachary Taylor in July, signed each bill, collectively known as the Compromise of 1850, into law (Map 13.2; see also "The Promise of Technology," page 458).

Actually, the Compromise of 1850 was not a true compromise at all. Douglas's parliamentary skill, not a spirit of conciliation, led to legislative success. Only by nimbly allying a small group of true compromisers with larger blocs of Northerners and Southerners who voted along sectional lines did Douglas gain a majority for each separate measure. Nor was the Compromise the "final settlement," as President Fillmore announced. The settlement resolved certain pesky conflicts, and it preserved the Union and peace for the moment— no small feat given the severity of the threats—but it scarcely touched the deeper conflict over slavery. Free-Soiler Salmon Chase was correct when he told Congress, "The question of slavery in the territories has been avoided. It has not been settled."

The Sectional Balance Undone

The words "final settlement" echoed through the halls of Congress like a magical phrase, but in reality the Compromise of 1850 began to come apart almost immediately. The thread that unraveled the Compromise was not slavery in the Southwest, the crux of the disagreement, but runaway slaves in New England, a part of the settlement that had received relatively little attention. Rather than restore calm, the Compromise brought the horrors of slavery into the North.

Millions of Northerners who never saw a runaway slave nevertheless confronted slavery in the early 1850s. Harriet Beecher Stowe's *Uncle Tom's Cabin*, a novel that vividly depicted the brutality

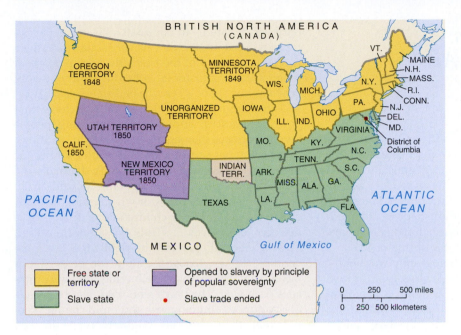

BRITISH NORTH AMERICA
(CANADA)

MAP 13.2

The Compromise of 1850
The patched-together sectional agreement was both clumsy and unstable. Few Americans—in either the North or the South— supported all five parts of the Compromise.

Free state or territory	Opened to slavery by principle of popular sovereignty
Slave state	Slave trade ended

0   250   500 miles

0   250 500 kilometers

and heartlessness of the South's "peculiar institution," aroused passions so deep that many found goodwill toward white Southerners nearly impossible. But no popular uprising forced Congress to reopen the slavery controversy: Politicians did it themselves. Four years after Congress delicately stitched the sectional compromise together, it ripped the threads out. It once again posed the question of slavery in the territories, the deadliest of all sectional issues.

The Fugitive Slave Act

The Fugitive Slave Act proved the most explosive of the Compromise measures. The issue of runaways was as old as the Constitution, which contained a provision for the return of any "person held to service or labor in one state" who escaped to another. In 1793, a federal law gave muscle to the provision by authorizing slave owners to enter other states to recapture their slave property. Proclaiming the 1793 law a license to kidnap free blacks, northern states in the 1830s began passing "personal liberty laws" that provided fugitives with some protection. Some northern communities also formed vigilance committees to help runaways and to obstruct white Southerners who came north to reclaim them. Each year, a few hundred slaves escaped into free states and found friendly northern "conductors" who put them aboard the "underground railroad," which

was not a railroad at all but a series of secret "stations" (hideouts) on the way to Canada.

Furious about northern interference, Southerners in 1850 insisted that any comprehensive settlement of sectional differences include an effective fugitive slave law. They got what they wanted in the stricter law passed as part of the Compromise. To seize an alleged slave, a slaveholder or his agent simply had to appear before a commissioner appointed by the court and swear that the runaway was his. The commissioner earned ten dollars for every black returned to slavery but only five dollars for those set free. Most galling to Northerners, the law stipulated that all citizens were expected to assist officials in apprehending runaways. Even individuals who had little sympathy for blacks resented being forced into the role of slave catcher. Others actively resisted the law. Theodore Parker, the clergyman and abolitionist, denounced the law as "a hateful statute of kidnappers" and headed a Boston vigilance committee that openly violated it. In February 1851, an angry crowd in Boston overpowered federal marshals and snatched a runaway named Shadrach from a courtroom, put him on the underground railroad, and whisked him off to Montreal, Canada.

Southerners viewed the Fugitive Slave Act as the one true concession they received in the Compromise. Now it seemed that fanatics of the "higher law" creed had whipped Northerners into a frenzy

Daguerreotypes: The "Sunbeam Art"

EARLY IN THE NINETEENTH CENTURY, several Europeans working separately discovered that the shadow of an object falling on a chemically treated surface remained after the light source was removed. In the late 1830s, Frenchman Louis Daguerre learned how to keep the "shadow" from fading. News of Daguerre's success in fixing an image arrived in New York City in the spring of 1839.

As Americans found, photography was not for amateurs. The daguerreotype photographic process was cumbersome and messy. Initially, a photographer's equipment included a large wooden box, glass lens, copper plates coated with silver, vials of chemicals, and fire for heat. Because picture taking required several minutes of exposure, candid shots were impossible. To ease the strain of sitting immobile for so long while facing the camera, an American photographer invented a vise to clamp the sitter's head from behind. The process tested patience and often led to photographs that captured grimaces and pained scowls.

Despite their considerable shortcomings, daguerreotypes were an instant success. Samuel Morris, the first American to see a daguerreotype, exclaimed, "The exquisite minuteness of the delineation cannot be conceived. No painting or engraving ever approached it." Another awed observer declared that the daguerreotype was a "perfect transcript of the thing itself." The hyperrealism of the images spooked country people, some of whom suspected magic. But by the early 1840s, photography was a booming business. Itinerant photographers rode the rural and small-town circuit, while in the cities photographic galleries sprang up. In 1850, one observer declared, "In our great cities a Daguerreotypist is to be found in almost every square; and there is scarce a county in the states that has not one or more of those industrious individuals busy at work catching 'the shadow' ere the 'substance fade.' "

Ordinary citizens could not afford to have their portraits painted, and thus few working people owned personal likenesses. Compared to paintings, daguerreotypes were cheap, and at midcentury one reporter claimed that "it is hard to find a man who has not gone through the operator's hands from once to half-a-dozen times, or who has not the shadowy faces of his wife & children done up in purple morocco and velvet. . . . Truly the sunbeam art is a most wonderful one, and the public feel it a great benefit." In the 1850s, the rage for photographs meant that Americans were buying millions of images each year. The new technology met the needs of a culture undergoing vast and rapid change. People kept their precious daguerreotypes in safe places, thankful that this "camera magic" preserved families so often parted by distance or death.

No early American photographer was more important than Mathew Brady. In 1844, he opened the Daguerrean Miniature Gallery at Broadway and Fulton Street in New York City. He sought to bend photography from merely personal to political ends. Brady declared that "from the first, I regarded myself as under obligation to my country to preserve the faces of its historic men and mothers." Seeing himself as a kind of historian of the nation, he shot portraits of distinguished citizens—presidents, congressmen, senators, and statesmen—as well as everyday people who walked into his gallery. Likenesses of illustrious Americans reflected Brady's devotion to the country, and he hoped that they would inspire patriotism in others. His elegant establishment was renowned as a meeting place where people of all classes mingled freely. "People used to stroll in there in those days," a writer remembered, "to see what new celebrity had been added to the

of massive resistance. Actually, the overwhelming majority of fugitives claimed before federal commissioners were reenslaved and shipped south peacefully. Many communities lost longtime African American residents. Spectacular rescues such as the one that saved Shadrach were rare. But brutal enforcement of the unpopular law had a radicalizing effect in the North, particularly in New England. Textile owner Amos A. Lawrence, a Cotton Whig eager for good relations with the South, said that "we went to bed one night old fashioned, conservative, Compromise Union Whigs & waked up little collection, and the last new portrait at Brady's was a standing topic of conversation."

In 1850, Brady sought to extend the public-spirited message of his photographs beyond his shop. He published *The Gallery of Illustrious Americans*— twelve portraits of famous statesmen, including John C. Calhoun, Daniel Webster, and Henry Clay. Anxiety framed the project. At that moment, Washington was embroiled in bitter sectional controversy, and the United States stood on the brink of disintegration. Accurate, realistic images of eminent public men, Brady figured, would capture the "genius" of the nation and rally citizens to their beleaguered Republic. *The Gallery* was a nonpartisan, nonsectional gesture that sought to embrace Whigs and Democrats, Northerners and Southerners, and

to urge them to overcome the disuniting elements in American life. The magic of daguerreotypes, Brady thought, would help bind citizens more directly, more personally to living statesmen and to the country they symbolized.

Technology, even technology married to art, could not save the nation. But such was the promise of early photography that some believed it might. Like Webster and Clay, *The Gallery* pleaded for compromise and national unity. In Brady's view, the new technology of photography would serve as a moral agent furthering political reconciliation and peace. By 1860, however, daguerreotypes had all but disappeared from American life, replaced by more efficient photographic processes, and the Union remained imperiled.

stark mad Abolitionists." He exaggerated, but it did seem to Southerners that Northerners had betrayed the Compromise. And as a Tennessee man warned in November 1850, "If the fugitive slave bill is not enforced in the north, the moderate men of the South . . . will be overwhelmed by the 'fire-eaters.'"

Uncle Tom's Cabin

The spectacle of shackled African Americans being herded south seared the conscience of every Northerner who witnessed such a scene. But even more Northerners were turned against slavery by a

THE MODERN MEDEA

In 1987 writer Toni Morrison published her award-winning **Beloved.** *The novel had historical origins. In 1855, a slave family—Robert Garner, his twenty-two-year-old wife Margaret, their four children, and his parents—fled Kentucky. Archibald Gaines, Margaret's owner, tracked them to a cabin in Ohio. Thinking that all was lost and that her children would be returned to slavery, Margaret seized a butcher knife and cut the throat of her two-year-old daughter. She was turning on her other children when slave catchers burst in and captured her. Garner's child-murder electrified the nation. Abolitionists claimed that the act revealed the horror of slavery and the tragic heroism of slave mothers. Defenders of slavery argued that the deed proved that slaves were savages. In 1867, Thomas Satterwhite Noble painted a defiant Margaret Garner standing over the bodies of two boys, a departure from history that the myth demanded. Noble's troubling title comes from a drama by Euripides, in which Medea kills her two children to spite her husband.*

Harper's Weekly, May 18, 1867.

fictional account, a novel. Harriet Beecher Stowe, a Northerner who had never seen a plantation, made the South's slaves into flesh-and-blood human beings almost more real than life.

The daughter of evangelist Lyman Beecher and a member of a famous clan of preachers, teachers, and reformers, Stowe despised the slave catchers and wrote to expose the sin of slavery. Beginning in June 1851 as a serial in an antislavery weekly, *Uncle*

Tom's Cabin, or Life among the Lowly made the author famous before the final installment was printed ten months later. Published as a book in March 1852, it sold 300,000 copies within a year and had become America's first literary blockbuster. By the end of the decade, more than three million copies had been sold at home and overseas.

Stowe's characters leaped from the page. Here was the gentle slave Uncle Tom, a Christian saint who forgave those who beat him to death; the courageous slave Eliza, who fled with her child across the frozen Ohio River; and the fiendish overseer Simon Legree, whose Louisiana plantation was a nightmare of torture and death. Herself the mother of seven children, Stowe aimed her most powerful blows at slavery's destructive impact on the family. Her character Eliza succeeds in keeping her son from being sold away, but other mothers are not so fortunate. When told that her infant has been sold, Lucy drowns herself. Driven half mad by the sale of a son and daughter, Cassy decides "never again [to] let a child live to grow up!" She gives her third child an opiate and watches as "he slept to death."

Responses to *Uncle Tom's Cabin* depended on geography. In the North, common people and literary giants alike shed tears and sang its praises. The poet John Greenleaf Whittier sent "ten thousand thanks for thy immortal book," and poet Henry Wadsworth Longfellow judged it "one of the greatest triumphs recorded in literary history." What Northerners accepted as truth, Southerners denounced as slander. Virginian George F. Holmes proclaimed Stowe a member of the "Woman's Rights" and "Higher Law" schools and dismissed the novel as a work of "intense fanaticism." Unfortunately, he said, this "maze of misinterpretation" had filled those who knew nothing about slavery "with hatred for that institution and those who uphold it." Holmes found only one character convincing: Simon Legree, whom Stowe had made a transplanted Yankee.

As Legree's northern origins suggest, the novel did not indict just the South. Stowe rebuked

THEATER POSTER
During the 1850s, at least ten individuals, including Harriet Beecher Stowe herself, dramatized the novel **Uncle Tom's Cabin.** *These plays, known as "Tom Shows," drew crowds in America and Britain. Stowe's moral indictment of slavery translated well to the stage. Scenes of Eliza crossing the ice with bloodhounds in pursuit, the cruelty of Legree, and Little Eva borne to heaven on puffy clouds gripped the imagination of audiences and fueled the growing antislavery crusade.*
Smithsonian Institution.

the entire nation for tolerating slavery. Although it is impossible to measure precisely the impact of a novel on public opinion, *Uncle Tom's Cabin* clearly helped to crystallize northern sentiment against slavery and to confirm white Southerners' suspicion that they no longer had any sympathy in the free states.

Responses to Uncle Tom's Cabin *depended on geography. . . . What Northerners accepted as truth, Southerners denounced as slander.*

Other writers—ex-slaves who knew life in slave cabins firsthand—also produced stinging indictments of slavery. Solomon Northup's compelling *Twelve Years a Slave* (1853) sold twenty-seven thousand copies in two years, and the powerful *Narrative of the Life of Frederick Douglass, as Told by Himself* (1845) eventually sold more than thirty thousand copies. But no work touched the North's conscience like the novel by the woman who had never set foot on a plantation. A decade after its publication, when Stowe visited Abraham Lincoln at the White House, he reportedly said, "So you are the little woman who wrote the book that made this great war."

The Election of 1852

As national elections approached in 1852, Democrats and Whigs sought to close the sectional rifts that had opened within their parties. For their presidential nominee, the Democrats turned to Franklin Pierce of New Hampshire. Pierce was an amiable veteran of the Mexican War and a former senator, but his most valuable asset was his well-known sympathy with southern views on public issues. His leanings caused northern critics to include him among the "doughfaces," northern men malleable enough to champion southern causes. The Whigs were less successful in compromising differences. They agreed to reject the incumbent, Millard Fillmore, but disagreed for fifty-two ballots on someone else. Finally, adopting the formula that had proved successful in 1848, they chose another Mexican War hero, General Winfield Scott of Virginia.

Hopelessly divided between Conscience and Cotton factions, the Whigs suffered a humiliating defeat in 1852. The Democrat Pierce carried twenty-seven states to Scott's four, 254 electoral votes to 42 (Table 13.1). In the afterglow of the Compromise, the Free-Soil Party lost almost half of the voters who had turned to it in the tumultuous atmosphere of 1848.

Eager to leave the sectional controversy behind, the new president turned swiftly to foreign expansion. Manifest Destiny remained robust. Pierce's major objective was Cuba, which was owned by Spain and in which slavery flourished. Earlier efforts by President Polk to purchase the island had failed. Private efforts by southern slaveholders to take Cuba by force met disaster. In 1851, Southerners bankrolled a Latin American adventurer, Narciso López, who invaded the island with five hundred American volunteers, several hundred of whom died in the aborted effort. Pierce's own clumsy diplomatic efforts to acquire Cuba galvanized antislavery Northerners, who denounced the

TABLE 13.1
THE ELECTION OF 1852

Candidate	Electoral Vote	Popular Vote	Percent of Popular Vote
Franklin Pierce (Democrat)	254	1,601,000	50.9
Winfield Scott (Whig)	42	1,385,000	44.1
John P. Hale (Free-Soil)	0	156,000	5.0

administration for promoting expansion on behalf of slavery and blocked Cuba's acquisition.

Although Pierce's foray in Cuba ended badly, his fortunes improved in Mexico. In 1853, he sent diplomat James Gadsden, a former army officer and railroad company president, to negotiate a $15 million purchase of some 30,000 square miles of territory south of the Gila River in present-day Arizona and New Mexico. The Gadsden Purchase stemmed from the dream of a transcontinental railroad to California. The burgeoning population of the Pacific coast made it obvious that the vast, loose-jointed republic needed a railroad to bind it together. Talk of a railroad ignited rivalries in cities from New Orleans to Chicago as they maneuvered to become the eastern terminus. Thus, the railroad became a sectional contest, which by the 1850s inevitably involved slavery.

Gadsden Purchase of 1853

The Kansas-Nebraska Act

No one played the railroad game more enthusiastically than Senator Stephen A. Douglas. The "Little Giant," as the public called him, was a "steam engine in britches," an energetic spokesman for western economic development. He badly wanted the transcontinental railroad for Chicago and his home state, Illinois. His chairmanship of the Senate Committee on Territories provided him with an opportunity. Any railroad that ran west from Chicago would pass through a region that Congress in 1830 had designated a "permanent" Indian reserve. Douglas proposed giving this vast area between the Missouri River and the Rocky Mountains an Indian name, Nebraska, and then nullifying Indian titles and throwing the Indians out. Once the region achieved territorial status, whites could survey and sell the land, establish civil government, and build a railroad.

Congress's promise to the Indians did not cause Douglas to hesitate, but another of its promises did. Nebraska lay within the Louisiana Purchase north of 36°30′, which, according to the Missouri Compromise of 1820, closed it to slavery. Since Douglas could not count on New England to back western economic development, he needed southern votes to pass his Nebraska legislation. But Southerners had no incentive to create another free territory or to help a northern city win the Pacific railroad. Douglas learned, however, that Southerners might agree to organize Nebraska—for a price: nothing less than the repeal of the Missouri Compromise. Southerners insisted that Congress organize Nebraska according to popular sovereignty, the formula it had used in 1850 in New Mexico and Utah. It meant giving slavery a chance in the Nebraska Territory and reopening the dangerous issue of slavery expansion that Douglas himself had so ably helped to resolve only four years earlier. A politician with presidential ambitions, a champion of his state's economic interests, a defender of western development, and a believer in popular sovereignty, Douglas persuaded himself that Nebraska was worth the price.

Congress's promise to the Indians did not cause Douglas to hesitate, but another of its promises did. Nebraska lay within the Louisiana Purchase north of 36°30′, which, according to the Missouri Compromise of 1820, closed it to slavery.

In January 1854, Douglas introduced his bill to organize the Nebraska Territory, leaving to the settlers themselves the decision about slavery. At southern insistence, and even though he knew it would "raise a hell of a storm," Douglas added an explicit repeal of the Missouri Compromise. Indeed, the Nebraska bill raised a storm of controversy. Free-Soilers wanted no part of a proposal that offered slavery a chance to expand. They branded Douglas's plan "a gross violation of a sacred pledge" and an "atrocious plot" to transform free land into a "dreary region of despotism, inhabited by masters and slaves."

As Douglas said later, he could have traveled from Washington back to Chicago by the light of his own burning effigies. But, coolest under fire, he skillfully shepherded the bill through Congress in May 1854. Nine-tenths of all southern members (Whigs and Democrats) and half of the northern

PAPAGO INDIANS
Major William Emory's Mexican boundary survey of the early 1850s provided Americans with glimpses of a little-known southwestern frontier. In this drawing, Papago Indian women in Arizona Territory use sticks to knock down cactus fruit.
The Center for American History, the University of Texas at Austin.

Realignment of the Party System

The Kansas-Nebraska Act marked a fateful escalation of the sectional conflict. Douglas's controversial measure had several consequences, none more crucial than the realignment of the nation's political parties. Since the rise of the Whigs in the early 1830s, Whigs and Democrats had organized and channeled political conflict in the nation. This party system dampened sectionalism and strengthened the Union. To achieve national political power, Whigs and Democrats had to retain strength in both the North and the South. Strong northern and southern wings required that each party compromise and find positions acceptable to both wings.

The Kansas-Nebraska controversy shattered this conservative political system. In place of two national parties with bisectional strength, the mid-1850s witnessed the development of one party heavily dominated by one section and another party entirely limited to the other section. Rather than "national" parties, the country had what one critic disdainfully called "geographic" parties. Parties now had the advantage of sharpening ideological and policy differences between the sections and no longer muffling moral issues, like slavery. But the new party system also thwarted political compromise and promoted political polarization instead. The breakup of the old party system of the 1830s and 1840s snapped one of what John C. Calhoun called the "cords of Union."

The Old Parties: Whigs and Democrats

Distress signals could be heard from the Whig camp as early as the Mexican War, when members clashed over the future of slavery in annexed Mexican lands. But the disintegration of the party dated from 1849–1850, when southern Whigs watched in stunned amazement as Whig president Zachary Taylor sponsored a plan for a free California. And above the Mason-Dixon line, the strains of the slavery issue split northern Whigs. The Conscience Whigs, who responded to slavery as a moral blight, gained a majority by 1852. The party could please the southern wing or the northern wing but not both. The Whigs' miserable showing in the election of 1852 made clear that they were no longer a strong national party. By

Democrats cast votes in favor. Like Douglas, these northern Democrats believed that popular sovereignty would make Kansas and Nebraska "free territories and free states, whether Congress shall prohibit slavery or not." Ominously, however, half of the northern Democrats broke with their party and opposed the bill. In its final form, the Kansas-Nebraska Act divided the huge territory in two: Nebraska west of the free state of Iowa and Kansas west of the slave state of Missouri (Map 13.3).

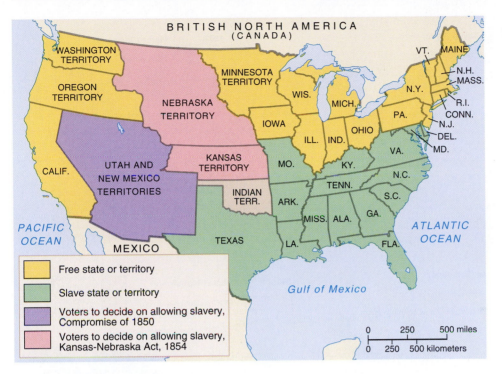

MAP 13.3

The Kansas-Nebraska Act, 1854
Americans hardly thought twice about dispossessing the Indians of lands guaranteed them by treaty, but many worried about the outcome of repealing the Missouri Compromise and opening up lands to slavery.

READING THE MAP: How many slave states and how many free states does the map show? Estimate the percentage of territory likely to be settled by slaveholders.
CONNECTIONS: Who would be more likely to support changes in government legislation to discontinue the Missouri Compromise, slaveholders or free-soil advocates? Why?

www.bedfordstmartins.com/tap   SEE THE ONLINE STUDY GUIDE for more help in analyzing this map.

1856, after more than two decades of contesting the Democrats, they were hardly a party at all (Map 13.4).

The decline and eventual collapse of the Whig Party left the Democrats as the country's only national party. Although the Democrats were not immune to the disruptive pressures of the territorial question, they discovered in popular sovereignty a doctrine that many Democrats could support. But popular sovereignty very nearly undid the party as well. When Stephen Douglas applied the doctrine to that part of the Louisiana Purchase where slavery had been barred, he divided northern Democrats and destroyed the dominance of the Democratic Party in the free states. Most of the northern Democrats in the

House who had cast ballots in support of Douglas's Kansas-Nebraska bill failed to be reelected the following year. As a result, northern Democratic representation in the House fell sharply, and after 1854 the Democrats became a southern-dominated party.

Nevertheless, Democrats remained the dominant party throughout the 1850s. Gains in the South more than balanced losses in the North. During the decade, Democrats elected two presidents and won majorities in Congress in almost every election. But national power required that the party maintain a northern and a southern wing, which in turn required that they avoid the issue of the expansion of slavery.

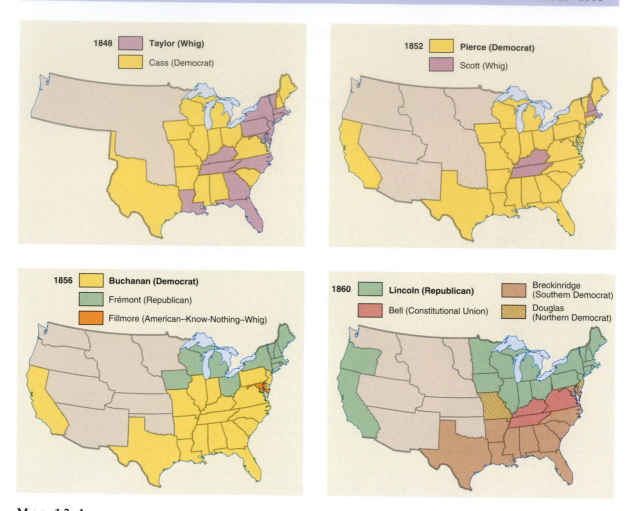

MAP 13.4

Political Realignment, 1848–1860

In 1848, slavery and sectionalism began hammering the country's party system. The Whig Party was an early casualty. By 1860, national parties—those that contended for votes in both the North and the South—had been replaced by regional parties.

The breakup of the Whigs and the disaffection of significant numbers of northern Democrats set many Americans politically adrift. As they searched for new political harbors, Americans found that the death of the old party system created a multitude of fresh political alternatives. The question was which party would attract the drifters.

The New Parties: Know-Nothings and Republicans

Among the new organizations that vied to replace the Whigs were splinter groups with such odd names as Anti-Nebraskaites, Fusionists, Rum Democrats, Hard Shell Democrats, Soft Shells, and Half Shells. Out of this confusion, two organizations emerged as true contenders. One grew out of the slavery controversy, a spontaneous coalition of indignant antislavery Northerners. The other arose from an entirely different split in American society, that between Roman Catholic immigrants and native Protestants.

The tidal wave of immigrants that broke over America in the decade from 1845 to 1855 produced a nasty backlash among Protestant Americans, who believed they were about to drown in a sea of

WHIG PARTY MEMBERS
On February 18, 1853, George Howe made this daguerreotype of the Log Cabin and Hard Cider Club of Portland, Maine. This Whig organization took its name and its emblem from William Henry Harrison's 1840 presidential campaign, a rousing effort to depict the tony Virginian as a man of the people. Well-heeled and respectable, these shop-keepers, bankers, and farm-ers made up the spine of the Whig Party. Soon, these solid citizens would be looking for a new party. Collections of the Maine Historical Society.

Roman Catholics from Ireland and Germany (see Figure 11.2). The new arrivals encountered economic prejudice, ethnic hostility, and religious antagonism. Because some of them displayed a taste for whiskey and beer, they also drew the wrath of the temperance movement. When the immigrants entered American politics, they largely became Democrats because they perceived that party as more tolerant of newcomers than were the Whigs. But even so, they met sharp political opposition. In the early 1850s, nativists (individuals who were anti-immigrant) began to organize, first into secret fraternal societies such as the Order of the Star-Spangled Banner, and then into a political party. Recruits swore never to vote for either foreign-born or Roman Catholic candidates and not to reveal any information about the organization. When questioned, they said: "I know nothing." Officially, they were the American Party, but most Americans called them Know-Nothings.

The Know-Nothings exploded onto the political stage in 1854 and 1855 with a series of dazzling successes. They captured state legislatures in the Northeast, West, and South and claimed dozens of seats in Congress. Their greatest triumph came in Massachusetts, a favorite destination for the Irish. Know-Nothings elected the Massachusetts governor, all of the state senators, all but two of the state representatives, and all of the congressmen. The American Party attracted both Democrats and Whigs, but with their party crumbling, more Whigs responded to the attraction. In 1855, an observer might reasonably have concluded that the Know-Nothings had emerged as the successor to the Whigs.

Know-Nothings were not the only new party making noise. Among the new antislavery organizations provoked by the Kansas-Nebraska Act, one called itself Republican. Republicans attempted to unite under their banner all the dissidents and political orphans—Whigs, Free-Soilers, anti-Nebraska Democrats, even Know-Nothings—who opposed the extension of slavery into any territory of the United States.

The Republican creed tapped basic beliefs and values of the northern public. Slave labor and free labor, Republicans argued, had spawned two incompatible civilizations. In the South, they said, slavery degraded the dignity of white labor by associating work with blacks and servility. Repression and tyranny laid heavily on every Southerner, except planter aristocrats. Those insatiable slave lords, whom antislavery Northerners called the Slave Power, now conspired to expand slavery, subvert liberty, and undermine the Constitution through the Democratic Party.

The Republican creed tapped basic beliefs and values of the northern public. Slave labor and free labor, Republicans argued, had spawned two incompatible civilizations.

Only by restricting slavery to the South, Republicans believed, could free labor flourish elsewhere. The system of free labor respected the dignity of work and provided anyone willing to toil an opportunity for a decent living and for advancement. These powerful images attracted a wide range of Northerners to the Republican cause.

The Election of 1856

By the mid-1850s, the Know-Nothings had emerged as the principal champion of nativism and the Republicans as the primary advocate of antislavery. Together, they had helped to break the Whigs and to bloody the Democrats. But the Republicans emerged as the Democrats' main challenger. The election of 1856 revealed that their political star was rising sharply, whereas that of the Know-Nothings was dead.

Slavery in the territories became the election's only issue. The Know-Nothings came apart when party leaders insisted on a platform that endorsed the Kansas-Nebraska Act, causing most Northerners to walk out. The Know-Nothings who remained nominated ex-president Millard Fillmore.

The Republicans, in contrast, adopted a platform that focused almost exclusively on "making every territory free." When they labeled slavery a "relic of barbarism," Republicans signaled that they had written off the South. For president, they nominated the dashing soldier and California adventurer John C. Frémont, "Pathfinder of the West." Though a celebrated explorer, Frémont lacked political credentials. Political know-how resided in his wife, Jessie, who, as a daughter of Senator Thomas Hart Benton of Missouri, knew the political map as well as her husband knew western trails. Although careful to maintain a proper public image, the vivacious thirty-two-year-old mother and antislavery zealot helped draw ordinary women into electoral politics. (See "Documenting the American Promise," page 470.) In Illinois, Abraham Lincoln once counted more than seventy mothers with nursing babies at a Frémont rally.

JOHN C. AND JESSIE BENTON FRÉMONT
The election of 1856 marked the first time a candidate's wife appeared on campaign items. Smart and ambitious, Jessie Benton Frémont made the breakthrough. Seen here on a silk ribbon with her husband, John C. Frémont, Republican Party presidential nominee, Jessie helped plan Frémont's campaign, coauthored his election biography, and drew northern women into political activity as never before. "What a shame that **women** *can't vote!" declared abolitionist Lydia Maria Child. "We'd carry 'our Jessie' into the White House on our shoulders,* **wouldn't** *we." Critics of Jessie's violation of women's traditional sphere ridiculed both Frémonts. A man who met the couple in San Francisco pronounced her "the better man of the two." Jessie Frémont was, as Abraham Lincoln observed ambivalently, "quite a female politician."*
Collection of Janice L. and David J. Frent.

The Democrats, successful in 1852 in bridging sectional differences by nominating a northern man with southern principles, chose another "dough-face," James Buchanan of Pennsylvania. The Democrats took refuge in the ambiguity of popular sovereignty and portrayed Republicans as extremists whose support for the Wilmot Proviso risked pushing the South out of the Union.

The Democratic strategy helped carry the day for Buchanan, but Frémont did astonishingly well. Buchanan won 174 electoral votes against Frémont's 114 and Fillmore's 8. Frémont carried all but five of the states north of the Mason-Dixon line. The election made clear that the Whigs had disintegrated, that the Know-Nothings would not ride nativism to national power, and that the Democrats were badly strained (see Map 13.4). But the big news was what the press called the "glorious defeat" of the Republicans. Despite being a brand-new party and purely sectional, Republicans challenged other par-

ties for national power. Sectionalism had fashioned a new party system, one that spelled danger for the Republic (Figure 13.1).

Freedom under Siege

The "glorious defeat" of the Republicans meant that the second party in the new two-party system was entirely sectional. It felt no compelling need to compromise, to conciliate, to keep a southern wing happy. Indeed, the Republican Party organized around the premise that the slaveholding South provided a profound threat to "free soil, free labor, and free men."

Events in distant Kansas Territory provided the young Republican organization with an enormous boost. Kansas reeled with violence between proslavery and antislavery settlers, which Republicans

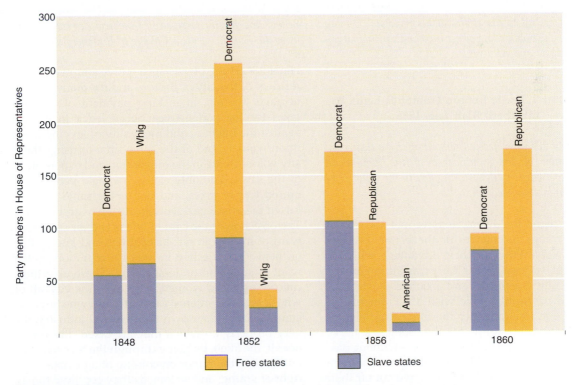

FIGURE 13.1

Changing Political Landscape, 1848–1860
The polarization of American politics between the free states and slave states occurred in little more than a decade.

Women's Politics

example & comfort in November for I don't think we will wear any but black feathers this year.

SOURCE: Pamela Herr and Mary Lee Spence, eds., *The Letters of Jessie Benton Frémont* (Urbana and Chicago: University of Illinois Press, 1993), 140.

*A*lthough women could not vote before the Civil War, many women nevertheless participated in public political activity. Uncle Tom's Cabin, Harriet Beecher Stowe's searing indictment of slavery, galvanized support for the Republican Party's campaign against the extension of slavery. The novel's moral power stemmed from its author's vivid description of how slavery assaulted cherished American institutions and values— Christian duty, female domesticity, and the family. Throughout her life, Jessie Benton Frémont sought to fulfill her domestic roles as wife and mother, even though she found them constraining. She also sought unabashedly to influence politics. She, like many other women, wrote to men of influence on behalf of her husband. "Do not suppose Sir, that I lightly interfere in a matter properly belonging to men," she began a letter to President James Polk in 1842, "but in the absence of Mr. Frémont I attend to his affairs at his request." During the 1850s, she became one of her husband's principal political analysts and advisers.

DOCUMENT 1. Jessie Benton Frémont's Letter to Elizabeth Blair Lee, 1856

On October 20, 1856, Jessie Frémont offered a clear-eyed interpretation of the significance of the Republican Party's paper-thin but devastating loss in the October 14 Pennsylvania state election.

I heartily regret the defeat we have met and do not look for things to change for the better. The Democrats will follow up their advantage with the courage of success & our forces are unorganized and just now surprised and inactive. I wish the cause had triumphed. I do wish Mr. Frémont had been the one to administer the bitter dose of subjection to the South for he has the coolness & nerve to do it just as it needs to be done—without passion & without sympathy—as coldly as a surgeon over a hospital patient would he have cut off their right hand Kansas from the old unhealthy southern body. . . . Tell your Father he must come to us for

DOCUMENT 2. Harriot K. Hunt's Letter "to . . . [the] Treasurer, and the Assessors, and other Authorities of the city of Boston, and the Citizens generally," 1852

Some activist women challenged the domesticity that Stowe and Frémont honored, however, arguing that women's equality depended on their liberation from tradition. These women not only attended women's rights conventions but also signed petitions asking legislators to change laws that discriminated against women and worked to put the ideas of equal rights into practice in their personal lives. Harriot K. Hunt protested having to pay taxes when she was prohibited from voting. A physician who had practiced medicine in Boston since 1835, Hunt had been refused admission to Harvard Medical School and finally received her medical degree in 1853 from the Female Medical College of Philadelphia.

Harriot K. Hunt, physician, a native and permanent resident of the city of Boston, and for many years a taxpayer therein, in making payment of her city taxes for the coming year, begs leave to protest against the injustice and inequality of levying taxes upon women, and at the same time refusing them any voice or vote in the imposition and expenditure of the same. The only classes of male persons required to pay taxes, and not at the same time allowed the privilege of voting, are aliens and minors. The objection in the case of aliens is their supposed want of interest in our institutions and knowledge of them. The objection in the case of minors, is the want of sufficient understanding. These objections can not apply to women, natives of the city, all of whose property interests are here, and who have accumulated, by their own sagacity and industry, the very property on which they are taxed. But this is not all; the alien, by going through the forms of naturalization, the minor on coming of age, obtain the right of voting; and so long as they continue to pay a mere poll-tax of a dollar and a half, they may continue to exercise it, though so ignorant as not to be able to sign their names, or read the very votes they put into the ballot-boxes. Even drunkards, felons, idiots, and lunatics, if men, may still enjoy that right of voting to which no woman, however large the amount of taxes she pays, however respectable her character, or useful her life, can ever attain. Wherein, your remonstrant would inquire, is the justice, equality, or wisdom of this?

SOURCE: Elizabeth Cady Stanton, Susan B. Anthony, and Matilda Joslyn Gage, eds., *History of Woman Suffrage*, vol. 1 (New York: Fowler & Wells, 1881), 259.

DOCUMENT 3. Elizabeth Cady Stanton's Letter on Women's Fashions, 1855

Stymied by male politicians' indifference to petitions like Hunt's, women's rights activists pondered how to translate their dedication to equality into arenas of life more directly under their personal control. In an 1855 letter to a friend, suffragist leader Elizabeth Cady Stanton explained how women's fashions could be tailored to promote equality.

I fully agree with you that woman is terribly cramped and crippled in her present style of dress. I have not one word to utter in its defense; but to me, it seems that if she would enjoy entire freedom, she should dress just like a man. Why proclaim our sex on the house-tops, seeing that it is a badge of degradation, and deprives us of so many rights and privileges wherever we go? . . . In male attire, we could travel by land or sea; go through all the streets and lanes of our cities and towns by night and day, without a protector; get seven hundred dollars a year for teaching, instead of three, and ten dollars for making a coat, instead of two or three, as we now do. All this we could do without fear of insult, or the least sacrifice of decency or virtue. If nature has not made the sex so clearly defined as to be seen through any disguise, why should we make the difference so striking? Depend upon it, when men and women in their every-day life see and think less of sex and more of mind, we shall all lead far purer and higher lives.

SOURCE: Elizabeth Cady Stanton, Susan B. Anthony, and Matilda Joslyn Gage, eds., *History of Woman Suffrage*, vol. 1 (New York: Fowler & Wells, 1881), 841.

DOCUMENT 4. Lucy Stone–Henry B. Blackwell Marriage Agreement, 1855

Marriage typically made women legally inferior to their husbands, but women's rights activists refashioned marriage vows to honor equality rather than subordination. When women's rights leader Lucy Stone married Henry B. Blackwell in 1855, both signed the following statement.

While acknowledging our mutual affection by publicly assuming the relationship of husband and wife, yet in justice to ourselves and a great principle, we deem it a duty to declare that this act on our part implies no sanction of, nor promise of voluntary obedience to such of the present laws of marriage, as refuse to recognize the wife as an independent, rational being, while they confer upon the husband an injurious and unnatural superiority, investing him with legal powers which no honorable man would exercise, and which no man should possess. We protest especially against the laws which give to the husband:

1. The custody of the wife's person.
2. The exclusive control and guardianship of their children.
3. The sole ownership of her personal [property], and use of her real estate. . . .
4. The absolute right to the product of her industry.
5. Also against laws which give to the widower so much larger and more permanent an interest in the property of his deceased wife, than they give to the widow in that of the deceased husband.
6. Finally, against the whole system by which "the legal existence of the wife is suspended during marriage," so that in most States, she neither has a legal part in the choice of her residence, nor can she make a will, nor sue or be sued in her own name, nor inherit property.

We believe that personal independence and equal human rights can never be forfeited, except for crime; that marriage should be an equal and permanent partnership, and so recognized by law; that until it is so recognized, married partners should provide against the radical injustice of present laws, by every means in their power. . . .   *(Continued)*

Thus reverencing law, we enter our protest against rules and customs which are unworthy of the name, since they violate justice, the essence of law.

(signed) Henry B. Blackwell
Lucy Stone

SOURCE: Elizabeth Cady Stanton, Susan B. Anthony, and Matilda Joslyn Gage, eds., *History of Woman Suffrage*, vol. 1 (New York: Fowler & Wells, 1881), 260–61.

QUESTIONS FOR ANALYSIS AND DEBATE

1. Jessie Frémont did not interpret the Republican defeat in Pennsylvania in 1856 as a "glorious defeat." Can you suggest possible reasons why she did not?
2. What legal disabilities for women was the marriage contract of Henry Blackstone and Lucy Stone designed to overcome?
3. On what grounds, according to Harriot Hunt, should women be accorded the vote? Do you agree with her argument? Why or why not?
4. Does Elizabeth Cady Stanton's early version of "dressing for success" make sense? Why or why not?

---

argued was southern in origin. They claimed that the Kansas frontier offered a window onto southern values and intentions. Republicans also pointed to the brutal beating by a Southerner of a respected northern senator on the floor of Congress. Even the Supreme Court, in the Republicans' view, reflected the South's drive toward tyranny and minority rule. Then, in 1858, the issues dividing North and South received an extraordinary airing in a senatorial contest in Illinois, when the nation's foremost Democrat debated a resourceful Republican.

"Bleeding Kansas"

Three days after the House of Representatives approved the Kansas-Nebraska Act, Senator William H. Seward of New York boldly challenged the South. "Come on then, Gentlemen of the Slave States," he cried, "since there is no escaping your challenge, I accept it in behalf of the cause of freedom. We will engage in competition for the virgin soil of Kansas, and God give the victory to the side which is stronger in numbers as it is in right." Because of Stephen Douglas, popular sovereignty would determine whether Kansas became slave or free. No one really expected New Mexico and Utah, with their harsh landscapes and dry climates, to become slave states when Congress instituted popular sovereignty there in 1850. But people disagreed

about Kansas. Kansas sat on the borderline, and many believed it could go either way. Free-state and slave-state settlers each sought majorities at the ballot box, claimed God's blessing, and kept their rifles ready.

In the North, emigrant aid societies sprang up to promote settlement from the free states. The most famous, the New England Emigrant Aid Company, sponsored some 1,240 settlers in 1854 and 1855. In the South, proslavery expansionists eagerly took up Seward's challenge. Tiny rural communities from Virginia to Texas raised money to support proslavery settlers. Missourians, already bordered on the east by the free state of Illinois and on the north by the free state of Iowa, especially thought it important to secure Kansas for slavery.

In theory, popular sovereignty meant an orderly tallying of ballots. In Kansas, however, elec-

"Bleeding Kansas," 1850s

FRAUDULENT VOTING
IN KANSAS
This drawing is a northern indictment of the corruption of popular sovereignty by Missourians. Rough frontier types, with pistols and knives tucked into their belts, rush to get free whiskey and then line up at the polling place, whose sign, DOWN WITH THE ABOLITIONISTS, *indicates that they voted the proslavery ticket.*
The Kansas State Historical Society, Topeka, Kansas.

www.bedfordstmartins.com
/tap SEE THE ONLINE STUDY GUIDE for more help in analyzing this image.

tions became circuses. Thousands of hell-for-leather frontiersmen from Missouri, egged on by Missouri senator David Rice Atchison, invaded Kansas. "There are eleven hundred coming over from Platte County to vote," Atchison reported, "and if that ain't enough we can send five thousand—enough to kill every God-damned abolitionist in the Territory." Not surprisingly, proslavery candidates swept the early elections. When the first territorial legislature met, it enacted some of the most severe proslavery laws in the nation. It became a felony merely to argue that slavery did not legally exist in Kansas. Antislavery men were barred from holding office or serving on juries. Assisting a runaway slave became a capital offense. Ever-pliant President Pierce endorsed the work of the fraudulently elected proslavery legislature. Free-state Kansans did not. They elected their own legislature, which promptly banned both slaves and free blacks from the territory and applied for admission to the Union as a free state. Organized into two rival govern-

ments and armed to the teeth, Kansans verged on civil war.

Fighting broke out on the morning of May 21, 1856, when a mob of several hundred proslavery men entered the town of Lawrence, the center of free-state settlement. Only one man died—a proslavery raider who was killed when a burning wall collapsed—but the "Sack of Lawrence," as free-soil forces called it, inflamed northern opinion. In Kansas, news of Lawrence provoked one free-soil settler, John Brown, to "fight fire with fire." Announcing that "it was better that a score of bad men should die than that one man who came here to make Kansas a Free State should be driven out," he led the posse that massacred five allegedly proslavery settlers along the Pottawatomie Creek. After that, guerrilla war engulfed the territory.

By providing graphic evidence of a dangerously aggressive Slave Power, "Bleeding Kansas" gave the fledgling Republican Party fresh ammunition. The Republicans received additional encouragement from an event that occurred in the national capital. On May 19 and 20, 1856, Senator Charles Sumner of Massachusetts delivered a scathing speech entitled "The Crime against Kansas." He damned the administration, the South, and proslavery Kansans. He also indulged in a scalding personal attack on the elderly South Carolina senator Andrew P. Butler, whom Sumner described as a "Don Quixote" who had taken as his mistress "the harlot, slavery."

> *Organized into two rival governments and armed to the teeth, Kansans verged on civil war.*

Preston Brooks, a young South Carolina member of the House and a kinsman of Butler, felt compelled to defend the honor of both his aged relative and his state. On May 22, armed with a walking cane, Brooks entered the Senate, where he found Sumner working at his desk. After accusing him of slander, Brooks began beating Sumner over the head with his cane. Within a minute, Sumner lay bleeding and unconscious on the Senate floor. Brooks resigned his seat in the House, only to be promptly reelected. In the North, the southern hero became an archvillain. Like Bleeding Kansas, "Bleeding Sumner" provided the Republican Party with a potent symbol of the South's twisted and violent "civilization."

The Dred Scott Decision

As the French visitor Alexis de Tocqueville observed in the 1830s, "Scarcely any question arises in the United States that is not resolved, sooner or later, into a judicial question." Because the Constitution lacked precision on the issue of slavery in the territories, political debate reflected sectional interests and party politics. Only the Supreme Court spoke definitively about the meaning of the Constitution. In 1857, in the *Dred Scott* case, the Court proved that it enjoyed no special immunity from the sectional and partisan passions that convulsed the land.

Dred Scott was born a slave in Virginia at the turn of the century and in 1818 had moved with his master, Peter Blow, to a cotton plantation in Alabama. Twelve years later, the Blow family and their six slaves moved to St. Louis. In 1833, Scott was sold

to Dr. John Emerson, an army doctor who took Scott with him as his personal servant to Fort Armstrong, Illinois. Two years later, Scott accompanied Emerson when he was transferred to Fort Snelling on the Minnesota River in Wisconsin Territory. Other moves followed, but in a few years Emerson returned Scott to St. Louis. On April 6, 1846, Dred Scott sued to prove that he, his wife Harriet, and their two daughters, Eliza and Lizzie, were legally entitled to their freedom. Dred Scott's claim was based on his travels and residences. He argued that living in Illinois, a free state, and in Wisconsin Territory, a free territory according to the Missouri Compromise of 1820, had made him and his family free; and once free, they remained free, even after returning to Missouri, a slave state.

Eleven years after the Scotts first sued for freedom, the U.S. Supreme Court ruled in the case. The justices could have simply settled the immediate issue of Scott's status as a free man or slave, but they saw the case as an opportunity to settle once and for all the vexing question of slavery in the territories. On the morning of March 6, 1857, Chief Justice Roger B. Taney read the majority decision of the Court. Taney hated Republicans and detested racial equality, and the Court's decision reflected those prejudices. First, the Court ruled that Dred Scott could not legally claim violation of his constitutional rights because he was not a citizen of the United States. At the time of the Constitution, Taney said, blacks "had for more than a century before been regarded as beings of an inferior order . . . so far inferior, that they had no rights which the white man was bound to respect." Second, the laws of Dred Scott's home state, Missouri, determined his status, and thus his travels in free areas did not make him free. Third, Congress's power to make "all needful rules and regulations" for the territories did not include the right to prohibit slavery. The Court then explicitly declared the Missouri Compromise unconstitutional, even though it had already been voided by the Kansas-Nebraska Act.

Republicans exploded in outrage. Taney's extreme proslavery decision ranged far beyond a determination of Dred Scott's freedom. By declaring unconstitutional the Republican program of federal exclusion of slavery in the territories, the Court had cut the ground from beneath the party. Moreover, as the *New York Tribune* lamented, the decision cleared the way for "all our Territories . . . to be ripened into Slave States." Particularly frightening to African Americans in the North was the Court's

THE DRED SCOTT FAMILY

*The **Dred Scott** case in 1857 not only produced a fierce political storm, but also fueled an enormous curiosity about the family suing for freedom. The correspondent for the popular **Frank Leslie's Illustrated** met Dred Scott in St. Louis and reported: "We found him on examination to be a pure-blooded African, perhaps fifty years of age, with a shrewd, intelligent, good-natured face, of rather light frame, being not more than five feet six inches high." But as this illustration makes clear, Northerners wanted to see all of the Scotts: Harriet, who was a slave when Dred Scott married her in Wisconsin Territory in about 1836; daughter Eliza, who was born in 1838 on board a ship traveling in free territory north of Missouri; and daughter Lizzie, born after the Scotts returned to St. Louis.*

Library of Congress.

declaration that blacks were not citizens and had "no rights which the white man was bound to respect."

The Republican rebuttal to Taney's decision relied heavily on the brilliant dissenting opinion of Justice Benjamin R. Curtis. Scott *was* a citizen of the United States, Curtis argued. At the time of the writing of the Constitution, free black men could vote in five states and participated in the ratification process. Scott *was* free: Because slavery was prohibited in Wisconsin, the "involuntary servitude of a slave, coming into the Territory with his master, should cease to exist." And the Missouri Compromise *was* constitutional. The Founders meant exactly what they said: Congress had the power to make "*all* needful rules and regulations" for the territories, including barring slavery.

Unswayed by Curtis's dissent, the Court's seven-to-two majority had validated the most extreme statement of the South's territorial rights. John C. Calhoun's claim that Congress had no authority to exclude slavery now became the law of the land. But what southern Democrats cheered, northern Democrats found profoundly disturbing. They feared that the *Dred Scott* decision annihilated not just the Wilmot Proviso but popular sovereignty as well. If Congress did not have the authority to exclude slavery, how could Congress's creation, a territorial government, assume that right? No one was in a tighter bind than Stephen A. Douglas. Civil war raged in Kansas at that very moment because Douglas's Kansas-Nebraska Act had opened the territory to popular sovereignty. Now, contrary to Douglas's promise, it appeared that a free-soil majority could not keep slavery out. No one could exclude slavery until the moment of statehood. By draining the last drop of ambiguity out of popular sovereignty, the *Dred Scott* decision jeopardized the ability of the Democratic Party to hold its northern and southern wings together.

John C. Calhoun's claim that Congress had no authority to exclude slavery now became the law of the land. But what southern Democrats cheered, northern Democrats found profoundly disturbing.

Ironically, the *Dred Scott* decision strengthened the young Republican Party by giving credence to its claim that a hostile Slave Power conspired against northern liberties. Only the capture of the Supreme Court by the "slavocracy," Republicans argued, could explain the tortured and historically inaccurate *Dred Scott* decision. As for Dred Scott, although the Court rejected his suit, he did in the end gain his freedom. In May 1857, Taylor Blow, the son of his first owner, purchased and freed Scott and his family. On September 17, 1858, Dred Scott died in obscurity.

Prairie Republican: Abraham Lincoln

The reigniting of sectional flames provided Republican politicians with fresh challenges and fresh opportunities. None proved more eager for them than Abraham Lincoln of Illinois. Lincoln had long since put behind him his hardscrabble log-cabin beginnings in Kentucky and Indiana. At the time of the *Dred Scott* decision, he lived in a fine two-story house in Springfield, brought in enough business from the Illinois Central Railroad to be known as the "railroad lawyer," and by virtue of his marriage into a well-to-do family and successful practice associated with men and women of reputation and standing.

The law provided Lincoln's living, but politics was his life. "His ambition was a little engine that knew no rest," observed his law partner William Herndon. At age twenty-six, he served his first term in the Illinois state legislature. Between 1847 and 1849, he enjoyed his only term in the House of Representatives, where he fired away at "Mr. Polk's War" and cast dozens of votes for free soil but otherwise served inconspicuously. When he returned to Springfield, he pitched into his law practice but kept his eye fixed on public office. As a young man, he had chosen as his political hero the Whig Henry Clay. On the vexing issues of Union, slavery, and race, Clay exemplified for Lincoln the reasonable moderate, the realistic pragmatist, and the effective compromiser.

But, like Whigs everywhere in the mid-1850s, Lincoln had no political home. With their party in shambles, a good many Illinois Whigs gravitated to the Know-Nothings. Mary Todd Lincoln, Lincoln's Kentucky-born wife, sympathized with the nativists, for she knew, she said, the burdens of "wild Irish" servants. But Lincoln was not a Know-Nothing. "How could I be?" he asked. "How can any one who abhors the oppression of negroes be in favor of degrading classes of white people?" Lincoln's credo—opposition to "the *extension* of slavery"—made the Democrats an impossible choice. The Republicans made free soil their principal tenet, and in 1856 Lincoln joined the party.

Convinced that slavery was a "monstrous injustice," a "great moral wrong," and an "unqualified evil to the negro, the white man, and the State," Lincoln was certain that Douglas's Kansas-Nebraska Act of 1854 had given slavery a new life. He admitted that the Constitution sanctioned slavery in those states where it existed, but he believed that the Founders planned to contain its spread. Penned in, plantation slavery would exhaust southern soil at the same time the number of slaves increased. Burdened with surplus slaves, slaveholders would have no choice but to end slavery themselves. By providing fresh, life-giving lands, however, Douglas put slavery "on the high road to extension and perpetuity." Lincoln conveniently forgot those moments when the Founders permitted slavery to expand westward, but he remained convinced that the "spirit of seventy-six and the spirit of Nebraska are utter antagonisms."

Just as Lincoln staked out the middle ground on antislavery, he held what were, for his times, moderate racial views. Like a majority of Republicans, Lincoln defended black humanity without challenging white supremacy. He denounced slavery as immoral and believed that it should end, but he also viewed black equality as impractical and unachievable. "Negroes have natural rights . . . as other men have," he said, "although they cannot enjoy them here." Insurmountable white prejudice made it impossible to extend full citizenship and equality to blacks in America. Freeing blacks and allowing them to remain in this country would lead to race war. In Lincoln's mind, social stability and black progress required that slavery end and that blacks leave the country.

Lincoln realized that because most Northerners lacked sympathy for blacks, humanitarian concern would not mobilize them to fight for free soil. Instead, he appealed to northern labor's self-interest. He described the territories as "places for poor people to go to, and better their conditions." He spoke to those millions of white Americans who wanted to make something of themselves: farmhands who wanted to become farm owners, clerks who aspired to be merchants, rail-splitters who dreamed of being lawyers. "The *free* labor system," he said, "opens the way for all—gives hope to all, and energy, and progress, and improvement of condition to all." In

Lincoln's view, slavery's expansion threatened this freedom to succeed.

Like a majority of Republicans, Lincoln defended black humanity without challenging white supremacy. He denounced slavery as immoral and believed that it should end, but he also viewed black equality as impractical and unachievable.

Lincoln became persuaded that slaveholders formed an aggressive and dangerous conspiracy to nationalize slavery. Evidence abounded. The Kansas-Nebraska Act repealed the restriction on slavery's advance in the territories. The *Dred Scott* decision denied Congress the right to impose fresh restrictions. The next step, Lincoln warned, would be "another Supreme Court decision, declaring that the Constitution of the United States does not permit a *State* to exclude slavery from its limits." Unless its citizens woke up, he warned, the Supreme Court would make "Illinois a slave State."

In Lincoln's view, the nation could not "endure, permanently half slave and half free." Either opponents of slavery would arrest its spread and place it on the "course of ultimate extinction" or its advocates would push it forward until it became legal in "*all* the States, *old* as well as *new—North* as well as *South.*" Lincoln's convictions that slavery was wrong, that Congress must stop its spread, and that it must be put on the road to extinction formed the core of the Republican ideology. By 1858, he had so impressed his fellow Republicans in Illinois that they put him forward to challenge the nation's premier Democrat, who was seeking reelection to the Senate.

The Lincoln-Douglas Debates

When Stephen Douglas learned that Abraham Lincoln would be his opponent for the Senate, he confided in a fellow Democrat: "He is the strong man of the party—full of wit, facts, dates—and the best stump speaker, with his droll ways and dry jokes, in the West. He is as honest as he is shrewd, and if I beat him my victory will be hardly won."

Not only did Douglas have to contend with a formidable foe, but he also carried the weight of a burden not of his own making. The previous year,

DISCUSSING THE NEWS
Newspapers permitted Midwesterners to keep up-to-date. Here a farmer takes a break from his task of cutting firewood to debate the latest news with his friends. He is so engrossed that he ignores the little girl tugging at his pants leg and trying to get him to notice the woman waving in the doorway. Men like these increasingly accepted Lincoln's portrait of the Republican Party as the guardian of the common people's liberty and economic opportunity. When Lincoln claimed that southern slaveholders threatened free labor and democracy, the midwestern farmers listened.
Copyright © 1971, The R. W. Norton Art Gallery, Shreveport, La. Used by permission. Painting by Arthur F. Tait.

the nation's economy experienced a sharp downturn. Prices plummeted, thousands of businesses failed, and unemployment rose. The causes of the panic of 1857 lay in the international economy, but Americans reflexively interpreted the panic in sectional terms. Northeastern businesses and industries suffered most, and Northerners blamed the southern-dominated Congress, which had just months before reduced tariff duties to their lowest levels in the nineteenth century. Given this invitation, Northerners believed, foreign competition ravaged the northern economy. Southerners, in contrast, had largely escaped hardship because cotton prices remained high. Although Illinois suffered less than the Northeast, Douglas had to go before the voters in 1858 as a member of the freshly accused, southern-dominated Democratic Party.

Douglas's response to another crisis in 1857, however, helped shore up his standing with his constituents. During the previous winter, proslavery forces in Kansas met in the town of Lecompton, drafted a proslavery constitution, and applied for statehood. Everyone knew that free-soilers outnumbered proslavery settlers by at least two to one, but President Buchanan blessed the Lecompton constitution and instructed Congress to admit Kansas as the sixteenth slave state. Republicans denounced the "Lecompton swindle." Douglas broke with the Democratic administration and came out against the proslavery constitution, not because it accepted slavery but because it violated the democratic requirement of popular sovereignty. In March 1858, despite Douglas's vigorous opposition, the Senate passed the Kansas statehood bill, but the northern majority in the House killed it. (When Kansans reconsidered the Lecompton constitution in an honest election, they rejected it six to one; Kansas entered the Union in 1861 as a free state.) In coming out against the constitution, Douglas declared his independence from the South and, he hoped, made himself acceptable at home.

A relative unknown and a decided underdog in the Illinois election, Lincoln challenged the incumbent Douglas to debate him face to face. Douglas agreed, and the two met in seven communities for what became a legendary series of debates. To the thousands who stood straining to see and hear, they must have seemed an odd pair. Douglas was five feet four inches tall, broad, and stocky; Lincoln was six feet four inches tall, angular, and lean. Douglas was in perpetual motion, darting across the platform, shouting, and jabbing the air. Lincoln stood still and spoke deliberately. Douglas wore the latest fashion and dazzled audiences with his flashy vests. Lincoln wore good suits but managed to look rumpled anyway. But their differences in physical appearance and style were of least importance. They showed the citizens of Illinois (and much of the nation because of widespread press coverage) the difference between an anti-Lecompton Democrat and a true Republican. They debated, often brilliantly, the central issue before the country: slavery and freedom.

Lincoln badgered Douglas with the question of whether he favored the spread of slavery. He tried to force Douglas into the damaging admission that the Supreme Court had repudiated his territorial solution, popular sovereignty. In the debate at Freeport, Illinois, Douglas admitted that settlers could not now pass legislation barring slavery, but he argued that they could ban slavery just as effectively by not passing protective laws. Without "appropriate police regulations and local legislation," such as those found in slave states, he explained, slavery could not live a day, an hour. Southerners condemned Douglas's "Freeport Doctrine" and charged him with trying to steal the victory they had gained with the *Dred Scott* decision. Lincoln chastised his opponent for his "don't care" attitude about slavery, for "blowing out the moral lights around us."

Lincoln and Douglas debated, often brilliantly, the central issue before the country: slavery and freedom.

For his part, Douglas worked the racial issue. He called Lincoln an abolitionist and an egalitarian enamored with "our colored brethren." Put on the defensive, Lincoln came close to staking out positions on abolition and race that were as conservative as Douglas's. Lincoln reiterated his belief that slavery enjoyed constitutional protection where it existed. He also reaffirmed his faith in white rule: "I will say, then, that I am not, nor ever have been, in favor of bringing about in any way the social and political equality of the white and black race." But unlike Douglas, who told racist jokes and spit out racial epithets, Lincoln was no negrophobe. He always tried to steer the debate back to what he considered the true issue: the morality and future of slavery. "Slavery is wrong," Lincoln repeated, because "a man has the right to the fruits of his own labor."

As Douglas predicted, the election was hard-fought. It was also closely contested. In the nineteenth century, citizens voted for state legislators, who in turn selected the U.S. senator. Since Democrats won a slight majority in the legislature, the new legislature chose to return Douglas to the Senate. But the debates thrust Lincoln, the prairie Republican, into the national spotlight.

The Union Collapses

Lincoln's thesis that the "slavocracy" conspired to make slavery a national institution now seems exaggerated. But from the northern perspective, the Kansas-Nebraska Act, the Brooks-Sumner affair, the *Dred Scott* decision, the panic of 1857, and the Lecompton constitution seemed irrefutable evidence of the South's aggressiveness. Southerners, of course, saw things differently. They were the ones who were under siege and had grievances, they declared. Which was the minority section? they asked. In a democracy, how could a minority hope to control the government? Signs were everywhere, they argued, that the North planned to use its numerical advantage to attack slavery, and not just in the territories. Republicans had already proved themselves unwilling to be bound by the Constitution as interpreted by the Supreme Court in the *Dred Scott* decision. After John Brown attempted to incite a slave insurrection in Virginia in 1859, Southerners argued that Northerners had also proven themselves unwilling to be bound by Christian decency and reverence for life.

Threats of secession increasingly laced the sectional debate. Talk of leaving the Union had been heard for years, but until the final crisis, Southerners used secession as a ploy to gain concessions within the Union, not to destroy the Union. But the 1850s delivered powerful blows to Southerners' confidence that they could remain Americans and protect slavery and their way of life. When the Republican Party won the White House in 1860, many Southerners concluded that national power had shifted permanently.

The Aftermath of John Brown's Raid

If John Brown had been killed during his raid on Harpers Ferry in 1859, his impact on history would probably have been minor. But he lived, stood trial in Virginia for treason and conspiracy to incite slave insurrection, and on December 2, 1859, was hanged. In life, "Old Brown" was a ne'er-do-well who failed at nearly everything he tried. He died, however, with courage, dignity, and composure. He wrote his wife that he was "determined to make the utmost possible out of a defeat." Resolute and calm, he uttered some of the most stirring words ever to issue from a courtroom: "If it is deemed necessary that I should forfeit my life for the furtherance of the ends of justice, and mingle my blood further with the blood of . . . millions in this slave country whose rights are disregarded by wicked, cruel, and unjust enactments, I say, let it be done." Implacable to the end, he refused to allow a Virginia minister to accompany him to the scaffold, saying "my knees will not bend with them while their hands are stained with the blood of souls."

Some Northerners grieved for John Brown. One abolitionist proclaimed Brown the "bravest and humanest man in all the country." In Boston, the essayist Ralph Waldo Emerson dubbed him "that new saint" who "will make the gallows glorious like the cross." On the eve of Brown's execution, writer Henry David Thoreau offered "A Plea for John Brown," in which he likened Brown to Christ and concluded, "He is not Old Brown any longer; he is an angel of light." Some abolitionists went beyond canonizing Brown to explicitly endorse his cause of slave rebellion. William Lloyd Garrison, who professed pacifism, announced, "I am prepared to say 'success to every slave insurrection at the South and in every country.'"

Generally, however, abolitionists did not condone violence, and northern opinion did not celebrate bloody slave insurrection. Most Northerners believed that John Brown had acted lawlessly, with unwarranted violence. Lincoln spoke for the majority when he endorsed Brown's antislavery stance but concluded that noble ideals could not "excuse violence, bloodshed, and treason."

Lincoln's sober voice failed to still a gathering fury in the South. A Mississippian denounced the bloodthirsty fiend whose mission was "to incite slaves to murder helpless women and children." Southerners contemplated what they had in common with people who "regard John Brown as a martyr and a Christian hero, rather than a murderer and robber." Many whites in the South could no longer distinguish between Northerners who opposed slavery, like Lincoln, and those who were willing to see it washed away in a river of blood, like Brown. Georgia senator Robert Toombs announced solemnly that Southerners must "never permit this Federal government to pass into the traitorous hands of the black Republican party." At that moment, the presidential election was only months away.

Republican Victory in 1860

Anxieties provoked by John Brown's raid flared for months as southern whites feverishly searched for

JOHN BROWN GOING TO HIS HANGING, HORACE PIPPIN, 1942

The grandparents of Horace Pippin, a Pennsylvania artist, had been slaves. His grand-mother had witnessed the hanging of John Brown, and here Pippin recalls the scene she so often described to him. He uses a muted palette to establish the bleak setting and to tell the grim story, but he manages to convey a striking intensity nevertheless. Tied and sitting erect on his coffin, Brown passes resolutely before the silent, staring white men. The black woman in the lower right corner is presumably Pippin's grandmother.

Romaire Bearden, a leading twentieth-century African American artist, recalled the place of John Brown in black memory: "Lincoln and John Brown were as much a part of the actuality of the Afro-American experience, as were the domino games and the hoe cakes for Sunday morning breakfast. I vividly recall the yearly commemorations for John Brown and see my grandfather reading Brown's last speech to the court, which was a regular part of the ceremony at Pittsburgh's Shiloh Baptist Church."

Pennsylvania Academy of Fine Arts. Lambert Fund Purchase, 1941.11.

abolitionists and whipped, tarred and feathered, and sometimes hanged those they suspected. More-over, other events in the eleven months between Brown's hanging and the presidential election heightened sectional hostility and estrangement.

First, a southern business convention meeting in Nashville shocked the country (including many Southerners) by calling for the reopening of the African slave trade, closed since 1808 and consid-ered an abomination everywhere in the Western

ABRAHAM LINCOLN

Lincoln actively sought the Republican presidential nomination in 1860. When in New York City to give a political address, he had his photograph taken by Mathew Brady. "While I was there I was taken to one of the places where they get up such things," Lincoln explained, sounding more innocent than he was, "and I suppose they got my shadow, and can multiply copies indefinitely." Multiply they did. Copies of the dignified photograph of Lincoln soon replaced the less flattering drawings. Later, Lincoln credited his victory to his New York speech and to Mathew Brady.

The Lincoln Museum, Fort Wayne, Indiana. Photo: #0-17; drawing: #2024.

world. Next, Chief Justice Taney provoked new indignation when the Supreme Court ruled northern personal liberty laws unconstitutional and reaffirmed the Fugitive Slave Act.

Then, in February 1860, the normally routine business of electing a Speaker of the House turned into one of the ugliest moments in the history of Congress. Two months of acrimonious debate left Republicans and Democrats deadlocked, and it looked for a while as if the congressmen would simply shoot it out. "The only persons who do not have a revolver and a knife are those who have two revolvers," observed a South Carolinian. The House

averted bloodshed when a few Know-Nothings finally pitched in with the Republicans to elect an old Whig. Finally, Mississippian Jefferson Davis demanded that the Senate adopt a federal slave code for the territories, a goal of extreme proslavery Southerners for several years. Not only was Congress powerless to block slavery's spread, he argued, but it must offer it all "needful protection."

When Democrats converged on Charleston for their convention in April 1860, Southerners gave notice that they intended to make their extreme position binding doctrine. Proud to be meeting only blocks from the grave of John C. Calhoun, southern fire-eaters denounced Stephen Douglas and demanded a platform that included federal protection of slavery in the territories. But northern Democrats needed a platform that they could take home, and northern voters would not stomach a federal slave code. When two platforms—one with a federal slave code and one with popular sovereignty—came before the delegates, popular sovereignty won. Representatives from the entire lower South and Arkansas stomped out of the convention. The remaining delegates adjourned to meet a few weeks later in Baltimore, where they nominated Douglas for president and adopted a platform that advocated little beyond congressional noninterference in the territories.

When southern Democrats met, they nominated Vice President John C. Breckinridge of Tennessee for president and approved a platform with a federal slave code. But southern moderates refused to hand over their section to Breckinridge and the fire-eaters. Senator John J. Crittenden of Kentucky and others formed a new party that would provide voters a Unionist choice. Instead of adopting a platform—which inevitably fanned controversy—the new Constitutional Union Party merely approved a vague resolution pledging "to recognize no political principle other than *the Constitution . . . the Union . . . and the Enforcement of the Laws.*" For president they picked former senator John Bell of Tennessee. Southern Democrats accused the new party of "insulting the intelligence of the American people" when it ignored "the slavery question. That issue must be met and settled."

The Republicans smelled victory. Four years earlier they had enjoyed "glorious defeat" to a Democratic Party that had since broken up. Still, Republicans estimated that they needed to carry nearly all the free states to win and therefore must broaden their appeal. In 1856, opponents had charged that the Republicans were a one-idea party. In 1860, the Republicans built a platform with more than a single antislavery plank. Free homesteads, a protective tariff, a Pacific railroad, and a guarantee of immigrant political rights defined an economic and social agenda broad enough to unify the North. While recommitting themselves to stopping the spread of slavery, they also denounced John Brown's raid as "among the gravest of crimes" and confirmed the security of slavery in the South.

Republicans cast about for a moderate candidate to go with their evenhanded platform. The foremost Republican, William H. Seward, had ene-

mies. His famous "higher law" doctrine and "irrepressible conflict" speech made conservatives shiver. Since bursting onto the national scene in 1858, Lincoln had demonstrated his clear purpose, good judgment, and solid Republican credentials on a speaking tour through the Midwest and East. That, combined with his rock-solid reputation for integrity and his residence in Illinois, a crucial state, made him attractive to the party. Masterful maneuvering by Lincoln's managers converted his status as the second choice of many delegates into a majority on the third ballot. Defeated by Douglas in a state contest less than two years earlier, Lincoln now stood ready to take him on for the presidency.

The election of 1860 was like none other in American politics. It took place in the midst of the nation's severest crisis. Moreover, four major candidates crowded the presidential field. Rather than a four-cornered contest, however, the election broke into two contests, each with two candidates. In the North, Lincoln faced Douglas, and in the South, Breckinridge confronted Bell. Southerners did not even permit Lincoln's name to appear on the ballot in ten of the fifteen slave states, so outrageous did they consider the Republican Party.

An unprecedented number of voters cast ballots on November 6, 1860. Approximately 82 percent of eligible northern men and nearly 70 percent of eligible southern men went to the polls. The Republican platform succeeded in attracting a broad coalition of northern interests, and Lincoln swept all of the eighteen free states except New Jersey, which split its votes between him and Douglas. While Lincoln received only 39 percent of the popular vote, he won easily in the electoral balloting, gaining 180 votes, 28 more than he needed for victory. Lincoln did not win because his opposition was splintered. Even if the votes of his three opponents were combined, Lincoln would still have won. Ominously, however, Breckinridge, running on a southern-rights platform, won the entire Lower South plus Delaware, Maryland, and North Carolina. Two fully sectionalized parties swept their regions, but the northern one won the presidency (Map 13.5).

Secession Winter

The telegraphs had barely stopped tapping out the news of Lincoln's victory when anxious Southerners began reappraising the value of the Union. Although Breckinridge had carried the South, a vote for "southern rights" was not necessarily a vote for

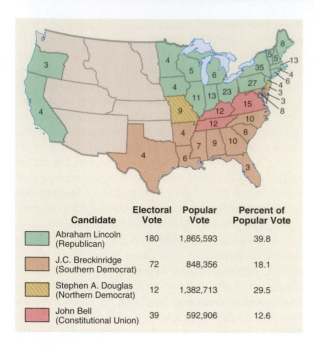

Candidate	Electoral Vote	Popular Vote	Percent of Popular Vote
Abraham Lincoln (Republican)	180	1,865,593	39.8
J.C. Breckinridge (Southern Democrat)	72	848,356	18.1
Stephen A. Douglas (Northern Democrat)	12	1,382,713	29.5
John Bell (Constitutional Union)	39	592,906	12.6

MAP 13.5
The Election of 1860

secession. In fact, Breckinridge steadfastly denied that he was a secession candidate. Besides, slightly more than half of the Southerners who voted cast ballots for Douglas and Bell, two stout defenders of the Union. "The people of the South have too much sense," Lincoln said, "to attempt the ruin of the government." During the winter of 1860–61, Southerners debated what to do.

Southern Unionists tried to calm the fears that Lincoln's election triggered. Let the dust settle, they pleaded, and then proceed deliberately. Extremists in both sections, they argued, had created the crisis. Former Congressman Alexander Stephens of Georgia eloquently defended the Union. He asked what Lincoln had done to justify something as extreme as secession. Had he not promised to respect slavery where it existed? In Stephens's judgment, the fire-eater cure would be worse than the Republican disease. Secession might lead to war, which would loosen the hinges of southern society, possibly even open the door to slave insurrection or a revolt by nonslaveholding whites. "Revolutions are much easier started than controlled," Stephens warned. "I consider slavery much more secure in the Union than out of it."

Secessionists emphasized the urgency of the moment and the dangers of delay. No Southerner should mistake Republican intentions, they argued. "Mr. Lincoln and his party assert that this doctrine of equality applies to the negro," former unionist Howell Cobb of Georgia asserted, "and necessarily there can exist no such thing as property in our equals." Lincoln had won the presidency without a single electoral vote south of the Mason-Dixon line. Now one party, hostile to slavery, could make decisions about the South's institutions, and Southerners' minority status made them helpless to defend themselves within the Union. Why wait, Cobb asked, for Lincoln to appoint Republican judges, marshals, customs collectors, and postmasters to federal posts throughout the South? Each one would become an abolitionist emissary spreading dangerous ideas among blacks and attempting to turn nonslaveholding whites against slaveholders. As for war, there would be none. The Union was a voluntary compact, and coerced patriotism was alien to America. If Northerners did resist secession with force, the conflict would be brief, for one southern woodsman could whip five of Lincoln's greasy mechanics.

For all their differences, southern whites were generally united in their determination to defend slavery, to take slave property into the territories, and to squeeze from the North an admission that they were good and decent people. They disagreed about whether the mere presence of a Republican in the White House made it necessary to exercise what they considered a legitimate right to secede.

The debate about what to do was briefest in South Carolina. It seceded from the Union on December 20, 1860. By February 1861, the six other Deep South states marched in South Carolina's footsteps. Only South Carolinians voted overwhelmingly in favor of secession, however; elsewhere, the vote was close. In general, the nonslaveholding inhabitants of the pine barrens and mountain counties displayed the greatest attachment to the Union. Slaveholders spearheaded secession. On February 4,

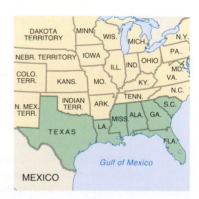

Secession of the Lower South, Dec. 1860–Feb. 1861

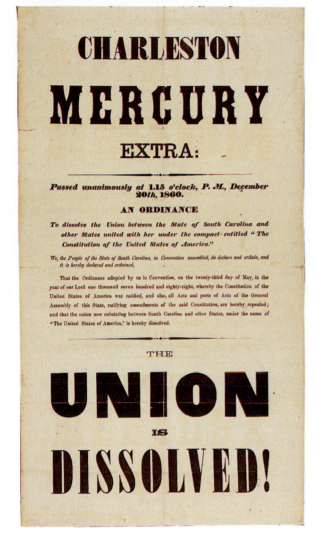

CHARLESTON MERCURY EXTRA:

Passed unanimously at 1.15 o'clock, P. M., December 20th, 1860.

AN ORDINANCE

To dissolve the Union between the State of South Carolina and other States united with her under the compact entitled "The Constitution of the United States of America."

We, the People of the State of South Carolina, in Convention assembled, do declare and ordain, and it is hereby declared and ordained,

That the Ordinance adopted by us in Convention, on the twenty-third day of May, in the year of our Lord one thousand seven hundred and eighty-eight, whereby the Constitution of the United States of America was ratified, and also, all Acts and parts of Acts of the General Assembly of this State, ratifying amendments of the said Constitution, are hereby repealed; and that the union now subsisting between South Carolina and other States, under the name of "The United States of America," is hereby dissolved.

THE UNION IS DISSOLVED!

"THE UNION IS DISSOLVED!"
On December 20, 1860, the **Charleston Mercury** *put out this special edition of the paper to celebrate South Carolina's secession from the Union. Six weeks earlier, upon hearing the news that Lincoln had won the presidency, it had predicted as much. "The tea has been thrown overboard," the* **Mercury** *announced. "The revolution of 1860 has been initiated."*
Chicago Historical Society.

representatives from South Carolina, Georgia, Florida, Alabama, Mississippi, Louisiana, and Texas met in Montgomery, Alabama, where three days later they celebrated the birth of the Confederate States of America. Jefferson Davis became president and Alexander Stephens, who had spoken so eloquently

about the dangers of revolution, became vice president.

Lincoln's election had split the Union. Now secession split the South. Seven slave states seceded during the winter, but eight did not. Citizens of the Upper South debated just as furiously whether the South could defend itself better inside or outside the Union, but they came down opposite the Lower South, at least for the moment. The fact was that the Upper South had a smaller stake in slavery. Just over half as many white families in the Upper South held slaves (21 percent) as did those in the Lower South (37 percent). Slaves represented twice as large a percentage of the population in the Lower South (48 percent) as in the Upper South (23 percent). Consequently, whites in the Upper South had fewer fears that Republican ascendancy meant economic catastrophe, racial war, and social chaos. Lincoln would need to do more than just be elected to provoke them into secession.

The nation had to wait until March 4, 1861, to see what Lincoln would do. (Presidents-elect waited four months to take office until 1933, when the Twentieth Amendment to the Constitution shifted the inauguration forward to January 20.) Throughout the winter, while Southerners debated the fate of the Union, Lincoln watched from Springfield. "Lame-duck" president James Buchanan watched from Washington. Buchanan firmly denied the constitutionality of secession but also denied that he had power to resist it. Buchanan demonstrated, William H. Seward said mockingly, that "it is the President's duty to enforce the laws, unless somebody opposes him."

Without leadership from the White House, the search for a peace-saving compromise shifted to Congress. To allay southern fears, a Senate committee hastily recommended a series of constitutional amendments, the most important of which revived the Missouri Compromise. Slavery would be prohibited in territories north of 36°30' and protected south of it. Lincoln, in private communications, counseled standing firm on Republican principles, and Republicans in Congress blocked the measure. But the Confederate states showed little interest in the proposal because they no longer focused on the territorial issue. Since the election of a Republican president, they had independence on their minds.

Finally, Lincoln arrived in Washington, forced to sneak in at night because of an assassination plot.

His entrance did nothing to build confidence in a nation that doubted that this odd-looking man with almost no national political experience would be up to the task before him. The frantic search for a sectional compromise had failed, and the Confederate States of America acted as if they were independent and assumed that the price of secession would be censure, nothing more.

Lincoln's election had split the Union. Now secession split the South.

In his inaugural address, Lincoln began with reassurances to the South. He had "no lawful right" to interfere with slavery where it existed, he said again, adding for emphasis that he had "no inclination to do so." There would be "no invasion—no using of force against or among the people anywhere." In filling federal posts, he would not "force obnoxious strangers" on the South. Conciliatory toward Southerners, Lincoln proved inflexible about the Union. The Union, he declared, is "perpetual." Secession was "anarchy" and "legally void." The Constitution required him to execute the law "in all the States." He would hold federal property, collect federal duties, and deliver the mails.

The decision for civil war or peace rested in the South's hands, Lincoln warned. "You can have no conflict, without being yourselves the aggressors. *You* have no oath registered in Heaven to destroy the government, while *I* shall have the most solemn one to 'preserve, protect, and defend' it." What Southerners in Charleston held in their hands at that very moment were the cords for firing the cannons that they aimed at the federal garrison at Fort Sumter.

Conclusion: The Failure of Compromise

Northerners and Southerners had clashed as early as the writing of the Constitution. As their economies, societies, and cultures diverged in the early nineteenth century, friction increased. Sectionalism then shifted into a new gear in 1846 when David Wilmot proposed banning slavery in any territory won in the Mexican War. "As if by magic," a Boston newspaper observed, "it brought to a head the great question that is about to divide the American people." During the extended crisis of the Union that stretched from 1846 to 1861, the nation's attention fixed on the expansion of slavery. From the beginning, though, both Northerners and Southerners recognized that the controversy had less to do with the expansion of slavery than with the future of slavery in America.

For more than seventy years, imaginative statesmen had found compromises that accepted slavery and preserved the Union. Citizens on both sides of the Mason-Dixon line took enormous pride in the national experiment in republican democracy, and few gave up the experiment easily. But accommodation had limits. In 1859, John Brown had pushed white Southerners to the edge. Lincoln's election in 1860 convinced whites in the Deep South that slavery and the society they had built on it were at risk in the Union, and they seceded. In his inaugural, Lincoln pleaded, "We are not enemies but friends. We must not be enemies." By then, however, the Deep South had ceased to sing what he called "the chorus of the Union." It remained to be seen whether disunion would mean war.

www.bedfordstmartins.com/tap SEE THE ONLINE STUDY GUIDE to test your mastery of the material covered in this chapter.

CHRONOLOGY

1846   Wilmot Proviso proposes barring slavery from all lands acquired in Mexican War.

1847   John C. Calhoun challenges Wilmot Proviso on constitutional grounds, stating that Congress has no power to exclude slavery from territories.

Senator Lewis Cass offers compromise of "popular sovereignty," allowing people of territories to determine fate of slavery.

1848   Opponents of expansion of slavery found Free-Soil Party.

Whig candidate General Zachary Taylor elected president of United States, defeating Democrat Lewis Cass and Free-Soil candidate Martin Van Buren.

1850s   Vigilance committees in North challenge and sometimes thwart Fugitive Slave Act.

1850   **July 9.** President Zachary Taylor dies; succeeded by Vice President Millard Fillmore.

Senator Henry Clay proposes Omnibus Bill to avert territorial crisis over slavery; bill ultimately defeated.

Senator Stephen Douglas's compromise bills (Compromise of 1850) pass Congress, signed into law by President Fillmore.

1852   Harriet Beecher Stowe's *Uncle Tom's Cabin* published in book form.

Democrat Franklin Pierce elected president of the United States, defeating Whig Winfield Scott.

1853   Gadsden Purchase adds 30,000 square miles of territory in present-day Arizona and New Mexico.

1854   American Party (Know-Nothings) emerges, advocating nativist positions.

Kansas-Nebraska Act opens the Kansas and Nebraska Territories to popular sovereignty.

Republican Party emerges on platform opposing extension of slavery in territories.

1856   Armed conflict between proslavery and antislavery forces erupts in Kansas.

Preston Brooks of South Carolina brutally assaults Charles Sumner of Massachusetts on Senate floor.

Democrat James Buchanan elected president of United States, defeating Republican John C. Frémont.

1857   *Dred Scott* decision declares that African Americans have no constitutional rights, that Congress cannot exclude slavery in the territories, and that the Missouri Compromise is unconstitutional.

Nation experiences economic downturn, panic of 1857.

1858   In Illinois senatorial campaign, Abraham Lincoln and Stephen A. Douglas debate slavery; Douglas defeats Lincoln for Senate seat.

1859   **October 16.** John Brown's attempt to foment slave uprising in Harpers Ferry, Virginia, further alienates South and moves nation toward war.

1860   Republican Abraham Lincoln elected president in four-way race that divides electorate along sectional lines.

December 20. South Carolina secedes from Union.

1861   Representatives of seven southern states, meeting in Montgomery, Alabama, form Confederate States of America.

BIBLIOGRAPHY

GENERAL WORKS

John Ashworth, *Slavery, Capitalism, and Politics in the Antebellum Republic* (1995).

Eric Foner, *Politics and Ideology in the Age of the Civil War* (1980).

Michael F. Holt, *Political Parties and American Political Development from the Age of Jackson to the Age of Lincoln* (1992).

Michael F. Holt, *The Rise and Fall of the American Whig Party: Jacksonian Politics and the Onset of the Civil War* (1999).

Bruce C. Levine, *Half Slave and Half Free: The Roots of Civil War* (1992).

Stephen E. Mazlish and John J. Kushman, eds., *Essays on American Antebellum Politics, 1840–1860* (1982).

James M. McPherson, *Ordeal by Fire: The Civil War and Reconstruction* (1982).

Allan Nevins, *Ordeal of the Union*, 2 vols. (1947).

Allan Nevins, *The Emergence of Lincoln*, 2 vols. (1950).

Roy F. Nichols, *Disruption of American Democracy* (1948).

David M. Potter, *The Impending Crisis, 1848–1861* (1976).

Anne C. Rose, *Voices of the Marketplace: American Thought and Culture, 1830–1860* (1995).

Kenneth M. Stampp, ed., *The Imperiled Union: Essays on the Background of the Civil War* (1980).

Kenneth M. Stampp, ed., *The Causes of the Civil War* (rev. ed., 1991).

Mark W. Summers, *The Plundering Generation: Corruption and the Crisis of the Union, 1849–1861* (1987).

SLAVERY IN THE TERRITORIES

Paul H. Bergeron, *The Presidency of James K. Polk* (1987).

Eugene H. Berwanger, *The Frontier against Slavery: Western Anti-Negro Prejudice and the Slavery Extension Controversy* (1967).

Don E. Fehrenbacher, *The Dred Scott Case: Its Significance in American Law and Politics* (1978).

Paul Finkelman, *An Imperfect Union: Slavery, Federalism, and Comity* (1981).

Holman Hamilton, *Prologue to Conflict: The Crisis and Compromise of 1850* (1964).

Michael F. Holt, *The Political Crisis of the 1850s* (1978).

Robert W. Johannsen, *Stephen A. Douglas* (1973).

Chaplain W. Morrison, *Democratic Politics and Sectionalism: The Wilmot Proviso Controversy* (1967).

James A. Rawley, *Race and Politics: "Bleeding Kansas" and the Coming of the Civil War* (1969).

Joseph G. Rayback, *Free Soil: The Election of 1848* (1970).

Kenneth M. Stampp, *America in 1857: A Nation on the Brink* (1990).

Gerald W. Wolff, *The Kansas-Nebraska Bill: Party, Section, and the Coming of the Civil War* (1977).

NORTHERN SECTIONALISM

Richard H. Abbott, *Cotton and Capital: Boston Businessmen and Antislavery Reform, 1854–1868* (1991).

Tyler Anbinder, *Nativism and Slavery: The Northern Know Nothings and the Politics of the 1850s* (1992).

Jean H. Baker, *Affairs of Party: The Political Culture of Northern Democrats in the Mid-Nineteenth Century* (1983).

R. J. M. Blackett, *Building an Antislavery Wall: Black Americans in the Atlantic Abolitionist Movement, 1830–1860* (1983).

Frederick J. Blue, *The Free Soilers: Third Party Politics, 1848–1854* (1973).

Stanley W. Campbell, *The Slave Catchers: Enforcement of the Fugitive Slave Law, 1850–1860* (1970).

Gary Lee Collison, *Shadrach Minkins: From Fugitive Slave to Citizen* (1997).

Robert F. Dalzell Jr., *Daniel Webster and the Trial of American Nationalism, 1843–1852* (1972).

David H. Donald, *Charles Sumner and the Coming of the Civil War* (1960).

Robert R. Dykstra, *Bright Radical Star: Black Freedom and White Supremacy on the Hawkeye Frontier* (1993).

Don E. Fehrenbacher, *Prelude to Greatness: Lincoln in the 1850s* (1962).

Eric Foner, *Free Soil, Free Labor, Free Men: The Ideology of the Republican Party before the Civil War* (1970).

George B. Forgie, *Patricide in the House Divided: A Psychological Interpretation of Lincoln and His Age* (1979).

Ronald P. Formisano, *The Birth of Mass Political Parties: Michigan, 1827–1861* (1971).

William E. Gienapp, *The Origins of the Republican Party, 1852–1856* (1987).

Thomas F. Gossett, *"Uncle Tom's Cabin" and American Culture* (1985).

Len Gougeon, *Virtue's Hero: Emerson, Antislavery, and Reform* (1990).

David Grimsted, *American Mobbing, 1828–1865: Toward Civil War* (1998).

Joan D. Hedrick, *Harriet Beecher Stowe: A Life* (1994).

Pamela Herr, *Jessie Benton Frémont: A Biography* (1987).

Pamela Herr and Mary Lee Spence, eds., *The Letters of Jessie Benton Frémont* (1993).

Harry V. Jaffa, *Crisis of the House Divided: An Interpretation of the Issues in the Lincoln-Douglas Debates* (1959).

Robert W. Johannsen, *Lincoln, the South, and Slavery: The Political Dimension* (1991).

Bruce C. Levine, *The Spirit of 1848: German Immigrants, Labor Conflict, and the Coming of the Civil War* (1992).

William S. McFeely, *Frederick Douglass* (1991).

John R. McKivigan, *The War against Proslavery Religion: Abolitionism and the Northern Churches, 1830–1865* (1984).

Thomas D. Morris, *Free Men All: The Personal Liberty Laws of the North, 1780–1861* (1974).

Stephen B. Oates, *To Purge This Land with Blood: A Biography of John Brown* (2nd ed., 1984).

Benjamin Quarles, *Allies for Freedom: Blacks and John Brown* (1974).

James A. Rawley, *Race and Politics: "Bleeding Kansas" and the Coming of the Civil War* (1969).

Anne C. Rose, *Victorian America and the Civil War* (1992).

Louis Ruchames, ed., *John Brown: The Making of a Revolutionary* (1959).

Richard H. Sewell, *Ballots for Freedom: Antislavery Politics in the United States, 1837–1860* (1976).

Thomas P. Slaughter, *Bloody Dawn: The Christiana Riot and Racial Violence in the Antebellum North* (1991).

James Brewer Stewart, *Holy Warriors: The Abolitionists and American Slavery* (1976).

James Brewer Stewart, *Wendell Phillips, Liberty's Hero* (1986).

Hans L. Trefousse, *The Radical Republicans: Lincoln's Vanguard for Racial Justice* (1969).

Wendy Hamand Venet, *Neither Ballots nor Bullets: Women Abolitionists and the Civil War* (1991).

Albert J. Von Frank, *The Trials of Anthony Burns: Freedom and Slavery in Emerson's Boston* (1998).

Ronald G. Walters, *The Antislavery Appeal: American Abolitionism after 1830* (1976).

Douglas L. Wilson, *Honor's Voice: The Transformation of Abraham Lincoln* (1998).

David Zarefsky, *Lincoln, Douglas, and Slavery: In the Crucible of Public Debate* (1990).

SOUTHERN SECTIONALISM

William L. Barney, *The Road to Secession: A New Perspective on the Old South* (1972).

John Barnwell, *Love of Order: South Carolina's First Secession Crisis* (1982).

Irving H. Bartlett, *John C. Calhoun: A Biography* (1993).

Tom Chaffin, *Fatal Glory: Narciso López and the First Clandestine U.S. War against Cuba* (1996).

William J. Cooper Jr., *The South and the Politics of Slavery, 1828–1856* (1978).

Drew Gilpin Faust, *James Henry Hammond and the Old South: A Design for Mastery* (1982).

Don E. Fehrenbacher, *The South and Three Sectional Crises* (1980).

Lacy K. Ford Jr., *Origins of Southern Radicalism: The South Carolina Upcountry, 1800–1860* (1988).

William W. Freehling, *The Road to Disunion,* Vol. 1, *Secessionists at Bay, 1776–1854* (1990).

Thelma Jennings, *The Nashville Convention: Southern Movement for Unity, 1848–1851* (1980).

Vicki Vaughn Johnson, *The Men and the Vision of the Southern Commercial Conventions, 1845–1871* (1992).

Robert E. May, *The Southern Dream of a Caribbean Empire, 1854–1861* (1973).

John McCardell, *The Idea of a Southern Nation: Southern Nationalists and Southern Nationalism, 1830–1860* (1979).

John Niven, *John C. Calhoun and the Price of Union: A Biography* (1988).

James Oakes, *Slavery and Freedom: An Interpretation of the Old South* (1990).

David M. Potter, *The South and the Sectional Conflict* (1968).

Mitchell Snay, *Gospel of Disunion: Religion and Separatism in the Antebellum South* (1993).

Ronald T. Takaki, *A Pro-Slavery Crusade: The Agitation to Reopen the African Slave Trade* (1971).

J. Mills Thornton III, *Politics and Power in a Slave Society: Alabama, 1800–1860* (1978).

Eric H. Walther, *The Fire-Eaters* (1992).

SECESSION

William L. Barney, *The Secessionist Impulse: Alabama and Mississippi in 1860* (1974).

Walter L. Buenger, *Secession and the Union in Texas* (1984).

Steven A. Channing, *Crisis of Fear: Secession in South Carolina* (1970).

Daniel W. Crofts, *Reluctant Confederates: Upper South Unionists in the Secession Crisis* (1989).

Dwight Lowell Dumond, *The Secession Movement, 1860–1861* (1931).

John Hope Franklin, *The Militant South, 1800–1861* (1956).

James L. Huston, *The Panic of 1857 and the Coming of the Civil War* (1987).

Michael P. Johnson, *Toward a Patriarchal Republic: The Secession of Georgia* (1977).

David M. Potter, *Lincoln and His Party in the Secession Crisis* (1942).

Kenneth M. Stampp, *And the War Came: The North and the Secession Crisis, 1860–61* (1960).

James M. Woods, *Rebellion and Realignment: Arkansas's Road to Secession* (1987).

Ralph A. Wooster, *The Secession Conventions of the South* (1962).

DAGUERREOTYPE OF UNION DRUMMER BOY

The Civil War is often called a "brother's war." Families sometimes split and offered up soldiers for both the Union and the Confederate armies. But the war was also a children's war, as this daguerreotype of the twelve-year-old Johnny Clem, a Union drummer boy, reminds us. Clem ran away from his Ohio home when he was ten, joined the Twenty-second Michigan Regiment, and fought with it in all its major battles from Shiloh to Atlanta. He became a hero in the North when, during the retreat of Union soldiers at Chickamauga, he shot and wounded a Confederate officer with a sawed-off musket cut down to his small size. When he retired from the U.S. Army in 1915, Major General John L. Clem was the last federal soldier who had fought in the Civil War. Clem's face shows no trace of the horrors he had seen, but even children who stayed at home often experienced the heartbreak of youth destroyed and innocence lost.

Library of Congress.

THE CRUCIBLE OF WAR
1861–1865

14

I N 1838, A TWENTY-YEAR-OLD MARYLAND SLAVE by the name of Frederick Bailey fled north to freedom. The young runaway took a new name, Frederick Douglass, and might understandably have settled into obscurity, content just to avoid the slave catchers and to live quietly as a free man. Instead, he chose to wage war against slavery. In 1841, an agent for the Massachusetts Anti-Slavery Society observed that "the public have itching ears to hear a colored man speak, and particularly a *slave*." Dozens of fugitive slaves brought to northern audiences the authority of hard personal experience. None stripped away the myth of the contented slave more eloquently than Frederick Douglass. In 1845, he published his immensely popular autobiography. In 1847, he began the *North Star*, an antislavery newspaper that reached thousands. Douglass's powerful denunciations of slavery and moving pleas for emancipation made him the most famous African American in the English-speaking world.

Throughout the 1840s and 1850s, Douglass remained optimistic in public, but in private he feared that he labored in vain. In his eyes, his two decades of speaking and writing had brought the country no closer to ending slavery. In some ways the situation had grown worse. When Douglass fled slavery in 1838, two million Americans were in bondage. By 1860, the number of slaves had doubled to four million. Every step forward—the birth of the Republican Party, for instance—was followed by a giant step back, such as the *Dred Scott* decision. To Douglass, the 1850s ended as they began, no closer to the eradication of slavery. "How long! How long! O Lord God of Sabbath!" he cried, "shall the crushed and bleeding bondsman wait?"

During the secession winter of 1860–61, Douglass found himself torn between hope and despair. Abraham Lincoln's election in November had revived his optimism in the wake of the *Dred Scott* decision. "The slaveholders know that the day of their power is over," Douglass exulted. But he realized that the Republican Party's free-soil principles fell short of abolition. Republicans opposed slavery's right to expand into the national territories, not slavery's right to exist in the South. Indeed, Douglass feared that the Republicans would become "the best protectors of slavery where it now is."

When news came from Charleston in April 1861 that Southerners had fired on the American flag, Douglass celebrated the outbreak of fighting. He realized that in going to war Lincoln was striking out against "treason and rebellion," but much earlier than most, he also understood that a war to save the Union would inevitably affect slavery. The South had initiated a "war for slavery," Douglass said, and it followed that a war to crush southern independence must become a war *against* slavery. Even though "the Government is not yet on the side of the oppressed, events mightier than the Government are bringing about that result," Douglass declared. "*Friends of freedom!*" he cried, "*be up and doing;—now is your time.*" Few Northerners, certainly not Abraham Lincoln, agreed that the outbreak of fighting marked mated 633,000 lives, nearly as many as in all of its other wars before and after. The war helped mold the modern American nation-state. The federal government emerged with new power and responsibility over national life. War furthered the emergence of a modern industrializing nation. But because the war to preserve the Union also became a war to destroy slavery, the northern victory had truly revolutionary meaning. Defeat and emancipation destroyed the slave society of the Old South and gave birth to a different society.

Years later, remembering the Civil War years, Douglass said, "It is something to couple one's name with great occasions." It *was* something—for millions of Americans. Whether they battled or defended the Confederacy, whether they labored behind the lines to produce goods for northern or southern soldiers, whether they kept the home fires burning for Yankees or rebels, all Americans experienced the crucible of war. But the war affected no group more than the four million African Americans who saw its beginning in 1861 as slaves and emerged in 1865 as free people.

FREDERICK DOUGLASS, 1852
Samuel J. Miller made this daguerreotype of Frederick Douglass in Akron, Ohio, a hotbed of abolitionism. Douglass self-consciously employed an aggressive posture and fiery expression to fashion his identity as a free man dead set on eradicating slavery. Fellow abolitionists understood that the "very look and bearing of Douglass are an irresistible logic against the oppression of his race."
Art Institute of Chicago.

the beginning of the end of slavery. For eighteen months, Union soldiers fought solely to uphold the Constitution and preserve the nation. But in 1863, as Douglass foresaw, the northern war effort took on a dual purpose: to save the Union and to free the slaves.

Even if the Civil War had not touched slavery, the conflict still would have transformed America. As the world's first modern war, it mobilized entire populations, harnessed the productive capacities of entire economies, and enlisted millions of troops, with single battles fielding 200,000 soldiers and producing casualties in the tens of thousands. The carnage lasted four years and cost the nation an esti-

"And the War Came"

New to high office, Abraham Lincoln faced the worst crisis in the history of the nation: the threat of disunion. Lincoln revealed his strategy on March 4, 1861, in his inaugural address, which was carefully crafted to combine firmness and conciliation. First, he would try to stop the contagion of secession. Eight of the fifteen slave states had said no to disunion, but they remained suspicious and skittish. Lincoln was determined to avoid any act that would push the Upper South (North Carolina, Virginia, Maryland, Delaware, Kentucky, Tennessee, Missouri, and Arkansas) into leaving. Second, he would buy time so that emotions could cool. By reassuring the Deep South (South Carolina, Georgia, Florida, Alabama, Mississippi, Louisiana, and Texas) that slavery would not be abolished, he would provide Unionists there the opportunity to reassert themselves and to overturn the secession decision. Always, Lincoln expressed his uncompromising will to oppose secession and to uphold the Union.

His counterpart, Jefferson Davis, fully intended to establish the Confederate States of America as an independent republic. To achieve permanence,

Davis had to sustain the secession fever that had carried the Deep South out of the Union and to dampen reunion sentiment. Even if the Deep South held firm, however, the Confederacy remained weak without additional states from the Upper South. Davis watched for opportunities to add new stars to the Confederate flag.

Neither man sought war. Both wanted to achieve their objectives peacefully. But as Lincoln later observed, "Both parties deprecated war, but one of them would *make* war rather than let the nation survive, and the other would *accept* war rather than let it perish. And the war came."

Attack on Fort Sumter

Fort Sumter's thick brick walls rose forty feet above the tiny island on which it perched at the entrance to Charleston harbor. Only four miles from the city, the fortress with its Union flag was a sight that infuriated Confederates. Major Robert Anderson and some eighty U.S. soldiers occupied what Charlestonians claimed as Confederate property. The fort became a hateful symbol of the nation Southerners had abandoned, and they wanted federal troops out. But Sumter was also a symbol to Northerners, a beacon affirming federal sovereignty in the seceded states.

The situation at Fort Sumter presented the new president with hard choices. Ordering the fort's evacuation would play well in the Upper South, whose edgy slave states threatened to bolt to the Confederacy if Lincoln resorted to military force. But yielding the fort would make it appear that Lincoln accepted the Confederacy's existence. Abandonment would divide the North, batter the new Republican administration, and magnify the rebel nation's status in the eyes of the world. Lincoln decided to hold Fort Sumter. But to do so, he had to provision it, for Anderson was running dangerously short of food. In the first week in April, Lincoln authorized a peaceful expedition to bring supplies, but not military reinforcements, to the fort. The president understood that he risked war, but his plan honored his inaugural promises to defend federal property and to avoid using military force unless first attacked. Masterfully, Lincoln had shifted the fateful decision of war or peace to Jefferson Davis.

On April 9, 1861, Jefferson Davis and his cabinet met to consider the situation in Charleston harbor. The territorial integrity of the Confederacy demanded the end of the federal presence, Davis argued. But his secretary of state, Robert Toombs of Georgia, pleaded against military action. "Mr. President," he declared, "at this time it is suicide, murder, and will lose us every friend at the North. You will wantonly strike a hornet's nest which extends from mountain to ocean, and legions now quiet will swarm out and sting us to death." Davis rejected Toombs's prophecy and sent word to General Pierre Gustave T. Beauregard, the Louisianan commanding Confederate troops in Charleston, to take the fort before the relief expedition arrived. Thirty-three hours of bombardment on April 12 and 13 reduced the fort to rubble, but, miraculously, not a single Union soldier died. On April 14, with the fort ablaze, Major Anderson offered his surrender. The Confederates had Fort Sumter, but they also had a war.

The fort became a hateful symbol of the nation Southerners had abandoned. But Sumter was also a symbol to Northerners, a beacon affirming federal sovereignty in the seceded states.

The response of the free states was thunderous. On April 15, Lincoln called for seventy-five thousand militia to serve for ninety days to put down the rebellion, and several times that number rushed to defend the flag. Lincoln asked Indiana for six regiments, and the governor wired that "without seriously repressing the ardor of the people, I can hardly stop short of twenty." Democrats responded as fervently as Republicans. Stephen A. Douglas, the recently defeated Democratic candidate for president, pledged his support. "There are only two sides to the question," he told a massive crowd in Chicago. "Every man must be for the United States or against it. There can be no neutrals in this war, *only patriots—or traitors.*" No one faced more acutely the dilemma of loyalty than the men and women of the Upper South.

The Upper South Chooses Sides

Lincoln's call for troops presented the Upper South with a horrendous choice: either to fight against the Lower South or to fight against the Union. Many who had only months earlier rejected secession now embraced the Confederacy. To oppose southern independence was one thing; to fight fellow Southerners was another. Thousands felt betrayed, believing that Lincoln had promised to achieve a peaceful reunion by waiting patiently for Unionists to reassert themselves in the seceding states. One man furiously denounced the conflict as a "politician's war," conceding that "this is no time now to discuss the causes, but it is the duty of all who regard Southern institutions of value to side with the South, make common cause with the Confederate States and sink or swim with them."

Some found the choice excruciating. Robert E. Lee, a career military officer and the son of one of Virginia's oldest families, denounced the Lower South's separation as the work of cotton-state hotheads. "I can anticipate no greater calamity for the country than a dissolution of the Union," he had told his son in January 1861. Still, he said, "a Union that can only be maintained by swords and bayonets . . . has no charm for me." Following the bombardment of Fort Sumter, Lee left his white-columned mansion in Arlington, Virginia, and crossed the Potomac River to Washington, D.C., where General Winfield Scott, the general-in-chief, on Lincoln's authority, offered him command of federal military forces. But Lee could not fight against the South. When he returned home, he learned that

Virginia had left the Union. He quickly penned his resignation from the U.S. army and declared, "Save in defense of my native State, I never desire again to draw my sword."

One by one the other states of the Upper South jumped off the fence. Within weeks, Arkansas, North Carolina, and Tennessee followed Virginia's lead (Map 14.1). But in the border states of Delaware, Maryland, Kentucky, and Missouri, Unionism triumphed. Only in Delaware, though, where slaves accounted for less than 2 percent of the population, was the victory easy. In Maryland, Unionism needed a helping hand. Rather than allow the state to secede and make Washington, D.C., a federal island in a Confederate sea, Lincoln suspended the writ of habeas corpus, essentially setting aside normal constitutional guarantees such as trial before a jury of peers, and marched troops into Baltimore. Maryland's legislature, frightened by the federal invasion and aware of the strength of Union sentiment in the western counties, rejected secession.

The struggle turned violent in the West. In Missouri, Unionists won a narrow victory, but southern-sympathizing guerrilla bands roamed the state for the duration of the conflict, wreaking bloody havoc on civilians and soldiers alike. In Ken-

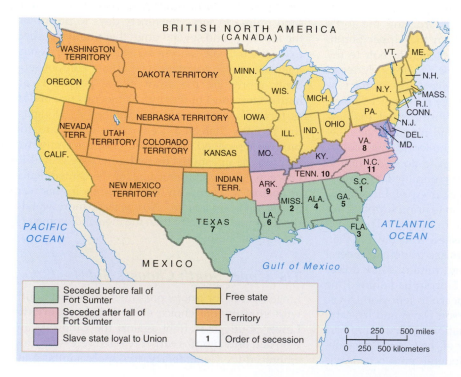

MAP 14.1

Secession, 1860–1861
After Lincoln's election, the fifteen slave states debated what to do. Seven states quickly left the Union, four left after the firing on Fort Sumter, and four refused to go.

tucky, as in Missouri, Unionists barely defeated secession and a prosouthern minority claimed that the state had severed its ties with the Union. The government that chose Richmond, Virginia, as its capital was not particularly fastidious in counting votes and eagerly made Missouri and Kentucky the twelfth and thirteenth Confederate states.

Throughout the border states, but especially in Kentucky, the Civil War was truly a "brother's war." Seven of Henry Clay's grandsons fought: four for the Confederacy and three for the Union. Lincoln understood that the border states—particularly Kentucky—not only contained indispensable resources, population, and wealth but also controlled major rivers and railroads. "I think to lose Kentucky is nearly the same as to lose the whole game," Lincoln said. "Kentucky gone, we can not hold Missouri, nor, as I think, Maryland. These all against us, . . . we would as well consent to separation at once."

Throughout the border states, but especially in Kentucky, the Civil War was truly a "brother's war."

In the end, only eleven of the fifteen slave states joined the Confederate States of America. Moreover, the four seceding Upper South states contained significant numbers of people who felt little affection for the Confederacy. Dissatisfaction was so rife in the western counties of Virginia that in 1863 citizens there voted to create the separate state of West Virginia, loyal to the Union. Still, the acquisition of four new Confederate states greatly strengthened the cause of southern independence.

The Combatants

Although fierce struggle continued in the border states and in some areas within the seceding states of the Upper South, most whites in the South chose to defend the Confederacy. For them, Yankee "aggression" was no longer a secessionist's abstraction; it was real, and it was at their door. For Northerners, rebel "treason" threatened to destroy the noble experiment of republican self-government. Men rallied behind their separate battle flags, fully convinced that they were in the right and that God was on their side.

While both sides claimed the lion's share of virtue, no one could argue that the South's resources and forces equaled the North's. A glance at the census figures contradicted such a notion. Yankees took heart at their superior power, but the rebels believed they had advantages that nullified every northern strength. Both sides mobilized swiftly in the spring and summer of 1861, and each devised what it believed would be a winning military and diplomatic strategy.

What They Fought For

Across the South, planters, yeomen, and artisans raced to enlist and to fight Yankees. Only slaveholders had a direct economic stake (estimated at some $3 billion in 1860) in preserving slavery, but almost all white Southerners—slaveholders and nonslaveholders alike—united in the defense of the institution. Slavery controlled blacks, whom they thought an inferior and potentially dangerous race. Moreover, the degraded and subjugated status of blacks was the basis of an elevated status for even the most humble whites. "It matters not whether slaves be actually owned by many or by few," one observer declared. "It is enough that one simply belongs to the superior and ruling race, to secure consideration and respect."

Rather than explicitly naming slavery as their reason for fighting, however, ordinary whites emphasized defending a special southern civilization from "subjugation" and protecting hearth and home from northern hordes bent on plunder and domination. Even planters and Confederate officials shied away from publicly identifying their cause with slavery. Instead, their rhetoric overflowed with lofty abstractions such as states' rights, self-determination, and liberty. But without slavery there would have been no distinctive southern civilization, no Republican Party to threaten it, and no reason to ensure it by creating a separate nation.

In 1861, white Southerners equated their position with that of American patriots in 1776. In both cases, they argued, a freedom-loving minority waged war to protect its liberty against the encroachments of a tyrannical central government. As one Georgia woman observed, Southerners wanted "nothing from the North but—*to be let alone*—and *they,* a people like ourselves whose republican independence was won by a rebellion, whose liberty was achieved by a secession, to think that they should attempt to coerce us—the idea is preposterous."

Northerners saw secession as an unconscionable attack on the best government on earth. The South's failure to accept the lawful election of a president and its firing on the nation's flag challenged the rule of law, the authority of the Constitution, and the ability of the people to govern themselves. Northerners believed that the South's effort to wreck the Republic threatened them in a personal way. As an Indiana soldier told his wife, a "good government is the best thing on earth. Property is nothing without it, because it is not protected; a family is nothing without it, because they cannot be educated."

Lincoln captured the Union's special magnetism. "This is essentially a People's contest," he declared on the first Fourth of July after the war began. The Union's cause, he said, was the preservation of the government "whose leading object is, to elevate the condition of man—to lift artificial weights from all shoulders—to clear the paths of laudable pursuit for all—to afford all, an unfettered start, and a fair chance, in the race of life." In short, secession menaced the life chances of millions of eager and aspiring individuals. Self-interest as well as patriotic fervor welded Northerners to the preservation of the nation.

How They Expected to Win

The balance sheet of northern and southern resources reveals enormous advantages for the Union (Figure 14.1). The twenty-three states remaining in the Union had a population of 22.3 million, while the eleven Confederate states had a population of only 9.1 million, of whom 3.67 million (40 percent) were slaves. The North had 22,000 miles of railroads; the South, only 9,280. The North manufactured more than 90 percent of the nation's industrial goods. It produced 13 times as much textiles; 32 times as much coal; 16 times as much iron; and 32 times as many firearms. The list is nearly endless. So overwhelming were the North's advantages that the question becomes why the South made war at all. Was not the South's cause lost before Confederates lobbed the first rounds at Fort Sumter? The answer quite simply is no. Southerners expected to win—and for some good reasons. They came very close to doing it.

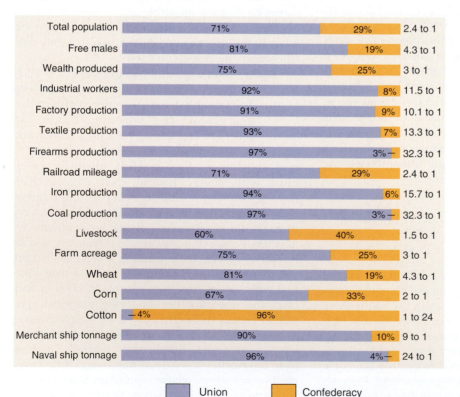

	Union	Confederacy	Ratio
Total population	71%	29%	2.4 to 1
Free males	81%	19%	4.3 to 1
Wealth produced	75%	25%	3 to 1
Industrial workers	92%	8%	11.5 to 1
Factory production	91%	9%	10.1 to 1
Textile production	93%	7%	13.3 to 1
Firearms production	97%	3%	32.3 to 1
Railroad mileage	71%	29%	2.4 to 1
Iron production	94%	6%	15.7 to 1
Coal production	97%	3%	32.3 to 1
Livestock	60%	40%	1.5 to 1
Farm acreage	75%	25%	3 to 1
Wheat	81%	19%	4.3 to 1
Corn	67%	33%	2 to 1
Cotton	4%	96%	1 to 24
Merchant ship tonnage	90%	10%	9 to 1
Naval ship tonnage	96%	4%	24 to 1

■ Union ■ Confederacy

FIGURE 14.1

Resources of the Union and Confederacy
The Union's enormous statistical advantages failed to convince Confederates that their cause was doomed.

Southerners believed that they would triumph because of their region's lofty cause, superior civilization, and unsurpassed character. They bucked the military odds, but hadn't the liberty-loving colonists in 1776, too? "Britain could not conquer three million," a Louisianan proclaimed, and "the world cannot conquer the South." How could anyone doubt the outcome of a contest between lean, hard, country-born rebel warriors defending family, property, and liberty, and soft, flabby, citified Yankee mechanics waging an unconstitutional war of aggression and subjugation? No wonder Southerners would claim

after the war that they had not been "whipped" but had "worn themselves out whipping Yankees."

The South's confidence also rested on its estimation of the economic clout of cotton. A war correspondent for the *London Times* found that "King Cotton" was "the fixed idea everywhere." For years Southerners had argued that northern prosperity depended on the South's cotton. Without southern cotton, New England textile mills would stand idle. Without southern planters purchasing northern manufactured goods, northern factories would drown in their own surpluses. Without the foreign exchange

BRIDGE ON THE ORANGE AND ALEXANDRIA RAILROAD
Confederate forces burned southern railroads and bridges to slow Union advances, cut federal supply lines, and protect Confederate retreats. West Point–trained Herman Haupt, seen here inspecting a rebuilt bridge, was in charge of the Union's efforts at railroad construction and repair. While the railroad had been used as an instrument of war in the Crimea in the 1850s, it was during the Civil War that the railroad took on revolutionary importance. Railroads helped set new standards of overland mobility, rapid maneuver, and concentration of forces.
Library of Congress.

earned by the overseas sales of cotton, the financial structure of the entire Yankee nation would collapse. One Virginian spoke for most Confederates when he declared that in the South's ability to "withhold the benefits of our trade, we hold a power over the North more powerful than a powerful army in the field."

Southerners believed that they would triumph because of their region's lofty cause, superior civilization, and unsurpassed character. They bucked the military odds, but hadn't the liberty-loving colonists in 1776, too?

King Cotton also could make Europe a powerful ally of the Confederacy. After all, Southerners said, England's economy (and to a lesser degree, France's) depended on cotton. Of the 900 million pounds of cotton England imported annually, more than 700 million came from the South. If the supply were interrupted, sheer necessity would make England (and perhaps France) a Confederate ally. And because the British navy ruled the seas, the North would find Britain a formidable foe.

Southerners' faith in their ability may seem naive today because that faith turned out to have been misplaced. But even tough-minded European military observers picked the South to win. Offsetting the North's power was the South's expanse. The North, Europeans predicted, could not conquer the vast territory (750,000 square miles) from the Potomac to the Rio Grande, with its rugged terrain and bad roads. It would require raising a massive invading army, supplying it with huge quantities of provisions and arms, and protecting supply lines that would stretch farther than any in modern history.

Indeed, the South enjoyed major advantages, and the Confederacy devised a military strategy to exploit them. Jefferson Davis called it an "offensive-defensive" strategy. It recognized that a Union victory required the North to defeat and subjugate the South. A Confederate victory required only that the South stay at home, blunt invasions, avoid battles that risked annihilating its army, and outlast the northern will to fight. When an opportunity presented itself, the South would strike the invaders. Like the American colonists, the South could win independence by not losing the war.

If the North did nothing, the South would by default establish itself as a sovereign nation. The Lincoln administration therefore adopted an offensive strategy. On April 19, four days after the president issued the proclamation calling for a militia to put down the rebellion, he issued another proclamation declaring a naval blockade of the Confederacy. He sought to deny the Confederacy the use of its most valuable commodity—cotton. Without the sale of cotton abroad, the South would have far fewer dollars to pay for war goods. Even before the North could mount an effective blockade, however, Jefferson Davis decided voluntarily to cease exporting cotton. He wanted to create a cotton "famine" that would enfeeble the northern economy and precipitate European intervention.

Southerners were not the only ones with illusions. Lincoln's call for seventy-five thousand men for ninety days illustrates his failure to predict the magnitude and duration of the war. He was not alone. Most Americans thought of war in terms of their most recent experience, the Mexican War in the 1840s. In Mexico, fighting had taken place between relatively small armies, had cost relatively few lives, and had inflicted only light damage on the countryside. Americans on the eve of the Civil War could not know that four ghastly years of bloodletting lay ahead. Early theories and strategies, however, like the expectations of military glory and fame, quickly confronted harsh reality.

Lincoln and Davis Mobilize

Mobilization required effective political leadership, and at first glance it appeared that the South had the decided advantage. An aristocrat from a Mississippi planter family, Jefferson Davis brought to the Confederate presidency a distinguished political career, including experience in the U.S. Senate. He was also a West Point graduate, a combat veteran of the Mexican War, and a former secretary of war. Dignified and erect, with "a jaw sawed in *steel*," Davis appeared to be everything a nation could want in a wartime leader.

In contrast, an Illinois lawyer-politician occupied the White House. He brought with him one lackluster term in the House of Representatives, where he had opposed the Mexican War in which Davis had served gallantly. He had almost no administrative experience, and his sole brush with anything military was as a captain in the militia in the Black Hawk War, a brief struggle in Illinois in 1832 in which whites expelled the last Indians from the state. Lincoln later joked about his service in the Black Hawk War as the time when he survived bloody encounters with mosquitoes and led raids on wild onion patches. The lanky, disheveled Westerner looked anything but military or presidential in his bearing, and even his friends feared that he was in over his head.

Davis, however, proved to be less than he appeared. Possessing little capacity for broad military strategy and yet vain about what he regarded as his own superior judgment, he intervened constantly in military affairs. He was an even less able political leader. Quarrelsome and proud, he had an acid tongue that made enemies the Confederacy could ill afford. The Confederacy's intimidating problems might have defeated an even more talented leader, however. For example, state sovereignty, which was enshrined in the Confederate constitution, made Davis's task of organizing a new nation and fighting a war difficult in the extreme. His wife, Varina Davis, reported that her husband "hardly takes time to eat his meals and works late at night," but his best efforts proved inadequate.

In Lincoln, however, the North got far more than met the eye. He proved himself a master politician and a superb leader. He never allowed personal feelings to get in the way of his objectives. When forming his cabinet, for example, Lincoln shrewdly appointed representatives of every Republican faction, men who were often his chief rivals and critics. He made Salmon P. Chase secretary of the treasury, knowing that Chase had presidential ambitions. As secretary of state, he chose his chief opponent for the Republican nomination in 1860, William H. Seward, who expected to twist Lincoln around his little finger and formulate policy himself. Despite his civilian background, Lincoln displayed an innate understanding of military strategy. In time, no one was more crucial in mapping the Union war plan. Further, Lincoln was an enormously eloquent man who reached out to the North's people, galvanizing them in defense of the nation he called "the last best hope of earth."

Guided by Lincoln and Davis, the North and South began gathering their armies. Southerners had the task of building almost everything from scratch, and Northerners had to mobilize their superior numbers and industrial resources for war. In 1861, the puny federal army numbered only sixteen thousand men, most of whom were scattered over the West subjugating Indians. One-third of the officers who wore Union blue followed Robert E. Lee's example, resigning their commissions and heading south. The navy was in better shape. Forty-two ships were in service, and a large merchant marine would in time provide more ships and sailors. Most of the officers and men were Northerners and loyal to the Union. Though it had strong leadership in its secretary of the navy, Stephen R. Mallory, the Confederate navy was never a match for the Union fleet, and thus the South pinned its hopes on its armies. Military companies sprang up everywhere. Since soldiers at first supplied their own uniforms, Confederate gray was just one of a rainbow of colors. Moreover, volunteers brought their own weapons, as often Bowie knives and shotguns as rifles and pistols.

In Lincoln the North got far more than met the eye. He proved himself a master politician and a superb leader.

From the beginning, the South exhibited more enthusiasm than ability to provide its soldiers with supplies and transportation. The Confederacy made prodigious efforts to build new factories to produce tents, blankets, shoes, and uniforms, but many soldiers slept in the open air without proper clothes and sometimes without shoes. Even when factories managed to produce what soldiers needed, southern railroads—constructed to connect plantations with ports—often could not deliver the goods. And with each year of the war, more railroads were captured, destroyed, or left in disrepair. Food production proved less of a problem, but food sometimes rotted before it reached the soldiers. The one bright spot was the Confederacy's Ordnance Bureau, headed by Josiah Gorgas, a near miracle worker when it came to manufacturing gunpower, cannons, and rifles. In April 1864, Gorgas observed: "Where three years ago we were not making a gun, a pistol nor a sabre, no shot nor shell . . .—a pound of powder—we now make all these in quantities to meet the demands of our large armies."

Recruiting and supplying huge armies required enormous public spending. Before the war, the federal government's tiny income had come primarily from tariff duties and the sale of public lands. Massive wartime expenditures made new revenues imperative. At first, both the North and the South resorted to selling war bonds, which essentially were loans from patriotic citizens. In time, both sides began printing paper money. Inflation soared, but the South suffered more because it financed a greater part of its wartime costs through the printing press. Prices in the North rose by about 80 percent during the war, while in the South inflation topped 9,000 percent. Eventually, the Union and the Confederacy turned to taxes, but whereas the North raised one-fifth of its wartime revenue from taxes, the South raised only one-twentieth.

Within months of the bombardment of Fort Sumter, both sides had found men to fight and people to supply and support them. But the underlying strength of the northern economy gave the Union the decided advantage. With their military and industrial muscles beginning to ripple, Northerners became itchy for action. Northerners wanted an invasion that would once and for all smash the rebellion. Horace Greeley's *New York Tribune* began the chant: "Forward to Richmond! Forward to Richmond!"

The Battlefields, 1861–1862

During the first year and a half of the war, armies fought major campaigns in two theaters: in Virginia-Maryland in the East and in Tennessee-Kentucky in the West. With the rival capitals of Richmond and Washington, D.C., only ninety miles apart and each threatened more than once with capture, the eastern campaign was more dramatic and commanded public attention. But the battles in the West proved more decisive. And as Yankee and rebel armies pounded each other on land, their navies fought it out on the seas and their diplomats sought advantage in the corridors of power in Europe. All the while, casualty lists reached appalling lengths.

Stalemate in the Eastern Theater

As commander in chief, Lincoln appointed Mexican War veteran Irvin McDowell to be commanding general of the army assembling outside Washington. McDowell had no thought of taking his raw recruits into battle during the summer of 1861, but Lincoln ordered McDowell to prepare his thirty thousand men for an attack on the Confederate army gathered at Manassas, a railroad junction in Virginia about thirty miles southwest of Washington. When McDowell complained, Lincoln replied,

"You are green, it is true, but they are green, also; you are all green."

Repeating to the last that he did not want to go, McDowell moved his greenhorn troops out on July 16. Five days later, the Union army forded Bull Run, a branch of the Potomac River, and engaged the southern forces effectively (Map 14.2). But fast-moving southern reinforcements blunted the Union attack and then counterattacked. What began as an orderly retreat turned into a panicky stampede. Demoralized soldiers ran over shocked civilians as they raced back to Washington.

By Civil War standards, casualties at Manassas (or Bull Run, as Northerners called the battle) were light; the significance of the battle lay in the lessons Northerners and Southerners drew from it. For Southerners, it confirmed the superiority of rebel fighting men and the inevitability of Confederate nationhood. Manassas was *"one of the decisive battles of the world,"* a Georgian proclaimed. It *"has* secured our independence." While victory lifted southern pride to new levels, defeat sobered Northerners. It was a major setback, admitted the *New York Tribune,* but, the writer added, "Let us go to work, then, with a will." Manassas taught Lincoln that victory would be neither quick nor easy. Within four days of the disaster, the president signed bills authorizing the enlistment of one million men for three years.

Lincoln also found a new general, replacing McDowell with the arrogant young George B. McClellan. Born in Philadelphia of well-to-do parents, educated in the best schools before graduating from West Point second in his class, the thirty-four-year-old McClellan believed that he was a great soldier and that Lincoln was a dunce, the "original Gorilla." A superb administrator and organizer, McClellan was brought to Washington as commander of the newly named Army of the Potomac. In the months following his appointment, McClellan energetically whipped his army of dispirited veterans and fresh recruits into shape. The troops cheered their boyish general when he rode among them, in part no doubt because of his reluctance to send them into battle. Lincoln said McClellan had a bad case of "the slows," and indeed McClellan, for all his energy, lacked decisiveness. Lincoln wanted a general who would advance, take risks, and fight, but McClellan went into winter quarters without budging from the Potomac. "If General McClellan does not want to use the army I would like to *borrow* it," Lincoln declared in frustration.

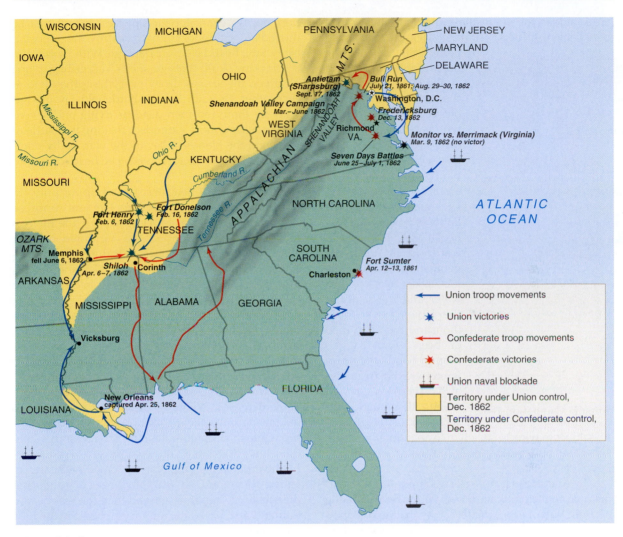

M A P   1 4 . 2
The Civil War, 1861–1862
*While eyes focused on the eastern theater, especially the tiny geography between the
two capitals of Washington and Richmond, strategic victories were being won by Union
troops in the West.*

Finally, in the spring of 1862, McClellan
launched his long-awaited offensive. He transported his highly polished army, now 130,000
strong, down the Chesapeake Bay to the mouth of
the James River and began moving up the peninsula
toward Richmond. McClellan took two and a half
months to advance sixty-five miles. When he was
within six miles of the Confederate capital, Confederate general Joseph Johnston hit him like a hammer. In the assault, Johnston was wounded and was

replaced by Robert E. Lee, the reluctant Confederate who would become the South's most celebrated
general. Lee named his command the Army of
Northern Virginia.

The contrast between Lee and McClellan could
hardly have been greater. McClellan overflowed
with conceit and braggadocio, while Lee was courteous and reserved. But on the battlefield, where Mc-
Clellan grew timid and irresolute, Lee became au-
daciously, even recklessly, aggressive. And Lee had

at his side in the peninsula campaign military men of real talent: General Thomas J. Jackson, nicknamed Stonewall for holding the line at Manassas, and James E. B. (Jeb) Stuart, the twenty-nine-year-old cavalry commander who wore a red-lined cape, yellow sash, and hat with ostrich-feather plume and rode circles around Yankee troops. Lee's assault initiated the Battle of Seven Days and began McClellan's backward march down the peninsula. By the time McClellan reached the water and the safety of the Union navy, thirty thousand men had died or been wounded. Although Southerners suffered twice the casualties of Northerners, Lee had saved Richmond and achieved a strategic success. Lincoln wired McClellan to abandon the peninsula campaign and replaced him with General John Pope.

Peninsula Campaign, 1862

In August, just north of Richmond, Pope had his own rendezvous with Lee. At the Second Battle of Bull Run, Lee's smaller army battered Pope's forces and sent them scurrying back to Washington. Lincoln ordered Pope to Minnesota to pacify Indians and again put McClellan in command. Lincoln had not changed his mind about McClellan's capacity as a warrior. Instead, he reluctantly concluded, "If he can't fight himself, he excels in making others ready to fight."

Lee could fight. Sensing that he had his enemy on the ropes, he sought to land the knockout punch. Lee pushed the Army of Northern Virginia across the Potomac and invaded Maryland. A victory on northern soil would dislodge Maryland from the Union, Lee reasoned, and might even cause Lincoln to sue for peace. On September 17, 1862, McClellan's forces finally engaged Lee's army at Antietam Creek (see Map. 14.2). Earlier, a Union soldier had found a copy of Lee's orders to his army wrapped around some cigars dropped by a careless Confederate officer. McClellan had a clear picture of Lee's position, but his characteristic slowness meant that he missed a great opportunity to destroy the opposing army. Still, he did it severe damage. With "solid shot . . . cracking skulls like egg-shells," according to one observer, the armies threw everything they had at each other. By nightfall the battlefield lay littered with six thousand men dead or dying and seventeen thousand more wounded, making the Battle of Antietam the bloodiest day of the war. Badly damaged and deeply disappointed, Lee headed back to Virginia.

But Lee remained alert for an opportunity to punish his enemy. In December, General Ambrose Burnside, yet another replacement for the ineffectual McClellan, provided the Virginian a fresh chance. At Fredericksburg, Virginia, Burnside's 122,000 Union troops faced 78,500 Confederates dug in behind a stone wall on the heights above the Rappahannock River. Half a mile of open ground lay between the armies. A Confederate artillery officer predicted that "a chicken could not live on that field when we open on it." Yet Burnside ordered a frontal assault, somehow convinced that Union soldiers could capture the heights. Wave after wave of bluecoats crashed against impregnable defenses. When the guns finally ceased, the federals counted nearly thirteen thousand casualties while the Confederates suffered fewer than five thousand. It was one of the Union's worst defeats. At the end of 1862, the North seemed no nearer to taking Richmond, to whipping Lee, or to ending the rebellion than it had been when the war began. Rather than checkmate, military struggle in the East had reached stalemate.

Union Victories in the Western Theater

While most eyes focused on the East, the decisive early encounters of the war took place between the Appalachian Mountains and the Ozarks. The West's rivers—the Mississippi, the Tennessee, and the Cumberland—became the keys to the military situation. Southerners looked northward along the rivers and spied Missouri and Kentucky, states they claimed but did not control. Looking southward, Northerners knew that by taking the Mississippi they would split Arkansas, Louisiana, and Texas from the Confederacy. And the Cumberland and Tennessee waterways penetrated Tennessee, one of the Confederacy's main producers of food, mules, and iron—all vital resources.

THE BATTLE OF SAVAGE'S STATION, ROBERT KNOX SNEDEN, 1862

In 1862, thirty-year-old Robert Sneden joined the 40th New York Volunteers and soon found himself in Virginia, part of George McClellan's peninsula campaign. A gifted artist in water colors, as well as an eloquent writer, Sneden captures here an early Confederate assault in what became known as the Seven Days Battle. "The immense open space in front of Savage's [house] was densely thronged with wagon trains, artillery, caissons, ammunition trains, and moving troops," Sneden observed. The "storm of lead was continuous and deadly on the approaching lines of the Rebels. They bravely rushed up, however, to within twenty feet of our artillery, when bushels of grape and canister from the cannon laid them low in rows." Over the next three years, Sneden produced hundreds of vivid drawings and eventually thousands of pages of remembrance, providing one of the most complete accounts of a Union soldier's Civil War experience.
Virginia Historical Society.

While most eyes focused on the East, the decisive early encounters of the war took place between the Appalachian Mountains and the Ozarks.

General Ulysses S. Grant became the key northern figure on the western battlefields. Although Grant had graduated from West Point, when war broke out he was a thirty-nine-year-old dry-goods clerk in Galena, Illinois. Gentle at home, he became pugnacious on the battlefield. "The art of war is simple," he said. "Find out where your enemy is, get at him as soon as you can and strike him as hard as you can, and keep moving on." Grant's philosophy of war as annihilation took a huge toll in human life, but it played to the North's strength: superior manpower. In time, the North fashioned victory from it. In his old uniform and slouch hat, with his tired, sad, nondescript face, Grant did not look much like a general. But Lincoln, who did not look much like a president, knew his worth. Later, to critics who wanted him to remove Grant from his command because of his drinking, Lincoln would say: *"I can't spare this man. He fights."*

In February 1862, operating in tandem with navy gunboats, Grant captured Fort Henry on the Tennessee River and Fort Donelson on the Cumberland (see Map 14.2). Defeat forced the Confederates to withdraw from all of Kentucky and most of Tennessee. Grant pushed after the retreating rebels until, on April 6, General Albert Sidney Johnston's army surprised him at Shiloh Church in Tennessee. Although his troops were badly mauled the first day, Grant remained cool and brought up reinforcements throughout the night. The next morning, the Union army counterattacked, driving the Confederates before it. The battle was terribly costly; there were twenty thousand casualties, including the death of Johnston. Manassas had disabused Lincoln of the illusion of a short war; and, after Shiloh, Grant "gave up all idea of saving the Union except by complete conquest."

Although no one knew it at the time, Shiloh inflicted a mortal wound to the Confederacy's bid to control the Western theater. In short order, the Yankees captured the strategic town of Corinth, Mississippi, the river city of Memphis, and the South's largest city, New Orleans. By the end of 1862, most—but not all—of the Mississippi Valley lay in Union hands.

War and Diplomacy in the Atlantic Theater

With a blockade fleet of only about three dozen ships at the beginning of the war and more than thirty-five hundred miles of southern coastline to patrol, the U.S. navy faced an impossible task. At first, rebel ships slipped in and out of port nearly at will. Taking on cargoes in the Caribbean, the sleek, fast blockade runners brought in vital supplies—guns and medicine—and also small quantities of luxury goods such as tea and liquor. But with the U.S. navy commissioning a new blockader almost weekly, the fleet eventually reached 150 ships on duty, and the Union navy dramatically improved its score.

Unable to build a conventional navy equal to the expanding federal fleet, the Confederates experimented with a radical new maritime design: the ironclad warship. At Norfolk, Virginia, they layered the wooden hull of the frigate *Merrimack* with two-inch-thick armor plate. Rechristened *Virginia,* it steamed out in March 1862 to engage the federal blockade. Within a few hours, it sank two large federal ships, killing at least 240 sailors. But when the

Virginia returned the following morning to finish its work, it found the *Monitor,* a federal ironclad that had arrived from Brooklyn during the night. The *Monitor,* a ship of even more radical design than the *Virginia,* was topped by a revolving turret containing two eleven-inch guns. Although the two ships hurled shells at each other for two hours, neither could penetrate the other's armor and the duel ended in a draw (see Map 14.2).

The Confederacy never found a way to break the blockade. Each month the northern navy tightened its noose until by 1865 the Union fleet intercepted about half of the southern ships that attempted to break through. Even more significant than the ships the Union fleet captured (about fifteen hundred total) were the ships that never sailed for fear of being captured. By 1863, the South had abandoned its embargo policy and desperately wanted to ship cotton to pay for imports it needed to fight the war. But the growing effectiveness of the federal blockade, a southern naval officer observed, "shut the Confederacy out from the world, deprived it of supplies, weakened its military and naval strength."

What they could not achieve on saltwater, Confederates sought through foreign policy. According to the theory of King Cotton, cotton-starved European nations had no choice but to break the blockade and recognize the Confederacy. The British and French briefly discussed joint action to lift the blockade, but it came to nothing. Although European nations granted the Confederacy "belligerent" status, which enabled it to buy goods and build ships in European ports, none recognized Confederate nationhood, a bolder act that would probably have drawn them into war with the United States.

King Cotton diplomacy failed for several reasons. A bumper cotton crop in 1860 meant that the warehouses of British textile manufacturers bulged with surplus cotton throughout 1861. In 1862, when Europe began to feel the pinch of the cotton famine, manufacturers found new sources of cotton in Egypt and India. In addition, a brisk trade developed between the Union and Britain—British war materiel for American grain and flour—which helped offset the decline in textiles and encouraged Britain to remain neutral. Even when the Union stepped hard on tender British toes, the British remained tolerant. In November 1861, a Union warship intercepted a British mail packet, the *Trent,* and illegally removed James Mason and John Slidell, Confederate diplomats on their way to Europe. Sentiment for war flared briefly in Britain, but when Lincoln ordered the Southerners' release, the British allowed the affair to end peacefully.

According to the theory of King Cotton, cotton-starved European nations had no choice but to break the blockade and recognize the Confederacy.

Europe's temptation to intervene disappeared for good in 1862. Union military successes on the rivers of the West made Britain and France think twice about linking their fates to the Confederacy. And in the fall of 1862, Lincoln announced a new policy that made an alliance with the Confederacy an alliance with slavery. The president finally acknowledged that it was impossible to fight for union without fighting against slavery.

Union *and* Freedom

Slavery and freedom had coexisted in North America for more than two centuries when the Civil War erupted. In his inaugural address in March 1861, Abraham Lincoln solemnly announced to the nation that he would not disturb that ancient relationship. He had "no legal right" and "no inclination" to interfere with slavery, he said. For a year and a half, Lincoln insisted that emancipation was not a goal; the war was strictly to save the Union.

Despite Lincoln's pronouncements, the war for union became a war for African American freedom. Each month the conflict dragged on, it became clearer that the Confederate war machine depended heavily on slavery. Rebel armies used slaves to build fortifications, haul materiel, tend horses, and perform camp chores. On the home front, slaves labored in ironworks and shipyards, and they grew the food that fed both soldiers and civilians. Slavery undergirded the Confederacy as certainly as it had the Old South. In the field among military commanders, in the halls of Congress, and in the White House, the truth gradually came into focus: To defeat the Confederacy, the North would have to destroy slavery. "I am a slow walker," Lincoln said, "but I never walk back."

From Slaves to Contraband

Personally, Lincoln detested human bondage, but as president he felt compelled to act prudently in the interests of the Union. He doubted his right under the Constitution to tamper with the "domestic institutions" of any state, even those in rebellion. An astute politician, Lincoln worked within the limits of public opinion, and in 1861 he believed those limits were tight. The issue of black freedom was particularly explosive in the loyal border states, where slaveholders threatened to jump into the arms of the Confederacy at even the hint of emancipation. Black freedom also attracted attention in the free states. The Democratic Party gave notice that emancipation would kill the bipartisan alliance and make the war strictly a Republican affair. Democrats were as ardent for union as Republicans, but they fought against treason—period. They marched under the banner "The Constitution As It Is, the Union As It Was."

Moreover, many white Northerners were not about to risk their lives to satisfy abolitionist "fanaticism." "We Won't Fight to Free the Nigger," one popular banner read. They feared that emancipation would propel "two or three million semi-savages" northward, where they would crowd into white neighborhoods, compete for white jobs, and mix with white "sons and daughters." A surge of anti-emancipation, antiblack sentiment, then, threatened to dislodge the loyal slave states from the Union, alienate the Democratic Party, deplete the armies, and perhaps even spark race warfare.

Yet proponents of emancipation pressed Lincoln as relentlessly as the anti-emancipation forces. Abolitionists argued that by seceding, Southerners had forfeited their right to the protection of the Constitution. Lincoln could now—as the price of treason—legally confiscate their property in slaves. When Lincoln refused, abolitionists scalded him. Frederick Douglass labeled Lincoln "the miserable tool of traitors and rebels." Abolitionists won increasing numbers of converts during the war, especially among the radical faction of the Republican Party, which came to believe that restoring the Union with the moral evil of slavery intact would make a mockery of the sacrifices of Union soldiers.

The Republican-dominated Congress refused to leave slavery policy entirely in Lincoln's hands. In August 1861, Congress approved the Confiscation Act, which allowed the seizure of any slave who was employed directly by the Confederate military. The House and the Senate also fulfilled the

CONTRABANDS
These refugees from slavery crossed the Rappahannock River in Virginia in August 1862 to seek the sanctuary of a federal army. Most slaves fled with little more than the clothes on their backs, but not all escaped slavery empty-handed. The oxen, wagon, and goods seen here could have been procured by a number of means—purchased during slavery, "borrowed" from the former master, or gathered during flight. Refugees who possessed draft animals and a wagon had much more economic opportunity than those who had only their labor to sell.
Library of Congress.

free-soil dream of prohibiting slavery in the territories and abolished slavery in Washington, D.C. Democrats and border-state representatives voted against even these mild measures, but little by little, Congress displayed a stiffening of attitude as it cast about for a just and practical slavery policy.

But slaves, not politicians, became the most insistent force for emancipation. By escaping their masters by the tens of thousands and running away to Union lines, they placed slavery on the North's wartime agenda. Union officials could not ignore the flood of fugitives, and runaways precipitated a series of momentous decisions on the part of the military, Congress, and the president. Were the runaways now free, or were they still slaves who, according to the fugitive slave law, had to be returned to their masters? At first, most Yankee military commanders believed that administration policy required them to send the fugitives back. But

Union armies needed laborers, and some officers accepted the runaways and put them to work. At Fort Monroe, Virginia, General Benjamin F. Butler not only refused to turn them over to their owners but also provided them with a new status. He called them "contraband of war," meaning "confiscated property." Congress established national policy in March 1862 when it forbade the practice of returning fugitive slaves to their masters. Slaves were still not legally free, but there was a tilt toward emancipation.

Gradually, Lincoln's policy of noninterference with slavery crumbled. To calm Northerners' racial fears, which he considered the chief obstacle to Union acceptance of emancipation, Lincoln offered colonization, the deportation of African Americans from the United States to Haiti, Panama, or elsewhere. In the summer of 1862, he defended colonization to a delegation of black visitors to the

White House. He told them that deep-seated racial prejudice made it impossible for them to achieve equality in this country. For blacks to be truly free, he said, they had to emigrate to countries where opportunities existed. An African American from Philadelphia spoke for the group when he told the president, "This is our country as much as it is yours, and we will not leave it." Congress voted a small amount of money to underwrite colonization, but after one miserable experiment on a small island near Haiti in the Caribbean, practical limitations and black opposition sank further efforts.

Slaves, not politicians, became the most insistent force for emancipation. By escaping their masters by the tens of thousands and running away to Union lines, they placed slavery on the North's wartime agenda.

At the same time that Lincoln was developing his own initiatives, he snuffed out actions he believed jeopardized northern unity. He was particularly alert to Union commanders who tried to dictate slavery policy from the field. In August 1861, when John C. Frémont, commander of federal troops in Missouri, impetuously freed the slaves belonging to Missouri rebels, Lincoln forced the general to revoke his edict and then removed him from command. (Never shy, Jessie Benton Frémont fired off a blistering letter to Lincoln defending her husband's "honor" and "integrity.") The following May, when General David Hunter issued a proclamation freeing the slaves in Georgia, Florida, and South Carolina, Lincoln countermanded his order. Events moved so rapidly, however, that Lincoln found it impossible to control federal policy on slavery. He had to hurry just to keep up.

From Contraband to Free People

On August 22, 1862, Lincoln replied to an angry abolitionist who demanded that he go after slavery. "My paramount objective in this struggle *is* to save the Union," Lincoln said deliberately, "and is *not* either to save or destroy slavery. If I could save the Union without freeing *any* slave I would do it, and if I could save it by freeing *all* the slaves I would do it; and if I could save it by freeing some and leaving others alone I would also do that." At first glance, it seemed

a restatement of his old position: that union was the North's sole objective. But what marked it as a radical departure was Lincoln's refusal to say that slavery was safe. Instead, he said that he would emancipate every slave if it would preserve the Union.

By the summer of 1862, events were tumbling rapidly toward emancipation. On July 17, Congress adopted a second Confiscation Act. The first had confiscated slaves employed by the Confederate military; the second declared all slaves of rebel masters "forever free of their servitude." In theory, this breathtaking measure freed most of the slaves in the Confederacy, for slaveholders formed the backbone of the rebellion. Congress had traveled far since the war began. Lincoln had too, but he wanted to blaze his own path. On July 21, the president informed his cabinet that he was ready "to take some definitive steps in respect to military action and slavery." The next day, he read a draft of a preliminary emancipation proclamation that promised to free all slaves in the seceding states on January 1, 1863.

Lincoln described emancipation as an "act of justice," but it was not the abolitionists' appeal to conscience that finally brought him around. It was the lengthening casualty lists. The duration and difficulty of the war eroded and then ended Lincoln's policy of noninterference. Emancipation, he declared, was "a military necessity, absolutely essential to the preservation of the Union." Only freeing the slaves would "strike at the heart of the rebellion." His cabinet favored Lincoln's plan but advised him to wait for a military victory before announcing it so that critics would not call it an act of desperation. On September 22, five days after the battle at Antietam, Lincoln served notice that if the rebel states did not lay down their arms and return to the Union by January 1, 1863, their slaves "shall be then, thenceforward, and forever free."

Lincoln described emancipation as an "act of justice," but it was not the abolitionists' appeal to conscience that finally brought him around. It was the lengthening casualty lists.

Abolitionists generally approved, but the limitations of the proclamation—it exempted the loyal border states and the Union-occupied areas of the Confederacy—caused some to ridicule the act. The *London Times* observed cynically, "Where he has no power Mr. Lincoln will set the negroes free, where he retains power he will consider them as slaves." But Lincoln had no power to free slaves in loyal states, and invading Union armies would liberate slaves in the Confederacy as they advanced.

By presenting emancipation as a "military necessity," Lincoln hoped he had disarmed his conservative critics. Emancipation would shorten the war and thus save lives. Instead, Democrats exploded with rage. They charged that the "shrieking and howling abolitionist faction" had captured the White House and made it "a nigger war." The fall elections were only weeks away, and Democrats sought to make political hay out of Lincoln's action. War-weariness probably had as much to do with the results as emancipation, but Democrats gained thirty-four congressional seats in 1862. When House Democrats proposed a resolution branding emancipation "a high crime against the Constitution," the Republicans, who maintained narrow majorities in both houses, beat it back. As promised, on New Year's Day, Lincoln issued the final Emancipation Proclamation. In addition to freeing the slaves in the states that were in rebellion, the edict also committed the federal government to the fullest use of African Americans to defeat the Confederate enemy.

War of Black Liberation

Even before Lincoln proclaimed freedom a Union war aim, African Americans in the North had volunteered to fight. But the War Department, doubtful of their abilities and fearful of white reaction to serving side by side with them, refused to make black men soldiers. Instead, the army employed black men as manual laborers; black women sometimes found employment—usually as laundresses and cooks—but less often. The navy, however, from the outset accepted blacks as sailors. They usually served in noncombatant roles, but within months a few blacks served on gun crews.

As the Union experienced manpower shortages, Northerners gradually and reluctantly turned to African Americans to fill blue uniforms. With the Militia Act of July 1862, Congress authorized enrolling blacks in "any military or naval service for which they may be found competent." Lingering resistance to black military service largely disappeared in 1863. After the Emancipation Proclamation, whites—like it or not—were fighting and

dying for black freedom, and few were likely to insist that blacks remain out of harm's way behind the lines. Indeed, rather than resist black military participation, whites insisted that blacks share the danger, especially after March 1863, when Congress resorted to the draft to fill the Union army.

Black soldiers discovered that the military was far from colorblind. The Union army established segregated black regiments, paid black soldiers $10 per month rather than the $13 it paid to whites, refused blacks the opportunity to become commissioned officers, punished blacks as if they were slaves, and assigned blacks to labor battalions rather than to combat units. But nothing deterred black recruits. When the war ended, 179,000 African American men had served in the Union forces, approximately 10 percent of the army total. An astounding 71 percent of black men ages eighteen to forty-five in the free states wore blue, a participation rate that was substantially higher than that of white men. More than 130,000 black soldiers came from the slave states, perhaps 100,000 of them ex-slaves.

In time, whites allowed blacks to put down their shovels and to shoulder rifles. At the battles of Port Hudson and Milliken's Bend on the Mississippi River and at Fort Wagner in Charleston harbor, black courage under fire finally dispelled notions that African Americans could not fight. More than thirty-eight thousand black soldiers died in the Civil War, a mortality rate that was higher than that of white troops. Blacks played a crucial role in the triumph of the Union and the destruction of slavery.

Even before Lincoln proclaimed freedom a Union war aim, African Americans had volunteered to fight.

From the beginning, African Americans viewed the Civil War as a revolutionary struggle for black liberation. They fought to overthrow slavery and to gain equality for their entire race. "Once let the black man get upon his person the brass letters, U.S.; let him get an eagle on his button, and a musket on his shoulder and bullets in his pocket," Frederick Douglass declared, "and there is no power on earth which can deny that he has earned the right of citizenship."

BAND OF THE 107TH U.S. COLORED INFANTRY, ARLINGTON, VIRGINIA, 1865

Photographed carrying their music and over-the-shoulder instruments, the members of this military band represent only a tiny fraction of the African Americans who served in the federal military during the Civil War. The Lincoln administration was slow to accept black soldiers, in part because of lingering doubts about their ability to fight. Colonial Thomas W. Higginson, a white Massachusetts clergyman and abolitionist, commanded the First South Carolina Infantry, which was made up of former slaves. After his regiment's first skirmish with Confederate soldiers, Higginson celebrated his men's courage: "No officer in this regiment now doubts that the key to the successful prosecution of this war lies in the unlimited employment of black troops. . . . Instead of leaving their homes and families to fight they are fighting for their homes and families." After the spring of 1863 the federal government did all it could to maximize the number of black soldiers. Throughout the war, however, policy required that blacks serve under white commissioned officers, such as the man on the left of this photograph. Library of Congress.

As Douglass predicted, when black men became liberators, they and their families gained new confidence, pride, and self-esteem. Military service taught them new skills, showed them more of the world than they had ever seen, and introduced them to political struggle as they battled for their rights within the army. War's experiences and lessons stood African Americans in good stead when the struggle for liberation was over and the battle for equality began. But first, there was the matter of the rebellion. Victory depended as much on what happened behind the lines as on the battlefields.

The South at War

During the secession winter of 1860–61, a Louisiana planter had declared confidently that the creation of the Confederate States of America would "guarantee order, security, tranquility, as well as liberty." The irony was staggering. By seceding, Southerners brought on themselves a firestorm of unimaginable fury. Monstrous losses on the battlefields nearly bled the Confederacy to death. But white Southerners at the home front were also under attack.

REBEL SOLDIER
Treasvant (Tris) D. Childers was twenty-seven years old in March 1862 when he enlisted as a private in Phelan's Battery, Alabama Light Artillery. He fought at Chickamauga, Missionary Ridge, Franklin, and Nashville—and survived. His older brothers William and Thomas died while fighting in Virginia. After the war, Childers moved to Arkansas and became a farmer. When he died in 1910, his widow, Emma McShan Childers, collected a state pension for her husband's service in the Civil War.
Private Collection.

The most surprising thrust came from their own government. Richmond's efforts to centralize power to fight the war effectively convinced many men and women that the Confederacy had betrayed them. Wartime economic changes hurt everyone, but some suffered more than others; by 1863, planters and yeomen who had stood together began to drift apart. Most disturbing of all, slaves became open participants in the destruction of slavery and the Confederacy.

Revolution from Above

When Jefferson Davis arrived in Richmond in 1861, he faced the gargantuan task of building an army and navy from scratch, supplying them from factories that were scarce and anemic, and paying for it all from a treasury that did not exist. The president agreed with one of his generals who observed that Southerners were engaged in a total war "in which the whole population and the whole production . . . are to be put on a war footing, where every institution is to be made auxiliary to war." Building the army proved easiest. Hundreds of officers defected from the federal army, and hundreds of thousands of eager young rebels volunteered to join them. Very quickly, the Confederacy developed formidable striking power.

The Confederacy's economy and finances proved tougher. Because of the Union blockade, the government had no choice but to build an industrial sector itself. Government-owned clothing and shoe factories, mines, arsenals, and powder works "sprung up almost like magic," according to one Mississippian. In addition, the government harnessed private companies, such as the huge Tredegar Iron Works in Richmond, to the war effort. The financial task proved most difficult because Southerners had invested their capital in land and slaves, which were not easily tapped for the war. Richmond came up with a mix of bonds, taxes, and paper money to finance the war effort.

Despite its bold measures, however, the Davis administration failed to transform the slave-labor, staple-producing agricultural economy into a modern industrial one. The Confederacy manufactured much more than many people imagined possible, but it never produced all that the South needed. Each month, the gap between the North's and the South's production widened. Moreover, the flood of paper money coming from Richmond caused debilitating inflation. By 1863, Charlestonians paid ten times more for food than they had at the start of the war. By Christmas 1864, a Confederate soldier's monthly pay no longer bought a pair of socks.

Richmond's war-making effort meant that government intruded in unprecedented ways into the private lives of Confederate citizens. In April 1862, the Confederate Congress passed the first conscription (draft) law in American history. All able-bodied white males between the ages of eighteen and thirty-five (later seventeen and fifty) were liable to serve in the rebel army for three years. The Confederate government adopted a policy of impressment, which allowed officials to confiscate food, horses, wagons, or whatever they wanted from private citizens and to pay for them at below-market rates. After March 1863, the Confederacy also legally impressed slaves, employing them as government military laborers. In addition, Richmond took control of the South's railroads and shipping. The war necessitated much of the government's unprecedented behavior, but citizens found it arbitrary and inequitable. In time, Southerners named Jefferson Davis as the politician they hated most, after Lincoln.

Hardship Below

Richmond's centralizing efforts ran head-on into the South's traditional values of states' rights and unfettered individualism. The states lashed out at what Georgia governor Joseph E. Brown denounced as the "dangerous usurpation by Congress of the reserved right of the States." A tug-of-war between Richmond and the states ensued for control of money, supplies, and soldiers, with damaging consequences for the war effort. Individual citizens also remembered that Davis had promised to defend southern "liberty" against Republican "despotism." Luckily for Davis, the Confederate constitution provided for a single, six-year term for the president, which meant he did not have to face an election during the war.

Hardships were widespread, but they fell most heavily on the poor. Inflation, for example, threatened the poor with starvation. Salt—necessary for preserving meat—shot up from $2 to $60 a bag during the first year of the war. Flour that cost three or four cents a pound in 1861 cost thirty-five cents in 1863. The draft depopulated yeomen farms of men, leaving the women and children to grow what they ate. A rampaging army, a drought, a sickness, a lame mule—any one calamity could cost a family a vital crop. When farm wives succeeded in bringing in a harvest, government agents took 10 percent of it as a "tax-in-kind" on agriculture. Like inflation, shortages also afflicted the entire population, but the rich lost luxuries while the poor lost necessities. In the spring of 1863, bread riots broke out in a dozen cities and villages across the South. In Richmond, a mob of nearly a thousand hungry women broke into shops and took what they needed.

Severe deprivation had powerful consequences. One southern leader observed in November 1862, "Men cannot be expected to fight for the Government that permits their wives & children to starve." A few wealthy individuals shared their bounty, the Confederacy made some efforts at so-

MARIA ISABELLA ("BELLE") BOYD, SPY
Most white southern women, in addition to keeping their families fed and safe, served the Confederate cause by sewing uniforms, knitting socks, rolling bandages, and nursing the sick and wounded. But Belle Boyd became a spy. Only seventeen when the war broke out, she became in the words of a northern journalist "insanely devoted to the rebel cause." Her first act for the Confederacy came on July 3, 1861, when she shot a drunken federal soldier who barged into her Virginia home and insulted her mother. Her relations with occupying northern troops improved, and soon this compelling young woman was eavesdropping on officers' conversations and slipping messages to Confederate armies. Boyd's information handed Stonewall Jackson an easy victory at Front Royal, Virginia, in May 1862. "I thank you," the general wrote Boyd, " . . . for the immense service that you have rendered your country today." Imprisoned several times for spying, Boyd took up a theatrical career when the war ended.
Warren Rifles Confederate Museum, Front Royal, Va. Photo by Larry Sherer.

CONFEDERATE SOLDIERS AND THEIR SLAVES
Soldiers of the Seventh Tennessee Cavalry pose with their slaves. Many slaveholders took "body servants" with them to war. These slaves cooked, washed, and cleaned for the white soldiers. In 1861, James H. Langhorne reported to his sister: "Peter . . . is charmed with being with me & 'being a soldier.' I gave him my old uniform overcoat & he says he is going to have his picture taken . . . to send to the servants." Do you think Peter was "puttin' on ol' massa" or just glad to be free of plantation labor?
Daguerreotype courtesy of Tom Farish.

cial welfare, and the states did even more, but every effort fell short. By some estimates, when the war ended, one-third of the soldiers had already gone home. A Mississippi deserter explained, "We are poor men and are willing to defend our country but our families [come] first." (See "Documenting the American Promise," page 516.)

The Confederacy also failed to persuade the suffering white majority that the war's burdens were being shared equally. Instead, yeomen saw a profound inequality of sacrifice. They called it "a rich man's war and a poor man's fight," and they had evidence. The original draft law permitted a man who had money to hire a substitute to take his place. Moreover, the "twenty-Negro law" exempted one white man on every plantation with twenty or more slaves. The government intended to provide protection for white women and to see that slaves tended the crops. But yeomen perceived rich men as evading military service. A slaveless Mississippian complained to his governor about stay-at-home planters who sent their slaves into the fields to grow cotton while in plain view "poor soldiers' wives are plowing with *their own* hands to make a subsistence for themselves and children—while their husbands are suffering, bleeding and dying for their country." In fact, most slaveholders went off to war, but the extreme suffering of common folk and the relative immunity of planters fueled class animosity.

Yeomen saw a profound inequality of sacrifice. They called it "a rich man's war and a poor man's fight," and they had evidence.

The Richmond government hoped that the crucible of war would mold a region into a nation. Officials and others worked tirelessly to promote a vibrant southern nationalism that, as one Confederate politician said, would "excite in our citizens an ardent and enduring attachment to our Government and its institutions." Clergymen assured their congregations that God had blessed slavery and the new nation. Jefferson Davis asked citizens to observe national days of fasting and prayer. Patriotic songwriters, poets, authors, and artists extolled southern culture. But it proved difficult to create a united slave republic in the midst of all-out war. Efforts to build consensus never succeeded in winning over thousands of die-hard Unionists. And friction between yeomen and planters increased rather than decreased. The war also threatened to rip the southern social fabric along its racial seam.

The Disintegration of Slavery

The legal destruction of slavery was the product of presidential proclamation, congressional legislation, and eventually constitutional amendment, but the practical destruction of slavery was the product of war, what Lincoln called war's "friction and abrasion." When the war ended in 1865, the institution had taken a heavy pounding, especially from within. More than 100,000 men fled bondage, took up arms, and attacked slavery directly. Other men and women stayed in the slave quarters, and as the slaveholders' grip loosened, they staked a claim to more freedom.

In dozens of ways, the war disrupted the routine, organization, and discipline of bondage. Almost immediately, it called the master away, leaving white women to assume managerial responsibilities. As one plantation mistress wrote to a newspaper, "Do impress upon the soldiers . . . that we are *working* for them, while they are *fighting* for us—and that their wants shall be supplied, as long as there is a *woman* or a *dollar* in the 'Southern Confederacy.'" But plantation mistresses could not maintain traditional standards of slave discipline. No one could. By stifling the production of cotton, war had divorced slaves from their principal work and thus from expected standards of behavior in general. Also, the government's impressment policy, extended to slaves, severed the personal relationship between masters and slaves. Moreover, as military action increasingly sliced through the South's farms and plantations, some slaveholders fled, leaving behind their slaves. Many more took their slaves with them, but flight meant additional chaos and offered slaves new opportunities to resist bondage.

In large parts of the South, the balance of power between master and slave gradually shifted. Slaveholders complained about the slaves' "demoralization" and "betrayal." Slaves got to the fields late, worked indifferently, and quit early. Some slaveholders responded violently; most saw no alternative but to strike bargains—offering gifts or part of the crop—to keep slaves at home and at work. An Alabama woman reported that she had to rely on "moral suasion" to "get them to do their duty." She "begged . . . what little is done." Changes in slave behavior shocked slaveholders. They had prided themselves on "knowing" their slaves, and they learned that they did not know them at all. When the war began, a North Carolina woman praised her slaves as "diligent and respectful." When it ended, she said, "As to the idea of a *faithful servant, it is all a fiction.*" But whites' greatest fear—black violence—rarely occurred. Instead, slaves undermined white mastery and expanded control over their own lives.

The North at War

Because rebel armies generally stayed within the Confederate borders, the North remained largely untouched by fighting. But Northerners could not avoid being touched by war. Almost every family had a son, a husband, a brother in uniform. Moreover, this war—a total war—blurred the distinction between home front and battlefield. As in the South, men marched off to fight, but preserving the country, either Union or Confederacy, was also women's

Home and Country

Husbands fighting for the Confederacy and wives back at home exchanged countless letters during the war. They wrote movingly of family, hardships, and battles, and they shared their deepest loves and fears. Their letters, which were uncensored, often revealed the conflicting tugs of home and country.

Christian Marion Epperly and his wife, Mary Epperly, lived in the Blue Ridge Mountains of Virginia. Although neither was an ardent secessionist, Marion entered the army as a private early in 1862. He saw action in both the eastern and western theaters of the war. He hated army life and longed for his wife and children. Mary was equally heartsick without Marion. The couple's letters reveal their limited schooling, but more important they show how plain folks wrestled with the tangled issues of personal and political loyalties and obligations.

DOCUMENT 1. Letter from Chickahominy Creek, Virginia, May 16, 1862

During the peninsula campaign in Virginia, as Union general George B. McClellan was approaching the Confederate capital of Richmond, Marion wrote to Mary from near the action.

I think the people will be bound to suffer for something to eat[;] the grain is all destroid and nearly all the fenses is burnt up from yorktown to Richmond: it looks distressing just to travel along the road: the wheat up waist hi some of it and horses and cattle has eat the most of it to the ground and I think the yankees will make a finish of the ballans [balance] that is left but the[y] cant doo much more damage than our army did[;] our own men killed all the cattle and hogs & sheep that the farmers had[,] even took ther chickens[;] every thing is totally destroid in this part of the State[.] I don't think the yankeys could doo much wors if they had a chanse[.]

I hope and pray this awful war will soon come to a close some way or another[,] any way to get pease in the world wonst more[;] it seems to me I had drather be at home and live on bred and water than to have this war hanging over us but I pray

god pease will soon be made[.] I dont think the war can last long.

DOCUMENT 2. Letter from Camp near Bells Bridge, Tennessee, August 15, 1863

By the summer of 1863, Marion's regiment had moved to Tennessee, where he notices increasing war weariness, desertions, and disillusionment with the Confederacy.

You don't know how glad I would be if I was just thar with you this morning to see the sun rise over the hills in Virginia again[,] for everry thing seames so sad and desolate here this morning; it seames like the absens of dear friends and the present condition of things has brought deep refletion and sadnes upon everry heart, and [men] are growing weary and getting out of heart and leaving the Army everry day. I cant tell wheather it will be for the better or wheather it will make things wors: but I hope it is a way god has provided to bring this war and time of sorrow to an end and to give us pease in our land again: Thoug I believe the south first started on a just course but our own wickedness and disobedians has brought us to what we are and I firmly believe wee will be bound to give up to subjugation[.] I don't think the south will stand much longer, and I am sorrow to say it for wee will be a ruined people while time ma [may] last, but wee ought to submit to any thing to have this awwful war ended.

DOCUMENT 3. Letter from Floyd County, Virginia, August 16, 1863

Mary longs for peace and argues that desertion will end the war.

Oh how much beter satisfied would I be if you was just hear with me this beatiful Sabath morning. I feel as if my troubles on earth would all be over if you was just at home to stay wonst more[,] but god sent it upon us and we will have to bear with it the best we can but I do pray that he may soon end this destressing time some way[.] I would be willing for it to end most any way just so it would end[.] Dear Marion I think if the head men dont soon end this war that the soldiers will for they are runing way from down east by hundreds[;] they was five hundard went though hear last weak and well armed and they say they wont go back any more and I dont blame them for it[.] I wish they would all runaway and these head men would be oblige to fight it out but as long as they can stay at home and speculate off of the poor soulders they dont care how long the war lasts[.] Serious Smith wrote a leter the 9 of this month and he wrote that they had to pay 15 dolars for a bushel of taters . . . how can the poor soulders make out and only get a leven [eleven] dolars a month[?] He wrote that they sawd very hard times down thare and had a heap of hard fighting to do[;] they had a fight the 1 and 4 of this month and he wrote that thare was five wounded and more killed and they was expecting a fight every hour.

Document 4. Letter from Floyd County, Virginia, December 4, 1863

Mary tells Marion that the Confederacy's new conscription law has thrown their neighborhood into turmoil.

It seams like things [are in] such a uproar that I cant keep my mind together long a nuff to write a leter as it aut to be wrote[;] people has never bin in such a uproar and confusion hear since the war as they are now[;] thare is orders now to take up every man between the age of 17 and 50 that hasent reported and if they hant [aren't] able to walk they have to hall them. . . . Dear Husban I expect they will pass a law yet to take the wimen for they have taken all the men and children almost ded and alive and the next I read I recon will be for the wiman. Dear Marion hour Country has got in a turable fix[;] thare is nothing but sorow and destress in this world any more[;] when I set and study about it and think if I could just take you and my dear litle children with me to heaven I would be willing to do to day but Dear Husban wee was born in this world to see trouble and wee will have to put up with it the best wee can and pray for a beter day to come which I hope is not fare off.

Document 5. Letter from Outskirts of Dalton, Georgia, March 25, 1864

As Marion's regiment is backing toward Atlanta, trying to fend off Sherman, he considers what has gone wrong with the Confederacy.

I dont think it will last much longer if the souldiers doo what they say they will doo[;] they are all verry tired of this war and the way it is carried on[.] I think wee all have stud it about as long as we can unless our leading men dos a heap better than they ever have yet: if they wer God fearing men I would think wee would prosper but so long as they [seek] the Bottom of a Whiskey Barl and frolick around bad places just so long we will hafto fight and suffer. . . . we was all Born in a free land and I think wee ought to stil be free and not be bound down wors than slaves[;] we wonst had a union and was living happy and had all man can wish for[;] now we are cut off from that union and what are wee nothing but a ruend people as long as we shal live . . . dissatisfaction and wickedness all over the south[;] may God show us our errors and put us in the rite way and Bring us Back to our old union again.

Document 6. Letter from Floyd County, Virginia, March 24, 1865

Mary expects a Yankee victory and says again that Confederate soldiers can end the war by deserting. Despite his doubts about the Confederacy and continued affection for the Union, Marion left the army without authorization only once, and after a few weeks at home in 1863, he returned to his regiment. Like many disillusioned soldiers, he fought in the rebel army to the very end.

Dear Marion they are looking every day for the yankees to take Richmond and Linchburg and I do wish from my hart that they had it now for I am not afrade of the yankeys treating us any worse nor not half as bad as our own men dos for they have taking all the men or tride to take all that is any acout [account] and are now taking the horses. . . . How much worse could the yankeys do than that[?] . . . It lais in the souldires hands now to make pease and I do wish that they may make it soon[;] our strongest sesess [secessionists] hear say that wee are whiped and they have nown [known] it for some time but was ashame to own it.

Source: Christian M. Epperly Correspondence, Gilder Lehrman Collection, Pierpont Morgan Library, New York.

(Continued)

work. For civilians as well as soldiers, for women as well as men, war was transforming.

The need to build and fuel the Union war machine caused the northern economy to boom. The North sent nearly two million men into the military and still increased production in almost every area. But because the rewards and burdens of patriotism were not evenly distributed, the North experienced sharp, even violent, divisions. Workers confronted employers, whites confronted blacks, and Republicans confronted Democrats. Still, Northerners on the home front remained fervently attached to the ideals of free labor and the Union.

The Government and the Economy

Democrats and Republicans traditionally disagreed about the best way to encourage economic growth. Democrats generally argued that in economic matters, the less government intrusion the better, while Republicans advocated government support to develop economic resources. Democratic domination of national politics for two decades before the war meant that the Republicans inherited a financial and economic structure that restricted government direction of the economy. When the war began, the United States had no national banking system, no national currency, and no federal income or excise taxes.

The secession of eleven slave states cut the Democrats' strength in Congress in half and destroyed their capacity to resist the Republican steamroller. The Republican platform of 1860 advocated an array of federal programs to encourage economic growth, and during the war Republicans had little trouble enacting their philosophy into law. In May 1862, Congress approved the Homestead Act, which offered 160 acres of public land to settlers who would live and labor on it. In time, the Homestead Act resulted in more than a million new farms in the West. July 1862 saw passage of the Pacific Railroad Act, which provided massive federal assistance for the building of a transcontinental railroad. When completed in 1869, the railroad ran from Omaha to San Francisco. Congress also enacted a higher tariff to increase protection for manufacturers against foreign competition.

The Legal Tender Act of February 1862 created a national currency, paper money that Northerners called "greenbacks." With passage of the National Banking Act in February 1863, Congress created a system of national banks that by the 1870s had largely replaced the antebellum system of decentralized state banks. Congress also enacted a series of sweeping tax laws that encompassed everything from incomes to liquor to billiard tables. The Internal Revenue Act created the Bureau of Internal Revenue to collect taxes. By revolutionizing the country's banking, monetary, and tax structures, the Republicans generated enormous economic power.

The secession of eleven slave states cut the Democrats' strength in Congress in half and destroyed their capacity to resist the Republican steamroller.

Two additional initiatives had long-term consequences for agriculture and industry. Congress created a Department of Agriculture and passed the Land-Grant College Act (also known as the Morrill

UNION ORDNANCE, YORKTOWN, VIRGINIA
As the North successfully harnessed its enormous industrial capacity to the needs of war, cannon, mortars, and shells poured out of its factories. A fraction of that abundance is seen here in 1862 at Yorktown, ready for transportation to Union troops in the field. Two years later, Abraham Lincoln observed that the Union was "gaining strength, and may if need be maintain the contest indefinitely. . . . Material resources are now more complete and abundant than ever. . . . The national resources are unexhausted, and, as we believe, inexhaustible."
Library of Congress.

www.bedfordstmartins.com /tap SEE THE ONLINE STUDY GUIDE for more help in analyzing this image.

Act after its sponsor, Representative Justin Morrill of Vermont), which set aside public lands to support universities that emphasized "agriculture and mechanical arts." Republicans defended their wartime legislation by arguing that additional economic muscle meant increased military might. Initiatives from Washington immeasurably strengthened the North's effort to win the war, but they were also permanently changing the nation.

Women and Work on the Home Front

With more than a million farm men called to the military, farm women added men's chores to their own. "I met more women driving teams on the road and saw more at work in the fields than men," a visitor to Iowa reported in the fall of 1862. Rising production figures testified to their success in plowing, planting, and harvesting. Rapid mechanization assisted farm women in their new roles. Cyrus Mc-

Cormick sold 165,000 of his reapers during the war years. The combination of high prices and increased production ensured that war and prosperity joined hands in the rural North.

While a few industries, such as textiles (which depended on southern cotton), declined during the war, many more grew. Huge profits prompted one Pennsylvania ironmaster to remark, "I am in no hurry for peace." With orders pouring in and a million nonfarm workers siphoned off into the military, unemployment declined and wages often rose. The boom proved friendlier to owners than to workers, however. In industry, as in agriculture, prewar trends continued to accelerate: specialization, mechanization, growth in the size of the workplace, and loss of worker control. Furthermore, inflation and taxes cut so deeply that workers' standard of living actually fell.

As on the farm, women in cities stepped into jobs vacated by men, particularly in manufacturing, and also into essentially new occupations such as government civil service. Often they had no choice because they could not make ends meet on their husbands' army pay. Women made up about one-quarter of the manufacturing workforce when the war began and one-third when it ended. But as more women entered the workforce, employers cut wages. By 1864, fourteen-hour days earned New York seamstresses only an average of $1.54 per week. As Cincinnati seamstresses explained to Abraham Lincoln, their wages were not enough "to sustain life." Urban workers resorted increasingly to strikes to try to wrench decent salaries from their employers, but their protests rarely succeeded. Nevertheless, tough times failed to undermine the patriotism of most workers, who took pride in their contribution to northern victory.

Middle-class white women were supposed to be homebodies, and hundreds of thousands contributed to the war effort in traditional ways. Like many southern white women, they wrapped bandages, labored long hours in sewing circles, and sold homemade goods at local fairs to raise money to aid the soldiers. Unpaid labor by women proved crucial in supplying the opposing war machines. But other women expressed their patriotism in an untraditional way—as wartime nurses. Thousands of women on both sides defied prejudices about female delicacy and volunteered to nurse the wounded. Many of the northern female volunteers worked through the U.S. Sanitary Commission, a civilian organization that bought and distributed clothing, food, and medicine and recruited doctors and nurses. Nursing meant working in the midst of unspeakable sights, sounds, and smells, but it brought the profound satisfaction of displaying competence and serving well. Katherine Wormeley of Rhode Island, who served three months as a volunteer nurse on a hospital ship in 1862, recorded in her diary, "We all know in our hearts that it is thorough enjoyment to be here,—it is life."

Some volunteers went on to become paid military nurses. In April 1861, Dorothea Dix, well known for her efforts to reform insane asylums, was named superintendent of female nurses; eventually, some three thousand women served under her. Most nurses worked in hospitals behind the battle lines, but some, like Clara Barton, who later founded the American Red Cross, worked in battlefield units. At Antietam, as Barton was giving a wounded man a drink, a bullet ripped through her sleeve and struck the man in the chest, killing him

U.S. SANITARY COMMISSION, BRANDY STATION, VIRGINIA, 1863
The burden of caring for the millions of Union soldiers was more than the government could shoulder. Private initiative in the form of the United States Sanitary Commission brought additional medical attention to the Union wounded and boosted the comfort and morale of soldiers in the camps. Volunteers like these northern women standing in front of the Commission's headquarters in Brandy Station, Virginia, offered soldiers some of the comforts of home—clean socks, new blankets, and fresh fruit. Do you suppose that the freshly painted white picket fence surrounding their building had symbolic value? If so, what did it symbolize?
National Archives.

instantly. Women who served in the war went on to lead the postwar movement to establish training schools for female nurses.

Politics and Dissent

At first, the bustle of economic and military mobilization seemed to silence politics, with Democrats supporting the Union as fervently as Republicans. But bipartisan unity did not last. Within a year, Democrats were labeling the Republican administration a "reign of terror," and Republicans were calling Democrats the party of "Dixie, Davis, and the Devil." As bruising as the political struggle became, the North's two-party system actually strengthened government. In the Confederacy, which had no well-organized parties, political disagreement spiraled down into fruitless bickering, but in the Union, parties helped to discipline and legitimize political debate. Fear of being driven from office by its rival's victory served to unify each party and to strengthen the political structure.

At first, the bustle of economic and military mobilization seemed to silence politics. But bipartisan unity did not last.

Nevertheless, Republican policy pushed the Democrats toward a dangerous alienation. Under Lincoln, the Republicans emancipated the slaves, subsidized private business, and expanded federal power at every turn. The Lincoln administration argued that the war required a loose interpretation of the Constitution, to which the Democrats countered, "The Constitution is as binding in war as in peace." Democrats had good evidence that Lincoln did not always reach first for a copy of the Constitution when he confronted a problem. In September 1862, in an effort to stifle opposition to the war, Lincoln placed under military arrest any person who discouraged enlistments, resisted the draft, or engaged in "disloyal" practices. Before the war ended, his administration had imprisoned nearly fourteen thousand individuals, most in the border states. The campaign fell short of a reign of terror, for the majority of the prisoners were not northern Democratic opponents but Confederate citizens, blockade runners, and foreign nationals (citizens of foreign countries), and most of the arrested gained quick release. Still, the administration's heavy-handed tactics did suppress free speech.

One Democratic dissenter, ex-congressman Clement L. Vallandigham of Ohio, proved indefatigable. He lambasted every Republican innovation, which meant most of Lincoln's conduct of the war. After the Emancipation Proclamation, Vallandig-

ham came out against the war itself. He denounced this "wicked, cruel and unnecessary war" waged "for the purpose of crushing out liberty and erecting a despotism . . . a war for the freedom of the blacks and the enslavement of the whites."

Was such talk protected by the right of free speech, or was it treason? In April 1863, General Ambrose Burnside decided that "the habit of declaring sympathy for the enemy will not be allowed" and arrested Vallandigham for treason. Lincoln had not ordered the arrest but decided to back his general, arguing that the Constitution permitted the military arrest of civilians during rebellions. "Must I shoot a simple-minded soldier boy who deserts, while I must not touch a hair of a wily agitator who induces him to desert?" Lincoln asked. Vallandigham's arrest and conviction in a military court sparked Democratic protest throughout the North. In 1866, a year after the war ended, the Supreme Court in *Ex parte Milligan* declared unconstitutional military trials of civilians where civil courts were still able to operate.

When the Republican-dominated Congress enacted the draft law in March 1863, Democrats had another grievance. Grim news from the battlefields had dried up the stream of volunteers, and the North, like the South a year earlier, turned to military conscription to fill the ranks. The law required that all men between the ages of twenty and forty-five enroll and make themselves available for a lottery, which would decide who went to war. What poor men found particularly galling were provisions that allowed a draftee to hire a substitute or simply to pay a $300 fee and get out of his military obligation. As in the South, common folk could be heard chanting, "A rich man's war and a poor man's fight."

Linking the draft and emancipation, Democrats argued that Republicans employed an unconstitutional means (the draft) to achieve an unconstitutional end (emancipation). In the summer of 1863, antidraft, antiblack mobs went on rampages in northern cities. New York experienced an explosion of unprecedented proportions. Solidly Democratic Irish workingmen, crowded into stinking, disease-ridden tenements, gouged by inflation, enraged by the inequities of the draft, and dead set against fighting to free blacks, erupted in four days of rioting. By the time police and soldiers restored order, at least 105 people, most of them black, lay dead and the Colored Orphan Asylum was a smoking ruin.

Linking the draft and emancipation, Democrats argued that Republicans employed an unconstitutional means (the draft) to achieve an unconstitutional end (emancipation).

The riots stunned black Northerners, but the racist mobs failed to achieve their purpose: the subordination of African Americans. Free black leaders had lobbied aggressively for emancipation, and after Lincoln's proclamation they fanned out over the North agitating for equality. They won some small wartime successes. Illinois and Iowa overturned laws that excluded blacks from entering the states. Illinois and Ohio began permitting blacks to testify in court. But defeat was more common. Indiana, for example, continued to forbid blacks to vote, testify, and attend public schools, and additional blacks were not allowed to enter the state.

Grinding Out Victory, 1863–1865

In the early months of 1863, the Union's prospects looked bleak, while the Confederate cause stood at high tide. But in July 1863, the tide began to recede. The military man who was most responsible for seeing that it never rose again was Ulysses S. Grant. Lifted from obscurity by brilliant successes in the West in 1862 and 1863, Grant became "*the* great man of the day," one man observed in July 1864, "perhaps of the age." Elevated to supreme command, Grant knit together a powerful war machine that integrated a sophisticated command structure, modern technology, and complex logistics and supply systems. But the arithmetic of this plain man remained unchanged: killing more of the enemy than he kills of you equaled "the complete overthrow of the rebellion."

The North ground out the victory, bloody battle by bloody battle. The balance tipped in the Union's favor in 1863, but if the Confederacy was beaten, Southerners clearly did not know it. The fighting reached new levels of ferocity in the last two years of the war. As national elections approached in the fall of 1864, a discouraged Lincoln expected a war-weary North to make him a one-term president. Instead, northern voters declared

their willingness to continue the war in the defense of the ideals of union and freedom.

Vicksburg and Gettysburg

Perched on the bluffs above the eastern bank of the Mississippi River, Vicksburg, Mississippi, bristled with cannon and dared Yankee ships to try to pass. This Confederate stronghold stood between Union forces and complete control of the river. Impenetrable terrain made it impossible to take the city from the north, and to get his army south of Vicksburg, Grant marched it down the western bank of the Mississippi. After four waterlogged failures, the troops made it through the swamps, but their supply wagons remained behind, up to their axles in the muck. Grant readied supply barges, and on the night of April 16, 1863, they ran the Confederate gauntlet. Rebel fire destroyed two vessels, but the rest rendezvoused with Grant's army below the city. Union forces crossed the Mississippi River, marched north more than one hundred miles, and attacked the city. When the Confederates beat back the assault, Grant began siege operations to starve out the enemy. Civilian inhabitants took to living in caves to escape incessant Union cannon bombardment, and to survive they soon began eating mules and rats.

Vicksburg Campaign, 1863

Eventually, the siege succeeded. On July 4, 1863, nearly thirty thousand rebels marched out of Vicksburg, stacked their arms, and surrendered unconditionally. A Yankee captain wrote home to his wife: "The backbone of the Rebellion is this day broken. The Confederacy is divided. . . . Vicksburg is ours. The Mississippi River is opened, and Gen. Grant is to be our next President."

On the same Fourth of July that a grateful nation received the news of Vicksburg, word arrived that Union forces had crushed General Lee at Gettysburg, Pennsylvania (Map 14.3). Lee's triumph two months earlier at Chancellorsville,

MAP 14.3

The Civil War, 1863–1865

Ulysses S. Grant's victory at Vicksburg divided the Confederacy at the Mississippi River. William Tecumseh Sherman's march from Chattanooga to Savannah divided it again. In northern Virginia, Robert E. Lee fought fiercely, but Grant's larger, better-supplied armies prevailed.

READING THE MAP: Describe the difference between Union and Confederate naval strength. Were the battles shown fought primarily in Union-controlled or Confederate-controlled territory?

CONNECTIONS: Did former slaves serve in the Civil War? If so, on which side(s)? Describe their efforts.

www.bedfordstmartins.com/tap   SEE THE ONLINE STUDY GUIDE for more help in analyzing this map.

Virginia, over Joseph "Fighting Joe" Hooker had revived his confidence, even though the battle cost him his favorite commander, the incomparable Stonewall Jackson, accidentally shot in the dark by his own troops. Lee wanted to relieve Virginia of the burden of the fighting, and he felt bold enough to think that he could deliver a morale-crunching defeat to the Yankees on their home turf.

On the same Fourth of July that a grateful nation received the news of Vicksburg, word arrived that Union forces had crushed General Lee at Gettysburg, Pennsylvania.

In June, Lee's seventy-five-thousand-man Army of Northern Virginia invaded Pennsylvania. On June 28, the Army of the Potomac, under its new commander, General George G. Meade, moved quickly to intercept it. Advanced units of both armies met at the small town of Gettysburg, where Union forces occupied the high ground. Three days of furious fighting, involving 165,000 soldiers, could not dislodge them from the ridges and hills. But Lee ached for a decisive victory, and on July 3 he ordered a major assault against the Union center on Cemetery Ridge. The open, rolling fields provided the dug-in Yankees with three-quarters of a mile of clear vision, and they raked the mile-wide line of Confederates with cannon and rifle fire. Time and again, the rebels closed ranks and raced on, until finally their momentum failed. Gettysburg cost Lee more than one-third of his army—twenty-eight thousand casualties. "It's all my fault," he said. In a drenching rain on the night of July 4, 1863, he marched his battered army back to Virginia.

Battle of Gettysburg, July 1863

The twin disasters at Vicksburg and Gettysburg proved to be the turning point of the war. The Confederacy could not replace the nearly sixty thousand soldiers who were captured, wounded, or killed. Lee never launched another major offensive north of the Mason-Dixon line. But it is hindsight that permits us to see the pair of battles as decisive. At the time, the Confederacy still controlled the heartland of the South, and Lee, back on the defensive in Virginia, still had a vicious sting. War-weariness threatened to erode the North's will to win before Union armies destroyed the Confederacy's ability to go on.

Grant Takes Command

In September 1863, Union general William Rosecrans placed his army in a dangerous situation in Chattanooga, Tennessee, where he had retreated after taking a whipping at the battle of Chickamauga (see Map 14.3). Rebels surrounded the disorganized bluecoats and threatened to starve them into submission. Ulysses S. Grant, whom Lincoln had made commander of all Union forces between the Mississippi River and the Appalachians, arrived in Chattanooga in October. Within weeks, he opened an effective supply line, broke the siege, and then (largely because troops disobeyed orders and charged wildly up Missionary Ridge) routed the Confederate army. The victory at Chattanooga had immense strategic value. It opened the door to Georgia. It also confirmed Lincoln's estimation of Grant. In March 1864, the president asked the commander to come east to become the general in chief of all Union armies.

In Washington, Grant implemented his grand strategy of a war of annihilation. He ordered a series of simultaneous assaults from Virginia to Louisiana. Two actions proved more significant than the others. In one, General William Tecumseh Sherman, whom Grant appointed his successor to command the western armies, plunged southeast toward Atlanta. In the other, Grant, who took control of the Army of the Potomac, went head-to-head with Lee for almost four straight weeks in Virginia.

Grant and Lee met in early May 1864 at the Wilderness, a dense tangle of scrub oaks and small pines that proved to be Lee's ally, for it helped offset the Yankees' numerical superiority. Often unable to see more than ten paces, the armies pounded away at each other until eighteen thousand Yankees and eleven thousand rebels had fallen. But the savagery of the Wilderness did not compare with that

GRANT AT COLD HARBOR
Seated next to his chief of staff, John A. Rawlins, at his Cold Harbor, Virginia, headquarters, Ulysses S. Grant plots his next move against Robert E. Lee. On June 3, 1864, Grant ordered frontal assaults against entrenched Confederate forces, resulting in enormous Union losses. "I am disgusted with the generalship displayed," young Brigadier General Emory Upton exclaimed. "Our men have, in many cases, been foolishly and wantonly slaughtered." Years later, Grant said that he regretted the assault at Cold Harbor, but in 1864 he kept pushing toward Richmond.
Chicago Historical Society.

at Spotsylvania Court House a few days later. Frenzied men fought hand to hand for eighteen hours in the rain. One veteran remembered men "piled upon each other in some places four layers deep, exhibiting every ghastly phase of mutilation." Spotsylvania cost Grant another eighteen thousand casualties and Lee ten thousand. But the Yankee bulldog would not let go. Grant kept moving and tangled with Lee again at Cold Harbor, where he lost thirteen thousand additional troops to Lee's five thousand. (See "Historical Question," page 526.)

Twice as many Union soldiers as rebel soldiers died in the four weeks of fighting in Virginia in the spring of 1864. Yet Grant did not consider himself defeated. Since Lee had only half the number of troops, he lost proportionally as many men as Grant. Ever the mathematician of war, Grant knew that the South could not replace the losses. Moreover, the campaign had carried Grant to the outskirts of Petersburg, just south of the Confederate capital. Since most of the major railroad lines supplying Richmond ran through Petersburg, Lee had little choice but to defend the city. Grant abandoned the costly tactic of the frontal assault and began a siege that immobilized both armies and dragged on for nine months.

There was no pause in "Uncle Billy" Sherman's invasion of Georgia. Grant had instructed Sherman to "get into the interior of the enemy's country as far as you can, inflicting all the damage you can against their War resources." In early May, while Grant thrashed in the Wilderness, Sherman moved 100,000 men south against the 65,000 rebels in the rugged mountains of northern Georgia. Skillful maneuvering, constant skirmishing, and one pitched battle (Kennesaw Mountain) brought Sherman to Atlanta, which fell on September 1.

Sherman was only warming up. Intending to "make Georgia howl," he marched out of Atlanta on November 15 with sixty-two thousand battle-hardened veterans, heading for Savannah, 285 miles away. Federal troops cut a swath from 25 to 60 miles wide. One veteran remembered, "[We] destroyed all we could not eat, stole their niggers, burned their cotton & gins, spilled their sorghum, burned & twisted their R. Roads and raised Hell generally." Sherman's scorched-earth campaign aimed at destroying the will of the southern people. A few weeks earlier, General Philip H. Sheridan had tried as much in the Shenandoah Valley, complying with Grant's order to turn the valley into "a barren waste . . . so that crows flying over it for the balance of

Why Did So Many Soldiers Die?

From 1861 to 1865, Americans killed Americans on a scale that had never before been seen. Not until the First World War, a half century later, would the world match (and surpass) the killing fields at Shiloh, Antietam, and Gettysburg (Figure 14.2). Why were the Civil War totals so huge? Why did 260,000 rebel soldiers and 373,000 Union soldiers die?

The balance between the ability to kill and the ability to save lives had tipped disastrously toward death. The sheer size of the armies—some battles involved more than 200,000 soldiers—ensured that battlefields would turn red with blood. Moreover, armies fought with antiquated strategy. In the generals' eyes, the ideal soldier remained the veteran of Napoleonic warfare, a man trained to advance with his comrades in a compact, close-order formation. Theory also emphasized frontal assaults. In classrooms at West Point and on the high plains of Mexico in the 1840s, men who would one day be officers in rival armies learned that infantry advancing shoulder to shoulder, supported by artillery, carried the day.

But by the 1860s, modern technology had made such strategy appallingly deadly. Weapons with ri-

WOUNDED MEN AT SAVAGE'S STATION
Misery did not end when the cannon ceased firing. This heap of mangled humanity strewn on the ground was but a fraction of the cost of General George McClellan's campaign on the Virginia peninsula in 1862.
Library of Congress.

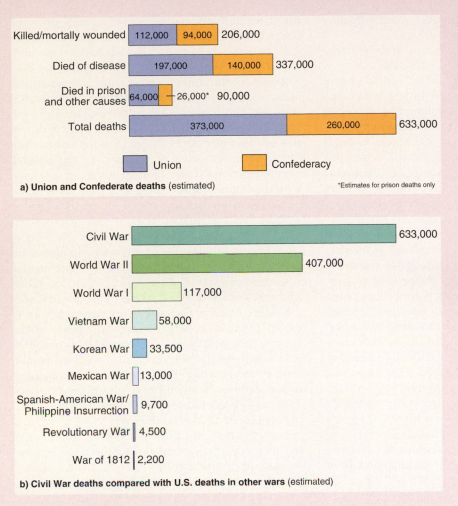

F I G U R E 14.2
Civil War Deaths
The loss of life in the Civil War was almost equal to the losses in all other American wars.

a) Union and Confederate deaths (estimated)

Killed/mortally wounded: 112,000 | 94,000 | 206,000

Died of disease: 197,000 | 140,000 | 337,000

Died in prison and other causes: 64,000 — 26,000* | 90,000

Total deaths: 373,000 | 260,000 | 633,000

■ Union   ■ Confederacy

*Estimates for prison deaths only

b) Civil War deaths compared with U.S. deaths in other wars (estimated)

Civil War: 633,000
World War II: 407,000
World War I: 117,000
Vietnam War: 58,000
Korean War: 33,500
Mexican War: 13,000
Spanish-American War/Philippine Insurrection: 9,700
Revolutionary War: 4,500
War of 1812: 2,200

fled barrels (that is, with spiral grooves cut into the bore) were replacing old smoothbore muskets. Whereas muskets had an effective range of only about eighty yards, rifles propelled spinning bullets four times as far. The rifle's greater range and accuracy, along with cannons firing canisters filled with flesh-ripping, bone-breaking steel shot, made sitting ducks of charging infantry units and gave enormous advantage to entrenched defensive forces. As a result, battles took thousands of lives in a single day. On July 2, 1862, the morning after the battle at Malvern Hill in eastern Virginia, a Union officer surveyed the scene: "Over five thousand dead and wounded men were on the ground . . . enough were alive and moving to give to the field a singular crawling effect."

Soldiers who littered the battlefields often lay for hours, sometimes days, without water or care of any kind. When the war began, no one anticipated casualty lists with thousands of names. Union and Confederate medical departments could not cope with skirmishes, much less large-scale battles. They had no ambulance corps to lift the wounded from the scene. They had no field hospitals to deliver them to. At first, the Quartermaster Department, which was responsible for constructing Union hospitals, answered demands that it do something by saying: "Men need guns, not beds." It took the shock of massive casualties to compel reform. Although a lack of resources meant that the South lagged behind the North, both North and South gradually organized effective ambulance *(Continued)* corps, built hospitals, and hired trained surgeons and nurses.

Soldiers did not always count speedy transportation to a field hospital as a blessing, however. As one Union soldier said, "I had rather risk a battle than the Hospitals." Real danger lurked behind the lines. While the technology of killing had advanced to very high standards, medicine remained primitive. Physicians gained a reputation as butchers, and soldiers dreaded the operating table more than they did entrenched riflemen. Serious wounds to the leg or arm usually meant amputation, the best way doctors knew to save lives. After major battles, surgeons worked among piles of wounded men's limbs.

The wounded man's real enemy was not doctors' callousness, but rather medical ignorance. Physicians had almost no knowledge of the cause and transmission of disease or the benefits of antiseptics. Not aware of basic germ theory, they spread infection almost every time they operated. Doctors wore the same bloody smock for days and washed their hands and their scalpels and saws in buckets of dirty water. When they had difficulty threading their needles, they wet the thread with their own saliva. Soldiers often did not survive amputations, not because of the operation but because of the infection that inevitably followed. Of the Union soldiers whose legs were amputated above the knee, more than half died. A Union doctor discovered in 1864 that bromine (previously used in combination with other elements as a sedative) arrested gangrene, but the best most amputees could hope for was maggots, which ate dead flesh on the stump and thus inhibited the spread of infection. During the Civil War, nearly one of every five wounded rebel soldiers died, and one in every six Yankees. A cen-

tury later, in Vietnam, the proportion of deaths was one wounded American soldier in four hundred.

Soldiers who avoided battlefield wounds and hospital infections still faced sickness. Deadly diseases swept through crowded army camps, where latrines were often in dangerous proximity to water supplies. The principal killers were dysentery and typhoid, but pneumonia and malaria also cut down thousands of men. Doctors did what they could, but their treatments often only added to the misery. They prescribed doses of turpentine for patients with typhoid, fought respiratory problems with mustard plasters, and attacked intestinal disorders with blisters and sulfuric acid.

Dorothea Dix, Clara Barton, Juliet Ann Opie Hopkins, and thousands of other female nurses in the North and South improved the wounded men's odds and alleviated their misery. Civilian relief agencies, such as the U.S. Sanitary Commission and the Women's Relief Society of the Confederacy, promoted hygiene in army camps and made some headway. Nevertheless, as Figure 14.2 shows, disease killed nearly twice as many soldiers as did combat. Many who died of disease were prisoners of war. Approximately thirty thousand Northerners died in Confederate prisons, and approximately twenty-six thousand Southerners died in Union prisons. No northern prison, however, could equal the horror of Andersonville in southern Georgia. In August 1864, about thirty-three thousand emaciated men lived in unspeakable conditions in a twenty-six-acre barren stockade with no shelter except what the prisoners were able to construct. More than thirteen thousand perished.

In the end, 633,000 northern and southern soldiers died, a staggering death toll.

this season will have to carry their provender [food] with them." When Sherman's troops entered an undefended Savannah in the third week of December, the general telegraphed Lincoln that he had "a Christmas gift" for him.

The Election of 1864

In the fall, white men in the Union states turned to the election of a president. Never before had a na-

tion held general elections in the midst of war. "We can not have free government without elections," Lincoln explained, "and if the rebellion could force us to forgo or postpone a national election, it might fairly claim to have already conquered and ruined us."

Lincoln's determination to hold elections is especially noteworthy because the Democratic Party smelled victory. The Union war effort had stalled during the summer. With Sherman temporarily

R. K. SNEDEN'S SHANTY AT ANDERSONVILLE PRISON, GA., ROBERT KNOX SNEDEN, JULY 15, 1864
The train carrying prisoner-of-war Robert Sneden arrived at Andersonville on the last
day of February 1864 just as the Confederates were completing the stockade that sur-
rounded their newest prison. Soon the sixteen and a half acres in southwestern Georgia
were crammed with humanity. By June the prison area had to be extended to twenty-six
and a half acres. Its 33,000 Union prisoners made Andersonville the fifth largest city in
the Confederacy. A talented water colorist, Sneden sketched this scene while a captive
and touched it up later. Smallpox, dysentery, scurvy, malnutrition, and infections took
the lives of thousands. "The flies are now here in millions," Sneden observed. "Every-
thing is covered with them, dense swarms like a cloud settle on the pile of dead which
are daily seen near the gates. The ground in the thickest part settled in the camp is
fairly alive and moves with maggots or lice! The filthy swamp undulates like small
waves with them, while the insufferable stench nearly takes away one's breath!"
Virginia Historical Society.

checked outside Atlanta and Grant bogged down in the siege of Petersburg, frustration had settled over the North. Rankled by inflation, the draft, the attack on civil liberties, and the commitment to blacks, Northerners appeared ready for a change. Lincoln himself concluded in the gloomy summer of 1864, "It seems exceedingly probable that this administration will not be re-elected."

Democrats were badly divided, however. "Peace" Democrats insisted on an armistice, while "war" Democrats supported the conflict but opposed Republican means of fighting it. They tried to paper over the chasm by nominating a war candidate, General George McClellan, but adopting a peace platform that demanded that "immediate efforts be made for a cessation of hostilities." Republicans labeled the peace plank a conspiracy of "Cop-

perheads" (after a deadly, easily concealed snake) to sell out the Union and claimed that it "virtually proposed to surrender the country to the rebels in arms against us."

"We can not have free government without elections," Lincoln explained, "and if the rebellion could force us to forgo or postpone a national election, it might fairly claim to have already conquered and ruined us."

Lincoln was no shoo-in for renomination, much less reelection. Conservatives believed he had acted precipitously in emancipating the slaves, and radicals criticized him for moving too slowly to free them and for failing to champion black equality. But frightened by the strength of the peace Democrats, the Republican Party stuck with Lincoln. In an effort to reach out to the largest number of voters, however, the Republicans made two changes. First, they chose a new name. As the Union Party, they made it easier for prowar Democrats to embrace Lincoln. Second, they chose a new vice presidential candidate. Dumping Hannibal Hamlin of Maine, the incumbent vice president, they turned to Andrew Johnson of Tennessee, the only southern senator to remain in Congress when his colleagues fled south in the winter of 1860–61. As a Southerner, a former slaveholder, and a former Democrat, Johnson personified the message that the party of Lincoln was broad enough to include any uncompromising Unionist.

Lincoln's pessimism about being reelected proved to be unfounded. The capture of Atlanta in September had turned the political tide in favor of the Republicans. Lincoln received 55 percent of the popular vote, but his electoral margin was a whopping 212 to McClellan's 21 (Map 14.4). The Republicans also stormed back in the congressional elections, gaining large margins over the Democrats in the Senate and the House. The Union Party bristled

with factions, but they united for a resounding victory. The victory gave Lincoln a mandate to continue the war until slavery and the Confederacy were dead.

The Confederacy Collapses

Jefferson Davis found little to celebrate as the new year of 1865 dawned in Richmond. Military disaster littered the Confederate landscape. With the destruction of John B. Hood's army at Nashville in November, the interior of the Confederacy lay in Yankee hands (see Map 14.3). Sherman's troops, resting momentarily in Savannah, eyed South Carolina hungrily. Only Lee's army remained, and Grant had it pinned down in Petersburg just a few miles from Richmond. Southerners took out their frustration and bitterness on their president. Kinder than most, Alexander Stephens, vice president of the Confederacy, likened Davis to "my poor old blind and deaf dog."

In the final months of the war, more and more whites turned their backs on the rebellion. News from the battlefields made it difficult not to conclude that the Yankees had beaten them. Soldiers' wives begged their husbands to return home to keep their families from starving, and the stream of deserters became a flood. In most cases, whites lost the will to continue not so much because they lost faith in southern independence but because they had been battered into submission. Despite all the divisions and conflicts within the Confederacy and the loss of heart in the final months, white Southerners had shown remarkable endurance for their cause. Half of the 900,000 Confederate soldiers had been killed or wounded, and ragged, hungry women and children had sacrificed for four years. Confederates had shown remarkable staying power through the bloodiest war then known to history. (See "Documenting the American Promise," page 516.)

But Jefferson Davis would not accept defeat. He concluded that there was one more arrow in the Confederate quiver. Slaves could become rebel soldiers. The Confederacy had used both slaves and free blacks in noncombatant military roles, but now Davis proposed arming slaves and, with a vague promise of freedom as an incentive, sending them to fight the Yankees. This bizarre notion reflects Richmond's desperation, but Lee approved, and in March 1865, so did the Confederate Congress. Slaveholders in the countryside, however, objected

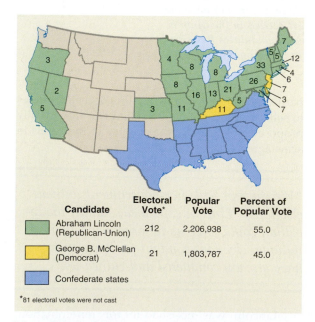

	Candidate	Electoral Vote*	Popular Vote	Percent of Popular Vote
(green)	Abraham Lincoln (Republican-Union)	212	2,206,938	55.0
(yellow)	George B. McClellan (Democrat)	21	1,803,787	45.0
(blue)	Confederate states			

*81 electoral votes were not cast

MAP 14.4

The Election of 1864

RUINS OF RICHMOND

A Union soldier and a small boy in a Union cap contemplate the silence and devastation of Richmond, Virginia, the Confederacy's capital. On their way out of the city on the evening of April 2, 1865, Confederate demolition squads set fire to tobacco warehouses and ammunition dumps. Huge explosions tore holes in the city, and windswept fires destroyed much of what was left standing. As one Confederate observed, "The old war-scarred city seemed to prefer annihilation to conquest."
Library of Congress.

to sacrificing slavery to win southern independence. A South Carolina planter asked who gave Richmond the right "to destroy that which it was created to protect and perpetuate." "No!" cried a plantation mistress, "freedom for whites, slavery for negroes, God has so ordained it!" Before the experiment got off the ground, time ran out for the Confederacy.

The end came with a rush. On February 1, 1865, Sherman's troops stormed out of Savannah into South Carolina, the "cradle of the Confederacy." But before Sherman could push through North Carolina and arrive at the rear of Lee's army at Petersburg, where he expected to crush the Confederates between his hammer and Grant's anvil, Lee abandoned the city. Davis fled Richmond, and the capital city fell a few days later. Grant pursued Lee for one hundred miles, until Lee surrendered on April 9, 1865, in a farmhouse near the town of Appomattox Court House, Virginia. The beaten man arrived in an immaculate full-dress uniform, complete with sash and sword; the victor came in his usual mud-splattered private's outfit. Grant offered a generous peace. He allowed Lee's men to return home and to take their horses to help "put in a crop to carry themselves and their families through the next winter." With Lee gone, the remaining ragtag Confederate armies lost hope and gave up. After four years, the war was over.

The day after Lee's surrender, a brass band led a happy crowd of three thousand to the White House, where they pleaded with Lincoln for a speech. He begged off and asked the band to strike up "Dixie." He knew that the rebels had claimed the tune as their own, he said, but it was one of his favorites, and now he was taking it back. The crowd roared its approval, and the band played "Dixie," following it with "Yankee Doodle." No one was more relieved than Lincoln that the war was over, but his celebration was restrained. He told his cabinet that his postwar burdens would weigh almost as heavily as those of wartime. But Lincoln had other things on his mind when he attended Ford's Theatre on the evening of Good Friday, April 14, 1865. While he and his wife, Mary, enjoyed *Our American Cousin*, a British comedy, John Wilkes Booth, an actor with southern sympathies, slipped into the president's box and mortally wounded Lincoln with a single shot to his head. The man who had led the nation through the war would not lead it in its postwar search for a just peace.

Conclusion: The Second American Revolution

The Civil War had a profound effect on the nation and its people. It devastated the South. Three-fourths of southern white men of military age served in the army, and at least half of them were captured, wounded, or killed or died of disease. The war destroyed two-fifths of the South's livestock, wrecked half of the farm machinery, and blackened dozens of cities and towns. The immediate impact of the war on the North was more paradoxical. Putting down the slaveholders' rebellion cost the North a heavy price: 373,000 lives. But rather than devastating the land, war set the countryside and cities humming with business activity.

A transformed nation emerged from the crucible of war. Antebellum America was decentralized politically and loosely integrated economically. To bend the resources of the country to a Union victory, Congress enacted legislation that reshaped the nation's political and economic character. It adopted policies that established the sovereignty of the federal government and the dominance of industrial capitalism. Moreover, the common sacrifice of northern people to save the nation created an even fiercer national loyalty. The shift in power from South to North and the creation of a national government, a national economy, and a national spirit led one historian to call the American Civil War the "Second American Revolution."

Most revolutionary of all, the war ended slavery. As Frederick Douglass had predicted, the South's war to preserve slavery killed it. Because that ancient labor and racial system was entangled in almost every aspect of southern life, slavery's uprooting would mean fundamental change. But the full meaning of abolition remained unclear in 1865. The task of determining the new economic, political, and social status of four million ex-slaves would be the principal task of the era known as Reconstruction.

www.bedfordstmartins.com/tap   SEE THE ONLINE STUDY GUIDE to assess your mastery of the material covered in this chapter.

CHRONOLOGY

1861 **April 12–13.** Confederate forces attack Fort Sumter, South Carolina, the opening engagement of Civil War.

April. Union nurse Dorothea Dix named superintendent of female nurses.

April–May. Four Upper South states secede and join Confederacy.

July. Union forces routed at Manassas, Virginia, in first major clash of war.

August. Congress approves first Confiscation Act, which allows seizure of any slave employed by Confederate military.

1862 **February.** Legal Tender Act creates first national currency, called "greenbacks."

Union forces in West under General Ulysses S. Grant capture Fort Henry and Fort Donelson and drive Confederates from Kentucky and most of Tennessee.

April. Battle of Shiloh in Tennessee results in huge casualties and ends Confederate bid to control Mississippi Valley.

Confederate Congress passes first draft law in American history.

May. Homestead Act offers western land to those who would live and labor on it.

May–July. General George McClellan's Union forces defeated during peninsula campaign in Virginia.

July. Congress approves second Confiscation Act, freeing all slaves of rebel masters.

Congress passes Militia Act, authorizing enrollment of blacks in Union military.

September 17. Battle of Antietam stops Lee's advance into Maryland, but Confederate forces escape back to Virginia.

September 22. Lincoln announces preliminary emancipation proclamation.

1863 **January 1.** Emancipation Proclamation becomes law, freeing slaves in areas still in rebellion.

February. National Banking Act creates system of national banks.

March. Congress authorizes draft.

July. Vicksburg falls to Union forces under Grant, effectively cutting Confederacy in two along Mississippi River.

Battle of Gettysburg results in Confederate defeat and Lee's last offensive into North.

1864 **March.** Grant appointed general in chief of all Union forces.

May–June. Grant's forces engage Confederates in Virginia in bloodiest fighting of war, from Wilderness campaign to beginnings of siege of Petersburg.

September. Atlanta falls to Union forces under General William Tecumseh Sherman.

November. Lincoln reelected president.

December. Sherman occupies Savannah after scorched-earth campaign in Georgia.

1865 **April 9.** Lee surrenders to Grant at Appomattox Court House, Virginia, essentially ending Confederate resistance.

April 14. Lincoln shot by John Wilkes Booth at Ford's Theatre in Washington. He dies on April 15, succeeded by Vice President Andrew Johnson.

BIBLIOGRAPHY

GENERAL WORKS

Jean Harvey Baker, David Herbert Donald, and Michael F. Holt, *The Civil War and Reconstruction* (2001).

James M. McPherson, *Battle Cry of Freedom: The Civil War Era* (1988).

Allan Nevins, *The War for the Union*, 4 vols. (1959–1971).

Roger L. Ransom, *Conflict and Compromise: The Political Economy of Slavery, Emancipation, and the American Civil War* (1989).

Charles P. Roland, *An American Iliad: The Story of the Civil War* (1991).

Russell F. Weigley, *A Great Civil War: A Military and Political History, 1861–1865* (2000).

THE COMBATANTS

Michael Barton, *Goodmen, the Character of Civil War Soldiers* (1981).

Richard E. Beringer et al., *Why the South Lost the Civil War* (1986).

Gabor S. Boritt, ed., *Why the Confederacy Lost* (1992).

Catherine Clinton and Nina Silber, eds., *Divided Houses: Gender and the Civil War* (1992).

Richard Nelson Current, *Lincoln's Loyalists: Union Soldiers from the Confederacy* (1992).

David Herbert Donald, *Lincoln* (1995).

David Herbert Donald, ed., *Why the North Won the Civil War* (1960).

Lesley J. Gordon, *General George E. Pickett in Life and Legend* (1998).

Randall C. Jimerson, *The Private Civil War: Popular Thought during the Sectional Conflict* (1988).

Gerald F. Linderman, *Embattled Courage: The Experience of Combat in the American Civil War* (1987).

John F. Marszalek, *Sherman: A Soldier's Passion for Order* (1993).

James Marten, *The Children's Civil War* (1998).

William S. McFeely, *Grant: A Biography* (1981).

Randall M. Miller, Harry S. Stout, and Charles Reagan Wilson, eds., *Religion and the American Civil War* (1998).

Reid Mitchell, *Civil War Soldiers: Their Expectations and Their Experiences* (1988).

Reid Mitchell, *The Vacant Chair: The Northern Soldier Leaves Home* (1993).

Mark E. Neely Jr., *The Last Best Hope of Earth: Abraham Lincoln and the Promise of America* (1993).

Alan T. Nolan, *Lee Considered: General Robert E. Lee and Civil War History* (1991).

Stephen B. Oates, *A Woman of Valor: Clara Barton and the Civil War* (1994).

James I. Robertson Jr., *Soldiers Blue and Gray* (1988).

Stephen W. Sears, *George B. McClellan: The Young Napoleon* (1988).

Brooks D. Simpson, *Ulysses S. Grant: Triumph over Adversity, 1822–1865* (2000).

Amy Dru Stanley, *From Bondage to Contract: Wage Labor, Marriage, and the Market in the Age of Slave Emancipation* (1998).

Emory M. Thomas, *Robert E. Lee: A Biography* (1995).

Bell I. Wiley, *The Life of Johnny Reb: The Common Soldier of the Confederacy* (1943).

Bell I. Wiley, *The Life of Billy Yank: The Common Soldier of the Union* (1952).

C. Vann Woodward, ed., *Mary Chesnut's Civil War* (1981).

MILITARY HISTORY

Gabor S. Boritt, ed., *Lincoln's Generals* (1994).

Bruce Catton, *The Centennial History of the Civil War*, 3 vols. (1961–1965).

Michael Fellman, *Inside War: The Guerilla Conflict in Missouri during the American Civil War* (1989).

Shelby Foote, *The Civil War: A Narrative*, 3 vols. (1958–1974).

Joseph T. Glatthaar, *The March to the Sea and Beyond: Sherman's Troops in the Savannah and Carolinas Campaigns* (1985).

Mark Grimsley, *The Hard Hand of War: Union Military Policy toward Southern Civilians, 1861–1865* (1995).

Herman Hattaway and Archer Jones, *How the North Won: A Military History of the Civil War* (1983).

Archer Jones, *Civil War Command and Strategy: The Process of Victory and Defeat* (1992).

Alvin M. Josephy Jr., *The Civil War in the American West* (1991).

Charles Royster, *The Destructive War: William Tecumseh Sherman, Stonewall Jackson, and the Americans* (1991).

Stephen W. Sears, *Landscape Turned Red: The Battle of Antietam* (1983).

Steven E. Woodworth, *Davis and Lee at War* (1995).

UNION AND FREEDOM

Herman Belz, *Emancipation and Equal Rights: Politics and Constitutionalism during the Civil War Era* (1978).

Ira Berlin et al., eds., *Freedom: A Documentary History of Emancipation, 1861–1867*, 3 vols. (1982–1990).

David W. Blight, *Frederick Douglass's Civil War: Keeping Faith in Jubilee* (1989).

Dudley Taylor Cornish, *The Sable Arm: Black Troops in the Union Army, 1861–1865* (1987).

LaWanda Cox, *Lincoln and Black Freedom: A Study in Presidential Leadership* (1981).

Louis S. Gerteis, *From Contraband to Freedman: Federal Policy toward Southern Blacks, 1861–1865* (1973).

Joseph T. Glatthaar, *Forged in Battle: The Civil War Alliance of Black Soldiers and White Officers* (1990).

Waldo E. Martin Jr., *The Mind of Frederick Douglass* (1984).

William S. McFeely, *Frederick Douglass* (1991).

James M. McPherson, *The Negro's Civil War: How American Negroes Felt and Acted during the War for the Union* (1965).

James M. McPherson, *Abraham Lincoln and the Second American Revolution* (1990).

Clarence L. Mohr, *On the Threshold of Freedom: Masters and Slaves in Civil War Georgia* (1986).

Edwin S. Redkey, ed., *A Grand Army of Black Men: Letters from African-American Soldiers in the Union Army, 1861–1865* (1992).

C. Peter Ripley, *Slaves and Freedmen in Civil War Louisiana* (1976).

C. Peter Ripley, ed., *Witness for Freedom: African American Voices on Race, Slavery, and Emancipation* (1993).

THE SOUTH AT WAR

Stephen V. Ash, *When the Yankees Came: Conflict and Chaos in the Occupied South, 1861–1865* (1995).

William A. Blair, *Virginia's Private War: Feeding Body and Soul in the Confederacy, 1861–1865* (1998).

William J. Cooper, *Jefferson Davis, American* (2000).

Mary A. DeCredico, *Patriotism for Profit: Georgia's Urban Entrepreneurs and the Confederate War Effort* (1990).

Charles B. Dew, *Ironmaker to the Confederacy: Joseph R. Anderson and the Tredegar Iron Works* (1966).

Wayne K. Durrill, *War of Another Kind: A Southern Community in the Great Rebellion* (1990).

Paul D. Escott, *After Secession: Jefferson Davis and the Failure of Confederate Nationalism* (1978).

Drew Gilpin Faust, *The Creation of Confederate Nationalism: Ideology and Identity in the Civil War South* (1988).

Drew Gilpin Faust, *Mothers of Invention: Women of the Slaveholding South in the American Civil War* (1996).

Ernest B. Furgurson, *Ashes of Glory: Richmond at War* (1996).

Gary W. Gallagher, *The Confederate War* (1997).

Charles M. Hubbard, *The Burden of Confederate Diplomacy* (1998).

Ervin L. Jordan Jr., *Black Confederates and Afro-Yankees in Civil War Virginia* (1995).

Robert Tracy McKenzie, *One South or Many? Plantation Belt and Upcountry in Civil War–Era Tennessee* (1994).

John Solomon Otto, *Southern Agriculture during the Civil War Era, 1860–1880* (1994).

Philip Shaw Paludan, *Victims: A True Story of the Civil War* (1981).

George C. Rable, *Civil Wars: Women and the Crisis of Southern Nationalism* (1989).

George C. Rable, *The Confederate Republic: A Revolution against Politics* (1994).

James L. Roark, *Masters without Slaves: Southern Planters in the Civil War and Reconstruction* (1977).

Daniel E. Sutherland, *Seasons of War: The Ordeal of a Confederate Community, 1861–1865* (1995).

Emory M. Thomas, *The Confederacy as a Revolutionary Experience* (1971).

Emory M. Thomas, *The Confederate Nation, 1861–1865* (1979).

Steven Elliott Tripp, *Yankee Town, Southern City: Race and Class Relations in Civil War Lynchburg* (1997).

Stephen R. Wise, *Lifeline of the Confederacy: Blockade Running during the Civil War* (1988).

THE NORTH AT WAR

Iver Bernstein, *The New York City Draft Riots: Their Significance for American Society and Politics in the Age of the Civil War* (1990).

George M. Fredrickson, *The Inner Civil War: Northern Intellectuals and the Crisis of the Union* (1965).

Earl J. Hess, *Liberty, Virtue, and Progress: Northerners and Their War for the Union* (1988).

Theodore J. Karamanski, *Rally 'Round the Flag: Chicago and the Civil War* (1993).

Ernest A. McKay, *The Civil War and New York City* (1990).

James H. Moorhead, *American Apocalypse: Yankee Protestants and the Civil War, 1860–1869* (1978).

Mark E. Neely Jr., *The Fate of Liberty: Abraham Lincoln and Civil Liberties* (1991).

Philip Shaw Paludan, *"A People's Contest": The Union and Civil War, 1861–1865* (1988).

Philip Shaw Paludan, *The Presidency of Abraham Lincoln* (1994).

Heather Cox Richardson, *The Greatest Nation of the Earth: Republican Economic Policies During the Civil War* (1997).

Joel H. Silby, *A Respectable Minority: The Democratic Party in the Civil War Era, 1860–1868* (1977).

ba be bi bo bu	ra re ri ro ru
da de di do du	sa se si so su
fa fe fi fo fu	ta te ti to tu
ka ke ki ko ku	va ve vi vo vu

Top. | Hen and chickens. | Drum.

la le li lo lu	ya ye yi yo yu
na ne ni no nu	*ca ce ci co cu
pa pe pi po pu	ga ge gi go gu

Bugle.

ab eb ib
ab ed id
af ef if
ag eg i

Zebra. | Hobby-horse.

Fire Engine. | Snake.

Turkey. | Hoopoe

Squirrel.

AMERICAN
ONE CENT
PRIMER.

NEW YORK:
KIGGINS & KELLOGG, PUBLISHERS,
Nos. 123 & 125 WILLIAM STREET,
Between John & Fulton.

ONE-CENT PRIMER

"The people are hungry and thirsty after knowledge," a former slave from South Carolina observed after the Civil War. Future African American leader Booker T. Washington remembered *"a whole race trying to go to school. Few were too young, and none too old, to make the attempt to learn."* Inexpensive elementary textbooks (this humble eight-page primer cost a penny) offered poor ex-slaves the basic elements of literacy—the letters of the alphabet and the sounds they make. For people who had been forbidden to learn to read and write as slaves, literacy symbolized freedom. It also meant that deeply religious people could experience the joy of reading the Bible. Literacy provided a crucial tool for negotiating the hostile world of the postwar South. Reading and writing permitted African Americans to understand labor agreements, sign contracts, and participate knowledgeably in politics.

The William Gladstone Collection.

RECONSTRUCTION
1863–1877

15

Y ORK DISAPPEARED on yesterday morning," David Golightly Harris noted in his journal on June 6, 1865. "I suppose that he has gone to the yankey. I wish they would give him a good whipping & hasten him back." York, a black field hand, had once belonged to Harris, a white slaveholder in Spartanburg District, South Carolina. When York "disappeared," however, the war had been over for two months, and York was a free man. In Harris's mind, however, simply declaring York free did not make him so. In July, Harris noted that another field hand, Old Will, had left "to try to enjoy the freedom the Yankey's have promised the negroes." Two weeks later black freedom still seemed in doubt. "There is much talk about freeing the negroes. Some are said already to have freed them," Harris declared. But Harris had not freed anyone. He did not inform his former slaves of their freedom until federal military authorities required him to. "*Freed the Negroes*," he announced on August 16, four months after Appomattox.

Like many ex-slaveholders, Harris had trouble coming to grips with emancipation. "Family well, Horses well, Cattle well, Hogs well & everything else are well so far as I know, if it was not for the free negroes," Harris wrote on September 17. "On their account everything is turned upside down. So much so that we do not know what to do with our land, nor who to hire if we want it worked. . . . We are in the midst of troublesome times & do not know what will turn up." Harris had owned ten slaves, and emancipation cost him more than $10,000 in lost capital, but the future concerned him more than the past. He faced what seemed to him an insoluble problem. He needed black labor to cultivate his farm, but like most whites he did not believe that blacks would work much when free. Some kind of compulsion would be needed. But slavery was gone, leaving the South upside down. Some white men in Harris's neighborhood sought to put it right again. "In this district several negroes have been badly whipped & several have been hung by some unknown persons," he noted in November. "This has a tendency to keep them in their proper bounds & make them more humble." But the violence did not keep ex-slaves from acting like free people. On Christmas Day 1865, Harris recorded, "The negroes leave today to hunt themselves a new home while we will be left to wait upon ourselves."

Across the South, ex-masters predicted that emancipation would mean economic collapse and social anarchy. Carl Schurz, a Union general who undertook a fact-finding mission to the ex-Confederate states in the summer of 1865, encountered this dire prediction often enough to conclude that the Civil War was a "revolution but half accomplished." Northern victory had freed the slaves, but it had not changed former slaveholders' minds about the need for slavery. Left to themselves, Schurz believed, whites would "introduce some new system of forced labor, not perhaps exactly slavery in its old form but something similar to it." To defend their freedom, blacks would need federal protection, land of their own, and voting rights, Schurz concluded. Until whites "cut loose from the past, it will be a dangerous experiment

BLACK WOMAN IN COTTON FIELDS, THOMASVILLE, GEORGIA

Few images of everyday black women during the era of reconstruction survive. This photograph was taken in 1895, but it nevertheless goes to the heart of the labor struggle after the Civil War. As slaves, black women worked in the fields, and white landlords wanted them to continue working there after emancipation. Freedom allowed some women to escape field labor, but not this Georgian, who no doubt worked to survive. Despite her plight, the photograph reveals a strong person with a clear sense of who she is. Although worn to protect her head and body from the fierce heat, her intricately wrapped headdress dramatically expresses her individuality.

Vanishing Georgia Collection, Georgia Department of Archives and History, Atlanta, Georgia.

to put Southern society upon its own legs." The end of the war did not mean the beginning of peace. Instead, the nation entered one of its most chaotic and conflicted eras—Reconstruction.

It was not that the Civil War failed to resolve anything. Northern victory doomed secession and slavery, but out of the war emerged two new divisive questions. First, what was the status of the defeated South within the Union? Would the eleven ex-Confederate states be quickly and forgivingly welcomed back, or would they be held at arm's length and required to reform before resuming their former places? Second, what would freedom mean for ex-slaves? Would they be left to make their place in the South on their own, or would the federal government guarantee free labor, full citizenship, and equality?

The political part of the debate took place in the nation's capital and in the state legislatures and county seats of the South. Politics was never simply a debate between whites. Blacks emerged from slavery with their own ideas, and they became active agents in the struggle to define freedom. The struggle also had social and economic dimensions. On farms and plantations from Virginia to Texas, ex-slaves like York and Old Will strove to escape bondage and to become free laborers and free people, while whites like David Golightly Harris resisted letting go of the Old South. In the midst of the flux and chaos, a small band of crusading women sought to achieve gender equality. The years of reconstruction witnessed an enormous contest to determine the consequences of Confederate defeat and emancipation. In the end white Southerners prevailed. They declared a "New South," but it was a very different South from the one Harris wished to return.

Wartime Reconstruction

Reconstruction did not wait for the end of war. As the odds of a northern victory increased, thinking about reunification quickened. Immediately, a question arose: Who had authority to devise a plan of reconstruction? The Founders had not anticipated such a problem, and so the Constitution stood silent. Lincoln believed firmly that reconstruction was a matter of executive responsibility. Congress just as firmly asserted its jurisdiction. Fueling the argument about who had authority to set the terms of reconstruction were significant differences about the terms themselves. Lincoln's primary aim was the restoration of national unity, which he sought through a program of speedy, forgiving political reconciliation. Congress feared that the president's program amounted to restoring the old southern ruling class to power. It wanted greater assurances of white loyalty and greater guarantees of black rights.

In their eagerness to formulate a plan for political reunification, neither Lincoln nor Congress gave much attention to the South's land and labor problems. But the war rapidly eroded slavery and traditional plantation agriculture, and Yankee military commanders in the Union-occupied areas of the Confederacy had no choice but to oversee the emergence of a new labor system. With little guidance from Washington, northern officials felt their way along, bumping heads with both planters and freedmen.

"To Bind Up the Nation's Wounds"

On March 4, 1865, President Abraham Lincoln delivered his second inaugural address. His words blazed with religious imagery as he surveyed the history of the long, deadly war and then looked ahead to peace. "With malice toward none; with charity for all; with firmness in the right, as God gives us to see the right," Lincoln said, "let us strive on to finish the work we are in; to bind up the nation's wounds . . . to do all which may achieve and cherish a just, and a lasting peace." Lincoln had contemplated reunion for nearly two years. Deep compassion for the enemy guided his thinking about peace. But kindness is not the key to understanding Lincoln's program. His reconstruction plan aimed primarily at shortening the war and ending slavery.

In his Proclamation of Amnesty and Reconstruction, issued in December 1863, when Union forces had finally gained the upper hand on the battlefield, Lincoln offered a full pardon to rebels willing to renounce secession and to accept the abolition of slavery. (Pardons were valuable because they restored all property, except slaves, and full political rights.) His offer excluded several groups of Confederates, such as high-ranking civilian and military officers, but the plan called for no mass arrests, no trials for treason, and no executions. Instead, when only 10 percent of men who had been qualified voters in 1860 had taken an oath of allegiance, they could organize a new state government. Lincoln's plan did not require ex-rebels to ex-

tend social or political rights to ex-slaves, nor did it anticipate a program of long-term federal assistance to freedmen. Clearly, the president sought to restore the broken Union, not to reform it.

Lincoln's easy terms enraged abolitionists like Bostonian Wendell Phillips, who charged that the president "makes the negro's freedom a mere sham." He "is willing that the negro should be free but seeks nothing else for him," Phillips declared. He compared Lincoln to the most passive of the Civil War generals: "What McClellan was on the battlefield—'Do as little hurt as possible!'—Lincoln is in civil affairs—'Make as little change as possible!'" Phillips and other northern radicals called instead for a thorough overhaul of southern society. Their ideas proved to be too drastic for most Republicans during the war years, but Congress agreed that Lincoln's plan was inadequate. In July 1864, Congress put forward a plan of its own.

As General William T. Sherman was marching on Atlanta, Congressman Henry Winter Davis of Maryland and Senator Benjamin Wade of Ohio jointly sponsored a bill that threw out Lincoln's "10 percent plan" and demanded that at least half of the voters in a conquered rebel state take the oath of allegiance before reconstruction could begin. Moreover, the Wade-Davis bill banned ex-Confederates from participating in the drafting of new state constitutions. Finally, the bill guaranteed the equality of freedmen before the law. Congress's reconstruction would be neither as quick nor as forgiving as Lincoln's. Still, the Wade-Davis bill angered radicals because it did not include a provision for black suffrage. When Lincoln exercised his right not to sign the bill and let it die instead, Wade and Davis published a manifesto charging the president with usurpation of power. They warned Lincoln to confine himself to "his executive duties—to obey and execute, not make the laws—to suppress by arms armed rebellion, and leave political organization to Congress."

Clearly, the president sought to restore the broken Union, not to reform it.

Undeterred, Lincoln continued to nurture the formation of loyal state governments under his own plan. Four states—Louisiana, Arkansas, Tennessee, and Virginia—fulfilled the president's requirements, but Congress refused to seat representatives from the "Lincoln states." In his last public address in April 1865, Lincoln defended his plan but stressed his willingness to be flexible. For the first time he expressed publicly his endorsement of suffrage for southern blacks, at least "the very intelligent, and . . . those who serve our cause as soldiers." The announcement demonstrated that Lincoln's thinking about reconstruction was still evolving. Four days later, he was dead.

Land and Labor

Of all the problems raised by emancipation, none proved more critical than the transition from slave to free labor. Slavery had been, at bottom, a labor system, and while Republicans agreed that free labor would replace forced labor, they disagreed about what free labor would mean in the South. As federal armies proceeded to invade and occupy the Confederacy during the war, hundreds of thousands of slaves became free workers. Moreover, northern occupation meant that Union armies controlled vast territories where legal title to land had become unclear. The wartime Confiscation Acts punished "traitors" by taking away their property. What to do with federally occupied land and how to organize labor on it engaged former slaves, former slaveholders, Union military commanders, and federal government officials long before the war ended.

Up and down the Mississippi valley, occupying federal troops announced a new labor code. The code required planters to sign contracts with ex-slaves and to pay wages. It also obligated employers to provide food, housing, and medical care. It outlawed whipping and other forms of physical punishment, but reserved to the army the right to discipline blacks who refused to work. The code required black laborers to enter into contracts, work diligently, and remain subordinate and obedient. Military leaders clearly had no intention of promoting a social or economic revolution. Instead, they sought to end coerced labor and to restore plantation agriculture with wage labor. The effort resulted in a hybrid system of "compulsory free labor" that satisfied no one. Depending on one's point of view, it either provided too little or too much of a break with the past.

Planters complained because the new system fell short of slavery. Blacks could not be "transformed by proclamation," a Louisiana sugar planter warned. Yet under the new system, blacks "are expected to perform their new obligations without coercion, & without the fear of punishment which is essential to stimulate the idle and correct the vicious." Without the right to whip, he concluded, the new labor system did not have a chance.

African Americans found the new regime too reminiscent of slavery to be called "free labor." Of its many shortcomings, none disappointed ex-slaves more than the failure to provide them land of their own. "What's the use of being free if you don't own land enough to be buried in?" one man asked. Freedmen believed they had a moral right to land because they and their ancestors had worked it without compensation for more than two centuries. Moreover, several wartime developments seemed to indicate that the federal government planned to link black freedom and landownership.

In January 1865, General Sherman had set aside for black settlement part of the coast south of Charleston. He devised the plan to relieve himself of the burden of thousands of impoverished blacks who trailed desperately after his army. By June 1865, some forty thousand freedmen sat on 400,000 acres of "Sherman land." In addition, in March 1865, Congress established the Bureau of Refugees, Freedmen, and Abandoned Lands. The Freedmen's Bureau, as it was called, distributed food and clothing to destitute Southerners and eased the transition of blacks from slaves to free persons. Congress also authorized the agency to divide abandoned and confiscated land into 40-acre plots, to rent them to freedmen, and eventually to sell them "with such title as the United States can convey." By June 1865, the bureau had situated nearly ten thousand black families on a half million acres that had been abandoned by fleeing South Carolina and Georgia planters. Hundreds of thousands of other ex-slaves eagerly anticipated farms of their own.

Despite the flurry of activity, wartime reconstruction had settled nothing. Two years of controversy had failed to produce agreement about whether the president or Congress had the authority to devise and direct policy or what proper policy should be. Lincoln had organized several new state governments, but Congress had not readmitted a single "reconstructed" state into the Union. There were hints of a revolution in landholding, but the "compulsory free labor" system that emerged on southern plantations suggested more continuity with antebellum traditions. Clearly, the nation faced dilemmas and difficulties almost as burdensome as those of the war.

The African American Quest for Autonomy

Although white politicians had difficulty agreeing, ex-slaves never had any doubt about what they wanted freedom to mean. They had only to contemplate what they had been denied as slaves. (See "Documenting the American Promise," page 542.) Slaves had to remain on their plantations; freedom allowed blacks to go wherever they pleased. Thus, in the first heady weeks after emancipation, freedmen often abandoned their plantations just to see what was on the other side of the hill and to feel freedom under their feet. Slaves had to be at work in the fields by dawn; freedom permitted blacks to taste the forbidden pleasure of sleeping through a sunrise. Slaves had to defer to whites; freedom saw them test the etiquette of racial subordination. "Lizzie's maid passed me today when I was coming from church *without speaking to me,*" huffed one plantation mistress.

To whites, it looked like pure anarchy. Without the discipline of slavery, they said, blacks had reverted to their natural condition: lazy, irresponsible, and wild. Actually, former slaves were experiment-

WASHINGTON MILLER AND FAMILY
After the Civil War, thousands of ex-slaves whose marriages had no legal standing under slavery rushed to formalize their unions. Natchez, Mississippi, home of cotton millionaires before the war, became the home of many black families after the war. Most ex-slaves worked as house servants, laundresses, gardeners, cooks, and day laborers, but some gained real economic independence. The proud and respectable Washington Miller family represents the achievement of middle-class African Americans. This sensitive photograph is the work of Henry C. Norman, a white Georgian who arrived in Natchez about 1870. Over the next four decades Norman made thousands of photographs of the black and white citizens who visited his studio.
Collection of Thomas H. Gandy and Joan W. Gandy.

The Meaning of Freedom

*O*n *New Year's Day 1863, President Abraham Lincoln issued the Emancipation Proclamation. It stated that "all persons held as slaves" within the states still in rebellion "are, and henceforward shall be, free." Although it did not in and of itself free any slaves, it transformed the character of the war. Despite often intolerable conditions, black people focused on the possibilities of freedom.*

DOCUMENT 1. Letter from John Q. A. Dennis to Edwin M. Stanton, July 26, 1864

John Q. A. Dennis, formerly a slave in Maryland, wrote to Secretary of War Edwin M. Stanton to ask his help in reuniting his family.

Boston

Dear Sir I am Glad that I have the Honour to Write you afew line I have been in troble for about four yars my Dear wife was taken from me Nov 19th 1859 and left me with three Children and I being a Slave At the time Could Not do Anny thing for the poor little Children for my master it was took me Carry me some forty mile from them So I Could Not do for them and the man that they live with half feed them and half Cloth them & beat them like dogs & when I was admitted to go to see them it use to brake my heart & Now I say again I am Glad to have the honour to write to you to see if you Can Do Anny thing for me or for my poor little Children I was keap in Slavy untell last Novr 1863. then the Good lord sent the Cornel borne [federal Colonel William Birney?] Down their in Marland in worsester Co So as I have been recently freed I have but letle to live on but I am Striveing Dear Sir but what I went too know of you Sir is it possible for me to go & take my Children from those men that keep them in Savery if it is possible will you pleas give me a permit from your hand then I think they would let them go. . . .

Hon sir will you please excuse my Miserable writeing & answer me as soon as you can I want get the little Children out of Slavery, I being Criple would like to know of you also if I Cant be permited to rase a Shool Down there & on what turm I Could be admited to Do so No more At present Dear Hon Sir

SOURCE: Ira Berlin, Joseph P. Reidy, and Leslie S. Rowland, eds., *Freedom: A Documentary History of Emancipation, 1861–1867*, ser. 1, vol. 1, *The Destruction of Slavery* (Cambridge: Cambridge University Press, 1985), 386.

DOCUMENT 2. Report from Reverend A. B. Randall, February 28, 1865

Freedom also prompted ex-slaves to seek legal marriages, which under slavery had been impossible. Writing from Little Rock, Arkansas, A. B. Randall, the white chaplain of a black regiment, in a report of February 1865 to the adjutant general of the Union army, affirmed the importance of marriage to freed slaves and emphasized their conviction that emancipation was just the first step toward full freedom.

Weddings, just now, are very popular, and abundant among the Colored People. They have just learned, of the Special Order No. 15. of Gen Thomas [Adjutant General Lorenzo Thomas] by which, they may not only be lawfully married, but have their Marriage Certificates, Recorded; in a book furnished by the Government. This is most desirable. . . . Those who were captured . . . at Ivy's Ford, on the 17th of January, by Col Brooks, had their Marriage Certificates, taken from them; and destroyed; and then were roundly cursed, for having such papers in their posession. I have married, during the month, at this Post; Twenty five couples; mostly, those, who have families; & have been living together for years. I try to dissuade single men, who are soldiers, from marrying, till their time of enlistment is out: as that course seems to me, to be most judicious.

The Colord People here, generally consider, this war not only; their exodus, from bondage; but the road, to Responsibility; Competency; and an honorable Citizenship—God grant that their hopes and expectations may be fully realized.

SOURCE: Ira Berlin, Joseph P. Reidy, and Leslie S. Rowland, eds., *Freedom: A Documentary History of Emancipation, 1861–1867*, ser. 2, *The Black Military Experience* (Cambridge: Cambridge University Press, 1982), 712.

DOCUMENT 3. Petition "to the Union Convention of Tennessee Assembled in the Capitol at Nashville," January 9, 1865

Early efforts at political reconstruction prompted petitions from former slaves demanding civil and political rights. In January 1865, black Tennesseans petitioned a convention of white Unionists debating the reorganization of state government.

We the undersigned petitioners, American citizens of African descent, natives and residents of Tennessee, and devoted friends of the great National cause, do most respectfully ask a patient hearing of your honorable body in regard to matters deeply affecting the future condition of our unfortunate and long suffering race.

First of all, however, we would say that words are too weak to tell how profoundly grateful we are to the Federal Government for the good work of freedom which it is gradually carrying forward; and for the Emancipation Proclamation which has set free all the slaves in some of the rebellious States, as well as many of the slaves in Tennessee. . . .

We claim freedom, as our natural right, and ask that in harmony and co-operation with the nation at large, you should cut up by the roots the system of slavery, which is not only a wrong to us, but the source of all the evil which at present afflicts the State. For slavery, corrupt itself, corrupted nearly all, also, around it, so that it has influenced nearly all the slave States to rebel against the Federal Government, in order to set up a government of pirates under which slavery might be perpetrated.

In the contest between the nation and slavery, our unfortunate people have sided, by instinct, with the former. We have little fortune to devote to the national cause, for a hard fate has hitherto forced us to live in poverty, but we do devote to its success, our hopes, our toils, our whole heart, our sacred honor, and our lives. We will work, pray, live, and, if need be, die for the Union, as cheerfully as ever a white patriot died for his country. The color of our skin does not lessen in the least degree, our love either for God or for the land of our birth. . . .

We know the burdens of citizenship, and are ready to bear them. We know the duties of the good citizen, and are ready to perform them cheerfully, and would ask to be put in a position in which we can discharge them more effectually. . . .

This is a democracy—a government of the people. It should aim to make every man, without regard to the color of his skin, the amount of his wealth, or the character of his religious faith, feel personally interested in its welfare. Every man who lives under the Government should feel that it is his property, his treasure, the bulwark and defence of himself and his family, his pearl of great price, which he must preserve, protect, and defend faithfully at all times, on all occasions, in every possible manner.

This is not a Democratic Government if a numerous, law-abiding, industrious, and useful class of citizens, born and bred on the soil, are to be treated as aliens and enemies, as an inferior degraded class, who must have no voice in the Government which they support, protect and defend, with all their heart, soul, mind, and body, both in peace and war. . . .

The possibility that the negro suffrage proposition may shock popular prejudice at first sight, is not a conclusive argument against its wisdom and policy. No proposition ever met with more furious or general opposition than the one to enlist colored soldiers in the United States army. The opponents of the measure exclaimed on all hands that the negro was a coward; that he would not fight; that one white man, with a whip in his hand could put to flight a regiment of them; that the experiment would end in the utter rout and ruin of the Federal army. Yet the colored man has fought so well, on almost every occasion, that the rebel government is prevented, only by its fears and distrust of being able to force him to fight for slavery as well as he fights against it, from putting half a million of negroes into its ranks.

The Government has asked the colored man to fight for its preservation and gladly has he done it. It can afford to trust him with a vote as safely as it trusted him with a bayonet.

SOURCE: Ira Berlin, Joseph P. Reidy, and Leslie S. Rowland, eds., *Freedom: A Documentary History of Emancipation, 1861–1867*, ser. 2, *The Black Military Experience* (Cambridge: Cambridge University Press, 1982), 811–16.

(Continued)

Document 4: Interview with Henry Baker, 1938

Henry Baker was born a slave in Alabama in 1854. In 1938, Thomas Monroe Campbell, a graduate of Tuskegee Institute and a black farm demonstration agent for the U.S. Department of Agriculture, visited Baker and recorded the interview. Here, Baker remembers his brush with formal education when he was a young man during Reconstruction.

'Gardin' muh education, I went tuh school once. It wuz de time dat I wuz workin' es wage han' fer ole man B. It wuz layin' by time en he sed ter me, "Now Henry yuh kin go 'head I haven't got enythin' fer yuh tuh do 'til time tuh start gatherin' de crops." This wuz all 'fore I mar'ied. So I 'cided tuh use dis time en goin' tuh school. So dere wuz er white man, named John Bradley. He wuz teachin' de "nigger" school. I went ter see him en he wuz glad tuh let me in. I went tuh school five days en muh landlord he'rd dat I wuz gwine tuh school so he sent fer me en tole me he had a job right away en he put me back tuh work. Yasser took me right outter school. 'Coase aftuh I mar'ed I did go tuh school three weeks dat wuz all. I wus a renter en uv coase I had so many obligations I couldn't keep up muh school work en look aftuh muh farm so I had tuh give hit up. So I went ter school in muh life, in all, three weeks en five days. I wuz not satisfied so I determined tuh better muh condition so I turned tuh Jesus Christ. . . . He'll teach yuh enythin yuh want ter know. He sho will.

Source: John W. Blassingame, ed., *Slave Testimony: Two Centuries of Letters, Speeches, Interviews, and Autobiographies* (Baton Rouge: Louisiana State University Press, 1977), 667.

QUESTIONS FOR ANALYSIS AND DEBATE

1. How does John Q. A. Dennis interpret his responsibility as a father?
2. Why do you think ex-slaves wanted their marriages legalized?
3. Why, according to the Union Convention of Tennessee, did blacks deserve voting rights?
4. How would you characterize Henry Baker's attitude toward education?

---

ing with freedom, in both trivial and profound ways. But poor black people could not long afford to roam the countryside, neglect work, and casually provoke whites. Soon, most were back on plantations, at work in the fields and kitchens.

Ex-slaves never had any doubt about what they wanted freedom to mean. They had only to contemplate what they had been denied as slaves.

But other items on ex-slaves' agenda of freedom endured. Freedmen did not easily give up their quest for economic independence. In addition, slavery had deliberately kept blacks illiterate, and freedmen emerged from slavery eager to read and write. Moreover, bondage had denied slaves secure family lives, and the restoration of their families became a persistent black aspiration. Although slave marriages and family relations had existed only at the master's whim, slaves had nevertheless managed to create deep, enduring family ties. Still, slave sales had often severed family connections. As a consequence, thousands of black men and women took to the roads in 1865 to look for relations who had been sold away. One northern journalist encountered a ragged freedman who had walked six hundred miles to North Carolina, where he had *heard* that his wife and children had been sold. Couples who emerged from slavery with their marriages intact often rushed to northern military chaplains to legalize their unions.

Another hunger that freedom permitted African Americans to satisfy was independent worship. Under slavery, blacks had often, like it or not, prayed with whites in biracial churches. Intent on religious independence, blacks greeted freedom with a mass exodus from white churches. Some joined the newly established southern branches of all-black northern churches, such as the African Methodist Episcopal Church. Others formed black versions of the major southern denominations, Baptists and Methodists. Slaves had viewed their tribulations through the lens of their deeply felt Christian faith, and freedmen comprehended the events of the Civil War and reconstruction as people of faith. It was not surprising that ex-slaves claimed Abraham Lincoln as their Moses.

Presidential Reconstruction

Abraham Lincoln died on April 15, 1865, just hours after John Wilkes Booth had shot him at a Washington, D.C., theater. Chief Justice Salmon P. Chase immediately administered the oath of office to Vice President Andrew Johnson. Lincoln's assassination thrust the Tennessean into leadership at a time of grave national crisis. Moreover, Congress had adjourned in March, which meant that legislators were away from Washington when Lincoln was killed. They would not reconvene until December. Throughout the summer and fall, therefore, the "accidental president" made critical decisions about the future of the South. Like Lincoln, Johnson believed that responsibility for restoring the Union lay with the president. With dizzying speed, he drew up and executed a plan of reconstruction.

Congress returned to the capital in December to find that, as far as the president and former Confederates were concerned, reconstruction was over. To most Republicans, Johnson's modest demands of ex-rebels made a mockery of the sacrifice of Union soldiers. In an 1863 speech dedicating the cemetery at Gettysburg, Lincoln had spoken of the "great task remaining before us . . . that we here highly resolve that these dead shall not have died in vain—that this nation, under God, shall have a new birth of freedom." Instead, Johnson had acted as midwife to the rebirth of the Old South. He had achieved political reunification at the cost of black liberty. To let his program stand, Republican legislators said, would mean that the North's dead had indeed died in vain.

Johnson's Program of Reconciliation

Born in 1808 in Raleigh, North Carolina, Andrew Johnson was the son of poor, illiterate parents. Un-

able to afford to send her son to school, Johnson's widowed mother apprenticed him to a tailor. Self-educated and ambitious, the young man ran away before completing his indenture and headed for Tennessee. There he worked as a tailor, accumulated a fortune in land, acquired five slaves, and built a career in politics championing the South's common white people and assailing its "illegitimate, swaggering, bastard, scrub aristocracy." The only senator from a Confederate state to remain loyal to the Union, Johnson held no grudge against the South's rebel yeomen. He believed they had been hoodwinked by slaveholding secessionists. Less than two weeks before he became president, he made it clear what he would do to the rascals if he ever had the chance: "I would arrest them—I would try them—I would convict them and I would hang them."

No wonder the South's elite trembled when Lincoln died. In reality, however, Johnson was no friend of northern radicals. A Democrat all his life, Johnson occupied the White House only because the Republican Party in 1864 had needed to broaden its appeal to loyal, Union-supporting Democrats. As a Tennessee congressman and senator, Johnson had favored traditional Democratic causes, vigorously defending states' rights (but not secession) and opposing Republican efforts to expand the power of the federal government, especially in the economic realm. He had voted against almost every federal appropriation, including a bill to pave the streets of Washington.

Moreover, Johnson had been a steadfast defender of slavery. He had owned slaves until 1862, when Tennessee rebels, angry at his Unionism, confiscated them. He only grudgingly accepted emancipation. When he did, it was more because of his hatred for slaveholders than sympathy for slaves. "Damn the negroes," he said. "I am fighting those traitorous aristocrats, their masters." At a time when the nation faced its moment of truth regarding black Americans, the new president harbored unshakable racist convictions. Africans, Johnson said, were "inferior to the white man in point of intellect—better calculated in physical structure to undergo drudgery and hardship." On the eve of his inauguration as vice president, he had reiterated his belief in a white man's government.

Johnson presented his plan of reconstruction as a continuation of Lincoln's plan, and in some ways it was. Like Lincoln, he stressed reconciliation between the Union and the defeated Confederacy and rapid restoration of civil government in the South. He offered to pardon most ex-rebels. Like Lincoln, Johnson excluded high-ranking ex-Confederates, but he also excluded all ex-rebels with property worth more than $20,000. The Tennessee tailor was apparently taking aim at his old enemy, the planter aristocrats. Wealthy individuals would have to apply directly to the president for pardons. Johnson recognized the state governments created by Lincoln and set out his own requirements for restoring the rebel states to the Union. All that the citizens of a state had to do was to renounce the right of secession, deny that the debts of the Confederacy were legal and binding, and ratify the Thirteenth Amendment abolishing slavery, which became part of the Constitution in December 1865. Johnson's plan ignored Lincoln's acceptance near the end of his life of some form of limited black voting.

Johnson's eagerness to normalize relations with southern states and his lack of sympathy for blacks also led him to instruct military and government officials to return to pardoned ex-Confederates all confiscated and abandoned land, even if it was in the hands of freedmen. Reformers were shocked. They had expected the president's vendetta against planters to mean the permanent confiscation of the South's plantations and the distribution of the land

to loyal freedmen. Instead, his instructions canceled the promising beginnings made by General Sherman and the Freedmen's Bureau to settle blacks on land of their own. As one freedman observed, "Things was hurt by Mr. Lincoln getting killed."

Southern Resistance and Black Codes

In the summer of 1865, delegates across the South gathered to draw up the new state constitutions required by Johnson's plan of reconstruction. While they had been defeated, clearly they had not been subdued. Rather than take their medicine, delegates choked on even the president's mild requirements. Refusing to declare their secession ordinances null and void, the South Carolina and Georgia conventions merely "repudiated" their ordinances, preserving in principle their right to secede. In addition, every state convention wrangled over the precise wording of the constitutional amendment ending slavery. In the end, Mississippi rejected the Thirteenth Amendment outright, and Alabama rejected it in part. Finally, South Carolina and Mississippi refused to repudiate their Confederate war debts. Despite these defiant acts, Johnson did not demand that Southerners comply with his lenient terms. By failing to draw a hard line, he rekindled southern

THE BLACK CODES
Entitled **Selling a Freeman to Pay His Fine at Monticello, Florida,** *this 1867 drawing from a northern magazine equates the black codes with the reinstitution of slavery. The laws stopped short of reenslavement, but they did sharply restrict blacks' freedom. In Florida, as in other southern states, certain acts, such as breaking a labor contract, were made criminal offenses, the penalty for which could be involuntary plantation labor for a year.* Library of Congress.

resistance. White Southerners began to think that by standing up for themselves they—not victorious Northerners—would shape the transition from slavery to freedom. In the fall of 1865, newly elected southern legislators set out to reverse the "retreat into barbarism" that followed emancipation.

Under the mantle of protectors of the freedmen, state governments across the South adopted a series of laws known as the *black codes.* While emancipation had brought freedmen important rights that they had lacked as slaves—to own property, to make contracts, to marry legally, and to sue and be sued in court—the black codes made a travesty of freedom. They sought to keep blacks subordinate to whites by subjecting blacks to every sort of discrimination. Several states made it illegal for blacks to own a gun. Mississippi made insulting gestures and language a criminal offense. Blacks were barred from jury duty. Not a single southern state granted any black—no matter how educated, wealthy, or refined—the right to vote.

At the core of the black codes, however, lay the matter of labor. Faced with the death of slavery and the disintegration of plantations, legislators sought to hustle freedmen back into traditional tasks. South Carolina attempted to limit blacks to either farmwork or domestic service by requiring them to pay annual taxes of $10 to $100 to work in any other occupation. Mississippi declared that blacks who did not possess written evidence of employment could be declared vagrants and be subject to fines or involuntary plantation labor. Most states allowed judges to bind black children—orphans and others whose parents they deemed unable to support them—to white employers. Under these so-called apprenticeship laws, courts bound out thousands of black children to planter "guardians." Legislators made every effort to resuscitate the traditional plantation economy and resurrect as nearly as possible the old regime.

While emancipation had brought freedmen important rights that they had lacked as slaves—to own property, to make contracts, to marry legally—the black codes made a travesty of freedom.

Johnson refused to intervene decisively. A staunch defender of states' rights, he believed that the citizens of every state, even those citizens who had attempted to destroy the Union, should be free to write their own constitutions and laws. Moreover, since Johnson was as eager as other white Southerners to restore white supremacy and black subordination, the black codes did not offend him.

But Johnson also followed the path he believed offered him the greatest political return. A conservative Tennessee Democrat at the head of a northern Republican Party, he began to look southward for political allies. Despite tough talk about punishing traitors, he issued more than fourteen thousand special pardons to wealthy or high-ranking ex-Confederates. By pardoning planters and Confederate officials, by acquiescing in the South's black codes, and by accepting the new southern governments even when they failed to satisfy his minimal demands, he won useful allies.

If Northerners had any doubts about the mood of the South, they evaporated in the elections of 1865. To represent them in Congress, white Southerners chose former Confederates, not loyal Unionists. Of the eighty senators and representatives they sent to Washington, fifteen had served in the Confederate army, ten of them as generals. Another sixteen had served in civil and judicial posts in the Confederacy. Nine others had served in the Confederate Congress. One—Alexander Stephens—had been vice president of the Confederacy. In December, this remarkable group arrived on the steps of the nation's Capitol building to be seated in Congress. As one Georgian later remarked: "It looked as though Richmond had moved to Washington."

Expansion of Black Rights and Federal Authority

Southerners had blundered monumentally. They had assumed that what Andrew Johnson was willing to accept, the northern public and Congress would accept as well. But southern intransigence compelled even moderate Republicans to conclude that ex-rebels were a "generation of vipers," still dangerous and untrustworthy.

The black codes in particular soured moderate Republicans on the South. The codes became a symbol of southern intentions not to accept the verdict of the battlefields, but instead to "restore all of slavery but its name." Northerners were hardly saints when it came to racial justice, but black freedom had become a hallowed war aim. "We tell the white men of Mississippi," the *Chicago Tribune* roared, "that the

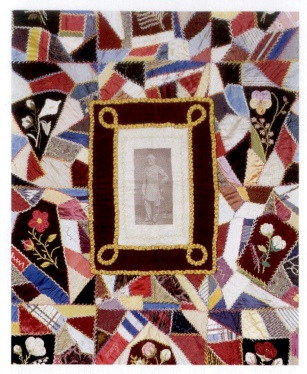

THE LOST CAUSE

While politicians in Washington, D.C., debated the future of the South, white Southerners were coming to grips with their emotions and history. They began to refer to their failure to secede from the Union as the "Lost Cause." They enshrined the memory of certain former Confederates, especially Robert E. Lee, whose nobility and courage represented the white South's image of itself. This quilt from about 1870, with Lee stitched in the center, illustrates how common whites incorporated the symbols of the Lost Cause into their daily lives. The maker of the quilt, a woman whose name is unknown, also included miniature Confederate flags and memorial ribbons.
Valentine Museum, Cook Collection.

men of the North will convert the State of Mississippi into a frog pond before they will allow such laws to disgrace one foot of the soil in which the bones of our soldiers sleep and over which the flag of freedom waves."

Moderates represented the mainstream of the Republican Party and wanted only assurance that slavery and treason were dead. They did not seek a revolution of the entire southern social order. They did not champion black equality or the confiscation of plantations or black voting, as did the Radicals, a minority faction within the Republican Party. In

December 1865, however, when Congress convened in Washington, it became clear that events in the South had succeeded in forging unity (at least temporarily) among Republican factions. Exercising Congress's right to determine the qualifications of its members, the moderate majority and the Radical minority came together to refuse to seat the southern representatives. Rather than accept Johnson's claim that the "work of restoration" was done, Congress countered his executive power. Congressional Republicans enjoyed a three-to-one majority over the Democrats, and if they could agree on a program of reconstruction, they could easily pass legislation and even override presidential vetoes.

The moderates took the initiative. Senator Lyman Trumbull of Illinois declared that the president's policy of trusting southern whites proved that the ex-slave would "be tyrannized over, abused, and virtually reenslaved without some legislation by the nation for his protection." Early in 1866, the moderates produced two bills that strengthened the federal shield. The first, the Freedmen's Bureau bill, prolonged the life of the agency established by the previous Congress. Since the end of the war, it had distributed food, supervised labor contracts, and sponsored schools for freedmen. Arguing that the Constitution never contemplated a "system for the support of indigent persons," President Andrew Johnson vetoed the Freedmen's Bureau bill. Congress failed by only a narrow margin to override the president's veto.

Johnson's shocking veto galvanized nearly unanimous Republican support for the moderates' second measure, the Civil Rights Act. Designed to nullify the black codes, it affirmed the rights of blacks to enjoy "full and equal benefit of all laws and proceedings for the security of person and property as is enjoyed by white citizens." Modest on its surface, the act boldly required the end of legal discrimination in state laws and represented an extraordinary expansion of black rights and federal authority. The president argued that the civil rights bill amounted to an "unconstitutional invasion of states' rights" and vetoed it. In essence, he denied that the federal government possessed authority to protect the civil rights of blacks.

Had Johnson's veto stood, reconstruction would have been over, and the president would have had the final word. But in April 1866, a thoroughly aroused Republican Party again pushed a civil rights bill through Congress and overrode another presidential veto. In July, it sustained another Freedmen's Bureau Act. For the first time in American history, Congress had overridden presidential vetoes of major legislation. As a worried South Carolinian observed, Johnson had succeeded in uniting the Republicans and probably touched off "a fight this fall such as has never been seen."

Congressional Reconstruction

By the summer of 1866, President Andrew Johnson and Congress had dropped their gloves and stood toe to toe in a bare-knuckled contest unprecedented in American history. Johnson had made it clear that he would not budge on either constitutional questions or policy. Moderate Republicans made a major effort to resolve the dilemma of reconstruction by amending the Constitution, but the obstinacy of Johnson and white Southerners pushed Republican moderates ever closer to the Radicals and to acceptance of additional federal intervention in the South.

Congressional reconstruction evolved haltingly and unevenly, but through it all black suffrage acted like a powerful magnet that steadily drew discussion its way. In time, white men in Congress debated whether to give the ballot to black men. Outside of Congress, blacks raised their voices on behalf of color-blind voting rights, while women argued to make voting sex-blind as well.

The Fourteenth Amendment and Escalating Violence

In April 1866, Republican moderates introduced the Fourteenth Amendment to the Constitution, which both houses of Congress approved in June by the necessary two-thirds majority. The amendment then went to the states for ratification. Although it took two years to gather approval from the required three-fourths of the states, the Fourteenth Amendment had immediate consequences.

The most important provisions of this complex amendment made all native-born or naturalized persons American citizens and prohibited states from abridging the "privileges and immunities" of citizens, depriving them of "life, liberty, or property without due process of law," and denying them "equal protection of the laws." Lawyers have battled ever since about the meaning of this broad

language, but by making blacks national citizens the amendment nullified the *Dred Scott* decision of 1857 and provided a national guarantee of equality before the law. In essence, it protected the rights of citizens against violation by their own state governments.

The Fourteenth Amendment also dealt with voting rights. Republicans revealed that while genuinely committed to black freedom, they were also alert to partisan advantage. Rather than explicitly granting the vote to blacks, as Radicals wanted, the amendment gave Congress the right to reduce the congressional representation of states that withheld suffrage from some of its adult male population. In other words, white Southerners could either allow their former slaves to vote or see their representation in Washington slashed.

> *By making blacks national citizens, the Fourteenth Amendment provided a guarantee of equality before the law. In essence, it protected the rights of citizens against violation by their own state governments.*

The Republicans drafted the Fourteenth Amendment in such a way that they could not lose. If southern whites caved in and granted voting rights to freedmen, the Republican Party, entirely a northern party since its birth, would gain valuable black votes, establish a wing in the South, and secure its national power. But if whites refused, southern representation in Congress would plunge, and Republicans would still gain immunity from southern Democratic political power. The Fourteenth Amendment's voting provision included northern states, where whites were largely hostile to voting rights for black Northerners. But northern states could continue to withhold suffrage and not suffer in Washington, for their black populations were too small to count in figuring representation. Radicals labeled the Fourteenth Amendment's voting provision "hypocritical" and a "swindle," but they understood that it was the best they could get at the time.

Tennessee approved the Fourteenth Amendment in July, and Congress promptly welcomed its representatives and senators back. Had Johnson counseled other southern states to ratify this relatively mild amendment and warned them that they

MEMPHIS RIOTS, MAY 1866
*On May 1, 1866, two carriages, one driven by a white man and the other by a black man, collided on a busy Memphis street. This minor incident spiraled into three days of bloody racial violence in which dozens of blacks and two whites died. Racial friction was common in postwar Memphis, and white newspapers routinely heaped abuse on black citizens. "Would to God they were back in Africa, or some other seaport town," the Memphis **Argus** shouted two days before the riot erupted, "anywhere but here." South Memphis, pictured in this lithograph from **Harper's Weekly**, was a shantytown where the families of black soldiers stationed at nearby Fort Pickering lived. The army commander refused to send troops to protect the soldiers' families and property, and white mobs ran wild.*
Library of Congress.

faced the fury of an outraged Republican Party if they refused, they might have listened. Instead, Johnson advised Southerners to reject the Fourteenth Amendment and to rely on him to trounce the Republicans in the fall congressional elections.

Johnson had decided to make the Fourteenth Amendment the overriding issue of the 1866 congressional elections and to gather its white opponents into a new conservative party, the National Union Party. In August, his supporters met in Philadelphia. Democrats came, but the slim Republican turnout made it clear that rather than drawing disgruntled Republicans to him, Johnson had united nearly the entire Republican Party against him.

The president's strategy had already suffered a setback two weeks earlier when whites in several

southern cities went on rampages against blacks. It was less an outbreak of violence than an escalation of the violence that had never ceased. In New Orleans, a mob assaulted delegates to a black suffrage convention, and thirty-four blacks died. In Memphis, white mobs hurtled through the black sections of town and killed at least forty-six people. The slaughter shocked Northerners and renewed skepticism about Johnson's claim that southern whites could be trusted. "Who doubts that the Freedmen's Bureau ought to be abolished forthwith," a New Yorker observed sarcastically, "and the blacks remitted to the paternal care of their old masters, who 'understand the nigger, you know, a great deal better than the Yankees can.'"

In a last-ditch effort, Johnson took his case directly to the people. In August, he made an ill-fated "swing around the circle," which took him from Washington to Chicago and St. Louis and back to Washington. However, the president embarrassed himself and his office. When hostile crowds hurled insults, he gave as good as he got. It was Johnson at his worst—intemperate, crude, undignified. Even a friend agreed that he had "made an ass of himself." Johnson's reception on the campaign trail foretold the fate of the National Union movement in the elections. Rather than witnessing the birth of a new conservative party, the elections pitted traditional rivals: Democrats (who lined up with Johnson) against Republicans (who lined up against him). The result was an overwhelming Republican victory in which the party retained its three-to-one congressional majority.

Johnson had bet that Northerners would not support federal protection of black rights. He expected a racist backlash to defeat the Fourteenth Amendment and blast the Republican Party. But the cautious (and ingenious) amendment was not radical enough to drive Republican voters into Johnson's camp. Besides, the war was still fresh in northern minds. As one Republican explained, southern whites "with all their intelligence were traitors, the blacks with all their ignorance were loyal."

Radical Reconstruction and Military Rule

The elections of 1866 should have taught southern whites the folly of relying on Andrew Johnson as a guide through the thicket of reconstruction. But when Johnson continued to urge Southerners toward rejection of the Fourteenth Amendment, one by one every southern state except Tennessee voted it down. "The last one of the sinful ten," thundered Representative James A. Garfield of Ohio, "has flung back into our teeth the magnanimous offer of a generous nation." In the void created by the South's rejection of the moderates' program, the Radicals seized the initiative.

Each act of defiance by southern whites had boosted the standing of the Radicals within the Republican Party. At the core was a small group of men who had cut their political teeth on the antebellum campaign against slavery, who had goaded Lincoln toward making the war a crusade for freedom, and who had carried into the postwar period the conviction that only federal power could protect the rights of the freedmen. Except for freedmen

themselves, no one did more to make freedom the "mighty moral question of the age." Men like Senator Charles Sumner, that pompous but sincere Massachusetts crusader, and Thaddeus Stevens, the caustic, cadaverous representative from Pennsylvania, did not speak with a single voice, but they united in calling for civil and political equality. They insisted on extending to ex-slaves the same opportunities that northern working people enjoyed under the free-labor system. The southern states were "like clay in the hands of the potter," Stevens declared in January 1867, and he called on Congress to begin reconstruction all over again.

In March 1867, after exhaustive debate, moderates joined the Radicals to overturn the Johnson state governments and initiate military rule of the South. The Military Reconstruction Act (and three subsequent acts) divided the ten unreconstructed Confederate states into five military districts. Congress placed a Union general in charge of each district and instructed him to "suppress insurrection, disorder, and violence" and to begin political reform. After the military had completed voter registration, which would include black men and exclude all those barred by the Fourteenth Amendment from holding public office, voters would elect delegates to conventions that would draw up new state constitutions. Each constitution would guarantee black suffrage. When the voters of each state had approved the constitution and the first legislature had ratified the Fourteenth Amendment, the state could submit its work to Congress. If Congress approved, the state's senators and representatives could be seated and political reunification would be accomplished.

Radicals proclaimed the provision for black suffrage "a prodigious triumph." The doggedness of the Radicals and of African Americans, along with the pigheadedness of Johnson and the white South, had swept the Republican Party far beyond the limited suffrage provisions of the Fourteenth Amendment. Republicans finally agreed with Sumner that only the voting power of ex-slaves could bring about a permanent revolution in the South. Indeed, suffrage provided blacks with a powerful instrument of change and self-protection. When combined with the disfranchisement of thousands of ex-rebels, it promised to cripple any neo-Confederate resurgence and guarantee Republican governments in the South.

Despite its bold suffrage provision, the Military Reconstruction Act of 1867 disappointed those who advocated the confiscation and redistribution of southern plantations. No one in Washington was more distressed than Thaddeus Stevens. Unlike Sumner, who conceived of reconstruction primarily in political terms, Stevens believed it was at bottom an economic problem. He agreed wholeheartedly with the ex-slave who said, "Give us our own land and we take care of ourselves, but without land, the old masters can hire us or starve us, as they please." But Johnson's offers of amnesty and pardon had reversed the small program of land transfer begun during the war. By early 1867, nearly all of the land had been returned to its ex-Confederate owners. Most Republicans believed they had already provided blacks with the critical tools: equal legal rights and the ballot. If blacks were to get forty acres, they would have to gain it themselves.

The doggedness of the Radicals and of African Americans, along with the pigheadedness of Johnson and the white South, had swept the Republican Party far beyond the limited suffrage of the Fourteenth Amendment.

Declaring that he would rather sever his right arm than sign such a formula for "anarchy and chaos," Andrew Johnson vetoed the Military Reconstruction Act. Congress overrode his veto the very same day, dramatizing the shift in power from the executive to the legislative branch of government. With the passage of the Reconstruction Acts of 1867, congressional reconstruction was virtually completed. Congress had left white folks owning most of the South's land, but in a radical departure it had given black men the ballot. More than any other provision, black suffrage justifies the term "radical reconstruction." In 1867, the nation began an unprecedented experiment in interracial democracy— at least in the South, for Congress's plan did not touch the North. Soon the former Confederate states

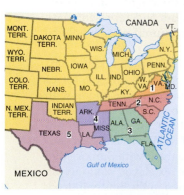

Reconstruction Military Districts, 1867

would become the primary theater for political struggle. But before the spotlight swung away from Washington, the president and Congress had one more scene to play.

Impeaching a President

Although Johnson had lost the support of the northern people and faced a hostile Republican majority in Congress, he had no intention of yielding control of reconstruction. As president, he was responsible for enforcing the laws that Congress enacted. As commander in chief, he oversaw the military rule of the South that Congress instituted. Yet in a dozen ways he sabotaged Congress's will and encouraged white belligerence and resistance. He issued a flood of pardons to undermine efforts at political and economic change. He waged war against the Freedmen's Bureau by removing officers who sympathized too fully with ex-slaves. And he replaced Union generals eager to enforce Congress's Reconstruction Acts with conservative men who were eager to defeat them. Johnson claimed that he was merely defending the "violated Constitution." At bottom, however, the president subverted congressional reconstruction to protect southern whites from what he considered the horrors of "Negro domination."

When Congress learned that overriding Johnson's vetoes did not ensure victory, it attempted to tie the president's hands. Congress required that all orders to field commanders pass through the General of the Army, Ulysses S. Grant, who Congress believed was sympathetic to southern freedmen, Unionists, and Republicans. It also enacted the Tenure of Office Act in 1867, which required the approval of the Senate for the removal of any government official who had been appointed with Senate consent. Republicans were seeking to protect Secretary of War Edwin M. Stanton, the lone cabinet officer who supported congressional policies. Some Republicans, however, believed that nothing less than removing Johnson from office could save reconstruction, and they initiated a crusade to impeach the president. According to the United States Constitution, the House of Representatives can impeach and the Senate can try any federal official for "TREASON, BRIBERY, or other high CRIMES and MISDEMEANORS."

As long as Johnson refrained from breaking a law, however, impeachment languished. Moderates interpreted "high CRIMES and MISDEMEANORS" to

ANDREW JOHNSON, WITH ADDITIONS
This dignified portrait by Currier and Ives of President Andrew Johnson appeared in 1868, the year of his impeachment trial. The portrait was apparently amended by a disgruntled citizen. Johnson's vetoes of several reconstruction measures passed by Congress caused his opponents to charge him with arrogant monarchical behavior. Johnson preferred the unamended image—that of a plain and sturdy statesman.
Museum of American Political Life.

mean violation of criminal statutes, and they did not believe that the president had committed an actual crime. Radicals argued that Johnson's abuse of constitutional powers and his failure to fulfill constitutional obligations were impeachable offenses. But in August 1867, Johnson suspended Secretary of War Stanton from office. As required by the Tenure of Office Act, he requested the Senate to consent to dismissal. When the Senate balked, the president removed Stanton anyway. "Is the President crazy, or only drunk?" asked a dumbfounded Republican moderate. "I'm afraid his doings will make us all favor impeachment."

News of Johnson's open defiance of the law did indeed convince every Republican in the House to vote for a resolution impeaching the president. Chief Justice Salmon Chase presided over the Senate trial, which lasted from March until May 1868. Chase refused to allow Johnson's opponents to raise the broad issues of misuse of power, his "high crimes," and forced them to argue their case exclusively on the narrow legal grounds of Johnson's removal of Stanton. Johnson's lawyers argued that he had not committed a criminal offense, that the Tenure of Office Act was unconstitutional, and that in any case it did not apply to Stanton, who had been appointed by Lincoln. When the critical vote came, seven moderate Republicans broke with their party and joined the Democrats in voting not guilty. With thirty-five in favor and nineteen opposed, the impeachment forces fell one vote short of the two-thirds needed to convict.

Republicans had put Johnson on trial because he threatened their efforts to remake the South. But some, including Chief Justice Chase, feared that impeachment for insufficient cause would permanently weaken the office of president. So Johnson survived, but he did not come through the ordeal unscathed. After his trial he called a truce, and for the remaining ten months of his term reconstruction proceeded unhindered by presidential interference.

The Fifteenth Amendment and Women's Demands

In February 1869, Republicans passed the Fifteenth Amendment to the Constitution. The amendment prohibited states from depriving any citizen of the right to vote because of "race, color, or previous condition of servitude." The Reconstruction Acts of 1867 had already required black suffrage in the South, but the Fifteenth Amendment extended black voting to the entire nation. Some Republicans felt morally obligated to do away with the double standard between North and South. Others believed that the freedman's ballot required the extra armor of a constitutional amendment to protect it from white counterattack. But partisan advantage also played an important role in the amendment's passage. Gains by northern Democrats in the 1868 elections worried Republicans, and black voters now represented the balance of power in several northern states. By giving ballots to northern blacks, Republicans could lessen their political vulnerability. As one Republican congressman observed, "Party expediency and exact justice coincide for once."

Some Republicans, however, found the final wording of the Fifteenth Amendment "lame and halting." Rather than absolutely guaranteeing the right to vote, the amendment merely prohibited exclusion on grounds of race. The distinction would prove to be significant. In time, inventive white Southerners would devise tests of literacy and property and other apparently nonracial measures that would effectively disfranchise blacks and yet not violate the Fifteenth Amendment. But an amendment that guaranteed the right to vote courted defeat in the North. Rising antiforeign sentiment—against the Chinese in California and against European immigrants in the Northeast—caused states to resist giving up control of suffrage requirements. In March 1870, after three-fourths of the states had ratified it, the Fifteenth Amendment became part of the Constitution. Republicans generally breathed a sigh of relief, confident that black suffrage had been "the last great point that remained to be settled of the issues of the war."

But the Republican Party's reappraisal of suffrage had ignored completely the small band of politicized and energized women who had emerged from the war demanding "the ballot for the two disenfranchised classes, negroes and women." Founding the Equal Rights Association in 1866, Susan B. Anthony and Elizabeth Cady Stanton lobbied for "a government by the people, and the whole people; for the people and the whole people." They felt betrayed when their old antislavery allies, who now occupied positions of national power, proved to be fickle and refused to work for their goals. "It was the Negro's hour," Frederick Douglass later explained. The Republican Party had to avoid anything that might jeopardize black gains, Charles Sumner declared. He suggested that woman suffrage could be "the great question of the future."

SUSAN B. ANTHONY
Like many outspoken suffragists, Anthony, depicted here in 1852, had begun her public career working on behalf of temperance and abolition. But she grew tired of laboring under the direction of male clergymen—"white orthodox little saints," she called them—who controlled the reform movements and who routinely dismissed the opinions of women. Anthony's continued passion for other causes—improving working conditions for labor, for example—led some conservatives to oppose women's political rights because they equated the suffragist cause with radicalism in general. Women could not easily overcome such views, and the long struggle for the vote eventually drew millions of women into public life.
Susan B. Anthony House, Inc.

The Republican Party's reappraisal of suffrage had ignored completely the small band of politicized and energized women who had emerged from the war demanding "the ballot for two disenfranchised classes, negroes and women."

It was not the first time women's expectations had been dashed. The Fourteenth Amendment had provided for punishment of any state that excluded voters on the basis of race but not on the basis of sex. It had also introduced the word *male* into the Constitution when it referred to a citizen's right to vote. Stanton had predicted that "if that word 'male' be inserted, it will take us a century at least to get it out." The Fifteenth Amendment proved to be no less disappointing. Although women fought hard to include the word *sex*, the amendment denied states the right to forbid suffrage only on the basis of race. Stanton and Anthony condemned the

Republicans' "negro first" strategy and concluded that woman "must not put her trust in man."

In a single decade, abolitionist William Lloyd Garrison declared, blacks had progressed from "the auction-block to the ballot-box." The Fifteenth Amendment, Congressman James A. Garfield of Ohio proclaimed, "confers upon the African race the care of its own destiny. It places their fortunes in their own hands." Even Wendell Phillips, that uncompromising crusader for equality, argued that the black man held "sufficient shield in his own hands. . . . Whatever he suffers will be largely now, and in future, his own fault." In essence, northern Republicans declared victory and scratched the "Negro question" from the agenda of national politics.

The Struggle in the South

While Northerners believed they had discharged their responsibilities with the Reconstruction Acts and the amendments to the Constitution, Southerners knew that the battle had just begun. Black suffrage and large-scale rebel disfranchisement that came with congressional reconstruction had destroyed traditional southern politics and established the foundation for the rise of the Republican Party. Gathering together outsiders and outcasts from traditional society, the Republicans in the South won elections, wrote new state constitutions, and formed new state governments.

Challenging the established class for political control was dangerous business. Equally dangerous were the confrontations that took place on farms and plantations from Virginia to Texas. In the countryside, blacks sought to give practical, everyday meaning to their newly won legal and political equality. But ex-masters like David Golightly Harris and other whites had their own ideas about the social and economic arrangements that should replace slavery. Freedom remained contested territory, and Southerners fought pitched battles with one another to determine the boundaries of their postemancipation world.

Freedmen, Yankees, and Yeomen

African Americans made up the majority of southern Republicans. Freedmen emerged from bondage illiterate and politically inexperienced, but they understood their own interests. They realized that without the ballot they were almost powerless, and they threw themselves into the suffrage campaign.

Southern blacks gained voting rights in 1867, and within months virtually every eligible black man had registered to vote. Blacks (like whites) did not have identical political priorities, but almost all voted Republican, and they united in their desire for education and equal treatment before the laws.

Northern whites who decided to make the South their home after the war were a second element of the South's Republican Party. Conservative white Southerners called any northern migrant a "carpetbagger," a man so poor that he could pack all his earthly belongings in a single carpet-sided suitcase and swoop southward like a buzzard to "fatten on our misfortunes." Some Northerners who moved south were scavengers, but most were restless, relatively well educated young men, often former Union officers and Freedmen's Bureau agents who looked upon the South as they did the West—as a promising place to make a living. Northerners in the southern Republican Party consistently supported programs that encouraged vigorous economic development along the lines of the northern free-labor model.

Southern whites made up the third element of the Republican Party in the South. Approximately one out of four white Southerners voted Republican. The other three cursed those who did. They condemned southern-born white Republicans as traitors to their region and their race and called them "scalawags," a term for runty horses and low-down, good-for-nothing rascals. Yeoman farmers in the piedmont accounted for the vast majority of white Republicans in the South. Many were Unionists who emerged from the war with bitter memories of Confederate persecution. Some small farmers also nursed long-standing grievances against planter domination and welcomed the Republican Party because it promised to end favoritism toward plantation interests. Yeomen usually supported initiatives for public schools and for expanding economic opportunity within a reinvigorated southern economy.

The Republican Party in the South, then, was made up of freedmen, Yankees, and yeomen—an improbable coalition. The mix of races, regions, and classes inevitably meant friction as each group maneuvered to define the party. Despite the stress and strain, reconstruction represents an extraordinary moment in American politics: Blacks and whites joined together to pursue political change. The Republican Party defended the political and civil equality of black Southerners and struggled to bring the South into the mainstream of American social and economic development. Formally, of course, only men participated in politics—casting ballots and holding offices—but women also played parts in the political struggle. Women joined in parades and rallies, attended stump speeches, and even campaigned. In 1868, black maids in Yazoo, Mississippi, shocked their white employers when they showed up for work boldly wearing buttons depicting the Republican candidate for president: Ulysses S. Grant.

Despite the stress and strain, reconstruction represents an extraordinary moment in American politics: Blacks and whites joined together to pursue political change.

Reconstruction politics was not for cowards. Any political act, even wearing a political button, took courage. Congress had introduced hundreds of thousands of ex-slaves into the southern electorate against the will of the white majority. Then, according to one Democrat, the Republican Party herded them to the polls like "senseless cattle." Most whites in the South condemned the entire political process as illegitimate and felt justified in doing whatever it took to stamp out Republicanism. Violence against blacks—the "white terror"—took brutal institutional form in 1866 with the formation of the Ku Klux Klan, a social club of Confederate veterans that quickly developed into a paramilitary organization armed against Republicans. The Klan went on a rampage of whipping, hanging, shooting, burning, and throat-cutting to defeat reconstruction and restore white supremacy. (See "Historical Question," page 558.) Rapid demobilization of the Union army after the war left only twenty thousand troops to patrol the entire South, a vast territory. Without effective military protection, southern Republicans had to take care of themselves.

Republican Rule

The Reconstruction Acts required southern states to draw up new constitutions before they could be readmitted to Congress. Beginning in the fall of 1867, states held elections for delegates to constitutional conventions. About 40 percent of the white electorate stayed home, either because they had been disfranchised or because they were boycotting

CONGRESSMAN JOHN R. LYNCH
Although whites almost always maintained control of reconstruction politics, over six hundred blacks served in legislatures in the South. Ex-slaves made up the majority of the black legislators. The Union Army freed John R. Lynch of Mississippi, and he gained an education at a Natchez freedmen's school. Lynch achieved power at an extraordinary age. He was only twenty-four when he became speaker of Mississippi's House. In 1872, he joined six other African Americans in Congress in Washington, D.C., where in support of civil rights legislation he told stories from his personal experience of being forced to occupy railroad smoking cars with gamblers and drunks. After reconstruction ended, Lynch practiced law and fought for an honest history of reconstruction legislatures, which he argued were the "best governments those States ever had." Natchez photographer Henry C. Norman took this powerful photograph, probably in the early 1870s.
Collection of Thomas H. Gandy and Joan W. Gandy.

politics. Republicans won three-fourths of the seats. About 15 percent of the Republican delegates were Northerners who had moved south, 25 percent were African Americans, and 60 percent were white

Southerners. As a British visitor observed, the elections reflected "the mighty revolution that had taken place in America." But Democrats described the conventions as zoos of "baboons, monkeys, mules . . . and other jackasses." David Golightly Harris despaired and asked, "What can be expected of a government framed by . . . black and ignorant negroes[?]" In fact, the conventions brought together serious, purposeful men who hammered out the legal framework for a new order.

The reconstruction constitutions introduced extensive changes into southern life. In general, changes fell into two categories: those that reduced aristocratic privilege and increased democratic equality and those that expanded the state's responsibility for the general welfare. In the first category, the constitutions adopted universal male suffrage, abolished property qualifications for holding office, and made more offices elective and fewer appointive. In the second category, they enacted prison reform; made the state responsible for caring for orphans, the insane, and the deaf and mute; and aided debtors by exempting their homes from seizure.

These forward-looking constitutions provided blueprints for a new South. But they stopped short of the specific reforms advocated by particular groups within southern Republicanism. Despite the wishes of virtually every former slave, no southern constitution confiscated and redistributed land. And despite the prediction of Unionists that unless all former Confederates were banned from politics they would storm back and wreck reconstruction, no constitution disfranchised ex-rebels wholesale.

But Democrats were blind to the limits of the Republican program. In their eyes, they stared at wild revolution. According to Democrats, Republican victories initiated "black and tan" (ex-slave and mulatto) governments. But the claims of "Negro domination" had almost no validity. Four out of five Republican voters were black men, but more than four out of five Republican officeholders were white. Southerners sent fourteen black congressmen and two black senators to Washington, but only 6 percent of Southerners in Congress during Reconstruction were black (Figure 15.1). With the exception of South Carolina, where blacks briefly held a majority in one house of the legislature, no state experienced "Negro rule," despite black majorities in the populations of three states.

In almost every state, voters ratified the new constitutions and swept Republicans into power. After they ratified the Fourteenth Amendment, the

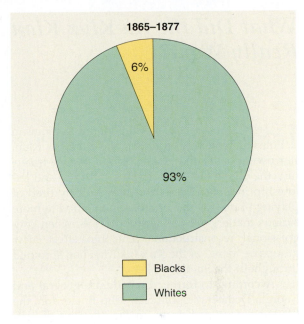

1865–1877

6%

93%

Blacks
Whites

FIGURE 15.1

Southern Congressional Delegations
The statistics contradict the myth of black domination of congressional representation during reconstruction.

former Confederate states were readmitted to Congress. Southern Republicans then turned to a staggering array of problems. Wartime destruction still littered the landscape. The South's share of the nation's wealth had fallen from 30 percent to only 12 percent. Manufacturing limped along at a fraction of prewar levels, agricultural production remained anemic, and the region's railroads had hardly advanced from the devastated condition in which Sherman had left them. Without the efforts of the Freedmen's Bureau, people would have starved. Moreover, reactionary violence and racial harassment dogged Southerners who sought reform. In this desperate context, Republicans struggled to breathe life into their new state governments.

Activity focused on three major areas. First, every state inaugurated a system of public education and began building schools and training teachers. Before the Civil War, whites had deliberately kept slaves illiterate, and planter-dominated governments rarely spent tax money to educate the children of yeomen. By 1875, half of Mississippi's and South Carolina's eligible children (the majority of whom were black) attended school. Persistent underfunding meant too few schools, dilapidated

What Did the Ku Klux Klan Really Want?

IN THE SUMMER OF 1866, six Confederate veterans in Pulaski, Tennessee, founded the Ku Klux Klan. Borrowing oaths and rituals from a college fraternity, the young men innocently sought fun and fellowship in a social club. But they quickly tired of playing pranks on one another and shifted to more serious matters. By the spring of 1868, when congressional reconstruction went into effect, new groups or "dens" of the Ku Klux Klan had sprouted throughout the South.

According to former Confederate general and Georgia Democratic politician John B. Gordon, the Klan owed its popularity to the "instinct of self-preservation . . . the sense of insecurity and danger, particularly in those neighborhoods where the Negro population largely predominated." Everywhere whites looked, he said, they saw "great crime." Republican politicians organized ignorant freedmen and marched them to the polls, where they blighted honest government. Ex-slaves drove overseers from plantations and claimed the land for themselves. Black robbers and rapists made white women cower behind barred doors. It was necessary, Gordon declared, "in order to protect our families from outrage and preserve our own lives, to have something that we could regard as a brotherhood—a combination of the best men of the country, to act purely in self-defense." According to Gordon and other conservative white Southerners, then, Klansmen were good men who stepped forward to do their duty, men who wanted nothing more than to guard their families and defend decent society from the assaults of degraded ex-slaves and a vindictive Republican Party.

Behind the Klan's high-minded and self-justifying rhetoric, however, lay another agenda. It was revealed in their actions, not their words. Klansmen embarked on a campaign to reverse history. Garbed in robes and hoods, Klansmen engaged in hit-and-run guerrilla warfare against free labor, civil equality, and political democracy. They aimed to terrorize their enemies—ex-slaves and white Republicans—into submission. As the South's chief terrorist organization between 1868 and 1871, the Klan whipped, burned, and shot in the name of white supremacy. Changes in four particular areas of southern life proved flash points for Klan violence: racial etiquette, education, labor, and politics.

The Klan punished those blacks and whites guilty of breaking the Old South's racial code. The Klan considered "impudence" a punishable offense. Asked to define "impudence" before a congressional investigating committee, one white opponent of the Klan responded: "Well, it is considered impudence for a negro not to be polite to a white man—not to pull off his hat and bow and scrape to a white man, as was done formerly." Klansmen whipped blacks for crimes that ranged from speaking disrespectfully and refusing to yield the sidewalk to raising a good crop and dressing well. Black women who "dress up and fix up like ladies" risked a midnight visit from the Klan. The Ku Klux Klan sought to restore racial subordination in every aspect of private and public life.

Klansmen also took aim at black education. White men, especially those with little schooling, found the sight of blacks in classrooms hard to stomach. Schools were easy targets, and scores of them went up in flames. Teachers, male and female, were flogged, or worse. Klansmen drove northern-born teacher Alonzo B. Corliss from North Carolina for "teaching niggers and making them like white men." In Cross Plains, Alabama, the Klan hanged an Irish-born teacher along with four black men. But not just ill-educated whites opposed black education. Planters wanted ex-slaves back in the fields, not at desks. Each student meant one less laborer. In 1869, an Alabama newspaper reported the burning of a black school and observed that it should be "a warning for them to stick hereafter to 'de shovel and de hoe,' and let their dirty-backed primers go."

Planters turned to the Klan as part of their effort to preserve plantation agriculture and restore labor discipline. An Alabama white admitted that in his area, the Klan was "intended principally for the negroes who failed to work." Masked bands "punished Negroes whose landlords had complained of

KU KLUX KLAN ROBE AND HOOD

The white robes that we associate with the Ku Klux Klan are a twentieth-century phenomenon. During reconstruction, Klansmen donned robes of various designs and colors. It is unlikely that the man who wore this robe about 1866—with its eye holes carefully trimmed with blue fabric—sewed it himself. Women did not participate in midnight raids, but mothers, wives, and daughters of Klansmen often shared their reactionary vision and did what they could to bring about the triumph of white supremacy.

Chicago Historical Society, Hope B. McCormick Center. Worn by Joseph Boyce Stewart, Lincoln County, Tenn., c. 1866. Gift of W. G. Dithmer.

them." Sharecroppers who disputed their share at "settling up time" risked a visit from the night riders. Klansmen murdered a Georgia blacksmith who refused to do additional work for a white man until he was paid for a previous job. It was dangerous for freedmen to consider changing employers. "If we got out looking for some other place to go," an ex-slave from Texas remembered, "them KKK they would tend to Mister negro good and plenty." In Marengo County, Alabama, when the Klan heard that some local blacks were planning to leave, "the disguised men went to them and told them if they undertook it they would be killed on their way." Whites had decided that they would not be "deprived of their labor."

Above all, the Klan terrorized Republican leaders and voters. Klansmen became the military arm of the Democratic Party. They drove blacks from the polls on election day and terrorized black officeholders. Klansmen gave Andrew Flowers, a black politician in Chattanooga, a brutal beating and told him that they "did not intend any nigger to hold office in the United States." Jack Dupree, president of the Republican Club in Monroe County, Mississippi, a man known to "speak his mind," had his throat cut and was disemboweled while his wife was forced to watch.

Between 1868 and 1871, political violence reached astounding levels. Arkansas experienced nearly three hundred political killings in the three months before the fall elections in 1868, including Little Rock's U.S. congressman, J. M. Hinds. Louisiana was even bloodier. Between the local elections in the spring of 1868 and the presidential election in the fall, Louisiana experienced more than one thousand killings. Political violence often proved effective. In Georgia, Republican presidential candidate Ulysses S. Grant received no votes at all in 1868 in eleven counties, despite black majorities. The Klan murdered three scalawag members of the Georgia legislature and drove ten others from their homes. As one Georgia Republican commented after a Klan attack: "We don't call them democrats, we call them southern murderers."

It proved hard to arrest Klansmen and harder still to convict them. "If a white man kills a colored man in any of the counties of this State," observed a Florida sheriff, "you cannot convict him." By 1871, the death toll had reached thousands. Federal intervention—in the Ku Klux Klan Acts of 1870 and 1871—signaled an end to much of the Klan's power but not to counterrevolutionary violence in the South. Other groups continued the terror.

facilities, and poorly trained teachers, but literacy rates rose sharply, nevertheless. Although public schools were racially segregated, education remained for many blacks a tangible, deeply satisfying benefit of freedom and Republican rule.

Second, states attacked racial discrimination and defended civil rights. Republicans especially resisted efforts by whites to establish separate facilities for blacks in public transportation. Texas replaced its law requiring segregation in its railroads with one that outlawed seating by race. Mississippi went further, levying fines of up to $1,000 and three years in jail for railroads, steamboats, hotels, and theaters that denied "full and equal rights" to all citizens. But passing color-blind laws was one thing; enforcing them was another. Segregation—the separation of blacks and whites in public places—developed at white insistence despite the law and became a feature of southern life long before the end of reconstruction.

Third, Republican governments launched ambitious programs of economic development. They envisioned a South of diversified agriculture, roaring factories, and booming towns. Republican legislatures chartered scores of banks and industrial companies, appropriated funds to fix ruined levees and to drain swamps, and went on a railroad-building binge, repairing old lines and adding some seven thousand miles of track. The mania for railroads and state-sponsored economic development fell far short of solving the South's economic troubles, however. Republican spending to stimulate economic growth also meant rising taxes and enormous debt that drained funds from schools and other programs.

Segregation developed at white insistence despite the law and became a feature of southern life long before the end of reconstruction.

The southern Republicans' record, then, was mixed. To their credit, the biracial Republican coalition had taken up an ambitious agenda to change the South. Success would have been difficult under the best circumstances. As it was, money was scarce. In addition, Democrats kept up a constant drumbeat of harassment, while factionalism threatened the party from within. Moreover, corruption infected Republican governments in the

South. Public morality reached new lows everywhere in the nation after the Civil War, and the chaos and disruption of the postwar South proved fertile soil for bribery, fraud, and influence peddling. Despite all of its problems and shortcomings, however, the Republican Party made headway in its efforts to purge the South of aristocratic privilege and racist oppression.

White Landlords, Black Sharecroppers

Reconstruction politics did not arise within a vacuum. Sharp dissatisfaction with conditions in the southern countryside politicized blacks and fueled political upheaval. Clashes occurred daily between ex-slaves who wished to take control of the conditions of their own labor and ex-masters who wanted to reinstitute old ways.

The system of agricultural labor that emerged in 1865 grew out of the labor program begun during the war by the federal military. When the war ended, supervision shifted to the Freedmen's Bureau, which renewed the army's campaign to restore production by binding black laborers and planters with wage contracts. Except for having to put down the whip and pay subsistence wages, planters were not required to offer many concessions to emancipation. Instead, they moved quickly to restore the antebellum world of work gangs, white overseers, field labor for black women and children, clustered cabins, minimal personal freedom, and even corporal punishment whenever they could get away with it.

Ex-slaves resisted every effort to roll back the clock. Land of their own would do much to end planters' involvement in their personal lives. They wanted, for example, to make their own decisions about whether women and children would labor in the fields. Indeed, within months after the war, perhaps one-third of black women abandoned field labor and began working full time within their own households. Whites claimed that black women were "acting the lady," but what whites meant was that black women were not acting like slaves. Instead, they behaved like free mothers and housewives, occupied with the same arduous domestic chores as poor white women. Moreover, hundreds of thousands of black children enrolled in school.

The freedmen's dream of landownership never came true. Congress and southern legislatures refused to confiscate the planters' land, and without political intervention, landownership proved to be beyond the reach of all but a small fraction of blacks. Without land, ex-slaves would have little choice but to work on plantations.

Although blacks were forced to return to the planters' fields, freedmen resisted efforts to restore slavelike conditions. In his South Carolina neighborhood, David Golightly Harris discovered that few freedmen were "willing to hire by the day, month or year." Instead of working for wages, "the negroes all seem disposed to rent land." By rejecting wage labor, by striking, and by abandoning the most reactionary employers, blacks sought to force concessions. A tug-of-war between white landlords and black laborers took place on thousands of farms and plantations and out of it emerged a new system of southern agriculture.

Sharecropping was a compromise that offered both ex-masters and ex-slaves something but satisfied neither. Under the new system, planters divided their cotton plantations into small farms of twenty-five to thirty acres that freedmen rented, paying with a share of each year's crop, usually half. Sharecropping gave blacks more freedom than wages and labor gangs and released them from the day-to-day supervision of whites. Black families abandoned the old slave quarters and scattered over plantations, building separate cabins on the patches of land they tilled (Map 15.1). David Golightly Harris reported in late 1867 that "much moveing is being done" and that "few negroes remain in their old homes." Black families now decided who would work, for how long, and how hard. Still, most blacks remained dependent on the white landlord, who retained the power to expel them at the end of each

MAP 15.1

A Southern Plantation in 1860 and 1881
The maps of the Barrow plantation in Georgia illustrate some of the ways that ex-slaves expressed their freedom. Former slaves deserted the clustered living quarters behind the big house, scattered over the plantation, built new family cabins, and farmed rented land. These ex-slaves also worked together to build a school and a church.

season. For planters, sharecropping offered a way to resume agricultural production, but it did not allow them to reinstitute the unified plantation system or to administer what they considered necessary discipline.

Sharecropping was a compromise that offered both ex-masters and ex-slaves something but satisfied neither.

Sharecropping also introduced a new figure—the country merchant—into the agricultural equation. While landlords supplied sharecroppers with land, mules, and tools, blacks needed someone to extend essential food and clothing on credit until they harvested their crops. Thousands of merchants at small crossroads stores sprang up to provide this service. Under an arrangement called a crop lien, local merchants advanced goods to sharecroppers in exchange for a lien, or claim, on the farmer's crop. Merchants sometimes charged exorbitant interest, as much as 60 percent, on the goods they sold—from seeds to needles to slabs of bacon. At "settling up time," after the landlord took half of the farmer's crop for rent, the merchant consulted his ledger. Invariably, the farmer's expenses exceeded the income from his half of the crop. It was a rare cropper who had two nickels to rub together at the end of a season. Empty-handed, he had no choice but to begin the cycle all over again.

An experiment at first, sharecropping spread quickly throughout the cotton South. While it never became the only system of agricultural labor, sharecropping soon dominated. By 1870, the old gang system, direct white supervision, and clustered black living quarters were fading memories. Soon, sharecropping ensnared small white farmers as well as black farmers.

Reconstruction Collapses

By 1870, Northerners looked forward to putting "the southern problem" behind them. They had written into the Constitution guarantees of civil and political rights for blacks and enacted a program of political reunification that had restored ex-Confederate states to the Union. Now, after a decade of engagement with the public issues of war and recon-

struction, they wanted to turn to their own affairs. Increasingly, practical business-minded men came to the forefront of the Republican Party, replacing the band of reformers and idealists who had been prominent in the 1860s. While northern resolve to defend black freedom withered, southern commitment to white supremacy intensified. Without northern protection, southern Republicans were no match for the Democrats' economic coercion, political corruption, and bloody violence. One by one, Republican state governments fell. The election of 1876 both confirmed and completed the collapse of reconstruction.

The Grant Regime: Cronies, Corruption, and Economic Collapse

Ulysses S. Grant was the obvious choice for the Republican Party's presidential nomination in 1868. When the Civil War ended, the general who beat Lee was easily the most popular man in the nation, at least north of the Mason-Dixon line. Radicals preferred someone with a deeper moral commitment to black equality, but Grant supported congressional reconstruction and that was enough for the Republican convention. The Democrats chose Horatio Seymour, former governor of New York. Their platform blasted congressional reconstruction as "a flagrant usurpation of power . . . unconstitutional, revolutionary, and void." Republicans answered by "waving the bloody shirt"; that is, they reminded voters that the Democrats were "the party of rebellion," the party that stubbornly resisted a just peace. During the campaign, the Ku Klux Klan erupted in another reign of terror, murdering hundreds of southern Republicans. Terrorist tactics cut into Grant's tally, but he gained a narrow 300,000-vote margin in the popular vote and a substantial victory (214 votes to 80) in the electoral college.

Grant understood that most Northerners had grown weary of reconstruction. Conservative business-minded Northerners had become convinced that recurrent federal intrusion was itself a major cause of instability. Eager to invest in the South and especially to resume the profitable cotton trade, they sought order, not disruption. A growing number of northern Republican leaders began to question the wisdom of their party's alliance with the South's lower classes—its small farmers and sharecroppers. Grant's secretary of the interior, Jacob D. Cox of Ohio, proposed allying with the "thinking

"I BEG TO REPEAT THAT THESE FRAUDS ON THE GOVERNMENT SHALL BE PROBED TO THE VERY BOTTOM."

TAMMANY RING
CANAL RING
WHISKEY RING
INDIAN RING
PRESS RING
STATE RING
COUNTY RING
TOWN RING
WARD RING

BELKNAP
FRAUD CLAIMS
BACK PAY GRAB
WHISKEY FRAUDS
BRIBERY
EMMA MINE

GRANT AND SCANDAL
This anti-Grant cartoon by the nation's most celebrated political cartoonist, Thomas Nast, shows the president falling headfirst into the barrel of fraud and corruption that tainted his administration. During Grant's eight years in the White House, many in his administration failed him. Sometimes duped, sometimes merely loyal, Grant stubbornly defended wrongdoers, even to the point of perjuring himself to keep an aide out of jail.
Library of Congress.

www.bedfordstmartins.com/tap SEE THE ONLINE STUDY GUIDE for more help in analyzing this image.

and influential native southerners . . . the intelligent, well-to-do, and controlling class."

The talents Grant had demonstrated on the battlefield—decisiveness, clarity, and resolution—deserted him in the White House. Unclear about his objectives, he grew tentative, unsure of himself, almost bewildered. Able advisers might have helped, but Grant surrounded himself with fumbling kinfolk and old cronies from his army days. He also made a string of dubious appointments that led to a series of damaging scandals. Charges of corruption tainted his vice president, Schuyler Colfax, and brought down his secretary of war and secretary of the navy as well as his private secretary. Grant's dogged loyalty to liars and cheats only compounded the damage. While never personally implicated in any scandal, Grant was aggravatingly naive and his administration filled with rot.

In 1872, disgusted anti-Grant Republicans bolted and launched a third party, the Liberal Republicans. The Liberals promised to create a gov-

ernment "which the best people of this country will be proud of." They condemned the Grant regime as a riot of vulgarity—crude graft, tasteless materialism, and blatant anti-intellectualism. To clean up the mess, they proposed ending the spoils system, by which victorious parties rewarded loyal workers with public office, and replacing it with a nonpartisan civil service commission that would oversee competitive examinations for appointment to office. Moreover, they demanded that the government remove federal troops from the South and restore "home rule." Democrats especially liked the southern policy of the Liberals, and the Democratic Party endorsed the Liberal presidential candidate, Horace Greeley, the longtime editor of the *New York Tribune*. Despite Grant's problems, however, the nation still felt enormous affection for the man who had saved the Union. In the 1872 election, voters gave him 56 percent of the popular vote, the most lopsided victory since Andrew Jackson swept into the White House forty-four years earlier.

In 1872, disgusted anti-Grant Republicans bolted and launched a third party, the Liberal Republicans. The Liberals promised to create a government "which the best people of this country will be proud of."

Grant was not without accomplishments during his eight years as president. Ironically, he scored his greatest triumph on an issue he cared little about: the settlement of the U.S. claim against Great Britain for wartime damages caused by British-built Confederate ships. When Britain denied any wrongdoing, tempers flared. But in 1872, Hamilton Fish, Grant's able secretary of state, skillfully orchestrated a peaceful settlement that paid the United States $15.5 million in damages.

Grant's great passion in foreign affairs—annexation of Santo Domingo in the Caribbean—ended in utter failure. Grant argued that the acquisition of this tropical land would permit the United States to expand its trade in the Caribbean and simultaneously provide a new home for the South's blacks, who were so desperately harassed by the Klan. Aggressive foreign policy had not originated with the Grant administration. Lincoln and Johnson's secretary of state, William H. Seward, had thwarted French efforts to set up a puppet empire under Maximilian in Mexico, and his purchase of Alaska ("Seward's Ice Box") from Russia in 1867 for only $7 million had fired Grant's imperial ambition. But the Republican Party split over the president's scheme to acquire Santo Domingo, and in the end Grant could not marshal the votes needed to approve the treaty of annexation.

Grant's Proposed Annexation of Santo Domingo

The Grant administration was caught up in a tangle of complicated problems, including a devastating economic depression that began in 1873. Railroads, which had fueled the postwar boom, led directly to the bust. A major Philadelphia bank, headed by Jay Cooke, had poured enormous sums into railroads, become overextended with debt, and

gone under, initiating the panic of 1873. Like dominoes, other companies failed, and soon the nation sank into its most severe depression to that time. More than eighteen thousand businesses collapsed in two years, and more than one million workers lost their jobs. Desperate times arrived at the doorsteps of most working people. Workers battled owners as industrial violence kept pace with economic hardship. The violence subsided as men and women returned to work, but only at the end of the decade did the depression lift. By then, southern Republican governments had fallen, and the experiment of reconstruction had ended.

Northern Resolve Withers

Although Northerners wanted desperately to shift their attention to the new issues, the old ones would not go away. When southern Republicans pleaded for federal protection from Klan violence, Congress enacted three laws in 1870 and 1871 that were intended to break the back of white terrorism. The severest of the three, the Ku Klux Klan Act, made interference with voting rights a felony and authorized the use of the army to enforce it. Intrepid federal marshals arrested thousands of suspected Klansmen. While the government came close to destroying the Klan, it did not end terrorism against blacks. Congress also passed the Civil Rights Act of 1875, which boldly outlawed racial discrimination in transportation, public accommodations, and juries. But federal authorities did little to enforce the law, and segregated facilities remained the rule throughout the South.

In reality, the retreat from reconstruction had begun in 1868 with Grant's election. Grant genuinely wanted to see blacks' civil and political rights protected, but he felt uneasy about an open-ended commitment that seemed to ignore constitutional limitations on federal power. Like his predecessor, he distributed pardons liberally and encouraged the passage of a general amnesty. In May 1872, Congress obliged and restored the right of officeholding to all but three hundred ex-rebels. Radicals did what they could to stiffen the North's resolve, but by the early 1870s reform had lost its principal spokesmen to death or defeat at the polls. Many Republicans had washed their hands of reconstruction, concluding that the quest for black equality was mistaken or hopelessly naive. Those who bolted to the Liberal Republican Party, for example, welcomed the South's "best people" back to power.

Traditional white leaders, it seemed to them, offered the best hope for honesty, order, and prosperity.

The North's abandonment of reconstruction rested on more than weariness, greed, and disillusionment. Underlying everything was unyielding racial prejudice. Emancipation failed to uproot racism in either the South or the North. During the war, Northerners had learned to accept black freedom, but deep-seated prejudice prevented many from equating freedom with equality. Even the actions they took on behalf of blacks often served partisan political advantage. Whether they expressed it quietly or boisterously, Northerners generally supported Indiana Senator Thomas A. Hendricks's declaration that "this is a white man's Government, made by the white man for the white man." Increasingly, when Radicals asked Northerners to remember reconstruction's victims, northern sympathy went out to white Southerners.

The U.S. Supreme Court also did its part to undermine reconstruction. From the first, Republicans had feared that the conservative Court would declare their southern policies unconstitutional. In the 1870s, a series of Court decisions significantly weakened the federal government's ability to protect black Southerners under the Fourteenth and Fifteenth Amendments. In the *Slaughterhouse* cases (1873), the Court distinguished between national and state citizenship and ruled that the Fourteenth Amendment protected only those rights that stemmed from the federal government, like voting in federal elections and interstate travel. Since the Court decided that most rights derived from the states, it sharply curtailed the federal government's authority to protect black citizens. Even more devastating, the *United States v. Cruikshank* ruling (1876) said that the reconstruction amendments gave Congress power to legislate only against discrimination by states, not by individuals. The "suppression of ordinary crime," such as assault, remained a state responsibility. The Supreme Court did not declare reconstruction unconstitutional, but it gradually undermined its legal foundation.

The mood of the North found political expression in the election of 1874, when for the first time in eighteen years the Democrats gained control of the House of Representatives. Voters blamed the Grant administration for the economic hard times that had begun the previous year, but they also sent a message about reconstruction. As one Republican observed, the people had grown tired of the "negro question, with all its complications, and the recon-

struction of the Southern States, with all its interminable embroilments."

Reconstruction had come apart in the North, and Congress gradually abandoned it. President Grant grew increasingly unwilling to enforce it. The Supreme Court busily denied the constitutionality of significant parts of it. And the people sent unmistakable messages that they were tired of it. Rather than defend reconstruction from its southern enemies, Northerners steadily backed away from the challenge. After the early 1870s, southern blacks faced the forces of reaction largely on their own.

White Supremacy Triumphs

Republican governments in the South attracted more bitterness and hatred than any other political regimes in American history. In the eyes of the majority of whites, each day of Republican rule produced fresh insults: Black militiamen patrolled town streets, black laborers negotiated contracts with former masters, black maids stood up to former mistresses, black voters cast ballots, and black legislators enacted laws. The northern retreat from reconstruction permitted southern Democrats to harness this white rage to politics. Taking the name "Redeemers," they promised to replace "bayonet rule" (some federal troops continued to be stationed in the South) with "home rule" (white southern control). They branded Republican governments a carnival of extravagance, waste, and fraud and promised that honest, thrifty Democrats would supplant the irresponsible tax-and-spend Republicans. Above all, Redeemers swore to save southern civilization from a descent into African "barbarism" and "negro rule." As one man put it, "We must render this either a white man's government, or convert the land into a Negro man's cemetery."

By the early 1870s, Democrats understood that race was their most potent weapon. They adopted a two-pronged racial strategy to overthrow Republican governments. First, they sought to polarize the parties around color, and, second, they relentlessly intimidated black voters. They went about gathering all the South's white voters into the Democratic Party, leaving the Republicans to depend on blacks. The "straight-out" appeal to whites promised great advantage because whites made up a majority of the population in every southern state except Mississippi, South Carolina, and Louisiana.

Democrats employed several devices to dislodge whites from the Republican Party. First and foremost, they fanned the flames of racial prejudice. In South Carolina, a Democrat crowed that his party appealed to the "proud Caucasian race, whose sovereignty on earth God has proclaimed." Ostracism also proved effective. Local newspapers published the names of whites who kept company with blacks. So complete was the ostracism that one of its victims said, "No white man can live in the South in the future and act with any other than the Democratic party unless he is willing and prepared to live a life of social isolation."

Above all, Redeemers swore to save southern civilization from a descent into African "barbarism" and "negro rule."

In addition, Democrats exploited the small white farmer's severe economic plight by blaming it on Republican financial policy. Government spending soared during reconstruction, and small farmers saw their tax burden skyrocket. Farms in Mississippi were taxed at four times the prewar level. When cotton prices fell by nearly 50 percent in the 1870s, yeomen farmers found cash in short supply. To pay their taxes, one man observed, "people are selling every egg and chicken they can get." In South Carolina, David Golightly Harris observed, "This is tax time. We are nearly all on our head about them. They are so high & so little money to pay with." He scraped together the $81.57 he owed, but those unable to pay lost their land. In 1871, Mississippi reported that one-seventh of the state's land—3.3 million acres—had been forfeited for nonpayment of taxes. The small farmer's economic distress had a racial dimension. Because few freedmen succeeded in acquiring land, they rarely paid taxes. In Georgia in 1874, blacks made up 46 percent of the population but paid only 2 percent of the taxes. From the perspective of the small white farmer, Republican rule meant not only that he was paying more taxes but that he was paying them to aid blacks. Democrats asked whether it was not time for hard-pressed yeomen to join the white man's party.

If racial pride, social isolation, and Republican financial policies proved insufficient to drive yeomen from the Republican Party, Democrats turned to terrorism. "Night riders" targeted scalawags as well as blacks for murder and assassination. By the early 1870s, then, only a fraction of southern whites any

IS THIS A REPUBLICAN FORM OF GOVERNMENT?
This powerful 1876 drawing by Thomas Nast depicts the end of reconstruction as the tragedy it was. As white supremacists in the South piled up more and more bodies, supporters of civil rights accused the Grant administration of failing to protect black Southerners and legitimately elected governments. They pointed specifically to the constitutional requirement that "[t]he United States shall guarantee to every State in this Union a Republican Form of Government, and shall protect each of them . . . against domestic violence" (Article IV, section 4). Library of Congress.

longer professed allegiance to the party of Lincoln. Racial polarization became a reality. Rich and poor whites united. Yeoman defection to the Redeemers proved a heavy blow to southern Republicanism.

The second prong of Democratic strategy—intimidation of black voters—proved equally devastating. Antiblack political violence escalated to unprecedented levels. In 1873 in Louisiana, a clash between black militiamen and gun-toting whites killed two white men and an estimated seventy black men. Half of the black men were slaughtered after they had surrendered. Although the federal government indicted more than one hundred white men, local juries failed to convict a single one of them.

Even before adopting the all-out white supremacist tactics of the 1870s, Democrats had already captured Virginia, Tennessee, and North Carolina. The new campaign brought fresh gains. The Redeemers retook Georgia in 1871, Texas in 1873, and Arkansas and Alabama in 1874. In 1876, Mississippi fell. The story in Mississippi was one of open, unrelenting, and often savage intimidation of black voters and their few remaining white allies. In a rampage by whites in Vicksburg, Mississippi, thirty-five blacks and two whites lost their lives. As the state election approached in 1876, Governor Adelbert Ames appealed to Washington for federal troops to control the violence, only to hear from the attorney general that the "whole public are tired of these annual autumnal outbreaks in the South." Abandoned, Mississippi Republicans succumbed to the Democratic onslaught in the fall elections. By 1876, only three Republican state governments—in Florida, Louisiana, and South Carolina—survived (Map 15.2).

An Election and a Compromise

The centennial year of 1876 witnessed one of the most tumultuous elections in American history. Its chaos and confusion provided a fitting conclusion to the experiment known as reconstruction. The election took place in November, but not until

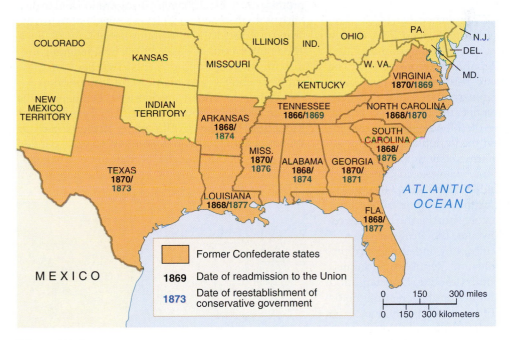

MAP 15.2

The Reconstruction of the South

Myth has it that Republican rule of the former Confederacy was not only harsh but long. In most states, however, conservative southern whites stormed back into power in only a matter of a few months or a very few years. By the election of 1876, Republican governments could be found in only three states. And they soon fell.

READING THE MAP: List in chronological order the readmission of former states to the Union. Which states reestablished conservative governments most quickly?

CONNECTIONS: What did the former Confederate states need to do in order to be readmitted to the Union? How did reestablished conservative governments react to reconstruction?

www.bedfordstmartins.com/tap   SEE THE ONLINE STUDY GUIDE for more help in analyzing this map.

March 2 of the following year, at 4 A.M., did the nation know who would be inaugurated president on March 4. For four months the country suffered through a constitutional and political crisis that jeopardized the peaceful transfer of power from one administration to the next. Sixteen years after Lincoln's election, Americans feared that a presidential contest would again precipitate civil war.

The centennial year of 1876 witnessed one of the most tumultuous elections in American history, a fitting conclusion to the experiment known as reconstruction.

The Democrats had nominated New York's reform governor, Samuel J. Tilden, who immediately targeted the corruption of the Grant administration and the despotism of Republican reconstruction. The Republicans put forward a reformer of their own, Rutherford B. Hayes, governor of Ohio. Privately, Hayes considered "bayonet rule" a mistake, but he concluded that waving the bloody shirt, as threadbare as it was, remained the Republicans' best political strategy." It leads people away from 'hard times,' which is our deadliest foe," Hayes said lamely.

On election day, Tilden tallied 4,284,000 votes to Hayes's 4,036,000. Yet in the all-important electoral college, Tilden fell one vote short of the majority required for victory. However, the electoral votes of three states remained in doubt and thus were uncounted. Both Democrats and Republicans claimed the nineteen votes of South Carolina, Louisiana, and Florida, the only remaining Republican strongholds in the South. To win, Tilden needed only one of the contested votes. Hayes had to have all of them to take the election. The two parties traded charges of fraud and intimidation. To be sure, Republicans had stuffed some southern ballot boxes, but stepped-up violence by the Democrats had kept hundreds of thousands of Republicans from the polls.

Congress had to decide who had actually won the elections in the three southern states and thus who would be president. The Constitution provided little guidance. Moreover, Democrats controlled the House, and Republicans the Senate. To break the deadlock, Congress created a special electoral commission to arbitrate the disputed returns. An odd and cumbersome compromise, the commission was made up of five representatives (two Republicans,

three Democrats), five senators (two Democrats, three Republicans), and five justices of the Supreme Court (two Republicans, two Democrats, and one justice who was considered an independent). But before the commission could meet, the Illinois legislature elected the independent justice to the Senate, and his place was filled with a Republican. The commissioners all voted the straight party line, giving every state to the Republican Hayes and putting him over the top in electoral votes (Map 15.3).

Some outraged Democrats vowed to resist Hayes's victory. But the impasse was broken when negotiations behind the scenes between Hayes's lieutenants and some moderate southern Democrats resulted in an informal understanding, known as the Compromise of 1877. In exchange for a Democratic promise not to block Hayes's inauguration and to deal fairly with the freedmen, Hayes vowed not to use the army to uphold the remaining Republican regimes. The South would also gain substantial federal subsidies for internal improvements. Two days later, the nation celebrated Hayes's peaceful inauguration.

Stubborn Tilden supporters bemoaned the "stolen election" and damned "His Fraudulency," Rutherford B. Hayes. Old-guard Radicals such as William Lloyd Garrison denounced Hayes's bargain as a "policy of compromise, of credulity, of weakness, of subserviency, of surrender." But the nation as a

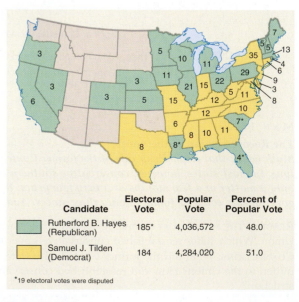

Candidate	Electoral Vote	Popular Vote	Percent of Popular Vote
Rutherford B. Hayes (Republican)	185*	4,036,572	48.0
Samuel J. Tilden (Democrat)	184	4,284,020	51.0

*19 electoral votes were disputed

MAP 15.3
The Election of 1876

whole celebrated, for the Republic had weathered a grave crisis. The Compromise of 1877 confirmed the conservatism that had been growing in the North for years. Even without a deal, Hayes would probably have withdrawn the troops. The last three Republican state governments fell quickly once Hayes abandoned them. Reconstruction had ended.

The nation's solution to the crisis of 1877 marked a return to the antebellum tradition of sectional compromise. As in previous crises, whites had found a way to bridge their differences and retain the peace, and again blacks had paid the price. Republicans followed a path of expediency and gained the presidency. Southern Democrats got home rule and a free hand in racial matters. Black Southerners were not completely subordinated to whites in 1877, but their prospects in the New South looked bleak.

Conclusion: "A Revolution but Half-Accomplished"

In 1865, when General Carl Schurz visited the South, he discovered "a revolution but half-accomplished." Defeat had not prepared the South for an easy transition from slavery to free labor, from white racial despotism to equal justice, and from white political monopoly to biracial democracy. Ex-masters like David Golightly Harris had trouble seeing former slaves like York and Old Will as free people. The old elite wanted to get "things back as near to slavery as possible," while ex-slaves and whites who had lacked power in the slave regime were eager to exploit the revolutionary implications of defeat and emancipation.

The northern-dominated Congress pushed the revolution along. Although it refused to provide an economic underpinning to black freedom, it required defeated Confederates to accept legal equality and share political power. But conservative whites fought ferociously to recover their power and privilege. When they regained control of politics, they used the power of the state, along with private violence, to wipe out many of the gains of reconstruction. So successful were the reactionaries that one observer concluded that the North had won the war but the South had won the peace.

But the Redeemer counterrevolution did not mean a return to slavery. Northern victory in the Civil War ensured abolition, and ex-slaves gained the freedom to not be whipped or sold, to send their children to school, to worship in their own churches, and to work independently on their own rented farms. The lives of impoverished sharecroppers overflowed with hardships, but even sharecropping provided more autonomy and economic welfare than bondage had. It was limited freedom, to be sure, but it was not slavery.

Emancipation set in motion the most profound upheaval in the nation's history, and nothing whites did entirely erased its revolutionary impact. War destroyed the richest and largest slave society in the New World. It cost masters $3 billion in lost property and destroyed the foundation of planter wealth. Abolition overturned the social and economic order that had dominated the region for nearly two centuries. The world of masters and slaves succumbed to that of landlords and sharecroppers. Even today, some Southerners divide history into "before the war" and "after the war."

The Civil War and emancipation mark a watershed not just in the South's history but in that of the entire nation. War served as midwife for the birth of a modern nation-state, and for the first time sovereignty rested uncontested in the federal government. Moreover, the South returned to the Union, but as a junior partner. The victorious North now possessed the power to establish the nation's direction, and it set its compass toward the expansion of industrial capitalism. War laid the foundation for the power of big business and its captains in postwar America.

Still, in one significant respect, the Civil War remained only a "half-accomplished" revolution. As such, reconstruction represents a tragedy of enormous proportions. The nation did not fulfill the promises that it seemed to hold out to black Americans at war's end. The revolution raced forward, halted, and then slipped back, coming to rest far short of equality and justice. The failure had enduring consequences. Almost a century after reconstruction, the nation would embark on what one observer called a "second reconstruction," another effort to fulfill nineteenth-century promises. The solid achievements of the Thirteenth, Fourteenth, and Fifteenth Amendments to the Constitution would provide a legal foundation for the renewed commitment. It is worth remembering, though, that it was only the failure of the first reconstruction that made a modern civil rights movement necessary.

www.bedfordstmartins.com/tap SEE THE ONLINE STUDY GUIDE to test your mastery of the material covered in this chapter.

CHRONOLOGY

1863 **December.** Lincoln issues Proclamation of Amnesty and Reconstruction.

1864 **July.** Congress offers more stringent plan for reconstruction, Wade-Davis bill.

1865 **January.** General William T. Sherman sets aside land in South Carolina for black settlement.

March 4. Lincoln sworn in for second term as president of United States.

March. Congress establishes Freedmen's Bureau.

April 14. Lincoln shot, dies on April 15, succeeded by Vice President Andrew Johnson.

Fall. Southern legislatures enact discriminatory black codes.

December. Thirteenth Amendment abolishing slavery becomes part of U.S. Constitution.

1866 **April.** Congress approves Fourteenth Amendment making native-born blacks American citizens and guaranteeing all American citizens "equal protection of the laws." Amendment becomes part of Constitution in 1868.

April. Congress passes Civil Rights Act over President Johnson's veto.

May. Susan B. Anthony and Elizabeth Cady Stanton found Equal Rights Association to lobby for vote for women.

July. Congress extends Freedmen's Bureau over President Johnson's veto.

Summer. Ku Klux Klan founded in Tennessee.

November. Republicans triumph over Johnson's Democrats in congressional elections.

1867 **March.** Overriding Johnson's veto, Congress passes Military Reconstruction Act imposing military rule on South and requiring states to guarantee vote to black men.

1868 **March–May.** Senate impeachment trial of President Johnson results in acquittal.

November. Ulysses S. Grant elected president of the United States.

1869 **February.** Congress approves Fifteenth Amendment prohibiting racial discrimination in voting rights. Amendment becomes part of Constitution in 1870.

1871 **April.** Congress enacts Ku Klux Klan Act in effort to end white terrorism in South.

1872 **November.** President Grant reelected.

1873 Economic depression sets in for remainder of decade.

1874 **November.** Elections return Democratic majority to House of Representatives.

1875 **February.** Civil Rights Act of 1875 outlaws racial discrimination, but federal authorities do little to enforce law.

1877 **March.** Special congressional committee awards disputed electoral votes to Republican Rutherford B. Hayes, making him president of United States; Hayes agrees to pull military out of South.

BIBLIOGRAPHY

GENERAL WORKS

David Herbert Donald, Jean H. Baker, and Michael F. Holt, *The Civil War and Reconstruction* (2000).

W. E. B. Du Bois, *Black Reconstruction, 1860–1880* (1935).

Eric Foner, *Reconstruction: America's Unfinished Revolution* (1988).

John Hope Franklin, *Reconstruction after the Civil War* (1961).

James M. McPherson, *Ordeal by Fire: The Civil War and Reconstruction* (3rd ed., 2000).

Kenneth M. Stampp, *The Era of Reconstruction, 1865–1877* (1965).

WARTIME RECONSTRUCTION

Richard H. Abbott, *The Republican Party and the South, 1855–1877: The First Southern Strategy* (1986).

Herman Belz, *Emancipation and Equal Rights: Politics and Constitutionalism in the Civil War Era* (1978).

Louis S. Gerteis, *From Contraband to Freedman: Federal Policy toward Southern Blacks, 1861–1865* (1973).

William S. McFeely, *Yankee Stepfather: General O. O. Howard and the Freedmen* (1968).

James M. McPherson, *The Struggle for Equality: Abolitionists and the Negro in the Civil War and Reconstruction* (1964).

Willie Lee Rose, *Rehearsal for Reconstruction: The Port Royal Experiment* (1964).

Brooks D. Simpson, *Let Us Have Peace: Ulysses S. Grant and the Politics of War and Reconstruction, 1861–1868* (1991).

THE MEANING OF FREEDOM

James D. Anderson, *The Education of Blacks in the South, 1860–1935* (1988).

Ira Berlin et al., eds., *Freedom: A Documentary History of Emancipation, 1861–1867,* 4 vols. to date (1982–).

Edmund L. Drago, *Black Politicians and Reconstruction in Georgia: A Splendid Failure* (1982).

Russell Duncan, *Freedom's Shore: Tunis Campbell and the Georgia Freedmen* (1986).

Barbara J. Fields, *Slavery and Freedom on the Middle Ground: Maryland during the Nineteenth Century* (1985).

Michael W. Fitzgerald, *The Union League Movement in the Deep South: Politics and Agricultural Change during Reconstruction* (1989).

Eric Foner, *Nothing but Freedom: Emancipation and Its Legacy* (1983).

Janet Sharp Hermann, *The Pursuit of a Dream* (1981).

Thomas C. Holt, *Black over White: Negro Political Leadership in South Carolina during Reconstruction* (1977).

Peter Kolchin, *First Freedom: The Responses of Alabama's Blacks to Emancipation and Reconstruction* (1972).

Leon F. Litwack, *Been in the Storm So Long: The Aftermath of Slavery* (1979).

William E. Montgomery, *Under Their Own Vine and Fig Tree: The African-American Church in the South, 1865–1900* (1992).

Lynda J. Morgan, *Emancipation in Virginia's Tobacco Belt, 1850–1870* (1992).

Robert Morris, *Reading, 'Riting and Reconstruction* (1981).

Howard N. Rabinowitz, *Race Relations in the Urban South, 1865–1890* (1978).

Roger L. Ransom and Richard Sutch, *One Kind of Freedom: The Economic Consequences of Emancipation* (1977).

C. Peter Ripley, *Slaves and Freedmen in Civil War Louisiana* (1976).

Julie Saville, *The Work of Reconstruction: From Slave to Wage Laborer in South Carolina, 1860–1870* (1994).

Clarence E. Walker, *A Rock in a Weary Land: The African Methodist Episcopal Church during the Civil War and Reconstruction* (1982).

Joel Williamson, *After Slavery: The Negro in South Carolina during Reconstruction, 1861–1877* (1965).

Joel Williamson, *The Crucible of Race: Black/White Relations in the American South since Emancipation* (1984).

THE POLITICS OF RECONSTRUCTION

Michael Les Benedict, *The Impeachment and Trial of Andrew Johnson* (1973).

Michael Les Benedict, *A Compromise of Principle: Congressional Republicans and Reconstruction* (1974).

Richard F. Bensel, *Yankee Leviathan: The Origins of Central State Authority in America, 1859–1877* (1990).

Michael Kent Curtis, *No State Shall Abridge: The Fourteenth Amendment and the Bill of Rights* (1986).

David H. Donald, *Charles Sumner and the Rights of Man* (1970).

Ellen Carol DuBois, *Feminism and Suffrage: The Emergence of an Independent Women's Movement in America* (1978).

William Gillette, *The Right to Vote: Politics and the Passage of the Fifteenth Amendment* (1965).

Victor B. Howard, *Religion and the Radical Republican Movement, 1860–1870* (1990).

Harold M. Hyman, *A More Perfect Union: The Impact of the Civil War and Reconstruction on the Constitution* (1973).

Michael L. Lanza, *Agrarianism and Reconstruction Politics: The Southern Homestead Act* (1990).

William S. McFeely, *Grant: A Biography* (1981).

Eric L. McKitrick, *Andrew Johnson and Reconstruction* (1960).

James C. Mohr, ed., *Radical Republicans in the North: State Politics during Reconstruction* (1976).

David Montgomery, *Beyond Equality: Labor and the Radical Republicans, 1862–1872* (1967).

William E. Nelson, *The Fourteenth Amendment: From Political Principle to Judicial Doctrine* (1988).

James E. Sefton, *Andrew Johnson and the Uses of Constitutional Power* (1980).

Joel H. Sibley, *A Respectable Minority: The Democratic Party in the Civil War Era, 1860–1868* (1977).

Hans L. Trefousse, *Andrew Johnson: A Biography* (1989).

THE STRUGGLE IN THE SOUTH

Stephen V. Ash, *Middle Tennessee Society Transformed, 1860–1870: War and Peace in the Upper South* (1988).

Dwight B. Billings Jr., *Planters and the Making of a "New South": Class, Politics, and Development in North Carolina, 1865–1900* (1979).

Randolph B. Campbell, *A Southern Community in Crisis: Harrison County, Texas, 1850–1880* (1983).

Dan T. Carter, *When the War Was Over: The Failure of Self-Reconstruction in the South, 1865–1867* (1985).

Barry A. Crouch, *The Freedmen's Bureau and Black Texans* (1992).

Richard N. Current, *Those Terrible Carpetbaggers: A Reinterpretation* (1988).

Jane E. Dailey, *Before Jim Crow: The Politics of Race in Postemancipation Virginia* (2000).

Laura F. Edwards, *Gendered Strife and Confusion: The Political Culture of Reconstruction* (1997).

W. McKee Evans, *Ballots and Fence Rails: Reconstruction on the Lower Cape Fear* (1966).

Gaines Foster, *Ghosts of the Confederacy: Defeat of the Lost Cause and the Emergence of the New South, 1865 to 1913* (1987).

Steven Hahn, *The Roots of Southern Populism: Yeoman Farmers and the Transformation of the Georgia Upcountry, 1850–1890* (1983).

William C. Harris, *Day of the Carpetbagger: Republican Reconstruction in Mississippi* (1979).

Elizabeth Jacoway, *Yankee Missionaries in the South: The Penn School Experiment* (1980).

Jacqueline Jones, *Soldiers of Light and Love: Northern Teachers and Georgia Blacks, 1865–1873* (1980).

Robert C. Kenzer, *Kinship and Neighborhood in a Southern Community: Orange County, North Carolina, 1849–1881* (1987).

Richard G. Lowe, *Republicans and Reconstruction in Virginia, 1865–1870* (1991).

Scott Reynolds Nelson, *Iron Confederacies: Southern Railways, Klan Violence, and Reconstruction* (1999).

Donald G. Nieman, *To Set the Law in Motion: The Freedmen's Bureau and the Legal Rights of Blacks, 1865–1868* (1979).

Michael Perman, *Reunion without Compromise: The South and Reconstruction, 1865–1868* (1973).

Michael Perman, *The Road to Redemption: Southern Politics, 1869–1879* (1984).

Lawrence N. Powell, *New Masters: Northern Planters during the Civil War and Reconstruction* (1980).

George C. Rable, *But There Was No Peace: The Role of Violence in the Politics of Reconstruction* (1984).

Philip N. Racine, ed., *Piedmont Farmer: The Journals of David Golightly Harris, 1855–1870* (1990).

James L. Roark, *Masters without Slaves: Southern Planters in the Civil War and Reconstruction* (1977).

Crandall A. Shifflett, *Patronage and Poverty in the Tobacco South: Louisa County, Virginia, 1860–1900* (1982).

Mark W. Summers, *Railroads, Reconstruction, and the Gospel of Prosperity: Aid under the Radical Republicans, 1865–1877* (1984).

Allen Trelease, *White Terror: The Ku Klux Klan Conspiracy and Southern Reconstruction* (1971).

Ted Tunnell, *Crucible of Reconstruction: War, Radicalism, and Race in Louisiana, 1862–1877* (1984).

Peter Wallenstein, *From Slave South to New South: Public Policy in Nineteenth-Century Georgia* (1987).

Michael Wayne, *The Reshaping of Plantation Society: The Natchez District, 1860–1880* (1983).

Jonathan M. Wiener, *Social Origins of the New South, 1860–1885* (1978).

Sara Woolfolk Wiggins, *The Scalawag in Alabama Politics, 1865–1881* (1977).

Gavin Wright, *Old South, New South: Revolutions in the Southern Economy since the Civil War* (1986).

THE COLLAPSE OF RECONSTRUCTION

William Gillette, *Retreat from Reconstruction, 1869–1879* (1979).

Otto H. Olsen, ed., *Reconstruction and Redemption in the South: An Assessment* (1980).

Ian Polakoff, *The Politics of Inertia: The Election of 1876 and the End of Reconstruction* (1973).

Terry L. Seip, *The South Returns to Congress: Men, Economic Measures, and Intersectional Relationships, 1868–1879* (1983).

John G. Sproat, *"The Best Men": Liberal Reformers in the Gilded Age* (1968).

Mark W. Summers, *The Era of Good Stealings* (1993).

Margaret S. Thompson, *The "Spider Web": Congress and Lobbying in the Age of Grant* (1985).

C. Vann Woodward, *Reunion and Reaction: The Compromise of 1877 and the End of Reconstruction* (1951).

THE DECLARATION OF INDEPENDENCE

In Congress, July 4, 1776,

THE UNANIMOUS DECLARATION OF THE
THIRTEEN UNITED STATES OF AMERICA

When in the course of human events, it becomes necessary for one people to dissolve the political bands which have connected them with another, and to assume, among the powers of the earth, the separate and equal station to which the laws of nature and of nature's God entitle them, a decent respect to the opinions of mankind requires that they should declare the causes which impel them to the separation.

We hold these truths to be self-evident, that all men are created equal; that they are endowed by their Creator with certain unalienable rights; that among these, are life, liberty, and the pursuit of happiness. That, to secure these rights, governments are instituted among men, deriving their just powers from the consent of the governed; that, whenever any form of government becomes destructive of these ends, it is the right of the people to alter or to abolish it, and to institute a new government, laying its foundation on such principles, and organizing its powers in such form, as to them shall seem most likely to effect their safety and happiness. Prudence, indeed, will dictate that governments long established, should not be changed for light and transient causes; and, accordingly, all experience hath shown, that mankind are more disposed to suffer, while evils are sufferable, than to right themselves by abolishing the forms to which they are accustomed. But, when a long train of abuses and usurpations, pursuing invariably the same object, evinces a design to reduce them under absolute despotism, it is their right, it is their duty, to throw off such government and to provide new guards for their future security. Such has been the patient sufferance of these colonies, and such is now the necessity which constrains them to alter their former systems of government. The history of the present King of Great Britain is a history of repeated injuries and usurpations, all having, in direct object, the establishment of an absolute tyranny over these States. To prove this, let facts be submitted to a candid world:

He has refused his assent to laws the most wholesome and necessary for the public good.

He has forbidden his governors to pass laws of immediate and pressing importance, unless suspended in their operation till his assent should be obtained; and, when so suspended, he has utterly neglected to attend to them.

He has refused to pass other laws for the accommodation of large districts of people, unless those people would relinquish the right of representation in the legislature; a right inestimable to them, and formidable to tyrants only.

He has called together legislative bodies at places unusual, uncomfortable, and distant from the depository of their public records, for the sole purpose of fatiguing them into compliance with his measures.

He has dissolved representative houses repeatedly for opposing, with manly firmness, his invasions on the rights of the people.

He has refused, for a long time after such dissolutions, to cause others to be elected; whereby the legislative powers, incapable of annihilation, have returned to the people at large for their exercise; the state remaining in the mean-time exposed to all the danger of invasion from without, and convulsions within.

He has endeavoured to prevent the population of these States; for that purpose, obstructing the laws for naturalization of foreigners, refusing to pass others to encourage their migration hither, and raising the conditions of new appropriations of lands.

He has obstructed the administration of justice, by refusing his assent to laws for establishing judiciary powers.

He has made judges dependent on his will alone, for the tenure of their offices, and the amount and payment of their salaries.

He has erected a multitude of new offices, and sent hither swarms of officers to harass our people, and eat out their substance.

He has kept among us, in times of peace, standing armies, without the consent of our legislature.

He has affected to render the military independent of, and superior to, the civil power.

He has combined, with others, to subject us to a jurisdiction foreign to our Constitution, and unacknowledged by our laws; giving his assent to their acts of pretended legislation:

For quartering large bodies of armed troops among us:

For protecting them by a mock trial, from punishment, for any murders which they should commit on the inhabitants of these States:

For cutting off our trade with all parts of the world:

For imposing taxes on us without our consent:

For depriving us, in many cases, of the benefit of trial by jury:

For transporting us beyond seas to be tried for pretended offences:

For abolishing the free system of English laws in a neighboring province, establishing therein an arbitrary government, and enlarging its boundaries, so as to render it at once an example and fit instrument for introducing the same absolute rule into these colonies:

For taking away our charters, abolishing our most valuable laws, and altering, fundamentally, the powers of our governments:

For suspending our own legislatures, and declaring themselves invested with power to legislate for us in all cases whatsoever.

He has abdicated government here, by declaring us out of his protection, and waging war against us.

He has plundered our seas, ravaged our coasts, burnt our towns, and destroyed the lives of our people.

He is, at this time, transporting large armies of foreign mercenaries to complete the works of death, desolation, and tyranny, already begun, with circumstances of cruelty and perfidy scarcely paralleled in the most barbarous ages, and totally unworthy the head of a civilized nation.

He has constrained our fellow citizens, taken captive on the high seas, to bear arms against their country, to become the executioners of their friends, and brethren, or to fall themselves by their hands.

He has excited domestic insurrections amongst us, and has endeavored to bring on the inhabitants of our frontiers, the merciless Indian savages, whose known rule of warfare is an undistinguished destruction of all ages, sexes, and conditions.

In every stage of these oppressions, we have petitioned for redress; in the most humble terms; our repeated petitions have been answered only by repeated injury. A prince, whose character is thus marked by every act which may define a tyrant, is unfit to be the ruler of a free people.

Nor have we been wanting in attention to our British brethren. We have warned them, from time to time, of attempts made by their legislature to extend an unwarrantable jurisdiction over us. We have reminded them of the circumstances of our emigration and settlement here. We have appealed to their native justice and magnanimity, and we have conjured them, by the ties of our common kindred, to disavow these usurpations, which would inevitably interrupt our connections and correspondence. They, too, have been deaf to the voice of justice and consanguinity. We must, therefore, acquiesce in the necessity which denounces our separation, and hold them as we hold the rest of mankind, enemies in war, in peace, friends.

We, therefore, the representatives of the United States of America, in general Congress assembled, appealing to the Supreme Judge of the world for the rectitude of our intentions, do, in the name, and by authority of the good people of these colonies, solemnly publish and declare, that these united colonies are, and of right ought to be, free and independent states: that they are absolved from all allegiance to the British Crown, and that all political connection between them and the state of Great Britain is, and ought to be, totally dissolved; and that, as free and independent states, they have full power to levy war, conclude peace, contract alliances, establish commerce, and to do all other acts and things which independent states may of right do. And, for the support of this declaration, with a firm reliance on the protection of Divine Providence, we mutually pledge to each other our lives, our fortunes, and our sacred honor.

The foregoing Declaration was, by order of Congress, engrossed, and signed by the following members:

JOHN HANCOCK

New Hampshire
Josiah Bartlett
William Whipple
Matthew Thornton

Massachusetts Bay
Samuel Adams
John Adams
Robert Treat Paine
Elbridge Gerry

New York
William Floyd
Phillip Livingston
Francis Lewis
Lewis Morris

New Jersey
Richard Stockton
John Witherspoon
Francis Hopkinson
John Hart
Abraham Clark

Rhode Island
Stephen Hopkins
William Ellery

Connecticut
Roger Sherman
Samuel Huntington
William Williams
Oliver Wolcott

Delaware
Caesar Rodney
George Read
Thomas M'Kean

Pennsylvania
Robert Morris
Benjamin Rush
Benjamin Franklin
John Morton
George Clymer
James Smith
George Taylor
James Wilson
George Ross

North Carolina
William Hooper
Joseph Hewes
John Penn

Maryland
Samuel Chase
William Paca
Thomas Stone
Charles Carroll,
   of Carrollton

Virginia
George Wythe
Richard Henry Lee
Thomas Jefferson
Benjamin Harrison
Thomas Nelson, Jr.
Francis Lightfoot Lee
Carter Braxton

South Carolina
Edward Rutledge
Thomas Heyward, Jr.
Thomas Lynch, Jr.
Arthur Middleton

Georgia
Button Gwinnett
Lyman Hall
George Walton

Resolved, That copies of the Declaration be sent to the several assemblies, conventions, and committees, or councils of safety, and to the several commanding officers of the continental troops; that it be proclaimed in each of the United States, at the head of the army.

THE ARTICLES OF CONFEDERATION AND PERPETUAL UNION

Agreed to in Congress, November 15, 1777
Ratified March 1781

BETWEEN THE STATES OF NEW HAMPSHIRE, MASSACHU-
SETTS BAY, RHODE ISLAND AND PROVIDENCE PLANTA-
TIONS, CONNECTICUT, NEW YORK, NEW JERSEY, PENN-
SYLVANIA, DELAWARE, MARYLAND, VIRGINIA, NORTH
CAROLINA, SOUTH CAROLINA, GEORGIA.*

Article 1

The stile of this confederacy shall be "The United States
of America."

Article 2

Each State retains its sovereignty, freedom and independence, and every power, jurisdiction, and right,
which is not by this confederation expressly delegated
to the United States, in Congress assembled.

Article 3

The said states hereby severally enter into a firm league
of friendship with each other for their common defence, the security of their liberties and their mutual
and general welfare; binding themselves to assist each
other against all force offered to, or attacks made upon
them, or any of them, on account of religion, sovereignty, trade, or any other pretence whatever.

Article 4

The better to secure and perpetuate mutual friendship
and intercourse among the people of the different
states in this union, the free inhabitants of each of these
states, paupers, vagabonds, and fugitives from justice
excepted, shall be entitled to all privileges and immunities of free citizens in the several states; and the people of each State shall have free ingress and regress to
and from any other State, and shall enjoy therein all
the privileges of trade and commerce, subject to the
same duties, impositions, and restrictions, as the inhabitants thereof respectively; provided, that such restrictions shall not extend so far as to prevent the removal of property, imported into any State, to any
other State of which the owner is an inhabitant; provided also, that no imposition, duties, or restriction,
shall be laid by any State on the property of the United
States, or either of them.

If any person guilty of, or charged with treason,
felony, or other high misdemeanor in any State, shall
flee from justice and be found in any of the United
States, he shall, upon demand of the governor or executive power of the State from which he fled, be delivered up and removed to the State having jurisdiction of his offence.

Full faith and credit shall be given in each of these
states to the records, acts, and judicial proceedings of
the courts and magistrates of every other State.

Article 5

For the more convenient management of the general interests of the United States, delegates shall be annually
appointed, in such manner as the legislature of each
State shall direct, to meet in Congress, on the 1st Monday in November in every year, with a power reserved
to each State to recall its delegates, or any of them, at
any time within the year, and to send others in their
stead for the remainder of the year.

No State shall be represented in Congress by less
than two, nor by more than seven members; and no
person shall be capable of being a delegate for more
than three years in any term of six years; nor shall any
person, being a delegate, be capable of holding any office under the United States, for which he, or any other
for his benefit, receives any salary, fees, or emolument
of any kind.

Each State shall maintain its own delegates in a
meeting of the states, and while they act as members
of the committee of the states.

In determining questions in the United States, in
Congress assembled, each State shall have one vote.

Freedom of speech and debate in Congress shall
not be impeached or questioned in any court or place
out of Congress: and the members of Congress shall
be protected in their persons from arrests and impris-
onments, during the time of their going to and from,
and attendance on Congress, except for treason, felony,
or breach of the peace.

---

*This copy of the final draft of the Articles of Confederation is taken
from the *Journals*, 9:907–925, November 15, 1777.

Article 6

No State, without the consent of the United States, in Congress assembled, shall send any embassy to, or receive any embassy from, or enter into any conference, agreement, alliance, or treaty with any king, prince, or state; nor shall any person, holding any office of profit or trust under the United States, or any of them, accept of any present, emolument, office or title, of any kind whatever, from any king, prince, or foreign state; nor shall the United States, in Congress assembled, or any of them, grant any title of nobility.

No two or more states shall enter into any treaty, confederation, or alliance, whatever, between them, without the consent of the United States, in Congress assembled, specifying accurately the purposes for which the same is to be entered into, and how long it shall continue.

No state shall lay any imposts or duties which may interfere with any stipulations in treaties entered into by the United States, in Congress assembled, with any king, prince, or state, in pursuance of any treaties already proposed by Congress to the courts of France and Spain.

No vessels of war shall be kept up in time of peace by any State, except such number only as shall be deemed necessary by the United States, in Congress assembled, for the defence of such State or its trade; nor shall any body of forces be kept up by any State, in time of peace, except such number only as, in the judgment of the United States, in Congress assembled, shall be deemed requisite to garrison the forts necessary for the defence of such State; but every State shall always keep up a well regulated and disciplined militia, sufficiently armed and accoutred, and shall provide, and constantly have ready for use, in public stores, a due number of field pieces and tents, and a proper quantity of arms, ammunition and camp equipage.

No State shall engage in any war without the consent of the United States, in Congress assembled, unless such State be actually invaded by enemies, or shall have received certain advice of a resolution being formed by some nation of Indians to invade such State, and the danger is so imminent as not to admit of a delay till the United States, in Congress assembled, can be consulted; nor shall any State grant commissions to any ships or vessels of war, nor letters of marque or reprisal, except it be after a declaration of war by the United States, in Congress assembled, and then only against the kingdom or state, and the subjects thereof, against which war has been so declared, and under such regulations as shall be established by the United States, in Congress assembled, unless such State be in-

fested by pirates, in which case vessels of war may be fitted out for that occasion, and kept so long as the danger shall continue, or until the United States, in Congress assembled, shall determine otherwise.

Article 7

When land forces are raised by any State for the common defence, all officers of or under the rank of colonel, shall be appointed by the legislature of each State respectively, by whom such forces shall be raised, or in such manner as such State shall direct; and all vacancies shall be filled up by the State which first made the appointment.

Article 8

All charges of war and all other expences, that shall be incurred for the common defence or general welfare, and allowed by the United States, in Congress assembled, shall be defrayed out of a common treasury, which shall be supplied by the several states, in proportion to the value of all land within each State, granted to or surveyed for any person, as such land and the buildings and improvements thereon shall be estimated according to such mode as the United States, in Congress assembled, shall, from time to time, direct and appoint.

The taxes for paying that proportion shall be laid and levied by the authority and direction of the legislatures of the several states, within the time agreed upon by the United States, in Congress assembled.

Article 9

The United States, in Congress assembled, shall have the sole and exclusive right and power of determining on peace and war, except in the cases mentioned in the 6th article; of sending and receiving ambassadors; entering into treaties and alliances, provided that no treaty of commerce shall be made, whereby the legislative power of the respective states shall be restrained from imposing such imposts and duties on foreigners as their own people are subjected to, or from prohibiting the exportation or importation of any species of goods or commodities whatsoever; of establishing rules for deciding, in all cases, what captures on land or water shall be legal, and in what manner prizes, taken by land or naval forces in the service of the United States, shall be divided or appropriated; of granting letters of marque and reprisal in times of peace; appointing courts for the trial of piracies and felonies committed on the high seas, and establishing courts for receiving and determining, finally, appeals in all cases of captures; provided, that no member of Congress shall be appointed a judge of any of the said courts.

The United States, in Congress assembled, shall also be the last resort on appeal in all disputes and differences now subsisting, or that hereafter may arise between two or more states concerning boundary, jurisdiction or any other cause whatever; which authority shall always be exercised in the manner following: whenever the legislative or executive authority, or lawful agent of any State, in controversy with another, shall present a petition to Congress, stating the matter in question, and praying for a hearing, notice thereof shall be given, by order of Congress, to the legislative or executive authority of the other State in controversy, and a day assigned for the appearance of the parties by their lawful agents, who shall then be directed to appoint, by joint consent, commissioners or judges to constitute a court for hearing and determining the matter in question; but, if they cannot agree, Congress shall name three persons out of each of the United States, and from the list of such persons each party shall alternately strike out one, the petitioners beginning, until the number shall be reduced to thirteen; and from that number not less than seven, nor more than nine names, as Congress shall direct, shall, in the presence of Congress, be drawn out by lot; and the persons whose names shall be so drawn, or any five of them, shall be commissioners or judges to hear and finally determine the controversy, so always as a major part of the judges who shall hear the cause shall agree in the determination; and if either party shall neglect to attend at the day appointed, without shewing reasons which Congress shall judge sufficient, or, being present, shall refuse to strike, the Congress shall proceed to nominate three persons out of each State, and the secretary of Congress shall strike in behalf of such party absent or refusing; and the judgment and sentence of the court to be appointed, in the manner before prescribed, shall be final and conclusive; and if any of the parties shall refuse to submit to the authority of such court, or to appear or defend their claim or cause, the court shall nevertheless proceed to pronounce sentence or judgment, which shall, in like manner, be final and decisive, the judgment or sentence and other proceedings begin, in either case, transmitted to Congress, and lodged among the acts of Congress for the security of the parties concerned: provided, that every commissioner, before he sits in judgment, shall take an oath, to be administered by one of the judges of the supreme or superior court of the State where the cause shall be tried, "well and truly to hear and determine the matter in question, according to the best of his judgment, without favour, affection, or hope of reward:" provided, also, that no State shall be deprived of territory for the benefit of the United States.

All controversies concerning the private right of soil, claimed under different grants of two or more states, whose jurisdictions, as they may respect such lands and the states which passed such grants, are adjusted, the said grants, or either of them, being at the same time claimed to have originated antecedent to such settlement of jurisdiction, shall, on the petition of either party to the Congress of the United States, be finally determined, as near as may be, in the same manner as is before prescribed for deciding disputes respecting territorial jurisdiction between different states.

The United States, in Congress assembled, shall also have the sole and exclusive right and power of regulating the alloy and value of coin struck by their own authority, or by that of the respective states; fixing the standard of weights and measures throughout the United States; regulating the trade and managing all affairs with the Indians not members of any of the states; provided that the legislative right of any State within its own limits be not infringed or violated; establishing and regulating post offices from one State to another throughout all the United States, and exacting such postage on the papers passing through the same as may be requisite to defray the expences of the said office; appointing all officers of the land forces in the service of the United States, excepting regimental officers; appointing all the officers of the naval forces, and commissioning all officers whatever in the service of the United States; making rules for the government and regulation of the said land and naval forces, and directing their operations.

The United States, in Congress assembled, shall have authority to appoint a committee to sit in the recess of Congress, to be denominated "a Committee of the States," and to consist of one delegate from each State, and to appoint such other committees and civil officers as may be necessary for managing the general affairs of the United States, under their direction; to appoint one of their number to preside; provided that no person be allowed to serve in the office of president more than one year in any term of three years; to ascertain the necessary sums of money to be raised for the service of the United States, and to appropriate and apply the same for defraying the public expences; to borrow money or emit bills on the credit of the United States, transmitting, every half year, to the respective states, an account of the sums of money so borrowed or emitted; to build and equip a navy; to agree upon the number of land forces, and to make requisitions from each State for its quota, in proportion to the number of white inhabitants in such State; which requisitions shall be binding; and thereupon, the legislature of each State shall appoint the regimental officers, raise the men, and cloathe, arm, and equip them in a soldier-like manner, at the expence of the United States; and the officers and men so cloathed, armed, and equipped, shall march to the place appointed and within the time agreed on by the United States, in Congress assembled; but if the United States, in Congress assembled, shall, on consideration of circumstances, judge proper that any State should not raise men, or should raise a smaller number than its quota, and that any other State should raise a greater number of men than the quota thereof, such extra number shall be raised, officered, cloathed, armed, and equipped in the same manner as the quota of such State, unless the legislature of such State shall judge that such extra number cannot be safely spared out of the same, in which case they shall raise, officer, cloathe, arm, and equip as many of such extra number as they judge can be safely spared. And the officers and men so cloathed, armed, and equipped, shall march to the place appointed and within the time agreed on by the United States, in Congress assembled.

The United States, in Congress assembled, shall never engage in a war, nor grant letters of marque and reprisal in time of peace, nor enter into any treaties or alliances, nor coin money, nor regulate the value thereof, nor ascertain the sums and expences necessary for the defence and welfare of the United States, or any of them: nor emit bills, nor borrow money on the credit of the United States, nor appropriate money, nor agree upon the number of vessels of war to be built or purchased, or the number of land or sea forces to be raised, nor appoint a commander in chief of the army or navy, unless nine states assent to the same; nor shall a question on any other point, except for adjourning from day to day, be determined, unless by the votes of a majority of the United States, in Congress assembled.

The Congress of the United States shall have power to adjourn to any time within the year, and to any place within the United States, so that no period of adjournment be for a longer duration than the space of six months, and shall publish the journal of their proceedings monthly, except such parts thereof, relating to treaties, alliances or military operations, as, in their judgment, require secrecy; and the yeas and nays of the delegates of each State on any question shall be entered on the journal, when it is desired by any delegate; and the delegates of a State, or any of them, at his, or their request, shall be furnished with a transcript of the said journal, except such parts as are above

excepted, to lay before the legislatures of the several states.

Article 10

The committee of the states, or any nine of them, shall be authorized to execute, in the recess of Congress, such of the powers of Congress as the United States, in Congress assembled, by the consent of nine states, shall, from time to time, think expedient to vest them with; provided, that no power be delegated to the said committee, for the exercise of which, by the articles of confederation, the voice of nine states, in the Congress of the United States assembled, is requisite.

Article 11

Canada acceding to this confederation, and joining in the measures of the United States, shall be admitted into and entitled to all the advantages of this union; but no other colony shall be admitted into the same, unless such admission be agreed to by nine states.

Article 12

All bills of credit emitted, monies borrowed and debts contracted by, or under the authority of Congress before the assembling of the United States, in pursuance of the present confederation, shall be deemed and considered as a charge against the United States, for payment and satisfaction whereof the said United States and the public faith are hereby solemnly pledged.

Article 13

Every State shall abide by the determinations of the United States, in Congress assembled, on all questions which, by this confederation, are submitted to them. And the articles of this confederation shall be inviolably observed by every State, and the union shall be perpetual; nor shall any alteration at any time hereafter be made in any of them, unless such alteration be agreed to in a Congress of the United States, and be afterwards confirmed by the legislatures of every State.

These articles shall be proposed to the legislatures of all the United States, to be considered, and if approved of by them, they are advised to authorize their delegates to ratify the same in the Congress of the United States; which being done, the same shall become conclusive.

THE CONSTITUTION OF THE UNITED STATES*

Agreed to by Philadelphia Convention, September 17, 1787. Implemented March 4, 1789.

Preamble

We the people of the United States, in order to form a more perfect union, establish justice, insure domestic tranquility, provide for the common defense, promote the general welfare, and secure the blessings of liberty to ourselves and our posterity, do ordain and establish this Constitution for the United States of America.

Article I

Section 1   All legislative powers herein granted shall be vested in a Congress of the United States, which shall consist of a Senate and a House of Representatives.

Section 2   The House of Representatives shall be composed of members chosen every second year by the people of the several States, and the electors in each State shall have the qualifications requisite for electors of the most numerous branch of the State Legislature.

No person shall be a Representative who shall not have attained to the age of twenty-five years, and been seven years a citizen of the United States, and who shall not, when elected, be an inhabitant of that State in which he shall be chosen.

Representatives and direct taxes shall be apportioned among the several States which may be included within this Union, according to their respective numbers, *which shall be determined by adding to the whole number of free persons, including those bound to service for a term of years and excluding Indians not taxed, three-fifths of all other persons.* The actual enumeration shall be made within three years after the first meeting of the Congress of the United States, and within every subsequent term of ten years, in such manner as they shall by law direct. The number of Representatives shall not exceed one for every thirty thousand, but each State shall have at least one Representative; *and until such enumeration shall be made, the State of New Hampshire shall be entitled to choose three, Massachusetts eight, Rhode Island and Providence Plantations one, Connecticut five, New York six, New Jersey four, Pennsylvania eight, Delaware one, Maryland six, Virginia ten, North Carolina five, South Carolina five, and Georgia three.*

When vacancies happen in the representation from any State, the Executive authority thereof shall issue writs of election to fill such vacancies.

The House of Representatives shall choose their Speaker and other officers; and shall have the sole power of impeachment.

Section 3   The Senate of the United States shall be composed of two Senators from each State, *chosen by the legislature thereof,* for six years; and each Senator shall have one vote.

Immediately after they shall be assembled in consequence of the first election, they shall be divided as equally as may be into three classes. The seats of the Senators of the first class shall be vacated at the expiration of the second year, of the second class at the expiration of the fourth year, and of the third class at the expiration of the sixth year, so that one-third may be chosen every second year; *and if vacancies happen by resignation or otherwise, during the recess of the legislature of any State, the Executive thereof may make temporary appointments until the next meeting of the legislature, which shall then fill such vacancies.*

No person shall be a Senator who shall not have attained to the age of thirty years, and been nine years a citizen of the United States, and who shall not, when elected, be an inhabitant of that State for which he shall be chosen.

The Vice-President of the United States shall be President of the Senate, but shall have no vote, unless they be equally divided.

The Senate shall choose their other officers, and also a President *pro tempore,* in the absence of the Vice-President, or when he shall exercise the office of President of the United States.

The Senate shall have the sole power to try all impeachments. When sitting for that purpose, they shall be on oath or affirmation. When the President of the United States is tried, the Chief Justice shall preside: and no person shall be convicted without the concurrence of two-thirds of the members present.

Judgment in cases of impeachment shall not extend further than to removal from the office, and disqualification to hold and enjoy any office of honor, trust or profit under the United States: but the party convicted shall nevertheless be liable and subject to indictment, trial, judgment and punishment, according to law.

Section 4   The times, places and manner of holding elections for Senators and Representatives shall be prescribed in each State by the legislature thereof; but the

---

*Passages no longer in effect are in italic type.

THE CONSTITUTION OF THE UNITED STATES

Congress may at any time by law make or alter such regulations, except as to the places of choosing Senators.

The Congress shall assemble at least once in every year, and such meeting *shall be on the first Monday in December, unless they shall by law appoint a different day.*

Section 5 Each house shall be the judge of the elections, returns and qualifications of its own members, and a majority of each shall constitute a quorum to do business; but a smaller number may adjourn from day to day, and may be authorized to compel the attendance of absent members, in such manner, and under such penalties, as each house may provide.

Each house may determine the rules of its proceedings, punish its members for disorderly behavior, and with the concurrence of two-thirds, expel a member.

Each house shall keep a journal of its proceedings, and from time to time publish the same, excepting such parts as may in their judgment require secrecy; and the yeas and nays of the members of either house on any question shall, at the desire of one-fifth of those present, be entered on the journal.

Neither house, during the session of Congress, shall, without the consent of the other, adjourn for more than three days, nor to any other place than that in which the two houses shall be sitting.

Section 6 The Senators and Representatives shall receive a compensation for their services, to be ascertained by law and paid out of the treasury of the United States. They shall in all cases except treason, felony and breach of the peace, be privileged from arrest during their attendance at the session of their respective houses, and in going to and returning from the same; and for any speech or debate in either house, they shall not be questioned in any other place.

No Senator or Representative shall, during the time for which he was elected, be appointed to any civil office under the authority of the United States, which shall have been created, or the emoluments whereof shall have been increased, during such time; and no person holding any office under the United States shall be a member of either house during his continuance in office.

Section 7 All bills for raising revenue shall originate in the House of Representatives; but the Senate may propose or concur with amendments as on other bills.

Every bill which shall have passed the House of Representatives and the Senate, shall, before it become a law, be presented to the President of the United States; if he approve he shall sign it, but if not he shall return it with objections to that house in which it shall have originated, who shall enter the objections at large on their journal, and proceed to reconsider it. If after such reconsideration two-thirds of that house shall agree to pass the bill, it shall be sent, together with the objections, to the other house, by which it shall likewise be reconsidered, and, if approved by two-thirds of that house, it shall become a law. But in all such cases the votes of both houses shall be determined by yeas and nays, and the names of the persons voting for and against the bill shall be entered on the journal of each house respectively. If any bill shall not be returned by the President within ten days (Sundays excepted) after it shall have been presented to him, the same shall be a law, in like manner as if he had signed it, unless the Congress by their adjournment prevent its return, in which case it shall not be a law.

Every order, resolution, or vote to which the concurrence of the Senate and House of Representatives may be necessary (except on a question of adjournment) shall be presented to the President of the United States; and before the same shall take effect, shall be approved by him, or being disapproved by him, shall be repassed by two-thirds of the Senate and House of Representatives, according to the rules and limitations prescribed in the case of a bill.

Section 8 The Congress shall have power

To lay and collect taxes, duties, imposts, and excises, to pay the debts and provide for the common defense and general welfare of the United States; but all duties, imposts and excises shall be uniform throughout the United States;

To borrow money on the credit of the United States;

To regulate commerce with foreign nations, and among the several States, and with the Indian tribes;

To establish an uniform rule of naturalization, and uniform laws on the subject of bankruptcies throughout the United States;

To coin money, regulate the value thereof, and of foreign coin, and fix the standard of weights and measures;

To provide for the punishment of counterfeiting the securities and current coin of the United States;

To establish post offices and post roads;

To promote the progress of science and useful arts by securing for limited times to authors and inventors the exclusive right to their respective writings and discoveries;

To constitute tribunals inferior to the Supreme Court;

To define and punish piracies and felonies committed on the high seas and offences against the law of nations;

To declare war, grant letters of marque and reprisal, and make rules concerning captures on land and water;

To raise and support armies, but no appropriation of money to that use shall be for a longer term than two years;

To provide and maintain a navy;

To make rules for the government and regulation of the land and naval forces;

To provide for calling forth the militia to execute the laws of the Union, suppress insurrections and repel invasions;

To provide for organizing, arming, and disciplining the militia, and for governing such part of them as may be employed in the service of the United States, reserving to the States respectively the appointment of the officers, and the authority of training the militia according to the discipline prescribed by Congress;

To exercise exclusive legislation in all cases whatsoever, over such district (not exceeding ten miles square) as may, by cession of particular States, and the acceptance of Congress, become the seat of the government of the United States, and to exercise like authority over all places purchased by the consent of the legislature of the State, in which the same shall be, for erection of forts, magazines, arsenals, dock-yards, and other needful buildings;—and

To make all laws which shall be necessary and proper for carrying into execution the foregoing powers, and all other powers vested by this Constitution in the government of the United States, or in any department or officer thereof.

Section 9 *The migration or importation of such persons as any of the States now existing shall think proper to admit shall not be prohibited by the Congress prior to the year one thousand eight hundred and eight; but a tax or duty may be imposed on such importation, not exceeding ten dollars for each person.*

The privilege of the writ of habeas corpus shall not be suspended, unless when in cases of rebellion or invasion the public safety may require it.

No bill of attainder or ex post facto law shall be passed.

No capitation, or other direct, tax shall be laid, unless in proportion to the census or enumeration herein before directed to be taken.

No tax or duty shall be laid on articles exported from any State.

No preference shall be given by any regulation of commerce or revenue to the ports of one State over those of another; nor shall vessels bound to, or from, one State be obliged to enter, clear, or pay duties in another.

No money shall be drawn from the treasury, but in consequence of appropriations made by law; and a regular statement and account of the receipts and expenditures of all public money shall be published from time to time.

No title of nobility shall be granted by the United States: and no person holding any office of profit or trust under them, shall, without the consent of the Congress, accept of any present, emolument, office, or title, of any kind whatever, from any king, prince, or foreign state.

Section 10 No State shall enter into any treaty, alliance, or confederation; grant letters of marque and reprisal; coin money; emit bills of credit; make anything but gold and silver coin a tender in payment of debts; pass any bill of attainder, ex post facto law, or law impairing the obligation of contracts, or grant any title of nobility.

No State shall, without the consent of Congress, lay any imposts or duties on imports or exports, except what may be absolutely necessary for executing its inspection laws: and the net produce of all duties and imposts, laid by any State on imports or exports, shall be for the use of the treasury of the United States; and all such laws shall be subject to the revision and control of the Congress.

No State shall, without the consent of Congress, lay any duty of tonnage, keep troops, or ships of war in time of peace, enter into any agreement or compact with another State, or with a foreign power, or engage in war, unless actually invaded, or in such imminent danger as will not admit of delay.

Article II

Section 1 The executive power shall be vested in a President of the United States of America. He shall hold his office during the term of four years, and, together with the Vice-President, chosen for the same term, be elected as follows:

Each State shall appoint, in such manner as the legislature thereof may direct, a number of electors, equal to the whole number of Senators and Representatives to which the State may be entitled in the Congress; but no Senator or Representative, or person holding an office of trust or profit under the United States, shall be appointed an elector.

The electors shall meet in their respective States, and vote by ballot for two persons, of whom one at least shall not be an inhabitant of the same State with themselves. And they shall make a list of all the persons voted for, and of the number of votes for each; which list they shall sign and certify, and transmit sealed to the seat of government of the United States, directed to the President of the Senate. The President of the Senate shall, in the presence of the Senate and House of Representatives, open all the certificates, and the votes shall then be counted. The person having the greatest number of votes shall be the President, if such number be a majority of the whole number of electors appointed; and if there be more than one who have such majority, and have an equal number of votes, then the House of Representatives shall immediately choose by ballot one of them for President; and if no person have a majority, then from the five highest on the list said house shall in like manner choose the President. But in choosing the President the votes shall be taken by States, the representation from each State having one vote; a quorum for this purpose shall consist of a member or members from two-thirds of the States, and a majority of all the States shall be necessary to a choice. In every case, after the choice of the President, the person having the greatest number of votes of the electors shall be the Vice-President. But if there should remain two or more who have equal votes, the Senate shall choose from them by ballot the Vice-President.

The Congress may determine the time of choosing the electors, and the day on which they shall give their votes; which day shall be the same throughout the United States.

No person except a natural-born citizen, *or a citizen of the United States at the time of the adoption of this Constitution,* shall be eligible to the office of President; neither shall any person be eligible to that office who shall not have attained to the age of thirty-five years, and been fourteen years a resident within the United States.

In cases of the removal of the President from office or of his death, resignation, or inability to discharge the powers and duties of the said office, the same shall devolve on the Vice-President, and the Congress may by law provide for the case of removal, death, resignation, or inability, both of the President and Vice-President, declaring what officer shall then act as President, and such officer shall act accordingly, until the disability be removed, or a President shall be elected.

The President shall, at stated times, receive for his services a compensation, which shall neither be increased nor diminished during the period for which he shall have been elected, and he shall not receive within that period any other emolument from the United States, or any of them.

Before he enter on the execution of his office, he shall take the following oath or affirmation:—"I do solemnly swear (or affirm) that I will faithfully execute the office of the President of the United States, and will to the best of my ability preserve, protect and defend the Constitution of the United States."

Section 2 The President shall be commander in chief of the army and navy of the United States, and of the militia of the several States, when called into the actual service of the United States; he may require the opinion, in writing, of the principal officer in each of the executive departments, upon any subject relating to the duties of their respective offices, and he shall have power to grant reprieves and pardons for offenses against the United States, except in cases of impeachment.

He shall have power, by and with the advice and consent of the Senate, to make treaties, provided two-thirds of the Senators present concur; and he shall nominate, and by and with the advice and consent of the Senate, shall appoint ambassadors, other public ministers and consuls, judges of the Supreme Court, and all other officers of the United States, whose appointments are not herein otherwise provided for, and which shall be established by law: but Congress may by law vest the appointment of such inferior officers, as they think proper, in the President alone, in the courts of law, or in the heads of departments.

The President shall have power to fill up all vacancies that may happen during the recess of the Senate, by granting commissions which shall expire at the end of their next session.

Section 3 He shall from time to time give to the Congress information of the state of the Union, and recommend to their consideration such measures as he shall judge necessary and expedient; he may, on extraordinary occasions, convene both houses, or either of them, and in case of disagreement between them, with respect to the time of adjournment, he may adjourn them to such time as he shall think proper; he shall receive ambassadors and other public ministers; he shall take care that the laws be faithfully executed, and shall commission all the officers of the United States.

Section 4 The President, Vice-President and all civil officers of the United States shall be removed from office on impeachment for, and on conviction of, treason, bribery, or other high crimes and misdemeanors.

Article III

Section 1 The judicial power of the United States shall be vested in one Supreme Court, and in such inferior courts as the Congress may from time to time ordain and establish. The judges, both of the Supreme and inferior courts, shall hold their offices during good behavior, and shall, at stated times, receive for their services a compensation which shall not be diminished during their continuance in office.

Section 2 The judicial power shall extend to all cases, in law and equity, arising under this Constitution, the laws of the United States, and treaties made, or which shall be made, under their authority;—to all cases affecting ambassadors, other public ministers and consuls;—to all cases of admiralty and maritime jurisdiction;—to controversies to which the United States shall be a party;—to controversies between two or more States;—*between a State and citizens of another State;*—between citizens of different States;—between citizens of the same State claiming lands under grants of different States, and between a State, or the citizens thereof, and foreign states, citizens or subjects.

In all cases affecting ambassadors, other public ministers and consuls, and those in which a State shall be party, the Supreme Court shall have original jurisdiction. In all the other cases before mentioned, the Supreme Court shall have appellate jurisdiction, both as to law and fact, with such exceptions, and under such regulations, as the Congress shall make.

The trial of all crimes, except in cases of impeachment, shall be by jury; and such trial shall be held in the State where said crimes shall have been committed; but when not committed within any State, the trial shall be at such place or places as the Congress may by Law have directed.

Section 3   Treason against the United States shall consist only in levying war against them, or in adhering to their enemies, giving them aid and comfort. No person shall be convicted of treason unless on the testimony of two witnesses to the same overt act, or on confession in open court.

The Congress shall have power to declare the punishment of treason, but no attainder of treason shall work corruption of blood, or forfeiture except during the life of the person attainted.

Article IV

Section 1   Full faith and credit shall be given in each State to the public acts, records, and judicial proceedings of every other State. And the Congress may by general laws prescribe the manner in which such acts, records, and proceedings shall be proved, and the effect thereof.

Section 2   The citizens of each State shall be entitled to all privileges and immunities of citizens in the several States.

A person charged in any State with treason, felony, or other crime, who shall flee from justice, and be found in another State, shall on demand of the executive authority of the State from which he fled, be delivered up, to be removed to the State having jurisdiction of the crime.

No Person held to service or labor in one State, under the laws thereof, escaping into another, shall, in consequence of any law or regulation therein, be discharged from such service or labor, but shall be delivered up on claim of the party to whom such service or labor may be due.

Section 3   New States may be admitted by the Congress into this Union; but no new State shall be formed or erected within the jurisdiction of any other State; nor any State be formed by the junction of two or more States, or parts of States, without the consent of the legislatures of the States concerned as well as of the Congress.

The Congress shall have power to dispose of and make all needful rules and regulations respecting the territory or other property belonging to the United States; and nothing in this Constitution shall be so construed as to prejudice any claims of the United States, or of any particular State.

Section 4   The United States shall guarantee to every State in this Union a republican form of government, and shall protect each of them against invasion; and on application of the legislature, or of the executive (when the legislature cannot be convened), against domestic violence.

Article V

The Congress, whenever two-thirds of both houses shall deem it necessary, shall propose amendments to this Constitution, or, on the application of the legislatures of two-thirds of the several States, shall call a convention for proposing amendments, which, in either case, shall be valid to all intents and purposes, as part of this Constitution, when ratified by the legislatures of three-fourths of the several States, or by conventions in three-fourths thereof, as the one or the other mode of ratification may be proposed by the Congress; provided *that no amendments which may be made prior to the year one thousand eight hundred and eight shall in any manner affect the first and fourth clauses in the ninth section of the first article*; and that no State, without its consent, shall be deprived of its equal suffrage in the Senate.

Article VI

All debts contracted and engagements entered into, before the adoption of this Constitution, shall be as valid against the United States under this Constitution, as under the Confederation.

This Constitution, and the laws of the United States which shall be made in pursuance thereof; and all treaties made, or which shall be made, under the authority of the United States, shall be the supreme law of the land; and the judges in every State shall be bound thereby, anything in the Constitution or laws of any State to the contrary notwithstanding.

The Senators and Representatives before mentioned, and the members of the several State legislatures, and all executive and judicial officers, both of the United States and of the several States, shall be bound by oath or affirmation to support this Constitution; but no religious test shall ever be required as a qualification to any office or public trust under the United States.

Article VII

The ratification of the conventions of nine States shall be sufficient for the establishment of this Constitution between the States so ratifying the same.

Done in convention by the unanimous consent of the States present, the seventeenth day of September in the year of our Lord one thousand seven hundred and eighty-seven and of the Independence of the United States of America the twelfth. In witness whereof we have hereunto subscribed our names.

GEORGE WASHINGTON
PRESIDENT AND DEPUTY FROM VIRGINIA

New Hampshire
John Langdon
Nicholas Gilman

Massachusetts
Nathaniel Gorham
Rufus King

Connecticut
William Samuel
   Johnson
Roger Sherman

New York
Alexander Hamilton

New Jersey
William Livingston
David Brearley
William Paterson
Jonathan Dayton

Pennsylvania
Benjamin Franklin
Thomas Mifflin
Robert Morris
George Clymer
Thomas FitzSimons
Jared Ingersoll
James Wilson
Gouverneur Morris

Delaware
George Read
Gunning Bedford, Jr.
John Dickinson
Richard Bassett
Jacob Broom

Maryland
James McHenry
Daniel of
   St. Thomas Jenifer
Daniel Carroll

Virginia
John Blair
James Madison, Jr.

North Carolina
William Blount
Richard Dobbs
   Spaight
Hugh Williamson

South Carolina
John Rutledge
Charles Cotesworth
   Pinckney
Charles Pinckney
Pierce Butler

Georgia
William Few
Abraham Baldwin

AMENDMENTS TO THE CONSTITUTION WITH ANNOTATIONS
(Including the six unratified amendments)

IN THEIR EFFORT TO GAIN Antifederalists' support for the Constitution, Federalists frequently pointed to the inclusion of Article 5, which provides an orderly method of amending the Constitution. In contrast, the Articles of Confederation, which were universally recognized as seriously flawed, offered no means of amendment. For their part, Antifederalists argued that the amendment process was so "intricate" that one might as easily roll "sixes an hundred times in succession" as change the Constitution.

The system for amendment laid out in the Constitution requires that two-thirds of both houses of Congress agree to a proposed amendment, which must then be ratified by three-quarters of the legislatures of the states. Alternatively, an amendment may be proposed by a convention called by the legislatures of two-thirds of the states. Since 1789, members of Congress have proposed thousands of amendments. Besides the seventeen amendments added since 1789, only the six "unratified" ones included here were approved by two-thirds of both houses and sent to the states for ratification.

Among the many amendments that never made it out of Congress have been proposals to declare dueling, divorce, and interracial marriage unconstitutional as well as proposals to establish a national university, to acknowledge the sovereignty of Jesus Christ, and to prohibit any person from possessing wealth in excess of ten million dollars.[1]

Among the issues facing Americans today that might lead to constitutional amendment are efforts to balance the federal budget, to limit the number of terms elected officials may serve, to limit access to or prohibit abortion, to establish English as the official language of the United States, and to prohibit flag burning. None of these proposed amendments has yet garnered enough support in Congress to be sent to the states for ratification.

Although the first ten amendments to the Constitution are commonly known as the Bill of Rights, only Amendments 1–8 actually provide guarantees of individual rights. Amendments 9 and 10 deal with the structure of power within the constitutional system. The Bill of Rights was promised to appease Antifederalists who refused to ratify the Constitution without guarantees of individual liberties and limitations to federal power. After studying more than two hundred amendments recommended by the ratifying conventions of the states, Federalist James Madison presented a list of seventeen to Congress, which used Madison's list as the foundation for the twelve amendments that were sent to the states for ratification. Ten of the twelve were adopted in 1791. The first on the list of twelve, known as the Reapportionment Amendment, was never adopted (see p. A-17). The second proposed amendment was adopted in 1992 as Amendment 27 (see p. A-26).

Amendment I

Congress shall make no law respecting an establishment of religion, or prohibiting the free exercise thereof; or abridging the freedom of speech, or of the press; or the right of the people peaceably to assemble, and to petition the government for a redress of grievances.

◆ ◆ ◆

The First Amendment is a potent symbol for many Americans. Most are well aware of their rights to free speech, freedom of the press, and freedom of religion and their rights to assemble and to petition, even if they cannot cite the exact words of this amendment.

The First Amendment guarantee of freedom of religion has two clauses: the "free exercise clause," which allows individuals to practice or not practice any religion, and the "establishment clause," which prevents the federal government from discriminating against or favoring any particular religion. This clause was designed to create what Thomas Jefferson referred to as "a wall of separation between church and state." In the 1960s, the Supreme Court ruled that the First Amendment prohibits prayer (see Engel v. Vitale, *p. A-51) and Bible reading in public schools.*

Although the rights to free speech and freedom of the press are established in the First Amendment, it was not until the twentieth century that the Supreme Court began to explore the full meaning of these guarantees. In 1919, the Court ruled in Schenck v. United States *(see p. A-50) that the government could suppress free expression only where it could cite a "clear and present danger." In a decision that continues to raise controversies, the Court ruled in 1990, in* Texas v. Johnson, *that flag burning is a form of symbolic speech protected by the First Amendment.*

---

[1] Richard B. Bernstein, *Amending America* (New York: Times Books, 1993), 177–81.

Amendment II

A well-regulated militia being necessary to the security of a free State, the right of the people to keep and bear arms shall not be infringed.

Fear of a standing army under the control of a hostile government made the Second Amendment an important part of the Bill of Rights. Advocates of gun ownership claim that the amendment prevents the government from regulating firearms. Proponents of gun control argue that the amendment is designed only to protect the right of the states to maintain militia units.

In 1939, the Supreme Court ruled in United States v. Miller *that the Second Amendment did not protect the right of an individual to own a sawed-off shotgun, which it argued was not ordinary militia equipment. Since then, the Supreme Court has refused to hear Second Amendment cases, while lower courts have upheld firearms regulations. Several justices currently on the bench seem to favor a narrow interpretation of the Second Amendment, which would allow gun control legislation. The controversy over the impact of the Second Amendment on gun owners and gun control legislation will certainly continue.*

Amendment III

No soldier shall, in time of peace, be quartered in any house without the consent of the owner, nor in time of war, but in a manner to be prescribed by law.

The Third Amendment was extremely important to the framers of the Constitution, but today it is nearly forgotten. American colonists were especially outraged that they were forced to quarter British troops in the years before and during the American Revolution. The philosophy of the Third Amendment has been viewed by some justices and scholars as the foundation of the modern constitutional right to privacy. One example of this can be found in Justice William O. Douglas's opinion in Griswold v. Connecticut *(see p. A-52).*

Amendment IV

The right of the people to be secure in their persons, houses, papers, and effects, against unreasonable searches and seizures, shall not be violated, and no warrants shall issue but upon probable cause, supported by oath or affirmation, and particularly describing the place to be searched, and the persons or things to be seized.

In the years before the Revolution, the houses, barns, stores, and warehouses of American colonists were ransacked by British authorities under "writs of assistance" or general warrants. The British, thus empowered, searched for seditious material or smuggled goods that could then be used as evidence against colonists who were charged with a crime only after the items were found.

The first part of the Fourth Amendment protects citizens from "unreasonable" searches and seizures. The Supreme Court has interpreted this protection as well as the words search *and* seizure *in different ways at different times. At one time, the Court did not recognize electronic eavesdropping as a form of search and seizure, though it does today. At times, an "unreasonable" search has been almost any search carried out without a warrant, but in the two decades before 1969 the Court sometimes sanctioned warrantless searches that it considered reasonable based on "the total atmosphere of the case."*

The second part of the Fourth Amendment defines the procedure for issuing a search warrant and states the requirement of "probable cause," which is generally viewed as evidence indicating that a suspect has committed an offense.

The Fourth Amendment has been controversial because the Court has sometimes excluded evidence that has been seized in violation of constitutional standards. The justification is that excluding such evidence deters violations of the amendment, but doing so may allow a guilty person to escape punishment.

Amendment V

No person shall be held to answer for a capital, or otherwise infamous crime, unless on a presentment or indictment of a grand jury, except in cases arising in the land or naval forces, or in the militia, when in actual service in time of war or public danger; nor shall any person be subject for the same offence to be twice put in jeopardy of life or limb; nor shall be compelled in any criminal case to be a witness against himself, nor be deprived of life, liberty, or property, without due process of law; nor shall private property be taken for public use without just compensation.

The Fifth Amendment protects people against government authority in the prosecution of criminal offenses. It prohibits the state, first, from charging a person with a serious crime without a grand jury hearing to decide whether there is sufficient evidence to support the charge and, second, from charging a person with the same crime twice. The best-known aspect of the Fifth Amendment is that it

prevents a person from being "compelled . . . to be a witness against himself." The last clause, the "takings clause," limits the power of the government to seize property.

Although invoking the Fifth Amendment is popularly viewed as a confession of guilt, a person may be innocent yet still fear prosecution. For example, during the Red-baiting era of the late 1940s and 1950s, many people who had participated in legal activities that were associated with the Communist Party claimed the Fifth Amendment privilege rather than testify before the House Un-American Activities Committee because the mood of the times cast those activities in a negative light. Since "taking the Fifth" was viewed as an admission of guilt, those people often lost their jobs or became unemployable. (See Chapter 25.) Nonetheless, the right to protect oneself against self-incrimination plays an important role in guarding against the collective power of the state.

Amendment VI

In all criminal prosecutions, the accused shall enjoy the right to a speedy and public trial, by an impartial jury of the State and district wherein the crime shall have been committed, which district shall have been previously ascertained by law, and to be informed of the nature and cause of the accusation; to be confronted with the witnesses against him; to have compulsory process for obtaining witnesses in his favor, and to have the assistance of counsel for his defence.

The original Constitution put few limits on the government's power to investigate, prosecute, and punish crime. This process was of great concern to the early Americans, however, and of the twenty-eight rights specified in the first eight amendments, fifteen have to do with it. Seven rights are specified in the Sixth Amendment. These include the right to a speedy trial, a public trial, a jury trial, a notice of accusation, confrontation by opposing witnesses, testimony by favorable witnesses, and the assistance of counsel.

Although this amendment originally guaranteed these rights only in cases involving the federal government, the adoption of the Fourteenth Amendment began a process of applying the protections of the Bill of Rights to the states through court cases such as Gideon v. Wainwright *(see p. A-51).*

Amendment VII

In suits at common law, where the value in controversy shall exceed twenty dollars, the right of trial by jury shall be preserved, and no fact tried by a jury shall be otherwise reexamined in any court of the United States, than according to the rules of the common law.

This amendment guarantees people the same right to a trial by jury as was guaranteed by English common law in 1791. Under common law, in civil trials (those involving money damages) the role of the judge was to settle questions of law and that of the jury was to settle questions of fact. The amendment does not specify the size of the jury or its role in a trial, however. The Supreme Court has generally held that those issues be determined by English common law of 1791, which stated that a jury consists of twelve people, that a trial must be conducted before a judge who instructs the jury on the law and advises it on facts, and that a verdict must be unanimous.

Amendment VIII

Excessive bail shall not be required, nor excessive fines imposed, nor cruel and unusual punishments inflicted.

The language used to guarantee the three rights in this amendment was inspired by the English Bill of Rights of 1689. The Supreme Court has not had a lot to say about "excessive fines." In recent years it has agreed that despite the provision against "excessive bail," persons who are believed to be dangerous to others can be held without bail even before they have been convicted.

Although opponents of the death penalty have not succeeded in using the Eighth Amendment to achieve the end of capital punishment, the clause regarding "cruel and unusual punishments" has been used to prohibit capital punishment in certain cases (see Furman v. Georgia, *p. A-52) and to require improved conditions in prisons.*

Amendment IX

The enumeration in the Constitution, of certain rights, shall not be construed to deny or disparage others retained by the people.

Some Federalists feared that inclusion of the Bill of Rights in the Constitution would allow later generations of interpreters to claim that the people had surrendered any rights not specifically enumerated there. To guard against this, Madison added language that became the Ninth Amendment. Interest in this heretofore largely ignored amendment revived in 1965 when it was used in a concurring opinion in Griswold v. Connecticut *(see p. A-52). While Justice William O. Douglas called on the Third Amendment to support the right to privacy in deciding that case, Justice Arthur Goldberg, in the concurring opinion, argued that the right to privacy regarding contraception was an*

unenumerated right that was protected by the Ninth Amendment.

In 1980, the Court ruled that the right of the press to attend a public trial was protected by the Ninth Amendment. While some scholars argue that modern judges cannot identify the unenumerated rights that the framers were trying to protect, others argue that the Ninth Amendment should be read as providing a constitutional "presumption of liberty" that allows people to act in any way that does not violate the rights of others.

Amendment X

The powers not delegated to the United States by the Constitution, nor prohibited by it to the States, are reserved to the States respectively, or to the people.

The Antifederalists were especially eager to see a "reserved powers clause" explicitly guaranteeing the states control over their internal affairs. Not surprisingly, the Tenth Amendment has been a frequent battleground in the struggle over states' rights and federal supremacy. Prior to the Civil War, the Democratic Republican Party and Jacksonian Democrats invoked the Tenth Amendment to prohibit the federal government from making decisions about whether people in individual states could own slaves. The Tenth Amendment was virtually suspended during Reconstruction following the Civil War. In 1883, however, the Supreme Court declared the Civil Rights Act of 1875 unconstitutional on the grounds that it violated the Tenth Amendment. Business interests also called on the amendment to block efforts at federal regulation.

The Court was inconsistent over the next several decades as it attempted to resolve the tension between the restrictions of the Tenth Amendment and the powers the Constitution granted to Congress to regulate interstate commerce and levy taxes. The Court upheld the Pure Food and Drug Act (1906), the Meat Inspection Acts (1906 and 1907), and the White Slave Traffic Act (1910), all of which affected the states, but struck down an act prohibiting interstate shipment of goods produced through child labor. Between 1934 and 1935, a number of New Deal programs created by Franklin D. Roosevelt were declared unconstitutional on the grounds that they violated the Tenth Amendment. (See Chapter 23.) As Roosevelt appointees changed the composition of the Court, the Tenth Amendment was declared to have no substantive meaning. Generally, the amendment is held to protect the rights of states to regulate internal matters such as local government, education, commerce, labor, and business, as well as matters involving families such as marriage, divorce, and inheritance within the state.

Unratified Amendment
Reapportionment Amendment (proposed by Congress September 25, 1789, along with the Bill of Rights)

After the first enumeration required by the first article of the Constitution, there shall be one Representative for every thirty thousand, until the number shall amount to one hundred, after which the proportion shall be so regulated by Congress, that there shall be not less than one hundred Representatives, nor less than one Representative for every forty thousand persons, until the number of Representatives shall amount to two hundred; after which the proportion shall be so regulated by Congress, that there shall not be less than two hundred Representatives, nor more than one Representative for every fifty thousand persons.

If the Reapportionment Amendment had passed and remained in effect, the House of Representatives today would have more than 5,000 members rather than 435.

Amendment XI
[Adopted 1798]

The judicial power of the United States shall not be construed to extend to any suit in law or equity, commenced or prosecuted against one of the United States by citizens of another State, or by citizens or subjects of any foreign state.

In 1793, the Supreme Court ruled in favor of Alexander Chisholm, executor of the estate of a deceased South Carolina merchant. Chisholm was suing the state of Georgia because the merchant had never been paid for provisions he had supplied during the Revolution. Many regarded this Court decision as an error that violated the intent of the Constitution.

Antifederalists had long feared a federal court system with the power to overrule a state court. When the Constitution was being drafted, Federalists had assured worried Antifederalists that section 2 of Article 3, which allows federal courts to hear cases "between a State and citizens of another State," did not mean that the federal courts were authorized to hear suits against a state by citizens of another state or a foreign country. Antifederalists and many other Americans feared a powerful federal court system because they worried that it would become like the British courts of this period, which were accountable only to the monarch. Furthermore, Chisholm v. Georgia prompted a series of suits against state governments by creditors and suppliers who had made loans during the war.

In addition, state legislators and Congress feared that the shaky economies of the new states, as well as the country as a whole, would be destroyed, especially if Loyalists who had fled to other countries sought reimbursement for land and property that had been seized. The day after the Supreme Court announced its decision, a resolution proposing the Eleventh Amendment, which overturned the decision in Chisholm v. Georgia, *was introduced in the U.S. Senate.*

Amendment XII
[Adopted 1804]

The electors shall meet in their respective States, and vote by ballot for President and Vice-President, one of whom, at least, shall not be an inhabitant of the same State with themselves; they shall name in their ballots the person voted for as President, and in distinct ballots the person voted for as Vice-President, and they shall make distinct lists of all persons voted for as President, and of all persons voted for as Vice-President, and of the number of votes for each, which lists they shall sign and certify, and transmit sealed to the seat of government of the United States, directed to the President of the Senate;—the President of the Senate shall, in the presence of the Senate and House of Representatives, open all the certificates and the votes shall then be counted;—the person having the greatest number of votes for President shall be the President, if such number be a majority of the whole number of electors appointed; and if no person have such majority, then from the persons having the highest numbers not exceeding three on the list of those voted for as President, the House of Representatives shall choose immediately, by ballot, the President. But in choosing the President, the votes shall be taken by States, the representation from each State having one vote; a quorum for this purpose shall consist of a member or members from two-thirds of the States, and a majority of all the States shall be necessary to a choice. And if the House of Representatives shall not choose a President whenever the right of choice shall devolve upon them, before *the fourth day of March* next following, then the Vice-President shall act as President, as in the case of the death or other constitutional disability of the President.

The person having the greatest number of votes as Vice-President shall be the Vice-President, if such number be a majority of the whole number of electors appointed; and if no person have a majority, then from the two highest numbers on the list the Senate shall choose the Vice-President; a quorum for the purpose shall consist of two-thirds of the whole number of Senators, and a majority of the whole number shall be necessary to a choice. But no person constitutionally ineligible to the office of President shall be eligible to that of Vice-President of the United States.

The framers of the Constitution disliked political parties and assumed that none would ever form. Under the original system, electors chosen by the states would each vote for two candidates. The candidate who won the most votes would become president, while the person who won the second-highest number of votes would become vice president. Rivalries between Federalists and Antifederalists led to the formation of political parties, however, even before George Washington had left office. Though Washington was elected unanimously in 1789 and 1792, the elections of 1796 and 1800 were procedural disasters because of party maneuvering (see Chapters 9 and 10). In 1796, Federalist John Adams was chosen as president, and his great rival, the Antifederalist Thomas Jefferson (whose party was called the Republican Party), became his vice president. In 1800, all the electors cast their two votes as one of two party blocs. Jefferson and his fellow Republican nominee, Aaron Burr, were tied with seventy-three votes each. The contest went to the House of Representatives, which finally elected Jefferson after thirty-six ballots. The Twelfth Amendment prevents these problems by requiring electors to vote separately for the president and vice president.

Unratified Amendment
Titles of Nobility Amendment (proposed by Congress May 1, 1810)

If any citizen of the United States shall accept, claim, receive or retain any title of nobility or honor or shall, without the consent of Congress, accept and retain any present, pension, office or emolument of any kind whatever, from any emperor, king, prince or foreign power, such person shall cease to be a citizen of the United States, and shall be incapable of holding any office of trust or profit under them, or either of them.

This amendment would have extended Article 1, section 9, clause 8 of the Constitution, which prevents the awarding of titles by the United States and the acceptance of such awards from foreign powers without congressional consent. Historians speculate that general nervousness about the power of the Emperor Napoleon, who was at that time extending France's empire throughout Europe, may have prompted the proposal. Though it fell one vote short of ratification, Congress and the American people thought the proposal had been ratified and it was included in many nineteenth-century editions of the Constitution.

The Civil War and Reconstruction Amendments (Thirteenth, Fourteenth, and Fifteenth Amendments)

In the four months between the election of Abraham Lincoln and his inauguration, more than two hundred proposed constitutional amendments were presented to Congress as part of a desperate attempt to hold the rapidly dissolving Union together. Most of these were efforts to appease the southern states by protecting the right to own slaves or by disfranchising African Americans through constitutional amendment. None were able to win the votes required from Congress to send them to the states. The relatively innocuous Corwin Amendment seemed to be the only hope for preserving the Union by amending the Constitution.

The northern victors in the Civil War tried to restructure the Constitution just as the war had restructured the nation. Yet they were often divided in their goals. Some wanted to end slavery; others hoped for social and economic equality regardless of race; others hoped that extending the power of the ballot box to former slaves would help create a new political order. The debates over the Thirteenth, Fourteenth, and Fifteenth Amendments were bitter. Few of those who fought for these changes were satisfied with the amendments themselves; fewer still were satisfied with their interpretation. Although the amendments put an end to the legal status of slavery, it took nearly a hundred years after the amendments' passage before most of the descendants of former slaves could begin to experience the economic, social, and political equality the amendments had been intended to provide.

Unratified Amendment
Corwin Amendment (proposed by Congress March 2, 1861)

No amendment shall be made to the Constitution which will authorize or give to Congress the power to abolish or interfere, within any State, with the domestic institutions thereof, including that of persons held to labor or service by the laws of said State.

Following the election of Abraham Lincoln, Congress scrambled to try to prevent the secession of the slaveholding states. House member Thomas Corwin of Ohio proposed the "unamendable" amendment in the hope that by protecting slavery where it existed, Congress would keep the southern states in the Union. Lincoln indicated his support for the proposed amendment in his first inaugural address. Only Ohio and Maryland ratified the Corwin Amendment before it was forgotten.

Amendment XIII
[Adopted 1865]

Section 1 Neither slavery nor involuntary servitude, except as a punishment for crime whereof the party shall have been duly convicted, shall exist within the United States, or any place subject to their jurisdiction.

Section 2 Congress shall have power to enforce this article by appropriate legislation.

Although President Lincoln had abolished slavery in the Confederacy with the Emancipation Proclamation of 1863, abolitionists wanted to rid the entire country of slavery. The Thirteenth Amendment did this in a clear and straightforward manner. In February 1865, when the proposal was approved by the House, the gallery of the House was newly opened to black Americans who had a chance at last to see their government at work. Passage of the proposal was greeted by wild cheers from the gallery as well as tears on the House floor, where congressional representatives openly embraced one another.

The problem of ratification remained, however. The Union position was that the Confederate states were part of the country of thirty-six states. Therefore, twenty-seven states were needed to ratify the amendment. When Kentucky and Delaware rejected it, backers realized that without approval from at least four former Confederate states, the amendment would fail. Lincoln's successor, President Andrew Johnson, made ratification of the Thirteenth Amendment a condition for southern states to rejoin the Union. Under those terms, all the former Confederate states except Mississippi accepted the Thirteenth Amendment, and by the end of 1865 the amendment had become part of the Constitution and slavery had been prohibited in the United States.

Amendment XIV
[Adopted 1868]

Section 1 All persons born or naturalized in the United States, and subject to the jurisdiction thereof, are citizens of the United States and of the State wherein they reside. No State shall make or enforce any law which shall abridge the privileges or immunities of citizens of the United States; nor shall any State deprive any person of life, liberty, or property, without due process of law; nor deny to any person within its jurisdiction the equal protection of the laws.

Section 2 Representatives shall be appointed among the several States according to their respective numbers, counting the whole number of persons in each

State, excluding Indians not taxed. But when the right to vote at any election for the choice of Electors for President and Vice-President of the United States, Representatives in Congress, the executive and judicial officers of a State, or the members of the legislature thereof, is denied to any of the male inhabitants of such State, being twenty-one years of age and citizens of the United States, or in any way abridged, except for participation in rebellion, or other crime, the basis of representation therein shall be reduced in the proportion which the number of such male citizens shall bear to the whole number of male citizens twenty-one years of age in such State.

Section 3   No person shall be a Senator or Representative in Congress, or Elector of President and Vice-President, or hold any office, civil or military, under the United States, or under any State, who, having previously taken an oath, as a member of Congress, or as an officer of the United States, or as a member of any State legislature, or as an executive or judicial officer of any State, to support the Constitution of the United States, shall have engaged in insurrection or rebellion against the same, or given aid or comfort to the enemies thereof. Congress may, by a vote of two-thirds of each house, remove such disability.

Section 4   The validity of the public debt of the United States, authorized by law, including debts incurred for payment of pensions and bounties for services in suppressing insurrection or rebellion, shall not be questioned. But neither the United States nor any State shall assume or pay any debt or obligation incurred in aid of insurrection or rebellion against the United States, or any claim for the loss or emancipation of any slave; but all such debts, obligations, and claims shall be held illegal and void.

Section 5   The Congress shall have power to enforce, by appropriate legislation, the provisions of this article.

◆◆◆

Without Lincoln's leadership in the reconstruction of the nation following the Civil War, it soon became clear that the Thirteenth Amendment needed additional constitutional support. Less than a year after Lincoln's assassination, Andrew Johnson was ready to bring the former Confederate states back into the Union with few changes in their governments or politics. Anxious Republicans drafted the Fourteenth Amendment to prevent that from happening. The most important provisions of this complex amendment made all native-born or naturalized persons American citizens and prohibited states from abridging the "privileges or immunities" of citizens; depriving them of "life, liberty, or
property, without due process of law"; and denying them "equal protection of the laws." In essence, it made all ex-slaves citizens and protected the rights of all citizens against violation by their own state governments.

As occurred in the case of the Thirteenth Amendment, former Confederate states were forced to ratify the amendment as a condition of representation in the House and the Senate. The intentions of the Fourteenth Amendment, and how those intentions should be enforced, have been the most debated point of constitutional history. The terms due process *and* equal protection *have been especially troublesome. Was the amendment designed to outlaw racial segregation? Or was the goal simply to prevent the leaders of the rebellious South from gaining political power?*

The framers of the Fourteenth Amendment hoped Article 2 would produce black voters who would increase the power of the Republican Party. The federal government, however, never used its power to punish states for denying blacks their right to vote. Although the Fourteenth Amendment had an immediate impact in giving black Americans citizenship, it did nothing to protect blacks from the vengeance of whites once Reconstruction ended. In the late nineteenth and early twentieth centuries, section 1 of the Fourteenth Amendment was often used to protect business interests and strike down laws protecting workers on the grounds that the rights of "persons," that is, corporations, were protected by "due process." More recently, the Fourteenth Amendment has been used to justify school desegregation and affirmative action programs, as well as to dismantle such programs.

Amendment XV
[Adopted 1870]

Section 1   The right of citizens of the United States to vote shall not be denied or abridged by the United States or by any State on account of race, color, or previous condition of servitude.

Section 2   The Congress shall have power to enforce this article by appropriate legislation.

◆◆◆

The Fifteenth Amendment was the last major piece of Reconstruction legislation. While earlier Reconstruction acts had already required black suffrage in the South, the Fifteenth Amendment extended black voting rights to the entire nation. Some Republicans felt morally obligated to do away with the double standard between North and South since many northern states had stubbornly refused to enfranchise blacks. Others believed that the freedman's ballot required the extra protection of a constitutional amendment to shield it from white counterattack. But partisan advantage also played an important role in the amendment's passage, since Republicans hoped that by giving the ballot to northern blacks, they could lessen their political vulnerability.

Many women's rights advocates had fought for the amendment. They had felt betrayed by the inclusion of the word male *in section 2 of the Fourteenth Amendment and were further angered when the proposed Fifteenth Amendment failed to prohibit denial of the right to vote on the grounds of sex as well as "race, color, or previous condition of servitude." In this amendment, for the first time, the federal government claimed the power to regulate the franchise, or vote. It was also the first time the Constitution placed limits on the power of the states to regulate access to the franchise. Although ratified in 1870, however, the amendment was not enforced until the twentieth century.*

The Progressive Amendments (Sixteenth–Nineteenth Amendments)

No amendments were added to the Constitution between the Civil War and the Progressive Era. America was changing, however, in fundamental ways. The rapid industrialization of the United States after the Civil War led to many social and economic problems. Hundreds of amendments were proposed, but none received enough support in Congress to be sent to the states. Some scholars believe that regional differences and rivalries were so strong during this period that it was almost impossible to gain a consensus on a constitutional amendment. During the Progressive Era, however, the Constitution was amended four times in seven years.

Amendment XVI
[Adopted 1913]

The Congress shall have power to lay and collect taxes on incomes, from whatever source derived, without apportionment among the several States, and without regard to any census or enumeration.

Until passage of the Sixteenth Amendment, most of the money used to run the federal government came from customs duties and taxes on specific items, such as liquor. During the Civil War, the federal government taxed incomes as an emergency measure. Pressure to enact an income tax came from those who were concerned about the growing gap between rich and poor in the United States. The Populist Party began campaigning for a graduated income tax in 1892, and support continued to grow. By 1909, thirty-three proposed income tax amendments had been presented in Congress, but lobbying by corporate and other special interests had defeated them all. In June 1909,

the growing pressure for an income tax, which had been endorsed by Presidents Roosevelt and Taft, finally pushed an amendment through the Senate. The required thirty-six states had ratified the amendment by February 1913.

Amendment XVII
[Adopted 1913]

Section 1   The Senate of the United States shall be composed of two Senators from each State, elected by the people thereof, for six years; and each Senator shall have one vote. The electors in each State shall have the qualifications requisite for electors of [voters for] the most numerous branch of the State legislatures.

Section 2   When vacancies happen in the representation of any State in the Senate, the executive authority of such State shall issue writs of election to fill such vacancies: Provided, that the Legislature of any State may empower the executive thereof to make temporary appointments until the people fill the vacancies by election as the Legislature may direct.

Section 3   This amendment shall not be so construed as to affect the election or term of any Senator chosen before it becomes valid as part of the Constitution.

The framers of the Constitution saw the members of the House as the representatives of the people and the members of the Senate as the representatives of the states. Originally senators were to be chosen by the state legislators. According to reform advocates, however, the growth of private industry and transportation conglomerates during the Gilded Age had created a network of corruption in which wealth and power were exchanged for influence and votes in the Senate. Senator Nelson Aldrich, who represented Rhode Island in the late nineteenth and early twentieth centuries, for example, was known as "the senator from Standard Oil" because of his open support of special business interests.

Efforts to amend the Constitution to allow direct election of senators had begun in 1826, but since any proposal had to be approved by the Senate, reform seemed impossible. Progressives tried to gain influence in the Senate by instituting party caucuses and primary elections, which gave citizens the chance to express their choice of a senator who could then be officially elected by the state legislature. By 1910, fourteen of the country's thirty senators received popular votes through a state primary before the state legislature made its selection. Despairing of getting a proposal through the Senate, supporters of a direct-election amendment had begun in 1893 to seek a convention of representatives from two-thirds of the states to propose an amendment that could then be ratified. By 1905, thirty-one of forty-five states had endorsed such an amendment. Finally, in 1911, despite extraordinary opposition, a proposed amendment passed the Senate; by 1913, it had been ratified.

Amendment XVIII
[Adopted 1919; Repealed 1933 by Amendment XXI]

Section 1   After one year from the ratification of this article the manufacture, sale, or transportation of intoxicating liquors within, the importation thereof into, or the exportation thereof from the United States and all territory subject to the jurisdiction thereof, for beverage purposes, is hereby prohibited.

Section 2   The Congress and the several States shall have concurrent power to enforce this article by appropriate legislation.

Section 3   This article shall be inoperative unless it shall have been ratified as an amendment to the Constitution by the legislatures of the several States, as provided by the Constitution, within seven years from the date of the submission thereof to the States by the Congress.

◆◆◆

The Prohibition Party, formed in 1869, began calling for a constitutional amendment to outlaw alcoholic beverages in 1872. A prohibition amendment was first proposed in the Senate in 1876 and was revived eighteen times before 1913. Between 1913 and 1919, another thirty-nine attempts were made to prohibit liquor in the United States through a constitutional amendment. Prohibition became a key element of the Progressive agenda as reformers linked alcohol and drunkenness to numerous social problems, including the corruption of immigrant voters. While opponents of such an amendment argued that it was undemocratic, supporters claimed that their efforts had widespread public support. The admission of twelve "dry" western states to the Union in the early twentieth century and the spirit of sacrifice during World War I laid the groundwork for passage and ratification of the Eighteenth Amendment in 1919. Opponents added a time limit to the amendment in the hope that they could thus block ratification, but this effort failed. (See also Amendment XXI.)

Amendment XIX
[Adopted 1920]

Section 1   The right of citizens of the United States to vote shall not be denied or abridged by the United States or by any State on account of sex.

Section 2   Congress shall have the power to enforce this article by appropriate legislation.

◆◆◆

Advocates of women's rights tried and failed to link woman suffrage to the Fourteenth and Fifteenth Amendments. Nonetheless, the effort for woman suffrage continued. Between 1878 and 1912, at least one and sometimes as many as four proposed amendments were introduced in Congress each year to grant women the right to vote. While over time women won very limited voting rights in some states, at both the state and federal levels opposition to an amendment for woman suffrage remained very strong. President Woodrow Wilson and other officials felt that the federal government should not interfere with the power of the states in this matter. Others worried that granting suffrage to women would encourage ethnic minorities to exercise their own right to vote. And many were concerned that giving women the vote would result in their abandoning traditional gender roles. In 1919, following a protracted and often bitter campaign of protest in which women went on hunger strikes and chained themselves to fences, an amendment was introduced with the backing of President Wilson. It narrowly passed the Senate (after efforts to limit the suffrage to white women failed) and was adopted in 1920 after Tennessee became the thirty-sixth state to ratify it.

Unratified Amendment
Child Labor Amendment (proposed by Congress June 2, 1924)

Section 1   The Congress shall have power to limit, regulate, and prohibit the labor of persons under eighteen years of age.

Section 2   The power of the several States is unimpaired by this article except that the operation of State laws shall be suspended to the extent necessary to give effect to legislation enacted by Congress.

◆◆◆

Throughout the late nineteenth and early twentieth centuries, alarm over the condition of child workers grew. Opponents of child labor argued that children worked in dangerous and unhealthy conditions, that they took jobs from adult workers, that they depressed wages in certain industries, and that states that allowed child labor had an economic advantage over those that did not. Defenders of child labor claimed that children provided needed income in many families, that working at a young age developed character, and that the effort to prohibit the practice constituted an invasion of family privacy.

In 1916, Congress passed a law that made it illegal to sell goods made by children through interstate commerce. The Supreme Court, however, ruled that the law violated the limits on the power of Congress to regulate interstate commerce. Congress then tried to penalize industries that used child labor by taxing such goods. This measure was also thrown out by the courts. In response, reformers set out to amend the Constitution. The proposed amendment was ratified by twenty-eight states, but by 1925, thirteen states had rejected it. Passage of the Fair Labor Standards Act in 1938, which was upheld by the Supreme Court in 1941, made the amendment irrelevant.

Amendment XX
[Adopted 1933]

Section 1   The terms of the President and Vice-President shall end at noon on the 20th day of January, and the terms of Senators and Representatives at noon on the 3rd day of January, of the years in which such terms would have ended if this article had not been ratified; and the terms of their successors shall then begin.

Section 2   The Congress shall assemble at least once in every year, and such meeting shall begin at noon on the 3rd day of January, unless they shall by law appoint a different day.

Section 3   If, at the time fixed for the beginning of the term of the President, the President-elect shall have died, the Vice-President-elect shall become President. If a President shall not have been chosen before the time fixed for the beginning of his term, or if the President-elect shall have failed to qualify, then the Vice-President-elect shall act as President until a President shall have qualified; and the Congress may by law provide for the case wherein neither a President-elect nor a Vice-President-elect shall have qualified, declaring who shall then act as President, or the manner in which one who is to act shall be selected, and such person shall act accordingly until a President or Vice-President shall have qualified.

Section 4   The Congress may by law provide for the case of the death of any of the persons from whom the House of Representatives may choose a President whenever the right of choice shall have devolved upon them, and for the case of the death of any of the persons from whom the Senate may choose a Vice-President whenever the right of choice shall have devolved upon them.

Section 5   Sections 1 and 2 shall take effect on the 15th day of October following the ratification of this article.

Section 6   This article shall be inoperative unless it shall have been ratified as an amendment to the Constitution by the Legislatures of three-fourths of the several States within seven years from the date of its submission.

Until 1933, presidents took office on March 4. Since elections are held in early November and electoral votes are counted in mid-December, this meant that more than three months passed between the time a new president was elected and when he took office. Moving the inauguration to January shortened the transition period and allowed Congress to begin its term closer to the time of the president's inauguration. Although this seems like a minor change, an amendment was required because the Constitution specifies terms of office. This amendment also deals with questions of succession in the event that a president- or vice president-elect dies before assuming office. Section 3 also clarifies a method for resolving a deadlock in the electoral college.

Amendment XXI
[Adopted 1933]

Section 1   The eighteenth article of amendment to the Constitution of the United States is hereby repealed.

Section 2   The transportation or importation into any State, Territory, or Possession of the United States for delivery or use therein of intoxicating liquors, in violation of the laws thereof, is hereby prohibited.

Section 3   This article shall be inoperative unless it shall have been ratified as an amendment to the Constitution by conventions in the several States, as provided in the Constitution, within seven years from the date of the submission thereof to the States by the Congress.

Widespread violation of the Volstead Act, the law enacted to enforce prohibition, made the United States a nation of lawbreakers. Prohibition caused more problems than it solved by encouraging crime, bribery, and corruption. Further, a coalition of liquor and beer manufacturers, personal liberty advocates, and constitutional scholars joined forces to challenge the amendment. By 1929, thirty proposed repeal amendments had been introduced in Congress, and the Democratic Party made repeal part of its platform in the 1932 presidential campaign. The Twenty-First Amendment was proposed in February 1933 and ratified less than a year later. The failure of the effort to enforce prohibition through a constitutional amendment has often been cited by opponents to subsequent efforts to shape public virtue and private morality.

Amendment XXII
[Adopted 1951]

Section 1 No person shall be elected to the office of the President more than twice, and no person who has held the office of President, or acted as President, for more than two years of a term to which some other person was elected President shall be elected to the office of President more than once. But this article shall not apply to any person holding the office of President when this Article was proposed by the Congress, and shall not prevent any person who may be holding the office of President, or acting as President, during the term within which this Article becomes operative from holding the office of President or acting as President during the remainder of such term.

Section 2 This article shall be inoperative unless it shall have been ratified as an amendment to the Constitution by the legislatures of three-fourths of the several States within seven years from the date of its submission to the States by the Congress.

George Washington's refusal to seek a third term of office set a precedent that stood until 1912, when former President Theodore Roosevelt sought, without success, another term as an independent candidate. Democrat Franklin Roosevelt was the only president to seek and win a fourth term, though he did so amid great controversy. Roosevelt died in April 1945, a few months after the beginning of his fourth term. In 1946, Republicans won control of the House and the Senate, and early in 1947 a proposal for an amendment to limit future presidents to two four-year terms was offered to the states for ratification. Democratic critics of the Twenty-Second Amendment charged that it was a partisan posthumous jab at Roosevelt.

Since the Twenty-Second Amendment was adopted, however, the only presidents who might have been able to seek a third term, had it not existed, were Republicans Dwight Eisenhower and Ronald Reagan, and Democrat Bill Clinton. Since 1826, Congress has entertained 160 proposed amendments to limit the president to one six-year term. Such amendments have been backed by fifteen presidents, including Gerald Ford and Jimmy Carter.

Amendment XXIII
[Adopted 1961]

Section 1 The District constituting the seat of Government of the United States shall appoint in such manner as the Congress may direct: A number of electors of President and Vice-President equal to the whole number of Senators and Representatives in Congress to which the District would be entitled if it were a State, but in no event more than the least populous State; they shall be in addition to those appointed by the States, but they shall be considered for the purposes of the election of President and Vice-President, to be electors appointed by a State; and they shall meet in the District and perform such duties as provided by the twelfth article of amendment.

Section 2 The Congress shall have the power to enforce this article by appropriate legislation.

When Washington, D.C., was established as a federal district, no one expected that a significant number of people would make it their permanent and primary residence. A proposal to allow citizens of the district to vote in presidential elections was approved by Congress in June 1960 and was ratified on March 29, 1961.

Amendment XXIV
[Adopted 1964]

Section 1 The right of citizens of the United States to vote in any primary or other election for President or Vice-President, for electors for President or Vice-President, or for Senator or Representative in Congress, shall not be denied or abridged by the United States or any State by reason of failure to pay any poll tax or other tax.

Section 2 The Congress shall have the power to enforce this article by appropriate legislation.

In the colonial and Revolutionary eras, financial independence was seen as necessary to political independence, and the poll tax was used as a requirement for voting. By the twentieth century, however, the poll tax was used mostly to bar poor people, especially southern blacks, from voting. While conservatives complained that the amendment interfered with states' rights, liberals thought that the amendment did not go far enough because it barred the poll tax only in national elections and not in state or local elections. The amendment was ratified in 1964, however, and two years later, the Supreme Court ruled that poll taxes in state and local elections also violated the equal protection clause of the Fourteenth Amendment.

Amendment XXV
[Adopted 1967]

Section 1 In case of the removal of the President from office or of his death or resignation, the Vice-President shall become President.

Section 2 Whenever there is a vacancy in the office of the Vice-President, the President shall nominate a Vice-President who shall take office upon confirmation by a majority vote of both Houses of Congress.

Section 3 Whenever the President transmits to the President pro tempore of the Senate and the Speaker of the House of Representatives his written declaration that he is unable to discharge the powers and duties of his office, and until he transmits to them a written declaration to the contrary, such powers and duties shall be discharged by the Vice-President as Acting President.

Section 4 Whenever the Vice-President and a majority of either the principal officers of the executive departments or of such other body as Congress may by law provide, transmit to the President pro tempore of the Senate and the Speaker of the House of Representatives their written declaration that the President is unable to discharge the powers and duties of his office, the Vice-President shall immediately assume the powers and duties of the office as Acting President.

Thereafter, when the President transmits to the President pro tempore of the Senate and the Speaker of the House of Representatives his written declaration that no inability exists, he shall resume the powers and duties of his office unless the Vice-President and a majority of either the principal officers of the executive department[s] or of such other body as Congress may by law provide, transmit within four days to the President pro tempore of the Senate and the Speaker of the House of Representatives their written declaration that the President is unable to discharge the powers and duties of his office. Thereupon Congress shall decide the issue, assembling within forty-eight hours for that purpose if not in session. If the Congress, within twenty-one days after receipt of the latter written declaration, or, if Congress is not in session, within twenty-one days after Congress is required to assemble, determines by two-thirds vote of both Houses that the President is unable to discharge the powers and duties of his office, the Vice-President shall continue to discharge the same as Acting President; otherwise, the President shall resume the powers and duties of his office.

◆◆◆

The framers of the Constitution established the office of vice president because someone was needed to preside over the Senate. The first president to die in office was William Henry Harrison, in 1841. Vice President John Tyler had himself sworn in as president, setting a precedent that was followed when seven later presidents died in office. The assassination of President James A. Garfield in 1881

posed a new problem, however. After he was shot, the president was incapacitated for two months before he died; he was unable to lead the country, while his vice president, Chester A. Arthur, was unable to assume leadership. Efforts to resolve questions of succession in the event of a presidential disability thus began with the death of Garfield.

In 1963, the assassination of President John F. Kennedy galvanized Congress to action. Vice President Lyndon Johnson was a chain smoker with a history of heart trouble. According to the 1947 Presidential Succession Act, the two men who stood in line to succeed him were the seventy-two-year-old Speaker of the House and the eighty-six-year-old president of the Senate. There were serious concerns that any of these men might become incapacitated while serving as chief executive. The first time the Twenty-Fifth Amendment was used, however, was not in the case of presidential death or illness, but during the Watergate crisis. When Vice President Spiro T. Agnew was forced to resign following allegations of bribery and tax violations, President Richard M. Nixon appointed House Minority Leader Gerald R. Ford vice president. Ford became president following Nixon's resignation eight months later and named Nelson A. Rockefeller as his vice president. Thus, for more than two years, the two highest offices in the country were held by people who had not been elected to them.

Amendment XXVI
[Adopted 1971]

Section 1 The right of citizens of the United States, who are eighteen years of age or older, to vote shall not be denied or abridged by the United States or by any State on account of age.

Section 2 The Congress shall have power to enforce this article by appropriate legislation.

◆◆◆

Efforts to lower the voting age from twenty-one to eighteen began during World War II. Recognizing that those who were old enough to fight a war should have some say in the government policies that involved them in the war, Presidents Eisenhower, Johnson, and Nixon endorsed the idea. In 1970, the combined pressure of the antiwar movement and the demographic pressure of the baby boom generation led to a Voting Rights Act lowering the voting age in federal, state, and local elections.

In Oregon v. Mitchell *(1970), the state of Oregon challenged the right of Congress to determine the age at which people could vote in state or local elections. The Supreme Court agreed with Oregon. Since the Voting Rights Act was ruled unconstitutional, the Constitution had to be amended to allow passage of a law that would lower the voting age. The amendment was ratified in a little more than three months, making it the most rapidly ratified amendment in U.S. history.*

Unratified Amendment

Equal Rights Amendment (proposed by Congress March 22, 1972; seven-year deadline for ratification extended June 30, 1982)

Section 1 Equality of rights under the law shall not be denied or abridged by the United States or by any State on account of sex.

Section 2 The Congress shall have the power to enforce, by appropriate legislation, the provisions of this article.

Section 3 This amendment shall take effect two years after the date of ratification.

In 1923, soon after women had won the right to vote, Alice Paul, a leading activist in the woman suffrage movement, proposed an amendment requiring equal treatment of men and women. Opponents of the proposal argued that such an amendment would invalidate laws that protected women and would make women subject to the military draft. After the 1964 Civil Rights Act was adopted, protective workplace legislation was removed anyway.

The renewal of the women's movement, as a byproduct of the civil rights and antiwar movements, led to a revival of the Equal Rights Amendment (ERA) in Congress. Disagreements over language held up congressional passage of the proposed amendment, but on March 22, 1972, the Senate approved the ERA by a vote of eighty-four to eight, and it was sent to the states. Six states ratified the amendment within two days, and by the middle of 1973 the amendment seemed well on its way to adoption, with thirty of the needed thirty-eight states having ratified it. In the mid-1970s, however, a powerful "Stop ERA" campaign developed. The campaign portrayed the ERA as a threat to "family values" and traditional relationships between men and women. Although thirty-five states ultimately ratified the ERA, five of those state legislatures voted to rescind ratification, and the amendment was never adopted.

Unratified Amendment

D.C. Statehood Amendment (proposed by Congress August 22, 1978)

Section 1 For purposes of representation in the Congress, election of the President and Vice-President, and article V of this Constitution, the District constituting

the seat of government of the United States shall be treated as though it were a State.

Section 2 The exercise of the rights and powers conferred under this article shall be by the people of the District constituting the seat of government, and as shall be provided by Congress.

Section 3 The twenty-third article of amendment to the Constitution of the United States is hereby repealed.

Section 4 This article shall be inoperative, unless it shall have been ratified as an amendment to the Constitution by the legislatures of three-fourths of the several states within seven years from the date of its submission.

The 1961 ratification of the Twenty-Third Amendment, giving residents of the District of Columbia the right to vote for a president and vice president, inspired an effort to give residents of the district full voting rights. In 1966, President Lyndon Johnson appointed a mayor and city council; in 1971, D.C. residents were allowed to name a nonvoting delegate to the House; and in 1981, residents were allowed to elect the mayor and city council. Congress retained the right to overrule laws that might affect commuters, the height of federal buildings, and selection of judges and prosecutors. The district's nonvoting delegate to Congress, Walter Fauntroy, lobbied fiercely for a congressional amendment granting statehood to the district. In 1978, a proposed amendment was approved and sent to the states. A number of states quickly ratified the amendment, but, like the ERA, the D.C. Statehood Amendment ran into trouble. Opponents argued that section 2 created a separate category of "nominal" statehood. They argued that the federal district should be eliminated and that the territory should be reabsorbed into the state of Maryland. Although these theoretical arguments were strong, some scholars believe that racist attitudes toward the predominantly black population of the city was also a factor leading to the defeat of the amendment.

Amendment XXVII
[Adopted 1992]

No law, varying the compensation for the services of the Senators and Representatives, shall take effect, until an election of Representatives shall have intervened.

While the Twenty-Sixth Amendment was the most rapidly ratified amendment in U.S. history, the Twenty-Seventh

Amendment had the longest journey to ratification. First proposed by James Madison in 1789 as part of the package that included the Bill of Rights, this amendment had been ratified by only six states by 1791. In 1873, however, it was ratified by Ohio to protest a massive retroactive salary increase by the federal government. Unlike later proposed amendments, this one came with no time limit on ratification. In the early 1980s, Gregory D. Watson, a University of Texas economics major, discovered the "lost" amendment and began a single-handed campaign to get state legislators to introduce it for ratification. In 1983, it was accepted by Maine. In 1984, it passed the Colorado legislature. Ratifications trickled in slowly until May 1992, when Michigan and New Jersey became the thirty-eighth and thirty-ninth states, respectively, to ratify. This amendment prevents members of Congress from raising their own salaries without giving voters a chance to vote them out of office before they can benefit from the raises.

THE CONSTITUTION OF THE CONFEDERATE STATES OF AMERICA

In framing the Constitution of the Confederate States, the authors adopted, with numerous small but significant changes and additions, the language of the Constitution of the United States, and followed the same order of arrangement of articles and sections. The revisions that they made to the original Constitution are shown here. The parts stricken out are enclosed in brackets, and the new matter added in framing the Confederate Constitution is printed in italics.

Adopted March 11, 1861

WE, the People of the [United States] *Confederated States, each State acting in its sovereign and independent character,* in order to form a [more perfect Union] *permanent Federal government,* establish Justice, insure domestic Tranquillity [provide for the common defense, promote the general Welfare], and secure the Blessings of Liberty to ourselves and our Posterity, *invoking the favor and guidance of Almighty God,* do ordain and establish this Constitution for the [United] *Confederate* States of America.

Article I

Section I   All legislative Powers herein [granted] *delegated,* shall be vested in a Congress of the [United] *Confederate* States, which shall consist of a Senate and House of Representatives.

Section II   The House of Representatives shall be composed of Members chosen every second Year by the People of the several States, and the Electors in each State shall *be citizens of the Confederate States, and* have the Qualifications requisite for Electors of the most numerous Branch of the State Legislature; *but no person of foreign birth, and not a citizen of the Confederate States, shall be allowed to vote for any officer, civil or political, State or federal.*

No Person shall be a Representative who shall not have attained to the Age of twenty-five Years, and [been seven Years a Citizen of the United] *be a citizen of the Confederate* States, and who shall not, when elected, be an Inhabitant of that State in which he shall be chosen.

Representatives and direct Taxes shall be apportioned among the several States which may be included within this [Union] *Confederacy,* according to their respective Numbers, which shall be determined by adding to the whole Number of free Persons, including those bound to Service for a Term of Years, and excluding Indians not taxed, three-fifths of all [other Persons] *slaves.* The actual Enumeration shall be made within three Years after the first Meeting of the Congress of the [United] *Confederate* States, and within every subsequent Term of ten Years, in such Manner as they shall by Law direct. The Number of Representatives shall not exceed one for every [thirty] *fifty* Thousand, but each State shall have at Least one Representative; and until such enumeration shall be made, the State of [New Hampshire shall be entitled to choose three, Massachusetts eight, Rhode Island and Providence Plantations one, Connecticut five, New York six, New Jersey four, Pennsylvania eight, Delaware one, Maryland six, Virginia ten, North Carolina five, South Carolina five, and Georgia three] *South Carolina shall be entitled to choose six, the State of Georgia ten, the State of Alabama nine, the State of Florida two, the State of Mississippi seven, the State of Louisiana six, and the State of Texas six.*

When vacancies happen in the Representation from any State, the Executive Authority thereof shall issue Writs of Election to fill such Vacancies.

The House of Representatives shall choose their Speaker and other Officers; and shall have the sole Power of Impeachment; *except that any judicial or other federal officer resident and acting solely within the limits of any State, may be impeached by a vote of two-thirds of both branches of the Legislature thereof.*

Section III   The Senate of the [United] *Confederate* States shall be composed of two Senators from each State, chosen by the Legislature thereof, for six Years, *at the regular session next immediately preceding the commencement of the term of service;* and each Senator shall have one Vote.

Immediately after they shall be assembled in Consequence of the first Election, they shall be divided as equally as may be into three Classes. The Seats of the Senators of the first Class shall be vacated at the Expiration of the second Year, of the second Class at the Expiration of the fourth Year, and of the third Class at the Expiration of the sixth Year, so that one-third may be chosen every second Year; and if Vacancies happen by Resignation, or otherwise, during the Recess of the Legislature of any State, the Executive thereof may make temporary Appointments until the next Meeting of the Legislature, which shall then fill such Vacancies.

No Person shall be a Senator who shall not have attained to the Age of thirty Years, and [been nine Years a Citizen of the United] *be a citizen of the Confederate* States, and who shall not, when elected, be an Inhabitant of that State for which he shall be chosen.

The Vice President of the [United] *Confederate* States shall be President of the Senate, but shall have no Vote, unless they be equally divided.

The Senate shall choose their other Officers, and also a President *pro tempore,* in the Absence of the Vice President, or when he shall exercise the Office of President of the United States.

The Senate shall have the sole Power to try all Impeachments. When sitting for that Purpose, they shall be on Oath or Affirmation. When the President of the [United] *Confederate* States is tried, the Chief Justice shall preside: And no Person shall be convicted without the Concurrence of two-thirds of the Members present.

Judgment in Cases of Impeachment shall not extend further than to removal from Office, and Disqualification to hold and enjoy any Office of honour, Trust or Profit under the [United] *Confederate* States; but the Party convicted shall nevertheless be liable and subject to Indictment, Trial, Judgment and Punishment, according to Law.

Section IV   The Times, Places and Manner of holding Elections for Senators and Representatives, shall be prescribed in each State by the Legislature thereof, *subject to the provisions of this Constitution;* but the Congress may at any time by Law make or alter such Regulations, except as to the *times and* places of choosing Senators.

The Congress shall assemble at least once in every Year, and such Meeting shall be on the first Monday in December, unless they shall by Law appoint a different Day.

Section V   Each House shall be the Judge of the Elections, Returns and Qualifications of its own Members, and a Majority of each shall constitute a Quorum to do Business; but a smaller Number may adjourn from day to day, and may be authorized to compel the Attendance of absent Members, in such Manner, and under such Penalties as each House may provide.

Each House may determine the Rules of its Proceedings, punish its Members for disorderly Behaviour, and, with the Concurrence of two-thirds *of the whole number* expel a Member.

Each House shall keep a Journal of its Proceedings, and from time to time publish the same, excepting such Parts as may in their Judgment require Secrecy; and the Yeas and Nays of the Members of either House on any question shall, at the Desire of one-fifth of those Present, be entered on the Journal.

Neither House, during the Session of Congress, shall, without the Consent of the other, adjourn for more than three days, nor to any other Place than that in which the two Houses shall be sitting.

Section VI   The Senators and Representatives shall receive a Compensation for their Services, to be ascertained by Law, and paid out of the Treasury of the [United] *Confederate* States. They shall in all Cases, except Treason [Felony] and Breach of the Peace, be privileged from Arrest during their Attendance at the Session of their respective Houses, and in going to and returning from the same; and for any Speech or Debate in either House, they shall not be questioned in any other Place.

No Senator or Representative shall, during the Time for which he was elected, be appointed to any civil Office under the Authority of the [United] *Confederate* States, which shall have been created, or the Emoluments whereof shall have been increased during such time; and no Person holding any Office under the [United] *Confederate* States, shall be a Member of either House during his Continuance in Office. *But Congress may, by law, grant to the principal officers in each of the executive departments a seat upon the floor of either House, with the privilege of discussing any measures appertaining to his department.*

Section VII   All Bills for raising Revenue shall originate in the House of Representatives; but the Senate may propose or concur with Amendments as on other Bills.

Every Bill which shall have passed [the House of Representatives and the Senate] *both Houses,* shall, before it become a Law, be presented to the President of the [United] *Confederate* States; If he approve he shall sign it, but if not he shall return it, with his Objections to that House in which it shall have originated, who shall enter the Objections at large on their Journal, and proceed to reconsider it. If after such Reconsideration two-thirds of that House shall agree to pass the Bill, it shall be sent, together with the Objections, to the other House, by which it shall likewise be reconsidered, and if approved by two-thirds of that House, it shall become a Law. But in all *such* Cases the Votes of both Houses shall be determined by Yeas and Nays, and the Names of the Persons voting for and against the Bill shall be entered on the Journal of each House respectively. If any Bill shall not be returned by the President within ten Days (Sundays excepted) after it shall have been presented to him, the Same shall be a law, in like Manner as if he had signed it, unless the Congress by their Adjournment prevent its return, in which Case it shall not be a Law. *The President may approve any appropriation and disapprove any other appropriation in the same bill. In such case he shall, in signing the bill, designate the appropriation disapproved, and shall return a copy of such appropriation, with his objections, to the House in which the bill shall have originated; and the same proceedings shall then be had as in case of other bills disapproved by the President.*

Every Order, Resolution, or Vote to which the Concurrence of [the Senate and House of Representatives] *both Houses* may be necessary (except on a question of Adjournment), shall be presented to the President of the [United] *Confederate* States; and before the Same shall take Effect, shall be approved by him, or being disapproved by him, [shall] *may* be repassed by two-thirds of [the Senate and House of Representatives] *both Houses,* according to the Rules and Limitations prescribed in the Case of a Bill.

Section VIII   The Congress shall have Power

To lay and collect Taxes, Duties, Imposts and *Excises, for revenue necessary* to pay the Debts [and], provide for the common Defense [and general Welfare of the United States; but], *and carry on the government of the Confederate States; but no bounties shall be granted from the treasury, nor shall any duties, or taxes, or importation from foreign nations be laid to promote or foster any branch of industry; and* all Duties, Imposts and Excises shall be uniform throughout the [United] *Confederate* States;

To borrow Money on the credit of the [United] *Confederate* States;

To regulate Commerce with foreign Nations, and among the several States, and with the Indian Tribes; *but neither this, nor any other clause contained in this Constitution, shall ever be construed to delegate the power to Congress to appropriate money for any internal improvement intended to facilitate commerce; except for the purpose of furnishing lights, beacons, and buoys, and other aids to navigation upon the coasts, and the improvement of harbors, and the removing of obstructions in river navigation; in all such cases such duties shall be laid on the navigation facilitated thereby, as may be necessary to pay the costs and expenses thereof;*

To establish an uniform Rule of Naturalization, and uniform Laws on the subject of Bankruptcies throughout the [United] *Confederate* States; *but no law of Congress shall discharge any debt contracted before the passage of the same;*

To coin Money, regulate the Value thereof, and of foreign Coin, and fix the Standard of Weights and Measures;

To provide for the Punishment of counterfeiting the Securities and current Coin of the [United] *Confederate* States;

To establish Post Offices and post [Roads] *routes; but the expenses of the Postoffice Department, after the first day of March, in the year of our Lord eighteen hundred and sixty-three, shall be paid out of its own revenues;*

To promote the progress of Science and useful Arts, by securing for limited Times to Authors and Inventors the exclusive Right to their respective Writings and Discoveries;

To constitute Tribunals inferior to the supreme Court;

To define and punish Piracies and Felonies committed on the high Seas, and Offences against the Law of Nations;

To declare War, grant Letters of Marque and Reprisal, and make Rules concerning Captures on Land and Water;

To raise and support Armies, but no Appropriation of Money to that Use shall be for a longer Term than two Years;

To provide and maintain a Navy;

To make Rules for the Government and Regulation of the land and naval Forces;

To provide for calling forth the Militia to execute the Laws of the [Union] *Confederate States,* suppress Insurrections and repel Invasions;

To provide for organizing, arming, and disciplining the Militia and for governing such Part of them as may be employed in the Service of the [United] *Confederate* States, reserving to the States respectively, the Appointment of the Officers, and the Authority of training the Militia according to the Discipline prescribed by Congress;

To exercise exclusive Legislation in all Cases whatsoever, over such District (not exceeding ten Miles square) as may, by Cession of particular States, and the Acceptance of Congress, become the Seat of the Government of the [United] *Confederate* States, and to exercise like Authority over all Places purchased by the Consent of the Legislature of the State in which the Same shall be, for the Erection of Forts, Magazines, Arsenals, Dock Yards, and other needful Buildings;—And

To make all Laws which shall be necessary and proper for carrying into Execution the foregoing Powers, and all other Powers vested by this Constitution in the Government of the [United] *Confederate* States or in any Department or Officer thereof.

Section IX   [The Migration or Importation of such Persons as any of the States now existing shall think proper to admit, shall not be prohibited by the Congress prior to the Year one thousand eight hundred and eight, but a Tax or Duty may be imposed on such Importation, not exceeding ten dollars for each Person.]

The importation of negroes of the African race from any foreign country other than the slaveholding States or territories of the United States of America, is hereby forbidden; and Congress is required to pass such laws as shall effectually prevent the same. Congress shall also have power to prohibit the introduction of slaves from any State not a member of, or territory not belonging to, this Confederacy.

The Privilege of the Writ of Habeas Corpus shall not be suspended, unless when in Cases of Rebellion or Invasion the public Safety may require it. No Bill of Attainder or ex post facto Law, *or law denying or impairing the right of property in negro slaves,* shall be passed.

No Capitation, or other direct, Tax shall be laid, unless in Proportion to the Census or Enumeration herein before directed to be taken.

No Tax or Duty shall be laid on Articles exported from any State, *except by a vote of two-thirds of both Houses.*

No Preference shall be given by any Regulation of Commerce or Revenue to the Ports of one State over those of another; nor shall Vessels bound to, or from, one State, be obliged to enter, clear, or pay Duties in another.

No Money shall be drawn from the Treasury, but in Consequence of Appropriations made by Law; and a regular Statement and Account of the Receipts and Expenditures of all public Money shall be published from time to time.

Congress shall appropriate no money from the Treasury except by a vote of two-thirds of both Houses, taken by yeas and nays, unless it be asked and estimated for by some one of the heads of departments and submitted to Congress by the President; or for the purpose of paying its own expenses and contingencies; or for the payment of claims against the Confederate States, the justice of which shall have been officially declared by a tribunal for the investigation of claims against the Government, which it is hereby made the duty of Congress to establish.

All bills appropriating money shall specify in Federal currency the exact amount of each appropriation and the purposes for which it is made; and Congress shall grant no extra compensation to any public contractor, officer, agent or servant, after such contract shall have been made or such service rendered.

No Title of Nobility shall be granted by the [United] *Confederate* States; and no Person holding any Office of Profit or Trust under them, shall, without the Consent of the Congress, accept of any present, Emolument, Office, or Title, of any kind whatever, from any King, Prince or foreign State.

[Here the framers of the Confederate Constitution insert the U.S. Bill of Rights.]

Congress shall make no law respecting an establishment of religion, or prohibiting the free exercise thereof; or abridging the freedom of speech, or of the press; or the right of the people peaceably to assemble, and to petition the Government for a redress of grievances.

A well-regulated Militia, being necessary to the security of a free State, the right of the people to keep and bear Arms shall not be infringed.

No Soldier shall, in time of peace, be quartered in any house, without the consent of the Owner, nor in time of war, but in a manner to be prescribed by law.

The right of the people to be secure in their persons, houses, papers, and effects, against unreasonable searches and seizures, shall not be violated, and no Warrants shall issue, but upon probable cause, supported by Oath or affirmation, and particularly describing the place to be searched, and the persons or things to be seized.

No person shall be held to answer for a capital, or otherwise infamous crime, unless on a presentment or indictment of a Grand Jury, except in cases arising in the land or naval forces, or in the Militia, when in actual service in time of War or public danger; nor shall any person be subject for the same offence to be twice put in jeopardy of life or limb; nor shall be compelled in any Criminal Case to be a witness against himself, nor be deprived of life, liberty or property without due process of law; nor shall private property be taken for public use, without just compensation.

In all criminal prosecutions, the accused shall enjoy the right to a speedy and public trial, by an impartial jury of the State and district wherein the crime shall have been committed, which district shall have been previously ascertained by law, and to be informed of the nature and cause of the accusation; to be confronted with the witnesses against him; to have Compulsory process for obtaining Witnesses in his favour, and to have the Assistance of Counsel for his defence.

In Suits at common law, where the value in controversy shall exceed twenty dollars, the right of trial by jury shall be preserved, and no fact tried by a jury shall be otherwise reexamined in any Court of the [United] *Confederate* States, than according to the rules of the common law.

Excessive bail shall not be required, nor excessive fines imposed, nor cruel and unusual punishments inflicted.

Every law or resolution having the force of law, shall relate to but one subject, and that shall be expressed in the title.

Section X No State shall enter into any Treaty, Alliance, or Confederation; grant Letters of Marque and Reprisal; coin Money; [emit Bills of Credit;] make any Thing but gold and silver Coin a Tender in Payment of Debts; pass any Bill of Attainder, *or* ex post facto Law, or Law impairing the Obligation of Contracts, or grant any Title of Nobility.

No State shall, without the consent of the Congress, lay any Imposts or Duties on Imports or Exports, except what may be absolutely necessary for executing its inspection Laws: and the net Produce of all Duties and Imposts, laid by any State on Imports or Exports, shall be for the Use of the Treasury of the [United] *Confederate* States; and all such Laws shall be subject to the Revision and Control of the Congress.

No State shall, without the Consent of Congress, lay any Duty of Tonnage, *except on sea-going vessels, for the improvement of its rivers and harbors navigated by the said vessels; but such duties shall not conflict with any treaties of the Confederate States with foreign nations; and any surplus of revenue thus derived shall, after making such improvement, be paid into the common treasury; nor shall any State* keep Troops, or Ships of War in time of Peace, enter into any Agreement or Compact with another State, or with a foreign Power, or engage in War, unless actually invaded, or in such imminent Danger as will not admit of Delay. *But when any river divides or flows through two or more States, they may enter into compacts with each other to improve the navigation thereof.*

Article II

Section I [The executive Power shall be vested in a President of the United States of America. He shall hold his Office during the Term of four Years, and, together with the Vice President, chosen for the same Term, be elected, as follows:] *The executive power shall be vested in a President of the Confederate States of America. He and the Vice President shall hold their offices for the term of six years; but the President shall not be re-eligible. The President and Vice President shall be elected as follows:*

Each State shall appoint in such Manner as the Legislature thereof may direct, a Number of Electors, equal to the whole Number of Senators and Representatives to which the State may be entitled in the Congress; but no Senator or Representative, or Person holding an Office of Trust or Profit under the [United] *Confederate* States, shall be appointed an Elector.

The Electors shall meet in their respective States, and vote by ballot for President and Vice President, one of whom, at least, shall not be an inhabitant of the same State with themselves; they shall name in their ballots the person voted for as President, and in distinct ballots the person voted for as Vice President, and they shall make distinct lists of all persons voted for as President, and of all persons voted for as Vice President, and of the number of votes for each, which lists they

shall sign and certify, and transmit sealed to the seat of the government of the [United] *Confederate* States, directed to the President of the Senate;—The President of the Senate shall, in the presence of the Senate and House of Representatives, open all the certificates and the votes shall then be counted;—The person having the greatest number of votes for President shall be the President, if such number be a majority of the whole number of Electors appointed; and if no person have such majority, then from the persons having the highest numbers not exceeding three on the list of those voted for as President, the House of Representatives shall choose immediately, by ballot, the President. But in choosing the President, the votes shall be taken by States, the representation from each State having one vote; a quorum for this purpose shall consist of a member or members from two-thirds of the States, and a majority of all the States shall be necessary to a choice. And if the House of Representatives shall not choose a President whenever the right of choice shall devolve upon them, before the fourth day of March next following, then the Vice President shall act as President, as in the case of the death or other constitutional disability of the President. The person having the greatest number of votes as Vice President shall be the Vice President, if such number be a majority of the whole number of Electors appointed, and if no person have a majority, then from the two highest numbers on the list the Senate shall choose the Vice President; a quorum for the purpose shall consist of two-thirds of the whole number of Senators, and a majority of the whole number shall be necessary to a choice. But no person constitutionally ineligible to the office of President shall be eligible to that of Vice President of the [United] *Confederate* States.

The Congress may determine the Time of choosing the Electors, and the Day on which they shall give their Votes; which Day shall be the same throughout the [United] *Confederate* States.

No Person except a natural-born Citizen [or a Citizen of the United States] *of the Confederate States, or a citizen thereof,* at the time of the Adoption of this Constitution, *or a citizen thereof born in the United States prior to the 20th of December, 1860,* shall be eligible to the Office of President; neither shall any Person be eligible to that Office who shall not have attained to the Age of thirty-five Years, and been fourteen Years a Resident within the [United States] *limits of the Confederate States, as they may exist at the time of his election.*

In Cases of the Removal of the President from Office, or of his Death, Resignation, or Inability to discharge the Powers and Duties of the said Office, the same shall devolve on the Vice President, and the Congress may by Law provide for the Case of Removal, Death, Resignation, or Inability, both of the President and Vice President, declaring what Officer shall then act as President, and such Officer shall act accordingly, until the Disability be removed, or a President shall be elected.

The President shall, at stated Times, receive for his Services, a Compensation, which shall neither be increased nor diminished during the Period for which he shall have been elected, and he shall not receive within that Period any other Emolument from the [United] *Confederate* States or any of them.

Before he enters on the Execution of his Office, he shall take the following Oath or Affirmation:—"I do solemnly swear (or affirm) that I will faithfully execute the Office of President of the [United] *Confederate* States, and will to the best of my Ability, preserve, protect and defend the Constitution [of the United States] *thereof.*"

Section II. The President shall be Commander in Chief of the Army and Navy of the [United] *Confederate* States, and of the Militia of the several States, when called into the actual Service of the [United] *Confederate* States; he may require the Opinion, in writing, of the principal Officer in each of the executive Departments, upon any Subject relating to the Duties of their respective Offices, and he shall have Power to grant Reprieves and Pardons for Offenses against the [United] *Confederate* States, except in Cases of Impeachment.

He shall have Power, by and with the Advice and Consent of the Senate, to make Treaties, provided two-thirds of the Senators present concur; and he shall nominate, and by and with the Advice and Consent of the Senate, shall appoint Ambassadors, other public Ministers and Consuls, Judges of the supreme Court, and all other Officers of the [United] *Confederate* States, whose Appointments are not herein otherwise provided for, and which shall be established by Law: but the Congress may by Law vest the Appointment of such inferior Officers, as they think proper, in the President alone, in the Courts of Law, or in the Heads of Departments. *The principal officer in each of the executive departments, and all persons connected with the diplomatic service, may be removed from office at the pleasure of the President. All other civil officers of the executive department may be removed at any time by the President, or other appointing power, when their services are unnecessary, or for dishonesty, incapacity, inefficiency, misconduct, or neglect of duty; and when so removed, the removal shall be reported to the Senate, together with the reasons therefor.*

The President shall have Power to fill [up] all Vacancies that may happen during the Recess of the Senate, by granting Commissions which shall expire at the End of their next Session.

Section III [He] *The President* shall from time to time give to the Congress Information of the State of the [Union] *Confederacy,* and recommend to their Consideration such Measures as he shall judge necessary and expedient; he may, on extraordinary Occasions, convene both Houses, or either of them, and in Case of Disagreement between them, with Respect to the Time of Adjournment, he may adjourn them to such Time as he shall think proper; he shall receive Ambassadors and other public Ministers; he shall take Care that the Laws be faithfully executed, and shall Commission all the officers of the [United] *Confederate* States.

Section IV The President, Vice President and all civil Officers of the [United] *Confederate* States, shall be removed from Office or Impeachment for, and Conviction of, Treason, Bribery, or other high Crimes and Misdemeanors.

Article III

Section I The judicial Power of the [United] *Confederate* States shall be vested in one [supreme] *Superior* Court, and in such inferior Courts as the Congress may from time to time ordain and establish. The Judges, both of the supreme and inferior Courts, shall hold their Offices during good Behavior, and shall, at stated Times, receive for their Services a Compensation, which shall not be diminished during their Continuance in Office.

Section II The judicial Power shall extend to all cases [in Law and Equity, arising under this Constitution], *arising under this Constitution, in law and equity,* the Laws of the [United] *Confederate* States, and Treaties made, or which shall be made, under their Authority;—to all Cases affecting Ambassadors, other public Ministers, and Consuls;—to all Cases of admiralty and maritime Jurisdiction;—to Controversies to which the [United] *Confederate* States shall be a Party;—to Controversies between two or more States; —between a State and Citizens of another State *where the State is plaintiff;—between* Citizens *claiming lands under grants* of different States,—[between Citizens of the same State claiming Lands under Grants of different States,] and between a State, or the Citizens thereof, and foreign States, Citizens or Subjects; *but no State shall be sued by a citizen or subject of any foreign State.*

In all Cases affecting Ambassadors, other public Ministers and Consuls, and those in which a State shall be Party, the supreme Court shall have original Jurisdiction. In all the other Cases before mentioned, the supreme Court shall have appellate Jurisdiction, both as to Law and Fact, with such Exceptions, and under such Regulations as the Congress shall make.

The Trial of all Crimes, except in Cases of Impeachment, shall be by Jury; and such Trial shall be held in the State where the said Crime[s] shall have been committed; but when not committed within any State, the Trial shall be at such Place or Places as the Congress may by Law have directed.

Section III   Treason against the [United] *Confederate* States shall consist only in levying War against them, or in adhering to their Enemies, giving them Aid and Comfort. No Person shall be convicted of Treason unless on the Testimony of two Witnesses to the same overt Act, or on Confession in open Court.

The Congress shall have Power to declare the Punishment of Treason, but no Attainder of Treason shall work Corruption of Blood, or Forfeiture except during the Life of the Person attainted.

Article IV

Section I   Full Faith and Credit shall be given in each State to the public Acts, Records, and judicial Proceedings of every other State. And the Congress may by general Laws prescribe the Manner in which such Acts, Records and Proceedings shall be proved, and the Effect thereof.

Section II   The Citizens of each State shall be entitled to all Privileges and Immunities of Citizens in the several States, *and shall have the right of transit and sojourn in any State of this Confederacy, with their slaves and other property; and the right of property in such slaves shall not be impaired.*

A Person charged in any State with Treason, Felony, or other Crime, who shall flee from Justice, and be found in another State, shall on Demand of the executive Authority of the State from which he fled, be delivered up, to be removed to the State having Jurisdiction of the Crime.

No *slave or* Person held to Service or Labor in [one State] *any State or Territory of the Confederate States* under the Laws thereof, escaping *or unlawfully carried* into another, shall, in Consequence of any Law or Regulation therein, be discharged from such Service or Labor, but shall be delivered up on Claim of the Party to whom such *slave belongs, or to whom such* Service or Labor may be due.

Section III   [New States may be admitted by the Congress into this Union;] *Other States may be admitted into*

this Confederacy by a vote of two-thirds of the whole House of Representatives and two-thirds of the Senate, the Senate voting by States; but no new State shall be formed or erected within the Jurisdiction of any other State; nor any State be formed by the Junction of two or more States, or Parts of States, without the Consent of the Legislatures of the States concerned as well as of the Congress.

The Congress shall have Power to dispose of and make all needful Rules and Regulations [respecting the Territory or other Property belonging to the United States; and nothing in this Constitution shall be so construed as to Prejudice any Claims of the United States, or of any particular State] *concerning the property of the Confederate States, including the lands thereof.*

The Confederate States may acquire new territory, and Congress shall have power to legislate and provide governments for the inhabitants of all territory belonging to the Confederate States lying without the limits of the several States, and may permit them, at such times and in such manner as it may by law provide, to form States to be admitted into the Confederacy. In all such territory the institution of negro slavery as it now exists in the Confederate States shall be recognized and protected by Congress and by the territorial government, and the inhabitants of the several Confederate States and territories shall have the right to take to such territory any slaves lawfully held by them in any of the States or Territories of the Confederate States.

[***Section IV***]   The [United] *Confederate* States shall guarantee to every State [in this Union] *that now is, or hereafter may become, a member of this Confederacy*, a Republican Form of Government, and shall protect each of them against Invasion; and on Application of the Legislature, or of the Executive (when the Legislature [cannot be convened] *is not in session*) against domestic Violence.

Article V

[The Congress, whenever two-thirds of both Houses shall deem it necessary, shall propose Amendments to this Constitution, or on the Application of the Legislatures of two-thirds of the several States, shall call a Convention for proposing Amendments, which, in either Case, shall be valid to all Intents and Purposes, as Part of this Constitution, when ratified by the Legislatures of three-fourths of the several States, or by Conventions in three-fourths thereof, as the one or the other Mode of Ratification may be proposed by the Congress; Provided that no Amendment which may be made prior to the Year one thousand eight hundred and eight shall in any Manner affect the first and fourth Clauses in the

Ninth Section of the first Article; and that no State, without its Consent, shall be deprived of its equal Suffrage in the Senate.]

Upon the demand of any three States, legally assembled in their several Conventions, the Congress shall summon a Convention of all the States, to take into consideration such amendments to the Constitution as the said States shall concur in suggesting at the time when the said demand is made; and should any of the proposed amendments to the Constitution be agreed on by the said Convention—voting by States—and the same be ratified by the Legislatures of two-thirds of the several States, or by Conventions in two-thirds thereof—as the one or the other mode of ratification may be proposed by the general Convention—they shall henceforward form a part of this Constitution. But no State shall, without its consent, be deprived of its equal representation in the Senate.

Article VI

The Government established by this Constitution is the successor of the Provisional Government of the Confederate States of America, and all laws passed by the latter shall continue in force until the same shall be repealed or modified; and all the officers appointed by the same shall remain in office until their successors are appointed and qualified or the offices abolished.

All Debts contracted and Engagements entered into, before the Adoption of this Constitution, shall be as valid against the [United] *Confederate* States under this Constitution, as under the [Confederation] *Provisional Government.*

This Constitution and the Laws of the [United] *Confederate* States [which shall be] made in Pursuance thereof; and all Treaties made, or which shall be made, under the authority of the [United] *Confederate* States, shall be the supreme Law of the Land; and the Judges in every State shall be bound thereby, any Thing in the Constitution or Laws of any State to the Contrary notwithstanding.

The Senators and Representatives before mentioned, and the Members of the several State Legislatures, and all executive and judicial Officers, both of the [United] *Confederate* States and of the several States, shall be bound by Oath or Affirmation, to support this Constitution; but no religious Test shall ever be required as a Qualification to any Office or public Trust under the [United] *Confederate* States.

The enumeration in the Constitution, of certain rights, shall not be construed to deny or disparage others retained by the people *of the several States.*

The powers not delegated to the [United] *Confederate* States by the Constitution, nor prohibited by it to the States, are reserved to the States respectively, or to the people.

Article VII

The Ratification of the Conventions of [nine] *five* States shall be sufficient for the Establishment of this Constitution between the States so ratifying the same.

When five States shall have ratified this Constitution, in the manner before specified, the Congress under the Provisional Constitution shall prescribe the time for holding the election of President and Vice President; and for the meeting of the electoral college; and for counting the votes and inaugurating the President. They shall also prescribe the time for holding the first election of members of Congress under this Constitution, and the time for assembling the same. Until the assembling of such Congress, the Congress under the Provisional Constitution shall continue to exercise the legislative powers granted them, not extending beyond the time limited by the Constitution of the Provisional Government.

[Done in Convention by the Unanimous Consent of the States present, the Seventeenth Day of September in the Year of our Lord one thousand seven hundred and eighty-seven and of the Independence of the United States of America the Twelfth.] *Adopted unanimously March 11, 1861.*

SENECA FALLS RESOLUTION

In 1848, leaders of the nascent women's movement took a critical step by calling a convention in Seneca Falls in upstate New York. Organized by Elizabeth Cady Stanton and Lucretia Mott, who had met at the World's Anti-Slavery Convention in 1840, and joined by a few sympathetic male abolitionists, the convention outlined for the first time a coherent program for women's equality. The delegates at Seneca Falls based their program on republican ideology, adopting resolutions patterned directly on the Declaration of Independence.

WHEREAS, The great precept of nature is conceded to be, that "man shall pursue his own true and substantial happiness." Blackstone in his Commentaries remarks, that this law of Nature being coeval with mankind, and dictated by God himself, is of course superior in obligation to any other. It is binding over all the globe, in all countries and at all times; no human laws are of any validity if contrary to this, and such of them as are valid, derive all their force, and all their validity, and all their authority, mediately and immediately, from this original; therefore,

Resolved, That such laws as conflict, in any way, with the true and substantial happiness of woman, are contrary to the great precept of nature and of no validity, for this is "superior in obligation to any other."

Resolved, That all laws which prevent woman from occupying such a station in society as her conscience shall dictate, or which place her in a position inferior to that of man, are contrary to the great precept of nature, and therefore of no force or authority.

Resolved, That woman is man's equal — was intended to be so by the Creator, and the highest good of the race demands that she should be recognized as such.

Resolved, That the women of this country ought to be enlightened in regard to the laws under which they live, that they may no longer publish their degradation by declaring themselves satisfied with their present position, nor their ignorance, by asserting that they have all the rights they want.

Resolved, That inasmuch as man, while claiming for himself intellectual superiority, does accord to woman moral superiority, it is pre-eminently his duty to encourage her to speak and teach, as she has an opportunity, in all religious assemblies.

Resolved, That the same amount of virtue, delicacy, and refinement of behavior that is required of woman in the social state, should also be required of man, and the same transgressions should be visited with equal severity on both man and woman.

Resolved, That the objection of indelicacy and impropriety, which is so often brought against woman when she addresses a public audience, comes with a very ill-grace from those who encourage, by their attendance, her appearance on the stage, in the concert, or in feats of the circus.

Resolved, That woman has too long rested satisfied in the circumscribed limits which corrupt customs and a perverted application of the scriptures have marked out for her, and that it is time she should move in the enlarged sphere which her great Creator has assigned her.

Resolved, That it is the duty of the women of this country to secure to themselves their sacred right to the elective franchise.

Resolved, That the equality of human rights results necessarily from the fact of the identity of the race in capabilities and responsibilities.

Resolved, therefore, That, being invested by the Creator with the same capabilities, and the same consciousness of responsibility for their exercise, it is demonstrably the right and duty of woman, equally with man, to promote every righteous cause by every righteous means, and especially in regard to the great subjects of morals and religion, it is self-evidently her right to participate with her brother in teaching them, both in private and in public, by writing and by speaking, by any instrumentalities proper to be used, and many assemblies proper to be held; and this being a self-evident truth growing out of the divinely implanted principles of human nature, any custom or authority adverse to it, whether modern or wearing the hoary sanction of antiquity, is to be regarded as a self-evident falsehood, and at war with mankind.

Resolved, That the speedy success of our cause depends upon the zealous and untiring efforts of both men and women, for the overthrow of the monopoly of the pulpit, and for the securing to woman an equal participation with men in the various trades, professions, and commerce.

"I HAVE A DREAM," MARTIN LUTHER KING JR.

On August 28, 1963, about 250,000 black and white demonstrators—the largest civil rights demonstration up to that time—gathered at the Lincoln Memorial in Washington, D.C. For many people, the speech that the Reverend Martin Luther King Jr. delivered was the high point of the March on Washington. King's eloquence and the sight of blacks and whites marching solemnly together did more than any other event to make the civil rights movement acceptable to white Americans.

Five score years ago, a great American, in whose symbolic shadow we stand signed the Emancipation Proclamation. This momentous decree came as a great beacon light of hope to millions of Negro slaves who had been seared in the flames of withering injustice. It came as a joyous daybreak to end the long night of captivity.

But one hundred years later, we must face the tragic fact that the Negro is still not free. One hundred years later, the life of the Negro is still sadly crippled by the manacles of segregation and the chains of discrimination. One hundred years later, the Negro lives on a lonely island of poverty in the midst of a vast ocean of material prosperity. One hundred years later, the Negro is still languishing in the corners of American society and finds himself an exile in his own land. So we have come here today to dramatize an appalling condition.

In a sense we have come to our nation's capital to cash a check. When the architects of our republic wrote the magnificent words of the Constitution and the Declaration of Independence, they were signing a promissory note to which every American was to fall heir. This note was a promise that all men would be guaranteed the inalienable rights of life, liberty, and the pursuit of happiness.

It is obvious today that America has defaulted on this promissory note insofar as her citizens of color are concerned. Instead of honoring this sacred obligation, America has given the Negro people a bad check which has come back marked "insufficient funds." But we refuse to believe that the bank of justice is bankrupt. We refuse to believe that there are insufficient funds in the great vaults of opportunity of this nation. So we have come to cash this check—a check that will give us upon demand the riches of freedom and the security of justice. We have also come to this hallowed spot to remind America of the fierce urgency of now. This is no time to engage in the luxury of cooling off or to take the tranquilizing drug of gradualism. Now

is the time to rise from the dark and desolate valley of segregation to the sunlit path of racial justice. Now is the time to open the doors of opportunity to all of God's children. Now is the time to lift our nation from the quicksands of racial injustice to the solid rock of brotherhood.

It would be fatal for the nation to overlook the urgency of the moment and to underestimate the determination of the Negro. This sweltering summer of the Negro's legitimate discontent will not pass until there is an invigorating autumn of freedom and equality. Nineteen sixty-three is not an end, but a beginning. Those who hope that the Negro needed to blow off steam and will now be content will have a rude awakening if the nation returns to business as usual. There will be neither rest nor tranquility in America until the Negro is granted his citizenship rights. The whirlwinds of revolt will continue to shake the foundations of our nation until the bright day of justice emerges.

But there is something that I must say to my people who stand on the warm threshold which leads into the palace of justice. In the process of gaining our rightful place we must not be guilty of wrongful deeds. Let us not seek to satisfy our thirst for freedom by drinking from the cup of bitterness and hatred.

We must forever conduct our struggle on the high plane of dignity and discipline. We must not allow our creative protest to degenerate into physical violence. Again and again we must rise to the majestic heights of meeting physical force with soul force. The marvelous new militancy which has engulfed the Negro community must not lead us to distrust of all white people, for many of our white brothers, as evidenced by their presence here today, have come to realize that their destiny is tied up with our destiny and their freedom is inextricably bound to our freedom. We cannot walk alone.

And as we walk, we must make the pledge that we shall march ahead. We cannot turn back. There are those who are asking the devotees of civil rights, "When will you be satisfied?" We can never be satisfied as long as our bodies, heavy with the fatigue of travel, cannot gain lodging in the motels of the highways and the hotels of the cities. We cannot be satisfied as long as the Negro's basic mobility is from a smaller ghetto to a larger one. We can never be satisfied as long as a Negro in Mississippi cannot vote and a Negro in New York believes he has nothing for which to vote. No, no, we are not satisfied, and we will not be satisfied until justice rolls down like waters and righteousness like a mighty stream.

I am not unmindful that some of you have come here out of great trials and tribulations. Some of you have come fresh from narrow cells. Some of you have come from areas where your quest for freedom left you battered by the storms of persecution and staggered by the winds of police brutality. You have been the veterans of creative suffering. Continue to work with the faith that unearned suffering is redemptive.

Go back to Mississippi, go back to Alabama, go back to Georgia, go back to Louisiana, go back to the slums and ghettos of our northern cities, knowing that somehow this situation can and will be changed. Let us not wallow in the valley of despair.

I say to you today, my friends, that in spite of the difficulties and frustrations of the moment, I still have a dream. It is a dream deeply rooted in the American dream.

I have a dream that one day this nation will rise up and live out the true meaning of its creed: "We hold these truths to be self-evident: that all men are created equal."

I have a dream that one day on the red hills of Georgia the sons of former slaves and the sons of former slaveowners will be able to sit down together at a table of brotherhood.

I have a dream that one day even the state of Mississippi, a desert state, sweltering with the heat of injustice and oppression, will be transformed into an oasis of freedom and justice.

I have a dream that my four children will one day live in a nation where they will not be judged by the color of their skin but by the content of their character.

I have a dream today.

I have a dream that one day the state of Alabama, whose governor's lips are presently dripping with the words of interposition and nullification, will be transformed into a situation where little black boys and black girls will be able to join hands with little white boys and white girls and walk together as sisters and brothers.

I have a dream today.

I have a dream that one day every valley shall be exalted, every hill and mountain shall be made low, the rough places will be made plain, and the crooked places will be made straight, and the glory of the Lord shall be revealed, and all flesh shall see it together.

This is our hope. This is the faith with which I return to the South. With this faith we will be able to hew out of the mountain of despair a stone of hope. With this faith we will be able to transform the jangling discords of our nation into a beautiful symphony of brotherhood. With this faith we will be able to work together, to pray together, to struggle together, to go to jail together, to stand up for freedom together, knowing that we will be free one day.

This will be the day when all of God's children will be able to sing with a new meaning, "My country, 'tis of thee, sweet land of liberty, of thee I sing. Land where my fathers died, land of the pilgrim's pride, from every mountainside, let freedom ring."

And if America is to be a great nation this must become true. So let freedom ring from the prodigious hilltops of New Hampshire. Let freedom ring from the mighty mountains of New York. Let freedom ring from the heightening Alleghenies of Pennsylvania!

Let freedom ring from the snowcapped Rockies of Colorado!

Let freedom ring from the curvaceous peaks of California!

But not only that; let freedom ring from Stone Mountain of Georgia!

Let freedom ring from Lookout Mountain of Tennessee!

Let freedom ring from every hill and every molehill of Mississippi. From every mountainside, let freedom ring.

When we let freedom ring, when we let it ring from every village and every hamlet, from every state and every city, we will be able to speed up that day when all of God's children, black men and white men, Jews and Gentiles, Protestants and Catholics, will be able to join hands and sing in the words of the old Negro spiritual, "Free at last! free at last! thank God Almighty, we are free at last!"

U.S. POLITICS AND GOVERNMENT

PRESIDENTIAL ELECTIONS

Year	Candidates	Parties	Popular Vote	Percentage of Popular Vote	Electoral Vote	Percentage of Voter Participation
1789	**GEORGE WASHINGTON (Va.)***				69	
	John Adams				34	
	Others				35	
1792	**GEORGE WASHINGTON (Va.)**				132	
	John Adams				77	
	George Clinton				50	
	Others				5	
1796	**JOHN ADAMS (Mass.)**	Federalist			71	
	Thomas Jefferson	Democratic-Republican			68	
	Thomas Pinckney	Federalist			59	
	Aaron Burr	Dem.-Rep.			30	
	Others				48	
1800	**THOMAS JEFFERSON (Va.)**	Dem.-Rep.			73	
	Aaron Burr	Dem.-Rep.			73	
	John Adams	Federalist			65	
	C. C. Pinckney	Federalist			64	
	John Jay	Federalist			1	
1804	**THOMAS JEFFERSON (Va.)**	Dem.-Rep.			162	
	C. C. Pinckney	Federalist			14	
1808	**JAMES MADISON (Va.)**	Dem.-Rep.			122	
	C. C. Pinckney	Federalist			47	
	George Clinton	Dem.-Rep.			6	
1812	**JAMES MADISON (Va.)**	Dem.-Rep.			128	
	De Witt Clinton	Federalist			89	
1816	**JAMES MONROE (Va.)**	Dem.-Rep.			183	
	Rufus King	Federalist			34	
1820	**JAMES MONROE (Va.)**	Dem.-Rep.			231	
	John Quincy Adams	Dem.-Rep.			1	
1824	**JOHN Q. ADAMS (Mass.)**	Dem.-Rep.	108,740	30.5	84	26.9
	Andrew Jackson	Dem.-Rep.	153,544	43.1	99	
	William H. Crawford	Dem.-Rep.	46,618	13.1	41	
	Henry Clay	Dem.-Rep.	47,136	13.2	37	
1828	**ANDREW JACKSON (Tenn.)**	Democratic	647,286	56.0	178	57.6
	John Quincy Adams	National Republican	508,064	44.0	83	

*State of residence when elected president.

Year	Candidates	Parties	Popular Vote	Percentage of Popular Vote	Electoral Vote	Percentage of Voter Participation
1832	**ANDREW JACKSON (Tenn.)**	Democratic	687,502	55.0	219	55.4
	Henry Clay	National Republican	530,189	42.4	49	
	John Floyd	Independent			11	
	William Wirt	Anti-Mason	33,108	2.6	7	
1836	**MARTIN VAN BUREN (N.Y.)**	Democratic	765,483	50.9	170	57.8
	W. H. Harrison	Whig			73	
	Hugh L. White	Whig	739,795	49.1	26	
	Daniel Webster	Whig			14	
	W. P. Magnum	Independent			11	
1840	**WILLIAM H. HARRISON (Ohio)**	Whig	1,274,624	53.1	234	80.2
	Martin Van Buren	Democratic	1,127,781	46.9	60	
	J. G. Birney	Liberty	7,069		—	
1844	**JAMES K. POLK (Tenn.)**	Democratic	1,338,464	49.6	170	78.9
	Henry Clay	Whig	1,300,097	48.1	105	
	J. G. Birney	Liberty	62,300	2.3	—	
1848	**ZACHARY TAYLOR (La.)**	Whig	1,360,967	47.4	163	72.7
	Lewis Cass	Democratic	1,222,342	42.5	127	
	Martin Van Buren	Free-Soil	291,263	10.1	—	
1852	**FRANKLIN PIERCE (N.H.)**	Democratic	1,601,117	50.9	254	69.6
	Winfield Scott	Whig	1,385,453	44.1	42	
	John P. Hale	Free-Soil	155,825	5.0	—	
1856	**JAMES BUCHANAN (Pa.)**	Democratic	1,832,995	45.3	174	78.9
	John C. Frémont	Republican	1,339,932	33.1	114	
	Millard Fillmore	American	871,731	21.6	8	
1860	**ABRAHAM LINCOLN (Ill.)**	Republican	1,865,593	39.8	180	81.2
	Stephen A. Douglas	Democratic	1,382,713	29.5	12	
	John C. Breckinridge	Democratic	848,356	18.1	72	
	John Bell	Union	592,906	12.6	39	
1864	**ABRAHAM LINCOLN (Ill.)**	Republican	2,206,938	55.0	212	73.8
	George B. McClellan	Democratic	1,803,787	45.0	21	
1868	**ULYSSES S. GRANT (Ill.)**	Republican	3,012,833	52.7	214	78.1
	Horatio Seymour	Democratic	2,703,249	47.3	80	
1872	**ULYSSES S. GRANT (Ill.)**	Republican	3,597,132	55.6	286	71.3
	Horace Greeley	Democratic; Liberal Republican	2,834,125	43.9	66	
1876	**RUTHERFORD B. HAYES (Ohio)**	Republican	4,036,572	48.0	185	81.8
	Samuel J. Tilden	Democratic	4,284,020	51.0	184	
1880	**JAMES A. GARFIELD (Ohio)**	Republican	4,454,416	48.5	214	79.4
	Winfield S. Hancock	Democratic	4,444,952	48.1	155	
1884	**GROVER CLEVELAND (N.Y.)**	Democratic	4,879,507	48.5	219	77.5
	James G. Blaine	Republican	4,850,293	48.2	182	
1888	**BENJAMIN HARRISON (Ind.)**	Republican	5,439,853	47.9	233	79.3
	Grover Cleveland	Democratic	5,540,309	48.6	168	
1892	**GROVER CLEVELAND (N.Y.)**	Democratic	5,555,426	46.1	277	74.7
	Benjamin Harrison	Republican	5,182,690	43.0	145	
	James B. Weaver	People's	1,029,846	8.5	22	

Year	Candidates	Parties	Popular Vote	Percentage of Popular Vote	Electoral Vote	Percentage of Voter Participation
1896	**WILLIAM McKINLEY (Ohio)**	Republican	7,104,779	51.1	271	79.3
	William J. Bryan	Democratic-People's	6,502,925	47.7	176	
1900	**WILLIAM McKINLEY (Ohio)**	Republican	7,207,923	51.7	292	73.2
	William J. Bryan	Dem.-Populist	6,358,133	45.5	155	
1904	**THEODORE ROOSEVELT (N.Y.)**	Republican	7,623,486	57.9	336	65.2
	Alton B. Parker	Democratic	5,077,911	37.6	140	
	Eugene V. Debs	Socialist	402,283	3.0	—	
1908	**WILLIAM H. TAFT (Ohio)**	Republican	7,678,908	51.6	321	65.4
	William J. Bryan	Democratic	6,409,104	43.1	162	
	Eugene V. Debs	Socialist	420,793	2.8	—	
1912	**WOODROW WILSON (N.J.)**	Democratic	6,293,454	41.9	435	58.8
	Theodore Roosevelt	Progressive	4,119,538	27.4	88	
	William H. Taft	Republican	3,484,980	23.2	8	
	Eugene V. Debs	Socialist	900,672	6.1	—	
1916	**WOODROW WILSON (N.J.)**	Democratic	9,129,606	49.4	277	61.6
	Charles E. Hughes	Republican	8,538,221	46.2	254	
	A. L. Benson	Socialist	585,113	3.2	—	
1920	**WARREN G. HARDING (Ohio)**	Republican	16,143,407	60.5	404	49.2
	James M. Cox	Democratic	9,130,328	34.2	127	
	Eugene V. Debs	Socialist	919,799	3.4	—	
1924	**CALVIN COOLIDGE (Mass.)**	Republican	15,725,016	54.0	382	48.9
	John W. Davis	Democratic	8,386,503	28.8	136	
	Robert M. LaFollette	Progressive	4,822,856	16.6	13	
1928	**HERBERT HOOVER (Calif.)**	Republican	21,391,381	58.2	444	56.9
	Alfred E. Smith	Democratic	15,016,443	40.9	87	
	Norman Thomas	Socialist	267,835	0.7	—	
1932	**FRANKLIN D. ROOSEVELT (N.Y.)**	Democratic	22,809,638	57.4	472	56.9
	Herbert Hoover	Republican	15,758,901	39.7	59	
	Norman Thomas	Socialist	881,951	2.2	—	
1936	**FRANKLIN D. ROOSEVELT (N.Y.)**	Democratic	27,751,597	60.8	523	61.0
	Alfred M. Landon	Republican	16,679,583	36.5	8	
	William Lemke	Union	882,479	1.9	—	
1940	**FRANKLIN D. ROOSEVELT (N.Y.)**	Democratic	27,244,160	54.8	449	62.5
	Wendell Willkie	Republican	22,305,198	44.8	82	
1944	**FRANKLIN D. ROOSEVELT (N.Y.)**	Democratic	25,602,504	53.5	432	55.9
	Thomas E. Dewey	Republican	22,006,285	46.0	99	
1948	**HARRY S. TRUMAN (Mo.)**	Democratic	24,105,695	49.5	303	53.0
	Thomas E. Dewey	Republican	21,969,170	45.1	189	
	J. Strom Thurmond	State-Rights Democratic	1,169,021	2.4	38	
	Henry A. Wallace	Progressive	1,156,103	2.4	—	
1952	**DWIGHT D. EISENHOWER (N.Y.)**	Republican	33,936,252	55.1	442	63.3
	Adlai Stevenson	Democratic	27,314,992	44.4	89	
1956	**DWIGHT D. EISENHOWER (N.Y.)**	Republican	35,575,420	57.6	457	60.6
	Adlai Stevenson	Democratic	26,033,066	42.1	73	
	Other	—	—	—	1	

Year	Candidates	Parties	Popular Vote	Percentage of Popular Vote	Electoral Vote	Percentage of Voter Participation
1960	**JOHN F. KENNEDY (Mass.)**	Democratic	34,227,096	49.9	303	62.8
	Richard M. Nixon	Republican	34,108,546	49.6	219	
	Other	—	—		15	
1964	**LYNDON B. JOHNSON (Tex.)**	Democratic	43,126,506	61.1	486	61.7
	Barry M. Goldwater	Republican	27,176,799	38.5	52	
1968	**RICHARD M. NIXON (N.Y.)**	Republican	31,770,237	43.4	301	60.9
	Hubert H. Humphrey	Democratic	31,270,533	42.7	191	
	George Wallace	American Indep.	9,906,141	13.5	46	
1972	**RICHARD M. NIXON (N.Y.)**	Republican	47,169,911	60.7	520	55.2
	George S. McGovern	Democratic	29,170,383	37.5	17	
	Other	—	—		1	
1976	**JIMMY CARTER (Ga.)**	Democratic	40,828,587	50.0	297	53.5
	Gerald R. Ford	Republican	39,147,613	47.9	241	
	Other	—	1,575,459	2.1	—	
1980	**RONALD REAGAN (Calif.)**	Republican	43,901,812	50.7	489	54.0
	Jimmy Carter	Democratic	35,483,820	41.0	49	
	John B. Anderson	Independent	5,719,722	6.6	—	
	Ed Clark	Libertarian	921,188	1.1	—	
1984	**RONALD REAGAN (Calif.)**	Republican	54,455,075	59.0	525	53.1
	Walter Mondale	Democratic	37,577,185	41.0	13	
1988	**GEORGE BUSH (Texas)**	Republican	47,946,422	54.0	426	50.2
	Michael S. Dukakis	Democratic	41,016,429	46.0	112	
1992	**WILLIAM J. CLINTON (Ark.)**	Democratic	44,908,254	42.3	370	55.9
	George Bush	Republican	39,102,282	37.4	168	
	H. Ross Perot	Independent	19,721,433	18.9	—	
1996	**WILLIAM J. CLINTON (Ark.)**	Democratic	47,401,185	49.2	379	49.0
	Robert Dole	Republican	39,197,469	40.7	159	
	H. Ross Perot	Independent	8,085,294	8.4	—	
2000	**GEORGE W. BUSH (Texas)**	Republican	50,456,062	47.8	271	51.2
	Al Gore	Democratic	50,996,862	48.4	267	
	Ralph Nader	Green Party	2,858,843	2.7	—	
	Patrick J. Buchanan	—	438,760	.4	—	

PRESIDENTS, VICE PRESIDENTS, AND SECRETARIES OF STATE

The Washington Administration (1789–1797)

Vice President	John Adams	1789–1797
Secretary of State	Thomas Jefferson	1789–1793
	Edmund Randolph	1794–1795
	Timothy Pickering	1795–1797

The John Adams Administration (1797–1801)

Vice President	Thomas Jefferson	1797–1801
Secretary of State	Timothy Pickering	1797–1800
	John Marshall	1800–1801

The Jefferson Administration (1801–1809)

Vice President	Aaron Burr	1801–1805
	George Clinton	1805–1809
Secretary of State	James Madison	1801–1809

The Madison Administration (1809–1817)

Vice President	George Clinton	1809–1813
	Elbridge Gerry	1813–1817
Secretary of State	Robert Smith	1809–1811
	James Monroe	1811–1817

The Monroe Administration (1817–1825)

Vice President	Daniel Tompkins	1817–1825
Secretary of State	John Quincy Adams	1817–1825

The John Quincy Adams Administration (1825–1829)

Vice President	John C. Calhoun	1825–1829
Secretary of State	Henry Clay	1825–1829

The Jackson Administration (1829–1837)

Vice President	John C. Calhoun	1829–1833
	Martin Van Buren	1833–1837
Secretary of State	Martin Van Buren	1829–1831
	Edward Livingston	1831–1833
	Louis McLane	1833–1834
	John Forsyth	1834–1837

The Van Buren Administration (1837–1841)

Vice President	Richard M. Johnson	1837–1841
Secretary of State	John Forsyth	1837–1841

The William Harrison Administration (1841)

Vice President	John Tyler	1841
Secretary of State	Daniel Webster	1841

The Tyler Administration (1841–1845)

Vice President	None	
Secretary of State	Daniel Webster	1841–1843
	Hugh S. Legaré	1843
	Abel P. Upshur	1843–1844
	John C. Calhoun	1844–1845

The Polk Administration (1845–1849)

Vice President	George M. Dallas	1845–1849
Secretary of State	James Buchanan	1845–1849

The Taylor Administration (1849–1850)

Vice President	Millard Fillmore	1849–1850
Secretary of State	John M. Clayton	1849–1850

The Fillmore Administration (1850–1853)

Vice President	None	
Secretary of State	Daniel Webster	1850–1852
	Edward Everett	1852–1853

The Pierce Administration (1853–1857)

Vice President	William R. King	1853–1857
Secretary of State	William L. Marcy	1853–1857

The Buchanan Administration (1857–1861)

Vice President	John C. Breckinridge	1857–1861
Secretary of State	Lewis Cass	1857–1860
	Jeremiah S. Black	1860–1861

The Lincoln Administration (1861–1865)

Vice President	Hannibal Hamlin	1861–1865
	Andrew Johnson	1865
Secretary of State	William H. Seward	1861–1865

The Andrew Johnson Administration (1865–1869)

Vice President	None	
Secretary of State	William H. Seward	1865–1869

The Grant Administration (1869–1877)

Vice President	Schuyler Colfax	1869–1873
	Henry Wilson	1873–1877
Secretary of State	Elihu B. Washburne	1869
	Hamilton Fish	1869–1877

The Hayes Administration (1877–1881)

Vice President	William A. Wheeler	1877–1881
Secretary of State	William M. Evarts	1877–1881

The Garfield Administration (1881)

Vice President	Chester A. Arthur	1881
Secretary of State	James G. Blaine	1881

The Arthur Administration (1881–1885)

Vice President	None	
Secretary of State	F. T. Frelinghuysen	1881–1885

The Cleveland Administration (1885–1889)

Vice President	Thomas A. Hendricks	1885–1889
Secretary of State	Thomas F. Bayard	1885–1889

The Benjamin Harrison Administration (1889–1893)

Vice President	Levi P. Morton	1889–1893
Secretary of State	James G. Blaine	1889–1892
	John W. Foster	1892–1893

The Cleveland Administration (1893–1897)

Vice President	Adlai E. Stevenson	1893–1897
Secretary of State	Walter Q. Gresham	1893–1895
	Richard Olney	1895–1897

The McKinley Administration (1897–1901)

Vice President	Garret A. Hobart	1897–1901
	Theodore Roosevelt	1901
Secretary of State	John Sherman	1897–1898
	William R. Day	1898
	John Hay	1898–1901

The Theodore Roosevelt Administration (1901–1909)

Vice President	Charles Fairbanks	1905–1909
Secretary of State	John Hay	1901–1905
	Elihu Root	1905–1909
	Robert Bacon	1909

The Taft Administration (1909–1913)

Vice President	James S. Sherman	1909–1913
Secretary of State	Philander C. Knox	1909–1913

The Wilson Administration (1913–1921)

Vice President	Thomas R. Marshall	1913–1921
Secretary of State	William J. Bryan	1913–1915
	Robert Lansing	1915–1920
	Bainbridge Colby	1920–1921

The Harding Administration (1921–1923)

Vice President	Calvin Coolidge	1921–1923
Secretary of State	Charles E. Hughes	1921–1923

The Coolidge Administration (1923–1929)

Vice President	Charles G. Dawes	1925–1929
Secretary of State	Charles E. Hughes	1923–1925
	Frank B. Kellogg	1925–1929

The Hoover Administration (1929–1933)

Vice President	Charles Curtis	1929–1933
Secretary of State	Henry L. Stimson	1929–1933

The Franklin D. Roosevelt Administration (1933–1945)

Vice President	John Nance Garner	1933–1941
	Henry A. Wallace	1941–1945
	Harry S. Truman	1945
Secretary of State	Cordell Hull	1933–1944
	Edward R. Stettinius Jr.	1944–1945

The Truman Administration (1945–1953)

Vice President	Alben W. Barkley	1949–1953
Secretary of State	Edward R. Stettinius Jr.	1945
	James F. Byrnes	1945–1947
	George C. Marshall	1947–1949
	Dean G. Acheson	1949–1953

The Eisenhower Administration (1953–1961)

Vice President	Richard M. Nixon	1953–1961
Secretary of State	John Foster Dulles	1953–1959
	Christian A. Herter	1959–1961

The Kennedy Administration (1961–1963)

Vice President	Lyndon B. Johnson	1961–1963
Secretary of State	Dean Rusk	1961–1963

The Lyndon Johnson Administration (1963–1969)

Vice President	Hubert H. Humphrey	1965–1969
Secretary of State	Dean Rusk	1963–1969

The Nixon Administration (1969–1974)

Vice President	Spiro T. Agnew	1969–1973
	Gerald R. Ford	1973–1974
Secretary of State	William P. Rogers	1969–1973
	Henry A. Kissinger	1973–1974

The Ford Administration (1974–1977)

Vice President	Nelson A. Rockefeller	1974–1977
Secretary of State	Henry A. Kissinger	1974–1977

The Carter Administration (1977–1981)

Vice President	Walter F. Mondale	1977–1981
Secretary of State	Cyrus R. Vance	1977–1980
	Edmund Muskie	1980–1981

The Reagan Administration (1981–1989)

Vice President	George H. W. Bush	1981–1989
Secretary of State	Alexander M. Haig	1981–1982
	George P. Shultz	1982–1989

The George H. W. Bush Administration (1989–1993)

Vice President	J. Danforth Quayle	1989–1993
Secretary of State	James A. Baker III	1989–1992
	Lawrence S. Eagleburger	1992–1993

The Clinton Administration (1993–2001)

Vice President	Albert Gore	1993–2001
Secretary of State	Warren M. Christopher	1993–1997
	Madeleine K. Albright	1997–2001

The George W. Bush Administration (2001–)

Vice President	Dick Cheney	2001–
Secretary of State	Colin Powell	2001–

ADMISSION OF STATES TO THE UNION

State	Date of Admission
Delaware	December 7, 1787
Pennsylvania	December 12, 1787
New Jersey	December 18, 1787
Georgia	January 2, 1788
Connecticut	January 9, 1788
Massachusetts	February 6, 1788
Maryland	April 28, 1788
South Carolina	May 23, 1788
New Hampshire	June 21, 1788
Virginia	June 25, 1788
New York	July 26, 1788
North Carolina	November 21, 1789
Rhode Island	May 29, 1790
Vermont	March 4, 1791
Kentucky	June 1, 1792
Tennessee	June 1, 1796
Ohio	March 1, 1803
Louisiana	April 30, 1812
Indiana	December 11, 1816
Mississippi	December 10, 1817
Illinois	December 3, 1818
Alabama	December 14, 1819
Maine	March 15, 1820
Missouri	August 10, 1821
Arkansas	June 15, 1836

State	Date of Admission
Michigan	January 16, 1837
Florida	March 3, 1845
Texas	December 29, 1845
Iowa	December 28, 1846
Wisconsin	May 29, 1848
California	September 9, 1850
Minnesota	May 11, 1858
Oregon	February 14, 1859
Kansas	January 29, 1861
West Virginia	June 19, 1863
Nevada	October 31, 1864
Nebraska	March 1, 1867
Colorado	August 1, 1876
North Dakota	November 2, 1889
South Dakota	November 2, 1889
Montana	November 8, 1889
Washington	November 11, 1889
Idaho	July 3, 1890
Wyoming	July 10, 1890
Utah	January 4, 1896
Oklahoma	November 16, 1907
New Mexico	January 6, 1912
Arizona	February 14, 1912
Alaska	January 3, 1959
Hawaii	August 21, 1959

SUPREME COURT JUSTICES

Name	Service	Appointed by
John Jay*	1789–1795	Washington
James Wilson	1789–1798	Washington
John Blair	1789–1796	Washington
John Rutledge	1790–1791	Washington
William Cushing	1790–1810	Washington
James Iredell	1790–1799	Washington
Thomas Johnson	1791–1793	Washington
William Paterson	1793–1806	Washington
John Rutledge†	1795	Washington
Samuel Chase	1796–1811	Washington
Oliver Ellsworth	1796–1799	Washington
Bushrod Washington	1798–1829	J. Adams
Alfred Moore	1799–1804	J. Adams
John Marshall	1801–1835	J. Adams
William Johnson	1804–1834	Jefferson
Henry B. Livingston	1806–1823	Jefferson
Thomas Todd	1807–1826	Jefferson
Gabriel Duval	1811–1836	Madison
Joseph Story	1811–1845	Madison
Smith Thompson	1823–1843	Monroe
Robert Trimble	1826–1828	J. Q. Adams
John McLean	1829–1861	Jackson
Henry Baldwin	1830–1844	Jackson
James M. Wayne	1835–1867	Jackson
Roger B. Taney	1836–1864	Jackson
Philip P. Barbour	1836–1841	Jackson
John Catron	1837–1865	Van Buren
John McKinley	1837–1852	Van Buren
Peter V. Daniel	1841–1860	Van Buren
Samuel Nelson	1845–1872	Tyler
Levi Woodbury	1845–1851	Polk
Robert C. Grier	1846–1870	Polk
Benjamin R. Curtis	1851–1857	Fillmore
John A. Campbell	1853–1861	Pierce
Nathan Clifford	1858–1881	Buchanan
Noah H. Swayne	1862–1881	Lincoln
Samuel F. Miller	1862–1890	Lincoln

*Chief Justices appear in bold type.
†Acting Chief Justice; Senate refused to confirm appointment.

Name	Service	Appointed by
David Davis	1862–1877	Lincoln
Stephen J. Field	1863–1897	Lincoln
Salmon P. Chase	1864–1873	Lincoln
William Strong	1870–1880	Grant
Joseph P. Bradley	1870–1892	Grant
Ward Hunt	1873–1882	Grant
Morrison R. Waite	1874–1888	Grant
John M. Harlan	1877–1911	Hayes
William B. Woods	1880–1887	Hayes
Stanley Matthews	1881–1889	Garfield
Horace Gray	1882–1902	Arthur
Samuel Blatchford	1882–1893	Arthur
Lucious Q. C. Lamar	1888–1893	Cleveland
Melville W. Fuller	1888–1910	Cleveland
David J. Brewer	1889–1910	B. Harrison
Henry B. Brown	1890–1906	B. Harrison
George Shiras	1892–1903	B. Harrison
Howell E. Jackson	1893–1895	B. Harrison
Edward D. White	1894–1910	Cleveland
Rufus W. Peckham	1896–1909	Cleveland
Joseph McKenna	1898–1925	McKinley
Oliver W. Holmes	1902–1932	T. Roosevelt
William R. Day	1903–1922	T. Roosevelt
William H. Moody	1906–1910	T. Roosevelt
Horace H. Lurton	1910–1914	Taft
Charles E. Hughes	1910–1916	Taft
Willis Van Devanter	1910–1937	Taft
Joseph R. Lamar	1911–1916	Taft
Edward D. White	1910–1921	Taft
Mahlon Pitney	1912–1922	Taft
James C. McReynolds	1914–1941	Wilson
Louis D. Brandeis	1916–1939	Wilson
John H. Clarke	1916–1922	Wilson
William H. Taft	1921–1930	Harding
George Sutherland	1922–1938	Harding

Name	Service	Appointed by
Pierce Butler	1923–1939	Harding
Edward T. Sanford	1923–1930	Harding
Harlan F. Stone	1925–1941	Coolidge
Charles E. Hughes	1930–1941	Hoover
Owen J. Roberts	1930–1945	Hoover
Benjamin N. Cardozo	1932–1938	Hoover
Hugo L. Black	1937–1971	F. Roosevelt
Stanley F. Reed	1938–1957	F. Roosevelt
Felix Frankfurter	1939–1962	F. Roosevelt
William O. Douglas	1939–1975	F. Roosevelt
Frank Murphy	1940–1949	F. Roosevelt
Harlan F. Stone	1941–1946	F. Roosevelt
James F. Byrnes	1941–1942	F. Roosevelt
Robert H. Jackson	1941–1954	F. Roosevelt
Wiley B. Rutledge	1943–1949	F. Roosevelt
Harold H. Burton	1945–1958	Truman
Frederick M. Vinson	1946–1953	Truman
Tom C. Clark	1949–1967	Truman
Sherman Minton	1949–1956	Truman
Earl Warren	1953–1969	Eisenhower
John Marshall Harlan	1955–1971	Eisenhower
William J. Brennan Jr.	1956–1990	Eisenhower
Charles E. Whittaker	1957–1962	Eisenhower
Potter Stewart	1958–1981	Eisenhower
Byron R. White	1962–1993	Kennedy
Arthur J. Goldberg	1962–1965	Kennedy
Abe Fortas	1965–1969	L. Johnson
Thurgood Marshall	1967–1991	L. Johnson
Warren E. Burger	1969–1986	Nixon
Harry A. Blackmun	1970–1994	Nixon
Lewis F. Powell Jr.	1972–1988	Nixon
William H. Rehnquist	1972–1986	Nixon
John Paul Stevens	1975–	Ford
Sandra Day O'Connor	1981–	Reagan
William H. Rehnquist	1986–	Reagan
Antonin Scalia	1986–	Reagan
Anthony M. Kennedy	1988–	Reagan
David H. Souter	1990–	Bush
Clarence Thomas	1991–	Bush
Ruth Bader Ginsburg	1993–	Clinton
Stephen Breyer	1994–	Clinton

SIGNIFICANT SUPREME COURT CASES

Marbury v. Madison (1803)

This case established the right of the Supreme Court to review the constitutionality of laws. The decision involved judicial appointments made during the last hours of the administration of President John Adams. Some commissions, including that of William Marbury, had not yet been delivered when President Thomas Jefferson took office. Infuriated by the last-minute nature of Adams's Federalist appointments, Jefferson refused to send the undelivered commissions out, and Marbury decided to sue. The Supreme Court, presided over by John Marshall, a Federalist who had assisted Adams in the judicial appointments, ruled that although Marbury's commission was valid and the new president should have delivered it, the Court could not compel him to do so. The Court based its reasoning on a finding that the grounds of Marbury's suit, resting in the Judiciary Act of 1789, were in conflict with the Constitution.

For the first time, the Court had overturned a national law on the grounds that it was unconstitutional. John Marshall had quietly established the concept of judicial review: The Supreme Court had given itself the authority to nullify acts of the other branches of the federal government. Although the Constitution provides for judicial review, the Court had not exercised this power before and did not use it again until 1857. It seems likely that if the Court had waited until 1857 to use this power, it would have been difficult to establish.

McCulloch v. Maryland (1819)

In 1816, Congress authorized the creation of a national bank. To protect its own banks from competition with a branch of the national bank in Baltimore, the state legislature of Maryland placed a tax of 2 percent on all notes issued by any bank operating in Maryland that was not chartered by the state. McCulloch, cashier of the Baltimore branch of the Bank of the United States, was convicted for refusing to pay the tax. Under the leadership of Chief Justice John Marshall, the Court ruled that the federal government had the power to establish a bank, even though that specific authority was not mentioned in the Constitution.

Marshall maintained that the authority could be reasonably implied from Article 1, section 8, which gives Congress the power to make all laws that are necessary and proper to execute the enumerated powers. Marshall also held that Maryland could not tax the national bank because in a conflict between federal and state laws, the federal law must take precedence. Thus he established the principles of implied powers and federal supremacy, both of which set a precedent for subsequent expansion of federal power at the expense of the states.

Scott v. Sandford (1857)

Dred Scott was a slave who sued for his own and his family's freedom on the grounds, that, with his master, he had traveled to and lived in free territory that did not allow slavery. When his case reached the Supreme Court, the justices saw an opportunity to settle once and for all the vexing question of slavery in the territories. The Court's decision in this case proved that it enjoyed no special immunity from the sectional and partisan passions of the time. Five of the nine justices were from the South and seven were Democrats.

Chief Justice Roger B. Taney hated Republicans and detested racial equality; his decision reflects those prejudices. He wrote an opinion not only declaring that Scott was still a slave but also claiming that the Constitution denied citizenship or rights to blacks, that Congress had no right to exclude slavery from the territories, and that the Missouri Compromise was unconstitutional. While southern Democrats gloated over this seven-to-two decision, sectional tensions were further inflamed and the young Republican Party's claim that a hostile "slave power" was conspiring to destroy northern liberties was given further credence. The decision brought the nation closer to civil war and is generally regarded as the worst decision ever rendered by the Supreme Court.

Butchers' Benevolent Association of New Orleans v. Crescent City Livestock Landing and Slaughterhouse Co. (1873)

The *Slaughterhouse* cases, as the cases docketed under the *Butchers'* title were known, were the first legal test of the Fourteenth Amendment. To cut down on cases of cholera believed to be caused by contaminated water, the state of Louisiana prohibited the slaughter of livestock in New Orleans except in one slaughterhouse, effectively giving that slaughterhouse a monopoly. Other New Orleans butchers claimed that the state had deprived them of their occupation without due process of law, thus violating the Fourteenth Amendment.

In a five-to-four decision, the Court upheld the Louisiana law, declaring that the Fourteenth Amendment protected only the rights of federal citizenship, like voting in federal elections and interstate travel. The federal government thus was not obliged to protect basic civil rights from violation by state governments. This decision would have significant implications for African Americans and their struggle for civil rights in the twentieth century.

United States v. E. C. Knight Co. (1895)

Also known as the *Sugar Trust* case, this was among the first cases to reveal the weakness of the Sherman Antitrust Act in the hands of a pro-business Supreme Court. In 1895, American Sugar Refining Company purchased four other sugar producers, including the E. C. Knight Company, and thus took control of more than 98 percent of the sugar refining in the United States. In an effort to limit monopoly, the government brought suit against all five of the companies for violating the Sherman Antitrust Act, which outlawed trusts and other business combinations in restraint of trade. The Court dismissed the suit, however, arguing that the law applied only to commerce and not to manufacturing, defining the latter as a local concern and not part of the interstate commerce that the government could regulate.

Plessy v. Ferguson (1896)

African American Homer Plessy challenged a Louisiana law that required segregation on trains passing through the state. After ensuring that the railroad and the conductor knew that he was of mixed race (Plessy appeared to be white but under the racial code of Louisiana was classified as "colored" because he was one-eighth black), he refused to move to the "colored only" section of the coach. The Court ruled against Plessy by a vote of seven to one, declaring that "separate but equal" facilities were permissible according to section 1 of the Fourteenth Amendment, which calls upon the states to provide "equal protection of the laws" to anyone within their jurisdiction. Although the case was viewed as relatively insignificant at the time, it cast a long shadow over several decades.

Initially, the decision was viewed as a victory for segregationists, but in the 1930s and 1940s civil rights advocates referred to the doctrine of "separate but

equal" in their efforts to end segregation. They argued that segregated institutions and accommodations were often *not* equal to those available to whites, and finally succeeded in overturning *Plessy* in *Brown v. Board of Education* in 1954 (see p. A-51).

Lochner v. New York (1905)

In this case, the Court ruled against a New York state law that prohibited employees from working in bakeries more than ten hours a day or sixty hours a week. The purpose of the law was to protect the health of workers, but the Court ruled that it was unconstitutional because it violated "freedom of contract" implicitly protected by the due process clause of the Fourteenth Amendment. Most of the justices believed strongly in a laissez-faire economic system that favored survival of the fittest. They felt that government protection of workers interfered with this system. In a dissenting opinion, Justice Oliver Wendell Holmes accused the majority of distorting the Constitution and of deciding the case on "an economic theory which a large part of the country does not entertain."

Muller v. Oregon (1908)

In 1905, Curt Muller, owner of a Portland, Oregon, laundry, demanded that one of his employees, Mrs. Elmer Gotcher, work more than the ten hours allowed as a maximum workday for women under Oregon law. Muller argued that the law violated his "freedom of contract" as established in prior Supreme Court decisions.

Progressive lawyer Louis D. Brandeis defended the Oregon law by arguing that a state could be justified in abridging freedom of contract when the health, safety, and welfare of workers was at issue. His innovative strategy drew on ninety-five pages of excerpts from factory and medical reports to substantiate his argument that there was a direct connection between long hours and the health of women and thus the health of the nation. In a unanimous decision, the Court upheld the Oregon law, but later generations of women fighting for equality would question the strategy of arguing that women's reproductive role entitled them to special treatment.

Schenck v. United States (1919)

During World War I, Charles Schenck and other members of the Socialist Party printed and mailed out flyers urging young men who were subject to the draft to oppose the war in Europe. In upholding the conviction of Schenck for publishing a pamphlet urging draft resistance, Justice Oliver Wendell Holmes established the "clear and present danger" test for freedom of speech. Such utterances as Schenck's during a time of national peril, Holmes wrote, could be considered the equivalent of shouting "Fire!" in a crowded theater. Congress had the right to protect the public against such an incitement to panic, the Court ruled in a unanimous decision. But the analogy was a false one. Schenck's pamphlet had little power to provoke a public firmly opposed to its message. Although Holmes later modified his position to state that the danger must relate to an immediate evil and a specific action, the "clear and present danger" test laid the groundwork for those who later sought to limit First Amendment freedoms.

Schechter Poultry Corp. v. United States (1935)

During the Great Depression, the National Industrial Recovery Act (NIRA), which was passed under President Franklin D. Roosevelt, established fair competition codes that were designed to help businesses. The Schechter brothers of New York City, who sold chickens, were convicted of violating the codes. The Supreme Court ruled that the NIRA unconstitutionally conferred legislative power on an administrative agency and overstepped the limits of federal power to regulate interstate commerce. The decision was a significant blow to the New Deal recovery program, demonstrating both historic American resistance to economic planning and the refusal of the business community to yield its autonomy unless it was forced to do so.

Brown v. Board of Education (1954)

In 1950, the families of eight Topeka, Kansas, children sued the Topeka Board of Education. The children were blacks who lived within walking distance of a whites-only school. The segregated school system required them to take a time-consuming, inconvenient, and dangerous route to get to a black school, and their parents argued that there was no reason their children should not be allowed to attend the nearest school. By the time the case reached the Supreme Court, it had been joined with similar cases regarding segregated schools in other states and the District of Columbia. A team of lawyers from the National Association for the Advancement of Colored People (NAACP), led by Thurgood Marshall (who would later be appointed to the Supreme Court), urged the Court to overturn the fifty-eight-year-old precedent established in *Plessy v. Ferguson*, which had enshrined "separate but equal" as the law of the land. A unanimous Court, led by Chief Justice Earl Warren, declared that "separate educa-

tional facilities are inherently unequal" and thus violate the Fourteenth Amendment. In 1955, the Court called for desegregation "with all deliberate speed" but established no deadline.

Roth v. United States (1957)

In 1957, New Yorker Samuel Roth was convicted of sending obscene materials through the mail in a case that ultimately reached the Supreme Court. With a six-to-three vote, the Court reaffirmed the historical view that obscenity is not protected by the First Amendment. Yet it broke new ground by declaring that a work could be judged obscene only if, "taken as a whole," it appealed to the "prurient interest" of "the average person."

Prior to this case, work could be judged obscene if portions were thought able to "deprave and corrupt" the most susceptible part of an audience (such as children). Thus, serious works of literature such as Theodore Dreiser's *An American Tragedy*, which was banned in Boston when first published, had received no protection. Although this decision continued to pose problems of definition, it did help to protect most works that attempt to convey ideas, even if those ideas have to do with sex, from the threat of obscenity laws.

Engel v. Vitale (1962)

In 1959, five parents with ten children in the New Hyde Park, New York, school system sued the school board. The parents argued that the so-called Regents' Prayer that public school students in New York recited at the start of every school day violated the doctrine of separation of church and state outlined in the First Amendment. In 1962, the Supreme Court voted six to one in favor of banning the Regents' Prayer.

The decision threw the religious community into an uproar. Many religious leaders expressed dismay and even shock; others welcomed the decision. Several efforts to introduce an amendment allowing school prayer have failed. Subsequent Supreme Court decisions have banned reading of the Bible in public schools. The Court has also declared mandatory flag saluting to be an infringement of religious and personal freedoms.

Gideon v. Wainwright (1963)

When Clarence Earl Gideon was tried for breaking into a poolroom, the state of Florida rejected his demand for a court-appointed lawyer as guaranteed by the Sixth Amendment. In 1963, the Court upheld his demand in a unanimous decision that established the obligation of states to provide attorneys for indigent defendants in felony cases. Prior to this decision, the right to an attorney had applied only to federal cases, not state cases. In its ruling in *Gideon v. Wainwright*, the Supreme Court applied the Sixth through the Fourteenth Amendments to the states. In 1972, the Supreme Court extended the right to legal representation to all cases, not just felony cases, in its decision in *Argersinger v. Hamlin*.

Griswold v. Connecticut (1965)

With a vote of seven to two, the Supreme Court reversed an "uncommonly silly law" (in the words of Justice Potter Stewart) that made it a crime for anyone in the state of Connecticut to use any drug, article, or instrument to prevent conception. *Griswold* became a landmark case because here, for the first time, the Court explicitly invested with full constitutional status "fundamental personal rights," such as the right to privacy, that were not expressly enumerated in the Bill of Rights. The majority opinion in the case held that the law infringed on the constitutionally protected right to privacy of married persons.

Although the Court had previously recognized fundamental rights not expressly enumerated in the Bill of Rights (such as the right to procreate in *Skinner v. Oklahoma* in 1942), *Griswold* was the first time the Court had justified, at length, the practice of investing such unenumerated rights with full constitutional status. Writing for the majority, Justice William O. Douglas explained that the First, Third, Fourth, Fifth, and Ninth Amendments imply "zones of privacy" that are the foundation for the general right to privacy affirmed in this case.

Miranda v. Arizona (1966)

In 1966, the Supreme Court, by a vote of five to four, upheld the case of Ernesto Miranda, who appealed a murder conviction on the grounds that police had gotten him to confess without giving him access to an attorney. The *Miranda* case was the culmination of the Court's efforts to find a meaningful way of determining whether police had used due process in extracting confessions from people accused of crimes. The *Miranda* decision upholds the Fifth Amendment protection against self-incrimination outside the courtroom and requires that suspects be given what came to be known as the "Miranda warning," which advises them of their right to remain silent and warns them that anything they say might be used against them in a court of law. Suspects must also be told that they have a right to counsel.

New York Times Co. v. United States (1971)

With a six-to-three vote, the Court upheld the right of the *New York Times* and the *Washington Post* to print materials from the so-called *Pentagon Papers*, a secret government study of U.S. policy in Vietnam, leaked by dissident Pentagon official Daniel Ellsberg. Since the papers revealed deception and secrecy in the conduct of the Vietnam War, the Nixon administration had quickly obtained a court injunction against their further publication, claiming that suppression was in the interests of national security. The Supreme Court's decision overturning the injunction strengthened the First Amendment protection of freedom of the press.

Furman v. Georgia (1972)

In this case, the Supreme Court ruled five to four that the death penalty for murder or rape violated the cruel and unusual punishment clause of the Eighth Amendment because the manner in which the death penalty was meted out was irregular, "arbitrary," and "cruel." In response, most states enacted new statutes that allow the death penalty to be imposed only after a postconviction hearing at which evidence must be presented to show that "aggravating" or "mitigating" circumstances were factors in the crime. If the postconviction hearing hands down a death sentence, the case is automatically reviewed by an appellate court.

In 1976, the Court ruled in *Gregg v. Georgia* that these statutes were not unconstitutional. In 1977, the Court ruled in *Coker v. Georgia* that the death penalty for rape was "disproportionate and excessive," thus allowing the death penalty only in murder cases. Between 1977 and 1991, some 150 people were executed in the United States. Public opinion polls indicate that about 70 percent of Americans favor the death penalty for murder. Capital punishment continues to generate controversy, however, as opponents argue that there is no evidence that the death penalty deters crime and that its use reflects racial and economic bias.

Roe v. Wade (1973)

In 1973, the Court found, by a vote of seven to two, that state laws restricting access to abortion violated a woman's right to privacy guaranteed by the due process clause of the Fourteenth Amendment. The decision was based on the cases of two women living in Texas and Georgia, both states with stringent anti-abortion laws. Upholding the individual rights of both women and physicians, the Court ruled that the Constitution protects the right to abortion and that states cannot prohibit abortions in the early stages of pregnancy.

The decision stimulated great debate among legal scholars as well as the public. Critics argued that since abortion was never addressed in the Constitution, the Court could not claim that legislation violated fundamental values of the Constitution. They also argued that since abortion was a medical procedure with an acknowledged impact on a fetus, it was inappropriate to invoke the kind of "privacy" argument that was used in *Griswold v. Connecticut* (see p. A-52), which was about contraception. Defenders suggested that the case should be argued as a case of gender discrimination, which did violate the equal protection clause of the Fourteenth Amendment. Others said that the right to privacy in sexual matters was indeed a fundamental right.

Regents of the University of California v. Bakke (1978)

When Allan Bakke, a white man, was not accepted by the University of California Medical School at Davis, he filed a lawsuit alleging that the admissions program, which set up different standards for test scores and grades for members of certain minority groups, violated the Civil Rights Act of 1964, which outlawed racial or ethnic preferences in programs supported by federal funds. Bakke further argued that the university's practice of setting aside spaces for minority applicants denied him equal protection as guaranteed by the Fourteenth Amendment. In a five-to-four decision, the Court ordered that Bakke be admitted to the medical school, yet it sanctioned affirmative action programs to attack the results of past discrimination as long as strict quotas or racial classifications were not involved.

Webster v. Reproductive Health Services (1989)

By a vote of five to four, the Court upheld several restrictions on the availability of abortions as imposed by Missouri state law. It upheld restrictions on the use of state property, including public hospitals, for abortions. It also upheld a provision requiring physicians to perform tests to determine the viability of a fetus that a doctor judged to be twenty weeks of age or older. Although the justices did not go so far as to overturn the decision in *Roe v. Wade* (see p. A-52), the ruling galvanized interest groups on both sides of the abortion issue. Opponents of abortion pressured state legislatures to place greater restrictions on abortions; those who favored availability of abortion tried to mobilize public action by presenting the decision as a major threat to the right to choose abortion.

Cipollone v. Liggett (1992)

In a seven-to-two decision, the Court ruled in favor of the family of Rose Cipollone, a woman who died of lung cancer after smoking for forty-two years. The Court rejected arguments that health warnings on cigarette packages protected tobacco manufacturers from personal injury suits filed by smokers who contract cancer and other serious illnesses.

Miller v. Johnson (1995)

In a five-to-four decision, the Supreme Court ruled that voting districts created to increase the voting power of racial minorities were unconstitutional. The decision threatens dozens of congressional, state, and local voting districts that were drawn to give minorities more representation as had been required by the Justice Department under the Voting Rights Act. If states are required to redraw voting districts, the number of black members of Congress could be sharply reduced.

Romer v. Evans (1996)

In a six-to-three decision, the Court struck down a Colorado amendment that forbade local governments from banning discrimination against homosexuals. Writing for the majority, Justice Anthony Kennedy said that forbidding communities from taking action to protect the rights of homosexuals and not of other groups unlawfully deprived gays and lesbians of opportunities that were available to others. Kennedy based the decision on the guarantee of equal protection under the law as provided by the Fourteenth Amendment.

Bush v. Palm Beach County Canvassing Board (2000)

In a bitterly argued five-to-four decision, the Court reversed the Florida Supreme Court's previous order for a hand recount of contested presidential election ballots in several counties of that battleground state, effectively securing the presidency for Texas Republican Governor, George W. Bush. The ruling ended a protracted legal dispute between presidential candidates Bush and Vice President Al Gore while inflaming public opinion: For the first time since 1888, a president who failed to win the popular vote took office. Critics charged that the Supreme Court had applied partisanship rather than objectivity to the case, pointing out that the decision went against this Court's customary interpretation of the Constitution to favor state over federal authority.

THE AMERICAN ECONOMY

THESE FOUR "SNAPSHOTS" of the U.S. economy show significant changes over the past century and a half. In 1849, the agricultural sector was by far the largest contributor to the economy. By the turn of the century, with advances in technology and an abundance of cheap labor and raw materials, the country had experienced remarkable industrial expansion and the manufacturing industries dominated. By 1950, the service sector had increased significantly, fueled by the consumerism of the 1920s and the post–World War II years, and the economy was becoming more diversified. Note that by 1990, government's share in the economy was more than 10 percent and activity in both the trade and manufacturing sectors had declined, partly as a result of competition from Western Europe and Asia.

Main Sectors of the U.S. Economy: 1849, 1899, 1950, 1997

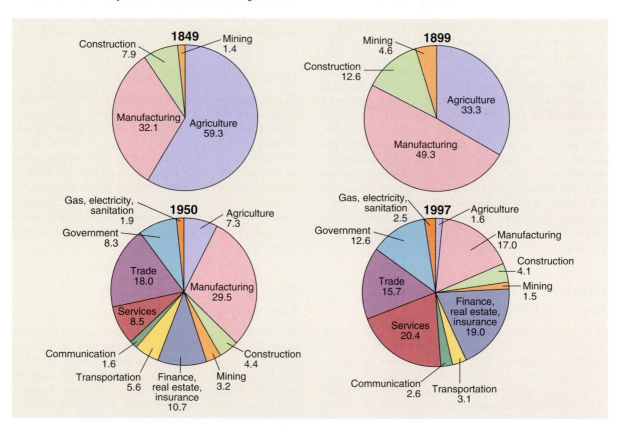

Source: Historical Statistics of the U.S., Colonial Times to 1970 (1975) and Statistical Abstract of the U.S., 1999 (1999).

Federal Spending and the Economy, 1790–1998

Year	Gross National Product (in billions)	Foreign Trade (in millions) Exports	Imports	Federal Budget (in billions)	Federal Surplus/Deficit (in billions)	Federal Debt (in billions)
1790	NA	20	23	0.004	0.00015	0.076
1800	NA	71	91	0.011	0.0006	0.083
1810	NA	67	85	0.008	0.0012	0.053
1820	NA	70	74	0.018	−0.0004	0.091
1830	NA	74	71	0.015	0.100	0.049
1840	NA	132	107	0.024	−0.005	0.004
1850	NA	152	178	0.040	0.004	0.064
1860	NA	400	362	0.063	−0.01	0.065
1870	7.4	451	462	0.310	0.10	2.4
1880	11.2	853	761	0.268	0.07	2.1
1890	13.1	910	823	0.318	0.09	1.2
1900	18.7	1,499	930	0.521	0.05	1.2
1910	35.3	1,919	1,646	0.694	−0.02	1.1
1920	91.5	8,664	5,784	6.357	0.3	24.3
1930	90.4	4,013	3,500	3.320	0.7	16.3
1940	99.7	4,030	7,433	9.6	−2.7	43.0
1950	284.8	10,816	9,125	43.1	−2.2	257.4
1960	503.7	19,600	15,046	92.2	0.3	286.3
1970	977.1	42,700	40,189	195.6	−2.8	371.0
1980	2,631.7	220,600	244,871	590.9	−73.8	907.7
1990	5,764.9	393,600	495,300	1,253.2	−221.2	3,266.1
1998	8,490.5	682,100	911,900	1,652.5	69.2	5,555.5

Source: Historical Statistics of the U.S., Colonial Times to 1970 (1975), Statistical Abstract of the U.S., 1996 (1996), and Statistical Abstract of the U.S., 1999 (1999).

A DEMOGRAPHIC PROFILE OF THE UNITED STATES AND ITS PEOPLE

POPULATION

FROM AN ESTIMATED 4,600 WHITE INHABITANTS IN 1630, the country's population grew to a total of just under 250 million in 1990. It is important to note that the U.S. census, first conducted in 1790 and the source of these figures, counted blacks, both free and slave, but did not include American Indians until 1860. The years 1790 to 1900 saw the most rapid population growth, with an average increase of 25 to 35 percent per decade. In addition to "natural" growth—birthrate exceeding death rate—immigration was also a factor in that rise, especially between 1840 and 1860, 1880 and 1890, and 1900 and 1910 (see table on page A-61). The twentieth century witnessed slower growth, partly a result of 1920s immigration restrictions and a decline in the birthrate, especially during the Depression era and the 1960s and 1970s. The U.S. population is expected to reach almost 300 million by the year 2010.

Population Growth, 1630–2000

Year	Population	Percent Increase
1630	4,600	—
1640	26,600	473.3
1650	50,400	89.1
1660	75,100	49.0
1670	111,900	49.1
1680	151,500	35.4
1690	210,400	38.9
1700	250,900	19.3
1710	331,700	32.2
1720	466,200	40.5
1730	629,400	35.0
1740	905,600	43.9
1750	1,170,800	30.0
1760	1,593,600	36.1
1770	2,148,100	34.8
1780	2,780,400	29.4
1790	3,929,214	41.3
1800	5,308,483	35.1
1810	7,239,881	36.4
1820	9,638,453	33.1
1830	12,866,020	33.5
1840	17,069,453	32.7
1850	23,191,876	35.9
1860	31,443,321	35.6
1870	39,818,449	26.6
1880	50,155,783	26.0
1890	62,947,714	25.5
1900	75,994,575	20.7
1910	91,972,266	21.0
1920	105,710,620	14.9
1930	122,775,046	16.1
1940	131,669,275	7.2
1950	150,697,361	14.5
1960	179,323,175	19.0
1970	203,302,031	13.4
1980	226,542,199	11.4
1990	248,718,301	9.8
2000	281,421,906	11.0

Source: Historical Statistics of the U.S. (1960), Historical Statistics of the U.S., Colonial Times to 1970 (1975), Statistical Abstract of the U.S., 1996 (1996), and United States Census, 2000 (2000).

VITAL STATISTICS

WITH SOME MINOR FLUCTUATIONS, the birthrate has been on a downward trend throughout the past century and a half, dipping especially low during the 1930s Depression years, when many economically hard-hit Americans postponed having children. A major exception to this decline was the steep but temporary rise nicknamed the "baby boom," which occurred during the relatively affluent post–World War II period. Improvements in health care and lifestyles have contributed to a decline in the death rate over the past century, which in turn has increased life expectancy figures. Over time, as people lived longer and the birthrate declined, the median age of Americans has increased from approximately seventeen in 1820 to thirty-three in 1990 and continues to rise.

Birthrate, 1820–2000

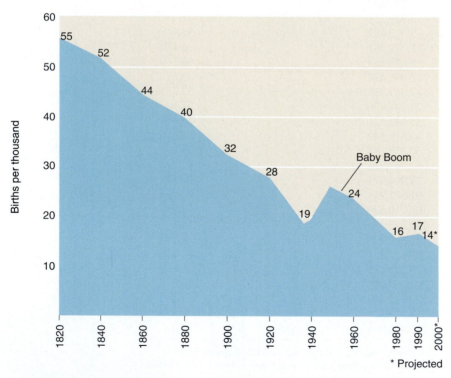

Source: Data from *Historical Statistics of the U.S., Colonial Times to 1970* (1975) and *Statistical Abstract of the U.S., 1996* (1996).

Death Rate, 1900–2000

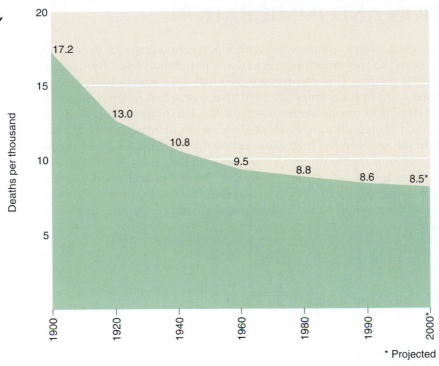

Source: *Historical Statistics of the U.S., Colonial Times to 1970* (1975) and
Statistical Abstract of the U.S., 1996 (1996).

Life Expectancy, 1900–2000

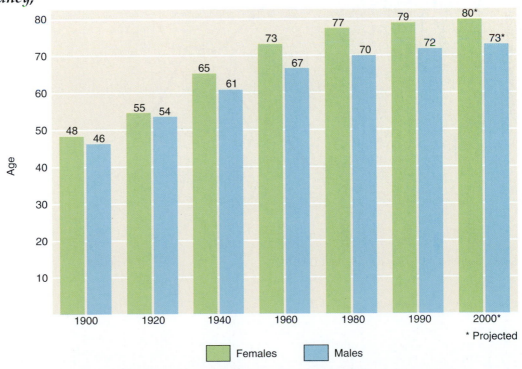

Source: *Historical Statistics of the U.S., Colonial Times to 1970* (1975) and
Statistical Abstract of the U.S., 1996 (1996).

MIGRATION AND IMMIGRATION

WE TEND TO ASSOCIATE INTERNAL MIGRATION with movement westward, yet equally significant has been the movement of the nation's population from the country to the city. In 1790, the first U.S. census recorded that approximately 95 percent of the population lived in rural areas. By 1990, that figure had fallen to less than 25 percent. The decline of the agricultural way of life, late-nineteenth-century industrialization, and immigration have all contributed to increased urbanization. A more recent trend has been the migration, especially since the 1970s, of people to the Sun Belt states of the South and West, lured by factors as various as economic opportunities in the defense and high-tech industries and good weather. This migration has swelled the size of cities like Houston, Dallas, Tucson, Phoenix, and San Diego, all of which in recent years ranked among the top ten most populous U.S. cities.

Rural and Urban Population, 1750–2000

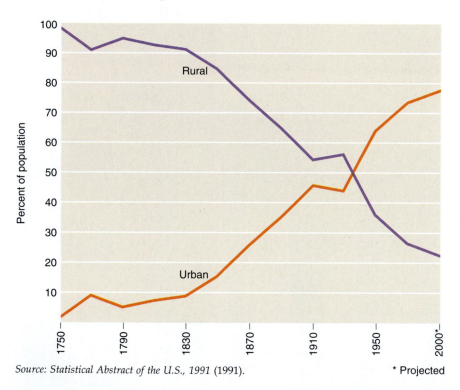

Source: Statistical Abstract of the U.S., 1991 (1991).   * Projected

A DEMOGRAPHIC PROFILE OF THE UNITED STATES AND ITS PEOPLE

THE QUANTITY AND CHARACTER OF IMMIGRATION to the United States has varied greatly over time. During the first major influx, between 1840 and 1860, newcomers hailed primarily from northern and western Europe. From 1880 to 1915, when rates soared even more dramatically, the profile changed, with 80 percent of the "new immigration" coming from central, eastern, and southern Europe. Following World War I, strict quotas reduced the flow considerably. Note also the significant falloff during the years of the Great Depression and World War II. The sources of immigration during the last half century have changed significantly, with the majority of people coming from Latin America, the Caribbean, and Asia. The latest surge during the 1980s brought more immigrants to the United States than in any decade except 1901–1910.

Rates of Immigration, 1820–1997

Year	Number	Percent of Total Population
1821–1830	151,824	1.6
1831–1840	599,125	4.6
1841–1850	1,713,521	10.0
1851–1860	2,598,214	11.2
1861–1870	2,314,824	7.4
1871–1880	2,812,191	7.1
1881–1890	5,246,613	10.5
1891–1900	3,687,546	5.8
1901–1910	8,795,386	11.6
1911–1920	5,735,811	6.2
1921–1930	4,107,209	3.9
1931–1940	528,431	0.4
1941–1950	1,035,039	0.7
1951–1960	2,515,479	1.6
1961–1970	3,321,677	1.8
1971–1980	4,493,300	2.2
1981–1990	7,338,100	3.0
1991	1,827,167	7.2
1992	973,977	3.8
1993	904,292	3.5
1994	804,416	3.0
1995	720,461	2.7
1996	915,900	3.5
1997	798,378	3.0

Source: Historical Statistics of the U.S., Colonial Times to 1970 (1975), Statistical Abstract of the U.S., 1996 (1996), and Statistical Abstract of the U.S., 1999 (1999).

Major Trends in Immigration, 1820–1998

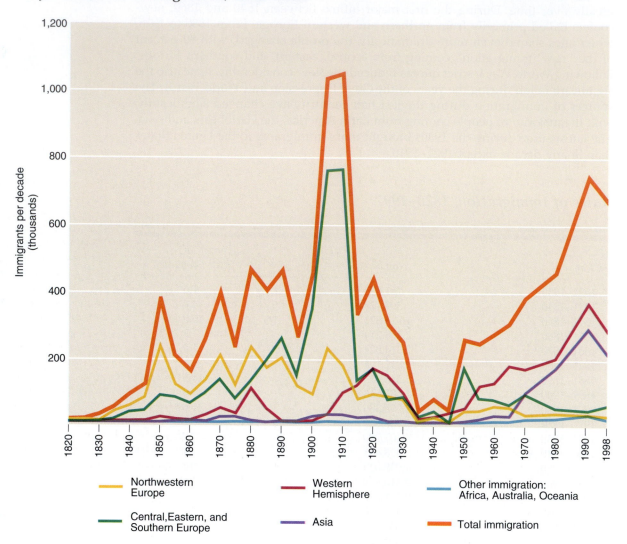

Source: *Historical Statistics of the U.S., Colonial Times to 1970 (1975)* and *Statistical Abstract of the U.S., 1999 (1999).*

Appendix III. Research Resources in U.S. History

While doing research in history, you will use the library to track down primary and secondary sources and to answer questions that arise as you learn more about your topic. This appendix suggests helpful indexes, references, periodicals, and sources of primary documents. It also offers an overview of electronic resources available through the Internet. The materials listed here are not carried at all libraries, but they will give you an idea of the range of sources available. Remember, too, that librarians are an extremely helpful resource. They can direct you to useful materials throughout your research process.

Bibliographies and Indexes

American Historical Association Guide to Historical Literature. 3rd ed. New York: Oxford University Press, 1995. Offers 27,000 citations to important historical literature, arranged in forty-eight sections covering theory, international history, and regional history. An indispensable guide recently updated to include current trends in historical research.

American History and Life. Santa Barbara: ABC-Clio, 1964–. Covers publications of all sorts on U.S. and Canadian history and culture in a chronological/regional format, with abstracts and alphabetical indexes. Available in computerized format. The most complete ongoing bibliography for American history.

Freidel, Frank Burt. *Harvard Guide to American History.* Cambridge: Harvard University Press, Belknap Press, 1974. Provides citations to books and articles on American history published before 1970. The first volume is arranged topically, the second chronologically. Though it does not cover current scholarship, it is a classic and remains useful for tracing older publications.

Prucha, Francis Paul. *Handbook for Research in American History: A Guide to Bibliographies and Other Reference Works.* 2nd rev. ed. Lincoln: University of Nebraska Press, 1994. Introduces a variety of research tools, including electronic ones. A good source to consult when planning an in-depth research project.

General Overviews

Dictionary of American Biography. New York: Scribner's, 1928–1937, with supplements. Gives substantial biographies of prominent Americans in history.

Dictionary of American History. New York: Scribner's, 1976. An encyclopedia of terms, places, and concepts in U.S. history; other more specialized sets include the *Encyclopedia of North American Colonies* and the *Encyclopedia of the Confederacy.*

Dictionary of Concepts in History. New York: Greenwood, 1986. Contains essays defining concepts in historiography and describing how the concepts were formed; excellent bibliographies.

Encyclopedia of American Social History. New York: Scribner's, 1993. Surveys topics such as religion, class, gender, race, popular culture, regionalism, and everyday life from pre-Columbian to modern times.

Encyclopedia of the United States in the Twentieth Century. New York: Scribner's, 1996. An ambitious overview of American cultural, social, and intellectual history in broad articles arranged topically. Each article is followed by a thorough and very useful bibliography for further research.

Specialized Information

Black Women in America: An Historical Encyclopedia. Brooklyn: Carlson, 1993. A scholarly compilation of biographical and topical articles that constitute a definitive history of African American women.

Carruth, Gordon. *The Encyclopedia of American Facts and Dates.* 10th ed. New York: HarperCollins, 1997. Covers American history chronologically from 986 to the present, offering information on treaties, battles, explorations, popular culture, philosophy, literature, and so on, mixing significant events with telling trivia. Tables allow for reviewing a year from a variety of angles. A thorough index helps pinpoint specific facts in time.

Cook, Chris. *Dictionary of Historical Terms.* 2nd ed. New York: Peter Bendrick, 1990. Covers a wide variety of terms—events, places, institutions, and topics—in history for all periods and places in a remarkably small package. A good place for quick identification of terms in the field.

Dictionary of Afro-American Slavery. New York: Greenwood, 1985. Surveys important people, events, and topics, with useful bibliographies; similar works include *Dictionary of the Vietnam War, Historical Dictionary of the New Deal,* and *Historical Dictionary of the Progressive Era.*

Knappman-Frost, Elizabeth. *The ABC-Clio Companion to Women's Progress in America.* Santa Barbara: ABC-Clio, 1994. Covers American women who were notable for their time as well as topics and organizations that have been significant in women's quest for equality. Each article is brief; there are a chronology and a bibliography at the back of the book.

United States Bureau of the Census. *Historical Statistics of the United States, Colonial Times to 1970.* Washington, D.C.: Government Printing Office, 1975. Offers vital statistics, economic figures, and social data for the United States. An index at the back helps locate tables by subject. For statistics since 1970, consult the annual *Statistical Abstract of the United States.*

Primary Resources

There are many routes to finding contemporary material for historical research. You may search your library catalog using the name of a prominent historical figure as an author; you may also find anthologies covering particular themes or periods in history. Consider also the following special materials for your research.

The Press

American Periodical Series, 1741–1900. Ann Arbor: University Microfilms, 1946–1979. Microfilm collection of periodicals from the colonial period to the turn of the century. An index identifies periodicals that focused on particular topics.

Herstory Microfilm Collection. Berkeley: Women's History Research Center, 1973. A microfilm collection of alternative feminist periodicals published between 1960 and 1980. Offers an interesting documentary history of the women's movement.

New York Times. New York: New York Times, 1851–. Many libraries have this newspaper on microfilm going back to its beginning in 1851. An index is available to locate specific dates and pages of news stories; it also provides detailed chronologies of events as they were reported in the news.

Readers' Guide to Periodical Literature. New York: Wilson, 1900–. This index to popular magazines started in 1900; an earlier index, *Poole's Index to Periodical Literature,* covers 1802–1906, though it does not provide such thorough indexing.

Diaries, Pamphlets, Books

The American Culture Series. Ann Arbor: University Microfilms, 1941–1974. A microfilm set, with a useful index, featuring books and pamphlets published between 1493 and 1875.

American Women's Diaries. New Canaan: Readex, 1984–. A collection of reproductions of women's diaries. There are different series for different regions of the country.

The March of America Facsimile Series. Ann Arbor: University Microfilms, 1966. A collection of more than ninety facsimiles of travel accounts to the New World published in English or English translation from the fifteenth through the nineteenth century.

Women in America from Colonial Times to the Twentieth Century. New York: Arno, 1974. A collection of reprints of dozens of books written by women describing women's lives and experiences in their own words.

Government Documents

Congressional Record. Washington, D.C.: Government Printing Office, 1874–. Covers daily debates and proceedings of Congress. Earlier series were called *Debates and Proceedings in the Congress of the United States* and *The Congressional Globe.*

Foreign Relations of the United States. Washington, D.C.: Department of State, 1861–. A collection of documents from 1861, including diplomatic papers, correspondence, and memoranda, that provides a documentary record of U.S. foreign policy.

Public Papers of the Presidents. Washington, D.C.: Office of the Federal Register, 1957–. Includes major documents issued by the executive branch from the Hoover administration to the present.

Serial Set. Washington, D.C.: Government Printing Office, 1789–1969. A huge collection of congressional documents, available in many libraries on microfiche, with a useful index.

Local History Collections

State and county historical societies often house a wealth of historical documents; consider their resources when planning your research—you may find yourself working with material that no one else has analyzed before.

Internet Resources

The Internet has been a useful place for scholars to communicate and publish information in recent years. Electronic discussion lists, electronic journals, and primary texts are among the resources available for historians. The following sources are good places to find historical information. You can also search the World Wide Web using any of a number of search engines. However, bear in mind that there is no board of editors screening Internet sites for accuracy or usefulness, and the search engines generally rely on free-text searches rather than subject headings. Be critical of all of your sources, particularly those found on the Internet. Note that when this book went to press, the sites listed below were active and maintained.

American Memory: Historical Collections for the National Digital Library Program. <http://rs6.loc.gov/amhome.html> An Internet site that features digitized primary source materials from the Library of Congress, among them African American pamphlets, Civil War photographs, documents from the Continental Congress and the Constitutional Convention of 1774–1790, materials on woman suffrage, and oral histories.

Supreme Court Collection. <http://supct.law.cornell.edu/supct> This database can be used to search for information on various Supreme Court cases. Although the site primarily covers cases that occurred after 1990, there is information on some earlier historic cases. The justices' opinions, as originally written, are also included.

Directory of Scholarly and Professional E-Conferences. <http://n2h2.com/KOVAKS> A good place to find out what electronic conversations are going on in a scholarly discipline. Includes a good search facility and instructions on how to connect to e-mail discussion lists, newsgroups, and interactive chat sites with academic content. Once identified, these conferences are good places to raise questions, find out what controversies are currently stirring the profession, and even find out about grants and jobs.

Douglass Archives of American Public Address. <http://douglass.speech.nwu.edu> An electronic archive of American speeches and documents by a variety of people from Jane Addams to Jonathan Edwards to Theodore Roosevelt.

Historical Text Archive. <http://www.geocities.com/djmabry/index.html> A Web interface for the oldest and largest Internet site for historical documents. Includes sections on Native American, African American, and U.S. history, in which can be found texts of the Declaration of Independence, the U.S. Constitution, the Constitution of Iroquois Nations, World War II surrender documents, photograph collections, and a great deal more. These can be used online or saved as files.

History Links from Yahoo! <http://dir.yahoo.com/Humanities/History> A categorically arranged and frequently updated site list for all types of history. Some of the sources are more useful than others, but this can be a helpful gateway to some good information.

Index of Civil War Information on the Internet. <http://www.cwc.lsu.edu/cwc/civlink.htm> Compiled by the United States Civil War Center, this index lists everything from diaries to historic battlefields to reenactments.

Index of Native American Resources on the Internet. <http://www.hanksville.org/NAresources> A vast index of Native American resources organized by category. Within the history category, links are organized under subcategories: oral history, written history, geographical areas, timelines, and photographs and photographic archives. A central place to come in the search for information on Native American history.

WWW-VL History Index. <http://www.ukans.edu/history/VL/> A vast list of more than 1,700 links to sites of interest to historians, arranged alphabetically by general topic. Some links are to sources for general reference information, but most are on historical topics. A good place to start an exploration of Internet resources.

Internet Archive of Texts and Documents. <http://history.hanover.edu/texts.html> As stated on its home page, the purpose of this site is to make primary sources available to students and faculty. Arranged chronologically, geographically, and by subject, the site lists speeches, reports, and other primary-document links. It also includes some secondary sources on each subject.

Internet Resources for Students of Afro-American History and Culture. <http://www.libraries.rutgers.edu/rul/rr_gateway/research_guides/history/afrores.shtml> A good place to begin research on topics in African American history. The site is indexed and linked to a wide variety of sources, including primary documents, text collections, and archival sources on African American history. Individual documents such as slave narratives and petitions, the Fugitive Slave Acts, and speeches by W. E. B. Du Bois, Booker T. Washington, and Martin Luther King Jr. are categorized by century.

The Martin Luther King Jr. Papers Project. <http://www.stanford.edu/group/King> Organized by Stanford University, this site gives information about Martin Luther King Jr. and offers some of his writings.

NativeWeb. <http://www.nativeweb.org> One of the best-organized and most-accessible sites available on

Native American issues, *NativeWeb* combines an events calendar and message board with history, statistics, a list of news sources, archives, new and updated related sites each week, and documents. The text is indexed and can be searched by subject, nation, and geographic region.

Perry-Castañeda Library Map Collection. <http://www.lib.utexas.edu/Libs/PCL/Map_collection/Map_collection.html> The University of Texas at Austin library has put over seven hundred United States maps on the Web for viewing by students and professors alike.

Smithsonian Institution. <http://www.si.edu> Organized by subject, such as military history or Hispanic/Latino American resources, this site offers selected links to sites hosted by Smithsonian Institution museums and organizations. Content includes graphics of museum pieces and relevant textual information, book suggestions, maps, and links.

United States History Index. <http://www.ukans.edu/~usa> Maintained by a history professor and arranged by subject, such as women's history, labor history, and agricultural history, this index provides links to a variety of other sites. Although the list is extensive, it does not include a synopsis of each site, which makes finding specific information a time-consuming process.

United States History Resources by Period. <http://www.cms.ccsd.k12.co.us/ss.history.htm> This list of links to a variety of history sites is arranged chronologically and updated periodically.

United States Holocaust Memorial Museum. <http://www.ushmm.org/learn.htm> This site contains information about the Holocaust Museum in Washington, D.C., in particular and the Holocaust in general, and it lists links to related sites.

Women's History Resources. <http://www.mcps.k12.md.us/curriculum/socialstd/Women_Bookmarks.html> An extensive listing of women's history sources available on the Internet. The site indexes resources on subjects as diverse as woman suffrage, women in the workplace, and celebrated women writers. Some of the links are to equally vast indexes, providing an overwhelming wealth of information.

INDEX

A note about the index:

Names of individuals appear in boldface; biographical dates are included for major historical figures.

Letters in parentheses following pages refer to:
- (i)   illustrations, including photographs and artifacts, as well as information in picture captions
- (f)   figures, including charts and graphs
- (m)   maps
- (b)   boxed features (such as "Historical Question")
- (t)   tables
- (n)   notes

Abenaki Indians, P-17
Abolitionists (abolitionist movement),
    347–349, 380–382
  during Civil War (1861–1865),
    507, 509
  expansion of slavery and, 452,
    455, 456
  John Brown and, 480
Abolition of slavery. *See also*
    Emancipation of slaves
  late eighteenth century, 229
Acoma pueblo (New Mexico), 27
Act of Supremacy (1534), 72
Adams, Abigail Smith (1744–1818),
    183, 184, 184(i), 189, 197
  on Sedition Bill, 278(b)
Adams, Charles Francis, 453
Adams, John (1735–1826), 111,
    162–163, 167
  1796 election, 275
  1800 election, 281, 289
  on Boston Tea Party, 169–170(b)
  as president (1797–1801),
    275–277, 275(i)
    foreign policy, 276, 278–280(b)
    France and, 276, 277, 281
    judicial appointments, 293
    Matthew Lyon's criticism of, 279(b)
  on property qualifications for
    suffrage, 227, 228
  during Revolutionary War, 176,
    183–184, 185, 189, 192
  as vice president, 257–258
Adams, John Quincy (1767–1848), 312
  1824 election, 312–315,
    313(i), 314(m)
  1828 election, 335–336
  as president (1825–1829),
    314–315, 325

Adams, Samuel (1722–1803), 163, 164,
    166, 167
  on Boston Tea Party, 170(b)
  during Revolutionary War, 185
  Shays's Rebellion (1786) and, 238
  Stamp Act of 1765 and,
    156–157, 156(i)
Adams-Onis Treaty (1819), 312
Adena people, P-16
Advice to American Women
    (Graves), 338
Advocate of Moral Reform, The
    (newspaper), 347
Africa
  emigration of freed slaves to, 347
  Portuguese exploration of, 7
African Americans (blacks). *See
    also* Civil rights; Free blacks;
    Racism; Reconstruction;
    Segregation; Slaves and slavery
  in armed forces during Civil War
    (1861–1865), 510–511, 511(i),
    521–522
  equality of. *See also* Civil rights
    Lincoln on, 477, 479, 509
    reconstruction and, 539, 548–551,
    552, 555, 564, 565
    slavery and principle of (late
    eighteenth century),
    228–229, 233
  Andrew Johnson's views of, 545
  population of
    eighteenth century, 112, 114,
    118–119
    nineteenth century (slaves),
    413–414, 414(f)
    seventeenth century, 62, 63, 64(f)
  religion and, during reconstruction,
    544–545

  in the South. *See* Reconstruction;
    Slaves and slavery
  voting rights (suffrage)
    Fifteenth Amendment, 553–555
    literacy tests, 554
    in Massachusetts, 229
    New Jersey, 258
    reconstruction and, 539, 540,
    543(b), 546, 547, 549,
    551–555
  women
    reconstruction and, 538(i), 556,
    558, 560
    as slaves, 113(i), 121, 423(i),
    426, 429
African culture, slaves and, 126, 434
African Methodist Episcopal
    Church, 545
Africans, 27
  in Chesapeake colonies, 56
  English colonists' view of, 54(b)
African slaves. *See* Slaves and
    slavery
African slave trade. *See* Slave trade
Agriculture. *See also* Farmers and
    farms; Plantations; Planters;
    and specific crops
  in 1790s, 260
  1840–1860, 367–369
  Civil War legislation, 518–519
  colonial period
    exports (1768–1772), 129(f)
    middle colonies, 114–115, 117
    New England, 109
  Columbian exchange and, 11–12
  Embargo Act of 1807 and, 300
  federal land policy and (1840–1860),
    368–369
  mechanization of, 519

THE TERRITORIAL GROWTH OF THE UNITED STATES

CANADA

MINNESOTA

WISCONSIN

MICHIGAN

Lake Superior

Lake Huron

Lake Michigan

Lake Ontario

Lake Erie

VERMONT

MAINE
(part of Mass.
until 1820)

NEW
HAMPSHIRE

NEW
YORK

MASS.

St. Lawrence R.

Connecticut R.

Hudson R.

RHODE
ISLAND

CONNECTICUT

IOWA

ILLINOIS

INDIANA

OHIO

PENN.

Susquehanna R.

Delaware R.

NEW JERSEY

DELAWARE

MARYLAND

*Chesapeake
Bay*

KANSAS

MISSOURI

Missouri R.

WEST
VIRGINIA

Ohio R.

KENTUCKY

Proclamation Line of 1763

Potomac R.

VIRGINIA

James R.

NORTH
CAROLINA

Cape Fear R.

ATLANTIC
OCEAN

OKLAHOMA

ARKANSAS

Arkansas R.

Mississippi R.

TENNESSEE

Cumberland R.

Tennessee R.

SOUTH
CAROLINA

THE ORIGINAL THIRTEEN COLONIES

Savannah R.

TEXAS

LOUISIANA

MISSISSIPPI

ALABAMA

GEORGIA

**THE ORIGINAL
THIRTEEN COLONIES
IN 1776**

0   150   300 miles

0   150   300 kilometers

Gulf of Mexico

FLORIDA

BAHAMAS

CUBA

CANADA

MAINE
(part of Mass.
until 1820)

VERMONT

NEW
HAMPSHIRE

NEW YORK

MASS.

RHODE
ISLAND

CONNECTICUT

NEW JERSEY

DELAWARE

MARYLAND

Chesapeake
Bay

Lake Superior

MINNESOTA

WISCONSIN

MICHIGAN

Lake Michigan

Lake Huron

Lake Ontario

Lake Erie

PENN.

St. Lawrence R.

Hudson R.

Connecticut R.

Delaware R.

Susquehanna R.

IOWA

OHIO

WEST
VIRGINIA

Potomac R.

James R.

VIRGINIA

KANSAS

MISSOURI

Missouri R.

KENTUCKY

**Gained by treaty
with Britain, 1783**

Ohio R.

NORTH
CAROLINA

Cape Fear R.

ARKANSAS

OKLAHOMA

Arkansas R.

Cumberland R.

Tennessee R.

TENNESSEE

Mississippi R.

SOUTH
CAROLINA

ATLANTIC
OCEAN

THE ORIGINAL THIRTEEN COLONIES

Proclamation Line of 1763

TEXAS

LOUISIANA

MISSISSIPPI

ALABAMA

GEORGIA

Savannah R.

**THE UNITED STATES
IN 1783**

0		150		300 miles
0	150		300 kilometers	

Gulf of Mexico

FLORIDA

BAHAMAS

CUBA

WASHINGTON

Columbia R.

OREGON

IDAHO

Snake R.

MONTANA

Missouri R.

**Area ceded by
Great Britain,
1818**

NORTH DAKOTA

SOUTH DAKOTA

**L O U I S I A N A
P U R C H A S E**
From France, 1803

WYOMING

Sacramento R.

San Joaquin R.

NEVADA

UTAH

Colorado R.

NEBRASKA

N. Platte R.

Platte R.

S. Platte R.

COLORADO

KANSAS

CALIFORNIA

ARIZONA

NEW
MEXICO

Red R.

TEXAS

PACIFIC
OCEAN

Rio Grande

M E X I C O

CANADA

MINNESOTA

WISCONSIN

MICHIGAN

Lake Superior

Lake Michigan

Lake Huron

Lake Ontario

Lake Erie

St. Lawrence R.

MAINE
(part of Mass.
until 1820)

VERMONT

NEW
HAMPSHIRE

NEW YORK

MASS.

Connecticut R.

Hudson R.

RHODE
ISLAND

CONNECTICUT

NEW JERSEY

IOWA

Missouri R.

ILLINOIS

INDIANA

OHIO

PENN.

Delaware R.

Susquehanna R.

DELAWARE

MARYLAND

*Chesapeake
Bay*

WEST
VIRGINIA

Potomac R.

James R.

THE ORIGINAL THIRTEEN COLONIES

VIRGINIA

Proclamation Line of 1763

MISSOURI

KENTUCKY

Ohio R.

**Gained by treaty
with Britain, 1783**

NORTH
CAROLINA

Cape Fear R.

Cumberland R.

Tennessee R.

TENNESSEE

OKLAHOMA

ARKANSAS

Arkansas R.

Mississippi R.

SOUTH
CAROLINA

ATLANTIC
OCEAN

MISSISSIPPI

ALABAMA

GEORGIA

Savannah R.

LOUISIANA

**Areas taken from Spain
in 1810, 1813**

FLORIDA

**THE UNITED STATES
IN 1819**

0   150   300 miles

0   150   300 kilometers

**FLORIDA,
Treaty with Spain,
1819**

Gulf of Mexico

BAHAMAS

CUBA

Area ceded by
Great Britain,
1818

WASHINGTON

Columbia R.

OREGON COUNTRY
Agreement with Britain,
1846

OREGON

IDAHO

Snake R.

MONTANA

NORTH DAKOTA

SOUTH DAKOTA

L O U I S I A N A
P U R C H A S E
From France, 1803

WYOMING

N. Platte R.

NEBRASKA

Platte R.

Missouri R.

Sacramento R.

NEVADA

UTAH

S. Platte R.

COLORADO

KANSAS

MEXICAN CESSION,
1848

San Joaquin R.

Colorado R.

CALIFORNIA

PACIFIC
OCEAN

ARIZONA

NEW
MEXICO

Red R.

TEXAS
Annexed, 1845

GADSDEN PURCHASE
From Mexico, 1853

TEXAS

Rio Grande

M E X I C O

M–6

CANADA

Lake Superior

Lake Huron

Lake Michigan

Lake Erie

Lake Ontario

St. Lawrence R.

MINNESOTA

WISCONSIN

MICHIGAN

MAINE

VERMONT

NEW HAMPSHIRE

NEW YORK

MASS.

RHODE ISLAND

CONNECTICUT

Hudson R.

Connecticut R.

IOWA

ILLINOIS

INDIANA

OHIO

PENN.

NEW JERSEY

DELAWARE

MARYLAND

Delaware R.

Susquehanna R.

Potomac R.

Chesapeake Bay

Missouri R.

MISSOURI

KENTUCKY

WEST VIRGINIA

VIRGINIA

James R.

Gained by treaty with Britain, 1783

Ohio R.

Proclamation Line of 1763

THE ORIGINAL THIRTEEN COLONIES

NORTH CAROLINA

Cape Fear R.

Cumberland R.

TENNESSEE

Tennessee R.

OKLAHOMA

ARKANSAS

Arkansas R.

SOUTH CAROLINA

Savannah R.

ATLANTIC OCEAN

Mississippi R.

LOUISIANA

MISSISSIPPI

ALABAMA

GEORGIA

THE UNITED STATES IN 1853

0   150   300 miles

0   150   300 kilometers

FLORIDA

**FLORIDA,
Treaty with Spain,
1819**

**Areas taken from Spain
in 1810, 1813**

Gulf of Mexico

BAHAMAS

CUBA

Area ceded by
Great Britain,
1818

WASHINGTON
★ Olympia

OREGON COUNTRY
Agreement with Britain,
1846

OREGON

Salem ★

Columbia R.

IDAHO
★ Boise

Snake R.

★ Helena   MONTANA

NORTH DAKOTA

Bismarck ★

Missouri R.

SOUTH DAKOTA
Pierre ★

LOUISIANA
PURCHASE
From France, 1803

WYOMING

NEBRASKA

Sacramento R.

★ Carson City
Sacramento ★

NEVADA

San Joaquin R.

Salt Lake
★ City

UTAH

Cheyenne
★

N. Platte R.

S. Platte R.

Platte R.

Denver
★

COLORADO

KANSAS

MEXICAN CESSION
1848

Colorado R.

CALIFORNIA

PACIFIC
OCEAN

ARIZONA

★ Phoenix

★ Santa Fe

NEW
MEXICO

TEXAS
Annexed, 1845

Red R.

TEXAS

GADSDEN PURCHASE
From Mexico, 1853

Rio Grande

MEXICO

ARCTIC OCEAN

RUSSIA

ALASKA
Purchased from
Russia, 1867

CANADA

Yukon R.

Bering
Sea

Gulf of
Alaska

Juneau ★

0   250   500 miles
0   250   500 kilometers

Honolulu HAWAII
★   Annexed, 1898

PACIFIC
OCEAN

0   50   100 miles
0   50   100 kilometers

M–8

CANADA

MINNESOTA
St. Paul ★

WISCONSIN

MICHIGAN
Lansing ★

Lake Superior

Lake Huron

Lake Michigan

Lake Erie

Lake Ontario

St. Lawrence R.

MAINE
Augusta ★

VERMONT
Montpelier ★

Concord ★
NEW HAMPSHIRE

NEW YORK
Albany ★

MASS.
Boston ★

Hartford ★
Providence ★
RHODE ISLAND
CONNECTICUT

Hudson R.
Connecticut R.

Madison ★

IOWA
Des Moines ★

Lincoln ★

Topeka ★

MISSOURI
Jefferson City ★

ILLINOIS
Springfield ★

INDIANA
Indianapolis ★

OHIO
Columbus ★

PENN.
Harrisburg ★

Trenton ★
NEW JERSEY

Dover ★
DELAWARE

Annapolis ★
MARYLAND
WASHINGTON, D.C.

Delaware R.
Susquehanna R.

Potomac R.

WEST VIRGINIA
Charleston ★

Frankfort ★
KENTUCKY

*Gained by treaty
with Britain, 1783*

Richmond ★
VIRGINIA

James R.

Chesapeake Bay

Ohio R.

Cumberland R.

Tennessee R.

Nashville ★

TENNESSEE

NORTH CAROLINA
Raleigh ★

Cape Fear R.

THE ORIGINAL THIRTEEN COLONIES

Proclamation Line of 1763

Oklahoma City ★

ARKANSAS
Little Rock ★

OKLAHOMA

Arkansas R.

Mississippi R.

Missouri R.

MISSISSIPPI
Jackson ★

ALABAMA
Montgomery ★

Atlanta ★

GEORGIA

SOUTH CAROLINA
Columbia ★

Savannah R.

ATLANTIC OCEAN

Austin ★

LOUISIANA

Baton Rouge ★

Tallahassee ★

FLORIDA

*FLORIDA,
Treaty with Spain,
1819*

*Areas taken
from Spain
in 1810, 1813*

Gulf of Mexico

BAHAMAS

U.S. Territories

ATLANTIC OCEAN

San Juan ★

VIRGIN ISLANDS
Acquired from
Denmark,
1916–1917

PUERTO RICO
Acquired from
Spain, 1898

Caribbean Sea

0   50   100 miles
0   50   100 kilometers

CUBA

THE CONTEMPORARY
UNITED STATES

0   150   300 miles
0   150   300 kilometers